Positive Psychology
in Practice

Positive Psychology in Practice

Edited by
P. Alex Linley and Stephen Joseph

WILEY

John Wiley & Sons, Inc.

Library of Congress Cataloging-in-Publication Data:

Positive psychology in practice / edited by P. Alex Linley and Stephen Joseph.
    p.   cm.
   Includes bibliographical references.
   ISBN 0-471-45906-2
   1. Positive psychology. I. Linley, P. Alex. II. Joseph, Stephen.
  BF204.6P67   2004
  150—dc22

                                                       2004043375

Printed in the United States of America.

10 9 8 7 6 5 4 3 2 1

We dedicate this volume to the memory of
Donald O. Clifton, PhD, 1924–2003.

"The father of strengths-based psychology and the grandfather
of positive psychology."
(Citation from the APA Presidential commendation made by
Philip G. Zimbardo, December 2002;
see http://www.apa.org/monitor/mar03/people.html.)

Contents

Foreword

IT HAS BEEN seven years since Nikki, age 5, told me that if she could stop whining, I could stop being such a grouch, and *positive psychology* (at least in my own mind) came into being (Seligman, 2002). In that moment, I acquired the mission of helping to build the scientific infrastructure of a field that would investigate what makes life worth living: positive emotion, positive character, and positive institutions. In these seven years, much has been accomplished, enough perhaps to call it a *movement* (but not, please, a *paradigm shift* since it uses the same tried and true methods of mainstream science to merely shed light on the relatively uninvestigated realm of happiness). Among the accomplishments are:

- A Positive Psychology Network that supports over 50 pods of scientists around the world
- An annual International Summit held at the Gallup headquarters in Washington the first weekend every October (mark your calendar now, please)
- A Classification of the Strengths and Virtues published by Oxford University Press and the American Psychological Association
- Measurement devices, psychometrically respectable, of many aspects of positive emotion, positive character, and positive institutions
- A substantial prize for the best research in positive psychology and a new, even more substantial prize in memory of Don Clifton to be announced this year for the best research on strengths and virtues
- Undergraduate, graduate, and even high school courses on positive psychology the world over, with several textbooks about to appear
- Positive Psychology Centers at several major universities, one of which will soon become degree granting (Pennsylvania)
- Many millions of dollars in research funding
- Active web sites for research and teaching in positive psychology:
  www.authentichappiness.org
  www.psych.upenn.edu/seligman
  www.bus.umich.edu/Positive
  www.authentichappinesscoaching.com
- Active Listserves in positive psychology
  FRIENDS-OF-PP@LISTS.APA.ORG
  POSITIVE-PSYCHOLOGY@LISTS.APA.ORG
  ppttf@lists.apa.org (Teaching Positive Psychology)
- The first Nobel Prize for a positive psychologist (Danny Kahneman)

- Empirically documented interventions that build happiness lastingly tested in random assignment placebo-controlled studies

So the science is well underway. The current challenge is to apply the science in the world. Analytic thinking and experimentation is only as good as the synthetic applications to practice. As my department was writing the ad for a social psychologist a few years ago, I got an e-mail note that gave me a sleepless night.

"Marty," my colleague Jon Baron wrote, "do you think it would be all right if one of the interests listed was industrial psychology?"

I wrote back, "Of course—the three great realms of life are work, love, and play, and industrial psychology is the psychology of work. I remember that Morris Viteles [who had just passed away at age 98] was a distinguished member of our department for 75 years and a founder of industrial psychology."

Then I couldn't get to sleep. It bothered me that my department did not have anyone whose main interest was work, love, or play. As I mentally ran through the rosters of several other fine academic departments, I couldn't think of anyone whose primary research was work or love or play. I happened to see Jerome Bruner the next day. Jerry, in his 80s, is still yeasty and going strong and is a walking history of modern psychology.

"How did this come to be?" I asked him.

"It actually happened at a moment in time," he replied. "About 60 years ago the chairmen [the gender is intentional] of Harvard, Princeton, and Penn got together at a meeting of the Society of Experimental Psychologists and agreed that they would hire no applied psychologists! This set the hiring pattern of many of the great departments to this very day."

This is a symptom of a larger problem. Complete scientific activity requires both analysis and synthesis. Synthesis is needed when you are not sure that the elements of your analysis carve nature at the joints. The only way to test the validity of your elements is by reconstructing natural phenomena with them. What entitles academic physics and chemistry to be almost solely analytic is their long, accompanying history of synthetic activity, which demonstrated the validity of their elements: predicting eclipses, tides, synthetic fibers, rockets, the green revolution, and computers. What those august chairmen forgot was that psychology did not have a history of engineering, so there was real danger that its laboratory elements might not be the elements out of which mind, emotion, behavior, and psychopathology are made.

There are a very large number of potential analysands, and the best way to tell which ones are valid is to apply them to real world practice and ask if they work. The scientific psychological literature of the twentieth century is littered with well-done analytic science that applied to nothing at all, and this is a fate that positive psychology must avoid.

Doing synthetic thinking to complement analytic thinking has several benefits: It moves *significance* claims from hand-waving toward rule-governed, rigorous discourse. It tests whether our analyses are valid. It helps link our findings to more complex phenomena as well as to simpler systems. It will help our scientists communicate effectively with the press, the public, and policymakers. And not least, it brings science and practice closer together.

Hence this volume. It contains the practical applications of the science of positive psychology to issues such as good versus bad materialism, optimal levels of choice and freedom, what makes people lastingly happier and what does not, exercise and the body, future mindedness and present mindedness, wisdom, teaching positive psychology, leadership, the successful and unsuccessful corporation, executive coaching, physical health and illness, positive therapy, clinical applications, building hope and optimism, posttraumatic growth, emotional intelligence, building gratitude, forgiveness, curiosity, eudaimonia, resilience, positive aging, rehabilitation of sex offenders, flow and optimal experience, and public policy.

This volume is the cutting edge of positive psychology and the emblem of its future.

MARTIN E. P. SELIGMAN

REFERENCE

Seligman, M. E. P. (2002). *Authentic happiness.* New York: Free Press.

Preface

IMAGINE A SCIENCE that is as interested in health and well-being as disease and disorder. A science that strives to promote flourishing and fulfillment at each of the individual, group, and social levels. A science that studies what makes life worth living. A science that holds meaningful lessons for all who choose to consider it. A science that speaks to us personally, as practitioners, as much as it does to the people for whom we practice. This is the science of positive psychology in practice and the subject matter of this volume.

Positive psychology is at the stage where solid theoretical foundations are being laid, experimental results are building, and attention is beginning to turn to the applications of this knowledge in real world contexts. However, there is no single resource to which psychologists may turn that provides them with a complete package of positive psychological theory, research, and application. This volume was designed to meet that need.

Positive psychology constitutes much of what the best professional psychologists already do in practice—however, until now, this *language of learned experience* has not been named, recognized, or celebrated. Our experience in talking to people about the practice of positive psychology is that it gives a voice to what they have always done, but never quite understood, or recognized, or named. Now positive psychology in practice can provide a language and identity that shape and define this implicit understanding.

Three strands are interwoven throughout the fabric of this volume: theory, research, and application. We asked our contributors to dedicate their efforts to producing a work that would define the emerging field of positive psychology in practice for the next five years. They have excelled themselves in doing so. Throughout the volume, you will find comprehensive reviews of the literature that are tailored toward questions of research and application. What is the state of current research in the field? What are the implications of this research for practice? What applied research is required that will best inform future practice? These are the questions that each of our contributors has striven to answer. The chapters of this volume serve as reviews of the theory and evidence, particularly as relevant to applications, but critically, they also provide concrete recommendations for applications and for the future research that will be necessary to underpin and guide these applications.

We are aware that the relationship between positive psychology and humanistic psychology has been a subject of debate. To be sure, there are differences between positive psychology and humanistic psychology, but we believe that these differences are far outweighed by their similarities. Hence, we have worked hard in this volume to speak to readers from the traditions of both positive psychology and humanistic psychology. Our knowledge will advance all the more quickly if we are able to acknowledge similarities, constructively explore our differences, and work together in the joint pursuit of our common goals.

But overall, it is up to you, as the readers, to judge this. We will judge the extent to which we have achieved our objectives by the measure of how much this volume contributes to the advancement of positive psychology in practice, with the goal of more fulfilled lives for all.

Finally, we are reminded that positive psychology is not only about our academic and professional practice and applications for other people but also tells us about how we can lead our own personal lives. May this volume inspire and help you in all these pursuits.

A NOTE TO THE READER

To guide you to further recommended reading in each of the topic areas, we have asked our authors to indicate a few key readings from their chapter reference lists. These key readings are indicated in each chapter reference list by asterisks. We hope that these key references will provide a valuable and informative guide to readers wishing to pursue their interests in the topic area.

P. ALEX LINLEY
STEPHEN JOSEPH

January 2004

Acknowledgments

THE GALLUP ORGANIZATION GENEROUSLY supported my attendance at three Positive Psychology Summits, facilitating many of the contacts that led to the ideas for this volume becoming reality. Stephen was a superb co-editor, and I thank him sincerely for that. I also thank my family for their continued love and support: my mother and father; my wife, Jenny; and my children, Jack, Lucy, and Sophie. For me, they bring positive psychology in practice to life.

P. A. L.

My thanks to Vanessa for her love and support and for her patience with me during the time this book was being prepared. Thanks also to Alex for making this project such an enjoyable collaboration and to friends and colleagues here at the University of Warwick and at Coventry University for their support.

S. J.

Martin E. P. Seligman's encouragement and support was instrumental in the formation of this volume, and we deeply appreciate this, together with his patronage of positive psychology in general.

We also wish to acknowledge Don Clifton's pioneering role in promoting the practice of strengths psychology and positive psychology. He is deeply missed.

Finally, we thank our editorial team at John Wiley & Sons, Tracey Belmont, Isabel Pratt, and Linda Witzling, together with the staff at Publications Development Company of Texas, for ensuring that this project evolved seamlessly from the outset.

P. A. L./S. J.

Contributors

Kara A. Arnold, PhD
Memorial University of
Newfoundland
St. John's, Newfoundland, Canada

Julian Barling, PhD
Queen's University
Kingston, Ontario, Canada

Nick Baylis, PhD (Cantab.) C.Psychol.
University of Cambridge
Cambridge, England

Ilona Boniwell, PhD Candidate
The Open University
Milton Keynes, United Kingdom

Giacomo Bono, PhD
University of Miami
Coral Gables, Florida

Kirk Warren Brown, PhD
University of Rochester
Rochester, New York

Roger Bretherton, BSc (Hons), ClinPsyD
Lincolnshire Partnership NHS Trust
Lincoln, United Kingdom

Chad M. Burton, BA
University of Missouri
Columbia, Missouri

Lawrence G. Calhoun, PhD
University of North Carolina
Charlotte, North Carolina

David Caruso, PhD
Work-Life Strategies
New Canaan, Connecticut

Donald O. Clifton, PhD
The Gallup Organization
Omaha, Nebraska

Michael A. Cohn, BA
University of Michigan
Ann Arbor, Michigan

Antonella Delle Fave, MD
Università degli Studi di Milano
Milano, Italy

Ed Diener, PhD
University of Illinois at Urbana-
Champaign
Champaign, Illinois

Lisa M. Edwards, PhD
University of Notre Dame
South Bend, Indiana

Jennifer Emilia Eells, MA
University of Missouri
Columbia, Missouri

Robert A. Emmons, PhD
University of California
Davis, California

Guy Faulkner, BEd (Hons), MSc., PhD
University of Toronto
Toronto, Canada

Giovanni A. Fava, MD
University of Bologna
Bologna, Italy

Amy C. Fineburg, MA
Spain Park High School
Hoover, Alabama

Frank D. Fincham, PhD
University of New York at Buffalo
Buffalo, New York

David Hansen, MS
University of Illinois
Urbana-Champaign, Illinois

Osnat Hazan, BA
The Hebrew University of Jerusalem
Jerusalem, Israel

Jane Henry, PhD
Open University
Milton Keynes, United Kingdom

Timothy D. Hodges, MS
The Gallup Organization
Omaha, Nebraska

Mark A. Hubble, PhD
The Institute for the Study of
   Therapeutic Change
Chicago, Illinois

Felicia A. Huppert, PhD, FBPS
University of Cambridge
Cambridge, England

Kelly Janowski, MS
University of Kansas
Lawrence, Kansas

Robin Jarrett, PhD
University of Illinois
Urbana-Champaign, Illinois

Ingvild S. Jørgensen, Cand. Psychol.
Sanderud Hospital
Ottestad, Norway

Stephen Joseph, PhD
University of Warwick
Coventry, United Kingdom

Todd B. Kashdan, MA
University of New York at Buffalo
Buffalo, New York

Tim Kasser, PhD
Knox College
Galesburg, Illinois

Carol Kauffman, PhD
Harvard Medical School
Cambridge, Massachusetts

Laura A. King, PhD
University of Missouri
Columbia, Missouri

Ute Kunzmann, Dr. phil.
Max Planck Institute for Human
   Development
Berlin, Germany

Reed Larson, PhD
University of Illinois
Urbana-Champaign, Illinois

P. Alex Linley, BSc (Hons)
University of Leicester
Leicester, United Kingdom

Shane J. Lopez, PhD
University of Kansas
Lawrence, Kansas

Sonja Lyubomirsky, PhD
University of California
Riverside, California

James E. Maddux, PhD
George Mason University
Fairfax, Virginia

Jeana L. Magyar-Moe, PhD
University of Wisconsin
Steven's Point, Wisconsin

Ruth Mann, BSc, MSc
Offender Programs Unit
London, England

Ann S. Masten, PhD
University of Minnesota
Minneapolis, Minnesota

Fausto Massimini, MD
Università degli Studi di Milano
Milano, Italy

John D. Mayer, PhD
University of New Hampshire
Durham, New Hampshire

Michael E. McCullough, PhD
University of Miami
Coral Gables, Florida

Scott D. Miller, PhD
Institute for the Study of Therapeutic
   Change
Chicago, Illinois

Nanette Mutrie, DPE, MEd, PhD
University of Glasgow
Scotland, United Kingdom

David G. Myers, PhD
Hope College
Holland, Michigan

Hilde Eileen Nafstad, Cand. Psychol.
University of Oslo
Oslo, Norway

**Roderick J. Ørner, BA, MA, Cert.
Dip. Psych., FBPS**
University of Lincoln
Lincoln, United Kingdom

Nansook Park, PhD
University of Rhode Island
Kingston, Rhode Island

William Pavot, PhD
Southwest Minnesota State University
Marshall, Minnesota

Nickki Pearce, MS
University of Illinois
Urbana-Champaign, Illinois

Jennifer Teramoto Pedrotti, PhD
Cal Poly
San Luis Opisbo, California

Christopher Peterson, PhD
University of Michigan
Ann Arbor, Michigan

Cindy Pressgrove, BS
University of Kansas
Lawrence, Kansas

Alina Reznitskaya, PhD
Montclair State University
Upper Montclair, New Jersey

Sonia Roccas, PhD
The Open University of Israel
Tel-Aviv, Israel

Chiara Ruini, PhD
University of Bologna
Bologna, Italy

Richard M. Ryan, PhD
University of Rochester
Rochester, New York

Lilach Sagiv, PhD
The Hebrew University of Jerusalem
Jerusalem, Israel

Peter Salovey, PhD
Yale University
New Haven, Connecticut

Barry Schwartz, PhD
Swarthmore College
Swarthmore, Pennsylvania

**Anne Scoular, BA (Hons),
PGDip Psychology**
Meyler Campbell Ltd
London, United Kingdom

Kennon M. Sheldon, PhD
University of Missouri
Columbia, Missouri

David K. Sherman, PhD
University of California
Santa Barbara, California

Niro Sivanathan, MSc
Northwestern University
Evanston, Illinois

C. R. Snyder, PhD
University of Kansas
Lawrence, Kansas

Robert J. Sternberg, PhD
Yale University
New Haven, Connecticut

Patrick Sullivan, MS
University of Illinois
Urbana-Champaign, Illinois

Shelley E. Taylor, PhD
University of California
Los Angeles, California

Richard G. Tedeschi, PhD
University of North Carolina
Charlotte, North Carolina

Nick Turner, PhD
Queen's University
Kingston, Ontario, Canada

Jerri L. Turner, MS
University of Kansas
Lawrence, Kansas

George E. Vaillant, MD
Harvard Medical School
Boston, Massachusetts

Ruut Veenhoven, PhD
Erasmus University
Rotterdam, Netherlands

Kathrin Walker, MS
University of Illinois
Urbana-Champaign, Illinois

Andrew Ward, PhD
Swarthmore College
Swarthmore, Pennsylvania

Tony Ward, MA (Hons), PhD,
DipClinPsych, MAPS
Victoria University of Wellington
Wellington, New Zealand

Natasha Watkins, MS
University of Illinois
Urbana-Champaign, Illinois

Dustin Wood, MS
University of Illinois
Urbana-Champaign, Illinois

Tuppett M. Yates, MA
University of Minnesota
Minneapolis, Minnesota

Philip G. Zimbardo, PhD
Stanford University
Stanford, California

PART I

THE APPLIED POSITIVE PSYCHOLOGY PERSPECTIVE

CHAPTER 1

Applied Positive Psychology: A New Perspective for Professional Practice

P. ALEX LINLEY and STEPHEN JOSEPH

POSITIVE PSYCHOLOGY HAS a research tradition that goes back decades. Yet despite this rich tradition, many topics that we would describe as within the scope of positive psychology have typically remained isolated from each other, lacking any shared language or common identity. The emergence of positive psychology has highlighted the common traditions of many working in these areas and has provided a conceptual home for researchers and practitioners interested in all aspects of optimal human functioning. In viewing the many different strands of research from which positive psychology is drawn, and seeing them as sharing a common core identity, psychologists have taken a sustained and serious interest in the study of human nature as a whole. This rich tradition provides the foundation on which applied positive psychology rests.

THE LINEAGE OF POSITIVE PSYCHOLOGY

Interest in what is good about humans and their lives and in optimal human functioning has long been a theme of human inquiry. From Aristotle's treatises on eudaimonia, through Aquinas' writings about virtue during the Renaissance, to the inquiries of modern psychology—whether in the guise of humanistic psychology or positive psychology—scholarly interest in the human potential for fulfillment has always existed. Within the very origins of modern psychology, James (1902) was interested in the role that transcendent experiences may play in stimulating optimal human functioning (see Rathunde, 2001). Jung's (1933) concept of individuation speaks much to people becoming all that they can be. This theme was echoed by Allport (1961) with his work on the mature individual, together with Jahoda's (1958) seminal thinking about what might constitute mental health

Many thanks to Chris Kent for preparing Figure 1.1.

in the true sense of the term. Similarly, the humanistic psychology movement speaks to our inherent potential as human beings (cf. Bugental, 1964), with Maslow's (1968) concept of self-actualization and Rogers' (1963) work around the fully functioning person typically invoked here. More recently, Ryff and her colleagues have integrated much of this literature in the concept of psychological well-being, defined as engagement with the existential challenges of life, and being distinct from (but typically associated with) subjective well-being, or the more generic happiness (e.g., Keyes, Shmotkin, & Ryff, 2002).

But these research trajectories have typically been diverse. There has been little integration (excepting Ryff, 1989), and still less broader recognition, of the themes that run consistently through them. Unlike clinical psychology and psychiatry, who share the common language of the *DSM*, for researchers and practitioners interested in human potential and fulfillment, there has been no integrative grouping, classification, language, or even collective identity with which to identify and to label our work and interests.

PROVIDING A COMMON LANGUAGE

The single most important contribution of positive psychology has been to provide a collective identity—a common voice and language for researchers and practitioners from all persuasions who share an interest in health as well as in sickness—in the fulfillment of potential as well as in the amelioration of pathology. Academic psychologists could be primarily working within abnormal, cognitive, developmental, or social areas, and yet still identify themselves as positive psychologists. Professional psychologists may work within settings that are primarily clinical, counseling, educational, forensic, health, industrial/organizational, and yet still consider themselves to be practitioners of positive psychology.

Positive psychology is unique in the ways that it transcends traditional dichotomies and divisions within psychology and offers ways of working that are genuinely integrative and applicable across settings. It is as natural for a neural scientist studying positive affect to identify themselves as a positive psychologist as it is for a social psychologist who studies varieties of religious experience, a developmental psychologist who studies resilience, or a health psychologist who works to promote health and well-being.

APPLIED POSITIVE PSYCHOLOGY— A WORKING DEFINITION

We start by offering this working definition:

> Applied positive psychology is the application of positive psychology research to the facilitation of optimal functioning.

Applied positive psychologists may work at the level of the individual, the group, the organization, the community, or the society. Applied positive psychologists work to promote optimal functioning across the full range of human functioning, from disorder and distress to health and fulfillment. We note six points to further elaborate on this definition:

1. *Facilitation:* Applied positive psychology, as we understand it, is not pre-scriptive in the sense that it dictates to people. Rather, it is facilitative in the way that it works to help people achieve their objectives. This approach is in keeping with the organismic valuing process that we believe to be a funda-mental assumption of positive psychology (see Linley & Joseph, Chapter 42, this volume).

2. *Optimal functioning:* We use this term as shorthand for a broad range of val-ued psychological processes and outcomes. These may be valued subjective experiences (such as well-being, hope, and flow), positive individual traits (such as forgiveness, emotional intelligence, and wisdom), or civic virtues that promote good citizenship (such as responsibility, nurturance, and altru-ism; see Seligman & Csikszentmihalyi, 2000). The optimal functioning of yourself and others may be facilitated through using positive character traits and acting as good citizens (positive processes); these processes will typi-cally lead to both individual and collective well-being (positive outcomes).

   The desired outcomes of positive psychology (i.e., optimal functioning) have been characterized in part as happiness and well-being (Seligman, 2002). Thus, we are careful to note the distinction here between subjective well-being and psychological well-being (Seligman & Csikszentmihalyi, 2000, also make this distinction using the terms *pleasure* and *enjoyment*, respectively). The terms *subjective well-being* and *psychological well-being* have been carefully delineated by Keyes et al. (2002; see also Christopher, 1999; Ryan & Deci, 2001; Waterman, 1993).

   Subjective well-being (SWB) is widely accepted as the sum of life satisfac-tion (the cognitive component) plus positive affect minus negative affect (the affective components). In common terms, this is everyday "happiness." In contrast, psychological well-being (PWB) reflects engagement with and full participation in the challenges and opportunities of life. SWB and PWB, although typically moderately correlated, are not the same. Further, al-though they may typically be representative of optimal functioning out-comes, again, this is not necessarily always so. Consider, for example, the case of a person who acts responsibly, but at detriment to their personal well-being. This raises the issue of the hierarchy of positive psychology val-ues. (See Linley & Joseph, Chapter 42, this volume, for a more extended dis-cussion of this issue.)

3. *Value position:* In talking of "the good life," "good citizenship," "positive indi-vidual traits," and "valued subjective experiences," we inevitably presuppose a value position. We emphasize three issues here: First, this assumption of a value position is inevitable however "value neutral" we claim science to be (cf. Christopher, 1996). Second, this value position should be stated explicitly so that it can be held open to scrutiny, criticism, and amendment (cf. Prillel-tensky, 1994). Third, in assuming a value position, we also explicitly note that this position should not be prescriptive in dictating to individuals the spe-cific ways in which they should lead their lives (see also Linley & Joseph, Chapter 42, this volume).

4. *Levels of application:* Applied positive psychology is relevant for individuals, groups, organizations, communities, and societies, being fully mindful of the social and cultural contexts in which our lives are embedded (cf. Christopher,

1999; Kekes, 1995; Markus & Kitayama, 1991). In this volume, you will find each of these levels represented.

5. *Full range of human functioning:* Applied positive psychologists may work both to alleviate distress and to promote optimal functioning. We do not see these as distinct or separate roles, but are mindful of the approach that has characterized much of psychology (counseling psychology sometimes providing an exception), that when the distress has been alleviated, or the symptoms treated, the role of the psychologist is complete. In contrast, we believe that is only half the job. Applied positive psychologists aim to facilitate optimal functioning by moving their clients *beyond* the zero point of psychopathology (cf. Joseph, Linley, Harwood, Lewis, & McCollam, in press). Their role is not complete when psychopathology is absent, but well-being is not present. Rather, applied positive psychologists aim to facilitate their clients' development more fully toward optimal functioning (i.e., the presence of well-being and other valued states and characteristics). This facilitation of optimal functioning is not only about the promotion of well-being. The approach also serves to buffer subsequent stresses, thereby serving an additional preventive function.

6. *A collective identity, not a new specialty:* Finally, we record an important proviso. In using the term *applied positive psychology* and *applied positive psychologist*, we are not seeking to create a new specialty within professional psychology—far from it. In contrast, our aim is to provide a collective identity and common language for professional psychologists who work in positive psychological ways, just as positive psychology has provided that collective identity for previously unconnected researchers and academics who nonetheless shared an interest in the brighter sides of human nature.

THE NEED FOR APPLIED POSITIVE PSYCHOLOGY

What is the need for the positive psychological perspective? A look at some statistics from the PsycINFO database reveals this need. In Figure 1.1, we have tracked the growth of research publications for each five-year period from 1978 up to and including September 2003 for the terms *depression, anxiety, subjective well-being,* and *psychological well-being.*

Research output on depression and anxiety exceeds the research output on subjective well-being and psychological well-being by several orders of magnitude. We are encouraged by the fact that research into subjective well-being has increased by a factor of almost 180 (from 6 publications by 1978 to 1,070 by September 2003). Further, research into psychological well-being has increased by a factor of 35 (from 93 publications by 1978 to 3,231 by September 2003). However, in spite of these encouraging trends, the gulf in research output remains enormous.

We could have selected any number of positive psychological constructs to compare with these two psychopathology constructs, and the results would have been essentially the same (cf. Fernandez-Ballesteros, 2003). Similarly, we may consider the number of professional journals dedicated to furthering our understanding of psychopathology (e.g., *Journal of Abnormal Psychology, Journal of Abnormal Child Psychology, Journal of Affective Disorders, Journal of Anxiety Disorders*). In contrast, there are barely any journals dedicated to furthering our understanding of well-being

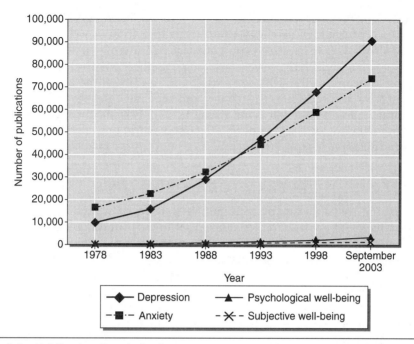

Figure 1.1   Publication Trends for Depression, Anxiety, Subjective Well-Being, and Psychological Well-Being, 1978 through September 2003

(the *Journal of Happiness Studies* being a notable exception). Clearly, positive psychology *is* necessary (Sheldon & King, 2001).

Does this focus on psychopathology mean that our fellow human beings are uninterested in their own health, well-being, and fulfillment? Far from it, as a cursory look at the self-help section of any bookstore will show. There is a vast array of material purporting to improve people's lives, to make them healthier, happier, or more fulfilled. And yet, psychologists—academic or professional—are rarely the authors of these volumes, and even more rarely are these prescriptions based on evidence that would withstand even the most cursory scientific scrutiny. Hence, psychologists appear largely silent on these issues, while any number of other "authorities" fill the void.

Positive psychology and specifically applied positive psychology are uniquely positioned to change this situation by offering scientifically rigorous—yet accessible and user-friendly—advice and guidance, as the success of Seligman's (2002) *Authentic Happiness* volume testifies. Also consider, for example, the history of the development of the Values In Action Classification of Strengths. By September 2003, over 175,000 individuals had completed this assessment battery in order to identify and learn about their signature strengths—this despite a typical time investment of 40 minutes, with no material incentive or obligation to participate (C. Peterson, personal communication, October 20, 2003).

Of increasing concern to us, as positive psychologists, both practicing and academic, should be the increasing psychiatric medicalization of everyday life experiences. The growth of diagnostic categories and labels in the *DSM* (e.g., American Psychiatric Association [APA], 1994) has been substantial (see Hubble & Miller,

Chapter 21, this volume; Maddux, Snyder, & Lopez, Chapter 20, this volume). Applied positive psychology provides what we believe to be a welcome alternative. Instead of attempting to capture varied nuances of human behavior as being representative of some underlying psychopathology, applied positive psychologists, instead, look to people's strengths, capacities, and resources, the key attributes and assets that have allowed them to survive, and in some cases flourish, despite the obstacles they have faced. That is not to say that illness and disorder are to be neglected, but simply that they should be regarded as but one aspect of the person's experience (Linley & Joseph, 2003).

THE PLAN FOR THIS VOLUME

In establishing the aims for this volume, we were faced with a daunting task: to provide state-of-the-art research evidence that underpinned practical recommendations for professional psychologists, while at the same time defining the parameters for future academic research. The result is a volume that bridges the theory, research, and application of positive psychology.

We encouraged our contributors to discuss the implications of their work for positive practice, outlining the evidence, evaluating applied research, and proposing the applications and research directions of the future. The contributors have brought to their chapters a broad range of knowledge, experiences, attitudes, and approaches from the perspectives of both academic and professional psychology. The result is a volume that brings together the current state of knowledge for many domains of applied positive psychology and offers clear directions for the field as it moves forward.

This volume was not prepared with a single defined constituency in mind, such as academic social psychologists or professional clinical psychologists—in fact, quite the opposite. Rather, we have consciously tried to produce a volume that cuts across these lines and demonstrates just how much psychologists have in common. Hence, it offers something of value for any professional psychologist and any academic psychologist who has an interest in the health and well-being of themselves, their family, their community, and their society.

Equally important, although written from the perspective of psychology, the questions with which this volume deals are in no way restricted to the professional or academic domain of psychology alone. The topics covered have implications that extend well beyond the laboratory or the consulting room. They deal with themes important to us all, such as the nature of how we should conduct our lives and the nature of how we as individuals, and members of groups or communities, consumers, learners, employees, clients, leaders or followers, policy makers or the subjects of policy, would wish to lead our lives. Hence, from this wider perspective, the volume transcends psychology to include the broader social sciences, such as economics, political science, and sociology, and stands in full support of a more positive social scientific practice.

THE CONTENT OF THIS VOLUME

In Part II (*Historical and Philosophical Foundations*), Ingvild Jørgensen and Hilde Nafstad (Chapter 2) deal more broadly with a number of antecedent developments in the history of psychology and science that have informed the development and epistemology of today's positive psychology. Laura King and colleagues (Chapter 3) address both professional and folk conceptions of the good life and consider some of the implications this has for practice.

In Part III (*Values and Choices in Pursuit of the Good Life*), Tim Kasser (Chapter 4) examines the question of our pursuit of "the good life or the goods life"—that is, psychological satisfaction or material success and its implications for personal and social well-being. Lilach Sagiv and colleagues (Chapter 5) consider three value pathways to fulfillment, looking specifically at the roles of healthy values, valued goal attainment, and the congruence between our own values and the values supported by our environment. Barry Schwartz and Andrew Ward (Chapter 6) address the paradox of choice, that is, how it can be that more choice is actually bad for us, and suggest ways in which we can act to counter this maladaptive influence. This theme is reflected by Kirk Warren Brown and Richard Ryan (Chapter 7), as they consider how adopting an attitude of mindfulness can facilitate autonomous thought and behavior that serves to facilitate more fully informed decisions with attendant positive psychological outcomes.

In Part IV (*Lifestyle Practices for Health and Well-Being*), Kennon Sheldon and Sonja Lyubomirsky (Chapter 8) discuss strategies for achieving sustained gains in happiness and well-being, noting that intentional activities may hold the key to this elusive pursuit. The role of physical activity in promoting both physical and psychological health is discussed by Nanette Mutrie and Guy Faulkner (Chapter 9), who show that relatively simple and available physical activity strategies can convey substantial benefits for well-being. Finally, in this section, Ilona Boniwell and Philip Zimbardo (Chapter 10) explore how the way in which we relate to the temporal aspects of our lives influences our choices, intentions, and behaviors, and what we can do to try and achieve a more optimal balanced time perspective.

In Part V (*Teaching and Learning: Methods and Processes*), Alina Reznitskaya and Robert Sternberg (Chapter 11) review the rationale and impact of their "Teaching for Wisdom" program with high school students, demonstrating how some of the key facets of wisdom can be facilitated through the high school history curriculum. Amy Fineburg (Chapter 12) shows the value of introducing positive psychology to the introductory psychology student, and provides several models for how this may be achieved. Nick Baylis (Chapter 13) shares his experiences of teaching dedicated positive psychology courses, offering techniques and inside tips on what has worked for him and why. In exploring the mechanisms of successful learning through upward social comparisons, Michael Cohn (Chapter 14) offers perspectives that inform not only educational practice, but also work and relationships.

In Part VI (*Positive Psychology at Work*), Niro Sivanathan and colleagues (Chapter 15) show how transformational leadership can positively affect all levels of an organization, from its employees and culture through to its leaders themselves. Tim Hodges and Don Clifton (Chapter 16) illustrate the powerful effects of strengths-based development, as developed and applied by the Gallup Organization throughout the world. The culture and functions of positive and creative organization are the subject of Jane Henry's chapter (Chapter 17), as she conveys how positive working practices can be fostered from the top-down. Carol Kauffman and Anne Scoular (Chapter 18) review executive coaching through the lens of positive psychology, and note the many possibilities for further research in this area.

In Part VII (*Health Psychology, Clinical Psychology, and Psychotherapy: A Positive Psychological Perspective*), Shelley Taylor and David Sherman (Chapter 19) elaborate on the integration of positive psychology and health psychology, showing how health psychologists have often worked in ways typical of positive psychological practice. James Maddux and colleagues (Chapter 20) critique the dominance of the *DSM* diagnostic system within clinical psychology, and provide recommendations for the development and practice of a positive clinical psychology. Mark Hubble and Scott Miller (Chapter 21) continue this theme within the domain of psychotherapy, showing how decades of research evidence all point to the client as the most powerful factor in therapeutic change. Further, they suggest that positive psychology needs to take account of this fact in its theorizing and applications. The implications of positive psychological research and assumptions form the basis of Stephen Joseph and Alex Linley's (Chapter 22) inquiry into what may constitute a positive therapy.

In Part VIII (*Positive Psychology in the Consulting Room*), Chiara Ruini and Giovanni Fava (Chapter 23) review well-being therapy, a psychotherapeutic approach that aims to facilitate sustainable increases in psychological well-being that go beyond the more traditional focus on just the treatment of presenting psychopathology. Shane Lopez and colleagues (Chapter 24) examine the role of hope as an agent of positive change, and focus on how hope might be facilitated within the consulting room and beyond. Dealing with the aftermath of trauma and adversity from a positive, growth-oriented perspective is the focus of Richard Tedeschi and Lawrence Calhoun's chapter (Chapter 25) on posttraumatic growth. Roger Bretherton and Roderick Ørner (Chapter 26) take up the issue of the existential themes raised, and consider how the focus of existential psychotherapy on the person's inherent strengths and capacities fits it well as a positive approach to psychotherapy.

In Part IX (*Strengths of Character in Practice*), Christopher Peterson and Nansook Park (Chapter 27) provide an overview of the VIA Strengths Classification project, and consider how this classification provides a solid basis for future applied work. Focusing on the specific strength of emotional intelligence, Peter Salovey and colleagues (Chapter 28) document its role in relationships, working environments, education, human resources, and executive coaching. Giacomo Bono and colleagues (Chapter 29) survey the role of gratitude in practice, demonstrating how it is a character strength reliably related to positive psychological outcomes and good lives. Todd Kashdan and Frank Fincham (Chapter 30) review the literature on curiosity, giving extensive consideration to the role that curiosity plays in facilitating positive outcomes across a range of settings. Ute Kunzmann (Chapter 31) describes her recent work on the emotional-motivational side of wisdom, a topic long neglected within psychology.

In Part X (*Positive Development across the Lifespan*), Tuppett Yates and Ann Masten (Chapter 32) explore the role of resilience theory in the practice of positive psychology with at-risk children. Reed Larson and colleagues (Chapter 33) describe their work in documenting what is positive and effective about youth development programs, and identify the processes through which these positive effects may come about. George Vaillant (Chapter 34) moves the focus toward the end of life with his analysis of what constitutes and facilitates positive aging—factors that are pertinent and applicable throughout the lifespan.

In Part XI (*Building Community through Integration and Regeneration*), Antonella Delle Fave and Fausto Massimini (Chapter 35) look at the role of optimal experiences in adjusting to and living with disability, demonstrating that to be disabled in no way represents the end of opportunities for optimal living. Tony Ward and Ruth Mann (Chapter 36) address positive treatment approaches with sex offenders, conveying how interventions that respect them as individuals lead to improved treatment compliance and lower recidivism. Frank Fincham and Todd Kashdan (Chapter 37) explore the role of forgiveness at group and community levels, offering a range of ways in which forgiveness can be facilitated to promote group and community healing and integration.

In Part XII (*Public Policy Initiatives: Good Governance and the Good Life*), David Myers (Chapter 38) explores the tension between individualism and community in facilitating good human connections and the attendant implications for public policy. Ruut Veenhoven (Chapter 39) outlines and debunks the objections to the greatest happiness principle, showing that greater happiness for people is a legitimate and achievable public policy aim. William Pavot and Ed Diener (Chapter 40) continue this theme, advocating national indices of subjective well-being that would be indicative of the nation's psychological health and complementary to the existing indicators of physical and economic health. In addressing health and well-being promotion from a public policy perspective, Felicia Huppert (Chapter 41) reviews how social interventions traditionally designed to prevent physical pathology can be adapted to promote well-being and prevent psychological disorder, with substantial consequences for the health and well-being of the nation.

Finally, in Part XIII (*Signposts for the Practice of Positive Psychology*), Alex Linley and Stephen Joseph (Chapter 42) conclude the volume by reviewing some of the key assumptions within positive psychology, identifying pertinent questions arising from these assumptions, and considering the implications of this for applied positive psychology.

This volume promises to be a valuable resource in the further development and evolution of applied positive psychology. We hope you will enjoy reading it as much as we have enjoyed preparing it.

REFERENCES

Allport, G. W. (1961). *Pattern and growth in personality.* New York: Holt, Rinehart and Winston.

American Psychiatric Association. (1994). *Diagnostic and statistical manual of mental disorders* (4th ed.). Washington, DC: Author.

Bugental, J. F. T. (1964). The third force in psychology. *Journal of Humanistic Psychology, 4,* 19–25.

Christopher, J. C. (1996). Counseling's inescapable moral visions. *Journal of Counseling and Development, 75,* 17–25.

Christopher, J. C. (1999). Situating psychological well-being: Exploring the cultural roots of its theory and research. *Journal of Counseling and Development, 77,* 141–152.

Fernandez-Ballesteros, R. (2003). Light and dark in the psychology of human strengths: The example of psychogerontology. In L. G. Aspinwall & U. M. Staudinger (Eds.), *A psychology of human strengths: Fundamental questions and future directions for a positive psychology* (pp. 131–147). Washington, DC: American Psychological Association.

Jahoda, M. (1958). *Current concepts of positive mental health.* New York: Basic Books.

James, W. (1902). *The varieties of religious experience: A study in human nature.* New York: Longmans, Green.

Joseph, S., Linley, P. A., Harwood, J., Lewis, C. A., & McCollam, P. (in press). Rapid assessment of well-being: The Short Depression-Happiness Scale. *Psychology and Psychotherapy: Theory, Research, and Practice.*

Jung, C. G. (1933). *Modern man in search of a soul.* New York: Harcourt, Brace & World.

Kekes, J. (1995). *Moral wisdom and good lives.* Ithaca, NY: Cornell University Press.

*Keyes, C. L. M., Shmotkin, D., & Ryff, C. D. (2002). Optimizing well-being: The empirical encounter of two traditions. *Journal of Personality and Social Psychology, 82,* 1007–1022.

*Linley, P. A., & Joseph, S. (2003). Putting it into practice [Special issue on Positive Psychology]. *The Psychologist, 16,* 143.

Markus, H. R., & Kitayama, S. (1991). Culture and the self: Implications for cognition, emotion, and motivation. *Psychological Review, 98,* 224–253.

Maslow, A. H. (1968). *Toward a psychology of being* (2nd ed.). New York: Van Nostrand Reinhold.

Prilleltensky, I. (1994). *The morals and politics of psychology: Psychological discourse and the status quo.* Albany: State University of New York Press.

Rathunde, K. (2001). Toward a psychology of optimal human functioning: What positive psychology can learn from the "experiential turns" of James, Dewey, and Maslow. *Journal of Humanistic Psychology, 41,* 135–153.

Rogers, C. R. (1963). The concept of the fully functioning person. *Psychotherapy: Theory, Research, and Practice, 1,* 17–26.

Ryan, R. M., & Deci, E. L. (2001). On happiness and human potentials: A review of research on hedonic and eudaimonic well-being. *Annual Review of Psychology, 52,* 141–166.

Ryff, C. D. (1989). Happiness is everything, or is it? Explorations on the meaning of psychological well-being. *Journal of Personality and Social Psychology, 57,* 1069–1081.

Seligman, M. E. P. (2002). *Authentic happiness: Using the new positive psychology to realize your potential for lasting fulfillment.* New York: Free Press.

*Seligman, M. E. P., & Csikszentmihalyi, M. (2000). Positive psychology: An introduction. *American Psychologist, 55,* 5–14.

*Sheldon, K. M., & King, L. (2001). Why positive psychology is necessary. *American Psychologist, 56,* 216–217.

Waterman, A. S. (1993). Two conceptions of happiness: Contrasts of personal expressiveness (eudaimonia) and hedonic enjoyment. *Journal of Personality and Social Psychology, 64,* 678–691.

PART II

HISTORICAL AND PHILOSOPHICAL FOUNDATIONS

Positive Psychology: Historical, Philosophical, and Epistemological Perspectives

INGVILD S. JØRGENSEN and HILDE EILEEN NAFSTAD

IN SCIENCE AND scientific work, and, therefore, for positive psychology, it is important to reflect on historical roots. There are at least three reasons for such analyses:

1. Historical analyses of roots and forerunners contribute to make visible the a priori, taken-for-granted suppositions, premises, or positions on human nature on which the field or tradition rests.
2. Historical analyses can explicate on which philosophical and philosophy of science traditions mainstream psychology builds and, thus, which perspectives and bases of knowledge contemporary psychology neglects or even excludes.
3. Looking back on historical roots, especially in a phase of reestablishing and reformulating themes and perspectives in psychology, may allow us to avoid reinventing the wheel: Most basic questions about human nature have indeed been raised in philosophy and psychology. It is, therefore, fruitful to identify and examine historical roots to see how various questions about core human nature have been formulated and discussed. (We use the concept *human nature* in this analysis because insofar as debates take place concerning underlying axioms and assumptions in mainstream psychology today, it is *human nature* that grasps and delimits the substantial core of these debates; see Gergen, 1982; Wrightsman, 1992.)

The philosopher of science Mendelsohn (1977, p. 3) maintains: "Science is an activity of human beings acting and interacting, thus a social activity." As a consequence, Mendelsohn emphasizes:

> Scientific knowledge is therefore fundamentally social knowledge. As a social activity, science is clearly a product of history and of processes that occurred in time and in place and involved human actors. These actors had lives not only in science, but in the wider societies of which they were members. (p. 4)

However, because psychology's subjects are historically anchored beings who are formed by their own times in quite another way compared to most other sciences' objects of study, psychology as a science becomes especially historically situated and formed by its (social) times (Allport, 1954; Gergen, 1973, 1985). Further, because the subject and the researchers themselves are always historically situated and formed by their own times' views on humanity and ways of viewing the world (*weltanschauung*), it is critically decisive for positive psychology's self-understanding to reflect on and analyze its historical and philosophical roots. Martin and Sugarman (2001, p. 370) formulate the historically situated nature of a priori assumptions more precisely: "because people are embedded inextricably within the world that they are compelled to make use of those assumptions, preconceptions, meanings, and prejudices provided by their historical, sociocultural contexts . . ."

The purpose of this chapter is to describe some of the underlying philosophical and historical assumptions and forerunners of positive psychology. We do this by exploring roots of the metatheoretical positions developed and/or revitalized by positive psychology because it is mainly on this level of scientific activity, the metatheoretical level, that positive psychology contributes to a reorientation. On other levels, positive psychology is, as is shown, more in line with mainstream psychology. Thus, we are undertaking an analysis of what the philosopher Lakatos (1970) terms *the hard core of science*, that is, scientific disciplines' or traditions' metatheories or the a priori basic assumptions. Analyses on this level constitute a most important and necessary task of scientific research.

A REVITALIZATION OF ARISTOTELIAN PHILOSOPHY

In his famous review of the history of social psychology, Gordon Allport (1954, p. 6) claimed: "one thing is certain: Platonic and Aristotelian strands of thought are found in all western theory, past and present." In fact, 50 years in advance, Allport was right, also, about positive psychology's philosophical roots: The Aristotelian tradition is a core root of positive psychology. Positive psychology concentrates on positive experiences and positive character or virtues. Hence, positive psychology strongly associates itself with the Aristotelian model of human nature. However, it is obvious that the ancient Greek philosophers formulated their frames of understanding of the human individual in a totally different social and material situation, without today's basic conditions characterized by threatening environmental pollution and a globalization that affects and changes every local culture (Arnett, 2002). Thus, parts of the basis of psychology's approaches to human beings must necessarily be formulated or reformulated as to contemporarily given conditions. Positive psychology is indeed well under way with this task (see Seligman, 2002; Seligman & Csikszentmihalyi, 2000; Snyder & Lopez, 2002). But even though positive psychology must shape its approaches and research questions based on human life situations and conditions of today, it is, as now underlined, necessary to inquire into historical roots and forerunners. Such exposure is especially important because psychology as a science has a long past, but a short history (Allport, 1954; Farr, 1996).

We, therefore, now trace positive psychology's central roots, in particular, the Aristotelian frame of reference. At the same time, we point out the state of today's mainstream psychology to show why positive psychology is needed as a corrective.

FROM A PATHOLOGY-ORIENTED UNDERSTANDING TO A PERSPECTIVE OF GROWTH AND POSITIVE DEVELOPMENT

Foucault (1972, 1980), a key postmodern philosopher, argues that science in different time periods develops what we might term *regimes of truth* about human nature. Foucault's (1973) works include critical analyses of how today's medical conceptual frameworks define and determine modes of human thought. Seligman and Csikszentmihalyi (2000) also maintain that contemporary psychology gives priority to a conception of human beings that to too great a degree is based on pathology, faults, and dysfunctions, that is, a medical-oriented psychology. Basic assumptions other than those that focus on lacks, dysfunctions, and crises have been given little possibility to direct and form contemporary (clinical) research. The ideology of illness is, thus, a priori given priority in today's psychology (Maddux, 2002; see also Maddux, Snyder, & Lopez, this volume). Seligman (2002, p. 21) also quotes the critical psychiatrist Thomas Szasz for having said: "Psychology is the racket that imitates the racket called psychiatry." Positive psychology attempts to be an important corrective and demands of predominant mainstream psychology not to continue to marginalize or exclude, but bring in again and revitalize the positive aspects of human nature: *positive subjective experiences, positive individual traits,* and *civic virtues* (Seligman & Csikszentmihalyi, 2000). Rather than taking the medical-oriented model as given, the human being should, as Seligman and Csikszentmihalyi maintain, be conceptualized and understood as a being with inherent potentials for developing positive character traits or virtues. This idea is the core of the actualizing tendency as described by Rogers (e.g., 1959) and self-actualization as described by Maslow (e.g., 1968).

For positive psychology, the concept of *good character* thus becomes the central concept. Referring explicitly to Abraham Lincoln's historical presidential inauguration speech with its oratorial expression, "the better angels of our nature," Seligman (2002, p. 125) formulates what may be termed the basic assumptions of positive psychology:

- There is a human "nature."
- Action proceeds from character.
- Character comes in two forms, both equally fundamental—bad character and good, virtuous (angelic) character.

Further, Seligman (2002, p. 125) states: "Because all of these assumptions have almost disappeared from the psychology of the twentieth century, the story of their rise and fall is the backdrop for my renewing the notion of good character as a core assumption of positive psychology." Seligman (p. 128) also maintains: "Any science that does not use character as a basic idea (or at least explain character and choice away successfully) will never be accepted as a useful account of human be-havior." At the same time, Seligman's point of view is that the individual has the capacity for both good and evil: "evolution has selected both sorts of traits, and any number of niches support morality, cooperation, altruism, and goodness, just as any number support murder, theft, self-seeking, and badness" (p. 211).

Thus, the major distinction between mainstream psychology and positive psy-chology is that mainstream psychology gives priority to negative behavior and various forms of dysfunctions. Positive psychology, on the other hand, concen-trates on positive experiences and positive character or virtues. Positive psychol-ogy is thus articulating the presumptions of the Aristotelian approach to human nature and development. This includes the view of the good person; the idea of the individual with a positive character, strengths, and given virtues; and the idea of the basic distinction between "man as he happens to be" and "man as he could be if he realized his essential nature" (MacIntyre, 1984, p. 52). This approach focus-ing on the positive human being is consequently at odds with the widely dissemi-nated medical model with its purely negative frame of reference emphasizing failure, fault, illness, and classification of mental disorders.

There are different approaches to positive psychology, but here we focus pri-marily on the approach put forward by Seligman (e.g., Seligman, 2002; Seligman & Csikszentmihalyi, 2000) as the foremost advocate of positive psychology. However, what is common to all approaches is this basic starting point: The human being has given potentials for a positive character or virtues. Or, as Sheldon and King (2001, p. 216) answer the question, What is positive psychology?: "Positive psychology revisits 'the average person,' with an interest in finding out what works, what is right, and what is improving."

FROM THE INDIVIDUAL AS ASOCIAL TO THE INDIVIDUAL AS SOCIALLY AND ETHICALLY RESPONSIBLE

The anthropologist Fiske (1992) is among those today concerned with analyzing fundamental starting points or cornerstones on which psychology and the social sciences rest. Fiske states concerning today's metatheoretical situation:

> From Freud to contemporary sociobiologists, from Skinner to social cognitionists, from Goffman to game theorists, the prevailing assumption in Western psychology has been that humans are by nature asocial individualists. Psychologists (and most other social scientists) usually explain social relationships as instrumental means to extrinsic, nonsocial ends, or as constraints on the satisfaction of individual de-sires. (p. 689)

Fiske ascertains that the predominant approach, in both psychology and the other social sciences, is the axiomatic postulate of human beings as asocial and egoistic individuals. A person is thus a priori defined as a self-interested being constantly preoccupied by consuming, using, or even exploiting the social, collective, and material world with the goal of gaining benefits or the best possible result, physi-cally as well as psychologically. Nafstad (2002, 2003) and van Lange (2000) draw similar conclusions about the prioritizing of this idea about asocial human nature in mainstream psychology. Van Lange concludes:

> Within the domain of psychological theory, this assumption of rational self-interest is embedded in several key constructs, such as reinforcement, the pursuit of pleasure, utility maximization (as developed in the context of behavioristic theory, including social learning theory), psychoanalytic theory, and theories of social decision making. (p. 299)

The individual is thus, as shown in contemporary psychology and the other social sciences, often a priori limited to a being constantly occupied by consuming the social and material world, with the goal of attaining the best possible situation for himself or herself, physically as well as psychologically. To keep order in this egoistically motivated consumption of the material and social world, society needs rules of morality. Without such moral rules or social norms, the individual as acting subject would not give any consideration to others as long as this might affect his or her own welfare and comfort negatively. It was the English philosopher Thomas Hobbes (1588–1679) who was first to argue in favor of such a view of human nature. The Greek philosophy that dominated until then held the view that human beings were positive and fundamentally social by nature. Hobbes, however, launched the doctrine that maintained that human beings were basically bad, and not much could be done about it. Thus, morality cannot be anything but social contracts between self-seeking and ruthless human beings. Morality is, therefore, the same as obedience to law. This view of human nature, often termed *psychological egoism*, is a deeply negative view of human nature.

The doctrine opposed to Hobbes', the view that human beings are born as moral beings with a potential for goodness, was proposed by Rousseau (1712–1778). In psychology, Spencer (1871–1939) and McDougall (1820–1903) around the turn of the previous century also attempted to oppose the negative position of psychological egoism. McDougall (1908) argued that human beings have an empathic instinct. However, this view did not gain approval. Thus, as Fiske (1992) and van Lange (2000) concluded, the perspective of the individual as egoistic and directed by self-interest has been, and still is, the a priori position on core human nature in theoretical psychology. However, egoism or hedonism within psychology is more than a historic and culture-bound ideology or a major assumption of human nature. It is also modern psychology's predominant theory of human motivation. According to mainstream psychology, the individual has only one motivation system (Darley, 1991; Nafstad, 2002, 2003). *Self-interest* is regarded as the primary and true motivation, the one from which other motives, including moral and social ones, derive.

Positive psychology, however, rejects this predominant negative assumption of human motivational nature. Positive psychology takes as its starting point the individual as a socially and morally motivated being. Seligman (2002, p. 211) argues this position very strongly: "Current dogma may say that negative motivation is fundamental to human nature and positive motivation merely derives from it, but I have not seen a shred of evidence that compels us to believe this." The task of psychology, therefore, must be also to describe and study positive individual and social character or virtues. As Seligman formulates this claim of an alternative presumption about the human being as a social and moral individual: "This unpacks the meaning of the claim that human beings are moral animals" (p. 133).

By taking the standpoint that humans are fundamentally social and moral, positive psychology places itself again in the midst of the Greek tradition and virtue ethics. In Greek philosophy, the individual was not considered to be such an enough-unto-itself-being—an individual concerned only with taking care of his or her own interests. Goods, resources, and advantages, Aristotle maintained (cf. *The Complete Works of Aristotle;* Barnes, 1984), were not mine and yours to such a great degree as is implied in our social time and culture. In the Aristotelian frame of reference, the person who acts egoistically is making a fundamental error, which in practice excludes the person from social relationships and, therefore, from the good life. Social relationships were concerned with sharing, giving, and taking care of each other (Vetlesen, 1994). For example, in the Aristotelian frame of understanding, a friendship would be a relationship of equality and mutuality, not a "one-way affair" (Vetlesen & Nortvedt, 2000) in which other people are considered to be a means for gaining something or becoming better off. As Vetlesen and Nortvedt described the social relationship of friendship in the Aristotelian approach: "friendship is inseparable from sharing with the other and reciprocating the feelings received" (p. 23). Aristotle thus maintained that individuals have characteristics that serve to preserve their own welfare, as well as *civic virtues* concerned with preserving the welfare of other(s). Central to Aristotle's philosophy of human nature is existence of a human core nature that entails positive relations and communal responsibility.

ON ARISTOTELIAN DEVELOPMENTAL THEORY

The philosopher Wartofsky (1986) argued that on a superordinate level, we may distinguish among three main approaches to the individual and human development in Western science:

1. The Aristotelian or essential frame of understanding of the individual as a virtuous creature.
2. The Darwinian or evolutionary perspective.
3. The social and cultural-historical or Marxist perspective.

Each of these major perspectives represents different a priori basic assumptions about human nature and human development. They are not neglected doctrines today but instead represent vitally ongoing projects in current science.

Positive psychology argues a Darwinian or evolutionary perspective (Seligman, 2002; Seligman & Csikszentmihalyi, 2000). However, as has been shown, positive psychology, with its fundamental idea of positive personal traits and individuals' desire to improve themselves as good people and to be living in truth according to their own potentials, represents an approach squarely in the Aristotelian tradition. Therefore, we next review some aspects of Aristotelian theory to explicate in more detail the philosophical roots and forerunners of positive psychology.

The Aristotelian model focuses on the virtuous individual and those inner traits, dispositions, and motives that qualify the individual to be virtuous. Moreover, in the Aristotelian model, the virtues of the soul are of two sorts: virtue of thought and virtue of character. "Virtue of thought arises and grows mostly from teaching; that is why it needs experience and time. Virtue of character (i.e., of *ethos*) results from habit (ethos)." Hence, it is also clear, as Aristotle states, "none of the virtues of character arise in us naturally" (*Nicomachean Ethics,* Book II, quoted in

Morgan, 2001, pp. 205–206). The topic of intellectual activities, giftedness, creativity, and exceptional cognitive performance is central to positive psychology. But equally important, positive psychology stresses that there are virtues of a different kind: The concept of *good character* constitutes, as shown, one of the conceptual cornerstones of positive psychology. Moreover, for positive psychology, wisdom, courage, humanity, justice, temperance, and transcendence are categories of virtue, which are postulated to be universal virtues (Dahlsgaard, Peterson, & Seligman, 2001; Peterson & Seligman, 2001; Seligman, 2002). Further, the individual normally undergoes continuous development or growth toward a realization of the given virtue potentials. Aristotle further maintains: "Since happiness is a certain sort of activity of the social in accord with complete virtue, we must examine virtue, for that will perhaps also be a way to study happiness better" (*Nicomachean Ethics*, Book I, quoted in Morgan, 2001, p. 204). It is also these ideas of a common core nature for all human beings and continuous development and realization of these human potentials as the source of well-being or happiness that are the central suppositions in positive psychology.

Moreover, in the Aristotelian model with its four causal factors (*causa materialis, causa formalis, causa efficiens,* and *causa finalis*), *growth* or *change* becomes a fundamental dimension of the object or phenomenon. The individual is thus understood as a being constantly driven forward by a dynamic principle, toward that which is better or more perfect. In Book I of the *Nicomachean Ethics*, Aristotle clarifies his perfectionism concept: "Every craft and every line of inquiry, and likewise every action and decision, seems to seek some good; that is why some people were right to describe the good as what everything seeks" (Morgan, 2001, p. 195). The good is what everything strives toward. Therefore, the Aristotelian frame of understanding is the perspective of a core human nature in which change(s) toward something good, better, or more perfect comprises a fundamental aspect. The individual is hence a being who introduces positive goals and values and strives to realize and reach them. The Aristotelian model then takes into account a teleological aspect: The individual as a being lives a life in which thoughts and ideas about future positive goals also influence the direction of actions here and now. The Aristotelian model introduces a distinction between the individual's *possibilities* or *potentials* on the one hand and the individual's *factual* characteristics or *realization* of these on the other hand. Aristotle's idea is, therefore, that we should habituate people to realization of their positive virtues in more perfect or complex ways, so that as a goal, moral and goodness become almost instinctive.

The individual is further, according to Aristotle, a being who is characterized by experiencing joy when exercising his or her inherent or acquired abilities and striving toward realizing them in ways that are experienced as better, more complex, or more perfect. As the philosopher Rawls (1976, p. 426) states on this positive or motivational dynamic principle that Aristotle formulated: "the Aristotelian Principle runs as follows: other things equal, human beings enjoy the exercise of their realized capacities (their innate or trained abilities), and this enjoyment increases the more the capacity is realized, or the greater the complexity." Thus, it is the *process* of *exercising* that is central in the Aristotelian frame of reference.

Positive psychology argues, as does Aristotle, that human beings enjoy the exercise of their capabilities. As Seligman and Csikszentmihalyi (2000, p. 12) reformulate this Aristotelian view on exercise:

Enjoyment, on the other hand, refers to the good feelings people experience when they break through the limits of homeostasis—when they do something that stretches them beyond what they were—in an athletic event, an artistic performance, a good deed, a stimulating conversation. Enjoyment, rather than pleasure, is what leads to personal growth and long term happiness. . . .

As shown, positive psychology clearly adopts and revitalizes an Aristotelian frame of reference and argues that the science of psychology should once again include assumptions about the good or essence-driven motivation and the good person within its hard-core basic assumptions of what a human being is. For positive psychology, in congruence with the Aristotelian model, goodness and morality thus do not come from outside the person. They do not arise from cultural sources nor from the moral rules of society, but from the potentials of the human being himself or herself. Positive psychology, therefore, in accordance with the Aristotelian root, takes as its point of departure that the human being is preprogrammed with a moral software of justice, courage, fairness, and so on. Aristotle, moreover, claims: "none of the virtues of character arise in us naturally . . . Rather we are by nature able to acquire them, and we are completed through habit" (*Nicomachean Ethics, Book II,* quoted in Morgan, 2001, p. 206). As the philosopher Vetlesen (1994, p. 30) formulates this Aristotelian view of human nature: "It is only through such an ongoing process of education and habituation that the individual acquires the virtues. . . ." Thus, it is up to the individual to realize his or her full potential. In addition, positive psychology (Seligman & Csikszentmihalyi, 2000) argues that strengths and virtues can be and must be cultivated. As Sheldon and King (2001, p. 217) advocated the position of positive psychology: "If psychologists allow themselves to see the best as well as the worst in people, they may derive important new understanding of human nature and destiny."

THE CONCEPT OF OPTIMAL OR MORE PERFECT FUNCTIONING IN MODERN PSYCHOLOGY

When an activity becomes cultivated, more complex, or optimal, what is implied? What does it mean to be stretching beyond what we are as psychological beings? What does it imply to flourish, for example, as a social being? In psychology, it was Gestalt psychology and Heinz Werner (1926/1957a) who first and most thoroughly inquired into this question. As Harvey (1997) summed up Gestalt psychology's idea that the individual continually strives to structure, to improve, or to be stretched: "A *Gestalt,* defined by Kohler as 'any segregated whole' (Kohler, 1929, p. 192) is rendered maximally distinctive through the processes of 'making precise' and 'leveling', terms used originally by Wulf to describe transitions of memory toward the attainment of good form, a better and more harmonious fit with the whole (Petermann, 1932, p. 247)." Werner's (1926/1957a) idea was that it is possible to postulate on a very general level that all individuals as cognitive, affective, and social beings go through a common developmental process toward what is better, more distinct, precise, or perfect. The hallmark of this general developmental process is, Werner (1957b, p. 126) maintained: "that wherever development occurs it proceeds from a state of relative globality and lack of differentiation to a state of increasing differentiation, articulation, and hierarchic integration." Werner's developmental principle, his orthogenetic principle, moreover postulates that positive change must always be assumed to shift from a diffuse state toward constantly more differentiation, variation, progression, and hierarchic integration. The orthogenetic principle represents the most systematic abstract attempt in modern psychology to describe optimal functioning (Baldwin, 1967). According to this principle, when actions become differentiated, that is, when development takes place, there is, moreover, simultaneously a hierarchic integration: Some functions and goals come first and are superordinate compared to others. Development toward the more mature and perfect action was then for Werner (1926/1957a) a process that moves from the simple to the more distinct, complex, or perfect action. This entails further a process that moves from a diffuse to a more ordered system of action, from an indistinct to a more articulated system of action, from a rigid to a more flexible system of action, and from a labile to a more stable and consistent system of action. Positive psychology also holds a fundamental assumption that living systems are self-organizing and oriented toward such an increasing differentiation and complexity. Deci and Ryan (2000, p. 230) maintained about this principle of more elaborate or complex functioning: "We suggest that it is inherent in people's nature to action in the direction of increased psychological differentiation and integration in terms of their capacities, their valuing processes, and their social connectedness." Or, as Massimini and Delle Fave (2000, p. 27) formulate this position of optimal functioning:

> . . . a person will search for increasingly complex challenges in the associated activities and will improve his or her skill accordingly. This process has been defined as *cultivation*; it fosters the growth of complexity not only in the performance of flow activities but in individual behavior as a whole. (original italics)

Consequently, from Aristotle, via Gestalt psychology, to positive psychology, cultivation, complexity, and optimal functioning are central concepts: Living organisms are oriented toward increasing complexity.

Further, in both the Aristotelian and the positive psychology approaches, the concept of optimal functioning is associated with the concept of *the good life, well-being*, or *happiness*. Aristotle's model of the good life, *eudaimonia*, is "the state of being well and doing well in being well" (MacIntyre, 1984, p. 148). Thus, for Aristotle, what constitutes the good for man "is a complete human life lived at its best, and the exercise of the virtues is a necessary and central part of such a life . . ." (p. 149). In positive psychology, however, there are two different approaches to *the good life*: hedonic approaches and eudaimonic approaches. Seligman (2002, p. 289) states, on his view of the differences between these two approaches, that we may: "divide research into hedonic approaches that concentrate on emotions, and eudaimonic approaches that concentrate on the fully functioning person" (cf. Rogers, 1963). Psychological hedonism, or the principle of utility, as the philosopher Bentham (1748–1832; see Bentham, 1789) calls it, is thus also part of positive psychology. However, far more positive psychologists take a eudaimonic approach to the good life (Seligman, 2002). The eudaimonic approach is concerned with the whole person and his or her optimal functioning and development in all areas of life. For instance, Ryan and Deci (2001) define the good life as "optimal functioning and experience" (p. 142) or as "the striving for perfection that represents the realization of one's true potential" (p. 144). Ryan and Deci thus maintain that the good life is well-being, which arises when the individual is functioning optimally. The good life is thus characterized by development from simple to more complex or optimal functioning. However, we next discuss how positive psychology has advanced the Aristotelian model on "the state of being well and doing well in being well."

THE EUDAIMONIC APPROACH TO *THE GOOD LIFE* IN POSITIVE PSYCHOLOGY

Having the Aristotelian model of a developmental continuum from the simple to the more complex as his point of departure, Seligman (2002) postulates a model of four different forms of the good life. Seligman terms the simplest of the four forms of good life as *a pleasant life*. Seligman describes the pleasant life as, "a life that successfully pursues the positive emotions about the present, past and future" (2002, p. 262). The pleasant life is characterized by positive emotions. The pleasant life is similar to an understanding of the good life characterized by a hedonic approach to the issue of what good life is. But in contrast to, for example, Diener's (2000) theory of subjective well-being, which focuses on positive emotions, absence of negative emotions and a judgment about an individual's life, Seligman focuses only on positive emotions in this form of the good life.

What Seligman (2002) terms *a good life* is more complex than the pleasant life. *A good life* is, according to Seligman: "using your signature strengths to obtain abundant gratification in the main realms of one's life." (p. 262). A good life is, therefore, a life in which you use your special character properties, "signature strengths," in important areas of life to experience "gratifications." *Authenticity* is an important concept for Seligman in this connection. Authenticity describes the experience that comes from using your own special character properties to obtain "gratifications." An authentic life is thus a prerequisite for a good life. Therefore, Seligman's standpoint is that the good life is to be using your signature strengths, being true to your own character or fundamental nature of virtues.

Seligman (2002) maintains further that a good life cannot be attained as a permanent state, but is a continuous development of the individual's strengths and values. A good life is, therefore, a life in continuous development or growth. Seligman thus takes the view that the individual is normally in a process of development, and the individual naturally has a given capacity for using his or her innate character traits. A good life is, therefore, not unattainable for human beings: Normally, they have the capacities that are necessary for this form of the good life.

The third form of the good life, which is closer to the optimally functioning individual, is for Seligman (2002) *the meaningful life.* The meaningful life adds, in addition to the good life, an affiliation to something "larger than yourself." Seligman defines the meaningful life in the following way: "The meaningful life: using your signature strengths and virtues in the service of something much larger than you are" (p. 263). Seligman, however, leaves the question of what can be conceived of as larger than yourself up to the individual to define. Moreover, it naturally follows that the most complex form of the good life is for Seligman *the full life.* This builds on all of the three previous forms of the good life and includes their characteristics. Seligman defines the full life: "Finally, a full life consists in experiencing positive emotions about the past and future, savoring positive feelings from pleasures, deriving abundant gratification from your signature strengths, and using these strengths in the service of something larger to obtain meaning" (p. 263). The full life is, therefore, for Seligman, a life in which the individual uses his or her capacities in an optimal way to serve something larger than himself or herself to give life meaning.

Accordingly, the full life is for Seligman (2002) the same as optimal functioning. This is how human beings are functioning at their best or most complex. At their best, individuals, furthermore, act both in concert with their own premises and capacities and in concert with the surroundings. Thus, positive psychology and Seligman explicitly both defend and revitalize the Aristotelian model with its emphasis on acting from both self-benefiting as well as other-benefiting virtues. Seligman also emphasizes that when the individual functions best, he or she has a good experience of life. The good life is thus not a fixed state, but for Seligman it is a life in striving toward the realization of your true positive human "potentials" in ever better ways. Positive psychology is, as now shown, clearly in accordance with an Aristotelian tradition in which the good life is one in which human beings are always in a process of development from the simple to the more complex or more perfect. Positive psychology, however, offers a more fully fledged life span theory of development of well-being or happiness, identifying and elaborating four different forms of the good life, varying from the simple to the more complex good life.

Might it be that such views of human nature, focusing on strengths and positive potentials, are just what psychology and the social sciences need when embarking on the huge and challenging problems of our time? To face the pressing problems of our civilization with knowledge based on the prevailing position of the individual as an asocial egoist is totally insufficient (Nafstad, 2002, 2003; Thurow, 1996). Moreover, to fight inequality, dehumanization, and a difficult life with the help of a psychology based on the predominant medical-oriented model focusing on sickness, weaknesses, and diagnostic categories is an endeavor bound to fail.

THE MULTICULTURAL PERSPECTIVE

In contemporary research, a multicultural perspective is maintained as an increasingly dominant and ethical imperative for psychological research and practice: "multiculturalism is, at its core, a moral movement that is intended to enhance the dignity, rights, and recognized worth of marginalized groups" (Fowers & Richardson, 1996, p. 609). One objection to the normative and universal ideals inherent in the Aristotelian position is that it does not accommodate the core principle of a multicultural perspective encompassing respect for all types of optimal functioning, development, and good life. Such a criticism was indeed made of Werner's perspective on optimal functioning when it was proposed (see Glick, 1992). An objection against the dynamic perspective, as Werner formulated it, is that every concrete actualization of such an ideal, abstract developmental principle of more complex activities inevitably will be influenced by predominant cultural, social, political, and personal values. Notions or ideas about ideal development are, in the end, inevitably created and formed in a subtle interplay between the values and ideals in society, the social and cultural conditions in which the researcher in question works, as well as the traditions of the discipline (Baumrind, 1982; Bruner, 1986; Cirillo & Wapner, 1986). Maintaining and giving priority to certain developmental goals and not others is thus an expression of the predominant values and power structures of the culture and time period in question (Bruner, 1986; Cirillo & Wapner, 1986; Foucault, 1972, 1978; Gergen, 1989, 1991). Seligman (2002) also argues that "fully functioning" is a culture-bound concept. An objection to Werner's orthogenetic principle was that it merely reflects the modern, dominant Western value pattern: modernism's ideal of just such a constantly greater progression toward more ordered, complex, articulated, and consistent developmental systems.

This type of criticism may also be directed toward positive psychology when attempting to establish parameters for development toward the good life. In fact, the concept of positive development as now demonstrated must be defined and analyzed in terms of five elements or dimensions: *motivation, action, goals, context,* and *(social) time.* Hence, when conceptualizing in terms of what is good or bad, wise or not wise, noble or ignoble, admirable or deplorable, positive psychology must decide how to deal with the influences of culture and social or historical time. Indeed, in the end, almost all discussions about approaches and paradigms in psychology thus are related in some way to this theme of the individual, history and social context(s), and/or the interaction among them (Blakar & Nafstad, 1982; Bronfenbrenner, 1979, 1992; Lewin, 1935; Nafstad, 1980, 1982; Pettigrew, 1997; Walsh, Craik, & Price, 1992).

THE HUMAN BEING: UNIVERSAL, LOCAL, OR UNIQUE?

In psychology, the Gestalt-oriented social psychologist Kurt Lewin's (1935) *field theory* has often been used as a frame of reference for discussing how theories take into account both personal and environmental factors and the interaction between them. In Lewin's schematic model, human actions or behavior (B) were conceptualized as a function (f) of both the person (P) and the environment (E): $B = f (P, E)$. Thus, a most crucial question for psychology throughout its history has been: Where are the defining and stabilizing forces of individual functioning to be found? in the individual? in the contexts? or in the interactions between them? As we have argued, dispositions, character, motivation, and goals represent central conceptual cornerstones of positive psychology. How person-centered is, then, positive psychology's approach? Is positive psychology arguing in favor of a universal psychology or for indigenous psychologies?

We again start our analysis by examining Aristotle's position. He argues that when we travel and meet people in different cultures, we nevertheless "can see how *every human being* is akin and beloved to a human being" (*Nicomachean Ethics,* Book VIII, quoted in Morgan, 2001, p. 268; italics added). Aristotle, thus, as demonstrated, argues the position of common features in different cultural groups. Parts of psychology and other social sciences have also always taken as a starting point that people in the past, present, and future have some given common capacities or characteristics. Furthermore, it has been assumed that *existing* and *adapting* are experiences that also give common characteristics and similarities (Darwin 1809–1882; see Darwin, 1859). The task then becomes to describe validly that which is common or universal to human beings. In such a universalist approach, groups of people are thus compared in order to illuminate aspects of the assumed common and homogeneous core. As Rohner (1975, p. 2) formulated the universalist position: "The universalist approach asks about the nature of human nature, or, more specifically, about researchable features of 'human nature.'"

In psychology and the other social sciences, however, some researchers adopted a fundamentally different point of departure on the individual: Every individual, every society is unique and different from all others. This assumption, the *idiographic tradition*, takes its principal arguments from, among others, Kierkegaard's (1813–1855) philosophy. Kierkegaard's (1843/1962, 1846/1968) philosophy did indeed represent a protest against the philosophy of his time, which was concerned only with what was common to all human beings. Kierkegaard's idea was, on the contrary, that it is the individual, the single person, who must be the frame of reference. Moreover, the individual as he or she exists and lives is more than the universal human being. The individual is thus a uniquely existing being. Consequently, it is not the species of mankind, but the single individual with whom we should be concerned. Thus, when studying human life and development, we must start with the individual or the person. All human beings are committed to their subjective truths, and it is always only the single individual who acts.

The idiographic position, with the idea of uniquely subjective experience as the basis of human actions, thus constitutes another important and central approach in psychological research. Gordon Allport was the first to be associated with this debate between nomothetic and idiographic approaches. Allport (1937/1961, 1946, 1960) maintained that both perspectives were legitimate but that an idiographic basis was to be preferred in studies of personality. Eysenck (1947, 1955, 1956, 1967) held, on the other hand, the opposite standpoint: Personality psychology, too, must be nomothetically oriented. Thus, the debate between a nomothetic and idiographic approach in psychology was primarily raised in the field of personality psychology.

Let us then consider the other central concept, the environment, in Lewin's (1935) formula. In anthropology, the unique or radical relativistic approach has maintained that no cultures are alike. Consequently, it is not possible to make generalizations. Hypotheses about cross-cultural or universal similarities and possible common claims of cause and effect are impossible (Benedict, 1934, 1946). Each culture must be considered as a unique configuration and may be understood only in its totality. A cultural element has no meaning except in its context. Thus, the single elements may be understood, and can only be understood, within the network of interpretations that the culture itself represents. The task of seeking what is common is thus meaningless. All cultures are special and unique. Nomothetic-oriented psychology and social science, consequently, represent an impossible idea.

In contemporary philosophy and psychology, there are many who argue that it is difficult or impossible to hold on to this idea of human nature having any such common core potentials (Bruner, 1986, 1990; Gergen, 1991, 1994; Kvale, 1992; Shotter & Gergen, 1989). The Aristotelian idea that the individual is preprogrammed with a personal and moral software of justice, wisdom, and so on, and, further, that it is up to the individual to realize, is thus not at all reasonable. Gergen (1982, 1994), therefore, argues in favor of a psychology concerned with understanding and attempting to account for social processes (in terms of social contexts and social and historical time) that create and fill a culture's concepts; for example, the concepts of human nature, the nature of human motivation, our personality or our self, and so on. Each culture thus creates at all times its own content of truth as to what human nature contains. The descriptions and concepts that psychology has at its disposal must not be understood as anything but what

they indeed are: cultural and historical objects. Every culture and every historical epoch creates its discourses, its forms of understanding, and its truths, for
example, about the concept of human nature and human virtues. The nomencla-
ture of psychology is thus not given its content through some form of more independent reality, for example, about how human nature *really* is. Consequently, the
task of seeking the common virtuous being, what is common and similar among
individuals, is not meaningful. Every culture creates its own content of meaning
as to what human nature is. Human nature, virtues, and individuality are thus
created by the prevailing concrete cultural patterns. People must adapt to, maintain, and reproduce this pattern of cultural values and images about what human
nature and personality is and should be.

Thus, the historical-cultural approach of today argued by the social construc-
tivists (e.g., Cushman, 1990; Gergen, 1989, 1994; Kvale, 1992; Shotter & Gergen,
1989) maintains that it is not a meaningful research issue to seek what is universal, common, and similar. The idea of ordered development, for example, from the
simple to the more complex, therefore, is rejected as being a typical idea from the
romantic and humanistic tradition in Western culture. And what would be, in
any case, better or more perfect development?

As previously discussed, positive psychology argues, in the same way as
Aristotle, that there are some common dimensions or dispositions in core
human nature. In fact, positive psychology argues in favor of a rather strong
universalism position. Human nature within positive psychology is to be understood more as a preprogrammed bundle of psychological software. The
human being is thus, for instance, programmed with a moral software of justice,
wisdom, humanity, courage, temperance, and transcendence. Human nature is,
therefore, not totally plastic and able to be formed by social time and culture.
However, this does not mean that positive psychology does not accept the idea
that human nature also is a product of history and cultural environment. As
Seligman and Csikszentmihalyi (2001, p. 90) contend: "We are acutely aware
that what one considers positive is, in part, a function of one's particular ethnic
tradition and social condition." But at the same time, Seligman and Csikszentmihalyi stress:

> . . . we believe that our common humanity is strong enough to suggest psychologi-
> cal goals to strive for that cut across social and cultural divides. Just as physical
> health, adequate nutrition, and freedom from harm and exploitation are univer-
> sally valued, so must psychologists ultimately aim to understand the positive
> states, traits and institutions that all cultures value. (p. 90)

Seligman and Csikszentmihalyi thus take as given and embrace the Aristotelian
basic position (1) ". . . what I strive toward as an individual is the perfection of
what it means to be a man" (Vetlesen, 1994, p. 30), and (2) what is good for me as
a unique person is what is good for humans as universal beings (cf. Rogers, 1964).
As a consequence, social practices for positive psychology will always be compared to and evaluated in the light of a core human nature of virtues that may,
and should, be developed and realized.

We might, therefore, conclude that positive psychology revitalizes not only
the Aristotelian idea of the positive individual but also the view of the universal
individual. The person, the P component in Lewin's classic formula, is given

more weight in positive psychology than is typical for large areas of contemporary psychology.

DIFFERENT LEVELS OF SCIENTIFIC ACTIVITY

Science may be divided into separate but related levels of activity. A pragmatic division of scientific levels of activity is to distinguish among: (1) metatheory, (2) theory, (3) design, (4) primary method, (5) data, and (6) phenomena. To succeed, a science or particular field of science must continually be concerned with reflection on and analysis of all of these levels of activity, systematically developing all levels and the relationships among them. To claim to be a new paradigm, any field of science must develop new perspectives and tools at each of these levels.

It is the metatheoretical level of positive psychology that we have analyzed. It is also primarily on the metatheoretical level that positive psychology distinguishes itself from contemporary mainstream psychology and attempts to constitute a corrective, demanding that contemporary psychology reflect on and change its views of human nature. However, we conclude that positive psychology does not demand a fundamental paradigm shift in psychology. Moreover, concerning the other levels of scientific activity, contrary to shifts in metatheoretical assumptions that positive psychology claims, Seligman and Csikszentmihalyi (2000, p. 13) state very clearly: "The same methods and in many cases the same laboratories and the next generation of scientists, with a slight shift of emphasis and funding, will be used to measure, understand, and build those characteristics that make life most worth living." Thus, when it comes to doing specific research, positive psychology connects to mainstream psychology. Positive psychology, therefore, concerns itself primarily with the attempt to change and redefine the basic a priori assumptions or perspectives on the nature of the individual and the interaction between the individual and its contexts.

In tracing the roots of positive psychology, it has to be emphasized that the positive about humans—human virtues, personal goals, and personal expressions—also constitute the core ideas of humanistic psychology (Jourard, 1974; Maslow, 1965, 1968; Moss, 1999; Rogers, 1959, 1980). However, inasmuch as the intimate relationships between positive psychology and humanistic psychology have already been extensively discussed (see, e.g., Taylor, 2001), we have chosen to try to identify and point out other central historical, philosophical, and epistemological roots of positive psychology. Moreover, because humanistic psychology, but also positive psychology, covers such a huge diversity of different approaches to psychology, a thorough analysis of these relationships would be beyond the scope of this chapter. However, while parts of humanistic psychology confront and reject mainstream psychology's approach in general and argue for fundamental shifts in all of the scientific levels mentioned previously, positive psychology as formulated by Seligman is more clearly in accordance with mainstream psychology as to general methodology (Jørgensen, 2003).

It is not just in positive psychology that the Aristotelian model of a virtuous human nature is being revitalized today. In the course of the past decade, ethical theory in philosophy has focused more and more on the assumption of the individual as having virtuous motives (Baron, Pettit, & Slote, 1997). As Slote (1997, p. 234) argues: "A truly moral person finds an appeal, say, to benevolence inherently forceful and attractive. . . ." Or, as the philosopher Tranøy (1998, p. 39, our translation) also maintains: "The two capabilities—the capability to acquire language and the capability to obtain morality—are closely interrelated with each other and together they are *constitutive for becoming a human being*" (original italics). Consequently, in philosophy and ethics today, some contend that the existence of human morality and goodness can a priori be taken for granted and does not need more foundation. As we have demonstrated, this is definitely not true in mainstream theoretical psychology. The foremost task of positive psychology so far has, consequently, been to argue in favor of, and legitimate in psychology, the very idea of the moral and good human being.

The strong interest for positive psychology and ethics in general and for positive character traits or virtues in particular, however, is hardly coincidental. Given the societal and ecological challenges of today, it is natural and important that someone begin to take responsibility for an imperative shift in psychology's predominantly negative bias toward a science of positive subjective experiences, positive individual traits, and positive social institutions and values (Nafstad, in press).

CONCLUDING REMARKS

One of the founders of modern psychology, William James (1842–1910), was concerned with the problem that Foucault (1972, 1980) conceived in terms of *regimes of truth*. James (1890/1962, 1909/1979) formulated what might be termed psychology's ethical imperative: not to exclude any views of human beings. James' (1909/1979, p. 19) point of departure was that human nature is so complex that psychology cannot afford to exclude any perspectives or points of view:

> We have so many different businesses with nature . . . The philosophic attempt to define nature so that no one's business is left out, so that no one lies outside the door saying "Where do I come in?" is sure in advance to fail. The most a philosophy can hope for is not to lock out any interest forever.

The obligation that James formulated here demands in practice that psychology continually try to identify and analyze its philosophical and historical roots as they constitute the perspectives or horizons that become our range of vision or our windows to the phenomena under study. Psychology needs the window to the human being as morally and socially good and positive to be reopened, so that this vital perspective is no longer a view "left outside the door."

REFERENCES

Allport, G. W. (1946). Geneticism versus ego-structure in theories of personality. *British Journal of Educational Psychology, 16*, 57–58.

Allport, G. W. (1954). The historical background of modern social psychology. In G. Lindzey (Ed.), *The handbook of social psychology* (Vol. 1, pp. 3–56). Reading, MA: Addison-Wesley.

Allport, G. W. (1960). *Personality and social encounter*. Boston: Beacon Press.

Allport, G. W. (1961). *Pattern and growth in personality*. New York: Holt; Rinehart and Winston. (Original work published 1937)

Arnett, J. J. (2002). The psychology of globalization. *American Psychologist, 57,* 774–783.

Baldwin, A. L. (1967). *Theories of child development.* New York: Wiley.

Barnes, J. (Ed.). (1984). *The complete works of Aristotle* (Vols. 1–2). Princeton, NJ: Princeton University Press.

*Baron, M. W., Pettit, P., & Slote, M. (Eds.). (1997). *Three methods of ethics.* Malden, MA: Blackwell.

Baumrind, D. (1982). Adolescent sexuality: Comments on William's and Silka's comments on Baumrind. *American Psychologist, 37,* 1402–1403.

Benedict, R. (1934). *Patterns of culture.* Boston: Houghton Mifflin.

Benedict, R. (1946). *The chrysanthemum and the sword: Patterns of Japanese culture.* Boston: Houghton Mifflin.

Bentham, J. (1789). *Introduction to the principles of morals and legislation.* London: Payne.

Blakar, R. M., & Nafstad, H. E. (1982). The family: A social-developmental framework for understanding psychopathology and deviant behavior. *Psychiatry and Social Science, 2,* 23–34.

Bronfenbrenner, U. (1979). *The ecology of human development: Experiments by nature and design.* Cambridge, MA: Harvard University Press.

Bronfenbrenner, U. (1992). Ecological systems theory. In R. Vasta (Ed.), *Six theories of child development* (pp. 185–246). Greenwich, CT: JAI Press.

Bruner, J. (1986). Value prepositions of developmental theory. In L. Cirillo & S. Wapner (Eds.), *Value presuppositions in theories of human development* (pp. 19–28). Hillsdale, NJ: Erlbaum.

Bruner, J. (1990). *Acts of meaning.* Cambridge, MA: Harvard University Press.

Cirillo, L., & Wapner, S. (Eds.). (1986). *Value presuppositions in theories of human development.* Hillsdale, NJ: Erlbaum.

Cushman, P. (1990). Why the self is empty: Toward a historically situated psychology. *American Psychologist, 45,* 599–611.

Dahlsgaard, K. A., Peterson, C., & Seligman, M. E. P. (2001). *Toward a classification of strengths and virtues: Lessons from history.* Unpublished manuscript, University of Pennsylvania, Philadelphia.

Darley, J. M. (1991). Altruism and prosocial behavior research: Reflections and prospects. In M. S. Clark (Ed.), *Prosocial behavior* (pp. 312–327). Newbury Park, CA: Sage.

Darwin, C. (1859). *On the origin of species.* London: Murray.

Deci, E. L., & Ryan, R. M. (2000). The "what" and "why" of goal pursuits: Human needs and the self-determination of behavior. *Psychological Inquiry, 11,* 227–268.

Diener, E. (2000). Subjective well-being: The science of happiness and a proposal for a national index. *American Psychologist, 55,* 34–43.

Eysenck, H. J. (1947). *Dimensions of personality.* London: Routledge & Keagan Paul.

Eysenck, H. J. (1955). The science of personality: Nomothetic! *Psychological Review, 61,* 339–342.

Eysenck, H. J. (1956). The inheritance of extraversion-introversion. *Acta Psychologica, 12,* 95–112.

Eysenck, H. J. (1967). *The biological basis of personality.* Springfield, IL: Thomas.

Farr, R. M. (1996). *The roots of modern social psychology.* Cambridge, MA: Blackwell.

Fiske, A. P. (1992). The four elementary forms of sociality: Framework for a unified theory of social relations. *Psychological Review, 99,* 689–723.

*Foucault, M. (1972). *The archeology of knowledge.* New York: Harper Colophon.

Foucault, M. (1973). *Birth of the clinic.* London: Tavistock.

Foucault, M. (1978). *The history of sexuality: An introduction* (Vol. 1). New York: Pantheon.

Foucault, M. (1980). *Power/knowledge.* New York: Pantheon.

Fowers, B. J., & Richardson, F. C. (1996). Why is multiculturalism good? *American Psychologist, 51,* 609–621.

Gergen, K. J. (1973). Social psychology as history. *Journal of Personality and Social Psychology, 26,* 309–320.

Gergen, K. J. (1982). *Toward transformation in social knowledge.* New York: Springer Verlag.

Gergen, K. J. (1985). The social constructionist movement in modern psychology. *American Psychologist, 40,* 266–275.

Gergen, K. J. (1989). Social psychology and the wrong revolution. *European Journal of Social Psychology, 19,* 463–484.

Gergen, K. J. (1991). *The saturated self: Dilemmas of identity in contemporary life.* New York: Basic Books.

Gergen, K. J. (1994). *Realities and relationships: Soundings in social construction.* Cambridge, MA: Harvard University Press.

Glick, J. (1992). Werner's relevance for contemporary developmental psychology. *Developmental Psychology, 28,* 558–565.

Harvey, O. J. (1997). Beliefs, knowledge, and meaning from the perspective of the perceiver: Need for structure-order. In C. McCarty & S. A. Haslam (Eds.), *The message of social psychology* (pp. 146–165). Cambridge, MA: Blackwell.

James, W. (1962). *Psychology: Briefer course.* New York: Collier Books. (Original work published 1890)

James, W. (1979). *A pluralistic universe.* Cambridge, MA: Harvard University Press. (Original work published 1909)

Jørgensen, I. S. (2003). *Positiv psykologi: En metateoretisk analyze* [Positive psychology: A metatheoretical analysis]. Unpublished Masters thesis, University of Oslo, Oslo, Norway.

Jourard, S. M. (1974). *The healthy personality: An approach from the viewpoint of humanistic psychology.* New York: MacMillan.

Kierkegaard, S. (1962). *Either/or* (Vol. 1). Princeton, NJ: Princeton University Press. (Original work published 1843)

Kierkegaard, S. (1968). *Concluding unscientific postscript.* Princeton, NJ: Princeton University Press. (Original work published 1846)

Kohler, W. (1929). *Gestalt psychology.* New York: Liveright.

Kvale, S. (Ed.). (1992). *Psychology and postmodernism.* Newbury Park, CA: Sage.

Lakatos, I. (1970). Falsification and the methodology of scientific research programs. In I. Lakatos & A. Musgrave (Eds.), *Criticism and growth of knowledge* (pp. 91–196). Cambridge, England: Cambridge University Press.

Lewin, K. (1935). *A dynamic theory of personality.* New York: McGraw-Hill.

MacIntyre, A. (1984). *After virtue: A study in moral theory.* Notre Dame, IN: University of Notre Dame Press.

Maddux, J. E. (2002). Stopping the "madness": Positive psychology and the deconstruction of the illness ideology and *DSM.* In C. R. Snyder & S. J. Lopez (Eds.), *Handbook of positive psychology* (pp. 13–25). New York: Oxford University Press.

Martin, J., & Sugarman, J. (2001). Modernity, postmodernity, and psychology. *American Psychologist, 56,* 370–371.

Maslow, A. H. (1965). A philosophy of psychology: The need for a mature science of human nature. In F. T. Severin (Ed.), *Humanistic viewpoints in psychology* (pp. 17–33). New York: McGraw-Hill.

Maslow, A. H. (1968). *Toward a psychology of being* (2nd ed.). New York: Van Nostrand Reinhold.

Massimini, F., & Delle Fave, A. (2000). Individual development in a bio-cultural perspective. *American Psychologist, 55,* 24–33.

McDougall, W. (1908). *An introduction to social psychology.* London: Methuen.

Mendelsohn, E. (1977). The social construction of scientific knowledge. In E. Mendelsohn, P. Weingert, & R. Whitley (Eds.), *The social production of scientific knowledge* (pp. 3–26). Dordrecht, The Netherlands: Reidel.

Morgan, M. L. (2001). *Classics of moral and political theory.* Cambridge, MA: Hackett.

*Moss, D. (Ed.). (1999). *Humanistic and transpersonal psychology: A historical and biographical sourcebook.* Westport, CT: Greenwood Press.

Nafstad, H. E. (1980). The child's development environment: The nursery school as a welfare component. *International Journal of Early Childhood, 12,* 17–22.

Nafstad, H. E. (1982). Preschool children: Inquiry into interconnections between social class, language and training programs. *Scandinavian Journal of Educational Research, 26,* 121–139.

*Nafstad, H. E. (2002). The neo-liberal ideology and the self-interest paradigm as resistance to change. *Radical Psychology, 3,* 3–21.

Nafstad, H. E. (2003). *Egoism and altruism: Values and assumptions defining psychology.* Manuscript submitted for publication.

Nafstad, H. E. (in press). Subject ethics: Integrating basic, applied and professional ethics in particular fields of practice. In R. Barnett, P. Jarvis, & J. Strain (Eds.), *Ethics, professions and higher education: Creating a discourse in the real world with real people.* London: University of Surrey Press.

Petermann, B. (1932). *The Gestalt theory and the problem of configuration.* New York: Harcourt Brace.

Peterson, C., & Seligman, M. E. P. (2001). *Values in action (VIA) classification of strengths.* Washington, DC: American Psychological Association.

Pettigrew, T. F. (1997). Personality and social structure: Social psychological contributions. In R. Hogan, J. Johnson, & S. Briggs (Eds.), *Handbook of personality psychology* (pp. 417–438). New York: Academic Press.

Rawls, J. (1976). *A theory of justice.* Oxford, England: Oxford University Press.

Rogers, C. R. (1959). A theory of therapy, personality, and interpersonal relationships, as developed in the client-centered framework. In S. Koch (Ed.), *Psychology: A study of a science* (Vol. 3, pp. 184–256). New York: McGraw-Hill.

Rogers, C. R. (1963). The concept of the fully functioning person. *Psychotherapy: Theory, Research, and Practice, 1,* 17–26.

Rogers, C. R. (1964). Toward a modern approach to values: The valuing process in the mature person. *Journal of Abnormal and Social Psychology, 68,* 160–167.

Rogers, C. R. (1980). *A way of being.* Boston: Houghton Mifflin.

Rohner, R. P. (1975). *They love me, they love me not: A worldwide study of the effects of parental acceptance and rejection.* New Haven, CT: HRAF Press.

Ryan, R. M., & Deci, E. L. (2001). On happiness and human potentials: A review of research on hedonic and eudaimonic well-being. *Annual Review of Psychology, 52,* 141–166.

Seligman, M. E. P. (2002). *Authentic happiness: Using the new positive psychology to realize your potential for lasting fulfillment.* New York: Free Press.

Seligman, M. E. P., & Csikszentmihalyi, M. (Eds.). (2000). Positive psychology. *American Psychologist, 55*(1).

Seligman, M. E. P., & Csikszentmihalyi, M. (2001). Reply to comments. *American Psychologist, 56,* 89–90.

Sheldon, K. M., & King, L. (2001). Why positive psychology is necessary. *American Psychologist, 56,* 216–217.

Shotter, J., & Gergen, K. J. (1989). *Texts of identity.* Newbury Park, CA: Sage.

Slote, M. (1997). Virtue ethics. In M. W. Baron, P. Pettit, & M. Slote (Eds.), *Three methods of ethics* (pp. 175–238). Malden, MA: Blackwell.

*Snyder, C. R., & Lopez, S. J. (Eds.). (2002). *Handbook of positive psychology.* New York: Oxford University Press.

Taylor, E. (2001). Positive psychology and humanistic psychology: A reply to Seligman. *Journal of Humanistic Psychology, 41,* 13–29.

Thurow, L. (1996). *The future of capitalism: How today's economic forces shape tomorrow's world.* London: Nicholas Brealey.

Tranøy, K. E. (1998). Om å oppgradere allmennmoralen [On upgrading general moral]. In J. Wetlesen (Ed.), *Hva er kasuistikk* [What is casuistic?] (pp. 30–39). Oslo, Norway: University of Oslo.

van Lange, P. A. M. (2000). Beyond self-interest: A set of propositions relevant to interpersonal orientations. In W. Stroebe & M. Hewstone (Eds.), *European review of social psychology* (Vol. 11, pp. 297–331). Chichester, England: Wiley.

Vetlesen, A. J. (1994). *Perception, empathy and judgment: An inquiry into the preconditions of moral performance.* University Park: Pennsylvania State University.

Vetlesen, A. J., & Nortvedt, P. (2000). *Følelser og moral* [Emotions and moral]. Oslo, Norway: Gyldendal Akademisk.

Walsh, W. B., Craik, K. H., & Price, R. H. (Eds.). (1992). *Person-environment psychology: Models and perspectives.* Hillsdale, NJ: Erlbaum.

Wartofsky, M. W. (1986). On the creation and transformation of norms of human development. In L. Cirillo & S. Wapner (Eds.), *Value presuppositions in theories of human development* (pp. 113–133). Hillsdale, NJ: Erlbaum.

Werner, H. (1957a). *Comparative psychology of mental development.* New York: International Universities Press. (Original work published 1926)

*Werner, H. (1957b). The concept of development from a comparative and organismic point of view. In D. B. Harris (Ed.), *The concept of development* (pp. 125–148). Minneapolis: University of Minnesota Press.

Wrightsman, L. (1992). *Assumptions about human nature: Implications for researchers and practitioners.* Newbury Park, CA: Sage.

CHAPTER 3

The Good Life, Broadly and Narrowly Considered

LAURA A. KING, JENNIFER EMILIA EELLS, and CHAD M. BURTON

MUCH OF THE field of psychology is occupied with the question of how to help human beings lead better lives. Researchers and practitioners have become increasingly interested in promoting lives that could be broadly defined as "good"—lives that are exemplary in a variety of ways—in terms of fulfillment, moral character, physical health, success, or excellence. Although for centuries philosophers have puzzled over the definition of "the good life" (cf. Aristotle, 1962; Becker, 1992; Cottingham, 1998), this question has rarely been broached explicitly in the field of psychology (with some exceptions, e.g., Keyes, Shmotkin, & Ryff, 2002; Ryan & Deci, 2001; Ryff & Singer, 1998; Waterman, 1993). Historically, some theorists have described the optimally functioning person. For example, Allport (1961) viewed the "healthy, mature person" as someone who possessed a variety of functional characteristics, including the capacity for close relationships, a positive view of himself or herself, common sense, objectivity about the self and others, the capacity for self-extension, and, perhaps most importantly, a unifying philosophy of life. Maslow (1954), likewise, described self-actualizers as individuals who maintained a capacity for awe and peak experiences; who were creative, democratic, and unpretentious; and who possessed a nonhostile sense of humor and a deep compassion for others. However, in contemporary research, the psychological definition of "the good life" remains largely *implicit* in the outcomes we choose to study and promote. In this chapter, we explore this implicit definition of the good life. In so doing, we first consider the role of positive mental states (i.e., happiness) in psychology's approach to the good life. Next, we consider research on folk concepts of the good life—to see how "just plain folk" approach the important question of what makes a life good. Finally, we consider, amidst all the focus on happiness, the role of unhappiness in the good life.

Preparation of this chapter and the research reported within were funded by NIMH Grant 54142 to Laura A. King.

IMPLICIT DEFINITIONS OF THE GOOD LIFE:
THE PROBLEM OF HAPPINESS

Perusing the psychological literature, in general, it may be difficult to argue with the idea that the psychological notion of the good life is the absence of mental illness. As has been argued by the founders of the positive psychology movement, the prevention and treatment of disease has occupied a large portion of empirical work in psychology (Seligman & Csikszentmihalyi, 2000; see also Ryff & Singer, 1998). An examination of the outcomes that we seek to track, predict, or enhance tells us that these outcomes are implicitly valued. Looking to these variables for the substance of the good life (rather than what it is *not*) leads, perhaps inevitably, to the question, "Is the good life, essentially, a happy life?" Psychological well-being, positive affect, feelings of satisfaction, and so on are common outcomes in a broad range of research areas. Furthermore, many of the other goods of life, aside from happiness, are, ultimately, associated with feeling happ*ier*. Indeed, the essential role of happiness in the contemporary psychological conception of the good life is demonstrated by the fact that measures of alternative constructs thought to be indicative of the goodness of life, such as meaning in life, autonomy, purposeful striving, optimism, and so on, tend to be lent construct validity by their associations with measures of happiness (see Keyes et al., 2002). Success in coping or negotiating life transitions is often gauged by a person's return to feeling good. It is not necessary to argue for the role of good feelings as a positive outcome—such outcomes are part and parcel of healthy psychological adjustment. Research on the content of goals and values demonstrates this focus on happiness is typical, not only of psychologists. King and Broyles (1997) found that when individuals were asked to make three wishes for anything at all, happiness was consistently nominated. Happiness is also a common theme in studies of goals and values (e.g., King & Broyles, 1997; Richards, 1966; Schwartz & Bilsky, 1987) and the ultimate goal of many self-help books.

Not surprisingly, an enormous body of evidence has been compiled tracing the occurrence, correlates, and causes of happiness (e.g., Diener & Diener, 1996; Diener & Seligman, 2002; Diener, Suh, Lucas, & Smith, 1999; Myers & Diener, 1995) in a variety of samples and settings. Happiness appears to be something of the natural state for human beings. Myers and Diener reviewed the literature and found that, in general, people tend to report themselves as pretty happy. Variables that might be thought of as related to lowered happiness have been found to be relatively unimportant (e.g., race, gender). Furthermore, life circumstances, such as income, also appear to be relatively unimportant to happiness (Myers, 1992; Myers & Diener, 1995).

Research has also addressed the potentially positive *outcomes* of short-term and long-term happiness (e.g., Lyubomirsky, King, & Diener, 2003). Though often thought of exclusively as an outcome of coping or life circumstances, happiness may itself predict a variety of positive outcomes. These include satisfying relationships (R. J. H. Russell & Wells, 1994), career success (Staw, Sutton, & Pelled, 1994), superior coping (Aspinwall, 1998; Carver, Pozo, Harris, & Noriega, 1993), and even physical health (e.g., Kubzansky, Sparrow, Vokonas, & Kawachi, 2001) and survival (Danner, Snowdon, & Friesen, 2001). Thus, happy people appear to be fortunate on a variety of fronts. Not only do the happy feel good much of the time (cf. Diener, Sandvik, & Pavot, 1991; Larsen & Ketelaar, 1991), these pleasant feelings may be associated with a variety of other goods in life. This burgeoning evidence suggests that there may be sound empirical support for the central place of positive mental states in (at least Western) psychology's implicit answer to the question, "What makes a life good?"

It has been argued that happiness may not be "everything" (cf. Ryff, 1989; Ryff & Singer, 1998). In their review of the occurrence of happiness, Myers and Diener (1995) concluded that "most people" are "pretty happy." Indeed, Ito and Cacioppo (1999) have suggested that in the absence of threat, human beings have evolved to tend toward a weak "approach" motivation. Thus, the status quo for a person is to feel mildly interested and engaged. It might be that asking why we value happiness is much like asking why we have 10 fingers and 10 toes. Happiness, at least to some extent, appears to be the general rule. Thus, it makes sense that unhappiness has captured so much of scientists' time and attention since unhappiness is likely to stand out against the backdrop of ubiquitous happiness.

Additionally, if happiness is an essential component of the good life, should we conclude that all happy lives are *good*? Depressing statistics about the rates of negative outcomes such as violence, depression, divorce, drug abuse, and so on lie somewhat paradoxically alongside statistics showing that people are generally happy. This juxtaposition may lead us to wonder if happiness is really the hallmark of the good life or if happiness alone can discriminate between good lives and lives that are lacking in essential ways.

Certainly, the role of happiness in the good life has been a central question of interest for humanity, in general (B. Russell, 1930/1960). Aristotle (1962) contrasted the pleasurable life with the good life and proposed the concept of eudaimonia as an alternative to sheer hedonism. While pleasure is a straightforward concept, eudaimonia refers to a type of enjoyment that is more complex, associated with cultivating and developing virtues. Pleasure is pleasurable for the person experiencing it—it is a wholly subjective state. In contrast, eudaimonia refers to a state in which the person meets more objective standards—an observer can judge whether an experience is purely hedonistic or is, in fact, eudaimonistic (Kraut, 1979). Waterman (1993) has translated Aristotle's conceptions of hedonism versus eudaimonia into psychological notions of simple pleasure versus expression of the self. From Waterman's perspective, eudaimonia can be understood as emerging in activities that express our essential selves. Similarly, Ryff (1995, p. 100) defined eudaimonia as "a striving for perfection that represents the realization of one's true potential." Hedonistic happiness can occur with no effort—sitting on the couch watching TV, one hand on the remote, and the other in a bag of chips. Eudaimonia apparently requires some effort. Have psychologists managed to successfully capture this seemingly crucial distinction? The answer to this question, like so many others in psychology, is "sort of" (see, e.g., Keyes et al., 2002; Ryan & Deci, 2001).

While a great deal of philosophizing about the contrast between hedonistic pleasure and eudaimonia has occurred, the role of happiness (e.g., under the guises of subjective well-being, life satisfaction, positive affectivity) in psychological notions of the good life is difficult to challenge. Although the variables that might be collected under the broad term "happiness" may be more complex than hedonistic pleasure, in general, these variables do not include a sense of effort or realizing one's potential, but rather tap into a general sense that one feels good. It is worth noting that even researchers who have focused their energies primarily on happiness do not argue that it is or should be considered the only true good in life. Indeed, no one in psychology appears to advocate a life of hedonism. It is true that humanistic traditions have taken a more benign view of pleasure, and for some, being happy is a sign that they are, in fact, engaged in activities that are for their betterment (Rogers, 1961; cf. Kasser, 2002). Often happiness is viewed as a good proxy measure for more complex variables such as intrinsic motivation, flow, and so on. Such variables will now be considered more fully. Note that these deeper or more complex positive emotional experiences are, still, positive.

OPTIMAL FUNCTIONING: EUDAIMONIA REVISITED

A number of constructs meant to capture "optimal experience" incorporate aspects of experience beyond enjoyment. For instance, a psychological variable that seems to resonate with Aristotle's concept of eudaimonia is intrinsic motivation. Most simply, intrinsic motivation is motivation for an activity that is innate in the activity itself. Intrinsic motivation has been identified as associated with activities that serve essential psychological needs of autonomy, competence, and relatedness (e.g., Deci & Ryan, 1985). Self Determination Theory (SDT; Deci & Ryan, 1985) holds that when individuals engage in activity that satisfies these central organismic needs, they experience genuine happiness, self-esteem, and so on. In contrast, activity that is directed at obtaining extrinsic rewards, such as material gain, promotes less fulfilling states. Clearly, SDT would hold that a good life is a life dedicated to the satisfaction of intrinsic needs. At the very least, research has shown that good days apparently are days that are occupied with such activity.

Sheldon and his colleagues have found that the fulfillment of autonomy, competence, and relatedness needs was associated with particular satisfaction for periods ranging from one day to an entire semester, across both Eastern and Western cultures (Reis, Sheldon, Gable, Roscoe, & Ryan, 2000; Sheldon, Elliot, Kim, & Kasser, 2001; Sheldon, Ryan, & Reis, 1996). Additional research inspired by SDT has shown that lives occupied with extrinsic need satisfaction (e.g., income, material possessions), to the detriment of more organismic concerns, are lives that are likely to be characterized by alienation and low self-actualization (Kasser, 2002).

Flow is a more specific type of intrinsically motivated state that also bears remarkable resemblance to Aristotle's notion of eudaimonia. Flow (Csikszentmihalyi, 1990) involves being optimally challenged by experience. In flow, the demands of a situation match the individual's abilities, and the individual is engaged fully in the act of doing. In flow, the person loses self-consciousness and a sense of the passing of time and enters a different level of experience. Flow is enjoyable; indeed we may think of it as a much desired state. Still, Csikszentmihalyi has noted that while flow is itself an attractive experience, it involves effort and as such may not be viewed as preferable to simply goofing off. For instance, although individuals are more likely to experience flow while at work, they are also more likely to say that while at work, they wish they were someplace else.

Although there is clearly more to intrinsic motivation than positive affect, it is nevertheless notable that positive emotions are strongly associated with such experiences. Often, enjoyment is used as a proxy measure for intrinsic motivation. This is a reasonable choice for researchers since, in the absence of clear demands or rewards, why would we do anything spontaneously, except that we like doing it? Indeed, research has shown a strong link between happiness and the experience of flow. Short-term positive feelings are often associated with feelings of flow (Hektner, 1997). In addition, individuals who are generally happy may be more likely to experience flow even during routine daily activities (Csikszentmihalyi & Wong, 1991). Thus, the empirical relationship between the conceptually distinct notions of hedonistic happiness and eudaimonia may not be as strong as Aristotle thought.

There are a variety of other important goods in life, goods for which happiness might be forsaken, at least temporarily. Close interpersonal relationships, good health, wisdom, maturity, charity, moral development, self-control, purposeful striving, creativity, and accomplishments represent just a few of these. Some (e.g., self-control) appear to be just the opposite of hedonism, and others (e.g., maturity) may require the sacrifice of happiness in the service of a larger goal. However, and importantly, these other aspects of life, when attained, are, again, often associated with heightened happiness. In addition, the absence of happiness in an individual's relationships or work may well be viewed as a signal that it's time to make a change in his or her life. If moods serve as information about how we are doing in areas we value (cf. Carver & Scheier, 1990), our level of happiness in life serves as a gauge of whether the decisions we've made, the activities in which we are engaged, and so on are indeed the ingredients for a fulfilling life.

One area in which there might be cause to reconsider the centrality of happiness to the good life is in the consideration of culture. Cross-cultural research has questioned the place of positive emotional states in determining whether a life is evaluated as good or not. People in individualistic nations base their quality of life on their emotional states, while the life satisfaction of those in collectivistic societies is based on not only emotional states but also societal norms (Suh, Diener, Oishi, & Triandis, 1998). Norms dictate which qualities should be important to a life well lived. Collectivists, more so than individualists, root their quality of life decisions in whether they are living up to societal standards. Individualists, in contrast, are more likely to be concerned solely with meeting their own personal standards, using their emotions as indicators of personal success. To make sense of quality of life judgments across cultures, it is important to focus on the differences in how cultures perceive the self. For individualists, the desirability of a life is based on the quality of his or her *own* life as an *individual.* For collectivists, the self is defined in relational terms (Markus & Kitayama, 1991, 1994). These differences in self-construal illuminate the findings that while both collectivist and individualist people value emotions, collectivists pay equal attention to normative value of a life in determining its quality. The more multidimensional nature of collectivists' quality of life judgments is corroborated by research examining the relations of positive and negative affect to life satisfaction across cultures. When positive and negative affective states are examined as correlates of life satisfaction, positive affect is significantly correlated with satisfaction in all cultures. However, negative affect is important to these judgments only in some collectivist societies (Suh et al., 1998).

Deciding that one's life is good or good enough is a complex decision. Traditionally, satisfaction with life has been understood as a consideration of the balance between positive and negative affect one experiences and an evaluation of that balance—is it ideal (Diener, Emmons, Larsen, & Griffin, 1985)? Moving this definition into the cross-cultural context, more recently, Diener, Napa Scollon, Oishi, Dzokoto, and Suh (2000) stated that satisfaction with life has two facets— one that incorporates cultural norms. The first focuses on specific life domains, such as health, finances, friends, family, and religion. The second facet is a global one, which varies according to a person's propensity to evaluate life positively. This positivity is related to personality and influenced by cultural norms and practices. For instance, the United States is a nation in which happiness is highly valued, and people in the United States tend to show a positivity bias in their life judgments. Positivity predicts satisfaction with life over the ratings of domain satisfaction within individuals. When comparing across individuals in a culture, domain satisfaction accounts for more variability in subjective well-being (SWB). However, cross-culturally, positivity accounts for more variability in well-being. On an individual level, both positivity and evaluations of specific domains are important. However, since positivity is at least partly culturally derived, when comparing across individuals in a culture, positivity remains fairly constant. On the other hand, positivity is an important variable to consider in examining cross-cultural differences in predicting satisfaction with life.

Even though collectivists rely less on emotional experience as a guide in making judgments of life quality, emotional states remain a significant predictor of these life judgments. Thus, for better or worse, the good life in the psychological literature typically begins and ends with a consideration of variables associated with psychological well-being. An important aspect of this research is that often results are presented as counterintuitive: as if people know or assume that, for instance, money leads to happiness, while research findings challenge these ideas (e.g., Kasser, 2002). Such findings are only truly counterintuitive if people's behaviors reveal underlying beliefs about what it is that makes a life good. Is it the case that "regular folk" have inaccurate notions of what makes a life good? Do people in general place the value on good feelings that psychologists seem to?

FOLK CONCEPTS OF THE GOOD LIFE

In addition to considering what philosophers and psychologists think about the content of the good life, it makes sense to consider what "just plain folk" think of this important construct. Folk notions of what makes a life good are valuable sources of information. When we ask people to tell us what they think makes a life good, we can compare their answers with those provided by the research literature to uncover places where people have toiled toward ends that are unlikely to lead to fulfillment. Furthermore, folk notions of the good life can help us to ground our research in the variables and values that matter to "real people," not just psychologists. If happiness, for instance, is indeed a key aspect of the good life and most people are happy, our participants may have a great deal to tell us about how they came to have such lives.

Over the past few years, research has begun to address what it is that people think makes a life good. In this work, typically, participants are shown a form that was, ostensibly, completed by another individual who rated his or her life on a variety of dimensions (see Appendix A for an example). After examining the target's life, participants are then asked to rate the life on a variety of scales tapping two general dimensions, desirability and moral goodness. By examining the effects of manipulating different aspects of the target's life, we can gauge the role of various characteristics in folk concepts of the good life.

DEFINING THE GOOD: DESIRABILITY AND MORAL GOODNESS

The term "good" is loaded with a variety of meanings. When we talk about the good life, we may be talking about a life that is filled with enjoyment—a life we'd like to have or a life that is morally good (Kekes, 1995). In research on folk concepts of the good life, we have examined both the desirability of a life and the moral goodness of that life.

Rating the desirability of a life involves making a fairly straightforward judgment of life quality (cf. Ditto, Druley, Moore, Danks, & Smucker, 1996). In this case, participants are simply asked if they would like to have the life in question, if the life seems like a good life, and to rate the overall quality of life of the target. This appears to be a fairly easy task, and we've never had a participant blanch at judging another's life in this way.

Perhaps more complicated is the question of how morally good a life is. We typically ask participants to rate the morality of a life but also to make a more provocative judgment of the life: "Do you think this person is going to heaven?" We include this question for a variety of reasons but, most importantly, because asking the question of moral judgment in this way taps into a gut instinct about the goodness of behaviors that may go beyond a rational decision. The individual may find a particular life superficially acceptable, but asking the question of the ultimate fate of the soul of the target may press the individual to make distinctions he or she wouldn't otherwise. Ironically, this question allows an individual to not appear judgmental while also making the ultimate judgment of another. The person can, in a sense, say, "This is fine with me, but God wouldn't like it" (Twenge & King, 2003, p. 10).

All of the studies we've conducted thus far have been in the United States. As such, we have relied primarily on the Judeo-Christian tradition to guide our hypotheses about how aspects of a life might relate to its judged moral goodness. Research beyond Western culture would surely provide fascinating information about the potentially culture-bound notions of the goods of life. In any case, given a methodology for assessing folk concepts of the good life, what has research shown the content of that life to be?

HAPPINESS, MEANING, AND MONEY IN FOLK CONCEPTS OF THE GOOD LIFE

In an initial investigation, King and Napa (1998) asked participants to judge a life that was manipulated to appear to be high or low in happiness, high or low in meaning, and high or low in wealth (see Appendix A). We chose these three variables as a starting point because all three have been well researched in the psychological literature.

As to the desirability of a life, there is good reason to expect all three of these variables—happiness, meaning in life, and wealth—to be strongly associated with judged desirability. Happiness was predicted to contribute to a life being considered both desirable as well as morally good. Happiness is clearly a desired commodity, as previously reviewed research would suggest. As to moral goodness, happiness may not be so clearly positive, but there is reason to believe happiness might be an indicator of moral goodness. In the Judeo-Christian tradition, there is some sense in which the image of the suffering servant is one who will find reward in heaven. Yet, there is also a sense in which a happy person is one who has found contentment or inner peace. In addition, the Bible encourages individuals to suffer in silence—to not display their suffering in outward appearance. Happiness may also be viewed as a reflection of leading a good life—the happy person has a clear conscience and has won God's favor (cf. Weber, 1930/1976).

Meaning in life was, likewise, predicted to contribute to judgments of a life as both desirable and morally good. Meaning in life typically involves having a sense of purpose, a feeling that one's life matters. Meaning in life is a strong correlate of subjective well-being (e.g., Antonovsky, 1987; Ryff, 1989; Zika & Chamberlain, 1992). In addition, concerning moral goodness, it is clear that devoting one's life to a meaningful purpose is considered a moral good.

Finally, as to wealth, predictions were mixed. Money is clearly a desirable commodity, at least to the extent that it allows people to meet the necessities of life. The desire for extreme wealth is also on the rise. Indeed, Myers (1992) reports that among college students the goal of making a lot of money has overtaken the goal of having an articulated philosophy of life. Wealth is also a common theme in values, private wishes, and goals (e.g., King & Broyles, 1997; Wicker, Lambert, Richardson, & Kahler, 1984). If folk concepts of the good life map onto these findings, it might demonstrate a serious flaw in the naïve public's notion of what makes a life good. Research on the relation between wealth and happiness, for instance, has demonstrated that the very wealthy are not much happier than others (Diener, Horwitz, & Emmons, 1985) and that the relation between wealth and happiness is very modest ($r = 0.12$; Diener, Sandvik, Seidlitz, & Diener, 1993). Furthermore, research has demonstrated that valuing the attainment of materialistic goals over goals such as autonomy, relatedness, and competence is associated with a variety of negative outcomes including mental illness, physical illness, alienation, interpersonal problems, and so on (e.g., Kasser, 2002; Kasser & Ryan, 1993, 1996). Thus, concerning the desirability of a life, we might expect to find that individuals give *too much* weight to the pleasures of a wealthy life.

A caveat is appropriate, however. Although SDT places extrinsic values in a negative light, it is worth considering that materialistic aspirations may supersede other values in life, particularly when people are impoverished. Oishi, Diener, Lucas, and Suh (1999) found that the strength of the association between home life satisfaction and overall life satisfaction was stronger in wealthier nations, for instance. Similarly, financial satisfaction was a stronger component of overall quality-of-life judgments in poorer nations. Satisfaction with self was a stronger predictor of overall satisfaction in wealthier nations. Thus, concern for personal happiness and other aspects of life may be viewed as luxuries—provided by living in relatively good conditions. When resources are low, the pursuit of materialistic goals may be a stronger predictor of overall quality of life.

As to judgments of the moral goodness of a wealthy life, predictions were even less straightforward. Although wealth may be valued (despite its lack of strong relation to well-being), the moral standing of the pursuit of wealth is less than wholly positive. The lavish lifestyles portrayed by televangelists notwithstanding, Biblical treatments of wealth are almost wholly negative. For instance, Jesus cautioned his followers that it is easier for "a camel to go through the eye of a needle, than for a rich man to enter into the Kingdom of God" (Matthew 19:24, King James Version).

In contrast, in his analysis of the Protestant Work Ethic, Weber (1930/1976) suggested that earthly economic success might be viewed as a sign of God's grace and, as such, it might serve as a proxy for an individual's moral standing. The wealthy might be viewed as more likely to go to heaven because God has clearly "allowed" them to enjoy earthly success.

Popular ideas about who is going to heaven appear to demonstrate a bit of this ambivalence about wealth. For instance, in a *U.S. News and World Report* survey ("Oprah," 1997) of over 1,000 Americans, 87% thought they themselves were going to heaven, followed by Mother Teresa at 79%, Oprah Winfrey at 66%, and Michael Jordan at 65%. Setting aside a sense of astonishment that a portion of individuals saw themselves as more likely to go to heaven than Mother Teresa, we can note, at least, that Mother Teresa appeared to represent the Biblical notion of the suffering servant—a person who led a rather impoverished life of dedication to a cause, but whose life was also marked by a sense of extreme joy. However, the ratings for Oprah Winfrey and Michael Jordan appear to more clearly indicate that earthly material success is indicative of a person's moral standing in the eyes of God.

The initial investigations of folk concepts of the good life demonstrated that naïve participants (104 college students in Study 1; 264 community adults in Study 2) tended to value happiness and meaning to a far greater extent than wealth in judgments of a life as either desirable or morally good. Results demonstrated across both samples that, though main effects for all three variables were found, the most preferred life was one high in meaning and happiness. In both studies, the main effects of happiness and meaning were considerably larger than the effect size for money. For instance, in Study 1, the multivariate effect sizes for the main effects of happiness and meaning on judgments of desirability were large (0.45 for happiness, .50 for meaning) while the multivariate effect size for money was nonsignificant (.01). As to moral goodness, only meaning showed a large effect (0.36). A similar pattern of findings emerged in Study 2 (King & Napa, 1998).

These results provide some evidence that folk concepts of the good life do, in fact, correspond considerably with the research literature in the area of well-being. People recognize the value of happiness and meaning in life and do not overestimate the importance of money in their evaluations of the goodness of a life. King and Napa (1998) concluded that people do seem to recognize the ingredients of a good life. The remaining mystery is why so few make choices that reflect this knowledge.

LOVE AND WORK IN FOLK CONCEPTS OF THE GOOD LIFE

Happiness and meaning, then, are important facets of the folk concept of the good life. It makes sense that the combination of meaning and happiness should be judged as most desirable—for isn't this combination indicative of a truly fulfilling life? Subsequent research sought to address if it matters *where* a person enjoys this kind of fulfillment. In the previous study, all targets were ostensibly describing their occupations. Does it matter if people find fulfillment in their job or in their personal life? In a series of studies, Twenge and King (2003) set out to examine the relative importance of love and work in evaluations of a life as desirable and morally good.

As in the previous studies, participants examined ratings that had ostensibly been made by targets describing their lives. In this case, the ratings were completed on items pertaining to the amount of fulfillment the person experienced at work or in relationships. For instance, items pertaining to relationship fulfillment included, "I gain a strong sense of personal fulfillment from my family relationships," and "I feel that my interpersonal relationships lack meaning." These items had been ostensibly endorsed to produce a profile of an individual high or low in relationship fulfillment. Similarly, items pertaining to work fulfillment included, "I gain a strong sense of personal fulfillment from my job," and "Working at my job is a source of personal meaning in my life." Again, items were filled in to reflect profiles of individuals high or low in work fulfillment. Participants rated these lives in both desirability and moral goodness.

Three studies were completed, using college samples and a community sample (n's = 161 students, 166 community adults, and 330 students and adults combined). The main result of this research, across all three samples (ranging from University of Michigan undergraduates to jurors in Dallas County, Texas), was that a life characterized by relationship fulfillment was judged as more desirable and morally superior. Work fulfillment also mattered at least for desirability—but in nearly every case, the effect size for relationship fulfillment was significantly stronger than the main effect for work fulfillment. At times, the effect for relationship fulfillment on desirability dwarfed the effect for work (e.g., Twenge & King, 2003; Study 1, ds = 0.45 versus 2.14 for work and relationship fulfillment, respectively, z = 6.44, for the difference in effect sizes). In addition, the pattern for those interactions that did emerge suggested that work fulfillment contributed to more positive evaluations of a life only when it was paired with high relationship fulfillment (Twenge & King, 2003). Work fulfillment was largely irrelevant to moral judgments of a life.

In the final study, Twenge and King (2003) explored the privileging of the personal domain over the work domain. In general, for both college students and community adults, the relationship domain was rated as the realm in which an individual's organismic or intrinsic needs (i.e., autonomy, relatedness, and competence) were more likely to be met. In addition, individuals who themselves generally experienced more intrinsic need satisfaction at work tended to judge the life high in relationship fulfillment more negatively, while those who rated themselves as experiencing need satisfaction in relationships tended to judge the life of fulfilling work more harshly.

Thus, folk concepts of the good life, as demonstrated in these results, seem to reflect the sense that people and relationships are what matter, not success (notably, there were no gender differences uncovered in these patterns), even in a presumably individualistic sample. These findings echo the common wisdom that "No one says on his or her death bed, 'if only I'd spent a few more hours at work'." In addition, these results demonstrate that people may not view the work domain as a place where important personal motives can be expressed. Such a perception may be realistic, or it may reflect a lack of awareness of the goods (besides money) that may be afforded by fulfilling work (e.g., opportunities for flow).

Note that in both sets of studies described so far, the folk concept of the good life appears to be uncannily on target—folk concepts of the good life tend to jibe well with psychological notions of the good life. Nonpsychologists seem to have a pretty wise idea of what it takes to make a life good. Yet, evidence from real life tends to question whether these ideas are actually put into practice. For instance, though happiness and meaning are highly valued, research has shown that in general the value placed on wealth has overcome that placed on seeking a unifying philosophy of life (Myers, 1992). In addition, many life decisions seem most reasonable and rational to us if they are justified for economic reasons (Miller, 1999). Furthermore, though Twenge and King (2003) found relationships to be valued over work, American workers have been spending increasingly more time at work (cf. Schor, 1991). Again, we are left with the impression that people have a sense of what it takes to make a fulfilling life, yet they continue to behave in ways that contradict these intuitions.

IS THE GOOD LIFE THE EASY LIFE?

Given the previous discussion of pleasure versus eudaimonia, it is perhaps fitting to consider this question as well: Does the folk concept of the good life imply simply hedonic pleasure, or does it incorporate effort, a requirement of eudaimonic happiness? In another set of studies, Scollon and King (in press) examined the role of hard work in folk concepts of the good life. Many psychological theories of optimal states require effort and sacrifice. Flow, intrinsic motivation, close relationships, and so on all require that an individual work hard. In three studies, participants (a total of 834 community adults and 186 college students) rated the desirability and moral goodness of a life characterized by high or low happiness, high or low meaning, and high or low effort. Results demonstrated that the place of effort in folk concepts of the good life depends on the type of effort considered. When effort was operationalized as working long hours, all participants preferred the easy life. When effort was operationalized as engagement in difficult, effortful activity that saps energy, a life of high effort was rated as more desirable (by students, but not adults) and as morally superior to a life of ease. Community adults showed a clear preference for a life of easy but meaningful activity. When effort was operationalized as chosen effortful engagement (not resource depletion), the hard life was rated as more desirable and morally superior. In addition, happiness interacted with effort on all measures of desirability such that individuals rated a life as more desirable and more meaningful if it included difficult work accompanied by joy. Finally, the individual engaged in a happy life of no hard work and little meaning was judged as most likely to be going to hell (Scollon & King, in press).

As to desirability, nonpsychologists come to eudaimonia with the same difficulty that plagues research psychologists. The role of hard work in the good life is difficult to appreciate. It is aversive, apparently, to think of a life of difficult labor that is devoid of happiness. As is the case for intrinsic motivation and flow, when hard work is paired with positive emotion, it becomes decidedly more palatable. In addition, folk concepts of the good life tend to incorporate hard work only when that work is operationalized as unrealistically easy (and perhaps even impossible): The preferred type of hard work was neither time consuming nor energy depleting. It is also notable, however, that folk concepts of moral goodness tended to view the pure hedonist negatively. An individual who leads an easy life of little meaning, who is still happy, appears poised for God's wrath.

This consideration of hard work in folk notions of the good life leads us to the conclusion that people have an inkling that the good life may be a difficult life, but, in general, the good life is viewed as a happy, meaningful one—ultimately, perhaps, as a fun and highly meaningful vacation. Such a conception of the good life seems to imply that the good life is lived during times of contentment and enjoyment. Yet, if our notions of the good life are to incorporate whole lives, they must not be limited to sun-filled weekends but include rainy days and Mondays as well. Good lives ought to include the various experiences that characterize all human life. When we think of the good life, can we incorporate the inevitability of sorrow?

THE ROLE OF SUFFERING: WHEN BAD THINGS HAPPEN TO GOOD LIVES

It probably reveals something about the naïve conception of the good life that when negative events occur in our lives, they are almost always deeply surprising. Misery and unhappiness are puzzlements—challenges to our sense of how things ought to be. Yet, unhappiness, though perhaps less common than happiness, is an inevitable part of life (cf. King, 2001). Throughout this chapter, we have examined the central role of happiness, among other values, in at least Western notions of the good life. Such a focus should not be taken to mean that good lives are happy lives all the time. What is the place of suffering or difficult times in the good life? Negative life experiences often motivate us to search for meaning, to make sense, and, often, to find something good that has come of even the bad events of life (e.g., Affleck & Tennen, 1996; Frankl, 1985; Janoff-Bulman & Berg, 1998; Linley & Joseph, in press). Indeed, looking on the bright side of negative life events has been shown to be related to enhanced adjustment (Affleck & Tennen, 1996), and experimental evidence demonstrates that instructing people to find the positives in traumatic life events causes health benefits as well (King & Miner, 2000). This evidence might lead us to conclude that the main focus of coping is, or should be, a return to happiness. Though the "pursuit of happiness" may well motivate the search for meaning, we argue that the search may lead to more significant changes in the person and, indeed, in the meaning of happiness itself.

One way to approach the place of difficult times in the good life is to look beyond happiness to alternative goods in life. One such variable is maturity. Most psychological definitions of maturity include the idea that the person is made more complex as a result of the maturation process (e.g., Block, 1982; Loevinger, 1976). Research has also shown that experiences with difficult life circumstances can foster the process of development (Helson, 1992; Helson & Roberts, 1994). Block (1982) used Piaget's ideas of assimilation and accommodation to capture the ways that experience may drive personality development. In assimilation, the developing person takes new experiences and interprets them via existing structures, avoiding any true change. When a person's existing meaning structure cannot incorporate new and challenging experiences, the person must invent new ways of understanding the self and world—this developmental process is accommodation. The outcome of accommodative process is a new way of existing in the world. In research on individuals who have experienced a broad range of life changes (e.g., parents of children with Down syndrome, divorced women, and gay men and lesbians), we have found that measures of accommodation (as revealed in narrative accounts of life change) relate to measures of personality development (King & Raspin, in press; King, Scollon, Ramsey, & Williams, 2000; King & Smith, in press). Furthermore, and importantly for the purposes of this chapter, neither personality development nor measure of accommodation are related to measures of happiness (cf. King, 2001).

Maturity is defined by the struggle to grasp the complexities of life and of one's place in the world of meaning. Because happiness and maturity are independent from each other—and these two goods of life are predicted by different processes (King et al., 2000)—we can consider the various lives in which all possible combinations of these variables exist (King, 2001; see also Keyes et al., 2002). The happy but immature person may be one who is generally content but who has a fairly simple view of himself or herself and the world. The unhappy immature person is one who is generally unhappy and who sees the world and himself or herself in very straightforward terms. The unhappy mature person might be someone who has confronted life's difficulties and come to experience the world in very complex ways but who has, perhaps, as a result, become overwhelmed by complexity or who has been rendered cynical by the vicissitudes of life. Finally, the happy mature person is one who has grappled with life's difficult circumstances and come to a sophisticated, complex view of self and world but who has also retained a capacity for joy and a sense of optimism (King, 2001; King et al., 2000). If both happiness and maturity are considered goods in life, it might be that the happy mature life represents the best possible scenario. Among the many differences that might be expected among these groups, we might also expect them to differ in their definitions of the good life itself. Certainly, it seems clear that the very experience of happiness might be rendered qualitatively different when it is experienced through the lens of maturity (King, 2001).

IN CONCLUSION: A MULTITUDE OF BEST LIVES?

This consideration of the combination of maturity and happiness and its implications for individuals' conceptualizations of the good life leads to the conclusion that there may not be one "good life" but rather a multitude of potentially good lives. There are likely to be exceptions to any rule about what makes a life good. If we decide that happiness is a requirement of a good life, we will certainly meet a miserable but successful scientist or artist who finds the pursuit of happiness utterly irrelevant to his or her life mission. Similarly, we might find someone who is extremely happy whom we would never view as "good" (cf. Becker, 1992). If we decide that diligence is a key component to the good life, inevitably, we will find a perfectly contented, kind, and generous person whose life simply doesn't conform to that standard. It is difficult to argue with the goodness of the variety of lives that we encounter in the world every day. The value placed on any one outcome must be viewed in the context of other important goods in life—happiness alongside cruelty means something quite different from happiness existing next to tireless work or a generous spirit. Perhaps the best we can say is that there are many paths to the life well lived, and some of the flagstones likely to be found along these paths include happiness, meaning, effortful engagement, relationships, maturity, and even difficult times. The precise layout of these many components on any given person's path varies according to his or her unique collection of dispositions, experiences, and cultural context.

APPENDIX A: SAMPLE SURVEY
FOR GOOD LIFE STUDIES

Career Survey

Name _____

Place of Employment _____

What is your highest level of education? (Check one)

Grade school _____	High school _____
Some college _____	B.A. degree _____
MA/MS _____	PhD _____ Other (explain) _____

What is your combined family income? (Check one)

Less than $10,000 _____	$11,000–20,000 _____	$21,000–30,000 _____
$31,000–40,000 _____	$41,000–50,000 _____	$51,000–70,000 _____
$71,000–100,000 _____	greater than $100,000 _____	

Rate the following items with regard to how much each is **true** of you in your job, using the scale below:

1	**2**	**3**	**4**	**5**
completely false of me			**completely true of me**	

_____ My work is very rewarding and I find it personally meaningful.

_____ I truly enjoy going to work every day.

_____ In my job I really feel like I am touching the lives of people.

_____ At my job, I feel happy most of the time.

_____ My job involves a lot of hassles.

_____ My work will leave a legacy for future generations.

Note: Participants had ostensibly completed these questionnaires in patterns indicating high vs. low income, happiness, and meaning.

REFERENCES

Affleck, G., & Tennen, H. (1996). Construing benefits from adversity: Adaptational significance and dispositional underpinnings. *Journal of Personality, 64,* 899–922.

Allport, G. W. (1961). *Pattern and growth in personality.* New York: Holt, Rinehart and Winston.

Antonovsky, A. (1987). *Unraveling the mystery of health.* San Francisco: Jossey-Bass.

Aristotle. (1962). *Nichomachean ethics* (Martin Oswald, Trans.). Indianapolis, IN: Bobbs-Merrill.

Aspinwall, L. G. (1998). Rethinking the role of positive affect in self-regulation. *Motivation and Emotion, 22,* 1–32.

Becker, L. (1992). Good lives: Prolegomena. *Social Philosophy and Policy, 9,* 15–37.

Block, J. (1982). Assimilation, accommodation, and the dynamics of personality development. *Child Development, 53,* 281–295.

Carver, C. S., Pozo, C., Harris, S. D., & Noriega, V. (1993). How coping mediates the effect of optimism on distress: A study of women with early stage breast cancer. *Journal of Personality and Social Psychology, 65,* 375–390.

Carver, C. S., & Scheier, M. F. (1990). Origins and functions of positive and negative affect: A control-process view. *Psychological Bulletin, 97,* 19–35.

Cottingham, J. (1998). *Philosophy and the good life.* Cambridge, England: Cambridge University Press.

*Csikszentmihalyi, M. (1990). *Flow: The psychology of optimal experience.* New York: HarperCollins.

Csikszentmihalyi, M., & Wong, M. M. (1991). The situational and personal correlates of happiness: A cross-national comparison. In F. Strack, M. Argyle, & N. Schwarz (Eds.), *Subjective well-being: An interdisciplinary perspective* (pp. 193–212). Oxford, England: Pergamon Press.

Danner, D. D., Snowdon, D. A., & Friesen, W. V. (2001). Positive emotions in early life and longevity: Findings from the nun study. *Journal of Personality and Social Psychology, 80,* 804–813.

Deci, E. L., & Ryan, R. M. (1985). *Intrinsic motivation and self-determination in human behavior.* New York: Plenum Press.

Diener, E., & Diener, C. (1996). Most people are happy. *Psychological Science, 7*(3), 181–185.

Diener, E., Emmons, R. A., Larsen, R. J., & Griffin, S. (1985). The Satisfaction With Life Scale. *Journal of Personality Assessment, 49,* 71–75.

Diener, E., Horwitz, J., & Emmons, R. A. (1985). Happiness of the very wealthy. *Social Indicators Research, 16,* 263–274.

Diener, E., Napa Scollon, C. K., Oishi, S., Dzokoto, V., & Suh, E. M. (2000). Positivity and the construction of life satisfaction judgments: Global happiness is not the sum of its parts. *Journal of Happiness Studies, 1,* 159–176.

Diener, E., Sandvik, E., & Pavot, W. (1991). Happiness is the frequency, not the intensity, of positive versus negative affect. In F. Strack, M. Argyle, & N. Schwarz (Eds.), *Subjective well-being: An interdisciplinary perspective* (pp. 119–139). Oxford, England: Pergamon Press.

Diener, E., Sandvik, E., Seidlitz, L., & Diener, M. (1993). The absolute relationship between income and subjective well-being: Relative or absolute? *Social Indicators Research, 28,* 195–223.

Diener, E., & Seligman, M. E. P. (2002). Very happy people. *Psychological Science, 13,* 81–84.

*Diener, E., Suh, E. M., Lucas, R. E., & Smith, H. L. (1999). Subjective well-being: Three decades of progress. *Psychological Bulletin, 125,* 276–302.

Ditto, P. H., Druley, J. A., Moore, K. A., Danks, J. H., & Smucker, W. D. (1996). Fates worse than death: The role of valued life activities in health-state evaluations. *Health Psychology, 15,* 332–343.

Frankl, V. (1985). *Man's search for meaning* (Rev. ed.). New York: First Washington Square Press.

Hektner, J. M. (1997). Exploring optimal personality development: A longitudinal study of adolescents. *Dissertation Abstracts International, 57*(11B), 7249. (UMI No. AAM9711187)

Helson, R. (1992). Women's difficult times and rewriting the life story. *Psychology of Women Quarterly, 16,* 331–347.

Helson, R., & Roberts, B. W. (1994). Ego development and personality change in adulthood. *Journal of Personality and Social Psychology, 66,* 911–920.

Ito, T. A., & Cacioppo, J. T. (1999). The psychophysiology of utility appraisals. In D. Kahneman, E. Diener, & N. Schwarz (Eds.), *Well-being: The foundations of hedonic psychology* (pp. 470–488). New York: Russell Sage Foundation.

Janoff-Bulman, R., & Berg, M. (1998). Disillusionment and the creation of value: From traumatic losses to existential gains. In J. Harvey (Ed.), *Perspectives on loss: A sourcebook* (pp. 35–47). Philadelphia: Brunner/Mazel.

Kasser, T. (2002). *The high price of materialism.* Cambridge, MA: MIT Press.

Kasser, T., & Ryan, R. M. (1993). A dark side of the American dream: Correlates of financial success as a central life aspiration. *Journal of Personality and Social Psychology, 65,* 410–422.

Kasser, T., & Ryan, R. M. (1996). Further examining the American dream: Differential correlates of intrinsic and extrinsic goals. *Personality and Social Psychology Bulletin, 22,* 280–287.

Kekes, J. (1995). *Moral wisdom and good lives.* Ithaca, NY: Cornell University Press.

Keyes, C. L. M., Shmotkin, D., & Ryff, C. D. (2002). Optimizing well-being: The empirical encounter of two traditions. *Journal of Personality and Social Psychology, 82,* 1007–1022.

*King, L. A. (2001). The hard road to the good life: The happy, mature person. *Journal of Humanistic Psychology, 41,* 51–72.

King, L. A., & Broyles, S. (1997). Wishes, gender, personality, and well-being. *Journal of Personality, 65,* 50–75.

King, L. A., & Miner, K. N. (2000). Writing about the perceived benefits of traumatic life events: Implications for physical health. *Personality and Social Psychology Bulletin, 26,* 220–230.

King, L. A., & Napa, C. K. (1998). What makes a life good? *Journal of Personality and Social Psychology, 75,* 156–165.

King, L. A., & Raspin, C. (in press). Lost and found possible selves, well-being and ego development in divorced women. *Journal of Personality.*

King, L. A., Scollon, C. K., Ramsey, C. M., & Williams, T. (2000). Stories of life transition: Happy endings, subjective well-being, and ego development in parents of children with Down Syndrome. *Journal of Research in Personality, 34,* 509–536.

King, L. A., & Smith, N. G. (in press). Gay and straight possible selves: Goals, identity subjective well-being, and personality development. *Journal of Personality.*

Kraut, R. (1979). Two conceptions of happiness. *Philosophical Review, 2,* 167–197.

Kubzansky, L. D., Sparrow, D., Vokonas, P., & Kawachi, I. (2001). Is the glass half empty or half full? A prospective study of optimism and coronary heart disease in the normative aging study. *Psychosomatic Medicine, 63,* 910–916.

Larsen, R. J., & Ketelaar, T. (1991). Personality and susceptibility to positive and negative emotional states. *Journal of Personality and Social Psychology, 61,* 132–140.

Linley, P. A., & Joseph, S. (2004). Positive change following trauma and adversity: A review. *Journal of Traumatic Stress, 17,* 11–21.

Loevinger, J. (1976). *Ego development: Conceptions and theories.* San Francisco: Jossey-Bass.

Lyubomirsky, S., King, L. A., & Diener, E. (2003). *The benefits of positive emotion.* Manuscript submitted for publication.

Markus, H. R., & Kitayama, S. (1991). Culture and the self: Implications for cognition, emotion, and motivation. *Psychological Review, 98,* 224–253.

Markus, H. R., & Kitayama, S. (Eds.). (1994). *Emotion and culture: Empirical studies of mutual influence.* Washington, DC: American Psychological Association.

Maslow, A. H. (1954). *Motivation and personality.* New York: Harper & Row.

Miller, D. T. (1999). The norm of self-interest. *American Psychologist, 54,* 1053–1060.

Myers, D. G. (1992). *The pursuit of happiness.* New York: Morrow.

Myers, D. G., & Diener, E. (1995). Who is happy? *Psychological Science, 6,* 10–19.

Oishi, S., Diener, E., Lucas, R. E., & Suh, E. M. (1999). Cross-cultural variations in predictors of life satisfaction: Perspectives from needs and values. *Personality and Social Psychology Bulletin, 25,* 980–990.

Oprah: A celestial being? (1997, March 31). *U.S. News and World Report, 112,* 18.

Reis, H. T., Sheldon, K. M., Gable, S. L., Roscoe, J., & Ryan, R. M. (2000). Daily well-being: The role of autonomy, competence, and relatedness. *Personality and Social Psychology Bulletin, 26,* 419–435.

Richards, J. M., Jr. (1966). Life goals of American college freshmen. *Journal of Counseling Psychology, 13,* 12–20.

Rogers, C. R. (1961). *On becoming a person.* Boston: Houghton Mifflin.

Russell, B. (1960). *The conquest of happiness.* London: Allen & Unwin. (Original work published 1930)

Russell, R. J. H., & Wells, P. A. (1994). Predictors of happiness in married couples. *Personality and Individual Differences, 17,* 313–321.

Ryan, R. M., & Deci, E. L. (2001). On happiness and human potentials: A review of research on hedonic and eudaimonic well-being. *Annual Review of Psychology, 52,* 141–166.

Ryff, C. D. (1989). Happiness is everything, or is it? Explorations on the meaning of psychological well-being. *Journal of Personality and Social Psychology, 57,* 1069–1081.

Ryff, C. D. (1995). Psychological well-being in adult life. *Current Directions in Psychological Science, 4,* 99–104.

*Ryff, C. D., & Singer, B. (1998). Contours of positive human health. *Psychological Inquiry, 9,* 1–28.

Schor, J. B. (1991). *The overworked American: The unexpected decline of leisure.* New York: Basic Books.

Schwartz, S. H., & Bilsky, W. (1987). Toward a universal psychological structure of human values. *Journal of Personality and Social Psychology, 53,* 550–562.

Scollon, C. K., & King, L. A. (in press). *Is the good life the easy life?* Social Indicators Research.

Seligman, M. E. P., & Csikszentmihalyi, M. (2000). Positive psychology: An introduction. *American Psychologist, 55,* 5–14.

Sheldon, K. M., Elliot, A. J., Kim, Y., & Kasser, T. (2001). What is satisfying about satisfying events? Testing 10 candidate psychological needs. *Journal of Personality and Social Psychology, 80,* 325–339.

Sheldon, K. M., Ryan, R. M., & Reis, H. T. (1996). What makes for a good day? Competence and autonomy in the day and in the person. *Personality and Social Psychology Bulletin, 22,* 1270–1279.

Staw, B. M., Sutton, R. I., & Pelled, L. H. (1994). Employee positive emotion and favorable outcomes at the workplace. *Organization Science, 5,* 51–71.

Suh, E. M., Diener, E., Oishi, S., & Triandis, H. C. (1998). The shifting basis of life satisfaction judgments across cultures: Emotions versus norms. *Journal of Personality and Social Psychology, 74,* 482–493.

Twenge, J., & King, L. A. (2003). *A good life is a good personal life: Relationship fulfillment and work fulfillment in judgments of life quality.* Manuscript submitted for publication.

Waterman, A. S. (1993). Two conceptions of happiness: Contrasts of personal expressiveness (eudaimonia) and hedonic enjoyment. *Journal of Personality and Social Psychology, 64*, 678–691.

Weber, M. (1976). *The Protestant ethic and the spirit of capitalism.* (T. Parsons, Trans.). London: Allen & Unwin. (Original work published 1930)

Wicker, F. W., Lambert, F. C., Richardson, F. C., & Kahler, J. (1984). Categorical goal hierarchies and classification of human motives. *Journal of Personality, 52*, 285–305.

Zika, S., & Chamberlain, K. (1992). On the relation of meaning in life and psychological well-being. *British Journal of Psychology, 83*, 133–145.

PART III

VALUES AND CHOICES IN PURSUIT OF THE GOOD LIFE

The Good Life or the Goods Life? Positive Psychology and Personal Well-Being in the Culture of Consumption

TIM KASSER

A T THIS POINT in the short history of positive psychology, one of the movement's key achievements has been its articulation of what it means to have *a good life.* Many thinkers have considered this issue over the course of recorded human thought, but positive psychology, in my view, has made two special contributions: First, rather than assuming that a good life is defined by the absence of psychopathology, many of the leaders of positive psychology have argued that happiness is a construct to be studied in its own right. Second, positive psychologists insist that conclusions about the meaning of a good life be based on sound empirical research, rather than on anecdotal observation or philosophical speculation. Excellent examples of these two contributions can be seen in the January 2000 issue of the *American Psychologist,* which was devoted to the topic of positive psychology and included several articles describing various approaches to understanding a good life. Although theorists differ in how they conceptualize and predict happiness and personal well-being, it is clear that variables such as life satisfaction, affective experience, good relationships, and feelings of meaning are among the important determinants (Csikszentmihalyi, 1999; Diener, 2000; Myers, 2000; Ryan & Deci, 2000; Ryff & Keyes, 1995; Seligman, 2002).

As positive psychology continues to make progress in both the articulation and (hopefully) the eventual actualization of its vision of a good life, I believe that it is crucially important to recognize that an opposing, better publicized vision of the good life is vying for space in people's minds. More specifically, every day and in many ways people are bombarded with powerful, psychologically sophisticated proclamations that the good life is "the goods life." Messages that happiness and well-being come from the attainment of wealth and the purchase and acquisition of goods and services is a pervasive and inescapable fact of modern life. Such messages are intertwined with governmental, educational, media, and business institutions, and are infused in our work, home, and leisure time. These messages are found not only in omnipresent advertisements, but also in the subtext of political debates, business decisions, educational practices, and life choices (see also Schwartz, 1994).

To investigate which of these two visions of the good life really fulfill their promises, my colleagues and I have been studying the content of people's values and goals. We have reasoned that people's values and goals provide an excellent way of understanding if their vision of the ideal (a standard definition of values, e.g., Rokeach, 1973) and the way they are attempting to organize their lives (a standard definition of goals, e.g., Emmons, 1989) is oriented toward the goods life or the good life. To reflect this dichotomy, we have described two types of goals and values (Kasser & Ryan, 1996, 2001). The first set, which we have called *extrinsic*, are goals and values that become prominent when people "buy into" the messages of consumer culture and organize their lives around the pursuit of money, possessions, image, and status. These types of goals are extrinsic in the sense that such pursuits are primarily focused on the attainment of external rewards and praise and are typically means to some other end. The second set of goals, which we have called *intrinsic*, involve striving for personal growth, intimacy, and contribution to the community, all values that are more closely associated with what positive psychologists typically include in their vision of the good life. We call this latter group of values intrinsic because they are inherently more satisfying to pursue and are more likely to satisfy the deeper psychological needs that are necessary for happiness and well-being (Kasser, 2002b; Ryan & Deci, 2000).

The next section briefly reviews empirical research demonstrating that when people organize their lives around the vision of the goods life promoted by consumer culture (i.e., extrinsic goals), personal well-being is actually diminished, whereas the reverse is true for the vision of the good life promoted by positive psychology (i.e., intrinsic pursuits). Refer to Kasser (2002a, 2002b) for a more extended discussion of this literature, as well as for a more detailed explanation as to why extrinsic values relate negatively to well-being. My objective here is to show that the two types of goals relate differently to a variety of measures of well-being and that this phenomenon is generalizable across a variety of methodologies and samples. This sets the stage for the practical suggestions that make up the remainder of the chapter.

VALUES AND PERSONAL WELL-BEING

Our initial study (Kasser & Ryan, 1993) assessed the relative importance that late adolescents placed on financial success (i.e., an extrinsic goal) in comparison to goals for self-acceptance, affiliation, and community feeling (i.e., intrinsic goals). Results showed that college students focused on this extrinsic goal reported lower levels of self-actualization and vitality and higher levels of depression and anxiety, whereas the reverse was true for intrinsic goals. Similarly, late adolescents scored lower on interviewers' ratings of overall functioning if they were extrinsically oriented than if they were intrinsically oriented. Since this initial study, the phenomenon has been replicated with a variety of different measures of both well-being and value orientation by various researchers and in several different types of samples.

Research shows that individuals who place relatively high importance on extrinsic compared to intrinsic goals also report lower quality of life on a variety of measures of well-being. For example, an extrinsic orientation is associated with lower life satisfaction, less happiness, fewer experiences of pleasant emotions, more physical symptomatology, more frequent experiences of unpleasant emotions, more drug and alcohol use, more narcissism, and more behavior disorders (Kasser & Ryan, 1996, 2001; Sheldon & Kasser, 1995; Williams, Cox, Hedberg, & Deci, 2000). These results have been demonstrated for surveys and diary reports of well-being and also hold up after controlling for socially desirable responding (Kasser & Ryan, 1996). The distinction between intrinsic and extrinsic orientations also has been assessed with a variety of methods, including both ratings and rankings of experimenter-provided aspirations and guiding principles (Kasser & Ryan, 1993, 1996, 2001), mixed idiographic-nomothetic goal striving methods (Sheldon & Kasser, 1995, 1998, 2001), and implicit methods based on reaction time (Schmuck, 2001; Solberg, Diener, & Robinson, 2004).

Researchers outside of our lab have independently reported similar results concerning the distinction between extrinsic and intrinsic values. In one major study, Cohen and Cohen (1996) found that adolescents who admired materialistic characteristics or put a high priority on being rich were especially likely to have a variety of *DSM* diagnoses, including conduct disorder, attention deficit disorder, separation anxiety disorder, and personality disorders (e.g., borderline, narcissistic). Several studies in the consumer research literature have also found that materialistic adults and college students report lower happiness and life satisfaction (Belk, 1985; Richins & Dawson, 1992; Sirgy, 1998).

Finally, the differential relationships between these types of goals and well-being have been documented in samples varying in age and nationality. Beyond the work with college students (Kasser & Ryan, 1993, 2001), lower well-being has been associated with strong extrinsic (relative to intrinsic) values in samples of adults (Kasser & Ryan, 1996; Schmuck, 2001; Sheldon & Kasser, 2001), adolescents (Cohen & Cohen, 1996; Kasser & Ryan, 1993), and business students and entrepreneurs (Kasser & Ahuvia, 2002; Srivastava, Locke, & Bortol, 2001). Results have also been replicated in nations outside of the United States, including Britain (Chan & Joseph, 2000), Germany (Schmuck, 2001; Schmuck, Kasser, & Ryan, 2000), Romania (Frost, 1998), Russia (Ryan et al., 1999), Singapore (Kasser & Ahuvia, 2002), and South Korea (Kim, Kasser, & Lee, 2003).

IMPLICATIONS FOR PRACTICE

As demonstrated earlier, the versions of the good life espoused by positive psychology and of the goods life espoused by consumer culture are not only at odds, but have very different outcomes. Whereas people who organize their lives around the intrinsic values of the good life are happier, those who pursue the extrinsic values of the goods life report more distress. Given these results, if positive psychology is to be successful, we have much work to do. Not only must we work to support the vision of the good life reflected in intrinsic values and positive psychology, but we must work to undermine and invalidate the vision of the goods life reflected in extrinsic values and our money-driven, consumer culture. To this end, I next discuss a variety of different interventions and initiatives that psychologists might undertake, all of which have the dual purpose of dislodging the psychic and social processes that encourage extrinsic values while at the same time supporting and nurturing the processes that encourage intrinsic values and goals.

CLINICAL PRACTICE

As reviewed earlier in the chapter, intrinsic and extrinsic values have been empirically associated with many of the psychological difficulties that clinicians see in their practices, including depression, anxiety, somatic complaints, personality disorders, substance abuse, and childhood disorders, not to mention the general malaise associated with diminished happiness and satisfaction with life. Other types of clinical problems may also be related to consumption. Probably the best researched is *compulsive consumption,* "a chronic, abnormal form of shopping and spending characterized in the extreme by an overpowering, uncontrollable, and repetitive urge to buy," (Edwards, 1992, p. 54; see Faber, 2004, for a review). Clinicians have also described difficulties such as *sudden wealth syndrome,* which involves "the emotional challenges and identity issues consequent of coming into money" (Goldbart, Jaffe, & DiFuria, 2004) and *acquisitive desire disorders,* which "include features of compulsive shopping, hoarding, greed, purchasing or collecting objects, and the neurotic pursuit of possessions" (Kottler, Montgomery, & Shepard, 2004).

Unfortunately, as noted by Kottler et al. (2004), clinicians frequently overlook the many ways that consumption and materialism interact with, and potentially cause, some of their clients' problems. Some of this may be because the current version of the *Diagnostic and Statistical Manual of Mental Disorders (DSM)* (American Psychiatric Association, 1994) does not recognize any disorders directly related to consumerism. Further, to my knowledge, no well-articulated clinical theories direct their practitioners to examine consumption-related issues such as spending patterns, debt, or materialism. Although space limits our discussion of this topic, there are two themes that might be particularly worth exploring with clients (see Kottler et al. [2004] for more treatment ideas).

The first theme concerns people's psychological needs. Substantial theorizing and research suggests that psychological well-being is enhanced when people have experiences that satisfy four psychological needs: security and safety; competence and efficacy; connection to others; and autonomy and authenticity (see Bandura, 1977; Baumeister & Leary, 1995; Kasser, 2002a; Maslow, 1954; Ryan & Deci, 2000; Sheldon, Elliot, Kim, & Kasser, 2001). Marketers and advertisers also recognize the importance of these needs when they use psychologically sophisticated and well-researched advertisements to associate the acquisition of products and services with the satisfaction of these needs. To take just the example of automobiles, advertisements show viewers that a sport utility vehicle can be used to protect you from dangerous conditions (i.e., safety), to show that you have made it in life (i.e., competence), to attract members of the opposite sex (i.e., relatedness), and to escape to wherever your heart desires (i.e., autonomy). The problem, however, is that these ads sell a false bill of goods. As reviewed elsewhere (Kasser, 2002a), research shows that when people organize their lives around attaining the extrinsic goals promoted by the goods life, they actually experience lower satisfaction of needs for safety (due largely to past experiences of threat), for competence and efficacy (as they have lower and a more contingent sense of self-esteem and are exposed to more upward social comparisons that make them dissatisfied with themselves), for connection (as they have shorter, more conflictual relationships) and for autonomy and authenticity (as they often feel more controlled and less free).

The second theme concerns the fact that some people habitually use acquisition, consumption, and other extrinsically oriented activities to try to cope with feelings of insecurity and unpleasant emotional states (Kasser, 2002a), including those that might result from poor need satisfaction. Like substance use, cutting one's body, sexual promiscuity, and other high-risk behaviors, obsessive acquisition and "retail therapy" are maladaptive ways that people try to cope with their unpleasant mood states. Indeed, compulsive buyers typically report that negative mood states precede their buying binges, and that when they feel bad, they like to shop (see Faber, 2004). Experimental manipulations similarly show that people become more materialistic and more desirous of consuming when they confront the fact of their own mortality (Kasser & Sheldon, 2000), when they are made aware that they have failed to live up to important ideals (Braun & Wicklund, 1989), and when feelings of isolation or meaninglessness are primed (Chang & Arkin, 2002). Although, like drinking and cutting, shopping and acquiring might temporarily distract people from their unpleasant feelings, such consumeristic behavior does little to help people actively confront and solve the problems that brought about the negative mood states in the first place. Additionally, such behavior can lead to increased debt, family conflicts, and even poorer need satisfaction, thus diminishing quality of life.

Clinicians might raise these themes with their clients and help them to explore the irrational thoughts, unpleasant feelings, and situational reinforcements that maintain an unsatisfying extrinsic value orientation. Once clients begin to realize that the promises of consumer culture are false and that retail therapy does little more than increase their credit card debt, they may become motivated to search out a different system of meaning in their lives. At this point, clinicians might introduce the idea of intrinsic values to help their clients reorganize their lives. For example, when stressed or insecure, clients might learn other, more adaptive coping strategies than shopping or watching television to actually help them to overcome these feelings. In particular, coping strategies that involve reaching out to other people and one's community or pursuing fun nonconsummatory activities (like painting, exercising, or playing music) should not only be more effective at alleviating unpleasant feelings, but should also help to build the values of affiliation, community feeling, and personal growth that are key intrinsic values. Similarly, helping individuals learn to satisfy their psychological needs through the pursuit of self-knowledge and self-acceptance, through close relationships with others, and through contribution to the community will not only dislodge extrinsic values, but also increase the likelihood that people will have the types of experiences that really do satisfy their psychological needs.

One last point to mention concerns *relapse prevention*. Like former alcoholics and overeaters who are every day tempted by social activities to return to their earlier problematic behaviors and thought patterns, therapists might help their clients recognize that they live in a world that is a veritable cornucopia of consumption that continually encourages a return to their previous, extrinsically oriented lifestyle. Discussing these issues before termination and helping clients develop ways of dealing with relapses helps ensure longer term success.

PREVENTION PRACTICES

Although psychotherapeutic efforts might be helpful, it would be better to prevent people from undervaluing intrinsic and overvaluing extrinsic goals in the first place. Psychologists can use their skills to develop many different types of interventions, including the two discussed next.

CHILDREN AND THEIR PARENTS

Children are like a holy grail for marketers and advertisers, since kids have a relatively large percentage of disposable income, can influence their parents' purchases through tactics such as whining and nagging, and might become lifelong consumers of a product if they are hooked early in their lives (Levin & Linn, 2004; Ruskin, 1999). Children are also particularly susceptible to messages tying security, self-worth, love, and freedom to the purchase of products, given that their cognitive skills are still in the process of developing and that they are often strongly motivated to fit in with their peers (who are usually consuming at equally high rates). Moreover, the enormous amount of time that children spend being exposed to commercial messages on television, the radio, and the Internet is now amplified by the spread of marketing strategies that connect the movies (e.g., Star Wars), toys (e.g., Star Wars action figures), and food (e.g., Star Wars Happy Meals) that children are encouraged to purchase (Levin & Linn, 2004). In sum, from the time they awake until they go to bed, children are increasingly exposed to a constant stream of psychologically sophisticated propaganda that propounds the worth of the goods life and of extrinsic values. It should thus be no surprise that between the late 1960s and the late 1990s, the percentage of first-year college students who believed that it is very important or essential to "be very well off financially" increased from around 40% to over 70% (Myers, 2000).

How might psychologists help stem this rising tide? First, we must recognize that some children are at higher risk than others for taking on the messages of the goods life. Research shows that children are more likely to emphasize extrinsic relative to intrinsic values if their parents are controlling or harsh, if they come from a divorced household, and if they are poorer (Cohen & Cohen, 1996; Kasser, Ryan, Zax, & Sameroff, 1995; Rindfleisch, Burroughs, & Denton, 1997). Additionally, African Americans and young girls are particularly targeted by marketers (Kilbourne, 2004; LaPoint & Hambrick-Dixon, 2004). Psychologists interested in prevention efforts with at-risk groups might do well to focus on these populations.

A variety of interventions might be developed and tested after choosing a particular population with whom to work. Among the most frequently used interventions are media literacy campaigns designed to help children understand the purposes and strategies of advertisements. Another possibility might be to "capitalize on" teenagers' sense of rebellion and educate them about the many ways that marketers attempt to manipulate and brand teens (Quart, 2003); teens' resulting anger might easily be turned against the marketers to help dethrone extrinsic values. Third, interventions based in cognitive-dissonance theory that have been developed for behaviors such as condom use (Aronson, Fried, & Stone, 1991) might be adapted. For example, many teens hold strong environmental beliefs, and if they can be shown how their consumption behavior is inconsistent with their ideals, dissonance might motivate a change in behavior. Finally, psychologists could develop any number of programs to help support and nurture intrinsic values; those that develop feelings of generosity and broader community feeling will probably have the strongest effects because they most oppose extrinsic values.

Because parents are important influences on children's value systems (Kasser et al., 1995), interventions might be developed with this group. For example, parents could be helped to examine how they inadvertently model extrinsic values to their children by each working 50 hours per week so that they can afford two large cars, a 3,000 square foot house, and a large-screen television with DVD player. Such behavior clearly sends children not-so-subtle messages about what is important in life. Helping parents model intrinsic values should not only increase their children's intrinsic values, but should also help to make the parents happier and healthier. Another aim of research could be to study the types of parenting practices that help build resilience in the face of consumer messages. For example, is it better to hit the mute button during commercials to demonstrate that commercials are unimportant and not worth listening to or is it better to leave the commercials on so that the parent can critique and decode the commercial messages? Some recent books provide advice about how to raise children who are living in a consumer culture (e.g., Taylor, 2003), but we need more empirical research and psychological theorizing to help guide parents.

VOLUNTARY SIMPLICITY INTERVENTIONS

Although movements toward a more materially simple life have been notable in U.S. history since the colonial era (Shi, 1985), *Voluntary Simplicity (VS)* has experienced a resurgence in recent years (Etzioni, 1998), with the publication of books like *Voluntary Simplicity* by Duane Elgin (1993), *Your Money or Your Life* by Joe Dominguez and Vicki Robin (1992) and the *Circle of Simplicity* by Cecile Andrews (1998). These and other books describe a lifestyle that rejects consumerism and instead focuses on a more "inwardly rich" life focused on personal growth, family, and volunteerism. Not surprisingly, then, Brown and Kasser (2003) found that, compared to a matched control group, people who self-identify as voluntary simplifiers place less emphasis on extrinsic and more emphasis on intrinsic aims.

Although the empirical literature on VS is sparse, the self-help literature is burgeoning and many types of workshops and programs have been designed to help people "downshift" and simplify their lives. Here are just two examples: First, *simplicity circles* have sprouted up around the world that act as support groups for those who are trying to simplify their lives (Andrews, 1998). The circles provide a place where people can talk with like-minded others about their struggles and challenges and can share ideas and resources in the form of co-operative and barter systems. Second, many workshops based on *Your Money or Your Life* (YMYL) are presented every year. These programs teach people how to live in an increasingly frugal manner while they save their extra earnings. Eventually a point of financial independence is reached when individuals are spending so little money each year that they can live off of the interest of the savings that have been accumulated (which is far below what most people consider necessary to have in their individual retirement accounts). At this time, they can quit their jobs and devote their time to their own growth, their families, and the community.

Simplicity circles and YMYL programs have attracted tens of thousands of adherents and provide well-designed interventions that can be used in randomized, controlled studies. Psychologists can now study how successfully people move away from extrinsic and toward intrinsic pursuits and how their well-being changes upon simplifying. If appropriately adapted, such interventions might even be useful for high school and college students before they move into the workforce.

PUBLIC POLICY INITIATIVES

Although all of the ideas described previously might have some potential, they all suffer from a problem analogous to what family therapists have recognized about therapy with children and what sociocultural theorists have recognized about psychopathology in general. Consider, for example, the likely efficacy of providing one hour of intervention per week to a child with oppositional-defiant disorder who lives in an abusive home with an alcoholic father in a poverty-stricken, gang-ridden neighborhood. As long as the broader family and social structures remain unchanged, the intervention is not likely to be very successful. In addition, acting as though the child is the one with the problem smacks of "blaming the victim," because his family, neighborhood, and broader social environment are the ones who are "sick" and largely responsible for his problems (although each would probably deny that this is so).

Analogously, then, we must wonder about the potential efficacy of any interventions as long as we remain in a culture where extrinsic values are continually encouraged, where intrinsic values are mentioned largely for marketing purposes, and where the media, government, and educational systems are all increasingly becoming outlets for corporate interests. If this is the state of our culture, is it reasonable to say that individuals should be solely responsible for being less materialistic? When children are targeted by marketers and pressured by peers to want the newest "in" product, is it reasonable to say that parents should just turn off the television and resist their children's complaints? In the face of the onslaught of the glorification of the goods life and statements by the U.S. president that people should "go shopping" after a national tragedy like 9/11 ("Excerpts," 2001), is it reasonable to believe that people can switch to a more materially simple lifestyle without being viewed as weird, unpatriotic, or subversive?

If we suspect that the broader social processes, structures, and agendas relevant to consumerism are indeed important to address, we psychologists must begin to overcome our disciplinary reticence to become involved in public policy issues (Kasser & Kanner, 2004) and begin to work for broader structural changes. There are a variety of areas of public policy psychologists might work on, including the three discussed next.

ADVERTISING

Advertising is one of the key ways in which extrinsic values are encouraged and intrinsic values are subverted. As such, one of the most important activities psychologists might undertake is to change the practices of advertising. Unfortunately, however, psychologists are probably more likely to go to work for advertising corporations and spread the materialistic mind-set than to actively work to change existing practices. One promising sign, however, is that the American Psychological Association has begun to consider whether it is unethical for psychologists to use their expertise to market to children (Clay, 2000), given that such behavior fails to support the discipline's endeavors to "apply and make public their knowledge of psychology in order to contribute to human welfare" (American Psychological Association, 1992).

Another reason psychologists should be particularly wary of the advertising industry is that there are currently no widely accepted ethical standards for the advertising industry nor institutional review boards, informed consent, or other standard ethical practices required for marketing and advertising research with children (Jacoby, Johar, & Morrin, 1998; Levin & Linn, 2004).

Psychologists have other reasons for opposing advertisements, particularly those directed at children. Many commercial messages not only encourage a materialistic value system, but also sell products that encourage violence, obesity, dissatisfaction with one's body, and hypersexuality (Kilbourne, 2004; LaPoint & Hambrick-Dixon, 2004; Levin & Linn, 2004). As such, psychologists interested in child welfare might work to pursue regulations on advertising such wares to children. For example, we could follow the lead of some European nations and ban commercial messages aimed at children (Ruskin, 1999). Although some corporations may cry that this will ruin their livelihood, we must ask whether economic progress or children's welfare should be our primary goal. The answer to this question is relevant to the distinction between extrinsic and intrinsic values.

EDUCATION

Advertisers have recognized that while children are in school they are a "captive audience" who cannot escape advertisements. One incident that demonstrates the aptness of this "captive" metaphor concerns Channel One, which is a corporation that broadcasts "teen-relevant news" in schools for several minutes every day, interspersed with several minutes of advertising. In an act of protest, two teenagers in Ohio walked out of class when Channel One came on in their class; in response, their principal placed them in a juvenile delinquency center for the day (Strickland, 2001). A similar incident occurred when a student in Georgia was suspended for wearing a Pepsi t-shirt on a day his school was hosting Coca-cola executives in the hopes of obtaining funds ("A Pepsi Fan," 1998).

These incidents only scratch the surface of demonstrating how children are exposed to multiple advertisements while in school. Pop machines stand in the hallways, scoreboards and sports team jerseys proclaim the names of corporate sponsors, and curricula use M&Ms to teach arithmetic. Some administrators claim that low levels of government funding force them to seek out and accept corporate donations in order to keep programs alive. Psychologists interested in this problem, and how it might be undermining the optimal education of children, might consider working for reforms to ensure that education remains for the purpose of enlightening minds and building skills, rather than for the promotion of extrinsic values and consumerism.

GOVERNMENT AND ECONOMICS

The United States and many other capitalist nations suffer from a fetish about economic growth, believing that the best measures of national progress derive from the gross national product (GNP) and the stock market. The nation is considered healthy if the economy is growing, and great faith is placed in the belief that economic growth will spur all sorts of wonderful outcomes and that the failure of growth will bring about calamities.

As it turns out, however, faith in economic progress is misplaced. Even though citizens in the United States are on average twice as wealthy today as in the 1950s, the percentage of people saying that they are very happy has remained stable (Myers, 2000); similar results are notable in other nations. Furthermore, during this same time, incidences of depression have risen (Cross-National Collaborative Group, 1992).

If a cognitive-behavioral therapist considered the beliefs of the U.S. government, certainly he or she would have to identify the belief that "economic growth equates with progress" as irrational given the large amount of evidence which contradicts it. But, like clients with other types of problems, our national leaders hold fast to their beliefs, sure that the same behavior that has failed in the past will magically bring about something good in the future. We psychologists might play a role here by continuing to disseminate the information that, at this point in our economic development, more wealth will apparently not bring greater happiness, and instead seems to be associated with multiple types of damage. Further, we can work to develop and validate other measures of national progress and health. Psychologists might have a role in this debate by studying alternative measures of economic progress (e.g., redefining progress), proposing noneconomic indicators of health and well-being (e.g., Diener, 2000), and studying nations that have decided to pursue policies that work for economic sustainability rather than growth.

CONCLUSION

In summary, consumer culture's vision of the goods life, as reflected in the pursuit of extrinsic aims for money, image, and popularity, is associated with a relatively low quality of life. In contrast, positive psychology's vision of the good life, as reflected in the pursuit of intrinsic values for personal growth, affiliation, and community contribution, fulfills its promises of happiness and enhanced well-being. Psychologists might help individuals and society move away from extrinsic and toward intrinsic values by developing and testing interventions with clients, children, or adults, and by working to change public policy relevant to advertising, education, and government. Such efforts might help to loosen the grip of the goods life and free people to pursue the truly good life.

REFERENCES

American Psychiatric Association. (1994). *Diagnostic and statistical manual of mental disorders* (4th ed.). Washington, DC: Author.

American Psychological Association. (1992). Ethical principles of psychologists and code of conduct. *American Psychologist, 46,* 1597–1611.

Andrews, C. (1998). *The circle of simplicity.* New York: Harper Collins.

Aronson, E., Fried, C., & Stone, J. (1991). Overcoming denial and increasing the intention to use condoms through the induction of hypocrisy. *American Journal of Public Health, 81,* 1636–1638.

Bandura, A. (1977). Self-efficacy: Toward a unifying theory of behavioral change. *Psychological Review, 84,* 191–215.

Baumeister, R. F., & Leary, M. R. (1995). The need to belong: Desire for interpersonal attachments as a fundamental human motivation. *Psychological Bulletin, 117,* 497–529.

Belk, R. W. (1985). Materialism: Trait aspects of living in the material world. *Journal of Consumer Research, 12,* 265–280.

Braun, O. L., & Wicklund, R. A. (1989). Psychological antecedents of conspicuous consumption. *Journal of Economic Psychology, 10,* 161–187.

Brown, K. W., & Kasser, T. (2003). *Are psychological and ecological well-being compatible? The role of values, mindfulness, and lifestyle.* Manuscript submitted for publication.

Chan, R., & Joseph, S. (2000). Dimensions of personality, domains of aspiration, and subjective well-being. *Personality and Individual Differences, 28,* 347–354.

Chang, L., & Arkin, R. M. (2002). Materialism as an attempt to cope with uncertainty. *Psychology and Marketing, 19,* 389–406.

Clay, R. A. (2000). Advertising to children: Is it ethical? *American Psychological Association Monitor on Psychology, 31,* 52–53.

Cohen, P., & Cohen, J. (1996). *Life values and adolescent mental health.* Mahwah, NJ: Erlbaum.

Cross-National Collaborative Group. (1992). The changing rate of major depression. *Journal of the American Medical Association, 268,* 3098–3105.

*Csikszentmihalyi, M. (1999). If we are so rich, why aren't we happy? *American Psychologist, 54,* 821–827.

Diener, E. (2000). Subjective well-being: The science of happiness and a proposal for a national index. *American Psychologist, 55,* 34–43.

Dominguez, J., & Robin, V. (1992). *Your money or your life.* New York: Viking Press.

Edwards, E. A. (1992). The measurement and modeling of compulsive buying behavior. *Dissertation Abstracts International, 53*(11-A).

*Elgin, D. (1993). *Voluntary simplicity.* New York: Morrow.

Emmons, R. A. (1989). The personal strivings approach to personality. In L. A. Pervin (Ed.), *Goal concepts in personality and social psychology* (pp. 87–126). Hillsdale, NJ: Erlbaum.

*Etzioni, A. (1998). Voluntary simplicity: Characterization, select psychological implications, and societal consequences. *Journal of Economic Psychology, 19,* 619–643.

Excerpts from the president's remarks on war on terrorism. (2001, October 12). *New York Times,* p. B4.

Faber, R. J. (2004). Self-control and compulsive buying. In T. Kasser & A. D. Kanner (Eds.), *Psychology and consumer culture: The struggle for a good life in a materialistic world* (pp. 169–187). Washington, DC: American Psychological Association.

Frost, K. M. (1998). *A cross-cultural study of major life aspirations and psychological well-being.* Unpublished doctoral dissertation, University of Texas at Austin.

Goldbart, S., Jaffe, D. T., & DiFuria, J. (2004). Money, meaning, and identity: Coming to terms with being wealthy. In T. Kasser & A. D. Kanner (Eds.), *Psychology and consumer culture: The struggle for a good life in a materialistic world* (pp. 189–210). Washington, DC: American Psychological Association.

Jacoby, J., Johar, G. V., & Morrin, M. (1998). Consumer behavior: A quadrennium. *Annual Review of Psychology, 49,* 319–344.

*Kasser, T. (2002a). *The high price of materialism.* Cambridge, MA: MIT Press.

Kasser, T. (2002b). Sketches for a self-determination theory of values. In E. L. Deci & R. M. Ryan (Eds.). *Handbook of self-determination research* (pp. 123–140). Rochester, NY: University of Rochester Press.

Kasser, T., & Ahuvia, A. C. (2002). Materialistic values and well-being in business students. *European Journal of Social Psychology, 32,* 137–146.

*Kasser, T., & Kanner, A. D. (2004). Where is the psychology of consumer culture. In T. Kasser & A. D. Kanner (Eds.), *Psychology and consumer culture: The struggle for a good life in a materialistic world* (pp. 3–7). Washington, DC: American Psychological Association.

Kasser, T., & Ryan, R. M. (1993). A dark side of the American dream: Correlates of financial success as a central life aspiration. *Journal of Personality and Social Psychology, 65,* 410–422.

Kasser, T., & Ryan, R. M. (1996). Further examining the American dream: Differential correlates of intrinsic and extrinsic goals. *Personality and Social Psychology Bulletin, 22,* 280–287.

Kasser, T., & Ryan, R. M. (2001). Be careful what you wish for: Optimal functioning and the relative attainment of intrinsic and extrinsic goals. In P. Schmuck & K. M. Sheldon (Eds.), *Life goals and well-being: Toward a positive psychology of human striving* (pp. 116–131). Goettingen, Germany: Hogrefe & Huber.

Kasser, T., Ryan, R. M., Zax, M., & Sameroff, A. J. (1995). The relations of maternal and social environments to late adolescents' materialistic and prosocial values. *Developmental Psychology, 31,* 907–914.

Kasser, T., & Sheldon, K. M. (2000). Of wealth and death: Materialism, mortality salience, and consumption behavior. *Psychological Science, 11,* 352–355.

Kilbourne, J. (2004). The more you subtract, the more you add: Cutting girls down to size. In T. Kasser & A. D. Kanner (Eds.), *Psychology and consumer culture: The struggle for a good life in a materialistic world* (pp. 251–270). Washington, DC: American Psychological Association.

Kim, Y., Kasser, T., & Lee, H. (2003). Self-concept, aspirations, and well-being in South Korea and the United States. *Journal of Social Psychology, 143,* 277–290.

Kottler, J., Montgomery, M., & Shepard, D. (2004). Acquisitive desire: Assessment and treatment. In T. Kasser & A. D. Kanner (Eds.), *Psychology and consumer culture: The struggle for a good life in a materialistic world* (pp. 149–168). Washington, DC: American Psychological Association.

LaPoint, V., & Hambrick-Dixon, P. J. (2004). Commercialism's influence on Black youth: The case of dress-related challenges. In T. Kasser & A. D. Kanner (Eds.), *Psychology and consumer culture: The struggle for a good life in a materialistic world* (pp. 233–250). Washington, DC: American Psychological Association.

Levin, D. E., & Linn, S. (2004). The commercialization of childhood: Understanding the problem and finding solutions. In T. Kasser & A. D. Kanner (Eds.), *Psychology and consumer culture: The struggle for a good life in a materialistic world* (pp. 213–232). Washington, DC: American Psychological Association.

Maslow, A. H. (1954). *Motivation and personality.* New York: Harper & Row.

Myers, D. G. (2000). The funds, friends, and faith of happy people. *American Psychologist, 55,* 56–67.

A Pepsi fan is punished in Coke's backyard. (1998, March 26). *New York Times,* p. D5.

Quart, A. (2003). *Branded: The buying and selling of teenagers.* Cambridge, MA: Perseus. Available from Redefining Progress (n.d.) http://www.rprogress.org.

Richins, M. L., & Dawson, S. (1992). A consumer values orientation for materialism and its measurement: Scale development and validation. *Journal of Consumer Research, 19,* 303–316.

Rindfleisch, A., Burroughs, J. E., & Denton, F. (1997). Family structure, materialism, and compulsive consumption. *Journal of Consumer Research, 23,* 312–325.

Rokeach, M. (1973). *The nature of human values.* New York: Free Press.

Ruskin, G. (1999, November/December). Why they whine: How corporations prey on our children. *Mothering,* 41–50.

Ryan, R. M., Chirkov, V. I., Little, T. D., Sheldon, K. M., Timoshina, E., & Deci, E. L. (1999). The American dream in Russia: Extrinsic aspirations and well-being in two cultures. *Personality and Social Psychology Bulletin, 25,* 1509–1524.

Ryan, R. M., & Deci, E. L. (2000). Self-determination theory and the facilitation of intrinsic motivation, social development, and well-being. *American Psychologist, 55,* 68–78.

Ryff, C. D., & Keyes, C. L. (1995). The structure of psychological well-being revisited. *Journal of Personality and Social Psychology, 69,* 719–727.

Schmuck, P. (2001). Life goal preferences measured by inventories, subliminal and supraliminal priming and their relation to well-being. In P. Schmuck & K. M. Sheldon (Eds.), *Life goals and well-being: Toward a positive psychology of human striving* (pp. 132–147). Goettingen, Germany: Hogrefe & Huber.

Schmuck, P., Kasser, T., & Ryan, R. M. (2000). Intrinsic and extrinsic goals: Their structure and relationship to well-being in German and, U.S. college students. *Social Indicators Research, 50,* 225–241.

Schwartz, B. (1994). *The costs of living: How market freedom erodes the best things in life.* New York: Norton.

Seligman, M. E. P. (2002). *Authentic happiness: Using the new positive psychology to realize your potential for lasting fulfillment.* New York: Free Press.

Sheldon, K. M., Elliot, A. J., Kim, Y., & Kasser, T. (2001). What is satisfying about satisfying events? Testing 10 candidate psychological needs. *Journal of Personality and Social Psychology, 80,* 325–339.

Sheldon, K. M., & Kasser, T. (1995). Coherence and congruence: Two aspects of personality integration. *Journal of Personality and Social Psychology, 68,* 531–543.

Sheldon, K. M., & Kasser, T. (1998). Pursuing personal goals: Skills enable progress but not all progress is beneficial. *Personality and Social Psychology Bulletin, 24,* 1319–1331.

Sheldon, K. M., & Kasser, T. (2001). Getting older, getting better: Personal strivings and psychological maturity across the life span. *Developmental Psychology, 37,* 491–501.

Shi, D. (1985). *The simple life.* New York: Oxford University Press.

Sirgy, M. J. (1998). Materialism and quality of life. *Social Indicators Research, 43,* 227–260.

Solberg, E. C., Diener, E., & Robinson, M. D. (2004). Why are materialists less satisfied. In T. Kasser & A. D. Kanner (Eds.), *Psychology and consumer culture: The struggle for a good life in a materialistic world* (pp. 29–48). Washington, DC: American Psychological Association.

Srivastava, A., Locke, E. A., & Bortol, K. M. (2001). Money and subjective well-being: It's not the money, it's the motives. *Journal of Personality and Social Psychology, 80,* 959–971.

Strickland, E. (2001, March/April). Watch or go to jail. *Adbusters,* 34.

Taylor, B. (2003). *What kids really want that money can't buy.* New York: Warner Books.

Williams, G. C., Cox, E. M., Hedberg, V. A., & Deci, E. L. (2000). Extrinsic life goals and health risk behaviors in adolescents. *Journal of Applied Social Psychology, 30,* 1756–1771.

CHAPTER 5

Value Pathways to Well-Being: Healthy Values, Valued Goal Attainment, and Environmental Congruence

LILACH SAGIV, SONIA ROCCAS, and OSNAT HAZAN

I N RECENT YEARS, extensive research has suggested that the American dream of monetary wealth has a dark side: Materialistic aspirations and goals may undermine well-being. Considering the centrality of materialism in the Western world (Derber, 1979), the question of whether valuing wealth promotes or reduces well-being is important in itself. However, it raises a much broader question: Does the content of the values an individual holds affect his or her well-being? Are there healthy or unhealthy values in terms of their impact on well-being?

Values are social-cognitive representations of motivational goals. They are desirable goals that vary in importance and serve as guiding principles in people's lives (Rokeach, 1973; Schwartz, 1992). Values influence individuals' perceptions and direct their decisions, choices, and behaviors (for review, see Schwartz & Bardi, 2001).

We examine the potential links between values and well-being from three perspectives. The first—the healthy values perspective—suggests that holding certain values or goals is likely to lead to positive well-being, while holding other values or goals may undermine well-being. The second emphasizes goal attainment, suggesting that well-being results from the attainment of goals that are pursued for intrinsic reasons, irrespective of the value content of those goals. The third—the congruency perspective—suggests that it is the congruency between

This project was supported by a grant from the Recanati Fund of the School of Business Administration at the Hebrew University to Lilach Sagiv. We thank Nir Halevy and Merav Hershkovitz for their comments on earlier drafts of this manuscript.

personal values and the values prevailing in the environment that lead to a positive sense of well-being.

We then discuss implications for the relations between values and well-being within the social context of immigration. We show how the different perspectives contribute to our understanding of immigrants' well-being. Finally, we present some practical implications of the three perspectives, exemplified within the context of career counseling, and discuss the ways in which individuals and society may rely on personal values to contribute to a positive sense of well-being.

THE HEALTHY VALUES PERSPECTIVE

We discuss next the three bodies of research that explored the relations of values to well-being from the healthy values perspective.

LIFE STRIVINGS AND WELL-BEING

Drawing on humanistic perspectives, self-determination theory (SDT; Deci & Ryan, 1985, 1991) asserts that some values, motives, and goals are inherently positively associated with well-being, while others might have a negative impact on well-being. Self-determination theory distinguishes between intrinsic and extrinsic motives. Intrinsic motives derive from basic psychological needs and have the inherent potential to lead to independent satisfaction. They reflect psychological growth and self-actualization needs that are inherently planted in humankind. Satisfying these needs is essential to well-being.

In contrast, extrinsic motives derive from the need to obtain other people's approval, admiration, and praise and from the need to avoid social censure and punishment. Extrinsic motives or goals usually do not stand for themselves; rather, they are a means to obtain others' approval or to avoid others' sanctions. As long as the potential benefit from attaining a goal depends on the approval of others, that goal is likely to be extrinsic. Striving for these goals does not promote well-being. Indeed, eventually, extrinsic strivings might undermine well-being because people who attribute high importance to extrinsic goals are at risk of neglecting their basic psychological needs of autonomy, relatedness, and competence.

Several studies have provided empirical evidence supporting the idea that emphasizing intrinsic goals or values over extrinsic ones is likely to have a positive effect on well-being and vice versa (e.g., Kasser & Ahuvia, 2002; Kasser & Ryan, 1993, 1996). These studies typically are surveys in which individuals state how important to them several life aspirations are and to what extent they expect to attain them. Life aspirations included both intrinsic goals (e.g., autonomy, relatedness, competence, and community) and extrinsic goals (e.g., financial success, attractiveness, and popularity). Well-being was measured with various cognitive, affective, and physical scales.

The findings of these studies show that the centrality of intrinsic goals in comparison to extrinsic goals correlated positively with some of the measures of positive well-being and negatively with some of the measures of negative well-being. For example, Kasser and Ryan (1993, 1996) found that the more importance attributed to intrinsic goals, the higher was the sense of self-actualization and vitality and the lower the frequency of physical symptoms and depression. In contrast, the higher the importance attributed to extrinsic goals, the lower was the sense of self-actualization and vitality and the higher was the frequency of physical symptoms and anxiety.

Additional support for the healthy values perspective was found in an earlier diary study (Emmons, 1991). Students wrote down their life aspirations; then, for 21 consecutive days, they reported two good events and two bad events that had happened to them during each day. These events were classified into one of three categories: interpersonal, achievement, or other. Twice a day, participants also reported their positive and negative affect, physical symptoms, and psychological and physical distress. Emmons found that power aspirations correlated positively with psychological and physical distress and with negative affect. In contrast, affiliation aspirations were positively correlated with positive affect.

Does the healthy values perspective fare similarly well in cultural groups outside the United States? Some evidence suggests that it does: Ryan (1999) found that emphasizing intrinsic goals over extrinsic materialistic goals correlated with various aspects of well-being among both American and Russian respondents. The associations were somewhat weaker for the Russian sample. Similarly, Schmuck, Kasser, and Ryan (2000) studied German and U.S. students and found that in both groups, respondents who were relatively intrinsically oriented in their aspirations reported greater self-actualization and lower anxiety. Finally, in a study on materialistic values and well-being of Singaporean business students, Kasser and Ahuvia (2002) found that the importance attributed to materialistic aspirations correlated negatively with several indicators of positive well-being and positively with indicators of poor well-being. In contrast, a relative focus on intrinsic aspirations of self-acceptance, affiliation, or community feeling was related to some indicators of positive well-being.

PERSONAL VALUES AND WELL-BEING

The most detailed categorization of goals and motives was proposed by Schwartz (1992). Studying universals in the content and structure of values, Schwartz presented a broader set of values. He identified 10 basic motivational goals that are relevant to all people in all societies. These motivations reflect basic needs of the individual as a biological organism, requirements of successful interaction among people, and requirements for the survival of groups and societies. Schwartz derived 10 distinct value types that represent the 10 basic motivations. This set of values was intended to be comprehensive of the main distinct motivations common to people in any society. Research offers considerable support for this claim of comprehensiveness (Schwartz, 1994; Schwartz & Sagiv, 1995).

The theory also explicates a structural aspect of values, namely, the dynamic relations among them (Schwartz, 1992). Actions in pursuit of any value have psychological, practical, and social consequences that may conflict or may be congruent with the pursuit of other values. For example, the pursuit of stimulation values may conflict with the pursuit of security values: Stimulation values reflect the motivation for seeking change and excitement and looking for novel and daring experiences. These strivings and actions are likely to obstruct goals and actions aimed at ensuring order, stability, and security. However, the pursuit of stimulation values may be compatible with the pursuit of self-direction values that emphasize autonomy of thought and action: Seeking novelty, change, and excitement may increase and be increased by expressing independence in thought and action.

The total pattern of relations of conflict and compatibility among value priorities yields a circular structure of values, or circumplex (see Figure 5.1). Competing value types emanate in opposing directions from the center; complementary types are in close proximity going around the circle.

Values can be classified as reflecting either intrinsic or extrinsic motives. Self-direction and stimulation can be viewed as largely reflecting autonomous needs, universalism and benevolence can be seen as reflecting relatedness, and achievement reflects competence. The other value types (power, security, conformity, and tradition) can be viewed as expressing extrinsic motivation (see Bilsky & Schwartz, 1994; Sagiv & Schwartz, 2000).

Sagiv and Schwartz (2000) examined the relations of the 10 value types to measures of cognitive and affective aspects of well-being. They studied three samples of university students and three adult samples from three cultures: West Germany, the former East Germany, and Israel. Findings were highly consistent both across the three cultural groups and across the two age groups. However, they differed substantially for the cognitive and affective aspects of subjective well-being.

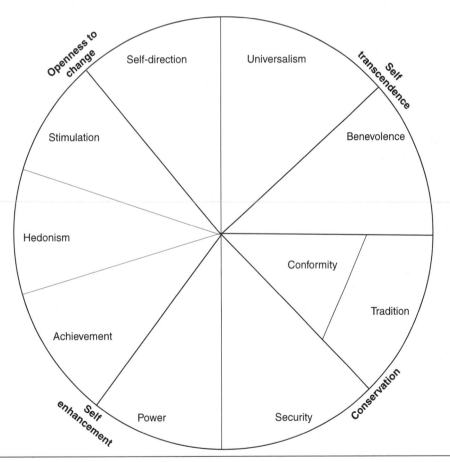

Figure 5.1   Schwartz's Model of the Structure of Personal Values. Reproduced by kind permission from "Are There Universal Aspects in the Content and Structure of Values?" by Shalom H. Schwartz, 1994, *Journal of Social Issues, 50*, pp. 19–45.

Specifically, achievement, self-direction, and stimulation values correlated positively, and tradition conformity and security values correlated negatively, with the *affective* aspect of well-being. The correlations were relatively weak ($r = 0.25$ or weaker), but they were consistent across the six samples. In contrast, there was no evidence for any relations between value priorities and the cognitive aspect of subjective well-being.

In another test of direct relations between values and well-being, Oishi, Diener, Suh, and Lucas (1999) found that the importance attributed to achievement and benevolence values did not correlate with subjective well-being in a sample of American university students. In a second part of their study, achievement values correlated positively with cognitive and affective subjective well-being. No other value type correlated significantly with any indicator of well-being.

Findings from Schwartz's work thus provide partial support for the healthy values perspective. Self-direction and achievement values, which emphasize autonomy and competence, respectively, correlated positively with well-being. Tradition and conformity values, which emphasize extrinsic motivation, correlated negatively with well-being. However, correlations were relatively weak and were found only for the affective aspect of well-being. Moreover, contrary to the healthy values perspective, benevolence and universalism values, which emphasize relatedness, and power values, which emphasize materialism, did not correlate with well-being at all. The marked different patterns of relations with values found for the cognitive and for the affective aspects of well-being call for further exploration of relations of values to additional aspects of well-being. In the studies described next, we present one such attempt: studying the relationships between values and worries.

VALUES AND WORRIES

Worries have been conceptualized as a subtype of anxiety and, hence, as an indicator of poor mental health (see Davey & Tallis, 1994; Eysenck, 1992). Boehnke, Schwartz, Stromberg, and Sagiv (1998) suggested the concept of worries is more complex: They distinguished between two types of worries, namely, micro and macro worries. Micro worries focus on the self or close others. For example, a person may worry that he will get cancer or lose his job. Macro worries focus on entities external to the self—the wider society, the world, or the universe. Thus, for example, a person may worry about unemployment in her country, about people in Africa dying from AIDS, or about nuclear disaster. In a study of worries in 14 cultures, Schwartz and Melech (2000) showed that micro worries correlated both with cognitive and affective indexes of poor mental health. Micro worries are, therefore, an indicator of negative well-being. Macro worries, on the other hand, were slightly, but consistently, related to positive well-being. Thus, worry about the welfare of others does not reflect poor well-being.

Schwartz, Sagiv, and Boehnke (2000) examined the relations of values with the two types of worries among seven samples from three cultures (students and adults from the former East Germany, West Germany, Israel, and a sample of adult immigrants to Israel from the former Soviet Union). Consistent with the healthy values perspective, having micro worries—an indicator of poor well-being—correlated positively with emphasizing power and hedonism values and negatively with emphasizing universalism values. In contrast, macro worries correlated positively with universalism values and, to a lesser degree, with benevolence values.

Having macro worries correlated negatively with attributing high importance to power, hedonism, achievement, and, to a lesser degree, stimulation values.

The healthy values perspective thus reasoned that motives, goals, and values have direct effects on well-being. Some studies indicate that indirect effects are likely as well, specifically, that well-being is affected by the extent to which people are able to attain the goals, motives, and values that are important to them. We discuss these studies next.

GOAL ATTAINMENT

Sheldon and Elliot (1999) presented the self-concordance model, which relates strivings to well-being. They suggested that a positive sense of well-being results from psychological need satisfaction. The latter is affected *indirectly* by the level of self-concordance of strivings or goals. They defined self-concordant goals as goals derived from intrinsic or identified motives, rather than introjected or extrinsic motives. This distinction draws on the model of *perceived locus of causality* (PLOC; Sheldon & Kasser, 2001).

Sheldon and Elliot (1999) contend that self-concordant goals originate in inherent basic psychological needs and differ from other goals in two ways: First, attainment of self-concordant goals contributed to an individual's sense of well-being more than attainment of other goals. Moreover, attainment of these goals is more likely, as individuals invest sustained effort in pursuing them (because they originate in inherent basic psychological needs).

Studying university students, Sheldon and Elliot (1999) provided empirical support for their model. In the beginning of the semester, students reported eight goals they had set for themselves, which would last at least one semester. In addition, they were asked about their motivation to pursue each goal. The researchers inferred self-concordance of each goal from the motivation that each participant gave for pursuing it (e.g., "You are striving for this goal because you would feel ashamed, guilty, or anxious if you didn't" was a measure of introjected motives). Three times throughout the semester, respondents reported the amount of effort put in to pursuing each goal and the extent of their attainment of that goal. The extent of self-concordance of goals significantly predicted the amount of effort students invested in pursuing that goal, which, in turn, largely predicted the attainment of that goal. Goal attainment led to an experience of psychological need satisfaction, which correlated with change in well-being during the semester. In addition, as suggested by the model, goal attainment predicted greater psychological need satisfaction, the greater the concordance of the goals attained. In some, the interaction between goal attainment and self-concordance correlated positively with psychological need satisfaction.

Sheldon and Houser-Marko (2001) replicated these findings and showed, in addition, that setting self-concordant goals at the beginning of the semester was related to setting future self-concordant goals, thus suggesting an upward spiral model. Note, however, that the latter was almost fully dependent on the success in goal attainment. Thus, setting self-concordant goals may have a longitudinal positive effect on well-being to the extent that these goals are successfully attained. The self-concordance model, therefore, suggests that attaining a goal—and not merely striving for it—is likely to improve well-being. The type of striving (i.e., the level of self-concordance) influences well-being, but only indirectly.

Sheldon and Elliot (1999) assume that intrinsic strivings (e.g., autonomy, relatedness, competence) are internal or identified, while extrinsic goals (i.e., materialism) are external or introjected. An alternative view suggests that any striving, goal, or value may be identified or introjected, and it is the extent of self-concordance that affects well-being and not the mere content of the goal. Carver and Baird (1998) presented a distinction between strivings (e.g., financial success, community involvement) and the reasons for those strivings—reasons that may be external, introjected, identified, or intrinsic. They showed that when material-istic goals of financial success were self-concordant, they led to a positive sense of well-being. Accordingly, when the intrinsic strivings of community involvement were external or introjected, they correlated negatively with well-being. In other words, it was the extent of self-concordance—and not the content of strivings—that led to positive well-being (Carver & Baird, 1998).

Recently, Chirkov, Ryan, Kim, and Kaplan (2003) took a similar view in stating: "a person is autonomous when his or her behavior is experienced as willingly en-acted and when he or she fully endorses the action in which he or she is engaged and/or the values expressed by them" (p. 98). Thus, any goal or value may lead to well-being, to the extent that it is self-concordant.

Support for the effect of goal attainment was found in another longitudinal study examining students' well-being during 23 consecutive days (Oishi et al., 1999). At the beginning of the study, the students reported the importance they attributed to achievement and benevolence values. Each day, students reported how satisfied they were with their achievements and with their social life that day. To measure daily well-being, students were asked each day how good or bad that day was. Consistent with the goal attainment perspective, participants' daily well-being was directly affected by daily satisfaction with their achievements and with their social life. Relations with values were more complex: Well-being did not correlate directly with the importance students attributed to achievement or benevolence values. The role of values became evident, however, when the in-teraction between values and satisfaction with achievements and social life was examined. Daily satisfaction with achievements was a stronger predictor of daily well-being for those who attributed high importance to achievement values than for those who attributed low importance to those values. Similarly, satisfaction with social life was a stronger predictor of well-being for those who emphasized benevolence values than for those who attributed relatively low importance to these values. Thus, individuals' day-to-day well-being was predicted by the satis-faction of those life domains that were important to them.

Oishi et al. (1999) further examined the moderating role of personal values in the relations between satisfaction with specific life domains and general satisfac-tion. Participants reported their satisfaction with their grades, family, and social life. Again, the relations between satisfaction with a specific life domain and gen-eral satisfaction were moderated by personal values. The more important achieve-ment values were held to be, the stronger was satisfaction with grades a predictor of general satisfaction. The more important conformity values were held to be, the stronger satisfaction with the family predicted general well-being. Finally, the more important benevolence values were held to be, the more satisfaction with so-cial life affected general satisfaction.

Further support for the goal attainment view was found by Brunstein, Schultheiss, and Grassman (1998). The researchers examined their participants' needs and characterized them as having relatively more agentic versus communal needs. They then followed participants during an academic semester and asked them which goals they had attained during that time period. Findings indicated that students who attained goals congruent with their main motive were likely to enjoy higher daily emotional well-being. That is, for students with agentic needs, positive well-being correlated with the attainment of agentic goals, while for students with communal needs, positive well-being correlated with the attainment of communal goals.

These findings support the notion that goal attainment leads to positive well-being. Moreover, they show that regardless of the type of values emphasized, people are happier when they attain the goals and values that are most important to them. The findings underscore the importance of identifying the factors that are most likely to increase the chances of goal attainment.

Environmental factors may play an important role in goal attainment. Ryan and Deci (2000) noted that while the existence of intrinsic motives is independent of environmental context, carrying them out, sustaining them, and enhancing them may well depend on circumstances. In the next section, we present a third perspective for the relations of values and well-being—the person-environment congruency perspective, which suggests that the more people emphasize the values that prevail in their environment, the more positive their well-being is likely to be.

PERSON-ENVIRONMENT VALUE CONGRUENCY

Several theories posit that congruency between individuals' value hierarchies and the values prevailing in their social environments is beneficial for their well-being (e.g., Feather, 1975; Furnham & Bochner, 1986; Segall, 1979). Sagiv and Schwartz (2000) named three mechanisms that may explain the process through which person-environment value congruency influences well-being.

ENVIRONMENTAL AFFORDANCES

The first mechanism relies on the effect of goal attainment on well-being discussed earlier. Sagiv and Schwartz (2000) underscored the impact the environments in which people operate have on their ability to attain their valued goals. Social environments offer sets of affordances (Gibson, 1979) of functional utilities or possibilities for action. Environments that are congruent with individuals' goals and values afford them with opportunities to attain their important goals. Incongruent environments, in contrast, do not provide people with opportunities to act on their values and, hence, block fulfillment of their important goals.

For example, the role of an accountant is highly structured and requires accuracy and precision. Accounting firms provide individuals with many opportunities to follow rules and regulations. Accountants who attribute high importance to values of conformity and order are likely to find many occasions to act on their values and attain their important goals. Conversely, working as an accountant provides individuals with few opportunities to express uniqueness and originality. In fact, this environment may block creativity and imagination. A person who emphasizes these values is, therefore, less likely to fulfill personal values and goals.

When people function in congruent environments, they are able to express their values and attain their important goals. As noted previously, such goal attainment is likely to lead to an experience of a positive sense of well-being. Brunstein et al. (1998), Carver and Baird (1998), and Oishi et al. (1999) found that positive well-being resulted from the attainment of *important* values, whether they were intrinsic or extrinsic. The congruency perspective takes the same view and suggests that any type of important value or goal may lead to positive well-being, provided that it is congruent with the values prevailing in the environment.

SOCIAL SANCTIONS

The second mechanism discussed by Sagiv and Schwartz (2000) is a mechanism of social support. Social support is an important source of positive well-being. Lazarus and Folkman (1984) suggested that social support is needed to cope effectively with stressors. Accordingly, studies found that the effects of stressors on well-being was buffered by perceived social support, which either reduced the perceived threat of the stressor or enhanced self-esteem, which, in turn, evoked adaptive responses to the stressor (Davis, Morris, & Kraus, 1998; Komproe, Rijken, Ros, Winnubst, & Hart, 1997).

Environments pose sets of expectations about the beliefs, values, and behaviors that are normative and desired. These expectations are backed by implicit or explicit sanctions (Getzels, 1969). In consensual environments—when most people share similar value hierarchies—clear messages are likely to be communicated about normative values (Holland, 1985; Schneider, 1987).

People who endorse the values prevailing in such consensual environments are likely to enjoy social support. They feel that their values are validated and that their opinions are well-founded. In contrast, individuals who express value hierarchies that oppose those prevailing in the environment are likely to experience some form of social sanctions: They may be ignored, ostracized, or punished (Holland & Gottfredson, 1976).

INTERNAL CONFLICT

Finally, the third mechanism proposed by Sagiv and Schwartz (2000) is a mechanism of intraperson consonance. According to this mechanism, personal well-being may be undermined by internal value conflict. This may happen when people enter new environments that differ substantially from those they come from. Consider, for example, a person who is the first of her family to start college or immigrants from a culture that differs markedly from the host society (we discuss the latter in more detail later). Individuals may internalize values advocated by their new environment, although these values may contradict values and goals they internalized earlier.

Consciously emphasizing incompatible sets of values is likely to provoke internal value conflict (Schwartz, 1992; Tetlock, 1986) because by pursuing one set of values, an individual necessarily acts in ways incompatible with the opposing set of values. Thus, acting in ways that are congruent with the whole set of important values may be impossible.

This mechanism has received support in several studies. For example, Burroughs and Rindfleisch (2002) showed that emphasizing materialism creates tension and threatens well-being—only for those who also emphasize values that conflict with materialism, such as religious and family values. Similarly,

Emmons (1986; Emmons & King, 1988) measured well-being 4 times a day for 3 weeks. Several measures of poor well-being related to both internal conflict (conceptualized as holding a goal whose attainment blocks the attainment of other goals held important) and ambivalence (conceptualized as a person's feeling that he or she will be simultaneously happy and unhappy if he or she attains that goal).

A recent line of research studied the impact of value-environment congruency on well-being directly by identifying the central values in various environments, or subcultures. In the first of this series of studies, Sagiv and Schwartz (2000) explored the values prevailing in different academic subcultures. They measured subjective well-being and value priorities of university students who studied management or psychology. They postulated that management students are exposed to an environment that promotes and encourages the attainment of power and achievement goals but blocks the attainment of goals of benevolence and universalism values. This environment differs markedly from the environment in which psychology students study. The latter are exposed to an environment that allows for fulfillment of benevolence and universalism values but limits or even blocks the attainment of power values.

Sagiv and Schwartz (2000) showed that neither students' values, nor the department they studied in, directly affected their subjective sense of well-being. The interaction between the two, however, had a significant effect on both cognitive and affective aspects of well-being. Specifically, different values affected students' well-being, depending on the environment in which they studied: Emphasizing power values correlated negatively with subjective well-being among psychology students, while it correlated positively among management students. The opposite pattern (although weaker) was found for universalism values.

Ivgi (2003) studied subjective well-being of religious teachers who taught in a religious high school. He analyzed the values endorsed in the teaching profession subculture and in the subculture of the religious school. On the basis of a review of the literature on the teaching profession and an analysis of cultural artifacts, such as reports of the ministry of education, and of the reward system of school employees, he suggested that teaching allows for the attainment of the goals reflected in benevolence values—expressing concern and care for others. He, therefore, expected subjective well-being to correlate positively with emphasizing benevolence values and negatively with emphasizing the opposing power values, which reflect the motivation to gain power and control over others. By reviewing cultural artifacts of the religious schools, such as rules and regulations, codex, and formal forms, Ivgi further concluded that the values prevalent in the subculture of these schools differ somewhat from those characterizing the teaching profession in general: Religious schools emphasize values of conformity and tradition. He, therefore, expected these values to correlate positively with well-being of teachers in the school.

As predicted, Ivgi (2003) found that job satisfaction and satisfaction with life correlated positively with attributing high importance to benevolence, conformity, and tradition values and with attributing low importance to power values. Relations with positive and negative affect were in the expected direction, but they were weak and insignificant.

In another study, conducted in the Israeli army, Jacobson (2003) compared two groups of female cadets. The cadets in the first group held commanding roles before the course and were intended to serve as commanding officers. The cadets in the second group had no commanding experience in their former roles and were intended for administrative positions. Power values, which reflect the motivation for power and control over other people and resources, are highly congruent with the environment of the commanding cadets, both prior and through their training. Power values were judged as less congruent (though not incongruent) with the environment in which the cadets in the administrative course worked before and during the course. As predicted, power values correlated positively with satisfaction of life among the former but not among the latter. In a regression equation, the interaction between course and values had a significant effect on satisfaction with life.

Finally, studying 45 accountants in the Israeli branch of a global high-tech firm, Kramer and Rosenfeld (2001) found that satisfaction with life correlated positively with emphasizing tradition values and negatively with emphasizing self-direction values. Correlations were also in the positive direction with conformity values and in the negative direction with stimulation values. These findings correspond to the nature of the accountancy profession, as discussed previously. Again, findings were weaker and less consistent as to affective well-being.

The studies reviewed here focused on only one of the many environments in which individuals spend time. Subjective well-being, however, is likely to be affected by the congruency between personal values and the values prevailing in the individual's family, group of close friends, social community, profession, organization, and many more. Does value congruency with each environment have equal effect on well-being? Probably not. Sagiv and Schwartz (2000) propose that the impact of value congruency with any environment depends on the relevance of the environment to the person's self-identity. The more important a given environment is for the person's self-identity, the stronger the impact that congruency with this environment will have on that person's well-being.

IMPLICATIONS FOR IMMIGRANTS' WELL-BEING

Our views of the links between values and well-being can help deepen our understanding of well-being in specific social situations. Consider, for example, the case of immigrants. The transition and adaptation to another culture involves major and challenging changes in the lives of immigrants. They are required to learn a new language, find a job, and generally master the skills necessary to effectively function in a new culture. These tasks are coupled with the need to cope with psychological changes: Immigrants need to adjust their identity to their new roles in the host society, to cope with a potential sense of social incompetence, and to deal with separation from people to whom they are emotionally attached (Chiu, Feldman, & Rosenthal, 1992; see Anderson, 1994, for a review).

Extensive research has been addressed at identifying factors affecting immigrants' well-being, and many such factors have received considerable empirical support. Here we apply the previously reviewed findings to better understand the effects of values on immigrants' well-being. We argue that values have both direct and indirect effects: Consistent with the healthy values approach, emphasizing certain values is likely to ease the process of immigration. Consistent with the person-environment congruency approach, immigrants' well-being is likely to be more positive when they move to a culture that endorses values similar to their own.

IMMIGRANTS' WELL-BEING AND THE HEALTHY VALUES PERSPECTIVE

Individuals' value hierarchies are likely to affect the extent to which the process of adaptation to a new culture is experienced as a series of overwhelming frustrations versus opportunities for personal development. Specifically, we suggest that attributing high importance to openness to change values is likely to facilitate immigrants' adaptation and enhance their well-being, while emphasizing conservatism values might hinder their adaptation.

People who value openness to change emphasize autonomy, self-direction, and independence of thought and action. They pursue novelty and excitement, esteem curiosity, and seek novel situations. Such value priorities are likely to lead people to perceive the changes they experience through the process of immigration as new opportunities for goal attainment and personal growth rather than stressful threats. People who value openness to change enjoy and appreciate the exposure to novel experiences and ideas. Learning the unfamiliar customs of the host society is experienced as exciting and challenging. In sum, placing high importance on values emphasizing personal autonomy and novelty may promote the subjective sense of well-being among immigrants.

In contrast, people who emphasize conservatism values attribute high importance to maintaining the status quo, adhering to traditional roles and familiar modes of thought. They are likely to feel stress in situations that seem to require personal change and uncertainty. Pressure to conform to new ideas, values, and attitudes is likely to be experienced as an intense threat to their identity. Moreover, the separation from previous interpersonal and group ties and limited integration in the social fabric are probably less problematic for individuals who place particular value on an autonomous individual identity rather than on an identity strongly embedded in a group.

The detrimental role of conservative values (specifically, conformity) on the well-being of immigrants was evident in a study that examined the discrepancies immigrants perceived between their own acculturation attitudes and the acculturation expectations of members of the host society (Roccas, Horenczyk, & Schwartz, 2000). Immigrants to Israel from the former Soviet Union believed that Israelis wanted them to relinquish their distinctive identity and to assimilate more than they themselves wished to do. The perceived pressure to assimilate correlated negatively with life satisfaction among those who valued conformity, but not among others. Thus, consistent with the healthy values approach, emphasizing conformity values threatened the immigrants' well-being.

IMMIGRANTS' WELL-BEING AND THE PERSON-ENVIRONMENT CONGRUENCY PERSPECTIVE

The person-environment congruency approach helps to identify conditions under which adherence to traditional values can also *enhance* immigrants' well-being. Value discrepancies between original and host cultures may affect intrafamily conflicts. Such conflicts result from the fact that the pace of acculturation is often much quicker for young immigrants than for their parents (e.g., Gil & Vega, 1996; Szapocznik & Kurtines, 1993). Consequently, discrepancies between norms and values of children and parents arise and are grounds for family disagreements and conflict, which, in turn, may undermine one of the important sources of social support (e.g., Gil & Vega, 1996; Rick & Forward, 1992; Szapocznik & Kurtines, 1993). Thus, the more adolescents are involved in their original culture and adhere to traditional values, the more positive their family functioning and personal well-being (e.g., Gil & Vega, 1996; Liebkind, 1994, 1996; Phalet & Hagendoorn, 1996; Sam, 1995).

A fit between the values important to immigrants and the values of the adopted culture affects well-being for an additional, possibly more obvious, reason: One of the major factors affecting successful acculturation is the immigrant's ability to function effectively in the new setting (e.g., Noels, Pon, & Clément, 1996; Ying, 1996). The higher the similarity between the culture of origin and the culture of the host society, the more likely immigrants are to be successful in operating effectively. Hence, the greater the similarity, the more immigrants are likely to succeed in attaining their important goals and maintaining a positive sense of well-being. Values play an important role in affecting immigrants' well-being because the extent of value discrepancy between the country of origin and the host country is one of the main indicators of the extent to which the new environment differs from the one immigrants are used to. Thus, the larger the value discrepancy, the more immigrants will face practices that are unfamiliar and possibly unmeaningful to them.

VALUE PATHWAYS TOWARD WELL-BEING

Each of the three perspectives presented in this chapter has practical implications for both individuals and society. By integrating all three views, we may suggest more fine-tuned implications for the role that socialization agents such as parents, educators, counselors, and leaders may play in individuals' striving for happiness.

The healthy values perspective suggests a simple path toward positive well-being: Values and strivings that are intrinsic by nature (e.g., autonomy) are likely to lead to positive well-being because they reflect self-actualization needs that are inherent to human beings. Parents, teachers, leaders, and therapists may all nurture such values and strivings by way of modeling and reinforcement. Note, however, that external rewards may lead to introjected or internalized goals at best, but they cannot lead to intrinsic motives that are most desired according to the healthy values perspective. Parents and teachers should, therefore, provide children with circumstances that offer them opportunities to develop intrinsic motivation.

Consider, for example, the case of career counseling. Sagiv (1999) proposed the distinction between two main products that counselors offer their clients: They can provide clients with direct guidance on the vocation most suitable to them (a process she named *giving answers*), or they can provide the clients with skills and tools that allow them to make decisions autonomously. Sagiv showed that the more clients were oriented to search for tools (i.e., they expressed independence, activity, and insightfulness) and the less they were oriented to look for answers (i.e., acted in a dependent and passive way), the more successful career counselors judged their counseling.

Similarly, well-being is not likely to increase when individuals adapt competence strivings during therapy because they want to please their therapist or gain the approval of their parents. Rather, a positive sense of well-being is more likely when therapy provides them with an accepting and supporting environment, where they can find out what their internal motives are and are encouraged to follow them. Correspondingly, parents may serve as models and may encourage and support their children for expressing autonomy or concern for others. Teachers may help students express independence, relatedness, or competence and create a learning environment that encourages them to follow their intrinsic motives and goals.

A second path toward happiness is suggested by the goal-attainment perspective: According to this view, individuals should fulfill their values and attain their important goals as means for positive well-being. Consider again the example of career counseling. Consistently with the goal attainment perspective, counselors may focus on helping clients to identify goals that they are likely to attain successfully. To identify such goals, counselors and clients may rely on intelligence and aptitude tests, on simulations, and on clients' successful past experiences. Once such desired and plausible goals have been identified, counselors may encourage clients to focus on these goals and neglect goals that are less probable.

Along these lines, societal agents and institutions may contribute to goal attainment in various ways. Parents, for example, may expose their children to suitable experiences, help them endorse those values that best suit their inner self, and encourage them to fulfill their internal goals. Education systems may be designed to allow students to identify and follow their academic interests, social perspectives, and life aspirations.

The third view discussed in this chapter—the person-environment congruency perspective—postulates that it is the *fit* between individuals and the environments they identify with that affects subjective well-being. Even truly intrinsic values may lead to a negative sense of well-being if a person holding such values highly identifies with an environment that rejects these values. Therefore, it is not enough to internalize intrinsic strivings—individuals have to find environments that are congruent with those strivings.

Again, we can readily apply this perspective to the example of career counseling. One of the main goals of career counseling is identifying an occupational environment that fits well with a client's personal characteristics, values, strivings, and goals. Thus, for example, counseling may help a person who emphasizes autonomy to choose an occupation where most people emphasize similar values and that affords many opportunities to express autonomy (e.g., artistic or investigative professions, according to Holland's 1985 typology) and to avoid occupations in which most people attribute low importance to autonomy values and that are highly structured and conservative (e.g., conventional professions).

The congruency perspective also suggests that when the environment is congruent, even extrinsic values may lead to positive well-being, because the environment offers individuals many opportunities to attain their important goals, because they may enjoy social support from those around them who endorse similar values, and because they hold a compatible set of values. This view of well-being thus underscores the importance of finding a meaningful environment (e.g., a profession, a social community, a spouse) that endorses values similar to their own.

Individuals and societies can use two types of processes in their efforts to seek and offer congruent environments: selection or socialization processes. Selection processes allow people to search and find those conditions, situations, and environments that may ease the attainment of their goals. Autonomous individuals in a collective culture may be active in social groups that are relatively autonomous (e.g., artists) while conservative individuals in an autonomous culture may join conservative communities (e.g., a religious community). Society may contribute to effective selection processes, too. Family members, teachers, and counselors may help individuals identify their basic motivations and recognize the circumstances that allow for their expression and attainment—for example, congruent schools, workplaces, social activities, and family lifestyles.

Socialization processes help individuals become more congruent with their environment. Individuals may change their own value system, so they come to internalize values and goals that may lead to well-being (e.g., values of autonomy or care for others). They may also choose to adopt values and goals that are more congruent with their environment. Finally, individuals may create or shape the environment or social situation in which they operate. Thus, for example, managers can allow employees to shape their working environment, determine the extent of autonomy they have in carrying out their tasks, and even influence their reward system.

CONCLUSION

Many paths may lead to happiness. In this chapter, we reviewed three paths, all of which regard happiness as an objective individuals may *actively* strive to achieve, and each entails different challenges for those who pursue it. The healthy values path requires that individuals be intrinsically motivated in their aspirations and their aspirations be of a certain form and nature. The goal attainment path requires individuals to invest sustained effort in pursuing the attainment of their goals. Finally, the congruent environment path requires individuals to either select or adapt to the environments important to them to produce the congruence beneficial to them. Pursuing some, or all, of these challenges increases individuals' chances to be happy and satisfied with their lives.

REFERENCES

Anderson, L. E. (1994). A new look at an old construct: Cross-cultural adaptation. *International Journal of Intercultural Relations, 18,* 293–328.

Bilsky, W., & Schwartz, S. H. (1994). Values and personality. *European Journal of Personality, 8,* 163–181.

Boehnke, K., Schwartz, S. H., Stromberg, C., & Sagiv, L. (1998). The structure and dynamics of worry: Theory, measurement, and cross-cultural replications. *Journal of Personality, 66,* 745–782.

Brunstein, J. C., Schultheiss, O. C., & Grassman, R. (1998). Personal goals and emotional well-being: The moderating role of motive dispositions. *Journal of Personality and Social Psychology, 75,* 494–508.

Burroughs, J. E., & Rindfleisch, A. (2002). Materialism and well-being: A conflict value perspective. *Journal of Consumer Research, 29,* 348–370.

Carver, C. S., & Baird, E. (1998). The American dream revisited: Is it *what* you want or *why* you want it that matters? *Psychological Science, 9,* 289–292.

Chirkov, V., Ryan, R. M., Kim, Y., & Kaplan, U. (2003). Differentiating autonomy from individualism and independence: A self-determination theory perspective on internalization of cultural orientations and well-being. *Journal of Personality and Social Psychology, 84,* 97–109.

Chiu, M. L., Feldman, S. S., & Rosenthal, D. A. (1992). The influence of immigration on parental behavior and adolescent distress in Chinese families residing in two Western nations. *Journal of Research on Adolescence, 2,* 205–239.

Davey, G. C. L., & Tallis, F. (Eds.). (1994). *Worrying: Perspectives on theory, assessment and treatment.* Chichester, England: Wiley.

Davis, M. H., Morris, M. M., & Kraus, L. A. (1998). Relationship-specific and global perceptions of social support: Associations with well-being and attachment. *Journal of Personality and Social Psychology, 74,* 468–481.

*Deci, E. L., & Ryan, R. M. (1985). *Intrinsic motivation and self-determination in human behavior.* New York: Plenum Press.

Deci, E. L., & Ryan, R. M. (1991). A motivational approach to self: Integration in personality. In R. Dienstbier (Ed.), *Nebraska Symposium on Motivation: Vol. 38. Perspectives on motivation* (pp. 237–288). Lincoln: University of Nebraska Press.

Derber, C. (1979). *The pursuit of attention: Power and individualism in everyday life.* Oxford, England: Oxford University Press.

Emmons, R. A. (1986). Personal strivings: An approach to personality and subjective well-being. *Journal of Personality and Social Psychology, 51,* 1058–1068.

Emmons, R. A. (1991). Personal strivings, daily life events, and psychological and physical well-being. *Journal of Personality, 59,* 453–472.

Emmons, R. A., & King, L. A. (1988). Conflict among personal strivings: Immediate and long-term implications for psychological and physical well-being. *Journal of Personality and Social Psychology, 54,* 1040–1048.

Eysenck, M. W. (1992). *Anxiety: The cognitive perspective.* London: Erlbaum.

Feather, N. T. (1975). *Values in education and society.* New York: Free Press.

Furnham, A., & Bochner, S. (1986). *Culture shock: Psychological reaction to unfamiliar environments.* London: Methuen.

Getzels, J. W. (1969). A social psychology of education. In G. Lindzey & E. Aronson (Eds.), *The handbook of social psychology* (Vol. 5, pp. 459–537). Reading, MA: Addison-Wesley.

Gibson, J. (1979). *The ecological approach to visual perception.* Boston: Houghton Mifflin.

Gil, A. G., & Vega, W. A. (1996). Two different worlds: Acculturation stress and adaptation among Cuban and Nicaraguan families. *Journal of Social and Personal Relationships, 13,* 435–456.

Holland, J. L. (1985). *Making vocational choices: A theory of careers.* Englewood Cliffs, NJ: Prentice-Hall.

Holland, J. L., & Gottfredson, G. D. (1976). Using a typology of persons and environments to explain careers: Some extensions and clarifications. *Counseling Psychologist, 6,* 20–29.

Ivgi, I. (2003). *Value congruency of teachers: Implications for well-being.* Unpublished master's thesis, The Hebrew University of Jerusalem.

Jacobson, Y. (2003). *Values and leadership style.* Unpublished master's thesis, The Hebrew University of Jerusalem.

Kasser, T., & Ahuvia, A. C. (2002). Materialistic values and well-being in business students. *European Journal of Social Psychology, 32,* 137–146.

*Kasser, T., & Ryan, R. M. (1993). A dark side of the American dream: Correlates of financial success as a central life aspiration. *Journal of Personality and Social Psychology, 65,* 410–422.

Kasser, T., & Ryan, R. M. (1996). Further examining the American dream: Differential correlates of intrinsic and extrinsic goals. *Personality and Social Psychology Bulletin, 22,* 280–287.

Komproe, I. H., Rijken, M., Ros, W. J. G., Winnubst, J. A. M., & Hart, H. (1997). Available support and received support: Different effects under stressful circumstances. *Journal of Social and Personal Relationships, 14,* 59–77.

Kramer, P., & Rosenfeld, R. (2001). *Value congruency and well-being in a hi-tech organization.* Unpublished seminar paper, The Hebrew University of Jerusalem.

Lazarus, R. S., & Folkman, S. (1984). *Stress, appraisal, and coping.* New York: Springer.

Liebkind, K. (1994). Ethnic identity and acculturative stress—Vietnamese refugees in Finland. *Migration, Nordic Issue, 23–24,* 155–177.

Liebkind, K. (1996). Acculturation and stress: Vietnamese refugees in Finland. *Journal of Cross-Cultural Psychology, 27,* 161–180.

Noels, K. A., Pon, G., & Clément, R. (1996). Language, identity, and adjustment: The role of linguistic self-confidence in the acculturation process. *Journal of Language and Social Psychology, 15,* 246–264.

*Oishi, S., Diener, E., Suh, E. M., & Lucas, R. E. (1999). Value as a moderator in subjective well-being. *Journal of Personality, 67,* 157–182.

Phalet, K., & Hagendoorn, L. (1996). Personal adjustment to acculturative transitions: The Turkish experience. *International Journal of Psychology, 31,* 131–144.

Rick, K., & Forward, J. (1992). Acculturation and perceived intergenerational differences among youth. *Journal of Cross-Cultural Psychology, 23,* 85–94.

Roccas, S., Horenczyk, G., & Schwartz, S. H. (2000). Acculturation discrepancies and well-being: The moderating role of conformity. *European Journal of Social Psychology, 30,* 323–334.

Rokeach, M. (1973). *The nature of human values.* New York: Free Press.

Ryan, R. M., Chirkov, V. I., Little, T. D., Sheldon, K. M., Timoshina, E., & Deci, E. L. (1999). The American dream in Russia: Extrinsic aspirations and well-being in two cultures. *Personality and Social Psychology Bulletin, 25,* 1509–1524.

Ryan, R. M., & Deci, E. L. (2000). Intrinsic and extrinsic motivations: Classic definitions and new directions. *Contemporary Educational Psychology, 25,* 54–67.

Sagiv, L. (1999). Searching for tools versus asking for answers: A taxonomy of counselee behavioral styles during career counseling. *Journal of Career Assessment, 7,* 19–34.

*Sagiv, L., & Schwartz, S. H. (2000). Values priorities and subjective well-being: Direct relations and congruity effects. *European Journal of Social Psychology, 30,* 177–198.

Sam, D. L. (1995). Acculturation attitudes among young immigrants as a function of perceived parental attitudes toward cultural change. *Journal of Early Adolescence, 15,* 238–258.

Schmuck, P., Kasser, T., & Ryan, R. M. (2000). The relationship of well-being to intrinsic and extrinsic goals in Germany and the U.S. *Social Indicators Research, 50,* 225–241.

Schneider, B. (1987). E=f(P,B): The road to a radical approach to person-environment fit. *Journal of Vocational Behavior, 31,* 353–361.

Schwartz, S. H. (1992). Universals in the content and structure of values: Theoretical advances and empirical tests in 20 countries. In M. P. Zanna (Ed.), *Advances in experimental social psychology* (Vol. 25, pp. 1–65). New York: Academic Press.

Schwartz, S. H. (1994). Are there universal aspects in the content and structure of values? *Journal of Social Issues, 50,* 19–46.

Schwartz, S. H., & Bardi, A. (2001). Value hierarchies across cultures: Taking a similarities perspective. *Journal of Cross-Cultural Psychology, 32,* 268–290.

Schwartz, S. H., & Melech, G. (2000). National differences in micro and macro worry: Social, economic and cultural explanations. In E. Diener & E. M. Suh (Eds.), *Culture and subjective well-being* (pp. 219–256). Cambridge, MA: MIT Press.

Schwartz, S. H., & Sagiv, L. (1995). Identifying culture-specifics in the content and structure of values. *Journal of Cross-Cultural Psychology, 26,* 92–116.

Schwartz, S. H., Sagiv, L., & Boehnke, K. (2000). Worries and values. *Journal of Personality, 68,* 309–346.

Segall, M. H. (1979). *Cross-cultural psychology: Human behavior in global perspective.* Monterey, CA: Brooks/Cole.

*Sheldon, K. M., & Elliot, A. J. (1999). Goal striving, need-satisfaction, and longitudinal well-being: The Self-Concordance Model. *Journal of Personality and Social Psychology, 76,* 482–497.

Sheldon, K. M., & Houser-Marko, L. (2001). Self-concordance, goal-attainment, and the pursuit of happiness: Can there be an upward spiral? *Journal of Personality and Social Psychology, 80,* 152–165.

Sheldon, K. M., & Kasser, T. (2001). Goals, congruence, and positive well-being: New empirical validation for humanistic ideas. *Journal of Humanistic Psychology, 41,* 30–50.

Szapocznik, J., & Kurtines, W. M. (1993). Family psychology and cultural diversity: Opportunities for theory, research, and application. *American Psychologist, 48,* 400–407.

Tetlock, P. E. (1986). A value pluralism model of ideological reasoning. *Journal of Personality and Social Psychology, 50,* 819–827.

Ying, Y. W. (1996). Immigration satisfaction of Chinese Americans: An empirical examination. *Journal of Community Psychology, 24,* 3–16.

CHAPTER 6

Doing Better but Feeling Worse: The Paradox of Choice

BARRY SCHWARTZ and ANDREW WARD

I N THE UNITED STATES, we live in a time and a place in which freedom and autonomy are valued above all else and in which expanded opportunities for *self-determination* are regarded as a sign of the psychological well-being of individuals and the moral well-being of the culture. We see *choice* as the critical sign that we have freedom and autonomy. It is axiomatic that choice is good, and that more choice is better. This chapter argues that choice, and with it freedom, autonomy, and self-determination, can become excessive, and that when that happens, freedom can be experienced as a kind of misery-inducing tyranny. Unconstrained freedom leads to paralysis. It is self-determination within significant constraints—within *rules* of some sort—that leads to well-being, to optimal functioning. The task for a future psychology of optimal functioning is to identify which constraints on self-determination are the crucial ones.

There is no denying that choice improves the quality of our lives. It enables us to control our destinies and to come close to getting exactly what we want out of any situation. Choice is essential to *autonomy*, which is absolutely fundamental to well-being. Healthy people want and need to direct their own lives. Whereas many needs are universal (food, shelter, medical care, social support, education, and so on), much of what we need to flourish is highly individualized. Choice is what enables each person to pursue precisely those objects and activities that best satisfy his or her own preferences within the limits of his or her resources. Any time choice is restricted in some way, there is bound to be someone, somewhere, who is deprived of the opportunity to pursue something of personal value.

As important as the instrumental value of choice may be, choice reflects another value that might be even more important. Freedom to choose has *expressive*

This research was facilitated by support from the Positive Psychology Network (M. Seligman, Director), an intramural grant from Swarthmore College to Barry Schwartz, and a sabbatical grant from the Solomon Asch Center for Study of Ethnopolitical Conflict to Andrew Ward.

value. Choice is what enables us to tell the world who we are and what we care about. Every choice we make is a testament to our autonomy. Almost every social, moral, or political philosopher in the Western tradition since Plato has placed a premium on such autonomy. Each new expansion of choice gives us another opportunity to assert our autonomy, and thus display our character. It is difficult to imagine a single aspect of our collective social life that would be recognizable if we abandoned our commitment to autonomy.

When people have no choice, life is almost unbearable. As the number of available choices increases, as it has in our consumer culture, the autonomy, control, and liberation this variety brings is powerful and seemingly positive. But the fact that *some* choice is good doesn't necessarily mean that *more* choice is better. As we will demonstrate, there is a cost to having an overabundance of choice. As the number of choices people face keeps increasing, negative aspects of having a multitude of options begin to appear. As the number of choices grows further, the negatives escalate until, ultimately, choice no longer liberates, but debilitates.

In this chapter, we examine some of the ways in which increased opportunities for choice, coupled with the goal of getting the best out of any situation can reduce well-being. We also offer some suggestions about how people can mitigate the negative psychological effects of the proliferation of options that the modern world provides.

THE EXPLOSION OF CHOICE

Modernity has provided an explosion of choice in two different respects: First, in areas of life in which people have always had choice, the number of options available to them has increased dramatically. Second, in areas of life in which there was little or no choice, significant options have now appeared.

To illustrate the first expansion of choice, consider the results of a recent trip to a local supermarket:

- 85 different varieties and brands of crackers
- 285 varieties of cookies
- 165 varieties of "juice drinks"
- 75 iced teas
- 95 varieties of snacks (chips, pretzels, etc.)
- 61 varieties of suntan oil and sunblock
- 80 different pain relievers
- 40 options for toothpaste
- 360 types of shampoo, conditioner, gel, and mousse
- 90 different cold remedies and decongestants
- 230 soups, including 29 different chicken soups
- 120 different pasta sauces
- 175 different salad dressings and if none of them suited, 15 extra-virgin olive oils and 42 vinegars to make your own
- 275 varieties of cereal

A typical American supermarket carries more than 30,000 items. That's a huge number to choose from. More than 20,000 *new* products hit the shelves every year (Cross, 2000).

In a consumer electronics store, there are:

- 45 different car stereo systems, with 50 different speaker sets to go with them.
- 42 different computers, most of which can be customized in various ways.
- 110 different televisions, offering high definition, flat screen, varying screen sizes and features, and various levels of sound quality.
- 30 different VCRs and 50 different DVD players.
- 74 different stereo tuners, 55 CD players, 32 tape players, and 50 sets of speakers. Given that these components can be mixed and matched in every possible way, that provides the opportunity to create 6,512,000 different stereo systems.

NEW DOMAINS FOR CHOICE

Here are some examples of how choice has grown in new domains in the United States:

- *Telephone service:* A generation ago, telephone service was a regulated monopoly. There were no choices to be made. With the break-up of the telephone monopoly came a set of options that has grown, over time, into a dizzying array—different possible long-distance providers, different possible plans, and still different local service providers. Cell phones have given us more choices, multiplying options yet again. Suddenly, phone service has become a decision to weigh and contemplate.
- *Retirement pensions:* The variety of pension plans offered to employees reflects the same change. Over the years, more and more employers have adopted "defined contribution" pension plans, in which employee and employer each contribute to some investment instrument. What the employee gets at retirement depends on the performance of the investment instrument. What began as a choice among a few alternative investment instruments has turned into choice among many. For example, a relative of one of the authors is a partner in a mid-sized accounting firm. The firm had previously offered its employees 14 pension options that could be combined in any way employees wanted. Just last year, several partners decided that this set of choices was inadequate, so they developed a retirement plan that has 156 options. Option Number 156 is that employees who don't like the other 155 can design their own.
- *Medical care:* Responsibility for medical care has landed on the shoulders of patients with a resounding thud. The tenor of medical practice has shifted from one in which the all-knowing, paternalistic doctor tells the patient what must be done—or just does it—to one in which the doctor arrays the possibilities before the patient, along with the likely plusses and minuses of each, and the patient makes a choice. There is no doubt that giving patients more responsibility for what their doctors do has greatly improved the quality of medical care they receive. But at least one physician suggests that the shift in responsibility has gone too far. Gawande (1999) reports that research has shown that patients commonly prefer to have others make their decisions for them. Although as many as 65% of people surveyed say that if they were to get cancer, they would want to choose their own treatment, in fact, among people who *do* get cancer, only 12% actually want to do so.

- *Choosing beauty:* What do you want to look like? Thanks to the options modern surgery provides, we can now transform our bodies and our facial features. In 1999, over one million cosmetic surgical procedures were performed on Americans—230,000 liposuctions, 165,000 breast augmentations, 140,000 eyelid surgeries, 73,000 face lifts, and 55,000 tummy tucks (Cottle, 2002; Kaminer, 2001). Cosmetic surgery is shifting from being a procedure that people gossip about to being a commonplace tool for self-improvement.

- *Choosing how to work:* The telecommunications revolution has created enormous flexibility about when and where many people work. Companies are slowly, if reluctantly, accepting the idea that people can do their jobs productively from home. Once people are in the position to be able to work at any time from any place, they face decisions every minute of every day about whether or not to be working. E-mail is just a modem away. Who do people work for? Here, too, people face increased choices. The average American 32-year-old has already worked for nine different companies. In an article about the increasingly peripatetic American workforce, *U.S. News and World Report* estimated that 17 million Americans would *voluntarily* leave their jobs in 1999 to take other employment (Clark, 1999).

- *Choosing how to love:* A range of life choices has been available to Americans for quite some time. But in the past, the "default" options were so powerful and dominant that few perceived themselves to be making choices. Whom we married was a matter of choice, but we knew that we would do it as soon as we could and have children, because that was something all people did. The anomalous few who departed from this pattern were seen as social renegades, subjects of gossip and speculation. These days, it's hard to figure out what kind of romantic choice would warrant such attention. Wherever we look, we see almost every imaginable arrangement of intimate relations. Though unorthodox romantic choices are still greeted with disapproval, in many parts of the world and in some parts of the United States, it seems clear that the general trend is toward ever greater tolerance of romantic diversity.

- *Choosing who to be:* We have another kind of freedom of choice in modern society that is surely unprecedented. We can choose our identities. Each person comes into the world with baggage from his or her ancestral past—race, ethnicity, nationality, religion, and social and economic class. All this baggage tells the world much about who we are. Or, at least, it used to. Not any more. Now, greater possibilities exist for transcending inherited social and economic class. Furthermore, because most of us possess multiple identities, we can highlight different ones in different contexts. The young New York immigrant woman from Mexico sitting in a college class in contemporary literature can ask herself, as the class discussion of a novel begins, whether she's going to express her identity as the Latina, the Mexican, the woman, the immigrant, or the teenager. Identity is much less a thing people "inherit" than it used to be (Sen, 2000).

CHOICE AND WELL-BEING

We have more choice, and presumably more freedom, autonomy, and self-determination, than ever before. It seems a simple matter of logic that increased choice improves well-being. And this, indeed, is the standard line among social scientists who study choice. If we're rational, they tell us, added options can only make us better off as a society. Those of us who want them will benefit, and those of us who don't can always ignore the added options. This view seems logically compelling; but empirically, it isn't true. As various assessments of well-being tell us, increased choice and increased affluence have been accompanied by *decreased* well-being (see Diener, 2000; Diener, Diener, & Diener, 1995; Diener & Suh, 2001; Diener, Suh, Lucas, & Smith, 1999; Inglehart, 1997; Lane, 2000; Myers, 2000). Not only do fewer people judge themselves to be happy than in previous generations, but the incidence of clinical depression and of attempted suicide have increased dramatically in this same period (Eckersley, 2002; Eckersley & Dear, 2002; Lane, 2000; Myers, 2000; Rosenhan & Seligman, 1995).

What assessments of well-being suggest is that the most important factor in providing happiness is close social relations. People who are married, who have good friends, and who are close to their families are happier than those who are not. In the context of a discussion of choice and autonomy, it is important to note that, in many ways, social ties actually *decrease* freedom, choice, and autonomy. Marriage, for example, is a commitment to a particular other person that curtails freedom of choice of sexual, and even emotional partners. To be someone's friend is to undertake weighty responsibilities and obligations that at times may limit your own freedom. Counterintuitive as it may appear, what seems to contribute most to happiness binds people rather than liberating them.

The case that increased choice leads to decreased well-being is highly inferential. However, there is some more specific evidence that people do not always find increased choice options attractive. Iyengar and Lepper (2000) report a series of studies that showed how choice can be "demotivating." One study was set in a gourmet food store in which the researchers set up a display featuring a line of exotic, high-quality jams. Customers who came by could taste samples, and then were given a coupon for a dollar off if they bought a jar. In one condition of the study, six varieties of the jam were available for tasting. In another, 24 varieties were available. In either case, the entire set of 24 varieties was available for purchase. The large array of jams attracted more people to the table than the small array, though in both cases people tasted about the same number of jams on average. When it came to buying, however, 30% of people exposed to the small array of jams actually bought a jar; only 3% of those exposed to the large array of jams did so.

In a second study, this time in the laboratory, college students were asked to evaluate a variety of gourmet chocolates. The students were then asked which chocolate—based on description and appearance—they would choose for themselves. Then they tasted and rated that chocolate. Finally, in a different room, the students were offered a small box of the chocolates in lieu of cash as payment for their participation. For one group of students, the initial array of chocolates numbered six, and for the other, it numbered 30. The key results of this study were that the students faced with the small array were more satisfied with their tasting than those faced with the large array. In addition, they were four times as likely to choose chocolate rather than cash as compensation for their participation.

This set of results is counterintuitive. Surely, you are more likely to find something you like from a set of 24 or 30 options than from a set of six. At worst, the extra options add nothing, but in that case, they should also take away nothing. Surely you are free to ignore as many of the options before you as you would like. But apparently, people find it difficult to do so.

THE GOALS OF CHOICE:
MAXIMIZING AND SATISFICING

Half a century ago, Simon (1955, 1956, 1957) argued that in choice situations individuals will often "satisfice," that is, choose the first option that surpasses some absolute threshold of acceptability, rather than attempt to optimize and find the best possible choice. Such a satisficing strategy was thought to make manageable the otherwise overwhelming task of evaluating options in terms of every possible piece of information that could potentially be known about them. Rather than attempt to engage in an exhaustive and ultimately limitless search for perfect information regarding a particular choice, satisficers would simply end their search as soon as an option was found that exceeded some criterion.

Such a strategy makes good sense in a world of ever-increasing freedom and choice. However, many would argue that attendant with increased choice has been a pressure to "maximize," that is, to seek the very best option available in a wide range of choice domains. It may well be the case that, for certain individuals, adding more choices to an existing domain simply makes choice more difficult, as they feel pressure to choose the "best" possible option from an overwhelming array of choices rather than simply settle for "good enough." After all, as the number of choices in a domain increases, so too does the cognitive work required to compare various options, along with the possibility of making a "wrong" or suboptimal choice. Thus, if you follow such a maximizing strategy, the more choices you face, the greater the potential to experience regret at having chosen suboptimally.

We undertook an investigation to determine whether some individuals are more likely to be these maximizers and, if so, if they are more unhappy than their satisficing peers (Schwartz et al., 2002). We designed a survey instrument, the Maximization Scale, to identify both maximizers and satisficers, and then examined the potential relation between various scores on the scale and a range of psychological correlates, including happiness, depression, optimism, self-esteem, perfectionism, neuroticism, and subjective well-being. We also explored whether these putative relationships might be mediated by a tendency for maximizers to experience more regret with regard to their choices than satisficers. Finally, we examined maximizers' versus satisficers' tendency to engage in social comparison. We reasoned that if maximizers are always on the lookout for the best possible option, one way to do so is to examine the choices of others, especially in domains in which no clear objective standard exists for what constitutes "the best" (cf. Festinger, 1954).

The Maximization Scale includes 13 items that assess a range of attitudes and behaviors that together comprise a tendency to maximize rather than satisfice. Thus, respondents are asked to endorse statements reflecting (1) the adoption of high standards (e.g., "No matter what I do, I have the highest standards for myself"); (2) actions that are consistent with maximizing tendencies ("When I am in the car listening to the radio, I often check other stations to see if something better is playing, even if I'm relatively satisfied with what I'm listening to"); and (3) choice behaviors aimed at seeking out the "best" option ("Renting videos is really difficult. I'm always struggling to pick the best one"). We administered the survey to over 1,700 participants in the United States and Canada who ranged in age from 16 to 81 and came from diverse ethnic backgrounds.

Different subsamples of our respondents also completed a number of other standard personality measures. Among these were the Subjective Happiness Scale

(Lyubomirsky & Lepper, 1999; $n = 1627$); the Beck Depression Inventory (BDI; Beck & Beck, 1972; $n = 1006$); a measure of dispositional optimism (Life Orientation Test; Scheier & Carver, 1985; $n = 182$); a neuroticism scale (John, Donahue, & Kentle, 1991; $n = 100$); a survey assessing subjective well-being (Satisfaction with Life Scale; Diener, Emmons, Larsen, & Griffin, 1985; $n = 100$); a self-esteem measure (Rosenberg, 1965; $n = 266$); and a subscale of the Multidimensional Perfectionism Scale (Hewitt & Flett, 1990, 1991; $n = 220$). Finally, we created a 5-item scale designed to assess a tendency to experience regret (e.g., "When I think about how I'm doing in life, I often assess opportunities I have passed up") and administered it to all of our participants.

In terms of self-reported happiness, there was a clear tendency for maximizers to report being significantly less happy and optimistic than satisficers. They were also less likely to report high subjective well-being scores and were more likely to be depressed. In one subsample, of the individuals whose BDI scores met the diagnostic criterion for mild depression, 44% also scored in the top quartile for maximization whereas only 16% scored in the bottom quartile. Maximizers also reported lower self-esteem scores and higher neuroticism scores than satisficers, although the latter relationship did not reach statistical significance in our sample, suggesting discriminant validity between the constructs of maximization and neuroticism. In addition, although we observed mildly significant correlations between maximizing and the related construct of perfectionism, the latter correlated positively with happiness in our sample, suggesting that, unlike maximizing, perfectionist tendencies are not necessarily associated with unhappiness. Finally, those who scored high on the Maximization Scale were also much more likely to report experiencing regret.

Statistical analyses showed that individuals' endorsement of the regret items appeared to at least partially mediate many of the relationships between maximizing and the other personality measures, including maximizers' tendency to be less happy and more depressed. It would seem that maximization constitutes a recipe for unhappiness, in that those individuals who search for the best possible option are more likely to regret a choice once made.

In a subsequent study (Schwartz et al., 2002; Study 4), the hypothesized tendency of maximizers to experience greater sensitivity to regret was investigated in a behavioral paradigm that made use of a version of the "ultimatum game" (Zeelenberg & Beattie, 1997). In the study, individuals had the opportunity to propose a division of funds to a second player (simulated by a computer) who could choose to accept or reject the offer. If the offer was accepted, the funds would be divided up as proposed. If the second player rejected the offer, however, neither player would receive any money. Participants played both a standard version of the game and a modified version, in which, after offering a division of funds, they got to learn the other player's "reservation price," that is, the minimal acceptable offer that the other player would have accepted. In short, this modified version created a greater potential for regret of your offer, because it carried the possibility of learning that you would not have needed to have been so generous in dividing up the provided funds.

As predicted, in the modified version (i.e., when participants expected to learn the other player's reservation price) maximizers made much more modest offers to their opponents than in the condition in which a participant never had to face the knowledge that a more meager offer would have been accepted. Satisficers did not show this pattern. It would appear that maximizers' greater tendency to experience regret extends to situations involving anticipated regret as well, as their behavior in this study appeared to be aimed at minimizing the possibility of later regret.

Maximizers were also hypothesized to engage in more social comparison than satisficers—especially upward comparison, in which an individual compares him or herself to someone who is better off, as such a person would presumably provide the best "evidence" that a maximizer has not yet achieved an optimal outcome. This tendency was investigated in two studies. In the first (Schwartz et al., 2002; Study 2), maximizers reported on a questionnaire measure that they were more likely to engage in social comparison—both upward and downward—than satisficers, and their greater frequency of upward comparison was associated with increased unhappiness (though their greater frequency of downward comparison did not predict enhanced happiness). The same study also probed respondents' experiences with consumer decisions and found that maximizers reported seeking more social comparison information in making purchases than did satisficers. They also reported engaging in more product comparisons and counterfactual thinking (thinking about alternatives not chosen) regarding buying decisions, along with heightened regret and diminished happiness with their purchases.

A second study (Schwartz et al., 2002; Study 3) examined social comparison tendencies in maximizers versus satisficers using a procedure developed by Lyubomirsky and Ross (1997). In the study, participants performed an anagram-solving task either much slower or much faster than a confederate posing as a fellow undergraduate. Maximizers were heavily affected by their peer's performance, especially when they were outperformed by the peer. They provided higher assessments of their ability to perform the task after working alongside a slower peer than a faster peer, and in the latter condition, their self-assessment declined and their negative affect increased significantly. Satisficers, by contrast, were barely affected by the performance of the other participant, and regardless of whether the situation provided an opportunity for downward comparison (i.e., outperforming a peer) or upward comparison (i.e., being outperformed by a peer), their assessment of their own ability and their affect level remained largely unaffected. In short, maximizers were sensitive to social comparison information and were made less happy when outperformed by a peer; satisficers showed little response to the social comparison information provided by the experimental situation, and their mood remained relatively stable throughout the study.

In sum, in both survey and experimental procedures, maximizers showed themselves to be less happy and more depressed than satisficers. They were more prone to regret, both experienced and anticipated, and they engaged in more social comparison, especially upward comparison, than satisficers. In their quest for the best option, they increased their own unhappiness and regretted their choices more than individuals who reported a willingness to settle for "good enough." For maximizers, "good enough" evidently was not, but at least in terms of their own psychological well-being, "the best" was far from ideal.

CHOICE AND WELL-BEING: WHY PEOPLE SUFFER

Several factors conspire to undermine the objective benefits that ought to come with increased choice. We will review them, and in each case, we'll show why the choice problem is exacerbated for maximizers (see Schwartz, 2004, for a more detailed discussion).

REGRET

Our research showed that regret mediated the relation between maximizing and various measures of life satisfaction. People with high regret scores are less happy, less satisfied with life, less optimistic, and more depressed than those with low regret scores. We also found that people with high regret scores tend to be maximizers. Concern about regret may be a major reason why individuals are maximizers. The only way to be sure that you won't regret a decision is by making the best possible decision. However, the more options you have, the more likely it is that you will experience regret.

Postdecision regret, sometimes referred to as *buyer's remorse,* induces second thoughts that rejected alternatives were actually better than the one we chose, or that there are better alternatives out there that haven't been explored. The bitter taste of regret detracts from satisfaction, whether or not the regret is justified.

Anticipated regret may be even worse, because it will produce not just dissatisfaction but paralysis. If someone asks herself how it would feel to buy this house only to discover a better one next week, she probably won't buy this house. Both types of regret—anticipated and postdecision—will raise the emotional stakes of decisions. Anticipated regret will make decisions harder to make and postdecision regret will make them harder to enjoy. (See Gilovich & Medvec, 1995; Landman, 1993; for thoughtful discussions of the determinants and consequences of regret.)

What makes the problem of regret much worse is that thinking is not restricted to objective reality. People can also think about states of affairs that don't exist. Studies of such counterfactual thinking have found that most individuals do not often engage in this process spontaneously. Instead, counterfactual thinking is usually triggered by the occurrence of something that itself produces a negative emotion. Counterfactual thoughts are generated in response to poor exam grades, to trouble in romantic relationships, and to the illness or death of loved ones. And when the counterfactual thoughts begin to occur, they trigger more negative emotions, like regret, which in turn trigger more counterfactual thinking, which in turn triggers more negative emotion. When they examine the actual content of counterfactual thinking, researchers find that individuals tend to focus on aspects of a situation that are under their control. The fact that counterfactual thinking seems to home in on the controllable aspects of a situation only increases the chances that the emotion a person experiences when engaging in counterfactual thinking will be regret (see Roese, 1997).

REGRET, MAXIMIZING, AND CHOICE POSSIBILITIES

We have seen that two of the factors affecting regret are personal responsibility for the result and how easily an individual can imagine a counterfactual, better alternative. The availability of choice exacerbates both of these factors. When there are no options, what can you experience? Disappointment, maybe; regret, no. When you have only a few options, you do the best you can, but circumstances simply may not allow you to do as well as you would like. When there are many options, the chances increase that there is a really good one out there, and you feel that you ought to be able to find it. When the option you actually settle on proves disappointing, you regret not having chosen more wisely. As the number of options continues to proliferate, making an exhaustive investigation of the possibilities impossible, concern that there may be a better option out there may induce you to anticipate the regret you will feel later on, when that option is discovered, and thus prevent you from making a decision at all. Landman (1993, p. 184) sums it up this way: "[R]egret may threaten decisions with multiple attractive alternatives more than decisions offering only one or a more limited set of alternatives . . . Ironically, then, the greater the number of appealing choices, the greater the opportunity for regret."

We have argued that the problem of regret will loom larger for maximizers than for satisficers. No matter how good something is, if a maximizer discovers something better, she'll regret having failed to choose it in the first place. Perfection is the only weapon against regret, and endless, exhaustive, paralyzing consideration of the alternatives is the only way to achieve perfection. For a satisficer, the stakes are lower. The possibility of regret doesn't loom as large, and perfection is unnecessary.

Opportunity Costs

Economists point out that the quality of any given option cannot be assessed in isolation from its alternatives. One of the "costs" of any option involves passing up the opportunities that a different option would have afforded. This is referred to as an *opportunity cost*. Every choice we make has opportunity costs associated with it.

According to standard economic assumptions, the only opportunity costs that should figure into a decision are the ones associated with the next best alternative, because you wouldn't have chosen the third, fourth, or *n*th best alternative in any event. This advice, however, is extremely difficult to follow. The options under consideration usually have multiple features. If people think about options in terms of their features rather than as a whole, different options may rank as second best (or even best) with respect to each individual feature. Even though there may be a single, second best option overall, each of the options may have some very desirable feature on which it beats its competition.

If we assume that opportunity costs take away from the overall desirability of the most preferred option, and that we will feel the opportunity costs associated with many of the options we reject, then the more alternatives there are from which to choose, the greater our experience of the opportunity costs will be. And the greater our experience of the opportunity costs, the less satisfaction we will derive from our chosen alternative.

This form of dissatisfaction was confirmed by a study in which people were asked how much they would be willing to pay for subscriptions to popular magazines, or to purchase videotapes of popular movies (Brenner, Rottenstreich, & Sood, 1999). Some participants were asked about individual magazines or videos. Others were asked about these same magazines or videos as part of a group with other magazines or videos. In almost every case, respondents placed a higher value on the magazine or the video when they were evaluating it in isolation than when they were evaluating it as part of a cluster. When magazines are evaluated as part of a group, opportunity costs associated with the other options reduce the value of each of them.

EFFECTS OF ADAPTATION

As Kahneman and various collaborators have shown (e.g., Kahneman, 1999), we appear to possess hedonic "thermometers" that run from negative (unpleasant), through neutral, to pleasant. When we experience something good, our pleasure "temperature" goes up, and when we experience something bad, it goes down. However, our responses to hedonic stimuli are not constant; repeated exposure results in adaptation (Frederick & Loewenstein, 1999).

In what is perhaps the most famous example of hedonic adaptation, respondents were asked to rate their happiness on a 5-point scale (Brickman, Coates, & Janoff-Bulman, 1978). Some of them had won between $50,000 and $1 million in state lotteries within the last year. Others had become paraplegic or quadriplegic as a result of accidents. Not surprisingly, the lottery winners were happier than those who had become paralyzed. What is surprising, though, is that the lottery winners were no happier than people in general. And what is even more surprising is that the accident victims, while somewhat less happy than people in general, still judged themselves to be happy.

Though hedonic adaptation is almost ubiquitous, people don't expect it (Loewenstein & Schkade, 1999). Thus, the ultimate result of adaptation to positive experiences appears to be disappointment. Faced with this inevitable disappointment, people will be driven to pursue novelty, to seek out new commodities and experiences whose pleasure potential has not been dissipated by repeated exposure. In time, these new commodities also will lose their intensity, but people still get caught up in the chase, a process that Brickman and Campbell (1971) labeled the "hedonic treadmill." Perhaps even more insidious than the hedonic treadmill is something that Kahneman (1999) calls the "satisfaction treadmill," which refers to the possibility that in addition to adapting to particular objects or experiences, people also adapt to particular levels of satisfaction.

The relevance of adaptation to the proliferation of choice is this: Imagine the search costs involved in a decision as being spread over the life of a decision. They may be very high in a world of overwhelming choice (especially for a maximizer), but if the results of the choice produce a long and sustained period of substantial satisfaction, their cumulative effects will be minimized. (The costs, in money and inconvenience, of painting your house may be substantial, but if you stay there for 10 years, enjoying the benefits, those costs will dissolve into insignificance.) If, however, the satisfaction with a decision is short-lived, because of adaptation (you get a job transfer and have to move two months after having painted your house), then the "amortization schedule" will be very much abbreviated and the initial costs will subtract much more from the total satisfaction.

HIGH EXPECTATIONS

When people evaluate an experience, they are performing one or more of the following comparisons (see Michalos, 1980, 1986):

1. Comparing the experience to what they hoped it would be
2. Comparing the experience to what they expected it to be
3. Comparing the experience to other experiences they have had in the recent past
4. Comparing the experience to experiences that others have had

As material and social circumstances improve, standards of comparison go up. As people have contact with items of high quality, they begin to suffer from "the curse of discernment." The lower quality items that used to be perfectly acceptable are no longer good enough. The hedonic zero point keeps rising, and expectations and aspirations rise with it. As a result, the rising quality of experience is met with rising expectations, and people are just running in place. As long as expectations keep pace with realizations, people may live better, but they won't *feel* better about how they live.

Social Comparison

Of all the sources we rely on when we evaluate experiences, perhaps nothing is more important than comparisons to other people. In many ways, social comparison parallels the counterfactual thinking process, but there is one very important difference. In principle, people have a great deal of control both over when they will engage in counterfactual thinking and what its content will be. People have less control over social comparison. There is always information available about how others are doing.

Though social comparison information is seemingly all-pervasive, it appears that not everyone pays attention to it, or at least, not everyone is affected by it. Lyubomirsky and her colleagues (e.g., Lyubomirsky & Ross, 1997, 1999; Lyubomirsky, Tucker, & Kasri, 2001) have conducted a series of studies that looked for differences among individuals in their responses to social comparison information, and what they found is that social comparison information has relatively little impact on dispositionally happy people. Happy people were only minimally affected by whether the person working next to them was better or worse at an anagram task than they were. In contrast, unhappy people showed increases in assessed ability and positive feelings after working beside a slower peer, and *decreases* in assessed ability and positive feelings if they'd been working beside a faster peer.

Such results parallel the findings we reported regarding maximizers, who seem more sensitive than satisficers to the behavior of others as a gauge of their own progress in obtaining "the best." Maximizers want the best, but how do you know that you have the best, except by comparison? And to the extent that we have more options, determining the "best" can become overwhelmingly difficult. The maximizer becomes a slave in her judgments to the experiences of other people. Satisficers don't have this problem. Satisficers can rely on their own internal assessments to develop those standards.

Learned Helplessness, Control, Depression, and Self-Blame

About 35 years ago, Seligman proposed that clinical depression may be the result of lack of control, or learned helplessness (see Maier & Seligman, 1976; Overmier & Seligman, 1967; Seligman, 1975; Seligman & Maier, 1967). The theory was subsequently modified by Abramson, Seligman, and Teasdale (1978), who suggested that important psychological steps intervene between the experience of helplessness and depression. According to these researchers, when people experience a lack of control, they look for causes and display a variety of predispositions to accept certain types of causes, quite apart from what the actual cause of the failure might be. There are three key dimensions to these predispositions, based on whether people view causes as being global or specific, chronic or transient (or what was labeled "stable versus unstable"), personal or universal (or "internal versus external"). The revised theory of helplessness and depression argued that helplessness induced by failure or lack of control leads to depression if a person's causal explanations for that failure are global, chronic, and personal. It is only then that people will have good reason to expect one failure to be followed by others.

Tests of this revised theory have yielded impressive results (e.g., Peterson & Seligman, 1984). People *do* differ in the types of predispositions they display. People who find chronic causes for failure expect failures to persist. People who find global causes for failure expect failure to follow them into every area of life. And people who find personal causes for failure suffer large losses in self-esteem.

Owing to the explosion of choice we outlined at the beginning of this chapter, the American middle class now experiences control and personal autonomy to a degree that people living in other times and places would find unimaginable. This fact, coupled with the helplessness theory of depression, might suggest that clinical depression in the United States should be disappearing. Instead, we see explosive *growth* in the disorder. Furthermore, depression seems to attack its victims at a younger age now than in earlier eras. Current estimates are that as many as 7.5% of Americans have an episode of clinical depression before they are 14. This is twice the rate seen in young people born only 10 years earlier (Angst, 1995; Klerman & Weissman, 1989; Klerman et al., 1985; Lane, 2000; Myers, 2000; Rosenhan & Seligman, 1995). The most extreme manifestation of depression—suicide—is also on the rise, and it, too, is happening to younger people. Suicide is the second leading cause of death (after accidents) among American high school and college students. In the past 35 years, the suicide rate among American college students has tripled. Throughout the developed world, suicide among adolescents and young adults is increasing dramatically (Eckersley, 2002; Eckersley & Dear, 2002). In an era of ever greater personal autonomy and control, what could account for this degree of personal misery?

We believe there are several answers to this question. First, increases in experienced control over the years have been accompanied, stride-for-stride, by increases in *expectations* about control. The more we are allowed to be the masters of our fates, the more we expect to be. Emphasis on freedom of choice, together with the proliferation of possibilities that modern life affords, have contributed to these unrealistic expectations.

Along with the pervasive rise in expectations, American culture also has become more individualistic than it was, perhaps as a by-product of the desire to have control over every aspect of life. Heightened individualism means that, not only do people expect perfection in all things, but they expect to produce this perfection themselves. When they (inevitably) fail, the culture of individualism biases people toward causal explanations that focus on personal rather than universal factors. That is, the culture has established a kind of officially acceptable style of causal explanation, and it is one that encourages the individual to blame himself for failure (see Weiner, 1985).

Unrealistically high expectations coupled with a tendency to take intense personal responsibility for failure make a lethal combination. This problem is especially acute for maximizers. As they do with missed opportunities, regret, adaptation, and social comparison, maximizers will suffer more from high expectations and self-blame than will satisficers. Maximizers will put the most work into their decisions and have the highest expectations about the results of those decisions, and thus will be the most disappointed.

Our research suggests that maximizers are prime candidates for depression. With group after group of people, varying in age, gender, educational level, geographical location, race, and socioeconomic status, we have found a strong positive relation between maximizing and measures of depression. Among people who score highest on our Maximization Scale, scores on the standard measure of depression are in the borderline clinical range. We find the same relation between maximizing and depression among young adolescents (Gillham, Ward, & Schwartz, 2001). High expectations, and personal attributions for failing to meet them, can apply to educational decisions, career decisions, and marital decisions just as they apply to decisions about where to eat. Even the trivial decisions add up. If the experience of disappointment is relentless, if virtually every choice you make fails to live up to expectations and aspirations, and if you consistently take personal responsibility for the disappointments, then the trivial looms larger and larger, and the conclusion that you can't do anything right becomes devastating.

FUTURE RESEARCH

We have only begun to investigate in a systematic fashion the behavior of maximizers versus satisficers. Future research will help determine the domain specificity of maximizing behaviors. No one pursues "the best" in every arena of life, and what distinguishes maximizers from satisficers may ultimately be the number of domains in which an individual attempts to obtain something that is optimal as opposed to merely acceptable. In addition, future studies will determine whether maximizers sometimes engage in behavior that looks similar to that of satisficers but reflects different motives. For example, if a maximizer is aware of his or her tendency to engage in an exhaustive, time-consuming, and ultimately disappointing search for the most attractive option, he or she may on occasion opt to restrict a choice set by simply selecting the first option available (a strategy pursued by the more maximizing of the two authors when he purchased his last car). In other words, there may be occasions in which maximizers "choose not to choose" rather than endure the misery and paralysis that can often follow their attempts to maximize. Such speculation implies that maximizers are aware of the negative psychological consequences that typically accompany their behavior, and that in and of itself (i.e., whether maximizers know that there is a psychological cost to be paid for their habitual "quest for the best") is worthy of further study.

Finally, additional research should investigate the origins of a maximizing versus satisficing style of choice behavior. We have speculated on the cultural pressures in a postindustrial capitalist society that might lead to the development of maximizing tendencies, especially in times of plenty (see Schwartz, 1994; Wieczorkowska & Burnstein, 1999, for further discussion). Although at times maximizing may produce superior material outcomes (a question worth pursuing in its own right), we believe that such a strategy leads individuals to inferior psychological outcomes. We should acknowledge, though, that the causal arrow may point in the opposite direction; that is, unhappy or depressed individuals may resort to a maximizing strategy in an attempt to improve their current psychological state. Regardless of the causal direction, however, a strategy of continually searching for the best option and then regretting one's choices once made does not appear to be a recipe for long-term happiness.

CHOICE, MAXIMIZING, AND MISERY: WHAT CAN BE DONE?

We have discussed why increased opportunities to choose can result in decreased well-being, and suggested that this inverse relation between choice and well-being is especially acute for people who are after the "best" in any choice situation. Next we offer some suggestions about what people can do to mitigate this problem (see Schwartz, 2004, for further discussion). None of them is easy to follow and all of them are speculative—that is, they are based on the arguments we offered rather than on evidence.

CHOOSE WHEN TO CHOOSE

Having the opportunity to choose is essential for well-being, but choice has negative features, and the negative features escalate as the number of choices increases. The benefits of having options are apparent with each particular decision people face, but the costs are subtle and cumulative. To manage the problem of excessive choice, people should decide where in life choice really matters and focus their time and energy there, letting other opportunities pass them by.

SATISFICE MORE AND MAXIMIZE LESS

It is maximizers who suffer most in a culture that provides too many choices. It is maximizers who have expectations that can't be met. It is maximizers who worry most about regret, about missed opportunities, and about social comparisons, and it is maximizers who are most disappointed when the results of decisions are not as good as they expect. Learning to accept "good enough" will simplify decision making and increase satisfaction. Though satisficers may do less well than maximizers according to certain objective standards, nonetheless, by settling for "good enough" even when the "best" may be just around the corner, satisficers will usually feel better about the decisions they make.

THINK LESS ABOUT OPPORTUNITY COSTS

When making a decision, it's usually a good idea to think about the alternatives we will pass up when choosing our most preferred option. Ignoring these "opportunity costs" can lead us to overestimate how good the best option is. On the other hand, the more we think about opportunity costs, the less satisfaction we'll derive from whatever we choose. So we should make an effort to limit how much we think about the attractive features of options we reject. Being a satisficer can help here. Because satisficers have their own standards for what is "good enough," they are less dependent than maximizers on comparison among alternatives. A "good investment" for a satisficer may be one that returns more than inflation. Will the satisficer earn less from investments than the maximizer? Perhaps. Will she be less satisfied with the results? Probably not. Will she have more time available to devote to other decisions that matter to her? Absolutely.

PRACTICE GRATITUDE

Our evaluation of our choices is profoundly affected by what we compare them with, including comparisons with alternatives that exist only in our imaginations. The same experience can have both delightful and disappointing aspects. Which of these we focus on may determine whether we judge the experience to be satisfactory or not. We can vastly improve our subjective experience by consciously striving to be grateful more often for what is good about a choice or an experience, and to be disappointed less by what is bad about it. The research literature suggests that gratitude does not come naturally to most of us most of the time (Emmons & Crumpler, 2000; McCullough, Kilpatrick, Emmons, & Larson, 2001). Usually, thinking about possible alternatives is triggered by dissatisfaction with what was chosen. When life is not too good, we think a lot about how it could be better. When life is going well, we tend not to think much about how it could be worse. But with practice, we can learn to reflect on how much better things are than they might be, which will in turn make the good things in life feel even better.

REGRET LESS

The sting of regret (either actual or potential) colors many decisions, and sometimes influences people to avoid making decisions at all. Whereas regret is often appropriate and instructive, when it becomes so pronounced that it poisons or even prevents decisions, people should make an effort to minimize it. We can mitigate regret by adopting the standards of a satisficer rather than a maximizer, reducing the number of options we consider before making a decision, and practicing gratitude for what is good in a decision rather than focusing on our disappointments with what is bad.

CONTROL EXPECTATIONS

Our evaluation of experience is substantially influenced by how it compares with expectations. So what may be the easiest route to increasing satisfaction with the results of decisions is to remove excessively high expectations about them. We can make the task of lowering expectations easier by reducing the number of options we consider, and, once again, by being satisficers rather than maximizers.

CURTAIL SOCIAL COMPARISON

We evaluate the quality of our experiences by comparing ourselves to others. Though social comparison can provide useful information, it often reduces our satisfaction. By comparing ourselves to others *less*, we will be satisfied *more*.

LEARN TO LOVE CONSTRAINTS

As the number of choices we face increases, freedom of choice eventually becomes a *tyranny* of choice. Routine decisions take so much time and attention that it becomes difficult to get through the day. In circumstances like this, we should learn to view limits on the possibilities we face as liberating, not constraining. Society provides rules, standards, and norms for making choices, and individual experience creates habits. By deciding to follow a rule (e.g., always wear a seat belt;

never drink more than two glasses of wine in one evening), we avoid having to make a deliberate decision again and again. This kind of rule following frees up time and attention that can be devoted to thinking about choices and decisions to which rules don't apply.

We probably would be deeply resentful if someone tried to take our freedom of choice away in any part of life that we really cared about and really knew something about. If it were up to us to choose whether or not to have choice, we would opt for choice almost every time. But it is the *cumulative* effect of these added choices that is causing substantial distress. We are trapped in what Hirsch (1976) called "the tyranny of small decisions." In any given domain, we say a resounding "yes" to choice, but we never cast a vote on the whole package of choices. Nonetheless, by voting yes in every particular situation, we are in effect voting yes on the package. The result, as we have suggested in this chapter, can be tyranny and misery rather than liberation and satisfaction.

REFERENCES

Abramson, L. Y., Seligman, M. E. P., & Teasdale, J. D. (1978). Learned helplessness in humans: Critique and reformulation. *Journal of Abnormal Psychology, 87,* 49–74.

Angst, J. (1995). The epidemiology of depressive disorders. *European Neuropsychopharmacology, 5,* 95–98.

Beck, A. T., & Beck, R. W. (1972). Screening depressed patients in a family practice: A rapid technique. *Postgraduate Medicine, 52,* 81–85.

Brenner, L., Rottenstreich, Y., & Sood, S. (1999). Comparison, grouping, and preference. *Psychological Science, 10,* 225–229.

Brickman, P., & Campbell, D. T. (1971). Hedonic relativism and planning the good society. In M. H. Appley (Ed.), *Adaptation-level theory: A symposium* (pp. 287–302). New York: Academic Press.

Brickman, P., Coates, D., & Janoff-Bulman, R. (1978). Lottery winners and accident victims: Is happiness relative? *Journal of Personality and Social Psychology, 36,* 917–927.

Clark, K. (1999, November 1). Why it pays to quit. *U.S. News and World Report,* 74–79.

Cottle, M. (2002, March 25). Bodywork. *New Republic,* pp. 16–19.

Cross, G. (2000). *An all-consuming century: Why commercialism won in modern America.* New York: Columbia University Press.

Diener, E. (2000). Subjective well-being: The science of happiness and a proposal for a national index. *American Psychologist, 55,* 34–43.

Diener, E., Diener, M., & Diener, C. (1995). Factors predicting the subjective well-being of nations. *Journal of Personality and Social Psychology, 69,* 851–864.

Diener, E., Emmons, R. A., Larsen, R. J., & Griffin, S. (1985). The Satisfaction With Life Scale. *Journal of Personality Assessment, 49,* 71–75.

Diener, E., & Suh, E. M. (Eds.). (2001). *Culture and subjective well-being.* Cambridge, MA: MIT Press.

*Diener, E., Suh, E. M., Lucas, R. E., & Smith, H. L. (1999). Subjective well-being: Three decades of progress. *Psychological Bulletin, 125,* 276–302.

Eckersley, R. (2002). Culture, health, and well-being. In R. Eckersley, J. Dixon, & B. Douglas (Eds.), *The social origins of health and well-being* (pp. 51–70). Cambridge, England: Cambridge University Press.

Eckersley, R., & Dear, K. (2002). Cultural correlates of youth suicide. *Social Science and Medicine, 55,* 1891–1904.

Emmons, R. A., & Crumpler, C. A. (2000). Gratitude as a human strength: Appraising the evidence. *Journal of Social and Clinical Psychology, 19,* 56–69.

Festinger, L. (1954). A theory of social comparison processes. *Human Relations, 7,* 114–140.

Frederick, S., & Loewenstein, G. (1999). Hedonic adaptation. In D. Kahneman, E. Diener, & N. Schwarz (Eds.), *Well-being: The foundations of hedonic psychology* (pp. 302–329). New York: Russell Sage Foundation.

Gawande, A. (1999, October 4). Whose body is it anyway? *New Yorker,* 83–95.

Gillham, J., Ward, A., & Schwartz, B. (2001). *Maximizing and depressed mood in college students and young adolescents.* Manuscript in preparation.

Gilovich, T., & Medvec, V. H. (1995). The experience of regret: What, when, and why. *Psychological Review, 102,* 379–395.

Hewitt, P. L., & Flett, G. L. (1990). Perfectionism and depression: A multidimensional analysis. *Journal of Social Behavior and Personality, 5,* 423–438.

Hewitt, P. L., & Flett, G. L. (1991). Perfectionism in the self and social contexts: Conceptualization, assessment, and association with psychopathology. *Journal of Personality and Social Psychology, 60,* 456–470.

Hirsch, F. (1976). *Social limits to growth.* Cambridge, MA: Harvard University Press.

Inglehart, R. (1997). *Modernization and postmodernization: Cultural, economic, and political changes in societies.* Princeton, NJ: Princeton University Press.

*Iyengar, S., & Lepper, M. (2000). When choice is demotivating: Can one desire too much of a good thing? *Journal of Personality and Social Psychology, 79,* 995–1006.

John, O. P., Donahue, E. M., & Kentle, R. L. (1991). *The "big five" inventory—Versions 4a and 54* [Technical report]. Berkeley, CA: Institute of Personality Assessment and Research.

Kahneman, D. (1999). Objective happiness. In D. Kahneman, E. Diener, & N. Schwarz (Eds.), *Well-being: The foundations of hedonic psychology* (pp. 3–25). New York: Russell Sage Foundation.

Kaminer, W. (2001, February 26). American beauty. *American Prospect,* 34–35.

Klerman, G. L., Lavori, P. W., Rice, J., Reich, T., Endicott, J., Andreasen, N. C., et al. (1985). Birth cohort trends in rates of major depressive disorder: A study of relatives of patients with affective disorder. *Archives of General Psychiatry, 42,* 689–693.

Klerman, G. L., & Weissman, M. M. (1989). Increasing rates of depression. *Journal of the American Medical Association, 261,* 2229–2235.

Landman, J. (1993). *Regret: The persistence of the possible.* New York: Oxford University Press.

*Lane, R. (2000). *The loss of happiness in market democracies.* New Haven, CT: Yale University Press.

Loewenstein, G., & Schkade, D. (1999). Wouldn't it be nice? Predicting future feelings. In D. Kahneman, E. Diener, & N. Schwarz (Eds.), *Well-being: The foundations of hedonic psychology* (pp. 85–108). New York: Russell Sage Foundation.

Lyubomirsky, S., & Lepper, H. S. (1999). A measure of subjective happiness: Preliminary reliability and construct validation. *Social Indicators Research, 46,* 137–155.

*Lyubomirsky, S., & Ross, L. (1997). Hedonic consequences of social comparison: A contrast of happy and unhappy people. *Journal of Personality and Social Psychology, 73,* 1141–1157.

Lyubomirsky, S., & Ross, L. (1999). Changes in attractiveness of elected, rejected, and precluded alternatives: A comparison of happy and unhappy individuals. *Journal of Personality and Social Psychology, 76,* 988–1007.

Lyubomirsky, S., Tucker, K. L., & Kasri, F. (2001). Responses to hedonically conflicting social comparisons: Comparing happy and unhappy people. *European Journal of Social Psychology, 31,* 1–25.

Maier, S. F., & Seligman, M. E. P. (1976). Learned helplessness: Theory and evidence. *Journal of Experimental Psychology: General, 105,* 3–46.

McCullough, M. E., Kilpatrick, S. D., Emmons, R. A., & Larson, D. B. (2001). Is gratitude a moral affect? *Psychological Bulletin, 127,* 249–266.

Michalos, A. C. (1980). Satisfaction and happiness. *Social Indicators Research, 8,* 385–422.

Michalos, A. C. (1986). Job satisfaction, marital satisfaction, and the quality of life: A review and a preview. In F. M. Andrews (Ed.), *Research on the quality of life* (pp. 57–83). Ann Arbor: University of Michigan, Institute for Social Research.

*Myers, D. G. (2000). *The American paradox: Spiritual hunger in an age of plenty.* New Haven, CT: Yale University Press.

Overmier, J. B., & Seligman, M. E. P. (1967). Effects of inescapable shock upon subsequent escape and avoidance behavior. *Journal of Comparative and Physiological Psychology, 63,* 23–33.

Peterson, C., & Seligman, M. E. P. (1984). Causal explanations as a risk factor for depression: Theory and evidence. *Psychological Review, 91,* 347–374.

Roese, N. J. (1997). Counterfactual thinking. *Psychological Bulletin, 121,* 133–148.

Rosenberg, M. (1965). *Society and the adolescent self-image.* Princeton, NJ: Princeton University Press.

Rosenhan, D. L., & Seligman, M. E. P. (1995). *Abnormal psychology.* New York: Norton.

Scheier, M. F., & Carver, C. S. (1985). Optimism, coping, and health: Assessment and implications of generalized outcome expectations. *Health Psychology, 4,* 219–247.

Schwartz, B. (1994). *The costs of living: How market freedom erodes the best things in life.* New York: Norton.

*Schwartz, B. (2004). *The paradox of choice: Why more is less.* New York: Ecco Press.

*Schwartz, B., Ward, A., Monterosso, J., Lyubomirsky, S., White, K., & Lehman, D. R. (2002). Maximizing versus satisficing: Happiness is a matter of choice. *Journal of Personality and Social Psychology, 83,* 1178–1197.

Seligman, M. E. P. (1975). *Helplessness: On depression, development, and death.* New York: Freeman.

Seligman, M. E. P., & Maier, S. F. (1967). Failure to escape traumatic shock. *Journal of Experimental Psychology, 74,* 1–9.

Sen, A. (2000, December 18). Other people. *New Republic,* 21–27.

Simon, H. A. (1955). A behavioral model of rational choice. *Quarterly Journal of Economics, 59,* 99–118.

Simon, H. A. (1956). Rational choice and the structure of the environment. *Psychological Review, 63,* 129–138.

Simon, H. A. (1957). *Models of man, social and rational: Mathematical essays on rational human behavior.* New York: Wiley.

Weiner, B. (1985). An attributional theory of achievement motivation and emotion. *Psychological Review, 92,* 548–573.

Wieczorkowska, G., & Burnstein, E. (1999). Adapting to the transition from socialism to capitalism in Poland: The role of screening strategies in social change. *Psychological Science, 10,* 98–105.

Zeelenberg, M., & Beattie, J. (1997). Consequences of regret aversion 2: Additional evidence for effects of feedback on decision making. *Organizational Behavior and Human Decision Processes, 67,* 63–78.

CHAPTER 7

Fostering Healthy Self-Regulation from Within and Without: A Self-Determination Theory Perspective

KIRK WARREN BROWN and RICHARD M. RYAN

Many theories view motivation as a unitary phenomenon that varies only in its strength. Yet, a deeper analysis readily shows that individuals vary not only in *how much* motivation they possess but also in the orientation or type of motivation that energizes behavior. For example, some people go to work each day because they find their jobs interesting, meaningful, even enjoyable, while others may do the same thing only because financial pressures demand it. Similarly, some students study out of a deep curiosity and an inner desire to learn, while others study only to obtain good grades or meet requirements. In these examples, both groups may be highly motivated, but the nature and focus of the motivation—that is, the *why* of the behavior—clearly varies, as do the consequences. For instance, the curious student may learn more than the required material, process it more deeply, talk more with others about it, and remember more enduringly. This difference may not show up immediately on a test score, but it may have many ramifications for the student's emotional and intellectual development.

Self-determination theory (SDT; Deci & Ryan, 1985; Ryan & Deci, 2000b) argues that motivational orientations that guide behavior have important consequences for healthy behavioral regulation and psychological well-being. Self-determination theory distinguishes between various types of motivation based on the reasons or goals that give impetus to behavior. Among the ways in which motivation varies, of primary consideration is the relative autonomy of an individual's activity. Autonomously motivated behavior is self-endorsed, volitional, and done willingly; that is, it is *self-determined*. In contrast, behavior that lacks autonomy is motivated by real or perceived controls, restrictions, and pressures, arising either from social contextual or internal forces.

The importance of the relative autonomy of motivated behavior is borne out by evidence suggesting that autonomy is endorsed as a primary need and source of satisfaction to people across diverse cultures (Sheldon, Elliot, Kim, & Kasser, 2001) and promotes positive outcomes in varied cultural contexts as well (e.g., Chirkov, Ryan, Kim, & Kaplan, 2003). The fundamental nature of this motivational dimension is also seen at the level of social groups. Over the course of recorded history, autonomy and self-determination have often been rallying cries among those seeking social change in the midst of oppressive or restrictive political or economic climates. Most importantly for the present discussion, however, the relative autonomy of behavior has important consequences for the quality of experience and performance in every domain of behavior, from health care to religious practice, and from education to work. In this chapter, we discuss the nature of motivation in terms of its relative autonomy and review evidence in support of its role in positive psychological and behavioral outcomes. In accord with the theme of this volume, a central focus of this discussion is the practical implications of this work—specifically, how to foster autonomy. We begin by describing variations in the orientation of motivations as outlined within SDT. We then address factors that impact motivation at two levels:

1. How motivators and social contexts can foster or undermine autonomous motivation, and
2. How individuals can best access and harness self-regulatory powers from within.

THE NATURE OF AUTONOMOUS REGULATION

For more than three decades, scholarship in motivation has highlighted the primary distinction between intrinsic and extrinsic reasons for behavioral engagement. *Intrinsic motivation* represents a natural inclination toward assimilation, exploration, interesting activity, and mastery. Activities are intrinsically motivated when they are done for the interest and enjoyment they provide. In contrast, extrinsically motivated activities are those done for instrumental reasons or performed as a means to some separable end. This basic motivational distinction has important functional value, but SDT takes a more nuanced view, postulating a spectrum model of regulation, wherein behavior can be guided by intrinsic motivation and by several forms of extrinsic motivation (Ryan & Deci, 2000a). These extrinsic motivations can range from those that entail mere passive compliance or external control to those that are characterized by active personal commitment and meaningfulness. That is, even extrinsic motives vary in the degree to which they are autonomous or self-determined and, therefore, according to SDT, have different consequences for well-being and the quality and persistence of action.

A subtheory within SDT, organismic integration theory (OIT), details this continuum of motivation and the contextual factors that either support or hinder internalization and integration of the regulation of behavior (Deci & Ryan, 1985; Ryan & Deci, 2000b). Figure 7.1 displays the taxonomy of motivational types described by OIT, arranged from left to right according to the extent to which behavior is externally or internally regulated. At the far left of the continuum is *amotivation,* representing a non-self-regulated state in which behavior is performed without intent or will or is not engaged in at all. Amotivation occurs when

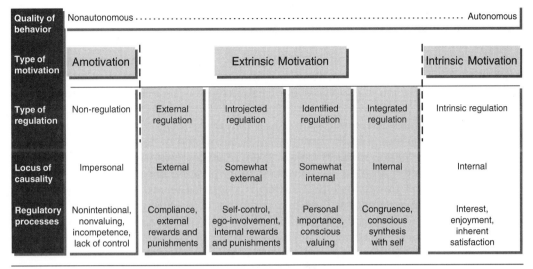

Quality of behavior	Nonautonomous . . . . Autonomous				
Type of motivation	Amotivation	Extrinsic Motivation			Intrinsic Motivation
Type of regulation	Non-regulation	External regulation	Introjected regulation	Identified regulation	Integrated regulation	Intrinsic regulation
Locus of causality	Impersonal	External	Somewhat external	Somewhat internal	Internal	Internal
Regulatory processes	Nonintentional, nonvaluing, incompetence, lack of control	Compliance, external rewards and punishments	Self-control, ego-involvement, internal rewards and punishments	Personal importance, conscious valuing	Congruence, conscious synthesis with self	Interest, enjoyment, inherent satisfaction

Figure 7.1   The Autonomy Continuum Showing Types of Motivation and Their Corresponding Regulatory Styles, Processes, and Loci of Causality

an individual can assign no meaning or value to the behavior, feels incompetent to perform it, or does not expect a desired outcome to result from performing it. The rest of the continuum displayed in Figure 7.1 outlines five conceptually and empirically distinct types of intentional behavioral regulation. At the far right is intrinsic motivation, the doing of an activity for its inherent enjoyment and interest. Such behavior is highly autonomous and represents a gold standard against which the relative autonomy of other forms of regulation is measured. Intrinsic motivation has been associated with a number of positive outcomes, including creativity (e.g., Amabile, 1996), enhanced task performance (Grolnick & Ryan, 1987), and higher psychological well-being (e.g., Csikszentmihalyi & Rathunde, 1993; Ryan, Deci, & Grolnick, 1995).

On the spectrum between amotivation and intrinsic motivation lie four types of extrinsic motivation that vary in the degree of autonomy that each affords. Least autonomous among these types of extrinsic motivation is *external regulation.* Externally regulated behaviors are performed in accord with some external contingency—to obtain reward or avoid punishment or to otherwise comply with a salient demand. The phenomenology of external regulation is one of feeling controlled by forces or pressures outside the self, or, in attributional terms, behavior is perceived as having an external locus of causality (DeCharms, 1968; Ryan & Deci, in press).

Behavior arising from *introjected regulation* is similar to that which is externally regulated in that it is controlled, but in this second form of extrinsic motivation, behavior is performed to meet self-approval-based contingencies. Thus, when operating from introjection, a person behaves to attain ego rewards such as pride or to avoid guilt, anxiety, or disapproval from self or others. Introjection has also been described as contingent self-esteem (e.g., Deci & Ryan, 1995; Ryan & Brown, 2003). A common manifestation of introjection is ego involvement (Ryan, 1982), in which an individual is motivated to demonstrate ability to maintain a sense of self-worth. Although ego involvement can be highly motivating under particular circumstances (e.g., Ryan, Koestner, & Deci, 1991), it is associated with a number of negative consequences, including greater stress, anxiety, self-handicapping, and unstable persistence.

Identified regulation is a more autonomous form of extrinsic motivation, wherein a behavior is consciously valued and embraced as personally important. For example, a person may write daily in a journal because he or she values the self-insight and clarity of mind that comes from that activity. Identification represents, in attributional terms, an internal perceived locus of causality—it feels relatively volitional or self-determined. Thus, identified motivation is associated with better persistence and performance compared to behaviors motivated by external or introjected regulations, as well as more positive affect. Finally, the most autonomous form of extrinsic motivation is *integrated regulation.* Behaviors that are integrated are not only valued and meaningful but also consciously assimilated into the self and brought into alignment with other values and goals. Like behaviors that are intrinsically motivated, integrated actions have an internal locus of causality and are self-endorsed; but because they are performed to obtain a separable outcome rather than as an end in themselves, they are still regarded as extrinsic.

Self-determination theory posits that as children grow older, most socialized behavior comes to be regulated in a more autonomous fashion because there is an overarching developmental tendency to seek the integration of behavioral regulation into the self (Chandler & Connell, 1987; Ryan, 1995). But this integrative process is not inevitable, and there are many factors that can disrupt or derail this tendency. Thus, the motivational model outlined in Figure 7.1 does not propose that individuals typically progress through the various forms of extrinsic motivation on their way to integrated or intrinsic regulation. Instead, when new behaviors are undertaken, any one of these motivational starting points may be predominant, as a function of the content of the goal and the presence of social and situational supports, pressures, and opportunities.

The greater internalization and integration of regulation into the self, the more self-determined is behavior felt to be. Early empirical support for this claim was obtained by Ryan and Connell (1989) in a study of achievement behaviors among elementary school children. Assessing external, introjected, identified, and intrinsic reasons for engaging in academically related behaviors (e.g., doing homework), they found that the four types of regulation were intercorrelated in a quasi-simplex or ordered pattern that lent empirical support to the theorized continuum of relative autonomy. The children's differing motivational styles for academic work were also related to their achievement-related attitudes and psychological adjustment. Students whose work was done for external reasons showed less interest and weaker effort, and they tended to blame teachers and others for negative academic outcomes. Introjected regulation was related to effort expenditure but also to higher anxiety and maladaptive coping with failure. Identified regulation was associated with more interest and enjoyment of school, greater effort, and a greater tendency to cope adaptively with stressful circumstances.

Recent research has extended these findings on motivational style and outcome, showing, for example, that more autonomous extrinsic motivation is associated with greater academic engagement and performance, lower dropout rates, higher quality learning, and greater psychological well-being across cultures (see Ryan & La Guardia, 2000, for review). Positive outcomes linked with higher

relative autonomy have also been found in the health care and psychotherapy domains, where greater internalization of treatment protocols has been associated
with higher levels of adherence and success. For example, Williams, Grow, Freedman, Ryan, and Deci (1996) showed that greater autonomy for participating in a
weight loss program, facilitated by support for autonomy from staff, was associated with better maintenance of weight loss among morbidly obese patients. A
number of studies relating autonomy to better compliance with addiction treatments have also emerged (e.g., Foote et al., 1998). These examples are drawn from
a growing body of literature on the positive impact of self-determination in clinical settings (Sheldon, Williams, & Joiner, 2003).

In fact, autonomous regulation of behavior has been associated with positive
outcomes in a wide variety of life domains, including relationships (e.g., Blais,
Sabourin, Boucher, & Vallerand, 1990), work (e.g., Deci et al., 2001), religion
(e.g., Baard & Aridas, 2001), political behavior (e.g., Koestner, Losier, Vallerand,
& Carducci, 1996), and environmental practices (Pelletier, 2002). These benefits
include greater persistence in, and effectiveness of, behavior and enhanced
well-being.

FOSTERING AUTONOMOUS FUNCTIONING
THROUGH SOCIAL SUPPORT

Considerable research has been devoted to examining social conditions that promote autonomous regulation, including both intrinsic motivation and more autonomous forms of extrinsic motivation. Despite the fact that the human organism
has evolved capacities and tendencies toward the autonomous regulation of behavior (Deci & Ryan, 2000), biological, social, and other environmental influences can
facilitate or undermine those tendencies. An understanding of the nature of these
influences is important because, as reviewed previously, autonomous versus het-
eronomous functioning has manifold personal consequences.

SUPPORTING INTRINSIC MOTIVATION

As already noted, intrinsic motivation represents a distinctly autonomous form of
functioning, in that behavior is performed for its own sake and is wholly self-
endorsed. Cognitive evaluation theory (CET), another subtheory within SDT, was
proposed by Deci and Ryan (1980, 1985) to specify the social contextual features
that can impact, both positively and negatively, intrinsic motivational processes.
Cognitive evaluation theory began with the assumption that while intrinsic motivation is a propensity of the human organism, it will be catalyzed or facilitated in
circumstances that support its expression and hindered under social circumstances
that undercut it. Among its major tenets, CET specifies that intrinsic motivation
depends on conditions that allow (1) an experience of autonomy or an internal perceived locus of causality, and (2) the experience of effectance or competence.

Factors that undermine the experiences of either autonomy or competence, therefore, undermine intrinsic motivation.

Among the most controversial implications of CET is the proposition that contexts in which rewards are used to control behavior undermine intrinsic motivation and yield many hidden costs that were unanticipated by reward-based
theories of motivation. Although much debated, the most definitive summary of

that research has shown that extrinsic rewards made contingent on task performance reliably weaken intrinsic motivation (Deci, Koestner, & Ryan, 1999). Cognitive evaluation theory specifies that this occurs because contingent rewards, as typically employed, foster the recipient's perception that the cause of their behavior lies in forces external to the self. Individuals come to see themselves as performing the behavior for the reward or the rewarding agent and thus not because of their own interests, values, or motivations. Accordingly, behavior becomes reward dependent, and any intrinsic motivation that might have been manifest is undermined. However, rewards are not the only type of influence that undermines intrinsic motivation. When motivators attempt to move people through threats, deadlines, demands, external evaluations, and imposed goals, intrinsic motivation is diminished (Deci & Ryan, 2000).

Evidence also highlights factors that can enhance intrinsic motivation. Laboratory and field research shows that the provision of choice and opportunities for self-direction and the acknowledgment of perspectives and feelings serve to enhance intrinsic motivation through a greater felt sense of autonomy. Such factors can yield a variety of salutary consequences. For example, evidence indicates that teachers who are autonomy-supportive (see Reeve, Bolt, & Cai, 1999, for specific teacher strategies) spark curiosity, a desire for challenge, and higher levels of intrinsic motivation in their students. In contrast, a predominantly controlling teaching style leads to a loss of initiative and less effective learning, especially when that learning concerns complex material or requires conceptual, creative processing (Ryan & La Guardia, 1999). In a similar vein, children of parents who are more autonomy-supportive show a stronger mastery orientation, manifest in greater spontaneous exploration and extension of their capacities, than children of more controlling parents (Grolnick & Apostoleris, 2002).

The support of autonomy in fostering intrinsic motivation is thus very critical. Yet, while autonomy-support is a central means by which intrinsic motivation is facilitated, CET specifies that supports for the other basic psychological needs proposed by SDT, namely competence and relatedness, are also important, especially when a sense of autonomy is also present. Deci and Ryan (1985) review evidence showing that providing optimal challenge, positive performance feedback, and freedom from controlling evaluations facilitate intrinsic motivation, while negative performance feedback undermines it. Vallerand and Reid (1984) found that these effects are mediated by the individual's own perceived competence.

Intrinsic motivation also appears to more frequently occur in relationally supportive contexts. This is so from the beginning of development. As Bowlby (1979) suggested and research has confirmed (e.g., Frodi, Bridges, & Grolnick, 1985), the intrinsic motivational tendencies evident in infants' exploratory behavior are strongest when a child is securely attached to a caregiver. Self-determination theory further argues that a sense of relatedness can facilitate intrinsic motivation in older children and adults, a claim also supported by research (e.g., Manoogian & Reznick, 1976; Ryan, Stiller, & Lynch, 1994). Practically, when teachers, parents, managers, and other motivators convey caring and acceptance, the motivatee is freed up to invest in interests and challenges that the situation presents.

In sum, research has supported CET by demonstrating how the expression of intrinsic motivation is supported by social conditions that promote a sense of autonomy, competence, and relatedness, which together make up the triad of basic psychological needs specified within SDT (Deci & Ryan, 2000; Ryan & Deci, 2000b). However, by definition, intrinsic motivation will be manifest only for activities that potentially offer inherent interest or enjoyment to the individual—for example, those that offer novelty, have aesthetic value, or produce excitement. For activities that do not carry such appeal, the principles of CET do not apply. However, the role of autonomy in positive experience is not limited to intrinsically motivated behavior, and, in fact, intrinsically motivated behavior may be comparatively rare in everyday life (Csikszentmihalyi & Rathunde, 1993; Ryan & Deci, 2000b). This brings us to a discussion of the wide range of behaviors that have an extrinsic motivational basis.

SUPPORTING MORE AUTONOMOUS EXTRINSIC MOTIVATION

Beginning in early childhood, the ratio of intrinsic to extrinsic motivation begins to shift dramatically in the direction of extrinsic activities. Indeed, as we grow older, most of us spend less and less time simply pursuing what interests us and more and more time pursuing goals and responsibilities that the social world obliges us to perform (Ryan, 1995). Given both the prevalence of extrinsic motivation and the positive consequences that accrue from autonomous functioning, an issue of key importance is how the self-regulation of these imposed activities can be facilitated by socializing agents such as parents, teachers, physicians, bosses, coaches, or therapists. Self-determination theory frames this issue in terms of how to foster the *internalization* and *integration* of the value and regulation of extrinsically motivated behavior. As noted already, internalization refers to the adoption of a value or regulation, and integration involves the incorporation of that regulation into the sense of self, such that the behavior feels self-endorsed and volitional.

Empirical research indicates that the presence of social supports for the psychological needs of competence, relatedness, and autonomy appears to foster not only the autonomous functioning seen in intrinsically motivated behavior but also the internalization and integration of behaviors focused on extrinsic goals. For example, when individuals do not have intrinsic reasons for engaging in a particular behavior, they do so primarily because the activity is prompted, modeled, or valued by another person or a group to which the individual feels, or wants to feel, in relationship. Organismic integration theory posits that internalization is more likely to occur when supports for feelings of relatedness or connectedness are present. For example, Ryan et al. (1994) found that children who felt securely attached to their parents and teachers showed more complete internalization of the regulation of academic behaviors.

There is a very close relationship between people's sense of relatedness, or secure attachment, and autonomy-support. Ryan and Lynch (1989) found that adolescents who experienced their parents as accepting and noncontrolling were those who felt securely attached. In a more recent examination of within-person, cross-relationship variations in security of attachment, La Guardia, Ryan, Couchman, and Deci (2000) found that autonomy-support was crucial to feeling securely attached or intimately related. Indeed, many studies support this connection, which itself is proposed in theories of attachment. As Bretherton (1987, p. 1075) argues, "In the framework of attachment theory, maternal respect for the child's autonomy is an aspect of sensitivity to the infant's signals." Within SDT, this connection between autonomy-support and intimacy is viewed as a lifelong dynamic (Ryan, 1993).

Research also indicates that perceived competence is important to the internalization of extrinsically motivated behaviors. Individuals who feel efficacious in performing an activity are more likely to adopt it as their own, and conditions that support the development of relevant skills, by offering optimal challenges and effectance-relevant feedback, facilitate internalization (Deci & Ryan, 2000). This analysis also suggests that activities that are too difficult for an individual to perform—those that demand a level of physical or psychological maturation that a child has not reached, for example—will likely be externally regulated or introjected at best.

Internalization also depends on supports for autonomy. Contexts that use controlling strategies such as salient rewards and punishments or evaluative, self-esteem-hooking pressures are least likely to lead people to value activities as their own. This is not to say that controls don't work to produce behavior—decades of operant psychology prove that they can. It is rather that the more salient the external control over a person's behavior, the more the person is likely to be merely externally regulated or introjected in his or her actions. Consequently, the person does not develop a value or investment in the behaviors, but instead remains dependent on external controls. Thus, parents who reward, force, or cajole their child to do homework are more likely to have a child who does so only when rewarded, cajoled, or forced. The salience of external controls undermines the acquisition of self-responsibility. Alternatively, parents who supply reasons, empathize with difficulties overcoming obstacles, and use a minimum of external incentives are more likely to foster a sense of willingness and value for work in their child (Grolnick & Apostoleris, 2002).

The internalization process depicted in Figure 7.1 can end at various points, and social contexts can facilitate or undermine the relative autonomy of an individual's motivation along this continuum. For instance, a teenager might initially introject the need to act a certain way in an attempt to enhance or maintain relatedness to a parent who values it. However, depending on how controlling or autonomy-supportive the context is, that introjection might evolve upward toward greater self-acceptance or integration, or downward toward external regulation. Similarly, a person who finds a behavior valuable and important, that is, regulated by identification, may, if contexts become too demanding, begin to feel incompetent and fall into amotivation.

The more integrated an extrinsic regulation, the more a person is consciously aware of the meaning and worth inherent in the conduct of a behavior and has found congruence, or an integral "fit" between that behavior and other behaviors in his or her repertoire (Sheldon, 2002). Integrated regulation reflects a holistic processing of circumstance and possibilities (Kuhl & Fuhrmann, 1998; Ryan & Deci, in press) and is facilitated by a perceived sense of choice, volition, and freedom from social and situational controls to think, feel, or act in a particular way. It is also facilitated by the provision of meaning for an extrinsic action—a nonarbitrary rationale for why something is important. Such supports for autonomy encourage the active endorsement of values, perceptions, and overt behaviors as the individual's own and are essential to identified or integrated behavioral regulation.

A number of laboratory and field research studies provide support for this theorizing and concrete examples of the integrative process described here. An experimental study by Deci, Eghrari, Patrick, and Leone (1994) showed that offering a meaningful rationale for an uninteresting behavior, in conjunction with supports for autonomy and relatedness, promoted internalization and integration. Grolnick and Ryan (1989) found that parents who were autonomy-supportive of their children's academic goals but also positively involved and caring fostered greater internalization of those goals and better teacher- and student-rated self-motivation. These and related findings have implications for efforts aimed at enhancing student motivation (see also Grolnick & Apostoleris, 2002; Vallerand, 1997).

The role of supportive versus undermining conditions also has practical significance in the fields of health care and psychotherapy, where issues of compliance with and adherence to treatment are of great concern, not only to front-line care providers with a vested interest in patients' health but also to those attentive to the financial and other consequences associated with treatment (non)compliance. Williams, Rodin, Ryan, Grolnick, and Deci (1998) found that patients who were more likely to endorse statements such as, "My doctor listens to how I would like to do things," showed better adherence to prescription medication regimens than patients who regarded their physicians as more controlling of their treatment plans. The patients' own autonomous motivation for medication adherence mediated the relation between perception of physician autonomy-support and actual adherence. Williams et al. (1996) found that perceived autonomy-support among care providers conduced to increases in autonomous motivation for weight loss among morbidly obese patients and to greater long-term weight loss maintenance. Longitudinal research currently underway is showing that the autonomy-supportiveness of counselors in a smokers' health program predicts declines in smoking frequency and higher quit rates, even among individuals lacking the intention to quit smoking at program entry (Williams et al., 2002).

The theoretical perspective of SDT also finds convergence with clinical practices emphasized in Miller and Rollnick's *Motivational Interviewing* (2002). Several investigators have suggested that some of the demonstrated clinical efficacy of motivational interviewing reflects the importance of this strategy's synergistic emphasis on autonomy-support, relatedness, and competency building (e.g., Foote et al., 1998; Markland, Ryan, Tobin, & Rollnick, 2003; Sheldon et al., 2003).

FOSTERING AUTONOMOUS REGULATION FROM THE INSIDE

To date, work on the promotion of autonomous functioning has been largely devoted to an examination of social contextual factors. That is, SDT has been preoccupied with the *social psychology* of motivation, or how supports for autonomy, competence, and relatedness facilitate self-motivation. Of equal importance is how processes within the psyche are associated with the promotion of autonomous regulation and how these processes can be facilitated. It is clear that even when environments provide an optimal motivational climate, autonomous regulation requires both an existential commitment to act congruently, as well as the cultivation of the potential possessed by almost everyone to reflectively consider their behavior and its fit with personal values, needs, and interests (Ryan & Deci, in press). We next discuss recent research on the role that internal resources centered in consciousness and pertaining to awareness can play in fostering more autonomous regulation. Discussion of this new research focuses particularly on the concept of *mindfulness* (Brown & Ryan, 2003).

A number of influential organismic and cybernetic theories of behavioral regulation place central emphasis on attention, the capacity to bring consciousness to bear on events and experience as they unfold in real time (e.g., Carver & Scheier, 1981; Deci & Ryan, 1985; Varela, Thompson, & Rosch, 1991). These perspectives agree that the power of awareness and attention lies in bringing to consciousness information and sensibilities necessary for healthy self-regulation to occur. The more fully an individual is apprised of what is occurring internally and in the environment, the more healthy, adaptive, and value-consistent his or her behavior is likely to be.

Just as social forces can both inhibit and enhance healthy behavioral regulation, so, too, can factors associated with the enhancement or diminishment of attention and awareness. As a regulatory tool, our usual day-to-day state of attention is limited in two important ways that have cognitive and motivational bases: First, the usual reach of attention is quite restricted. Under normal circumstances, we are consciously aware of only a small fraction of our perceptions and actions (Varela et al., 1991). Evidence for such *attentional limits* comes from research on automatic or implicit processes. Automatic cognitive and behavioral processes are those that are activated and guided without conscious awareness. Accumulating research shows that much of our cognitive, emotional, and overt behavioral activity is automatically driven (Bargh, 1997).

The second way in which attention is limited pertains to its *motivated selectivity*. Among the information that is allowed into awareness, a high priority is placed on that which is relevant to the self, with the highest priority given to information that is relevant to self-preservation, in both biological and psychological terms. In developed societies, where threats to the biological organism are not usually at the forefront of concern, *self-concept* preservation is a primary motivation, within which is implicated our general tendency to evaluate events and experiences as good or bad for the self (Langer, 2002). Reviewing the self-regulation literature, Baumeister, Heatherton, and Tice (1994) noted that, in general, individuals give relatively low priority to accurate self-knowledge. Instead, they pay most attention to information that enhances and validates the self-concept. The invested nature of attention can thus lead to the defensive redirection of attention away from phenomena that threaten the concept of self.

Both attentional limits and selectivity biases can have adaptive value in many circumstances, but they also can hinder optimal regulation of behavior. Information we do not want to be conscious of can be actively and conveniently displaced from focal attention and even from the wider field of awareness, in favor of other information more agreeable to the self. Attentional limits and biases provide ripe conditions for compartmentalization or fracturing of the self, wherein some aspects of self are placed on the stage of awareness and play a role in an individual's behavior, while others are actively kept backstage, out of the spotlight of attention. For purposes of behavioral regulation, the cost of such motivated attentional limits and biases lies in the controlled nature of behavior that can result, in which the aim is to remain responsive to internal and external forces or pressures toward ego-enhancement and preservation, rather than the sense of valuing, interest, and enjoyment that characterizes autonomous functioning. An ego-invested motivational orientation uses attention to select and shape experiences or distort them in memory in a way that defends and protects against ego-threat and clings to experiences or an interpretation of them that affirms the ego (e.g., Hodgins & Knee, 2002). The self-centered use of attention outlined here hinders the openness to events and experience that could allow for an integration of self-aspects that could permit fuller, more authentic functioning.

MINDFULNESS AND THE ENHANCEMENT OF BEHAVIORAL REGULATION

The limits and biases of attention discussed here are not immutable. Regarding automatic processes, recent research has provided a detailed cognitive specification of the conditions under which behavior can be implicitly triggered (see Bargh & Ferguson, 2000). But research has also begun to show how such behavior can be modified or overridden (e.g., Dijksterhuis & van Knippenberg, 2000; Macrae & Johnston, 1998). Ample evidence indicates that the enactment of automatic, habitual behavior depends on a lack of attention to one's behavior and the cues that activate it. As Macrae and Johnston note, habitual action can unfold when the "lights are off and nobody's home." Similarly, automatic thought patterns thrive while they remain out of the field of awareness (Segal, Williams, & Teasdale, 2002).

Conversely, there is evidence to indicate that enhanced attention and awareness can interfere with the development and unfoldment of automatic, habitual responses. An early demonstration was provided by Hefferline, Keenan, and Harford (1959). Using a conditioning paradigm in which individuals were reinforced for a subtle hand movement, they demonstrated that those who were unaware that conditioning was taking place showed the fastest rates of learning. Individuals who were told in a vague way that they were being conditioned showed slower learning of the response. Those who were explicitly instructed to learn the movement response that was being reinforced displayed the slowest learning. Thus, the more conscious individuals were of the conditioning, the more difficult was the development of automatized behavior. More recently, Dijksterhuis and van Knippenberg (2000) compared the ease with which stereotypes about politicians, college professors, and soccer hooligans could be activated through priming, depending on whether subjects' attention to the prime-response situation and awareness of themselves in that situation were induced. Heightened attention and self-awareness were shown to override the behavioral effects of activation of all three stereotypes examined. Evidence also suggests that the enhancement of awareness through training can intervene between the initial activation of an implicit response and the consequences that would typically follow. For example, Gollwitzer (1999) describes research showing that individuals who were made aware of their automatic stereotypic reactions to elderly people and then trained to mentally counteract them when they arose through implementation intentions no longer showed an automatic activation of stereotypic beliefs.

Collectively, this research suggests that consciousness, when brought to bear on present realities, can introduce an element of self-direction in what would otherwise be nonconsciously regulated, controlled behavior. But if behavior is to be regulated in a self-directed or self-endorsed manner on an ongoing, day-to-day basis, a dispositionally elevated level of attention and awareness would seem essential. Several forms of trait self-awareness have been examined over the years, including self-consciousness (Fenigstein, Scheier, & Buss, 1975) and reflection (Trapnell & Campbell, 1999), but such "reflexive consciousness" constructs (Baumeister, 1999) reflect cognitive operation on the contents of consciousness, rather than a perceptual sensitivity to the mind's contents. Neither are they designed to tap attention to and awareness of an individual's behavior and ongoing situational circumstances.

Mindfulness   Deci and Ryan (1980) suggested that a quality of consciousness termed *mindfulness* can act as an ongoing conscious mediator between causal stimuli and behavioral responses to them, leading to dispositional resistance to shifts away from self-determined, autonomous functioning in the presence of salient primes and other behavioral controls. Recently, we (e.g., Brown & Ryan, 2003) began an intensive investigation of mindfulness, which we define as an open or receptive awareness of and attention to what is taking place in the present moment. It has similarly been described as "the clear and single-minded awareness of what actually happens to us and in us at the successive moments of perception" (Nyanaponika Thera, 1972, p. 5) and, more simply, as "keeping one's consciousness alive to the present reality" (Hanh, 1976, p. 11). The construct has a long pedigree, having been discussed for centuries in Eastern philosophy and psychology and more recently in Western psychology (e.g., Kabat-Zinn, 1990; Langer, 1989; Linehan, 1993; Teasdale, Segal, & Williams, 1995). Aside from the apparent role of present attention and awareness in the "de-automatization" of behavior (Safran & Segal, 1990), Wilber (2000) notes that bringing this quality of consciousness to bear on facets of the self and its experience that have been alienated, ignored, or distorted is theorized by a number of personality traditions to convert "hidden subjects" into "conscious objects" that can be differentiated from, transcended, and integrated into the self. In this sense, the quality of consciousness that is mindfulness conduces to the view that "all the facts are friendly," which Rogers (1961, p. 25) believed necessary for "full functioning."

As a monitoring function, mindfulness creates a mental distance between the "I," or self (cf. James, 1890/1999) and the contents of consciousness (thoughts, emotions, and motives), one's behavior, and the environment. One consequence of this observant stance, we argue, is enhanced self-awareness and the provision of a window of opportunity to choose the form, direction, and other specifics of action; that is, to act in an autonomous manner.

Brown and Ryan (2003) developed the Mindful Attention Awareness Scale (MAAS) to assess this "presence of mind." They found that mindfulness was associated with a number of facets of the openness to experience dimension of personality (Costa & McCrae, 1992). It was also related to "emotional intelligence" (Salovey, Mayer, Goldman, Turvey, & Palfai, 1995), particularly a greater clarity of emotional experience, which reflects emotional self-knowledge. Another study examined the degree of congruence between implicit, or nonconscious emotional state, and its explicit, or self-reported counterpart (Brown & Ryan, 2003). Using the Implicit Association Test (IAT) to measure implicit affective state (Greenwald, McGhee, & Schwartz, 1998), this study found that mindfulness predicted greater congruence between the two measures. Because implicit measures are not susceptible to conscious control and manipulation, this study suggested that more mindful individuals are more attuned to their implicit emotions and reflect that knowledge in their explicit, affective self-descriptions. More research is needed to test this proposal, but this study's finding, along with other findings presented in this section, is consistent with theory positing that present-centered awareness and attention facilitates self-knowledge, a crucial element of integrated functioning.

Awareness of self, including one's feelings, needs, and values, is theorized to be an important facilitator of self-determined behavioral regulation (Deci & Ryan, 1985), and evidence for the role of mindfulness in the autonomous regulation of behavior comes from several studies. Brown and Ryan (2003) found that the MAAS was positively correlated with dispositional autonomy (as well as competence and relatedness, collectively, the three basic psychological needs specified by SDT). To examine the role of mindfulness in facilitating autonomous behavior in daily life, the authors asked students and working adults to complete the MAAS and then to record the relative autonomy of their behavior (based on the conceptual model in Figure 7.1) at the receipt of a pager signal. This occurred three times a day on a quasi-random basis over a two-week (students) and three-week (adults) period. In both groups, higher scores on the MAAS predicted higher levels of autonomous behavior on a day-to-day basis.

This study also included a state measure of mindfulness. Participants specifically rated how attentive they were to the activities that had also been rated for their relative autonomy. Individuals who were more mindfully attentive to their activities also experienced more autonomous motivation to engage in those activities. The effects of trait and state mindfulness on autonomy were independent in this study, indicating that the regulatory benefits of mindfulness were not limited to those with a mindful disposition. The fact that state mindfulness and autonomous behavior were correlated in these samples bears some similarity to the intrinsically motivated autotelic, or "flow" experience (Csikszentmihalyi, 1990), in which awareness and action merge. In fact, Csikszentmihalyi (1997) suggests that key to the autotelic personality is the individual's willingness to be present to his or her ongoing experience.

This view of the human capacity for autonomy stands in contrast to the position that most behavior is automatically driven and that conscious will may be illusory (e.g., Wegner, 2002). Although, as we noted, it is clear that much behavior is automatic, we believe this issue is more complex than it may appear (see Ryan & Deci, in press). Although automatic processes may activate behaviors in any given moment, we contend that mindfulness of motives and the actions that follow from them can lead to an overriding or redirection of such processes (see also Bargh, 1997; Westen, 1998). For example, Levesque and Brown (2003) examined whether mindfulness could shape or override the behavioral effects of implicit, low levels of autonomy. As with other motivational orientations, such as achievement, intimacy, and power (McClelland, Koestner, & Weinberger, 1989), Levesque and Brown (2003) hypothesized that individuals would differ not only in self-attributed relative autonomy but also in the extent to which they implicitly or nonconsciously associate themselves with autonomy. Using the IAT to assess relative levels of implicit autonomy, Levesque and Brown found that MAAS-measured dispositional mindfulness moderated the degree to which implicit relative autonomy predicted day-to-day autonomy, as measured through experience-sampling. Specifically, among less mindful individuals, implicit-relative autonomy positively predicted day-to-day motivation for behavior. Among such persons, those who implicitly associated themselves with control and pressure manifested the same kind of behavioral motivation in daily life, while individuals with high levels of implicit autonomy behaved in accord with this automatic self-association. However, among more mindful individuals, the relation between the automatic motivational association and daily behavior was null. Mindfulness thus served an overriding functioning, such that it facilitated self-endorsed behavior, regardless of the type of implicit motivational tendency that individuals held.

In this vein, it is important to note that the effect of mindfulness lies not necessarily in *creating* psychological experiences, many of which are conditioned phenomena (Wegner, 2002) that arise spontaneously (Dennett, 1984), but in allowing for choicefulness in whether to endorse or veto the directives that consciousness brings to awareness, thereby permitting the direction of action toward self-endorsed ends (Libet, 1999; Ryan & Deci, in press). Indeed, by definition, self-endorsement requires a consciousness of one's needs or values and the role of anticipated action in meeting or affirming them (Deci & Ryan, 1985). Relatedly, an individual may be aware of several competing motives at a given time, all of which cannot be satisfied. Mindfulness creates an opportunity for choices to be made that maximize the satisfaction of needs and desires within the parameters of the situation at hand (Deci & Ryan, 1980).

Mindfulness appears not only to foster self-endorsed activity at the level of day-to-day behavior but also to encourage the adoption of higher order goals and values that reflect healthy regulation. Kasser and colleagues (e.g., Kasser, this volume; Kasser & Ryan, 1996) have shown that intrinsic values—for personal development, affiliation, and community contribution, for example—have an inherent relationship to basic psychological need satisfaction; that is, they directly fulfill needs for autonomy, competence, and relatedness. Extrinsic values, in contrast, including aspirations for wealth, popularity, and personal image, are pursued for their instrumental value and typically fulfill basic needs only indirectly, at best. Moreover, extrinsic goals are often motivated by introjected pressures or external controls (Kasser, 2002). Accordingly, accumulating research indicates that the relative centrality of intrinsic and extrinsic values has significant consequences for subjective well-being, risk behavior, and other outcomes (see Kasser, this volume). It is thus noteworthy that recent research has shown that mindfulness is associated with a stronger emphasis on intrinsic aspirations, and this values orientation is in turn related to indicators of subjective well-being and healthy lifestyle choices (Brown & Kasser, 2003). While mindfulness directly predicts higher well-being (Brown & Ryan, 2003), this research also shows that its salutary effects come by facilitating self-regulation.

Cultivating Mindfulness   Research conducted over the past 25 years indicates that mindfulness can be enhanced through training (Kabat-Zinn, 1990). In such training, individuals learn, through daily practice, to sharpen their inherent capacities to attend to and be aware of presently occurring internal, behavioral, and environmental events and experience. Mindfulness training is associated with a variety of lasting positive psychological and somatic well-being outcomes (see Baer, 2003). Research has yet to show whether such training conduces to more self-determined behavior, but a first step in this direction is being taken by studies currently under way in our laboratory that are examining whether the experimental induction of mindful states leads to more autonomous behavior. Given the apparent covariation of dispositional and state mindfulness with both trait and state autonomous functioning, the enhancement of mindfulness through training may enhance behavioral regulation.

CONCLUSION

This chapter has attempted to demonstrate that autonomous regulation of inner states and overt behavior is key to a number of positive outcomes that reflect healthy behavioral and psychological functioning. The practical value of autonomy has been demonstrated through research in a number of important life domains, including child development and education, health behavior, sport and exercise, and others. Decades of research also show that when people act autonomously, whether motivated intrinsically or extrinsically through more internalized and integrated regulation, their quality of action and sense of well-being benefits.

Judgment as to the practical utility of research on autonomy relies on evidence that this regulatory style can be promoted. We have shown here that autonomy can be facilitated both from without—through social supports—and from within, through the receptive attention and awareness to present experience that defines mindfulness. While significant in themselves, these two sources of support are not necessarily separate and may, in fact, interact to enhance autonomous regulation. For example, an individual in a position to influence the motivation of another person or group may do so more effectively and positively when mindfulness about the effects of his or her communication style and behavior is present. Just as an individual seeking to change his or her regulatory style can benefit from greater awareness of self and attention to behavior, reason suggests that parents, teachers, supervisors, and others may draw on their own mindful capacities to facilitate the support of healthy, growth-promoting regulation in others.

Research reviewed here indicated that mindfulness can enhance self-knowledge and action that accords with the self, both of which are key to authentic action (Harter, 2002). Enhanced attention and awareness also appear to undermine the effects of past and present conditioning and the external control of behavior that it may entail. It might then be possible that a greater dose of mindfulness helps to inoculate individuals against social and cultural forces acting to inhibit or undermine choicefulness and the self-endorsement of values, goals, and behaviors. In fact, it may be difficult in today's society to live autonomously without mindfulness, considering the multitude of forces, internal and external, that often pull us in one direction or another. In a world where commercial, political, economic, and other messages seeking to capture attention, allegiance, and wallets have become ubiquitous, mindful reflection on the ways in which we wish to expend the limited resource of life energy that all of us are given seems more important than ever.

REFERENCES

Amabile, T. M. (1996). *Creativity in context.* New York: Westview Press.

Baard, P. P., & Aridas, C. (2001). *Motivating your church: How any leader can ignite intrinsic motivation and growth.* New York: Crossroad.

Baer, R. A. (2003). Mindfulness training as a clinical intervention: A conceptual and empirical review. *Clinical Psychology: Science and Practice, 10,* 125–143.

Bargh, J. A. (1997). Automaticity in social psychology. In E. T. Higgins & A. W. Kruglanski (Eds.), *Social psychology: Handbook of basic principles* (pp. 169–183). New York: Guilford Press.

Bargh, J. A., & Ferguson, M. J. (2000). Beyond behaviorism: On the automaticity of higher mental processes. *Psychological Bulletin, 126,* 925–945.

Baumeister, R. F. (1999). The nature and structure of the self: An overview. In R. F. Baumeister (Ed.), *The self in social psychology* (pp. 1–20). Philadelphia: Psychology Press.

Baumeister, R. F., Heatherton, T. F., & Tice, D. M. (1994). *Losing control: How and why people fail at self-regulation.* San Diego, CA: Academic Press.

Blais, M. R., Sabourin, S., Boucher, C., & Vallerand, R. J. (1990). Toward a motivational model of couple happiness. *Journal of Personality and Social Psychology, 59,* 1021–1031.

Bowlby, J. (1979). *The making and breaking of affectional bonds.* London: Tavistock.

Bretherton, I. (1987). New perspectives on attachment relations: Security, communication and internal working models. In J. Osofsky (Ed.), *Handbook of infant development* (pp. 1061–1100). New York: Wiley.

Brown, K. W., & Kasser, T. (2003). *Are psychological and ecological well-being compatible? The role of values, mindfulness, and lifestyle.* Manuscript submitted for publication.

*Brown, K. W., & Ryan, R. M. (2003). The benefits of being present: Mindfulness and its role in psychological well-being. *Journal of Personality and Social Psychology, 84,* 822–848.

Carver, C. S., & Scheier, M. F. (1981). *Attention and self-regulation: A control theory approach to human behavior.* New York: Springer-Verlag.

Chandler, C. L., & Connell, J. P. (1987). Children's intrinsic, extrinsic and internalized motivation: A developmental study of children's reasons for liked and disliked behaviors. *British Journal of Developmental Psychology, 5,* 357–365.

Chirkov, V., Ryan, R. M., Kim, Y., & Kaplan, U. (2003). Differentiating autonomy from individualism and independence: A self-determination theory perspective on internalization of cultural orientations and well-being. *Journal of Personality and Social Psychology, 84,* 97–109.

Costa, P. T., Jr., & McCrae, R. R. (1992). *Revised NEO personality inventory (NEO PI-R) and NEO five-factor inventory (NEO-FFI): Professional manual.* Odessa, FL: Psychological Assessment Resources.

Csikszentmihalyi, M. (1990). *Flow: The psychology of optimal experience.* New York: HarperCollins.

Csikszentmihalyi, M. (1997). *Finding flow: The psychology of engagement with everyday life.* New York: Basic Books.

Csikszentmihalyi, M., & Rathunde, K. (1993). The measurement of flow in everyday life: Toward a theory of emergent motivation. In J. E. Jacobs (Ed.), *Nebraska Symposium on Motivation: Vol. 40. Developmental perspectives on motivation* (pp. 57–97). Lincoln: University of Nebraska Press.

DeCharms, R. (1968). *Personal causation.* New York: Academic Press.

Deci, E. L., Eghrari, H., Patrick, B. C., & Leone, D. R. (1994). Facilitating internalization: The self-determination theory perspective. *Journal of Personality, 62,* 119–142.

Deci, E. L., Koestner, R., & Ryan, R. M. (1999). A meta-analytic review of experiments examining the effects of extrinsic rewards on intrinsic motivation. *Psychological Bulletin, 125,* 627–668.

Deci, E. L., & Ryan, R. M. (1980). Self-determination theory: When mind mediates behavior. *Journal of Mind and Behavior, 1,* 33–43.

*Deci, E. L., & Ryan, R. M. (1985). *Intrinsic motivation and self-determination in human behavior.* New York: Plenum Press.

Deci, E. L., & Ryan, R. M. (1995). Human autonomy: The basis for true self-esteem. In M. Kernis (Ed.), *Efficacy, agency, and self-esteem* (pp. 31–49). New York: Plenum Press.

Deci, E. L., & Ryan, R. M. (2000). The "what" and "why" of goal pursuits: Human needs and the self-determination of behavior. *Psychological Inquiry, 11,* 227–268.

Deci, E. L., Ryan, R. M., Gagné, M., Leone, D. R., Usunov, J., & Kornazheva, B. P. (2001). Need satisfaction, motivation, and well-being in the work organizations of a former Eastern bloc country: A cross-cultural study of self-determination. *Personality and Social Psychology Bulletin, 27,* 930–942.

Dennett, D. (1984). *Elbow room: The varieties of free will worth wanting.* Oxford, England: Clarendon Press.

Dijksterhuis, A. P., & van Knippenberg, A. D. (2000). Behavioral indecision: Effects of self-focus on automatic behavior. *Social Cognition, 18,* 55–74.

Fenigstein, A., Scheier, M. F., & Buss, A. H. (1975). Public and private self-consciousness: Assessment and theory. *Journal of Consulting and Clinical Psychology, 43,* 522–527.

Foote, J., DeLuca, A., Magura, S., Warner, A., Grand, A., Rosenblum, A., et al. (1998). A group motivational treatment for chemical dependency. *Journal of Substance Abuse Treatment, 17,* 181–192.

Frodi, A., Bridges, L., & Grolnick, W. S. (1985). Correlates of mastery-related behavior: A short-term longitudinal study of infants in their second year. *Child Development, 56,* 1291–1298.

Gollwitzer, P. M. (1999). Implementation intentions: Strong effects of simple plans. *American Psychologist, 54,* 493–503.

Greenwald, A. G., McGhee, D. E., & Schwartz, J. L. K. (1998). Measuring individual differences in implicit cognition: The Implicit Association Test. *Journal of Personality and Social Psychology, 74,* 1464–1480.

Grolnick, W. S., & Apostoleris, N. H. (2002). What makes parents controlling. In E. L. Deci & R. M. Ryan (Eds.), *Handbook of self-determination research* (pp. 161–181). Rochester, NY: University of Rochester Press.

Grolnick, W. S., & Ryan, R. M. (1987). Autonomy in children's learning: An experimental and individual difference investigation. *Journal of Personality and Social Psychology, 52,* 890–898.

Grolnick, W. S., & Ryan, R. M. (1989). Parent styles associated with children's self-regulation and competence in school. *Journal of Educational Psychology, 81,* 143–154.

Hanh, T. N. (1976). *Miracle of mindfulness.* Boston: Beacon Press.

Harter, S. (2002). Authenticity. In C. R. Snyder & S. J. Lopez (Eds.), *Handbook of positive psychology* (pp. 382–394). New York: Oxford University Press.

Hefferline, R. F., Keenan, B., & Harford, R. A. (1959). Escape and avoidance conditioning in human subjects without their observation of the response. *Science, 130,* 1338–1339.

*Hodgins, H. S., & Knee, C. R. (2002). The integrating self and conscious experience. In E. L. Deci & R. M. Ryan (Eds.), *Handbook of self-determination research* (pp. 87–100). Rochester, NY: University of Rochester Press.

James, W. (1999). The self. In R. F. Baumeister (Ed.), *The self in social psychology* (pp. 9–77). Philadelphia: Psychology Press. (Original work published 1890)

Kabat-Zinn, J. (1990). *Full catastrophe living: Using the wisdom of your body and mind to face stress, pain and illness.* New York: Delacourt Press.

Kasser, T. (2002). Sketches for a self-determination theory of values. In E. L. Deci & R. M. Ryan (Eds.), *Handbook of self-determination research* (pp. 123–140). Rochester, NY: University of Rochester Press.

Kasser, T., & Ryan, R. M. (1996). Further examining the American dream: Differential correlates of intrinsic and extrinsic goals. *Personality and Social Psychology Bulletin, 22,* 280–287.

Koestner, R., Losier, G. F., Vallerand, R. J., & Carducci, D. (1996). Identified and introjected forms of political internalization: Extending self-determination theory. *Journal of Personality and Social Psychology, 70,* 1025–1036.

Kuhl, J., & Fuhrmann, A. (1998). Decomposing self-regulation and self-control. In I. Heckhausen & C. Dweck (Eds.), *Motivation and self-regulation across the life span* (pp. 15–49). New York: Cambridge University Press.

La Guardia, J. G., Ryan, R. M., Couchman, C. E., & Deci, E. L. (2000). Within-person variation in security of attachment: A self-determination theory perspective on attachment, need fulfillment, and well-being. *Journal of Personality and Social Psychology, 79,* 367–384.

Langer, E. (1989). *Mindfulness.* Reading, MA: Addison-Wesley.

Langer, E. (2002). Well-being: Mindfulness versus positive evaluation. In C. R. Snyder & S. J. Lopez (Eds.), *Handbook of positive psychology* (pp. 214–230). New York: Oxford University Press.

Levesque, C. S., & Brown, K. W. (2003). *Overriding motivational automaticity: Mindfulness as a moderator of the influence of implicit motivation on day-to-day behavior.* Unpublished manuscript, Southwest Missouri State University, Springfield.

Libet, B. (1999). Do we have free will? *Journal of Consciousness Studies, 6,* 47–57.

Linehan, M. M. (1993). *Cognitive-behavioral treatment of borderline personality disorder.* New York: Guilford Press.

Macrae, C. N., & Johnston, L. (1998). Help, I., need somebody: Automatic action and inaction. *Social Cognition, 16,* 400–417.

Manoogian, S. T., & Reznick, J. S. (1976). The undermining and enhancing of intrinsic motivation in preschool children. *Journal of Personality and Social Psychology, 34,* 915–922.

Markland, D., Ryan, R. M., Tobin, V., & Rollnick, S. (2003). *Motivational interviewing and Self-Determination Theory.* Unpublished manuscript, University of Wales, Bangor.

McClelland, D. C., Koestner, R., & Weinberger, J. (1989). How do self-attributed and implicit motives differ? *Psychological Review, 96,* 690–702.

Miller, W. R., & Rollnick, S. (2002). *Motivational interviewing: Preparing people to change* (2nd ed.). New York: Guilford Press.

Nyanaponika Thera. (1972). *The power of mindfulness.* San Francisco: Unity Press.

Pelletier, L. G. (2002). A motivational analysis of self-determination for pro-environmental behaviors. In E. L. Deci & R. M. Ryan (Eds.), *Handbook of self-determination research* (pp. 205–232). Rochester, NY: University of Rochester Press.

Reeve, J., Bolt, E., & Cai, Y. (1999). Autonomy-supportive teachers: How they teach and motivate students. *Journal of Educational Psychology, 91,* 537–548.

Rogers, C. R. (1961). *On becoming a person.* Boston: Houghton Mifflin.

Ryan, R. M. (1982). Control and information in the intrapersonal sphere: An extension of cognitive evaluation theory. *Journal of Personality and Social Psychology, 43,* 450–461.

Ryan, R. M. (1993). Agency and organization: Intrinsic motivation, autonomy, and the self in psychological development. In J. E. Jacobs (Ed.), *Nebraska Symposium on Motivation: Vol. 40. Developmental perspectives on motivation* (pp. 1–56). Lincoln: University of Nebraska Press.

Ryan, R. M. (1995). Psychological needs and the facilitation of integrative processes. *Journal of Personality, 63,* 397–427.

Ryan, R. M., & Brown, K. W. (2003). Why we don't need self-esteem: On fundamental needs, contingent love, and mindfulness. *Psychological Inquiry, 14,* 71–76.

Ryan, R. M., & Connell, J. (1989). Perceived locus of causality and internalization: Examining reasons for acting in two domains. *Journal of Personality and Social Psychology, 57,* 749–761.

Ryan, R. M., & Deci, E. L. (2000a). Intrinsic and extrinsic motivations: Classic definitions and new directions. *Contemporary Educational Psychology, 25,* 54–67.

*Ryan, R. M., & Deci, E. L. (2000b). Self-determination theory and the facilitation of intrinsic, motivation, social development, and well-being. *American Psychologist, 55,* 68–78.

*Ryan, R. M., & Deci, E. L. (in press). Autonomy is no illusion: Self-determination theory and the empirical study of authenticity, awareness, and will. In J. Greenberg, S. Koole, & T. Pyszczynski (Eds.), *Handbook of experimental existential psychology.* New York: Guilford Press.

Ryan, R. M., Deci, E. L., & Grolnick, W. S. (1995). Autonomy, relatedness, and the self: Their relation to development and psychopathology. In D. Cicchetti & D. J. Cohen (Eds.), *Developmental psychopathology: Theory and methods* (pp. 618–655). New York: Wiley.

Ryan, R. M., Koestner, R., & Deci, E. L. (1991). Ego-involved persistence: When free-choice behavior is not intrinsically motivated. *Motivation and Emotion, 15,* 185–205.

Ryan, R. M., & La Guardia, J. G. (1999). Achievement motivation within a pressured society. Intrinsic and extrinsic motivations to learn and the politics of school reform. *Advances in Motivation and Achievement, 11,* 45–85.

Ryan, R. M., & La Guardia, J. G. (2000). What is being optimized? Self-determination theory and basic psychological needs. In S. H. Qualls & N. Abeles (Eds.), *Psychology and the aging revolution: How we adapt to longer life* (pp. 145–172). Washington, DC: American Psychological Association.

Ryan, R. M., & Lynch, J. (1989). Emotional autonomy versus detachment: Revisiting the vicissitudes of adolescence and young adulthood. *Child Development, 60,* 340–356.

Ryan, R. M., Stiller, J., & Lynch, J. H. (1994). Representations of relationships to teachers, parents, and friends as predictors of academic motivation and self-esteem. *Journal of Early Adolescence, 14,* 226–249.

Safran, J. D., & Segal, Z. V. (1990). *Interpersonal process in cognitive therapy.* New York: Basic Books.

Salovey, P., Mayer, J. D., Goldman, S. L., Turvey, C., & Palfai, T. F. (1995). Emotional attention, clarity, and repair: Exploring emotional intelligence using the trait meta-mood scale. In J. W. Pennebaker (Ed.), *Emotion, disclosure, and health* (pp. 125–154). Washington, DC: American Psychological Association.

Segal, Z., Williams, J. M. G., & Teasdale, J. D. (2002). *Mindfulness-based cognitive therapy for depression: A new approach to preventing relapse.* New York: Guilford Press.

Sheldon, K. M. (2002). The self-concordance model of healthy goal striving: When personal goals correctly represent the person. In E. L. Deci & R. M. Ryan (Eds.), *Handbook of self-determination research* (pp. 65–86). Rochester, NY: University of Rochester Press.

Sheldon, K. M., Elliot, A. J., Kim, Y., & Kasser, T. (2001). What is satisfying about satisfying events? Testing 10 candidate psychological needs. *Journal of Personality and Social Psychology, 80,* 325–339.

Sheldon, K. M., Williams, G., & Joiner, T. (2003). *Self-determination theory in the clinic.* New Haven, CT: Yale University Press.

Teasdale, J. D., Segal, Z., & Williams, J. M. G. (1995). How does cognitive therapy prevent depressive relapse and why should attentional control (mindfulness) training help? *Behavior Research and Therapy, 33,* 25–39.

Trapnell, P. D., & Campbell, J. (1999). Private self-consciousness and the five factor model of personality: Distinguishing rumination from reflection. *Journal of Personality and Social Psychology, 76,* 284–304.

Vallerand, R. J. (1997). Toward a hierarchical model of intrinsic and extrinsic motivation. In M. P. Zanna (Ed.), *Advances in experimental social psychology* (Vol. 29, pp. 271–360). San Diego, CA: Academic Press.

Vallerand, R. J., & Reid, G. (1984). On the causal effects of perceived competence on intrinsic motivation: A test of cognitive evaluation theory. *Journal of Sport Psychology, 6,* 94–102.

Varela, F. J., Thompson, E., & Rosch, E. (1991). *The embodied mind: Cognitive science and human experience.* Cambridge, MA: MIT Press.

Wegner, D. M. (2002). *The illusion of conscious will.* Cambridge, MA: MIT Press.

Westen, D. (1998). Unconscious thought, feeling and motivation: The end of a century-long debate. In R. F. Bornstein & J. M. Mesling (Eds.), *Empirical perspectives on the psychoanalytic unconscious* (pp. 1–43). Washington, DC: American Psychological Association.

Wilber, K. (2000). *Integral psychology: Consciousness, spirit, psychology, therapy.* Boston: Shambhala.

Williams, G. C., Grow, V. M., Freedman, Z., Ryan, R. M., & Deci, E. L. (1996). Motivational predictors of weight loss and weight-loss maintenance. *Journal of Personality and Social Psychology, 70,* 115–126.

Williams, G. C., Minicucci, D. S., Kouides, R. W., Levesque, C. S., Chirkov, V. I., Ryan, R. M., et al. (2002). Self-determination, smoking, diet, and health. *Health Education Research, 17,* 512–521.

Williams, G. C., Rodin, G. C., Ryan, R. M., Grolnick, W. S., & Deci, E. L. (1998). Autonomous regulation and long-term medication adherence in adult outpatients. *Health Psychology, 17,* 269–276.

PART IV

LIFESTYLE PRACTICES FOR HEALTH AND WELL-BEING

CHAPTER 8

Achieving Sustainable New Happiness: Prospects, Practices, and Prescriptions

KENNON M. SHELDON and SONJA LYUBOMIRSKY

Happiness depends upon ourselves.

—Aristotle

It is not God's will merely that we should be happy, but that we should make ourselves happy.

—Immanuel Kant

Like swimming, riding, writing, or playing golf, happiness can be learned.

—Boris Sokoloff

HAPPINESS IS A central criterion of mental health (Jahoda, 1958; Taylor & Brown, 1988) and has been found to be associated with numerous tangible benefits, such as enhanced physical health, reduced psychopathology, superior coping skills, and even longer life (see Lyubomirsky, King, & Diener, 2003, for a review). Thus, an important goal for positive psychology is advancing knowledge about how to help people increase their levels of happiness, positive mental health, and personal thriving. As others have noted (Seligman & Csikszentmihalyi, 2000; Sheldon & King, 2001), this issue has received very little research attention because mental health interventions have primarily focused on ameliorating suffering, weakness, and anxiety, rather than on increasing happiness and well-being.

This work was supported in part by grants from the Positive Psychology Network.

The assumption of such interventions appears to be that if we can relieve a person's suffering, well-being will result. However, this reasoning appears erroneous—that is, relieving people's suffering may only return them "back to zero" and do nothing to help them achieve their optimum happiness potentials.

How is it possible to help people go *beyond* zero, beyond the hedonic neutral point—that is, to lift them and sustain them above this point, thereby helping them attain their highest possible levels of happiness? Immediately, we encounter a paradox: Perhaps it is not possible. Indeed, some contemporary theories of well-being seem to indicate that trying to increase a person's happiness level is futile—an endeavor doomed to failure from the start. As described next, this pessimism is rooted in several assumptions about the nature of psychological well-being, including the notion of a genetic set point for happiness, the concept of hedonic adaptation, and the idea that there is much longitudinal stability for well-being-related personality traits. All of these views imply that, although they might become happier or more satisfied in the short term, people are destined to return to their original level in the long term. If this is true, perhaps people should give up on the idea of becoming happier!

In this chapter, we first consider the idea that it is impossible to sustainably increase our level of well-being. Then, we present evidence suggesting that there may be reason for hope after all. To illustrate, we present our own formal model of sustainable gains in well-being, which focuses on the distinction among the genetic set point, the positive circumstantial changes that a person undergoes, and the positive activity changes that a person enacts. We show that sustainable gains in well-being are indeed possible, *if* the person makes the right kind of changes in his or her life (i.e., activity changes), and we describe some new data to support this proposition. We then consider some specific *types* of volitional or activity changes that a person might make, such as resolving to regularly count his or her blessings, pursue meaningful personal goals, or commit random acts of kindness. In the final part of the chapter, we discuss how to best frame and conduct interventions to allow for the best chance of success.

WHY IT MAY BE IMPOSSIBLE TO INCREASE A PERSON'S HAPPINESS LEVEL

Considerable behavioral-genetic research indicates that permanently changing a person's happiness levels is very difficult, if not impossible. In other words, it appears there is a *genetically determined set point for happiness*. Lykken and Tellegen (1996) provided twin and adoption data to suggest that the heritability of well-being may be as high as 80% (although a more widely accepted figure is 50%; Braungart, Plomin, DeFries, & Fulker, 1992; Tellegen et al., 1988; cf. Diener, Suh, Lucas, & Smith, 1999). This suggests that each person has a built-in *attractor* for happiness, which he or she can orbit around but never leave behind (Vallacher & Nowak, 2002). In other words, the set point remains the most likely or expected value in a person's temporal distribution of happiness across the life span. Consistent with this idea, Headey and Wearing (1989) found, in a four-wave panel study, that participants tended to keep returning to their own baselines over time (see also Suh, Diener, & Fujita, 1996).

A related source of pessimism comes from research on personality traits. Traits are cognitive, affective, and behavioral complexes that are, by definition, consistent across situations and across the life span (Allport, 1955). Therefore, they may account for part of the stability of well-being. For example, McCrae and Costa (1990) have shown impressive long-term stability for neuroticism and extraversion, the two Big Five traits most closely related to well-being. Based on such data, McCrae and Costa argued that people also tend to maintain the same relative level of happiness over time (see also Costa, McCrae, & Zonderman, 1987; Diener & Lucas, 1999).

A third source of pessimism arises from the concept of *hedonic adaptation* (Frederick & Loewenstein, 1999) or the *hedonic treadmill* (Brickman & Campbell, 1971). Humans quickly adapt to changes, positive or negative (Kahneman, 1999; Scitovsky, 1976; Tversky & Griffin, 1991). Thus, although new circumstances may temporarily cause people to become happier or sadder, the effect of these new circumstances on happiness diminishes quickly or even disappears entirely, once people habituate to it. In support of this idea, Brickman, Coates, and Janoff-Bulman (1978) showed that after one year, lottery winners were no happier than controls and recent paralysis victims were not as unhappy as we might expect. The notion of habituation brings to mind the image of people walking up a descending escalator; although the improving circumstances of their life may propel them upward toward greater happiness, the process of adaptation eventually forces them back to their initial state.

These three ideas all suggest that "what goes up must come down." If so, instead of seeking an upward spiral, perhaps people would be better off simply accepting their current personality and happiness levels (McCrae & Costa, 1994). By doing so, they might avoid experiencing upsetting fluctuations and instabilities in their mood and self-feelings (Kernis, Brown, & Brody, 2000) and the disappointment of realizing that nothing really makes a difference (Gaskins, 1999).

WHY IT MAY BE POSSIBLE TO INCREASE A PERSON'S HAPPINESS LEVEL AFTER ALL

If the previous considerations are true, the very linchpin of the American ideology (and Western ideology more generally)—namely, that a person can take action to pursue and attain new happiness—becomes suspect. These considerations also have troubling implications for the positive psychology movement and its avowed goal of enhancing personal and social well-being. However, we believe that these arguments are overstated and that most people have considerable room for improvement in their chronic levels of happiness. We outline counterarguments next.

First, some researchers have had success in using interventions to increase happiness (e.g., Fava, Rafanelli, Cazzaro, Conti, & Grandi, 1998; Fordyce, 1977, 1983; Langer & Rodin, 1976; Lichter, Haye, & Kammann, 1980; Sheldon, Kasser, Smith, & Share, 2002). Recent research in the positive psychology tradition has identified several promising interventions, including prompting participants to pursue meaningful personal goals (Sheldon & Elliot, 1999), to seek out and forgive transgressors (McCullough, Pargament, & Thoresen, 2000), and to count their blessings on a regular basis (Emmons & McCullough, 2003). Notably, however, most of this research has not examined the stability of these changes in the long term.

Second, research documenting the long-term effectiveness of cognitive and behavioral strategies to ameliorate negative affect and depression has encouraging implications for the possibility of elevating long-term happiness (Gillham &

Reivich, 1999; Gloaguen, Cottraux, Cucherat, & Blackburn, 1998; Jacobson et al., 1996). Furthermore, evidence that psychotherapeutic outcomes can be stable in the long term supports the idea that gains in happiness might also be stable.

Another reason that genes are not necessarily destiny is that they influence happiness only indirectly—that is, by shaping the kinds of experiences and environments a person has or seeks to have. Thus, unwanted effects of genes could be minimized by active efforts to steer yourself away from problematic situations or to avoid maladaptive behaviors (Lykken, 2000). In addition, heritability coefficients describe covariations, not mean levels. Thus, even a high heritability coefficient for a particular trait (such as happiness) does not rule out the possibility that the mean level of that trait for a specific population can be elevated. Under the right conditions, everyone might become happier than they were before, even if their rank ordering relative to others remains stable.

Finally, longitudinal investigations of personal goal-pursuit suggest that happiness may be sustainably boosted. For example, Sheldon and Houser-Marko (2001) conducted a four-wave study of college freshmen, covering the entire first academic year. They showed that students who attained their goals over the first semester experienced an increase in their global well-being scores. Although some of these students had regressed to their original starting point by the end of the second semester, other students maintained their earlier gain—specifically, those who continued to do very well in their personal goals during the second semester. Thus, consistent with our theoretical model, these results suggest that new (in this case, goal-based) activities can first boost well-being and then maintain it at the new level, to the extent that the person remains successful in the activities. Sheldon and Lyubomirsky (2003) revisited this freshman goals sample at the end of their senior year and found that the doubly successful group had maintained their initial gain throughout their entire college career. Presumably, their initially successful activity instigated a cascading series of positive experiences throughout their undergraduate years.

A NEW CONCEPTUAL MODEL OF HAPPINESS

Which of these perspectives is true? Are sustainable gains in well-being possible, or are they impossible? We simply do not know. Indeed, there has been a remarkable paucity of longitudinal research on happiness. Instead, most of the existing literature concerns the cross-sectional associations of various factors (such as income, gender, traits, attitudes, and goals) with concurrent well-being. In other words, most well-being research focuses on between-subject (cross-person) differences, rather than within-subject (cross-time) differences. While this may be due in part to the difficulty of conducting longitudinal studies, part of it is rooted in the considerable scientific pessimism, described earlier, over whether sustainable happiness increases are possible. The assumption seems to have been that because lasting within-subject variations are impossible, between-subject variations tell us all we need to know.

In contrast to this view, our model (Sheldon, Lyubomirsky, & Schkade, 2003), described next, focuses explicitly on within-subject variations, making the assumption that it is possible to achieve, and maintain, a level of happiness greater than a person's set point. Before turning to the model, we first offer a conceptual definition of happiness.

DEFINITION OF HAPPINESS

Happiness is defined here as it is often defined empirically—that is, via people's direct ratings of their happiness, long-term balance of positive and negative affect, or life satisfaction (Diener, 1984; Lyubomirsky, 2001). Because these terms are not readily separable (Lyubomirsky & Lepper, 1999; Stones & Kozma, 1985), we use them interchangeably in this chapter. All three constructs are inherently subjective; therefore, they are usually assessed via self-report. Although this may be construed as a methodological weakness, we believe it essential to rely on an individual's own perspective. Indeed, it would make little sense to pronounce a particular person as happy unless that person thought so himself or herself.

Our primary focus in this chapter is on a person's characteristic level of happiness during a particular period in his or her life, which we term the *current happiness level.* We define happiness this way to enable us to identify a quantity that is more enduring than momentary or daily happiness, but that is also somewhat malleable over time and thus amenable to meaningful pursuit. Operationally, we might define a person's current happiness level in terms of his or her retrospective summary judgments about some recent period (such as the last 2, 6, or 12 months) or as the average of momentary judgments of happiness generated at multiple times during that period.

DETERMINANTS OF HAPPINESS

Our model identifies three primary factors that influence a person's current happiness level: The happiness set point, circumstantial/contextual factors in the person's life, and volitional/activity-based factors in the person's life (see Figure 8.1).

Set Point The *set point* is genetically determined and essentially constant. In a sense, it represents the level of happiness a person is likely to experience when all other factors in the model are equal to zero. In other words, the set point is analogous to the intercept in a within-subject regression equation, a constant

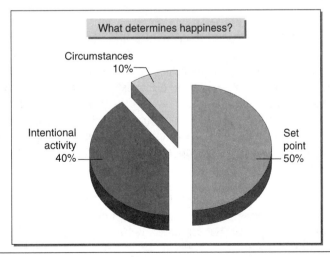

Figure 8.1 Three Primary Factors Influencing the Chronic Happiness Level

that always contributes to the output value and that determines it exactly when the other factors in the model have no influence or have canceling influences.

The regression equation metaphor suggests an interesting possibility—that the set point is not really a set *point*, but rather, a set *range*. That is, people may have considerable latitude to be located *above* the central point, depending on the other factors in the model. An example involving an analogy with the intelligence quotient (IQ): Although an average individual's potential range of IQ may be largely determined at birth (i.e., between 85 and 115), exactly where he or she ends up in the range may depend on other factors. In a stimulating and nurturing environment, the child may achieve an IQ near the top of his or her potential (e.g., 112), and in a nonsupportive environment, the child may be at the bottom of his or her potential range (e.g., 87).

However, happiness is not really like IQ, which is largely rooted in cognitive development. Because achieved cognitive abilities are unlikely to be lost (except in the case of disease or advanced age), high IQ, once attained, is not likely to be lost. In contrast, happiness may be inherently more unstable than IQ, such that high levels relative to the set point may not be maintainable. Again, however, we believe this argument overstates the case. To illustrate, it is necessary to consider the critical differences between life circumstances and life activities.

Life Circumstances　According to our model, positive life changes relevant to happiness fall into two broad categories—those based on changes in the circumstances, settings, and facts of a person's life and those based on changes in a person's intentional activities in life. "Circumstances" refers to demographic variables, such as age, marital status, employment status, and income. They also refer to geographic and contextual variables, such as the home and region in which the person lives, the conveniences a person enjoys, and the person's possessions. All of these examples share an important feature in common—they tend to remain relatively static and stable, becoming part of the background of the person's life or, as Henry James (1909) eloquently put it, "the whole envelope of circumstance." Our model assumes that people relatively quickly adapt to positive circumstantial changes precisely because of their static character.

According to this view, a person's new flat screen television, relocation to California, or new income level may all give a temporary boost, but the boost will likely fade after the person habituates to the constant new situation. Or, a within-subject regression equation such as that described previously would need to include a *time elapsed* variable as a moderator of the effect of circumstantial changes. That is, the more time that has gone by since the new circumstance arose, the smaller influence the circumstance would be expected to have on the predicted level of well-being at a particular point in time. Again, Headey and Wearing's (1989) four-wave panel study of the transitory influence of life circumstances on changes in well-being supports this idea, as do Brickman and colleagues' (1978) findings on the fleeting effects of winning the lottery.

Intentional Activities　In contrast, *activities* refers to the intentional and effortful practices in which a person engages. Such practices may be cognitive (i.e., regularly adopting an optimistic or positive attitude), behavioral (i.e., regularly being kind to others or regularly engaging in physical exercise), or volitional (i.e., identifying and striving for meaningful personal goals). Common to all of these is the notion of intentional effort and commitment in service of particular desired objectives or experiences.

Because of their intentional character, activities are more resistant to the effects of adaptation. In other words, a person can deliberately vary his or her activities, such that they continually provide new experiences and results. Indeed, some intentional activities (such as meditation or pausing to count your blessings) can serve to directly counter adaptation. Furthermore, intentional activity can create a self-sustaining cycle of positive change, in which invested effort leads the person to further opportunities for satisfying actions and accomplishments. The person can also perform an activity robotically, without variation, or fail to sensitively apply or enact the strategy. In such cases (described in more detail later), the benefits of the activity are likely to fade over time, just as the impact of positive circumstantial changes dampens. Still, activities have the *potential* to create sustained positive change because of their more dynamic and varying nature and because of their capacity to produce a steady stream of positive and rich experiences. If anything can do it, activities can.

The boundary between activity changes and circumstantial changes is somewhat fuzzy. For example, bringing about many circumstantial changes undoubtedly takes intentional effort, and, conversely, circumstantial changes may enable or afford new types of activity. Furthermore, some kinds of circumstances (i.e., the demographic factor of marital status) doubtless involve activity (i.e., the person acts within the marital relationship). Nevertheless, the data we describe next suggests that the basic distinction between the two types of factors is meaningful and important.

TESTING THE MODEL

Sheldon and Lyubomirsky (2004) conducted a three-wave longitudinal study of 666 undergraduates. Students rated their well-being at the beginning of an academic semester, using a variety of standard measures. Midway through the semester, they rated the extent to which they had experienced both positive activity and positive circumstantial changes since the beginning of the semester and rated their well-being again. They rated their well-being a final time at the end of the semester. Sheldon and Lyubomirsky predicted that both positive activity changes and positive circumstantial changes would predict enhanced well-being from Time 1 to Time 2 but that only activity changes would predict maintained gains at Time 3.

The activity and circumstance measures each consisted of a single item, with which participants rated their agreement. The circumstances item read:

> Please rate the extent to which there has been some significant positive change in the *circumstances* of your life since the beginning of the semester, which has given you a boost since it occurred. "Circumstances" means "facts" about your life, such as living arrangement, monetary situation, or course load. For example, you may have moved to a better dorm or better roommate, received an increase in financial support so you can have more fun, or dropped a course that you were really going to have trouble with.

The activity item read:

> Please rate the extent you have adopted some significant positive new *goal or activity* since the beginning of the semester, which has given you a boost since it occurred. "Goal/activity" means something you chose to do or get involved in, which takes effort on your part. For example, you may have joined a rewarding new group, club, or sports team; decided on a major or career direction which makes it clear what to focus on; or taken on some other important new project or goal in your life.

Figure 8.2 reproduces a longitudinal path model that well-fit the data. As expected, both positive activity and circumstantial changes predicted increased happiness at Time 2. However, only activity changes predicted happiness at Time 3, indicating that the earlier activity-based gains had been maintained, whereas the earlier circumstance-based gains had been attenuated. Parenthetically, the two change variables correlated .34 with each other, suggesting that some overlap does indeed exist between the two categories. Again, however, only the activity change variable accounted for maintained change in well-being. These results suggest that, at least in the short term, it is possible to increase well-being above the set point and to maintain it there.

Two other findings from this research program deserve mention. First, Sheldon and Lyubomirsky (2004) found, in a separate study using the same two change measures, that activity changes are associated with more varied experiences and less of a sense of getting used to (i.e., adapting to) the change, compared to circumstantial changes. This finding supports an important premise of our longitudinal model—namely, that activity changes induce more varied experiences and less hedonic adaptation, relative to circumstantial changes. Again, we believe these characteristics of activity help account for its potential long-term effect on happiness.

Second, Sheldon and Lyubomirsky (2004) found in the longitudinal study that competence and relatedness need-satisfaction (Deci & Ryan, 2000; Sheldon, Elliot, Kim, & Kasser, 2001) *mediated* the sustained activity effects. In other words, the reason that newly adopted activities at Time 1 produced sustained gains in well-being at Time 3 is that participants felt more competent in their daily lives during the semester and felt more related to others during the semester. These findings make sense, given the kinds of activity changes participants listed; for example: "When I

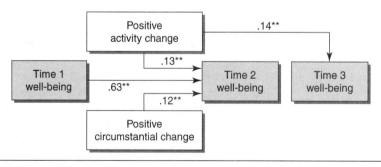

** = p < .01.

Figure 8.2 Longitudinal Path Model Predicting Maintained Changes in Well-Being

first got here, my classes seemed hard and I didn't study as much as I should have. I set myself a goal to study for at least five hours a day and now my classes are going a lot better for me"; "I used to not ever go to church but now I am going to Campus Crusade for Christ meetings, and God is more a part of my life than He ever has been"; and "I made a goal for myself that I would get involved and spend mostly all of my free time working on homecoming for my fraternity."

In contrast, circumstantial changes tend to be more superficial and bring less opportunity to fulfill deeper psychological needs. Consider some typical circumstantial changes people listed: "I learned that I won't have to be in a lottery in order to get in my Broadcast 1 class (which is required)," "My roommate at the beginning of the semester was a cocaine addict. She is no longer my roommate," and "I was recently initiated into my fraternity. The stress level of my life has now decreased because I no longer have to worry about initiation requirements." In short, the limited relevance of circumstantial changes for psychological need-satisfaction may be another reason such changes have limited influence on well-being, in addition to the reason that people more quickly habituate to altered circumstances.

Notably, the mediational findings are consistent with bottom-up models of well-being, which posit that global judgments of well-being are made by summating across the person's recent positive experiences. We believe that daily feelings of competence and relatedness, induced by activity, are important sources of such judgments. However, we also believe that changing your activities can create positive top-down influences on happiness. Top-down models of well-being propose that a person's global attitudes, expectancies, or self-concept may positively color all of his or her well-being judgments. Successful activity is a potentially important route to enhanced life expectancies and self-concepts—for example, the student described previously, who now studies five hours a day and is succeeding in her classes, may now think of herself as an excellent student who can achieve whatever she aspires.

HAPPINESS-INDUCING INTERVENTIONS

Lyubomirsky, Tkach, and Yelverton (2004) conducted two different happiness-enhancing interventions, attempting to sustainably boost college students' well-being. This endeavor builds on earlier intervention work by Fordyce (1977, 1983) but also draws from the contemporary positive psychology tradition and its attempt to identify essential human strengths and virtues (Seligman, 2002). Specifically, the two interventions experimented with prompting participants to practice, on a regular basis, either random acts of kindness (Study 1) or counting your blessings (Study 2).

Committing random acts of kindness is a behavioral happiness-enhancing strategy that was expected to boost temporary moods and long-lasting well-being, based on prior theory and research. For example, individuals who reported a greater interest in helping people, a tendency to act in a prosocial manner, or intentions to perform altruistic or courteous behaviors were more likely to rate themselves as dispositionally happy (Feingold, 1983; Lucas, 2000; Rigby & Slee, 1993; Williams & Shiaw, 1999). Although no experimental tests of the associations between happiness and generosity are available, acts of kindness can conceivably boost happiness in a variety of ways. Such acts may promote a charitable perception of other people and a person's social community, a heightened sense of interdependence and cooperation, and a perception of good fortune. In addition, people who commit acts of kindness may begin to view themselves as generous people, as well as feel more confident, efficacious, in control, and optimistic about their ability to help (Clark & Isen, 1982; Cunningham, 1988). Furthermore, acts of kindness can inspire greater liking by others, as well as appreciation, gratitude, and prosocial reciprocity (Trivers, 1971), all of which are valuable in times of stress and need. Finally, acts of kindness may help satisfy a basic human need for relatedness (Baumeister & Leary, 1995), thereby contributing to increased happiness, as in the Sheldon and Lyubomirsky (2004) study described previously.

In their intervention, Lyubomirsky and colleagues (Lyubomirsky, Tkach, et al., 2004) asked students to perform five random acts of kindness per week, over the course of six weeks. Such acts were described as behaviors that benefit others or make others happy, typically at some cost to themselves (e.g., dropping coins into a stranger's parking meter, donating blood, helping a friend with a problem set, visiting a sick relative, or writing a thank-you note to a former teacher). A no-treatment control group simply completed the measures of well-being—first, immediately before the intervention and last, immediately after the intervention. The findings, shown in the top panel of Figure 8.3, support the hypothesis that a short-term happiness-enhancing activity can increase well-being. While the control

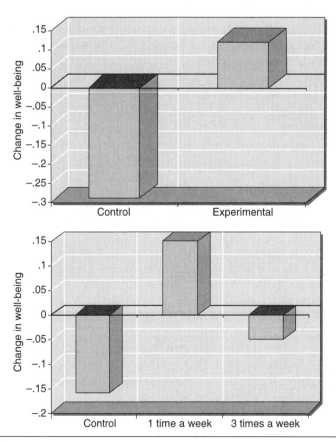

Figure 8.3 Changes in Well-Being over the Six-Week Intervention for Study 1 (Top Panel) and Study 2 (Bottom Panel)

group (left) experienced a reduction in happiness over the course of the six-week period, the experimental group (right) experienced an increase.

The second intervention tested a cognitive happiness-increasing practice. Emmons and McCullough showed that practicing gratitude on a regular basis can enhance well-being (Emmons & McCullough, 2003; McCullough, Kilpatrick, Emmons, & Larson, 2001). Grateful thinking promotes the savoring of positive life experiences and situations, so that the maximum satisfaction and enjoyment is extracted from the person's circumstances. As noted previously, this activity may directly counteract the effects of hedonic adaptation by helping people to distill as much appreciation from the good things in their lives as possible. In addition, the capacity to appreciate their life circumstances may also be an adaptive coping strategy by which people positively reinterpret problematic life experiences, bolster coping resources, and strengthen social relationships. Finally, the practice of gratitude is incompatible with negative emotions; thus, it may reduce feelings of envy, anger, or greed.

In Lyubomirsky and colleagues' (Lyubomirsky, Tkach, et al., 2004) second intervention, also for six weeks, students were instructed to engage in self-guided exercises involving counting their blessings either once a week or three times a week. Examples of blessings listed by students included "getting through my first set of midterms," "having supportive friends," "the car my dad bought me," "my parents telling me that they love me," and "AOL instant messenger." As in Study 1, control participants, by contrast, completed only the happiness assessments. The results again supported the predictions of our model—first, that short-term increases in happiness are possible and, second, that optimal timing is important. In sum, students who regularly expressed gratitude showed increases in well-being over the course of the study, relative to controls, but those increases were evident only for those students who performed the activity only once a week (see the bottom panel of Figure 8.3). Perhaps counting their blessings several times a week led them to tire of the practice, finding it less fresh and meaningful over time.

The results of these two interventions are encouraging, suggesting a promising program of research that has vast applications for the possibility of increasing happiness in the larger population. Notably, however, these studies did not test the *sustainability* of the well-being increases for the experimental (i.e., "kindness" and "blessings") groups and did not examine the effects of key moderators of activity effects. These moderators are described next.

FUTURE RESEARCH AND RECOMMENDATIONS FOR INTERVENTIONS

The model and theory reviewed previously suggest a number of fruitful research avenues. Next, we consider several potentially important issues.

POTENTIAL MODERATORS OF ACTIVITY EFFECTS

Our theoretical model (Sheldon et al., 2003) goes beyond specifying three classes of determinants of happiness (i.e., set point, circumstances, and activities). It additionally makes several as-yet untested assumptions, which are briefly considered here because they may be relevant to the long-term task of developing maximally effective happiness interventions. We first consider the question of how to *choose* a particular happiness-boosting activity, then the question of how such activity may be *initiated,* and last the question of how the activity can be *maintained* over time to produce a sustained increase in the chronic level of happiness. In the process, we discuss the issue of person-strategy fit, the meaning and nature of effort, the definition and role of habits, the importance of social support, and the influence of the individual's cultural membership.

Choosing an Activity: The Role of Person-Activity Fit   Not all activities will help a particular person become happier. People have enduring strengths, interests, values, and inclinations, which predispose them to benefit more from some activities than others. This general "matching" hypothesis (Harackiewicz & Sansone, 1991; Snyder & Cantor, 1998) is supported by work showing that the positive effects of goal-attainment on subjective well-being are moderated by goal-person fit (Brunstein, Schultheiss, & Grassman, 1998; Diener & Fujita, 1995; Sheldon & Elliot, 1999; Sheldon & Kasser, 1998). It is also supported by past well-being intervention research. For example, in several studies that instructed participants to apply 14 different techniques to raise their personal happiness, the most effective happiness-increasing strategies varied greatly from one individual to another and appeared to be determined by each participant's needs and specific areas of weakness (Fordyce, 1977, 1983).

The Role of Effort   We assume that performing an activity necessitates at least two different kinds of effort—first, the effort needed to *initiate* the activity and, second, the effort needed to *carry out* and *maintain* the activity. The first kind of effort refers to the difficulty of overcoming inertia or getting over the hump so that the person starts doing an activity. For example, meditating in the morning, making time to work on at least one important project during the day, or dropping by the gym at the end of the day can have significant benefits, but only if the person can remember to do them and overcome any obstacles to initiating them. We assume that this kind of self-regulatory effort requires considerable self-discipline and willpower to exert. Furthermore, such effort may constitute a limited resource. In Muraven and Baumeister's (2000) terms, self-regulatory will is like a "muscle," which has a limited capacity in a given unit of time and must be used strategically to avoid fatigue.

Some activities are intrinsically more appealing and easier to jump-start—indeed, this is undoubtedly one advantage of selecting an activity that fits the person's personality. For example, rather than jogging around the block, a fitness-seeking wilderness lover might instead choose to run on a trail through the woods, thereby feeling much less initial resistance to beginning the activity. Or, rather than expressing gratitude and appreciation in a diary, a visually oriented individual might instead choose to express himself or herself through painting, and a musical individual might instead choose to write a song. Such choices would enhance the intrinsic appeal of sitting down to engage in the activity.

As these examples illustrate, finding intrinsically motivated activities may be crucial not only for the person's ability to *initiate* the activity but also for his or her ability to *keep on doing* the activity in the long term. If the activity becomes boring, the person may stop doing it. In this light, an important factor influencing activity's effect on happiness likely concerns how the person *varies* his or her activities. For example, by shifting attention among several projects at work, by exploring new trails in the state park, or by focusing gratitude on different aspects of his or her life, a person's activities should remain intrinsically enjoyable and conducive to many rewarding "flow" experiences (Csikszentmihalyi, 1990). Another factor may be the *timing* of activity; if the person does the activity too often or not often enough or at the wrong times, it may lose its efficacy. For example, Lyubomirsky, Tkach, et al. (2004) found that counting your blessings once a week may be the optimal rate or schedule.

The Role of Social Support   Social support is believed to be another important factor in enacting happiness changes. Following through on your volitional intentions can be tough, and the task can be made easier if others are in the same boat. Indeed, many groups and organizations, such as Alcoholics Anonymous or Weight-Watchers, emphasize the import of having "teammates" during abstinence attempts. Thus, we assume that interpersonal support can aid an individual both in *initiating* a potential happiness-increasing activity and in *maintaining* it. In addition, because social support is an important correlate of psychological well-being in its own right (e.g., Baldassare, Rosenfield, & Rook, 1984; Henderson & Brown, 1988), performing an intentional activity as a group or with the support of close others is likely to promote greater and more sustained happiness change than "bowling alone" (Putnam, 2000).

The Role of Habitual Activity   If activities such as maintaining an optimistic outlook about the future, spending time on the things that matter, or pursuing a meaningful life goal can indeed enhance and sustain new happiness, it would arguably be a good idea to make a habit of doing them. However, at first glance, habits appear to present a paradox for our model. By acquiring a habit, doesn't a person necessarily turn a formerly conscious activity into an unconscious one, which is practiced routinely, automatically, and without variation? If so, isn't the person likely to experience hedonic adaptation to that activity, such that it loses its happiness-boosting potential?

Perhaps not. However, to illustrate, we must distinguish between two different types of habits—first, the habit of *regularly initiating* a potentially beneficial activity, and, second, the habit of *implementing it the same way every time*. The first type of habit is likely to be a valuable and beneficial one because it can help a person continually get over the hurdle. For example, a woman might make running or yoga an automatic part of her daily routine, thus deriving considerable benefit. In contrast, the second type of habit is likely to be problematic because it is most likely to foster boredom and ultimately lead to hedonic adaptation. For example, the woman might run the same route every day and begin to get tired of running. To overcome this, as suggested previously, people should mindfully attend to optimal timing and variety in the ways they practice an activity. For example, the woman might want to vary the route, time of day, and duration and pace of her running to help forestall the effects of adaptation.

The Role of Cultural Membership   Another potential moderator of activity effects on happiness may be the norms and traditions of the culture in which the individual resides. There is little doubt that the "pursuit of happiness" is an important and well-supported element of U.S. culture. However, in cultural settings that deemphasize individual happiness or striving or perhaps actively disapprove of them, it may be more difficult to take action to increase your happiness level. Alternatively, in collectivist cultures, happiness-relevant activity may merely require a somewhat different focus. In these settings, it may be more effective to act in service of others rather than act in service of personal achievements and goals. In terms of the Sheldon and Lyubomirsky (2003) data described previously, activities that provide relatedness need-satisfaction may be more important in such cultures than activities providing competence need-satisfaction (Sheldon et al., 2001). These important questions await future research.

FACTORS INFLUENCING PARTICIPANTS' ACCEPTANCE OF INTERVENTIONS

The previous section concerned some potentially important *dynamic* factors that may influence the effect of activity on sustained well-being. In this section, we consider some potentially important *contextual* factors that may influence the extent to which participants take maximal advantage of happiness-enhancing opportunities.

One factor concerns the manner in which participants are prompted to take part in the presented activity or opportunity. Self-determination theory (Deci & Ryan, 1985, 2000) examines in detail the approaches by which teachers, coaches, bosses, and parents can best motivate their charges, focusing in particular on *autonomy support*. Supporting autonomy means taking the target's perspective, providing as much choice as possible, and supplying a meaningful rationale when choice-provision is not possible. In contrast, *controlling behavior* involves "must" or "should" language, insensitivity to the perspective of the one being motivated, and lack of concern with providing a sense of choice to the one being motivated. This analysis suggests that when enrolling people in happiness intervention programs, it is very important not to imply that they "have" to do it or that they "must" or "should" become happier.

This analysis also raises important issues concerning how to properly *test* the happiness-inducing potential of a particular program or intervention. Ideally, double-blind procedures would be used, in which neither the participant nor the experimenter is aware of the treatment being given and in which the participant has no conception of the experimental hypothesis. But is this reasonable or desirable when the intervention concerns encouraging people to take intentional action that may enhance their personal well-being? Perhaps such interventions can work only if the participant is fully aware of what the research is about. Although this possibility raises potential methodological problems concerning placebo and demand effects, such problems may be surmounted with appropriate control groups. In addition, the issues of autonomy-support and person-strategy fit suggest that participants be given the choice of what intervention to enact, rather than being randomly assigned to interventions. Such self-selection procedures may once again threaten conventional methodological standards, but again, the problem may be offset by careful experimental design.

A related issue is how happiness-enhancing programs or practices should be labeled. Should their potential relation to happiness be acknowledged directly, or should they instead be simply introduced as positive life practices involving kindness, gratitude, physical exercise, or what have you? The latter content-based approach may be preferable, for several reasons. First, as discussed previously, the explicit happiness label approach is more likely to create demand effects that may obscure whatever real changes are occurring for participants. Second, inducements such as, "Do you want to be happy?" might not appeal to a segment of potential participants, who might object to associations with self-help gurus and popular psychology how-to books or for whom the term *happiness* denotes unrealistic and wrongheaded positivity and optimism. Third, content-based (rather than happiness-based) labeling may sidestep another possible barrier to intervention efficacy—namely, that active and conscious attempts to increase happiness might backfire altogether if the person becomes too focused on this goal (i.e., "Are we having fun yet?"; Schooler, Ariely, & Loewenstein, in press). In other words, it is probably better to be fully engaged in the activities of your life, without frequently pausing to ask, "Am I happy?" In this case, happiness may come as a natural by-product of a life well lived.

RECOMMENDATIONS FOR HAPPINESS

What are the most general recommendations for increasing happiness suggested by our model? Simply, that happiness seekers might be advised to find new activities to become engaged in—preferably activities that fit their values and interests. They should make a habit of initiating the activity, while at the same time varying the way they implement the activity and aiming for the optimal timing of the activity. People might be advised to avoid basing their happiness on the acquisition of particular circumstances or objects (e.g., buy a luxury car, arrange for cosmetic surgery, or move to California) because they will tend to habituate to such stable factors. However, if they can remember to appreciate or actively engage with the object or circumstance (i.e., pause to savor their new Mercedes or take advantage of the California weather), stable objects and circumstances may not be stable after all from a phenomenological perspective.

CONCLUSION

More than 227 years ago, the American Declaration of Independence proclaimed "the pursuit of happiness" as a God-given right. Today, after decades of scientific research into subjective well-being, we still do not know if such pursuit is possible, much less how best to effect it. Given the breadth of beneficial effects that follow from subjective well-being, for both the individual and those around him or her (Lyubomirsky, King, et al., 2003), it seems vital to undertake such research. Fortunately, there are emerging reasons to believe that "the pursuit of happiness" is indeed a practical and attainable goal. In this chapter, we described these reasons and presented our own model depicting the architecture of sustainable gains in happiness. We also made a number of suggestions about what kinds of interventions and activities are expected to be most effective. Finally, we described some important factors that are likely to influence the effectiveness of any adopted activity, such as person-activity fit, appropriate effort, positive habits, and social support. We hope these ideas will stimulate researchers to take up the gauntlet of better understanding longitudinal well-being.

REFERENCES

Allport, G. W. (1955). *Becoming: Basic considerations for a psychology of personality.* New Haven, CT: Yale University Press.

Baldassare, M., Rosenfield, S., & Rook, K. S. (1984). The types of social relations predicting elderly well-being. *Research on Aging, 6,* 549–559.

Baumeister, R. F., & Leary, M. R. (1995). The need to belong: Desire for interpersonal attachments as a fundamental human motivation. *Psychological Bulletin, 117,* 497–529.

Braungart, J. M., Plomin, R., DeFries, J. C., & Fulker, D. W. (1992). Genetic influence on tester-rated infant temperament as assessed by Bayley's Infant Behavior Record: Nonadoptive and adoptive siblings and twins. *Developmental Psychology, 28,* 40–47.

Brickman, P., & Campbell, D. T. (1971). Hedonic relativism and planning the good society. In M. H. Appley (Ed.), *Adaptation-level theory: A symposium* (pp. 287–302). New York: Academic Press.

Brickman, P., Coates, D., & Janoff-Bulman, R. (1978). Lottery winners and accident victims: Is happiness relative? *Journal of Personality and Social Psychology, 36,* 917–927.

Brunstein, J. C., Schultheiss, O. C., & Grassman, R. (1998). Personal goals and emotional well-being: The moderating role of motive dispositions. *Journal of Personality and Social Psychology, 75,* 494–508.

Clark, M. S., & Isen, A. M. (1982). Toward understanding the relationship between feeling states and social behavior. In A. H. Hastorf & A. M. Isen (Eds.), *Cognitive social psychology* (pp. 71–108). New York: Elsevier.

Costa, P. T., McCrae, R. R., & Zonderman, A. B. (1987). Environmental and dispositional influences on well-being: Longitudinal follow-up of an American national sample. *British Journal of Psychology, 78,* 299–306.

Csikszentmihalyi, M. (1990). *Flow: The psychology of optimal experience.* New York: HarperCollins.

Cunningham, M. R. (1988). What do you do when you're happy or blue? Mood, expectancies, and behavioral interest. *Motivation and Emotion, 12,* 309–331.

Deci, E. L., & Ryan, R. M. (1985). *Intrinsic motivation and self-determination in human behavior.* New York: Plenum Press.

*Deci, E. L., & Ryan, R. M. (2000). The "what" and "why" of goal pursuits: Human needs and the self-determination of behavior. *Psychological Inquiry, 11,* 227–268.

Diener, E. (1984). Subjective well-being. *Psychological Bulletin, 95,* 542–575.

Diener, E., & Fujita, F. (1995). Resources, personal strivings, and subjective well-being: A nomothetic and idiographic approach. *Journal of Personality and Social Psychology, 68,* 926–935.

Diener, E., & Lucas, R. E. (1999). Personality and subjective well-being. In D. Kahneman, E. Diener, & N. Schwartz (Eds.), *Well-being: The foundations of hedonic psychology* (pp. 213–229). New York: Russell Sage Foundation.

*Diener, E., Suh, E. M., Lucas, R. E., & Smith, H. L. (1999). Subjective well-being: Three decades of progress. *Psychological Bulletin, 125,* 276–302.

Emmons, R. A., & McCullough, M. E. (2003). Counting blessings versus burdens: An experimental investigation of gratitude and subjective well-being in daily life. *Journal of Personality and Social Psychology, 84,* 377–389.

Fava, G. A., Rafanelli, C., Cazzaro, M., Conti, S., & Grandi, S. (1998). Well-being therapy: A novel psychotherapeutic approach for residual symptoms of affective disorders. *Psychological Medicine, 28,* 475–480.

Feingold, A. (1983). Happiness, unselfishness, and popularity. *Journal of Psychology, 115,* 3–5.

Fordyce, M. W. (1977). Development of a program to increase happiness. *Journal of Counseling Psychology, 24,* 511–521.

Fordyce, M. W. (1983). A program to increase happiness: Further studies. *Journal of Counseling Psychology, 30,* 483–498.

Frederick, S., & Loewenstein, G. (1999). Hedonic adaptation. In D. Kahneman, E. Diener, & N. Schwarz (Eds.), *Well-being: The foundations of hedonic psychology* (pp. 302–329). New York: Russell Sage Foundation.

Gaskins, R. W. (1999). "Adding legs to a snake": A reanalysis of motivation and the pursuit of happiness from a Zen Buddhist perspective. *Journal of Educational Psychology, 91,* 204–215.

Gillham, J. E., & Reivich, K. J. (1999). Prevention of depressive symptoms in school children: A research update. *Psychological Science, 10,* 461–462.

Gloaguen, V., Cottraux, J., Cucherat, M., & Blackburn, I. (1998). A meta-analysis of the effects of cognitive therapy in depressed patients. *Journal of Affective Disorders, 49,* 59–72.

Harackiewicz, J. M., & Sansone, C. (1991). Goals and intrinsic motivation: You can get there from here. In M. L. Maehr & P. R. Pintrich (Eds.), *Advances in motivation and achievement* (Vol. 7, pp. 21–49). Greenwich, CT: JAI Press.

Headey, B., & Wearing, A. (1989). Personality, life events, and subjective well-being: Toward a dynamic equilibrium model. *Journal of Personality and Social Psychology, 57,* 731–739.

Henderson, A. S., & Brown, G. W. (1988). Social support: The hypothesis and the evidence. In A. S. Henderson & G. D. Burrows (Eds.), *Handbook of social psychiatry* (pp. 73–85). Amsterdam: Elsevier.

Jacobson, N. S., Dobson, K. S., Truax, P. A., Addis, M. E., Koerner, K., Gollan, J. K., et al. (1996). A component analysis of cognitive-behavioral treatment for depression. *Journal of Consulting and Clinical Psychology, 64,* 295–304.

Jahoda, M. (1958). *Current concepts of positive mental health.* New York: Basic Books.

James, H. (1909). *The portrait of a lady.* Boston: Houghton Mifflin.

Kahneman, D. (1999). Objective happiness. In D. Kahneman, E. Diener, & N. Schwarz (Eds.), *Well-being: The foundations of hedonic psychology* (pp. 3–25). New York: Russell Sage Foundation.

Kernis, M. H., Brown, A. C., & Brody, G. H. (2000). Fragile self-esteem in children and its associations with perceived patterns of parent-child communication. *Journal of Personality, 68,* 225–252.

Langer, E., & Rodin, J. (1976). The effects of choice and enhanced personal responsibility for the aged: A field experiment in an institutional setting. *Journal of Personality and Social Psychology, 34,* 191–198.

Lichter, S., Haye, K., & Kammann, R. (1980). Increasing happiness through cognitive retraining. *New Zealand Psychologist, 9,* 57–64.

Lucas, R. E. (2000). *Pleasant affect and sociability: Toward a comprehensive model of extraverted feelings and behaviors.* Unpublished doctoral dissertation, University of IL, Urbana.

*Lykken, D. (2000). *Happiness: The nature and nurture of joy and contentment.* New York: St. Martin's Griffin.

Lykken, D., & Tellegen, A. (1996). Happiness is a stochastic phenomenon. *Psychological Science, 7,* 186–189.

*Lyubomirsky, S. (2001). Why are some people happier than others? The role of cognitive and motivational processes in well-being. *American Psychologist, 56,* 239–249.

Lyubomirsky, S., King, L. A., & Diener, E. (2003). *Is happiness a good thing? A theory of the benefits of long-term positive affect.* Manuscript submitted for publication.

Lyubomirsky, S., & Lepper, H. S. (1999). A measure of subjective happiness: Preliminary reliability and construct validation. *Social Indicators Research, 46,* 137–155.

Lyubomirsky, S., Tkach, C., & Yelverton, J. (2004). *Pursuing sustained happiness through random acts of kindness and counting one's blessings: Tests of two six-week interventions.* Unpublished data, University of California, Riverside, Department of Psychology.

McCrae, R. R., & Costa, P. T. (1990). *Personality in adulthood.* New York: Guilford Press.

McCrae, R. R., & Costa, P. T. (1994). The stability of personality: Observations and evaluations. *Current Directions in Psychological Science, 3,* 173–175.

McCullough, M. E., Kilpatrick, S. D., Emmons, R. A., & Larson, D. B. (2001). Is gratitude a moral affect? *Psychological Bulletin, 127,* 249–266.

McCullough, M. E., Pargament, K. I., & Thoresen, C. E. (Eds.). (2000). *Forgiveness: Theory, research, and practice.* New York: Guilford Press.

Muraven, M., & Baumeister, R. F. (2000). Self-regulation and depletion of limited resources: Does self-control resemble a muscle? *Psychological Bulletin, 126,* 247–259.

Putnam, R. D. (2000). *Bowling alone: The collapse and revival of American community.* New York: Simon & Schuster.

Rigby, K., & Slee, P. T. (1993). Dimensions of interpersonal relation among Australian children and implications for psychological well-being. *Journal of Social Psychology, 133,* 33–42.

Schooler, J. W., Ariely, D., & Loewenstein, G. (in press). The explicit pursuit and assessment of happiness can be self-defeating. In J. Carrillo & I. Brocas (Eds.), *Psychology and economics.* Oxford, England: Oxford University Press.

Scitovsky, T. (1976). *The joyless economy: The psychology of human satisfaction.* New York: Oxford University Press.

Seligman, M. E. P. (2002). *Authentic happiness: Using the new positive psychology to realize your potential for lasting fulfillment.* New York: Free Press.

Seligman, M. E. P., & Csikszentmihalyi, M. (2000). Positive psychology: An introduction. *American Psychologist, 55,* 5–14.

Sheldon, K. M., & Elliot, A. J. (1999). Goal striving, need-satisfaction, and longitudinal well-being: The Self-Concordance Model. *Journal of Personality and Social Psychology, 76,* 482–497.

Sheldon, K. M., Elliot, A. J., Kim, Y., & Kasser, T. (2001). What is satisfying about satisfying events? Testing 10 candidate psychological needs. *Journal of Personality and Social Psychology, 80,* 325–339.

*Sheldon, K. M., & Houser-Marko, L. (2001). Self-concordance, goal-attainment, and the pursuit of happiness: Can there be an upward spiral? *Journal of Personality and Social Psychology, 80,* 152–165.

Sheldon, K. M., & Kasser, T. (1998). Pursuing personal goals: Skills enable progress but not all progress is beneficial. *Personality and Social Psychology Bulletin, 24,* 1319–1331.

Sheldon, K. M., Kasser, T., Smith, K., & Share, T. (2002). Personal goals and psychological growth: Testing an intervention to enhance goal-attainment and personality integration. *Journal of Personality, 70,* 5–31.

Sheldon, K. M., & King, L. (2001). Why positive psychology is necessary. *American Psychologist, 56,* 216–217.

Sheldon, K. M., & Lyubomirsky, S. (2004). *Achieving sustainable increases in happiness: Change your actions, not your circumstances.* Manuscript submitted for publication.

Sheldon, K. M., Lyubomirsky, S., & Schkade, D. (2003). *Pursuing happiness: The architecture of sustainable change.* Manuscript submitted for publication.

Snyder, M., & Cantor, N. (1998). Understanding personality and social behavior: A functionalist strategy. In D. T. Gilbert & S. T. Fiske (Eds.), *The handbook of social psychology* (4th ed., Vol. 1, pp. 635–679). New York: McGraw-Hill.

Stones, M. J., & Kozma, A. (1985). Structural relationships among happiness scales: A second order factorial study. *Social Indicators Research, 17,* 19–28.

Suh, E. M., Diener, E., & Fujita, F. (1996). Events and subjective well-being: Only recent events matter. *Journal of Personality and Social Psychology, 70,* 1091–1102.

Taylor, S. E., & Brown, J. D. (1988). Illusion and well-being: A social psychological perspective on mental health. *Psychological Bulletin, 103,* 193–210.

Tellegen, A., Lykken, D. T., Bouchard, T. J., Wilcox, K. J., Segal, N. L., & Rich, S. (1988). Personality similarity in twins reared apart and together. *Journal of Personality and Social Psychology, 54,* 1031–1039.

Trivers, R. (1971). The evolution of reciprocal altruism. *Quarterly Review of Biology, 46,* 35–57.

Tversky, A., & Griffin, D. (1991). Endowment and contrast in judgments of well-being. In F. Strack, M. Argyle, & N. Schwarz (Eds.), *Subjective well-being: An interdisciplinary perspective* (pp. 101–118). Oxford, England: Pergamon Press.

Vallacher, R. R., & Nowak, A. (2002). The dynamical perspective in personality and social psychology. *Personality and Social Psychology Review, 6,* 264–273.

Williams, S., & Shiaw, W. T. (1999). Mood and organizational citizenship behavior: The effects of positive affect on employee organizational citizenship behavior intentions. *Journal of Psychology, 133,* 656–668.

CHAPTER 9

Physical Activity: Positive Psychology in Motion

NANETTE MUTRIE and GUY FAULKNER

SELIGMAN (2002) SUGGESTED THAT the goal of positive psychology is to "learn how to build the qualities that help individuals and communities not just endure and survive but also flourish" (p. 8). We argue that physical activity is one human behavior that will help both individuals and communities survive and flourish. At an individual level, we show that physical activity has the capacity to prevent mental illness, to foster positive emotions, and to buffer individuals against the stresses of life. At a community level, we suggest that a community in which physical activity is seen as the social norm may be healthier and increase the social capital of communities.

We use physical activity (PA) as a general term that refers to any movement of the body that results in energy expenditure above that of resting level (Caspersen, Powell, & Christenson, 1985). *Exercise* is often (incorrectly) used interchangeably with PA, but this term refers to a subset of PA in which the activity is structured, often supervised and undertaken with the aim of maintaining or improving physical fitness or health. Examples of exercise include going to the gym, jogging, taking an aerobics class, or taking part in a recreational sport for fitness.

In the past couple of decades, interest in sports and exercise science has expanded from a focus on the high-intensity, high-volume physical activity that athletes are required to undertake to reach peak fitness levels for sports performance, toward an interest in much lower levels of physical activity that can be derived from making active choices (such as walking instead of driving for short journeys or choosing the stairs instead of the escalator) in everyday life. This expansion of interest reflects the growing concern that physical inactivity is a public health problem, and the study of the determinants and consequences of physical activity in the developing field of exercise psychology has increased dramatically over the past decade (see the special edition of *The Psychologist* [2002, vol. 15, no. 8] for an overview of sports and exercise psychology).

In the field of exercise science, there are well-established, evidence-based guidelines about the amount of physical activity required to gain health benefits but with the majority of evidence derived from studies focusing on physical diseases such as coronary disease and diabetes (Pate et al., 1995). Current guidelines recommend that adults accumulate 30 minutes (and children 60 minutes) of moderate-intensity physical activity (equivalent to brisk walking) on most days of the week. These bouts could be one period of sustained activity but may be accumulated through the day in shorter units, for example, three 10-minute walks.

If we take an evolutionary look at our beginnings, we see a life in which high levels of physical activity were required for survival. Even one century ago, most people needed to be physically active to work, to travel, and to take care of homes and families. Our modern world has engineered such activity out of our lives. There are fewer manual jobs, we do not need to travel on foot, we do not need to hunt and harvest for our food, and many domestic chores have been mechanized. While these changes have created many benefits for our longevity and quality of life, they have also created many problems. Lack of sufficient physical activity has now been linked to at least 17 unhealthy conditions, almost all of which are chronic diseases or considered risk factors for chronic diseases (Booth, Gordon, Carlson, & Hamilton, 2000). Hardman (2001, p. 1195) has summarized this serious situation for public health: "Physical inactivity is a waste of human potential for health and well-being."

We cannot and would not want to return to the lifestyles of our ancestors, but we do need to take a positive approach to creating lifestyles that include physical activity. Many people who are physically inactive are not diseased or ill, but their health (both physically and mentally) could benefit from regular activity. The aim of this chapter is to provide an up-to-date review of what is known about the effects of physical activity on psychological function and to raise awareness of this knowledge among psychologists. This chapter develops the principle that the body is important to how we think, feel, and behave. The principles of psychosomatic medicine have established the idea that how we think and feel will affect the functioning of the body. However, our task in this chapter is to show that the reverse is also true—that there is a somatopsychic principle (Harris, 1973) that is very much in line with the principles of positive psychology. The somatopsychic principle is neatly displayed in the well-known phrase *mens sana in corpore sano* (a healthy mind in a healthy body).

Seligman (2002) talks of building strength as one of the key principles of positive psychology. If we examine physical strength as part of this concept, we can begin to see the somatopsychic principles working. Gaining physical strength or capacity allows us to feel more confident in our ability to do everyday tasks, perhaps provides us with a more positive perception of our physical selves, and thus can influence our self-esteem. Seligman further argues that building strength should be at the forefront of treating mental illness, and we show that this building of physical strength has a somatopsychic impact on those people who are suffering from mental ill health. Overall, we develop the evidence that shows the positive link between psychological well-being and regular physical activity.

PHYSICAL ACTIVITY AND PSYCHOLOGICAL WELL-BEING

Despite frequent reports of psychological benefits from regular exercisers and the intuitive holistic link between physical and mental well-being, researchers have only recently begun to systematically examine the impact of physical activity on mental health outcomes. As a result of this research, we now have a convincing evidence base that supports the existence of a strong relationship between physical activity and psychological well-being (Biddle, Fox, & Boutcher, 2000). This relationship may be critical. The literature indicates that mental health outcomes motivate people to persist in physical activity while also having the potentially positive impact on well-being (Biddle & Mutrie, 2001). Without regular participation, both mental and physical benefits will not accrue. The physiological and psychological benefits of physical activity that have good evidence to support them are shown in Table 9.1.

The existing evidence suggests four main functions of physical activity for impacting mental health (Fox, Boutcher, Faulkner, & Biddle, 2000). First, physical activity may prevent mental health problems. Second, exercise has been examined as a treatment or therapy for existing mental illness. Third, exercise may improve the quality of life for people with mental health problems. The final function concerns the role of physical activity in improving the psychological well-being of the general public. All four of these functions have elements of positive psychology in that there is a clear preventative function, a clear function for enhancing positive emotions, even for those with existing mental illness, and a clear role in a positive approach to treating mental illness. We now examine each of these functions in turn before focusing on the relationship between physical activity and psychological well-being in the general population.

Table 9.1

The Physiological and Psychological Benefits of Regular Physical Activity

---

Regular physical activity:

Reduces the risk of dying prematurely.

Reduces the risk of dying prematurely from heart disease.

Reduces the risk of developing diabetes.

Reduces the risk of developing high blood pressure.

Reduces the risk of developing colon cancer.

Reduces feelings of depression and anxiety.

Helps control weight.

Helps reduce blood pressure in people who already have high blood pressure.

Helps build and maintain healthy bones, muscles, and joints.

Helps older adults become stronger and better able to move about without falling.

Promotes psychological well-being.

Adapted from U.S. Surgeon General's Report on Physical Activity and Health, available at: http://www.cdc.gov/nccdphp/sgr/sgr.htm.

THE PREVENTATIVE FUNCTION

In terms of psychological functioning, the strongest evidence supporting the role of physical activity comes in the area of depression. There are at least four epidemiological studies that show that physical inactivity increases the likelihood of developing clinically defined depression (Camacho, Roberts, Lazarus, Kaplan, & Cohen, 1991; Farmer et al., 1988; Paffenbarger, Lee, & Leung, 1994; Strawbridge, Deleger, Roberts, & Kaplan, 2002). Such studies involve large numbers of people and measure physical activity status before the incidence of depression. For example, Camacho et al. found an association between inactivity and incidence of depression in a large population from Alameda County in California, who provided baseline data in 1965 and were followed up in 1974 and 1983. Physical activity was categorized as low, medium, or high. In the first wave of follow-up (1974), the odds ratios (OR) of developing depression were significantly greater for both men and women who were low active in 1965 (OR 1.8 for men, 1.7 for women) compared to those who were high active (see Figure 9.1).

There are three further epidemiological studies that do not show this association (Cooper-Patrick, Ford, Mead, Chang, & Klag, 1997; Kritz-Silverstein, Barret-Connor, & Corbeau, 2002; Weyerer, 1992). However, they have rather small numbers (fewer than 1,000 participants) and restrictive measures of physical activity, which focuses mostly on sports and vigorous activity. There could be

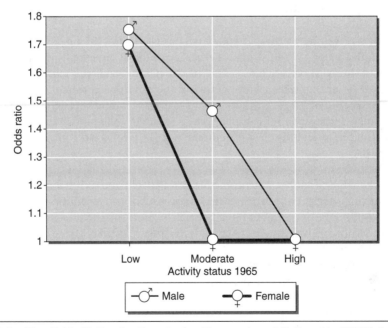

Figure 9.1   The Odds Ratios for Developing Depression at Follow-Up (1974) from Different Levels of Baseline Physical Activity (1965). Adapted from "Physical Activity and Depression: Evidence from the Alameda County Study," by T. C. Camacho, R. E. Roberts, N. B. Lazarus, G. A. Kaplan, and R. D. Cohen, 1991, *American Journal of Epidemiology, 134,* pp. 220–231.

alternative explanations of the positive findings such as bias, confounding, or chance. Bias is unlikely in these former large studies, and careful checks of non-respondents are made to ensure they do not differ from the responders. All of these studies take account of a wide range of possible confounding factors, such as disability, body mass index, smoking, alcohol, and social status, in the statistical modeling; and the relationship between physical activity and a decreased risk of depression remains. All studies show significance at the normal level, and perhaps what we should be more concerned about is whether the studies that do not show this relationship have insufficient power and are perhaps committing Type 2 statistical errors. Therefore, the weight of the good evidence favors a causal connection (Mutrie, 2000) for regular activity preventing depression.

The evidence for a preventative role for physical activity in other mental illnesses is not convincing at this point, possibly because large-scale epidemiological studies do not often measure clinically defined anxiety and the incidence of other mental illnesses is often small. Thus, if we accept that one of the key principles in positive psychology is to identify preventative strategies, then, at least for depression, enabling individuals to be physically active is a central target.

THE THERAPY FUNCTION

The possibility that physical activity could be used as a treatment in mental illness has long been recognized, but it has not been well researched until more recent times. For example, physical activity was seen as a popular and effective treatment for alcoholism as far back as the nineteenth century, as the following quotation from Cowles (1898) illustrates:

> The benefits accruing to the patients from the well-directed use of exercise and baths is indicated by the following observed symptoms: increase in weight, greater firmness of muscles, better colour of skin, larger lung capacity, more regular and stronger action of the heart, clearer action of the mind, brighter and more expressive eye, improved carriage, quicker responses of nerves, and through them of muscle and limb to stimuli. All this has become so evident to them that only a very few are unwilling to attend the classes and many speak freely of the great benefits derived. (p. 108)

More recently, consensus statements in the United Kingdom suggested a role for physical activity in alleviating depression and anxiety (Biddle, Fox, & Boutcher, 2000). Positive effects have been recorded for individuals with schizophrenia and those rehabilitating from drug and alcohol abuse, but these areas need more research.

As with the preventative function, the most compelling evidence comes from studies in the area of clinical depression. For example, two meta-analyses reported effects sizes of 0.72 (Craft & Landers, 1998) and 1.1 (Lawlor & Hopker, 2001) for exercise compared to no treatment for depression, and both meta-analyses showed effects for exercise similar to those found from other psychotherapeutic interventions. One study has also shown that exercise equaled the effect found from a standard antidepressant drug after 16 weeks (Blumenthal et al., 1999); and after six months, there was some indication that those who

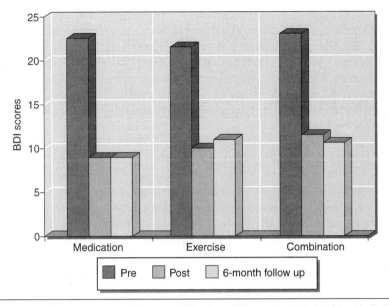

Figure 9.2 BDI Scores Pre- and Post-16 Weeks of Treatment and 6-Month Follow-Up. *Data sources:* Weeks of Treatment adapted from "Effects of Exercise Training on Older Patients with Major Depression," by J. A. Blumenthal et al., 1999, *Archives of Internal Medicine, 159,* pp. 2349–2356; Follow-Up adapted from "Exercise Treatment for Major Depression: Maintenance of Therapeutic Benefit at 10 Months," by M. Babyak et al., 2000, *Psychosomatic Medicine, 62,* pp. 633–638.

had continued to exercise had additional benefits in comparison (Babyak et al., 2000; see Figure 9.2).

In the United Kingdom, the National Health Service web site (May 03, http://cebmh.warne.ox.ac.uk/cebmh/elmh/depression/new.html) has listed exercise as one of the array of treatments that might help people with depression. It may be that the evidence for the use of exercise is beginning to filter through to practice despite resistance from psychologists who may not think physical activity is a suitable topic for therapeutic treatment (e.g., Faulkner & Biddle, 2001; McEntee & Halgin, 1996).

Physical Activity for Quality of Life and Coping with Mental Disorders

For people with severe and enduring mental health problems, improvement in quality of life tends to enhance individuals' ability to cope with and manage their disorder. Preliminary evidence suggests that regular physical activity can improve positive aspects of mental health (such as psychological quality of life and emotional well-being) in people with mental disorders. Positive psychological effects from physical activity in clinical populations have been reported even among those individuals who experience no objective diagnostic improvement (Carter-Morris & Faulkner, 2003; Faulkner & Biddle, 1999).

A recent study described a football project that was established to promote the social well-being of service users with enduring mental health problems in Birmingham, United Kingdom (Carter-Morris & Faulkner, 2003). For one participant, participation in the project offered a safe environment to reclaim an old and salient identity as a footballer but, more importantly, allowed him to escape from his identity as someone with a mental illness. As he described:

> When you have had a bad day . . . then you can go out for football for an hour and a half with complete strangers and they don't know what I do, they just know me to play football with and that's how I like it. I've got friends who know about my illness but these people don't know nothing about me, they just respect that I am a good footballer and they like me because of that. It's kind of a therapy for myself because I don't have to justify who I am and what I have done in the past in terms of illness and they just respect me for being a damn fine soccer player because I am the captain of the team. I can just go and kick a ball around you don't need to mention your mental health. You're accepted for being part of that group. (p. 27)

Importantly, this service user had chosen to engage in this project, which built on his existing strengths and interests as an individual.

Improved quality of life is particularly important for individuals with severe and enduring mental health problems when complete remission may be unrealistic (Faulkner & Sparkes, 1999). For example, there is a potential role for exercise in the treatment of schizophrenia. Faulkner and Biddle (1999) concluded that exercise may alleviate secondary symptoms of schizophrenia such as depression, low self-esteem, and social withdrawal.

The Feel Good Function

Often when we ask people why they exercise, they respond: "Because it makes me feel good." Current consensus clearly supports an association between physical activity and numerous domains of mental health in the general population. This has largely been addressed through studies assessing the impact of physical activity on variables such as subjective well-being, mood, and/or affect, stress, self-esteem, and self-perceptions (see Biddle, Fox, & Boutcher, 2000). The effect of physical activity and exercise on sleep and cognitive performance is also briefly addressed.

Subjective Well-Being, Mood, and Affect   Feeling good during and/or after physical activity is motivational, serves as an important health outcome in itself, and contributes to quality of life. Evidence is consistent across a wide range of meta-analyses, randomized control trials (RCTs), and large-scale epidemiological surveys that physical activity can make people feel better (Biddle, 2000). This has been established through measures of subjective well-being, mood (the global set of affective states individuals experience on a day-to-day basis), and emotions or affect (specific feeling states generated in reaction to exercise). Evidence shows that there are immediate benefits from a single bout of exercise (acute effects), as well as more enduring benefits (chronic effects) from exercise training programs (Biddle, 2000).

Positive relationships have been found between physical activity and subjective well-being in five epidemiological surveys in the United Kingdom although not all groups report positive benefit (Biddle, 2000). Experimental studies, including five controlled trials in the United Kingdom, report small, but consistent, positive effects on subjective well-being following exercise. A recent large RCT in the United States supported a causal relationship between increases in physical activity and enhanced subjective well-being (Rejeski et al., 2001). Meta-analyses support the predicted temporal sequencing of exercise preceding improvements in mood (Arent, Landers, & Etnier, 2000; McDonald & Hodgdon, 1991).

In a meta-analysis examining older adults (Arent et al., 2000), exercise produced, on average, small improvements in mood (effect size = 0.34) in studies comparing an exercise training group with a control group. This seems to work for both the reduction of negative moods and the enhancement of positive mood states (effect size = 0.35 and 0.33, respectively) while both acute and chronic exercise are associated with effect sizes significantly greater than zero. Effects of a similar, small to moderate magnitude are reported in populations of all ages and seem to be independent of socioeconomic or health status (Biddle, 2000). Simply, exercise can help people *feel good.*

Stress   Stress is a common feature of life for many of us. Often of a subclinical nature, it has a negative impact on quality of life and health, and it is a major source of sickness-related absence from work. Stress can manifest itself in emotional states such as anxiety that reflects negative cognitive appraisal and physiological responses such as increased blood pressure. A single session of exercise has been considered as a strategy to reduce immediate anxiety feelings (state anxiety), and a period of exercise training can reduce a predisposition to act anxiously (trait anxiety).

Cross-sectional and prospective surveys in the United States and Canada (Iwasaki, Zuzanek, & Mannell, 2001; Stephens, 1988), Finland (Hassmen, Koivula, & Uutela, 2000), and the United Kingdom (Steptoe & Butler, 1996) indicate that more active individuals self-report fewer symptoms of anxiety or emotional distress. Overall, six meta-analyses of trials also indicate that exercise is significantly related to a reduction in anxiety. The effect sizes in these reviews range from "small" to "moderate" (effect size = −0.15 to −0.56) while the largest effects are found for unfit, high-anxious individuals. It is important that the strongest effects are shown in RCTs (Taylor, 2000).

In his narrative review, Taylor (2000) identified 24 experimental studies involving acute exercise, and only three (12.5%) failed to show an anxiety-reducing effect on self-report measures from pre- to postexercise. Twenty-seven studies involving chronic exercise were also identified, with nine (33%) failing to show any anxiety-reducing effect. Research confirms that exercise training can help people feel less anxious in general (trait anxiety), and single exercise sessions can help individuals feel less anxious afterwards (state anxiety; Taylor, 2000).

Another focus for research concerns the effectiveness of fitness and/or regular physical activity on the mental and physical ability to cope with stress. While results are mixed, Taylor (2000) reviewed 14 experimental studies and concluded that single sessions of moderate exercise can reduce short-term physiological reactivity to and enhance recovery from brief psychosocial stressors. An earlier meta-analysis found an overall effect size of 0.48 for reduced reactivity to stressors (Crews & Landers, 1987). Specifically, reduced reactivity to stressors (e.g., systolic and diastolic blood pressure, skin conductivity, muscle tension, self-reported psychological symptoms) or a faster recovery following a stressor were generally found for those who were fitter or improved their fitness with training or who had undertaken a single exercise session, compared with baseline measures or a control group. Larger effects were found for randomized studies. Taylor further identified 12 studies since this meta-analysis. Six showed no effect while six showed some positive effect of exercise training on psychological and physiological measures during and/or after a stressor. While there are some inconsistencies, exercise may act as a *buffer* or coping strategy for psychosocial stress.

Self-Esteem and Self-Perceptions   Self-esteem is often regarded as the single most important indicator of psychological well-being. High self-esteem is associated with a number of important life adjustment qualities whereas low self-esteem is associated with poor health behavior decisions and is characteristic of many mental disorders such as depression (Fox, 1997). Self-esteem or the degree to which an individual experiences overall positive self-worth is thought to be derived from a personal combination of judgments about qualities, competencies, and actions in several life domains such as social, academic, work, family, and physical aspects of living. Moderate to high correlations ($r = 0.5–0.7$) between ratings of the self in the physical domain (such as physical self-worth, body satisfaction, or physical competence) and self-esteem are consistently found in studies of participants in Western cultures (Fox, 1997). Since 1970, at least 40 RCTs have been identified that address the effect of some form of exercise or sports program on self-esteem and/or self-perceptions (Fox, 2000). A meta-analysis of studies examining the impact of exercise on self-esteem found a weak positive effect size of 0.22 (Spence & Poon, 1997).

Fox (2000) concluded that exercise promotes physical self-worth and other important physical self-perceptions, such as improved body image. That is, exercise can make people feel better about themselves physically. For some people, in some situations, this generalizes to improvements in global self-esteem. Given the array of factors that influence global self-esteem, it is probably optimistic to expect exercise participation to reliably improve self-perceptions beyond the physical domain. However, direct links have been found between physical self-worth and mental health indicators independent of global self-esteem (Sonstroem & Potts, 1996). Increasing evidence suggests that these specific physical self-perception variables mediate the effects of exercise on self-esteem or subjective well-being (e.g., Rejeski et al., 2001).

Sleep   Exercise has been suggested as one nonpharmacological strategy for improving sleep quality. Two meta-analyses report small to moderate effects (0.18 to 0.52) for single exercise bouts on certain parameters of sleep (slow wave sleep, REM, REM latency, and total sleep time; Kubitz, Landers, Petruzzello, & Han, 1996; Youngstedt, O'Connor, & Dishman, 1997). Effect sizes for REM sleep were larger for women and less fit people and when the exercise was aerobic (while anaerobic exercise had a negative effect). Kubitz et al. also examined the effect of regular exercise and found a similar trend for fitter individuals in comparison to unfit individuals. That is, exercising individuals fall asleep faster and sleep longer and deeper than nonexercising individuals. Both meta-analyses did not find study quality to be a moderating variable. Exercise may, consequently, be of moderate benefit in improving well-being in the population by improving sleep quality.

Cognitive Functioning   Cognitive functioning can be viewed as functions of the brain that include memory, abstract reasoning, and spatial ability. Attention, information processing speed, and perceptions are examples of processes of cognition that support the cognitive functions (Spirduso, 1994). While not inevitable, some decline in cognitive performance might be associated with aging. Research has examined the role of exercise in preventing and alleviating this decline. Better cognitive performance in older age (particularly in those tasks that are attention demanding and rapid) is associated with fitness, physical activity, and sports participation (Boutcher, 2000). Recent research suggests that physical activity is protective against problems of serious cognitive impairment in old age as experienced in some forms of dementia and Alzheimer's disease. Using prospective data on more than 9,000 randomized adults age 65 or over from the Canadian Study of Health and Aging, Laurin, Verreault, Lindsay, MacPherson, and Rockwood (2001) demonstrated that high levels of physical activity reduced by half the risk of cognitive impairment, Alzheimer's disease, and dementia.

Small but significant improvements in cognitive functioning have been reported as a result of exercise participation although measurement difficulties have hindered research in this area (Biddle & Faulkner, 2003; Boutcher, 2000). An early meta-analysis of studies (Etnier et al., 1997) indicated a small effect size (*ES* = 0.19) for adults ages 60 to 90. However, there are very few good studies available to support the hypothesis that physical activity improves academic performance in youth (Mutrie & Parfitt, 1998). Conversely, there is evidence that devoting substantially increased school time to health-related physical education does *not* have detrimental effects on students' academic performance, while conferring significant health benefits (Sallis et al., 1999).

MECHANISMS: A PROCESS ORIENTATION

There is considerable agreement that the underlying mechanisms that relate to the positive effects from exercise on mental health are not yet known (Biddle & Mutrie, 2001; O'Neal, Dunn, & Martinsen, 2000; Plante, 1993). Several possible mechanisms, including biochemical changes such as increased levels of neurotransmitters (such as endorphins or serotonin) as a result of exercise, physiological changes such as improved cardiovascular function or thermogenesis, and psychological changes such as an increased sense of mastery, have been proposed (Petruzzello, Landers, Hatfield, Kubitz, & Salazar, 1991).

Rather than describing all of the plausible biochemical, physiological, or psychological mechanisms for mental health change through physical activity, we briefly discuss a *process* orientation for understanding the causes of such change, which we believe is indicative of the principles of positive psychology (see Carless & Faulkner, 2003). In acknowledging the huge diversity of potential triggers (such as exercise type, environment, social context) and individual circumstances (such as state of mental health, needs, preferences, and personal background), Fox (1999) suggests that several mechanisms most likely operate in concert, with the precise combination being highly individual-specific. That is, different processes operate for different people at different times. Studying the process of mental health change as a result of physical activity participation must, therefore, allow for the diverse range of biological and psychosocial factors that influence an individual's sense of psychological well-being. The isolation of a specific mechanism cannot realistically address the large number of potential psychological influences that may be experienced through physical activity. It is more realistic for a process-oriented approach to allow for the broad range of potential influences and, therefore, provide a more complete explanation of the causes of psychological change.

For example, Deci and Ryan (1985) have proposed that the basic needs for competence, autonomy, and relatedness must be satisfied across the life span for an individual to experience an ongoing sense of integrity and well-being (see also Ryan & Deci, 2000). These three basic needs are commonly reported outcomes of physical activity interventions. As discussed, existing research suggests that physical competence and self-perceptions can be improved through physical activity and that this can have a positive mental health effect (Fox, 1997). Exercise self-efficacy can be increased through interventions and is associated with positive exercise emotion (Biddle & Mutrie, 2001). Autonomy, or perceptions of personal control, is reported to be frequently lacking among people with depression, where feelings of powerlessness and helplessness are common (Seligman, 1975). Physical activity offers a potential avenue where meaningful control can be gradually taken, as the individual assumes responsibility for the organization of his or her exercise schedule or feels in control of how his or her body looks or performs. When we make progress in our physical capacity, it is difficult for even the most pessimistic to attribute this progress to anything but their own efforts and abilities. Thus, we suggest physical activity programs have the potential to contribute to learned optimism training, which Seligman (2002) suggests as a proactive program to enhance positive psychology. It might be that autonomy gained through exercise generalizes to other areas of life through feelings of empowerment (Fox, 1997). Finally, the provision of physical activity in a supportive group environment represents one approach to providing opportunity for positive social interaction that may be valuable. Experimentally, the social relations developed within the exercise components of an RCT in the United States were related to increases in satisfaction with life and reductions in loneliness in a sample of 174 adults (McAuley et al., 2000).

No *single* theory is likely to adequately explain the mental health benefits of physical activity (Salmon, 2001). Process theories, such as self-determination theory (Deci & Ryan, 1985), allow for a broader theoretical stance in understanding the mechanisms underpinning the physical activity and psychological well-being relationship while also suggesting how motivation to be active can be facilitated (Carless & Faulkner, 2003). Specifically, we argue that structuring the exercise experience to support feelings of autonomy, competence, and social relatedness is a good basis for promoting adherence to exercise and enhancing psychological well-being.

HOW CAN PEOPLE GET MORE ACTIVE?

A sedentary lifestyle is now the normal lifestyle for the majority of the populations in developed countries, and relapse from regular physical activity is also high (Department of Culture, Media and Sport [DCMS], 2002; The Scottish Office, 2000; U.S. Department of Health and Human Services, 1996). For example, two-thirds of the European population are not doing sufficient activity to meet current recommendations. However, a high proportion of individuals believe in the efficacy of physical activity for obtaining and promoting good health; more than 90% of the populations in each of 15 European countries believed that physical activity had numerous health benefits, and there was little variation in this belief by age or socioeconomic status (Kearney, de Graff, Damkjaer, & Magnus Engstrom, 1999). Mutrie and Woods (2003) suggested that getting people more active is a problem waiting to be solved because there is still a big gap between the belief that physical activity and exercise might provide health benefits and actual physical activity behavior.

Recent summaries of evidence-supported interventions to encourage more physical activity (Blamey & Mutrie, in press; Kahn et al., 2002) suggest the following five guidelines:

1. Point of decision prompts to encourage stair use.
2. Large-scale, high-visibility, multistrand communitywide campaigns.
3. Strengthening local support networks through buddy systems, walking groups, and exercise contacts.
4. Personalized health behavior-change programs, tailored to an individual's specific stage of behavior or interest.
5. Improved access to opportunities and active environments (e.g., walking or biking trails, local activities in local centers and workplaces, educational counseling, risk screening, and workshops), along with educational activities connected to these opportunities.

Additional interventions in schools and primary care are building evidence bases for what kind of approaches work best, but at this time there is insufficient knowledge to make conclusions (Blamey & Mutrie, in press). One area that may be particularly appealing for practicing psychologists to consider is the concept of exercise counseling for individuals. Loughlan and Mutrie (1995) provided guidelines on how to undertake such counseling. Some of the key issues involve understanding the client's physical activity history, discussing the pros and cons of becoming more active, finding social support for activity, and setting realistic activity goals. Psychologists and other mental health workers can use these guidelines with clients who could benefit from increasing physical activity. Most people could follow a graduated walking program, over a four- to six-week period, which should allow them to reach the recommended 30 minutes of activity on most days of the week.

Is there an Exercise Dosage for Psychological Well-Being?

Identifying a dose-response relationship between physical activity and enhanced mood and subjective well-being is still not possible. Effects are likely to be highly individualized and depend on preferences, experiences, and setting conditions (Fox, 1999). However, current guidelines for physical activity are supported in terms of their potential for improving psychological well-being. Evidence is most convincing concerning moderate-intensity exercise that lasts between 20 and 60 minutes, but high-intensity exercise may also be effective for some individuals and may be indicative of a differential temporal pattern of change according to intensity. Aerobic and nonaerobic forms of exercise may be equally effective, although larger effects have been found for resistance training in the elderly (a form of exercise that may use weights or a person's own body weight as resistance to movement and, therefore, enhance strength: average gains $ES = 0.80$; Arent et al., 2000). Furthermore, short bouts (10 to 15 minutes) of moderate walking have been shown to induce significant affective changes in experimental studies (Ekkekakis, Hall, VanLanduyt, & Petruzzello,2000). Randomized controlled trials in community settings also support the mood-elevating effects of brisk walking (e.g., King, Baumann, O'Sullivan, Wilcox, & Castro, 2002; Lee et al., 2001). Limited evidence supports a relationship between improved mood and accumulated bouts of moderate exercise (Hansen, Stevens, & Coast, 2001).

In the absence of a single definitive exercise dosage for psychological well-being, standard recommendations of accumulating 30 minutes of moderate physical activity on most or all days should apply equally to mental health promotion. Critically, a range of exercise modes and intensities should be recommended based on the participant's previous exercise experiences, personal preferences, strengths, and goals.

ACTIVE COMMUNITIES

The potential role of physical activity in reducing social exclusion is an emerging area of interest (Coggins, Swanston, & Crombie, 1999). This remains an underresearched area of study. Less is known about the rich potential of physical activity in alleviating social exclusion (individuals or communities that suffer from a combination of problems such as poor education, housing, employment, and health) or enhancing social outcomes such as increased social interaction and feelings of community. This is an important gap in the research base because good social networks and relationships are often associated with lower mortality risk and greater well-being (Acheson, 1998). Physical activity is certainly a process that allows for meaningful social interaction while also acting as a healthy vehicle to points of social interaction and networking in community settings.

Coggins et al. (1999) described a number of ways in which physical activity might have a role to play in addressing broader determinants of health:

- *Reducing social exclusion* through group physical activity programs that aim to promote social interaction among isolated groups
- *Reducing crime* through projects for young offenders that aim to relieve boredom, provide a social focus, and stimulate participation in enjoyable activities
- *Increasing family play* through activity schemes that encourage parents and children to engage with one another in a healthy context
- *Building a sense of community* through activity projects that aim to increase social contact and promote neighborhood networks
- *Improving the physical environment* through projects that reduce environmental barriers to physical activity by developing active transport or recreation opportunities
- *Creating respite opportunities* through the provision of active opportunities for groups who find activity and leisure time difficult

Despite such potential, there has been a lack of systematic monitoring and evaluation of the presumed positive outcomes of sports and physical activity-based projects. In a comprehensive narrative review, Coalter (2001) concluded that it is most likely that sports and physical activity are in themselves not *the* solution. As part of wider ranging development initiatives, they could be *part* of the solution when addressing issues of crime, education and employment initiatives, and community development and social exclusion (Coalter, 2001).

CONCLUSION

The recently published *National Physical Activity and Mental Health Consensus Statements* offer compelling evidence as to the positive relationship between physical activity and mental health in clinical and nonclinical populations (Biddle, Fox, Boutcher, & Faulkner, 2000). Physical activity can benefit healthy people of all ages by improving subjective well-being. While methodological concerns do exist (e.g., Biddle, Fox, Boutcher, & Faulkner, 2000; Lawlor & Hopker, 2001), we contend that the potential of psychological benefits accruing through exercise far outweighs the potential risk that no effect will occur. Because physical activity is an effective method for improving important aspects of physical health, such as obesity, cardiovascular fitness, and hypertension (see Bouchard, Shephard, & Stephens, 1994), the promotion of exercise for psychological well-being can be seen as a win-win situation with both mental and physical health benefits accruing (Mutrie & Faulkner, 2003). Less convincing evidence currently exists to support the notion that active communities can reduce social exclusion and increase the social capital of communities. A sedentary lifestyle is still the norm for the majority of populations in developed countries. By helping to develop environments that facilitate increased physical activity, we should expect substantial improvements in community health, transport, and the environment (Kerr, Eves, & Carroll, 2003).

Overall, we believe that physical activity participation epitomizes the principles of positive psychology. Drawing from unpublished data collected during a recent study (Faulkner & Biddle, 2004), one participant described this positive psychology in motion:

> It [exercise] means a feeling of enjoyment, of your whole body in motion, of every part, the way you're actually feeling all parts of your body, particularly say if you're running for instance. Every part of your body's in use and you can feel it all and that's exhilarating and you feel charged up . . . it makes me feel much more powerful, both physically and emotionally. It's like a kind of animal enjoyment of the body, you know, an animal feeling of power.

While the mental health benefits associated with physical activity can be complex and idiosyncratic (Faulkner & Biddle, 2004), we concur that "From the cradle to the grave, regular physical activity appears to be an essential ingredient for human well-being" (Boreham & Riddoch, 2003, p. 24).

REFERENCES

Acheson, D. (Chairman). (1998). *Independent inquiry into inequalities in health report*. London: The Stationery Office.

Arent, S. M., Landers, D. M., & Etnier, J. L. (2000). The effects of exercise on mood in older adults: A meta-analytic review. *Journal of Aging and Physical Activity, 8,* 407–430.

Babyak, M., Blumenthal, J. A., Herman, S., Khatri, P., Doraiswamy, M., Moore, K., et al. (2000). Exercise treatment for major depression: Maintenance of therapeutic benefit at 10 months. *Psychosomatic Medicine, 62,* 633–638.

Biddle, S. J. H. (2000). Emotion, mood and physical activity. In S. J. H. Biddle, K. R. Fox, & S. H. Boutcher (Eds.), *Physical activity and psychological well-being* (pp. 63–87). London: Routledge.

Biddle, S. J. H., & Faulkner, G. (2003). Psychological and social benefits of physical activity. In K. Chan, W. Chodzko-Zajko, W. Frontera, & A. Parker (Eds.), *Active aging* (pp. 89–164). Hong Kong, China: Williams & Wilkins.

*Biddle, S. J. H., Fox, K. R., & Boutcher, S. H. (Eds.). (2000). *Physical activity and psychological well-being.* London: Routledge.

Biddle, S. J. H., Fox, K. R., Boutcher, S. H., & Faulkner, G. (2000). The way forward for physical activity and the promotion of psychological well-being. In S. J. H. Biddle, K. R. Fox, & S. H. Boutcher (Eds.), *Physical activity and psychological well-being* (pp. 154–168). London: Routledge.

*Biddle, S. J. H., & Mutrie, N. (2001). *Psychology of physical activity: Determinants, well-being and interventions.* London: Routledge.

Blamey, A., & Mutrie, N. (in press). Changing the individual to promote health enhancing physical activity: The difficulties of producing evidence and translating it into practice. *Journal of Sports Sciences.*

Blumenthal, J. A., Babyak, M. A., Moore, K. A., Craighead, E., Herman, S., Khatri, P., et al. (1999). Effects of exercise training on older patients with major depression. *Archives of Internal Medicine, 159,* 2349–2356.

Booth, F., Gordon, S., Carlson, C., & Hamilton, M. (2000). Waging war on modern chronic diseases: Primary prevention through exercise biology. *Journal of Applied Physiology, 88,* 774–787.

Boreham, C., & Riddoch, C. (2003). Physical activity and health through the lifespan. In J. McKenna & C. Riddoch (Eds.), *Perspectives on health and exercise* (pp. 11–32). London: Palgrave Macmillan.

Bouchard, C., Shephard, R. J., & Stephens, T. (Eds.). (1994). *Physical activity, fitness and health: International consensus proceedings.* Champaign, IL: Human Kinetics.

Boutcher, S. H. (2000). Cognitive performance, fitness, and aging. In S. J. H. Biddle, K. R. Fox, & S. H. Boutcher (Eds.), *Physical activity and psychological well-being* (pp. 118–129). London: Routledge.

Camacho, T. C., Roberts, R. E., Lazarus, N. B., Kaplan, G. A., & Cohen, R. D. (1991). Physical activity and depression: Evidence from the Alameda county study. *American Journal of Epidemiology, 134,* 220–231.

*Carless, D., & Faulkner, G. (2003). Physical activity and psychological health. In J. McKenna & C. Riddoch (Eds.), *Perspectives on health and exercise* (pp. 61–82). London: Palgrave Macmillan.

Carter-Morris, P., & Faulkner, G. (2003). A football project for service users: The role of football in reducing social exclusion. *Journal of Mental Health Promotion, 2,* 24–30.

Caspersen, C. J., Powell, K. E., & Christenson, G. M. (1985). Physical activity, exercise and physical fitness: Definitions and distinctions for health-related research. *Public Health Reports, 100,* 126–131.

Coalter, F. (2001). *Realising the potential of cultural services: The case for sport.* London: Local Government Association.

Coggins, A., Swanston, D., & Crombie, H. (1999). *Physical activity and inequalities: A briefing paper.* London: Health Education Authority.

Cooper-Patrick, L., Ford, D. E., Mead, L. A., Chang, P. P., & Klag, M. J. (1997). Exercise and depression in midlife: A prospective study. *American Journal of Public Health, 87,* 670–673.

Cowles, E. (1898). Gymnastics in the treatment of inebriety. *American Physical Education Review, 3,* 107–110.

Craft, L. L., & Landers, D. M. (1998). The effect of exercise on clinical depression and depression resulting from mental illness: A meta-analysis. *Journal of Sport and Exercise Psychology, 20,* 339–357.

Crews, D. J., & Landers, D. M. (1987). A meta-analytic review of aerobic fitness and reactivity to psychosocial stressors. *Medicine and Science in Sports and Exercise, 19*(Suppl.), S114–S120.

Department of Culture, Media and Sport. (2002). *Game plan: A strategy for delivering government's sport and physical activity objectives.* London: Cabinet Office.

Deci, E. L., & Ryan, R. M. (1985). *Intrinsic motivation and self-determination in human behavior.* New York: Plenum Press.

Ekkekakis, P., Hall, E. E., VanLanduyt, L. M., & Petruzzello, S. J. (2000). Walking in (affective) circles: Can short walks enhance affect? *Journal of Behavioral Medicine, 23,* 245–75.

Etnier, J. L., Salazar, W., Landers, D. M., Petruzzello, S. J., Han, M., & Nowell, P. (1997). The influence of physical fitness and exercise upon cognitive functioning: A meta-analysis. *Journal of Sport and Exercise Psychology, 19,* 249–274.

Farmer, M., Locke, B., Moscicki, E., Dannenberg, A., Larson, D., & Radloff, L. (1988). Physical activity and depressive symptoms: The NHANES 1 epidemiological follow-up study. *American Journal of Epidemiology, 128,* 1340–1351.

Faulkner, G., & Biddle, S. J. H. (1999). Exercise as an adjunct treatment for schizophrenia: A review of the literature. *Journal of Mental Health, 8,* 441–457.

Faulkner, G., & Biddle, S. J. H. (2001). Exercise as therapy: It's just not psychology! *Journal of Sports Sciences, 19,* 433–444.

Faulkner, G., & Biddle, S. J. H. (2004). Physical activity and depression: Considering contextuality and variability. *Journal of Sport and Exercise Psychology.*

Faulkner, G., & Sparkes, A. (1999). Exercise as therapy for schizophrenia: An ethnographic study. *Journal of Sport and Exercise Psychology, 21,* 52–69.

Fox, K. R. (1997). The physical self and processes in self-esteem development. In K. R. Fox (Ed.), *The physical self: From motivation to well-being* (pp. 111–140). Champaign, IL: Human Kinetics.

Fox, K. R. (1999). The influence of physical activity on mental well-being. *Public Health Nutrition, 2,* 411–418.

Fox, K. R. (2000). The effects of exercise on self-perceptions and self-esteem. In S. J. H. Biddle, K. R. Fox, & S. H. Boutcher (Eds.), *Physical activity and psychological well-being* (pp. 88–117). London: Routledge.

Fox, K. R., Boutcher, S. H., Faulkner, G., & Biddle, S. J. H. (2000). The case for exercise in the promotion of mental health and psychological well-being. In S. J. H. Biddle, K. R. Fox, & S. H. Boutcher (Eds.), *Physical activity and psychological well-being* (pp. 1–9). London: Routledge.

Hansen, C. J., Stevens, L. C., & Coast, J. R. (2001). Exercise duration and mood state: How much is enough to feel better? *Health Psychology, 20,* 267–275.

Hardman, A. E. (2001). Physical activity and health: Current issues and research needs. *International Journal of Epidemiology, 30,* 1193–1197.

Harris, D. V. (1973). *Involvement in sport: A somatopsychic rationale.* Philadelphia: Lea & Febiger.

Hassmen, P., Koivula, N., & Uutela, A. (2000). Physical exercise and psychological well-being: A population study in Finland. *Preventive Medicine, 30,* 17–25.

Iwasaki, Y., Zuzanek, J., & Mannell, R. C. (2001). The effects of physically active leisure on stress-health relationships. *Canadian Journal of Public Health, 92,* 214–218.

Kahn, E. B., Ramsey, L. T., Brownson, R. C., Heath, G. W., Howze, E. H., Powell, K. E., et al. (2002). The effectiveness of interventions to increase physical activity—A systematic review. *American Journal of Preventive Medicine, 22,* 73–107.

Kearney, J. M., de Graff, C., Damkjaer, S., & Magnus Engstrom, L. (1999). Stages of change toward physical activity in a nationally representative sample in the European Union. *Public Health Nutrition, 2,* 115–124.

Kerr, J., Eves, F., & Carroll, D. (2003). The environment: The greatest barrier. In J. McKenna & C. Riddoch (Eds.), *Perspectives on health and exercise* (pp. 203–225). London: Palgrave Macmillan.

King, A. C., Baumann, K., O'Sullivan, P., Wilcox, S., & Castro, C. (2002). Effects of moderate-intensity exercise on physiological, behavioral, and emotional responses to family caregiving: A randomised controlled trial. *Journals of Gerontology: Series A, Biological Sciences and Medical Sciences, 57,* M26–M36.

Kritz-Silverstein, D., Barret-Connor, E., & Corbeau, C. (2002). Cross sectional and prospective study of exercise and depressed mood in the elderly: The Rancho Bernardo study. *American Journal of Epidemiology, 153,* 596–603.

Kubitz, K. A., Landers, D. M., Petruzzello, S. J., & Han, M. (1996). The effects of acute and chronic exercise on sleep: A meta-analytic review. *Sports Medicine, 21,* 277–291.

Laurin, D., Verreault, R., Lindsay, J., MacPherson, K., & Rockwood, K. (2001). Physical activity and risk of cognitive impairment and dementia in elderly persons. *Archives of Neurology, 58,* 498–504.

Lawlor, D. A., & Hopker, S. W. (2001). The effectiveness of exercise as an intervention in the management of depression: Systematic review and meta-regression analysis of randomised controlled trials. *British Medical Journal, 322,* 1–8.

Lee, R. E., Goldberg, J. H., Sallis, J. F., Hickmann, S. A., Castro, C. M., & Chen, A. H. (2001). A prospective analysis of the relationship between walking and mood in sedentary ethnic minority women. *Women and Health, 32,* 1–15.

Loughlan, C., & Mutrie, N. (1995). Conducting an exercise consultation: Guidelines for health professionals. *Journal of the Institute of Health Education, 33,* 78–82.

McAuley, E., Blissmer, B., Marquez, D. X., Jerome, G. J., Kramer, A. F., & Katula, J. (2000). Social relations, physical activity, and well-being in older adults. *Preventive Medicine, 31,* 608–617.

McDonald, D. G., & Hodgdon, J. A. (1991). *Psychological effects of aerobic fitness training: Research and theory.* New York: Springer-Verlag.

McEntee, D. J., & Halgin, R. P. (1996). Therapists' attitudes about addressing the role of exercise in psychotherapy. *Journal of Clinical Psychology, 52,* 48–60.

Mutrie, N. (2000). The relationship between physical activity and clinically defined depression. In S. J. H. Biddle, K. R. Fox, & S. H. Boutcher (Eds.), *Physical activity and psychological well-being* (pp. 46–62). London: Routledge.

Mutrie, N., & Faulkner, G. (2003). Physical activity and mental health. In T. Everett, M. Donaghy, & S. Fever (Eds.), *Physiotherapy and occupational therapy in mental health: An evidence based approach* (pp. 82–97). Oxford, England: Butterworth-Heinemann.

Mutrie, N., & Parfitt, G. (1998). Physical activity and its link with mental, social and moral health in young people. In S. Biddle, J. Sallis, & N. Cavill (Eds.), *Young and active? Young people and health-enhancing physical activity: Evidence and implications* (pp. 49–68). London: Health Education Authority.

*Mutrie, N., & Woods, C. (2003). How can we get people to be more active? A problem waiting to be solved. In J. McKenna & C. Riddoch (Eds.), *Perspectives on health and exercise* (pp. 131–152). London: Palgrave Macmillan.

O'Neal, H. A., Dunn, A. L., & Martinsen, E. W. (2000). Depression and exercise. *International Journal of Sport Psychology, 31,* 110–135.

Paffenbarger, R. S., Lee, I.-M., & Leung, R. (1994). Physical activity and personal characteristics associated with depression and suicide in American college men. *Acta Psychiatrica Scandinavica, 89,* 16–22.

Pate, R. R., Pratt, M., Blair, S. N., Haskell, W. L., Macera, C. A., Bouchard, C., et al. (1995). Physical activity and public health: A recommendation from the Centers for Disease Control and Prevention and the American College of Sports Medicine. *Journal of the American Medical Association, 273,* 402–407.

Petruzzello, S. J., Landers, D. M., Hatfield, B. D., Kubitz, K. A., & Salazar, W. (1991). A meta-analysis on the anxiety-reducing effects of acute and chronic exercise: Outcomes and mechanisms. *Sports Medicine, 11,* 143–182.

Plante, T. G. (1993). Aerobic exercise in prevention and treatment of psychopathology. In P. Seraganian (Ed.), *Exercise psychology: The influence of physical exercise on psychological processes* (pp. 358–379). New York: Wiley.

Rejeski, W. J., Shelton, B., Miller, M., Dunn, A. L., King, A. C., & Sallis, J. F. (2001). Mediators of increased physical activity and change in subjective well-being: Results from the Activity Counseling Trial (ACT). *Journal of Health Psychology, 6,* 159–168.

Ryan, R. M., & Deci, E. L. (2000). Self-determination theory and the facilitation of intrinsic motivation, social development, and well-being. *American Psychologist, 55,* 68–78.

Sallis, J. F., McKenzie, T. L., Kolody, B., Lewis, M., Marshall, S., & Rosengard, P. (1999). Effects of health-related physical education on academic achievement: Project SPARK. *Research Quarterly for Exercise and Sport, 70,* 127–134.

Salmon, P. (2001). Effects of physical exercise on anxiety, depression, and sensitivity to stress: A unifying theory. *Clinical Psychology Review, 21,* 33–61.

The Scottish Office. (2000). *The Scottish Health Survey 1998.* Edinburgh, Scotland: The Stationery Office.

Seligman, M. E. P. (1975). *Helplessness: On depression, development, and death.* New York: Freeman.

Seligman, M. E. P. (2002). Positive psychology, positive prevention and positive therapy. In C. R. Snyder & S. J. Lopez (Eds.), *Handbook of positive psychology* (pp. 3–9). New York: Oxford University Press.

Sonstroem, R. J., & Potts, S. A. (1996). Life adjustment correlates of physical self-concepts. *Medicine and Science in Sports and Exercise, 28,* 619–625.

Spence, J. C., & Poon, P. (1997). The effect of physical activity on self-concept: A meta-analysis. *Alberta Center for Well-Being: Research Update, 4,* 4.

Spirduso, W. W. (1994). *Physical dimensions of aging.* Champaign, IL: Human Kinetics.

Stephens, T. (1988). Physical activity and mental health in the United States and Canada: Evidence from four population surveys. *Preventive Medicine, 17,* 35–47.

Steptoe, A., & Butler, N. (1996). Sports participation and emotional well-being in adolescents. *Lancet, 347,* 1789–1792.

Strawbridge, W. J., Deleger, S., Roberts, R. E., & Kaplan, G. A. (2002). Physical activity reduces the risk of subsequent depression for older adults. *American Journal of Epidemiology, 156,* 328–334.

Taylor, A. H. (2000). Physical activity, anxiety, and stress. In S. J. H. Biddle, K. R. Fox, & S. H. Boutcher (Eds.), *Physical activity and psychological well-being* (pp. 10–45). London: Routledge.

U.S. Department of Health and Human Services. (1996). *Physical activity and health: A report of the Surgeon General.* Atlanta, GA: U.S. Department of Health and Human Services, Centers for Disease Control and Prevention, National Center for Chronic Disease Prevention and Health Promotion.

Weyerer, S. (1992). Physical inactivity and depression in the community: Evidence from the Upper Bavarian Field Study. *International Journal of Sports Medicine, 13,* 492–496.

Youngstedt, S. D., O'Connor, P. J., & Dishman, R. K. (1997). The effects of acute exercise on sleep: A quantitative synthesis. *Sleep, 20,* 203–214.

CHAPTER 10

Balancing Time Perspective in Pursuit of Optimal Functioning

ILONA BONIWELL and PHILIP G. ZIMBARDO

CENTRAL TO THE discipline of *positive psychology* (Seligman & Csikszentmihalyi, 2000) is the answer to the question of what makes life worth living, or simply: What is a good life? What constitutes a good life is a multifaceted issue that positive psychology sets out to study across three levels: positive subjective experience, positive individual characteristics, and qualities that contribute to a good society (Seligman, 1999). One key to learning how to live a fulfilling life is discovering how to achieve a balanced temporal perspective (Boniwell & Zimbardo, 2003).

The construct of a balanced time perspective provides a unique way of linking positive psychology's three levels of research. The study of time perspective investigates how the flow of human experience is parceled into temporal categories, or time frames, usually of past, present, and future. The relative emphasis or habitual focus on any of these frames is often biased toward overusing some of them while underusing others. These learned temporal biases are influenced by culture, education, religion, social class, and other conditions. A balanced time perspective is the state and the ongoing process of being able to switch flexibly among these time frames as most appropriate to the demands of the current behavioral setting (Zimbardo & Boyd, 1999). Time perspective is a basic aspect of individual subjective experience. It also influences individual choices and actions and can become a dispositional characteristic when an individual's biased time perspective becomes a dominant way of responding. At positive psychology's third level (the good society), time perspective is both influenced by cultural values and processes and can have a major impact on social behavior as well as on cultural discourses in society. Learning to overcome our temporal biases that limit optimal, healthy functioning, and discovering how to achieve a balanced time perspective should be a mandate for all of us. We believe it should be a central component in the agenda of positive psychology.

Dealing with time is a fundamental feature of the human experience, both objective, or so-called clock time, and subjective, personal constructions of time. The invention of huge clocks on impressive towers in most European town squares was a great feat of human creativity. They served to coordinate many community activities—religious, agricultural, business, and social commerce—in the many years before individual time pieces became commonplace. At first, time was controlled locally, but that meant there were almost as many time systems as there were communities (Lofy, 2000). It was only relatively recently, at the end of nineteenth century, when time became coordinated across geographical regions following the necessity to establish railway timetables. The impact of quantifying and standardizing time cannot be underestimated. The development of mechanical devices for measuring time changed the dominant representation of time in the West from cyclical to linear, from never-ending to irreplaceable. The unification and coordination of time, essential and beneficial for the development of economies, became a regulating structure of much human behavior.

Time not only underlies and regulates our social behavior but also penetrates the very fabric of our consciousness. The theme of time permeates poetry, songs, proverbs, homilies, metaphors, and even childhood fairy tales. An image of Cinderella, having to win over a prince's heart within very tight temporal constraints, and mindful that present pleasures are transient, is likely to be embedded in the consciousness of many Western children. Similarly, the moral of the tale of *The Three Little Pigs* is not lost on most children, who recognize that the lazy pig who builds his house quickly of straw is not the match for the fearsome wolf as is his future-oriented brother pig, who takes the time and effort to build his fortress of bricks. In some cultural constructions, time translates into a concept like rubber that can be stretched to fit human affairs, while in other more industrialized societies, human affairs are subordinated to temporal demands. In idiomatic use, time has become a commodity that can be saved, spent, used, found, lost, wasted, or maximized.

It is surprising to us that in spite of the obvious importance of temporal processes in our lives, their systematic exploration has received relatively little attention from psychology and the social sciences. The psychological study of subjective time has focused on time estimation, perceived duration of experiences, perceived rate of change, pace of life, and reaction time (RT). The use of RT as a major dependent variable in experimental and cognitive psychology blends objective recording of clock time and subjective responding. Time has also been conceived of as a key methodological factor that needs to be accounted for in study designs and measurement techniques or in assessing an experiment's validity (McGrath, 1988).

The focus of this chapter is the construct of *time perspective* (TP), which is viewed as an integral part of the subjective or personal experience of "Lived Time" (Gorman & Wessman, 1977). Time perspective represents an individual's way of relating to the psychological concepts of past, present, and future. Time and its dimensions are not viewed as objective stimuli that exist independently of the person, but as psychological concepts constructed and reconstructed by the individual (Block, 1990).

One of the broadest definitions of *time orientation*, given by Hornik and Zakay (1996, p. 385), is the "relative dominance of past, present or future in a person's thought." Lennings (1996) gives a somewhat more specific definition of TP as "a cognitive operation that implies both an emotional reaction to imagined time zones (such as future, present or past) and a preference for locating action in some temporal zone . . ." (p. 72).

One literature review identifies up to 211 different ways of approaching the concept of TP (McGrath & Kelly, 1986). Such a multiplicity of approaches has resulted in various definitions and numerous methods of assessing dimensions of time orientation. Thus, we can find some researchers focusing on emotional valence of the past or the future; others, on time dominance or dwelling on the past or the future; and some dealing with continuities among the past, present, and future, time relatedness, and many other facets of temporal perspective.

Time perspective is considered to have cognitive, emotional, and social components. The formation of TP is influenced by a host of factors, some learned in the process of socialization, such as an individual's cultural values and dominant religious orientation, kind and extent of education, socioeconomic status, and family modeling. But TP can also be influenced throughout a person's life course development by the nature of his or her career, economic or political instability, personal experiences with mind-altering substances, traumatic events, or personal successes. Further, TP is regarded as an expression of a person's own system of meanings that allows him or her to develop a coherent framework for living (Lennings, 1998). This central aspect of human nature can be shown to affect attention, perception, decision making, and a variety of mundane and significant personal actions. Time perspective is one of the most powerful influences on virtually all aspects of human behavior. It can shape the quality of life of individuals and even the destinies of nations, such as when a majority of individuals adopt a biased temporal orientation that overly promotes a focus on the past, or the future, or the present.

Gorman and Wessman (1977) suggest that it is possible to regard temporal orientation, attitudes, and experiences as persisting personality traits. Zimbardo and Boyd (1999) further agree that although TP may be affected by situational forces, such as inflation, being on vacation, or under survival stresses, it can also become a relatively stable dispositional characteristic when a particular temporal bias comes to predominate a person's outlook and response hierarchy.

The study of TP has often focused on one temporal zone, usually that of the future, or of the present in other studies. Limited examples of research focus on the combination of the three dominant time zones (Rappaport, 1990). Furthermore, the majority of studies have failed to provide a multidimensional picture of TP, focusing on either time orientation as a preferred temporal region or time extension—the length of time projected into the past or the future. The few earlier empirical studies that investigated all three time zones in the same group of subjects produced scarce and inconsistent findings (Carr, 1985).

MEASUREMENT OF TIME PERSPECTIVE

There have been several attempts to develop a measuring instrument of TP on the basis of combination of past, present, and future orientations. These endeavors have included, among others, the Circles Test (Cottle, 1976), Time Structure Questionnaire (Bond & Feather, 1988), and Time Lines (Rappaport, 1990). However, the majority of these instruments exhibited low reliability and scoring difficulties and measured only one or two temporal regions, with the past TP being largely ignored (Kazakina, 1999). The Stanford Time Perspective Inventory (STPI), developed by

Zimbardo (1992), included five predominant orientations: past regret orientation, future achievement orientation, two types of present orientation—hedonistic and fatalistic—and time press factor. However, this factor structure proved to be relatively unstable with subsequent factor analyses yielding four, five, or seven factors (Lennings, 2000a, 2000b).

The Zimbardo Time Perspective Inventory (ZTPI) is the latest modification of the STPI, which has addressed the shortcomings of the previous scales (Zimbardo & Boyd, 1999). This single, integrated scale for measuring TP has suitable psychometric properties and is reliable, valid, and easy to use. Five main factors underlie this empirically derived factor structure: Future, Past-Positive, Past-Negative, Present-Hedonistic, and Present-Fatalistic. These factors were derived from an extensive series of exploratory studies (including interviews, focus groups, feedback from participants, theoretical consideration, and others) and have been continuously empirically refined for more than a decade (Gonzalez & Zimbardo, 1985; Zimbardo & Boyd, 1999; Zimbardo & Gonzalez, 1984). Essentially, the scale provides a profile of relative values on each of these five factors for individuals or, when aggregated, for groups. The same factor structure has emerged from recent translations and replications with French, German, and Turkish samples. In practice, researchers typically highlight and compare individuals whose TP biases mark them as very high on one of these factors and low on others.

The ZTPI consists of 56 items that are assessed on a five-point Likert scale ranging from very uncharacteristic (1) to very characteristic (5) of the respondent. A consistent five-factor structure was revealed through exploratory principal component factor analysis and further supported by confirmatory factor analysis. Thirty-six percent of the total variance is explained by these factors. The ZTPI was demonstrated to have high test-retest reliability, ranging from 0.70 to 0.80 for the different factors (Zimbardo & Boyd, 1999). The convergent and discriminant validity of the instrument was established through predicted correlational patterns of each of the five factors with measures of aggression, depression, conscientiousness, ego-control, impulse control, state-trait anxiety, self-esteem, preference for consistency, reward dependence, sensation seeking, novelty seeking, and consideration of future consequences. The results confirmed associations between individual factors of the ZTPI and predicted scales in combination with low associations with inappropriate scale constructs. For example, the Present-Hedonistic factor was found to be associated with a lack of consideration of future consequences, a low preference for consistency, low ego or impulse control, but very high interest in novelty and sensation seeking, as well as not correlating with any past or future-oriented constructs. To ensure that ZTPI items are not reflecting the same underlying dimensions as the preceding psychological constructs, Zimbardo and Boyd carried out further tests of discriminant validity by examining robust correlations between depression and conscientiousness with Past-Negative and Future ZTPI factors. It was concluded that despite significant correlations between these two pairs of constructs, they remain distinct and not entirely overlapping.

TIME PERSPECTIVE PROFILES AND FINDINGS FROM TIME PERSPECTIVE RESEARCH

A brief overview of features found to be characteristic of individuals who reveal a dominant bias on each of the five TP factors may help put substance on these conceptual bones. It should be clear that each of these factors may have some personal value to given individuals in particular contexts, but when they come to be an excessive orientation that excludes or minimizes the others, they may become dysfunctional.

Items on the Future TP scale include, among others: "I am able to resist temptations when I know that there is work to be done," and "When I want to achieve something, I set goals and consider specific means for reaching those goals." The future-oriented person always has an eye toward consequences, contingencies, and probable outcomes of present decisions and actions. He or she is dedicated to working for future goals and their attendant rewards, often at the expense of present enjoyment, delaying gratification, and avoiding time-wasting temptations. Such individuals live in a world of cognitive abstraction, suppressing the reality of the present for the imagined reality of an idealized future world. At micro levels of behavior, they differ from those in other TP categories by being more likely to floss their teeth, eat healthful foods regardless of flavor, get medical checkups regularly, and solve puzzles well. They tend to be more successful than others, both academically and in their careers. The third little pig who built his house from bricks, estimating the possible dangers and uncertainties of a wolf-filled future instead of partying with his quick-and-easy, straw-house-building brother, was surely a future-oriented pig. The downside of excessive future orientation is minimizing the need for social connections, not taking time for occasional self indulgence, and not being grounded in a sense of community and cultural traditions.

The Past TP is associated with focus on family, tradition, continuity of self over time, and a focus on history. This can be either positive or negative. The Past-Positive TP reflects a warm, pleasurable, often sentimental and nostalgic view of the person's past with emphasis on maintaining relationships with family and friends. These individuals have the highest sense of self-esteem and happiness of those dominant on the other factors. Past-Positive scale contains items such as: "It gives me pleasure to think about my past," and "I get nostalgic about my childhood." The Past-Negative TP is characterized by items such as: "I often think of what I should have done differently in my life" and is associated with focusing on personal experiences that were aversive or noxious. In general, a past orientation has the downside of being excessively conservative, cautious, avoiding change and openness to new experiences and cultures, and sustaining the status quo even when it is not in the person's best interest.

A body of research marks present-oriented individuals living in Western societies as at risk for failure of all kinds. The ZTPI distinguishes between two very different ways of being focused on the present. The Present-Hedonistic person lives in the moment, values hedonistic pleasures, enjoys high-intensity activities, seeks thrills and new sensations, and is open to friendships and sexual adventures. He or she would score highly on items such as: "It is important to put excitement in my life." That kind of person acts with little concern for the consequences of his or her actions by avoiding cost-benefit analyses and contingency planning. Indeed, all of us were such creatures as infants and children, essentially biologically driven, whose behavior is determined by physical needs, emotions, strong situational stimuli, and social input. Life is about seeking pleasure and avoiding pain. The downside of this orientation is that behavior does have consequences, as behaviorist B. F. Skinner taught us so well. Present-Hedonists are at risk for succumbing to the temptations leading to virtually all addictions, for accidents and injuries, and for academic and career failure.

The Present-Fatalistic TP, on the other hand, is associated with hopelessness and immutable beliefs that outside forces control the person's life, such as spiritual or governmental forces. It may be a rather realistic orientation for those living in poverty in ghettoes or refugee camps. It is not uncommon for the parents of poor children—living the hedonistic life—to become fatalistically resigned to be helpless in changing or improving the quality of their life. This TP orientation is expressed by statements such as: "Since whatever will be will be, it doesn't really matter what I do," and "My life path is controlled by forces I cannot influence."

Zimbardo and Boyd (1999) demonstrate that both Past-Negative and Present-Fatalistic perspectives are associated with strong feelings of depression, anxiety, anger, and aggression. Such temporal perspectives create a negative self-image that handicaps attempts at constructive actions. Even though they may be reality-based in their origin, it is their maintenance and elevation to dominance in an individual's temporal hierarchy that makes them dysfunctional and nonadaptive among middle-class high school and college students functioning in schools in the United States.

The TP construct has been found to be related to many attitudes, values, and status variables, such as educational achievement, health, sleep and dreaming patterns, and romantic partner choices. It is also predictive for a wide range of behaviors, including risky driving and other forms of risk taking, delinquency and sexual behaviors (Zimbardo, Keough, & Boyd, 1997), and substance abuse of beer, alcohol, and drugs (Keough, Zimbardo, & Boyd, 1999). Furthermore, it appears that scores on the ZTPI factors are indicative of choice of food, health choices, parental marital state, desire to spend time with friends, and perceived time pressure, among other factors. For a full depiction of the role of TP in health and risk taking, see Boyd and Zimbardo (in press). It even predicts the extent to which unemployed people living in shelters use their time constructively to seek jobs (future-oriented) or waste time watching TV and engaging in other noninstrumental activities and avoidant coping strategies (present-oriented; Epel, Bandura, & Zimbardo, 1999).

Extension of such research data on individuals to the role of TP among nations and cultures is obviously more sociological, historical, and epidemiological, but they reveal some fascinating patterns. Protestant nations tend to be more future-oriented than Catholic nations (due to the enduring legacy of the Calvinistic focus on earthly success as an indicator of being chosen for heavenly rewards). In turn, the gross national product indexes are higher among Protestant than Catholic nations. Within countries, those living in southern sections tend to be more present-oriented than those in northern regions above the equator. Cultures with more individualistic focus tend to be more future-oriented than do those emphasizing collectivism. Western ways of life have become predominantly goal-focused and future-oriented in the service of capitalist values. The new trend toward globalization implicitly promotes a future-oriented market economy of the major industrial nations on developing nations that have been more present- or past-oriented.

However, an excessive emphasis on any given TP type at the expense of the other orientations leads to an imbalance that may not be optimal for individuals nor ideal in the long run for nations. There are costs and sacrifices associated with valuing achievement-oriented, workaholic, future TP traits over and above personal indulgences and civic and social engagement. Westerners are now spending less time on the following vital activities: family, friends, churchgoing, recreation, hobbies, and even household chores (Myers, 2000).

It looks as though Puritan values, recapitulated in "Waste of time is the first and in principle the deadliest of sins" (Weber, 1930/1992, p. 157), have finally won the game of modern life—with a minor drawback of God heading the list of time-wasters. The rituals and narratives essential to a sense of family, community, and nation are endangered and undermined, together with a sense of personal identity, by those living such totally work-focused lives.

BALANCED TIME PERSPECTIVE

The ideal of a *balanced time perspective* comes into play as a more positive alternative to living life as a slave to any particular temporal bias. A blend of temporal orientations would be adaptive, depending on external circumstances and optimal in terms of psychological and physiological health. "In an optimally balanced time perspective, the past, present, and future components blend and flexibly engage, depending on a situation's demands and our needs and values" (Zimbardo, 2002, p. 62). A curious finding emerged from a cross-cultural comparison of TP between U.S. and South African student samples. One of the temporal factors for South Africans consisted of a complex blend of items characteristic of separate future, past positive, and present hedonistic factors in U.S. populations (Zimbardo, 2001). For these respondents, a balanced or integrated TP, which we have considered to be an ideal blend, constituted a single dominant factor and not three separate ones.

Some theorists have attempted to define a personality that is balanced in terms of its relationship with time. Litvinovic (1998), for instance, speaks of *productive time orientation*. She argues that it includes a positive evaluation of the past and of the future, not dwelling on the past, and a sense of continuity among the past, present, and the future. This construct appears to be similar to that of a balanced time orientation, although it does not include a positive present orientation but, instead, argues for continuity between the positive past and positive future.

Lennings (1998) distinguishes an *actualizer* profile of TP, which combines a positive attitude to time, strong sense of time awareness, and temporal structure with personality variables, such as high achievement and self-control. He argues that this profile is optimal in terms of time functioning. Shostrom (1974) identified a notion of *time competence* as a necessary component of a self-actualizing personality:

> The self-actualizing person is primarily Time Competent and thus appears to live more fully in the here-and-now. Such a person is able to tie the past and the future to the present in meaningful continuity; appears to be less burdened by guilts, regrets and resentments from the past than is a non-self-actualizing person, and aspirations are tied meaningfully to present working goals. There is an apparent faith in the future without rigid or over-idealistic goals. (p. 13)

Shostrom (1968) also highlights the inadequacies of particular temporal biases. For instance, he talks of future-oriented individuals as identifying themselves with their goals and unable to accept themselves for who they are. The past-oriented individual is incapable of seeing that the solution for any problem can be found only in the here-and-now. The Time Competence Scale is yet another attempt to measure both balance and continuity in an individual's TP (Boyd-Wilson, Walkey, & McClure, 2002).

People with a balanced TP are capable of operating in a temporal mode appropriate to the situation in which they find themselves. When they spend time with their families and friends, they are fully with them and value the opportunity to share a common past. When they take a day off work, they get involved in recreation rather than feel guilty about the work they haven't done. However, when working and studying, they may well put on their more appropriate future TP hat and work more productively. Indeed, when work is to be done and valued, the balanced TP person may get into the flow of enjoying being productive and creative—a present-hedonistic state for a future-focused activity. That is when work becomes play as the worker becomes engaged with the process of the activity and not only with a focus on the product of his or her labors.

Flexibility and "switch-ability" are essential components of a balanced TP, in our view. "The optimal time perspective depends upon the demands of the situation and its task and reward structure" (Epel et al., 1999, p. 590). These researchers argue that among the unemployed living in homeless shelters and experiencing pressure to find other affordable accommodations, it may be better to be present-oriented when dealing with an acute crisis. While future TP allows a greater degree of self-efficacy and fosters optimism for future gains, present orientation may be more effective in allowing yourself to be open to finding immediate solutions to current challenges. While evidence seems to suggest that temporal flexibility is important for dealing with extreme circumstances, it doesn't tell us much as to why such flexibility may be important in dealing with the hassles of everyday life. Are people with a balanced TP likely to be happier than the rest of us? There is no consistent empirical data we can rely on for a firm "yes," but reasonable conjecture pushes us in that direction.

TIME PERSPECTIVE AND WELL-BEING

Over the years, there have been various attempts to establish a relationship between TP and well-being. However, taking into account the variety and complexity of measures of both TP and well-being, it is hardly surprising that the findings are inconsistent and often contradictory. A number of scholars hypothesized that a time orientation with a focus on the present is a necessary prerequisite for well-being. Among them are Csikszentmihalyi (1992), Maslow (1971), and Schopenhauer (1851), with their emphasis on the value of here-and-now experiences (see Boyd-Wilson et al., 2002). Some empirical support for this claim has been found in correlations between present orientation and various measures of well-being, including general happiness (Kammann & Flett, 1983) and life satisfaction (Diener, Emmons, Larsen, & Griffin, 1985). Furthermore, in a study with an older adult sample, Lennings (2000a) found optimism to be positively correlated with both stable time orientation and future avoidance factors (which are essentially a present TP). Similarly, in another sample of older adults, Kazakina (1999) established a relationship between positive past orientation and life satisfaction and between present positive perspective and positive affect. Carstensen and her collaborators have developed a scale that reflects changing conceptions of time over the life course in support of her theory of socioemotional selectivity (Carstensen,

Issacowitz, & Charles, 1999). As people become elderly, they narrow their social choices and intensify their emotional ties to a limited set of people because of their awareness of the preciousness of limited time resources.

While such research on past and present time factors is a welcome addition to our knowledge, most of the literature highlights the positive correlations between various future orientation measures and well-being. Some authors argue that a focus on futurity is fundamental to well-being and positive functioning (Kazakina, 1999). This relationship can be seen in the study of Wessman and Ricks (1966), where happy male college students were significantly more likely to be future-oriented than less happy peers. The *density* of the future zone, usually measured by the number of plans, commitments, and anticipated experiences, has been found to be positively correlated with well-being (Kahana & Kahana, 1983). The dimension of *emotional valence,* or positive attitudes toward the future, was consistently found to be associated with indicators of subjective well-being among older people. A positive future orientation is often viewed as the essence of personal optimism, which is conceptualized as the anticipation of positive changes in the future (Kazakina, 1999).

Wills, Sandy, and Yaeger (2001) examined the relationship between TP and early-onset substance use in elementary school students. The ZTPI was administered alongside the measures from stress-coping theory (esteem and control, resistance efficacy, coping patterns, substance use, recent negative events, positive and negative affectivity). Future orientation was found to be related to higher levels of perceived control and positive well-being (positive affect). Present orientation, by contrast, was related to perceived lack of control and negative affect. Furthermore, Zaleski, Cycon, and Kurc (2001) found that future TP, and especially possession of long-term goals, positively correlated with virtually all aspects of well-being, especially a meaningful life, social self-efficacy, and realism/persistence. On the other hand, higher levels of present preoccupation were associated with greater degrees of emotional distress and hopelessness.

Bohart (1993) argues that the ability of humans to be future-oriented is fundamental for human development because it allows the sense of possibility, of being agentic, of taking responsibility, and of making choices. The association of future orientation with a greater sense of personal power and control has been supported by empirical research. However, Bohart stresses the importance of the optimality of a balance between time perspectives, which would allow people to move into the future having reconciled with their past experiences while staying grounded in the system of meanings derived from the present.

Finally, a small number of studies have looked at the relationships between various measures of a generalized balanced TP and measures related to subjective well-being. Kazakina's (1999) literature review indicates that dimensions of *temporal continuity* and *temporal balance,* which characterize TP as a whole, have been theoretically and empirically shown to be associated with well-functioning (Rappaport, Sandy, & Yaeger, 1985). Temporal continuity, for instance, has been shown to correlate with intelligence, achievement needs, ego strength, self-actualization, purpose in life, and positive perception of time. It has been confirmed that scores on the Time Competence Scale (Shostrom, 1968) positively correlate with purpose in life and positive evaluation of the present (Robertson, 1978), as well as with creativity and positive perception of time (Yonge, 1975). A significant relationship between a productive time orientation and well-being in adulthood is shown in the research of Litvinovic (1998). Kazakina has examined the temporal balance among the past, present, and future across multiple dimensions of temporal orientation, density, extension, and emotional valence in older adults. Although she failed to find an association between temporal balance and well-being, this null outcome can be explained by the use of measurement tools with questionable psychometric properties (e.g., the Temporal Balance Scale and the Affect Balance Scale).

CRITIQUES AND FUTURE RESEARCH DIRECTIONS

Although there have been recent attempts to examine relationships between TP and well-being, the majority of studies have continued to focus either on one of the temporal zones (that of past, present, or future) or on one of the dimensions of TP (density, emotional valence, etc.). A small number of studies have used often-arbitrary measures of a balanced TP that are difficult to compare directly. Similarly, the construct of well-being has been arbitrarily and selectively defined, with researchers focusing either on the emotional (positive and/or negative affect) or on the cognitive (satisfaction with life) components of subjective well-being (Argyle, 2001)—rather than on the totality of this construct. The current state of inconsistency and ambiguity of findings points to the need for standardization in constructs and measurements before further examination of the relationship between TP and well-being.

It should not be surprising that various unrelated studies point to positive patterns of association between virtually all temporal zones and differing aspects of well-being—precisely because all three general factors of a balanced TP are important for different aspects of positive functioning. Operating in past-positive and present-hedonistic modes enhances individuals' chances of developing happy personal relationships, which is a key factor in enhancing their well-being, according to research on exceptionally happy people (Diener & Seligman, 2002). Yet, future TP is correlated with many factors that are strongly or moderately associated with well-being, such as optimism, hope, and internal locus of control. We strongly suspect the construct of a balanced TP will show a consistent correlation with well-being. Further research is urgently needed to examine this relationship between balanced TP and the sense of well-being, using multidimensional, valid, and reliable measures.

Moreover, we need research to operationalize the concept of a balanced TP. It is also essential to conduct additional exploratory case studies with the aim of developing a working, rather than hypothetical, profile of individuals with an optimal or balanced TP. There is almost no research that deals with multifaceted constructs, such as TP, using profile analyses of the complex of factor scores for each individual. Another needed venue for researchers and practitioners is the development of intervention strategies that empower individuals to overcome the limitations of their learned, narrow temporal biases and to acquire a balanced temporal orientation. We turn next to the potential applications of the concept of TP in the real world.

APPLICATIONS OF TIME PERSPECTIVE

Despite being conceived primarily at a theoretical level, the constructs of TP and a balanced TP offer considerable potential for practical interventions in clinical and occupational psychology. However, such implementations are conspicuous by their absence. Possible avenues of practical implementations can range from time-based clinical interventions with depressed patients, to rehabilitation programs with disabled persons, and to time management counseling with elderly clients.

Consider the development of clinical interventions designed for people with cognitive distortions associated with recurrent depression. Often, these clients are negatively past-focused, with global attributions, which taken together render them vulnerable to depressive ruminative cycles. An intervention program would focus on teaching them how to reconstruct past negative experiences by either neutralizing them or discovering some hidden positive elements in them. Clients could be given a slide-show metaphor training in which they learn to switch away from replaying the old slides of past negative experiences by inserting new slides into their tray and then viewing these encouraging perspectives of current positive experiences and imagined slides of a better future.

Persons suffering from disabilities typically must undergo long periods of physical rehabilitation that is effortful and painful. Many discontinue this critical treatment before it has had a chance to improve their condition, precisely because of these aversive aspects of the retraining. We believe that time therapy focused on building an enriched future orientation while minimizing the present would benefit such clients. It is only with a sense of hope of improvement, of belief that present suffering will pay off in the future, that anyone can continue in rehabilitation programs that have few immediate rewards and much pain (see Zimbardo, in press).

Knowledge and understanding of TP can be a useful tool in psychological counseling. An insight into how clients think and feel about past, present, and future experiences and about their connectedness and disconnections serves as a starting point for therapeutic explorations. Extending the ideas we have championed throughout this chapter, we believe that a strong, narrowly selective temporal bias in a client should alert a counselor or therapist of a fundamental platform on which many presenting problems are erected. Seemingly disparate problems may then be seen as symptomatic of a common underlying temporal misbalance, thus the need for temporal adjustment and rebalancing (see Kazakina, 1999).

There are some rare examples of qualitative investigations of people's psychological attitudes and perception of time that reveal how discussions about time have had unexpectedly positive therapeutic effects (Elliot, 1999; Rappaport, 1990). An exploration of an individual's relationship with time has the potential to direct awareness toward fuller evaluations of his or her life, toward finding the links and connections between past and present events. Doing so helps to develop a sense of continuity between temporal zones and facilitates the process of finding deeper meaning in his or her existence. Such potential can be invaluable in working with specific categories of clients in clinical psychology, including the elderly and terminally ill. It is plausible that achieving a temporal balance can facilitate the sense of fuller involvement with life, which some believe to be paramount for successful aging (Kazakina, 1999).

The concept of balanced TP can also be fruitfully implemented in an organizational context. It is our belief that the current pressures being experienced by workers in offices and factories around the world will not be resolved by more time-management techniques. Normative experience is that within about six months following a time-management training program, participants revert to their own practices of time management. We believe this happens for two reasons.

First, these programs are promoted by management and essentially are designed to make workers more future-oriented, more productive, and less wasteful of company time. But much of the sense of time press and work urgency comes from workers who are already overly future-oriented. They need very different time training. Secondly, most time-management techniques are not tied to the actual psychology of people's understanding of time. The construct of TP has a potential to provide a theoretical underpinning for time management interventions. The focus of time management techniques can shift from advocating generalized time management strategies—such as taking time off or putting more focus on their work—to developing interventions based on an understanding of workers' TP profiles. Doing so would help in recognizing the associated internal states and TP cognitive biases that unconsciously dominate workers. Such techniques can be useful in reducing and, ideally, preventing occupational stress. They can also be invaluable in solving the eternal dilemma of balancing the dialectic of work and play/leisure or of work as a source of personal engagement versus a source of job burnout (Maslach & Leiter, 1997).

CONCLUSION

Working hard when it's time to work, playing intensively when it's time to play, enjoying listening to grandma's old stories while she is still alive, meaningfully connecting with your friends, viewing children through the eyes of wonder with which they see the world, laughing at jokes and life's absurdities, indulging in desire and passions, saving for a rainy day and spending it when it's sunny, recognizing the social and sexual animal in each of us, taking fuller control of your life—these are all part of the benefits of learning to achieve a balanced time perspective. They are the keys to unlocking personal happiness and finding more meaning in life despite the relentless, indifferent movement of life's time clock toward its final ticking for each of us. The value of the concept of a balanced time perspective is that it both suggests novel approaches to a wide range of psychological interventions, while offering yet another answer to positive psychology's enduring question—what is a good life, and how can we pursue it?

REFERENCES

Argyle, M. (2001). *The psychology of happiness* (2nd ed.). London: Routledge.

Block, R. A. (1990). Introduction. In R. A. Block (Ed.), *Cognitive models of psychological time* (pp. xiii–xix). Hillsdale, NJ: Erlbaum.

Bohart, A. C. (1993). Emphasizing the future in empathy responses. *Journal of Humanistic Psychology, 33,* 12–29.

*Bond, M., & Feather, N. (1988). Some correlates of structure and purpose in the use of time. *Journal of Personality and Social Psychology, 55,* 321–329.

Boniwell, I., & Zimbardo, P. G. (2003). Time to find the right balance. *The Psychologist, 16,* 129–131.

Boyd, J. N., & Zimbardo, P. G. (in press). Time perspective, health. and risk taking. In A. Strathman & J. Joireman (Eds.), *Understanding behavior in the context of time: Theory, research, and applications in social personality, health, and environmental psychology.*

Boyd-Wilson, B. M., Walkey, F. H., & McClure, J. (2002). Present and correct: We kid ourselves less when we live in the moment. *Personality and Individual Differences, 33,* 691–702.

Carr, M. A. (1985). *The effects of aging and depression on time perspective in women.* Unpublished doctoral dissertation, New York, Columbia University, Teachers College.

Carstensen, L., Issacowitz, D. M., & Charles, S. T. (1999). Taking time seriously: A theory of socioemotional selectivity. *American Psychologist, 54,* 165–181.

Cottle, T. J. (1976). *Perceiving time.* New York: Wiley.

Csikszentmihalyi, M. (1992). *Flow: The psychology of happiness.* London: Rider.

Diener, E., Emmons, R. A., Larsen, R. J., & Griffin, S. (1985). The Satisfaction With Life Scale. *Journal of Personality Assessment, 49,* 71–75.

Diener, E., & Seligman, M. E. P. (2002). Very happy people. *Psychological Science, 13,* 81–84.

Elliot, M. K. (1999). *Time, work, and meaning.* Unpublished doctoral dissertation, Pacifica Graduate Institute, Carpinteria, California.

Epel, E., Bandura, A., & Zimbardo, P. G. (1999). Escaping homelessness: The influences of self-efficacy and time perspective on coping with homelessness. *Journal of Applied Social Psychology, 29,* 575–596.

Gonzalez, A., & Zimbardo, P. G. (1985). Time in perspective: A *Psychology Today* survey report. *Psychology Today, 19,* 21–26.

Gorman, B. S., & Wessman, A. E. (1977). Images, values, and concepts of time in psychological research. In B. S. Gorman & A. E. Wessman (Eds.), *The personal experience of time* (pp. 218–264). New York: Plenum Press.

Hornik, J., & Zakay, D. (1996). Psychological time: The case of time and consumer behavior. *Time and Society, 5,* 385–397.

Kahana, E., & Kahana, B. (1983). Environmental continuity, futurity, and adaptation of the aged. In G. D. Rowles & R. J. Ohta (Eds.), *Aging and milieu* (pp. 205–228). New York: Haworth Press.

Kammann, R., & Flett, R. (1983). Affectometer 2: A scale to measure current level of general happiness. *Australian Journal of Psychology, 35,* 259–265.

*Kazakina, E. (1999). *Time perspective of older adults: Relationships to attachment style, psychological well-being and psychological distress.* Unpublished doctoral dissertation, Columbia University, New York.

Keough, K. A., Zimbardo, P. G., & Boyd, J. N. (1999). Who's smoking, drinking, and using drugs? Time perspective as a predictor of substance use. *Basic and Applied Social Psychology, 21,* 149–164.

Lennings, C. J. (1996). Self-efficacy and temporal orientation as predictors of treatment outcome in severely dependent alcoholics. *Alcoholism Treatment Quarterly, 14,* 71–79.

Lennings, C. J. (1998). Profiles of time perspective and personality: Developmental considerations. *Journal of Psychology, 132,* 629–642.

Lennings, C. J. (2000a). Optimism, satisfaction and time perspective in the elderly. *International Journal of Aging and Human Development, 51,* 168–181.

Lennings, C. J. (2000b). The *Stanford Time* Perspective Inventory: An analysis of temporal orientation for research in health psychology. *Journal of Applied Health Behavior, 2,* 40–45.

*Litvinovic, G. (1998). *Perceived change, time orientation, and subjective well-being through the life span in Yugoslavia and the United States.* Unpublished doctoral dissertation, University of North Carolina, Chapel Hill.

Lofy, M. M. (2000). *A matter of time: Power, control, and meaning in people's everyday experience of time.* Unpublished doctoral dissertation, The Fielding Institute, Santa Barbara, California.

Maslach, C., & Leiter, M. (1997). *The truth about burnout: How organizations cause personal stress and what to do about it.* San Francisco: Jossey-Bass.

Maslow, A. H. (1971). *Farther reaches of human nature.* New York: Viking Penguin.

McGrath, J. E. (Ed.). (1988). *The social psychology of time: New perspectives* (Vol. 1). New York: Sage.

McGrath, J. E., & Kelly, J. (1986). *Time and human interaction: Toward a social psychology of time.* New York: Guilford Press.

Myers, D. G. (2000). *The American paradox: Spiritual hunger in an age of plenty.* New Haven, CT: Yale University Press.

Rappaport, H. (1990). *Making time.* New York: Simon & Schuster.

Rappaport, H., Sandy, J. M., & Yaeger, A. M. (1985). Relation between ego identity and temporal perspective. *Journal of Personality and Social Psychology, 48,* 1609–1620.

Robertson, S. A. (1978). Some personality correlates of time competence, temporal extension, and temporal evaluation. *Perceptual and Motor Skills, 46,* 743–750.

Schopenhauer, A. (1851). *The wisdom of life* [English translation 1890]. London: Swan Sonnenschein & Co.

Seligman, M. E. P. (1999). *Mission statement and conclusion of Akumal 1.* Retrieved January 9, 1999, from http://psych.upenn.edu/seligman/pospsy.htm.

Seligman, M. E. P., & Csikszentmihalyi, M. (2000). Positive psychology: An introduction. *American Psychologist, 55,* 5–14.

*Shostrom, E. L. (1968). *Man, the manipulator: The inner journey from manipulation to actualization.* New York: Bantam Books.

Shostrom, E. L. (1974). *Manual for the Personal Orientation Inventory.* San Diego, CA: Educational and Industrial Testing Service.

Weber, M. (1992). *The protestant ethic and the rise of capitalism.* London: Routledge. (Original work published 1930)

Wessman, A. E., & Ricks, D. F. (1966). *Mood and personality.* New York: Holt, Rinehart and Winston.

Wills, T. A., Sandy, J. M., & Yaeger, A. M. (2001). Time perspective and early onset substance use: A model based on stress-coping theory. *Psychology of Addictive Behaviors, 15,* 118–125.

Yonge, C. D. (1975). Time experiences, self-actualizing values and creativity. *Journal of Personality Assessment, 39,* 601–606.

Zaleski, Z., Cycon, A., & Kurc, A. (2001). Future time perspective and subjective well-being in adolescent samples. In P. Schmuck & K. M. Sheldon (Eds.), *Life goals and well-being: Toward a positive psychology of human striving* (pp. 58–67). Goettingen, Germany: Hogrefe & Huber.

Zimbardo, P. G. (1992). *Draft Manual,* Stanford Time *Perspective Inventory.* Stanford, CA: Stanford University.

Zimbardo, P. G. (2001, October). *Achieving a balanced time perspective as a life goal.* Paper presented at the Positive Psychology Summit, Washington, DC.

Zimbardo, P. G. (2002). Just think about it: Time to take our time. *Psychology Today, 35,* 62.

Zimbardo, P. G. (in press). Enriching psychological research on disability. In D. F. Thomas & F. E. Menz (Eds.), *Bridging gaps: Refining the disability research agenda for rehabilitation and the social sciences—Conference Proceedings.* Menomonie: University of Wisconsin-Stout, Stout Vocational Rehabilitation Institute, Research and Training Center.

*Zimbardo, P. G., & Boyd, J. N. (1999). Putting time in perspective: A valid, reliable individual-differences metric. *Journal of Personality and Social Psychology, 77,* 1271–1288.

Zimbardo, P. G., & Gonzalez, A. (1984). A *Psychology Today* reader survey: *Psychology Today, 18,* 53–54.

Zimbardo, P. G., Keough, K. A., & Boyd, J. N. (1997). Present time perspective as a predictor of risky driving. *Personality and Individual Differences, 23,* 1007–1023.

PART V

TEACHING AND LEARNING: METHODS AND PROCESSES

CHAPTER 11

Teaching Students to Make Wise Judgments: The "Teaching for Wisdom" Program

ALINA REZNITSKAYA and ROBERT J. STERNBERG

THE OFTEN HARSH realities of today's life, ranging from school shootings to prolonged international conflicts, force us to rethink the primary goals of general education. From both academic circles (e.g., Costa, 2001a; Damon, 2002; DeRoche & Williams, 1998) and presidential speeches (e.g., Bush, 2002; Clinton, 1996), we hear that schools must foster both the cognitive and the moral development of their students. Unfortunately, these two educational objectives are often considered separately. The critical thinking movement (e.g., Ennis, 1993; Nickerson, 1986) places its emphasis on cognitive and analytic abilities, while the character education initiative (e.g., Berkowitz, 2002; Lickona, 1991) is primarily concerned with social and moral competencies.

In this chapter, we propose an educational approach that integrates cognitive and moral objectives, giving equal and simultaneous attention to both critical thinking and character development. This approach is based on Sternberg's balance theory of wisdom (Sternberg, 1998, 2001). We first review Sternberg's theory and discuss its pedagogical implications. We then illustrate how this theory can be used for the development of a middle school history curriculum. Finally, we suggest directions for further research and applications of the balance theory of wisdom.

The preparation of this chapter and the research herein were supported by a grant from the W. T. Grant Foundation.

THE BALANCE THEORY OF WISDOM

Sternberg (2001) defines *wisdom* as:

> the application of tacit as well as explicit knowledge as mediated toward the achievement of a common good through a balance among a) intrapersonal, b) interpersonal, and c) extra-personal interests, over the a) short- and b) long-terms to achieve a balance among a) adaptation to existing environments, b) shaping of existing environments, and c) selection of new environments. (p. 231)

The visual presentation of this conception of wisdom is shown in Figure 11.1.

Multiple factors constitute this model of wise decision making. First, the definition draws heavily on the idea of *balance:* the balance among multiple interests, immediate and lasting consequences, and environmental responses. Importantly,

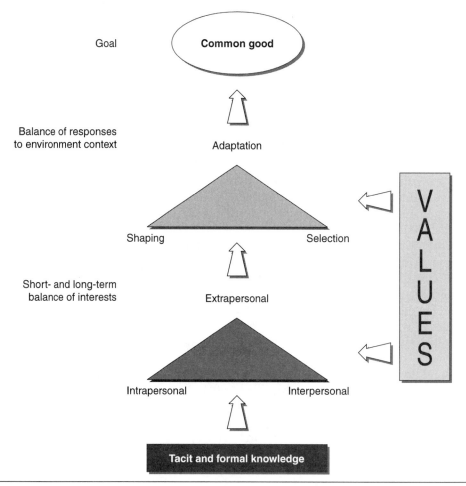

Figure 11.1 Wisdom as Value-Mediated Tacit Knowledge Balancing Goals, Responses, and Interests. Reprinted from "Why Schools Should Teach for Wisdom: The Balance Theory of Wisdom in Educational Settings," by R. J. Sternberg, 2001, *Educational Psychologist, 36*, pp. 227–245. Used with permission.

the balance in Sternberg's theory of wisdom does not mean that each interest, consequence, or response is weighted equally. The relative weightings are determined by the extent to which a particular alternative contributes to the achievement of a common good. For example, when working out a solution, self-interests (intrapersonal) can be weighted less than the interests of others (interpersonal), although both are considered in the final decision. To illustrate, when deciding whether to smoke a cigarette at a dinner party, an individual may consider the self-interest of craving a cigarette as well as the interests of other people at the party (i.e., nonsmokers, children, or people with allergies). An individual may also think of short-term consequences (i.e., the pleasant experience of smoking) and of the longer term consequences (i.e., the house smelling of cigarette smoke, the serious illnesses caused by smoking). A wise person takes into account all of these considerations. Moreover, he or she tries to balance multiple interests and consequences in a way that maximizes a common good. For example, a person can decide to step outside to smoke or to abandon smoking altogether, therefore weighting self-interest and immediate satisfaction less, although not necessarily ignoring them altogether.

What is evident, even from the preceding trivial example, is that choosing the right balance depends on your system of values. In fact, *values* lie at the core of wise decision making. In Sternberg's theory, values not only establish what constitutes the common good but also influence the relative weightings of the various interests, conflicting consequences, and alternative responses to environment.

The central place of values in Sternberg's theory brings up the question of who determines what the *right* values are. We know that people's values are not the same in different cultures and at different points in history. In fact, our own democratic values dictate that we respect others' differences in deciding what is right or wrong. The danger here is of succumbing to moral relativism and proclaiming that any value framework is equally justifiable and that there is no principle to distinguish right from wrong. We would argue that although there could be more than one acceptable value system, there are also those that must be rejected on the grounds of failing to acknowledge fundamental human freedoms. In other words, the respect for others' differences must not extend beyond the respect for the core human values, such as life or fairness. In addition, although we do not claim to define the exhaustive list of values that should be held and recognized by every culture, we reserve the right to explicitly set apart certain values, such as disrespect for human life, as unacceptable and unwise.

Tacit knowledge is another crucial component of wise decision making. The term, first introduced by Polanyi (1966), describes knowledge that is (1) implicit, or acquired without instructional support or even conscious awareness, (2) procedural, or "knowing how" rather than "knowing what," and (3) instrumental to obtaining a particular goal (Sternberg et al., 2000). Tacit knowledge allows people to appreciate the nuances of a given situation that are not obtainable from any formalized, or even verbalized, set of rules. It is the ability to be attuned to the unique complexities of their rich environment and to flexibly use the understanding of these complexities to reach the desired objectives. Although it is important, tacit knowledge is not a substitute for other types of knowledge, such as declarative or explicit procedural knowledge. Tacit knowledge helps to inform wise decision making in combination with other types of explicit knowledge.

When faced with a problem, wise individuals rely on their values and knowledge to help them find a solution that balances conflicting intrapersonal, interpersonal, and extrapersonal interests over short and long terms. *Intrapersonal interests* affect only the individual. They have to do with an individual's own sense of identity and may include concerns such as the desire for self-actualization, popularity, prestige, power, prosperity, or pleasure. In the previous smoking example, the cigarette craving and the willingness to stay healthy can be considered conflicting intrapersonal interests.

Interpersonal interests involve other people. They relate not only to the individual's sense of self but also to desirable relationships with others. *Extrapersonal interests* are those that affect a wider organization, community, country, or environment. For instance, the smoker might have an interpersonal interest in maintaining a good relationship with the guests at a dinner party as well as an extrapersonal interest in not wanting to pollute the environment with cigarette smoke. In addition to multiple interests, the consequences of each decision are assessed to balance short- and long-term objectives.

Sternberg's conceptual model of wisdom is not a matter of an esoteric intellectual exercise. Rather, it is oriented toward action. Applying relevant values and knowledge, together with considering multiple interests and consequences, must lead to choosing a particular behavior. Here, again, the theory draws on the idea of balance: a balance among adaptation, shaping, and selection of environments. *Adaptation* involves changing yourself to fit the already existing environment. For example, smokers may decide to quit smoking to adjust to the nonsmoking constraints of their work or social environments. *Shaping* is the opposite behavior, which involves modifying parts of the environment to fit your own interests. For instance, smokers may request that their company provide a smoking section in the company cafeteria. Finally, when people cannot adapt to an existing environment or change the environment to meet their needs, they can *select* a new environment. Smokers might choose to leave the nonsmoking restaurant and go to one where smoking is allowed. A particular solution may also combine several of the environmental responses, such as adaptation and shaping, as when you concurrently change a part of yourself and a part of your environment.

It may seem that the balancing act among interests, consequences, and responses to environment has by now become overwhelmingly complex and will not help us understand the psychological processes and outcomes involved in wise decision making. However, each decision takes place in a particular context, where there is, realistically, a finite number of competing interests, possible consequences, and available environmental responses. The balance theory of wisdom provides a framework for evaluating a decision within a specific context by considering all the factors enumerated and described in the conceptual model of the decision-making process. For example, a decision to step outside to smoke will get a high score on balancing intrapersonal and interpersonal interests but will score lower on taking into account long-term consequences. Thus, although the balance theory of wisdom cannot determine a wise answer to any problem, it can help to assess how well a particular solution meets the theory specifications in a given context.

It could be rightly argued that formulating a wise solution to a problem may not necessarily lead to acting on it. We may think of personal examples when a clear awareness of potentially harmful long-term consequences did not preclude us from performing an action that was in some way attractive at the moment. This mismatch between insight and behavior is addressed through the inclusion of intrapersonal interests in the model. A wise *action,* as well as a wise solution, requires a balance among intrapersonal interests, which may include resolving the tension between various affective and cognitive appeals. Perkins (2002) describes several strategies for confronting behaviors that an individual considers unwise, but nevertheless finds too irresistible to abandon. For example, behaviors such as impulsiveness, procrastination, indulgence, or indecisiveness can be diminished and even eliminated with the use of deliberate conditioning and self-management techniques (Perkins, 2002).

The balance theory of wisdom relates to several psychological and philosophical constructs previously discussed in the wisdom literature. The idea of balance, central to Sternberg's theory, can also be found in other contemporary formulations of wisdom. For example, Birren and Fisher (1990) define wisdom as "a balance between the opposing valences of intense emotion and detachment, action and inaction, knowledge and doubts" (p. 326). Labouvie-Vief (1990) suggests that wisdom constitutes a balancing of *logos,* which are objective and logical processes, and *mythos,* which represent subjective and organismic processes. Similarly, Kramer (1990) argues that wisdom involves integration of cognition and affect, resulting in a "well-balanced personality, where conscious and unconscious processes do not stand in powerful opposition." Balance is also well recognized in the philosophical writings on wisdom, such as in the Middle Way concept of Buddhist teachings (e.g., Hartshorne, 1987). Setting aside philosophical conceptions, the psychological theories of wisdom presented earlier propose a balance of only one component from Sternberg's theory—intrapersonal interests. In contrast, Sternberg's theory applies the idea of balance to the interactions within and between people and within their environment. In other words, the balance needs to exist not only for intrapersonal interests, but also for interpersonal and extrapersonal interests, as well as among the environmental responses.

Values, the mediating force of wise decision making in Sternberg's model, have also been considered in other theories of wisdom. According to Brent and Watson (1980, as cited in Holliday & Chandler, 1986), one of the five dimensions of wisdom is "moral-ethical." For Csikszentmihalyi and Rathunde (1990), "wisdom becomes the best guide for what is the *summum bonum,* or 'supreme good.' The knowledge of how causes and effects are connected shows the way for action and is the basis for morality" (p. 32). Similarly, Pascual-Leone (1990) regards "moral feelings and ethical evaluations (right-wrong or bad-good judgments) of motives and possible acts (e.g., morality)" as an important component of wisdom (p. 267).

In addition to balance and values, traditional and contemporary conceptions of wisdom consistently incorporate knowledge, both tacit and explicit. The connection between knowledge and wisdom has a long tradition. It can be traced back to the writings of Aristotle, who claimed that "wisdom is knowledge about certain principles and causes. . . . The wise man knows all things, as far as possible, although he has not knowledge of each of them in detail" (Ross, 1908, p. 981). The persistent association of various types of knowledge with wisdom is evident from the typical contemporary usage of the word *wisdom,* which, according to the dictionary, is defined as the "power of judging rightly and following the soundest course of action, based on knowledge, experience, understanding, etc." (*Webster's New World College Dictionary,* 1997, p. 1533). In the psychological literature, Holliday and Chandler (1986) suggest that wisdom requires an "exceptional understanding of ordinary experience," as well as "general competencies." These factors resemble the ideas of the tacit and formal knowledge in Sternberg's theory. Similarly, the five wisdom-related criteria proposed by Baltes and Smith (1990) are:

1. Rich factual knowledge,
2. Rich procedural knowledge,
3. Life-span contextualization, or an understanding of life development and events,
4. Relativism, or knowledge about the differences in individual and cultural priorities, and
5. Uncertainty, or appreciation of the probabilistic nature of knowledge.

Thus, the presence of balance, values, and knowledge in a conceptualization of wise thinking is not unique to Sternberg's theory. What is unique is the proposition to combine these and other components into one model. Sternberg's theory attempts to include all the relevant factors involved in making wise judgments, as well as to explain the relationship among these factors.

The all-inclusiveness of the model has been criticized by Paris (2001), who claims that the model mystifies rather than clarifies the phenomenon by including "all possible sources of influence" (p. 259). However, we argue that the breadth of the model represents its strength, rather than its weakness. The value of the balance theory of wisdom comes from its comprehensiveness in describing one of the most sophisticated acts of a human mind. Rather than dissecting wise thinking into conveniently manageable fractions, the theory depicts a general system that preserves the complexity of "real behavior" in "real environments." The richness of the theory allows it to escape the common trap of contemporary psychology, where authenticity of the process is often sacrificed for the sake of precision and control. For instance, the typical preference for rigor over meaning is exemplified by the dominance of the Watson selection task paradigm in the study of deductive reasoning (for reviews, see Evans, Newstead, & Byrne, 1993; Johnson-Laird, 1999). After numerous investigations using the most bizarre variations of the four-card problem, its computer simulations, and volumes of published research, how much do we really know about people's inferential abilities, especially in naturalistic settings? If we want to study the psychology of wise thinking, we need to start with a model that is nontrivial, broad, and all-inclusive. The questions of model underspecification can be addressed through further research of particular model components.

The balance theory of wisdom is still in its early stages of development. For now, it aims to provide a meaningful starting point for the study of wise thinking. Each component of the model, as well as the relationships among the components, needs to be elaborated further through theoretical advances and empirical research. Yet, even in its current form, the model offers a useful guide to understanding and assessing people's decisions and actions. How well did the taken action balance multiple interests and consequences? Was the decision maker trying to reach a common good? Was there a balance among adaptation, shaping, and selection of the environment?

In addition, the balance theory of wisdom has already been successfully applied to the context of schooling. In the following sections, we describe the pedagogical implications of Sternberg's theory and explain how it was used to guide the design of the middle school curriculum intended to help students develop their ability to make wise and sound judgments.

WISDOM THEORY AND EDUCATION

At a first glance, Sternberg's model of wisdom may appear unsuitable for formal education. The heavy emphasis placed in the balance theory on values, tacit knowledge, and context-specific interactions between the person and the environment may seem to preclude its application in a classroom setting. How can teachers help their students develop all the explicit and implicit insights requisite for the display of wisdom?

The goal of teaching for wisdom can be achieved by providing students with *educational contexts*, where students can formulate their own understanding of what constitutes wise thinking. In other words, teaching for wisdom is not accomplished through a didactic method of *imparting* information *about wisdom* and subsequently assessing students with multiple-choice questions. Instead, students need to actively experience various cognitive and affective processes that underlie wise decision making.

What are these processes and how can they be introduced into the classroom? Sternberg (2001) outlines 16 pedagogical principles and 6 procedures derived from the theory of wisdom. The fundamental idea behind all these educational guidelines is that "one teaches children not *what* to think, but, rather, *how* to think. There is no place, when one teaches for wisdom, for teaching doctrinaire beliefs or ideologies" (Sternberg, 2001, p. 237). Thus, the development of wise thinking calls for an ongoing and systematic exercise of mind and emotion carried out by the student and supported by the teacher only when necessary. More specifically, students need to engage in activities that promote their ability to think reflectively, dialogically, and dialectically. The teacher's role is to provide scaffolding for the students' development of the various types of thinking. In addition, teachers must use the opportunities naturally arising in a classroom to encourage and model wise thinking. We next consider the desirable student and teacher practices in more detail.

In *reflective thinking*, an individual's functioning becomes an object of reflection, which allows for the monitoring and control of various processes. Importantly, our notion of reflective thinking is not limited to the awareness and regulation of cognitive processes. Rather, it is similar to Flavell's (1987) broadened concept of metacognition, which involves perception and knowledge of cognitive functioning, as well as emotions, motives, and motor acts. Wisdom not only implies a clear awareness of your psychological state but also requires an ability to detect and regulate the tensions among conflicting values and interests, such as between an urge to have a cigarette and a desire to protect your health by not smoking. "One cannot be wise and at the same time impulsive and mindless in one's judgments" (Sternberg, 2001).

In addition, wisdom is based on tacit knowledge and, thus, calls for an exceptional sensitivity to implicit contextual clues. A wise decision maker purposefully seeks to pick up the unstated rules and assumptions of a particular environment and to effectively use his or her understanding of the environmental conditions to achieve a desired goal. Because wise decision making is strategic and goal-oriented, it necessarily involves an ongoing monitoring of selected strategies, as well as an ability to flexibly modify less successful strategies to better fit the situational demands.

An awareness of your values, an effective management of conflicting interests, including self-management, an ability to gain insight into the subtleties of a particular situation and to use this insight for devising a useful strategy—all represent processes that require reflection. Teachers can help students practice reflective thinking by designing instructional activities that allow students to explore and shape their own values. In addition, students can be explicitly instructed in useful metacognitive strategies such as self-questioning or the use of self-monitoring checklists. Instruction in such strategies improves student performance in a variety of ways, including better allocation of resources, an improved transfer performance, and a deeper understanding of the content (e.g., Bender, 1986; Chi, De Leeuw, Chiu, & LaVancher, 1994; Cross & Paris, 1988; Gourgey, 1998).

In addition to reflective thinking, wisdom requires an ability to think *dialogically*. As argued by Paul (1986), "messy" problems that do not have right answers cannot be solved monologically, that is, using a single framework with defined logical rules. They require a different kind of thinking, the thinking that transcends a solitary frame of reference, forcing a person to recognize that "it is perfectly possible to have an overwhelming inner sense of correctness of one's views and still be wrong" (Paul, 1986, p. 130). In dialogical thinking, an individual uses multiple frames of reference to generate and deliberate about various perspectives on the issue. Solutions come from careful weighting of alternatives, rather than from following the prescribed course of action.

The development of dialogical thinking can be best fostered in supportive educational settings that are, themselves, dialogical. For example, dialogical thinking can be promoted through reading and discussion of multiple viewpoints. "Thinkers must hear several voices within their own heads representing different perspectives on the issue. The ability and disposition to take more than one perspective arises from participating in discussions with others who hold different perspectives" (Anderson et al., 2001, p. 2). A few empirical studies that investigated the effectiveness of student discussions for the development of dialogical thinking were able to show improvements in students' abilities to resolve ill-structured problems, following their participation in the discussions (Kuhn, Shaw, & Felton, 1997; Reznitskaya et al., 2001). For example, having participated in group discussions on controversial topics raised in their readings, elementary school students performed better on an individual writing task requiring them to choose a course of action in a difficult-to-resolve situation. Specifically, student essays contained a greater number of reasons for and against the chosen action than the essays of comparable students who did not have group discussions (Reznitskaya et al., 2001). A qualitative analysis of the essays revealed that at least some students who engaged in discussions wrote about the problem in a dialogical manner, consistently anticipating and exploring the alternative perspectives on the issue.

Whereas dialogical thinking revolves around consideration of multiple points of view, *dialectical thinking* emphasizes dynamic integration of opposing perspectives. Dialectical thinking is an understanding of how ideas and situations evolve. It is a concept dating back to Hegel (1807/1931) that involves, essentially, becoming your own "devil's advocate." In dialectical thinking, knowledge is constructed by finding a resolution to contradictions. First, a *thesis* is considered; for example, someone might propose banning smoking altogether. Second, an *antithesis* or a negation of the original statement is considered; for example, someone might suggest allowing people to make their own decisions about smoking. Finally, a *synthesis* or reconciliation of the two seemingly opposing statements is developed; for example, you might decide that while people should be free to decide on the issue of smoking, some restrictions are necessary, such as prohibiting smoking in certain public places or forbidding the sale of cigarettes to minors. Importantly, the process does not stop when the two opposing views are reconciled. A synthesis becomes a new thesis, which is, again, negated in a new round of dialectical thinking.

Dialectical thinking fosters wisdom by making salient the limitations of a single solution, the existence of alternatives, and the possibility of integration of seemingly opposing views to form a new and, perhaps, more complex and wiser reconciliation. In addition, dialectical thinking allows you to abandon a static and fixed notion of knowledge, supporting the acquisition of more sophisticated epistemological commitments. In dialectical thinking, knowledge is conceived as malleable and fluid. It is constructed through the dynamic interaction of alternative views. Dialectical thinking shifts the focus of the source of knowledge from authority to self and views knowledge as complex, relative, and evolving. Such conceptions of knowledge and its origins have been shown to relate to (1) active engagement in learning (e.g., McDevitt, 1990), (2) persistence in performing a task (e.g., Dweck & Leggett, 1988), and (3) deeper comprehension and integration of the material (e.g., Qian & Alvermann, 2000; Songer & Linn, 1991).

Dialectical thinking is fostered in a classroom when students are given opportunities to construct their own understanding of the material, rather than when teachers transmit knowledge in the form of known facts. In addition, students need assignments that require an integration of the material, where they can overcome the artificial boundaries between the content areas, such as literature, history, art, or science. Finally, students should study shifting paradigms present in any content area in order to discover the dynamic nature of knowledge.

In addition to providing contexts for students to engage in reflective, dialogical, and dialectical thinking, teachers must look for naturally arising opportunities in and outside the classroom to *model* and *encourage* wise thinking. For example, a teacher might use a conflict situation, such as two students getting into a fight, as a way to demonstrate how an individual can approach a similar situation in a more constructive way. For example, a teacher can model wise thinking by saying: "When I get into situations like this, I try to see the dispute from the perspective of the other person and I think about whether my own behavior contributed to the situation. Was there anything I could have done differently to prevent this confrontation? Is there a solution to our disagreement that is acceptable to both of us?"

In addition, teachers should not miss the opportunity to recognize and praise good judgments made by students. For example, when students exhibit behaviors that show their consideration for others, teachers should acknowledge their progress. "We teach who we are," and it is difficult to overestimate the importance of creating classroom communities where wisdom is practiced, rather than preached. Students need to experience that wise decision making is real, it can be accomplished, and it can lead to a better, more harmonious existence.

Sternberg's proposal to teach for wisdom is consistent with several other contemporary approaches to education. Most notably, it relates to the educational initiatives designed to promote critical thinking and character development. The notions of critical thinking and character development have undergone multiple interpretations over the years, and it is difficult to assess what each entails. Nevertheless, it can be observed that, more often than not, education for critical thinking primarily constitutes the teaching of analytical and reasoning abilities, whereas the emphasis in character education programs is on social and moral development. For example, Ennis (1993) defines critical thinking as "reasonable and reflective thinking focused on deciding what to believe or do" (p. 180). Ennis's taxonomy of 12 critical thinking abilities includes:

1. Focusing on a question
2. Analyzing arguments
3. Asking and answering questions of clarification and/or challenge
4. Judging the credibility of a source
5. Observing and judging observation reports
6. Deducing and judging deductions
7. Inducing and judging inductions
8. Making value judgments
9. Defining terms and judging definitions in three dimensions: form, definitional strategy, and content
10. Identifying assumptions
11. Deciding on an action
12. Interacting with others (Ennis, 1986, p. 12)

Of these 12 abilities described by Ennis, only two—making value judgments and interacting with others—can be considered as targeting something other than formal and informal reasoning. Notably, by "interacting with others," Ennis means "a) employing and reacting to fallacy labels, b) logical strategies, c) rhetorical strategies, and d) argumentation" (Ennis, 1986, p. 15). This, again, illustrates the primary focus of critical thinking education on argumentation and reasoning.

Character education, on the other hand, is defined as "a concerned effort . . . to educate children and youth about an agreed-upon set of values" (DeRoche & Williams, 1998). The various "value lists" generally include ethical values such as honesty, integrity, fairness, responsibility, and respect for self and others (for a review, see DeRoche & Williams, 1998).

Thus, critical thinking and character development emphasize different aspects of education, with the former initiative primarily focusing on intellectual skills, and the latter emphasizing social and moral competencies. Sternberg's proposal of teaching for wisdom integrates the important educational objectives of intellectual and sociomoral development into a single, theoretically motivated approach. Wisdom involves knowledge and critical thinking, but it also has an ethical and prosocial quality. People who skillfully use their reasoning abilities to merely benefit themselves can be considered good critical thinkers, but they cannot be considered wise.

In the following section, we illustrate how the balance theory of wisdom can be used to design a middle school curriculum that aims to help students develop their intellectual abilities as well as to form and practice core ethical values.

THEORY INTO PRACTICE

We have used the pedagogical guidelines derived from the balance theory of wisdom to design a curriculum for middle school students in the subject matter of American history. Before describing specific instructional activities from the curriculum, we briefly discuss two additional educational principles used in its development. First, the design of the curriculum is informed by the educational model of cognitive apprenticeship (Collins, Brown, & Newman, 1989; Coy, 1989; Lave & Wenger, 1991). Throughout the curriculum, students are invited to experience and solve the problems faced by actual practitioners of the discipline of history. For example, students engage in age-appropriate activities that require them to apply the typical inquiry methods adopted by historians, such as formulating historical questions and studying primary sources to find answers. While necessarily simpler than the research done by historians, these activities preserve the authenticity of the professional practice. Engagement in such activities allows students not only to learn the content but also to think through the content in the same way experts do.

Second, many activities in the curriculum are performed in groups or in pairs because research shows that students of the same age can and do learn from one another (e.g., Anderson et al., 2001; Johnson, Johnson, & Holubec, 1993; Slavin, 1995; Stahl, 1994). Working in groups increases student achievement and motivation (Johnson, Johnson, Stanne, & Garibaldi, 1990; Slavin, 1995; Stahl, 1994). It improves the social climate in a classroom and supports the development of the cognitive, moral, and social competencies we would like to foster in the curriculum (Johnson et al., 1993; Slavin, 1995; Stahl, 1994).

Recalling the pedagogical implications of the balance theory of wisdom, teaching for wisdom should provide students with opportunities to engage in reflective, dialogical, and dialectical thinking. We next consider several examples from the curriculum that illustrate each kind of thinking. The first example comes from the section of the curriculum in which students study the ideas of the intellectual movement of the Enlightenment and the character of Benjamin Franklin. In this activity, students first read Franklin's maxims, such as, "Whatever is begun in anger ends in shame," "Be slow in choosing a friend, slower in changing," "Well done is better than well said," and so on (Franklin, 1983). Next, students work in pairs to describe to their partners their own past experiences where one of Franklin's maxims could apply. Students are then invited to think of a maxim that they have learned from their own past and to continue writing their maxims in a notebook or a journal throughout the school year.

From this activity, students learn about the benefits of reflecting on their life experiences and thinking about a general rule, or a maxim, that they can apply to the new situations. Wisdom involves an ability to learn from the past, whether your own or that of other people. Reflective thinking about their life experiences is an important skill that students get to practice in this activity. In addition, having students generate their own maxims throughout the year helps to make reflection on various life experiences become a habit of mind.

In the homework related to the preceding activity, students study an excerpt from Franklin's autobiography, where Franklin describes his plan to achieve moral perfection. Having read Franklin's plan, students choose three values that they consider important and develop their own plan to improve their characters. Students then monitor their behavior for a period of one week and record in a journal their successes and failures at practicing the chosen values. This activity allows students to explore, form, and apply their own values. In addition, students are given an opportunity to monitor events in their daily lives and to recognize the connections between values and actions.

A good example of an activity that fosters the development of dialogical thinking comes from the historical topic of British colonial polices in the late eighteenth century. In this activity, students read the multiple accounts of the events during the Boston Massacre. The reports include an excerpt from a colonial newspaper, an account by a captain of the British troops, and an interview with a Boston shoemaker. Students discuss the origins of the differences among the accounts and evaluate the relative credibility of the sources. They are also invited to write their own account of the Boston Massacre events and to consider how their own frames of reference affect their descriptions. From this activity, students learn to appreciate the importance of multiple standpoints, the constructed nature of knowledge, and the powerful influences of an individual's perspective on his or her view of the world.

An example of an activity where students get to practice their dialectical thinking comes from a related historical topic. In this activity, students first study the writings of Thomas Paine and Charles Inglis, who express two opposing views on the question of whether America should break away from England. Next, students consider a compromise solution proposed by Joseph Galloway, in which he attempts to reconcile the two conflicting positions. Students then discuss the notion of compromise and propose their own resolutions to the British-American conflict. Through this activity, students practice synthesizing the opposing perspective. They also learn to recognize that the same questions can be answered differently at different points at time.

The preceding examples of student activities demonstrate that it is possible to design instructional activities consistent with the theoretical tenets of the balance theory of wisdom. In fact, our biggest discovery when developing the curriculum was the abundance of opportunities to integrate teaching for wise thinking into the subject matter of history. Regardless of the historical topic we were working on, we found multiple opportunities for incorporating instructional activities that would allow students to develop their ability to make just and sound judgments.

The development of this curriculum is part of a larger project that aims to evaluate the application of Sternberg's balance theory of wisdom to education. We plan to assess the effectiveness of the curriculum using a quasi-experimental design, where 36 classrooms will be assigned to one of the three conditions. In the first experimental condition, the teachers will use the curriculum previously described or the Wisdom Curriculum. Teachers in the second condition will use a Critical Thinking Curriculum. The Critical Thinking Curriculum represents a modified Wisdom Curriculum, in which we take out the specific content and activities intended to teach wisdom-related thinking. We leave in the material that teaches only critical thinking and replace the wisdom-related instruction with additional teaching of critical thinking. Thus, we are able to isolate the educational value of wisdom-related content and activities, while equating the Wisdom and the Critical Thinking curricula on the amount of material and classroom time.

In the third condition, called Historical Sources, students will be taught using the regular methods adopted by their teachers. Teachers will also be provided with primary and secondary historical sources to supplement their instruction. These historical sources will be identical to those used in Wisdom and Critical Thinking conditions. The Historical Sources condition allows us to assess the instructional contributions due to the use of the novel and engaging source materials. In other words, in the third condition, we are able to separate the value of educational contexts and activities dealing with wise and critical thinking from the value of the historical documents used in the activities. Students' performance in all conditions will be evaluated using identical assessment instruments. Specifically, we will assess students' progress in wise thinking, critical thinking, and knowledge of history.

An example of an assessment that we plan to employ to evaluate wise thinking is a life-problem measure that uses social-context dilemmas. In this measure, students are given four short scenarios that describe a problematic life situation relevant to middle school learners. For the first two scenarios, students are required to provide open-ended responses as to how to resolve the situations. For the remaining two scenarios, students are asked to indicate whether a given resolution represents a poor or a good choice, using a rating scale. Thus, the evaluation of student competencies includes open-ended and multiple-choice/rating assessments, which are expected to increase both validity and reliability of the measure.

The quasi-experimental design involving three conditions allows us to empirically investigate the controversial question of whether wisdom can be taught. In addition, by comparing the Wisdom and Critical Thinking conditions, we will test our assumption that wise decision making involves more than just critical thinking. We expect to find that students who are taught for wisdom will show greater increases in wisdom-related skills from pre- to posttest than those who are taught only for critical thinking and knowledge. However, the possibility of teaching for wisdom and the effectiveness of the specific Wisdom Curriculum described here are, for now, empirical questions, which are best addressed through rigorous future empirical research.

DIRECTIONS FOR FUTURE RESEARCH

The balance theory of wisdom is still in its early stages of development. There are plenty of questions to be answered about the multiple factors enumerated in Sternberg's model, as well as their relations. For example, what psychological processes underlie the search for a common good? What individual characteristics influence an individual's ability to balance among conflicting interests, consequences, and environmental responses? What are the features of the environments that support or oppose wise decision making? What are the dynamics of the model: Is there a particular progression in relation to considering multiple interests, consequences, and environmental responses, as well as in applying values and knowledge? Are the processes that make up wise thinking sequential, parallel, circular, or mixed? Sternberg's model provides a useful basis for launching an exploration of the complicated phenomenon of wise thinking. The challenge now is to further elaborate the theoretical constructs and to design and implement multiple studies that can put the theory to an empirical test.

The educational implications of the balance theory of wisdom also need to be examined in further detail. The evaluation of the Wisdom Curriculum described previously will provide some answers to the questions of whether teaching for wisdom is possible and how the instruction for wisdom should be accomplished. However, many more questions remain. For example, when educational programs are being evaluated as a whole, information about the relative contribution of the various instructional practices is often lost. Namely, it is unclear if the curriculum *worked* because of its emphasis on fostering reflective, dialogical, or dialectical thinking or because the teacher effectively modeled and encouraged wise behaviors. The information about the relative usefulness of various pedagogical practices is important for theoretical and practical reasons. We need to test the advocated pedagogical practices of teaching for wisdom and, possibly, extend and modify the theory. Educators involved in curriculum development need to rely on instructional practices that have been carefully tested in empirical studies.

In addition, an important research direction related to reorienting school instruction toward teaching for wisdom is teacher education. We believe that change in students' learning starts with changes in teachers' teaching. Teachers' beliefs, knowledge, and ways of understanding the material are directly tied to student learning (Cole & Knowels, 2000; Costa, 2001b; Jetton & Alexander, 1997). This relationship may be especially strong when teachers are trying to promote students' competencies in wise thinking. More research is needed to identify effective ways of preparing teachers to understand the theories underlying wisdom and to develop pedagogical strategies allowing them to conduct their lessons in accordance with the theories. Without significant changes in knowledge, skills, and attitudes, teachers may teach a new program, but they model and expect traditional performance from their students, with the result that they get traditional performance from these students.

Teaching for wisdom is an ambitious goal. However, we believe that it can be accomplished, given that pedagogy of wise thinking relies on clear theoretical structure and is supported by sound empirical research. Considering the potential benefits to individuals and society, we must accept and address the challenges of teaching students to be wise in their judgments. The "Teaching for Wisdom" program is an important first step in that direction.

REFERENCES

Anderson, R. C., Nguyen-Jahiel, K., McNurlen, B., Archodidou, A., Kim, S., Reznitskaya, A., et al. (2001). The snowball phenomenon: Spread of ways of talking and ways of thinking across groups of children. *Cognition and Instruction, 19,* 1–46.

Baltes, P. B., & Smith, J. (1990). Toward a psychology of wisdom and its ontogenesis. In R. J. Sternberg (Ed.), *Wisdom: Its nature, origins, and development* (pp. 87–120). New York: Cambridge University Press.

Bender, T. A. (1986). Monitoring and the transfer of individual problem-solving. *Contemporary Educational Psychology, 11,* 161–169.

Berkowitz, M. W. (2002). The science of character education. In W. Damon (Ed.), *Bringing in a new era in character education* (pp. 43–63). Stanford, CA: Hoover Institution Press.

Birren, J. E., & Fisher, L. M. (1990). The elements of wisdom: Overview and integration. In R. J. Sternberg (Ed.), *Wisdom: Its nature, origins, and development* (pp. 317–332). New York: Cambridge University Press.

Bush, G. (2002, June 19). Speech at White House Conference on Character and Community, Washington, DC: Retrieved from http://www.whitehouse.gov/news/releases/2002/06/20020619-22.html.

Chi, M., De Leeuw, N., Chiu, M., & LaVancher, C. (1994). Eliciting self-explanations improves understanding. *Cognitive Science, 18,* 439–377.

Clinton, B. (1996, January 23). Fourth State of the Union Address. Retrieved from http://clinton4.nara.gov/WH/New/other/stateunion-top.html.

Cole, A. L., & Knowels, J. G. (2000). *Researching teaching.* Boston: Allyn & Bacon.

Collins, A., Brown, J. S., & Newman, S. E. (1989). Cognitive apprenticeship: Teaching the crafts of reading, writing and mathematics. In L. B. Resnick (Ed.), *Knowing, learning, and instruction: Essays in honor of Robert Glaser* (pp. 453–494). Hillsdale, NJ: Erlbaum.

*Costa, A. L. (2001a). Habits of mind. In A. B. Costa (Ed.), *Developing minds: A resource book for teaching thinking* (pp. 80–86). Alexandria, VA: Association for Supervision and Curriculum Development.

Costa, A. L. (2001b). Teacher behaviors that enable student thinking. In A. B. Costa (Ed.), *Developing minds: A resource book for teaching thinking* (pp. 359–369). Alexandria, VA: Association for Supervision and Curriculum Development.

Coy, M. W. (1989). *Apprenticeship: From theory to method and back again.* Albany: State University of New York Press.

Cross, D. R., & Paris, S. G. (1988). Developmental and instructional analyses of children's metacognition and reading comprehension. *Journal of Educational Psychology, 83,* 35–42.

*Csikszentmihalyi, M., & Rathunde, K. (1990). The psychology of wisdom: An evolutionary interpretation. In R. J. Sternberg (Ed.), *Wisdom: Its nature, origins, and development* (pp. 25–51). New York: Cambridge University Press.

Damon, W. (Ed.). (2002). *Bringing in a new era in character education.* Stanford, CA: Hoover Institution Press.

DeRoche, E. F., & Williams, M. M. (1998). *Educating hearts and minds: A comprehensive character education framework.* Thousand Oaks, CA: Corwin Press.

Dweck, C. S., & Leggett, E. L. (1988). A social-cognitive approach to motivation and personality. *Psychological Review, 95,* 256–273.

*Ennis, R. H. (1986). A taxonomy of critical thinking dispositions and abilities. In J. B. Baron & R. J. Sternberg (Eds.), *Teaching thinking skills: Theory and practice* (pp. 9–26). New York: Freeman.

Ennis, R. H. (1993). Critical thinking assessment. *Theory into Practice, 32,* 179–186.

Evans, J., Newstead, S., & Byrne, R. (1993). *Human reasoning: The psychology of deduction.* Hillsdale, NJ: Erlbaum.

Flavell, J. H. (1987). Speculations about the nature and development of metacognition. In F. E. Wienert & R. H. Kluwe (Eds.), *Metacognition, motivation, and understanding* (pp. 21–29). Hillsdale, NJ: Erlbaum.

Franklin, B. (1983). *Poor Richard's Almanack.* White Plains, NY: Peter Pauper Press. (Original work published 1733)

Gourgey, A. F. (1998). Metacognition in basic skills instruction. *Instructional Science, 26,* 81–96.

Hartshorne, C. (1987). *Wisdom as moderation: A philosophy of the middle way.* Albany: State University of New York Press.

Hegel, G. W. F. (1931). *The phenomenology of the mind* (2nd ed., J. D. Baillie, Trans.). London: Allen & Unwin. (Original work published 1807)

Holliday, S. G., & Chandler, M. J. (1986). *Wisdom: Explorations in adult competence.* Basel, Switzerland: Karger.

Jetton, T. L., & Alexander, P. A. (1997). Instructional importance: What teachers value and what students learn. *Reading Research Quarterly, 32,* 290–308.

Johnson, D. W., Johnson, R. T., & Holubec, E. J. (1993). *Circles of learning: Cooperation in the classroom* (4th ed.). Edina, MN: Interaction Book.

Johnson, D. W., Johnson, R. T., Stanne, M., & Garibaldi, A. (1990). The impact of group processing on achievement in cooperative groups. *Journal of Social Psychology, 130,* 507–516.

Johnson-Laird, P. (1999). Deductive reasoning. *Annual Review of Psychology, 50,* 109–135.

Kramer, D. A. (1990). Conceptualizing wisdom: The primacy of affect-cognition relations. In R. J. Sternberg (Ed.), *Wisdom: Its nature, origins, and development* (pp. 52–83). New York: Cambridge University Press.

Kuhn, D., Shaw, V., & Felton, M. (1997). Effects of dyadic interaction on argumentative reasoning. *Cognition and Instruction, 15,* 287–315.

Labouvie-Vief, G. (1990). Wisdom as integrated thought: Historical and developmental perspectives. In R. J. Sternberg (Ed.), *Wisdom: Its nature, origins, and development* (pp. 52–83). New York: Cambridge University Press.

Lave, J., & Wenger, E. (1991). *Situated learning: Legitimate peripheral participation.* Cambridge, England: Cambridge University Press.

Lickona, T. (1991). *Educating for character: How our schools can teach respect and responsibility.* New York: Bantam Books.

McDevitt, T. M. (1990). Mothers' and children's beliefs about listening. *Child Study Journal, 20,* 105–128.

Nickerson, R. S. (1986). Why teach thinking? In J. B. Baron & R. J. Sternberg (Eds.), *Teaching thinking skills: Theory and practice* (pp. 27–38). New York: Freeman.

Paris, S. G. (2001). Wisdom, snake oil, and the educational marketplace. *Educational Psychologist, 36,* 257–260.

Pascual-Leone, J. (1990). An essay on wisdom: Toward organismic processes that make it possible. In R. J. Sternberg (Ed.), *Wisdom: Its nature, origins, and development* (pp. 244–278). New York: Cambridge University Press.

Paul, R. W. (1986). Dialogical thinking: Critical thought essential to the acquisition of rational knowledge and passions. In J. B. Baron & R. J. Sternberg (Eds.), *Teaching thinking skills: Theory and practice* (pp. 127–148). New York: Freeman.

Perkins, D. (2002). The engine of folly. In R. J. Sternberg (Ed.), *Why smart people can be so stupid* (pp. 233–243). New Haven, CT: Yale University Press.

Polanyi, M. (1966). *The tacit dimensions.* Garden City, NY: Doubleday.

Qian, G., & Alvermann, D. E. (2000). Relationship between epistemological beliefs and conceptual change learning. *Reading and Writing Quarterly, 16,* 59–74.

Reznitskaya, A., Anderson, R. C., McNurlen, B., Nguyen-Jahiel, K., Archodidou, A., & Kim, S. (2001). Influence of oral discussion on written argument. *Discourse Processes, 32,* 155–175.

Ross, W. D. (Ed.). (1908). *The works of Aristotle* (Vol. 8). Oxford, England: Oxford University Press.

Slavin, R. (1995). *Cooperative learning: Theory, research and practice* (2nd ed.). Boston: Allyn & Bacon.

Songer, N. B., & Linn, M. C. (1991). How do views of science influence knowledge integration. *Journal of Research in Science Teaching, 28,* 761–784.

Stahl, R. J. (1994). *Cooperative learning in social studies: A handbook for teachers.* Menlo Park, CA: Addison-Wesley.

*Sternberg, R. J. (1998). A balance theory of wisdom. *Review of General Psychology, 2,* 347–365.

*Sternberg, R. J. (2001). Why schools should teach for wisdom: The balance theory of wisdom in educational settings. *Educational Psychologist, 36,* 227–245.

Sternberg, R. J., Forsythe, G. B., Hedlund, J., Horvath, J. A., Wagner, R. K., Williams, W. M., et al. (2000). *Practical intelligence in everyday life.* Cambridge, MA: Cambridge University Press.

Webster's New World College Dictionary (3rd ed.). (1997). New York: Simon & Schuster.

CHAPTER 12

Introducing Positive Psychology to the Introductory Psychology Student

AMY C. FINEBURG

POSITIVE PSYCHOLOGY HAS emerged as an antithesis to *negative psychology*—instead of studying the psychological disorders that plague us, positive psychology seeks to understand the qualities that strengthen, build, and foster us. The study of the positive has long been controversial and yet timely as each generation seeks the answers to questions about life, happiness, and fulfillment. Psychology in general is a discipline that attracts people who are seeking the answers to life's questions, and up to this point, the answers psychology has provided mainly center on the explanation and suppression of mental illness and deviancy. Common domain areas studied in psychology include methodology, biological bases of behavior, cognition, social-cultural psychology, and development (Maitland et al., 2000). These domain areas have evolved as psychology has rapidly evolved as a discipline. Introductory psychology texts of the late 1970s did not include the cognitive perspective in the schools of thought section while texts of the 1980s had little to say about cross-cultural issues, and behavior genetics and evolutionary psychology were rarely covered in textbooks until the mid- to late 1990s (Ernst & Fineburg, 2003). Yet, all of these new, evolving areas are more concerned with the negative rather than the positive.

This emphasis on the negative rather than the positive in textbooks almost requires teaching from a negative psychology perspective. Introductory psychology teachers, whose curriculum is less specialized, must give students an overview of what psychology has studied in the past and what current directions the discipline is engaged in exploring. As psychology grows as a science, the amount of material to be covered in a traditional introductory course increases as well. Time forces instructors to make a choice about what to cover. Because study of the negative is supported by a wealth of scientific inquiry, it is well supported in textbooks. Thus, the canon of introductory psychology is more inclusive of well-established concepts in negative psychology rather than newer positive psychology constructs. Griggs and Mitchell (2002) surveyed introductory psychology textbooks to see what terms were most commonly used, citing those terms that appeared in at least 67% of the introductory textbooks' glossaries. While the majority could be considered neutral (i.e., reliability, validity, hormones, conditioned response), a lack of terms related to positive psychology is apparent. Consider only those chapters where positive psychology would naturally fit—therapy, social psychology, personality, and motivation/emotion. Terms most represented in the therapy chapters center mostly around psychoanalytic concepts of repression, resistance, transference, and free association. In personality chapters, psychoanalytic concepts dominate as well, with seven of nine terms. In the social psychology chapter, six terms are cited—aggression, attitude, norm, prejudice, social psychology, and stereotype. Only drive, emotion, and motivation are terms most often used in introductory textbooks in the motivation/emotion chapter. Where is flow? Optimism? Hope? With this level of representation of negative psychology, there is little wonder that positive psychology is an afterthought.

But what effect does learning about negative psychology have on students' perceptions of psychology in general? VanderStoep, Fagerlin, and Feenstra (2000) surveyed introductory psychology students to see what concepts were recalled most after taking the course. The concepts most often recalled were overwhelmingly related to negative psychology and the illness model. Students most often remembered learning about Phineas Gage and his brain injury, systematic desensitization, narcolepsy, Milgram's obedience study, attitudes influencing behavior (presented through a "controversial issue" debate), and two disorders—dissociative identity disorder and schizophrenia. The other ideas recalled—"psychic" powers, altered visual perception, neuron firing, and classical conditioning—could be considered neutral, but not specifically positive. Many introductory psychology students do not continue to higher levels of psychology, so their overall perceptions of psychology center around the disease and illness model that has dominated for the past half century.

On the upper and graduate levels, positive psychology is taught as its own course. Upper-level undergraduate and graduate-level courses in positive psychology have been offered at U.S. institutions as varied as University of Pennsylvania, Harvard Medical School, University of Michigan, Middle Tennessee State University, University of Kentucky, University of Montana, and University of Alabama at Birmingham. Courses have also been offered at University of Cambridge and University of Warwick in the United Kingdom. These courses typically provide a general overview of positive psychology, covering a wide range of researched topics such as optimism, hope, flow, and human strengths. With an entire course to devote to teaching positive psychology, coverage of these issues can be comprehensive and deep. Students in these courses often read primary source material and popular-press books written by researchers in the field. They also participate in activities that challenge them to apply positive psychology to their lives. The freedom of the devoted course enables instructors on the upper and graduate levels to immerse students in positive psychology, cultivating future positive psychologists in both practice and research.

The challenge, then, for instructors of introductory level psychology courses is to determine when and how to teach positive psychology. An entire course is not likely to be devoted to positive psychology at the high school or freshman level since the study of negative psychology has been the focus of most of the discipline's explorations. Ignoring negative psychology for the positive and vice versa is not the end goal of the positive psychology movement. Positive psychology seeks a balance with negative psychology, hoping students will get a complete picture of the human experience where both good and bad experiences interact. But the problems of teaching positive psychology in the introductory course are numerous. As noted, mention of positive concepts is scant, with the exception of newer books that emphasize positive psychology (see Blair-Broeker & Ernst, 2003; Myers, 2001). Well-established concepts in the disease and illness model of psychology are considered fundamental for understanding principles taught in more specialized upper-level courses. Graduate-school entrance exams and licensing exams expect students to know and apply principles of negative psychology. Limited time in introductory classes also necessitates picking and choosing concepts to teach. Thus, to abandon these foundational, yet negative, principles would be irresponsible.

Positive psychology can and should be taught to introductory students. Are these problems insurmountable? Is positive psychology defined clearly enough to be taught reliably to introductory students? Is it important to teach positive psychology when the curricula is already full to capacity? How can positive psychology be taught without compromising what students are already expected to know? What benefits can result from teaching positive psychology? I address these issues in the following sections.

POSITIVE PSYCHOLOGY: A WELL-ESTABLISHED MOVEMENT

Positive psychology has been around for as long as humans have existed. People have always been curious about what makes life good, how to be successful, and what the purpose of life is. Aristotle called it *eudaemonia*. Epicureans believed people should "eat, drink, and be merry" to live the good life. For centuries, people have sought and still seek answers to life's burning questions through religion, relationships, service, power, and glory. Questions about what makes people happy and fulfilled have burned in the thoughts of philosophers, politicians, theologians, and scientists. Why do we believe that helping others is an important duty to fulfill? Why do we cry out against those who seek to harm others? Why do we seek cures and treatments for our ills? We do these things to have the good life, to be happy, to "live long and prosper."

In psychology, the study of the positive has been around since the discipline's inception in 1879. As Seligman and Csikszentmihalyi (2000) described, psychology had three goals before World War II:

1. To cure mental illness
2. To make people's lives more productive and fulfilling
3. To encourage genius and high talent

As world events came to shape a new worldview in the mid-twentieth century, psychology's goals became reshaped as well. The horrors of the Great Depression in the United States and of World War II made people all too aware of how far individuals and groups would go to inflict pain, suffering, and damage to others. The study of the positive became associated with eugenics and elitism as the motives behind Hitler's "Final Solution" became public. How do we stop the evils of war and genocide? How do we help people who've seen the horrors of war to recover to their former selves? To stop these ills and promote healing, funding became available to study why people behave the way they do in adverse situations and to explore the workings of the diseased mind so that cures and treatments can be found. The Veterans Administration, the National Institute of Mental Health, Stanley Milgram's obedience study, Solomon Asch's conformity study, and Philip Zimbardo's prison-guard study all emerged from this model of studying the negative (Seligman & Csikszentmihalyi, 2000).

The wealth of information and knowledge that stemmed from these organizations and individuals has proven to be priceless. According to Seligman & Csikszentmihalyi (2000), more than 14 different disorders have been effectively understood as a result of the money, time, and effort poured into research and treatment of mental illness. Can we even imagine a time when schizophrenia was treated with a lobotomy or when bloodletting and rest in a sanatorium purported to alleviate depression? We cannot, and we owe a debt of gratitude to those who still seek to understand mental illness. Stigmas still exist, as do the disorders they accompany, so the work still remains.

BENEFITS OF TEACHING POSITIVE PSYCHOLOGY

But what of the other two goals? The shelves of bookstores are crowded with self-help books that tout the answers to life's burning questions. These books, along with radio and television advertisements, lead people to believe the answers are simple—take this pill, read this book, eat (or do not eat) this food, drink this potion, do this exercise, buy this and this, and it will all be better for you and yours. But what psychology has taught us since the very beginning of the field is that life's answers are not simple. For psychology to leave its other two goals to nonscientific avenues of inquiry is both dangerous and shameful. What really does make people's lives more productive and fulfilling? Is genius inherited or learned? How do we encourage high talent? If we leave these questions to self-help gurus, marketing executives, and those who only wish to make a buck, we are in danger of allowing the prejudices of the past century to creep back into public consciousness. Surely the recipes for happiness, fulfillment, and purpose can be systematically explored through careful study and scientific reflection. And if this study and reflection can occur, the concepts generated from them can and should be taught to students. The benefits of teaching positive psychology are numerous. Students gain critical thinking skills and knowledge of how to facilitate wellness in themselves and others while educators are reinforced in their beliefs about effective teaching and instructional practices.

BENEFITS TO STUDENTS

Possessing critical thinking skills about the scientific process will help students to be better consumers of information about positive psychology. While scholarly journals and publications represent scientific research well, the popular press often misconstrues, perhaps unintentionally, these studies. Studies that yield correlational results are represented as establishing cause-and-effect relationships. Print and television media provide only condensed summaries of the vast wealth of knowledge scientific study offers the public. And the power of the media over our beliefs about how people behave at times supercedes research-based wisdom. Psychology teachers must take the responsibility to educate students in the value of critical thinking, especially about reports of scientific studies. Since many of these studies involve positive psychology concepts, teaching critical thinking skills about achieving the good life is just as important as teaching about recovering from hardship and disease. Thus, instead of believing that men and women come from different planets or that the key to happiness is making money or being thin, students will be able to evaluate these claims, separating the dubious ones from the validated.

Educating students about positive psychology can promote healing instead of just suppressing illness. Seligman (2002) proposed that negative psychology focuses mainly on firefighting and not fire prevention. A psychology that emphasizes diagnosing and treating illness is more equipped to deal with problems after they have afflicted patients rather than advising people on how to avoid getting ill in the first place. The value of being able to diagnose mental illness reliably is immeasurable, considering the state of mental illness care before World War II. But for the vast majority of people, mental illness is likely preventable. Studies in optimism have shown that middle school students can be trained in how to adopt a more optimistic explanatory style. This training yields a 100% decrease in the incidence of depression in these adolescents (Seligman, Reivich, Jaycox, & Gillham, 1995). Consider how much in insurance dollars and personal anguish were saved with the implementation of a 12-week course in optimistic thinking for middle school students. Certainly, services for adolescents and adults who suffer from depression must be reliable and effective. However, understanding the mechanisms of preventing illness is cost effective in terms of both financial and personal capital. The vast majority of college students take introductory psychology, and teaching these students about positive psychology will give them the tools they need to prevent mental illness in their own lives and the lives of their friends and families. Students who are exposed to positive psychology on the introductory level will have a clear picture about both sides of psychology. They will be more effective individuals, being less likely to succumb to destructive thinking. They could encourage optimism, hope, and fulfillment among those they touch in daily life.

BENEFITS TO EDUCATORS

The goals of positive psychology mirror the goals of educators. Ask any group of educators why they went into teaching, and most will say something to the effect of "to make a difference in the lives of students." What sustains teachers through the trials and tribulations involved in leading students to learn is the reinforcement of seeing students thrive and perform at optimal levels. Seligman and Csikszentmihalyi (2000, p. 6) described positive psychology as valuing:

> positive individual traits: the capacity for love and vocation, courage, interpersonal skill, perseverance, forgiveness, originality, future mindedness, spirituality, high talent, and wisdom. At the group level, it is about civic virtues and the institutions that move individuals toward better citizenship: responsibility, nurturance, altruism, moderation, tolerance, and work ethic.

What teacher hasn't wanted to instill and inspire such strengths in students? The golden moments of teaching come when students "get it," when they thank you for changing their way of viewing things, or when they use the knowledge they gained from you to become a better learner and person. Teaching students the goals of positive psychology exposes them to the science of individual achievement and ful-fillment, giving them insight into their own lives and making the actual lessons taught more meaningful.

Positive psychology principles can give educators insight into the motivational problems inherent in the teaching process. While teachers can take their horses to water, they cannot make them drink. It takes creativity, inspiration, and hard work to prepare lessons that will reach the intellectual level of each student. But even when teachers prepare outstanding lessons that appeal to a wide variety of stu-dents, motivational issues that could prevent students from learning and appreciat-ing what is taught can distract them. If students have pessimistic beliefs about their academic ability, they may not learn. Therefore, teachers need to consider not only content and pedagogy but also motivational issues that may hinder the learning process. Positive psychology provides insight into some questions teachers should be asking about lesson planning in addition to content and pedagogy:

- How optimistic are our students about their abilities as learners? Pes-simistic students are more hostile toward school (Boman & Yates, 2001). If students could be taught to be more optimistic about school, they would be more likely to succeed.
- What goals have our students set for this class and how realistic are their plans for achieving them? When students set realistic goals about school, de-velop plans to achieve those goals, and believe their goals can be achieved, they will likely achieve, earning higher grades and scores on achievement tests (Snyder, 2000).
- How do students' comparisons of their achievement to others in the class af-fect their learning? Students who receive a higher grade than expected both feel good and praise the teacher, whereas those who receive a lower grade than expected both feel lousy and trash the teacher. Thus, a B grade could mean something quite different to the student who expected an F as com-pared to a student who expected an A, thus changing levels of satisfaction with the class (Fineburg, 2003; Snyder & Clair, 1976).
- How can we make learning a flow experience for our students? Flow activi-ties involve freely invested attention, challenge with requisite skill, and lack of worry about failure (Csikszentmihalyi, 1990). If students can experience learning as flow, their enjoyment and intellectual stimulation about learn-ing will likely be enhanced.

By developing lessons that address these questions, teachers can help make stu-dents' experiences under their tutelage more effective, helpful, and encouraging as students realize how to become better learners.

STRATEGIES FOR TEACHING
POSITIVE PSYCHOLOGY

Because the evolution of psychology as a scientific discipline has grown far be-yond the three forces of psychoanalysis, behaviorism, and humanistic psychol-ogy, there seems to be no time to add more content without sacrificing other important concepts. Yet, it also seems important to expose students to cutting-edge areas of study so they can be aware of where the discipline is going. Positive psychology can be taught from several pedagogical perspectives, depending on the time available.

INFUSING POSITIVE PSYCHOLOGY

One way to teach positive psychology involves infusing it into the existing psychology curriculum. Even though positive psychology concepts are not part of the common language of introductory psychology, positive psychology does fit in with several well-established content areas and can be blended in seamlessly with the curriculum that is already being taught. Two current introductory textbooks—one directed at high school students (Blair-Broeker & Ernst, 2003) and one directed at advanced placement and introductory students (Myers, 2001)—have positive psychology woven into the fabric of the content. Both also highlight positive psychology specifically as a new movement, and perhaps perspective, in psychology's history. Many of the principles that have been addressed in different topic areas in introductory classes are positive psychology concepts, but research into these concepts has only recently been emphasized to a greater extent.

As the positive psychology movement endures, more introductory textbooks will include it and related concepts, encouraging future generations of psychologists to explore not only the illnesses that plague humanity but also the experiences that enrich humanity. Teaching from an infusion perspective doesn't require a complete overhaul of an instructor's lesson plans for a course. Infusion also serves to recognize the growing emphasis on the good in life and how positive psychology is not limited to one topic area of specialty. Students and researchers interested in a wide range of psychological concepts can approach their interests from a positive perspective without ignoring or sacrificing the contributions of traditional models of psychological thought.

TEACHING POSITIVE PSYCHOLOGY SEPARATELY

While infusion is the more efficient and holistic way of teaching positive psychology, using a stand-alone unit on positive psychology is not without its merits. Positive psychology may get lost in the myriad concepts students must absorb in the typical introductory course. Instead of encouraging interest in positive psychology, students may equate the study of the positive with other, more established schools of thought. Teaching a stand-alone unit in positive psychology will emphasize the study of the positive as a subdiscipline of psychology that is worthy of concentrated focus.

Not until late 2000 did any kind of summary document that was dedicated to classroom use exist. A seven-day unit plan for positive psychology, designed for high school teachers, was written to provide a framework for teachers to use to teach this new field (Fineburg, 2003). Focusing on positive subjective experiences, this unit plan divided these experiences into those of the past, present, and future, highlighting two fundamental concepts in each area. The only framework in existence at that time was a "Network Concept Paper" by Seligman and Csikszentmihalyi, which established the goals and structure of the positive psychology movement in its infancy. This document outlined three pillars of positive psychology: positive subjective experience (now known as *positive emotions*), positive individuals, and positive institutions. At the inaugural meeting of the

Positive Psychology Teaching Task Force in April 2000 in Philadelphia, Pennsylvania, a group of high school teachers, college professors, and researchers gathered to discuss how to disseminate positive psychology through teaching. Among the goals of this group was to create a lesson plan for positive psychology that high school teachers could use, thereby introducing the subject to students at the earliest levels of introductory psychology and creating a demand for more knowledge of the subject as those students became undergraduate and graduate students (i.e., Fineburg, 2003). The only course that existed at that time was one taught by Martin Seligman at University of Pennsylvania, which he described in an article in the APA's *Monitor on Psychology* newsmagazine while he was president of the Association (Seligman, 1999). Going with an early framework and one college class as models, I set to work writing the unit plan. Little did I realize that I would be creating one of the only summaries of positive psychology available. It is a daunting task to cull the original research of pioneering individuals, hoping to represent their work adequately to an audience that is unfamiliar with the topic to begin with. What I discovered was that the wealth of knowledge in positive psychology has been forming for several decades, and the concepts in positive psychology were not just recent developments but had been carefully and rigorously studied. Seligman, the champion of positive psychology as APA president, had been formulating his theories of learned optimism for at least 20 years. C. R. Snyder has been researching hope and uniqueness since the late 1970s. Ed Diener had been focusing on subjective well-being and Mihaly Csikszentmihalyi had been working on the concept of flow for many years as well.

The reception of the unit plan was overwhelming and positive. Not only did high school teachers find it helpful, but college instructors on all levels were interested in using the unit plan for their classes. Clinicians and educators from several countries requested electronic copies of the unit plan to use with their work as well. In 2003, Teachers of Psychology in Secondary Schools, the high school teacher affiliate group of the APA, published the unit plan as part of its series of unit plans focusing on different content areas studied in high school psychology (Fineburg, 2003). Psychology students of the future will know about positive psychology as an area of research focus as teachers at the introductory level include it in their current curriculum.

But the time challenge of teaching introductory psychology still remains, even when positive psychology is added to course content. For high school teachers of psychology, adding positive psychology is an easier task than for undergraduate instructors. Typically, high school psychology courses last an entire school year while introductory psychology is offered only during a semester. Finding a seven-day time period within a year is easier than in a semester. Teachers who teach Advanced Placement (AP) Psychology (a college-level course taught on the high school level) may want to teach positive psychology but feel they do not have time to fit it in before the AP exam. They may find that teaching positive psychology fits in well after students have taken the AP exam in mid-May when school doesn't end until late May or June. Standardized testing that occurs on the high school level also interferes with the flow of lessons periodically throughout the year, and a unit in positive psychology may work when a teacher sees some of his or her students only part of the day or all students part of the day. College instructors may have a more difficult time fitting in an extra unit in positive psychology in the traditional introductory course, but since the application of positive psychology to students' lives can be a time-consuming process, introducing stand-alone lessons periodically throughout the course may be useful. Students who are challenged to volunteer to demonstrate strengths or who need to create flow in their lives will need time outside class to accomplish these goals.

Consider having periodic positive psychology seminars where students can discuss, learn, and apply positive psychology as they learn about other traditional concepts in psychology. Treat the lessons on wellness as a discussion of positive psychology. Be creative in highlighting positive psychology without sacrificing the rich material contained in the rest of the introductory curriculum.

The question of infusion versus stand-alone may be a matter of preference and comfort. Some instructors may prefer to focus classroom lectures and discussion on cutting-edge concepts while having students read the foundational material in the textbook on their own. Some teachers may feel more comfortable integrating positive psychology into areas they already have knowledge about. Others may want to see positive psychology promoted as a separate perspective on the level of behaviorism, psychoanalysis, and humanistic psychology. Whatever the preference or comfort, positive psychology is a beneficial addition to any introductory psychology course. By teaching positive psychology in introductory psychology courses on the high school and undergraduate levels, students will get a balanced picture of psychology as it is studied today. They will realize that mental health is different from mental illness and, it is hoped, become inspired to study positive psychology throughout their lives.

NEW DIRECTIONS IN TEACHING ABOUT POSITIVE PSYCHOLOGY

As an educator, I am concerned about the state of my profession. Teachers are both heralded for their dedication and blamed for society's ills. Parents and the general public both trust implicitly and distrust explicitly public school teachers. Many problems exist in public education today. Lack of resources, funding, and support erode the ability of teachers to educate students. Higher standards and accountability both help and hurt teachers as they struggle to fulfill the variety of expectations that today's high school and college graduates must meet. Teachers and students are frustrated with rising expectations, less time, and more pressure to succeed. I have hope, though, that positive psychology may offer some of the answers to the problems public schools face. Curricular and pedagogical changes incorporating positive psychology could assist educators in strengthening students' learning experiences.

OPTIMISTIC TEACHING

Convincing teenagers that school is important when they've decided that it isn't is an imposing challenge. But teachers are a generally optimistic group (Smith, Hall, & Woolcock-Henry, 2000). Good teachers believe that every student can learn. But getting students to take advantage of opportunities is a daunting task. Take my personal experience: I allow my students to take a make-up test for each test they take during the school year. The regular tests are multiple-choice or matching tests—common tests of recognition. They are challenging, so often students find they want to raise their grades on my tests. The make-up tests are short answer, changing to recall instead of recognition to encourage students to find the answers they do not know. I feel that offering a make-up test opportunity helps students realize that a test is not the end-all, be-all of their intellectual lives. They can have opportunities to make up for a bad day, a busy week, or a lack of understanding the first time around. But I do not end there. I allow my students to retake the make-up tests as many times as they'd like until they get the grade they want for that test. I offer this for every test. For my students, it ain't over until the grades are turned in.

You may think that I have a hard time keeping up with the mounds of papers this system creates. But I'm sad to say that I do not. The only students who consistently return to take advantage of my policy are those who are striving for an A for the term. Usually, these students already have an A, but they want a higher one. To me, these are the very students who don't need make-up tests. They usually do relatively well on the tests anyway. They understand how to do well in school and achieve. The students who consistently fail do not come back. They complain that the make-up tests are too difficult. They say they know they'll fail that test as well as the original. Why bother if they're only going to fail? It is sad to see parents come for conferences to discuss their children's grades. I tell them of my policy, and they are grateful for my generosity. But they grow sad when they see their child pass up the opportunity to make a better grade. Why won't my child take advantage of this? I often hear the comment, "I wish I had you as my teacher when I was in school. I'd have made all A's."

I am not alone in my generosity with students. Teachers bend over backwards to help students who want to succeed. It may involve taking work that is late or spending time after school tutoring a student who has fallen behind. And still, students fail. These students who accept failure at school have become my personal challenge. Why have students become so pessimistic about school and their own abilities to succeed? What is it about our education system that allows these students to wallow through? I believe that part of the answer lies in positive psychology.

Teachers are equipped to instruct students in the content they teach. To be highly qualified, teachers must take certain classes that prepare them to teach whatever content area they are certified in, be it my areas of psychology and English or other areas of math, science, or history. Teachers are taught how to manage a classroom, how to integrate technology into lessons, and how to develop lessons that systematically guide students through a concept. But teachers are not taught how to motivate students who are refusing to be motivated. What do you do with a student who refuses to learn? Send him or her to the office? Give detention? Give more homework? Teachers are not taught how to address the underlying motivational and attributional problems students possess as they muddle through school.

Optimism research shows that mothers pass on their levels of optimism to their children (Seligman, 1998). But as children enter school, they spend less time with their mothers and more time with their teachers. If teachers are generally optimistic, will students pick up optimistic thinking from their teachers? The research on this is scarce if it exists at all. Scherer and Kimmel (1993) led teachers through a one-day optimism workshop that increased teachers' overall optimism scores. But how does this increased optimism affect student performance and achievement? Can an optimistic teacher help a pessimistic student feel less negative about school? It is hoped that these questions will be answered as positive psychology becomes more prominent. During the 2003–2004 school year, a Values in Action (VIA) Strengths and Virtues grant will fund a research project in which high school teachers will participate in optimism training and student achievement will be monitored to see if any relationship exists between teacher optimism and increased student performance. If students are better learners with optimistic teachers, optimism training could become part of teacher education programs, giving teachers some of the tools they need to reach every student, enabling them to make a difference more often.

Stand-alone lessons in positive psychology are also successful in fostering positive traits in students. The Penn Optimism Program, as described in Seligman et al.'s (1995) book *The Optimistic Child*, involves a stand-alone curriculum that teaches middle school students about changing pessimistic thinking into optimistic thinking. The success of the program is well documented, showing the aforementioned 100% decrease in student depression later in high school. Going even further, in 2003, a group of researchers from University of Pennsylvania and Swarthmore College developed and implemented a positive language arts curriculum for ninth graders, with funding coming from a multimillion-dollar Department of Education grant (lead investigators: Karen Reivich, University of Pennsylvania; Jane Gillham, Swarthmore College/University of Pennsylvania; Martin Seligman, University of Pennsylvania; Chris Peterson, University of Michigan; Sharon Parker, superintendent of Wallingford-Swarthmore School District). Working with teachers, the researchers have developed stand-alone lessons that will teach students about a wide range of positive psychology concepts—gratitude, forgiveness, altruism, flow, optimism—while challenging them to apply these principles to their lives. The hope of the project lies in creating more positive students but using a more light-handed approach. Instead of pulling students out of class to learn about positive thinking, positive thinking will become part of the day-to-day dialogue within the classroom. Positive psychology concepts will be seen less as an addition to the curriculum but rather an important enhancement. The results of this work will be explored throughout the students' high school careers.

A MORE POSITIVE HUMANITIES CURRICULUM

Teaching positive psychology will likely become infused not only in the introductory psychology curriculum but also throughout the disciplines that comprise liberal arts education. Traditional psychology is already infused into critical and analytical thinking about literature and history. Courses in both high school and college explore the psychological issues of characters and themes in literature. Scholars debate the psychological factors inherent in historical movements such as war, economic policy, and politics. If this level of analysis occurs with negative psychology concepts, imagine the possibilities of encouraging a discourse that spoke the language of positive psychology.

Changing an entire, established curriculum is a challenging endeavor. Those who teach the humanities often consider sacrosanct what is taught in it. Instructors wonder whether students can truly be well rounded if they haven't read *Death of a Salesman* by Arthur Miller (1998) or if they don't know when the Japanese bombed Pearl Harbor. Cultural literacy demands knowing about the tragedy of slavery and the sorrow of a man chasing a white whale. Not that this history and literature isn't important or good. An old adage warns about the dangers of forgetting the past.

Reading *The Scarlet Letter* by Nathaniel Hawthorne (1997) or *The Great Gatsby* by F. Scott Fitzgerald (1995) helps students understand the world of early American Puritans and the rebels of the Jazz Age. And certainly reinventing history to put a positive spin on events is more dangerous than learning only about the devastation of war. But governments and school systems across the country realize that students are not getting a balanced view of what life is all about. Drugs and violence pervade in the media and in school. Legislators in several states have enacted mandatory character education—specific instruction in character traits such as citizenship, patience, caring, and generosity. What students are not getting through the curriculum they must now get in addition to it.

Just as psychology needs a balance of the positive and negative, so does the humanities curriculum. The same questions that challenge introductory psychology educators also challenge liberal arts teachers. Does an effort to include the positive mean sacrificing the negative? How can more information be taught in an already full curriculum? And like the answers to a more positive introductory curriculum, so the answers to a more positive humanities curriculum fall into both infusion and stand-alone models.

Infusing the positive into the humanities is the most efficient means available. Fortunately, the literature that is so often associated with death, tragedy, and scandal also contains characters and themes that overcome, resist evil, and triumph. While the themes of tragedy are easy to spot and often well presented, the themes of triumph are also necessary to glean from literature. Why does Nick Carroway not turn out like Jay Gatsby? Does Biff Loman's optimism keep him from becoming like his father, Willy? How does Hester Prynne serve as a model of strength, courage, and virtue? History as well can be taught from a positive perspective as paragons of virtue are highlighted in each unit. George Washington's leadership, Harriet Tubman's courage, Dorothea Dix's compassion, Franklin Roosevelt's hardiness, and Jimmy Carter's humanitarianism can all be emphasized as examples of how the evils of history don't necessarily need to be repeated. These emphases can just as easily be included without throwing out the traditional curriculum.

CONCLUSION

Teaching psychology and teaching in general can be revolutionized by positive psychology. Psychology is a young science, and this emergence of positive psychology likely signals the next phase of psychology's development. Psychology has moved from a strict focus on *consciousness* to a strict focus on observable behavior to an emphasis on eclecticism. But all of these movements have centered on figuring out what makes people mentally ill. Now, as a new millennium dawns, psychology is addressing questions of how life can be lived well in addition to how to address mental illness. Psychology teachers are in a prime position to communicate this emphasis on balance and encourage a change in perspective not only in their own field but throughout the educational spectrum.

REFERENCES

Blair-Broeker, C. T., & Ernst, R. M. (2003). *Thinking about psychology.* New York: Worth.

Boman, P., & Yates, G. C. R. (2001). Optimism, hostility, and adjustment in the first year of high school. *British Journal of Educational Psychology, 71,* 401–411.

*Csikszentmihalyi, M. (1990). *Flow: The psychology of optimal experience.* New York: Harper-Collins.

Ernst, R. M., & Fineburg, A. C. (2003, April). Thinking about positive psychology. *Excellence in Teaching Essays, 5.* Distributed on the Psych-News listserv.

Fineburg, A. C. (2003). *Positive psychology: A seven-day unit plan for high school psychology.* Washington, DC: American Psychological Association.

Fitzgerald, F. S. (1995). *The great Gatsby.* New York: Scribner Paperback Fiction.

Griggs, R. A., & Mitchell, M. C. (2002). In search of psychology's classic core vocabulary. *Teaching of Psychology, 29,* 144–147.

Hawthorne, N. (1997). *The scarlet letter.* New York: International Thomson.

Maitland, L. L., Anderson, R. M., Blair-Broeker, C. T., Dean, C. J., Ernst, R. M., Halonen, J. S., et al. (2000). *National standards for the teaching of high school psychology.* Washington, DC: American Psychological Association.

Miller, A. (1998). *Death of a salesman.* New York: Penguin.

Myers, D. G. (2001). *Psychology: Myers in modules* (6th ed.). New York: Worth.

Scherer, M. E., & Kimmel, E. (1993, March) *Modifying teachers' attributions: An education-consultation approach.* Paper presented at the annual meeting of the Southeastern Psychological Association, Atlanta, Georgia.

*Seligman, M. E. P. (1998). *Learned optimism: How to change your mind and your life* (2nd ed.). New York: Pocket Books.

Seligman, M. E. P. (1999, July/August). Teaching positive psychology. *American Psychological Association Monitor, 30.* Retrieved April 24, 2003, from http://www.apa.org/monitor/julaug99/speaking.html.

Seligman, M. E. P. (2002, October). *Welcome to positive psychology.* Address to the First International Positive Psychology Summit, Washington, DC.

Seligman, M. E. P., & Csikszentmihalyi, M. (2000). Positive psychology: An introduction. *American Psychologist, 55,* 5–14.

*Seligman, M. E. P., Reivich, K., Jaycox, L., & Gillham, J. (1995). *The optimistic child: A proven program to safeguard children against depression and build lifelong resilience.* New York: Harper Perennial.

Smith, B. P., Hall, H. C., & Woolcock-Henry, C. (2000). The effects of gender and years of teaching experience on explanatory style of secondary vocational teachers. *Journal of Vocational Education Research, 25,* 21–33.

Snyder, C. R., & Clair, M. (1976). The effects of expected and obtained grades on teacher evaluation and attribution of performance. *Journal of Educational Psychology, 68,* 75–82.

*Snyder, C. R. (2000). The past and possible futures of hope. *Journal of Social and Clinical Psychology, 19,* 11–28.

VanderStoep, S. W., Fagerlin, A., & Feenstra, J. S. (2000). What do students remember from introductory psychology? *Teaching of Psychology, 27,* 89–92.

CHAPTER 13

Teaching Positive Psychology

NICK BAYLIS

I N SPRING 1999, at the University of Pennsylvania, Martin Seligman taught the first undergraduate lecture course in the emerging science of positive psychology. The Outstanding Syllabus Award (see Teaching Resources at www .positivepsychology.org) has recently become a pool for good practice in teaching this new subject at the high school and college level, and I offer this chapter as a complement to that resource. I'm assuming that you know what you wish to teach in terms of a syllabus and a reading list, and my role is simply to suggest some of the evidence-based strategies that might help students engage more effectively with our field.

In *Talented Teenagers: The Roots of Success and Failure,* Csikszentmihalyi, Rathunde, and Whalen (1997, p. 195) wrote: "We cannot expect our children to become truly educated until we ensure that teachers know not only how to provide information, but also how to spark the joy of learning." In this endeavor, educators might be glad to learn that Werner (1993) found that all of the resilient children of the Kauai Longitudinal Study who had successfully endured high risk, had at least one teacher who was a source of support. A positive psychologist is unusually well placed to be this support to his or her students.

Hence, the first part of this chapter introduces some key topics of positive psychology largely through facilitating their in-vivo deployment in classroom and homework assignments. The second part of the chapter addresses some lessons learned from experience. Finally, I consider positive psychology as one part of the science of well-being.

POSITIVE PSYCHOLOGY IN PRACTICE IN THE CLASSROOM

A host of potent psychological techniques and principles can be deployed to enhance the learning experience for student and teacher alike.

FOSTER CALM FOR CLEAR THINKING

Thinking is inhibited when emotions are high, so teaching strategies can benefit from having a reduction of emotional arousal as their precursor (Vass, 2003). When we are emotionally calm, we are more able to problem-solve, and one of the best ways to achieve this calm in ourselves is through strategic use of slow and gentle breathing combined with a systematic relaxation of the body (Griffin & Tyrrell, 2003; Levine, 2000). When our slow, deep exhalation is considerably longer than our slow deep inhalation, the parasympathetic nervous system is stimulated, bringing about the relaxation response. To this end, each class might begin with everyone sharing two minutes of a breathing and relaxation induction.

FOSTER INTRINSIC MOTIVATION

Deci and Ryan (1985) observed how people pursue an activity if they enjoy doing it and that people tend to enjoy what they can do well. In a study of Nobel laureates as well as other leading artists and scientists, there was a consensus that "enjoyment of work" was the characteristic most responsible for their success—more important than 32 other traits including creativity, competence, and breadth of knowledge (Griessman, 1987).

One means of fostering intrinsic enjoyment is through inviting students to play to their "signature strengths" when designing their own assignments (Seligman, 2003). Signature strengths are those half-dozen or so activities, mental or physical, that feel so good to do that it's almost as if you were made for them. These are the skills we learn quickly, yearn to do, and they energize rather than exhaust us. There is mounting support for the idea that giving full rein to such strengths would be a far more productive and personally rewarding strategy than focusing on trying to shore up your weaknesses. Indeed, Gardner advises that we ignore our weaknesses and simply ask, "In which ways can I use my own strengths in order to gain a competitive advantage in the domain in which I have chosen to work?" (Gardner, 1997, p. 148). However, The Gallup Organization interviewed *two million* successful people in 60 countries about how and when they work at their best, from which Buckingham and Clifton (2000) concluded that barely 20% of employees in large organizations said they got to play to their strengths each day; and yet that key factor turned out to be strongly correlated with staff turnover, sick days, accidents, productivity, and customer satisfaction.

FOSTER AN INTERNAL LOCUS OF CONTROL

An internal locus of control has long been regarded as a key factor creating resilience in the face of extreme adversity (Werner & Smith, 1982), of high achievement in the face of social disadvantage (Harrington & Boardman, 1997), and of happiness (Myers, 1992). Moreover, feeling that you have the power to carve your own future is a highly beneficial characteristic well supported by the empirical evidence of Gardner (1997) and Howe (1990a, 1990b, 1997, 1999). They argue that an individual of average learning ability is capable of acquiring virtually any exceptional skill or professional expertise. There is simply no evidence to support the commonly held belief that some innate lack of talent prevents us from achieving a high level of competence in math or languages, music or science, art or athletics. Yes, genes play a role in our abilities, but even with a lifetime's effort, we're unlikely to hit the upper limits of our inborn potential. No, we can't set out to produce works of genius, but we can, in principle, attain nationally competitive proficiency in most any field of endeavor, whether the guitar, speaking Italian as a second language, surgery . . . or positive psychology. It is the number of hours of practice that is the primary factor differentiating the levels of attainment; and as we see later, better still if that practice is "mindful" (Langer, 1989).

On a similar note, Gould (1984) cautions us not to attribute too much power to a notion of genetic determination: "Few tragedies can be more extensive than the stunting of life, few injustices deeper than the denial of an opportunity to strive or even to hope, by a limit imposed from without, but falsely identified as lying within" (Gould, 1984, pp. 28–29). Thus, in choosing their homework assignments, students can be reminded how "the expression of many genes is only possible given the right kind of experience" (Robertson, 2000, p. 281), so they should seek out environments and experiences that will be catalysts for their growth.

Foster Respect for Happiness

Far from being a luxury, happiness is a state that will greatly benefit well-being in many of life's arenas, not least of all learning (Hallowell, 2002). Putnam (2000) reminds us that "extracurricular activities and involvement in peer social networks are powerful predictors of college dropout rates and college success" (Putnam, 2000, p. 306). Moreover, happiness at college is strongly correlated with future well-being. A 15-year longitudinal study of many thousands of Australian teenagers in the 1980s and 1990s (Marks & Fleming, 1999) showed that their self-reported happiness as *teenagers* made future employment and higher incomes more likely as *adults*. This evidence is consistent with the work of Harker and Keltner (2001). A genuine smile (a so-called Duchenne smile), in contrast to a forced grin, of women college graduates in their yearbook photos was a good predictor of their future happiness several decades later. Moreover, the study of 180 Catholic nuns by Danner, Snowdon, and Friesen (2001) revealed that although the nuns lived all but identical lives in terms of diet and lifestyle, those who exuded happiness in their self-report diary at barely 20 years of age died a full 9 years older than their fellow nuns who had exuded *unhappiness* in their self-reports. There is mounting evidence, then, that happiness is a powerful preventative and remedial medicine, as well as better enabling us to thrive and flourish. Hence, putting happiness at the top of our to-do list makes very good sense, and the real challenge is to pursue excellence in our vocations *without* spoiling our life or the lives of those who love us.

In pursuit of greater happiness as a bedrock for better learning, Diener and Seligman (2002) found that the happiest 10% of 222 college undergraduates were distinguished from their "average" and "unhappy" peers by their rich and fulfilling social life. This suggests an appropriate class exercise may be for students to team up with one another to design field experiments based on the intervention implications that these studies have for their own college lifestyles.

Foster Mindfulness and Flow

In contrast to the rigid, habitual, automatic-pilot thinking that characterizes mindlessness, *mindfulness* is characterized by our ability to draw novel distinctions between one situation and another. It is a flexible state of mind in which we are very much focused in the present activity, but rather than simply focusing on something, we're deliberately varying our focus on that thing or activity and are open to new ways of doing and perceiving. To learn maximally from a situation, we not only must pay our undivided attention, but must also mentally manipulate the subject matter (Langer, 2002).

To help each student make connections to his or her existing passions and strengths and to mindfully manipulate and explore the concepts to be learned, we can ask of students what feature films most successfully exude some of the spirit of positive psychology, because movies are such a commonly shared part of the majority of young adult lives. In which films, for instance, is sheer *joie de vivre* conveyed; and in which films are specific aspects of strengths and virtues the focus of the drama? Check out the old-time classics such as *The 39 Steps, Casablanca, Singin' in the Rain, It's a Wonderful Life, To Kill a Mockingbird, What's Up Doc, The Producers,* and *The Italian Job* and, more recently, *Cyrano de Bergerac, Ferris Bueller's Day Off, Forrest Gump, Groundhog Day, Toy Story, Good Will Hunting, American Pie, American Beauty,* and *Goodbye Lenin.* And don't forget the award-winning documentaries, *Into the Arms of Strangers: Stories of the Kindertransport* and *Bowling for Columbine.*

This classroom exercise may promote flow as students recall and recount for the class their strongest responses to favorite films. Csikszentmihalyi et al. (1997) wrote: "A deeply involving flow experience usually happens when there are clear goals and when the person receives immediate and unambiguous feedback on the activity" (p. 14). This film challenge can lead to the question: Which psychologically positive works of art would *your* list include? For instance, is it hope that is embodied in Johnny Mercer's lyrics to Henry Mancini's melody for "Moon River" as sung by Audrey Hepburn in *Breakfast at Tiffany's?* Exercises such as this present opportunities to illustrate the themes of positive psychology with 30-second video-clips and musical extracts chosen by the students.

Another means of fostering mindfulness is the work by James Pawelski at Vanderbilt University (personal communication, July 2003) in his teaching of character development. He encourages his students to use "somatic awareness" exercises to illustrate the observation coined by Myers that "going through the *motions* can trigger the *emotions*" (1992, p. 105). Pawelski's students strategically experiment with their own physiology, such as willfully smiling and assuming a confident open posture to *initiate* positive feelings, rather than as a response to them (cf. Fredrickson, 2001).

Seligman (2003) recounts a similar form of experiential learning from his teaching experiences at the University of Pennsylvania: "Unlike the other courses I teach [in Positive Psychology classes], there are real world assignments that are meaningful and even life-changing" (Seligman, 2003, p. 72), and he cites the example of the student who suggested a "gratitude night" in which students, if they so chose, made a public statement of gratitude to someone special in their life. (The power of gratitude has been empirically explored by Emmons & McCullough, 2003.) We can extrapolate from Seligman's example to challenge our students to empirically explore within their own lives. What is the positive potential of altruism, or using a signature strength, or savoring a good memory, or turning off the TV to team up with other people in a rewarding activity? Students can report back the following week with a one-minute account to the class.

LESSONS LEARNED FROM EXPERIENCE

After three years offering lectures in positive psychology to Cambridge University's undergraduates, graduates, and faculty, I've finally begun to polish a few chestnuts.

CLARIFICATION OF COMMON MISUNDERSTANDINGS

I find it helpful to address from the outset some common sources of uncertainty and misunderstanding.

First, positive psychology is not uncommonly mistaken for *positive thinking*. However, while positive psychology is an entire field of scientific inquiry (see, e.g., this volume; Snyder & Lopez, 2002), positive thinking is merely a thinking technique probably most closely associated with Seligman's (1991) seminal work, *Learned Optimism*. I also note to my classes that positive psychology is a field in its own right and a distinctive approach to our science precisely because it has been so marginalized since World War II (Seligman & Csikszentmihalyi, 2000).

Second, as far as positive psychology is concerned, the absence of illness is not a sufficient criterion for health, even though the strongly prevailing medical model of health has acted as though it is. Health is an organism thriving and flourishing, not simply surviving. Hence, though the by-products of positive psychology may assist in the prevention and cure of illness and pathology, the field's defining goal is to help our *ordinary life* improve and excel. On this issue, I quote Chris Peterson (from his 2002 University of Michigan syllabus, available under Teaching Resources at www.positivepsychology.org):

> Positive psychology calls for as much focus on strength as on weakness, as much interest in building the best things in life as in repairing the worst, and as much attention to fulfilling the lives of healthy people as to healing the wounds of the distressed. The concern of psychology with human problems is understandable. It will not and should not be abandoned. Positive psychologists are merely saying that the psychology of the past sixty years is incomplete. But as simple as this proposal sounds, it demands a sea change in perspective. Psychologists interested in promoting human potential need to start with different assumptions and to pose different questions from their peers who assume a disease model.

PREVAILING OMISSIONS IN MAINSTREAM LITERATURE

As far back as 1937, at the birth of the Grant Study of Adult Development (Vaillant, 1977), two of its three founding fathers, Grant and Bock, observed: "Very few have thought it pertinent to make a systematic inquiry into the kinds of people who *are* well and *do* well" (Heath, 1945, p. 4). But even when there have been studies of distinctly positive lives, we should note that they, too, rarely find recognition in the mainstream literature. To establish for our students of positive psychology the current state of affairs, it is pertinent that we note how mainstream general texts on normal adolescent psychosocial development (e.g., Santrock, 1998; Schaffer, 1999; Seifert & Hoffnung, 1997) may frequently cite criminologists and psychiatrists studying mental disorder, but the same texts rarely, if ever, cite researchers who have studied high achievement (e.g., Csikszentmihalyi et al., 1997; Gardner, 1983; Howe, 1997; Vaillant, 1995).

One explanation for these long-held omissions is perhaps to be found in *Psychosocial Disorders in Young People* (Rutter & Smith, 1995), where the authors explain in their introduction: "Happiness and well-being isn't studied because it can't be defined well-enough." Positive psychologists would categorically disagree.

INSPIRATIONAL LIFE STORIES

"Self-analysis can serve as a basis for raising legitimate questions that require more systematic research," wrote Yale's director of clinical psychology, Jerome Singer (1975, p. 16). It is with respect to this proposition that I encourage students to consider what in their own lives has most intrigued them because their own most heartfelt life experiences can be wonderful sources of motivation and insight for their scientific explorations.

For example, it was through reflection on his up-bringing in the poverty of the postwar South Bronx, that led Philip G. Zimbardo to speculate that many of his family and friends may have been prisoners of a self-inhibiting time perspective, whereas his own forward-looking orientation was a means for growth and freedom (Zimbardo & Boyd, 1999). And it was only when the rookie philosophy graduate, Martin E. P. Seligman, walked into University of Pennsylvania research laboratories in 1964 that he recognized, in the learning behavior of dogs, something akin to his own father's stroke-induced helplessness (Seligman, 1991). George E. Vaillant was just 10 years old when *his* father died. At 13, George found himself fascinated while reading an alumni magazine about how members of his father's college class of 1922 were faring 25 years after graduation; this was to be a foreshadowing of George's own 36-year career studying adult life development (Vaillant, 2002; see also Vaillant, this volume). And finally, Robert J. Sternberg, who was told as a child that he had a low IQ, and was told as a college freshman that he had no aptitude for psychology (Sternberg, 1997). Even so, he was elected the 2003 president of the American Psychological Association and is recognized as a leading authority on research domains as diverse as intelligence, love, wisdom, and creativity.

By using the biographies and even the photos of these individuals as young men (drawn from their web sites), I try to illustrate for my students how each of these pioneers began their illustrious careers in the face of adversity, simply as very inquisitive and determined undergraduates (often sporting hilarious hairstyles).

To help restore a balance to the cumulative perspective of our psychological science (noting the omissions in the literature cited in the preceding section), I urge each new student to be the Lara Croft or Indiana Jones of positive psychology, blowing holes in the accepted wisdoms, as did the groundbreaking scientists just described. To bring this point to life, I quote from *Lessons Learned from a Life in Psychological Science* (Morgeson, Seligman, Sternberg, Taylor, & Manning, 1999):

WHO SAID: Good science is, by and large, courageous science. It is unpopular science. It is science that no one did before and thought should not be done.
ANSWER: Marty Seligman.
WHO SAID: As I have gotten older, I have spent successively more time thinking about the question and less about the answer. Namely, *is this a good question to ask in the first place?* Why should I or anyone else care what the answer is?
ANSWER: Bob Sternberg.

CONCLUSION: POSITIVE PSYCHOLOGY AS ONE PART OF THE SCIENCE OF WELL-BEING

By vocation and training, I am a positive psychologist engaged in the study and encouragement of lives that are happy, healthy, and helpful. However, in urging students to conceptually locate this movement in relation to other scientific approaches, I view this specialty as only one of *four* supporting pillars of a broader movement that my Cambridge colleagues and I have called *The Science of Well-Being* (Huppert, Keverne, & Baylis, in press). I define *well-being* as any positively healthy state in which people or things thrive and flourish, and its science is the cross-disciplinary study of life going well and incorporates under one holistic umbrella the life of the mind, body, social environment, and physical environment. Hence, the science of well-being is the rightful domain of not only psychologists, but also medics, sociologists, technologists, architects, economists, and many others—all those who can contribute to our insight into how individuals and their communities can best be helped to attain a vigorous and sustainable positive living, not simply the fragile absence of pathology. Seen in this context, positive psychology has been vanguard for the broader movement of the science of well-being.

REFERENCES

Buckingham, M., & Clifton, D. O. (2001). *Now, discover your strengths.* New York: Free Press.

Csikszentmihalyi, M. (1990). *Flow: The psychology of optimal experience.* New York: Harper-Collins.

Csikszentmihalyi, M., Rathunde, K., & Whalen, S. (1997). *Talented teenagers: The roots of success and failure.* New York: Cambridge University Press.

Danner, D. D., Snowdon, D. A., & Friesen, W. V. (2001). Positive emotions in early life and longevity: Findings from the nun study. *Journal of Personality and Social Psychology, 80,* 804–813.

Deci, E. L., & Ryan, R. M. (1985). *Intrinsic motivation and self-determination in human behavior.* New York: Plenum Press.

Diener, E., & Seligman, M. E. P. (2002). Very happy people. *Psychological Science, 13,* 81–84.

Emmons, R. A., & McCullough, M. E. (2003). Counting blessings versus burdens: An experimental investigation of gratitude and subjective well-being in daily life. *Journal of Personality and Social Psychology, 84,* 377–389.

Fredrickson, B. L. (2001). The role of positive emotions in positive psychology: The broaden-and-build theory of positive emotions. *American Psychologist, 56,* 218–226.

Gardner, H. (1983). *Frames of mind: The theory of multiple intelligences.* New York : Basic Books.

Gardner, H. (1997). *Extraordinary minds: Portraits of exceptional individuals and an examination of our extraordinariness.* London: Weidenfeld & Nicolson.

Gould, S. (1984). *The mismeasure of man.* New York: Norton.

Griessman, B. (1987). *The achievement factors.* New York: Dodd, Mead & Co.

Griffin, G., & Tyrrell, I. (2003). *Human givens: The new approach to emotional health and clear thinking.* Chalvington, England: Human Givens.

*Hallowell, E. (2002). *The childhood roots of adult happiness.* London: Vermillion.

Harker, L., & Keltner, D. (2001). Expressions of positive emotions in women's college yearbook pictures and their relationship to personality and life outcomes across adulthood. *Journal of Personality and Social Psychology, 80,* 112–124.

Harrington, C., & Boardman, S. (1997). *Paths to success: Beating the odds in American society.* Cambridge, MA: Harvard University Press.

Heath, C. W. (1945). *What people are.* Cambridge, MA: Harvard University Press.

Howe, M. J. A. (1990a). *The development of exceptional abilities and talents.* Leicester, England: British Psychological Society.

Howe, M. J. A. (1990b). *The origins of exceptional abilities.* Oxford, England: Blackwell.

Howe, M. J. A. (1997). *IQ in question: The truth about intelligence.* London: Routledge.

*Howe, M. J. A. (1999). *Genius explained.* Cambridge, England: Cambridge University Press.

*Huppert, F. A., Keverne, E. B., & Baylis, N. V. K. (in press). *Philosophical transactions of the Royal Society: The science of well-being.* London: The Royal Society.

Langer, E. (1989). *Mindfulness.* Reading, MA: Addison-Wesley.

Langer, E. (2002). Well-being: Mindfulness versus positive evaluation. In C. R. Snyder & S. J. Lopez (Eds.), *Handbook of positive psychology* (pp. 214–230). New York: Oxford University Press.

Levine, M. (2000). *The positive psychology of Buddhism and yoga.* Mahwah, NJ: Erlbaum.

Marks, G. N., & Fleming, N. (1999). Influences and consequences of well-being among Australian young people: 1980–1995. *Social Indicators Research, 46,* 301–323.

Morgeson, F., Seligman, M., Sternberg, R., Taylor, S., & Manning, C. (1999). Lessons learned from a life in psychological science. *American Psychologist, 54,* 106–116.

Myers, D. G. (1992). *The pursuit of happiness.* New York: Basic Books.

Putnam, R. D. (2000). *Bowling alone: The collapse and revival of American community.* New York: Simon & Schuster.

Robertson, I. (2000). *Mind sculpture.* London: Bantam Books.

Rutter, M., & Smith, D. (1995). *Psychosocial disorders in young people: Time trends and their causes.* Chichester, England: Wiley.

Santrock, J. (1998). *Adolescence.* Boston: McGraw-Hill.

Schaffer, D. (1999). *Childhood and adolescence.* New York: Brooks/Cole.

Seifert, K. L., & Hoffnung, R. J. (1997). *Childhood and development.* Boston: Houghton Mifflin.

Seligman, M. E. P. (1991). *Learned optimism.* New York: Alfred A. Knopf.

Seligman, M. E. P. (2003). *Authentic happiness* (2nd ed.). London: Nicholas Brealey.

Seligman, M. E. P., & Csikszentmihalyi, M. (2000). Positive psychology: An introduction. *American Psychologist, 55,* 5–14.

Singer, J. (1975). *Daydreaming and fantasy.* New York: Oxford University Press.

Snyder, C. R., & Lopez, S. J. (Eds.). (2002). *Handbook of positive psychology.* New York: Oxford University Press.

*Sternberg, R. J. (1997). *Successful intelligence.* New York: Plume.

Vaillant, G. E. (1977). *Adaptation to life.* Cambridge, MA: Harvard University Press.

Vaillant, G. E. (1995). *Adaptation to life* (2nd ed.). Cambridge, MA: Harvard University Press.

*Vaillant, G. E. (2002). *Aging well: Surprising guideposts to a happier life from the landmark Harvard Study of Adult Development.* Boston: Little, Brown.

Vass, A. (2003). Human Givens and education. In J. Griffin & I. Tyrrell (Eds.), *Human Givens: A new approach to emotional health and clear thinking* (pp. 391–400). Chalvington, England: Human Givens.

Werner, E. E. (1993). Risk, resilience and recovery: Perspectives from the Kauai Longitudinal Study. *Development and Psychopathology, 5,* 503–515.

Werner, E. E., & Smith, R. (1982). *Vulnerable but invincible: A longitudinal study of resilient children and youth.* New York: McGraw-Hill.

*Zimbardo, P. G., & Boyd, J. N. (1999). Putting time in perspective: A valid, reliable individual-differences metric. *Journal of Personality and Social Psychology, 77,* 1271–1288.

CHAPTER 14

Rescuing Our Heroes: Positive Perspectives on Upward Comparisons in Relationships, Education, and Work

MICHAEL A. COHN

S TUDENTS OF THE science of happiness and fulfillment are natural supporters of the movement against consumer culture and unchecked materialism. We are familiar with the evidence that higher salaries, bigger cars, and more *stuff* are unlikely to produce lasting fulfillment and that the real enemy is dissatisfaction itself. Positive psychology authors variously blame our dissatisfaction on envy of other people (Myers, 1992, pp. 56–67) or of wealthier nations (Diener, 2000), unrealistic expectations (Parducci, 1995), extrinsically motivated work (Csikszentmihalyi, 1990), and failure to appreciate what we already have (Seligman, 2002). All approach the same conclusion: Upward comparisons, those involving people who are superior to us, give rise to dissatisfaction and greed. We should instead focus on downward comparisons to foster reasonable expectations and a sense of gratitude.

But if that were the whole story, we would also be compelled to throw out decades of research on mentoring, modeling, and teaching, all of which involve setting ourselves alongside a superior other. There are nuances differentiating jealousy and inferiority from admiration and inspiration—nuances these authors seem to understand implicitly. Their popular works make liberal use of anecdotes about individuals who put positive psychological concepts into practice, and the *Values In Action (VIA) Classification of Strengths* being created by Peterson and Seligman (2003b) goes so far as to cite famous exemplars of each strength in its formal definitions.

What makes the difference? How can we meet knowledge of our own shortcomings with interest, efficacy, and even excitement? How can we create social structures that engender beneficial comparisons and do away with ones that turn us against one another? In this chapter, I briefly review past research on social comparisons and then use this research to envision ways in which we can integrate beneficial upward comparisons into our thoughts, our relationships, and the systems in which we live and work.

SOCIAL COMPARISON RESEARCH

In his early and hugely influential paper, Festinger (1954) theorized that social comparison was fundamentally about information and served as a second-best way of assessing our skill when objective tests were not available. Subsequent research has borne out some of his theorems regarding social comparison and social group cohesion, but has also demonstrated that social comparison information is compelling in itself. People prefer to learn their standing relative to others even when only objective performance is relevant (reviewed in Wood & Wilson, 2002). However, both of these views focus on social comparison as a useful source of information about an individual's performance, not merely a way of changing his or her self-esteem.

The interaction between affect and information-seeking was conceptualized by Brickman and Bulman (1977) as a painful dilemma: When we want to learn how we might improve, we must swallow the bitter pill of our own inferiority; when we want to enhance our self-esteem, we must pay the price of foregoing useful information. However, we can escape this double bind as long as we believe that we are capable of remedying the situation. Lockwood and Kunda (1997) demonstrated that when students were exposed to a profile of a graduating senior who was superior to them in achievement and popularity, the self-esteem of graduating seniors declined, but the self-esteem of first-year students, who could see such achievements in their future, increased. Other studies (Buunk & Brenninkinmeijer, 2001; Buunk, Ybema, Gibbons, & Ipenburg, 2001) have similarly demonstrated that *attainability* is a crucial element of positive upward comparisons.

Attainability, however, can cut both ways. If the similarity of an inferior target* becomes salient, the downward comparison can result in reduced self-esteem and increased anxiety (Buunk, Taylor, Collins, VanYperen, & Dakof, 1990). Instead of thinking, "It could be worse," subjects think, "It could *get* worse"—the existence of someone similar to themselves in an undesirable position indicates that they, too, could end up there. In addition to direction, then, comparisons can be categorized into *contrasts* and *assimilations*. Contrasts naturally pair with downward comparisons in which we want to emphasize our difference from the target, while assimilation is for upward comparisons in which we emphasize our ability to be like the target. Circumstances may push us toward less-preferred forms of comparison, however, giving rise to feelings of inferiority or anxiety (see Figure 14.1).

Taylor and Lobel (1989) uncovered exactly this asymmetry in their study of social comparisons by women with breast cancer. Downward comparisons were generally contrasts, while upward comparisons were what they termed contacts. Subjects appreciated contact with their upward comparison targets but had no desire to meet their targets of downward comparison on either physical health or coping; they wanted just enough information to know that they were doing comparatively well. Generally, downward comparison tends to function as an affect-regulation strategy

---

* The person making a social comparison is referred to as the *subject*, and the person to whom they compare themselves as the *target*.

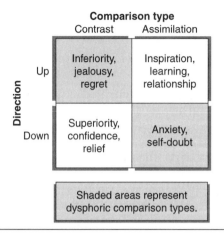

Figure 14.1 Upward Assimilation, Downward Contrast

(e.g., Buunk et al., 1990; Friend & Gilbert, 1973; Wills, 1981) and involves little personal concern with its targets. In contrast, women in Taylor & Lobel's study described their upward comparison targets as sources of inspiration and hope, as well as practical social support.

Contact with upward comparison targets is not just a form of social support. Research on comparisons involving *self-improvement* goals indicates that we can enter into a comparison not for the purpose of judging ourselves or the target, but for the purpose of *observing* the target to learn how we can improve our own skills (Lockwood, Jordan, & Kunda, 2002; Taylor, Neter, & Wayment, 1995). Rather than an imagined or metaphorical assimilation, we may literally be taking their qualities into ourselves.

Another route to affectively positive upward comparisons involves reducing the significance of the domain. There is little cost in learning that we are not good at something we never cared about to begin with, although there may be significant benefits: When members of our in-group do well, we can feel good about our association with them, a phenomenon referred to as "reflected glory"* (Major, Sciacchitano, & Crocker, 1993; Tesser, Millar, & Moore, 1988). Our own self-image begins to overlap with the image of the group (as in Brewer, 1991). Thus, reflected glory may also be seen as a form of assimilation. This effect is diminished if the subject feels a sense of competition with the target, replacing reflected glory with jealousy or negative self-focus.

The factors contributing to self-improving upward comparisons are drawn together by the mutability-by-distinctiveness model (Stapel & Koomen, 2000). Information about a comparison target is assimilated into the self if two conditions are met:

1. The subject's self-image is malleable rather than fixed (high versus low mutability).

---

*More charitably, this behavior might be thought of as "vicarious joy." If we consider compassion (literally, "shared suffering") is a virtue, there is no reason to denigrate its hedonically-positive counterpart.

2. The subject attends to the relevant *qualities* of the target, rather than to the target as an individual (low versus high distinctiveness).

When self-mutability is high and target distinctiveness is low, information about the target's performance can be incorporated into the subject's own self-image. This can give rise to inspiration and learning with upward comparisons or insecurity and negative influence with downward comparisons. If the two conditions are not met, comparisons are more like contrasts, leading to a judgment of the subject's standing compared to the target's. Stapel and Koomen (2000) demonstrated this by manipulating mutability of self and perceived distinctiveness of others using a variety of priming tasks; they also treated mutability as a stable personal trait using Dweck's (1999) model of entity and incremental theories.

POSITIVE UPWARD COMPARISONS

There is ample evidence that positive psychology's goals of fostering optimism, resilience, and adaptive ways of relating to the world can be served by attending to individuals who outperform us in some way. Upward comparisons are a valuable resource for learning about ourselves, improving our performance, and receiving social support from others who are well situated to offer it. Additionally, because naturalistic surveys indicate that social comparison is ubiquitous (Buunk et al., 1990; Wheeler & Miyake, 1992) and potentially involuntary (Kalma, 1991; Wood & Wilson, 2002), it is a fertile area for interventions to improve day-to-day coping and emotional experience across many, if not all, populations.

Simply avoiding the dangers of upward comparison is easy: We should attend only to domains that are unimportant to us and only to targets who differ from us enough that they are not valid sources of information about our own potential. Unfortunately, this latter strategy ends up warning against mentorship, role modeling, Taylor and Lobel's (1989) "upward contacts," and any other situation in which we might benefit from associating with people to whom we are inferior. Attending conferences would be incredibly dangerous! In reality, comparison targets that are superior in our particular field of interest are the ones who have the most to offer us. To pursue our goals of fostering skills and increasing fulfillment across the life span, we need to delve into the other side of social comparison: the side that is personally relevant, emotionally risky, and potentially beneficial.

Upward comparisons are rewarding when we focus on another's performance—on the information contained in his or her superior outcomes—and assimilate these observations into ourselves. I next discuss the attitudes and circumstances that help us make assimilation comparisons and suggest techniques that can help bring these conditions about. I then focus on specific domains of life such as work, school, and personal relationships and discuss more systematic ways in which we can reduce the threat and increase the pleasure, excitement, and informational value of upward comparisons.

ELEMENTS OF POSITIVE UPWARD COMPARISON

Our attentional focus and initial attitude during a comparison can make the difference between contrast and assimilation, between an affective experience and an informative one, and between humiliation and resilience. I have condensed from the literature four elements that contribute to positive upward comparisons: a mutable self-image, a detailed and nuanced understanding of the comparison target, an appropriate choice of comparisons, and an appropriate choice of valued domains.

Mutable Self-Image   For upward comparison to be a resource for change, persons making the comparison need to believe that they are able to change. Without a mutable self-image, we can respond to upward comparisons only by feeling irremediably inferior or by defensively discounting the domain or the target. The association between mutability and positive response to challenge has been extensively researched by Carol Dweck, using the rubric of entity and incremental theories of intelligence (reviewed in Dweck, 1999). People holding entity theories believe that traits such as intelligence, morality, and sociability are difficult or impossible to change and, consequentially, that an individual's performance on a wide range of tasks is immutably constrained to a restricted range. Incremental theorists believe that traits emerge from experience and practice and that performance can usually be improved by effort. Individuals who make effort attributions show more resilience in the face of failure than those making innate-ability attributions (Anderson & Jennings, 1980; Fowler & Peterson, 1981). This includes "failure" relative to your peers and is similar to learning that a close other presents an upward comparison target. Indeed, Stapel and Koomen (2000) found that Dweck's test of incremental theories strongly predicted an assimilation response to an upward comparison.

An incremental theory of intelligence is clearly beneficial if you want to receive an initially negative piece of information (i.e., that you could be doing better) and use it as a spur to improvement. But are theories of intelligence amenable to intentional change? Dweck's research (e.g., 1999) has generated robust and highly replicated effects simply by telling subjects about one of the two theories, either indirectly through stories or directly through faked psychology journal articles. It appears, then, that people wishing to make better use of superior peers can start with a relatively simple program of self-education. Research on grade school, middle school, and college students shows that brief, limited interventions aimed at altering self-theories can have effects on both theory and academic outcomes over the following year (Andrews & Debus, 1978; J. Aronson, Fried, & Good, 2002; Blackwell, Dweck, & Trzesniewski, 2003). Research in cognitive therapy has demonstrated even longer term change in related constructs such as pessimistic attribution style and black-and-white thinking (Segal, Gemar, & Williams, 1999; Teasdale et al., 2001; Whisman, 1993). In addition to education focusing explicitly on self-theories, techniques developed in clinical psychology to help clients dispute the assumption of an immutable (and failed) self may be of use in helping us to imagine ourselves becoming like our friends, role models, and heroes.

Understanding of Target   A mutable self-image is helpful only if the target of an upward comparison offers plausible ways in which to change. An affective, judgmental comparison can be made simply by noting that the target differs on some concrete outcome (e.g., number of cars owned, number of pounds lifted, number of articles published), but an informational comparison requires observing *how* they succeeded. Thus, the optimal comparison is with an individual whom we know well and whom we have ample opportunity to observe in action.

Lockwood and Kunda (1997) speculated that the early results showing negative effects for upward comparison were a result of paradigms in which subjects were told only that an unknown individual had outperformed them. The effect has been reversed when subjects have been given enough information about the comparison target to feel that they can learn from them or at least assess the target's validity as a benchmark for the self. In the mutability-by-distinctiveness paradigm, closeness serves to reduce the other's distinctness. The other seems less like a closed black box and more like an understandable person.

Finally, choosing a close other as a comparison target maximizes the opportunities for social contact. We have not only more opportunities to observe the target's behavior but also more opportunities for personal conversation, direct inspiration, and the giving and receiving of support.

Choice of Comparisons　This element of comparison encompasses both the choice of a comparison target and the choice of a measure for comparison. Choosing a target whose circumstances are too similar to ours offers us nothing to target for improvement, while choosing one who is too different makes the comparison irrelevant. Both extremes violate the same principle: We must be able to see some way of moving from our present state to the state of the target.

The need for mobility is also expressed in our choice of a measure for comparison. Some measures inherently encourage contrast and differentiation, while others are information-rich and encourage improvement. Myers (1992, 2000), Diener (2000), and other positive psychology authors may depict upward comparison as invidious and dissatisfying largely because their paradigmatic comparison dimensions are wealth, status, and possessions, ones that are not compatible with a self-improvement goal. Imagine a salesperson who wants to become better at her job. She feels capable of improving her skills and has identified a close coworker with whom to compare herself. However, if the only comparison information she attends to is that her colleague makes more money than she does, she will not be able to have a positive upward comparison experience. Salary is a decontextualized quantity, carrying no information about *how* her coworker came to earn that amount. The comparison provides a failure experience but no information as to the cause, context, or remediability of the failure. Even a dyed-in-the-wool incremental theorist, for whom every setback is a new challenge, would be hard pressed not to be discouraged.

Better comparisons come with information. If our salesperson ignores her colleague's superior outcomes and instead focuses on single elements of the colleague's technique, such as choice of clients, language, and persuasive techniques, she can emulate the colleague, request practical advice, and aspire to similar achievements. This strategy is more complex in that observations of behavior are richer than observations of single outcome measures, but it is also simpler in that each element of the target's behavior offers a clear goal to work towards, whereas earnings are determined by many factors, ground up and mashed together so that reconstructing useful information is all but impossible.

This does not suggest that overall outcomes such as salary are unimportant. If the salesperson hadn't had any overall measure of success, she might not have been able to tell that her coworker was surpassing her in some ways. It is important, however, to focus on the steps leading to an outcome rather than the outcome itself.

Choice of Domains　I have discussed different types of comparison measures, but there are also differences in the underlying qualities we can choose to measure. On a personal level, the domain should be one in which we are interested and motivated to achieve—otherwise, all the self-improvement information in the world won't lead us to improve.

Intrinsically, some domains also involve more room for improvement than others. This is important because while we can habituate to many pleasures (Parducci, 1995)—the "hedonic treadmill" concept, which is often blamed for constant dissatisfaction and acquisitiveness (e.g., Seligman, 2002, pp. 47–50) becoming accustomed to a given level of achievement is not a difficulty if higher levels of achievement are always just within our reach. We would do well to choose to value domains in which there is a very wide range of possible skill levels and a great deal of progress to be made before effort begins to produce diminishing returns. This is the type of activity Csikszentmihalyi (1990, 1997) endorses as producing *flow*, a state of intense interest in which our ever-growing skills can be matched with ever-increasing challenges. And, because flow is achieved through effort and immersion rather than an activity's ultimate outcome, it also helps protect us against any impulse to competition we may feel when observing someone who is consistently superior to us.

This lack of concern with evaluation shifts attention away from scores, salaries, and other uninformative measures and onto direct observation of performance. Meanwhile, the reduced focus on self (which more imaginative authors [e.g., Weil, 1972] have gone so far as to refer to as "ego-loss") readies us to assimilate information about others rather than seeing ourselves and them as distinct and competing entities—even if we actually are in conflict. This adds up to a competitive advantage to ignoring competition and may be one of the reasons academics and businesspeople who demonstrate little interest in zero-sum competition may outperform colleagues who focus highly on it (Helmreich, Beane, Licker, & Spence, 1978).

INTRAPSYCHIC TECHNIQUES FOR POSITIVE UPWARD COMPARISON

This section discusses techniques for positive upward comparison that individuals can use covertly, at the moment a comparison situation arises, and across a variety of circumstances. They include selective attention to adaptive aspects of the situation, using priming and automatic behavior as an alternative to conscious comparison, distinguishing between teachers and role models or heroes, and making comparisons with individuals who differ from the self on important aspects of identity. All of these tools can be taught and rehearsed in psychotherapy, but in the spirit of using our knowledge to improve ordinary life as well as heal sickness, I present them in a more general context.

Salience Manipulation   This technique amounts to performing the experimental manipulations described previously. While subjects generally have some manipulation-independent orientation on the variables affecting comparison outcome (Buunk & Brenninkinmeijer, 2001; Lockwood et al., 2002; Stapel & Koomen, 2000), relatively simple instructional manipulations of attentional focus, self-concept, or cognitive set are able to generate significant effects (e.g., Lockwood & Kunda, 1999; Mussweiler, 2001; Oyserman, Gant, & Ager, 1995). An individual who is preparing to observe a superior target would be advised to focus on similarities between them that make the target's experience and skills relevant but on differences that make the target's state still attainable. During the observation, it is better not to focus on the target at all, but on his or her actions. To whatever extent the subject engages in internal monologue, he or she can reinforce this focus by practicing technique-observations such as, "That was a good answer to that question," rather than person-observations such as, "She answered that question well." Furthermore, he or she can search for specific and informative elements of the technique to think about. For example, "That was a *good* answer to that question" is a less useful observation than "That answer *did a good job of reconciling different perspectives* on that question." Technique-focused and information-rich observations give us the material we need to make upward comparisons with a sense of competence, hope, and inspiration.

Priming   The apparent difficulty of retrospectively reporting day-to-day episodes of social comparison (Wood & Wilson, 2002) suggests that comparison may sometimes be involuntary and automatic (although it appears easier to report them immediately after they occur [Wheeler & Miyake, 1992]). The possibility of an automatic and efficient faculty for comparison is supported by evolutionary accounts of the origins of comparison (P. Gilbert, Price, & Allen, 1995) and by research showing that interpersonal dominance judgments can be made nearly instantaneously (Kalma, 1991). Furthermore, the literature on priming and behavioral automaticity suggests that subtle exposure to comparison targets can cause substantial assimilation of their traits (Bargh, Chen, & Burrows, 1996; Dijksterhuis & van Knippenberg, 1998), attitudes (Kawakami, Dovidio, & Dijksterhuis, 2003), and behaviors (Chartrand & Bargh, 1998). For example, experimental participants asked to think about professors' activities and hobbies showed better intellectual performance than participants asked to think about soccer hooligans, and participants completing a scrambled-sentence task with words relating to the elderly walked more slowly when leaving the lab.

These results show intriguing parallels to our guidelines for upward comparisons: They focus on the relevant behavior rather than on a distinct target, they avoid activating any self-concept that might reduce mutability, and they use ambiguous stimuli that can be interpreted by the subject to avoid irrelevance or unattainability. Furthermore, they go beyond many explicit social-comparison studies in that they demonstrate concrete effects on performance-relevant behavior, rather than merely changing responses on a self-report measure.

Participants in these experiments do not typically report awareness of the manipulation's purpose or its effect. Practically speaking, however, it is unlikely that people can prime themselves without their own awareness. But we may be able to access a similar attentive-but-unaware state when we are engaged in absorbing activities. The task-focus and lack of self-consciousness reported by individuals experiencing flow states (Csikszentmihalyi, 1990) resemble the state of the priming subjects, in that they are both responding to material they are not deliberately and effortfully processing. It may well be that flow activities are also particularly good times to observe superior targets because the idea of a distinct self is in the background, and the focus on performance-related activities undermines any observation of the target as a distinct other. This suggests that any activity performed in a group, whether it be sports, negotiations, collaborative problem solving, or simple conversation, will automatically lead to assimilation as long as it is sufficiently absorbing. Noncompetitive activities are probably superior because they remove any intrusive negative evaluation of others' success.

We can also evoke targets for this type of comparison symbolically, by exposing ourselves to indirectly-related stimuli (as when Bargh et al. [1996] used words like "wise" and "Florida" to evoke the concept of elderly people), or by appropriating aspects of the target's speech or dress.

It appears that the beneficial aspects of upward comparison (learning and inspiration) can occur peripherally and automatically, whereas the negative aspects require conscious attention and self-focus. Thus, we can see engagement and interest in valued tasks as a tool for positive upward comparison and an antidote to jealousy and dysphoria. While it seems a truism that we are likely to become better at whatever we do by giving it our full attention, this suggests that social comparison can be an integral part of improvement—and that one of the most effective ways to perform positive upward comparisons involves trying not to make them at all.

Distinguishing Role Models from Teachers Sometimes too much information can spoil a good assimilation. This occurs when the general idea or aesthetic of our target is inspiring, but the details cause a focus on differences and difficulties (Buunk & Brenninkinmeijer, 2001; Lockwood & Kunda, 1999). This chapter primarily discusses targets we can learn from and interact with, but we should also acknowledge the value of heroes and role models. Comparisons with inspiring-but-distant individuals work when the domain is general and affective, but not when we're trying to iron out details of performance. A young basketball player might keep a poster of Michael Jordan on her wall, but concrete improvement will come from interacting with her teammates. This is not to say that the same target can never serve both roles; a young writer who idolizes Virginia Woolf could also learn specific literary techniques by reading her books.

Incommensurate Comparisons We benefit from being around those who are superior to us, but how do they feel about this arrangement? People who are downward comparison targets may not be desirable company if they are perceived as envious (Brickman & Bulman, 1977; Exline & Lobel, 2001) or if they evoke our own fears of failure (Buunk et al., 1990). This difficulty can be remedied if we learn to make asymmetric comparisons, so that our upward targets do not necessarily see us as downward targets. For the cancer patients in Taylor and Lobel's (1989) study, upward contacts with cancer survivors may have worked out because the patients saw cancer status as a relevant comparison dimension, while individuals who had recovered did not. In fact, if a recovered individual were able to admire the courage or resilience of a cancer patient, each might come to see the other as an upward contact. The idea that specifically focusing on virtues can help us make these mutual upward comparisons is discussed further in the section on comparisons in close relationships.

UPWARD COMPARISONS IN LEARNING, WORK, AND LOVE

In this section, we take the principles of positive upward comparison and carry them into the social situations that we move through every day. I discuss ways to implement the elements of positive upward comparisons in school, in work, and among friends and family.

UPWARD COMPARISON IN SCHOOL

From preschool to college, we are met with a continuous stream of assessment experiences, opportunities for learning, and relevant peers with whom to compare ourselves in both directions. Moreover, school is a relatively controlled environment in which interventions or changes in organization can have a powerful and pervasive effect. Academics is a valuable domain in which to learn positive social comparison techniques not only because of its intrinsic value but also because it is the source of much of our early socialization, providing a test bed in which to learn the cognitive strategies we will use elsewhere in life.

Maintaining a Mutable Self-Image   Dweck's (1999) work on entity and incremental self-theories discussed earlier mostly involved academic achievement and is directly relevant to this discussion. Intuitively, we can see how people who believe that the self is unchangeable would see little value in attempting to assimilate the qualities of others, and there is evidence that they are less willing to try to improve their performance in general (Anderson & Jennings, 1980; Fowler & Peterson, 1981).

To allow students to learn from one another, we should encourage them to see their abilities as fluid rather than fixed. This may be challenging in an environment built around grades, standardized tests, and grouping students by ability level (ultimately leading to grouping by opportunities for higher education). Teachers can make a substantial difference by avoiding ability praise ("You're very smart!") and substituting effort praise ("You worked very hard on that!") or specific feedback about a student's techniques and strategies ("You did a good job of organizing that paper!") (Dweck, 1999). Grades should also be rendered less final by offering students opportunities to correct past assignments and review poorly learned material (see Fineburg, this volume). Finally, students should be exposed to the success stories of peers who initially struggled with a class but went on to master it.

Deeply Understanding the Target   Students will not be able to learn from their peers unless they know what they are doing and how they're doing it. This, too, is somewhat incompatible with traditional teaching arrangements: When the teacher is lecturing and the students are working independently, the variety of techniques and types of understanding in the classroom are camouflaged. A long-lived and robust body of research suggests that cooperative and small-group learning strategies are more effective than individual work or competition, in groups ranging from grade-schoolers to college undergraduates (for meta-analyses, see D. W. Johnson, Maruyama, Johnson, & Nelson, 1981; Springer, Stanne, & Donovan, 1999). Students should be encouraged to share their knowledge and ideas with one another. Another option is for the teacher to identify students who understand the material and ask them to explain some part of it to the class. This technique exploits the value of similarity: Students can assimilate the self-image of a peer who understands the material, whereas the self-image of a grown-up is more incongruous. A student presenter may also restate the material in a way that is more accessible to the students because of their similar age, culture, and cognitive level. This goes beyond a diffuse inspiration effect to make the student a powerful upward contact as well.

In addition to being allowed to observe their peers' techniques, students can benefit from getting to know one another in a more general sense. Greater knowledge about a comparison target helps prevent common attribution errors (D. Gilbert & Malone, 1995) and may also help prevent contrast comparisons in cases where the subject is inclined to believe that the target belongs to some distinct and unattainable category (e.g., nerd, genius, Asian). Competitive situations have been found to reduce this kind of detailed knowledge (Tjosvold, Johnson, & Johnson, 1984) and to encourage students to attribute their successes and others' failures to immutable personal characteristics (Stephan, Kennedy, & Aronson, 1977). Competition in general reduces opportunities to make detailed comparisons with others (Kohn, 1992), while students are able and willing to learn from peers who outperform them (and those peers are able and willing to make information about themselves available) when the classroom involves some degree of cooperation. R. T. Johnson and Johnson (1994) note that competition may be beneficial when students are in teams and can learn from and cohere with their teammates. The same benefits come from purely cooperative work, in which small groups of students share goals and perceive one another's success as positively correlated (Johnson & Johnson and E. Aronson & Patnoe [1997] offer detailed suggestions for creating these situations). In sum, friendship and social contact make students more likely to have the detailed knowledge of one another, which is vital to informationally useful comparisons.

These techniques do have the potential to backfire if a student chosen as a comparison target does have knowledge or cognitive abilities that are beyond the grasp of his or her classmates. Teachers must take care to ensure that the comparison targets they select represent *attainable* comparisons. Extremely bright students can still provide assistance in teaching and explaining material, but they may not provide an appropriate basis on which to set their classmates' proximate goals. It may also be that while this argument calls for some degree of heterogeneity in the classroom, a coarse degree of ability separation is also beneficial, especially if it offers the brighter students more opportunities to make beneficial upward comparisons.

Appropriate Choice of Comparison Measure   This is the area in which standard education practices fail most starkly. Students can most readily compare their success with others based on their grades, which are ubiquitous in teachers' and parents' exhortations, in every calculation of their academic success, and in large bold print at the top of every assignment returned. Yet, grades are exactly the kind of information-poor measure that encourages contrast. There's nothing else we can do with them. It is possible that students can be inspired by seeing others like them succeed, and there is evidence that comparing grades with classmates whose grades are slightly superior leads to better future performance (Huguet, Dumas, Monteil, & Genestoux, 2001). However, grades still offer no opportunities for students to learn from or be helped by others who outperform them. Moreover, students who receive grades much higher than their classmates may still evoke a contrast response, even if they did so by using habits or strategies that could allow their classmates to perform at a similar level.

Teachers and students should both attempt to frame upward comparisons in a more informative fashion. A simple change would be to honor students who put forth extreme effort, participate well in class, study efficiently, are helpful to their peers, or otherwise excel in a manner that can be explained and inculcated in others. Similarly, the concept of an *honor roll* based solely on grades could be replaced by rewarding students for specific achievements or special projects to reduce the impression that being on the honor roll indicates some irreducible quality of intelligence. The goal is not to eliminate rewards for success, for all students still have the same ultimate goal of developing intellectually and doing well at their work. Instrumentally, however, this goal is best served by studying the details of high achievement rather than by rewarding it in an abstract and holistic sense.

Appropriate Choice of Comparison Domain   In a broad sense, students have little choice in deciding whether to value academic achievement. The penalties, both intrinsic and socially imposed, for doing otherwise are high—although the fact that many children still choose to disengage from school should discourage us from relying on that. The goal of making academic success a valued and upward-comparison-friendly domain requires us to think broadly about how learning is structured.

The most useful change we can make may be to reduce or eliminate fear in the classroom. The perceived negative consequences of poor performance can be reduced by encouraging an incremental theory of intelligence, as discussed previously. This is a direct prerequisite for upward comparison because of the evidence that fear of negative evaluation disposes people toward prevention goals and affect-regulating downward comparisons rather than potentially educational upward comparisons (Friend & Gilbert, 1973; Lockwood et al., 2002). Additionally, anxiety has been shown to narrow our available range of thoughts and actions, whereas positive emotions produce a cognitive state more conducive to mental and behavioral flexibility (Losada, 1999) and ultimate growth (Fredrickson, 2001). The result is that students who fear losing face or looking dumb if they show weakness are more likely to persevere with ineffective courses of action and less likely to seek contact with those who can help them.

We also need to take responsibility for the actual negative consequences of poor performance. Students may be completely justified in fearing punishment or reduced future prospects if they receive a poor grade, and this, too, can lead to maladaptive anxiety-driven responses. This provides another reason for us to make grades and evaluations as preliminary and changeable as possible. Students should be able to see a grade as helpful feedback, not as a final and potentially damning judgment.

UPWARD COMPARISON IN WORK

As adults, we move from school into the less arbitrary and (if we are fortunate) more intrinsically valued domain of work. Many of the personal issues involved in succeeding at work resemble those facing students, but the shared goals of one's workplace and the financial consequences of success or failure present new challenges as well.

Maintaining a Mutable Self-Image   Like the grades we give students, the evaluations we give and receive at work can be either a valuable resource or a dreaded punishment. Certainly being called in to talk to the boss is an icon of modern-day anxiety.

Evaluations that are frequent and forgiving of mistakes may help make the recipients willing to learn from one another, rather than striving to hide weaknesses.

Mutability can also be maintained on a higher level by keeping in mind that the job itself is changeable. It is possible that the value of mentorship rests partially on the image of upward mobility presented by the (attainable) success of the mentor, as opposed to the homogeneity and stasis implied by interacting only with others in your own job position. We can also remember that over the past decades, it has become increasingly common to leave your job mid-life and find another employer, another specialty, or another field entirely. The increasing number of people who enter the workforce briefly, then leave to pursue further education, presents a mutable self-image writ large: It's never too late to learn more. Potential comparison targets become more numerous and varied—anyone, in any job, can serve as a role model or an image of a possible future. And because their professions are different enough that direct comparison on job outcomes is meaningless, such comparisons present less threat of negative self-evaluation than do comparisons with coworkers.

Finally, this type of mutability can help prevent a tedious or highly specialized job from robbing us of the benefits of a diverse self-image. Students are encouraged to take part in a variety of activities and remain well-rounded, but a job may involve spending the entire day on one type of task and one personal role. If only one role and one task are salient, when we see ourselves as inferior to others it becomes more difficult to mobilize the defenses of shifting to an alternate domain and seeking alternative self-affirmations (Friend & Gilbert, 1973; Koole, Smeets, van Knippenberg, & Dijksterhuis, 1999; Mussweiler, Gabriel, & Bodenhausen, 2000). Maintaining a mutable self-image allows us to make comparisons across multiple domains and maintain flexibility in our contingencies of self-worth. While it is not beneficial to always ignore or devalue a domain in which we have failed, these strategies can provide temporary emotional relief so that it becomes easier to mobilize long-term learning strategies such as self-improvement comparisons with coworkers who outperform us.

Deeply Understanding the Target   As mentioned previously, being called in to talk to a superior is a powerful anxiety-evoking situation. But shouldn't the boss also be an ideal comparison target for learning how we can advance? This is the idea behind mentoring, a practice in which successful, older individuals offer advice and resources to younger individuals in their field. Mentoring has been found to provide substantial benefits to both parties in a variety of professions (e.g., Mobley, Jaret, Marsh, & Lim, 1994; Orpen, 1995), but this would not be true if it were unfailingly depressing to be situated next to an individual with more status, money, or power than ourselves. This suggests that some element of the mentoring relationship assists the junior member in making assimilative comparisons. Indeed, Burke, McKenna, and McKeen (1991) found that mentors in the high-tech industry did not offer more feedback or pragmatic advice to their protégés than to other employees under their supervision, but they did offer more psychosocial support and make more personal disclosures. Personal closeness is not a direct advantage in improving your performance, but it does contribute to seeing your upward comparison target as more open and understandable and allows you to observe them more closely. Additionally, it may be that these disclosures transmit information about dealing with setbacks and weaknesses. Such a nuanced understanding of your superiors provides a more information-rich and emulatable comparison than simply observing their level of performance.

Are there ways we can extend these benefits to workers in a broader range of jobs? One obvious response is to offer mentoring at all levels and all positions in an organization. Even the most "unskilled" jobs involve domain-specific knowledge and rely on basic skills such as literacy or manual dexterity. Helping new employees to make positive upward comparisons will allow them to open themselves to receiving both knowledge about the job and inspiration to improve their skills. Aside from the obvious benefits to employers, this situation is also likely to improve job satisfaction and subjective well-being by encouraging workers to challenge themselves and seek mastery experiences (as well as by fostering enjoyable personal relationships).

Organizations can also encourage adaptive upward comparisons by paying close attention to how they honor exceptional employees. Simply bestowing raises, promotions, or employee-of-the-month awards may encourage others to emulate the honoree's behavior, but it may also cause them to think of the honoree as categorically different or unattainably superior, leading to dissatisfaction, dysphoria, and disengagement from work. Rather, employees who excel should be encouraged to explicitly discuss their techniques. Perhaps they should even be temporarily reassigned to work as roving trainers, helping their coworkers improve their own skills.

These techniques also bring us back to the arguments against creating a competitive environment. Employees can't be expected to share their skills and knowledge if holding back their coworkers improves their own security and future prospects. Employers should reward all workers when a unit improves and should consider group cohesion and cooperation to be a significant outcome that figures into their bottom line. To whatever extent promotions and raises are limited resources, they should be awarded to employees who are able to teach, support, and inspire others.

Appropriate Choice of Comparison Measure   Perhaps the worst comparison measure imaginable is salary. Comparison with a coworker on the basis of salary provides a single number, completely without context or explanation. Individuals who want to improve their work performance need to compare themselves on information-rich dimensions such as effort and domain-specific skills; they need to see comparison as a way of learning how to perform like the comparison target.

Appropriate Choice of Comparison Domain   A different set of individuals may be more interested in comparing themselves with their coworkers to see who is happier, more fulfilled, or "doing better" in life. Here again, an individual's salary is singularly uninformative. Comparisons can focus on personal satisfaction, match/mismatch with strengths and talents, or social success in the workplace. The goal is to move away from simple, convenient types of comparison and to focus on those that are personally meaningful and directly contribute to a good life. The Gallup Organization has addressed this issue through its strengths model (Clifton & Anderson, 2002), which encourages workers to find jobs that capitalize on their deepest personal qualities. In this context, social comparison may not be competitive or even work-focused; rather, it is a way of determining what skills allow others to flourish in their professions and whether further attempts to improve at their jobs are warranted or whether it would be best to seek changes or leave entirely.

Upward Comparisons in Relationships

We compare ourselves to others at work and in school, but we also interact informally with friends and family, and they, too, may provide opportunities to evaluate ourselves. Much research in social comparison has dealt with the question of how we can weather these comparisons without feelings of condescension on one hand or inferiority and jealousy on the other. This quandary encompasses sibling rivalry, friends who, deliberately or inadvertently, measure one another's success, and couples who experience tension as one member succeeds in his or her career goals while the other flounders. Most of the principles discussed previously still apply to these situations, but when the comparison target is a valued individual who is part of our lives, the risks, benefits, and latitude in our behavior are all heightened.

An important difference between job comparisons and friendship comparisons is that our friends are usually different from us in at least some socially important performance domains. We may share interests and values, but we have different professions and educations, meaning that straightforward observation is less likely to lead to straightforward improvement on tests or job performance. My discussion of personal relationships follows two divergent paths: one that prevents invidious and inappropriate comparisons through differentiation and another that fosters valuable comparisons by seeking out deep similarities.

Differentiation: Doing Away with Keeping Score   I have already mentioned the defensive tactics of devaluing a domain or switching our attention to an alternate domain when it appears that we may be outperformed. These tactics are not appropriate long-term responses to experiencing an upward comparison in school or work, but they may be so when two criteria are fulfilled: First, when we are unable or not inclined to improve to the target's level, and second, when our relationship with the target has value independent of the comparison. If one of my old friends becomes a Fortune 500 CEO, it's reasonable to see how I might become envious of her fame and riches (or she of my journal publications and teaching position). Even if we were to make a well-informed psychological effort to assimilate each other's techniques, the results would be discouraging: There are few good ways for psychologists to become billionaires, and CEOs rarely get to lecture undergraduates. In this case, it would be more helpful to emphasize to ourselves the differences between us, our histories, and our roles and opportunities. Each of us would see the other as a less appropriate comparison target, and thus the implied attainability of our success would diminish. Simple and deliberate instructions to ourselves may be sufficient to achieve this (Mussweiler, 2001; Oyserman et al., 1995).

When the differences between ourselves and our friends are not so categorical, we can elaborate on or even create smaller differences. For example, we can develop new skills or interests, which overlap only partially with those of our friends, thus allowing us to find a niche free of competition. If we are achieving in different fields, it becomes more difficult to keep score on the type of information-poor, unidimensional measures that create harmful comparisons. But is there any danger that emphasizing dissimilarity will cause us to become distant from our friends? On the contrary, social comparison research suggests that when we are not making these direct comparisons, we are freer to share our friends' triumphs through reflected glory (Tesser et al., 1988). Furthermore, specialization within personal networks can increase cohesion by allowing all members to experience value and mastery and may also be desirable because it increases the total capability of the group (Wegner, 1995; Wegner, Erber, & Raymond, 1991). On the other hand, friendships and romantic relationships clearly do involve shared interests, beliefs, and values (e.g., Grover & Brockner, 1989). I now turn to the ways in which we can benefit from our similarities.

Assimilation: Finding Deep Commonalities   Earlier, I used the example of a friend who is a Fortune 500 CEO and thus presents a thoroughly unreasonable comparison standard for wealth. Let us imagine that, instead, my friend is a professional dancer and I envy her grace and agility. This type of comparison differs in two ways: First, physical grace may be valued for its own sake, while wealth is valued only because we assume (often mistakenly) that it is a good predictor of life satisfaction (Myers, 2000). Second, while I am no more likely to attain the grace of a dancer than I am the wealth of a CEO, it is possible for me to observe the dancer and substantially improve my agility, without needing to make major changes to my career and life course. That is, the dancer can act as a source of inspiration or a role model. Such comparisons fail to attain the attainability criterion literally, but it may be that the attainment of *progress* is more significant than the attainment of a final level of excellence comparable to the comparison target. This would be consistent with the demonstrable superiority, on both performance and affective dimensions, of holding goals related to learning and challenge as opposed to goals related to reaching a certain level of performance (Dweck, 1999; Kaplan & Maehr, 1999). Comparisons of this type can offer a powerful incentive for self-improvement, especially if interspersed with genuinely attainable comparisons, or masterful performance in comparison-free niche domains, to buffer against potential feelings of inferiority.

Another possibility for friendship comparisons is that I might look at my dancer friend, or my CEO friend, and choose to admire the devotion, vision, ingenuity, or interpersonal skills that allowed them to attain their success. Now the comparison has become both attainable and self-relevant, for people in all fields can benefit from this kind of general strength. This is the concept behind Peterson and Seligman's work on a taxonomy of ubiquitous strengths (Peterson & Seligman, 2003a; Seligman, 2002), which is conceived as a counterpart to the *Diagnostic and Statistical Manual of Mental Disorders (DSM)* taxonomy of flaws and pathologies. It is not always easy to identify the deep personal characteristics that underlie an impressive individual's success, which is why this aspect of comparison is discussed in the section on love and friendship. While close relationships make comparison and outperformance emotionally hazardous (Brickman & Bulman, 1977; Exline & Lobel, 2001; Tesser et al., 1988), they also afford us the time, comfort, and interpersonal access to learn about the deep characteristics of our upward comparison targets that underlie their success. Additionally, as in the case of mentorship (Burke et al., 1991), people we are close to are more likely to provide specific useful information about dealing with weakness and setbacks, as opposed to presenting a facade of perfection.

CONCLUSION

In this chapter, I have attempted to run the gamut from simple personal techniques to ambitious long-term goals. In crafting beneficial upward comparisons, we are mapping out paths of human relationship, learning to experience joy and shared learning when we are in danger of falling into feelings of inferiority and conflict. We can change failure and defeat into enjoyable opportunities for learning, assimilate the qualities of others without even being aware of it, and, though it may initially seem paradoxical, create relationships in which each partner looks up to the other. The study of social comparison allows us to apply subtle interventions to the very fabric of our everyday interactions, creating growth, pleasure, and excellence seemingly out of nothing.

REFERENCES

Anderson, C., & Jennings, D. (1980). When experiences of failure promote expectations of success: The impact of attributing failure to ineffective strategies. *Journal of Personality, 48*, 393–407.

Andrews, G., & Debus, R. (1978). Persistence and the causal perception of failure: Modifying cognitive attributions. *Journal of Educational Psychology, 70*, 154–166.

Aronson, E., & Patnoe, S. (1997). *The jigsaw classroom: Building cooperation in the classroom.* New York: Longman.

Aronson, J., Fried, C., & Good, C. (2002). Reducing the effects of stereotype threat on African American college students by shaping theories of intelligence. *Journal of Experimental Social Psychology, 38*, 113–125.

Bargh, J., Chen, M., & Burrows, L. (1996). Automaticity of social behavior: Direct effects of trait construct and stereotype activation on action. *Journal of Personality and Social Psychology, 71*, 230–244.

Blackwell, L., Dweck, C., & Trzesniewski, K. (2003). *Implicit theories of intelligence predict achievement across an adolescent transition: A longitudinal study and an intervention.* Manuscript in preparation, Columbia University.

Brewer, M. B. (1991). The social self: On being the same and different at the same time. *Personality and Social Psychology Bulletin, 17*, 475–482.

Brickman, P., & Bulman, R. (1977). Pleasure and pain in social comparison. In J. Suls & R. Miller (Eds.), *Social comparison processes* (pp. 149–186). Washington, DC: Hemisphere Publishing Corporation.

Burke, R., McKenna, C., & McKeen, C. (1991). How do mentorships differ from typical supervisory relationships? *Psychological Reports, 68*, 459–466.

Buunk, B., & Brenninkinmeijer, V. (2001). When individuals dislike exposure to an actively coping role model: Mood change as related to depression and social comparison orientation. *European Journal of Social Psychology, 31*, 537–548.

*Buunk, B., Taylor, S., Collins, R., VanYperen, N., & Dakof, G. (1990). The affective consequences of social comparisons: Either direction has its ups and downs. *Journal of Personality and Social Psychology, 59*, 1238–1249.

Buunk, B., Ybema, J., Gibbons, F., & Ipenburg, M. (2001). The affective consequences of social comparison as related to professional burnout and social comparison orientation. *European Journal of Social Psychology, 31*, 337–51.

Chartrand, T. L., & Bargh, J. A. (1999). The chameleon effect: The perception-behavior link and social interaction. *Journal of Personality and Social Psychology, 76*, 893–910.

Clifton, D. O., & Anderson, E. (2002). *StrengthsQuest: Discover and develop your strengths in academics, career, and beyond.* Washington, DC: The Gallup Organization.

Csikszentmihalyi, M. (1990). *Flow: The psychology of optimal experience.* New York: Harper-Collins.

Csikszentmihalyi, M. (1997). *Finding flow: The psychology of engagement with everyday life.* New York: Basic Books.

Diener, E. (2000). Subjective well-being: The science of happiness and a proposal for a national index. *American Psychologist, 55,* 34–43.

Dijksterhuis, A. P., & Van Knippenberg, A. D. (1998). The relation between perception and behavior, or how to win a game of trivial pursuit. *Journal of Personality and Social Psychology, 74,* 865–877.

*Dweck, C. S. (1999). *Self-theories: Their role in motivation, personality, and development.* Philadelphia: Psychology Press.

Exline, J., & Lobel, M. (2001). Private gain, social strain: Do relationship factors shape responses to outperformance? *European Journal of Social Psychology, 31,* 593–607.

Festinger, L. (1954). A theory of social comparison processes. *Human Relations, 7,* 114–140.

Fowler, J., & Peterson, P. (1981). Increasing reading persistence and altering attributional style of learned helpless children. *Journal of Educational Psychology, 73,* 251–260.

Fredrickson, B. L. (2001). The role of positive emotions in positive psychology: The broaden-and-build theory of positive emotions. *American Psychologist, 56,* 218–226.

Friend, R., & Gilbert, J. (1973). Threat and fear of negative evaluation as determinants of locus of social comparison. *Journal of Personality, 41,* 328–340.

Gilbert, D., & Malone, P. (1995). The correspondence bias. *Psychological Bulletin, 117,* 21–38.

Gilbert, P., Price, J., & Allen, S. (1995). Social comparison, social attractiveness, and evolution: How might they be related? *New Ideas in Psychology, 15,* 149–165.

Grover, S., & Brockner, J. (1989). Empathy and the relationship between attitudinal similarity and attraction. *Journal of Research in Personality, 23,* 469–79.

Helmreich, R., Beane, W., Licker, W., & Spence, T. (1978). Achievement motivation and scientific attainment. *Personality and Social Psychology Bulletin, 4,* 222–226.

Huguet, P., Dumas, F., Monteil, J., & Genestoux, N. (2001). Social comparison choices in the classroom: Further evidence for students' upward comparison tendency and its beneficial impact on performance. *European Journal of Social Psychology, 31,* 557–578.

Johnson, D. W., Maruyama, G., Johnson, R. T., & Nelson, D. (1981). Effects of cooperative, competitive, and individualistic goal structures on achievement: A meta-analysis. *Psychological Bulletin, 89,* 47–62.

*Johnson, R. T., & Johnson, D. W. (1994). *Learning together and alone: Cooperative, competitive, and individualistic learning.* Needham Heights, MA: Allyn & Bacon.

Kalma, A. (1991). Hierarchisation and dominance assessment at first glance. *European Journal of Social Psychology, 21,* 165–181.

Kaplan, A., & Maehr, M. (1999). Achievement goals and student well-being. *Contemporary Educational Psychology, 24,* 330–58.

Kawakami, K., Dovidio, J., & Dijksterhuis, A. (2003). Effect of social category priming on personal attitudes. *Psychological Science, 14*(4), 315–319.

Kohn, A. (1992). *No contest: The case against competition.* Boston: Houghton Mifflin.

Koole, S., Smeets, K., van Knippenberg, A., & Dijksterhuis, A. (1999). The cessation of rumination through self-affirmation. *Journal of Personality and Social Psychology, 77,* 111–125.

Lockwood, P., Jordan, C., & Kunda, Z. (2002). Motivation by positive or negative role models: Regulatory focus determines who will inspire us. *Journal of Personality and Social Psychology, 83,* 854–864.

*Lockwood, P., & Kunda, Z. (1997). Superstars and me: Predicting the impact of role models on the self. *Journal of Personality and Social Psychology, 73,* 91–103.

Lockwood, P., & Kunda, Z. (1999). Increasing the salience of one's best selves can undermine inspiration by outstanding role models. *Journal of Personality and Social Psychology, 76,* 214–228.

Losada, M. (1999). The complex dynamics of high performance teams. *Mathematical and Computer Modeling, 30,* 179–192.

Major, B., Sciacchitano, A., & Crocker, J. (1993). In-group versus out-group comparisons and self-esteem. *Personality and Social Psychology Bulletin, 19,* 711–721.

Mobley, G., Jaret, C., Marsh, K., & Lim, Y. (1994). Mentoring, job satisfaction, gender, and the legal profession. *Sex Roles, 31,* 79–98.

Mussweiler, T. (2001). "Seek and ye shall find": Antecedents of assimilation and contrast in social comparison. *European Journal of Social Psychology, 31,* 499–509.

Mussweiler, T., Gabriel, S., & Bodenhausen, G. (2000). Shifting social identities as a strategy for deflecting threatening social comparisons. *Journal of Personality and Social Psychology, 79*(3), 398–409.

Myers, D. G. (1992). *The pursuit of happiness.* New York: Basic Books.

Myers, D. G. (2000). The funds, friends, and faith of happy people. *American Psychologist, 55,* 56–67.

Orpen, C. (1995). The effects of mentoring on employees' career success. *Journal of Social Psychology, 135,* 667–668.

Oyserman, D., Gant, L., & Ager, J. (1995). A socially contextualized model of African American identity: Possible selves and school persistence. *Journal of Personality and Social Psychology, 69,* 1216–1232.

Parducci, A. (1995). *Happiness, pleasure, and judgment: The contextual theory and its applications.* Mahwah, NJ: Erlbaum.

Peterson, C., & Seligman, M. E. P. (2003a). *Values In Action (VIA) classification of strengths: Introduction.* Retrieved April 25, 2003, from University of Pennsylvania, Martin Seligman Research Alliance web site: http://www.positivepsychology.org/viamanualintro.pdf.

Peterson, C., & Seligman, M. E. P. (2003b). *Values In Action (VIA) classification of strengths: Section introductions.* Retrieved April 25, 2003, from University of Pennsylvania, Martin Seligman Research Alliance web site: http://www.positivepsychology.org/taxonomy.htm.

Segal, Z., Gemar, M., & Williams, S. (1999). Differential cognitive response to a mood challenge following successful cognitive therapy or pharmacotherapy for unipolar depression. *Journal of Abnormal Psychology, 108,* 3–10.

Seligman, M. E. P. (2002). *Authentic happiness: Using the new positive psychology to realize your potential for lasting fulfillment.* New York: Free Press.

Springer, L., Stanne, M., & Donovan, S. (1999). Effects of small-group learning on undergraduates in science, math, engineering, and technology: A meta-analysis. *Review of Educational Research, 69,* 21–51.

*Stapel, D., & Koomen, W. (2000). Distinctness of others, mutability of selves: Their impact on self-evaluation. *Journal of Personality and Social Psychology, 79,* 1068–1087.

Stephan, C., Kennedy, J. C., & Aronson, E. (1977). The effects of friendship and outcome on task attribution. *Sociometry, 40,* 107–111.

*Taylor, S., & Lobel, M. (1989). Social comparison activity under threat: Downward evaluation and upward contacts. *Psychological Review, 96,* 569–575.

Taylor, S., Neter, E., & Wayment, H. (1995). Self-evaluation processes. *Personality and Social Psychology Bulletin, 21,* 1278–1287.

Teasdale, J., Scott, J., Moore, R., Hayhurst, H., Pope, M., & Paykel, E. (2001). How does cognitive therapy prevent relapse in residual depression? Evidence from a controlled trial. *Journal of Consulting and Clinical Psychology, 69,* 347–357.

Tesser, A., Millar, M., & Moore, J. (1988). Some affective consequences of social comparison and reflection processes: The pain and pleasure of being close. *Journal of Personality and Social Psychology, 54,* 49–61.

Tjosvold, D., Johnson, D., & Johnson, R. (1984). Influence strategy, perspective-taking, and relationships between high- and low-power individuals in cooperative and competitive contexts. *Journal of Psychology, 116,* 187–202.

Wegner, D. (1995). A computer network model of human transactive memory. *Social Cognition, 13,* 319–339.

Wegner, D., Erber, R., & Raymond, P. (1991). Transactive memory in close relationships. *Journal of Personality and Social Psychology, 61*(6), 923–929.

Weil, A. (1972). *The natural mind.* Boston: Houghton Mifflin.

Wheeler, L., & Miyake, K. (1992). Social comparison in everyday life. *Journal of Personality and Social Psychology, 62,* 760–773.

Whisman, M. (1993). Mediators and moderators of change in cognitive therapy of depression. *Psychological Bulletin, 114,* 248–265.

Wills, T. (1981). Downward comparison principles in psychology. *Psychological Bulletin, 90,* 245–271.

Wood, J., & Wilson, E. (2002). How important is social comparison. In M. Leary & J. Tangney (Eds.), *Handbook of self and identity* (pp. 344–366). New York: Guilford Press.

PART VI

POSITIVE PSYCHOLOGY AT WORK

CHAPTER 15

Leading Well: Transformational Leadership and Well-Being

NIRO SIVANATHAN, KARA A. ARNOLD,
NICK TURNER, and JULIAN BARLING

YOU DON'T HAVE to look far in either the popular media or academic research literature to find accounts of poor leadership (e.g., Dutton, Frost, Worline, Lilius, & Kanov, 2002; Tepper, 2000), and we are now beginning to understand just how negative such leadership can be for people trapped in these organizational relationships. Thankfully, at the other end of the spectrum, there are countless stories about positive leadership, embedded both in states of crisis (e.g., Giuliani, 2002) and in the routines and rhythms of everyday organizational life. What is missing from this dialogue, however, is a body of knowledge about positive leadership—leadership that has the potential to elevate followers in the long term, such that followers can achieve greater levels of both well-being and effectiveness themselves. We have a limited appreciation of the comprehensive benefits that can be derived from leadership (Turner, Barling, & Zacharatos, 2002), and transformational leadership represents a set of behaviors that have the potential to fill this void.

The organizational effectiveness of transformational leadership is not in question. Studies routinely demonstrate its effectiveness in diverse situations, ranging from profit-oriented organizations (Barling, Weber, & Kelloway, 1996), trade unions (Kelloway & Barling, 1993), young workers (Barling, Loughlin, & Kelloway, 2002; Sivanathan, Barling, & Turner, 2003), sports teams (Charbonneau, Barling, & Kelloway, 2001; Zacharatos, Barling, & Kelloway, 2000), educational contexts (Koh, Steers, & Terborg, 1995), self-managed teams (Arnold, Barling, & Kelloway, 2001), to military organizations (Bass, 1998). Understanding exactly

All of the authors contributed equally to this manuscript. A version of this chapter was presented at the Second International Positive Psychology Summit, Washington, DC. Financial support from the Queen's School of Business and the Social Sciences and Humanities Research Council of Canada helped to make this collaboration possible.

what constitutes transformational leadership not only enables us to appreciate its effects on these organizations but also aids in knowing precisely why transformational leadership might enhance well-being.

To explore these connections, we have organized our discussion here into several parts. First, we define *well-being*. Second, we outline both the nature of transformational leadership and the rich background of research that has documented its effects, which leads us to the surprisingly few research studies that have empirically documented leadership in relation to well-being. Third, we speculate on several psychological processes that we believe underpin the effects of transformational leadership on well-being. Finally, we chart some directions for future research and some issues about putting the link between transformational leadership and well-being into practice.

WHAT IS WELL-BEING?

Like the medical model of health, many studies of individual health in organizations have focused on psychological and physical ill health (Warr, 1987). However, like a number of recent contributors to the field (e.g., Hofmann & Tetrick, 2003; Snyder & Lopez, 2002), we believe that well-being (at least in Westernized cultures) goes beyond the absence of ill health to include aspirations to learn, being reasonably independent, and possessing confidence. In the same way, physical well-being at work goes beyond evading workplace injury and disease to include personal initiatives that aim to improve physical health. We define *job-related well-being* as the promotion of both psychological and physical health at work, and we discuss this in more detail later.

We focus on the effects of job-related well-being in this chapter for two reasons. First, a broad concept of job-related well-being is now well defined in the literature and provides a *positive* basis from which to examine healthy work. For example, Warr (1987, 1990) identifies three assessable aspects of affective well-being on two orthogonal dimensions (pleasure and level of arousal):

1. An axis of pleasure or displeasure, often measured in terms of satisfaction or happiness
2. An axis ranging from anxiety (low pleasure, high arousal) to comfort (high pleasure, low arousal)
3. An axis from depression (low pleasure, low arousal) to enthusiasm (high pleasure, high arousal)

Measures of affective well-being that assess anxiety, depression, psychological distress, and psychosomatic symptoms aim to detect ill health, as opposed to positive mental health. Measures of positive mental health, on the other hand, capture high arousal–high pleasure states such as enthusiasm.

Job satisfaction (i.e., a pleasurable emotional state resulting from the appraisal of your job experiences) can be considered either an indicator of poor mental health (e.g., job dissatisfaction) or an indicator of positive mental health (e.g., job satisfaction). According to Warr (1999), however, job satisfaction is a rather "passive" form of mental health because most measures of job satisfaction assess only the degree of pleasure or displeasure derived from the job and do not include the arousal state. Indeed, Bruggeman, Groskurth, and Ulich (1975) describe a state of "resigned" job satisfaction, in which employees, while "happy," may also experience little aspiration and acquiesce to job constraints. Given the scope of this chapter, we do not discuss evidence that explores transformational leadership and job satisfaction (for examples of this research, see Pillai, Scandura, & Williams, 1999; Sparks & Schenk, 2001). Instead, we focus on evidence about explicit indicators of mental and physical ill health and active mental and physical health.

Warr (1987) also identified a number of other types of mental health that may persevere and represent more active states and behaviors than most traditional indicators of well-being. These variously include positive self-regard (e.g., high self-esteem), perceived competence (e.g., effective coping), aspiration (e.g., goal directedness), autonomy (e.g., proactivity), and integrated functioning (e.g., balance, harmony, and internal relatedness). These indicators can influence a person's affective well-being (e.g., reduced anxiety through effective coping), and in this chapter we discuss a number of these components as the mechanisms that might enable transformational leadership to affect well-being.

Our first reason for focusing on job-related well-being, as we have just discussed, is its rich conceptual and empirical foundation. Second, the experience of work translates directly into other health outcomes (e.g., Amick et al., 2002; Kelloway & Barling, 1991). There is evidence that job-related well-being affects employees' overall life satisfaction (e.g., Hart, 1999; Higginbottom, Barling, & Kelloway, 1993; Judge & Watanabe, 1993), and maintaining physical health at work (e.g., staying injury-free and helping to keep coworkers safe) affects life beyond the workplace (Hofmann & Tetrick, 2003). Although this interdependence between work and nonwork domains warrants prominent attention in emergent positive psychology scholarship, our focus in this chapter is on how transformational leadership, which we describe in more detail next, promotes well-being in the workplace.

WHAT IS TRANSFORMATIONAL LEADERSHIP?

Transformational leadership comprises four separate elements, or perhaps more accurately, four different types of behaviors (idealized influence, inspirational motivation, intellectual stimulation, and individualized consideration; Bass, 1985, 1998). Any or all of these four have the potential to advance well-being.

Idealized influence reflects behaviors that leaders enact because they choose to do what is right, rather than what is expedient, simple, or cost-effective. Leaders are guided to engage in these behaviors because of their moral commitment to both their own actions and to their followers (Turner, Barling, Epitropaki, Butcher, & Milner, 2002). Employees respect leaders who engage in behaviors that reflect idealized influence because they know that their leaders have chosen to behave in this way; they are not behaving this way just because they have to. Indeed, any positive benefits would be minimized to the extent to which followers perceive leaders as having no choice to behave any other way. Employees who see their leaders as doing the right thing and, therefore, manifesting idealized influence are likely to accord their leaders high levels of trust and respect and to have positive perceptions of interpersonal justice (Turner, Barling, & Zacharatos, 2002).

Leaders evidence *inspirational motivation* when they inspire their followers to be their very best and to greater levels than the followers themselves ever thought possible. Unlike many popular, and perhaps populist notions of inspiration, inspirational motivation does not require that the leader display stereotypical charismatic behaviors. Instead, inspirational motivation within a transformational leadership context is achieved by convincing employees that they can break through previously perceived performance barriers, whether self- or externally imposed. Leaders do so by instilling in their employees realistic feelings of self-efficacy, feelings of what can be accomplished rather than fears of what cannot be accomplished. They frequently use symbols and stories to convey positive messages.

Using *intellectual stimulation,* leaders no longer provide all the answers for others. They challenge employees to think more for themselves and to continuously question their long-held and cherished assumptions. This is critical in the development of well-being, first, because followers will become more confident and, second, because this enhances their self-efficacy.

Finally, *individualized consideration* is reflected through those behaviors in which leaders show their concern for their employees' development and physical and psychological safety. They do this by listening, caring, empathizing, and being compassionate, perhaps especially during the most difficult of times when employees need them the most. It is through individualized consideration that leaders develop and cement a relationship with their followers.

TRANSFORMATIONAL LEADERSHIP AND WELL-BEING

Transformational leadership may have important, positive effects on both leaders' and followers' well-being. Although transformational leadership has garnered more empirical attention than all other leadership paradigms combined over the past decade (Judge & Bono, 2000), there is surprisingly little empirical research linking it with facets of well-being. One facet of well-being that has recently received attention with respect to the effects of transformational leadership is workplace safety. Recent research shows that transformational leadership enhances employees' safety performance in correlational (Barling et al., 2002) and quasi-experimental investigations (Sivanathan et al., 2003; Zohar, 2002).

However, we suggest that the four components of transformational leadership are also especially relevant in terms of psychological well-being. Idealized influence takes place when leaders do what is proper and ethical, rather than what is effortless, and when they are guided by their moral commitment to their followers and go beyond the interests of the organization. During times of crisis, leaders who manifest idealized influence are able to forego organizational pressures for short-term financial outcomes and instead focus their efforts on the long-term health and well-being of their employees (Walsh, 2001). Leaders exhibiting inspirational motivation inspire their employees to achieve more than what was once thought possible. These leaders inspire employees to surmount psychological setbacks and instill in them the strength to tackle future hurdles. Leaders who manifest intellectual stimulation help employees to question their own commonly held assumptions, reframe problems, and approach matters in innovative ways. Given the autonomy to arrive at their own personal strategies to tackle psychological setbacks, employees become more confident of developing and protecting their own well-being. Finally, individual consideration occurs when leaders pay special attention to employees' needs for achievement and development; they provide needed empathy, compassion, and guidance that employees may seek for their well-being. In doing so, leaders establish the basis for a relationship within which their other leadership behaviors are more likely to be accepted.

We also hypothesize that being a transformational leader has the potential to enhance the leader's well-being. The logic underlying this hypothesis is that when leaders feel trusted by their own employees because of their own leadership behaviors, when they experience reciprocal care and consideration from their followers, they in turn develop higher levels of well-being. While intriguing, this remains but an interesting proposition that awaits empirical testing.

PSYCHOLOGICAL MECHANISMS LINKING TRANSFORMATIONAL LEADERSHIP AND WELL-BEING

In articulating the nature of the relationship between components of transformational leadership and well-being, we have implied a number of psychological processes that deserve further attention. More specifically, we believe that followers' self-efficacy, trust in management, meaning derived from work, and way of identifying with their work and their leader enable the effects of transformational leadership on well-being. We describe each of these potential mechanisms in more detail in the following sections.

SELF-EFFICACY

Self-efficacy reflects the judgment of an individual's ability to accomplish a certain level of performance (Bandura, 1997). Self-efficacy has attracted considerable research scrutiny and has been shown to be positively related to job attitudes (Saks, 1995), motivation on the job (Prussia & Kinicki, 1996), and job performance (Stajkovic & Luthans, 1998). At the same time, research findings also show consistently that feelings of self-efficacy enable individuals to confront formerly fear- and anxiety-provoking stimuli (see Bandura, 1997). For example, Jex and Bliese's (1999) findings that self-efficacy buffers the negative impact of work stressors on employee psychological well-being are to be expected because individuals high in self-efficacy are more likely to confront their stressors, while those low in self-efficacy are more likely to consume their time worrying about them (Kinicki & Latack, 1990). Therefore, by relying on their problem-focused coping, employees higher in self-efficacy are better equipped to have more adaptive responses to setbacks and stressors in their work environment and thus are more likely to maintain healthy levels of psychological well-being.

Successful accomplishments, vicarious experiences, and verbal persuasion have been found to facilitate the development of the individual's self-efficacy (Bandura, 1997). These results suggest that the cognitive and affective processes that shape an individual's self-efficacy can be positively shaped by psychosocial factors such as the quality of leadership. We believe that by (1) inspiring their followers to greater heights (verbal persuasion), (2) manifesting positive behaviors that followers want to emulate (vicarious experience), (3) exhorting their followers to think of challenges in ways that make it possible to confront them (verbal persuasion), and (4) providing a supportive climate in which this is all possible (successful accomplishments), transformational leaders affect their followers' self-efficacy.

Preliminary evidence for this claim comes from a laboratory study in which Kirkpatrick and Locke (1996) found that the effects of charismatic/transformational leaders' vision on followers' performance were mediated by self-efficacy. Thus, we suggest that transformational leadership positively affects employee self-efficacy, which in turn enhances employee well-being.

Trust in Management

Mayer, Davis, and Schoorman (1995) view trust as an individual's willingness to be vulnerable to another individual. Extending this to the workplace, trust in management can be viewed as the willingness of employees to be vulnerable to their leader. Trust in management, and, perhaps more specifically, the process by which employees are willingly vulnerable to their leader, has been defined as being comprised of a cognitive component (a belief that the leader is capable of carrying out his or her tasks) and an affective component (a belief that the leader will not act in a manner to harm employees; Cook & Wall, 1980; McAllister, 1995). Not surprisingly, the development of *trust in leader* has been identified as a crucial element in the effectiveness of leaders, individuals, and their organization (Bass, 1990; Fleishman & Harris, 1962). Given its importance in organizations, surprisingly little research has focused on illuminating the positive effects trust in leadership has on employee well-being.

Our hypothesis that trust in management mediates the relationship between transformational leadership and employee well-being derives from two separate sources: The first has received substantial empirical support; the second, as mentioned previously, has received no empirical scrutiny and is thus more speculative. First, being able to rely on the skills, abilities, and intentions of those in supervisory positions (i.e., trust in leadership) has been argued to be one of the most important predictors of positive organizational outcomes (Kouzes & Posner, 1995; Yukl, 1998). Empirical findings support this notion: Trust in leadership is associated, for example, with higher work satisfaction (Butler, Cantrell, & Flick, 1999), citizenship behaviors (Pillai, Schriesheim, & Williams, 1999), and performance (Dirks, 2000). Of specific importance to this chapter, transformational leadership has been shown to be associated with higher levels of trust in management in several different studies (Jung & Avolio, 2000; Pillai, Schriesheim, et al., 1999; Podsakoff, Mackenzie, Moorman, & Fetter, 1990). These consistently positive findings suggest that by acting as role models who consistently do what is moral and right and not personally beneficial, transformational leaders gain the respect and trust of their followers.

In contrast, we are not aware of any empirical inquiry to date on the relationship between trust in management and psychological well-being. Nonetheless, we suggest that such a link exists for two reasons. First, positive individual outcomes are consistently associated with trust in management (Arthur, 1994; see Kramer, 1999). Second, as organizations face changes of the nature and severity experienced in the past decade, individuals experience uncertainty, anxiety, and fear (Yukl, 1998), all of which have potentially detrimental effects on an individual's well-being. Under such circumstances, high levels of trust in leadership would enable employees to feel less threatened, thereby exerting positive effects on their well-being.

Thus, we propose that by acting as role models, being committed to employee needs, empowering and encouraging employees to think on their own, and motivating their followers to achieve more than what was thought possible, transformational leaders gain their followers' trust and heighten followers' self-efficacy beliefs. In turn, employees' trust in management and self-efficacy beliefs are associated with their own well-being.

Meaningful Work

A transformational leader can also enable individuals to find positive meaning in their work. We propose that the meaning that individuals make of their work is another one of the mechanisms through which transformational leadership exerts its positive effects on individual well-being. First, we briefly describe the various ways that meaningful work has been conceptualized and measured; then we discuss the research that leads us to suggest that meaningful work mediates this relationship.

The meaning of work is generally conceptualized as the aim or purpose that people have for working. Early research into the meaning that people make of their work found that the economic function of work is but one of many meanings that work may have (Morse & Weiss, 1955) and is, in fact, not generally the most salient meaning of work (Morse & Weiss, 1955; MOW International Research Team, 1987).

Meaning has been conceptualized and measured in many different ways. While we cannot summarize this body of literature adequately here, we point to a few of the main conceptualizations. Meaning may be conceptualized as existing on multiple levels. Individuals may find a certain specific meaning in their current job (i.e., job involvement; Kanungo, 1982). They may also espouse meaning in relation to work in general (work involvement, Kanungo, 1982; work centrality, Paullay, Alliger, & Stone-Romero, 1994; or work values, Nord, Brief, Atieh, & Doherty, 1988). These measures entail a broader sense of what work should provide in terms of purpose, as well as some indication of the value of work in relation to other aspects of life. Orientation toward work has been conceptualized as intrinsic versus extrinsic motivation (Robertson, 1990). In the job characteristics model (Hackman & Oldham, 1980), meaningful work is conceptualized as a critical psychological state resulting from a job that is high in task significance, task identity, and skill variety. The commonality among all of these measures of meaning is that they all focus on a purpose to work that somehow transcends the financial one. We posit that it is this *higher* purpose that a transformational leader instills in followers, and, as we discuss later, it is this connection that we believe contributes to enhanced well-being.

The theory of transformational leadership suggests several avenues through which the meaning of work can be positively transformed. Transformational leaders raise followers' levels of morality to "more principled levels of judgment" (Burns, 1978, p. 455; Turner, Barling, Epitropaki, et al., 2002) and activate higher order needs in followers (Bass, 1985). The intellectual stimulation dimension of transformational leadership allows the transformation of crises or stressful situations to challenges (Bass, 1998). Finally, stress levels of followers may be reduced because of a sense of identity with a social support network that is created through the use of individualized consideration (Bass, 1998). The respect that a transformational leader exhibits for each follower as an individual also applies to the work that each follower is engaged in. The verbal cues that individuals in the environment give us about our work are very powerful (see the social information processing literature:

Salancik & Pfeffer, 1978; White & Mitchell, 1979). The transformational leader is likely to provide positive verbal cues to followers.

Research has established an association between transformational leadership and various measures of meaningful work. Transformational leadership has been found to have a positive impact on congruence of values between leaders and followers (Jung & Avolio, 2000; Kirkpatrick & Locke, 1996), on intrinsic motivation (Charbonneau et al., 2001), on belief in a higher purpose of work (Sparks & Schenk, 2001), and indirectly on job involvement through procedural justice perceptions (Beeler, 1997). Transformational leadership has also been shown to be negatively associated with work alienation (consisting of the dimensions of powerlessness, meaninglessness, & self-estrangement; Sarros, Tanewski, Winter, Santora, & Densten, 2002).

Evidence of a positive link between the meaning of work and well-being is mixed. Some studies have found that job involvement may exacerbate negative health outcomes in certain cases (cf. Frone, Russell, & Cooper, 1995). Yet, there are also studies that find a positive link between the meaning of work and well-being. Experiencing higher job involvement has been found to be negatively related to burnout (Paullay, 1991), and in a recent longitudinal study, the meaning of work (defined as "being engaged in important and relevant work") was found to explain 32% of the variance in psychological benefits derived from the experience of deployment in Bosnia (Britt, Adler, & Bartone, 2001). These studies suggest that a positive link between meaningful work and well-being is possible. Future research is necessary to confirm these associations and to establish empirically our belief that transformational leadership affects well-being via enhancing the meaning of work.

ORGANIZATIONAL AND OCCUPATIONAL IDENTITY

A final mediating mechanism through which we believe transformational leadership enhances well-being is organizational and/or occupational identity. Social identity theory states that an individual's self-concept is composed of a personal identity, which encompasses idiosyncratic characteristics, and a social identity, which encompasses the salient groups to which an individual belongs (Ashforth & Mael, 1989). Social identification is "the perception of belongingness to a group classification" (Mael & Ashforth, 1992, p. 104). An individual possessing a positive self-concept (i.e., positive personal and social identity) potentially experiences more positive well-being. Hence, we hypothesize that enhancing organizational or occupational identity (both potentially salient aspects of social identity) in turn positively affects well-being.

In terms of an individual's sense of belonging in the work domain, two of the salient groups to which we belong are the organization and our occupation. *Organizational identification* has been defined as "a perceived oneness with an organization and the experience of the organization's successes and failures as one's own" (Mael & Ashforth, 1992, p. 103). We define occupational identity in a similar fashion: a sense of oneness with an occupational group. We know little, if anything, about how these two identities may interact because of a limited focus in the literature on potential interactions that exist between organizations and occupations (Barley & Tolbert, 1991; Van Maanen & Barley, 1984).

To our knowledge, there have been no empirical investigations of the links between transformational leadership and occupational or organizational identity. Yet, theoretically, transformational leaders have the potential to positively influence how individuals perceive the defining characteristics of the organization as well as the occupational group to which they belong. Indeed, with respect to organizational identification, it is "through the manipulation of symbols such as traditions, myths, metaphors, rituals, sagas, heroes, and physical setting, [that] management can make the individuals' membership salient and provide compelling images of what the . . . organization represents" (Ashforth & Mael, 1989, p. 28). Through transformational leadership, the needs, values, preferences, and aspirations of followers evolve from self- to collective interests (Shamir, House, & Arthur, 1993). Specifically, Bass (1998, p. 23) suggests that the charismatic dimensions transform participation in organizational efforts from satisfying the self-interests of the follower to an "expression of membership and identity with a social collective." The dimensions of idealized influence and inspirational motivation are most likely to inspire positive identification—whether with the organization or the occupation.

The positive impact of organizational identification on well-being of individuals and organizations has been recognized in past research (Brown, 1969; Hall & Schneider, 1972; O'Reilly & Chapman, 1986). However, because of a lack of attention to occupations in organizational research (Van Maanen & Barley, 1984), there have been fewer investigations of occupational identity. There is indirect evidence that occupational identity impacts positively on well-being. One study of cancer patients found that being able to return to a work role that was important gave people a sense of control (Peteet, 2000). Possession of positive student identity was also found to be positively related to self-esteem in another study (Shields, 1995). Theory would suggest that the more positively and strongly that we feel *at one* with the organization and the occupation we work in, the more positive our self-concept is, and hence our well-being is enhanced. The influence of transformational leadership on this process is conceptually plausible, yet remains empirically untested.

SUMMARY OF OUR MODEL

Based on the previous discussion, Figure 15.1 shows a model for linking transformational leadership and well-being. This model draws on and aims to integrate existing research on the outcomes of transformational leadership, as well as the determinants of well-being summarized thus far.

Two broader features of this model are worth noting in summary. First, well-being is broadly defined to include both traditional, mainly negative, indicators of well-being (e.g., distress, strain, injuries), as well as more positive indicators. This approach is consistent with more established research approaches (e.g., Warr, 1987) and burgeoning interest in broader conceptualizations of health in organizations (e.g., Hofmann & Tetrick, 2003). Second, the model proposes that transformational leadership influences well-being via four key psychological mechanisms: self-efficacy (i.e., belief in your ability to perform), trust in management (i.e., belief in your leader), meaningful work (i.e., a sense of making a valuable contribution), and identity with your organization and occupation (i.e., a sense of belonging to an important collective). Although it is likely that there are stronger links between some of these mechanisms and different indicators of well-being, these more specific suggestions are not depicted in this initial version of the model. We also suggest that the mechanisms may influence one another. For example, if a person believes

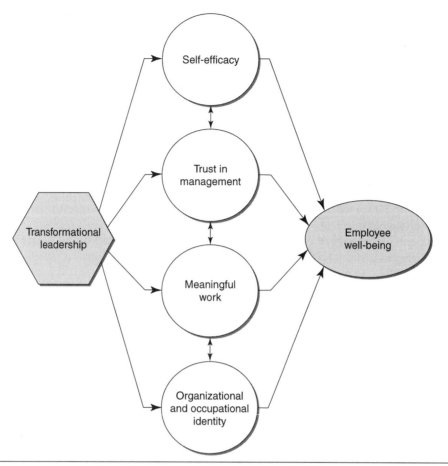

Figure 15.1 Proposed Indirect Effects of Transformational Leadership on Employee Well-Being

in her ability to perform to a certain level (e.g., high self-efficacy), it is likely that she also derives considerable meaning from the target of her efforts (e.g., meaningful work). Likewise, feeling connected with the organization (e.g., organizational identification) may also manifest itself with a simultaneous belief in the capabilities of the organization's leaders (i.e., trust in management). Taken together, these mechanisms help to articulate the empirical black box between transformational leadership and well-being.

RESEARCH DIRECTIONS AND PUTTING IT INTO PRACTICE

As with all emerging fields, the arena of positive psychology at work has many avenues for future research. With respect to transformational leadership and well-being, one aspect that future research must incorporate is more rigorous research designs. Not only is there the usual call for more longitudinal studies, but also combining multiple wave studies with multiple levels of analyses will help to rule out alternative explanations. For example, the predominant approach to studying transformational leadership is an individual level of analysis (i.e., subordinates' perceptions of a supervisor's leadership behaviors) and using formal supervisors as the source of transformational leadership behaviors. While formal supervisors can clearly play a role in employee well-being (e.g., Barling et al., 2002), exploring the effects of transformational leadership on group-level constructs (e.g., group-level safety climate; Zohar, 2000, 2002) over time and the emergent role of informal leaders in a work group remain important research directions in this domain. Future research might also explore more positive aspects of well-being, in line with a broader conceptualization of health (Hofmann & Tetrick, 2003). One such avenue might be to distinguish the effects of transformational leadership on context-specific well-being (i.e., job-related mental health) versus general well-being (e.g., life satisfaction). This could be of importance to the larger study of positive psychology, given the growing evidence of job-related well-being spilling over to well-being in life (Judge & Watanabe, 1993), and have implications for what organizations view as positive consequences of leadership development and training.

Given evidence that transformational leadership is trainable (Barling et al., 1996), an important and practical focus should be the well-being of young people. Young workers make up a growing percentage of the workforce, and research on transformational leadership has shown the validity of this leadership theory to young people (e.g., Charbonneau et al., 2001; Sivanathan et al., 2003; Zacharatos et al., 2000). If organizations bolster the well-being of young workers, this will have a positive impact on future effectiveness, in terms of both healthy workers and organizations as these young/part-time workers join the full-time workforce.

A more underresearched population on which to focus the positive effects of transformational leadership on well-being is "dirty workers" (Ashforth & Kreiner, 1999). Dirty work has been defined as work that is considered disgusting and/or degrading and is stigmatized by society (Ashforth & Kreiner, 1999; Hughes, 1951). This could include various physically tainted work roles (e.g., janitors, funeral directors), socially tainted work roles (e.g., prison guards), and morally tainted work roles (e.g., sex workers). Individuals who hold these types of work roles are potentially at higher risk for experiencing negative well-being (Arnold & Barling, in press). These workers must expend extra effort to overcome the stigma of their work roles and to be able to define their work in a more positive light. If individuals are not able to reframe their work in positive terms (Ashforth & Kreiner, 1999), their well-being is potentially negatively affected. Transformational leadership may exert even more positive effect in these marginalized groups, and empirical research is necessary to explore this question.

It is our wish that researchers continue to address the call for research on work and well-being through the lens of positive psychology. Orienting the study of work and well-being in this way has the potential to amplify our knowledge and practice of work through which employees and their leaders have a chance to truly flourish.

REFERENCES

Amick, B. C., III, McDonough, P., Chang, H., Rogers, W. H., Duncan, G., & Pieper, C. (2002). The relationship between all-cause mortality and cumulative working life course psychosocial and physical exposures in the United States labor market from 1968–1992. *Psychosomatic Medicine, 64,* 370–381.

Arnold, K. A., & Barling, J. (in press). Prostitution: An illustration of occupational stress in "dirty" work. In M. Dollard, A. Winefield, & H. Winefield (Eds.), *Occupational stress in the service professions.* London: Taylor & Francis.

Arnold, K. A., Barling, J., & Kelloway, E. K. (2001). Transformational leadership or the iron cage: Which predicts trust, commitment and team efficacy? *Leadership and Organization Development Journal, 22,* 315–320.

Arthur, J. B. (1994). Effects of human resource systems on manufacturing performance and turnover. *Academy of Management Journal, 37,* 670–687.

Ashforth, B. E., & Kreiner, G. E. (1999). How can you do it? Dirty work and the challenge of constructing a positive identity. *Academy of Management Review, 24,* 413–434.

Ashforth, B. E., & Mael, F. (1989). Social identity theory and the organization. *Academy of Management Review, 14,* 20–39.

Bandura, A. (1997). *Self-efficacy: The exercise of control.* New York: Freeman.

Barley, S. R., & Tolbert, P. S. (1991). Introduction: At the intersection of organizations and occupations. In P. S. Tolbert & S. R. Barley (Guest Eds.), *Research in the sociology of organizations* (Vol. 8, pp. 1–13). Greenwich, CT: JAI Press.

*Barling, J., Loughlin, C. A., & Kelloway, E. K. (2002). Development and test of a model linking safety-specific transformational leadership and occupational injuries. *Journal of Applied Psychology, 87,* 488–496.

Barling, J., Weber, T., & Kelloway, E. K. (1996). Effects of transformational leadership training on attitudinal and financial outcomes: A field experiment. *Journal of Applied Psychology, 81,* 827–832.

Bass, B. M. (1985). *Leadership and performance beyond expectations.* New York: Free Press.

Bass, B. M. (1990). *Bass & Stogdill's handbook of leadership: Theory, research, and managerial applications* (3rd ed.). New York: Free Press.

Bass, B. M. (1998). *Transformational leadership: Industrial, military, and educational impact.* Mahwah, NJ: Erlbaum.

Beeler, J. D. (1997, Winter). A survey report of job satisfaction and job involvement among governmental and public auditors. *Government Accounts Journal, 45,* 26–31.

Britt, T. W., Adler, A. B., & Bartone, P. T. (2001). Deriving benefits from stressful events: The role of engagement in meaningful work and hardiness. *Journal of Occupational Health Psychology, 6,* 53–63.

Brown, M. (1969). Identification and some conditions of organizational involvement. *Administrative Science Quarterly, 14,* 346–355.

Bruggeman, A., Groskurth, P., & Ulich, E. (1975). *Arbeitszufriedenheit* [Work satisfaction]. Bern, Switzerland: Huber.

Burns, J. M. (1978). *Leadership.* New York: Harper & Row.

Butler, J. K., Cantrell, R. S., & Flick, R. J. (1999). Transformation leadership behaviors, upward trust, and satisfaction in self-managed work teams. *Organization Development Journal, 17,* 13–28.

Charbonneau, D., Barling, J., & Kelloway, E. K. (2001). Transformational leadership and sports performance: The mediating role of intrinsic motivation. *Journal of Applied Social Psychology, 31,* 1521–1534.

Cook, J., & Wall, T. D. (1980). New work attitudes measures of trust, organizational commitment and personal need nonfulfillment. *Journal of Occupational Psychology, 53,* 39–52.

Dirks, K. T. (2000). Trust in leadership and team performance: Evidence from NCAA basketball. *Journal of Applied Psychology, 85,* 1004–1012.

*Dutton, J. E., Frost, P. J., Worline, M. C., Lilius, J. M., & Kanov, J. M. (2002). Leading in times of trauma. *Harvard Business Review, 80,* 55–61.

Fleishman, E., & Harris, E. F. (1962). Patterns of leadership behavior related to employee grievances and turnover. *Personnel Psychology, 15,* 43–56.

Frone, M. R., Russell, M., & Cooper, M. L. (1995). Job stressors, job involvement and employee health: A test of identity theory. *Journal of Occupational and Organizational Psychology, 68,* 1–11.

Giuliani, R. W. (2002). *Leadership.* New York: Miramax.

Hackman, J. R., & Oldham, G. R. (1980). *Work redesign.* Reading, MA: Addison-Wesley.

Hall, D. T., & Schneider, B. (1972). Correlates of organizational identification as a function of career pattern and organizational type. *Administrative Science Quarterly, 17,* 340–350.

Hart, P. M. (1999). Predicting employee life satisfaction: A coherent model of personality, work and nonwork experiences, and domain satisfaction. *Journal of Applied Psychology, 84,* 564–584.

Higginbottom, S., Barling, J., & Kelloway, E. K. (1993). Linking retirement experiences and marital satisfaction: A mediational model. *Psychology and Aging, 8,* 508–516.

*Hofmann, D. A., & Tetrick, L. E. (Eds.). (2003). *Health and safety in organizations: A multilevel perspective.* San Francisco: Jossey-Bass.

Hughes, E. C. (1951). Work and the self. In J. H. Rohrer & M. Sherif (Eds.), *Social psychology at the crossroads: The University of Oklahoma lectures in social psychology* (pp. 313–323). New York: Harper & Brothers.

Jex, S. M., & Bliese, P. D. (1999). Efficacy beliefs as moderator of the impact of work-related stressors: A multilevel study. *Journal of Applied Psychology, 86,* 349–361.

Judge, T. A., & Bono, J. E. (2000). Five-factor model of personality and transformational leadership. *Journal of Applied Psychology, 85,* 751–765.

Judge, T. A., & Watanabe, S. (1993). Another look at the job satisfaction-life satisfaction relationship. *Journal of Applied Psychology, 78,* 939–948.

Jung, D. I., & Avolio, B. J. (2000). Opening the black box: An experimental investigation of the mediating effects of trust and value congruence on transformational and transactional leadership. *Journal of Organizational Behavior, 21,* 949–964.

Kanungo, R. N. (1982). Measurement of job and work involvement. *Journal of Applied Psychology, 67,* 341–349.

Kelloway, E. K., & Barling, J. (1991). Job characteristics, role stress, and mental health. *Journal of Occupational Psychology, 64,* 291–304.

Kelloway, E. K., & Barling, J. (1993). Member's participation in local union activities: Measurement, prediction, replication. *Journal of Applied Psychology, 78,* 262–279.

Kinicki, A. J., & Latack, J. C. (1990). Explication of the construct of coping with involuntary job loss. *Journal of Vocational Behavior, 36,* 339–360.

Kirkpatrick, S. A., & Locke, E. A. (1996). Direct and indirect effects of three core charismatic leadership components on performance and attitudes. *Journal of Applied Psychology, 81,* 36–51.

Koh, W. L., Steers, J. M., & Terborg, J. R. (1995). The effects of transformational leadership on teacher attitudes and student performance in Singapore. *Journal of Organizational Behavior, 16,* 319–333.

Kouzes, J. M., & Posner, B. Z. (1995). *The leadership challenge: How to keep getting extraordinary things done in organizations* (2nd ed.). San Francisco: Jossey-Bass.

Kramer, R. M. (1999). Trust and distrust in organizations: Emerging perspectives, enduring questions. *Annual Review of Psychology, 50,* 569–598.

Mael, F., & Ashforth, B. E. (1992). Alumni and their alma mater: A partial test of the re-formulated model of organizational identification. *Journal of Organizational Behavior, 13,* 103–123.

Mayer, R. C., Davis, J. H., & Schoorman, F. D. (1995). An integrative model of organizational trust. *Academy of Management Review, 20,* 709–734.

McAllister, D. J. (1995). Affect- and cognition-based trust as foundations for interpersonal cooperation in organizations. *Academy of Management Journal, 38,* 24–59.

Morse, N. C., & Weiss, R. W. (1955). The function and meaning of work and the job. *American Sociological Review, 20,* 191–198.

MOW International Research Team. (1987). *The meaning of working.* New York: Academic Press.

Nord, W. R., Brief, A. P., Atieh, J. M., & Doherty, E. M. (1988). Work values and the conduct of organizational behavior. *Research in Organizational Behavior, 10,* 1–42.

O'Reilly, C., & Chapman, J. (1986). Organizational commitment and psychological attachment: The effects of compliance, identification, and internalization on prosocial behavior. *Journal of Applied Psychology, 71,* 492–499.

Paullay, I. M. (1991). *Clarification of the job involvement and work centrality constructs and their relationship to job burnout.* Unpublished doctoral dissertation, State University of New York, Albany.

Paullay, I. M., Alliger, G. M., & Stone-Romero, E. F. (1994). Construct validation of two instruments designed to measure job involvement and work centrality. *Journal of Applied Psychology, 79,* 224–228.

Peteet, J. R. (2000). Cancer and the meaning of work. *General Hospital Psychiatry, 22,* 200–205.

Pillai, R., Scandura, T. A., & Williams, E. A. (1999). Leadership and organizational justice: Similarities and differences across cultures. *Journal of International Business Studies, 30,* 763–779.

Pillai, R., Schriesheim, C. A., & Williams, E. S. (1999). Fairness perceptions and trust as mediators for transformational and transactional leadership: A two-sample study. *Journal of Management, 25,* 897–933.

Podsakoff, P. M., Mackenzie, S. B., Moorman, R. H., & Fetter, R. (1990). Transformational leader behaviors and their effects on followers' trust in leader, satisfaction, and organizational citizenship behaviors. *Leadership Quarterly, 1,* 107–142.

Prussia, G. E., & Kinicki, A. J. (1996). A motivational investigation of group effectiveness using social-cognitive theory. *Journal of Applied Psychology, 81,* 187–198.

Robertson, L. (1990). Functions of work meanings: Work meanings and work motivation. In A. P. Brief & W. R. Nord (Eds.), *Meanings of occupational work: A collection of essays* (pp. 107–134). Toronto, Ontario, Canada: Butterworth.

Saks, A. M. (1995). Longitudinal field investigation of the moderating and mediating effects of self-efficacy on the relationship between training and newcomer adjustment. *Journal of Applied Psychology, 80,* 211–225.

Salancik, G. R., & Pfeffer, J. (1978). A social information processing approach to job attitudes and task design. *Administrative Science Quarterly, 23,* 224–253.

Sarros, J. C., Tanewski, G. A., Winter, R. P., Santora, J. C., & Densten, I. L. (2002). Work alienation and organizational leadership. *British Journal of Management, 13,* 285–304.

Shamir, B., House, R. J., & Arthur, M. B. (1993). The motivational effects of charismatic leadership: A self-concept based theory. *Organization Science, 4,* 577–594.

Shields, N. (1995). The link between student identity, attributions, and self-esteem among adult, returning students. *Sociological Perspectives, 38,* 261–272.

Sivanathan, N., Barling, J., & Turner, N. (2003). *Leading others to safety: Effects of transformational leadership training on occupational safety.* Manuscript in preparation, Queen's University, Kingston, Ontario, Canada.

Snyder, C. R., & Lopez, S. J. (Eds.). (2002). *Handbook of positive psychology.* New York: Oxford University Press.

Sparks, J. R., & Schenk, J. A. (2001). Explaining the effects of transformational leadership: An investigation of the effects of higher-order motives in multilevel marketing organizations. *Journal of Organizational Behavior, 22,* 849–869.

Stajkovic, A. D., & Luthans, F. (1998). Self-efficacy and work-related performance: A meta-analysis. *Psychological Bulletin, 42,* 240–261.

Tepper, B. K. (2000). Consequences of abusive supervision. *Academy of Management Journal, 43,* 178–190.

Turner, N., Barling, J., Epitropaki, O., Butcher, V., & Milner, C. (2002). Transformational leadership and moral reasoning. *Journal of Applied Psychology, 87,* 304–311.

*Turner, N., Barling, J., & Zacharatos, A. (2002). Positive psychology at work. In C. R. Snyder & S. J. Lopez (Eds.), *Handbook of positive psychology* (pp. 715–728). New York: Oxford University Press.

Van Maanen, J., & Barley, S. R. (1984). Occupational communities: Culture and control in organizations. *Research in Organizational Behavior, 6,* 287–365.

Walsh, C. (2001). *Leadership on 9/11: Morgan Stanley's challenge.* Retrieved August 20, 2002, from http://hbswk.hbs.edu/item.jhtml?id=2690&t=leadership&sid=0&pid=0.

Warr, P. B. (1987). *Work, unemployment, and mental health.* Oxford, England: Oxford University Press.

Warr, P. B. (1990). The measurement of well-being and other aspects of mental health. *Journal of Occupational Psychology, 63,* 193–210.

*Warr, P. B. (1999). Well-being and the workplace. In D. Kahneman, E. Diener, & N. Schwarz (Eds.), *Well-being: The foundations of hedonic psychology* (pp. 392–412). New York: Russell Sage Foundation.

White, S. E., & Mitchell, T. R. (1979). Job enrichment versus social cues: A comparison and competitive test. *Journal of Applied Psychology, 64,* 1–9.

Yukl, G. (1998). *Leadership in organizations* (4th ed.). Upper Saddle River, NJ: Prentice-Hall.

Zacharatos, A., Barling, J., & Kelloway, E. K. (2000). Development and effects of transformational leadership in adolescents. *Leadership Quarterly, 11,* 211–226.

Zohar, D. (2000). A group-level model of safety climate: Testing the effect of group climate on microaccidents in manufacturing jobs. *Journal of Applied Psychology, 85,* 587–596.

Zohar, D. (2002). Effects of leadership dimensions, safety climate, and assigned priorities on minor injuries in work groups. *Journal of Organizational Behavior, 78,* 85–97.

CHAPTER 16

Strengths-Based
Development in Practice

TIMOTHY D. HODGES and DONALD O. CLIFTON

People don't change that much. Don't waste time trying to put in what was left out.
Try to draw out what was left in. That is hard enough.

—Buckingham and Coffman, 1999, p. 57

THESE WORDS, SUMMARIZED from the interviews of tens of thousands of great managers studied by Gallup, articulate the simple notion underpinning strengths-based development. Rather than spending time helping their associates become well-rounded, many of the world's best managers have instead invested time in learning about the individual talents of each of their associates and managing with those unique talents in mind. This concept applies to not only managers but also educators, administrators, students, salespeople, leaders of faith communities, and essentially all who desire to heighten their self-awareness and change their paradigm from one of becoming average in many things to excelling in a few areas.

If many of the world's best managers agree on this simple premise, then everyone must think that way, right? Gallup asked the following question around the world: "Which would help you be more successful in your life—[rotated] knowing what your weaknesses are and attempting to improve your weaknesses, or knowing what your strengths are and attempting to build on your strengths?" (See Figure 16.1.) Those who chose to focus on their strengths and manage around their weaknesses were a minority in the United States, United Kingdom, Canada, France, Japan, and China—every country in Gallup's study.

The authors wish to thank Jim Harter, Tom Rath, Piotrek Juszkiewicz, and Connie Rath for their encouragement and suggestions during the writing of this chapter.

256

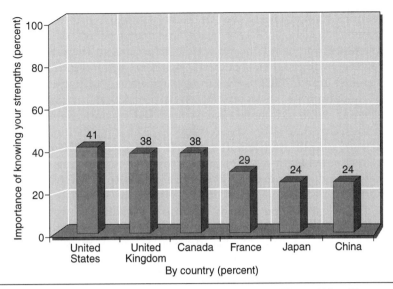

Figure 16.1   Results of a Global Gallup Poll Indicate That Those Who Choose to Focus on Their Strengths to Achieve Success in Life Are in the Minority. Reprinted with the permission of The Gallup Organization.

As is presented in this chapter, strengths-based development has potential that is just beginning to be realized. There is clearly a need to educate the world about positive psychology in practice and the importance of understanding and focusing on strengths. This chapter reviews the theory behind strengths-based development, introduces an instrument that has enabled hundreds of thousands of individuals to identify their themes of talent, reviews the impact of several strengths-based development interventions, and describes future research directions for strengths-based development.

THE THEORY AND PRACTICE OF STRENGTHS-BASED DEVELOPMENT

While the opening statement of this chapter presents strengths-based development in simple terms, fully understanding the concept requires further explanation of associated terms, including strength, theme, and talent:

> A strength is the ability to provide consistent, near-perfect performance in a given activity. The key to building a strength is to first identify your dominant themes of talent, then to discover your specific talents within those themes, and to lastly refine them with knowledge and skills. Talents are naturally recurring patterns of thought, feeling, or behavior that can be productively applied. One of the three "raw materials" used in strengths building, talent naturally exists within you, while skills and knowledge must be acquired. (Clifton & Hodges, in press)

Talent is defined as naturally recurring. The field of neuroscience further clarifies this notion. Roughly, between the ages of 3 and 15, the human brain organizes itself by strengthening the synaptic connections used often, while infrequently used connections weaken over time. Dr. Harry Chugani, professor of pediatrics, neurology, and radiology at Wayne State University School of Medicine, made the following statement about the synaptic connections in the brain: "Roads with the most traffic get widened. The ones that are rarely used fall into disrepair" (Coffman & Gonzalez-Molina, 2002, p. 21). Stronger synapses within the network of connections in the brain continue to strengthen, while weaker connections fade away. After about age 15, an individual's unique network of synaptic connections does not change significantly. While this doesn't imply that people cannot change, it does provide scientific backup for the notion that their talents, or recurring patterns of thought, feeling, or behavior—don't significantly change over time. Individuals can develop a heightened self-awareness, they can stabilize their values and beliefs, and they can add knowledge and skills on the way to developing their talents into strengths. Still, it seems that their greatest return on their investment into development comes from focusing on the synaptic connections that are already strong.

At the individual level, strengths-based development involves three stages: identification of talent, integration into how the individual views himself or herself, and behavioral change (Clifton & Harter, 2003). This process involves many steps, including identifying things done at excellence, claiming them as strong points, naming them, sharing them with others, consciously thinking about how performance can be maximized if behaviors and talents are aligned, adding necessary knowledge and skills, and actively using the talents whenever possible.

In the identification of talent phase, individuals increase their level of self-awareness. They capitalize on opportunities to claim particular themes of talent. In the integration phase, individuals are more able to explain the behaviors that take place because of their top talents. They begin to define who they are in terms of their talents. Finally, in the behavior change phase, individuals tie their successes back to their themes of talent. Further, they report increases in satisfaction, productivity, and other outcomes as a result of their focus on what they do best.

Traces of talents can be identified in several ways, including spontaneous reactions, yearnings, rapid learning, and satisfaction (Buckingham & Clifton, 2001). Spontaneous reactions are subconscious, immediate responses to a given situation. These glimpses of talent may be observed in a person who naturally takes charge of a situation without being asked to do so, a new employee who quickly introduces herself to her coworkers, and a student who willingly volunteers to stay after class to help a fellow student with his homework. Yearnings may also provide clues to talent. A passion for a new hobby, a need to keep things neat and tidy, and a desire to learn a new language could be indications of talent. Others identify talents through examples of rapid learning, whether it is in a new role at work, geometry class, or violin lessons. Finally, satisfactions from positive activities provide clues to talent. If someone enjoys the process of planning a family reunion, reading a technical paper, or giving a speech to a large audience, the chances are that they are appealing to one or more of their talents.

Monitoring thoughts and behavior over a period of time can provide important insights into identifying themes of talent. Other means of talent identification are available as well. The Gallup Organization designed a web-based assessment called the StrengthsFinder (available at http://www.strengthsfinder.com) to assist in the talent discovery process by measuring the predictability of patterns of behavior within individuals. The StrengthsFinder presents individuals with pairs of statements, sorts the responses, and presents the results in the form of dominant patterns of behavior, or themes of talent. Thirty-four themes of talent have been identified to capture prevalent patterns of behavior recognized through Gallup's study of excellence. These themes are areas where the greatest potential exists for strengths building.

The conceptual basis of StrengthsFinder is grounded in more than three decades of the study of success across a wide variety of functions and more than 30 countries. StrengthsFinder identifies an individual's themes of talent, which, when supplemented with relevant knowledge and skills, can be developed into strengths. For this reason, StrengthsFinder serves as a starting point for self-discovery in strengths-based developmental programs. This initial diagnostic tool provides insights that are reported back as themes and supplemented with developmental suggestions customized to the individual's top themes and his or her role. The themes help individuals form a language of success on which they are able to articulate what they do well. Specific developmental programs are tailored to meet the unique needs of clients. In addition, audience-specific books have been published and are available in the popular press for employees (Buckingham & Clifton, 2001), salespeople (Smith & Rutigliano, 2003), students (Clifton & Anderson, 2002), and members of faith communities (Winseman, Clifton, & Liesveld, 2003).

Strengths-based development has been applied in several different settings, with programs designed for leaders, managers, salespeople, customer service representatives, nurses, teachers, students, and more. The StrengthsFinder assessment is available in several languages and, at the time of writing, had been completed by nearly one million individuals from more than 40 countries. Strengths-based developmental programs vary depending on the audience. Various programs may include the StrengthsFinder assessment, online learning, classroom instruction, and one-on-one consulting or executive coaching (visit http://www.gallup.com/university/ for a partial listing of strengths-based developmental programs).

OUTCOMES OF STRENGTHS-BASED DEVELOPMENT

Strengths-based development has been linked to positive outcomes in a variety of studies across a range of domains. Individuals participating in strengths-based development report changed behaviors in follow-up surveys. More direct relationships between strengths-based development and attendance, grades, and per-person productivity have been identified. In other cases, strengths-based development has been linked to increases in employee engagement, which has been meaningfully linked to business outcomes including profitability, turnover, safety, customer satisfaction, and more (Harter, Schmidt, & Hayes, 2002). Still other studies arrive at increases in positive psychological or positive organizational behavior capacities such as hope, subjective well-being, and confidence. This section reviews several studies that provide evidence of the impact of strengths-based development on positive outcomes.

FOLLOW-UP SURVEYS

Gallup researchers conducted brief web-based surveys to study the impact of strengths awareness on participant behaviors (Hodges, 2003). E-mail invitations were sent to study participants 75 days following their completion of the Strengths-Finder assessment through the *Now, Discover Your Strengths* web site (http://www

.strengthsfinder.com). Invitations were sent to participants who provided a valid e-mail address and consented to being contacted in the future. A total of 459 surveys were completed during a period of several weeks in the autumn of 2002. The survey consisted of open-ended items as well as five-point "strongly disagree" to "strongly agree" Likert-type items.

Three survey items were written to serve as indicators of behavioral change as a result of the participants' strengths awareness. The first item was written to broadly measure the impact of strengths awareness on lifestyle. Fifty-nine percent of respondents agreed or strongly agreed with the statement, "Learning about my strengths has helped me to make better choices in my life." The second behavioral change survey item focused more specifically on individual productivity as an outcome measure, with 60% of respondents stating that they agreed or strongly agreed with the statement, "Focusing on my strengths has helped me to be more productive." The third survey item is closely aligned with the field of positive psychology. Through this item, 63% of respondents indicated that they agreed or strongly agreed with the statement, "Learning about my strengths has increased my self-confidence." Other studies on the relationship between strengths and self-confidence are reviewed later in this chapter.

While the study results point in a favorable direction, it should be noted that these study participants took part in a very minimal strengths-based developmental intervention, consisting only of having had the opportunity to read *Now, Discover Your Strengths,* complete the StrengthsFinder assessment, and receive a printed copy of their top five themes of talent. Participants in more intensive strengths-based developmental interventions are currently being invited to complete the survey items identified in this review. Preliminary results show that more intensive interventions, including classroom instruction and individual coaching with a trained consultant, yield a higher magnitude of positive results on each survey item than in the minimal intervention reviewed here.

DIRECT IMPACT ON OUTCOMES

Several recent research studies have explored the impact of strengths-based development across various contexts. The following section reviews examples from both education and the workplace.

Education   Strengths-based developmental interventions have also been shown to positively impact educational outcomes. Gallup researchers conducted a 4-year study at a Midwestern U.S. urban high school from 1994 to 1997 (Harter, 1998). These studies involved training a random selection of teachers to administer talent-based interviews to incoming freshmen in each of the four years of the intervention. Following the interviews, the teachers provided individualized feedback to the students, highlighting their patterns of strongest talent identified through the interviews. The research team tracked absenteeism, tardiness, and grades for all of the students associated with the study during this important first semester of high school. Weighted average effect size correlations were calculated to measure the impact across the four years of the semester-long strengths-based interventions. Meaningful differences were observed between the study group of 807 students and the control group of 841 students on all three outcome measures. The study group had 3.8 fewer days absent per student (0.33 standard score units), 0.78 fewer times tardy per student (0.31 standard score units), and grade point averages that were 0.15 standard score units higher than the control group.

Colleges and universities have also served as a context for strengths-based development. A recent study was conducted with college freshmen enrolled at a private, faith-based university (Williamson, 2002). The researcher set out to determine if there was a difference between a study group of students introduced to strengths-based development and a control group who was not. A random sample of first-year English writing students was invited to participate in the program. This study group of 32 students participated in an intervention, including the administration of the StrengthsFinder assessment during a summer orientation program, participation in two one-hour presentations on strengths theory and presentation of individual StrengthsFinder results, and a one-on-one advising session with a trained StrengthsCoach. A control group of 40 students, randomly selected from the same sections of the English writing course, completed the StrengthsFinder survey during the summer orientation program but did not receive feedback on their results or participate in any group or individual strengths-based advising. First-semester college student success at the study site is defined as, at a minimum, completing 12 credit hours of coursework with a 2.0 GPA or higher. Although the high school GPA and ACT scores for the study and contrast groups were not statistically different, the first-semester college academic results differed among the two groups. Only 2 of the 32 students in the group participating in the strengths-based intervention failed to meet the minimum standards expected of first-semester students, while 8 of the 40 control group students failed to meet these standards. Further, the college GPAs were significantly higher for the study group ($p < .05$) at the conclusion of the first semester.

Workplace Strengths-based developmental interventions have taken place in various workplace domains, including a Southern California auto parts warehouse. The Toyota North American Parts Center California (NAPCC), composed of 400 employees on 54 work teams, underwent a strengths-based intervention with an objective to build effective work teams (Connelly, 2002). The intervention began with warehouse associates completing the StrengthsFinder to identify their themes of talent. Many lunchtime learning sessions were conducted to answer any questions and to deliver StrengthsFinder results to individual associates. Next, NAPCC managers attended a 4-day course designed to introduce them to the theory and practice of managing themselves and their teams according to their strengths. Finally, warehouse associates at NAPCC came together on a Saturday at 6:00 A.M. for a half-day team-blend session designed to move individuals from thinking about their own strengths to thinking about the strengths of their team members to optimize team relationships and performance. Quantifiable business results were attributed to the strengths-based intervention when, within a year of the intervention, per-person-productivity at the warehouse increased by 6%. These results were in sharp contrast to the previous three years, when quarterly productivity figures varied either positively or negatively by less than 1%. Further, two teams who underwent a more intensive strengths-based developmental program realized a 9% productivity increase over a period of just 6 months.

IMPACT ON EMPLOYEE ENGAGEMENT

Many strengths-based developmental interventions have led to a quantifiable impact on the employee engagement metric. Employee engagement is measured by 12 questions (Buckingham & Coffman, 1999) selected for their comprehensiveness, performance-relatedness, and actionability (Harter, 2000). The employee engagement metric is designed to enable managers to take necessary steps toward increased levels of engagement and improved performance in response to employee ratings. Employee engagement is measured at the business-unit level and has been meaningfully linked to performance outcomes, including customer satisfaction, productivity, profit, employee turnover, and accidents (Harter, Schmidt, & Hayes, 2002).

While several studies have shown linkages between strengths-based development and the entire employee engagement metric, one employee engagement item in particular, "opportunity to do what I do best," has a strong conceptual relationship to strengths-based development. This item also has strong research evidence linking it to success, defined as above the median performance within an individual's company, across work units. A recent meta-analysis of more than 10,000 work units and more than 300,000 employees in 51 companies indicates that work units scoring above the median on the "opportunity to do what I do best" item have 38% higher probability of success on productivity measures and 44% higher probability of success on customer loyalty and employee retention (Harter & Schmidt, 2002).

To further illustrate the impact of strengths-based development on employee engagement and business outcomes, Clifton and Harter (2003) reviewed data from 65 organizations, all of which were involved in employee engagement interventions. A study group consisted of four companies that had used strengths-based development, and a control group was made up of 61 organizations that had not. The study group exceeded the control group on employee engagement from year 1 to year 2 ($d = 0.65$) and even more dramatically so from year 1 to year 3 ($d = 1.15$). Utility analyses, conducted to determine the difference between the study and control groups, yielded an increase in annual per employee productivity of more than $1,000. This equates to more than $1 million for an organization of 1,000 employees and more than $5.4 million for the average-size company in the study. Further tangible value from the study may be realized through further utility analyses on other performance outcomes, including turnover, profit, safety, and customer satisfaction. Focus groups and follow-up interviews with staff participating in strengths-based development programs widely report an increased understanding and respect for their coworkers and report that they work together better as a result of knowing, accepting, and working to develop the strengths that their peers bring to the table.

An example of an increase in employee engagement in response to strengths-based development is found at St. Lucie Medical Center in Florida (Black, 2001). This 150-bed hospital was the place of work for 700 nurses, clinicians, and support staff. High turnover and low morale were barriers to the hospital's success. In 1998, the hospital ranked in the bottom quartile of Gallup's worldwide employee engagement database. However, a closer look revealed that, although the overall hospital scores were low, there were several engaged work groups within St. Lucie. The leadership of St. Lucie decided to study the talents of the top leaders, and eventually of employees across functions, through structured talent inventory interviews. This information was used to build teams that allowed each employee to flourish according to his or her innate talents. Just two years into the strengths-based development and employee engagement intervention, St. Lucie's staff turnover had declined by almost 50% and the employee engagement scores had jumped to the top quartile of Gallup's database. Furthermore, the hospital's percentile ranking for patient satisfaction jumped by 160% in comparison to its peers.

As with the employee engagement metric, research on congregational engagement indicates that members of faith-based communities who regularly have the opportunity to do what they do best within their faith communities are more engaged than those who do not. Further, engaged members have higher life satisfaction, give more money, volunteer more, and are more likely to invite others to participate in their congregations (Winseman, 2002). In a 2001 study of congregational members, 66% of congregation members who had invited someone to participate in their congregation within the last month also strongly agreed with the statement, "I regularly have the opportunity to do what I do best." Further, 50% of those polled who volunteered two or more hours per week also stated that they regularly had the opportunity to do what they do best. The benefits of strengths-based development seem clear and quantifiable through the congregational engagement metric within the context of faith-based communities.

IMPACT ON OTHER POSITIVE PSYCHOLOGICAL MEASURES

Empirical research suggests that strengths-based developmental interventions have a positive impact on positive psychological and positive organizational behavioral constructs. The field of positive psychology, defined as "the scientific study of optimal human functioning" (Sheldon, Frederickson, Rathunde, & Csikszentmihalyi, 2000), has grown in popularity over the past several years. Several researchers have applied positive psychology to the workplace (Cameron, Dutton, & Quinn, 2003). Building from the foundation of the positive psychology movement, recent attention has been paid to positive organizational behavior (POB), defined as "the study and application of positively oriented human resource strengths that can be measured, developed, and effectively managed for performance improvement in today's workplace" (Luthans, 2002, p. 59). Three POB constructs receiving recent attention have been hope, subjective well-being, and confidence.

Hope Hope is a positive psychological capacity consisting of two components: agency, or goal-directed determination, and pathways, or planning ways to meet goals (Snyder et al., 1991). State hope (Snyder et al., 1996) describes an individual's present goal-directed thinking. State hope can be developed and has been used as a measure of ongoing goal-related activities in many domains (Snyder, 2000), including the workplace (Peterson & Luthans, 2003). Suggestions for developing hope include clarification of goals, simplifying the goals into smaller steps, developing alternative plans, taking pleasure in the process, and being strategic in overcoming obstacles (Luthans & Jensen, 2002).

Two empirical studies offer evidence that strengths-based developmental interventions can increase levels of state hope. A three-month study consisted of undergraduate business students participating in a strengths-based intervention over the course of the academic term. At the beginning of the semester, a pretest with several positive psychological assessments, including the six-item State Hope Scale (Snyder et al., 1996), was administered to the students. Next, students completed the StrengthsFinder assessment and were provided access to online learning about strengths. Then, the students took part in 30-minute one-on-one consulting calls with an individual trained to administer strengths feedback. Finally, at the conclusion of the semester (approximately two months following the consulting calls), students completed a posttest identical to the pretest given at the beginning of the academic term. Analysis of the pretest-posttest data revealed that state hope scores increased by 0.36 standard score units over the three-month interval.

The second strengths-based intervention providing evidence for the development of state hope is from a study conducted at a Midwestern United States rehabilitation hospital. This study involved an organizationwide pretest with items designed to measure self-awareness, hope, and subjective well-being. The pretest was administered to hospital employees via the Internet in May 2002. Employees then had an opportunity to complete the StrengthsFinder and receive a printed report of their top five themes of talent with suggested action statements associated with each theme. Twenty-four hospital employees were trained as Strengths-Coaches. The coaches' names and contact information were made available to associates, and the associates were encouraged to schedule and complete feedback sessions designed to teach them more about their themes of talent and how they could build them into strengths. Approximately one year later, hospital employees were invited to complete the online posttest (identical to the pretest with the exception of an additional item at the end asking employees to rate the extent to which they received feedback on their StrengthsFinder results within the past year). A total of 488 employees completed both the pretest and the posttest. Forty percent of the 488 employees strongly agreed with the statement, "In the last year, I have received feedback on my StrengthsFinder results." These 40% were identified as having actively participated in the strengths-based developmental intervention. While the overall level of state hope at the hospital remained relatively unchanged from the pretest to the posttest, the 40% of associates who received feedback on their StrengthsFinder results increased in hope significantly more than the other 60% of employees ($p < .001$). In fact, the group of associates who actively participated in the strengths-based intervention was the only group who increased in state hope from the pretest to the posttest.

Subjective Well-Being   Subjective well-being (Diener, 1984) can be distilled into three components: positive affect, negative affect, and life satisfaction (Andrews & Withey, 1976). The life satisfaction component is of particular interest to workplace research as it has been linked to job satisfaction (Judge & Watanabe, 1993; Tait, Padgett, & Baldwin, 1989). Further, job satisfaction has been linked to job performance (Judge, Thoresen, Bono, & Patton, 2001). Emerging research suggests that workplace well-being and performance are "complimentary and dependent components of a financially and psychologically healthy workplace" (Harter, Schmidt, & Keyes, 2003, p. 221). Life satisfaction scores have been shown to increase over periods of outpatient therapy (Pavot & Diener, 1993), suggesting that it is state-like and able to be developed.

The strengths-based intervention at a Midwestern rehabilitation hospital described earlier also served as a test site for changes in the satisfaction with life component of subjective well-being. The pretest and posttest included the five-item Satisfaction with Life Scale (Diener, Emmons, Larsen, & Griffin, 1985). Again, of the 488 employees who completed both the pretest and posttest, 40% strongly agreed when asked if they had received feedback on their Strengths-Finder results within the past year. The group of employees who maximally participated in the program increased in satisfaction with life significantly more than the other 60% of employees ($p < 0.05$).

Confidence   Confidence draws heavily from Bandura's (1982) work with self-efficacy. *Self-efficacy* is defined as, "an individual's conviction (or confidence) about his or her abilities to mobilize the motivation, cognitive resources, and courses of action needed to successfully execute a specific task within a given context" (Stajkovic & Luthans, 1998b, p. 66). Self-efficacy, or confidence, can be developed through positive feedback, mastery experiences or performance attainments, vicarious learning, and physiological or psychological arousal (Bandura, 1997). A meta-analysis illustrated a strong link between confidence and work-related performance (Stajkovic & Luthans, 1998a).

A recent study with 212 UCLA students provides evidence that increased confidence may be an outcome of strengths-based development. This study took place in the fall semester of 2002. Students completed a pretest, participated in the strengths-based developmental intervention, and then completed a posttest. The intervention consisted of several classroom activities and homework assignments facilitated by the course professor, a trained strengths coach. The pretest and posttest consisted of identical surveys with items designed to measure participants' awareness of strengths, direction about the future, and level of confidence (Clifton, 1997; Rath, 2002). Ten items from the survey comprised a subscale measure of confidence, including items such as, "I am confident in my ability to build friendships," and "I am an academically confident person." The posttest scores on the confidence subscale were significantly higher than the pretest scores ($p < 0.001$), with an increase of 0.23 standard score units.

THE ROAD AHEAD

Strengths-based development involves the identification of talents, integration into individuals' view of themselves, and resulting changes in behavior (Clifton & Harter, 2003). This chapter reviewed several studies that illustrate the impact of strengths-based development on various outcomes, including productivity, educational performance, employee engagement, hope, subjective well-being, and confidence, across several domains, including education, health care, and the workplace.

While there are several examples of the impact of strengths-based development presented in this chapter, there is still much research that needs to be conducted on the topic. Numerous strengths-based developmental studies are currently underway. Longitudinal studies are being conducted to measure the impact of development over time. Several variations of developmental programs are being tested with various audiences to determine the most effective intervention for each audience. Strengths-based development is also being tested against the *Barnum effect*, defined as the tendency for people to accept very vague or general feedback as accurate (see Snyder, Shenkel, & Lowery, 1977, for a review of the Barnum effect).

Future research should explore relationships between strengths-based development and other positive psychological/positive organizational behavioral constructs, such as resiliency. The Pygmalion effect, a self-fulfilling prophecy where subordinates perform better when expected to do so by their superiors, has been explored in education (Rosenthal, 1994; Rosenthal & Jacobson, 1968) and management (Eden, 1990; White & Locke, 2000). Studies comparing strengths-based development and Pygmalion effects should be considered.

Further controlled experiments should be conducted to measure the impact of strengths-based developmental programs. Advanced statistical models, including path analysis, should be applied to measure causality and explore possible mediators in the relationship between strengths-based development and desired outcomes. Future research is expected to uncover further breakthroughs concerning the importance of strengths-based development and its linkage to performance improvement. Strengths-based development stands at the forefront of positive psychology in practice and offers much to professional psychologists, educators, managers, and others who wish to work from a positive psychological perspective.

CONCLUSION

The Positive Psychology movement has come about partially in response to the realization that, since World War II, the field of psychology has focused primarily on weakness-fixing and the treatment of psychological disorders. Global surveys indicate that individuals elect to focus on improving weaknesses to achieve success in life.

Current research indicates that there may be a better way. This chapter reviewed theory and empirical studies that offer support for strengths-based development as a means for performance improvement across various contexts. Our hope is that future developmental interventions will build from this solid research base and will focus primarily on the more positive strengths-based approach.

REFERENCES

Andrews, F. M., & Withey, S. B. (1976). *Social indicators of well-being: America's perception of life quality.* New York: Plenum Press.

Bandura, A. (1982). Self-efficacy mechanism in human agency. *American Psychologist, 37,* 122–147.

Bandura, A. (1997). *Self-efficacy: The exercise of control.* New York: Freeman.

Black, B. (2001). The road to recovery. *Gallup Management Journal, 1*(4), 10–12.

*Buckingham, M., & Clifton, D. O. (2001). *Now, discover your strengths.* New York: Free Press.

Buckingham, M., & Coffman, C. (1999). *First, break all the rules: What the world's greatest managers do differently.* New York: Simon & Schuster.

Cameron, K. S., Dutton, J. E., & Quinn, R. E. (Eds.). (2003). *Positive organizational scholarship.* San Francisco: Berrett-Koehler.

Clifton, D. O. (1997). *The self-reflection scale.* Princeton, NJ: The Gallup Organization.

*Clifton, D. O., & Anderson, E. (2002). *StrengthsQuest: Discover and develop your strengths in academics, career, and beyond.* Washington, DC: The Gallup Organization.

*Clifton, D. O., & Harter, J. K. (2003). Strengths investment. In K. S. Cameron, J. E. Dutton, & R. E. Quinn (Eds.), *Positive organizational scholarship* (pp. 111–121). San Francisco: Berrett-Koehler.

Clifton, D. O., & Hodges, T. D. (in press). Strengths. In J. M. Burns (Ed.), *The encyclopedia of leadership.* Thousand Oaks, CA: Sage.

*Coffman, C., & Gonzalez-Molina, G. (2002). *Follow this path: How the world's greatest organizations drive growth by unleashing human potential.* New York: Warner Books.

Connelly, J. (2002). All together now. *Gallup Management Journal, 2*(1), 13–18.

Diener, E. (1984). Subjective well-being. *Psychological Bulletin, 95,* 542–575.

Diener, E., Emmons, R. A., Larsen, R. J., & Griffin, S. (1985). The Satisfaction with Life Scale. *Journal of Personality Assessment, 49,* 71–75.

Eden, D. (1990). *Pygmalion in management: Productivity as a self fulfilling prophecy.* Washington, DC: Lexington.

Harter, J. K. (1998). *Gage Park High School research study.* Princeton, NJ: The Gallup Organization.

Harter, J. K. (2000). Managerial talent, employee engagement, and business-unit performance. *Psychologist-Manager Journal, 4,* 215–224.

Harter, J. K., & Schmidt, F. L. (2002). *Employee engagement, satisfaction, and business-unit-level outcomes: Meta-analysis.* Princeton, NJ: The Gallup Organization.

*Harter, J. K., Schmidt, F. L., & Hayes, T. L. (2002). Business-unit-level relationship between employee satisfaction, employee engagement, and business outcomes: A meta-analysis. *Journal of Applied Psychology, 87,* 268–279.

*Harter, J. K., Schmidt, F. L., & Keyes, C. L. M. (2003). Well-being in the workplace and its relationship to business outcomes: A review of the Gallup studies. In C. L. M. Keyes & J. Haidt (Eds.), *Flourishing: Positive psychology and the life well-lived* (pp. 205–224). Washington, DC: American Psychological Association.

Hodges, T. D. (2003). *Results of 2002 StrengthsFinder follow-up surveys.* Princeton, NJ: The Gallup Organization.

Judge, T. A., Thoresen, C. J., Bono, J. E., & Patton, G. K. (2001). The job satisfaction-job performance relationship: A qualitative and quantitative review. *Psychological Bulletin, 127,* 376–407.

Judge, T. A., & Watanabe, S. (1993). Another look at the job satisfaction-life satisfaction relationship. *Journal of Applied Psychology, 78,* 939–948.

Luthans, F. (2002). Positive organizational behavior: Developing and managing psychological strengths. *Academy of Management Executive, 16,* 57–72.

Luthans, F., & Jensen, S. M. (2002). Hope: A new positive strength for human resource development. *Human Resource Development Review, 3,* 304–322.

Pavot, W., & Diener, E. (1993). Review of the satisfaction with life scale. *Psychological Assessment, 5,* 164–172.

Peterson, S. J., & Luthans, F. (2003). The positive impact and development of hopeful leaders. *Leadership and Organizational Development Journal, 24,* 26–31.

Rath, T. C. (2002). *Measuring the impact of Gallup's strengths-based development program for students.* Princeton, NJ: The Gallup Organization.

Rosenthal, R. (1994). Interpersonal expectancy effects: A 30-year perspective. *Current Directions in Psychological Science, 3,* 176–179.

Rosenthal, R., & Jacobson, L. (1968). *Pygmalion in the classroom: Teacher expectation and pupils' intellectual development.* New York: Holt, Rinehart and Winston.

Sheldon, K., Frederickson, B., Rathunde, K., & Csikszentmihalyi, M. (2000). *Positive psychology manifesto* (Rev. ed.). Available from http://www.positivepsychology.org/akumalmanifesto.htm.

Smith, B., & Rutigliano, T. (2003). *Discover your sales strengths: How the world's greatest salespeople develop winning careers.* New York: Warner Books.

Snyder, C. R. (Ed.). (2000). *The handbook of hope*. San Diego, CA: Academic Press.

Snyder, C. R., Harris, C., Anderson, J. R., Holleran, S. A., Irving, L. M., Sigmon, S. T., et al. (1991). The will and the ways: Development and validation of an individual-differences measure of hope. *Journal of Personality and Social Psychology, 60*, 570–585.

Snyder, C. R., Shenkel, R. J., & Lowery, C. R. (1977). Acceptance of personality interpretations: The "Barnum effect" and beyond. *Journal of Consulting and Clinical Psychology, 45*, 104–114.

Snyder, C. R., Sympson, S. C., Ybasco, F. C., Borders, T. F., Babyak, M. A., & Higgins, R. L. (1996). Development and validation of the state hope scale. *Journal of Personality and Social Psychology, 70*, 321–335.

Stajkovic, A. D., & Luthans, F. (1998a). Self-efficacy and work-related performance: A meta-analysis. *Psychological Bulletin, 124*, 240–261.

Stajkovic, A. D., & Luthans, F. (1998b). Social cognitive theory and self-efficacy: Going beyond traditional motivational and behavioral approaches. *Organizational Dynamics, 26*, 62–74.

Tait, M., Padgett, M. Y., & Baldwin, T. T. (1989). Job satisfaction and life satisfaction: A reexamination of the strength of the relationship and gender effects as a function of the date of the study. *Journal of Applied Psychology, 74*, 502–507.

White, S. S., & Locke, E. A. (2000). Problems with the Pygmalion effect and some proposed solutions. *Leadership Quarterly, 11*, 389–415.

Williamson, J. (2002). *Assessing student strengths: Academic performance and persistence of first-time college students at a private, church affiliated college*. Unpublished doctoral dissertation, Mount Vernon Nazarene University, Mount Vernon, OH.

Winseman, A. L. (2002). Doing what they do best. *Gallup Management Journal, 2*(3), 1–4.

Winseman, A. L., Clifton, D. O., & Liesveld, C. (2003). *Living your strengths: Discover your God-given talents, and inspire your congregation and community*. Washington, DC: The Gallup Organization.

CHAPTER 17

Positive and Creative Organization

JANE HENRY

T HIS CHAPTER OUTLINES the application of positive approaches in organizational practice. It discusses the role of work in the *good life* and some of the main strategies used in attempts to develop and sustain a positive and creative organizational culture. It introduces some of the main forms of organizational intervention at individual, team, organizational, and interorganization levels, such as addressing motivation, aiding personal development, building teams, introducing participatory working practices, empowering staff, developing and sustaining creativity, and encouraging networking.

The chapter notes that though much organizational practice and research is negatively oriented, many organizational interventions take a more positive orientation. It suggests that organizations can be accused of inclining toward a naive positivity in their acceptance of organizational interventions as curative. It argues that certain aspects of good personal and professional training go beyond either a purely negative or positive orientation to teach a metacognitive perspective that helps facilitate wise behavior. It concludes that work is important for well-being and that certain organizational practices can enhance satisfaction and aid performance, while noting that different practices may be needed for different personalities, sectors, and cultures.

WELL-BEING AT WORK

Work has long been recognized as a very important avenue for enhancing well-being and studies of life satisfaction often report higher levels of satisfaction among the employed than the unemployed (Warr, 1987, 1999). Exceptions include the healthy, voluntarily early retired with ample finances (Haworth, 1997).

Research into *flow* supports the notion that work provides opportunities for experiencing a state of well-being. Flow is a psychological state associated with well-being that entails the exercise of challenging skills (Csikszentmihalyi & Csikszentmihalyi, 1988). In several studies, Haworth (1997) and colleagues have found flow was more common in work than leisure. In contrast, Delle Fave (2001)

269

reported finding flow in all areas of life including work and leisure, though less commonly at work among white-collar workers than professionals such as doctors and teachers.

The centrality of work to well-being is not surprising when you think of the number of benefits it offers, notably: an identity, opportunities for social interaction and support, purpose, time filling, engaging challenges, and possibilities for status apart from the provision of income. Jahoda (1982) went further and argued that it is mainly work that supplies time structure, social contact, collective purpose, social identity and status, and regular activity—five factors whose presence she found to be central to a sense of well-being.

Warr and his colleagues from the Institute of Work Psychology at the University of Sheffield have investigated well-being at work in a range of settings. Warr (1987) concludes that a combination of personal and environmental influences act to facilitate or constrain individual well-being. The environmental influences center on opportunity for control, environmental clarity (including feedback and predictability), opportunity for skill use, externally generated goals, variety, opportunity for interpersonal contact, valued social position, availability of money, and physical security. A key feature of this model is the variable effect of these features according to the degree to which they are present. For example, while some opportunity for control and skill use generally improves well-being, too much can be experienced as coercion and the sense of well-being diminishes.

Job-related well-being is known to interrelate with general life satisfaction (Judge & Watanabe, 1993). It also appears to be affected by dispositional variables. In a study using longitudinal data, Straw, Bell, and Clausen (1986) found that affective disposition in junior high school was a fair predictor of attitudes to work in middle life (40 to 60 years) with a correlation of about 0.3 to 0.4.

Surprisingly, though GDP has gone up threefold and working conditions have improved markedly since World War II, life satisfaction ratings have shown relatively little change over that period (Myers, 2000). This finding has led to the idea that above a certain basic minimum level of comfort, such as that provided by income from a steady job, it is other factors that account for high levels of satisfaction. Key contenders include the level of control individuals have over their life and the amount of coherence among their values, goals, and activities (see Kasser, Chapter 4, this volume; Sagiv, Roccas, & Hazan, Chapter 5, this volume).

ORGANIZATIONAL DEVELOPMENT

Business managers are under pressure to enhance performance and make their mark. As a consequence, organizations have a long history of attempting to intervene at the individual, group, and organizational level in the hope of making the workplace a more efficient and pleasant environment. Recent interventions involving practices, such as worker participation, open cultures, supportive supervision, team empowerment, and looser organizational structures, seem to accord with the ethos of positive psychology.

We next consider some of the practices and interventions that aim at more positive organization. Note that many of the practices taken up by organizations are not theory driven and have little empirical work to back them up. We look at individual-, group-, and organizational-level interventions in turn.

INDIVIDUAL LEVEL I: JOB SATISFACTION AND PERFORMANCE

Among the practices that have been employed to enhance well-being at work at the individual level are attempts to enrich jobs, offer feedback, improve and align motivation, increase responsibility, and offer focused development.

Some interventions, such as job redesign, aim to improve performance directly. Others seek to improve working conditions and satisfaction at work and indirectly improve performance. Hertzberg (1966) and the human relations school stressed the idea that the happy worker was an efficient one, though the degree to which satisfaction enhances performance has been contested. Judge, Thoresen, Bono, and Patton's (2001) meta-analysis of more than 300 groups covering approximately 55,000 people estimated the correlation between job satisfaction and performance to be around 0.3. They also found that global measures of job satisfaction produced a higher correlation than facet measures.

Job Variety   Early attempts at enhancing individual well-being at work focused on *enhancing job variety and challenge* (Hackham & Oldham, 1980). A well-known example comes from Volvo, the Swedish car manufacturer. Volvo famously restructured two of its factories to enhance job variety for the factory workers. Instead of working on one stage of the production process, workers worked in self-governing teams that could follow the cars they worked on through different production processes. This did enhance job interest as expected, but it also increased expense, with the result that these experimental factories were eventually shut down (Pettinger, 1996). However, times change, and much of the routine work in car manufacturing is now done by robots. Now, cell manufacturing—where groups of multiskilled workers take responsibility for sequences of production on a particular product or product group—is commonplace.

Motivation   There have been various attempts to enhance motivation at work. Early attempts focused on external rewards ranging from recognition for good work in the form of an award and financial recompense for productive innovations to bonuses when the firm did well. More attention has been paid recently to the role of *intrinsic* motivation. Recognizing that intrinsic motivation is a key factor in job satisfaction and performance among creative scientists, some organizations have a policy of granting scientists free time and, in some cases, genesis grants to work on pet projects. For example, 3M has allowed scientists up to 15% of working time to work on such projects (Mitchell, 1991). Such practices are not just a matter of company largesse. The ubiquitous Post-It Notes, the semisticky notepads currently found on most office desks, emerged from just such a project (Nayak & Ketteringham, 1991). Oldham (1996) argues that a high degree of control over work and feedback on performance enhance motivation for a job.

Confidence   *Confidence* in your ability to do tasks tends to aid performance on that task. Bandura (1982) has conducted many studies showing the importance of confidence or self-efficacy—how able individuals believe themselves to be to perform a particular task or group of tasks. Confidence has been shown to affect goal aspiration positively (Bandura, 2000). Stajkovic and Luthans (1998) found a stronger relationship between self-efficacy and work-related performance than many other variables, including goal setting, feedback, job satisfaction, and conscientiousness.

Bandura (2000) has also shown how confidence can be developed in the workplace through mastery experiences, modeling, positive feedback on progress, and arousal. Many management training techniques include elements that aim to reframe negative experiences as learning and/or positive experiences. For example, negative mind-sets are a recognized limitation, and organizations go to considerable lengths to persuade staff to keep their aspirations high. The *yes and* technique encourages people to accept difficulties and see how they can work toward a goal despite the difficulties. Adventure training takes managers offsite and presents teams with various physical challenges such as abseiling, crossing cold streams, and engaging in outdoor games. Proponents argue that the team spirit that clicks in ensures participants help one another complete the various challenges and that the increased confidence from completing tasks that they previously found fearful, or deemed beyond their competence, has a positive payoff in workplace activities.

Hope   Hope has not been investigated much in workplace settings, but there is some evidence suggesting that the hopeful fair better in stressful occupations than the less hopeful (Kirk & Koesk, 1995; Taylor & Brown, 1988). This is one area that deserves more scrutiny (see Lopez et al., Chapter 24, this volume, for strategies to accentuate hope).

INDIVIDUAL LEVEL II: PERSONAL DEVELOPMENT

In organizations, there is a general appreciation of the centrality of people problems, even in technical spheres. Perhaps this is one reason that much of the training offered to managers, professionals, and specialist staff is concerned with psychologically oriented *personal, interpersonal, and group skills* such as listening, communication, and group process skills. Most managers complete a number of personality inventories designed to analyze their problem solving, decision making, and learning styles, for example, and take part in numerous role plays designed to help them relate to staff more sensitively and effectively.

The importance of an element of individualized personal and professional development is also now institutionalized in kitemarks such as Investors in People (IIP). Among other things, IIP ensures that attention is given to employees' personal and professional development needs by requiring that these needs be specified annually through an individual development plan, normally now included in the annual staff appraisal. This requirement sometimes turns an appraisal into more of a coaching session, where the employee has a chance to voice his or her own development needs. An element of continuous professional development is now compulsory for most professionals in the West. This may involve the commitment of, for example, five days a year to training and updating. As part of a process of building trust, some companies have given employees money to undertake any training course they wish.

Currently, training is often built around the notion of *competencies*. Competencies derive from a model of education that presumes skills can be acquired and transferred to other settings by inputting knowledge in which the individual is deficient. The use of a competency-based approach, though endorsed by governments and taken up by most management organizations, is not without its critics—not least among human resource professionals. One critique is that knowledge and skill are situated and do not transfer readily to other situations, so the idea of generalized competencies transferring to new settings is suspect (see Sparrow, 2002, for a review).

However, it would be a mistake to think that organizational development is entirely oriented to fixing the negative. Organizations tend to be quick to take up new approaches, such as the idea of *emotional intelligence* (Salovey & Mayer, 1990; see also, Salovey, Caruso, & Mayer, Chapter 28, this volume). In discussing emotional intelligence, Goleman (1995) highlights the importance of self-awareness, self-regulation, motivation, empathy, and social skill in management capability. As it is taught in organizations, emotional intelligence typically reframes material that was previously presented as social skills. Nevertheless, it serves to highlight strengths as well as weaknesses and to draw attention to noncognitive aspects of interpersonal relating.

Strengths As in clinical settings, until recently, organizations tended to give relatively little overt attention to the idea of building on an individual's *strengths*. However, considerable attention was given to correcting any perceived deficiencies through training and the notion of organizational fit, that is, fitting someone with the appropriate abilities, style, experience, and inclination to the position concerned.

Aiming for work that complements the individual's natural talents and developing areas that exploit these talents have found a ready audience in organizations. The Gallup Organization has been championing the idea of building on strengths for many years (see Hodges & Clifton, Chapter 16, this volume). They list 34 talents, grouped under four themes (Coffman & Gonzalez-Molina, 2002):

1. Relating: for example, communication, empathy
2. Thinking: for example, analytical, strategic
3. Striving: for example, adaptability, focus
4. Impact: for example, positivity, command

The strengths approach has been well received by organizations in countries such as the United States, the United Kingdom, and India. The appeal is not so much the specified talents, which are similar to the traits and capabilities that managers are familiar with, but the idea of building on and developing an individual's strengths. Even where managers already take account of employee's strengths intuitively, the development of the strengths rhetoric helps organizations to legitimize a more overtly positive approach to staff selection and development (see Hodges & Clifton, Chapter 16, this volume).

Style To date, positive psychology has stressed the benefits of apparent virtues but has given little attention to any downside of such traits. For example, I have a colleague who is playful. This trait makes him entertaining, but it can also get him into trouble. A good deal of personal development education goes beyond focusing on the need to make good deficiencies or drawing on the merits of innate virtues and talents. Rather, it teaches the *metaperspective* that there is a positive and negative to all things and that constructives response take account of the situation and participants' worldviews. Going beyond a purely positive or a negative orientation offers a mature approach to personal development that can lead to increased tolerance, acceptance, and balance.

For example, most training programs include work on self- and other awareness. Typically, managers are given personality inventories such as the Myers-Briggs Type Indicator (MBTI; Briggs Myers & McCauley, 1989), the Kirton Adaption Innovation Inventory (KAI; Kirton, 1987), and the Learning Styles Inventory (LSI; Honey & Mumford, 1985). The great merit of many of these instruments is that they are concerned with cognitive style or preference—not ability. This teaches people to appreciate the strengths and weaknesses, opportunities, and threats that are inherent in any style or situation.

The most widely used organizational inventory in the world is the MBTI (Briggs Myers & McCauley, 1989). The MBTI employs four bipolar dimensions (extraversion-introversion, sensing-intuiting, thinking-feeling, and judging-perceiving). These correlate with their respective Big Five dimensions as follows: extraversion 0.7, openness 0.7, agreeableness 0.5, and conscientiousness 0.5 (Bayne, 1994). However, unlike the Big Five, which are normally presented as traits, neither pole of the MBTI types is favored over the other. For example, MBTI judgers (high conscientiousness on the Big Five) may be focused and well-organized and, therefore, good at meeting deadlines, but adaptability may be more of a weakness. In contrast, on the MBTI, perceivers (low conscientiousness on the Big Five) may maintain a number of diverse interests and be late handing over material as a consequence, but they are usually good at adapting to change (Hirsch, 1985). The key message is that people are different, with tendencies to attend to different aspects of the environment and to excel in different areas and that groups in organizations are more productive if they harness a variety of styles.

The popular *360 degree* training also offers people the chance to assess themselves and compare their own self-assessment to appraisals of the same areas completed by one or more peers, superiors, and sometimes junior staff. This type of training offers important feedback on the accuracy of self-perception and the impact of self-presentation.

Much personal and professional development and training offers practices that encourage staff to treat one another with respect and integrity. Such training emphasizes understanding yourself, realizing that others are different, appreciating that all have a role to play, and encouraging ways of relating to people that make it more likely that they will be heard. This approach can be seen as one that teaches the rudiments of *wisdom*. One characteristic of wisdom is relativistic thinking, the ability to see a situation from the other's point of view and to see ramifications for different parties (see Kunzmann, Chapter 31, this volume). Personal and professional development practices can help facilitate *relativistic* thinking and the outcome of associated management training can enhance tolerance, acceptance, and respect for self and other.

GROUP LEVEL

Most organizational endeavor is accomplished by groups, and these groups often have to compete for scarce resources. Perhaps for this reason there is an appreciation that many organizational problems are *people* problems. Groups are central to most organizations' endeavors and are increasingly important as organizations decentralize and push responsibility down to multidisciplinary project teams.

Much of the benefit gained from work may be attributed to its social opportunities. Team membership can provide social support and satisfy a need to belong. Various studies suggest that working in a team leads to improved well-being for its members (Sonnentag, 1996). On the basis of a series of studies with health workers, Carter and West (1999) found that employees in well-defined teams reported better psychological health than those working in ambiguously defined teams and those who worked alone.

Team Building Organizations appreciate that group dynamics are important. Most managers are familiar with the idea that new groups may be expected to go through stages, colorfully known, for example, as forming, storming, norming, and performing. Because teams need time to coalesce into a working unit, new project teams commonly go off-site for team-building exercises to aid the process—an event that may involve leisure rather than work-related activities. Such activities afford time for the development of interpersonal relationships; the goal being to build the individuals' commitment to one another and to the team.

Group Processes Some of the personal, interpersonal, and group skills that are accepted as helping organizational groups to function well include listening to others, acknowledging the other's position, affording recognition for good work, adopting a win-win attitude to negotiation, and applying principles of conflict resolution where parties disagree.

Like personal and professional development, group process training shows a certain psychological maturity, notably in the stress on valuing and working with *diversity.* The emphasis on valuing diversity can be traced in part to the popularization of empirical work, which showed that successful work groups were more likely to contain a mix of personality types and that groups containing too many of one particular personality type, for example, shapers (task leaders), could flounder (Belbin, 1981). Belbin produced a team role inventory claiming to identify people's preference for these different roles. The use of personality inventories and team-role inventories in work settings can lead group members to a better appreciation of the consequences of cognitive style and personality type for ways of working and of the importance of differing roles. This in turn tends to lead to greater respect for and tolerance of others.

Diversity of knowledge is known to be important for successful innovation. In a series of studies, West and colleagues found that commitment to the group and participation in decision making enhanced innovation, whereas formalized rules restricted creativity and innovation (West, 2000; West & Anderson, 1996). Some work suggests that when the group is working on innovative products, it is more effective to reward the group as a whole, rather than the individual participants.

Resilience The ability to bounce back from adversity seems an obvious trait to investigate in terms of how people cope with group pressures at work. However, it does not seem to have received much attention in workplace settings (Coutu, 2002). This area is worth future investigation.

ORGANIZATIONAL LEVEL I: STRUCTURE

One variable that has long been associated with well-being is control over your own life. Control over one's activities is generally associated with higher levels of well-being. Lack of control over one's activities in work and elsewhere is generally associated with higher levels of stress and lower levels of satisfaction. Traditional organizational structures seemed to offer staff very little control indeed. Bureaucracies have rigid organizational hierarchies that place the manager as captain deciding what the workers will do and when they will do it, with the power to check to see that orders have been carried out and implement sanctions if they have not.

As far back as 1957, Argyris noted the incongruity between the demands of the traditional "command and control" organization and the needs of the individual (Argyris, 1957). Features such as task specification, chains of command, and lack of delegated authority promote passivity and dependence, in effect assuming that workers are in a state of immaturity and treating them like children who need to be told what to do (Semler, 1994). This form of organization does not appear at face value to offer much scope for well-being at work because it offers workers little control and autonomy over their working lives.

Changing Environment   However, over the past 50 years, organizational practices have been radically transformed, largely in response to increasing competition. Organizations now need to respond more quickly to shorter product life cycles and compete with ever more cost-efficient organizations on a global scale. Bureaucratic chains of command have proven too slow and expensive, and many organizations have introduced more participatory working practices, pushing responsibility down to multidisciplinary teams. Pressure to reduce costs has led to lean, downsized organizations where the remaining staff usually have to do more with less resources.

There is a long-term trend away from hierarchically organized bureaucratic structures toward more decentralized structures where front-line staff have more control. Organizing companies in divisions based around product groupings is common, though some large, heavily decentralized companies such as Hewlett Packard found they needed to recentralize certain functions to ensure compatibility across different product types (Ashkenas, Ulrich, Jick, & Kerr, 1995). Project-based management, where multidisciplinary teams come together to work on particular projects, is the rule in sectors such as film-making and construction, which are organized around temporary project groupings (DeFillippi & Arthur, 1998).

Many manufacturing companies have shifted to cell manufacturing, where *multidisciplinary teams* are responsible for particular product types. Such teams may have representatives from sales and marketing, as well as design and engineering. Data from Japan and elsewhere suggest that production organized in this way is more efficient in the long run. Although such groups may take longer to agree on a way to proceed, the agreed-on plans are executed more quickly, so the process is more efficient in the long run (Clark & Fujimoto, 1991). However, working with people from different disciplines with their different languages does not necessarily make life easy. There may be more conflict than before and greater challenges as a result. Whether the greater responsibility in these decentralized structures is perceived as beneficial depends partly on the personality of the workers and their commitment to the job.

The changes to practice have so transformed many organizations that the manager is now more commonly pictured as the *conductor* drawing out the best in his or her staff, coordinating as much as controlling workplace activities. In some organizations, a more participatory ethos grants staff considerable responsibility for deciding when and how they set about work goals. Many staff now benefit from flextime—flexible working hours—and in certain sectors, an increasing number of white-collar staff opt to telework—at home or on the move for a portion of the working week, keeping in touch with work via e-mail, the Internet, fax, and phone. Such practices seem to allow for more mature adult behavior where individuals are trusted to be active and independent, making their own decisions and being treated as equals in terms of the value placed on ideas and opinions they might offer.

Given this move toward more *participatory working practices* that seem to afford staff more control over their actions at work, you might expect job satisfaction to have increased. However, recent measures of satisfaction at work seem to have shown a decline, thought to be because of increased pressures at work. The switch to more participatory practices has often been accompanied by increasing workload, which has led to greater stress for many workers. The demise of layers of middle management has led to fewer opportunities for promotion in some areas, and the perceived increase in project-based and temporary working has led to a decline in perceived job security. The move to formalized quality control systems has brought in a form of employee scrutiny that can lead to a climate of distrust (White, 2001). Taken together, these factors seem to go a long way toward accounting for the decline in satisfaction levels (Taylor, 2002).

Orientation   Despite these changes, much of the organizational framework within which practices are considered tends to orient toward *fixing the negative*. For example, managers solve problems and troubleshoot, training is dominated by a competency framework that aims to input the skills in which staff are deficient, and stress is perceived as a major problem. Empirical work is very largely directed at negative aspects of the working environment, such as the effects of downsizing, job insecurity, problems with stress and burnout, and lack of career development in a world with less full-time employment.

Organizational Level II: Culture

In contrast, many of the organizational interventions of the past few decades have a *positive orientation*. The popular organizational literature is dominated by tales of the practices of *successful* people and organizations. For example, Covey (1990) talks of the seven habits of highly effective people. (He argues that these are proactivity, beginning with the end in mind, putting first things first, thinking win-win, seeking to understand before being understood, synergizing, and balanced self-renewal.)

Managers are encouraged to be proactive rather than reactive—to take time to gain buy-in and commitment upfront, rather than try to mop up resistance to change after the event. Organizations have visions and mission statements (language borrowed from spiritual discourse) that define where they would like to see themselves going and the values they espouse en route. Positive behavior such as recognizing and praising staff for good work is normal practice, and open climates where mistakes are forgiven are encouraged. Some commentators argue that the best staff gravitate to organizations that share their values, rather than opting to work for organizations with better pay and prospects that do not share their values (Handy, 2001).

Management Fads and Good Practice   Organizations are continually on the lookout for practices that will improve their performance. However, empirical work suggests organizational development is typically a difficult, lengthy, and time-consuming process. Nevertheless managers—at least those in Anglo-Saxon countries—have tended to maintain a remarkable faith in the possibility of a quick fix for their organizational ills.

Indeed, the past 50 years of organizational development have been characterized by a succession of so-called management *fads,* such as management by objectives, continuous improvement, quality, reengineering, the learning organization, empowerment, and knowledge management (Mintzberg, 1983; Pascale, 1990). Many of these organizational interventions derive not from academic *research* but from practices perceived to have been effective in other organizations.

One popular approach is *benchmarking,* which aims to compare the processes and practices of one's own organization with those in successful competitor organizations (Zairi, 1996). Sober examination after the event shows that companies lauded for good practice and exceptional performance at one time have not necessarily looked so rosy when examined 10 or even 5 years down the road. High-profile examples include the downfall of a number of companies praised by Peters in his bestseller *In Search of Excellence* (Peters & Waterman, 1982).

Indeed, in their haste to take up the latest *good practice* and management fad, organizations can be faulted for an overly *naive* acceptance of the positive and a failure to appreciate what works in one situation may not transplant to another so happily. Further, other unwanted effects may occur because the ramifications of any organizational development intervention tend to be considerable.

Pascale (1999) argues that 80% of organizational change efforts fail. Robertson, Roberts, and Porras's (1992) meta-analysis found that multipronged organizational change that sought to change a number of different subsystems had a better chance of success. Nadler (1988) suggests organizational change efforts are more likely to succeed if they involve key players, get participation in the process, and build in feedback.

Some long-term trends in organizational structure, culture, and employment patterns are discernible. Together, these present a shift to a more participatory form of management.

Open Culture   Perhaps the main shift in organizational practice over the past century has been the change in culture. Gone are the days where status differences were emphasized; the go-ahead organization seeks a culture where *trust* is sufficient for employees to feel able to challenge established practices and to innovate. Managers are urged to forgive mistakes and walk the talk, though reality does not always match the rhetoric. Various studies have shown that in sectors such as information technology (IT), innovative companies that had open cultures have fared well (Jelinek & Schoonhaven, 1991). However, such cultures are not without cost, since they typically involve staff in many meetings and a good deal of confrontation.

Many organizations have gone to great lengths to try to change their culture from a more conservative to a more open culture, a process that normally takes many years. The Norwegian-based Karmoy, the largest aluminum plant in Europe, provides an example. Karmoy used a gardening metaphor (which they hoped staff would easily identify with) to visualize the past, present, and future state of the company. A series of group meetings was held, in which they gave all staff a chance to voice their aspirations for the company. Subsequent to this intervention, the company found health improved, absenteeism reduced, and the number of employee suggestions for organizational improvement substantially increased, all measures of an improved climate (Parker, 1990). However, in culture change programs, middle managers often end up with less power than previously. This loss of power is not to everyone's taste, and many culture change programs find they lose a proportion of staff who are unable or unwilling to adapt to the new approach (Henry, 1994).

Great claims have been made for organizational culture change as a means of improving organizational performance and climate, but it has been objected that some high-profile culture change efforts, such as that undertaken at British Airways in the 1980s, had short-lived effects. Legge's (1994) review questions whether the benefits of moves to more enterprising cultures have been as substantial as generally claimed.

There is some evidence that different personality types and different departments favor different organizational cultures. Ekvall (1997) found that production staff preferred a climate where rules are clear and people work in tried and tested ways. In contrast, people in research departments tended to favor a more open, easy-going climate where staff were freer to pursue what they perceived as important.

Empowerment and Self-Organization   A consequence of more participatory working practices in many organizations is that the worker is empowered to a greater degree than before. However, in some cases, the empowerment offered is a travesty of the term, as in MacDonald's workers being allowed to modify the standard customer greeting.

At the other end of the spectrum, some companies have empowered their staff to the point where they *self-organize*. Dutton, a small-scale engineering works in the United Kingdom, and Semco, a medium-size pump manufacturing concern in Brazil, are two examples. Semco employees set their own hours, get their own parts, have control of their expenses, and, in some cases, decide on their share of the profits. The company has abolished many standard corporate departments such as quality and personnel and allows staff to hire employees for their areas directly. They also have a policy of limiting all memos to a page. Semco uses upward appraisal where staff use a simple satisfaction measure to appraise their bosses every six months. Often, such companies also practice open accounting where detailed information about company finances is available to employees.

Dutton's self-managed teams deal directly with the customer and design cost and set delivery dates (Lewis & Lytton, 1995). In short, these companies abolish most of the red tape traditionally associated with organizations and treat their staff like adults able to organize their own lives.

Staff who work in these firms become very committed to the company, very few if any abuses of the system are reported, and levels of satisfaction and performance are high (Semler, 1994; www.semco.com). However, self-organizing companies tend to be small or medium. Such practices are more difficult to incorporate in large multinationals where a need for coordination across departments usually necessitates some "red-tape."

Although participatory working practices accord with individualistic Western values, this is not true of all nations. We can question to what extent these practices are suited to more hierarchical cultures such as those found in South India, Malaysia, and much of Africa, where high power-distance between subordinates and superiors is the norm (Hofstede, 1984).

INTERORGANIZATION LEVEL

The type of practice advocated depends partly on the unit of analysis under scrutiny. We have looked at the individual, team, and organizational levels, assuming interventions at all these levels can aid job satisfaction and the bottom line. These days a number of interventions are directed outside the organization at an interorganizational level, for example, partnerships across the supply chain. The boundaries between companies have become more fluid.

Typically, large private companies form long-term relationships with suppliers rather than accepting the lowest tender each year. This enables the suppliers to build a relationship with the companies they are supplying. Nissan sends engineers to help underperforming suppliers improve, rather than change suppliers, for example. Though these partnership *networks* give greater prominence to trust and a committed relationship than solely cost, they perform well compared to traditional tendering systems when all costs are taken into account. (Henry, 2002, amplifies on different approaches to organizational level intervention.)

CREATIVE ORGANIZATION

One area that has been receiving considerable attention recently is how to make an organization more creative and how to sustain high levels of creativity. Organizations have adopted markedly different policies to achieve this end, and the practices adopted follow from beliefs about the cause of creativity (see Table 17.1 and Henry, 2001).

Table 17.1

Relationship between Perceived Cause of Creativity and Resulting Policy

Perceived Cause of Creativity	Resulting Policy
Ability	Select for subset of creative individuals.
Style	Nurture adaptive creativity in all staff.
Mental skill	Send employees on creative problem-solving course.
Experience	Allow employees freedom to follow their hunches.
Motivation	Support individuals' ideas, provide some resources.
Emergent property	Facilitate networking.

ABILITY OR STYLE

The traditional view sees creativity as a property of a subset of the population and seeks to identify and attract such creative individuals to work for the organization (MacKinnon, 1961). The intervention here may involve the use of pencil and paper inventories that supposedly measure an individual's creative ability. Research suggests that in the specialized environment of exploratory science, the caliber of the scientists involved is important.

Western conceptions of creativity have tended to glorify revolutionary breakthrough innovations and associate that creativity with a particular heroic individual. Yet, most innovations are evolutionary and build on what has gone before, for example computers, cars, cameras, and phones have evolved almost beyond recognition from the first example of their kind. Kirton (1989) has drawn attention to this kind of adaptive creativity that has previously received little attention. He notes the difference in cognitive style between innovative individuals who favor challenging assumptions and the status quo, essentially doing things differently, and adaptors, who favor improving tried and tested practices, essentially doing things better. (This dimension correlates with openness on the Big Five.) The latter may be more inclined to excel at evolutionary creativity.

Simultaneously, organizational interest has shifted away from focusing on a subset of privileged individuals toward ways of engaging the creative input of the workforce as a whole in a process of continual improvement (or adaptive creativity).

Research suggests that creative companies tend to have more open climates where people feel able to challenge the way things are done and are able to try new approaches. Many culture change programs aim to build a climate of trust where people feel able to make suggestions and act on them. This may be formalized into some kind of suggestion scheme, often with financial or other forms of recognition for the best ideas and sometimes with innovation development personnel available to assist staff to develop their ideas (e.g., Rosenfeld & Servo, 1991).

SKILL AND EXPERIENCE

Another strand of thinking sees creativity as a mental skill that is based around lateral thinking (De Bono, 1984; Osborn, 1953). Western culture, it is argued, emphasizes rational thinking, in which the individual is expected to justify each step logically. The assumption is that this logical step by step thinking can diminish the number of options considered and lead to premature closure. Many organizations send staff on creative problem-solving courses, centered around exercises such as brainstorming, mapping, and visualization, which are designed to teach staff how to think creatively. Whether such courses succeed has been a matter of debate in the literature. A number of studies have found that a greater variety of ideas are produced when participants brainwrite individually than if they brainstorm by voicing ideas aloud in groups (e.g., Bouchard & Hare, 1970).

At the same time, cognitive psychologists have been investigating creative individuals in various fields. Studies suggest that individuals who have made a substantive contribution to their field have been working in it a long time, suggesting that experience in the area concerned is critical (Weisburg, 1983). Research also suggests that creativity, like knowledge, is situated so an individual may be creative in a field he or she is knowledgeable about but not necessarily in other fields. The theory here is that creativity is a form of expert recognition. We know experts chunk and process knowledge differently than novices, and this leads them to notice and attend to different aspects than novices including critically important problems. For example, Fleming attended to the odd reaction on his petri dishes, which led to the discovery of penicillin precisely because he had a developed map of possible reactions from years of looking at them. In the popular mind, creativity is associated with ideas, but studies of creative people show that they take longer to decide which problem is worth addressing—a phenomena known as *problem finding* (e.g., Getzels & Csikszentmihalyi, 1976). Allowing staff to work on projects they are interested in and have experience of can help them to capitalize on such tacit knowledge and intuitive understanding.

MOTIVATION AND EMERGENCE

Generally, creative ideas involve challenging the status quo, and, often, it takes a lot of work to move from the idea through a working model to implementation. If an individual cares about something, it is likely to be easier to make the concessions needed, put up with the extra effort required, and deal with the criticism that new ideas often receive. Hence, it is perhaps no surprise that successful people tend to love their work, and creative people are usually motivated intrinsically (Amabile, 1983; Perkins, 1981). In terms of interventions, it seems that supervisory support can be important in helping to nurture ideas in organizations (Amabile, 1991). Amabile has also shown that creative endeavor normally happens when motivation, experience, and a degree of mental flexibility conjoin.

The programs previously described locate the source of creativity in the individual's head and seek to facilitate the explication and development of tacit creativity in individuals. An alternative perspective looks at the systems within which creativity emerges. Csikszentmihalyi (1996) has emphasized that three elements are necessary for creativity to emerge:

1. An individual with sufficient mental flexibility to be alert to new possibilities
2. Expertise in a particular domain
3. Openness on the part of the field's gatekeepers to these new ideas

Complexity theory has also been applied to creativity with proponents arguing that creativity is a natural property of adaptive living systems (Stacy, 1996). Interventions arising from these systems views stress the importance of facilitating networking among those with related interests inside and outside the organization and providing resources to enable them to pursue their interests (Wheatley, 1994).

The idea that creativity is best achieved by facilitating networking of those with common interests is a different approach from the aforementioned strategies of selecting highly innovative individuals, fostering creativity throughout the workforce, sending staff on creative thinking courses, sustaining an open organizational climate, and nurturing new ideas. Those seeking to build creative and positive organizations would be well advised to pursue all of these strategies as well as encouraging networking.

CONCLUSION

Most people spend much of their life at work in organizations, and a major source of well-being typically comes from work. Sustaining a sense of the good life can be more difficult in large organizations than small ones, but certain participatory organizational practices can help.

The increase in participation, moves toward more open cultures, and emphasis placed on personal development suggest that organizations have become more positive places over the past 30 years. However, satisfaction measures suggest that this is not universally so. It is thought that increasing workload, the increased policing inherent in many quality schemes, increasing stress, and uncertainty over future employment opportunities may account for this decline in satisfaction, despite the enhanced autonomy and control afforded through practices such as empowerment and multidisciplinary team working.

In terms of much of their day-to-day practice, mainstream organizations seem to operate from a negative orientation, that is, hierarchical structures, a problem-solving orientation, and a competency framework for development. However, much personal, group, and organizational development have been framed more positively with the accent on success, good practice, intrinsic motivation, recognition, learning from mistakes, the need for a vision, empowerment, and respectful relations.

In this chapter, I have argued that much management training rises above either a purely negative or positive orientation to take a metaperspective that recognizes that strengths and weaknesses are inherent in any style or situation, even apparently positive ones. The best development in organizations already encourages a positive approach to learning about self and others; an approach that can lead to enhanced respect, acceptance, and tolerance for others; and one that affords a good basis for wise organization.

REFERENCES

Amabile, T. (1983). *The social psychology of creativity.* New York: Springer Verlag.

Amabile, T. (1991, September/October). How to kill creativity. *Harvard Business Review,* 77–87.

Argyris, C. (1957). *On personality and learning.* New York: Harper & Row.

Ashkenas, R., Ulrich, D., Jick, T., & Kerr, S. (1995). *The boundary-less organization: Breaking the chains of organizational structure.* San Francisco: Jossey-Bass.

Bandura, A. (1982). Self-efficacy mechanism in human agency. *American Psychologist, 37,* 122–147.

Bandura, A. (2000). Cultivate self-efficacy for personal and organizational effectiveness. In E. A. Locke (Ed.), *Blackwell handbook of principles of organizational behavior* (pp. 120–136). Oxford, England: Blackwell.

Bayne, R. (1994). The Big Five versus the Myers-Briggs. *The Psychologist, 7,* 14–16.

Belbin, R. M. (1981). *Management teams: Why they succeed or fail.* Oxford, England: Heinemann.

Bouchard, T. J., & Hare, M. (1970). Size, potential and performance in brainstorming groups. *Journal of Applied Psychology, 54,* 51–55.

Briggs Myers, I., & McCauley, M. H. (1989). *Manual: A guide to the development and use of the Myers-Briggs Type Indicator.* Palo Alto, CA: Consulting Psychologists Press.

Carter, A. J., & West, M. A. (1999). Sharing the burden: Teamwork in health-care settings. In R. L. Payne & J. Firth-Cozens (Eds.), *Stress in health care professionals* (pp. 191–202). Chichester, England: Wiley.

Clark, K., & Fujimoto, T. (1991). Reducing time to market: The case of the world auto industry. In J. Henry & D. Walker (Eds.), *Managing innovation* (pp. 106–117). London: Sage.

*Coffman, C., & Gonzalez-Molina, G. (2002). *Follow this path: How the world's greatest organizations drive growth by unleashing human potential.* New York: Warner Books.

Coutu, D. L. (2002, May). How resilience works. *Harvard Business Review, 46–55.*

Covey, S. R. (1990). *The seven habits of highly effective people.* New York: Fireside.

Csikszentmihalyi, M. (1996). *Creativity: Flow and the psychology of discovery and invention.* New York: HarperCollins.

Csikszentmihalyi, M., & Csikszentmihalyi, I. S. (Eds.). (1988). *Optimal experience: Psychological studies of flow in consciousness.* New York: Cambridge University Press.

De Bono, E. (1984). *Lateral thinking for management.* London: Penguin.

DeFillippi, R. J., & Arthur, M. B. (1998, Winter). Paradox in project based enterprise: The case of film-making. *California Management Review, 10, 2.*

Delle Fave, A. (2001, December). *Flow and optimal experience.* Paper presented to ESRC Individual and Situational Determinants of Well-Being, Seminar 2: Work, employment, and well-being. Manchester, England, Manchester Metropolitan University.

Ekvall, G. (1997). Organizational conditions and level of creativity. *Creativity and Innovation Management, 6, 195–205.*

Getzels, J., & Csikszentmihalyi, M. (1976). *The creative vision: A longitudinal study of creativity in art.* New York: Wiley.

Goleman, D. (1995). *Emotional intelligence.* New York: Bantam Books.

Hackham, J. R., & Oldham, G. R. (1980). *Work redesign.* Reading, MA: Addison-Wesley.

Handy, C. (2001). The citizen company. In J. Henry (Ed.), *Creative management* (2nd ed., pp. 240–251). London: Sage.

Haworth, J. (1997). *Work, leisure and well-being,* London: Routledge.

Henry, J. (1994). *Creative management media book.* Milton Keynes, England: Open University Press.

Henry, J. (2001). *Creativity and perception in management.* London: Sage.

Henry, J. (with Gardiner, P., Grugulis, I., & Mayle, D.). (2002). *Organizing for innovation.* Milton Keynes, England: Open University Press.

Hertzberg, F. (1966). *Work and the nature of man.* Chicago: World Publishing.

Hirsch, S. K. (1985). *Using the Myers-Briggs Type Indicator in organizations,* Oxford, England: Oxford Psychologists Press.

Hofstede, G. (1984). *Culture's consequences: International differences in work-related values.* Beverly Hills, CA: Sage.

Honey, P., & Mumford, A. (1985). *The manual of learning styles.* Maidenhead, England: Peter Honey.

Jahoda, M. (1982). *Employment and unemployment: A social psychological analysis.* Cambridge, England: Cambridge University Press.

Jelinek, M., & Schoonhaven, C. B. (1991). Strong culture and its consequences. In J. Henry & D. Walker (Eds.), *Managing innovation* (pp. 80–89). London: Sage.

Judge, T. A., Thoresen, C. J., Bono, J. E., & Patton, G. K. (2001). The job satisfaction-job performance relationship: A qualitative and quantitative review. *Psychological Bulletin, 127, 376–407.*

Judge, T. A., & Watanabe, S. (1993). Another look at the job satisfaction-life satisfaction relationship. *Journal of Applied Psychology, 78, 939–948.*

Kirk, S., & Koesk, G. (1995). The fate of optimism: A longitudinal study of managers' hopefulness and subsequent morale. *Research in Social Work Practice, 86,* 80–92.

Kirton, M. J. (1987). *Adaption—Innovation Inventory (KAI) manual* (2nd ed.). Hatfield, England: Occupational Research Center.

Kirton, M. J. (1989). *Adaptors and innovators: Styles of creativity and problem solving.* London: Routledge.

Legge, K. (1994). Managing culture: Fact or fiction. In K. Sisson (Ed.), *Personnel management.* Oxford, England: Blackwell.

Lewis, K., & Lytton, S. (1995). *How to transform your company and enjoy it.* Oxford, England: Management Books.

MacKinnon, D. W. (1961). *The creative person.* Berkeley: University of California, Institute of Personality Assessment Research.

Mintzberg, H. (1983). *Structure in fives: Designing effective organizations.* Englewood Cliffs, NJ: Prentice-Hall.

Mitchell, R. (1991). Masters of innovation: How 3M keeps its products coming. In J. Henry & D. Walker (Eds.), *Managing innovation* (pp. 171–181). London: Sage.

Myers, D. G. (2000). The funds, friends and faith of happy people. *American Psychologist, 55,* 56–67.

Nadler, D. A. (1988). Concepts for the management of organizational change. In M. L. Tushman & W. L. Moore (Eds.), *Readings in the management of innovation* (pp. 718–732). London: Harper Business.

Nayak, R. M., & Ketteringham, J. (1991). 3M's little yellow postit pads: Never mind I'll do it myself. In J. Henry & D. Walker (Eds.), *Managing innovation* (pp. 215–223). London: Sage.

Oldham, G. R. (1996). Job design. In C. Cooper & I. T. Robertson (Eds.), *International review of industrial and organizational psychology* (pp. 33–60). Chichester, England: Wiley.

Osborn, A. F. (1953). *Applied imagination.* New York: Scribner's.

Parker, M. (1990). *Creating shared vision.* Clarendon Hills, IL: Dialog.

Pascale, R. (1990). *Managing on the edge.* London: Penguin.

Pascale, R. (1999). *From complexity and the unconscious: Creativity, innovation and change* [CD-Rom 1]. Milton Keynes, England: Open University Press.

Perkins, D. (1981). *The mind's best work.* Cambridge, MA: Harvard University Press.

Peters, T., & Waterman, R. H. (1982). *In search of excellence.* London: Harper & Row.

Pettinger, R. (1996). *Introduction to organizational behavior.* London: MacMillan.

Robertson, P. J., Roberts, D. R., & Porras, J. I. (1992). An evaluation of a model of planned organizational change: Evidence from a meta-analysis. In R. W. Woodman & W. A. Pasmore (Eds.), *Research in organizational change and development* (Vol. 7). Greenwich, CT: JAI Press.

Rosenfeld, R., & Servo, J. C. (1991). Facilitating innovation in large organizations. In J. Henry & D. Walker (Eds.), *Managing innovation* (pp. 28–38). London: Sage.

Salovey, P., & Mayer, J. D. (1990). Emotional intelligence. *Imagination, Cognition and Personality, 9,* 185–211.

*Semler, R. (1994). *Maverick.* London: Arrow.

Sonnentag, S. (1996). Work group factors and individual well-being. In M. A. West (Ed.), *The handbook of work-group psychology* (pp. 346–367). Chichester, England: Wiley.

Sparrow, P. (2002). To use competencies or not to use competencies, that is the question. In M. Pearn (Ed.), *Individual differences and development in organization* (pp. 107–130). Chichester, England: Wiley.

Stacy, R. (1996). *Complexity and creativity in organizations,* San Francisco: Berrett-Koehler.

Stajkovic, A. D., & Luthans, F. (1998). Self-efficacy and work-related performance: A meta-analysis. *Psychological Bulletin, 124,* 240–261.

Straw, B. M., Bell, N. E., & Clausen, J. A. (1986, March). The dispositional approach to job satisfaction. *Administrative Science Quarterly,* 40–53.

Taylor, R. (2002). *The future of work-life balance.* London: ESRC.

Taylor, S., & Brown, J. D. (1988). Illusion and well-being. *Psychological Bulletin, 103,* 193–210.

Warr, P. B. (1987). *Work, unemployment and mental health.* Oxford, England: Clarendon Press.

*Warr, P. B. (1999). Well-being and the workplace. In D. Kahneman, E. Diener, & N. Schwartz (Eds.), *Well-being: The foundations of hedonic psychology* (pp. 392–412). New York: Russell Sage Foundation.

Weisburg, R. W. (1983). *Creativity: Genius and other myths.* San Francisco: Freeman.

West, M. (2000). Creativity and innovation at work. *The Psychologist, 13,* 460–464.

West, M., & Anderson, N. (1996). Innovation in top management teams. *Journal of Applied Psychology, 81,* 680–693.

*Wheatley, M. (1994). *Leadership and the new science.* San Francisco: Berrett-Koehler.

White, M. (2001, December). *Conditions for well-being in working life: Evidence from Working in Britain 2000 survey.* Paper presented at the ESRC Social and Individual Determinants of Well-being, Seminar 2: Work, employment and well-being, Manchester, England, Manchester Metropolitan University.

Zairi, M. (1996). *Benchmarking for best practice.* Oxford, England: Butterworth-Heinemann.

CHAPTER 18

Toward a Positive Psychology of Executive Coaching

CAROL KAUFFMAN and ANNE SCOULAR

A S POSITIVE PSYCHOLOGY is becoming more accepted by the mainstream, it's potential contribution to clinical, consulting, and coaching psychology is becoming evident. Until now, the underlying assumptions of executive coaching have been steeped in the medical model. Inherent in this orientation is a hierarchical relationship between a "well" coach and a presumably skilled, but "less well" client who receives individualized skill development training by the coach. The strength-based and positive psychology perspectives pull from an entirely different model, one where the client is already "whole" and skilled. From this standpoint, the coach functions as a catalyst to help the client access and develop his or her inherent strengths. While a positive psychological perspective does not pretend that all clients are paragons of mental health and virtue, it does provide a completely different filter through which to view the client's skills and wishes (Buckingham & Clifton, 2001).

In this chapter, we describe some of the current theoretical orientations of coaching and examine how these might be related to applications of positive psychology. We then make more explicit what a positive psychology model of coaching might entail. In addition, we explore how the field of coaching can be enriched by drawing upon the rigorous research and theoretical solidity provided by the traditions of scientific inquiry.

EXECUTIVE COACHING: A GENERATION CHANGE

After 20 years of executive coaching in both the United States and the United Kingdom, we believe we are now moving from what we call "first-generation" to "second-generation" coaching. The first generation of coaches established the existence of

The authors thank James O. Pawelski, PhD, for his helpful comments on directions for future research.

the profession; brought it to the attention of the business world; and established basic models of application. Those who did this best brought enthusiasm, inspiration, and the ability to bring fresh new skills to jaded executives. This is the guru generation, which often has exceptional command and communication skills (see Buckingham & Clifton, 2001) but on occasion has created closed systems where their own talents and experience are the sine qua non of their approach. As such, they are ultimately limited (Storr, 1996).

We are now seeing the emergence of a second generation, who face very different challenges as interventions are becoming more complex and clients are becoming more sophisticated in their expectations of what executive coaching can offer. The field needs to become an open system, not one based on the personal strengths of a few visionaries. To achieve this, the theory and practice of executive coaching need to be based on explicit psychological principles and built on the foundation of solid empirical research.

One task of the new wave in coaching is to re-examine the theoretical bases of the work being done. As we discuss in this chapter, positive psychology and a strengths-based orientation provide a more appropriate model for executive coaching.

For the past two decades, the medical model has been the implicit basis of the majority of coaching interventions. When reviewing the literature, most of the stated differences between coaching "versus" therapy seem to be fairly superficial with the contrasts focusing on the structure of the sessions and the depths to which one explores issues (Hart, Blattner, & Leipsic, 2001). Yet, as Kiel, Rimmer, Williams, and Doyle (1996) note, only one-fourth of executive coaches are in need of "remedial" assistance to improve performance. Three-fourths are doing quite well and request coaching to help negotiate increases in responsibility as they are moving up the organizational ladder, often quite quickly. Wasylyshyn (2003) also found that a vast majority of executive coaching clients want to focus on their career success. These bright, accomplished individuals don't want diagnoses or proclamations; they want *data* about themselves and their subordinates that they can use as feedback. In addition, they value and benefit from having an independent sounding board to help them develop, challenge, and enhance their strengths.

Positive psychology and the strengths-based approach provide a theoretical framework that suggests an alternative to the medical model. This is the "co-active" (Whitworth, Kimsey-House, & Sandahl, 1998) or "egalitarian" (Greene & Grant, 2003) model. In these frameworks, the perspective shifts and the client is no longer a high-level *patient*. Instead, the client is a co-active, equal *partner*. The coach's job is to pull as much relevant material as possible from the client and those in the organization, using the armamentaria of interview techniques, psychometrics, personality instruments, and business data. Then coach and coachee can work together as co-researchers and decide how best to harness this information and put it to use.

THE PRAGMATICS: WHAT IS EXECUTIVE COACHING?

At its simplest, executive coaching is a service provided to those in business who want individual assistance to enhance their performance, skills, and achievement (Douglas & McCauley, 1999). It was originally geared for top-level executives for whom it was considered a "perk" and an indication that one was being groomed for promotion.

The structure of a coaching session usually takes the form of regularly scheduled one-on-one interviews. The number of sessions can vary from one session to many. For example, a one-time consultation for a particular task, a few sessions focusing on specific performance enhancement issues, or open-ended "developmental" contracts where the coaching team helps the organization move through a series of transitions. Coaching is usually one-on-one and may include group training as well. In some cases, the "360-degree" model is used (Wasylyshyn, 2003), where the executive and subordinates, peers, and even family members are interviewed to provide feedback information.

Since the 1980s, the executive coaching field has exploded in popularity and the provision of services has trickled down from top management to other client groups. It is now a basic offering and part of many management training and development services. As coaching received huge amounts of media attention (Garman, Whiston, & Zlatoper, 2000) small businesses, entrepreneurs, and professionals, including lawyers, doctors, and architects (Judge & Cowell, 1997) began taking advantage of these kinds of services. It is now available to virtually anyone who desires to improve his or her work performance and/or career satisfaction. Particularly in the United States, individuals now hire executive coaches just as they choose their own therapists. At present, tens of thousands of people who call themselves coaches (Hall, Otazo, & Hollenbeck, 1999) provide executive, performance enhancement, and life coaching for an ever-growing segment of the population.

WHO PROVIDES THESE SERVICES?

The chaos of the field is quite stunning. While huge amounts of money change hands, the industry is without enforceable regulation, professional standards, required certification, practice benchmarks, or safety procedures (Grant, 2001; Scoular, 2001). Shockingly to those of us steeped in science, there are very few efficacy studies. Nonpsychologists do much of the work often with a "one-size-fits-all" approach to their clients. As a result, much of the first-generation coaching culture is largely untrammelled by the psychological mandates of peer-review and scientific assessment. Until recently, there have been few publications on the theoretical sources of coaching and even fewer descriptions of how interventions are conceived or operationalized. In short, anyone who can sell his or her services as an executive coach is free to do so.

TOWARD A NEW SYNTHESIS: POSITIVE PSYCHOLOGY AND COACHING

In spirit, executive coaching and positive psychology are natural partners. The goal of coaching has always been to maximize the potential of the client by building his or her strengths and skills. In practice, however, the so-called positive orientation of executive coaching has often simply been a preamble to the real work: fixing the executive's problems. This mixed perspective is a natural effect of the nature of applied psychology over the past 50 years, namely to identify and treat the ill (Seligman & Csikszentmihalyi, 2000). Until very recently, coaching literature has consisted primarily of grafting applications of techniques developed from clinical or counseling psychology onto performance enhancement work with athletes, performers, and high-level executives. Having few other resources from which to draw, most executive (and life) coaches creatively altered treatment models to fit a normal population interested in optimal performance.

While it was not their intent, these practitioners point out a very important trend for the future of positive psychology. Deeply embedded in many theoretical orientations are kernels of truth about what forms the best in us. As we build an integrated theoretical basis for the positive psychology of coaching, we can explore potential models of normal and optimal health from biological, cognitive, emotion-focused, humanistic, existential, systems, cultural relational, and neopsychoanalytic models. At times, this requires a reversal of what these theories have focused on (etiology of illness) and what they can shed light on, but have chosen to overlook (etiology of strength and resilience).

Seligman (2003) recently described the differences between therapy and coaching as follows: "In therapy, you look for the underlying source of the problem to help the client fix it. In coaching you look for what is right with the person and work on how to enhance it." Positive psychology and strength-based coaching are based on the assumption that the client has everything he or she needs to address the challenge.

This orientation is illustrated in Whitworth et al.'s (1998) *Co-Active Coaching,* a training manual widely used in the United States. According to Whitworth and her colleagues, the work of coaching (life or executive) is to assume the client is whole and proceed to help them articulate and follow their own agenda, design an optimal relationship, and hold the client accountable in the manner he or she has chosen. Then the coach can help the client "tap into, and actualize, their deepest vision of who they are" (Dean, 2001). A positive psychology theoretical base does not assume that everything goes smoothly. When coach and client hit obstacles, or the inner sabotaging voice that can undermine the client's agenda, the coach actively listens and uses curiosity and intuition to find the powerful questions that will help the client to re-access their strengths, deepen their learning, and move toward fulfillment (Whitworth et al., 1998). In addition, new models of change, and resistance to change, based on the difficulties inherent in striving for excellence, rather than simply the result of psychopathology, need to be developed (Kauffman, in press).

In the United Kingdom, Whitmore's (1996) model of coaching also assumes the existence of an actualizing tendency that the coach calls forth. He suggests, "We are more like an acorn, which contains within it all the potential to be a magnificent oak tree. We need nourishment, encouragement, and the light to reach toward, but the 'oaktreeness' is already within" (p. 9). Joseph and Linley (Chapter 22, this volume) examine what psychological principles support the actualizing model.

COACHING TECHNIQUES AND INTERVENTIONS AND THEIR UNDERLYING THEORY

If positive psychology has value to offer executive coaching, what is the existing methodology and theoretical base from which it might suffuse? We discuss some of the many strands of current executive coaching practice—and note that in recent years approaches consonant with, or directly based on, positive psychology have steadily increased their market share of coaching approaches.

BEHAVIORAL APPROACHES

The techniques that executive and life coaches have pulled from behavior psychology include relaxation techniques; methods developed from systematic desensitization and stress management interventions. These interventions have been modified for high performance athletes and executives needing to operate successfully despite stressful circumstances (Karageorghis, 2002). The foundations of learning theory, however, were originally based on observation and study of normal behavior, and it has enormous potential for the field of positive psychology. Learning to enhance relaxation responses in the face of stress is an extraordinarily useful skill that top-level executives can tap into, as is diaphragmatic breathing and mindfulness meditation.

COGNITIVE BEHAVIOR THERAPY

Cognitive behavior therapy-based coaching takes techniques proven useful with anxious and depressed clients and applies them to those seeking self and performance enhancement. The literature is new, and there is emerging support for its effectiveness (Dendato & Diener, 1986; McCombs, 1988; Zimmerman & Paulson, 1995). The kinds of interventions used with high performers include cognitive restructuring (Davis, 1991), attribution training, and visualization.

MULTIMODAL THERAPY

The coaching potential of the Lazarus (1976, 1997) multimodal therapy has been discussed by Richard (1999) who suggests that executive coaching should be "integrative and holistic in approach." To achieve this, the coach evaluates seven dimensions of the client's life in terms of their "BASIC ID": Behavior, Affect Sensation, Imagery, Cognition, Interpersonal Relationships, and Drug/Biology modality. While opening up various modalities for coaching skills is useful, the tone of Richard's work is extremely medical and has a remedial focus. In the spirit of the positive psychology, you could use these dimensions as potential reservoirs of strength or as seven "intelligences" that the executive could tap into to enhance performance (Kauffman, in press).

SYSTEMS THEORY

Systems theory is another theoretical reservoir that has been used by coaching psychologists. Laske (1999) harnesses insights from family systems theory and constructive-developmental psychology in working with executives. Kilburg (1996, 2000) has developed a highly complex model of executive coaching based on systems theory, psychodynamic theory, and models of change that include elements of applications from chaos theory. While his work is complex, with a 17-dimensional model, his extensive experience and integrative approach has been used to train many American executive coaches. In Britain, systems theory is more commonly brought into coaching directly from management writers such as Senge (1990). Miller uses both systems theory and emergent change/complexity work to help people articulate bigger possibilities than previously thought and identify steps toward achieving them (Pascale & Miller, 1999).

SOLUTION-FOCUSED COACHING

Solution-focused coaching (Greene & Grant, 2003) is a promising orientation to developing a coherent psychology of coaching. Their approach is based on an integration of cognitive behavior therapy and brief solution-focused therapy (O'Connell, 1998). Greene and Grant have what they see as the first model of coaching psychology. The assumptive base of solution-focused coaching is very congruent with, though not identical to, positive psychology. Grant (2001) cites O'Connell's (1998) description of the core assumptions as including:

1. It challenges to optimal performance stem from constriction of the client's skill base, not signs of pathology.
2. The work of the coach/therapist is to participate in joint construction of solutions versus a focus on exploring deficits.
3. The orientation is toward helping clients access and develop unrecognized skills and resources.
4. It teaches clients how to use lessons drawn from other aspects of their life experience.
5. Solution-focused coaching is future- versus past-oriented.
6. Goals are clear, specific, and tailor-made by each coach/client match.

THE MYERS-BRIGGS TYPE INDICATOR

The Myers-Briggs Type Indicator (MBTI) is an application of Jungian theory that is used by thousands of management and executive coaches around the world. The extraordinarily popular self-assessment tool, the Myers-Briggs Personality Indicator, has been widely adopted within human resources management and is administered to over two million people a year worldwide (Consulting Psychologists Press, personal communication, 2003).

Much of its powerful draw stems from its inherent positive psychological premise—all personality profiles are healthy. The Myers-Briggs shares with positive psychology an assumption that anyone can learn to recognize and develop their preferred strengths. In addition, the model suggests anyone can learn to build up their less preferred side if they so wish, but these "weak" areas do not signify pathology. Like the Seligman and Clifton strengths approaches, it emphasizes that no single pattern is inherently good or bad, but rather that organizations need representation from all types if they are to function at their best.

The four dimensions of the MBTI (Myers & Myers, 1980) are Extrovert/Introvert; Sensor/Intuiter (specific, hands-on focus versus brush-stroke and overview); Thinkers/Feelers (preference for objective versus subjective information); and Perceiver/Judgers (those who prefer to explore data versus those who use it to form conclusions). Sixteen personality types are possible, for example, one could be an: Extrovert, Intuitor, Thinker, Judger. The four-by-four matrix of types is well known to most of the business community. There are a huge number of studies correlating various personality types with choice and success at different professions. Myers-Briggs trained coaches help their clients identify their profiles and learn what kinds of management styles fit best with their subordinates based on their MBTI personality profiles. The MBTI is also very useful in giving clients and organizations a depersonalized and readily accessible language with which to discuss otherwise sensitive or difficult areas, such as interpersonal conflict, in a constructive way.

EMOTIONAL INTELLIGENCE

Although not a psychological school of thought in itself, Goleman's (1995, 1998) work on emotional intelligence has had a significant impact on executive coaching (see also Salovey, Caruso, & Mayer, Chapter 28 this volume). His five areas of emotional intelligence lend themselves easily to becoming goals toward which the executive can aspire. His five basic emotional and social competencies include self-awareness, self-regulation, motivation, empathy, and social skills. In theory, Goleman's orientation, which builds also on Gardner's (1983) classic *Frames of Mind,* is compatible with positive psychology's emphasis on multiple and diverse intelligences and strengths. In its application, however (e.g., Goleman, 1998), it is often used to separate the superstar "haves" from the drone "have-nots" of emotional intelligence.

TRANSTHEORETICAL MODEL OF CHANGE

The Transtheoretical Model of Change, developed by J. O. Prochaska, Norcross, and DiClemente (1994) has also become a resource used by many executive and life coaches. Prochaska et al. suggest six stages of change. The stages are Precontemplation, Contemplation, Preparation, Action, Maintenance, and Termination. Clients are not expected to move through these in a linear fashion. The normal course of change is described as a repeated spiral through the early stages, until the client can enter into an action mode, eventually achieving maintenance of the targeted skill set, and finally moving through termination and pursuit of a new goal area. It is crucial, as Dean (2004) emphasizes, to create stage-matched interventions rather than to assume that all clients are ready to move into action. J. M. Prochaska, Prochaska, and Levesque (2001) examine in more detail how to apply the stages of change to development within organizations, in order to reduce resistance to change and to synthesize models of change.

POSITIVE PSYCHOLOGY AND STRENGTHS BUILDING

The newest wave of coaching is directly based on positive psychology (Seligman & Dean, 2003) and the strengths-building perspective (Buckingham & Clifton, 2001). The model is quite simple, but radical. In sum, it asserts that you should focus on strengths and values, rather than weaknesses. When assessing how an executive is performing in the workplace, you examine his or her taxonomy of strengths in order to assess how these are (or are not) being utilized in the work setting.

The strengths-based model suggests that the effort of building up weaknesses is a misplaced goal, as it takes enormous effort to get "up" to an average level, if that skill is not easily available to the worker. In contrast, building strengths is much more effective and greatly increases performance and job satisfaction (Buckingham & Clifton, 2001). For example, instead of forcing a creative, visionary thinker to build up his or her "detail-oriented" skills, you should instead, match that person with an assistant or coworker whose detail-oriented skills are a natural strength. While this seems obvious, it is not prevalent practice.

Over the past decade, the Gallup Organization has developed a strengths-finder instrument for specific application to the workplace (see Hodges & Clifton, this volume). This questionnaire assesses the top 5 (of 34) strengths such as action, accountability, connectedness, command, and many others. The Gallup strengths-based work is used by many Fortune 500 companies and is nearly always part of an extensive, companywide program. Their goal is to create a strengths-based corporate culture that will permeate all executive, management, and online employees. First, top executives receive intensive training in the strength-finder model. Then the entire staff of the corporation, usually numbering a minimum of 1,000 employees, takes the strengths assessment instrument (and possibly other measures). Each member of the staff then receives a telephone interview describing their top five strengths and an overview of their assessment. One goal is to shift the focus of the entire organization to a strengths rather than a deficit model of functioning (Stone, personal communication, October 2003). Further outcome studies are forthcoming, but the preliminary indications are positive (see Hodges & Clifton, this volume).

In positive psychology, Seligman's understanding of signature strengths is just now being developed for application by life coaches and in the work setting (Seligman & Dean, 2003). This model has enormous potential to be harnessed by executive coaches who may not have the power to change the orientation of the entire company, but can help clients alter the ways in which they approach their careers. Clients can take the Values in Action questionnaire and learn their top five strengths and virtues. Coaches can then brainstorm ways to "recraft" their jobs to "deploy their strengths and virtues every day" (Seligman, 2002, p. 166). Preliminary research suggests that using these strengths at work increases emotional well-being and job satisfaction. Because there are many different routes a person can take toward task completion, finding those that are more congruent with your core strengths is a manageable task that quickly becomes rewarding.

A related area of positive psychology, Csikszentmihalyi's (1991) study of flow has enormous potential for use by executive coaches. *Flow* is the state where a person becomes utterly absorbed in a task, to the extent that he loses track of time. Csikszentmihalyi has elaborated "nine conditions of flow" including the optimal balance between challenge and skill, immediate feedback, and a task being autotelic, inherently satisfying. This extensively researched area is a rich reservoir of resource for executive coaches. For example, clients can learn to identify the nine conditions and change their working practice or environment to increase the likelihood of having more flow work experiences. The benefits of being fully engaged in and experiencing flow have been examined in many studies (e.g., Csikszentmihalyi, 1997).

HOW SMALL DIFFERENCES IN PERSPECTIVE CAN HAVE A HUGE IMPACT

Executive coaches are starting to utilize a positive psychology approach with initially promising results. Gerhard Huhn, for example (personal communication, October 2003), described how a pilot coaching intervention designed to highlight and foster strengths turned the work experience around for a number of the highest level management officers in an international corporation. One executive described how his repeated lateness (five minutes) to meetings with the CEO or the board had hung over his head, made people angry with him, and how quickly they forgot that it was his innovations that made the company and these same individuals millions and millions of dollars. A strength-focused approach helped put his behavior in a more reality-based context. As a result, the client felt much better about himself and hopeful that he could impact the organization productively. Similar results were seen with a small group of executives and this small pilot intervention provided a new framework for those in charge to re-examine their assumptions about work effectiveness. This multinational organization is now considering full-scale implementation of a strengths-based approach.

To date, a Positive Psychology 360-degree intervention has yet to be described in the literature. We wonder what the impact would be of a figure-ground reversal of highlighting the strengths and virtues of chief executive officers and building on their strengths. The problem of narcissistic leadership does exist (Berglas, 2002). However, it is also true that corporations adapt (as in adapting to a level of noise or light so it is no longer heard as loud or seen as bright) to the strengths of their leaders, so that they no longer see the strengths that their leaders have to offer.

THE RESEARCH CONUNDRUM

When executive coaching is so prevalent and based on established theoretical sources and methods, why are there so few studies of its effectiveness? Many people are convinced of its utility, but the contrast between the thousands and thousands of articles and books on providing these services, and the few dozen outcome studies is startling. We consider the effectiveness of executive coaching in three parts. First, we consider the scientific research primarily in the psychology literature. Second, we consider the business research on the effectiveness of coaching and explore some of the issues raised by the findings in both areas. Finally, we explore future research directions.

SCIENTIFIC RESEARCH

There have been numerous studies in the psychology literature that seem to indicate that coaching is effective. Grant (2001) surveyed the peer-reviewed journals in psychology in 2001 and found 1,435 citations, but of these only 17 represented actual scientific studies of coaching interventions with adult normal people. However, many of these are one-subject studies. For example, Tobias (1996) in a single case found coaching improved performance; Peterson (1996) found that a 360-degree intervention improved performance evaluations and self-report indicated improvement; and Diedrich (1996), Kilburg (1996), and Richard (1999) also reported single case improvements.

Individual Differences   There has been very little research on personality differences and executive coaching, which given the heavy reliance by coaches on the MBTI in particular as noted earlier, is astonishing. Brown (2000) has examined personality correlates of leadership and gender using the Jackson Personality Inventory-Revised and the Leadership Competencies 360-Degree Rating Form. Although the study was conducted in the context of executive coaching, the implications for coaching are not developed. Thompson (1994) and Swain (1998) have written briefly on coaching and the MBTI, and Fitzgerald (1999) and particularly

Pearman (1999, 2000) have offered fuller consideration of it, but from an applied rather than an evaluative perspective. Scoular (2001) found statistically significant differences between MBTI types in an analytical task in a coaching simulation, but this study has not yet been replicated. If it is, and the findings hold, it will point to considerable work to be done to examine the many issues raised, such as whether or not some people are more suited to receiving coaching than other development options and whether coaches with certain personality preferences provide better services, in particular, for example, those who are MBTI Intuitive types (having a preference for the overview versus specifics).

Group Studies   While limited in scope, group studies also show some effects. The most cited study is by Olivero, Bane, and Kopelman (1997). Their action research found that the productivity of managers who had received training plus eight posttraining sessions of one-to-one coaching significantly increased productivity compared with the control group. Barling, Weber, and Kelloway (1996) found that the mean sales performance of managers following training plus coaching intervention improved by 38% compared with a 9% *decline* over the same time period in the control group. These results are startlingly large, and require replication. Although the potential of coaching to clarify goals and develop strengths could have effects of this magnitude, the studies noted are mostly action research with small sample sizes, and the kinds of rigorous studies with random assignment, double blind raters, and so on that we take for granted in most treatment outcome studies don't yet exist for the emerging executive coaching field.

BUSINESS RESEARCH

In the academic business journals, we found a similar pattern to that in the psychology literature. Information abounds on the pragmatics of executive coaching, but there is far less information assessing its effectiveness. There is also a more troubling aspect: Who is studying whether or not the service is working? Often it is the provider of the service, and some research looks more like quantified marketing statements than objective assessments.

Business community research is treated very differently than in academia. In the positivist scientific literature, research is ideally shared, designed to be replicable, and intended ultimately to answer questions such as "why?" As a result, issues such as correlation, causation, mediating variables, or covariance are important. The attempts by business-driven research to evaluate the effectiveness take place in a very different context. Evaluation is usually assessed within the organization and is not to be shared if it is seen as a source of competitive advantage. Therefore, much of the most valuable information on effectiveness is not published.

Despite the lack of outcome studies or the sharing of what is seen as "insider" information, most members of the business world are clear about what is effective. The data they use are the well-known matrixes of corporate health and include: have sales improved, have profits improved, have customer satisfaction ratings improved, is the corporation expanding, and of course, what is its showing on the stock markets. If the answers tilt the correct way, the intervention is deemed to be a success (Cusumano, personal communication, 2003; Stone, personal communication, October 2003).

These issues raise a number of challenges facing those who want to comprehensively evaluate the effectiveness of executive coaching. In practice, it straddles the two worlds of psychology and business. Therefore, those who wish to provide and assess these services would do well to be familiar with the ethos and mores of both cultures.

FUTURE RESEARCH DIRECTIONS

Turning to possible future directions for research, given the newness of the field and marked paucity of existing data, there are remarkable and nearly endless research opportunities for psychologists and business researchers—perhaps even working together. It would be extraordinarily useful if psychologists could present possible research protocols to conferences attended by those who practice executive coaching (such as the *American Society of Industrial and Organizational Psychologists*). These coaches are often inundated by the fast-paced demands of their work. If presented with possible outcome-assessment packages, many might be willing to add these to their own assessments.

What topics might this research usefully investigate? Fully conceptualizing a considered research program must itself be high on the list. In the absence at this point of such a program, we simply offer a number of questions, which we believe merit consideration, and give an example or two of specific studies that could be initiated.

1. What Are Some Research Methodologies That Can Be Developed to Study Coaching? At this point in time, any rigorous research whatsoever would be a significant and valued addition to the field. Possible research directions run the gamut from focusing on the organization, to the coaches, clients, or the many potential outcome measures one could use to assess effectiveness. The field is wide open to many levels of research, from demographic and descriptive data collection, to questionnaires. There have been few studies of content analysis of coaching sessions, exploring just what is being talked about, and how. To our knowledge there have been no interaction studies exploring the behavioral and/or interaction style of executive coach and coachee. In this field, even studies with extremely small sample sizes are published and at this point are useful for hypothesis generation.

Other kinds of research the field could use include narrative analysis, content analysis of structured interviews, and factor analyses of more extensive data collection. And, of course, any kind of random assignment studies measuring outcome of coaching interviews with blind raters is as yet unknown in executive coaching.

At present there are few, if any, true observational studies of coaching. Researchers could randomly pick a number of coaches and have them tape record a series of sessions. These tapes could be analyzed in a number of ways: Transcriptions could be divided into utterance units and coded for type of speech such as; interrogatives, imperatives, and declaratives. We could also perform content analysis of the sessions by dividing the utterance units into categories. The categories might include relationship support statements, goal articulation, value clarification, movement into action, or any category of interest to the researcher. The information collected could be used for descriptive analysis or correlated with outcome measures.

Stepping back from the coach-coachee dyad, studies can also be addressed at the team or organization level, studying the impact not just on individuals but also on groups of individuals and on business measures such as the bottom line (i.e., company profits).

Positive psychology research offers many potential avenues for study and includes excellent research instruments such as those measuring optimism, levels of happiness, and core strengths (see, e.g., Seligman, 2002; and the web site www.AuthenticHappiness.org). We could also employ the research methodologies similar to those used in the study of flow (Csikszentmihalyi, 1991) including random measurement of subjective experience and the study of subjective well-being and happiness (Diener & Diener, 1996).

2. What Factors Might Predict Coaching Effectiveness? There is a great need for basic research on coaching effectiveness. In particular, we need to methodically explore what variables might predict greater effectiveness. The potential range of studies is very wide. For example, we may explore the characteristics of the coach and client, and how these interact. Variables of interest might include gender, age, experience, signature strengths, personality variables, or motivation.

We could also examine the role of coaching activities. Does the specific content of sessions predict the efficacy of coaching? Do certain interventions work better than others? We could devise a categorization of coaching interventions such as support, being a sounding board for strategy, asking the client powerful questions (versus giving advice), identifying and developing signature strengths, active problem solving, or the specific use of behavioral, cognitive, or affect-based interventions. Then the relationship of these variables to coaching outcome measures could be explored.

In addition, researchers could examine if practicing from a theoretical orientation impacts on coaching effectiveness. If so, what orientation or intervention issues are relevant? Do those emphasizing strengths and positive psychology coaches fare better than coaches using more traditional approaches?

Other kinds of questions regarding characteristics of coaching style could also be addressed. For example, some forms of executive coaching are more open ended, directed toward the whole life of the client. Others are more specific and solution focused. Comparative success of these different orientations could be assessed by multiple outcome measures including client satisfaction, multirater assessment, and changes in performance evaluations.

Coaching is often associated with helping the client reach specific goals. However, do we know if goal attainment actually increases job satisfaction and well-being? The phenomenon of the hedonistic treadmill suggests that individuals "adapt" to new experiences of success. Does this occur in executive coaching? Are increases in self-report or performance ratings associated with increased job satisfaction and well-being at work? And if so, are these effects sustained, and if so, for how long a period? Descriptive or observational-based study of how the coach and coachee determine goals could be examined. We could assess how intrinsic or extrinsic these are, and see what role this might have in increasing satisfaction, well-being at work, and job stability.

An additional specific issue is that of the short-term versus long-term effects of coaching. Many coaches believe the effects of coaching continue after the relationship is over, believing that the lessons learned are internalized. Is this true?

There are few longitudinal studies of executive coaching and this kind of research is crucial to judging the lasting effects of coaching efficacy. In addition, we could explore if the effects of coaching are generalized beyond the specific work demands. Does quality of life improve outside of the work setting? Are those who are coached more resilient than those who are not coached?

A different specific issue that has received some attention but needs more inquiry is the question of whether internal coaches (from within the organization) help more, or differently compared with external coaches? As the demand for coaching increases, corporations are saving money by hiring internal coaches. The pros and cons of internal (versus external) coaches could be explored via interviewing coachees regarding their satisfaction with the process and by assessing comparative outcome measures. Interaction effects (certain types of challenges do better with internal or do better with external) could also be explored.

Another avenue for potential research is an exploration of contextual and cross-cultural variables that might influence outcome. What is the impact of the organization on coaching outcomes? Do companies that invest in corporatewide coaching interventions (such as those provided by the Gallup Organization; see Hodges & Clifton, Chapter 16 this volume) show improved receptivity and greater effectiveness than individuals receiving more individualized coaching that is not a part of a larger effort? What are the cross-cultural differences in how coaching is received or offered? Do cultures have different philosophies of "failure" that would impact on coaching services and outcome?

In medicine, physicians are trained to do no harm. The same must be true for coaches. Therefore, we should determine if there are ways that coaching may in fact prove harmful. Questions should include the possible predictors of negative outcomes of coaching, and particular qualities of the coach, such as underdeveloped relational or technical skills that lower success rates? Are certain client qualities predictive of poor outcome such as low motivation or certain character or value variables? Or is there an interaction effect that suggests certain "matches" may be contraindicated. In addition, some influential factors may lie well outside the coach-client dyad, such as unrealistic time constraints, lack of support from the organization, or choosing goals that are out of synchrony with the corporate culture.

These questions and more await the second generation of coaches. We hope those who value scientific research as a basis for a coaching psychology will use these ideas and develop their own projects. We also hope for future collaborations similar to what the authors experienced in preparing this chapter. One of us is in academia, with a private practice that includes executive coaching. The other works full-time in executive coaching with extensive experience in the business world. The field would be well served by more joint ventures integrating the strengths and virtues from those both in the academic and the corporate community.

There is extraordinary opportunity for theory development and research in the area of executive coaching. There are huge numbers of busy practitioners who could benefit enormously from the kind of theory building and research that psychologists can provide. The incorporation of positive psychology and strengths-based coaching into the mainstream of executive coaching has a number of potential benefits. Moving beyond the medical model and its focus on weakness, toward an appreciation and fostering of strengths, is finding both initial empirical support and an enthusiastic reception from the executives who are benefiting from it.

REFERENCES

*Barling, J., Weber, T., & Kelloway, E. K. (1996). Effects of transformational leadership training on attitudinal and financial outcomes: A field experiment. *Journal of Applied Psychology, 81,* 827–832.

Berglas, S. (2002, Spring). The very real dangers of executive coaching. *Harvard Business Review,* 87–92.

Brown, M. E. (2000). Personality correlates of leadership behavior. *Dissertation Abstracts International, 60*(12), 6402-B.

*Buckingham, M., & Clifton, D. O. (2001). *Now, discover your strengths.* New York: Free Press.

*Csikszentmihalyi, M. (1991). *Flow: The psychology of optimal experience.* New York: HarperCollins.

Csikszentmihalyi, M. (1997). *Finding flow: The psychology of engagement with everyday life.* New York: Basic Books.

Davis, K. (1991). Performance enhancement program for a college tennis player. *International Journal of Sport Psychology, 22,* 140–153.

Dean, B. (2001, January/February). The sky's the limit. *Psychotherapy Networker,* 36–44.

Dean, B. (2004). *The mentorcoach training program foundations manual.* Bethesda, MD: MentorCoach.

Dendato, K. M., & Diener, D. (1986). Effectiveness of cognitive/relaxation therapy and study-skills training in reducing self-reported anxiety and improving the academic performance of test-anxious students. *Journal of Counseling Psychology, 33,* 131–135.

Diedrich, R. C. (1996). An iterative approach to executive coaching. *Consulting Psychology Journal: Practice and Research, 48,* 61–66.

Diener, E., & Diener, C. (1996). Most people are happy. *Psychological Science, 7*(3), 181–185.

Douglas, C. A., & McCauley, C. D. (1999). Formal development relationships: A study of organizational practices. *Human Resource Development Quarterly, 10,* 203–220.

Fitzgerald, C. R. (1999). *In support of complexity, paradox, and wisdom in leaders: How type development theory offers guidance for coaching midlife executives.* Presentation at the third biennial International Conference on Leadership of the Center for Applications of Psychological Type, Washington, DC.

Gardner, H. (1983). *Frames of mind.* New York: Basic Books.

Garman, A., Whiston, D., & Zlatoper, K. (2000). Media perceptions of executive coaching and the formal preparation of coaches. *Consulting Psychology Journal: Practice and Research, 52,* 201–205.

Goleman, D. (1995). *Emotional intelligence.* New York: Bantam Books.

Goleman, D. (1998). *Working with emotional intelligence.* New York: Bantam Books.

Grant, A. M. (2001). *Toward a psychology of coaching.* Unpublished manuscript, University of Sydney, Australia, Coaching Psychology Unit. Retrieved from www.psychcoach.org.

*Greene, J., & Grant, A. (2003). *Solution focused coaching.* Essex, England: Pearson Education.

Hall, D. T., Otazo, K. K., & Hollenbeck, G. P. (1999). Behind closed doors: What really happens in executive coaching. *Organizational Dynamics, 27,* 39–52.

Hart, V., Blattner, J., & Leipsic, S. (2001). Coaching versus therapy: A perspective. *Consulting Psychology Journal: Practice and Research, 53,* 229–237.

Judge, W. Q., & Cowell, J. (1997). The brave new world of executive coaching. *Business Horizons, 40,* 71–77.

Karageorghis, C. (2002). *Entering "the zone": A guide for coaches.* Retrieved November 17, 2002, from www.thesportjournal.org.

Kauffman, C. (in press). *Pivot points: Small choices change your life.* New York: M. Evans Press.

Kiel, F., Rimmer, E., Williams, K., & Doyle, M. (1996). Coaching at the top. *Consulting Psychology Journal: Practice and Research, 48,* 67–77.

Kilburg, R. (1996). Toward a conceptual understanding and definition of executive coaching. *Consulting Psychology Journal: Practice and Research, 48,* 134–144.

*Kilburg, R. (2000). *Executive coaching: Developing managerial wisdom in a world of chaos.* Washington, DC: American Psychological Association.

Laske, O. E. (1999). An integrated model of developmental coaching. *Consulting Psychology Journal: Practice and Research, 51,* 139–159.

Lazarus, A. (1976). *Multimodal behavior therapy.* New York: Springer.

Lazarus, A. (1997). *Brief but comprehensive psychotherapy: The multimodal way.* New York: Springer.

McCombs, B. L. (1988). Motivational skills training: Combining metacognitive, cognitive, and affective learning strategies. In C. E. Weinstein, E. T. Goetz, & P. A. Alexander (Eds.), *Learning and study strategies: Issues in assessment, instruction and evaluation* (pp. 141–169). San Diego, CA: Academic Press.

Myers, I. B., & Myers, P. B. (1980). *Gifts differing.* Palo Alto, CA: Consulting Psychologists Press.

O'Connell, B. (1998). *Solution-focused therapy.* London: Sage.

*Olivero, G., Bane, K. D., & Kopelman, R. E. (1997). Executive coaching as a transfer of training tool: Effects on productivity in a public agency. *Public Personnel Management, 26,* 461–469.

Pascale, R. T., & Miller, A. H. (1999, Spring). The action lab: Creating a greenhouse for organizational change. *Strategy and Business, 64–72.*

Pearman, R. R. (1999). *Enhancing leadership effectiveness through psychological type.* Gainsville, FL: Center for Applications of Psychological Type.

Pearman, R. R. (2000). *Leadership coaching: Strategies for unleashing type development for effectiveness.* Paper presented to Oxford Psychologists Press MBTI Masterclass, Oxford, England.

Peterson, D. (1996). Executive coaching at work: The art of one-on-one change. *Consulting Psychology Journal: Practice and Research, 48,* 78–86.

Prochaska, J. M., Prochaska, J. O., & Levesque, D. A. (2001). A transtheoretical approach to changing organizations. *Administration and Policy in Mental Health, 28,* 247–260.

Prochaska, J. O., Norcross, J. C., & DiClemente, C. C. (1994). *Change for good.* New York: Morrow.

Richard, J. (1999). Multimodal therapy: A useful model for the executive coach. *Consulting Psychology Journal: Practice and Research, 51,* 24–30.

Scoular, P. A. (2001). *Is U.K. business coaching based on testable psychological theory?* Unpublished doctoral dissertation, Guildhall University, London.

Seligman, M. E. P. (2002). *Authentic happiness: Using the new positive psychology to realize your potential for lasting fulfillment.* New York: Free Press.

Seligman, M. E. P. (2003, October). *Values in Action Symposium.* Paper presented at the second International Positive Psychology Summit, Washington, DC.

Seligman, M. E. P., & Csikszentmihalyi, M. (2000). Positive psychology: An introduction. *American Psychologist, 55,* 5–14.

Seligman, M. E. P., & Dean, B. (2003, October). *Authentic happiness coaching.* Handout presented at the second International Positive Psychology Summit, Washington, DC.

Senge, P. M. (1990). *The fifth discipline: The art and practice of the learning organization.* London: Century Business.

Storr, A. (1996). *Feet of clay: A study of gurus.* London: HarperCollins.

Swain, M. (1998, February). Type: An executive coaching tool. *TypeWorks, 21,* 1–3.

Thompson, G. (1994, October). Using type in executive coaching. *TypeWorks, 1,* 4–5.

Tobias, L. L. (1996). Coaching executives. *Consulting Psychology Journal: Practice and Research, 48,* 87–95.

Wasylyshyn, K. (2003). Executive coaching: An outcome study. *Consulting Psychology Journal: Practice and Research, 55,* 94–106.

*Whitmore, J. (1996). *Coaching for performance* (2nd ed.). London: Nicholas Brealey.

Whitworth, L., Kimsey-House, H., & Sandahl, P. (1998). *Co-active coaching: New skills for coaching people toward success in work and life.* Palo Alto, CA: Davies-Black.

Zimmerman, B. J., & Paulson, A. S. (1995). Self-monitoring during collegiate studying: An invaluable tool for academic self-regulation. In P. Pintrich (Ed.), *New directions for teaching and learning* (Vol. 63, pp. 13–27). San Francisco: Jossey-Bass.

PART VII

HEALTH PSYCHOLOGY, CLINICAL PSYCHOLOGY, AND PSYCHOTHERAPY: A POSITIVE PSYCHOLOGICAL PERSPECTIVE

CHAPTER 19

Positive Psychology and Health Psychology: A Fruitful Liaison

SHELLEY E. TAYLOR and DAVID K. SHERMAN

Positive psychology has been a highly generative initiative, both in its implications for basic theory and laboratory research and in its implications for practice. There is perhaps no field as clearly a beneficiary of this thrust than health psychology. Health psychology and its intellectual antecedent, behavioral medicine, began in earnest in the 1970s, although there was related research before that time. Virtually from its inception, health psychology has been an arena in which the contributions of positive psychology have been evident, yielding insights that, in turn, have helped to refine the theories that give birth to applications. In this chapter, we pursue this theme with reference to several subfields within health psychology: health behaviors, social support, psychological control, adjustment to illness, and psychological cofactors in the course of illness.

HEALTH BEHAVIORS

Health behaviors are important, not only because they directly affect health, but because they can become habitual and influence susceptibility to the course of illness across the lifespan. Accordingly, health psychologists have been concerned with the factors that influence the practice of health behaviors, especially those factors that may help people change behaviors known to compromise health, such as smoking, poor diet, and lack of exercise.

Not surprisingly, some of the earliest approaches to this problem emphasized the negative incentives that may lead people to change their behaviors. An impressive program of research examined the role of fear and feelings of vulnerability on changing health habits, the underlying assumption being that as fear

This research was supported by NIMH grant MH056880. The second author was supported, in part, by NIMH training grant 15750.

increases, people will be increasingly motivated to make necessary behavior changes. Research drawing on fear appeals demonstrated only modest relations to health behavior change, however (Becker & Janz, 1987; H. Leventhal, 1970). Persuasive messages that elicit too much fear may actually undermine health behavior change (Becker & Janz, 1987). Moreover, fear may not produce long-lasting change in health habits unless it is coupled with recommendations for action or information about the efficacy of the health behavior for eliminating threat (Self & Rogers, 1990). Building on this research, the Health Belief Model (Rosenstock, 1966), as well as related models (e.g., Ajzen & Madden, 1986), proposed that feelings of vulnerability, coupled with beliefs about the efficacy of a particular health behavior for reducing vulnerability, were among the key variables needed to motivate people to engage in behavior change. While there is manifold evidence for this approach, positive psychology has suggested a very different way of addressing the same issues.

Research on the self has been brought to bear on understanding health habits and has yielded a particularly significant insight: Positive beliefs may actually help people come to grips with health threats and adopt better health behaviors. This counterintuitive observation was originally made in research on optimism. In the past, researchers had expressed the fear that optimism about one's health might interfere with the ability to process negative health-related information appropriately (e.g., Weinstein, 1984). Aspinwall and her colleagues, however, found that optimistic college students were actually *more* receptive to negative information about the risks of health behaviors in which they were currently engaging than less optimistic students (e.g., Aspinwall & Brunhart, 1996). In one study, female sunbathers were given information about skin cancer that was either highly relevant (the average skin cancer patient was someone their age) or less highly relevant (the average skin cancer patient was much older). Optimists were more accepting of the highly relevant health information than the pessimists, and were less likely to argue against the health information (Aspinwall & Brunhart, 1996; see Armor & Taylor, 1998, for a review).

Situations that make people feel more secure and positive about themselves can also lead to greater acceptance of threatening health information. This is an important insight, because people are often resistant to highly relevant health information suggesting that they should change their behavior (Ditto & Lopez, 1992; Liberman & Chaiken, 1992). In fact, people who have the most to gain from health communications are often the least likely to accept them. For example, studies have found that coffee drinkers are more critical than noncoffee drinkers of scientific evidence linking caffeine to breast cancer, and they are much more accepting of information disconfirming that link (Kunda, 1987).

In a series of studies, Sherman and colleagues have found that leading people to engage in self-affirming experiences, such as reflecting on important values, helps decrease defensiveness about health risks, and motivates people to change their health behaviors (Sherman, Nelson, & Steele, 2000; see Sherman & Cohen, 2002, for a review). In one study, women who were either coffee drinkers or noncoffee drinkers reviewed a scientific report linking caffeine consumption to breast cancer. The article strongly urged women to reduce their caffeine consumption to avoid breast cancer. As in earlier research (e.g., Kunda, 1987), coffee drinkers were more critical of the health information and thus more resistant to the message as a whole than were noncoffee drinkers. Yet, among self-affirmed participants, who had reflected upon a personally important value, coffee drinkers were more open to the information contained in the report than were noncoffee drinkers, and they intended to reduce their coffee drinking accordingly. When people who would otherwise feel threatened by a health message affirmed an alternative source of self-worth, their responses to the self-relevant threatening information proved more balanced and open than was true for people who had not self-affirmed (see also Raghunathan & Trope, 2002; M. B. Reed & Aspinwall, 1998).

Health information about AIDS can be particularly threatening because the disease is highly stigmatized, and people do not want to think that they have put themselves and their partners at risk for the disease by their sexual behavior. Consequently, people are often very resistant to AIDS-educational messages. One study found that sexually active college students saw themselves as being less at risk for HIV after seeing an AIDS-educational video (Morris & Swann, 1996), suggesting that the educational message may have prompted a defensive response. However, research has shown self-affirmations can reduce this defensiveness and promote positive health behaviors. In one study, sexually active undergraduates completed a self-affirmation prior to viewing an AIDS-educational video. Relative to participants in a control condition, students who wrote an essay about an important value, thereby affirming a valued self-image, were more likely to see themselves as being at risk for HIV and were also more likely to purchase condoms (Sherman et al., 2000).

Positive beliefs about the self among optimists have also been shown to promote AIDS preventive behaviors. One longitudinal study of gay, HIV-seropositive men found that those men who were optimistic about not developing AIDS reported greater efforts to maintain their health through diet and exercise (Taylor et al., 1992; see also Carver et al., 1993). These positive health habits in the face of disease can reinforce individuals' optimism, thereby creating a positive feedback loop.

Given the benefits of being optimistic in the face of health threats (Scheier & Carver, 1985), an important issue is whether social psychological interventions can make pessimistic people more optimistic. A study by Mann (2001) addressed this topic in a sample of HIV-infected women on combination therapies that required them to take many medications. The women in the study wrote about a positive future in which their medical treatment was simpler than their current reality. They wrote on this topic in a journal twice a week for four weeks. Compared to pessimists in a nonwriting control group, pessimists who wrote about a positive future had greater optimism, increased self-report adherence to medications, and reduced distress from the side effects of the medicine (Mann, 2001). Writing about a positive future in the face of a serious health threat, then, conferred on the pessimists the health benefits of being optimistic.

Why do positive experiences like self-affirmation or positive qualities like optimism help people to confront negative health information and promote positive health behaviors? Several models have proposed that positive experiences and self-affirmations work as a resource upon which individuals can draw in time of need (M. B. Reed & Aspinwall, 1998; Sherman & Cohen, 2002; Steele, 1988; Taylor, Lerner, Sherman, Sage, & McDowell, 2003a, 2003b; Trope & Pomerantz, 1998). People rely on their strengths in one domain to deal with potential weaknesses in other domains. At an affective level, when people are in a more positive affective state, they can confront information and events that might otherwise put them into a more negative mood (Carver, 2003; Isen, 2000). In this view, positive self-feelings serve as a psychological resource from which people can draw to confront negative health information (Raghunathan & Trope, 2002).

SOCIAL SUPPORT

The role of close relationships in health behavior change and in adjustment to illness has been an important topic within health psychology. Much of the early work focused on the potential problems or complications that can arise when social relationships are adversely affected by the looming threat of advancing illness. For example, early work on cardiovascular disease and the rehabilitative process emphasized many of the strains that can arise in families when the heart patient returns home from the hospital and discussed ways to anticipate and head off these adverse developments (Croog & Levine, 1977). Similarly, research on the interpersonal relationships experienced by cancer patients focused on experiences of "victimization," that is, rejection and avoidance from acquaintances, friends, and even intimates (e.g., Wortman & Dunkel-Schetter, 1979). A strong emphasis within the clinical literature on family relationships and illness stressed the potential maladaptive dynamics of family systems that could exacerbate or prolong illness experiences (Minuchen, 1977). The risks to interpersonal relationships that illness poses are undeniably important and merit investigation and clinical intervention when warranted. Such a focus, however, can obscure the important and growing recognition that social relationships play a positive critical role in the illness experience as well.

Social support is defined as the perception or experience that one is loved and cared for by others, esteemed and valued, and part of a social network of mutual assistance and obligations (Wills, 1991). Social support may involve specific transactions whereby one person receives advice, instrumental support, or emotional solace from another, or it may be experienced primarily via the perception that help and support is potentially available from those with whom one is close.

A substantial body of research has examined the relation of perceived and actual social support to mental health and health outcomes and found strongly positive associations (e.g., Thoits, 1995). Social support consistently reduces psychological distress, such as depression and anxiety, during times of stress, and it promotes psychological adjustment to chronically stressful conditions, including coronary artery disease (Holahan, Moos, Holahan, & Brennen, 1997), diabetes, HIV infection (Turner-Cobb et al., 2002), cancer (Stone, Mezzacappa, Donatone, & Gonder, 1999), rheumatoid arthritis (Goodenow, Reisine, & Grady, 1990), and many more disorders.

Social support contributes to physical health and survival as well. For example, in a classic study by Berkman and Syme (1979), social contacts predicted an average 2.8 years increased longevity among women and 2.3 years among men. Most significant is the fact that the positive impact of social ties on morbidity and mortality is as powerful or more powerful a predictor of health and longevity than well-established risk factors for chronic diseases and mortality, such as smoking, blood pressure, lipids, obesity, and physical activity (House, Landis, & Umberson, 1988). Studying the process of how social support serves as a resource for positive health has, as a result, been an important priority for health psychology.

The benefits of social support for health appear to operate at all points in the health/illness experience. Many forms of social support are helpful for encouraging good health behaviors (Taylor, 2003). Social support may help people to stave off illness altogether. For example, Cohen, Doyle, Skoner, Rabin, and Gwaltney (1997) intentionally infected healthy community volunteers with a cold or flu virus by swabbing the inside of their nasal passages with virus-soaked cotton swabs. They found that people who had more social ties were less likely to become ill following exposure to the virus and, if they did become ill, they were able to recover more quickly than those with fewer social ties. Indeed, the impact of social support on course of illness and recovery shows consistent beneficial effects.

More recently, research has examined the connection between interpersonal relationships and indicators of allostatic load, that is, the accumulating adverse changes in biological stress regulatory systems that can result from long-term exposure to chronic or recurring stress (McEwen & Steller, 1993). Allostatic load is, in essence, a preclinical state with implications for health later in life. A study by Ryff and colleagues (Ryff, Singer, Wing, & Love, 2001) examined adults in mid-life and their relationships with close others. Using a longitudinal methodology, they compared adults who had positive and negative relationship pathways. Negative relationship pathways were operationalized as having a negative evaluation of both mother and father in childhood or of having a negative evaluation in important domains (intellectual, sexual, recreational) of a person's ties to a spouse. Positive relationship pathways were defined as having at least one positive relationship with a parent or at least one positive evaluation of an important domain of ties with a person's spouse. Adults who had positive relationship pathways were less likely to have high allostatic load (as assessed by a composite including blood pressure, waist-hip ratio, total and cholesterol levels, and levels of cortisol, epinephrine, norepinephrine, and DHEA-S; Seeman, Singer, Horwitz, & McEwen, 1997).

In response to evidence like this, a broad array of clinical interventions have arisen, both to close gaps in social support that people with chronic stressors may experience, and to supplement supportive relationships with education and stressor-specific types of social support that may provide additional benefits. Experimental research that has provided social support to hospitalized people, for example, has found it to be associated with better adjustment and/or faster recovery (e.g., Kulik & Mahler, 1993). Specifically, Kulik and Mahler (1987) developed a social support intervention for patients about to experience cardiac surgery. Some of the patients were assigned to a roommate who was also awaiting surgery, whereas others were assigned to a roommate who had already had surgery. The surgery was either similar or dissimilar to their own. They found that patients who had a postoperative roommate profited from these contacts, whether the surgery was the same or different from the patients' own surgeries. The patients were less anxious preoperatively, were more ambulatory postoperatively, and were released more quickly from the hospital than were patients who were paired with a roommate who was awaiting surgery. This subtle social support manipulation may have provided patients with relevant information about the postoperative period, and/or the roommate may have acted as a role model for how one might feel and react postoperatively. Alternately, those awaiting surgery may simply have been relieved to see someone who had gone through the surgery and come out all right. Nonetheless, the benefits were clear, providing a strong basis for intervention.

Social support can also be critical for helping patients manage chronic conditions. For example, when a person has been diagnosed with a chronic disability or illness, the family's participation in an intervention may be enlisted to improve the diagnosed patient's adjustment. Involving the family in health behavior change, such as dietary change that may be required for the management of heart disease, is often beneficial for the effective management of chronic disorders, and it can also be educational and soothing for family members.

Social support groups have arisen as low-cost, efficient vehicles for supplementing social support needs that may be generated by specific stressors. Recent estimates are that about 25 million individuals participate in support groups at some point during their life (Kessler, Mickelson, & Zhao, 1997). Such groups can be a vital resource for the chronically ill and for helping people manage chronic stressors, such as obesity, alcoholism, or a family member's illness. They provide a format for discussions of mutual concern, provide specific information for how others have dealt with similar problems, and provide people with the opportunity to share their emotional responses with others who are going through the same problem (Gottlieb, 1988). A large number of studies have evaluated the efficacy of social support groups by comparing participants with those who have been waitlisted for participation, and these studies find beneficial effects (Hogan & Najarian, 2002).

So beneficial have self-help groups proven to be, that such groups are now available on the Internet (Davison, Pennebaker, & Dickerson, 2000). Although virtual support groups do not provide the benefits of face-to-face social contact, they are logistically easy to access, they are inexpensive, they provide opportunities to come and go at will and at times of personal need, and they offer answers to many specific questions. As such, Internet-based support groups are a rapidly growing means of providing social support, especially to individuals with chronic conditions or to those who are socially isolated from others like themselves, by virtue of disability or geography. Internet social support has also proven to be a valuable intervention for children (Hazzard, Celano, Collins, & Markov, 2002).

Thus, across the lifespan, nurturant, supportive contact with others, a sense of belonging or mattering, and participation in social groups have been tied to a broad array of mental health and health benefits. Perhaps no field better exemplifies the tangible benefits to health and longevity that positive resources can provide.

PSYCHOLOGICAL CONTROL

The experience of illness and its treatment can be disorienting and frightening. At one time, these adverse changes were accepted as simply part of the unfortunate consequences of the illness experience. Relatively early in health psychology's history, however, researchers learned that it is possible to harness the intrinsic psychologically adaptive qualities of the person in the service of adjustment to treatment and its aftermath.

Psychologist Irving Janis (1958) conducted a landmark study that changed completely how patients awaiting surgery were treated. Janis observed that patients varied in how well they understood and used the information that the hospital staff gave them to help them cope with the after-effects of surgery. Patients who were highly fearful and anxious showed many adverse effects of surgery, including vomiting, pain, urinary retention, and the inability to eat. Patients who were initially low in fear also showed unfavorable reactions after surgery, often becoming angry or upset or complaining, because of the unexpected problems they encountered. Moderately fearful patients, however, coped with postoperative distress most favorably. Janis reasoned that this group was vigilant enough by virtue of their fearfulness, but not overwhelmed by their fear so that they were able to develop realistic expectations of what their postsurgery reactions would be. When they later encountered these sensations and reactions, they expected them and were ready to deal with them.

Janis's seminal work sparked an interest in enlisting patient cooperation in the procedures that they would undergo, through enhanced understanding and participation. These interventions articulated and drew on the concept of *psychological control,* that is, the sense that one is prepared for and has psychological or behavioral measures one can undertake to cope with an impending stressful event. An early example of research drawing on this principle was conducted with patients facing intra-abdominal surgery (Egbert, Battit, Weleb, & Bartlett, 1964). Half the patients were alerted to the likelihood of postoperative pain and were given information about its normality, duration, and severity. They were also taught breathing exercises that would help them control the pain. The other half of the patients received no such instructions. When evaluated postoperatively, patients in the instruction group showed better postoperative adjustment, required fewer narcotics, and were able to leave the hospital sooner than were the patients who had not received the preparatory instructions. Many subsequent studies have examined the role of preparatory information and coping techniques and adjustment to surgery, and the effects are consistently beneficial.

The fact that patients who feel prepared and somewhat in control do so well has led to automated interventions for patients to prepare them for upcoming procedures. In one study (Mahler & Kulik, 1998), patients awaiting coronary artery bypass graft (CABG) were exposed to one of three preparatory videotapes or to no information. One videotape contained information about the procedure conveyed by a health care expert; the second videotape featured the health care expert and also included clips of interviews with patients who reported on their progress; a third videotape presented information from a health care expert coupled with patients who reported on their recovery, both its ups and its downs. Overall, patients who saw the videotapes—any videotape—felt significantly better prepared for the recovery period, reported higher self-efficacy during that period, and were more adherent to recommended dietary and exercise changes during their recovery. They were also released from the hospital sooner, compared to patients who did not receive videotape preparation. Similar interventions have been employed successfully for patients awaiting other medical procedures (e.g., Doering et al., 2000) including gastroendoscopic examinations (e.g., Johnson & Leventhal, 1974), childbirth (e.g., E. A. Leventhal, Leventhal, Shacham, & Easterling, 1989), the management of peptic ulcers (e.g., Putt, 1970), and chemotherapy (Burish & Lyles, 1979), with similar success.

Reviews of this literature have suggested that the combination of information, relaxation, and modest cognitive behavioral interventions, such as learning to think differently about the unpleasant sensations of a procedure, or developing behavioral coping techniques, such as breathing exercises, account for the success in reducing anxiety, improving coping, and fostering recovery (e.g., Ludwick-Rosenthal & Neufeld, 1988). The beneficial effects of interventions based on psychological control do have limits. People who have a high desire for control in their lives may especially benefit from control-based interventions (e.g., Burger, 1989), but control may be aversive to people who prefer to put themselves in the hands of others when awaiting distressing medical procedures. It is possible to give people too much control, such as multiple coping techniques to undertake or too much information (e.g., Mills & Krantz, 1979; Thompson, Cheek, & Graham, 1988). Nonetheless, the field of psychological control remains a particular achievement of health psychology. Interventions that have drawn on psychological control have recognized the great potential for recruiting and harnessing a latent and often untapped resource that most people have: the resilient capacity to grapple with and adjust to the stressful aspects of their lives.

ADJUSTMENT TO THE ILLNESS EXPERIENCE

For decades, psychologists and medical researchers have explored the factors that influence illness-related quality of life. For the most part, this research has been heavily oriented toward measuring survival, course of disease, compliance with medications, and determinants of psychological distress (Taylor & Aspinwall, 1990). Psychological research has focused disproportionately on the negative fallout from acute and chronic illness. Much attention, for example, has been paid to the factors associated with denial, anxiety, and depression in response to illness (Taylor, 2003). Clinical interventions have addressed the adverse consequences of illness as well, including physical and psychosocial rehabilitation, problems in body image, and vocational issues.

Although many people experience at least short-term anxiety and depression in response to the diagnosis of a chronic illness or disorder, very commonly and perhaps surprisingly, people find benefits in these experiences and report an improved quality of life, better relationships, and positive changes in their values and priorities (e.g., Affleck & Tennen, 1996; Linley & Joseph, 2004; Taylor, 1983; Tedeschi, Park, & Calhoun, 1998; Updegraff & Taylor, 2000). Evidence of benefit-finding, meaning, positive illusions, and growth in the wake of chronic and terminal illness has been found in populations as diverse as cancer patients (e.g., Taylor, 1983), low-income women infected with HIV (e.g., Updegraff, Taylor, Kemeny, & Wyatt, 2002), caregivers of the terminally ill (e.g., Folkman, 1997), and people coping with traumatic events (e.g., Wortman & Silver, 1987).

In their studies of adjustment to chronic conditions, Petrie, Buick, Weinman, and Booth (1999), for example, found considerable evidence of positive changes following a myocardial infarction or diagnosis of cancer. As Figure 19.1 shows, many benefits were experienced by both of these patient groups, although their specific nature varied somewhat. Most of the benefits reported by the myocardial infarction patients reflected lifestyle changes, perhaps indicative of the fact that the course of heart disease is directly tied to changes in personal health habits. The cancer patients, in contrast, reported more changes in their social relationships and in the meaning they attached to their life activities, perhaps because cancer may not be as directly influenced by health habit changes as is true of heart disease, but may be amenable to finding purpose or meaning in life.

In the past, the benefits reported by patients in response to illness experiences have sometimes been dismissed by researchers and practitioners as inconsequential, short-lived, or trivial (Aspinwall & Clark, in press). However, psychological

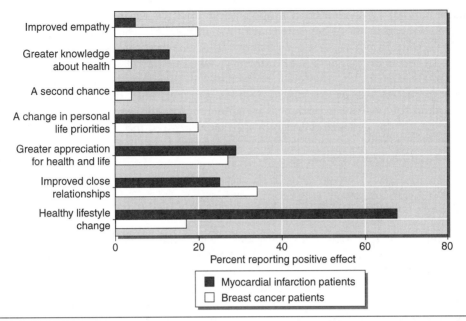

Figure 19.1   This Figure Shows the Positive Life Changes Experienced by Patients Who Survived a Myocardial Infarction and by Cancer Patients in Response to Their Illness. *Source:* "Positive Effects of Illness Reported by Myocardial Infarction and Breast Cancer Patients," by K. J. Petrie, D. L. Buick, J. Weinman, and R. J. Booth, 1999, *Journal of Psychosomatic Research, 47,* pp. 537–543. Reprinted with permission from Elsevier.

theories that emphasize the benefits of these positive experiences have provided a basis for viewing these insights not only as real, but as critical for subsequent adjustment. Research has now verified that benefit-finding in chronic and terminal illness is common and associated with lower levels of psychological distress (e.g., Folkman, 1997; see Updegraff & Taylor, 2000, for a review) and with greater attentiveness to actions that may improve health (e.g., Carver et al., 1993; Taylor et al., 1992). Such work provides a yield to practitioners, as they observe and attempt to respond to the often paradoxical positive changes they see in their patients' responses to illness. Rather than feeling concern that their patients may be defensively ignoring the legitimate risks their health problems pose, practitioners may have some assurance that these positive perceptions are adaptive, fostering psychological adjustment and attentive self-care.

In addition, how people cope with disease can affect their subsequent psychological health and illness-related behavior. For example, Annette Stanton's program of research has examined the relationship between finding benefits in medical illness and subsequent well-being. In one study with women who had breast cancer, Stanton and colleagues found that benefit-finding in the cancer experience was associated with better adjustment (Stanton & Snider, 1993). Subsequent research examined whether an intervention that promoted benefit finding would lead to more positive physical and psychological outcomes. In this study (Stanton & Danoff-Burg, 2002), women with early-stage breast cancer were randomly assigned to one of three writing conditions: (1) an emotional expression condition in which they wrote about their deepest thoughts and feelings regarding breast cancer; (2) a condition emphasizing positive thoughts and feelings, in which they wrote about benefits that they had found in the experience; and (3) a control group in which they wrote about their psychological and physical symptoms. In terms of psychological outcomes, women (particularly those who were high in avoidance) who wrote about the benefits they found in their cancer experience reported less psychological distress. Further, both the emotional writing group and the positive experiences writing group made significantly fewer visits to the doctor for cancer-related morbidities at a three-month check up. This research demonstrates a causal link between finding benefits in illness and psychological and health-related outcomes.

PSYCHOLOGICAL COFACTORS IN THE COURSE OF ILLNESS

The yield of positive psychology for health issues has expanded to include a consideration of psychological cofactors in the course of illness. Considered preposterous at one time, the idea that positive states of mind may slow the course of illness and facilitate recovery is coming to be widely acknowledged.

Positive beliefs, such as the ability to find meaning in threatening events, have been tied to a slower course of illness among people infected with HIV (Bower, Kemeny, Taylor, & Fahey, 1998). Positive affect is associated with lower risk of AIDS mortality (Moskowitz, in press). Optimism, even unrealistic optimism (G. M. Reed, Kemeny, Taylor, & Visscher, 1999; G. M. Reed, Kemeny, Taylor, Wang, & Visscher, 1994; G. M. Reed, Taylor, & Kemeny, 1993) has been associated with a slower course of illness among people infected with HIV. Among men and women recovering from coronary heart disease, those with greater self-esteem and optimism were less likely to suffer from an additional heart attack or need additional angioplasty (Helgeson & Fritz, 1999). A study by Levy, Slade, Kunkel, and Kasl (2002) found that older individuals who held more positive self-perceptions of aging (measured 23 years earlier) lived seven and a half years longer than those with less positive self-perceptions of aging in earlier life. The advantages associated with these positive beliefs remained in place after controlling for potential demographic and health-related confounds.

Such findings have led to an interest in the biopsychosocial pathways by which such impressive effects may be mediated. Positive beliefs may have beneficial effects on the cardiovascular, endocrine, and immune systems (e.g., Seeman & McEwen, 1996; Taylor et al., 2003b; Uchino, Cacioppo, & Kiecolt-Glaser, 1996) and these effects, in turn, may moderate disease course. Helgeson and Fritz (1999) for example, suggest that self-esteem and optimism may promote better health outcomes among coronary heart disease patients because they are associated with reduced neuroendocrine and autonomic responses to stress. Evidence consistent with this pathway comes from laboratory research examining whether extremely positive self views (self-enhancement) are associated with positive or negative biological responses to stress (Taylor et al., 2003b). They found that participants who were high self-enhancers, that is, who saw themselves as possessing many positive characteristics and traits, responded to a stressful task with lower autonomic activity, as assessed by heart rate and blood pressure, relative to low self-enhancers. In addition, high self-enhancers had lower baseline cortisol levels than low self-enhancers, which suggests that their hypothalamic-pituitary-adrenocortical axis may be less chronically activated or less recurrently activated in response to stress as well.

Insights from positive psychology have been invaluable in bringing to light the mechanisms whereby psychosocial cofactors affect the course of illness, and without these insights, such knowledge would have been slow to develop. Although the intervention implications of these findings have yet to be fully explored, the strong empirical basis for relating positive states of mind to illness progression suggests considerable intervention potential (cf. Stanton & Danoff-Burg, 2002).

CONCLUSION

We have focused on only a few of the rich and varied examples of how insights from positive psychology provide both a scientific understanding of health, illness, and their determinants and course, as well as a theoretical basis for clinical intervention and practice. Numerous other examples are actively being pursued by health psychologists. As such, the bridges between positive psychology and health psychology are manifold, robust, and extremely fruitful.

REFERENCES

Affleck, G., & Tennen, H. (1996). Construing benefits from adversity: Adaptational significance and dispositional underpinnings. *Journal of Personality, 64,* 899–922.

Ajzen, I., & Madden, T. J. (1986). Prediction of goal-directed behavior: Attitudes, intentions, and perceived behavioral control. *Journal of Experimental Social Psychology, 22,* 453–474.

Armor, D. A., & Taylor, S. E. (1998). Situated optimism: Specific outcome expectancies and self-regulation. In M. P. Zanna (Ed.), *Advances in experimental social psychology* (Vol. 30, pp. 309–379). New York: Academic Press.

*Aspinwall, L. G., & Brunhart, S. M. (1996). Distinguishing optimism from denial: Optimistic beliefs predict attention to health threats. *Personality and Social Psychology Bulletin, 22,* 933–1003.

Aspinwall, L. G., & Clark, A. (in press). Taking positive changes seriously: Toward a positive psychology of cancer survivorship and resilience. *Cancer.*

Becker, M. H., & Janz, N. K. (1987). On the effectiveness and utility of health hazard/health risk appraisal in clinical and nonclinical settings. *Health Services Research, 22,* 537–551.

Berkman, L. F., & Syme, S. L. (1979). Social networks, host resistance, and mortality: A nine-year follow-up study of Alameda County residents. *American Journal of Epidemiology, 109,* 186–204.

Bower, J. E., Kemeny, M. E., Taylor, S. E., & Fahey, J. L. (1998). Cognitive processing, discovery of meaning, CD 4 decline, and AIDS-related mortality among bereaved HIV-seropositive men. *Journal of Consulting and Clinical Psychology, 66,* 979–986.

Burger, J. M. (1989). Negative reactions to increases in perceived personal control. *Journal of Personality and Social Psychology, 56,* 246–256.

Burish, T. G., & Lyles, J. N. (1979). Effectiveness of relaxation training in reducing the aversiveness of chemotherapy in the treatment of cancer. *Journal of Behavior Therapy and Experimental Psychiatry, 10,* 357–361.

Carver, C. S. (2003). Pleasure as a sign you can attend to something else: Placing positive feelings within a general model of affect. *Cognition and Emotion, 17,* 241–261.

Carver, C. S., Pozo, C., Harris, S. D., Noriega, V., Scheier, M. F., Robinson, D. S., et al. (1993). How coping mediates the effect of optimism on distress: A study of women with early stage breast cancer. *Journal of Personality and Social Psychology, 65,* 375–390.

Cohen, S., Doyle, W. J., Skoner, D. P., Rabin, B. S., & Gwaltney, J. M., Jr. (1997). Social ties and susceptibility to the common cold. *Journal of the American Medical Association, 277,* 1940–1944.

Croog, S. H., & Levine, S. (1977). *The heart patient recovers.* New York: Human Sciences Press.

Davison, K. P., Pennebaker, J. W., & Dickerson, S. S. (2000). Who talks? The social psychology of illness support groups. *American Psychologist, 55,* 205–217.

Ditto, P. H., & Lopez, D. F. (1992). Motivated skepticism: Use of differential decision criteria for preferred and nonpreferred conclusions. *Journal of Personality and Social Psychology, 63,* 568–584.

Doering, S., Katzleberger, F., Rumpold, G., Roessler, S., Hofstoetter, B., Schatz, D. S., et al. (2000). Videotape preparation of patients before hip replacement surgery reduces stress. *Psychosomatic Medicine, 62,* 365–373.

Egbert, L. D., Battit, C. E., Weleb, C. E., & Bartlett, M. K. (1964). Reduction of postoperative pain by encouragement and instruction of patients. A study of doctor-patient rapport. *New England Journal of Medicine, 270,* 825–827.

Folkman, S. (1997). Positive psychological states and coping with severe stress. *Social Science and Medicine, 45,* 1207–1221.

Goodenow, C., Reisine, S. T., & Grady, K. E. (1990). Quality of social support and associated social and psychological functioning in women with rheumatoid arthritis. *Health Psychology, 9,* 266–284.

Gottlieb, B. H. (Ed.). (1988). *Marshalling social support: Formats, processes, and effects.* Newbury Park, CA: Sage.

Hazzard, A., Celano, M., Collins, M., & Markov, Y. (2002). Effects of STARBRIGHT World on knowledge, social support, and coping in hospitalized children with sickle cell disease and asthma. *Children's Health Care, 31,* 69–86.

*Helgeson, V. S., & Fritz, H. L. (1999). Cognitive adaptation as a predictor of new coronary events after percutaneous transluminal coronary angioplasty. *Psychosomatic Medicine, 61,* 488–495.

Hogan, B. E., & Najarian, B. (2002). Social support interventions: Do they work? *Clinical Psychology Review, 22,* 381–440.

Holahan, C. J., Moos, R. H., Holahan, C. K., & Brennan, P. L. (1997). Social context, coping strategies, and depressive symptoms: An expanded model with cardiac patients. *Journal of Personality and Social Psychology, 72,* 918–928.

House, J. S., Landis, K. R., & Umberson, D. (1988). Social relationships and health. *Science, 241,* 540–545.

Isen, A. M. (2000). Positive affect and decision making. In M. Lewis & J. M. Haviland-Jones (Eds.), *Handbook of emotions* (2nd ed., pp. 417–435). New York: Guilford Press.

Janis, I. L. (1958). *Psychological stress.* New York: Wiley.

Johnson, J. E., & Leventhal, H. (1974). Effects of accurate expectations and behavioral instructions on reactions during a noxious medical examination. *Journal of Personality and Social Psychology, 29,* 710–718.

Kessler, R. C., Mickelson, K. D., & Zhao, S. (1997). Patterns and correlates of self-help group membership in the United States. *Social Policy, 27,* 27–46.

Kulik, J. A., & Mahler, H. I. M. (1987). Effects of preoperative roommate assignment on preoperative anxiety and recovery from coronary-bypass surgery. *Health Psychology, 6,* 525–543.

Kulik, J. A., & Mahler, H. I. M. (1993). Emotional support as a moderator of adjustment and compliance after coronary artery bypass surgery: A longitudinal study. *Journal of Behavioral Medicine, 16,* 54–64.

Kunda, Z. (1987). Motivated inference: Self-serving generation and evaluation of causal theories. *Journal of Personality and Social Psychology, 53,* 636–647.

Leventhal, E. A., Leventhal, H., Shacham, S., & Easterling, D. V. (1989). Active coping reduces reports of pain from childbirth. *Journal of Consulting and Clinical Psychology, 57,* 365–371.

Leventhal, H. (1970). Findings and theory in the study of fear communications. In L. Berkowitz (Ed.), *Advances in experimental social psychology* (Vol. 5, pp. 120–186). New York: Academic Press.

Levy, B. R., Slade, M. D., Kunkel, S. R., & Kasl, S. V. (2002). Longevity increased by positive self-perceptions of aging. *Journal of Personality and Social Psychology, 83,* 261–270.

Liberman, A., & Chaiken, S. (1992). Defensive processing of personally relevant health messages. *Personality and Social Psychology Bulletin, 18,* 669–679.

Linley, P. A., & Joseph, S. (2004). Positive change following trauma and adversity: A review. *Journal of Traumatic Stress, 17,* 11–21.

Ludwick-Rosenthal, R., & Neufeld, R. W. J. (1988). Stress management during noxious medical procedures: An evaluative review of outcome studies. *Psychological Bulletin, 104,* 326–342.

*Mahler, H. I. M., & Kulik, J. A. (1998). Effects of preparatory videotapes on self-efficacy beliefs and recovery from coronary bypass surgery. *Annals of Behavioral Medicine, 20,* 39–46.

Mann, T. (2001). Effects of future writing and optimism on health behaviors in HIV-infected women. *Annals of Behavioral Medicine, 23,* 26–33.

McEwen, B. S., & Stellar, E. (1993). Stress and the individual: Mechanisms leading to disease. *Archives of Internal Medicine, 153,* 2093–2101.

Mills, R. T., & Krantz, D. S. (1979). Information, choice, and reactions to stress: A field experiment in a blood bank with laboratory analogue. *Journal of Personality and Social Psychology, 37,* 608–620.

Minuchen, S. (1977). *Psychosomatic diabetic children and their families.* (DHEW Publication No. ADM 77-477). Washington, DC: U.S. Government Printing Office.

Morris, K. A., & Swann, W. B. (1996). Denial and the AIDS crisis: On wishing away the threat of AIDS. In S. Oskamp & S. Thompson (Eds.), *Safer sex in the '90s: Understanding and preventing HIV risk behavior* (pp. 57–79). New York: Sage.

Moskowitz, J. T. (in press). Positive affect predicts lower risk of AIDS mortality. *Psychosomatic Medicine.*

*Petrie, K. J., Buick, D. L., Weinman, J., & Booth, R. J. (1999). Positive effects of illness reported by myocardial infarction and breast cancer patients. *Journal of Psychosomatic Research, 47,* 537–543.

Putt, A. M. (1970). One experiment in nursing adults with peptic ulcers. *Nursing Research, 19,* 484–494.

Raghunathan, R., & Trope, Y. (2002). Walking the tightrope between feeling good and being accurate: Mood as a resource in processing persuasive messages. *Journal of Personality and Social Psychology, 83,* 510–525.

Reed, M. B., & Aspinwall, L. G. (1998). Self-affirmation reduces biased processing of health-risk information. *Motivation and Emotion, 22,* 99–132.

Reed, G. M., Kemeny, M. E., Taylor, S. E., & Visscher, B. R. (1999). Negative HIV-specific expectancies and AIDS-related bereavement as predictors of symptom onset in asymptomatic HIV-positive gay men. *Health Psychology, 18,* 354–363.

*Reed, G. M., Kemeny, M. E., Taylor, S. E., Wang, H.-Y. J., & Visscher, B. R. (1994). "Realistic acceptance" as a predictor of decreased survival time in gay men with AIDS. *Health Psychology, 13,* 299–307.

Reed, G. M., Taylor, S. E., & Kemeny, M. E. (1993). Perceived control and psychological adjustment in gay men with AIDS. *Journal of Applied Social Psychology, 23,* 791–824.

Rosenstock, I. M. (1966). Why people use health services. *Milbank Quarterly, 44,* 94.

Ryff, C. D., Singer, B. H., Wing, E., & Love, G. D. (2001). Elective affinities and uninvited agonies: Mapping emotion with significant others onto health. In C. D. Ryff & B. H. Singer (Eds.), *Emotion, social relationships, and health: Series in affective science* (pp. 133–175). London: Oxford University Press.

Scheier, M. F., & Carver, C. S. (1985). Optimism, coping, and health: Assessment and implications of generalized outcome expectancies. *Health Psychology, 4,* 219–247.

Seeman, T. E., & McEwen, B. S. (1996). Impact of social environment characteristics on neuroendocrine regulation. *Psychosomatic Medicine, 58,* 459–471.

Seeman, T. E., Singer, B., Horwitz, R., & McEwen, B. S. (1997). The price of adaptation—Allostatic load and its health consequences: MacArthur studies of successful aging. *Archives of Internal Medicine, 157,* 2259–2268.

Self, C. A., & Rogers, R. W. (1990). Coping with threats to health: Effects of persuasive appeals on depressed, normal, and antisocial personalities. *Journal of Behavioral Medicine, 13,* 343–358.

Sherman, D. A. K., Nelson, L. D., & Steele, C. M. (2000). Do messages about health risks threaten the self? Increasing the acceptance of threatening health messages via self-affirmation. *Personality and Social Psychology Bulletin, 26,* 1046–1058.

Sherman, D. K., & Cohen, G. L. (2002). Accepting threatening information: Self-affirmation and the reduction of defensive biases. *Current Directions in Psychological Science, 11,* 119–123.

Stanton, A. L., & Danoff-Burg, S. (2002). Emotional expression, expressive writing, and cancer. In S. J. Lepore & J. M. Smyth (Eds.), *The writing cure: How expressive writing promotes health and emotional well-being* (pp. 31–51). Washington, DC: American Psychological Association.

Stanton, A. L., & Snider, P. R. (1993). Coping with a breast cancer diagnosis: A prospective study. *Health Psychology, 12,* 16–23.

Steele, C. M. (1988). The psychology of self-affirmation: Sustaining the integrity of the self. In L. Berkowitz (Ed.), *Advances in experimental social psychology, Vol. 21: Social psychological studies of the self: Perspectives and programs* (pp. 261–302). San Diego, CA: Academic Press.

Stone, A. A., Mezzacappa, E. S., Donatone, B. A., & Gonder, M. (1999). Psychosocial stress and social support are associated with prostate-specific antigen levels in men: Results from a community screening program. *Health Psychology, 18,* 482–486.

Taylor, S. E. (1983). Adjustment to threatening events: A theory of cognitive adaptation. *American Psychologist, 38,* 1161–1173.

Taylor, S. E. (2003). *Health psychology* (5th ed.). New York: McGraw-Hill.

Taylor, S. E., & Aspinwall, L. G. (1990). Psychological aspects of chronic illness. In G. R. VandenBos & P. T. Costa Jr. (Eds.), *Psychological aspects of serious illness* (pp. 3–60). Washington, DC: American Psychological Association.

*Taylor, S. E., Kemeny, M. E., Aspinwall, L. G., Schneider, S. G., Rodriguez, R., & Herbert, M. (1992). Optimism, coping, psychological distress, and high-risk sexual behavior among men at risk for AIDS. *Journal of Personality and Social Psychology, 63,* 460–473.

Taylor, S. E., Lerner, J. S., Sherman, D. K., Sage, R. M., & McDowell, N. K. (2003a). Portrait of the self-enhancer: Well-adjusted and well-liked or maladjusted and friendless? *Journal of Personality and Social Psychology, 84,* 165–176.

Taylor, S. E., Lerner, J. S., Sherman, D. K., Sage, R. M., & McDowell, N. K. (2003b). Are self-enhancing beliefs associated with healthy or unhealthy biological profiles? *Journal of Personality and Social Psychology, 85,* 605–615.

Tedeschi, R. G., Park, C. L., & Calhoun, L. G. (Eds.). (1998). *Posttraumatic growth: Positive changes in the aftermath of crisis.* Mahwah, NJ: Erlbaum.

Thoits, P. A. (1995). Stress, coping, and social support processes: Where are we? What next? *Journal of Health and Social Behavior* [Extra issue], 53–79.

Thompson, S. C., Cheek, P. R., & Graham, M. A. (1988). The other side of perceived control: Disadvantages and negative effects. In S. Spacapan & S. Oskamp (Eds.), *The social psychology of health: The Claremont applied social psychology conference* (Vol. 2, pp. 69–94). Beverly Hills, CA: Sage.

Trope, Y., & Pomerantz, E. M. (1998). Resolving conflicts among self-evaluation motives: Positive experience as a resource for overcoming defensiveness. *Motivation and Emotion, 22,* 53–72.

Turner-Cobb, J. M., Gore-Felton, C., Marouf, F., Koopman, C., Kim, P., Israelski, D., et al. (2002). Coping, social support, and attachment style as psychosocial correlates of adjustment in men and women with HIV/AIDS. *Journal of Behavioral Medicine, 25,* 337–353.

Uchino, B. N., Cacioppo, J. T., & Kiecolt-Glaser, J. K. (1996). The relationship between social support and physiological processes: A review with emphasis on underlying mechanisms and implications for health. *Psychological Bulletin, 119,* 488–531.

Updegraff, J. A., & Taylor, S. E. (2000). From vulnerability to growth: The positive and negative effects of stressful life events. In J. H. Harvey & E. D. Miller (Eds.), *Loss and trauma* (pp. 3–28). Philadelphia: Taylor & Francis.

Updegraff, J. A., Taylor, S. E., Kemeny, M. E., & Wyatt, G. E. (2002). Positive and negative effects of HIV-infection in women with low socioeconomic resources. *Personality and Social Psychology Bulletin, 28,* 382–394.

Weinstein, N. D. (1984). Why it won't happen to me: Perceptions of risk factors and susceptibility. *Health Psychology, 3,* 431–457.

Wills, T. A. (1991). Social support and interpersonal relationships. In M. S. Clark (Ed.), *Prosocial behavior* (pp. 265–289). Newbury Park, CA: Sage.

Wortman, C. B., & Dunkel-Schetter, C. (1979). Interpersonal relationships and cancer: A theoretical analysis. *Journal of Social Issues, 35,* 120–155.

Wortman, C. B., & Silver, R. C. (1987). Coping with irrevocable loss. In G. R. VandenBos & B. K. Bryant (Eds.), *Cataclysms, crises, and catastrophes: Psychology in action* (pp. 189–235). Washington, DC: American Psychological Association.

CHAPTER 20

Toward a Positive Clinical Psychology: Deconstructing the Illness Ideology and Constructing an Ideology of Human Strengths and Potential

JAMES E. MADDUX, C. R. SNYDER, and SHANE J. LOPEZ

THIS CHAPTER IS concerned with the ways that clinical psychologists think about or *conceive* psychological illness and wellness, and especially how they conceive the *difference* between psychological wellness and illness. More specifically, it is concerned with how clinical psychologists traditionally *have conceived* the difference between psychological illness and wellness and how positive psychology suggests they *should conceive* this difference. Thus, the major purpose of this chapter is to challenge traditional conceptions of psychological wellness and illness and to offer a new conception based on positive psychology, with a corresponding statement of a new mission for and vision of clinical psychology.

A *conception* of the difference between wellness and illness is not a *theory* of either wellness or illness (Wakefield, 1992). A conception of the difference between wellness and illness attempts to define these terms—to delineate which human experiences are to be considered "well" or "ill." More specifically, a conception of *psychopathology* does not try to explain the psychological phenomena that are considered pathological, but instead tells us what psychological phenomena are considered pathological and thus need to be explained. A theory of psychopathology, however, is an attempt to explain those psychological phenomena and experiences that have been identified by the conception as pathological (see also Maddux, Gosselin, & Winstead, in press).

Conceptions are important for a number of reasons. As medical philosopher Lawrie Reznek (1987) said: "Concepts carry consequences—classifying things one way rather than another has important implications for the way we behave toward such things" (p. 1). In speaking of the importance of the conception of *disease*, Reznek wrote:

> The classification of a condition as a disease carries many important consequences. We inform medical scientists that they should try to discover a cure for the condition. We inform benefactors that they should support such research. We direct medical care toward the condition, making it appropriate to treat the condition by medical means such as drug therapy, surgery, and so on. We inform our courts that it is inappropriate to hold people responsible for the manifestations of the condition. We set up early warning detection services aimed at detecting the condition in its early stages when it is still amenable to successful treatment. We serve notice to health insurance companies and national health services that they are liable to pay for the treatment of such a condition. Classifying a condition as a disease is no idle matter. (p. 1)

To label is to classify. If we substitute the labels *psychopathology* or *mental disorder* for the label *disease* in this paragraph, Reznek's message still holds true. How we conceive psychological illness and wellness has wide-ranging implications for individuals, medical and mental health professionals, government agencies and programs, and society at large. It determines what behaviors we consider it necessary to explain with our theories, thus determining the direction and scope of our research efforts. It also determines how we conceive the subject matter of clinical psychology, the roles and functions of clinical psychologists, and the people with whom they work.

Unlike theories of psychological wellness and illness, conceptions of psychological wellness and illness cannot be subjected to empirical validation. We cannot conduct research on the validity of a construction of psychological wellness and illness. They are *social constructions* grounded in values, not science, and socially constructed concepts cannot be proven true or false. (We return to this issue later in this chapter.) Because this chapter deals with socially constructed conceptions, it offers no new facts or research findings intended to persuade the reader of the greater value of one conception of psychological wellness and illness over another. Instead, this chapter offers a different perspective based on a different set of values. More than anything else, it offers a mission statement and a vision.

THE ILLNESS IDEOLOGY AND CLINICAL PSYCHOLOGY

Words can exert a powerful influence over thought. Long after the ancient roots of the term *clinical psychology* have been forgotten, they nevertheless continue to influence our thinking about the discipline. *Clinical* derives from the Greek *klinike* or "medical practice at the sickbed," and *psychology* derives from *psyche*, meaning "soul" or "mind" (*Webster's Seventh New Collegiate Dictionary*, 1976). Although few clinical psychologists today literally practice at people's bedsides, many practitioners and most of the public still view clinical psychology as a kind of medical practice for people with sick souls or sick minds. The discipline is still steeped not only in an *illness metaphor* but also an *illness ideology*—as evidenced by the fact that the language of clinical psychology remains the language of medicine and pathology. Terms such as *symptom, disorder, pathology, illness, diagnosis, treatment, doctor, patient, clinic, clinical,* and *clinician* are all consistent with the ancient assumptions captured in the term *clinical psychology* and with an ideology of illness and disease (Maddux, 2002). Although the illness *metaphor* (also referred to as the *medical model*) prescribes a certain way of thinking about psychological problems (e.g., a psychological problem is like a biological disease), the illness *ideology* goes beyond this and tells us to what aspects of human behavior we should pay attention. Specifically, it dictates that the focus of our attention should be disorder, dysfunction, and disease rather than health. Thus, it narrows our focus on what is weak and defective about people to the exclusion of what is strong and healthy.

This illness ideology emphasizes abnormality over normality, poor adjustment over healthy adjustment, and sickness over health. It promotes dichotomies between normal and abnormal behaviors, between clinical and nonclinical problems, and between clinical and nonclinical populations. It locates human adjustment and maladjustment inside the person rather than in the person's interactions with the environment and encounters with sociocultural values and societal institutions. Finally, this ideology and its language portray people who seek help as passive victims of intrapsychic and biological forces beyond their direct control. As a result, they are relegated to the passive reception of an expert's care.

Despite clinical psychology's long and deeply entrenched association with the illness ideology, it is time for a change in the way that clinical psychology views itself and the way it is viewed by the public. We believe that the illness ideology has outlived its usefulness for clinical psychology. Decades ago, the field of medicine began to shift its emphasis from the treatment of illness to the prevention of illness; moreover, more recently, medicine has moved from the prevention of illness to the enhancement of health (Snyder, Feldman, Taylor, Schroeder, & Adams, 2000). Furthermore, over two decades ago, the new field of health psychology acknowledged the need to emphasize illness prevention and health promotion. Unless clinical psychology embraces a similar change in emphasis, it will struggle for identity and purpose in much the same manner as psychiatry has for the last two or three decades (Wilson, 1993). We believe that it is time to abandon the illness ideology and replace it with a *positive clinical psychology* grounded in positive psychology's ideology of health, happiness, and human strengths.

HISTORICAL ROOTS OF THE ILLNESS IDEOLOGY IN CLINICAL PSYCHOLOGY

Despite the illness ideology's current hold on clinical psychology, the discipline was not steeped in the illness ideology at its start. Some historians of psychology trace the beginning of the profession of clinical psychology in the United States back to the 1886 founding of the first "psychological clinic" in the United States at the University of Pennsylvania by Lightner Witmer (Reisman, 1991). Witmer and the other early clinical psychologists worked primarily with children who had learning or school problems—not with "patients" with "mental disorders" (Reisman, 1991; Routh, 2000). Thus, they were more influenced by psychometric theory and its emphasis on careful measurement than by psychoanalytic theory and its emphasis on psychopathology and illness. Following Freud's momentous 1909 visit to Clark University, however, psychoanalysis and its derivatives dominated both psychiatry and clinical psychology (Barone, Maddux, & Snyder, 1997; Korchin, 1976). Psychoanalytic theory, with its emphasis on hidden intrapsychic processes and sexual and aggressive urges, provided a fertile soil into which the illness ideology deeply sank its roots.

Several other factors encouraged clinical psychologists to devote their attention to psychopathology and thereby strengthened the hold of the illness ideology on the field. First, although clinical psychologists were trained academically in universities, their practitioner training occurred primarily in psychiatric hospitals and clinics (Morrow, 1946). In these settings, clinical psychologists worked primarily as psycho-diagnosticians under the direction of psychiatrists trained in medicine and psychoanalysis. Second, after World War II, the United States Veterans Administration was founded and soon joined the American Psychological Association in developing training centers and standards for clinical psychologists. Because these early training centers were in Veterans Administration hospitals, the training of clinical psychologists continued to occur primarily in psychiatric settings, which were steeped in both biological models and psychoanalytic models. Third, the United States National Institute of Mental Health (NIMH) was founded in 1947. Given the direction that the NIMH took from the beginning, perhaps it should have been named the National Institute for Mental *Illness*. Regardless of the name, very soon, "thousands of psychologists found out that they could make a living treating mental illness" (Seligman & Csikszentmihalyi, 2000, p. 6).

By the 1950s, clinical psychologists in the United States had come "to see themselves as part of a mere subfield of the health professions" (Seligman & Csikszentmihalyi, 2000, p. 6). By this time, the practice of clinical psychology was grounded firmly in the illness ideology and was characterized by four basic assumptions, described next, about its scope and nature of psychological adjustment and maladjustment (Barone et al., 1997).

First, clinical psychology would be concerned with *psychopathology*—deviant, abnormal, and maladaptive behavioral and emotional conditions. Thus, the focus was not on facilitating mental health but on alleviating mental illness; not on the everyday problems in living experienced by millions, but on severe conditions experienced by a relatively small number of people. Common problems in living became the purview of counseling psychology, social work, and child guidance. Counseling psychology, in fact, because of its concern with everyday problems in living, gradually shifted away from an intrapsychic illness approach and toward interpersonal theories (Tyler, 1972), thus making counseling psychologists less enamored with the illness ideology.

Second, psychopathology, clinical problems, and clinical populations differ in kind, not just in degree, from normal problems in living, nonclinical problems, and nonclinical populations. Psychopathologies are *disorders,* not merely extreme variants of common problems in living and expected human difficulties and imperfections. As such, understanding psychopathology requires theories different from those theories that explain normal problems in living and effective psychological functioning. This separation became concretely evident in 1965 when the *Journal of Abnormal and Social Psychology* was split into the *Journal of Abnormal Psychology* and the *Journal of Personality and Social Psychology.*

Third, psychological disorders are analogous to biological or medical diseases in that they reflect distinct conditions *inside* the individual; moreover, these internal conditions cause people to think, feel, and behave maladaptively. This illness analogy does not hold that psychological disorders are necessarily directly caused by biological dysfunction. Instead, it holds that the causes of emotional and behavioral problems are located inside the person, rather than in the person's interactions with his or her environment (including his or her relationships with other people and society at large). Thus, to understand psychological problems, it is more important to understand and measure the fixed properties of people (e.g., personality traits) than to understand and assess the complex interactions between the person and the wide range of his or her life situations.

Fourth, following from the illness analogy, the psychological clinician's task, similar to the medical clinician's task, is to identify (diagnose) the disorder (disease) inside the person (patient) and to prescribe an intervention (treatment) for eliminating (cure) the internal disorder (disease). This treatment consists of alleviating conditions, either biological or psychological, that reside inside the person and are thought to be responsible for the symptoms. Even if the attempt to alleviate the problem is a purely verbal attempt to educate or persuade, it is still referred to as *treatment* or *therapy*, unlike often equally successful attempts to educate or persuade on the part of teachers, ministers, friends, and family (see also Szasz, 1978). In addition, these psychotherapeutic interactions between clinicians and their patients are thought to differ in quality from helpful and distress-reducing interactions between the patient and other people in his or her life, and understanding these psychotherapeutic interactions requires special theories.

Once clinical psychology became pathologized, there was no turning back. Albee (2000) suggests that "the uncritical acceptance of the medical model, the organic explanation of mental disorders, with psychiatric hegemony, medical concepts, and language" (p. 247) was the "fatal flaw" of the standards for clinical psychology training in the United States. These standards were established in 1950 by the American Psychological Association at a conference in Boulder, Colorado. At this same conference, the scientist-practitioner model of clinical psychology training was established. Albee argues that this fatal flaw "has distorted and damaged the development of clinical psychology ever since" (p. 247).

Little has changed since 1950. The basic assumptions of the illness ideology continue as implicit guides to clinical psychologists' activities, and they permeate the view of clinical psychology held by the public and policymakers. In fact, the influence of the illness ideology has grown over the past two and a half decades as clinical psychologists have fallen more and more deeply under the spell of the American Psychiatric Association's *Diagnostic and Statistical Manual of Mental Disorders (DSM;* APA, 2000). First published in the early 1950s (APA, 1952), the *DSM* is now in its fourth edition (actually, the sixth if we count as editions the revisions of the third and fourth editions, in 1987 and 2000, respectively), and its size and influence have increased with each revision. Through the first two editions (1952 and 1968), the influence of the *DSM* on research, practice, and clinical training was negligible, but it increased exponentially after the publication of the greatly expanded third edition in 1980.

The influence of the *DSM* has increased with the increasing size of the subsequent revisions. The *DSM* now provides the organizational structure for almost all textbooks and courses on abnormal psychology and psychopathology, as well as almost all books on the assessment and treatment of psychological problems for practicing clinical psychologists. The growth in the role of third-party funding for mental health services in the United States during this same period fueled the growth of the influence of the *DSM* as these third parties began requiring a *DSM* diagnostic label as a condition for payment or reimbursement for mental health services. Nowhere is the power of the illness ideology over clinical psychology more evident than in the dominance of the *DSM*. (Although we acknowledge the international importance and influence of the World Health Organization's *International Classification of Disease* [*ICD-10*; WHO, 1992], it has not generated the heated ideological and professional controversies that have been sparked by the *DSM*.)

Although most of the previously noted illness ideology assumptions are explicitly disavowed by the *DSM-IV*'s introduction (APA, 1994), practically every word thereafter is inconsistent with this disavowal. For example, *mental disorder* is defined as "a clinically significant behavioral or psychological syndrome or pattern that occurs *in an individual*" (p. xxi, emphasis added), and numerous common problems in living are viewed as mental disorders. So steeped in the illness ideology is the *DSM-IV* that, for example, *affiliation, anticipation, altruism,* and *humor* are described as "defense mechanisms" (p. 752). So closely aligned are the illness ideology and the *DSM* and so powerful is the influence of the *DSM* over clinical psychology (at least in the United States) that clinical psychology's rejection of the illness ideology must go hand in hand with its rejection of *DSM* as the best way to conceive of psychological difficulties.

THE SOCIAL CONSTRUCTION OF CONCEPTIONS OF PSYCHOLOGICAL WELLNESS AND ILLNESS

Positive clinical psychology rejects the illness ideology as the most accurate or effective approach for conceiving of the psychologically problematic aspects of human life. As such, positive clinical psychology refutes the illness ideology's premise that normal problems in living are symptoms of psychopathologies—that is, psychological illness or disease. This refutation is based on the assumption that the illness perspective is not a scientific theory or set of facts but rather a *socially constructed ideology*. The process of *social constructionism* involves "elucidating the process by which people come to describe, explain, or otherwise account for the world in which they live" (Gergen, 1985, pp. 3–4; see also Gergen, 1999). Social constructionism is concerned with "examining ways in which people understand the world, the social and political processes that influence how people define words and explain events, and the implications of these definitions and explanations— who benefits and who loses because of how we describe and understand the world" (Muehlenhard & Kimes, 1999, p. 234). From this perspective, our ways of thinking about human behavior and our explanations for human problems in living "are products of particular historical and cultural understandings rather than . . . universal and immutable categories of human experience" (Bohan, 1996, p. xvi). Because the prevailing views depend on who has the power to determine them, universal or "true" conceptions and perspectives do not exist. The people who are privileged to define such views usually are people with power, and their conceptions reflect and promote their interests and values (Muehlenhard & Kimes, 1999). Therefore, "When less powerful people attempt to challenge existing power relationships and to promote social change, an initial battleground is often the words used to discuss these problems" (p. 234). Because the interests of people and institutions are based on their values, debates over the definition of concepts often become clashes between deeply and implicitly held beliefs about the way the world should work and about the difference between right and wrong.

The social constructionist perspective can be contrasted with the *essentialist* perspective that is inherent in the illness ideology. Essentialism assumes that there are natural categories and that all members of a given category share important characteristics (Rosenblum & Travis, 1996). For example, the essentialist perspective views our categories of race, sexual orientation, and social class as objective categories that are independent of social or cultural processes. It views these categories as representing "empirically verifiable similarities among and differences between people" (p. 2). In the social constructionist view, however, "reality cannot be separated from the way that a culture makes sense of it" (p. 3). In social constructionism, such categories represent not what people *are* but rather the ways that people think about and attempt to make sense of differences among people. Social processes also determine what differences among people are more important than other differences (Rosenblum & Travis, 1996).

Thus, from the essentialist perspective, the distinctions between psychological wellness and illness and among various so-called psychopathologies and mental disorders are natural distinctions that can be discovered and described. From the social constructionist perspective, however, these distinctions are abstract ideas that are defined by people and thus reflect cultural, professional, and personal values. The social constructionist view of the illness ideology and its various presumed psychopathologies and mental disorders is that they are not scientifically verifiable facts or even scientifically testable theories. Instead, they are abstract ideas that have been constructed by people with particular personal, professional, and cultural values. The meanings of these and other concepts are not *revealed* by the methods of science but are *negotiated* among the people and institutions of society who have an interest in their definitions. What people often call "facts" are not truths but reflect reality negotiations (or social constructions) by those people who have an interest in using "the facts" (see Snyder & Higgins, 1997).

Not surprisingly, we typically refer to psychological concepts as *constructs* because their meanings are constructed and negotiated rather than discovered or revealed (Maddux, 1999). The ways in which conceptions of basic psychological constructs such as the "self" (Baumeister, 1987) and "self-esteem" (Hewitt, 2002) have changed over time and the different ways they are conceived by different cultures (e.g., Cross & Markus, 1999; Cushman, 1995; Hewitt, 2002) illustrate this process. Thus, in social constructionism, "all categories of disorder, even physical disorder categories convincingly explored scientifically, are the product of human beings constructing meaningful systems for understanding their world" (Raskin & Lewandowski, 2000, p. 21).

Therefore, our basic thesis is that conceptions of psychological normality and abnormality, along with our specific diagnostic labels and categories, are not facts about people but *social constructions*—abstract concepts reflecting shared worldviews that were developed and agreed on collaboratively over time by the members of society (e.g., theorists, researchers, professionals, their clients, the media, and the culture in which all are embedded). For this reason, the illness ideology, its conception of mental disorder, and the various specific categories of mental disorders found in traditional psychiatric diagnostic schemes (such as the *DSM* and *ICD*) are not psychological facts about people, nor are they testable scientific theories. Instead, they are heuristic social artifacts that serve the same sociocultural goals as do our constructions of race, gender, social class, and sexual orientation—maintaining and expanding the power of certain individuals and institutions, as well as maintaining the social order as defined by those in power (Beall, 1993; Becker, 1963; Parker, Georgaca, Harper, McLaughlin, & Stowell-Smith, 1995; Rosenblum & Travis, 1996). As are these other social constructions, our concepts of psychological normality and abnormality are tied ultimately to social values—in particular, the values of society's most powerful individuals, groups, and institutions—and the contextual rules for behavior derived from these values (Becker, 1963; Parker et al., 1995; Rosenblum & Travis, 1996).

Reznek (1987) has demonstrated that even our definition of *physical disease* "is a normative or evaluative concept" (p. 211) because to call a condition a disease "is to judge that the person with that condition is less able to lead a good or worthwhile life" (p. 211). If this is true of physical disease, it certainly is true of psychological disease. Because our notions of psychological normality-abnormality and health-illness are social constructions that serve sociocultural goals and values, they are linked to our assumptions about how people should live their lives and what makes life worth living.

The socially constructed illness ideology and associated traditional psychiatric diagnostics schemes, also socially constructed, have led to the proliferation of "mental illnesses" and to the pathologization of human existence. Given these precursors, it comes as no surprise that a highly *negative* clinical psychology evolved during the twentieth century. The increasing heft and weight of the *DSM*, which has been accompanied by its increasing influence over clinical psychology, provides evidence for this. From 1952 to 1994, the *DSM* increased from 86 to almost 900 pages, and the number of mental disorders increased from 106 to 297. As the socially constructed boundaries of "mental disorder" have expanded with each *DSM* revision, more relatively mundane human behaviors have become pathologized; as a result, the number of people with diagnosable mental disorders has continued to grow. This growth has occurred largely because mental health professionals have not been content to label only the obviously and blatantly dysfunctional patterns of behaving, thinking, and feeling as mental disorders. Instead, mental health professionals have gradually pathologized almost every conceivable human problem in living. As a result of the growing dominance of the illness ideology among both professionals and the public, eventually everything that human beings think, feel, do, and desire that is not perfectly logical, adaptive, or efficient will become a mental disorder.

The powerful sociocultural, political, professional, and economic forces that constructed the illness ideology now continue to sustain it. In this ongoing saga, however, the debate over the conception of psychological wellness and illness is not a search for truth. Rather, it is a struggle over the definition of a socially constructed abstraction and over the personal, political, and economic benefits that flow from determining what and whom society views as normal and abnormal. The most vivid and powerful embodiment of the illness ideology is the *DSM*, and the struggle is played out in the continual debates involved in its revision (see Kirk & Kutchins, 1992; Kutchins & Kirk, 1997).

These debates and struggles are described in detail by Allan Horwitz in *Creating Mental Illness* (2002):

> The emergence and persistence of an overly expansive disease model of mental illness was not accidental or arbitrary. The widespread creation of distinct mental diseases developed in specific historical circumstances and because of the interests

of specific social groups. . . . By the time the *DSM-III* was developed in 1980, thinking of mental illnesses as discrete disease entities . . . offered mental health professionals many social, economic, and political advantages. In addition, applying disease frameworks to a wide variety of behaviors and to a large number of people benefited a number of specific social groups including not only clinicians but also research scientists, advocacy groups, and pharmaceutical companies, among others. The disease entities of diagnostic psychiatry arose because they were useful for the social practices of various groups, not because they provided a more accurate way of viewing mental disorders. (p. 16)

Psychiatrist Mitchell Wilson (1993) offered a similar view. He argued that a noncategorical dimensional/continuity view of psychological wellness and illness posed a basic problem for psychiatry because it "did not demarcate clearly the well from the sick" (p. 402). He also argued that psychosocial modes of psychological difficulties posed a problem for psychiatry because "if conceived of psychosocially, psychiatric illness is not the province of medicine, because psychiatric problems are not truly medical but social, political, and legal" (p. 402). According to Wilson, the *DSM-III* gave psychiatry a means for marking its professional territory. Kirk and Kutchins (1992; Kutchins & Kirk, 1997) reached the same conclusion from their review of the papers, letters, and memos of the various *DSM* working groups—namely, that many of the most important decisions made about the inclusion or exclusion of certain disorders or certain symptoms were political decisions arrived at through negotiation and compromise rather than through an objective analysis of scientific facts.

THE ILLNESS IDEOLOGY AND THE CATEGORIES VERSUS DIMENSIONS DEBATE

Embedded in the illness ideology's conception of psychological wellness and illness is a *categorical model* in which individuals are determined to either have or not have a disorder—that is, to be either psychologically well or psychologically ill. An alternative model is the *dimensional model*, which assumes that normality and abnormality, wellness and illness, and effective and ineffective psychological functioning lie along a continuum. In this dimensional approach, so-called psychological disorders are simply extreme variants of normal psychological phenomena and ordinary problems in living (Keyes & Lopez, 2002; Widiger, in press). The dimensional model is concerned not with classifying people or disorders but with identifying and measuring individual differences in psychological phenomena such as emotion, mood, intelligence, and personal styles (e.g., Lubinski, 2000). Great differences among individuals on the dimensions of interest are expected, such as the differences we find on formal tests of intelligence. As with intelligence, divisions made between normality and abnormality may be demarcated for convenience or efficiency, but they are *not* to be viewed as reflecting a true discontinuity among types of phenomena or types of people.

Empirical evidence for the validity of a dimensional approach to psychological adjustment can be found in research on personality disorders (Coker & Widiger, in press; Costello, 1996; Maddux & Mundell, in press), the variations in normal emotional experiences (e.g., Oatley & Jenkins, 1992), adult attachment patterns in relationships (Fraley & Waller, 1998), self-defeating behaviors

(Baumeister & Scher, 1988), children's reading problems or dyslexia (Shaywitz, Escobar, Shaywitz, Fletcher, & Makuch, 1992), attention deficit/hyperactivity disorder (Barkeley, 1997), posttraumatic stress disorder (Anthony, Lonigan, & Hecht, 1999), depression (Costello, 1993a), and schizophrenia (Claridge, 1995; Costello, 1993b). Even the inventor of the term *schizophrenia*, Eugene Bleuler, viewed so-called pathological conditions as being continuous with so-called normal conditions, and he noted the occurrence of schizophrenic symptoms among normal individuals (Gilman, 1988). In fact, Bleuler referred to the major symptom of schizophrenia, thought disorder, as simply *ungewohnlich*, which in German means "unusual," not "bizarre," as it was translated in the first English version of Bleuler's classic monograph (Gilman, 1988).

Understanding the research supporting the dimensional approach is important because the vast majority of this research undermines the illness ideology's assumption that we can make clear, scientifically based distinctions between the psychologically well or healthy and the psychological ill or disordered. Inherent in the dimensional view is the assumption that these distinctions are not natural demarcations that can be discovered; instead, they are created or constructed.

SOCIAL CONSTRUCTIONISM AND SCIENCE IN CLINICAL PSYCHOLOGY

A social constructionist perspective is not necessarily antiscience. To insist that conceptions of psychological wellness and illness are socially constructed rather than scientifically derived is not to say that human psychological distress and suffering are not real. Nor is it to say that the patterns of thinking, feeling, and behaving that society decides to label as *ill* cannot be studied objectively and scientifically. Instead, it is to acknowledge that science can no more determine the proper or correct conceptions of psychological wellness and illness than it can determine the proper and correct conception of other social constructions such as beauty, justice, race, and social class. We nonetheless can use science to study the psychological phenomena that our culture refers to as *well* or *ill*. We can use the methods of science to understand a culture's conception of psychological wellness and illness, how this conception has evolved, and how it affects individuals and society. We also can use the methods of science to understand the origins of the patterns of thinking, feeling, and behaving that a culture considers psychopathological and to develop and test ways of modifying those patterns.

The science of medicine is not diminished by acknowledging that the notions of health and illness are socially constructed (Reznek, 1987), nor is the science of economics diminished by acknowledging that the notions of poverty and wealth are socially constructed. Likewise, the science of clinical psychology will not be diminished by acknowledging that its basic concepts are socially and not scientifically constructed. We agree with Lilienfeld and Marino (1995) that it is important to "make the value judgments underlying these decisions more explicit and open to criticism" (p. 418). We also agree that "heated disputes would almost surely arise concerning which conditions are deserving of attention from mental health professionals. Such disputes, however, would at least be settled on the legitimate basis of social values and exigencies, rather than on the basis of ill-defined criteria of doubtful scientific status" (pp. 418–419).

BEYOND THE ILLNESS IDEOLOGY: POSITIVE CLINICAL PSYCHOLOGY

The solution to this problem is not to move even closer to pathology-focused psychiatry, but instead to join the positive psychology movement. The viability of clinical psychology depends on our ability to build a *positive clinical psychology*. Heretofore, clinical psychologists always have been "more heavily invested in intricate theories of failure than in theories of success" (Bandura, 1998, p. 3). If we are to change our paradigm, we need to acknowledge that "much of the best work that [we] already do in the counseling room is to amplify strengths rather than repair the weaknesses of their clients" (Seligman & Csikszentmihalyi, 2000). The illness ideology and its medicalizing and pathologizing language are inconsistent with positive psychology's view that "Psychology is not just a branch of medicine concerned with illness or health; it is much larger. It is about work, education, insight, love, growth, and play" (Seligman & Csikszentmihalyi, 2000, p. 7).

In building a positive clinical psychology, we must adopt not only a new ideology but also a new language for talking about human behavior. This new ideology also offers a new language for talking about human behavior. In this new language, ineffective patterns of behaviors, cognitions, and emotions are construed as problems in living, not as disorders or diseases. Likewise, these problems in living are construed not as located inside individuals but in the interactions between the individual and other people, including the larger culture. Also, those who seek assistance in enhancing the quality of their lives are clients or students, not patients. The professionals who specialize in facilitating psychological health are teachers, counselors, consultants, coaches, or even social activists, not clinicians or doctors. Strategies and techniques for enhancing the quality of lives are educational, relational, social, and political interventions, not medical treatments. Finally, the facilities to which people will go for assistance with problems in living are centers, schools, or resorts, not clinics or hospitals. Such assistance might even take place in community centers, public and private schools, churches, and people's homes rather than in specialized facilities.

The positive psychology ideology emphasizes goals, well-being, satisfaction, happiness, interpersonal skills, perseverance, talent, wisdom, and personal responsibility. It is concerned with understanding what makes life worth living, with helping people become more self-organizing and self-directed, and with recognizing that "people and experiences are embedded in a social context" (Seligman & Csikszentmihalyi, 2000, p. 8).

These principles offer a conception of psychological functioning that gives at least as much emphasis to mental health as to mental illness and at least as much emphasis to identifying and understanding human strengths and assets as to human weaknesses and deficits (see Lopez & Snyder, 2003). More specifically, a positive clinical psychology is as much concerned with understanding and enhancing subjective well-being and effective functioning as it is with alleviating subjective distress and maladaptive functioning.

Consistent with our social constructionist perspective, we are not arguing that the positive psychology ideology is more true than the illness ideology. Both ideologies are socially constructed views of the world, not scientific theories or bodies of facts. We argue, however, that positive psychology offers an ideology that is more useful to clinical psychology than the obsolete illness ideology. As Bandura (1978) has observed:

Relatively few people seek cures for neuroses, but vast numbers of them are desirous of psychological services that can help them function more effectively in their everyday lives. . . . We have the knowledge and the means to bring benefit to many. We have the experimental methodology with which to advance psychological knowledge and practice. But to accomplish this calls for a broader vision of how psychology can serve people, and a fundamental change in the uses to which our knowledge is put. (pp. 99–100)

CONCLUSION

As we indicated at the beginning, this chapter has presented no new facts or research findings intended to persuade the reader of the greater efficacy of clinical psychological interventions grounded in positive psychology over those grounded in the illness ideology. Conceptions themselves do not offer new facts and findings; instead, they are concerned with what we view as facts and as findings, how we organize existing facts and findings, and, perhaps most important, what questions we consider worthy of attention. The illness ideology is more concerned with telling us what should be changed than with how it should be changed. The same is true of positive psychology. The greater utility of the positive psychology ideology for clinical psychology is found in its expanded view of what is important about human behavior and what we need to understand about human behavior to enhance people's quality of life. Unlike a negative clinical psychology based on the illness ideology, a positive clinical psychology is concerned not just with identifying weaknesses and treating or preventing disorders but also with identifying human strengths and promoting mental health. It is concerned not just with alleviating or preventing "suffering, death, pain, disability, or an important loss of freedom" (APA, 2000, p. xxxi) but also with promoting health, happiness, physical fitness, pleasure, and personal fulfillment through the free pursuit of chosen and valued goals.

A clinical psychology that is grounded not in the illness ideology but in a positive psychology ideology rejects:

- The categorization and pathologization of humans and human experience;
- The assumption that so-called mental disorders exist in individuals rather than in the relationships between the individual and other individuals and the culture at large; and
- The notion that understanding what is worst and weakest about us is more important than understanding what is best and bravest.

Psychological assessments and clinical interventions grounded in positive psychology will not differ from those grounded in the illness ideology as much in the *how* as in the *what*. The most important differences are not in strategies or tactics of assessments and interventions. Instead, they are in the domains of psychological functioning that are the focus of assessment and in the kinds of changes in human psychological functioning that interventions are designed to facilitate. Positive psychological assessment will emphasize the evaluations of people's strengths and assets along with their weaknesses and deficiencies (Keyes & Lopez, 2002; Lopez, Snyder, & Rasmussen, 2003; Wright & Lopez, 2002). More often than not, strategies and tactics for assessing strengths and assets will borrow from the strategies and tactics that have proven useful in assessing human weaknesses and deficiencies

(Lopez et al., 2003). Positive psychological interventions will emphasize the enhancement of people's strengths and assets in addition to, and at times instead of, the amelioration of their weaknesses and deficiencies, secure in the belief that strengthening the strengths will weaken the weaknesses. The interventions most often will derive their strategies and tactics from traditional treatments of traditional psychological disorders. The efficacy of this new focus in improving the human condition remains to be examined. The major change for clinical psychology, however, is not a matter of strategy and tactic, but a matter of vision and mission.

REFERENCES

Albee, G. W. (2000). The Boulder model's fatal flaw. *American Psychologist, 55,* 247–248.

American Psychiatric Association. (1952). *Diagnostic and statistical manual of mental disorders.* Washington, DC: Author.

American Psychiatric Association. (1968). *Diagnostic and statistical manual of mental disorders* (2nd ed.). Washington, DC: Author.

American Psychiatric Association. (1980). *Diagnostic and statistical manual of mental disorders* (3rd ed.). Washington, DC: Author.

American Psychiatric Association. (1987). *Diagnostic and statistical manual of mental disorders* (3rd ed., rev.). Washington, DC: Author.

American Psychiatric Association. (1994). *Diagnostic and statistical manual of mental disorders* (4th ed.). Washington, DC: Author.

American Psychiatric Association. (2000). *Diagnostic and statistical manual of mental disorders* (4th ed., text rev.). Washington, DC: Author.

Anthony, J. L., Lonigan, C. J., & Hecht, S. A. (1999). Dimensionality of post-traumatic stress disorder symptoms in children exposed to disaster: Results from a confirmatory factor analysis. *Journal of Abnormal Psychology, 108,* 315–325.

Bandura, A. (1978). On paradigms and recycled ideologies. *Cognitive Therapy and Research, 2,* 79–103.

Bandura, A. (1998, August). *Swimming against the mainstream: Accenting the positive aspects of humanity.* Invited address presented at the annual meeting of the American Psychological Association, San Francisco.

Barkeley, R. A. (1997). *ADHD and the nature of self-control.* New York: Guilford Press.

Barone, D. F., Maddux, J. E., & Snyder, C. R. (1997). *Social cognitive psychology: History and current domains.* New York: Plenum Press.

Baumeister, R. F. (1987). How the self became a problem: A psychological review of historical research. *Journal of Personality and Social Psychology, 52,* 163–176.

Baumeister, R. F., & Scher, S. J. (1988). Self-defeating behavior patterns among normal individuals: Review and analysis of common self-destructive tendencies. *Psychological Bulletin, 104,* 3–22.

Beall, A. E. (1993). A social constructionist view of gender. In A. E. Beall & R. J. Sternberg (Eds.), *The psychology of gender* (pp. 127–147). New York: Guilford Press.

Becker, H. S. (1963). *Outsiders.* New York: Free Press.

Bohan, J. (1996). *The psychology of sexual orientation: Coming to terms.* New York: Routledge.

Claridge, G. (1995). *Origins of mental illness.* Cambridge, MA: Malor Books.

Coker, L. A., & Widiger, T. A. (in press). Personality disorders. In J. E. Maddux & B. A. Winstead (Eds.), *Psychopathology: Contemporary issues, theory, and research.* Mahwah, NJ: Erlbaum.

Costello, C. G. (1993a). *Symptoms of depression.* New York: Wiley.

Costello, C. G. (1993b). *Symptoms of schizophrenia.* New York: Wiley.

Costello, C. G. (1996). *Personality characteristics of the personality disordered.* New York: Wiley.

Cross, S. E., & Markus, H. R. (1999). The cultural constitution of personality. In L. A. Pervin & O. P. John (Eds.), *Handbook of personality: Theory and research* (2nd ed., pp. 378–396). New York: Guilford Press.

Cushman, P. (1995). *Constructing the self, constructing America.* New York: Addison-Wesley.

Fraley, R. C., & Waller, N. G. (1998). Adult attachment patterns: A test of the typological model. In J. A. Simpson & W. S. Rholes (Eds.), *Attachment theory and close relationships* (pp. 77–114). New York: Guilford Press.

*Gergen, K. J. (1985). The social constructionist movement in modern psychology. *American Psychologist, 40,* 266–275.

Gergen, K. J. (1999). *An invitation to social construction.* Thousand Oaks, CA: Sage.

Gilman, S. L. (1988). *Disease and representation: Images of illness from madness to AIDS.* Ithaca, NY: Cornell University Press.

Hewitt, J. P. (2002). The social construction of self-esteem. In C. R. Snyder & S. J. Lopez (Eds.), *Handbook of positive psychology* (pp. 135–147). New York: Oxford University Press.

*Horwitz, A. V. (2002). *Creating mental illness.* Chicago: University of Chicago Press.

Keyes, C. L., & Lopez, S. J. (2002). Toward a science of mental health: Positive directions in diagnosis and interventions. In C. R. Snyder & S. J. Lopez (Eds.), *Handbook of positive psychology* (pp. 45–59). New York: Oxford University Press.

*Kirk, S. A., & Kutchins, H. (1992). *The selling of DSM: The rhetoric of science in psychiatry.* New York: Aldine de Gruyter.

Korchin, S. J. (1976). *Modern clinical psychology.* New York: Basic Books.

Kutchins, H., & Kirk, S. A. (1997). *Making us crazy: DSM: The psychiatric bible and the creation of mental disorder.* New York: Free Press.

Lilienfeld, S. O., & Marino, L. (1995). Mental disorder as a Roschian concept: A critique of Wakefield's "harmful dysfunction" analysis. *Journal of Abnormal Psychology, 104,* 411–420.

Lopez, S. J., & Snyder, C. R. (Eds.). (2003). *Positive psychological assessment: A handbook of models and measures.* Washington, DC: American Psychological Association.

Lopez, S. J., Snyder, C. R., & Rasmussen, H. N. (2003). Striking a vital balance: Developing a complementary focus on human weakness and strength through positive psychological treatment. In S. J. Lopez & C. R. Snyder (Eds.), *Positive psychological assessment: A handbook of models and measures* (pp. 3–20). Washington, DC: American Psychological Association.

Lubinski, D. (2000). Scientific and social significance of assessing individual differences: Sinking shafts at a few critical points. *Annual Review of Psychology, 51,* 405–444.

Maddux, J. E. (1999). The collective construction of collective efficacy: Comment on Paskevich, Brawley, Dorsch, and Widmeyer. *Group Dynamics: Theory, Research, and Practice, 3,* 1–4.

Maddux, J. E. (2002). Stopping the madness: Positive psychology and the deconstruction of the illness ideology and the *DSM.* In C. R. Snyder & S. J. Lopez (Eds.), *Handbook of positive psychology* (pp. 13–25). New York: Oxford University Press.

Maddux, J. E., Gosselin, J. T., & Winstead, B. A. (in press). Conceptions of psychopathology: A social constructionist perspective. In J. E. Maddux & B. A. Winstead (Eds.), *Psychopathology: Contemporary issues, theory, and research.* Mahwah, NJ: Erlbaum.

Maddux, J. E., & Mundell, C. E. (in press). Disorders of personality: Diseases or individual differences. In V. J. Derlega, B. A. Winstead, & W. H. Jones (Eds.), *Personality: Contemporary theory and research* (2nd ed., pp. 541–571). Chicago: Nelson-Hall.

Morrow, W. R. (1946). The development of psychological internship training. *Journal of Consulting Psychology, 10,* 165–183.

Muehlenhard, C. L., & Kimes, L. A. (1999). The social construction of violence: The case of sexual and domestic violence. *Personality and Social Psychology Review, 3,* 234–245.

Oatley, K., & Jenkins, J. M. (1992). Human emotions: Function and dysfunction. *Annual Review of Psychology, 43,* 55–85.

*Parker, I., Georgaca, E., Harper, D., McLaughlin, T., & Stowell-Smith, M. (1995). *Deconstructing psychopathology.* London: Sage.

Raskin, J. D., & Lewandowski, A. M. (2000). The construction of disorder as human enterprise. In R. A. Neimeyer & J. D. Raskin (Eds.), *Constructions of disorder: Meaning-making frameworks for psychotherapy* (pp. 15–40). Washington, DC: American Psychological Association.

Reisman, J. M. (1991). *A history of clinical psychology.* New York: Hemisphere.

Reznek, L. (1987). *The nature of disease.* London: Routledge & Kegan Paul.

Rosenblum, K. E., & Travis, T. C. (1996). Constructing categories of difference: Framework essay. In K. E. Rosenblum & T. C. Travis (Eds.), *The meaning of difference: American constructions of race, sex and gender, social class, and sexual orientation* (pp. 1–34). New York: McGraw-Hill.

Routh, D. K. (2000). Clinical psychology training: A history of ideas and practices prior to 1946. *American Psychologist, 55,* 236–240.

Seligman, M. E. P., & Csikszentmihalyi, M. (2000). Positive psychology: An introduction. *American Psychologist, 55,* 5–14.

Shaywitz, S. E., Escobar, M. D., Shaywitz, B. A., Fletcher, J. M., & Makuch, R. (1992). Evidence that dyslexia may represent the lower tail of a normal distribution of reading ability. *New England Journal of Medicine, 326,* 145–150.

Snyder, C. R., Feldman, D. B., Taylor, J. D., Schroeder, L. L., & Adams, V., III. (2000). The roles of hopeful thinking in preventing problems and enhancing strengths. *Applied and Preventive Psychology, 15,* 262–295.

Snyder, C. R., & Higgins, R. L. (1997). Reality negotiation: Governing oneself and being governed by others. *General Psychology Review, 4,* 336–350.

Szasz, T. (1978). *The myth of psychotherapy.* Syracuse, NY: Syracuse University Press.

Tyler, L. (1972). Reflecting on counseling psychology. *Counseling Psychologist, 3,* 6–11.

Wakefield, J. C. (1992). The concept of mental disorder: On the boundary between biological facts and social values. *American Psychologist, 47,* 373–388.

Widiger, T. A. (in press). Classification and diagnosis: Historical development and contemporary issues. In J. E. Maddux & B. A. Winstead (Eds.), *Psychopathology: Contemporary issues, theory, and research.* Mahwah, NJ: Erlbaum.

*Wilson, M. (1993). *DSM-III* and the transformation of American psychiatry: A history. *American Journal of Psychiatry, 150,* 399–410.

World Health Organization. (1992). *The ICD-10 classification of mental and behavioral disorders: Clinical descriptions and diagnostic guidelines.* Geneva, Switzerland: Author.

Wright, B. A., & Lopez, S. J. (2002). Widening the diagnostic focus: A case for including human strengths and environmental resources. In C. R. Snyder & S. J. Lopez (Eds.), *Handbook of positive psychology* (pp. 26–44). New York: Oxford University Press.

CHAPTER 21

The Client: Psychotherapy's Missing Link for Promoting a Positive Psychology

MARK A. HUBBLE and SCOTT D. MILLER

O N REFLECTION, THE term *positive psychology* merits serious consideration as an oxymoron. Setting aside the many subdisciplines that comprise the grand field of psychology (e.g., human factors, engineering, perception and sensation, environmental, developmental), the tone of professional discourse, particularly as it applies to clinical assessment and intervention, has been and remains decidedly negative. That this is so can hardly be surprising when it is recalled that Sigmund Freud (1918/1996) himself, the presumptive father of modern psychotherapy, asserted: "I have found little that is 'good' about human beings on the whole. In my experience most of them are trash . . ."

No matter the reception extended to Freud or his many convictions, his censorious, even cynical position on humanity has become much like a ghost in the machine. The dominant language of therapy unquestionably is based on a vocabulary of deficiency and despair. *Clients* (or for the more medically minded, *patients*) are variously portrayed as impaired, maladjusted, disturbed, regressed, addicted, psychotic, neurotic, or character-disordered. If a single classification is not enough, in recent years, it has become fashionable to invoke dual and multiaxial diagnoses. Because of the wide and imaginative assortment of these characterizations, a reasonable person might conclude that psychotherapists have nothing good to recount about the very people who support their livelihoods (Hubble, Duncan, & Miller, 1999a). Sad to say, our theories of therapy are principally theories of psychopathology (Held, 1991).

DSMING THE CLIENT AND PRACTICE ECONOMICS

Over the years, sociologists and psychologists alike have decried the use of labels. Scheff (1966), for example, warned that a categorization such as mental illness becomes an identity, thus stabilizing and reinforcing role adoption as a mentally ill person. Despite the efforts of highly visible personalities, such as Rosalyn Carter and Tipper Gore, to advocate for those ultimately described as mentally ill, the public has considerable difficulty in accepting patients and ex-patients as employees, neighbors, tenants, or spouses. For their part, insurance companies, by placing strict limits and exclusions on mental health treatments, reinforce the belief that mental conditions are somehow beyond the pale—different, ineligible by most actuarial standards, and thus, less treatable (Ganguli, 2000). Curiously, data indicate that people diagnosed with schizophrenia find their most stigmatizing experiences occur within the mental health provider community (Stuart & Arboleda-Flôrez, 2001).

Combining the evidence that stigma powerfully compromises social adjustment with other results showing that psychiatric diagnoses provide little value in predicting the differential effects of therapy outcome (Beutler, 1989; Brown, Dreis, & Nace, 1999; Duncan, Hubble, & Miller, 1997; Hubble & Miller, 2001), one has to wonder why the field's appetite grows for these linguistic contrivances. Even a quick look at the history of the American Psychiatric Association's *Diagnostic and Statistical Manual of Mental Disorders* (DSM) reveals that the number of categories blossomed from 66 in the first edition to more than 250 in the fourth (American Psychiatric Association, 1952, 1994). Additionally, this boom, it should be remembered, is *not* taking place in the context of a real decline in the mental health of the American public (Hubble, Duncan, & Miller, 1999b). If diagnostic descriptors fail to relieve suffering in any practical or measurable way, other explanations must account for their persistence and growing popularity. In this regard, population dynamics suggest an avenue for understanding the phenomenon; that is, the population dynamics of therapists, not the clientele (S. D. Miller & Hubble, 2002; S. D. Miller & Hubble, in press).

Since the mid-1980s, the number of therapists has increased by 275% (S. D. Miller, Duncan, & Hubble, 1997). Consumers now choose among psychiatrists, psychologists, psychoanalysts, Jungian analysts, family therapists, social workers, marriage and family counselors, licensed professional counselors, alcoholism and addiction counselors, pastoral counselors, psychiatric nurses, and other therapists of every description and stripe (Hubble et al., 1999b).

The data are telling. In the United States, for instance, research by Brown and his associates (Brown et al., 1999) showed that the country has twice the number of therapists needed. Without a doubt, the supply is exceeding demand. It is also apparent that if the demand for services does not exist to match existing supply, for survival, the demand must be created.

With the preceding in mind, psychiatric diagnoses are proliferating because the mental health disciplines are promoting an agenda to render the world their oyster. In short, aggressive efforts are pursued to convert every aspect of living into a problem amenable to therapy (Hubble et al., 1999b). As Woodward (1995) commented:

> The APA has always argued that the *DSM* must include any condition that might be the focus of psychiatric treatment. Got to have that diagnosis number before we can cough up the cash! Everything that goes wrong must be treated! (p. 22)

Put another way, what Freud called the "psychopathology of everyday life," the foibles, peccadilloes, and daily problems of living, is being converted to pathology period (Woodward, 1995).

When the *DSM-IV* was about to make its appearance, psychologists, the proponents and defenders of the scientist-practitioner model, spoke out loudly against it. Resnick (1993), for instance, wrote that the *DSM-IV* had all the pitfalls of its predecessors and, in that sense, was of no help. He also noted, "There are more and more disorders with biological etiologies without adequate evidence to support such contentions. . . . We would all be better served, . . . if the publishers of such manuals would aspire to science" (p. 6). Yet, by 1997, approximately two-thirds of the articles published in the *Journal of Consulting and Clinical Psychology* were organized around a psychiatric diagnosis (Hubble & Miller, 2001). As did psychiatry, professional psychology apparently found that money talks—the science notwithstanding.

In the overpopulated practice environment, the now decades-old commentary of Johns Hopkins University's Jerome Frank (the renowned psychiatrist who published the classic *Persuasion and Healing*) carries additional weight. He wryly observed that psychotherapy might be the only treatment that creates the illness it treats (Frank, 1973).

TRUTH OR HEGEMONY?

It is affirmed—therapy works (Asay & Lambert, 1999; Lambert & Bergin, 1994; Wampold, 2001). At least, as to its general effectiveness, few believe that therapy need be put to the test any longer. More than 40 years of outcome research, meta-analyses, and scholarly reviews of published studies attest to the usefulness of psychologically-based or informed interventions (Hubble et al., 1999b). Indeed, across a variety of treatments and presenting problems, the average person receiving therapy is better off than 80% of the untreated sample (Asay & Lambert, 1999; Wampold, 2001).

Certain projects and preoccupations of psychotherapists, unfortunately, have overshadowed the good news about therapy's efficacy and, thereby, hindered movement toward a positive psychology. Though hardly unique to this profession, intense political or factional rivalry abounds. A subtext of our history is the story of how the proponents of the various models or schools sought to achieve ascendancy and usurp the influence of their competitors. Freud, for instance, believed that he had discovered the ultimate truth about the human psyche and that he possessed the intellect and will to convert others to his vision (Grosskurth, 1991). He was determined to create a structure that would remain fixed and firm. He even went so far as to discourage his closest followers from "burdening him with their ideas on the pretense that he found it difficult to follow another's train of thought" (p. 17). In the face of this pressure, or perhaps, precisely because of it, the cadre of his faithful fractured. Soon, Jung, Adler, Stekel, Rank, and Ferenczi proclaimed their theoretical differences with Freud, if not independence, promoting their own versions of mental life and therapy. The parting was not pleasant.

Since those turbulent days, the divisions rapidly multiplied. Dating from the 1960s, the number of approaches has grown approximately 600% (S. D. Miller, Hubble, & Duncan, 1996). Although the tally varies among observers, it is estimated that more than 200 models now exist. Techniques, associated with the various therapies, exceed 400 (Garfield & Bergin, 1994).

After overcoming the early taboo against observing and investigating therapy, researchers joined the fray. The age of comparative clinical trials began. In the ensuing years, the "more mature interests of inquiry" (Bergin & Lambert, 1978, p. 162) were set aside in favor of identifying winners and losers. As Bergin and Lambert described this period, "Presumably, the one shown to be most effective will prove that position to be correct and will serve as a demonstration that the 'losers' should be persuaded to give up their views" (p. 162). Thus, behavior, psychoanalytic, client-centered or humanistic, rational-emotive, cognitive, time-limited and unlimited, drug, and other therapies were pitted against one another in a great battle of the brands (Hubble et al., 1999b).

However, no one therapy emerged the victor (more on this finding later). This result, as robust as it is, goes largely ignored and in some professional circles, is regarded as downright controversial. So, no surprise, the scramble for the top continues. The phrase *comparative clinical trials* has eventually given way to a much catchier tagline: empirically validated treatments (or empirically supported treatments). These empirically validated, empirically supported, evidence-based practices, or other scientific sounding catch phrases, assign a particular treatment for a particular disorder. It is said that they represent the latest and best findings and, therefore, should be adopted as a standard of care.

Hard to dispute, the prospect of having a specific psychological intervention for a given type of problem is appealing. The idea that therapists might possess the psychological equivalent of a pill for emotional distress is also one that resonates strongly with the public and government policymakers. Additionally, no one could argue with the success of the idea of problem-specific interventions in the field of medicine (e.g., surgery for acute appendicitis). This point was not lost on movers and shakers in the American Psychological Association. In his 1996 article in the *American Psychologist,* the official house organ of the American Psychological Association, researcher *and* cognitive-behavior therapist David Barlow submitted:

> . . . the evidence is now incontrovertible that there are effective psychological interventions for a large number of (but by no means all) psychological disorders . . . Numerous studies and subsequent meta-analyses have demonstrated that any number of specific psychotherapeutic approaches, . . . are more effective than credible alternative psychological interventions. (p. 1051)

Nevertheless, Barlow's assessment is much like men's and women's bikini wear: interesting for what it reveals, but essential for what it conceals (Hubble et al., 1999a).

Dating back as it does to the early 1980s, the finding that psychotherapy is effective is not particularly newsworthy. Accordingly, what Barlow (1996) means when he says, "the evidence is now incontrovertible that there are effective psychological interventions for a large number of . . . disorders" is less clear. His subsequent citation of studies on specific treatment approaches (e.g., cognitive-behavior therapy, dialectical-behavior therapy) for specific problems (e.g., panic, depression, borderline personality disorder) might lead an uninformed reader to conclude that specific brands of therapy exist that are *differentially* more effective than others. As is discussed in greater depth, this is patently untrue. Barlow's statements can only be taken to mean that some treatment approaches have had the privilege of being investigated and others have not—a conclusion hardly worth noting (Hubble et al., 1999a).

In all, the *Sturm und Drang* in our field may have served a purpose in the past, but they are now inhibiting efforts to advance understanding. Yes, therapy works. This is a positive and affirmative finding. It is time to identify the power behind it. Where this ultimately leads turns out to be quite surprising.

WHITHER THE CLIENT?

Historically, consumers have taken a back seat amid all the economic and partisan competition. As it turns out, overlooking the client is a mistake. In this respect, the field is finally gaining a real appreciation of the extent of the client's contribution to positive outcomes. How has this development come about and what are we learning?

The understanding of what the client brings to therapy can be traced, in part, to the failure of the comparative clinical trials to yield differential effects. As reported earlier, though therapy is superior to no treatment, apparently no psychotherapy is superior to any other. "This is really quite remarkable," noted Weinberger (1995), "given the claims of unique therapeutic properties made by advocates of the various treatments available today" (p. 45). The finding of no difference, incidentally, has been called the *dodo bird verdict* (Luborsky, Singer, & Luborsky, 1975; Rosenzweig, 1936). Borrowed from Lewis Carroll's *Alice in Wonderland*, it says, "Everyone has won and so all must have prizes."

More than 20 years have passed since the dodo verdict was rendered. Since that time, many attempts have been made to overturn it. The results have been consistent. The verdict has yet to be seriously challenged (Hubble et al., 1999b). In addition, evidence continues to mount in its support. For instance, in a recent study, 17 meta-analyses of comparisons of active treatments with one another were examined. The effect size for the treatments was small and nonsignificant. When the already small differences between treatments were corrected for the therapeutic allegiance of the researchers involved in comparing the different therapies, the differences even further reduced in size and significance (Luborsky et al., 2002, p. 2).

Left with "little evidence to recommend the use of one type [of therapy] over another in the treatment of specific problems" (Norcross & Newman, 1992, p. 9), investigators redirected their attention. A less provincial stance toward therapy was adopted (e.g., Garfield, 1992). Breaking with the tradition of saying, "Mine's better," efforts were then made to identify the pantheoretical or shared elements that made the various treatments effective. The organizing question became: If therapies work, but their efficacy has nothing to do with their bells and whistles, what are the *common* therapeutic factors (Hubble et al., 1999b; S. D. Miller, Hubble, & Duncan, 1995)?

Interestingly enough, this formulation is not new. The possibility that therapies have more in common than less was broached more than 60 years ago. In 1936, Saul Rosenzweig, writing in the *Journal of Orthopsychiatry*, suggested that the effectiveness of different therapy approaches had more to do with their common elements than with the theoretical tenets on which they were based (Goldfried & Newman, 1992, p. 48). Looking back, Luborsky (1995) says that Rosenzweig's paper "deserves a laurel in recognition of its being the first systematic presentation of the idea that common factors across diverse forms of psychotherapy are so omnipresent that comparative treatment studies *should* show nonsignificant differences in outcomes" (p. 106). Though without any way of knowing, Rosenzweig anticipated the recent interest in the therapeutic alliance as a critical pantheoretical factor. In particular, he indicated that one of the most common factors across therapies was the relationship between the client and clinician.

If Rosenzweig wrote the first note of the call to the common factors, Johns Hopkins University's Jerome Frank composed an entire symphony. In all three editions of *Persuasion and Healing: A Comparative Study of Psychotherapy* (1961, 1973; Frank & Frank, 1991), Frank placed therapy within the larger family of projects designed to bring about healing. He (with his psychiatrist daughter, Julia, in the last edition) looked for the threads joining different activities such as traditional psychotherapy, group and family therapies, inpatient treatment, drug therapy, medicine, religio-magical healing in nonindustrialized societies, cults, and revivals. In their analysis, the Franks (1991) concluded that therapy in its various forms should be thought of as "a single entity." They proposed this analogy:

> . . . two such apparently different psychotherapies as psychoanalysis and systematic desensitization could be like penicillin and digitalis—totally different pharmacological agents suitable for totally different conditions. On the other hand, the active therapeutic ingredient of both could be the same analogous to two aspirin-containing compounds marketed under different names. We believe the second alternative is closer to the truth. (p. 39)

They also identified four features shared by all effective therapies: (1) "an emotionally charged, confiding relationship with a helping person," (2) "a healing setting," (3) "a rationale, conceptual scheme, or myth that provides a plausible explanation for the patient's symptoms and prescribes a ritual or procedure for resolving them," and (4) "a ritual or procedure that requires the active participation of both patient and therapist and that is believed by both to be the means of restoring the patient's health" (Frank & Frank, 1991, pp. 40–43). Weinberger (1995) observed that after 1980, an outpouring of writing began to appear on the common factors. Until that time, Frank's work stood virtually alone. Now, a flood of "views on and lists of common factors" may be found with a positive relationship existing between the year of publication and the number of common factors proposals offered (pp. 44–45).

With so many schemes vying for attention, knowing which one to adopt or endorse proves difficult. Therefore, in 1997, we (S. D. Miller et al., 1997) proposed a plan for organizing and understanding common factors, including their clinical implications that provided the following benefits. First, it offered the advantages of both economy and flexibility. Second, it weighed the relative importance of the common factors based on their estimated contribution to treatment outcomes. Third, it gave a direction for future investigations into the relationship between common factors and effective therapy.

In 1992, Brigham Young University's Michael Lambert proposed four therapeutic factors—extratherapeutic, common factors, expectancy or placebo, and techniques—as the principal elements accounting for improvement in clients. Though not derived from a strict statistical analysis, he wrote that they embody what empirical studies suggest about psychotherapy outcome. Lambert added that the research base for this interpretation of the factors was extensive, spanned decades, dealt with a wide range of adult disorders, and a variety of research designs, including naturalistic observations, epidemiological studies, comparative clinical trials, and experimental analogues (Lambert, 1992, pp. 96–98).

Inspired by Lambert's specification of a "big four," we turned to the literature with the purpose of selecting the major components or ingredients of therapy that provided the best bridge between the various schools. The result of this effort builds on Lambert's important work and significantly broadens the base of what has traditionally been called the *common factors* (i.e., "nonspecific factors"; Duncan et al., 1997; Hubble et al., 1999b; S. D. Miller et al., 1997). The four factors are summarized in the following sections.

CLIENT/EXTRATHERAPEUTIC FACTORS

Without a client, therapy does not exist. These factors, unquestionably the most common and powerful of the common factors in therapy, are part of the client or the client's life circumstances that aid in recovery despite the client's formal participation in therapy. They consist of the client's strengths, supportive elements in the environment, and even chance events. Examples of these factors include persistence, faith, a supportive grandmother, membership in a religious community, sense of personal responsibility, a new job, a good day at the tracks, and a crisis successfully managed (Duncan et al., 1997). Lambert (1992) estimates that the client/extratherapeutic factors account for 40% of outcome variance. This hefty percentage represents a departure from convention, considering that most of what is written about therapy celebrates the might of the therapist, therapist's model, or technical prowess (Tallman & Bohart, 1999).

RELATIONSHIP FACTORS

The next class of factors comes in with 30% of the outcome variance (Lambert, 1992) and largely coincides with what has been typically called the *common factors* in the literature. These represent a wide range of relationship-mediated variables found among therapies regardless of the therapist's theoretical persuasion. Caring, empathy, warmth, acceptance, mutual affirmation, and encouragement of risk taking and mastery are but a few. Except what the client brings to therapy, these variables are probably responsible for most of the gains resulting from psychotherapy interventions (Lambert & Bergin, 1994). True to the position of Rosenzweig and the Franks, investigators have recently expended much time and energy in researching the therapeutic alliance as one of the more important relationship factors (Norcross, 2002).

PLACEBO, HOPE, AND EXPECTANCY

Following extratherapeutic and relationship factors comes placebo, hope, and expectancy. Lambert (1992) puts their contribution to psychotherapy outcome at 15%. In part, this class of therapeutic factors refers to the portion of improvement deriving from clients' knowledge of being treated and assessment of the credibility of the therapy's rationale and related techniques. The curative effects, therefore, are not thought to derive specifically from a given treatment procedure; they come from the positive and hopeful expectations that accompany the use and implementation of the method.

MODEL/TECHNIQUE FACTORS

Models and techniques are the last of the four factors. Lambert (1992) suggests that they, like expectancy, account for 15% of improvement in therapy. In a narrow sense, model/technique factors may be regarded as beliefs and procedures *unique* to specific treatments. The miracle question in solution-focused brief therapy, the use of the genogram in Bowenian family therapy, hypnosis, systematic desensitiza-tion, biofeedback, transference interpretations, and the respective theoretical premises attending these practices are exemplary.

In concert with the Franks, we interpret model/technique factors more broadly as therapeutic or healing rituals (Hubble et al., 1999a; S. D. Miller et al., 1997). They include a rationale, an explanation for the client's difficulties, and a variety of strategies or procedures to follow for resolving them. Depending on the clinician's theoretical orientation, different content is emphasized. Nevertheless, most thera-peutic methods or tactics share the common quality of preparing clients to take some action to help themselves. In particular, therapists expect their clients to do something different—to develop new understandings, feel different emotions, face fears, or alter old patterns of behavior (Hubble, 1993; S. D. Miller et al., 1997).

Now that the review of the four factors is complete, the title for this section— "Whither the Client?"—can be changed to "The Client Found." The evidence points to the client, figuratively speaking, as the mighty engine that makes therapy work. It is not the field's many suppositions and models. In fact, in one major study of therapeutic outcomes performed in a managed care setting, "differences in treat-ment methods, diagnoses, and even length of treatment" accounted for less than 5% of the outcome variance (Brown et al., 1999, p. 390). Improvement is surely de-pendent on the client.

There is more. After publishing our survey and analysis of the common factors (Hubble et al., 1999a; S. D. Miller et al., 1997), Wampold (2001) conducted and pub-lished a series of meta-analyses of the research literature. Based on his results, the percentage-wise contribution of each of the four factors can be revised. First, the total portion of the outcome variance attributable to treatment-mediated vari-ables markedly attenuated. That is, therapeutic modality (the therapist's model and technique) fell from 15% to only 8%. In contrast, the variance attributable to the client/extratherapeutic factors (those parts of the client or the client's life cir-cumstances that aid in recovery despite the client's formal participation in therapy) increased from 40% to 87%, a change of more than 100%. If anything, Wampold's work shows that the client's contribution to positive outcomes is even greater than previously believed.

The empirical findings bearing on the common factors stand conventional wis-dom on its head. Knowing that only 13% (100 [total variance] minus 87 [client/extratherapeutic factors] equals 13) of what therapists do influences outcome requires a revision of our doctrines and practices. The profession's earlier pursuits, trying harder to draft a definitive nosology (a *DSM-I, -II, -III, -IV, -IV-TR*) and derive distinct, "empirically validated" treatments for each classification (genera-tion after generation of prescriptive treatments), loom as a waste of time. When the temptation arises to try again, it would be well to remember that in the past 30 years of outcome research, not one interaction theoretically derived from hypothesized client deficits has been documented robustly (Wampold, 2001). It is no exaggeration to say that serious doubts—born in the field's very own research—surround our diagnostic systems and weaken faith in the specificity of psychological treatments. For all that, the field continues to stumble on, blithely ignoring the results.

Though we call the client the "missing link" in the chapter subtitle, this is a misnomer. Clients have never been missing. Instead, it is the field's acknowledgment and understanding of what therapists can do to support clients that have been long absent. Joining our work with their efforts in service of enhancing outcomes is the task before us all. To this issue we now turn particular attention.

OPERATIONALIZING THE COMMON FACTORS

On hearing the findings on the common factors, therapists express either relief and validation, or, more often, disbelief. The latter reaction is not surprising, as professional training has historically headlined the authority and power of theories and methods. Even so, once the dust settles, questions about the utility of a common factors perspective quickly come to mind. A sampling of the many heard include: "What do I do with this knowledge?" "How do I translate these findings into my daily work?" "Should I restructure my practice?" "Does this mean I continue to do what I have been doing all along?"

The authors, too, grappled with the same questions, each of us having undergone extensive training in a specific (and different) therapeutic approach. This prompted us to begin investigating the link between common factors and effective therapy. Our goal was to determine how therapists could directly support the therapeutic action of the common factors.

Owing to the overwhelming importance of the client and extratherapeutic factors, we reasoned that whatever we did (or did not do) as clinicians must place the client first. On the surface, this stance might look like an endorsement of strengths-based treatments, such as solution-focused or solution-oriented therapy. Recall, these therapies maintain that the task for the practitioner is to flush out, like a wise fox in hiding, the latent or unrecognized strengths and solutions of the client. Once identified, therapy becomes simple and straightforward—help clients do more of what they are already doing that works.

Although it was not our intent to emulate this model, in the end, the result turned out much the same. After proposing a set of principles or guidelines for enhancing the action of the client/extratherapeutic factors (e.g., become change-focused, potentiate change for the future, mind the client's competence), we then suggested for each principle a set of interventions and interviewing strategies (Hubble et al., 1999a; S. D. Miller et al., 1997). Once done, we placed ourselves in an inescapable conundrum. To recommend a set of technical operations is, in reality, a tacit endorsement of the very factor that research shows has the weakest relationship with outcome. Techniques are techniques, no matter their theoretical underpinnings or inferred relationship with the most potent curative factors. Clients, it bears emphasizing, almost never mention techniques as the defining element for change (Metcalf, Thomas, Duncan, Miller, & Hubble, 1996). Some other approach was needed to operationalize the client factors.

Toward this end, we surmised that the client factors could be enhanced by exploring and working within the client's worldview or frame of reference. That is, instead of imposing our own theories and techniques on the process (or therapy as traditionally practiced), adopting the *client's* frame of reference as the defining theory for the therapy would provide a catalyst for the client factors (Duncan & Miller, 2000a; Duncan & Moynihan, 1994; Duncan, Solovey, & Rusk, 1992; Hubble et al., 1999a). Our hope was to remove the therapist as "the leading character" and ennoble the "client as the star of the therapeutic stage" (Hubble et al., 1999a, p. 425). After all, if client factors account for 87% of the outcome variance (Wampold, 2001), the client's preexisting beliefs about problem formation, maintenance, and resolution should directly inform and influence the therapy. To do otherwise would exclude the person most responsible for positive change.

This development in our thinking fit with a major finding from the extant, process-outcome research literature. Orlinsky, Grawe, and Parks (1994) reported that the most important determinant for therapeutic success is the quality of the client's participation. In addition, the same body of findings showed that the therapeutic alliance, "especially as perceived by the patient," is "importantly involved" in mediating the link between participation and outcome (p. 361). By this reckoning, what better way to enlist the client's partnership with and openness to the therapist (an alliance) than by accommodating the client's preexisting beliefs about change, the goals, and the tasks of therapy— what we termed the *client's theory of change* (Duncan & Miller, 2000a; Hubble et al., 1999a, p. 431)? Blaise Pascal (1670/1970), the seventeenth-century French philosopher and mathematician, voiced a similar view in his famous observation on human nature, "People are generally better persuaded by the reasons which they have themselves discovered than by those which come into the minds of others." In short, we postulated that by having the client's theory take pride of place in the treatment process, therapy could be transformed from an exercise in colonization to one of discovery.

In practical terms, adopting the client's theory first entailed using the client's language. The rationale was that speaking the client's language (idioms, expressions, phrasing, etc.) would accomplish two related aims:

1. Prevent the client from being trapped in and influenced by the therapist's preferred theories
2. Increase the chances that changes initiated in session would more easily generalize outside therapy

Second, clients were asked to identify *their* goals. What they wanted for treatment was viewed as superseding any goal derived in the therapist's mind. Third, therapeutic conversation was oriented around the client's ideas about goal attainment— their solutions (i.e., ones that worked in the past, ones they believed would work in the future). The second and third steps in the work were seen as most important for gaining an understanding of the client's theory of change. Over time, as the theory became clear, the therapist could then assist clients in implementing their identified solutions. Alternatively, the therapists could make suggestions that both conformed to the theory and provided possibilities for change, taking care to offer them as suggestions rather than must-do directives (Duncan & Miller, 2000a; Hubble et al., 1999a).

As much *face validity* as discovering *the client's theory of change* possessed, it was still out of step with the cold, hard facts from the psychotherapy outcome literature. Yes, at first blush, it seemed to support the client factors. No matter how abstractly the ideas might be presented, whether defined as principles rather than mandates, closer examination made clear that any attempt to operationalize them merely led to the creation of another model for how to do therapy. As shown throughout this chapter, models—be they client-directed, client-centered, technique-intensive, and so on—ultimately matter little.

Other problems became manifest. For example, research has provided little reason to believe that training therapists to focus on alliance building improves treatment outcome (Horvath, 2001). Similarly, using treatment manuals, a popular and recent answer to how to teach therapists to be better therapists, does not improve success and may undermine alliance formation (S. J. Miller & Binder, 2002; Wampold, 2001). As to the latter, Henry, Strupp, Butler, Schacht, and Binder (1993) established that using treatment manuals adversely affected therapists' helpfulness. Indeed, therapists became less approving, supportive, and more pessimistic, defensive, and authoritarian. Such findings challenge the supposition that therapists can be coached to learn and use the client's theory of change reliably as a bridge to a better alliance and better outcome. The goal was ambitious, but misplaced.

Another difficulty is that clinical experience strongly indicates that it is impossible for therapists to suspend their own biases and theoretical preferences long enough to learn a client's theory of change. Further, no matter how accurate therapists may believe their perceptions of clients to be, research demonstrates that what the client perceives matters much more for the process and outcome of treatment. Finally, learning a client's worldview in no way guarantees interpersonal comfort and compatibility. It is highly unlikely that therapists will get along with everyone who comes for their help. Gender, ethnicity, age, personal background, life experiences, values, pet peeves, and unanticipated idiosyncrasies intrude in ways that can be neither predicted nor controlled. Outside therapy, everyone knows no one marries every person he or she dates.

POSITIVE PSYCHOLOGY: TOWARD A CONTEXTUAL PARADIGM FOR CLINICAL PRACTICE

Over the past 100 years, remarkable effort has been extended in the search for *the* specific ingredients of good therapeutic process. Forever hopeful, an endless array of explanations and methods have been offered: uncovering "hidden" trauma, working through transference, resolution of the Oedipal complex, identifying secondary gain, confronting dysfunctional thoughts, and realigning energy meridians, to name but a few. Despite such efforts, however, legions of theoreticians, researchers, and clinicians—ourselves included—have failed to isolate the elements of therapeutic process that everyone can use to achieve success. Instead, the dodo bird verdict reigns supreme: *All have won and, therefore, all deserve prizes.* Perhaps it is time for the field to come to grips with this reality.

Over the past 20 years, moreover, the field has become increasingly medicalized (Wampold, 2001). As a paradigm, the *medical model* operates virtually unquestioned. Indeed, in Western society—and in America in particular—it is equated with Truth. In powerful ways, the medical view not only shapes the way clinicians think about their work but also directs the very questions that therapists and researchers ask.

Few would debate the success of the medical model in improving the health and well-being of the general public. Improvements in the identification of illness and pathogens, coupled with the development of treatments containing *specific* therapeutic ingredients, have led to the near extinction of a number of once-fatal diseases. Claims and counterclaims notwithstanding, psychotherapy, in spite of a hundred years of research and development, can boast of no similar accomplishment—a finding that is unlikely to change if the field's theories and techniques suddenly start focusing on client strengths and resilience. Yet another series of randomized clinical trials comparing strength-based and traditional treatment approaches will likely suffer the same fate as all of the studies that have come before. That is, positive psychology is not the key to unlocking the door to effectiveness that has eluded everyone else. It is not a diamond in the rough that, once polished and refined, will inspire awe, interest, and envy. Whether positive or negative in nature, the exclusive focus on process in professional discourse and practice will only beget more of the same.

Fortunately, an alternative to the medical paradigm exists: a framework that fits the findings from more than 40 years of research on psychotherapy outcome research, while simultaneously honoring the central role of the client in the treatment process. As opposed to repeating the failures of the past by attempting to determine a priori what approach works best for which problem, the contextual paradigm for clinical practice takes advantage of three robust findings from the treatment literature (Duncan & Miller, 2000b; Wampold, 2001). First, treatment works mostly because of the *client*. Remember, large-scale meta-analytic studies have consistently found that the average person receiving therapy is better off than 80% of the untreated sample (Asay & Lambert, 1999; Wampold, 2001). The same research further shows that between 40% and 87% of the variance in treatment outcome is attributable to the client. By contrast, techniques and models account for between 8% and 15% (Duncan & Miller, 2000b; S. D. Miller et al., 1997; Wampold, 2001).

The second consistent finding is that the *client's* rating of the therapeutic alliance is one of the best predictors of engagement in treatment. Research shows that the quality of the relationship between client and therapist is not solely a by-product of success but rather an active factor (Gaston, Marmar, Thompson, & Gallagher, 1991; Lambert & Bergin, 1994). Moreover, across studies of different treatment approaches, the client's experience of the quality of the therapeutic relationship accounts for more than half of any beneficial effects (Horvath, 2001; Orlinsky et al., 1994).

Third, and finally, a growing body of data shows that the *client's* subjective experience of change *early* in the treatment process is one of the best predictors of eventual success between any particular pairing of client and therapist or treatment system (Brown et al., 1999; Garfield, 1994; Haas, Hill, Lambert, & Morrell, 2002; Howard, Kopte, Krause, & Orlinsky, 1986; Howard, Moras, Brill, Martinovich, & Lutz, 1996; Lambert, Okiishi, Finch, & Johnson, 1998; Lambert et al., 2001; Lebow, 1997; Steenbarger, 1992). For example, in a study of more than 2,000 therapists and thousands of clients, researchers found that therapeutic relationships in which no improvement occurred by the third visit did not on average result in improvement over the entire course of treatment (Brown et al., 1999). The study further found that clients who worsened by the third visit were twice as likely to drop out than those reporting progress. The researchers note that variables such as diagnosis, severity, family support, and type of therapy were "not . . . as important [in predicting eventual outcome] as knowing whether or not the treatment being provided is actually working" (p. 404).

In practice, such findings indicate that clients are anything but mere repositories of resilience waiting to be tapped by strength-based therapists. Such a view, as already noted, maintains the focus of professional discourse and practice on therapeutic process—specifically, one in which clients are dependent on the expert machinations of therapists to unleash their potential. The data makes abundantly clear that therapy does not make clients work, but rather clients make therapy work. Indeed, if the research reviewed previously is taken at face value, therapists are dependent on their clients to tell them both whether they are aligned properly and if that relationship is leading to the kinds of changes desired. Within the contextual paradigm, rather than assuming that good process leads to favorable results, outcome—as determined by the client's rating of the alliance and experience of improvement—is used to steer process.

In finding what fits and works for a client, therapists are limited only by practical and ethical considerations and by their creativity. Available data indicate that therapists have, whatever the popular trends, always worked in this fashion anyway; that is, drawing on their personal as well as professional knowledge, being "sensitive to the particular, contextual, and changing situation characteristic of therapy practice" (Polkinghorne, 1999, p. 1429). The common factors as defined in the earlier sections of this chapter may serve as organizing principles for clinical practice. After all, a therapist must start someplace. However, the proof of the pudding is, as the old saying goes, in the tasting. If the client does not like the flavor or the results, a change of recipes and ingredients is a must. In some cases, a new kitchen or cook may be required.

From the consumer's perspective, taste is the paramount issue—a mercurial and highly idiosyncratic variable—not recipe. Because of the number of treatment approaches currently vying for attention and the affinity for eclecticism among experienced clinicians, we have to wonder if the practice of therapy has not always implicitly operated in the way being described. In practice, therapists have acted as though models and techniques constitute empathic possibilities. Instead of representing truth in some grand (i.e., contextless) sense, the myriad approaches provide clinicians with a variety of ways to connect with the diverse people seeking their services. At the same time, client feedback, albeit historically gathered informally, provides clues for finding something that appeals to the individual.

Several studies show that the formal, ongoing use of feedback regarding the client's rating of the alliance and experience of change early in treatment improves treatment outcome. As to the latter, Lambert et al. (2001) found that cases most at risk for premature termination or negative outcome were significantly better off when their therapists had access to formal feedback about their clients' subjective experience of progress in treatment. Indeed, clients in the feedback condition were better off than approximately 65% of those in the control condition. In another study, Whipple et al. (2003) found that clients whose therapists had access to outcome *and* alliance information were less likely to deteriorate, more likely to stay longer, and twice as likely to achieve a clinically significant change.

If these results are not enough, consider research by S. D. Miller, Duncan, Brown, Sorrell, and Chalk (in press). Using two brief, four-item scales to provide feedback to therapists about clients' experience of the process and outcome of treatment, these researchers documented a 150% improvement in change scores in a single calendar year. The average effect size of services at the agency where the measures were employed shifted from 0.5 to 0.8. A closer analysis of the data from more than 12,000 cases indicates that the improvement was due to a combination of decreasing negative outcomes, increasing positive outcomes, and including a shift in overall outcome for therapists working at the clinic. More importantly, perhaps, these results were obtained *without* training the staff in any new treatment models or techniques.

A detailed description of the methods involved in the development of a feedback system similar to those employed in the studies reviewed previously is beyond the scope of this chapter but may be found in several sources (Duncan & Miller, 2000b, in press; IsHak, Burt, & Sederer, 2002; Lyons, Howard, O'Mahoney, & Lish, 1997; Ogles, Lambert, & Masters, 1996). The first step, however, begins with finding measures of outcome and process that are valid, reliable, and feasible for the context in which the tools will be employed. A period then follows during which the instruments are piloted, data is collected, and norms for the particular setting are established. Thereafter, statistical analysis of the results is used to determine the usual pattern of alliance development and outcome for therapists and clients at the given agency. Finally, depending on the degree of technological sophistication, an automated data entry and feedback system may be developed.

Developing an outcome-informed therapeutic practice need not be complicated, expensive, or time-consuming. Neither is a background in statistics nor sophisticated research methodology required. Therapists can simply choose from among the many paper-and-pencil rating scales available either in the public domain or for a nominal cost. (The process and outcome tools employed in the study by S. D. Miller, Duncan, Brown, Sorrell, and Chalk [in press] are available gratis at www.talkingcure.com.) The key is not the method per se but rather the access to valid and reliable feedback from clients that can be used to inform the process in the context in which services are being offered.

Becoming outcome-informed in clinical practice offers other advantages in addition to improving outcome. The first is an immediate decrease in the process-oriented paperwork and external management schemes that have come to dominate modern clinical practice. As will be news to no therapist on the front lines of treatment, the number of forms, authorizations, and other oversight procedures has exploded in recent years, consuming an ever-increasing amount of time and resources. Where a single HCFA 1500 form once sufficed, clinicians now have to contend with pretreatment authorization, intake interviews, treatment plans, and ongoing quality assurance reviews—procedures that were originally designed to ensure "right" process, but have succeeded in adding an estimated $200 to $500 to the cost of each case (Johnson & Shaha, 1997).

In the past few years, two large companies, PacifiCare Behavioral Health (PCBH), a managed care company, and Resources for Living (RFL), a telephonically-based employee assistance and disease management firm, have eliminated virtually all paperwork and oversight other than a simple, ongoing assessment of treatment outcome and process. In both systems, clinicians receive ongoing feedback about client progress with minimal intrusion from the companies and an absence of service limits traditionally associated with managed care. Recently, PCBH automated the treatment authorization process based on the submission of the outcome tool. Both systems are working a similar system for reimbursement.

Experience with the system in these and other settings point to another benefit of becoming outcome-informed: increased client engagement. First, it eliminates the paper curtain that all too often has served as a barrier rather than the entryway to services. Second, use of formal client feedback invites client participation in every aspect and decision about his or her mental health care. The study by S. D. Miller et al. (in press), for example, found that clients whose therapists failed to assess the alliance were two times more likely to drop out and three to four times more likely to have a negative or null outcome if they did return. The same research found that therapists who were slow to incorporate feedback into their practices on balance had the poorest outcomes. Such clinicians lacked a basic quality essential to effective clinical work: listening skills.

The last finding points to one final benefit of becoming outcome-informed. Depending on the reliability of the scales employed, gathering data on outcome and process eventually allows for comparisons of therapists and, in large systems, clinics or even whole agencies. Research shows that therapists differ significantly in effectiveness even when practicing the same approach and working with similar cases. The same is true of different treatment settings (Johnson & Miller, 2003). Importantly, awareness of differences between sites and clinicians allows for the delivery of context-specific training and supervision. The result is that rather than being subjected to evidence-based, empirically-supported treatments, clients meet with empirically-supported clinicians in settings identified by practice-based evidence.

CONCLUSION

Imagine a mental health system in which clients are full and complete partners in their care, where their voices are used to structure and direct treatment. Gone and gladly forgotten will be the dominion of paper. Notes and documentation will report events in the treatment that bear directly on outcome. The countless hours devoted to the generation of histories, interview protocols, and treatment plans will be freed for more productive services and activities. Gone, too, will be an attitude that therapists know what is best for their clients. When it is more important to know whether change is occurring in any given circumstance, theories of therapy and the many diagnostic labels they have sponsored become distractions. Therapists will no longer be evaluated on how well they talk the talk, at best a dubious standard for competence, but by how they walk the walk. For those reared on the belief that change, should it occur at all, is an internal and arcane experience long in coming, perhaps unmeasurable, the client's input from one session to the next may feel disconcerting, even suspect. And yet, as Carl Rogers once said, "The facts are always friendly." Better to know what is working or not in the here and now than mere failure down the road. At length, liberated from the traditional focus on process, be it positive or negative, therapists will be achieving what they always claimed to have been in the business of doing—assisting change. In our estimation, that would be a truly positive psychology for all.

REFERENCES

American Psychiatric Association. (1952). *Diagnostic and statistical manual of mental disorders.* Washington, DC: Author.

American Psychiatric Association. (1994). *Diagnostic and statistical manual of mental disorders* (4th ed.). Washington, DC: Author.

Asay, T. P., & Lambert, M. J. (1999). The empirical case for the common factors in therapy: Quantitative findings. In M. A. Hubble, B. L. Duncan, & S. D. Miller (Eds.), *The heart and soul of change: What works in therapy* (pp. 33–56). Washington, DC: American Psychological Association.

Barlow, D. H. (1996). Health care policy, psychotherapy research, and the future of psychotherapy. *American Psychologist, 51,* 1050–1058.

Bergin, A. E., & Lambert, M. J. (1978). The evaluation of therapeutic outcomes. In S. L. Garfield & A. E. Bergin (Eds.), *Handbook of psychotherapy and behavior change* (2nd ed., pp. 139–189). New York: Wiley.

Beutler, L. E. (1989). Differential treatment selection: The role of diagnosis in psychotherapy. *Psychotherapy, 26,* 271–281.

Brown, J., Dreis, S., & Nace, D. K. (1999). What really makes a difference in psychotherapy outcome? Why does managed care want to know? In M. A. Hubble, B. L. Duncan, & S. D. Miller (Eds.), *The heart and soul of change: What works in therapy* (pp. 389–406). Washington, DC: American Psychological Association.

Duncan, B. L., Hubble, M. A., & Miller, S. D. (1997). Stepping off the throne. *Family Therapy Networker, 21*(3), 22–31, 33.

Duncan, B. L., & Miller, S. D. (2000a). The client's theory of change: Consulting the client in the integrative process. *Journal of Psychotherapy Integration, 10,* 169–187.

Duncan, B. L., & Miller, S. D. (2000b). *The heroic client: Doing client-directed, outcome-informed therapy.* San Francisco: Jossey-Bass.

Duncan, B. L., & Miller, S. D. (in press). *The heroic client: Doing client-directed, outcome-informed therapy* (Rev. ed.). San Francisco: Jossey-Bass.

Duncan, B. L., & Moynihan, D. (1994). Applying outcome research: Intentional utilization of the client's frame of reference. *Psychotherapy, 31,* 294–301.

Duncan, B. L., Solovey, A., & Rusk, G. (1992). *Changing the rules: A client-directed approach to therapy.* New York: Guilford Press.

Frank, J. D. (1961). *Persuasion and healing: A comparative study of psychotherapy.* Baltimore: Johns Hopkins University Press.

Frank, J. D. (1973). *Persuasion and healing: A comparative study of psychotherapy* (2nd ed.). Baltimore: Johns Hopkins University Press.

Frank, J. D., & Frank, J. B. (1991). *Persuasion and healing: A comparative study of psychotherapy* (3rd ed.). Baltimore: Johns Hopkins University Press.

Freud, S. (1996). NUMBER: 23091. In R. Andrews, M. Biggs, & M. Seidel (Eds.), *Columbia world of quotations* (Letter dated October 9, 1918, "Psycho-analysis and faith: The letters of Sigmund Freud and Oskar Pfister," no. 59, from the International Psycho-Analytical Library in 1963, New York: Columbia University Press).

Ganguli, R. (2000). *Mental illness and misconceptions: Understand the weak link between mental illness and violent behavior.* Retrieved March 19, 2003, from http://www.postgazette.com/forum/20000318gang1.asp.

Garfield, S. L. (1992). Eclectic psychotherapy: A common factors approach. In J. C. Norcross & M. R. Goldfried (Eds.), *Handbook of psychotherapy integration* (pp. 169–201). New York: Basic Books.

Garfield, S. L. (1994). Research on client variables in psychotherapy. In A. E. Bergin & S. L. Garfield (Eds.), *Handbook of psychotherapy and behavior change* (4th ed., pp. 190–228). New York: Wiley.

Garfield, S. L., & Bergin, A. E. (1994). Introduction and historical overview. In A. E. Bergin & S. L. Garfield (Eds.), *Handbook of psychotherapy and behavior change* (4th ed., pp. 3–18). New York: Wiley.

Gaston, L., Marmar, C. R., Thompson, L. W., & Gallagher, D. (1991). Alliance prediction of outcome: Beyond in-treatment symptomatic change as psychotherapy progresses. *Psychotherapy Research, 1,* 104–112.

Goldfried, M. R., & Newman, C. F. (1992). A history of psychotherapy integration. In J. C. Norcross & M. R. Goldfried (Eds.), *Handbook of psychotherapy integration* (pp. 46–93). New York: Basic Books.

Grosskurth, P. (1991). *The secret ring: Freud's inner circle and the politics of psychoanalysis.* Reading, MA: Addison-Wesley.

Haas, E., Hill, R. D., Lambert, M. J., & Morrell, B. (2002). Do early responders to psychotherapy maintain treatment gains? *Journal of Clinical Psychology, 58,* 1157–1172.

Held, B. S. (1991). The process/content distinction revisited. *Psychotherapy, 28,* 207–218.

Henry, W. P., Strupp, H. H., Butler, S. F., Schacht, T. E., & Binder, J. L. (1993). Effects of training in time-limited dynamic psychotherapy: Changes in therapists behavior. *Journal of Consulting and Clinical Psychology, 61,* 434–440.

Horvath, A. O. (2001). The alliance. *Psychotherapy, 38,* 365–372.

Howard, K. I., Kopte, S. M., Krause, M. S., & Orlinsky, D. E. (1986). The dose-effect relationship in psychotherapy. *American Psychologist, 41,* 159–164.

Howard, K. I., Moras, K., Brill, P. L., Martinovich, Z., & Lutz, W. (1996). Evaluation of psychotherapy: Efficacy, effectiveness, and patient progress. *American Psychologist, 51,* 1059–1064.

Hubble, M. A. (1993). Therapy research: The bonfire of the uncertainties. *Family Psychologist: Bulletin of the Division of Family Psychology, 9*(2), 14–16.

*Hubble, M. A., Duncan, B. L., & Miller, S. D. (1999a). Directing attention to what works. In M. A. Hubble, B. L. Duncan, & S. D. Miller (Eds.), *The heart and soul of change: What works in therapy* (pp. 407–448). Washington, DC: American Psychological Association.

Hubble, M. A., Duncan, B. L., & Miller, S. D. (1999b). Introduction. In M. A. Hubble, B. L. Duncan, & S. D. Miller (Eds.). *The heart and soul of change: What works in therapy* (pp. 1–19). Washington, DC: American Psychological Association.

Hubble, M. A., & Miller, S. D. (2001). In pursuit of folly. *Academy of Clinical Psychology Bulletin, 7,* 2–7.

IsHak, W. W., Burt, T., & Sederer, L. (2002). *Outcome measurement in psychiatry: A critical review.* Washington, DC: American Psychological Association.

Johnson, L. D., & Miller, S. D. (2003). *Effective and ineffective clinical settings: Management strategy, supervision, and emotional intelligence.* Manuscript in preparation.

Johnson, L. D., & Shaha, S. H. (1997, July). Upgrading clinicians' reports to MCOs. *Behavioral Health Management,* 42–46.

Lambert, M. J. (1992). Implications of outcome research for psychotherapy integration. In J. C. Norcross & M. R. Goldfried (Eds.), *Handbook of psychotherapy integration* (pp. 94–129). New York: Basic Books.

Lambert, M. J., & Bergin, A. E. (1994). The effectiveness of psychotherapy. In A. E. Bergin & S. L. Garfield (Eds.), *Handbook of psychotherapy and behavior change* (4th ed., pp. 143–189). New York: Wiley.

Lambert, M. J., Okiishi, J. C., Finch, A. E., & Johnson, L. D. (1998). Outcome assessment: From conceptualization to implementation. *Professional Psychology: Practice and Research, 29,* 63–70.

Lambert, M. J., Whipple, J. L., Smart, D. W., Vermeersch, D. A., Nielsen, S. L., & Hawkins, E. (2001). The effects of providing therapists with feedback on patient progress during psychotherapy: Are outcomes enhanced? *Psychotherapy Research, 11,* 49–68.

Lebow, J. (1997). New science for psychotherapy: Can we predict how therapy will progress? *Family Therapy Networker, 21*(2), 85–91.

Luborsky, L. (1995). Are common factors across different psychotherapies the main explanation for the dodo bird verdict that "Everyone has won so all shall have prizes"? *Clinical Psychology: Science and Practice, 2,* 106–109.

Luborsky, L., Rosenthal, R., Diguer, L., Andrusyna, T. P., Berman, J. S., Levitt, J. T., et al. (2002). The dodo verdict is alive and well—mostly. *Clinical Psychology: Science and Practice, 9,* 2–12.

Luborsky, L., Singer, B., & Luborsky, L. (1975). Comparative studies of psychotherapies: Is it true that "Everybody has won and all must have prizes"? *Archives of General Psychiatry, 32,* 995–1008.

Lyons, J., Howard, K., O'Mahoney, M. T., & Lish, J. D. (1997). *The measurement and management of clinical outcomes in mental health.* New York: Wiley.

Metcalf, L., Thomas, F. N., Duncan, B. L., Miller, S. D., & Hubble, M. A. (1996). What works in solution-focused brief therapy: A qualitative analysis of client and therapist perceptions. In S. D. Miller, M. A. Hubble, & B. L. Duncan (Eds.), *Handbook of solution-focused brief therapy* (pp. 335–349). San Francisco: Jossey-Bass.

Miller, S. D., Duncan, B. L., Brown, J., Sorrell, R., & Chalk, M. B. (in press). Using outcome to inform and improve treatment process: An analysis of 12,000 cases in a real world clinical context. *Journal of Brief Therapy.*

Miller, S. D., Duncan, B. L., & Hubble, M. A. (1997). *Escape from Babel: Toward a unifying language for psychotherapy practice.* New York: Norton.

Miller, S. D., & Hubble, M. A. (2002). Report from Planet Drrxx-3977 on the therapists: An archaeological dig. *Psychotherapy in Australia, 9,* 2–9.

Miller, S. D., & Hubble, M. A. (in press). Further archaeological and ethnological findings on the obscure, late twentieth century, quasi-religious Earth group known as "the therapists": Imagining the future of psychotherapy. *Journal of Psychotherapy Integration.*

Miller, S. D., Hubble, M. A., & Duncan, B. L. (1995). No more bells and whistles. *Family Therapy Networker, 19*(2), 52–58, 62–63.

Miller, S. D., Hubble, M. A., & Duncan, B. L. (1996, March). *Psychotherapy is dead, long live psychotherapy.* Workshop presented at the 19th annual Family Therapy Network Symposium, Washington, DC.

Miller, S. J., & Binder, J. L. (2002). The effects of manual based training on treatment fidelity and outcome: A review of the literature on adult individual psychotherapy. *Psychotherapy, 39,* 184–198.

Norcross, J. C. (2002). *Psychotherapy relationships that work.* Oxford, England: Oxford University Press.

Norcross, J. C., & Newman, C. F. (1992). A history of psychotherapy integration. In J. C. Norcross & M. R. Goldfried (Eds.), *Handbook of psychotherapy integration* (pp. 3–45). New York: Basic Books.

Ogles, B., Lambert, M. J., & Masters, K. S. (1996). *Assessing outcome in clinical practice.* Needham Heights, MA: Allyn & Bacon.

Orlinsky, D. E., Grawe, K., & Parks, B. K. (1994). Process and outcome in psychotherapy—*noch einmal*. In A. E. Bergin & S. L. Garfield (Eds.), *Handbook of psychotherapy and behavior change* (4th ed., pp. 270–376). New York: Wiley.

Pascal, B. (1970). *The international thesaurus of quotations* (R. T. Tripp, Compiler). New York: Perennial Library. (Original work published 1670)

Polkinghorne, D. E. (1999). Traditional research and psychotherapy practice. *Journal of Clinical Psychology, 55,* 1429–1440.

Resnick, R. J. (1993). *DSM-IV:* It is to be but does it help? *Register Report, 19*(2), 1–2, 6.

Rosenzweig, S. (1936). Some implicit common factors in diverse methods in psychotherapy. *Journal of Orthopsychiatry, 6,* 412–415.

Scheff, T. (1966). *Being mentally ill: A sociological theory.* Chicago, IL: Aldine.

Steenbarger, B. N. (1992). Toward science-practice integration in brief counseling and therapy. *Counseling Psychologist, 20,* 403–450.

Stuart, H., & Arboleda-Flôrez, J. (2001). Community attitudes toward people with schizophrenia. *Canadian Journal of Psychiatry, 46,* 245–252.

Tallman, K., & Bohart, A. C. (1999). The client as a common factor: Clients as self-healers. In M. A. Hubble, B. L. Duncan, & S. D. Miller (Eds.), *The heart and soul of change: What works in therapy* (pp. 91–131). Washington, DC: American Psychological Association.

*Wampold, B. E. (2001). *The great psychotherapy debate: Models, methods, and findings.* Mahwah, NJ: Erlbaum.

Weinberger, J. (1995). Common factors aren't so common: The common factors dilemma. *Clinical Psychology: Science and Practice, 2,* 45–69.

Whipple, J. L., Lambert, M. J., Vermeersch, D. A., Smart, D. W., Nielsen, S. L., & Hawkins, E. J. (2003). Improving the effects of psychotherapy: The use of early identification of treatment and problem-solving strategies in routine practice. *Journal of Counseling Psychology, 50,* 59–68.

Woodward, J. R. (1995, March/April). A place for everyone, and everyone in place: A history of the *Diagnostic and Statistical Manual of Mental Disorders. Disability Rag and Resource,* 17–22.

CHAPTER 22

Positive Therapy: A Positive Psychological Theory of Therapeutic Practice

STEPHEN JOSEPH and P. ALEX LINLEY

IN THIS CHAPTER, we explore the relevance of positive psychology to therapy. We are interested in what positive psychology has to offer in how we think about the ways we work with people, whether in clinical and health care settings or other applied psychological settings. First, we describe what we see as a fundamental assumption of positive psychology. Second, we discuss the implication of this assumption for therapy practice. It is not our intention to advocate new ways of working therapeutically, but rather to ask what it is to work therapeutically within a positive psychology framework. Can some therapies be considered positive therapies? Our answer to this is yes. In particular, those therapies based on the theoretical premise of an organismic valuing process and an actualizing tendency appear to be most consistent with what the positive psychology research is now telling us.

As therapists, we have many choices as to how to respond to what a person tells us. We can give advice, ask questions, make diagnoses, reassure, listen, administer tests, interpret—to name but a few ways we might respond in our endeavor to assist the person to make changes in his or her life. Therapy must be informed by scientific research, but, in our view, the practice of therapy is also an art. As Wampold (2001) put it:

> The performer's grounding in music theory is invisible to the audience unless the canons of composition are violated in such a way as the performance is discordant. Similarly, the master therapist, informed by psychological knowledge and theory

Grateful thanks to Delia Cushway, Carol Kauffman, and Jacky Knibbs for their advice and comments on this chapter.

and guided by experience, produces an artistry that assists clients to move ahead in their lives with meaning and health. (p. 225)

How we decide our artistry depends ultimately on our fundamental assumptions about human nature (Joseph, 2001).

POSITIVE PSYCHOLOGY AND FUNDAMENTAL ASSUMPTIONS

Broadly speaking, our view of human nature falls into one of two camps: basically negative and destructive or positive and constructive. It has been suggested that the fundamental assumptions of mainstream psychology are those of the former. As Seligman (2003) has said:

> This "rotten-to-the-core" view pervades Western thought, and if there is any doctrine positive psychology seeks to overthrow it is this one. Its original manifestation is the doctrine of original sin. In secular form, Freud dragged this doctrine into 20th-century psychology where it remains fashionably entrenched in academia today. For Freud, all of civilization is just an elaborate defence against basic conflicts over infantile sexuality and aggression. (p. 126)

Positive psychology has made explicit the fact that psychology has traditionally rested on a fundamental assumption that emphasizes human nature as negative in orientation and in need of being controlled (see Hubble & Miller, Chapter 21, this volume; Maddux, 2002; Maddux, Snyder, & Lopez, Chapter 20, this volume). Having discarded the "rotten-to-the-core" view of human nature, positive psychologists are now casting around for new ways of conceptualizing human nature. Like Seligman, another past president of the American Psychological Association, Carl Rogers, also questioned the fundamental assumptions of mainstream psychology in his day, proposing instead the view that human beings are organismically motivated toward developing to their full potential:

> I have little sympathy with the rather prevalent concept that man is basically irrational, and thus his impulses, if not controlled, would lead to destruction of others and self. Man's behavior is exquisitely rational, moving with subtle and ordered complexity toward the goals his organism is endeavoring to achieve. (Rogers, 1969, p. 29)

Deep down, Rogers proposed, human beings are striving to become all that they can be. Rogers (1959) referred to this directional force of becoming as the actualizing tendency:

> This is the inherent tendency of the organism to develop all its capacities in ways which serve to maintain or enhance the organism. It involves not only the tendency to meet what Maslow terms "deficiency needs" for air, food, water, and the like, but also more generalized activities. It involves development toward the differentiation of organs and of functions, expansion in terms of growth, expansion of effectiveness through the use of tools, expansion and enhancement through reproduction. It is development toward autonomy and away from heteronomy, or control by external forces. (p. 196)

Rogers (1959) was conceptualizing the basic directionality of the actualizing tendency as toward the development of autonomous determination, expansion and effectiveness, and constructive social behavior. Rogers was not the only psychologist to discuss the concept of the actualizing tendency, although his writings on the topic are probably the most well known. Other theorists who have proposed some form of actualization tendency include Adler (1927), Angyal (1941), Goldstein (1939), Horney (1950), Jung (1933), Maslow (1968), and Rank (1936). The concept of an actualizing tendency has a distinguished heritage.

It is refreshing for our profession that positive psychology has provided the impetus for us to now reexamine our fundamental assumptions about human nature, particularly concerning the actualizing tendency as the core motivational force for optimal human development. We next argue that the fundamental assumption of an inherent actualizing tendency provides the foundation for a positive therapy.

THE ORGANISMIC VALUING PROCESS AND PERSON-CENTERED THEORIES

What we do as therapists, whether it is to give advice, interpret, reassure, listen, ask questions, or whatever else, is contextualized by our view of human nature. What needs to be emphasized is the paradigmatic difference between the two fundamental assumptions previously described and how an individual's approach to the artistry of therapy inevitably follows from his or her view of human nature. If people's nature is essentially driven by destructive impulses as suggested by Freud, the role of therapists is to help keep tight the constraints on those impulses. If people's nature is essentially driven by constructive impulses as suggested by Rogers, our role is to loosen the constraints on those impulses.

Although a mainstay of person-centered psychology (see Bozarth, 1998), the actualizing tendency has been a controversial concept in mainstream psychology (see Ryan, 1995). The concept of the actualizing tendency implies that people can trust themselves to know their own best directions in life (Joseph, 2003). Rogers (1964) talked about the organismic valuing process (OVP). The OVP refers to people's innate ability to know what is important to them and what is essential for a fulfilling life. Rogers' view was that human organisms can be relied on through their physiological processes to know what they need from their environment and what is right for them for the self-actualization of their potentialities.

To illustrate the concept of the OVP, Maslow (1971) made this suggestion:

> I sometimes suggest to my students that when they are given a glass of wine and asked how they like it, they try a different way of responding. First, I suggest that they not look at the label on the bottle. Thus they will *not* use it to get any cue about whether or not they *should* like it. Next, I recommend that they close their eyes if possible and that they "make a hush." Now they are ready to look within themselves and try to shut out the noise of the world so that they may savor the wine on their tongues and look to the "Supreme Court" inside themselves. (pp. 44–45)

In recent years, the concept of the OVP has been reexamined by positive psychology theorists (see Ryan, 1995). What positive psychologists are able to bring to the ideas of earlier theorists such as Maslow and Rogers are the research techniques of current mainstream psychology (see Sheldon & Kasser, 2001). We are beginning to see research that is supportive of the concept of the OVP. In a series of three studies, for example, Sheldon, Arndt, and Houser-Marko (2003) examined how people changed their minds over time about what goals and values to pursue. Their rationale was that evidence for the existence of an OVP would be demonstrated by people's tendency to move toward well-being-related outcomes, such as those to do with intrinsic goals as opposed to extrinsic goals. Their results show that participants evidenced relatively greater ratings shifts toward goals that are more likely to be beneficial to their well-being. Other work into the longitudinal effects of self-concordant goal selection shows that those with more self-concordant goals (i.e., those who pursue goals for intrinsic rather than extrinsic reasons) put more sustained effort into those goals, which enables them to better attain those goals. Goal attainment in turn is associated with stronger feelings of autonomy, competence, and relatedness, which in turn lead to greater well-being (Sheldon & Elliot, 1999). The evidence suggests that people grow when there is contact with the OVP.

Much further research work into the existence of an OVP remains to be conducted. However, we believe that the emerging positive psychology research in this area suggests that the organismic valuing process might be set central stage as the fundamental pillar of positive therapy. This approach is very much consistent with the findings from positive psychology research traditions. For example, the positive influence on well-being created by intrinsic aspirations (Kasser & Ryan, 1993, 1996; Kasser, Chapter 4, this volume), intrinsic motivation (Deci & Ryan, 1985, 1991, 2000; Ryan & Deci, 2000), intrinsic yearning to use your signature strengths (Peterson & Seligman, 2003), and the concept of flow (Csikszentmihalyi, 1997) have all been extensively documented. We concur with Sheldon and Elliot (1999), who wrote:

> . . . along with Rogers (1961), we believe that individuals have innate developmental trends and propensities that may be given voice by an organismic valuing process occurring within them. The voice can be very difficult to hear, but the current research suggests that the ability to hear it is of crucial importance for the pursuit of happiness. (p. 495)

Critics of Rogers' ideas have seen his emphasis on the actualizing tendency as evidence of his Pollyanna theorizing. If humans do have an innate ability to know what is important to them and what is essential for a fulfilling life, how is it that so many are distressed and dysfunctional? But this is to misunderstand the concept of the actualizing tendency and the OVP as it is developed in the person-centered theory proposed by Rogers, an issue to which we now turn.

PERSON-CENTERED THEORY

Two important concepts in person-centered theory are *conditions of worth* and *the fully functioning person*. Below, we will describe these concepts and how they provide the basis for understanding psychopathology.

Conditions of Worth   Rogers (1959) was saying that although there is a universal motivational force toward growth and development, this directional force becomes thwarted by our social environment. In person-centered theory, social environments characterized by conditional positive regard thwart the OVP. An example of conditional positive regard is a parent giving a child the message that to be loved, she must do well at school. The child internalizes this message, which is said to be a condition of worth for her. In a social environment characterized by conditional positive regard, people self-actualize not in a direction consistent with their actualizing tendency but in a direction consistent with their conditions of worth:

> This, as we see it, is the basic estrangement in man. He has not been true to himself, to his natural organismic valuing of experience, but for the sake of preserving the positive regard of others has now come to falsify some of the values he experiences and to perceiving them in terms based only on their value to others. Yet this has not been a conscious choice, but a natural—and tragic—development in infancy. (p. 226)

Fully Functioning Psychological maladjustment develops through the internalization of conditions of worth. In contrast, in a social environment characterized by unconditional positive regard, people self-actualize in a direction consistent with their actualizing tendency toward becoming what Rogers referred to as fully functioning human beings:

> "The fully functioning person" is synonymous with optimal psychological adjustment, optimal psychological maturity, complete congruence, complete openness to experience.... Since some of these terms sound somewhat static, as though such a person "had arrived" it should be pointed out that all the characteristics of such a person are *process* characteristics. The fully functioning person would be a person-in-process, a person continually changing. (Rogers, 1959, p. 235; see also Rogers, 1963)

The fully functioning person is an ideal, and we have all, to varying extents, self-actualized incongruently to our actualizing tendency. For some, their incongruence is minimum; for others, more substantial; and the more we struggle to hear our inner voice, the more we can be said to be in a state of incongruence. According to this view, many of the psychological problems people experience are manifestations of the internalization of conditions of worth.

SELF-DETERMINATION THEORY

Positive psychologists—as we have seen—are reexamining the concept of the actualizing tendency and suggesting that the available evidence is consistent with the existence of an OVP. Positive psychologists such as Ryan (1995) are also in agreement that the OVP is either supported or undermined by the social environment. However, whereas Rogers emphasized the need for unconditional positive regard from the social environment, Ryan has emphasized how the social environment must provide the nutrients to provide for individuals' needs for autonomy, relatedness, and competence. Self-determination theory (SDT; Deci & Ryan, 1985, 1991, 2000; Ryan & Deci, 2000) was developed to be consistent with person-centered theory and embraces the concept of the actualizing tendency and provides a theoretical perspective on how the self is actualized. Self-determination theory posits three basic psychological needs—autonomy, competence, and relatedness—and theorizes that fulfillment of these needs is essential for growth. It, therefore, defines the nutrients that the social environment must provide for intrinsic motivation to take place. Deci and Ryan agree that the social environment does not always meet these needs. Whereas Rogers talked generally about condition of worth—those ways of behaving that we have learned from experience that make us acceptable to others—Deci and Ryan have provided a more sophisticated account of the ways in which extrinsic motivations become integrated. They distinguish among external regulations (e.g., doing something out of fear of punishment), introjected regulations (e.g., doing something to avoid feeling guilty), and identified regulations (e.g., doing something because the values are endorsed).

Self-determination theory and person-centered theory obviously share much common ground, and we are left with some questions for future research and theoretical discussion. It is not clear from the writings of Deci and Ryan whether an unconditionally and positively regarding social environment as posited by Rogers (1957, 1959) sufficiently provides the organism with the nutrients to develop autonomy, competence, and relatedness. Empirically, some research into Deci and Ryan's conceptualization of need satisfactions might be interpreted as evidence for the role of unconditional positive regard. For example, sample items (from La Guardia, Ryan, Couchman, & Deci, 2000) used to measure autonomy (e.g., My mother allows me to decide things for myself), competence (e.g., My mother puts time and energy into helping me), and relatedness (e.g., My mother accepts me and likes me as I am) could also be conceptualized as measuring the broader concept of unconditional positive regard. The difference between unconditional positive regard and need satisfactions might simply be terminological, an issue that requires further theoretical and empirical clarification.

We began this section by asking how we should decide on our artistry as therapists. If we assume the existence of the OVP, our task as therapists is to facilitate the OVP and to assist clients in hearing their own inner voice. How do we go about helping people to hear the voice within themselves? What positive psychology tells us about personality processes leads us to formulate a framework for therapy that is largely consistent with the person-centered approaches to therapy. The critical point here is that the locus of responsibility for the direction of the therapy is with the client rather than the therapist.

THERAPEUTIC IMPLICATIONS

In this section, we first describe in some detail what client-centered therapy looks like and how it relates to some current positive psychology constructs. As to what the client-centered therapist does to facilitate clients in hearing their own inner voice, Rogers (1957) stated that there were six necessary and sufficient conditions, which, when present, provided the social environment that facilitated the OVP:

1. Two persons are in psychological contact.
2. The first, whom we shall call the client, is in a state of incongruence, being vulnerable or anxious.
3. The second person, whom we shall call the therapist, is congruent or integrated in the relationship.
4. The therapist experiences unconditional positive regard for the client.

5. The therapist experiences an empathic understanding of the client's internal frame of reference and endeavors to communicate this experience to the client.

6. The communication to the client of the therapist's empathic understanding and unconditional positive regard is to a minimal degree achieved (Rogers, 1957, p. 96).

Conditions 3, 4, and 5 are referred to as the core conditions and describe the practice of the client-centered therapist—they endeavor to be congruent, empathic, and to experience unconditional positive regard for their client. Relating this statement of Rogers (1957) to current terminology, we would describe client-centered therapy as a profound experiential approach founded on the emotional intelligence of the therapist.

EMOTIONAL INTELLIGENCE

The basis of the client-centered therapeutic approach is condition 3, the therapist's congruence. Congruence refers to persons' awareness of their underlying thoughts and feelings and their ability to express these thoughts and feelings appropriately in the context (Bozarth, 1998). That is to say, there is congruence between the internal cognitive and emotional states of the person, their conscious awareness of those states, and their ability to articulate the expression of those states. Congruence, when combined with condition 5, empathic understanding, would involve all four facets of emotional intelligence as discussed by Salovey, Caruso, and Mayer (Chapter 28, this volume; Salovey, Mayer, & Caruso, 2002). Congruent therapists who have an empathic understanding of the client's frame of reference are perceptive of how the client is feeling and of how they themselves are feeling. They are able to manage their own emotions and to use their own emotions creatively in the service of the therapeutic relationship. They are able to understand emotions and to label them appropriately. What this means in practice is that client-centered therapists have a deep understanding of themselves and are able to be present in an authentic way with the client. Therapists strive to understand the client's world from the client's perspective, and they are accepting of the client's directions in life without imposing their own agenda. This latter point, accepting the client's directions without imposing their own, is the crux of client-centered therapy (i.e., condition 4) and is communicated through therapists' congruence and empathy (see Bozarth, 1998).

AUTHENTIC RELATIONSHIP

What we emphasize most of all is how client-centered therapy allows for tremendous variety and spontaneity in ways of working. For example, positive psychology research tells us the importance of helping our clients realize their strengths. One of the questions we have been asked recently is: How do we help people realize their strengths in client-centered therapy? It is inevitable that the therapist who is endeavoring to be congruent and empathic will have opportunities to provide support to clients in exploring their strengths. In this climate, strengths will naturally be found. As Peterson and Seligman (2003) describe, an individual's signature strengths convey a sense of ownership and authenticity, an intrinsic yearning to use them, and a feeling of inevitability in doing so. Using your signature strengths is concordant with your intrinsic interests and values; hence, in a supportive environmental context, the client's strengths will become evident. This does not typically happen in a prescriptive way, such as by having the client complete a strengths inventory, but it occurs spontaneously in the relationship, as illustrated by the following examples showing how the congruent and empathic therapist is inevitably drawn toward identifying strengths:

> Carol, I can see how awful you feel because it seems to you like you let Bob down, and I just want to say, too, how much I value your compassion and sensitivity as a person . . .
>
> You're angry with me for what I said last week, and I'm thinking how much courage it must have taken you to tell me that . . .

Client-centered therapy is about the authentic quality of the relationship between the therapist and client. Decades of therapy research suggest that Rogers' (1957) statement was close to the mark in pointing to the central importance of the therapeutic relationship (see Martin, Garske, & Davis, 2000; Wampold, 2001). What we do know with as much certainty as it is possible to have is that successful therapy is not due to particular therapeutic techniques, levels of training, or the use of diagnosis. Rather, it is the therapeutic relationship and the client's own inner resources that are important. This is a conclusion now reached by many researchers (e.g., Bozarth, 1998; Duncan & Miller, 2000; Hubble & Miller, Chapter 21, this volume; Martin et al., 2000; Wampold, 2001). We hesitate, therefore, to recommend particular therapeutic techniques. However, drawing on positive psychology research, there are a tremendous amount of intervention strategies that clients might sometimes find useful (see, e.g., Lopez & Snyder, 2003). The use of intervention techniques is a contentious issue in client-centered therapy. However, we see no reason that positive therapists should not draw on the wider resources available to them as long as they are able to articulate how the use of particular tests or techniques are helping to facilitate the clients' OVP (see Bozarth, 1991). As Yalom (2001) writes:

> . . . the flow of therapy should be spontaneous, forever following unanticipated riverbeds: it is grotesquely distorted by being packaged into a formula . . . I try to avoid technique that is prefabricated and do best if I allow my choices to flow spontaneously . . . (pp. 34–35)

OTHER THERAPEUTIC APPROACHES

Although we have talked here about client-centered therapy as a form of positive therapy, we would not want to prescribe what it is to be a positive therapist in terms of what the therapist says or does. Other therapeutic approaches that also emphasize the client as the active agent might be equally good candidates as positive therapies (see Follette, Linnerooth, & Ruckstuhl, 2001; Resnick, Warmoth, & Serlin, 2001).

Seligman (2002) and Seligman and Peterson (2003) have discussed what they see as positive therapy and positive clinical psychology. Their central contention is that much of what makes therapy successful is what they refer to as the "deep strategies," such as instilling hope, providing narration, and building strengths, all of which are employed, instinctively and intuitively, by successful therapists. However, the problem arises, they suggest, in that these deep strategies are not named or specifically recognized; hence, they are not researched, trained for, or developed.

More recently, however, there has been a surge of interest in more positive therapies. Mindfulness-based approaches provide possible means of fostering self-determination and self-awareness (see Brown & Ryan, 2003, Chapter 7, this volume). Further examples include the work by Fava and colleagues (e.g., Fava, 1997, 1999; Ruini & Fava, Chapter 23, this volume), who have developed a therapeutic approach based on Ryff's (e.g., 1989; Ryff & Singer, 1996) research on psychological well-being. Clients are helped to identify areas of their psychological well-being that may be improved; then the therapist proceeds to work with the client on these areas as well as the presenting symptoms of disorder (for a fuller discussion, see Ruini & Fava, Chapter 23, this volume). Tedeschi and Calhoun (Chapter 25, this volume; Calhoun & Tedeschi, 1999) are explicit in noting that therapy that seeks to facilitate posttraumatic growth is always client-led, moving at the client's pace and in the client's direction. The therapist acts as a co-traveler who, when appropriate, may note certain developments or offer alternative interpretations. Similarly, from an existential therapy background, Bretherton and Ørner (2003) write:

> . . . the most obvious way in which the existential approach parallels positive psychotherapy is in its preoccupation with what is presented by the client rather than with global models of deficit and disorder. Using the phenomenological method, therapists attempt to "bracket" (put to one side) many of the assumptions and reactions they have with regard to clients (including the desire for therapeutic progress) so as to better engage with a client's way of being. By stepping back from their own prejudices and stereotypes, existential therapists can identify client's possibilities as well as their limitations . . . The existentialists suggest that by identifying the constellations of meaning by which we relate to the world, we give ourselves the opportunity of decision—to decide whether to alter our way of being in the world. (p. 136; see also Bretherton & Ørner, Chapter 26, this volume)

Our stance, therefore, is that it is not what the therapist *does* (i.e., their technique) that determines whether a therapy is a good candidate as a positive therapy. Rather, it is what the therapist *thinks* (i.e., his or her fundamental assumptions) that is important. The crux of being a positive therapist is that the therapist adopts a way of thinking that fully embraces the notion that his or her task is to facilitate the client's actualizing tendency. It is our ideas about human nature that make us the psychotherapists we are. As Yalom (2001) writes:

> When I was finding my way as a young psychotherapy student, the most useful book I read was Karen Horney's *Neurosis and Human Growth*. And the single most useful concept in that book was the notion that the human being has an inbuilt propensity toward self-realization. If obstacles are removed, Horney believed, the individual will develop into a mature, fully realized adult, just as an acorn will develop into an oak tree. "Just as an acorn develops into an oak . . ." What a wonderful liberating and clarifying image! It forever changed my approach to psychotherapy by offering me a new vision of my work: My task was to remove obstacles blocking my patient's

path. I did not have to do the entire job; I did not have to inspirit the patient with the desire to grow, with curiosity, will, zest for life, caring, loyalty, or any of the myriad of characteristics that make us fully human. No, what I had to do was to identify and remove obstacles. The rest would follow automatically, fueled by the self-actualizing forces within the patient. (p. 1)

This quote from Yalom captures for us the essence of what we would call positive therapy. It is the client and not the therapist who knows best. But we would not want the reader to come away thinking that we are saying that the inner voice of clients is easily articulated. On the contrary, it is a difficult path. Although there are a variety of new prefabricated therapeutic approaches that embrace the ideas we have been discussing, what we find particularly appealing is the more classical approach to client-centered therapy. We say this because our understanding of Rogers' (1957, 1959) approach permits for a broad and flexible way of working, which is not wedded to one particular set of techniques, but rather it is about working in a way that is individual for each client. Like Yalom (2001), we would advise against sectarianism and advocate therapeutic pluralism.

Finally, there is also the *positive psychotherapy* developed by Peseschkian and colleagues (e.g., Peseschkian & Tritt, 1998). However, this approach is not drawn from the positive psychology tradition, but instead notes that the "positive" in its title is drawn from the word " 'positum', i.e., from what is factual and given" (Peseschkian & Tritt, 1998, p. 94). Hence, while its title may be misleading, we would not consider Peseschkian's positive psychotherapy to be a positive psychotherapy within the positive psychological sense.

UNDERSTANDING PSYCHOPATHOLOGY

Positive therapy represents something of a sea change in mainstream psychological practice because it rejects the medical model orientation of viewing psychological problems in the same way as medical conditions, that is, a series of discrete conditions, each requiring a particular form of treatment. Researchers are now beginning to doubt the validity of the medical model for understanding psychological problems (see Hubble & Miller, Chapter 21, this volume; Maddux, Gosselin, & Winstead, in press). Instead, we propose the adoption of a conceptual model based on our inherent tendency toward actualization. This view of human nature represents a different paradigm to the medical model that underlies much of contemporary clinical and counseling psychology.

In talking about the ways we can work therapeutically to facilitate movement toward becoming more fully functioning, the impression might be given that positive therapy is just for the promotion of well-being and would not be suitable for people with severe and chronic psychological problems. In this chapter, we have not discussed the various psychological problems associated with *DSM* diagnostic categories because the actualizing tendency is an alternative paradigm to the medical model. Psychological problems are seen as resulting from the thwarting of the tendency toward actualization, and the nature of individuals' psychological problems can be understood when we know more about their developmental social-environmental conditions and the values and beliefs that they have internalized. In working to facilitate the actualizing tendency, the therapist is both helping to alleviate psychopathology and to promote well-being. As Rogers (1961) writes:

> I am quite aware that out of defensiveness and inner fear individuals can and do behave in ways which are incredibly cruel, horribly destructive, immature, regressive, antisocial, hurtful. Yet one of the most refreshing and invigorating parts of my experience is to work with such individuals and to discover the strongly positive directional tendencies which exist in them, as in all of us, at the deepest levels. (p. 27)

The actualizing tendency provides a holistic framework that simultaneously spans psychopathology and well-being. In facilitating the actualizing tendency, the therapist is both alleviating psychopathology and promoting well-being. We are not saying that we need to reject the medical approach altogether when thinking about psychological problems: Some psychopathology might be best considered as disorder and treated within the medical field by psychiatrists and clinical psychologists. For example, schizophrenia, bipolar disorders, temporal lobe epilepsy, and organic brain diseases may fall into this category. Similarly, as Seligman and Peterson (2003) note, there may be some clear specific treatments for some specific disorders, such as applied tension for blood and injury phobia, cognitive therapy for panic, and exposure for obsessive-compulsive disorder (for a review, see Seligman, 1994). However, the idea that all psychological problems are best understood through the lens of the medical model and require specific treatments is an unfounded assumption. Like many other writers (see, e.g., Hubble & Miller, Chapter 21, this volume; Maddux, 2002; Maddux et al., Chapter 20, this volume; Yalom, 2001), we are increasingly concerned about the inappropriate medicalization of psychological problems. A positive therapy stands in sharp contrast to attempts that seek to classify every problem of living as a psychological disorder.

In summary, we propose that the actualizing tendency provide a model for understanding the continuum between ill-being and well-being. Through viewing so-called psychological disorders as manifestations of the extent to which our inherent tendency toward actualization has been thwarted, we can comprehend ill-being and well-being as a continuum of experience rather than distinct categories (see also Maddux, 2002; Maddux et al., Chapter 20, this volume).

SOCIAL AND POLITICAL CONTEXT

In moving away from the medical approach to understanding psychopathology toward an emphasis on the client rather than the therapist, positive therapeutic approaches are revolutionary in the current social and political climate. All therapy takes place within a social and political context. If we adopt the assumption that our task is to help our clients hear their own inner voice, sometimes we find ourselves helping to facilitate personal change that is at odds with the social and political context. For example, Western society places greater emphasis on extrinsic values than intrinsic values. We grow up internalizing values about how to lead our lives and what values to hold. Most of us in Western society will have grown up internalizing values about the importance of achieving financial success and material wealth. In general, a person who is not financially successful or materially wealthy is not as valued in our society as someone who is (see Kasser, 2002, Chapter 4, this volume). Theoretically, client-centered therapy should facilitate movement in a person away from materialistic aspirations and towards intrinsic aspirations. In helping people explore the values that are important to them, the implication is that therapy is not about social adjustment but about personal change. Much of the work that is carried out by clinical and counseling psychologists is aimed at social adjustment. This becomes a political agenda when personal change is in conflict with social adjustment.

In turning our attention to the political agenda behind the practice of therapy, we are aware that similar ideas have been previously expressed by others. Jung talked of how the process of individuation leads eventually to the improvement of society (Donlevy, 1996). Rogers (1978) talked of the *quiet revolution* to describe the political agenda of how personal change leads to social change. Fromm (1976), in his book *To Have or To Be,* argued that the more fulfilling life was to be had through "being" as opposed to "having." Looked at in this way, it's also evident that the answer to the question of how to do therapy is not necessarily just an evidence-based one but also a question of values and morality (see Christopher, 1996):

> When, as counselors, we interact with clients or engage in research or theorizing, we will be adopting a stance. This stance will be a moral stance, presupposing a moral vision. Whether we admit it or not in our work with clients, we are engaging in conversation about the good. Ultimately, counseling is part of a cultural discussion about ethos and world view, about the good life and the good person, and about moral visions. (p. 24)

We are excited at the thought of the new possibilities for practice that the positive psychology approach promises to open up. We can imagine a very different health care system if it were based on the principles of positive psychology and the view that it is the client and not the therapist who knows best. In addition, the positive therapy approach raises questions about the nature of therapist training programs. The conclusions that we reach about the nature of therapy lead us to think that much of current professional psychology training is misguided with its emphasis on diagnosis and technique. Rather, what we would want to see is emphasis on the congruence of therapists and their ability to develop authentic relationships. Personal development should be central to training. There is no one path to congruence, although experiential learning methods are often employed. More recent work within the positive psychology literature suggests that mindfulness training might help in the pursuit of greater congruence (see Brown & Ryan, Chapter 7, this volume).

Finally, there is also the recognition that we have been here before. The general principles of positive psychology—that we ought to think also about human potential, fulfillment, growth, development, and so on—is not new. These topics are at the core of humanistic psychology, although the relationship between humanistic psychology and positive psychology has sometimes been a contentious one (see Greening, 2001; Taylor, 2001). Humanistic psychology is a broad church, and there are parts of it we would not recognize as positive psychology; but in our view, the ideas of the main humanistic psychology writers, such as Rogers and Maslow, deserve to be set center stage within positive psychology. Theirs was an empirical stance, explicitly research-based, albeit lacking in the sophistication of current psychological research methods. We ought to respect this lineage, and we encourage those who are not familiar with this earlier work to visit it.

CONCLUSION

When we ask about the implications of positive psychology for therapy, we find that the current positive psychology movement raises questions about our fundamental assumptions about human nature. We propose a positive therapeutic approach based on the concept of the actualizing tendency as the motivational force for optimal human development. This approach to therapy has a lineage to the humanistic psychology tradition and to the work of Carl Rogers and Abraham Maslow in particular. The idea that the psyche contains its own natural or inherent principles that promote growth, integration, and the resolution of psychological inconsistencies and conflicts is, as we have shown, not a new one. However, it is a powerful idea that resonates with positive psychological principles and is supported by emerging research evidence. It is an idea with revolutionary implications for therapy, suggesting as it does that the task of the therapist is to help clients hear their own voices. We believe that therapy based on positive psychology needs to be self-reflective of its fundamental assumptions, holistic and integrative of the negative and positive aspects of human experience, and aware of its social and political context. Finally, we are left with a research agenda around the nature of an innate motivational tendency toward growth and development and the social environmental conditions that are able to release this inner tendency. These are research questions of profound value, since they offer insights into the fundamentals of human nature as viewed from a positive psychological perspective.

REFERENCES

Adler, A. (1927). *The practice and theory of individual psychology.* New York: Harcourt, Brace & World.

Angyal, A. (1941). *Foundations for a science of personality.* New York: Commonwealth Fund.

Bozarth, J. D. (1991). Person-centered assessment. *Journal of Counseling and Development, 69,* 458–461.

*Bozarth, J. D. (1998). *Person-centered therapy: A revolutionary paradigm.* Ross-on-Wye, England: PCCS Books.

Bretherton, R., & Ørner, R. (2003). Positive psychotherapy in disguise. *The Psychologist, 16,* 136–137.

Brown, K. W., & Ryan, R. M. (2003). The benefits of being present: Mindfulness and its role in psychological well-being. *Journal of Personality and Social Psychology, 84,* 822–848.

Calhoun, L. G., & Tedeschi, R. G. (1999). *Facilitating posttraumatic growth: A clinician's guide.* Mahwah, NJ: Erlbaum.

Christopher, J. C. (1996). Counseling's inescapable moral visions. *Journal of Counseling and Development, 75,* 17–25.

Csikszentmihalyi, M. (1997). *Finding flow: The psychology of engagement with everyday life.* New York: Basic Books.

Deci, E. L., & Ryan, R. M. (1985). *Intrinsic motivation and self-determination in human behavior.* New York: Plenum Press.

Deci, E. L., & Ryan, R. M. (1991). A motivational approach to self: Integration in personality. In R. Dienstbier (Ed.), *Nebraska Symposium on Motivation: Vol. 38. Perspectives on motivation* (pp. 237–288). Lincoln: University of Nebraska Press.

Deci, E. L., & Ryan, R. M. (2000). The "what" and "why" of goal pursuits: Human needs and the self-determination of behavior. *Psychological Inquiry, 11,* 227–268.

Donlevy, J. G. (1996). Jung's contribution to adult development: The difficult and misunderstood path of individuation. *Journal of Humanistic Psychology, 36,* 92–108.

Duncan, B., & Miller, S. (2000). *The heroic client: Doing client-directed, outcome informed therapy.* San Francisco: Jossey-Bass.

Fava, G. A. (1997). Conceptual obstacles to research progress in affective disorders. *Psychotherapy and Psychosomatics, 66,* 283–285.

Fava, G. A. (1999). Well-being therapy. *Psychotherapy and Psychosomatics, 68,* 171–178.

Follette, W. C., Linnerooth, P. J. N., & Ruckstuhl, L. E. (2001). Positive psychology: A clinical behavior analytic perspective. *Journal of Humanistic Psychology, 41,* 102–134.

Fromm, E. (1976). *To have or to be?* New York: Harper & Row.

Goldstein, K. (1939). *The organism.* New York: American Books.

Greening, T. (2001). Commentary. *Journal of Humanistic Psychology, 41,* 4–7.

Horney, K. (1950). *Neurosis and human growth: The struggle toward self-realization.* New York: Norton.

Joseph, S. (2001). *Psychopathology and therapeutic approaches: An introduction.* Houndmills, England: Palgrave Macmillan.

*Joseph, S. (2003). Client-centered psychotherapy: Why the client knows best. *The Psychologist, 16,* 304–307.

Jung, C. G. (1933). *Modern man in search of a soul.* New York: Harcourt, Brace & World.

Kasser, T. (2002). *The high price of materialism.* Cambridge, MA: MIT Press.

Kasser, T., & Ryan, R. M. (1993). A dark side of the American dream: Correlates of financial success as a central life aspiration. *Journal of Personality and Social Psychology, 65,* 410–422.

Kasser, T., & Ryan, R. M. (1996). Further examining the American dream: Differential correlates of intrinsic and extrinsic goals. *Personality and Social Psychology Bulletin, 22,* 280–287.

La Guardia, J. G., Ryan, R. M., Couchman, C. E., & Deci, E. L. (2000). Within-person variation in security of attachment: A self-determination theory perspective on attachment, need fulfilment, and well-being. *Journal of Personality and Social Psychology, 79,* 367–384.

Lopez, S. J., & Snyder, C. R. (Eds.). (2003). *Positive psychological assessment: A handbook of models and measures.* Washington, DC: American Psychological Association.

Maddux, J. E. (2002). Stopping the "madness": Positive psychology and the deconstruction of the illness ideology and the *DSM.* In C. R. Snyder & S. J. Lopez (Eds.), *Handbook of positive psychology* (pp. 13–25). New York: Oxford University Press.

Maddux, J. E., Gosselin, J. T., & Winstead, B. A. (in press). Conceptions of psychopathology: A social constructionist perspective. In J. E. Maddux & B. A. Winstead (Eds.), *Psychopathology: Contemporary issues, theory, and research.* Mahwah, NJ: Erlbaum.

Martin, D. J., Garske, J. P., & Davis, M. K. (2000). Relation of the therapeutic alliance with outcome and other variables: A meta-analytic review. *Journal of Consulting and Clinical Psychology, 68,* 438–450.

Maslow, A. H. (1968). *Toward a psychology of being* (2nd ed.). New York: Van Nostrand Reinhold.

Maslow, A. H. (1971). *Farther reaches of human nature.* New York: Penguin Arkana.

Peseschkian, N., & Tritt, K. (1998). Positive psychotherapy: Effectiveness study and quality assurance. *European Journal of Psychotherapy, Counseling, and Health, 1,* 93–104.

Peterson, C., & Seligman, M. E. P. (2003). *Values in Action (VIA) classification of strengths* [Draft dated January 4, 2003]. Retrieved January 15, 2003, from www.positivepsychology.org/strengths.

Rank, O. (1936). *Truth and reality: A life history of the human will.* New York: Knopf.

Resnick, S., Warmoth, A., & Serlin, I. A. (2001). The humanistic psychology and positive psychology connection: Implications for psychotherapy. *Journal of Humanistic Psychology, 41,* 73–101.

Rogers, C. R. (1957). The necessary and sufficient conditions of therapeutic personality change. *Journal of Consulting Psychology, 21*, 95–103.

*Rogers, C. R. (1959). A theory of therapy, personality and interpersonal relationships, as developed in the client-centered framework. In S. Koch (Ed.), *Psychology: A study of a science: Vol. 3. Formulations of the person and the social context* (pp. 184–256). New York: McGraw-Hill.

Rogers, C. R. (1961). *On becoming a person.* Boston: Houghton Mifflin.

Rogers, C. R. (1963). The concept of the fully functioning person. *Psychotherapy: Theory, Research, and Practice, 1*, 17–26.

*Rogers, C. R. (1964). Toward a modern approach to values: The valuing process in the mature person. *Journal of Abnormal and Social Psychology, 68*, 160–167.

Rogers, C. R. (1969). *Freedom to learn.* Columbus, OH: Merrill.

*Rogers, C. R. (1978). *Carl Rogers on personal power: Inner strength and its revolutionary impact.* London: Constable.

Ryan, R. M. (1995). Psychological needs and the facilitation of integrative processes. *Journal of Personality, 63*, 397–427.

Ryan, R. M., & Deci, E. L. (2000). Self-determination theory and the facilitation of intrinsic motivation, social development, and well-being. *American Psychologist, 55*, 68–78.

Ryff, C. D. (1989). Happiness is everything, or is it? Explorations on the meaning of psychological well-being. *Journal of Personality and Social Psychology, 57*, 1069–1081.

Ryff, C. D., & Singer, B. H. (1996). Psychological well-being: Meaning, measurement, and implications for psychotherapy research. *Psychotherapy and Psychosomatics, 65*, 14–23.

Salovey, P., Mayer, J. D., & Caruso, D. R. (2002). The positive psychology of emotional intelligence. In C. R. Snyder & S. J. Lopez (Eds.), *Handbook of positive psychology* (pp. 159–171). New York: Oxford University Press.

Seligman, M. E. P. (1994). *What you can change and what you can't.* New York: Knopf.

Seligman, M. E. P. (2002). Positive psychology, positive prevention and positive therapy. In C. R. Snyder & S. J. Lopez (Eds.), *Handbook of positive psychology* (pp. 3–9). New York: Oxford University Press.

Seligman, M. E. P. (2003). Positive psychology: Fundamental assumptions. *The Psychologist, 16*, 126–127.

Seligman, M. E. P., & Peterson, C. (2003). Positive clinical psychology. In L. G. Aspinwall & U. M. Staudinger (Eds.), *A psychology of human strengths: Fundamental questions and future directions for a positive psychology* (pp. 305–317). Washington, DC: American Psychological Association.

Sheldon, K. M., Arndt, J., & Houser-Marko, L. (2003). In search of the organismic valuing process: The human tendency to move toward beneficial goal choices. *Journal of Personality, 71*, 835–886.

Sheldon, K. M., & Elliot, A. J. (1999). Goal striving, need satisfaction, and longitudinal well-being: The Self-Concordance Model. *Journal of Personality and Social Psychology, 76*, 482–497.

*Sheldon, K. M., & Kasser, T. (2001). Goals, congruence, and positive well-being: New empirical validation for humanistic ideas. *Journal of Humanistic Psychology, 41*, 30–50.

Taylor, E. (2001). Positive psychology and humanistic psychology: A reply to Seligman. *Journal of Humanistic Psychology, 41*, 13–29.

Wampold, B. E. (2001). *The great psychotherapy debate: Models, methods, and findings.* Mahwah, NJ: Erlbaum.

*Yalom, I. D. (2001). *The gift of therapy: Reflections on being a therapist.* London: Piatkus.

PART VIII

POSITIVE PSYCHOLOGY IN THE CONSULTING ROOM

CHAPTER 23

Clinical Applications of Well-Being Therapy

CHIARA RUINI and GIOVANNI A. FAVA

T HE CONCEPT OF psychological well-being has received increasing attention in clinical psychology. Recent investigations have documented the complex relationship among well-being, distress, and personality traits, both in clinical (Fava, Rafanelli, et al., 2001) and nonclinical populations (Ruini et al., 2003). The findings show that psychological well-being could not be equated with the absence of symptomatology, nor with personality traits. It is thus particularly important to analyze the concept of well-being in clinical settings, with emphasis on changes in well-being occurring during psychotherapy.

A relevant methodological issue encountered in literature is the broad definition of psychological well-being and optimal functioning. A recent review by Ryan and Deci (2001) has shown that research on well-being has followed two main directions: (1) happiness and hedonic well-being and (2) development of human potential (eudaimonic well-being). In the first realm, all studies dealing with concepts of subjective well-being (Diener, Suh, Lucas, & Smith, 1999), life satisfaction (Neugarten, Havinghurst, & Tobin, 1961), and positive emotions (Fredrickson, 2002) can be included. The concept of well-being here is equated with a cognitive process of evaluation of an individual's life or with the experience of positive emotions.

In clinical settings, however, the concept of eudaimonic well-being has received important support. In humanistic psychology, concepts such as self-realization (Maslow, 1968), full functioning (Rogers, 1961), maturity (Allport, 1961), and individuation (Jung, 1933) have been proposed. In 1958, Jahoda outlined positive criteria for defining mental health, but all these aspects of psychological well-being

This chapter was supported in part by a grant from the Mental Health Evaluation Project (Istituto Superiore di Sanità, Rome, Italy) and a grant from the Ministero dell'Università e della Ricerca Scientifica e Tecnologica (MURST, Rome, Italy). Dr. Carol D. Ryff's work, criticism, and guidance were instrumental in developing the psychotherapeutic technique described in this chapter.

have been neglected for a long time because the development of psychotherapeutic strategies that may lead to symptom reduction has been the main focus of research. Such developments have been particularly impressive for cognitive-behavioral therapies (CBT; Fava, 2000). Even though Parloff, Kelman, and Frank suggested as early as 1954 that the goals of psychotherapy were increased personal comfort and effectiveness, these latter achievements were viewed only as by-products of the reduction of symptoms or as a luxury that clinical investigators could not afford. Four converging developments have recently modified this stance:

1. *Relapse in affective disorders:* There has been increasing awareness of the bleak long-term outcome of mood and anxiety disorders (Fava, 1996), particularly in unipolar major depression (Fava, 1999a; Labbate & Doyle, 1997). Various follow-up studies, in fact, have documented relapses and recurrence in affective disorders (Ramana et al., 1995). As a result, the challenge of treatment of depression today appears to be the prevention of relapse more than the attainment of recovery. Thunedborg, Black, and Bech (1995) found that quality-of-life measurement, and not symptomatic ratings, could predict recurrence of depression. It has thus become a legitimate question to wonder whether an increase in psychological well-being may protect against relapse and recurrence.

2. *Response versus recovery:* There is increasing awareness that clinicians and researchers in clinical psychiatry confound response to treatment with full recovery (Fava, 1996). A substantial residual symptomatology (anxiety, irritability, interpersonal problems) was found to characterize the majority of patients who were judged to be remitted according to *DSM* criteria and no longer in need of active treatment. Further, we have argued that psychological well-being needs to be incorporated into the definition of recovery (Fava, 1996). Ryff and Singer (1996) have suggested that the absence of well-being creates conditions of vulnerability to possible future adversities and that the route to enduring recovery lies not exclusively in alleviating the negative, but in engendering the positive. Interventions that bring the person out of the negative functioning (e.g., exposure treatment in panic disorder with agoraphobia) are one form of success, but facilitating progression toward the restoration of positive functioning is quite another (Ryff & Singer, 1996).

3. *Quality of life and positive health:* There has been an upsurge of interest in quality-of-life assessment in health care (Fava & Sonino, 2000; Frisch, 1998) and in the concept of positive health (Ryff & Singer, 2000). Clinical researchers have turned their attention to quality-of-life assessment as a means of broadening the evaluation of treatment outcome encompassing satisfaction, functioning, and objective life circumstances (Gladis, Gosch, Dishuk, & Crits-Christoph, 1999). This creates the necessity of multidimensional instruments (Gladis et al., 1999). Such directions in health care call for strategies to enhance the well-being that underlies these constructs.

4. *The growth of positive psychology:* There is increasing interest in positive psychology within clinical psychology and psychotherapy (Gillham & Seligman, 1999). Issues such as the building of human strength in different psychotherapeutic strategies and the characteristics of subjective well-being have become increasingly important in psychological research (Diener et al., 1999; Gillham & Seligman, 1999) as outlined in this volume. In particular, Ryff's model of psychological well-being, encompassing autonomy, personal growth, environmental mastery, purpose in life,

positive relations, and self-acceptance has been found to describe specific impairments of patients with affective disorders (Fava, Rafanelli, et al., 2001; Rafanelli et al., 2000, 2002; Ruini et al., 2002).

These four developments have paved the way for well-being-enhancing psychotherapeutic strategies in clinical medicine. However, there has been a very limited response to these emerging needs. Notable exceptions are Ellis and Becker's (1982) guide to personal happiness, Fordyce's (1983) program to increase happiness, Padesky's (1994) work on schema change processes, Frisch's (1998) quality-of-life therapy, and Horowitz and Kaltreider's (1979) work on positive states of mind. Unfortunately, these approaches have not affected clinical practice more broadly, for three main reasons.

First—as Ryff and Singer (1996) remark—historically, mental health research is dramatically weighted on the side of psychological dysfunction, and health is equated with the absence of illness rather than the presence of wellness. In a naive conceptualization, yet the one implicitly endorsed by the *DSM*, well-being and distress may be seen as mutually exclusive (i.e., well-being is lack of distress). According to this model, well-being should result from removal of distress. Yet, there is evidence both in psychiatric (Rafanelli et al., 2000) and psychosomatic (Fava, Mangelli, & Ruini, 2001) research to call such views into question. A second reason is concerned with the conceptual model that a psychotherapeutic approach should refer to. To justify therapeutic efforts aimed at increasing psychological well-being, we should demonstrate impaired levels of psychological well-being in a clinical population. This was achieved by using the Psychological Well-Being Scales (PWB) developed by Ryff (1989).

In a controlled investigation (Rafanelli et al., 2000), 20 remitted patients with mood or anxiety disorders displayed significantly lower levels in all six dimensions of well-being according to the PWB compared to healthy control subjects matched for sociodemographic variables. It is obvious, however, that the quality and degree of impairment may vary from patient to patient and within the same patient, according to clinical status. Further, Fava, Rafanelli, et al. (2001) administered the PWB to 30 remitted patients with panic disorder and 30 matched controls and found impairments in some specific areas, but not in others. The model described by Ryff (1989) and Ryff and Keyes (1995) was thus found to satisfactorily describe the variations in psychological well-being that may occur in a clinical setting. The concept of *salutogenesis* developed by the medical sociologist Antonovsky (1987) was an important, yet partial, element.

Finally, until recently, it was unclear what types of clinical applications might be feasible for a well-being-enhancing psychotherapy because therapeutic efforts were aimed only at the acute phase of psychiatric disorders, and subclinical symptomatology was viewed as devoid of substantial clinical interest (Fava, 1997). The application of a well-being-enhancing psychotherapeutic strategy as a relapse prevention measure was thus not envisioned. The helpfulness of positive cognitions within cognitive therapy has only recently been highlighted by a number of investigators (e.g., MacLeod & Moore, 2000). This clinical and conceptual framework was thus instrumental in developing a well-being-enhancing psychotherapeutic strategy, defined as well-being therapy (Fava, 1999b; Fava, Rafanelli, Cazzaro, Conti, & Grandi, 1998).

PROTOCOL OF WELL-BEING THERAPY

Well-being therapy (WBT) is a short-term psychotherapeutic strategy that extends over eight sessions and may take place every week or every other week. The duration of each session may range from 30 to 50 minutes. It is a technique that emphasizes self-observation (Emmelkamp, 1974), with the use of a structured diary, and interaction between patients and therapists. Well-being therapy is based on Ryff's cognitive model of psychological well-being (Ryff, 1989). This model was selected on the basis of its easy applicability to clinical populations (Fava, Rafanelli, et al., 2001; Rafanelli et al., 2000). Well-being therapy is structured, directive, problem-oriented, and based on an educational model. The development of sessions is described in the following sections.

INITIAL SESSIONS

These sessions are simply concerned with identifying episodes of well-being and setting them into a situational context, no matter how short lived they were. Patients are asked to report the circumstances surrounding their episodes of well-being in a structured diary, rated on a 0 to 100 scale, with 0 being absence of well-being and 100 the most intense well-being that could be experienced. When patients are assigned this homework, they often object that they will bring a blank diary, because they never feel well. It is helpful to reply that these moments do exist but tend to pass unnoticed. Patients should, therefore, monitor them anyway.

Meehl (1975) described:

> . . . how people with low hedonic capacity should pay greater attention to the "hedonic book keeping" of their activities than would be necessary for people located midway or high on the hedonic capacity continuum. That is, it matters more to someone cursed with an inborn hedonic defect whether he is efficient and sagacious in selecting friends, jobs, cities, tasks, hobbies, and activities in general. (p. 305)

This initial phase generally extends over a couple of sessions. Yet, its duration depends on the factors that affect any homework assignment, such as resistance and compliance.

INTERMEDIATE SESSIONS

Once the instances of well-being are properly recognized, the patient is encouraged to identify thoughts and beliefs leading to the premature interruption of well-being. The similarities with the search for irrational, tension-evoking thoughts in Ellis and Becker's rational-emotive therapy (1982) and automatic thoughts in cognitive therapy (Beck, Rush, Shaw, & Emery, 1979) are obvious. The trigger for self-observation is, however, different, being based on well-being instead of distress.

This phase is crucial because it allows the therapist to identify areas of psychological well-being that are unaffected by irrational or automatic thoughts and areas saturated with them. The therapist may challenge these thoughts with appropriate questions, such as, "What is the evidence for or against this idea?" or "Are you thinking in all-or-none terms?" (Beck et al., 1979). The therapist may also reinforce and encourage activities that are likely to elicit well-being (e.g., assigning the task of undertaking particular pleasurable activities for a certain time each day). Such reinforcement may also result in graded task assignments (Beck et al., 1979). However, the focus of this phase of WBT is always on self-monitoring of moments and feelings of well-being. The therapist refrains from suggesting conceptual and technical alternatives, unless a satisfactory degree of self-observation (including irrational or automatic thoughts) has been achieved. This intermediate phase may extend over two or three sessions, depending on the patient's motivation and ability, and it paves the way for the specific well-being-enhancing strategies.

FINAL SESSIONS

The monitoring of the course of episodes of well-being allows the therapist to realize specific impairments in well-being dimensions according to Ryff's conceptual framework. An additional source of information may be provided by Ryff's PWB Scales, an 84-item self-rating inventory (Ryff, 1989). Ryff's six dimensions of psychological well-being are progressively introduced to the patients, as long as the material recorded lends itself to it. For example, the therapist could explain that autonomy consists of possessing an internal locus of control, independence, and self-determination or that personal growth consists of being open to new experience and considering self as expanding over time, if the patient's attitudes show impairments in these specific areas. Errors in thinking and alternative interpretations are then discussed.

CONCEPTUAL FRAMEWORK OF WELL-BEING THERAPY

Cognitive restructuring in WBT follows Ryff's conceptual framework (Ryff & Singer, 1996). The goal of the therapist is to lead the patient from an impaired level to an optimal level in the six dimensions of psychological well-being (see Table 23.1).

ENVIRONMENTAL MASTERY

Environmental mastery is the most frequent impairment that emerges. A patient expressed it as follows: "I have got a filter that nullifies any positive achievement (I was just lucky) and amplifies any negative outcome, no matter how much expected. (This once more confirms I am a failure.)" This lack of sense of control leads the patient to miss surrounding opportunities, with the possibility of subsequent regret over them.

PERSONAL GROWTH

Patients often tend to emphasize their distance from expected goals much more than the progress that has been made toward goal achievement. A basic impairment that emerges is the inability to identify the similarities between events and situations that were handled successfully in the past and those that are about to come (transfer of experiences). Impairments in perception of personal growth and

Table 23.1
Modification of the Six Dimensions of Psychological
Well-Being According to Ryff's (1989) Model

Dimensions	Impaired Level	Optimal Level
Environmental mastery	The subject has or feels difficulties in managing everyday affairs; feels unable to change or improve surrounding context; is unaware of surrounding opportunities; lacks sense of control over the external world.	The subject has a sense of mastery and competence in managing the environment; controls external activities; makes effective use of surrounding opportunities; is able to create or choose contexts suitable to personal needs and values.
Personal growth	The subject has a sense of personal stagnation; lacks a sense of improvement or expansion over time; feels bored and uninterested with life; feels unable to develop new attitudes or behaviors.	The subject has a feeling of continued development; sees self as growing and expanding; is open to new experiences; has a sense of realizing own potential; sees improvement in self and behavior over time.
Purpose in life	The subject lacks a sense of meaning in life; has few goals or aims, lacks a sense of direction, does not see purpose in past life; has no outlooks or beliefs that give life meaning.	The subject has goals in life and a sense of directedness; feels there is meaning to present and past life; holds beliefs that give life purpose; has aims and objectives for living.
Autonomy	The subject is overconcerned with the expectations and evaluation of others; relies on judgment of others to make important decisions; conforms to social pressures to think or act in certain ways.	The subject is self-determining and independent; able to resist social pressures; regulates behavior from within; evaluates self by personal standards.
Self-acceptance	The subject feels dissatisfied with self; is disappointed with what has occurred in past life; is troubled about certain personal qualities; wishes to be different from what he or she is.	The subject has a positive attitude toward the self; accepts his or her good and bad qualities; feels positive about his or her past life.
Positive relations with others	The subject has few close, trusting relationships with others; finds it difficult to be open and is isolated and frustrated in interpersonal relationships; is not willing to make compromises to sustain important ties with others.	The subject has warm and trusting relationships with others; is concerned about the welfare of others; is capable of strong empathy, affection, and intimacy; understands the give and take of human relationships.

environmental mastery thus tend to interact in a dysfunctional way. A university student who is unable to realize the common contents and methodological similarities between the exams he or she successfully passed and the ones that are to be given shows impairments in both environmental mastery and personal growth.

PURPOSE IN LIFE

An underlying assumption of psychological therapies (whether pharmacological or psychotherapeutic) is to restore premorbid functioning. In treatments that emphasize self-help, such as cognitive-behavioral therapies, therapy itself offers a sense of direction and hence a short-term goal. However, this does not persist when acute symptoms abate and/or premorbid functioning is suboptimal. Patients may perceive a lack of sense of direction and may devalue their function in life. This particularly occurs when environmental mastery and a sense of personal growth are impaired.

AUTONOMY

It is a frequent clinical observation that patients may exhibit a pattern whereby a perceived lack of self-worth leads to unassertive behavior. For instance, patients may hide their opinions or preferences, go along with a situation that is not in their best interests, or consistently put their needs behind the needs of others. This pattern undermines environmental mastery and purpose in life; these, in turn, may affect autonomy, since these dimensions are highly correlated in clinical populations. Such attitudes may not be obvious to the patients, who hide their considerable need for social approval. A patient who tries to please everyone is likely to fail to achieve this goal, and the unavoidable conflicts that may ensue result in chronic dissatisfaction and frustration.

SELF-ACCEPTANCE

Patients may maintain unrealistically high standards and expectations, driven by perfectionistic attitudes (that reflect lack of self-acceptance) and/or endorsement of external instead of personal standards (that reflect lack of autonomy). As a result, any instance of well-being is neutralized by a chronic dissatisfaction with self. A person may set unrealistic standards for his or her performance. For instance, it is a frequent clinical observation that patients with social phobia tend to aspire to outstanding social performances (being sharp, humorous, etc.) and are not satisfied with average performances—despite the fact that the latter would not put them under the spotlight, which could be seen as their apparent goal.

POSITIVE RELATIONS WITH OTHERS

Interpersonal relationships may be influenced by strongly held attitudes of which the patient may be unaware and that may be dysfunctional. For instance, a young woman who recently got married may have set unrealistic standards for her marital relationship and find herself frequently disappointed. At the same time, she may avoid pursuing social plans that involve other people and may lack sources of comparison. Impairments in self-acceptance (with the resulting belief of being rejectable and unlovable) may also undermine positive relations with others.

PRELIMINARY VALIDATION STUDIES

Well-being therapy, according to the format previously outlined, has been employed in several clinical studies. Other studies are currently in progress.

RESIDUAL PHASE OF AFFECTIVE DISORDERS

The effectiveness of WBT in the residual phase of affective disorders has been tested in a small controlled investigation (Fava, Rafanelli, Cazzaro, et al., 1998). Twenty patients with affective disorders (major depression, panic disorder with agoraphobia, social phobia, generalized anxiety disorder, obsessive-compulsive disorder), who had been successfully treated by behavioral (anxiety disorders) or pharmacological (mood disorders) methods, were randomly assigned to either a well-being therapy or cognitive-behavioral treatment of residual symptoms. Both WBT and CBT were associated with a significant reduction of residual symptoms, as measured by the Clinical Interview for Depression (CID; Paykel, 1985) and in PWB well-being. However, when the residual symptoms of the two groups were compared after treatment, a significant advantage of WBT over cognitive-behavioral strategies was observed with the CID. Well-being therapy was associated also with a significant increase in PWB well-being, particularly in the Personal Growth subscale. The small number of subjects suggests caution in interpreting this difference and the need for further studies with larger samples of patients with specific affective disorders. However, these preliminary results point to the feasibility of WBT in the residual stage of affective disorders.

The improvement in residual symptoms may be explained on the basis of the balance between positive and negative affect (Fava, Rafanelli, Cazzaro, et al., 1998). If treatment of psychiatric symptoms induces improvement of well-being—and indeed subscales describing well-being are more sensitive to drug effects than subscales describing symptoms (Kellner, 1987)—it is conceivable that changes in well-being may affect the balance of positive and negative affect. In this sense, the higher degree of symptomatic improvement that was observed with WBT in this study is not surprising: In the acute phase of affective illness, removal of symptoms may yield the most substantial changes, but the reverse may be true in its residual phase.

PREVENTION OF RECURRENT DEPRESSION

Well-being therapy was a specific and innovative part of a cognitive-behavioral package that was applied to recurrent depression (Fava, Rafanelli, Grandi, Conti, & Belluardo, 1998). Here, *recurrent depression* was defined as the occurrence of three or more episodes of unipolar depression, with the immediately preceding episode being no more than 2.5 years before the onset of the current episode (Frank et al., 1990). This package included also cognitive-behavioral treatment of residual symptoms (Fava, Grandi, Zielezny, Canestrari, & Morphy, 1994; Fava, Grandi, Zielezny, Rafanelli, & Canestrari, 1996) and lifestyle modification (Fava, Rafanelli, Grandi, et al., 1998).

Forty patients with recurrent major depression, who had been successfully treated with antidepressant drugs, were randomly assigned to either this cognitive-behavioral package including WBT or clinical management. In both groups, antidepressant drugs were tapered and discontinued. The group that received CBT had a significantly lower level of residual symptoms after drug discontinuation in comparison with the clinical management group. Cognitive-behavioral therapy also resulted in a significantly lower relapse rate (25%) at a two-year follow-up than did clinical management (80%). At a six-year follow-up (unpublished findings), the relapse rate was 40% in the CBT group and 90% in the clinical management group. Further, the group treated with CBT had a significantly lower number of recurrences when multiple relapses were taken into account. Since well-being therapy here was only a part of the cognitive-behavioral package and, therefore, was associated with two other main ingredients (cognitive behavioral treatment of residual symptoms and lifestyle modification), it is inconclusive from this study whether it yielded a significant contribution.

Loss of Clinical Effect

The return of depressive symptoms during maintenance antidepressant treatment is a common and vexing clinical phenomenon (Baldessarini, Ghaemi, & Viguera, 2002). A number of pharmacological strategies have been suggested for addressing loss of antidepressant efficacy, but with limited success (Schmidt et al., 2002). Ten patients with recurrent depression who relapsed while taking antidepressant drugs were randomly assigned to dose increase or to a sequential combination of CBT and WBT (Fava, Ruini, Rafanelli, & Grandi, 2002). Four of five patients responded to a larger dose, but all relapsed again on that dose by one-year follow-up. Four of the five patients responded to psychotherapy and only one relapsed. The data suggest that application of WBT may counteract loss of clinical effect during long-term antidepressant treatment. Tolerance to antidepressant treatment has been associated with activation of the hypothalamic-pituitary-adrenal (HPA) axis (Sonino & Fava, 2003). In a single case report, WBT induced a normalization of the HPA axis (Sonino & Fava, 2003). It is thus conceivable that WBT may, through this mechanism, restore and maintain remission with antidepressant drugs when response fails or is about to fail.

Treatment of Generalized Anxiety Disorder

Well-being therapy has recently been applied for the treatment of generalized anxiety disorder (GAD; Ruini & Fava, 2002). Twenty patients with *DSM-IV* GAD were randomly assigned to eight sessions of CBT or the sequential administration of four sessions of CBT followed by another four sessions of WBT. Both treatments were associated with a significant reduction of anxiety. However, significant advantages of the WBT-CBT sequential combination over CBT were observed, both in terms of symptom reduction and psychological well-being improvement. These preliminary results suggest the feasibility and clinical advantages of adding WBT to the treatment of GAD. A possible explanation of these findings is that self-monitoring of episodes of well-being may lead to a more comprehensive identification of automatic thoughts than that entailed by the customary monitoring of episodes of distress in cognitive therapy (Beck & Emery, 1985), thus resulting in a more effective cognitive restructuring. These results lend support to a sequential use of treatment components for achieving a more sustained recovery.

EXAMPLES OF ADDITIONAL POTENTIAL CLINICAL APPLICATIONS

Well-being therapy was originally designed as a specific psychotherapeutic strategy for the residual phase of affective disorders (Fava, Rafanelli, Cazzaro, et al., 1998). The application of this therapy to the acutely ill patient, whose life is dominated by mental pain and suffering, indeed appeared to be difficult. While this remains its most important clinical application, there are several other areas that may be potentially beneficial.

COGNITIVE-BEHAVIORAL TREATMENT PACKAGES

Well-being therapy may not be necessarily used on its own; it may become a part of a more complex, symptom-oriented cognitive-behavioral strategy. By adding monitoring of episodes of well-being, it may provide a more comprehensive coverage of automatic thoughts and dysfunctional schemas. Our investigation on GAD (Ruini & Fava, 2002) would support this inclusion.

TREATMENT RESISTANCE IN AFFECTIVE DISORDERS

There is increasing awareness of the high proportion of patients with affective disorders who fail to respond to standard pharmacological and psychotherapeutic treatments (Pollack, Otto, & Rosenbaum, 1996). Compliance, particularly in cognitive-behavioral settings, requires the patient's endurance and motivation. It is thus conceivable that WBT may either complete the degree of improvement afforded by symptom-oriented treatments or increase compliance or both. This was found in a preliminary study on three patients with panic disorder associated with agoraphobia who failed three sequential trials of exposure, imipramine, and cognitive therapy (Fava, 1999b). There has been little exploration, outside the psychodynamic realm, of psychological factors affecting progression to full recovery in affective illness (Strean, 1985). Yet, clinical phenomena such as refusal to comply with basic requests are common observations in this setting. The strategies for handling psychological resistances derive from psychodynamic psychotherapy. It is possible that Ryff's conceptual framework and WBT may provide an empirically based approach to the understanding and treatment of these clinical phenomena. For instance, a low level of self-acceptance may affect the initial phase of exposure treatment: The patient may perceive the difficulties and ups and downs of treatment as a demonstration of his or her poor personal qualities, instead of as unavoidable drawbacks of the process of graded exposure.

BODY IMAGE DISTURBANCES

Even though there is little specific investigation in the area of body image disorders, psychological dimensions related to well-being may be related to them, with particular reference to body dysmorphic disorder. Current treatment of body image disorder appears to lack specific therapies (Jaeger et al., 2002), aside from cognitive restructuring of unrealistic thoughts on an individual's appearance. Well-being therapy may have therapeutic potential in this area. If specific impairments in psychological well-being are demonstrated in body dysmorphic disorder, they may be amenable to improvement, which may lead either to a more effective contrast of body-image-related automatic thoughts or to a decrease in the patient's perceived importance. Such a study is currently in progress.

HEALTH PSYCHOLOGY

Ryff and Singer (1998) discussed the contours of positive human health and how it is rooted in a biopsychosocial consideration of the patient (Engel, 1997). An extensive body of evidence suggests the influence of psychological well-being in altering individual vulnerability to disease (Mangelli, Gribbin, Buchi, Allard, & Sensky, 2002; Ryff & Singer, 1998) or quality of life (Fava & Sonino, 2000; Ryff & Singer, 2000). An increase in psychological well-being may counteract the feelings of demoralization and loss that are part of chronic disease and thus improve individual coping. It is thus conceivable that WBT may yield clinical benefits in improving quality of life, coping style, and social support in chronic and life-threatening illnesses, as has been shown for cognitive-behavioral strategies (Emmelkamp & Van Oppen, 1993). Disorders related to somatization—defined as the tendency to experience and communicate psychological distress in the form of physical symptoms and to seek medical help for them (Lipowski, 1987)—may also derive some benefit from well-being-enhancing strategies. For example, there is extensive evidence (Ryff & Singer, 2000) that levels of psychological well-being may affect vulnerability to medical illness, its course of development, and illness behavior. In a recent investigation (Ruini et al., 2003), Ryff's dimensions of psychological well-being displayed a negative correlation with intensity of somatization.

OBSESSIVE-COMPULSIVE DISORDER

Intrusive anxiety-provoking thoughts are a core feature of obsessive-compulsive disorder (Marks, 1997). Amir, Cashman, and Foa (1997) suggested that obsessive patients use punishment, worry, reappraisal, and social control as techniques of thought control more frequently than healthy subjects. Punishment appears to be the strongest discriminator (Amir et al., 1997). Clinical observation suggests that anxiety-provoking thoughts may often be preceded by instances of well-being in obsessive-compulsive disorder. These patients may thus have a low threshold for well-being-related anxiety. The following clinical example illustrates this point.

Case Study

Tom is a 23-year-old philosophy student with a severe obsessive illness, fulfilling the *DSM-IV* criteria, and refractory to drug treatment (fluvoxamine up to 200 mg per day and clomipramine 150 mg per day) and cognitive-behavioral therapy. (He dropped out of treatment after six sessions.) He is being treated with well-being therapy. After the first two sessions, he is able to identify that obsessions start when well-being ensues. Adding an observer's interpretation column makes the patient realize that an effective contrast of preobsessive thoughts triggered by well-being may prevent obsessions and ruminations (see Table 23.2). As long as

Table 23.2
Prevention of Obsessive Thoughts by Cognitive Restructuring

Situation	Feeling of Well-Being	Interrupting Thoughts	Observer's Interpretation
Lunch with family	Maybe I am getting better and my life will change.	A terrible crisis is on its way. I feel it . . .	To acknowledge some progress does not mean asking for trouble. The problem is that you do not believe you can feel well. You are afraid of being well, because you do not think it is possible.

therapy goes on (one session every other week), the intensity and perceived importance of obsessions decrease. After eight sessions, the patient no longer meets *DSM-IV* criteria for obsessive-compulsive disorder and feels much better. He is able to finish his studies. He no longer reports obsessive-compulsive disturbances at a four-year follow-up.

INTERVENTIONS IN THE ELDERLY

A vast literature has accumulated on interventions aimed at increasing subjective well-being in the elderly (Okun, Olding, & Cohn, 1990). Interventions seem to have a significant immediate posttreatment beneficial influence, but such gains fade in subsequent months. The use of WBT in an elderly population may yield more enduring effects. Ryff's conceptual model of psychological well-being encompasses biopsychosocial modifications and aging processes in defining positive functioning (Ryff & Singer, 2000). Controlled studies should test the efficacy of WBT compared to other interventions for increasing subjective well-being in elderly populations.

PREVENTION

Well-being therapy could play an important role in preventive interventions, for example, with children or adolescents. The hypothesis is that improving their levels of psychological well-being could be crucial in the development of their personality and could provide protection against future adversity and against health-risk behavior (i.e., smoking, alcohol, or drug abuse). These positive preventive interventions could be performed at school, with teenager groups, and in other social contexts (Seligman, 2002).

CLINICAL ISSUES

The techniques that are used in overcoming impairments in psychological well-being may include cognitive restructuring (modification of automatic or irrational thoughts), scheduling of activities (mastery, pleasure, and graded task assignments), assertiveness training, and problem solving (Beck et al., 1979; Ellis & Becker, 1982; Pava, Fava, & Levenson, 1994; Weissman & Markowitz, 1994).

The goal of the therapist is to lead the patient through the transitions outlined in Table 23.1. As happens with symptom-oriented CBT, at times, the simple discovery of untested standards and assumptions for well-being may lead to challenge and growth. Other times, modification of these patterns may be time consuming and require working on repeated instances through the structured diary. However, it is only when such insights about these impairments in well-being dimensions are translated into behavioral terms that a significant improvement has been made, as the following case study shows.

Case Study

A patient after his third recurrent episode of major depression may learn how his lack of autonomy leads his workmates to consistently take advantage of him. This situation results in a workload that, because of its diverse nature, undermines his environmental mastery and constitutes a significant stress, also in terms of working hours. The situation is accepted by virtue of a low degree of self-acceptance: The patient claims that this is the way he is, but at the same time he is dissatisfied with himself and chronically irritable. When he learns to say no to his colleagues (assertiveness training) and consistently endorses this attitude, a significant degree of distress ensues, linked to perceived disapproval by others. However, as time goes by, his tolerance for self-disapproval gradually increases, and, in the last session, he is able to make the following remark: "Now my workmates say that I am changed and have become a bastard. In a way I am sorry, since I always tried to be helpful and kind to people. But in another way I am happy, because this means that—for the first time in my life—I have been able to protect myself." The patient had no further relapse at a six-year follow-up, while being medication free.

This clinical picture illustrates how an initial feeling of well-being (being helpful to others), which was identified in the diary, was likely to lead to overwhelming distress. Its appraisal and the resulting change in behavior initially led to more distress, but then yielded a lasting remission. The example clarifies that a similar behavioral change might have been achieved by distress-oriented psychotherapeutic strategies (indeed, the approach that was used to tackle this specific problem was no different). However, these changes would not have been supported by specific modifications of well-being dimensions.

The standard format that has been outlined involves eight sessions; however, the number of sessions may vary according to the patient's needs and collaboration with therapy. In certain cases, 12 to 16 sessions may be necessary; in other cases (when, for instance, the patient already underwent a traditional, symptom-oriented CBT and is thus familiar with daily homework and the diary), the number of sessions may be shortened.

A question may arise: What differentiates WBT from standard cognitive therapies, which may also involve positive thinking (MacLeod & Moore, 2000)? A main difference is the focus (in WBT, the focus is on instances of emotional well-being, whereas in cognitive therapy, the focus is psychological distress). A second important distinction is that in cognitive therapy, the goal is the abatement of distress through automatic thought control or contrast, whereas in WBT, the goal is the promotion of psychological well-being along Ryff's (1989) dimensions (see Table 23.1). Since both may share similar techniques and therapeutic ingredients, WBT may be conceptualized as a specific strategy within the broad spectrum of self-therapies (Fava, 2000). A final distinction is the fact that, unlike cognitive-behavioral frameworks, WBT refrains from explaining its rationale and strategies to the patient at the outset but relies on his or her progressive appraisals of a positive self. The patient who struggles against anxiety, for instance, may be helped to view anxiety as an unavoidable element of everyday life, which can be counteracted by a progressive increase in environmental mastery and self-acceptance.

Well-being therapy's effectiveness may be based on two distinct, yet ostensibly related, clinical phenomena. The first concerns the fact that an increase in psychological well-being may have protective effect in terms of vulnerability to chronic and acute life stresses (Ryff & Singer, 1998, 2000). The second concerns the complex balance of positive and negative affects. Extensive research—reviewed in detail elsewhere (Rafanelli et al., 2000; Ruini et al., 2003)—indicates a certain degree of inverse correlation between positive and negative affects. As a result, changes in well-being may induce a decrease in distress and vice versa. In the acute phase of illness, removal of symptoms may yield the most substantial changes, but the reverse may be true in its residual phase. An increase in psychological well-being may decrease residual symptoms that direct strategies (whether cognitive-behavioral or pharmacological) would be unlikely to affect.

Further, it has been suggested that cognitive-behavioral psychotherapy may work at the molecular level to alter stress-related gene expression and protein synthesis or influence mechanisms implicated in learning and memory acquisition in neuronal structures (Goddard & Charney, 1997). For instance, in one study, sadness and happiness affected different brain regions: Sadness activates limbic and paralimbic structures, whereas happiness was associated with temporal parietal decreases in cortical activity (George et al., 1995). Such effects were not merely opposite activity in identical brain regions. The pathophysiological substrates of WBT may thus be different compared to symptom-oriented cognitive-behavioral strategies, to the same extent that well-being and distress are not merely opposites (Rafanelli et al., 2000).

CONCLUSION

Well-being therapy is obviously at a very preliminary stage. Adequate validation studies are required that elucidate further its specific role in clinical and health psychology. Well-being therapy is rooted on constructs derived from the positive psychology literature (Fava, 1999b; Seligman, 2002). Even though the goal of WBT may appear ambitious, its theoretical implications are that wellness and healthy living can be promoted by helping people to realize their true potential, to be fully engaged with others, and to achieve optimal functioning. Further, it suggests that psychological distress may be counteracted, and even prevented, by increasing levels of well-being.

REFERENCES

Allport, G. W. (1961). *Pattern and growth in personality*. New York: Holt, Rinehart and Winston.

Amir, N., Cashman, L., & Foa, E. B. (1997). Strategies of thought control in obsessive-compulsive disorder. *Behavior Research and Therapy, 35,* 775–779.

Antonovsky, A. (1987). *Unraveling the mystery of health.* San Francisco: Jossey-Bass.

Baldessarini, R. J., Ghaemi, S. N., & Viguera, A. C. (2002). Tolerance in antidepressant treatment. *Psychotherapy and Psychosomatics, 71,* 177–179.

Beck, A. T., & Emery, G. (1985). *Anxiety disorders and phobias.* New York: Basic Books.

Beck, A. T., Rush, A. J., Shaw, B. F., & Emery, G. (1979). *Cognitive therapy of depression.* New York: Guilford Press.

Diener, E., Suh, E. M., Lucas, R. E., & Smith, H. L. (1999). Subjective well-being: Three decades of progress. *Psychological Bulletin, 125,* 276–302.

Ellis, A., & Becker, I. (1982). *A guide to personal happiness.* Hollywood, CA: Melvin Powers Wilshire Book Company.

Emmelkamp, P. M. G. (1974). Self-observation versus flooding in the treatment of agoraphobia. *Behavior Research and Therapy, 12,* 229–237.

Emmelkamp, P. M. G., & Van Oppen, P. (1993). Cognitive interventions in behavioral medicine. *Psychotherapy and Psychosomatics, 59,* 116–130.

Engel, G. L. (1997). From biomedical to biopsychosocial. *Psychotherapy and Psychosomatics, 66,* 57–62.

Fava, G. A. (1996). The concept of recovery in affective disorders. *Psychotherapy and Psychosomatics, 65,* 2–13.

Fava, G. A. (1997). Conceptual obstacles to research progress in affective disorders. *Psychotherapy and Psychosomatics, 66,* 283–285.

Fava, G. A. (1999a). Subclinical symptoms in mood disorders: Pathophysiological and therapeutic implications. *Psychological Medicine, 29,* 47–61.

*Fava, G. A. (1999b). Well-being therapy. *Psychotherapy and Psychosomatics, 68,* 171–178.

Fava, G. A. (2000). Cognitive behavioral therapy. In M. Fink (Ed.), *Encyclopedia of stress* (pp. 484–497). San Diego, CA: Academic Press.

Fava, G. A., Grandi, S., Zielezny, M., Canestrari, R., & Morphy, M. A. (1994). Cognitive behavioral treatment of residual symptoms in primary major depressive disorder. *American Journal of Psychiatry, 151,* 1295–1299.

Fava, G. A., Grandi, S., Zielezny, M., Rafanelli, C., & Canestrari, R. (1996). Four year outcome for cognitive behavioral treatment of residual symptoms in major depression. *American Journal of Psychiatry, 153,* 945–947.

Fava, G. A., Mangelli, L., & Ruini, C. (2001). Assessment of psychological distress in the setting of medical disease. *Psychotherapy and Psychosomatics, 70,* 171–179.

Fava, G. A., Rafanelli, C., Cazzaro, M., Conti, S., & Grandi, S. (1998). Well-being therapy: A novel psychotherapeutic approach for residual symptoms of affective disorders. *Psychological Medicine, 28,* 475–480.

*Fava, G. A., Rafanelli, C., Grandi, S., Conti, S., & Belluardo, P. (1998). Prevention of recurrent depression with cognitive behavioral therapy. *Archives of General Psychiatry, 55,* 816–820.

Fava, G. A., Rafanelli, C., Ottolini, F., Ruini, C., Cazzaro, M., & Grandi, S. (2001). Psychological well-being and residual symptoms in remitted patients with panic disorder and agoraphobia. *Journal of Affective Disorders, 31,* 899–905.

Fava, G. A., Ruini, C., Rafanelli, C., & Grandi, S. (2002). Cognitive behavior approach to loss of clinical effect during long-term antidepressant treatment. *American Journal of Psychiatry, 159,* 2094–2095.

Fava, G. A., & Sonino, N. (2000). Psychosomatic medicine: Emerging trends and perspectives. *Psychotherapy and Psychosomatics, 69,* 184–197.

Fordyce, M. W. (1983). A program to increase happiness. *Journal of Counseling Psychology, 30*, 483–498.

Frank, E., Kupfer, D. J., Perel, J. M., Cornes, C., Jarrett, D. B., Mallinger, A. G., et al. (1990). Three year outcomes for maintenance therapies in recurrent depression. *Archives of General Psychiatry, 47*, 1093–1099.

Fredrickson, B. L. (2002). Positive emotions. In C. R. Snyder & S. J. Lopez (Eds.), *Handbook of positive psychology* (pp. 120–134). New York: Oxford University Press.

Frisch, M. B. (1998). Quality of life therapy and assessment in health care. *Clinical Psychology: Science and Practice, 5*, 19–40.

George, M. S., Ketter, T. A., Parekh, P. I., Horowitz, B., Herscovitch, P., & Post, R. M. (1995). Brain activity during transient sadness and happiness in healthy women. *American Journal of Psychiatry, 152*, 341–351.

Gillham, J. E., & Seligman, M. E. P. (1999). Footsteps on the road to a positive psychology. *Behavior Research and Therapy, 37*(Suppl.), 163–173.

Gladis, M. M., Gosh, E. A., Dishuk, N. M., & Crits-Christoph, P. (1999). Quality of life: Expanding the scope of clinical significance. *Journal of Consulting and Clinical Psychology, 67*, 320–331.

Goddard, A. W., & Charney, D. S. (1997). Toward an integrated neurobiology of panic disorder. *Journal of Clinical Psychiatry, 58*(Suppl. 2), 4–11.

Horowitz, M. J., & Kaltreider, N. B. (1979). Brief therapy of the stress response syndrome. *Psychiatric Clinics of North America, 2*, 365–377.

Jaeger, B., Ruggiero, G. M., Edlund, B., Gomez-Perrett, C., Lang, F., Mohammadkhani, P., et al. (2002). Body dissatisfaction and its interrelations with other risk factors for bulimia nervosa in 12 countries. *Psychotherapy and Psychosomatics, 71*, 54–61.

Jahoda, M. (1958). *Current concepts of positive mental health.* New York: Basic Books.

Jung, C. G. (1933). *Modern man in search of a soul.* New York: Harcourt, Brace and World.

Kellner, R. (1987). A symptom questionnaire. *Journal of Clinical Psychiatry, 48*, 269–274.

Labbate, L. A., & Doyle, M. E. (1997). Recidivism in major depressive disorder. *Psychotherapy and Psychosomatics, 66*, 145–149.

Lipowski, Z. J. (1987). Somatization. *Psychotherapy and Psychosomatics, 47*, 160–167.

*MacLeod, A. K., & Moore, R. (2000). Positive thinking revisited: Positive cognitions, well-being and mental health. *Clinical Psychology and Psychotherapy, 7*, 1–10.

Mangelli, L., Gribbin, N., Buchi, S., Allard, S., & Sensky, T. (2002). Psychological well-being in rheumatoid arthritis. *Psychotherapy and Psychosomatics, 71*, 112–116.

Marks, I. (1997). Behavior therapy for obsessive-compulsive disorder: A decade of progress. *Canadian Journal of Psychiatry, 42*, 1021–1027.

Maslow, A. H. (1968). *Toward a psychology of being* (2nd ed.). New York: Van Nostrand Reinhold.

Meehl, P. E. (1975). Hedonic capacity: Some conjectures. *Bulletin of the Menninger Clinic, 39*, 295–307.

Neugarten, B. L., Havinghurst, R. J., & Tobin, S. S. (1961). The measurement of life satisfaction. *Journal of Gerontology, 16*, 134–143.

Okun, M. A., Olding, R. W., & Cohn, C. M. G. (1990). A meta-analysis of subjective well-being interventions among elders. *Psychological Bulletin, 108*, 257–266.

Padesky, C. A. (1994). Schema change processes in cognitive therapy. *Clinical Psychology and Psychotherapy, 1*, 267–278.

Parloff, M. B., Kelman, H. C., & Frank, J. D. (1954). Comfort, effectiveness, and self-awareness as criteria of improvement in psychotherapy. *American Journal of Psychiatry, 11*, 343–351.

Pava, J. A., Fava, M., & Levenson, J. A. (1994). Integrating cognitive therapy and pharmacotherapy in the treatment and prophylaxis of depression. *Psychotherapy and Psychosomatics, 61,* 211–219.

Paykel, E. S. (1985). The clinical Interview for depression. *Journal of Affective Disorders, 9,* 85–96.

Pollack, M. H., Otto, M. W., & Rosenbaum, J. F. (Eds.). (1996). *Challenges in clinical practice.* New York: Guilford Press.

Rafanelli, C., Conti, S., Mangelli, L., Ruini, C., Ottolini, F., Fabbri, S., et al. (2002). Psychological well-being and residual symptoms in patients with affective disorders, II. *Rivista di Psichiatria, 37,* 179–183.

Rafanelli, C., Park, S. K., Ruini, C., Ottolini, F., Cazzaro, M., & Fava, G. A. (2000). Rating well-being and distress. *Stress Medicine, 16,* 55–61.

Ramana, R., Paykel, E. S., Cooper, Z., Hayburst, H., Saxty, M., & Surtees, P. G. (1995). Remission and relapse in major depression. *Psychological Medicine, 25,* 1161–1170.

Rogers, C. R. (1961). *On becoming a person.* Boston: Houghton Mifflin.

Ruini, C., & Fava, G. A. (2002, August 9–15). *Well-being therapy of generalized anxiety disorder.* Paper presented at the 2nd Positive Psychology Summer Institute, Philadelphia.

Ruini, C., Ottolini, F., Rafanelli, C., Tossani, E., Ryff, C. D., & Fava, G. A. (2003). The relationship of psychological well-being to distress and personality. *Psychotherapy and Psychosomatics, 72,* 268–275.

Ruini, C., Rafanelli, C., Conti, S., Ottolini, F., Fabbri, S., Tossani, E., et al. (2002). Psychological well-being and residual symptoms in patients with affective disorders, I. *Rivista di Psichiatria, 37,* 171–178.

Ryan, R. M., & Deci, E. L. (2001). On happiness and human potentials: A review of research on hedonic and eudaimonic well-being. *Annual Review of Psychology, 52,* 141–166.

Ryff, C. D. (1989). Happiness is everything, or is it? Explorations on the meaning of psychological well-being. *Journal of Personality and Social Psychology, 57,* 1069–1081.

Ryff, C. D., & Keyes, C. L. M. (1995). The structure of psychological well-being revisited. *Journal of Personality and Social Psychology, 69,* 719–727.

*Ryff, C. D., & Singer, B. H. (1996). Psychological well-being: Meaning, measurement, and implications for psychotherapy research. *Psychotherapy and Psychosomatics, 65,* 14–23.

Ryff, C. D., & Singer, B. H. (1998). The contours of positive human health. *Psychological Inquiry, 9,* 1–28.

*Ryff, C. D., & Singer, B. H. (2000). Biopsychosocial challenges of the new millennium. *Psychotherapy and Psychosomatics, 69,* 170–177.

Schmidt, M. E., Fava, M., Zhang, S., Gonzales, J., Rante, N. J., & Judge, R. (2002). Treatment approaches to major depressive disorder relapse. *Psychotherapy and Psychosomatics, 71,* 190–194.

Seligman, M. E. P. (2002). Positive psychology, positive prevention, and positive therapy. In C. R. Snyder & S. J. Lopez (Eds.), *Handbook of positive psychology* (pp. 3–9). New York: Oxford University Press.

Sonino, N., & Fava, G. A. (2003). Tolerance to antidepressant treatment may be overcome by ketoconazole. *Journal of Psychiatric Research, 37,* 171–173.

Strean, H. S. (1985). *Resolving resistances in psychotherapy.* New York: Wiley.

Thunedborg, K., Black, C. H., & Bech, P. (1995). Beyond the Hamilton depression scores in long-term treatment of manic-melancholic patients: Prediction of recurrence of depression by quality of life measurements. *Psychotherapy and Psychosomatics, 64,* 131–140.

Weissman, M. M., & Markowitz, J. C. (1994). Interpersonal psychotherapy. *Archives of General Psychiatry, 51,* 599–606.

CHAPTER 24

Strategies for Accentuating Hope

SHANE J. LOPEZ, C. R. SNYDER, JEANA L. MAGYAR-MOE,
LISA M. EDWARDS, JENNIFER TERAMOTO PEDROTTI, KELLY JANOWSKI,
JERRI L. TURNER, and CINDY PRESSGROVE

PEOPLE SOMEHOW SUMMON enough mental energy to set the goal of seeking a therapist or other healer. Likewise, they identify pathways to the desired helper and muster the requisite energy to build a working alliance with their newfound agent of change. In essence, self-referred clients already have demonstrated hope in their pursuit of therapeutic support by the time they reach their therapist. In turn, therapists can help clients to name and to nurture the hope that they already possess.

In this chapter, we identify formal strategies for accentuating the hope that people possess. We discuss the effectiveness data, where available, associated with these strategies. Given that most therapists are eclectic, we also describe informal strategies that could be implemented within any therapeutic framework; moreover, we address common strategies that can be assigned to clients as homework. We begin by outlining hope theory and discuss hope's role as an active ingredient in psychological change.

HOPE THEORY

According to hope theory, hope reflects individuals' perceptions of their capacities to (1) clearly conceptualize goals; (2) develop the specific strategies to reach those goals (pathways thinking); and (3) initiate and sustain the motivation for using those strategies (agency thinking).

The pathways and agency components are both necessary, but neither by itself is sufficient to sustain successful goal pursuit. As such, pathways and agency thoughts are additive, reciprocal, and positively related, but they are not synonymous (Snyder, 1989, 1994, 2000a, 2000b, 2002; Snyder et al., 1991). According to hope theory, a goal can be anything that an individual desires to experience, create, get, do, or become. As such, a goal may be a significant, lifelong pursuit (e.g., developing a comprehensive theory of human motivation), or it may be mundane and brief (e.g., getting a ride to school). Goals also may vary in terms of having perceived probabilities of attainment that vary from very low to very high. On this point, high-hope individuals prefer *stretch goals* that are slightly more difficult than previously attained goals.

Whereas other positive psychology concepts such as goal theory (Covington, 2000; see also Dweck, 1999), optimism (Scheier & Carver, 1985), self-efficacy (Bandura, 1982), and problem-solving (Heppner & Petersen, 1982) give differentially weighted emphases to the goal itself or to the future-oriented agency- or pathways-related processes, hope theory equally emphasizes all of these goal-pursuit components (Snyder, 1994). For detailed comparisons of the similarities and differences between hope theory and other theories (e.g., achievement motivation, flow, goal setting, mindfulness, optimism, optimistic explanatory style, problem solving, resiliency, self-efficacy, self-esteem, Type A behavior pattern), see Magaletta and Oliver (1999), Peterson (2000), Snyder (1994, 2002), and Snyder, Rand, and Sigmon (2002).

HOPE AS AN AGENT OF CHANGE

The power of hope as a motivating force has been discussed throughout modern time and, for the past century, has been examined by medical and psychological scholars. Over the past 40 years, Jerome Frank's (1968, 1975) work has conceptualized hope as a process that is common to all psychotherapy approaches. Karl Menninger (1959), in his academic lecture on hope when he was president of the American Psychiatric Association, issued a call for more rigorous examination of the role of hope in change. As a response to Menninger's request, Snyder's operationalization of this robust construct has facilitated, over the past two decades, the scholarly inquiry into hope as a change agent. Indeed, whatever the system of psychotherapy, beneficial change may be attributable, in part, to hope. According to Snyder, Ilardi, Cheavens, et al. (2000), change occurs because people learn more effective agentic and pathways and goal-directed thinking:

> In particular, the agency component is reflected in the placebo effect (i.e., the natural mental energies for change that clients bring to psychotherapy). The particular psychotherapy approaches that are used to provide the client with a route or process for moving forward to attain positive therapeutic goals reflect the pathways component. (p. 267)

Furthermore, Snyder and his colleagues (Snyder, Ilardi, Cheavens, et al., 2000; Snyder, Ilardi, Michael, & Cheavens, 2000) have offered detailed hypotheses about how hope, and agency and pathways in particular, might help to explain the role of common and specific treatment factors in psychotherapy. Before any specific treatment strategies are applied, the primary source of change is the client's expectancy that therapy will make a positive difference in his or her life. These initial improvements are analogous to increases in the agency component of hope—determination that an individual can make improvements in his or her life. Therefore, it is believed that increases in agency, as opposed to increases in pathways thinking, will be related to positive change in the first stages of therapy. The positive changes that occur in these early stages of therapy have been described elsewhere as "remoralization" (Howard, Krause, Saunders, & Koptka, 1997), and they are characterized by enhanced subjective well-being. More specifically, clients begin to experience relief from distress and have renewed hope that their situation can and will improve. Increased well-being even may take place before the client steps into the therapy room; that is, an initial phone call to set up the appointment may engender feelings of relief from distress.

From this perspective on hope, it is conceivable that hope is malleable and that it can be the spark for and pathway to change. Likewise, beneficial change may lead to more hope for creating a good life. Because most people have the capacity to hope (they possess the basic components of the cognitive skills needed to generate a hopeful line of thought), accentuating this change agent requires naming and nurturing this personal strength in the context of supportive helping relationships.

We propose that hope finding, bonding, enhancing, and reminding are the essential strategies for accentuating hope. *Hope finding* can strengthen clients' expectations that the therapists can and will help them. Bolstering clients' expectations for assistance simultaneously may instill hope in change and enhance the therapeutic bond between client and therapist. *Hope bonding* is the formation of a sound hopeful therapeutic alliance; it grounds the client in a hopeful therapeutic context. Therapists possessing high levels of hope may be most facile at meeting the important therapeutic goal of establishing an emotionally charged connection. They also may be best at collaborating on mutually agreed-on goals by engaging in productive tasks. *Hope-enhancing* strategies typically involve enlisting clients in tasks that are designed to:

- Conceptualize reasonable goals more clearly
- Produce numerous pathways to attainment
- Summon the energy to maintain pursuit
- Reframe insurmountable obstacles as challenges to be overcome

Hope reminding is the promotion of effortful daily use of hopeful cognitions. Goal thoughts and barrier thoughts are identified cognitive cues that stimulate the client to incorporate therapeutic techniques that have previously enhanced hopeful thought. Next, we describe the formal and informal strategies for accentuating hope by finding, bonding, enhancing, and reminding.

HOPE FINDING

Hope can exist as a relatively stable personality disposition (i.e., a trait) or as a more temporary frame of mind (i.e., a state). Similarly, hopeful thought can occur at various levels of abstraction. For example, individuals can be hopeful about achieving:

- Goals in general (i.e., a trait)
- Goals in a certain life arena (i.e., domain-specific)
- One goal in particular (i.e., goal-specific)

Finding the hope that each person possesses is essential to building personal resources in preparation for the therapeutic change process. Naming and measuring the type of hope most relevant to a client's goal pursuit can be achieved via formal and informal means.

FORMAL STRATEGIES

Brief, valid measures of hope can be used during initial phases of therapy to find an individual's hope. Snyder et al. (1997) developed the Children's Hope Scale (CHS) as a trait hope measure for children ages 7 through 14 years (see Appendix A). The CHS is composed of three agency and three pathways items, and it has demonstrated satisfactory psychometric properties: (1) internal consistency reliabilities (overall alphas from 0.72 to 0.86); (2) test-retest reliabilities of 0.71 to 0.73 over 1 month; and (3) convergent and discriminant validities. Furthermore, this scale has been used with physically and psychologically healthy children from public schools, boys diagnosed with attention-deficit/hyperactivity disorder, children with various medical problems, children under treatment for cancer or asthma, child burn victims, adolescents with sickle-cell disease, and early adolescents exposed to violence (Snyder et al., 1997).

To measure the trait aspect of hope in adolescents and adults, ages 15 and higher, Snyder et al. (1991) developed the Hope Scale (see Appendix B). This scale consists of four items measuring agency, four items measuring pathways, and four distracter items. Having been used with a wide range of samples, the Hope Scale has exhibited acceptable reliability and validity: (1) internal consistency reliabilities (overall alphas from 0.74 to 0.88, agency alphas of 0.70 to 0.84, and pathways alphas of 0.63 to 0.86); (2) test-retest reliabilities ranging from 0.85 for 3 weeks to 0.82 for 10 weeks; and (3) concurrent and discriminant validity (Snyder et al., 1991). (Lopez, Ciarlelli, Coffman, Stone, & Wyatt, 2000, provide an in-depth coverage of these formal measures, including the development and validation of additional self-report, observational, and narrative measures of hope.)

INFORMAL STRATEGIES

Narrative approaches often have been used to illustrate the theory of hope to children, adolescents, and adults in individual therapy and psychoeducational programs. By telling stories of fictitious and real characters, therapists engage clients in thinking about goals, agency, and pathways. Furthermore, with time, clients tell stories about their goal pursuits, thereby making hope more personally relevant. Hope-related themes are captured when clinicians explore the following 14 aspects of clients' stories:

1. How did the client generate goals?
2. What was the motivation?
3. How attainable or realistic were the goals?
4. How were the goals perceived?
5. What was the client's mood/attitude during the process?
6. How was movement toward goals initiated?
7. How was movement maintained?
8. What were the biggest barriers to reaching the goals?
9. What emotions did these barriers elicit?

10. How were barriers overcome, and what steps were taken to reach the goals?
11. Were the goals attained?
12. How does the client feel about the outcome?
13. If the client were to attempt the same goal today, what would he or she do differently?
14. Can the client recast the experience in more hopeful terms (i.e., by identifying lessons learned that can facilitate future efforts)?

It may be necessary to offer some suggestions to direct the client's attention to hopeful elements in their stories. These narratives should support a sense of movement rather than stagnant rumination. The benefits of narrative techniques come from the integration of these cognitive and emotional elements of the client's stories.

Another informal strategy, *hope profiling*, is a semistructured intervention in which the therapist requests that the client write (or audiotape) brief stories about past and current goal pursuits to uncover the hope that is part of a person's psychological makeup. Typically, five stories (two to five pages) detailing goal pursuits in various life domains reveal the requisite pathways and agency involved in hopeful pursuits. Review of these stories in the therapeutic context can help clients to realize that they have the resources necessary to make positive changes. In addition, clients learn the language of hope by identifying the goal thoughts, pathway thinking, and agency sources referred to in their narrative.

HOPE BONDING

Bordin (1979) defined the *working alliance* as the collaboration between the therapist and client that is based on their agreement on the goals and tasks of counseling and on the development of a personal attachment bond. As described previously, Snyder's (1994) conceptualization of hope suggests a model composed of three cognitive components: goals, agency, and pathways. Goals are considered the targets or endpoints of mental action sequences and, as such, form the anchor of hope theory (Snyder, Ilardi, Michael, et al., 2000). Pathways, which are the routes toward desired goals, are necessary to attain goals and navigate around obstacles. Finally, agency taps the motivation that is necessary to begin and sustain movement toward goals. Given these definitions, it seems plausible that working alliance goals coincide with hope goal thoughts, tasks coincide with pathways, and the bond translates to agency (Lopez, Floyd, Ulven, & Snyder, 2000). Indeed, empirical research has supported this theoretical relationship between the working alliance and hope and their components (i.e., tasks and pathways, bond and agency; Magyar-Moe, Edwards, & Lopez, 2001). Although the causality cannot be determined through correlational data, the large amount of shared variance ($r = 0.48$) between these two models suggests that increasing an individual's level of hope also may increase working alliance ratings and vice versa. Thus, working to build hopeful alliances seems appropriate, given the many positive correlations among the working alliance, hope, and various positive outcomes (Horvath & Greenberg, 1994; Martin, Garske, & Davis, 2000; Snyder, 2000b).

FORMAL STRATEGIES

Working alliance and hope researchers have outlined what it takes to form a productive therapeutic relationship and have described how a sound relationship is associated with beneficial change. Indeed, Bordin (1994) stated that negotiation between the client and therapist about the change goal that is most relevant to the client's struggle is essential. Such negotiation depends largely on the bonding component, defined as the positive personal attachment between the client and the therapist that results from working together on a shared activity. Bonding in therapy usually is expressed in terms of liking, trusting, and respect for one another, in addition to a feeling of mutual commitment and understanding in the activity (Bordin, 1994). Such a relationship mirrors that required for begetting hope. According to Snyder et al. (1997), hope flourishes when people develop a strong bond to one or more caregivers, allowing the person to perceive himself or herself as having some sense of control in the world. "As social creatures, we need to confide in someone about our dreams and goals" (Rodriguez-Hanley & Snyder, 2000, p. 46). Thus, it seems that for both the therapeutic alliance and for hope to develop, a supportive environment is needed in which people receive basic instruction in goal pursuits from a positive model (Snyder, 2000b).

Building the working alliance based on hope theory principles seems in order, given that the goal of connecting with other people is fundamental, that the seeking of an individual's goals almost always occurs within the context of social commerce (Snyder et al., 2002), and that goal-directed thinking virtually always develops in the context of other people who teach hope (Snyder, 2000b). Indeed, Lopez, Floyd, et al. (2000) state that hope-enhancement strategies "are designed to help clients in conceptualizing clearer goals, producing numerous pathways to attainment, summoning the mental energy to maintain the goal pursuit, and reframing insurmountable obstacles as challenges to be overcome. The hopeful therapeutic relationship facilitates these hope components" (p. 123).

Taken together, the working alliance and hope literature suggests that building a hopeful alliance involves:

- Respectfully negotiating flexible therapeutic goals
- Generating numerous and varied pathways to goal attainment
- Translating the sense of connectedness between therapist and client into the mental energy necessary to sustain pursuit toward therapeutic goals

INFORMAL STRATEGIES

Based on the assumption that hope begets more hope, hopeful familial relationships and friendships could serve as hope-enhancing agents. Clients could benefit from evaluating their relationships and determining which generate mental energy that facilitates coping and those that drain this energy. Though data about hope in friendships, siblingships, and marriages have not been collected, the infectious nature of hope in such contexts has been assumed (Snyder, 1994). Therefore, therapists should encourage the development of new relationships that increase the hope in an individual's life. Associating with individuals who are supportive of goal pursuits, who challenge their peers to pursue stretch goals, and who encourage those peers to overcome barriers may help people crystallize their hopeful thought.

HOPE ENHANCING

All individuals inherently possess hope (Snyder et al., 1991, 1997). Nevertheless, there is variability in terms of the level of hope that one individual might possess as compared to a peer. Research has shown that children, adolescents, and adults with higher levels of hope do better in school and athletics, have better health, have better problem-solving skills, and are more adjusted psychologically (Snyder, 2002; Snyder, Cheavens, & Michael, 1999). As such, enhancing hope may have much benefit for these individuals. As people chart their own paths through life, a sense of hope can assist them in making good decisions about their goals.

FORMAL STRATEGIES

One of the first interventions aimed at increasing hope in children was developed by McDermott and Hastings (2000). This program involved eight weekly sessions with first- through sixth-grade students at a culturally diverse elementary school. During each week of this program, students were presented with information about hope and goal-setting, as well as stories about high-hope children. Through hearing and discussing these stories each week for 30 minutes, children had the opportunity to identify goals in the lives of protagonists, as well as to apply the hope concepts to their own lives. Evaluation of the program was conducted through comparing pre- and posttest hope scores for the intervention group to a control group of students, and results demonstrated that there were modest gains. Furthermore, teacher ratings of students' levels of hope were significantly higher at posttest, suggesting that they perceived increases in their students' levels of hopeful thinking. McDermott and Hastings concluded that an eight-week session was not sufficient time to instill high hope, but they considered their results promising.

Another elementary school intervention, *Making Hope Happen for Kids* (Edwards & Lopez, 2000), was developed to enhance hope in fourth-grade students. This five-session program, based on the general format of the junior high school program (described subsequently), involves age-appropriate activities and lessons related to learning about hope and applying this construct to children's lives. During this five-session program, which was conducted in several classrooms, two graduate student cofacilitators led groups of 7 to 10 students in various activities and lessons.

The first week of the program involved learning about the hope model and acting out the parts of the model with laminated props. Students pretended to be goals, obstacles, pathways, and willpower (i.e., agency) in a brief psychodrama depicting meaningful goal pursuits. In the second week, children were introduced to a story that described a young girl navigating obstacles as she worked toward the goal of learning lines for her school play. The third week of the program involved the *Hope Game* (a board game depicting multiple goal pursuits), during which children identified obstacles, pathways, and agency thoughts as they worked in teams to accomplish a shared goal. During the fourth week, children designed hope cartoons, emphasizing hopeful language. Finally, during the last week of the program, children were asked to write hope stories describing the goals on which they had been working and then share their stories with one another; they then enjoyed snacks to celebrate the end of the program.

Evaluation of the program was conducted at the end of the first and second years. The Children's Hope Scale (Snyder et al., 1997) was administered before and after delivery of the intervention with all children. While the evaluation of this program did not include a control group, comparisons of means at pre- and posttest demonstrated significant gains in hope scores in the fourth-grade students. Thus, hope was enhanced in these young children.

Pedrotti, Lopez, and Krieshok (2000) developed a program for seventh graders designed to enhance hope through five weekly 45-minute sessions. Assistance from classroom teachers allowed this version of the *Making Hope Happen* program to be integrated into the regular school day as a part of a family consumer sciences course. Groups consisting of 8 to 12 students were formed, and each was facilitated by two graduate student leaders. The program was designed to enhance the hope inherent in these youth by teaching them about the hope model.

The five sessions were developed to take these adolescents through the hope model step by step. During the first session, students were taught about the hope model in general, through the use of posters and cartoons. Pictorial representations were used to exemplify the different components to help students to commit these to memory. In addition, in this first session, two narratives depicting characters with high levels of hope were read. Group discussions followed in which the children delineated the behaviors that the characters had exhibited that corresponded to these hope components. Students also were placed in partnerships called *Hope Buddies* on this first day. These pairs were designed to help students to work with a peer to talk about their goals for the future. Finally, participants formed their own goals on which to work for the coming weeks. Goals varied from student to student, with some being very long term ("I want to graduate from an Ivy League college"), and others more short term ("I will keep my locker clean for five weeks"). All goals were treated as equal in terms of importance, and an emphasis was placed on the *process* as opposed to the actual *achievement* of the goal.

In week two, the tenets learned during the first week were reemphasized through the use of more narratives and exercises. Youth were taught about G-POWER this week as well. Each letter of this acronym was used to remind students of the various components of the hope model and to emphasize the goal-seeking process. Each letter was accompanied by a question designed to assist participants as they talked through this process (see Table 24.1).

During the third week, the components of the hope model were reinforced through other forms of media—including the use of a board game (*The Hope Game*) developed specifically for use in the program. Differing forms of media were used throughout the program to tap into the many different learning styles. In week four, the group moved to a more individual focus to work more closely on goals relevant for each student. During this week, the concept of *Hope Talk* was introduced in which group leaders explained that the statements we tell ourselves about our goals often influence our goal pursuit process in general. Participants were then asked to determine if particular statements made by historical figures, book characters, and sports stars were of a hopeful or unhopeful nature. Individual worksheets emphasizing hopeful language were also completed during this portion of the program.

Table 24.1
G-POWER

G	What is the character's **G**oal?
P	Which **P**athways does the character identify to use to move toward his or her stated goal?
O	What **O**bstacles lay in the character's pathway?
W	What source of **W**illpower is keeping the character energized in this process?
E	Which pathway did the character **E**lect to follow?
R	**R**ethink the process—would you have made the same decisions and choices?

In the last activity of the fourth session, the students began to write their personal hope stories. From the goals formed during the first session, the students were asked to think about each of the components in the hope model. Separate paragraphs were written for each session, and the finished product was a short essay that told the story of students' progress and listed their future steps toward this goal. Each student read his or her hope story to the group during the fifth and final session.

As to program evaluation, before the first session, all participants were administered the CHS (Snyder et al., 1997). At the conclusion of the program, the CHS again was administered to the junior high students. Scores were then compared to those found on the CHS given to a group who had not participated in the program. When analyzed statistically, the participants in the program had significantly higher levels of hope in comparison to their counterparts who did not participate in the program. As such, the program appeared to enhance the hope in these children. In a follow-up study, the higher hope levels were maintained after six months, pointing to the robustness of the intervention results even after the program was completed. Therefore, apparently, the participants continued to use the tools taught to them during the *Making Hope Happen* program.

Group and individual hope enhancement strategies for adults also have been developed and evaluated. Three groups (Cheavens, Gum, Feldman, Michael, & Snyder, 2001; Irving et al., in press; Klausner et al., 1998) have conducted intervention studies. Klausner et al. demonstrated that depressed older adults benefited from group therapy focused on goal setting and increasing the production of pathways and agency through actual work on reasonable goals, discussion of the process, and weekly homework assignments. Hopelessness and anxiety lessened significantly, whereas state hope increased reliably. Moreover, in comparison to members of a reminiscence therapy group, members of the hope-focused group experienced a more substantial decrease in depressive symptomatology. Irving et al. demonstrated that a five-week pretreatment orientation group focusing on hope had benefits for a group of incoming clients who were in need of assistance. Those lower in hope reported the greater responsiveness (as suggested by scores on measures of well-being, level of functioning, coping, and symptomatology) to the hope-focused orientation. Cheavens et al., in their work with college-age distressed adults, implemented an eight-session, closed group that was successful in reducing depressive and anxious symptoms and increasing hope.

Hope interventions also may be used with adults in relationship enrichment (Worthington et al., 1997). This type of intervention focuses on a mutual goal as defined by the presenting couple and enhances the relationship via growth, communication, and a mutual level of commitment to the identified goal. Outcomes of this program include increased partner satisfaction of adjustment and quality of couple skills, and higher satisfaction was maintained at a three-week follow-up. An additional follow-up study (Ripley & Worthington, 2002) indicated that the hope-focused intervention was particularly effective in increasing the ratio of positive to negative communications between couples.

INFORMAL STRATEGIES

It is probable that many clinicians already have incorporated hope theory tenets into their interventions. Hence, we encourage clinicians to reflect on their practice and identify those strategies that work to enhance hopeful thinking. Sharing a list with other clinicians can serve to improve your strategies and generate more resources.

Snyder, McDermott, Cook, and Rapoff's (2002) *Hope for the Journey: Helping Children through Good Times and Bad* and McDermott and Snyder's (1999) *Making Hope Happen: A Workbook for Turning Possibilities into Realities* and *The Great Big Book of Hope* (2000) provide well-conceptualized examples of how to engage clients and students in a therapeutic process focused on hope. For convenience, we have summarized the basic principles and steps of an informal approach to enhancing hope in the therapeutic context in Table 24.2.

The Psychology of Hope, Snyder's (1994) first book on the topic, provides numerous recommendations for enhancing hope that a clinician can share with a client. Table 24.3 provides suggestions for increasing pathways thinking. Agency thinking, which can be stimulated by having clients engage in the behavior that engenders the energy needed to pursue goals along selected pathways, is also addressed in Table 24.3.

HOPE REMINDING

Hope reminding could be thought of as a feedback loop for the therapeutic process. It is this strategy that encourages clients to become their own hope-enhancing agents. Over the course of therapy or psychoeducational sessions, clients become facile at finding hope through narratives and assessment, at bonding with their therapists and others who generate hopeful thoughts, and at enhancing their levels of hope through narrative, solution-focused, and cognitive-behavioral techniques. With the use of hope-reminding strategies, effortful daily use of hopeful cognitions is promoted.

FORMAL STRATEGIES

Being able to identify goal thoughts as well as barrier thoughts is a key element of the hope-reminding process. These thoughts serve as cues for the client to initiate the cognitive feedback loop. Self-monitoring techniques can be used to respond to these cues and for facilitating hopeful reminding. When the client has become adept at identifying cognitive cues of goal and barrier thoughts (this may occur

Table 24.2
Steps to Enhancing Hope in Adult Clients

I. Administration of the Adult Hope Scale (trait)

The first step in this process is the completion of the Adult Hope Scale. The therapist then tallies the total score and computes subscale scores for both pathway and agency.

II. Learning about Hope

Once a baseline hope score is determined, the therapist can then discuss hope theory with the client and its relevance to the therapy process and to positive outcomes.

III. Structuring Hope for the Client

In this step, the client creates a list of important life components, determines which areas are most important, and discusses the level of satisfaction within those areas.

IV. Creating Positive and Specific Goals

Using the important life components identified above, the client and therapist work together to create workable goals that are both positive and specific. These goals should be salient to the client and attainable. Additionally, the client develops multiple pathways for each goal and identifies agency thoughts for each goal.

V. Practice makes Perfect

Once the client and therapist have agreed on these goals, clients should visualize and verbalize the steps to reach their goals. With this practice, the client and therapist can collaborate on the most effective pathways and the agency behind the goals.

VI. Checking In

Clients incorporate these goals, pathways, and agency into their lives and report back to the therapist on the process of goal attainment. Again, collaboration can occur to adjust or modify any disparities in actions or thinking that may hinder the successful achievement of their desired goals.

This process is cyclical and requires continual assessment by both the client and the therapist. Once clients have grasped the concepts of hope theory, however, they can then assume the bulk of responsibility in the implementation of hope theory to their unique experiences.

---

early in treatment, or it may be a treatment goal that is difficult to attain), the therapist should encourage the client to use mini-interventions in sessions and outside of sessions. These mini-interventions should be selected by the therapist and the client on the basis of what has worked for the client in the past. Examples of mini-interventions include:

- Reviewing a favorite hope narrative
- Constructing and completing a brief automatic thought record that refines goals and confronts barrier thoughts
- Reviewing the personal hope statement
- Bonding with a hopeful person and meeting to discuss current goals and barriers

Table 24.3

Checklist for Enhancing Pathways and Agency in Adults

Pathways

DO

Break a long-range goal into steps or subgoals.

Begin your pursuit of a distant goal by concentrating on the first subgoal.

Practice making different routes to your goals and select the best one.

Mentally rehearse scripts for what you would do should you encounter a blockage.

If you need a new skill to reach your goal, learn it.

Cultivate two-way friendships where you can give and get advice.

DON'T

Think you can reach your big goals all at once.

Be too hurried in producing routes to your goals.

Be rushed to select the best or first route to your goal.

Overthink with the idea of finding one perfect route to your goal.

Conclude you are lacking in talent or are no good when an initial strategy fails.

Get into friendships where you are praised for not coming up with solutions to your problems.

Agency

DO

Tell yourself that you have chosen the goal, so it is your job to go after it.

Learn to talk to yourself in positive voices (e.g., I can do this!).

Recall your previous successful goal pursuits, particularly when you are in a jam.

Be able to laugh at yourself, especially if you encounter some impediment to your goal pursuits.

Find a substitute goal when the original goal is blocked solidly.

Enjoy the process of getting to your goals and do not focus only on the final attainment.

DON'T

Allow yourself to be surprised repeatedly by roadblocks that appear in your life.

Try to squelch totally any internal put-down thoughts because this may only make them stronger.

Get impatient if your willful thinking doesn't increase quickly.

Conclude that things never will change, especially if you are down.

Engage in self-pity when faced with adversity.

Stick to a blocked goal when it is truly blocked.

Constantly ask yourself how you are doing to evaluate your progress toward a goal.

Clients can use these interventions on a daily basis each time they become aware of a significant goal thought or barrier thought.

INFORMAL STRATEGIES

Increasing clients' cognizance of goal and barrier thoughts, effectively modeling full-scale versions of interventions during sessions, and helping clients choose and refine mini-interventions are the therapists' "how to's" of hope reminding. Clients make effortful daily use of hopeful cognitions by responding to cognitive cues with hope-assessing and hope-enhancing interventions. (See Tennen & Affleck, 1999, for a discussion of benefit-finding and -reminding, processes that influenced the development of the hope-reminding strategy.)

CONCLUDING COMMENTS AND RECOMMENDATIONS

Strategies for accentuating hope have been incorporated into a clinical approach called *hope therapy* (Lopez, Floyd, Ulven, & Snyder, 2000). Hope therapy was developed in response to a call by clinicians for a systematic application of hope theory principles in a therapeutic context. Though it may be considered a manualized intervention, it is undergirded by the assumption that common factors account for psychological change (see, e.g., Luborsky et al., 2002).

Despite the existence of dozens of strategies for accentuating hope, the development of hope therapy, and 15 years of scientific examination of hope theory and its application, many clinical needs and questions are yet to be rigorously considered. Our recommendations for future work in the area are arranged according to the categories of strategies: finding, bonding, enhancing, and reminding.

Hope Finding

- Develop and validate a children's version of the state hope scale to account for static changes in hopeful thinking and to round out the selection of hope measures.
- Identify novel methods of detecting hope during clinical intake and orientation procedures.

Hope Bonding

- Examine the possible cause-effect relationship associated with high-hope therapists sharing agency with low-hope clients.
- Determine if a hope contagion exists among high-hope groups of friends.

Hope Enhancing

- Refine techniques to orient clients to the hopeful pursuit of therapeutic goals via low cost, brief video, CD-ROM, or web-based psychoeducation that could be administered before the first therapy session.
- Examine the effectiveness of hope therapy as a specific clinical approach.

Hope Reminding

- Develop and examine hope booster sessions that could be facilitated during a brief office visit or over the telephone or other media.

- Identify effective hope-reminding procedures that clients have developed over the six-month course following the termination of therapy.

Continued focus on hope as a change agent and the effectiveness of hope-accentuating strategies is needed. Hope is a human strength that fuels our pursuit of the good life. The more we understand about hope, the closer we get to a good life for all.

APPENDIX A

Children's Hope Scale

Directions: Read each item carefully. Using the scale shown below, please select the number that best describes YOU and put that number in the blank provided.

1	2	3	4	5	6
None of the time	A little of the time	Some of the time	A lot of the time	Most of the time	All of the time

_____ 1. I think I am doing pretty well.

_____ 2. I can think of many ways to get the things in life that are most important to me.

_____ 3. I am doing just as well as other kids my age.

_____ 4. When I have a problem, I can come up with lots of ways to solve it.

_____ 5. I think the things I have done in the past will help me in the future.

_____ 6. Even when others want to quit, I know that I can find ways to solve the problem.

Note: From "The development and validation of the Children's Hope Scale," by C. R. Snyder, B. Hoza, W. E. Pelham, M. Rapoff, L. Ware, M. Danovsky, et al., 1997, *Journal of Pediatric Psychology, 22,* pp. 399–421. Reprinted with permission.

APPENDIX B

Adult Dispositional Hope Scale

Directions: Read each item carefully. Using the scale shown below, please select the number that best describes YOU and put that number in the blank provided.

1 = Definitely False   2 = Mostly False   3 = Mostly True   4 = Definitely True

_____ 1. I can think of many ways to get out of a jam.

_____ 2. I energetically pursue my goals.

_____ 3. I feel tired most of the time.

_____ 4. There are lots of ways around any problem.

_____ 5. I am easily downed in an argument.

_____ 6. I can think of many ways to get the things in life that are most important to me.

_____ 7. I worry about my health.

_____ 8. Even when others get discouraged, I know I can find a way to solve the problem.

_____ 9. My past experiences have prepared me well for my future.

_____10. I've been pretty successful in life.

_____11. I usually find myself worrying about something.

_____12. I meet the goals that I set for myself.

Notes: When we administer this scale, we call it the "Goals Scale" rather than the "Hope Scale" because on some initial occasions when giving the scale, people became interested in the fact that hope could be measured and wanted to discuss this issue rather than take the scale. No such problems have been encountered with the rather mundane "Goals Scale." Items 3, 5, 7, and 11 are distracters and are not used for scoring. The pathways subscale score is the sum of items 1, 4, 6, and 8; the agency subscale is the sum of items 2, 9, 10, and 12. Hope is the sum of the four pathways and four agency items. In our original studies, we used a four-point response continuum, but to encourage more diversity in scores in our more recent studies, we have used the eight-point scale:

1 = Definitely False	2 = Mostly False	3 = Somewhat False	4 = Slightly False
5 = Slightly True	6 = Somewhat True	7 = Mostly True	8 = Definitely True

Scores using the four-point continuum can range from a low of 8 to a high of 32. For the eight-point continuum, scores can range from a low of 8 to a high of 64.

Note: From "The Will and the Ways: Development and Validation of an Individual Differences Measure of Hope," by C. R. Snyder, C. Harris, J. R. Anderson, S. A. Holleran, L. M. Irving, S. T. Sigmon, L. Yoshinobu, J. Gibb, C. Langelle, and P. Harney, 1991, *Journal of Personality and Social Psychology, 60,* pp. 570–585. The scale can be used for research or clinical purposes without contacting the author. Reprinted with permission of the American Psychological Association and the senior author of the scale.

REFERENCES

Bandura, A. (1982). Self-efficacy mechanism in human agency. *American Psychologist, 37,* 122–147.

Bordin, E. S. (1979). The generalizability of the psychoanalytic concept of the working alliance. *Psychotherapy: Theory, Research, and Practice, 16,* 252–260.

Bordin, E. S. (1994). Theory and research on the therapeutic working alliance: New directions. In A. O. Horvath & L. S. Greenberg (Eds.), *The working alliance: Theory, research, and practice* (pp. 13–37). New York: Wiley.

Cheavens, J., Gum, A., Feldman, D. B., Michael, S. T., & Snyder, C. R. (2001, August). *A group intervention to increase hope in community sample.* Poster presented at the annual convention of the American Psychological Association, San Francisco.

Covington, M. V. (2000). Goal theory, motivation, and school achievement: An integrative review. *Annual Review of Psychology, 51,* 171–200.

Dweck, C. S. (1999). *Self-theories: Their role in motivation, personality, and development.* Philadelphia: Psychology Press.

Edwards, L. M., & Lopez, S. J. (2000). *Making hope happen for kids.* Unpublished protocol, University of Kansas, Lawrence.

Frank, J. D. (1968). The role of hope in psychotherapy. *International Journal of Psychiatry, 5,* 383–395.

Frank, J. D. (1975). The faith that heals. *Johns Hopkins Medical Journal, 137,* 127–131.

Heppner, P. P., & Petersen, C. H. (1982). The development and implications of a personal problem-solving inventory. *Journal of Counseling Psychology, 29,* 66–75.

Horvath, A. O., & Greenberg, L. S. (Eds.). (1994). *The working alliance: Theory, research, and practice.* New York: Wiley.

Howard, K. I., Krause, M. S., Saunders, S. M., & Koptka, S. M. (1997). Trials and tribulations in the meta-analysis of treatment differences: Comment on Wampold et al. (1997). *Psychological Bulletin, 122,* 221–225.

Irving, L. M., Cheavens, J., Snyder, C. R., Gravel, L., Hanke, J., Hilberg, P., et al. (in press). The relationships between hope and outcomes at pretreatment, beginning, and later phases of psychotherapy. *Journal of Psychotherapy Integration.*

Klausner, E. J., Clarkin, J. F., Spielman, L., Pupo, C., Abrams, R., & Alexopoulos, G. S. (1998). Late-life depression and functional disability: The role of goal-focused group psychotherapy. *International Journal of Geriatric Psychiatry, 13,* 707–716.

Lopez, S. J., Ciarlelli, R., Coffman, L., Stone, M., & Wyatt, L. (2000). Diagnosing for strengths: On measuring hope building blocks. In C. R. Snyder (Ed.), *Handbook of hope: Theory, measures, and interventions* (pp. 57–85). San Diego, CA: Academic Press.

*Lopez, S. J., Floyd, R. K., Ulven, J. C., & Snyder, C. R. (2000). Hope therapy: Helping clients build a house of hope. In C. R. Snyder (Ed.), *Handbook of hope: Theory, measures, and applications* (pp. 123–166). San Diego, CA: Academic Press.

Luborsky, L., Rosenthal, R., Diguer, L., Andrusnya, T. P., Berman, J. S., Levitt, J. T., et al. (2002). The dodo verdict is alive and well—mostly. *Clinical Psychology: Science and Practice, 9,* 2–12.

Magaletta, P. R., & Oliver, J. M. (1999). The hope construct, will, and ways: Their relations with self-efficacy, optimism, and general well-being. *Journal of Clinical Psychology, 55,* 539–551.

Magyar-Moe, J. L., Edwards, L. M., & Lopez, S. J. (2001, March). *A new look at the working alliance: Is there a connection with hope?* Paper presented at the Division 17 National Counseling Psychology Conference, Houston, Texas.

Martin, D. J., Garske, J. P., & Davis, M. K. (2000). Relation of the therapeutic alliance with outcome and other variables: A meta-analytic review. *Journal of Consulting and Clinical Psychology, 68,* 438–450.

McDermott, D., & Hastings, S. (2000). Children: Raising future hopes. In C. R. Snyder (Ed.), *Handbook of hope: Theory, measures, and interventions* (pp. 185–199). San Diego, CA: Academic Press.

McDermott, D., & Snyder, C. R. (1999). *Making hope happen.* Oakland, CA: New Harbinger.

McDermott, D., & Snyder, C. R. (2000). *The great big book of hope: Help your children achieve their dreams.* Oakland, CA: New Harbinger.

Menninger, K. (1959). The academic lecture on hope. *American Journal of Psychiatry, 190,* 481–491.

Pedrotti, J. T., Lopez, S. J., & Krieshok, T. (2000). *Making hope happen: A program for fostering strengths in adolescents.* Manuscript submitted for publication.

Peterson, C. (2000). The future of optimism. *American Psychologist, 55,* 44–55.

Ripley, J. S., & Worthington, E. L. (2002). Hope-focused and forgiveness-based group interventions to promote marital enrichment. *Journal of Counseling and Development, 80,* 452–463.

Rodriguez-Hanley, A., & Snyder, C. R. (2000). The demise of hope: On losing positive thinking. In C. R. Snyder (Ed.), *Handbook of hope: Theory, measures, and applications* (pp. 39–56). San Diego, CA: Academic Press.

Scheier, M. F., & Carver, C. S. (1985). Optimism, coping, and health: Assessment and implications of generalized outcome expectancies. *Health Psychology, 4,* 219–247.

Snyder, C. R. (1989). Reality negotiation: From excuses to hope and beyond. *Journal of Social and Clinical Psychology, 8,* 130–157.

*Snyder, C. R. (1994). *The psychology of hope: You can get there from here.* New York: Free Press.

*Snyder, C. R. (Ed.). (2000a). *Handbook of hope: Theory, measures, and applications.* San Diego, CA: Academic Press.

*Snyder, C. R. (2000b). The past and possible futures of hope. *Journal of Social and Clinical Psychology, 19,* 11–28.

Snyder, C. R. (2002). Hope theory: Rainbows in the mind. *Psychological Inquiry, 13,* 249–275.

Snyder, C. R., Cheavens, J., & Michael, S. T. (1999). Hoping. In C. R. Snyder (Ed.), *Coping: The psychology of what works* (pp. 205–231). New York: Oxford University Press.

Snyder, C. R., Harris, C., Anderson, J. R., Holleran, S. A., Irving, L. M., Sigmon, S. T., et al. (1991). The will and the ways: Development and validation of an individual-differences measure of hope. *Journal of Personality and Social Psychology, 60,* 570–585.

Snyder, C. R., Hoza, B., Pelham, W. E., Rapoff, M., Ware, L., Danovsky, M., et al. (1997). The development and validation of the Children's Hope Scale. *Journal of Pediatric Psychology, 22,* 399–421.

Snyder, C. R., Ilardi, S., Cheavens, J., Michael, S. T., Yamhure, L., & Sympson, S. (2000). The role of hope in cognitive behavior therapies. *Cognitive Therapy and Research, 24,* 747–762.

*Snyder, C. R., Ilardi, S., Michael, S. T., & Cheavens, J. (2000). Hope theory: Updating a common process for psychological change. In C. R. Snyder & R. E. Ingram (Eds.), *Handbook of psychological change: Psychotherapy processes and practices for the 21st century* (pp. 128–153). New York: Wiley.

Snyder, C. R., McDermott, D., Cook, W., & Rapoff, M. (2002). *Hope for the journey* (Rev. ed.). Clinton Corners, NY: Percheron Press.

Snyder, C. R., Rand, K. L., & Sigmon, D. R. (2002). Hope theory: A member of the positive psychology family. In C. R. Snyder & S. J. Lopez (Eds.), *Handbook of positive psychology* (pp. 257–266). New York: Oxford University Press.

Tennen, H., & Affleck, G. (1999). Finding benefits in adversity. In C. R. Snyder (Ed.), *Coping: The psychology of what works* (pp. 279–304). New York: Oxford University Press.

Worthington, E. L., Jr., Hight, T. L., Ripley, J. S., Perrone, K. M., Kurusu, T. A., & Jones, D. R. (1997). Strategic hope-focused relationship-enrichment counseling with individual couples. *Journal of Counseling Psychology, 44,* 381–389.

CHAPTER 25

A Clinical Approach to Posttraumatic Growth

RICHARD G. TEDESCHI and LAWRENCE G. CALHOUN

FOR ALMOST 20 years, we have been examining a phenomenon that has been recognized since ancient times: Suffering sometimes yields strengthening and growth (Tedeschi & Calhoun, 1995). It is a theme of many literary works, both ancient and modern, in religion and philosophy, and, more recently, it has been reported in the social and behavioral science literature. Pioneering thinkers such as Caplan (1964) and Frankl (1963) recognized the possibility that positive psychological change could occur in the context of highly stressful circumstances. In earlier empirical reports, growth associated with attempts to adapt to highly challenging events was examined as a peripheral factor (e.g., Andreasen & Norris, 1972; Lopata, 1973). More recently, we have considered how this process occurs in attempts to cope with bereavement (Calhoun & Tedeschi, 1989–1990; Calhoun, Tedeschi, Fulmer, & Harlan, 2000; Tedeschi & Calhoun, 2004; Tedeschi, Calhoun, Morrell, & Johnson, 1984), physical disability (Tedeschi & Calhoun, 1988), and war (Powell, Rosner, Butollo, Tedeschi, & Calhoun, 2003; Tedeschi, Calhoun, & Engdahl, 2001) and looked at how this process may affect entire societies (Tedeschi, 1999). The available data suggest that at least a significant minority of individuals facing a wide array of traumas, including loss of a home in a fire, divorce, the birth of a medically vulnerable child, sexual assault, bone marrow transplantation, military combat and captivity, diagnosis with HIV, and others, report some aspect of personal growth, and we have reviewed these reports in other places (Tedeschi & Calhoun, 1995, in press; Tedeschi, Park, & Calhoun, 1998; see also Linley & Joseph, 2004).

In this chapter, we briefly review the literature that shows that growth occurs in the aftermath of a variety of life crises and summarize ways of understanding how this growth occurs. We then explore how the therapy relationship can be a vehicle to promoting growth and noticing and enhancing personal strength at a time of vulnerability. We encourage therapists to use an existential-narrative-cognitive framework for approaching growth in clients.

THE CONCEPT OF POSTTRAUMATIC GROWTH

We coined the term *posttraumatic growth* (Tedeschi & Calhoun, 1996) to refer to these reports of positive changes in individuals that occur as the result of attempts to cope in the aftermath of traumatic life events. Other terms have been applied to the phenomenon of posttraumatic growth, including *stren conversion* (Finkel, 1974, 1975), *positive psychological changes* (Yalom & Lieberman, 1991), *perceived benefits* or *construing benefits* (Calhoun & Tedeschi, 1991; McMillen, Zuravin, & Rideout, 1995; Tennen, Affleck, Urrows, Higgins, & Mendola, 1992), *stress-related growth* (Park, Cohen, & Murch, 1996), *discovery of meaning* (Bower, Kemeny, Taylor, & Fahey, 1998), *positive emotions* (Folkman & Moskowitz, 2000), *flourishing* (Ryff & Singer, 1998), and *thriving* (O'Leary & Ickovics, 1995). Taylor and Brown (1988) have labeled similar outcomes as *positive illusions*. Coping mechanisms of *positive reinterpretation* (Scheier, Weintraub, & Carver, 1986), *drawing strength from adversity* (McCrae, 1984), and *transformational coping* (Aldwin, 1994; Pargament, 1996) have also been described. The term posttraumatic growth appears to capture the essentials of this phenomenon better than others because (1) it occurs most distinctively in conditions of severe crisis rather than lower-level *stress*; (2) it is often accompanied by transformative life changes that appear to go beyond *illusion*; (3) it, therefore, is experienced as an outcome rather than a *coping mechanism*; and (4) it requires a shattering of basic assumptions about an individual's life that *thriving* or *flourishing* does not imply.

Our conceptualization of posttraumatic growth and of the inclusion of these elements into psychological intervention relies on two elements: the growing, but still limited, literature on this phenomenon and our combined clinical experiences as practicing clinical psychologists. The empirical literature focused specifically on posttraumatic growth is rather recent and still small. And, when we rely on clinical experience, the possibility of inadvertent bias always exists. However, since our conceptualizations about posttraumatic growth have some data to support them, this way of thinking appears to offer a potentially helpful expansion of the way in which psychological interventions are done with persons struggling with trauma and its aftermath.

THE PARADOXICAL CHANGES OF POSTTRAUMATIC GROWTH

The kinds of positive changes individuals experience in their struggle with trauma are reflected in a measure of posttraumatic growth that we developed based on interviews with many trauma survivors (Tedeschi & Calhoun, 1996): improved relationships, new possibilities for their lives, a greater appreciation for life, a greater sense of personal strength, and spiritual development. There appears to be a basic paradox that is apprehended by trauma survivors who report these aspects of posttraumatic growth: *Their losses have produced something of value.*

We also find that other paradoxes are involved. For example, "I am more vulnerable, yet stronger." Individuals who experience negative life events not surprisingly tend to report an increased sense of vulnerability, congruent with the fact that they have suffered in ways they may not have been able to control or prevent (Janoff-Bulman, 1992). However, a common theme in the experience of persons who have faced major life challenges *is an increased sense of their own capacities to survive and prevail* (Calhoun & Tedeschi, 1999).

Another paradox often reported is that in the midst of suffering through the worst times in life, trauma survivors discover both the worst and best in others. People talk about finding out "who their real friends are" or "whom you can really count on." People often find themselves disappointed in the responses of some of those persons with whom they may have been close but, on the other hand, pleasantly surprised by the helpfulness of others they may not have been particularly close to. A need to talk about the traumatic events sets in motion tests of interpersonal relationships—some pass, others fail. Another aspect of this self-disclosure is that trauma survivors find themselves becoming *more comfortable with intimacy*. A further component of the interpersonal elements of posttraumatic growth is the experience of *greater sense of compassion* for others who experience life difficulties. Although this increased sense of compassion may extend to other persons generally, it seems to be particularly the case for others who experience similar life difficulties.

Individuals who face trauma, particularly trauma that reminds them of the mortality of themselves and others, may be more likely to become cognitively engaged with fundamental existential questions about death and the purpose of life. A commonly reported change is for the individual to *value the smaller things in life more* and the apparently more important things less. For example, family, friends, and small daily pleasures can be viewed as more important than before and perhaps are now seen as more important than others, such as working long hours at an occupation.

Issues of mortality that are faced through trauma also can produce important changes in the *religious, spiritual, and existential* components of philosophies of life. The specific content varies, contingent on the individual's initial belief system and the cultural contexts within which the struggle with a life crisis occurs. A common theme, however, is that after a period of spiritual or existential quest, individuals often report that *their philosophies of life are more fully developed, satisfying, and meaningful* to them. It appears that for many trauma survivors, a period of questioning their beliefs is ushered in because existential or spiritual issues have become more salient and less abstract. Although firm answers to the questions raised by trauma—Why do traumatic events happen? What is the point to my life now that this trauma has occurred? Why should I continue to struggle?—are not necessarily found, grappling with these issues often produces a satisfaction in trauma survivors that they are experiencing life at a deeper level of awareness. This may be part of a developing life wisdom (cf. Linley, 2003), particularly in terms of the "fundamental pragmatics of life" (Baltes & Freund, 2003; Baltes & Smith, 1990) and the further development of the individual's own life narrative (McAdams, 1993; Tedeschi & Calhoun, 1995). The reflections on traumas and their aftermath are often unpleasant, although necessary in reconstructing the life narrative and establishing a wiser perspective on living that accommodates these difficult circumstances. Therefore, posttraumatic growth does not *necessarily* yield less emotional distress.

POSTTRAUMATIC GROWTH, PSYCHOLOGICAL
COMFORT, AND SELF-ENHANCEMENT.

One of the areas in which there is some inconsistency in the empirical data is on the relationship between posttraumatic growth and the sense of psychological comfort (Park, 1998). Although some studies find some relationship between measures of distress and measures of growth, others do not. It appears that the experience of posttraumatic growth, and psychological distress and comfort, may be essentially separate dimensions. This is relevant to the clinical context, because individuals who experience significant levels of posttraumatic growth will not necessarily experience a commensurate decrease in their levels of distress nor an increase in their levels of happiness. Furthermore, the maintenance of the growth experienced may require periodic, unpleasant cognitive reminders of what has been lost, so in an apparently paradoxical way, what has been gained remains in focus as well. Posttraumatic growth may lead to a more fulfilling and meaningful life, but it seems not to be the same as simply being carefree, happy, or feeling good. Living a life at a deeper level of personal, interpersonal, and spiritual awareness is not necessarily the same as feeling good (cf. King, Eells, & Burton, Chapter 3, this volume).

Given that survivors of trauma may reflect on any of these aspects of posttraumatic growth, clinicians need to be prepared to grapple together with their clients as they address these issues. Clinicians need to appreciate paradox and ambiguity, the usefulness of thinking dialectically, and the patience necessary to process these concerns. Clinicians may also recognize some elements of self-enhancing bias at work in the experience of posttraumatic growth (McFarland & Alvaro, 2000). Our view, however, is that the clinician should approach such experiences on the part of their patients by accepting the reality of the experience for the individual. In addition, the available empirical evidence suggests that the self-ratings of growth on the part of individuals facing significant life challenges tend to be correlated with the ratings given to them by others (Park et al., 1996; Weiss, 2002), indicating that the experience of posttraumatic growth is more than the mere manifestation of a self-enhancing cognitive bias.

A CLARIFICATION ABOUT VIEWING TRAUMA AS BENEFICIAL

We interrupt our discussion with a perhaps unnecessary reminder that these traumatic events tend to produce a variety of distressing responses in the persons who experience them. These responses are almost always unpleasant, sometimes long lasting, and, for some people, the traumatic sets of circumstances may lead to the development of identifiable psychiatric disorders. It would be a misunderstanding to think that trauma is good—*we most certainly are not saying that.* What we are saying is that despite these distressing experiences, people often report positive transformations, what we have called posttraumatic growth. An important way to think about this, which has implications for clinical practice, is that the traumatic events set in motion attempts to cope and that the struggle in the *aftermath* of the trauma, *not the trauma itself,* produces the posttraumatic growth. In addition, the empirical evidence indicates that posttraumatic growth is common but certainly not universal, and as clinicians, we should never have the expectation that every trauma survivor will experience growth or that it is a necessary outcome for full trauma recovery.

THE PROCESS OF POSTTRAUMATIC GROWTH

A central theme of the life challenges that are the focus here is their *seismic* nature (Calhoun & Tedeschi, 1998). Much like earthquakes can impact the physical environment, the events that represent major life crises are those that severely shake, challenge, or sometimes shatter the individual's way of understanding the world (Janoff-Bulman, 1992). These seismic circumstances, characterized by their unusual, uncontrollable, potentially irreversible, and threatening qualities, can produce a severe upheaval in individuals' major assumptions about the world, their place in it, and how they make sense of their daily lives. When this shaking of the foundations of the individual's assumptive world (Parkes, 1970) reaches a sufficient catastrophic threshold, the individual can be thought of as experiencing a traumatic event. In our model of posttraumatic growth (Calhoun & Tedeschi, 1998; Tedeschi & Calhoun, 1995, in press), we emphasize that events must be of great enough impact to force individuals to reconsider the basic assumptions about who they are, what people around them are like, what kind of world they live in, or what the future may hold. In this reconsideration, there are the seeds for new perspectives on all these matters and a sense that valuable, though painful, lessons have been learned. From a narrative perspective, the story of an individual's life has been divided into before and after the traumatic event, and the person after is quite different from the person before (McAdams, 1993; Tedeschi & Calhoun, 1995). This is particularly so when trauma has produced a very strong challenge to, or has invalidated, higher order goals or schemas (Carver, 1998).

COGNITIVE ENGAGEMENT AND COGNITIVE PROCESSING

Shattered assumptive worlds, or schemas, must be reconstructed so that people have useful guides for their behaviors and choices. The necessity of rebuilding a more resilient set of schemas leads people who have experienced trauma to think repeatedly about their circumstances, a form of cognitive processing that is characterized by "making sense, problem solving, reminiscence, and anticipation" (Martin & Tesser, 1996, p. 192). In the encounter with a traumatic event, the individual's *cognitive engagement,* recurring ruminative thought, tends to reflect the lack of fit between what has happened and the individual's reaction on the one hand and the organizing schemas, beliefs, and life goals on the other hand. This repeated cognitive engagement with the elements that have been made salient by the crisis can lead to the recognition that certain life goals are no longer attainable, certain schemas no longer accurately reflect what is, and certain beliefs (e.g., *My world is safe.*) are no longer valid.

As individuals come to recognize that some goals are no longer attainable and some components of the assumptive world cannot assimilate the reality of the aftermath of the trauma, it is possible for them to begin to formulate new goals and to revise major components of the assumptive world in ways that acknowledge their changed life circumstances. To the extent that cognitive engagement produces these kinds of changes and the individual begins to experience a movement toward the achievement of new life goals, increased life satisfaction might be expected as a result (Little, 1998).

Individuals who face trauma often experience high levels of emotional distress, which for some persons can be debilitating. Our assumption is that for many persons, the level of emotional distress, which tends to be higher in the time following trauma, tends also to be accompanied by cognitive engagement that tends to be more automatic than deliberate. These are automatic processes of coping with negative emotional states, which, at the earlier stages, are more likely to have intrusive thoughts and intrusive images. As the individual's adaptive mechanisms become more effective at managing the high levels of emotional distress, eventually the reduction of distress and the process of ongoing cognitive engagement with trauma can lead to the adaptive disengagement from the goals and fundamental beliefs and assumptions that are no longer tenable. However, remember that for some persons, this process will take a long time, perhaps months or years. And, it is possible that for some persons, the attempt at adaptation to loss or trauma will never achieve a fully satisfactory psychological outcome (Wortman & Silver, 2001).

For many persons faced with major crises and losses, their circumstances tend to lead them to become cognitively engaged in two general domains: making sense of the immediate circumstances and making sense of the more fundamental elements of significance raised by the circumstances (Calhoun, Selby, & Selby, 1982; Davis, Nolen-Hoeksema, & Larson, 1998). The first domain reflects the process of attempting to understand the particular sequence of events that produced the set of circumstances with which the person must now cope. For example, what led a loved one to commit suicide, or what sequence of events produced a transportation accident? The second general domain reflects broader and more abstract concerns, often existential or spiritual in nature, about the fundamental meaning of circumstances of a person's life as they exist in the aftermath of a trauma. These two domains of making sense of trauma are interwoven to some degree, although dealing successfully with the first probably allows the trauma survivor to focus more on the second. Cognitive processing of trauma is not a neat process that can be easily reduced to a formula. There are many recursive and iterative aspects to it.

We are following the model of Martin and Tesser (1996), who describe this cognitive processing as conscious, that is, easily cued, but also occurring without direct cueing and involving attempts to make sense, problem solve, reminisce, or anticipate. There is some empirical suggestion that this kind of cognitive processing can be related to higher levels of posttraumatic growth. In one study, for example, young adults who had experienced major life stressors tended to report greater levels of posttraumatic growth when also reporting higher levels of cognitive engagement and processing recalled as occurring soon after crisis events (Calhoun, Cann, Tedeschi, & McMillan, 2000). In a study of the effects of journaling (Ullrich & Lutgendorf, 2002), university students who had been instructed to cognitively process their emotional responses, as compared to those instructed to focus on the facts or the associated emotions alone, reported higher levels of posttraumatic growth after four weeks. Although these sorts of findings are only suggestive, they are congruent with the view that significant cognitive engagement and processing of crisis-related elements tend to be associated with higher levels of posttraumatic growth.

DISCLOSURE, SUPPORT, AND NARRATIVE

The individual's cognitive engagement with and cognitive processing of trauma may be assisted by the disclosure of that internal process to others in socially supportive environments. The available evidence suggests that such disclosure, in the form of written communications, can have useful health benefits (Pennebaker, 1997). Written disclosure of trauma-related material can also have an impact on the extent of posttraumatic growth experienced when the focus is on the processing of cognitive and emotional elements (Ullrich & Lutgendorf, 2002). The degree to which individuals perceive their social contexts to either encourage and accept or inhibit and sanction their disclosure of trauma-related thoughts and feelings may play an important role in the process of posttraumatic growth. When persons affected by trauma perceive their significant others as not wanting to hear about their difficulties, cognitive processing may be inhibited. And, to the extent that the processes of cognitive engagement with crisis-related material are limited, it might be expected that crisis-related growth is less likely (Cordova, Cunningham, Carlson, & Andrykowski, 2001).

The experience of social constraints that inhibit the disclosure of trauma-related thoughts, particularly those thoughts that are troubling and intrusive, produces a reliable relationship between the occurrence of those thoughts and depression (Lepore & Helgeson, 1998; Lepore, Silver, Wortman, & Wayment, 1996). Persons who are engaging in significant levels of trauma-related cognitive processing, but who experience social constraints limiting or prohibiting such disclosure, appear to be at higher risk for dysphoric emotions in the aftermath of a major life crisis. Trauma survivors who are supported when they engage in the disclosure of their cognitive processing may not only be less likely to experience depression but also experience somewhat higher levels of posttraumatic growth (Nolen-Hoeksema & Larson, 1999). In addition, *the presence of a social environment that explicitly addresses and encourages growth* may be an important factor in promoting posttraumatic growth. The availability of examples of growth narratives in the immediate social environment, perhaps in stories about how others have been changed positively by their encounters with trauma or by exposure to others who have experienced similar difficulties and exhibit or describe ways in which their struggles have changed them, may enhance the likelihood that the individual will experience posttraumatic growth.

COGNITIVE PROCESSING, THE LIFE NARRATIVE, AND WISDOM

As individuals weave the experience of posttraumatic growth into the fabric of their life narratives (McAdams, 1993), the way they understand themselves and their lives can change. Trauma can become incorporated into the individual's own life story as a "reckoning time" that sets the stage for some fundamental changes in outlook (Tedeschi & Calhoun, 1995) or at least as "redemption sequences" (McAdams, Reynolds, Lewis, Patten, & Bowman, 2001) that are incorporated into life narratives. At some point, trauma survivors may be able to engage in a sort of metacognition, or reflection on their own processing of their life events, seeing themselves as having spent time making a major alteration of their understanding of themselves and their lives. This becomes part of the life narrative and includes an appreciation for new, more sophisticated ways of grappling with life events. This is part of how posttraumatic growth develops dynamically over time, and the processes that lead to its maintenance, and, for some, perhaps its abatement over time are dynamic also.

WAYS CLINICIANS CAN FACILITATE THE PROCESS OF POSTTRAUMATIC GROWTH

With a basic understanding of the variables involved in the process of posttraumatic growth, we can consider how a clinician can affect this process in useful ways. We have talked about clinicians playing roles as facilitators of this process, because posttraumatic growth is likely to be inhibited by heavy-handed attempts to move trauma survivors toward understandings they have not yet directly experienced (Calhoun & Tedeschi, 1999). The changes that trauma produces are experiential, not merely intellectual, which makes those changes so powerful for many trauma survivors. This is the same for posttraumatic growth—there is a compelling affective or experiential flavor to it that is important for the clinician to honor. Therefore, we see the clinician's role as often subtle in this facilitation. The clinician must be well attuned to the client when the client may be in the process of reconstructing schemas, thinking dialectically, recognizing paradox, and generating a revised life narrative. What follows here are some general guidelines for this process. See Calhoun and Tedeschi (1999) for more extensive discussion and case examples.

We emphasize that the clinical activity we recommend does not constitute a technique to be employed, nor is this a proposal for a new therapy school. The recommendation is that clinicians broaden their clinical perspectives so that elements of posttraumatic growth and the possibility of helping clients further develop it are part of the general clinical perspective they employ when trying to understand and assist persons who have been psychologically affected by a variety of events that might be considered traumatic for particular clients. Attention to elements of posttraumatic growth is compatible with a wide variety of the approaches that are currently used to provide help to persons dealing with trauma. Initially, clinicians should address high levels of emotional distress, providing the kind of support that can help make this distress manageable (Tedeschi & Calhoun, 1995). Allowing a distressed client to regain the ability to cognitively engage the aftermath of the trauma in a rather deliberate fashion will promote the possibility for posttraumatic growth. Then, it is likely that the domain the clinician may find most productive for a possible focus on elements of posttraumatic growth is the process of cognitive engagement, cognitive processing, and cognitive change, including narrative reconstruction.

GENERAL CONSIDERATIONS IN FACILITATING POSTTRAUMATIC GROWTH

Particularly when working with trauma survivors, who may be very distressed and vulnerable, it is important to use best clinical practices. These practices are critical to the facilitation of posttraumatic growth. We next highlight the relationship between these practices and how the clinician can act as a facilitator.

The Framework of the Trauma Survivor   Although for most clinicians the reminder is unnecessary, it is probably useful to repeat a general recommendation to make a good effort to understand the client's way of thinking about his or her trauma. We emphasize three aspects of the client's perspective that need to concern clinicians. First, it is imperative that *clinicians listen carefully to the language of crisis and psychological response that clients use and that they judiciously join the client in this form of communication.* Second, it is useful for clinicians to feel comfortable and willing to help their clients process their cognitive engagement with existential or spiritual matters. It is important *for clinicians to respect and work within the existential framework that clients have developed or are trying to rebuild in the aftermath of a trauma.* Another way in which the clinician should respect the client's framework, particularly when issues of posttraumatic growth are the focus, regards the acceptance of what the clinician may view as "positive illusions" (Taylor & Brown, 1988). Human beings generally tend to operate with certain benign cognitive distortions, and persons facing major crisis are probably not an exception. When working with clients dealing with traumatic circumstances, *clinicians may need to have some degree of tolerance and respect for the use of some benign cognitive biases.* Although the evidence tends to support the veracity of the posttraumatic growth, some clinicians may still be somewhat skeptical about the realistic foundations of the client's experience of growth. Although there certainly can be exceptions, our assumption is that clinical attempts to directly modify cognitions so that the benign "illusory" elements are corrected are likely to do psychological harm rather than to produce psychological benefit.

The Value of Effective Listening   As we have suggested, individuals in the aftermath of trauma exhibit a high level of cognitive engagement with and cognitive processing of their life situation. Such cognitive processes can lay the foundation for the development of the elements of posttraumatic growth. In addition, a skilled listener, who can encourage the individual to engage in disclosure of the trauma-related cognitive processing, can encourage the kinds of cognitive changes that not only enhance coping generally but also may promote posttraumatic growth. Although individual clients may need additional specific interventions designed to alleviate crisis-related psychological symptoms, we think that the clinical guideline of *listen without necessarily trying to solve* (Calhoun & Tedeschi, 1999) can be a helpful one. In fact, one way of ensuring that you practice this sort of approach is to relate to the trauma survivor in such a way that his or her story affects you personally. Being changed yourself as a result of listening to the story of the trauma and its aftermath communicates the highest degree of respect for clients and encourages them to see the value in their own experience. This acknowledged value is a short step away from posttraumatic growth.

Individuals who have been exposed to trauma may find it useful to tell their story repeatedly, and the clinician may need to listen patiently as the client repeats the story of what has happened. The individual's repetition of the account of the difficult experience can serve a safe exposure function when the difficulty is associated with an identifiable stimulus array, and this alone can have therapeutic value. The retelling of the account can also help the individual engage in the kinds of cognitive actions that can help the individual accommodate cognitive structure to the undeniable events, and in this process the possibility of discovering posttraumatic growth exists.

Although we are encouraging what may seem to be a rather passive clinical stance, the way the clinician listens and what the clinician listens to and attends to can have significant therapeutic consequences. Our assumption is that the clinician needs to be skilled at deciding the types of responses to make and what to encourage the client to say and do. For example, in listening to the repeated tellings of stories, clinicians may highlight the subtle changes in the tellings—details never included before, differences in the descriptors used, changes in the perspective taken, shifts in the affect displayed. Any such elements can be pointed out, especially when there is a hint of an emerging aspect of posttraumatic growth. Although compared to more structured approaches—what is suggested here does lack a certain degree of prescriptiveness—this general framework can certainly be woven into even rather prescriptive, manual-driven psychological interventions designed to help persons coping with the aftermath of trauma.

Listen For and Label Posttraumatic Growth

Clients routinely and spontaneously articulate ways in which their struggle has produced highly meaningful changes in them, without clinicians prompting them. However, our experience has been that only rarely do clients identify such changes as a representation of posttraumatic growth. A small but very useful change that clinicians can make in their work with persons who are dealing with trauma, then, is simply to *listen for themes of posttraumatic growth* in what their clients say. When clinicians notice and label as positive the positive changes that clients relate, this can be a therapeutic cognitive experience for the client. The clinician must have good knowledge of the domains and elements of posttraumatic growth, listen for and attend to the client's account of the experience of growth, and label the experience in a way that makes the growth experience cognitively salient for the client. However, *the clinician must guard against the mechanistic offering of empty platitudes* that tell the client, for example, what wonderful opportunities for growth are offered by the experience of trauma. If the clinician has listened well to the client's account of the circumstances and of the client's personal reactions, including affective, cognitive, and behavioral components, the insensitive and inappropriate offering of platitudes becomes extremely unlikely. What we are suggesting is that the clinician should respond in ways that reflect discoveries that their clients themselves are making. As we have implied, however, the way in which the client has cognitively constructed the posttraumatic experience may only implicitly reflect the experience of growth, and the clinician can highlight these statements that imply growth.

How and when a clinician chooses to highlight the posttraumatic growth that is emerging in a client is an important consideration. Just as a clinician could make insensitive remarks that come across as platitudes, getting the timing of remarks wrong can also have a counterproductive effect. Our experience suggests to us that very early in the posttrauma process is usually not a good time for attention to be directed toward the possibility of posttraumatic growth. The immediate aftermath of tragedy is a time during which clinicians must be particularly sensitive to the psychological needs of the patient and never engage in the insensitive introduction of didactic information or trite comments about growth coming from suffering. This is not to say that systematic treatment programs designed for trauma survivors should not include growth-related components, since these may indeed be helpful (Antoni et al., 2001). We have also described ways in which a posttraumatic growth perspective can be used even in critical incident stress management (Calhoun & Tedeschi, 2000). But we tend to think that, even as part of a systematic intervention program, matters related to growth are best addressed after the individual has had sufficient time to adapt to the aftermath of the trauma.

The Focus on the Struggle Rather Than the Trauma

For some trauma survivors, what has happened to them may have been so horrible and the aftermath may be so devastating that the very concept of posttraumatic growth may be repellant. Clinicians should respect that perspective. The available data, however, indicate that some individuals coping with even the most horrible events can experience some degree of posttraumatic growth (Tedeschi &

Calhoun, 1995). The clinician who is interested in the encouragement of growth that some clients may experience, then, must perform what on the surface may be a paradoxical task—to acknowledge the reality that for some persons the very discussion of growth coming from the struggle may be unacceptable given the horrific nature of what they have undergone; but, at the same time, the clinician should be open to the possibility that clients themselves may experience growth from their struggle with even the most tragic and traumatic sets of circumstances. To try to address this issue, a clinician may say, "You may have heard people say that they have found some benefit in their struggle with trauma. Given what has happened to you, do you think that is possible?" Also notice that in this question, the clinician makes a clear distinction between the events that have happened and the individual's *struggle* to survive psychologically and adapt to his or her painful circumstances. A useful way to speak of the possibility of growth is to use words that indicate that the experience of growth the patient may have undergone is a result *of the struggle* to adapt to the trauma and not to the situation itself.

Clinicians who work with trauma survivors often find themselves using metaphors in conversations with these clients because description of the traumatic events and their effects may be difficult to achieve in more straightforward language. Listening for metaphors a client uses or introducing metaphors that might be particularly salient for an individual allows for discussions of posttraumatic growth in these more indirect ways, allowing trauma survivors to acknowledge things that otherwise would be difficult. For example, we have described a case in which a photographer whose son died could recognize changes in himself as photos emerging from developing fluid (Calhoun & Tedeschi, 1999).

EXPOSURE TO MODELS OF POSTTRAUMATIC GROWTH

As we mentioned previously, trauma survivors may be better able to develop an ability to recognize, or even aspire to posttraumatic growth, if they are exposed to other survivors who have responded in this way. We have thus favored the use of group treatments for many trauma survivors (Tedeschi & Calhoun, 1995, 2004), with the expectation that the mutual help exchanged in such groups may also give trauma survivors an opportunity to experience the power of their own gifts of empathy and compassion learned from their trauma. We also have recommended a number of books and other resources that include growth themes in trauma survival (Calhoun & Tedeschi, 1999; Tedeschi & Calhoun, 1995, 2004).

A LITTLE PUSH TOWARD GROWTH

Without announcing to clients that we have any expectations for them to experience posttraumatic growth, we sometimes offer assignments that may allow them to begin to notice aspects of growth in their struggles. Writing assignments that encourage narrative development are often useful for trauma survivors (Resick & Calhoun, 2001), and in these narratives growth can emerge. We also have suggestions for assignments that involve self-monitoring of changing beliefs in the aftermath of trauma (Calhoun & Tedeschi, 1999). Focus on these assignments in subsequent therapy sessions can allow clinicians an opportunity to highlight emerging growth perspectives.

Caveats and Reminders

To clarify the clinical perspective in focusing on posttraumatic growth, we offer these reminders. Posttraumatic growth occurs in the context of suffering and significant psychological struggle, and a focus on this growth should not come at the expense of empathy for the pain and suffering of trauma survivors. For most trauma survivors, posttraumatic growth and distress coexist. Second, trauma is not necessary for growth. Individuals can mature and develop in meaningful ways without experiencing tragedy or trauma. Third, in no way are we suggesting that trauma is good. We regard life crises, loss, and trauma as undesirable, and our wish would be that nobody would have to experience such life events. We regard traumatic events as indeed negative, but the evidence suggests that individuals who struggle with them can experience highly meaningful personal changes. Fourth, posttraumatic growth is neither universal nor inevitable. Although a majority of individuals experiencing a wide array of highly challenging life circumstances experience posttraumatic growth, a significant number of persons experience little or no growth in their struggle with trauma. This sort of outcome is acceptable—we are not raising the bar on trauma survivors so that they are to be expected to show posttraumatic growth before being considered recovered.

CONCLUSION

Work with survivors of traumatic events from the growth perspective we have outlined is highly rewarding for clinicians. In listening to clients with respect for their strength and ability to change, we find ourselves changed for the better. We learn lessons along with our clients and find that many of our colleagues can also identify this vicarious posttraumatic growth (Arnold, Calhoun, Tedeschi, & Cann, 2000; Linley, Joseph, & Loumidis, 2003; Profitt, Calhoun, Tedeschi, & Cann, 2002). The model we have outlined allows us to share both the suffering and the possibilities with those who are being tempered by the fire.

REFERENCES

Aldwin, C. M. (1994). *Stress, coping, and development.* New York: Guilford Press.

Andreasen, N. L., & Norris, A. S. (1972). Long-term adjustment and adaptation mechanisms in severely burned adults. *Journal of Nervous and Mental Diseases, 154,* 352–362.

Antoni, M. H., Lehman, J. M., Kilbourn, K. M., Boyers, A. E., Yount, S. E., Culver, J. L., et al. (2001). Cognitive-behavioral stress management intervention decreases the prevalence of depression and enhances the sense of benefit among women under treatment for early stage breast cancer. *Health Psychology, 20,* 20–32.

Arnold, D., Calhoun, L. G., Tedeschi, R. G., & Cann, A. (2000, August). *Vicarious transformation in psychotherapy with trauma survivors.* Poster presented at the annual convention of the American Psychological Association, Washington, DC.

Baltes, P. B., & Freund, A. M. (2003). Human strengths as the orchestration of wisdom and selective optimization with compensation. In L. G. Aspinwall & U. M. Staudinger (Eds.), *A psychology of human strengths* (pp. 23–35). Washington, DC: American Psychological Association.

Baltes, P. B., & Smith, J. (1990). Toward a psychology of wisdom and its ontogenesis. In R. J. Sternberg (Ed.), *Wisdom: Its nature, origins, and development* (pp. 87–120). New York: Cambridge University Press.

Bower, J. E., Kemeny, M. E., Taylor, S. E., & Fahey, J. L. (1998). Cognitive processing, discovery of meaning, CD 4 decline, and AIDS-related mortality among bereaved HIV-seropositive men. *Journal of Consulting and Clinical Psychology, 66,* 979–986.

Calhoun, L. G., Cann, A., Tedeschi, R. G., & McMillan, J. (2000). A correlational test of the relationship between posttraumatic growth, religion, and cognitive processing. *Journal of Traumatic Stress, 13,* 521–527.

Calhoun, L. G., Selby, J. W., & Selby, L. E. (1982). The psychological aftermath of suicide: An analysis of current evidence. *Clinical Psychology Review, 2,* 409–420.

Calhoun, L. G., & Tedeschi, R. G. (1989–1990). Positive aspects of critical life problems: Recollections of grief. *Omega, 20,* 265–272.

Calhoun, L. G., & Tedeschi, R. G. (1991). Perceiving benefits in traumatic events: Some issues for practicing psychologists. *Journal of Training and Practice in Professional Psychology, 5,* 45–52.

Calhoun, L. G., & Tedeschi, R. G. (1998). Posttraumatic growth: Future directions. In R. G. Tedeschi, C. L. Park, & L. G. Calhoun (Eds.), *Posttraumatic growth: Positive change in the aftermath of crisis* (pp. 215–238). Mahwah, NJ: Erlbaum.

*Calhoun, L. G., & Tedeschi, R. G. (1999). *Facilitating posttraumatic growth: A clinician's guide.* Mahwah, NJ: Erlbaum.

*Calhoun, L. G., & Tedeschi, R. G. (2000). Early posttraumatic interventions: Facilitating possibilities for growth. In J. M. Volanti, D. Paton, & C. Dunning (Eds.), *Posttraumatic stress intervention: Challenges, issues and perspectives* (pp. 135–152). Springfield, IL: Charles C Thomas.

Calhoun, L. G., Tedeschi, R. G., Fulmer, D., & Harlan, D. (2000, August). *Parental grief: The relation of rumination, distress, and posttraumatic growth.* Poster presented at the annual convention of the American Psychological Association, Washington, DC.

Caplan, G. (1964). *Principles of preventive psychiatry.* New York: Basic Books.

Carver, C. S. (1998). Resilience and thriving: Issues, models, and linkages. *Journal of Social Issues, 54,* 245–266.

Cordova, M. J., Cunningham, L. L. C., Carlson, C. R., & Andrykowski, M. A. (2001). Posttraumatic growth following breast cancer: A controlled comparison study. *Health Psychology, 20,* 176–185.

Davis, C. G., Nolen-Hoeksema, S., & Larson, J. (1998). Making sense of loss and benefiting from the experience: Two construals of meaning. *Journal of Personality and Social Psychology, 75,* 561–574.

Finkel, N. J. (1974). Strens and traumas: An attempt at categorization. *American Journal of Community Psychology, 2,* 265–273.

Finkel, N. J. (1975). Strens, traumas and trauma resolution. *American Journal of Community Psychology, 3,* 173–178.

Folkman, S., & Moskowitz, J. T. (2000). Stress, positive emotion, and coping. *Current Directions in Psychological Science, 9,* 115–118.

Frankl, V. E. (1963). *Man's search for meaning.* New York: Pocket Books.

Janoff-Bulman, R. (1992). *Shattered assumptions.* New York: Free Press.

Lepore, S. J., & Helgeson, V. S. (1998). Social constraints, intrusive thoughts, and mental health after prostate cancer. *Journal of Social and Clinical Psychology, 17,* 89–106.

Lepore, S. J., Silver, R. C., Wortman, C. B., & Waymant, H. A. (1996). Social constraints, intrusive thoughts, and depressive symptoms among bereaved mothers. *Journal of Personality and Social Psychology, 70,* 271–282.

Linley, P. A. (2003). Positive adaptation to trauma: Wisdom as both process and outcome. *Journal of Traumatic Stress, 16,* 601–610.

Linley, P. A., & Joseph, S. (2004). Positive change following trauma and adversity: A review. *Journal of Traumatic Stress, 17,* 11–21.

Linley, P. A., Joseph, S., & Loumidis, K. (2003). *Trauma work, sense of coherence, and therapist changes: Direct and moderational relations.* Manuscript submitted for publication.

Little, B. R. (1998). Personal project pursuit: Dimensions and dynamics of personal meaning. In P. T. P. Wong & P. S. Fry (Eds.), *The human quest for meaning: A handbook of psychological research and clinical applications* (pp. 193–212). Mahwah, NJ: Erlbaum.

Lopata, H. Z. (1973). Self-identity in marriage and widowhood. *Sociological Quarterly, 14,* 407–418.

Martin, L. L., & Tesser, A. (1996). Clarifying our thoughts. In R. S. Wyer (Ed.), *Ruminative thought: Advances in social cognition* (Vol. 9, pp. 189–209). Mahwah, NJ: Erlbaum.

McAdams, D. P. (1993). *The stories we live by: Personal myths and the making of the self.* New York: Morrow.

McAdams, D. P., Reynolds, J., Lewis, M., Patten, A. H., & Bowman, P. J. (2001). When bad things turn good and good things turn bad: Sequences of redemption and contamination in life narrative and their relations to psychosocial adaptation in midlife adults and in students. *Personality and Social Psychology Bulletin, 27,* 474–485.

McCrae, R. R. (1984). Situational determinants of coping responses: Loss, threat, and challenge. *Journal of Personality and Social Psychology, 46,* 919–928.

McFarland, C., & Alvaro, C. (2000). The impact of motivation on temporal comparisons: Coping with traumatic events by perceiving personal growth. *Journal of Personality and Social Psychology, 79,* 327–343.

McMillen, C., Zuravin, S., & Rideout, G. (1995). Perceived benefits from child sexual abuse. *Journal of Consulting and Clinical Psychology, 63,* 1037–1043.

Nolen-Hoeksema, S., & Larson, J. (1999). *Coping with loss.* Mahwah, NJ: Erlbaum.

O'Leary, V. E., & Ickovics, J. R. (1995). Resilience and thriving in response to challenge: An opportunity for a paradigm shift in women's health. *Women's Health: Research on Gender, Behavior, and Policy, 1,* 121–142.

Pargament, K. I. (1996). Religious methods of coping: Resources for the conservation and transformation of significance. In E. P. Shafranske (Ed.), *Religion and the clinical practice of psychology* (pp. 215–240). Washington, DC: American Psychological Association.

Park, C. L. (1998). Implications of posttraumatic growth for individuals. In R. G. Tedeschi, C. L. Park, & L. G. Calhoun (Eds.), *Posttraumatic growth: Positive change in the aftermath of crisis* (pp. 153–177). Mahwah, NJ: Erlbaum.

Park, C. L., Cohen, L., & Murch, R. (1996). Assessment and prediction of stress-related growth. *Journal of Personality, 64,* 71–105.

Parkes, C. M. (1970). Psycho-social transitions: A field for study. *Social Science and Medicine, 5,* 101–115.

Pennebaker, J. W. (1997). *Opening up: The healing power of expressing emotions.* New York: Guilford Press.

Powell, S., Rosner, R., Butollo, W., Tedeschi, R. G., & Calhoun, L. G. (2003). Posttraumatic growth after war: A study with former refugees and displaced people in Sarajevo. *Journal of Clinical Psychology, 59,* 71–83.

Profitt, D. H., Calhoun, L. G., Tedeschi, R. G., & Cann, A. (2002, August). *Clergy and crisis: Correlates of posttraumatic growth and well-being.* Poster presented at the annual convention of the American Psychological Association, Chicago.

Resick, P. A., & Calhoun, K. S. (2001). Posttraumatic stress disorder. In D. H. Barlow (Ed.), *Clinical handbook of psychological disorders* (3rd ed., pp. 60–113). New York: Guilford Press.

Ryff, C. D., & Singer, B. (1998). The role of purpose in life and personal growth in positive human health. In P. T. P. Wong & P. S. Fry (Eds.), *The human quest for meaning: A handbook of psychological research and clinical applications* (pp. 213–235). Mahwah, NJ: Erlbaum.

Scheier, M. F., Weintraub, J. K., & Carver, C. S. (1986). Coping with stress: Divergent strategies of optimists and pessimists. *Journal of Personality and Social Psychology, 51,* 1257–1264.

Taylor, S. E., & Brown, J. D. (1988). Illusion and well-being: A social psychological perspective on mental health. *Psychological Bulletin, 103,* 193–210.

Tedeschi, R. G. (1999). Violence transformed: Posttraumatic growth in survivors and their societies. *Aggression and Violent Behavior, 4,* 319–341.

Tedeschi, R. G., & Calhoun, L. G. (1988, August). *Perceived benefits in coping with physical handicaps.* Paper presented at the annual meeting of the American Psychological Association, Atlanta, GA.

Tedeschi, R. G., & Calhoun, L. G. (1995). *Trauma and transformation: Growing in the aftermath of suffering.* Thousand Oaks, CA: Sage.

Tedeschi, R. G., & Calhoun, L. G. (1996). The Posttraumatic Growth Inventory: Measuring the positive legacy of trauma. *Journal of Traumatic Stress, 9,* 455–471.

*Tedeschi, R. G., & Calhoun, L. G. (2004). *Helping the bereaved parent: A clinician's guide.* New York: Brunner-Routledge.

Tedeschi, R. G., & Calhoun, L. G. (in press). Posttraumatic growth: Conceptual foundations and empirical evidence. *Psychological Inquiry.*

Tedeschi, R. G., Calhoun, L. G., & Engdahl, B. E. (2001). Opportunities for growth in survivors of trauma. *National Center for PTSD Clinical Quarterly, 10,* 23–25.

Tedeschi, R. G., Calhoun, L. G., Morrell, R. W., & Johnson, K. A. (1984, August). *Bereavement: From grief to psychological development.* Paper presented at the annual meeting of the American Psychological Association, Toronto, Ontario, Canada.

*Tedeschi, R. G., Park, C. L., & Calhoun, L. G. (Eds.). (1998). *Posttraumatic growth: Positive change in the aftermath of crisis.* Mahwah, NJ: Erlbaum.

Tennen, H., Affleck, G., Urrows, S., Higgins, P., & Mendola, R. (1992). Perceiving control, construing benefits, and daily processes in rheumatoid arthritis. *Canadian Journal of Behavioral Science, 24,* 186–203.

Ullrich, P. M., & Lutgendorf, A. K. (2002). Journaling about stressful events: Effects of cognitive processing and emotional expression. *Annals of Behavioral Medicine, 24,* 244–250.

Weiss, T. (2002). Posttraumatic growth in women with breast cancer and their husbands: An intersubjective validation study. *Journal of Psychosocial Oncology, 20,* 65–80.

Wortman, C. B., & Silver, R. C. (2001). The myths of coping with loss revisited. In M. S. Stroebe, R. O. Hansson, W. Stroebe, & H. Schut (Eds.), *Handbook of bereavement research: Consequences, coping and care* (pp. 405–429). Washington, DC: American Psychological Association.

Yalom, I. D., & Lieberman, M. A. (1991). Bereavement and heightened existential awareness. *Psychiatry, 54,* 334–345.

CHAPTER 26

Positive Psychology and Psychotherapy: An Existential Approach

ROGER BRETHERTON and RODERICK J. ØRNER

A N EXISTENTIAL APPROACH to psychotherapy maintains that human potential can be developed even in confronting the irreversible difficulties of life. It is in this sense that an existential perspective can be considered a positive approach in therapeutic psychology—not because it concentrates solely on the good things in life, but rather by suggesting that vigor and passion in living emerge from courageously confronting unavoidable challenges such as death, isolation, loss of control, and meaninglessness. Any perspective on life that elevates the rich possibilities of existence without reference to its limiting factors perpetuates a fantasy. The ability of existential philosophers and psychotherapists to glean profound insights from adversity suggests that a truly positive psychology does not deliver us from our troubles but speaks to us in them.

AN OUTLINE OF EXISTENTIAL THOUGHT

This chapter provides a broad idea of what existentialism is by identifying some of the historical contributors to existential thinking. We seek to draw out applications by which these philosophical considerations can serve the process of psychotherapy and highlight some of the direct avenues by which existential thought became applied to therapeutic practice in the twentieth century. We then present a brief case study, in which the specific methodology and theoretical concepts of existential psychotherapy are examined in their capacity to offer a positive approach to the activity of helping people therapeutically.

A Brief Definition

Mary Warnock (1970) sums up the central concern of existential philosophy:

Broadly speaking, we can say that the common interest which unites Existential philosophers is the interest in human freedom . . . for Existentialists the problem of freedom is in a sense a practical problem. They aim, above all, to show people *that they are free,* to open their eyes to something which has always been true, but which for one reason or another may not always have been recognized, namely that men are free to choose, not only what to do on a specific occasion, but what to value and how to live. (pp. 1–2, original italics)

She tells us first that the great theme that unites existential philosophers, and particularly those thinking and writing in Continental Europe during the 1940s and 1950s, is human freedom. To put it more directly, at the heart of the existential inquiry lies the human ability to decide. Second, the philosophers of the existential tradition devote themselves to a specific methodology in examining human freedom, in that they seek to examine human freedom from the inside out. They aim to describe what it is like to be a human being who is able to make choices and the implications of this capacity for choice on our interaction with the world. Third, and perhaps most importantly as far as the therapeutic endeavor is concerned, Warnock (1970) draws our attention to the missionary zeal of the existentialists. They are not content with mere rational proof of their assertions, but rather aim to bring their readers into a living experience, a new way of seeing the world.

EXISTENTIAL BEGINNINGS: PASCAL, KIERKEGAARD, AND NIETZSCHE

It is difficult to pinpoint precisely the historical beginnings of modern existential philosophy. Many of the themes of later existential thought can be detected in the writings of the French philosopher Blaise Pascal (1623–1662). He described his dramatic conversion to Christianity as a breaking away from the "god of the philosophers" into a *relational* apprehension of the divine in which he could know God in experience, but not by dispassionate thought (Rogers, 1998). Pascal's insight into the failure of the academic philosophy of his time to give an account of human existence has been a recurrent motif in existential thinking to the present day.

Søren Kierkegaard (1813–1855), the Danish intellectual whom many would consider to be one of the first existentialist thinkers (Gardiner, 1988), forged many of his ideas in direct opposition to the philosophical views of his contemporaries. In a similar tone, but from a different perspective, Friedrich Nietzsche (1844–1900), the German atheistic existentialist, lamented the philosophers of his day who dedicated their prodigious output to thinking about the world without reference to the pains and passions of being human (Tanner, 1994). In his writing, Kierkegaard pillories the tendency to construct elegant systems of thought that do not correspond to everyday human experience. He compares it to a man who builds a magnificent mansion, yet lives in a shack next door (Kierkegaard, 1849/1989) or, in another passage, to a king who turns everything to gold and then dies of starvation (Kierkegaard, 1843/1985).

Existential thinking, therefore, from the beginning, has always been interested in the lived experience of human beings, and it is this that enables it to inform psychotherapy. It could be argued that the writings of Pascal, Kierkegaard, and Nietzsche, with their persuasive and varied attempts to convince their readers and with their astute insights into the human condition, offer a therapeutic prototype, a means of helping others to make sense of the world.

THREE TWENTIETH-CENTURY EXISTENTIALISTS

The three major twentieth-century existential philosophers we wish to focus on are Paul Tillich (1886–1965), Martin Heidegger (1889–1976), and Jean-Paul Sartre (1905–1980). Our reason for this emphasis is not that they were the only existential thinkers of that period, but rather that they best illustrate the application of existential thought to therapeutic practice and, during their lifetimes, made direct contributions to psychiatry and psychotherapy.

Paul Tillich   In 1933, the philosopher and theologian Paul Tillich was dismissed from teaching theology in German universities because of his opposition to the Nazi regime. The same year, he accepted an invitation to join the staff of Union Theological Seminary in New York, where he had a profound effect on those who came under his influence.

Most notably as far as existential psychotherapy is concerned, he supervised a PhD thesis by Rollo May, which was later published as *The Meaning of Anxiety* (May, 1950) in which the concept of nonpathological anxiety was espoused as the accompaniment to human freedom. Arguing from previous existential thinkers, such as Kierkegaard, May asserted that existential anxiety resulted from the awareness of the full scope of human freedom and the enormous responsibility this places on us as human beings. This led to a responding volume by Tillich (1952), called *The Courage to Be*, in which he elaborated the value of *self-affirmation* for fulfilled human existence. Rollo May was instrumental in introducing the Anglophone world to many of the continental existential psychotherapists by arranging the translation and editing of an anthology of papers entitled *Existence* (May, Angel, & Ellenberger, 1958). His concern not just with the individual, but with society as a whole, was the direct result of his interaction with Tillich and has become a hallmark of existential psychotherapy.

Martin Heidegger   Heidegger's seminal work, published in 1927, was *Being and Time*, which was, according to the existential psychotherapist Hans Cohn:

> . . . to a great extent, the analysis of the Being of human beings which [Heidegger] sees as radically different from the Being of other beings. It is just because human beings can be aware of their Being and have always already some understanding of it, however vague, that they are also able to forget it. (Cohn, 2000, p. 2)

For a first-time reader, this quotation may be confusing, but the basic gist of Cohn's précis is that we as human beings differ from rocks, trees, and flowers in our ability to be conscious of ourselves and to choose how we relate to ourselves. A rock cannot know that it is a rock, but a human being can not only be aware that it is a human being but also consider what it means to be so. Throughout *Being and Time*, therefore, Heidegger refers to human beings using the German word *Dasein*, literally meaning "being-there," indicating that we as human beings understand ourselves, to some degree explicitly (Heidegger, 1927/1962). This understanding of what it means to be human is of vital importance to psychotherapists because it is often the awareness that something is wrong or undesirable that initially motivates a person to seek out psychotherapy or counseling; and from Heidegger's perspective, this ability to be aware of ourselves is a uniquely human characteristic.

Heidegger made an explicit impression on the development of existential psychotherapy when, from 1959 to 1969, he conducted a series of seminars at the home of Medard Boss, a Swiss psychoanalyst, in which he outlined his thinking for psychotherapists (Cohn, 2000, 2002). Boss went on to develop *Daseinsanalysis* (Boss, 1963), which can be detected as an influence in many of the more recent writings of existential psychotherapists (Cohn, 1997; van Deurzen-Smith, 1988; Yalom, 1980). Viktor Frankl, the Viennese psychiatrist and founder of logotherapy, also describes conversing with Heidegger (Frankl, 1969), and his therapeutic approach could be considered a synthesis of existential thought with religious belief.

Jean-Paul Sartre   Jean-Paul Sartre's philosophical treatise, published in 1943, was entitled *Being and Nothingness* as a direct acknowledgment of Heidegger's earlier manuscript; it contains possibly the most well-known passage in existential philosophy:

> What do we mean by saying that existence precedes essence? We mean that first of all man exists, encounters himself, surges up in the world—and defines himself afterwards. If man as the existentialist sees him is not definable, it is because to begin with he is nothing. He will not be anything until later, and then he will be what he makes of himself. (1943/1956, p. 28)

Sartre identified radical freedom with being human, and his assertion that existence precedes essence means that man is not determined, he has no essential self, and is, therefore, free to make of himself what he will. With reference to psychotherapy, it has been argued that the principle aim of any effective therapeutic approach is to enable individuals who come feeling confined or limited to regain an appreciation of their freedom as human beings (May, 1981).

In addition, many of the ideas developed in *Being and Nothingness* can be discerned in embryonic form in Sartre's earlier *Sketch for a Theory of the Emotions* (Sartre, 1939/1962). In this, he demonstrates his radical view of human freedom, by suggesting that emotions do not just happen to us but that we choose them as a way of altering our way of perceiving the world. He draws a distinction between reflected and unreflected emotions: those of which we are aware and those that we express unknowingly. *Sketch for a Theory of the Emotions* is, therefore, a prime source for Sartre's views on the nature of psychology (Warnock, 1994) and has been influential among contemporary existential psychotherapists (e.g., Strasser, 1999).

THE CASE OF MEREDITH

Having set the scene by reviewing some of the main historical figures in existential philosophy and the channels by which much of their thinking has trickled into the practice of existential psychotherapy, we now turn to a brief case study. The case of Meredith identifies many of these existential themes in the context of therapy and demonstrates how an existential approach can be the catalyst for a positive outcome.

Meredith (names have been changed) was referred to the department of clinical psychology by her family doctor with a letter stating that she suffered from high blood pressure and panic attacks. Over the course of the first three sessions, she gave an account of how her anxiety began with the birth of her first and only child,

Toby, six years before seeking therapy. The birth had been an intensely difficult experience, with numerous complications both for her and the infant requiring a prolonged stay in the hospital, during which she was not always informed precisely what was going on. She was, therefore, left feeling helpless and bewildered as various intravenous medications for high blood pressure were administered, and on more than one occasion, the child was whisked away from her for tests. After several weeks in the hospital, she and Toby were discharged, but following discharge, she developed frequent spells of dizziness and was returned to the hospital for observation lasting a further week.

However, the way she reported her story seemed unusual. Throughout her account of the traumatic events surrounding the birth of Toby, she showed very little emotion, she did not cry or become angry, and almost every time she reached a natural pause in her narration of the episode, she broke out into an incongruous smile: a smile that was, however, marred by a spasm in her lips, which seemed to signal that immense energy was being exerted in an attempt to conceal powerful emotions.

Meredith was seen for long-term individual psychotherapy, which focused not on direct techniques for alleviating her anxious symptomatology, but on elaborating and clarifying the way in which she related to the world generally. Many significant dilemmas were confronted using this approach. These included her need to conceal her emotions to feel safe in the presence of other people, the anxiety elicited by situations in which she was required to make decisions, her frequent inability to know what she wanted, and the fear of being left alone following the death of her mother. As Meredith explored and clarified her attitudes to these areas of her life, she began to gain the freedom to choose her response to them. As her sense of freedom increased, her courage in confronting the problems presented by life increased also. What began as a referral for panic became a complete reexamination of the values by which she lived. Discussing her difficulty in relating to some of the irreversible givens of human existence allowed her to take the opportunity to make changes in her relationships with people, her occupational direction, and her understanding of the world.

POSITIVE ASPECTS OF THE EXISTENTIAL APPROACH

As shown with Meredith, there are numerous ways in which an existential perspective can be used to shed positive light on the human condition

Adversarial Growth

The existential approach is positive in the way it responds to traumatic events. It is in this respect that work on posttraumatic growth (PTG; Tedeschi, Park, & Calhoun, 1998) has often used existential theory as a starting point for its empirical study (Bretherton & Ørner, 2001; Linley, 2003). By facing the questions posed by suffering, existential psychotherapy lends itself to the understanding of people, like Meredith in the case study, who are confronting the extreme challenges of life. Other examples may include HIV (Milton, 1997) or terminal cancer (Jacobsen, Joergensen, & Joergensen, 2000). (See Linley & Joseph, 2004; and Tedeschi & Calhoun, Chapter 25, this volume, for reviews of adversarial growth.) The existential approach can, therefore, be considered a positive approach in therapeutic psychology in its recognition of human potential, even given the prospect of irreversible difficulty.

THE PHENOMENOLOGICAL METHOD

In terms of methodology, the existential approach parallels positive psychology in not being principally concerned with global models of deficit and disorder, but rather with what is presented by the patient. In meeting the patient, practitioners of existential psychotherapy use what is known as the phenomenological method: a way of attending to the world originally proposed by the philosopher Edmund Husserl (1859–1938). Husserl suggested that all knowledge consists of a *what* (which he called the *noema*) and a *how* (which he called the *noesis*). In other words, knowing something is not just about the content (noema) of what is known, but also the process (noesis) through and by which it is known. Adams (2001) illustrates this with reference to the consciousness of a pint of milk, in which the milk itself is the noema, that is, the content of the experience, and the bottle is the noesis, that is, the form or process in which the experience appears. Spinelli (1989) applies this distinction to a phenomenon more applicable to the therapeutic situation of Meredith, namely, listening to someone speak, in which what is said is the content, but the various cognitive and affective biases of the listener form the interpretation of the experience.

Given this bipolar understanding of knowledge, Husserl devised three rules to get at, as far as possible, "things in themselves." These three rules are a common feature of psychotherapy conducted from an existential perspective (e.g., Strasser & Strasser, 1997) and form the phenomenological method.

Rule 1: Bracketing   This rule suggests that, as much as possible, the therapist should put to one side prejudices, assumptions, and stereotypes. The therapist, therefore, notes but does not settle on certain conclusions concerning the patient, including strong emotional responses or desires and the interpretation of these that the therapist might otherwise be partial to take as decisive. The desire for therapeutic progress itself may even be bracketed at times. Meredith, for example, was referred with specific complaints concerning panic and high blood pressure, but bracketing these presenting symptoms allowed the recognition and examination of other significant aspects of her way of being.

Rule 2: Description   The second rule proposes that that which is presented (the phenomena) is described, rather than inferring an underlying essence or cause. Sticking as closely as possible to that which presents itself is, according to existential thinking, the means by which truth is found. Ernesto Spinelli explains: ". . . 'truth' for Heidegger, does not mean what we have grown to suppose. It is not, 'the correctness of an assertion.' Rather, Heidegger points out that the original meaning of truth was derived from the Greek term *aletheia*—meaning the unconcealedness, the transparent presence, of beings" (Spinelli, 2000, p. 14). And in the therapeutic encounter, as with Meredith, the existential psychotherapist adheres tightly to what is presented by the patient to better engage with his or her way of being.

Rule 3: Equalization   The rule of equalization suggests that every phenomenon is possibly as any other. No particular fact or perception should necessarily be given precedence over another. Equalizing in this way leaves the therapist open to discover alternative clusters of meaning in the patient's presentation, rather than settling with the usual suspects.

The phenomenological method is positive in that, by stepping back from his or her own prejudices and stereotypes, the existential therapist can identify patients' possibilities as well as their limitations and their strengths as well as their weaknesses (van Deurzen-Smith, 1988), rather than being attuned principally to the signs and symptoms of psychological disorder. The existentialists suggest that by identifying the constellations of meaning by which we relate to the world, we afford ourselves the opportunity of decision—to decide to alter our way of being.

A further positive correlate of using the phenomenological method in psychotherapy is that the existential approach has been instrumental in facilitating the integration of many of the modern psychotherapy traditions. Largely because of its use of the phenomenological method rather than a theory-driven approach to the therapy situation, it has been able to transcend the lines of demarcation that have habitually divided the different therapeutic orientations (Corey, 1996; see also Hubble & Miller, Chapter 21, this volume).

Possibility and Necessity

Necessity refers to the givens of life, the things that are unavoidable, such as death and the existence of other human beings. With reference to the necessities of life, Heidegger (1962) described existence as having the quality of "thrownness." That is, we do not choose many of the givens of life, for example, our parents and the way the world is; nor do we choose to be born, but rather we are thrown into life and, therefore, have to do with it as best we can. In our case study, Meredith was being confronted with many of the unavoidable givens of life, such as her mother's death, her difficulty in relating to others (especially her baby), and the need in life to make decisions.

It is the unashamed manner with which these nonnegotiable givens are confronted that has, at times, led to the attribution of a rather morbid reputation to existential thinking. In his paper *Logotherapy and the Challenge of Suffering*, Viktor Frankl (1967) responds to the accusation of morbidity as follows:

> It has become fashionable to blame existential philosophy for overemphasising the tragic aspects of human existence. Logotherapy, which is considered one of the schools of existential psychiatry, has become the target of the same reproaches. Logotherapy, it is true, centers on issues such as dying and suffering. This, however, must not be interpreted as evidence of a pessimistic slant and bias. What we rather have to deal with is an optimistic position; namely, the conviction that even dying and suffering are potentially meaningful. (p. 87)

It is the freedom to choose a response to the givens of life that, according to Frankl, makes an existential perspective positive. Even from a less optimistic perspective, Emmy van Deurzen-Smith (1988) notes the propensity for existential philosophers to draw strength from confrontation with necessity:

> The European existential philosophers . . . never intended to create the illusion of being able to solve the human dilemma. There is nothing in their writing that

suggests the prospect of a paradise on earth, inhabited by self-actualised individuals. Their aim has been to gain insight into the unavoidable paradoxes that life presents and to gain strength from that knowledge. (p. viii)

In contrast to necessity (what is given) stands possibility (what we can make of it). *Possibility* refers to the openness of existence—that humans are free to choose the way they relate to life, how they define themselves, and the way they understand the world. The existential dual concern with both possibility and limitation, therefore, provides a framework within which the practice of positive psychology can recognize human potential without succumbing to an unrealistic optimism.

Optimism represents the expectation of a favorable outcome whereas hope, being more flexible, recognizes situations in which a favorable outcome is less likely and, therefore, maintains an openness to the difficulty of the experience and a flexibility of response to its challenges (Calhoun & Tedeschi, 1998). The existential approach is, therefore, to adjust Frankl's terminology, neither pessimistic nor optimistic, but it can be profoundly hopeful by finding meaning even in the face of the unchangeable givens of life such as pain, guilt, and death.

Values and Meaning

Seligman (2003) referred to positive psychology as being concerned with the pleasant life, the good life, and the meaningful life. He described the meaningful life as, "the use of your strengths and virtues in the service of something much larger than you are" (p. 127). The existential approach is also concerned with living meaningfully by engaging with life (Yalom, 1980) and acting consistently with our values (Frankl, 1986). In our case study, Meredith used her period of crisis to reexamine her life and thereby increase her sense of meaning by acting more in keeping with the things she valued. Our values are those things for which we are prepared to give up other things (van Deurzen-Smith, 1988). One way of understanding the difference between rules and values is that whereas a rule is to be obeyed, values are realized or fulfilled. That is, we bring them into reality when we act on them. Therefore, the way we relate to ourselves, the world, and others both discloses and is dictated by the values we hold.

Viktor Frankl (1986) places values at the center of logotherapy. He categorizes human values into three distinct clusters: creative, aesthetic, and attitudinal. Creative values are realized by what we produce or the ways we transform our environments. Aesthetic values involve the appreciation of things that are already given. Attitudinal values become most relevant in situations that cannot be changed or appreciated, but to which we can still adapt ourselves through a change in attitude or in the position we adopt toward them. Frankl suggests that meaning in life is attained by the realization of values and refers to his ability to find meaning even in the Nazi concentration camp by quoting Nietzsche's maxim, "He who has a why to live for can endure almost any how" (Frankl, 1959).

However, whereas Frankl and others suggest that the meaning of life is out there to be found, more atheistic thinkers suggest that life in itself is meaningless and that the best we can do, therefore, is create meaning for ourselves, particularly through engagement with life (e.g., Yalom, 1980). But whichever is the case, it may be that the activity of discovering or of making meaning may involve the same creative process. For example, when reading a novel, it could be argued that finding the author's meaning can be achieved only by creatively constructing it from the text, but, having done this, it may be that the reader has not created the meaning but only identified what the author had intended to communicate. Either way, the positive aspect is that fulfillment in life can be gained from realizing values; no matter what situation we are placed in, we can still realize or adopt attitudinal values and, from this rationale, as Frankl (1959) says, life remains meaningful to the last gasp.

Concern for Society

A final positive aspect of existential psychotherapy is its concern not just with the individual but with the person in society. Rollo May (1973), having been influenced by the profound cultural analysis of Paul Tillich, came to the view that Western society is at a point of transition and change. He argued that while this produces an atmosphere of anxiety and uncertainty, it also prompts vast creativity on the part of those who feel the tension of such a transition. One of the implications is that therapy should not aim to conform its beneficiaries to society if society itself is unstable, but rather see its task as enabling individuals to transcend the confusing cultural challenges in which they find themselves. It was from this perspective that May could write cogently about the place of sexual behavior in society and the difficulties this poses to the individual (May, 1969).

More recently, Emmy van Deurzen (1998) has made a case in the strongest terms that existential therapy could be at the forefront of a changing society:

> It is an outrageous state of affairs that there are so many casualties of post-modern society, including the nearly a quarter of a million people who try to kill themselves every year in this country alone. We need to take extremely seriously the role of counseling and psychotherapy in remedying the situation. The therapeutic profession needs to claim its proper place in the world of professions and will come into its own only if it is willing to take up its role of secular and postscientific religion. (van Deurzen, 1998, p. 126)

She traces the etymology of the word *religion* to the Latin verb *religare*, meaning to bind together. The assertion that psychotherapy should occupy previously religious territory may be debatable, but the ultimately positive aspiration of the existential psychotherapy movement is well stated. In a society suffering fragmentation and lacking in direction, the existential approach aims to act as a force for clarity and cohesion, to enable individuals and communities to thrive.

CONCLUSION

It is therefore our assertion that a therapeutic approach derived from existential thinking can be profoundly positive and hopeful, in spite of the morbid and pessimistic reputation occasionally associated with the existential approach. The positive aspects outlined are not intended to be an exhaustive list. It is rather, an indication of the benefits found in an approach that does not shy away from acknowledging the difficulties of life, yet recognises the courage of the human spirit that directly confronts these givens of existence. It is our hope, therefore, that in the further development of positive psychology, the contributions of the existential therapies will not be side-lined, but emphasized as a possible source of positive insights into the human condition.

REFERENCES

Adams, M. (2001). Practicing phenomenology: Some reflections and considerations. *Journal of the Society for Existential Analysis, 12*(1), 65–84.

Boss, M. (1963). *Psychoanalysis and daseinsanalysis.* New York: Basic Books.

Bretherton, R., & Ørner, R. J. (2001). The professor confronts Achilles: Positive adjustments following trauma. In N. Retterstøl & M. S. Mortensen (Eds.), *Disasters and after effects: Disaster psychiatry in a troubled world* (pp. 135–146). Oslo, Norway: Atlantic Press.

Calhoun, L. G., & Tedeschi, R. G. (1998). Posttraumatic growth: Future directions. In R. G. Tedeschi, C. L. Park, & L. G. Calhoun (Eds.), *Posttraumatic growth: Positive changes in the aftermath of crisis* (pp. 215–238). Mahwah, NJ: Erlbaum.

*Cohn, H. W. (1997). *Existential thought and therapeutic practice: An introduction to existential psychotherapy.* London: Sage.

Cohn, H. W. (2000). Heidegger's way to psychotherapy. *Journal of the Society for Existential Analysis, 11*(2), 2–10.

Cohn, H. W. (2002). *Heidegger and the roots of existential therapy.* London: Continuum International.

Corey, G. (1996). *Theory and practice of counseling and psychotherapy* (5th ed.). New York: Brooks/Cole.

Frankl, V. E. (1959). *Man's search for meaning.* London: Washington Square.

Frankl, V. E. (1967). Logotherapy and the challenge of suffering. In V. E. Frankl (Ed.), *Psychotherapy and existentialism: Selected papers on logotherapy* (pp. 87–94). Hammondsworth, England: Penguin.

*Frankl, V. E. (1969). *The will to meaning: Foundations and applications of logotherapy.* New York: Meridian.

Frankl, V. E. (1986). *The doctor and the soul: From psychotherapy to logotherapy* (3rd ed.). New York: Vintage.

Gardiner, P. (1988). *Kierkegaard.* Oxford, England: Oxford University Press.

Heidegger, M. (1962). *Being and time* (J. Macquarrie & E. S. Robinson, Trans.). Oxford, England: Blackwell. (Original work published 1927)

Jacobsen, B., Joergensen, S. D., & Joergensen, E. (2000). The world of the cancer patient from an existential perspective. *Journal of the Society for Existential Analysis, 11*(1), 122–135.

Kierkegaard, S. (1985). *Fear and trembling* (A. Hannay, Trans.). Hammondsworth, England: Penguin. (Original work published 1843)

Kierkegaard, S. (1989). *The sickness unto death* (A. Hannay, Trans.). Hammondsworth, England: Penguin. (Original work published 1849)

Linley, P. A. (2003). Positive adaptation to trauma: Wisdom as both process and outcome. *Journal of Traumatic Stress, 16,* 601–610.

Linley, P. A., & Joseph, S. (2004). Positive change following trauma and adversity: A review. *Journal of Traumatic Stress, 17,* 11–21.

May, R. (1950). *The meaning of anxiety.* New York: Norton.

May, R. (1969). *Love and will.* New York: Norton.

May, R. (1973). *Paulus: A personal portrait of Paul Tillich.* New York: Harper & Row.

May, R. (1981). *Freedom and destiny.* London: Norton.

*May, R., Angel, E., & Ellenberger, H. F. (Eds.). (1958). *Existence.* New York: Aronson.

Milton, M. (1997). Roberto: Living with HIV—Issues of meaning and relationship in HIV-related psychotherapy. In S. du Plock (Ed.), *Case studies in existential psychotherapy and counseling* (pp. 42–58). Chichester, England: Wiley.

Rogers, B. (1998). *Pascal: In praise of vanity.* London: Phoenix.

Sartre, J.-P. (1956). *Being and nothingness* (H. Barnes, Trans.). London: Routledge. (Original work published 1943)

Sartre, J.-P. (1962). *Sketch for a theory of the emotions* (P. Mairet, Trans.). London: Routledge. (Original work published 1939)

Seligman, M. E. P. (2003). Positive psychology: Fundamental assumptions. *The Psychologist, 16,* 126–127.

Spinelli, E. (1989). *The interpreted world: An introduction to phenomenological psychology.* London: Sage.

Spinelli, E. (2000). Creation and being: Existential-phenomenological challenges to psycho-analytic theories of artistic creativity. *Journal of the Society for Existential Analysis, 11*(1), 2–20.

Strasser, F. (1999). *Emotions: Experiences in existential psychotherapy and life.* London: Duckworth.

Strasser, F., & Strasser, A. (1997). *Existential time-limited therapy.* Chichester, England: Wiley.

Tanner, M. (1994). *Nietzsche: A very short introduction.* Oxford, England: Oxford University Press.

Tedeschi, R. G., Park, C. L., & Calhoun, L. G. (Eds.). (1998). *Posttraumatic growth: Positive changes in the aftermath of crisis.* Mahwah, NJ: Erlbaum.

Tillich, P. (1952). *The courage to be.* Cambridge, MA: Yale University Press.

van Deurzen, E. (1998). *Paradox and passion in psychotherapy: An existential approach to therapy and counseling.* Chichester, England: Wiley.

*van Deurzen-Smith, E. (1988). *Existential counseling in practice.* London: Sage.

Warnock, M. (1970). *Existentialism* (Rev. ed.). Oxford, England: Oxford University Press.

Warnock, M. (1994). Preface [J.-P. Sartre, 1939]. *Sketch for a theory of the emotions* (P. Mairet, Trans.). London: Routledge. (Original work published 1962)

*Yalom, I. D. (1980). *Existential psychotherapy.* New York: Basic Books.

PART IX

STRENGTHS OF CHARACTER IN PRACTICE

CHAPTER 27

Classification and Measurement of Character Strengths: Implications for Practice

CHRISTOPHER PETERSON and NANSOOK PARK

THE FLEDGLING FIELD of positive psychology calls for as much focus on strength as on weakness, as much interest in building the best things in life as in repairing the worst, and as much concern with fulfilling the lives of healthy people as healing the wounds of the distressed (Seligman, 2002; Seligman & Csikszentmihalyi, 2000). The past concern of psychology with human problems is understandable and will not be abandoned in the foreseeable future, but psychologists interested in promoting human potential need to pose different questions from their predecessors who assumed a disease model (Peterson & Park, 2003b).

As positive psychology becomes its own field, the attention of some has turned to interventions intended to cultivate and to sustain the good life. Skeptics might worry that the field is too new to inspire interventions, but we have a different opinion. We agree with Kurt Lewin's sentiment expressed decades ago that the best way to understand a psychological phenomenon is to try to change it. By this view, intervention research is not something that follows basic research at a polite distance but is instead its inherent complement. In any event, interventions are going to be mounted by some regardless of the caution of others, and it makes sense to us that rigorous evaluation be built into interventions from the beginning.

The example of psychotherapy is instructive. "Talking cures" of many stripes proliferated for almost a century before anyone could say with certainty that therapy actually works and that all forms of therapies show about the same effectiveness

We thank Martin Seligman for his help and acknowledge the encouragement and support of the Manuel D. and Rhoda Mayerson Foundation in creating the Values in Action Institute, a nonprofit organization dedicated to the development of a scientific knowledge base of human strengths.

(Smith & Glass, 1977). Think of how much effort and energy went into developing and defending different systems of psychotherapy when the data eventually showed that the more productive strategy would have been to search for common ingredients (cf. Frank, 1974; see also Hubble & Miller, Chapter 21, this volume). We envision something better for positive psychology interventions and propose that the slow-to-arrive gold standard of psychotherapy—empirical validation—be adopted sooner rather than later as the criterion for positive psychology interventions (Nathan & Gorman, 2002; Patrick & Olson, 2000).

Nevertheless, requiring that interventions be empirically validated before they are used with anyone can freeze innovation and progress. Experimentation with new interventions must be legitimized at the same time that empirical validation is advanced as a goal.[1] The good news is that people like participating in "experimental" programs (cf. Wortman, Hendricks, & Hillis, 1976). It, therefore, behooves positive psychology practitioners to be honest with clients about what is known and not known about the effectiveness of interventions. We also note that insurance companies and HMOs do not reimburse interventions that target the good life. For the time being, positive psychology clients will pay their own fare, and it further behooves positive psychology practitioners to offer their services—especially when they involve experimental techniques—at a modest cost.

The most critical tools for positive psychologists interested in evaluating interventions are a vocabulary for speaking about the good life and assessment strategies for investigating its components. For the past several years, we have focused our attention on positive traits[2]—strengths of character such as curiosity, kindness, and hope. What are the most important of these, and how can they be measured as individual differences? So long as we fail to identify the specifics, different groups in our society—despite common concern for human goodness—will simply talk past one another when attempting to address the issue of character. For instance, is character defined by what someone does *not* do, or is there a more active meaning? Is character a singular characteristic of an individual, or is it composed of different

---

[1] Our own experience as positive psychology practitioners has involved out-of-class "happiness" and "gratification" exercises with college students enrolled in our positive psychology courses. In the spirit of informed experimentation, they are invited to try out an exercise and then evaluate it. No student has ever felt cheated or misled by an exercise that did not work as intended. For example, our students have written and delivered *gratitude letters* to individuals who have been kind to them but never received explicit thanks. This exercise was successful in that it created lingering feelings of satisfaction for all parties. In another example, our students have written (but not delivered) *forgiveness letters* to individuals who had hurt them but never received explicit absolution. This exercise was unsuccessful because almost all of the students felt that delivering the letter to an individual who had never requested forgiveness would create more bad feelings than good ones. On reflection, they believed that in many cases they themselves had contributed to the hurt (e.g., painful romantic breakups) and that forgiving the other party would imply that they had been but innocent victims as opposed to co-conspirators. This unsuccessful exercise was nonetheless informative, and in the future, we will limit this exercise to cases in which an apology had been tendered. We also plan to experiment with *apology letters*.

[2] Positive traits are just one outcome of interest to positive psychology. Just as important, given the goal of an intervention, might be happiness, pleasure, gratification, fulfillment, life satisfaction, or serenity, for both the individual per se and the individual in an interpersonal or institutional context: friendship, marriage, family, work, and community. We focus here on positive traits but note in passing that positive psychology interventions that target happiness and its cognates are challenged by the fact that most people most of the time are already satisfied with their lives (Myers & Diener, 1995). In other words, there may be a ceiling effect for happiness, not to mention a biologically determined set-point that interventions cannot readily change.

aspects? Is character socially constructed and laden with idiosyncratic values, or are there universals suggesting a more enduring basis? Does character—however we define it—exist in degrees, or is it just something that an individual happens to have or not have? How does character develop? Can it be learned? Can it be taught, and who might be the most effective teacher? What roles are played by families, schools, peers, youth development programs, the media, religious institutions, and the larger culture?

THE VALUES IN ACTION
CLASSIFICATION OF STRENGTHS

With funding from the Mayerson Foundation, we have laid the groundwork that will allow these questions to be answered. Our project—the *VIA (Values in Action) Classification of Strengths*—means to complete what the *Diagnostic and Statistical Manual (DSM)* of the American Psychiatric Association (APA, 1987) has begun, by focusing on what is right about people and, specifically, about the strengths of character that make the good life possible (Peterson & Seligman, 2004). We are following the example of *DSM* and its collateral creations by proposing a classification scheme and by devising assessments for its entries.

We recognize the components of good character as existing at different levels of abstraction. Virtues are the core characteristics valued by moral philosophers and religious thinkers: wisdom, courage, humanity, justice, temperance, and transcendence. These six broad categories of virtue emerge consistently from historical surveys (Dahlsgaard, Peterson, & Seligman, 2002). We speculate that these are universal, perhaps grounded in biology through an evolutionary process that selected for these predispositions toward moral excellence as means of solving the important tasks necessary for survival of the species (cf. Bok, 1995; Schwartz, 1994).

Character strengths are the psychological ingredients—processes or mechanisms—that define the virtues. That is, character strengths are distinguishable routes to displaying one or another of the virtues. For example, the virtue of wisdom can be achieved through strengths such as curiosity and love of learning, open-mindedness, creativity, and what we call *perspective*—having a big picture on life. These strengths are similar in that they all involve the acquisition and use of knowledge, but they are also distinct. Again, we regard these strengths as ubiquitously recognized and valued, although a given individual will rarely, if ever, display all of them (Walker & Pitts, 1998). We regard character strengths as dimensional traits—individual differences—that exist in degrees.

We generated the entries for the VIA Classification by reviewing pertinent literatures that addressed good character—from psychiatry, youth development, character education, religion, philosophy, organizational studies, and psychology. From the many candidate strengths identified, we winnowed the list by combining redundancies and applying the following seven criteria:

1. *A strength needs to be manifest in the range of an individual's behavior—thoughts, feelings, and/or actions—in such a way that it can be assessed.* In other words, a character strength should be trait-like in the sense of having a degree of generality across situations and stability across time.
2. *A strength contributes to various fulfillments that comprise the good life, for the self and for others.* Although strengths and virtues no doubt determine how an individual copes with adversity, our focus is on how they fulfill an

individual. In keeping with the broad premise of positive psychology, strengths allow the individual to achieve more than the absence of distress and disorder. They "break through the zero point" of psychology's traditional concern with disease, disorder, and failure to address quality-of-life outcomes (Peterson, 2000).

3. *Although strengths can and do produce desirable outcomes, each strength is morally valued in its own right, even in the absence of obvious beneficial outcomes.* To say that a strength is morally valued is an important qualification, because there exist individual differences that are widely valued and contribute to fulfillment but still fall outside our classification. Consider intelligence or athletic prowess. These talents and abilities are cut from a different cloth than character strengths such as valor or kindness. The latter are valued more for their tangible consequences (acclaim, wealth) than are the former. Someone who "does nothing" with a talent such as a high IQ or physical dexterity courts eventual disdain. In contrast, we never hear the criticism that a person did nothing with his or her hope or authenticity. Talents and abilities can be squandered, but strengths and virtues cannot.

4. *The display of a strength by one person does not diminish other people in the vicinity but rather elevates them.* Onlookers are impressed, inspired, and encouraged by their observation of virtuous action. Admiration is created but not jealousy, because character strengths are the sorts of characteristics to which all can—and do—aspire. The more people surrounding us who are kind, or curious, or playful, the greater our own likelihood of acting in these ways.

5. *As suggested by Erikson's (1963) discussion of psychosocial stages and the virtues that result from their satisfactory resolutions, the larger society provides institutions and associated rituals for cultivating strengths and virtues.* These can be thought of as simulations: trial runs that allow children and adolescents to display and develop a valued characteristic in a safe (as-if) context in which guidance is explicit.

6. *Yet another criterion for a character strength is the existence of consensually recognized paragons of virtue.* Paragons of character display what Allport (1961) called a *cardinal trait*, and the ease with which we can think of paragons in our own social circles gives the lie to the claim that virtuous people are either phony or boring (Wolf, 1982). Certainly, the virtuous people we each know are neither. In one of our preliminary strategies of validating assessment strategies (see later discussion), we asked our research assistants to nominate people of their acquaintance who are paragons of virtue and prevail on them—without full disclosure why—to complete our measures. No one has had any difficulty thinking of appropriate respondents.

7. *A final criterion is that the strength is arguably unidimensional and not able to be decomposed into other strengths in the classification.* For example, the character strength of *tolerance* meets most of the other criteria enumerated but is a complex blend of open-mindedness and fairness. The character strength of *responsibility* seems to result from perseverance and teamwork. And so on.

When we applied these criteria to the candidate strengths identified through literature searches and brainstorming, what resulted were 24 positive traits organized under six broad virtues (see Table 27.1). We hasten to add that there are other positive traits that a positive psychology practitioner might wish to

Table 27.1
VIA Classification of Character Strengths

---

1. **Wisdom and knowledge**—cognitive strengths that entail the acquisition and use of knowledge.

   Creativity: Thinking of novel and productive ways to do things; includes artistic achievement but is not limited to it.

   Curiosity: Taking an interest in all ongoing experience; finding all subjects and topics fascinating; exploring and discovering.

   Judgment/critical thinking: Thinking things through and examining them from all sides; *not* jumping to conclusions; being able to change your mind in light of evidence; weighing all evidence fairly.

   Love of learning: Mastering new skills, topics, and bodies of knowledge, whether on your own or formally. Obviously related to the strength of curiosity but goes beyond it to describe the tendency to add *systematically* to what you know.

   Perspective: Being able to provide wise counsel to others; having ways of looking at the world that make sense to the self and to other people.

2. **Courage**—emotional strengths that involve the exercise of will to accomplish goals in the face of opposition, external or internal.

   Bravery: Not shrinking from threat, challenge, difficulty, or pain; speaking up for what is right even if there is opposition; acting on convictions even if unpopular; includes physical bravery but is not limited to it.

   Industry/perseverance: Finishing what you start; persisting in a course of action in spite of obstacles; "getting it out the door"; taking pleasure in completing tasks.

   Authenticity: Speaking the truth but more broadly presenting yourself in a genuine way; being without pretense; taking responsibility for your feelings and actions.

   Zest: Approaching life with excitement and energy; *not* doing things halfway or half-heartedly; living life as an adventure; feeling alive and activated.

3. **Love**—interpersonal strengths that involve "tending" and "befriending" others (Taylor et al., 2000).

   Intimacy: Valuing close relations with others, in particular those in which sharing and caring are reciprocated; being close to people.

   Kindness: Doing favors and good deeds for others; helping them; taking care of them.

   Social intelligence: Being aware of the motives and feelings of other people and the self; knowing what to do to fit in to different social situations; knowing what makes other people tick.

4. **Justice**—civic strengths that underlie healthy community life.

   Citizenship/teamwork: Working well as member of a group or team; being loyal to the group; doing your share.

   Fairness: Treating all people the same according to notions of fairness and justice; *not* letting personal feelings bias decisions about others; giving everyone a fair chance.

   Leadership: Encouraging a group of which you are a member to get things done and at the same time good relations within the group; organizing group activities and seeing that they happen.

(Continued)

Table 27.1 *Continued*

5. **Temperance**—strengths that protect against excess.

Forgiveness/mercy: Forgiving those who have done wrong; giving people a second chance; *not* being vengeful.

Modesty/humility: Letting your accomplishments speak for themselves; *not* seeking the spotlight; *not* regarding yourself as more special than you are.

Prudence: Being careful about your choices; *not* taking undue risks; *not* saying or doing things that might later be regretted.

Self-control/self-regulation: Regulating what you feel and do; being disciplined; controlling your appetites and emotions.

6. **Transcendence**—strengths that forge connections to the larger universe and provide meaning.

Awe/appreciation of beauty and excellence: Noticing and appreciating beauty, excellence, and/or skilled performance in all domains of life, from nature to art to mathematics to science to everyday experience.

Gratitude: Being aware of and thankful for the good things that happen; taking time to express thanks.

Hope: Expecting the best in the future and working to achieve it; believing that a good future is something that can be brought about.

Playfulness: Liking to laugh and tease; bringing smiles to other people; seeing the light side; making (not necessarily telling) jokes.

Spirituality: Having coherent beliefs about the higher purpose and meaning of the universe; knowing where you fit within the larger scheme; having beliefs about the meaning of life that shape conduct and provide comfort.

encourage among clients—for example, ambition, autonomy, patience, and tolerance, to name but a few—and their absence in the VIA Classification reflects only our judgment that these are not as universally valued as the included entries. The VIA Classification is only a tool and cannot tell practitioners or their clients what the goals of an intervention should be.

ASSESSMENT OF THE VIA STRENGTHS

What distinguishes the VIA Classification from previous attempts to articulate good character is its simultaneous concern with assessment, and in the remainder of this chapter, we describe our work to date on measurement. Sophisticated social scientists sometimes respond with suspicion when they hear our goal, reminding us of the pitfalls of self-report and the validity threat posed by *social desirability* (Crowne & Marlow, 1964). We do not dismiss these considerations out of hand, but their premise is worth examining from the vantage point of positive psychology. We seem to be willing, as researchers and practitioners, to trust what individuals say about their problems. With notable exceptions such as substance abuse and eating disorders, in which denial is part-and-parcel of the problem, the preferred way to measure psychological disorder relies on self-report, either in the form of symptom questionnaires or structured interviews. So why not ascertain wellness in the same way? Perhaps we accept self-reports about the negative but not the positive because we do not believe that the positive really exists. That is the pervasive assumption that positive psychology urges us to reject.

Suppose that people really do possess moral virtues. Most philosophers emphasize that virtuous activity involves choosing virtue in light of a justifiable life plan (Yearley, 1990). In more psychological language, this characterization means that people can reflect on their own virtues and talk about them to others. They may be misled and/or misleading, but virtues are not the sort of entities that are, in principle, outside the realm of self-commentary (cf. Nisbett & Wilson, 1977). Furthermore, character strengths are not contaminated by a response set of social desirability; they *are* socially desirable, especially when reported with fidelity.

We can point to previous research that measured character strengths with self-report questionnaire batteries (e.g., Cawley, Martin, & Johnson, 2000; Greenberger, Josselson, Knerr, & Knerr, 1975; Ryff & Singer, 1996). In no case did a single methods factor order the data. Rather, different clusters of strengths always emerged. External correlates were sensible. These conclusions converge with what we have learned from our own attempts to measure the VIA Strengths among young people and adults with self-report questionnaires. We acknowledge the possibility that some strengths of character lend themselves less readily to self-report than do others, but it is easy to understand why. Almost by definition, strengths such as authenticity and bravery are not the sorts of traits individuals usually attribute to themselves. But this consideration does not preclude the use of self-report to assess other strengths of character.

As part of the VIA Classification, we commissioned literature reviews by expert social scientists about what was known about each of the 24 strengths currently in the classification (Peterson & Seligman, 2004). These experts followed a common format, focusing on definition, theory, enabling factors and causes, consequences, and correlates. Of relevance to the present proposal, each expert also summarized what was known about the assessment of a strength as an individual difference. Space does not permit a strength-by-strength summary of assessment, so here are the summarized conclusions from these reviews:

- In most cases, there exist reliable and valid ways of measuring these strengths as individual differences, not a surprising conclusion given that we deliberately included strengths already of interest to psychologists.
- However, there are some exceptions. Modesty and humility have eluded reliable assessment, although nomination procedures have been used to identify modest/humble paragons. And there seem to be no extant self-report measures of bravery, although, again, nomination procedures have been used by previous researchers.
- In most cases, the assessment strategy of choice is a self-report questionnaire, although these have different formats and lengths, which would work against the creation of an inclusive battery that would be practical to use.
- However, again, there are some exceptions, which make sense given the nature of the strength. In these cases, additional or alternative techniques of assessment are needed. For example, scenario methods are often used to assess fairness; respondents are provided with a brief story in which a moral dilemma is posed and then asked to describe how they would respond. Along these lines, open-mindedness is often measured by asking people to

write or speak about some complex issue and then having expert judges score their responses for the use of multiple perspectives.

- Most existing measures are intended for use with adults. When measures for younger individuals exist, they make no contact with measures of analogous strengths among adults, thus precluding longitudinal studies that span developmental stages. So, there is a need for parallel measures across the lifespan that are at the same time developmentally appropriate. The ways in which young people show curiosity or bravery, for example, differ from the ways of adults, and assessment devices need to reflect these differences.

With these insights as a starting point, we set about creating measures that allow the character strengths in the VIA Classification to be assessed among English speakers in the contemporary Western world. (Our collaborators in other countries are beginning the process of translating our measures, but these projects are too preliminary to discuss in this chapter.) We were wary of becoming so fixated on issues of reliability—which are important—that we neglected the even more important issues of validity.

The assessment strategy we have most extensively developed to date entails self-report surveys to be completed by respondents in a single session. We have devised separate inventories for adults and for young people (ages 10 to 17). Although the expert literature reviews we commissioned concluded that some small number of the VIA Strengths have not and perhaps cannot be measured with self-report, we nonetheless attempted to create self-report scales for each of the 24 strengths. Our inventory for adults is better validated than the one for children, so we focus on it here (but see Peterson & Park, 2003a).

THE VIA INVENTORY OF STRENGTHS

The VIA Inventory of Strengths (VIA-IS) is intended for use by adults and has already been completed in four different incarnations by more than 75,000 individuals. The VIA-IS is a face-valid self-report questionnaire that uses five-point Likert-style items to measure the degree to which respondents endorse items reflecting the various strengths of character that comprise the VIA Classification (see sample items in Table 27.2). There are 10 items per strength (240 total). We have created versions with and without reverse-scored items and have found that they are psychometrically similar and have much the same factor structures. Paper copies are available as well as a Web-based version that provides immediate feedback about signature strengths directly to respondents. Consistent with comparative studies by other researchers, we find no psychometric differences between paper and Web versions of the questionnaire (Birnbaum, 2000). The Web-based questionnaire has an option that allows identification numbers to be included so that respondents can be tracked.

The Web-based questionnaire has proven enormously useful to us as we developed the VIA-IS. On any given day, at least 10 to 15 individuals complete the measure, and on some days, hundreds of individuals do so. We do not pay any of these respondents, and there is no evidence whatsoever (based on inspection of the ITP addresses) that the same individual responds more than once to the survey. About 85% of the respondents are from the United States; virtually all others are from English-speaking nations (the United Kingdom, Canada, Australia)

Table 27.2
Sample Items for Selected VIA-IS Scales

Curiosity
Q030 I am never bored.

Judgment
Q201 I always weigh the pros and cons.

Love of learning
Q186 I read all of the time.

Bravery
Q012 I have taken frequent stands in the face of strong opposition.

Industry
Q181 I do not procrastinate.

Gratitude
Q099 At least once a day, I stop and count my blessings.

Note: Numbers in front of items refer to placement within the questionnaire.

although we have had a smattering of respondents from Asia, Africa, Central and South America, the Middle East, and continental Europe. About two-thirds of the respondents are women. The ethnic makeup of the U.S. sample approximates that of the country as a whole. The typical respondent is 35 years of age, is married, is employed, and has completed some schooling post-high school, although there is great variation across all such sociodemographic contrasts. Given the need for computer literacy and access, our respondents are not a perfect match to the U.S. or world population but arguably much closer than convenience samples otherwise obtained by psychology researchers (e.g., college sophomores enrolled in an introductory psychology course). The efficiency and economy of Web-based research seems to offset concerns about the makeup of the samples. We can complete a given study (VIA-IS + other surveys) with more than adequate power in little more than a few weeks and then begin another study.

Here is what we know so far about the reliability and validity of the VIA-IS:

- All scales have satisfactory alphas (> 0.70).
- Test-retest correlations for all scales over a four-month period are substantial (> 0.70) and, in almost all cases, approach their internal consistencies.
- Demographic correlations are modest but sensible. For example, women score higher than men on all of the humanity strengths. Younger adults score higher than older adults on the scale for playfulness. Married individuals are more forgiving than divorced people. And so on.
- A single-item measure of political stance (conservative versus liberal) correlates with but one VIA Strength; conservative individuals are more likely to score higher on spirituality.
- We have found few ethnic differences among the major U.S. census groupings (African American, Asian American, European American, Latino/a, Native American) on the VIA scales.
- Self-nomination of strengths correlates substantially ($rs = 0.5$) with the matching scale scores.

- "Other" nomination of strengths (by friends or family members) correlate modestly ($rs = 0.3$) with the matching scale scores for most of the 24 strengths.
- Marlow-Crowne social desirability scores do not significantly correlate with scale scores, with the exception of prudence ($r = 0.44$) and spirituality ($r = 0.30$).
- NEO-PI Big Five correlations are substantial and sensible: that is, openness correlates with awe ($r = 0.65$), curiosity ($r = 0.73$), and love of learning ($r = 0.58$); agreeableness with teamwork ($r = 0.42$); and conscientiousness with perseverance ($r = 0.73$) and self-regulation ($r = 0.55$).
- Individuals scoring high on a measure of serenity not surprisingly score high as well on the VIA scale of spirituality but, more interestingly, even higher on our scale of forgiveness.
- In a series of three large sample studies ($ns > 600$), we explored correlations between the VIA scales and rewarding aspects of work, love (friendship, romance), and play (recreation, leisure). Again, the correlates we found are modest but congruent with the meanings of the strengths. For example, individuals scoring high on the strength of kindness particularly enjoy jobs in which they can mentor others. Those high in curiosity prefer sexually experienced romantic partners. Those high on love of learning appreciate gardening. And so on.
- In the immediate aftermath of the September 11, 2001, terrorist attacks, VIA scale scores significantly increased for intimacy, kindness, gratitude, citizenship/teamwork, hope, and spirituality (Peterson & Seligman, 2003).
- Individuals who have successfully recovered from serious physical or psychological difficulties score higher on several scales: appreciation of beauty, gratitude, and hope.
- Students ($n = 20$) enrolled in a positive psychology class at the University of Pennsylvania showed reliable increases in the strengths of love, prudence, gratitude, perspective, and spirituality, all strengths explicitly targeted by classroom discussions and out-of-class exercises.
- Preliminary factor analyses of scale scores suggest five factors, which we tentatively identify as cognitive strengths (e.g., love of learning, creativity, curiosity), emotional strengths (e.g., playfulness, zest, intimacy, and hope), conative strengths (e.g., open-mindedness, industry, prudence, and self-regulation), interpersonal strengths (e.g., leadership, forgiveness, teamwork, and kindness), and transcendence strengths (e.g., awe, gratitude, and spirituality). These factors are not identical to our a priori classification (Table 27.1) but represent a coherent psychological structure that we may eventually adopt as our overarching scheme.
- Each factor correlates independently and robustly with subjective well-being, with the exception of cognitive strengths. This finding is interesting because our schools typically emphasize the development of these sorts of strengths but not the others, which helps explain why schooling is not an automatic pathway to a fulfilling life (Myers, 1993).

IMPLICATIONS FOR PRACTICE

Our work is in progress, but we can still draw some conclusions about the assessment of character and its implications for practice. Almost all of the strengths in the VIA Classification have been the subject of empirical research using various strategies of assessment (Peterson & Seligman, 2004). However, despite likely links, these lines of research have been conducted in isolation from one another, in part because an efficient battery of strength measures has not existed. We could assemble such a battery by collating existing measures, but respondent burden would quickly become prohibitive as more and more surveys are added. The VIA-IS, in contrast, allows 24 different strengths to be assessed in an efficient way, making research possible that looks at the joint and interactive effects of character strengths. Furthermore, the VIA-IS allows an investigator to control for one strength when ascertaining the correlates, causes, or consequences of another. Conclusions can thereby become crisper. For example, a researcher using the VIA-IS would be able to say that spirituality has (or does not have) consequences above and beyond contributions of associated strengths such as awe, kindness, or hope, a conclusion not possible if only measures of spirituality are used in a study.

The VIA-IS can obviously be used to evaluate interventions that target the good life. Consider character education, positive youth development, life coaching, workplace wellness promotion, and the like. Hundreds of thousands of people participate in such programs every year, with virtually no empirical checks on their effectiveness (Eccles & Goorman, 2002). In some cases, strengths of character are the explicit outcome of interest, and in other cases, one or another character strength is proposed as a mediator or moderator of the effects of the intervention on other outcomes. The availability of the VIA-IS (and the parallel measure for youth) will allow such interventions to be rigorously evaluated and perhaps will lead to the discovery of unanticipated effects of interventions. At this early stage in the development of positive psychology, we suspect that unanticipated effects will be common, which implies that a broad outcome net should be cast.

The VIA measures may have some utility—theoretical and practical—when scored ipsatively.[3] That is, rather than using someone's kindness score in comparisons and contrasts with the kindness scores of others, it can be used to judge that individual's kindness relative to his or her other strengths. We have speculated that most individuals have "signature strengths" (Peterson & Seligman, 2004) and that use of these strengths at work, love, and play provides a route to the psychologically fulfilling life (Seligman, 2002). These are empirical questions that we are just beginning to answer. But we suspect that a positive psychology client is probably not interested in becoming the kindest person in the world but simply in having kindness be a more salient trait than it has been.

Along these lines, within-subjects comparisons may reduce the potential problem created by the fact that almost all the VIA Strength scores are skewed to the right and, thus, crowd the ceiling. Whether this skew reflects inherent human nature (the essential goodness of most people assumed by humanists) or a peculiarity of the VIA-IS is unclear, but it does mean that positive psychology interventions

---

[3] Appreciate that the ipsative assessment of character strengths is not the same thing as the specification of cutpoints—for example, decreeing that someone who scores above 4.5 on a VIA curiosity scale is curious, whereas someone who scores below 4.5 is not. Indeed, our conceptualization of character strengths as traits—dimensions or continua—argues against the use of cutpoints except as a shorthand way of saying that individuals score relatively high or relatively low in a strength. This is hardly a novel conclusion; modern personality theories no longer posit "types" of people, despite the intuitive appeal of being able to speak about someone as an introvert or an optimist (Peterson, 1992).

that target character strengths may not have much room for change. Within-subjects comparisons provide a more statistically powerful means of detecting what may necessarily be small effect sizes, and positive psychology practitioners should probably ascertain baseline measures.

If the VIA measures are used in program evaluation, certain pitfalls need to be anticipated and avoided. We have argued that self-report is a valid way to measure character strengths, but questionnaires are not foolproof if incentives are in place for confirming results. Practitioners may teach to the test, and clients may shade their responses to justify the investments they have made as participants. These are not reasons to forego use of the VIA measures, but they do imply the need for ongoing validity checks—like reports of objective informants.

Rigorous evaluation research must be adequately powered—that is, outcomes studies must have a sample size that allows effects to be reliably detected. Although exact ways of determining adequate sample sizes are readily available (cf. Cohen's, 1992, power primer), they are all too frequently ignored by both basic and applied researchers. It would be not only bad science but a societal loss if a positive psychology intervention were deemed unsuccessful simply because it was tested with too few participants.

Although we believe that positive traits can be strengthened, there is no reason to think that this is simple or easy for practitioners or clients. Theorists as far back as Aristotle argued that virtue is the product of habitual action. One-shot positive psychology interventions can probably jump-start the process, but it is only sustained practice that will make changes permanent. As described, the events of September 11, 2001, increased several VIA-IS scores for people in the United States, but note that these were small in absolute magnitude and detectable only because our research used a very large sample (Peterson & Seligman, 2003). Furthermore, a year after September 11, those strengths that did change had started to return to their pre-September 11 levels.

Although we have concluded that the measures we have developed are efficient, they are not as quick as exit interviews. Our surveys take about 30 to 45 minutes to complete, and some respondents require supervision to prevent break-off effects due to wandering attention. Practitioners looking for "single indicators" of character strengths will not adopt our measures. However, we believe strongly that most character strengths are sufficiently complex that a single-indicator approach to their assessment is doomed. (There may be exceptions to this assertion for a few of the strengths in the VIA Classification. For example, *reading constantly* might suffice as a single item measuring love of learning.) We offer this conclusion without apology. Anyone interested in assessing strengths needs to appreciate that there is no shortcut to measuring good character, any more than there is a shortcut to measuring intellectual achievement or ability. As noted, self-nominations of given strengths—for example, *I am [or am not] religious*—tend to converge with the corresponding scale scores. Nevertheless, we do not recommend that these brief questions be substituted for the scales themselves because it is patently more valid to ask about thoughts, feelings, and actions that reflect a given strength as opposed to abstract trait labels that might be applied idiosyncratically or capriciously. Consider that grade point averages and achievement test scores probably converge impressively with answers to the question, "Are you smart—yes or no," but we would not want to substitute this single-item indicator for the SATs.

We will eventually create shorter versions of both our youth and adult surveys, not by eliminating items from a given scale but by collapsing scales following factor analyses indicating redundancy. For example, scales measuring curiosity and love of learning do not appear distinct, so there is probably no good reason to sustain their distinction.

Although our goal has been to create a battery of measures, we can imagine researchers or practitioners administering only selected VIA scales if they so desire. However, we offer the caveat that presenting respondents with 8 or 10 items measuring—for example—forgiveness and nothing else might create a demand for socially desirable responses that the full batteries seem to avoid by allowing all respondents to say something positive about themselves. Furthermore, as already noted, selective use of the VIA scales may preclude discovery of unanticipated results, so we recommend the full inventory unless there is a strong reason to the contrary. Let the interventions begin.

CONCLUSION

The new field of positive psychology requires equally new perspectives on theories, methods, and applications. As much as traditional approaches can contribute to the goals of positive psychology, there are important issues that must be considered when one's subject matter entails what is best about people. In the present contribution, we discussed these issues and how they come to the forefront when the focus is on character strengths. Good character matters, to positive psychology and to the larger society. The VIA project is the first major project explicitly inspired by positive psychology. We hope that the VIA Classification and the measures it suggests for measuring positive traits will allow psychologists to participate in an informed discussion of this topic.

REFERENCES

Allport, G. W. (1961). *Pattern and growth in personality.* New York: Holt, Rinehart and Winston.

American Psychiatric Association. (1987). *Diagnostic and statistical manual of mental disorders* (3rd ed., rev.). Washington, DC: Author.

Birnbaum, M. H. (Ed.). (2000). *Psychological experiments on the Internet.* San Diego, CA: Academic Press.

Bok, S. (1995). *Common values.* Columbia: University of Missouri Press.

*Cawley, M. J., Martin, J. E., & Johnson, J. A. (2000). A virtues approach to personality. *Personality and Individual Differences, 28,* 997–1013.

Cohen, J. (1992). A power primer. *Psychological Bulletin, 112,* 155–159.

Crowne, D. P., & Marlow, D. (1964). *The approval motive: Studies in evaluative dependence.* New York: Wiley.

Dahlsgaard, K. A., Peterson, C., & Seligman, M. E. P. (2002). *Virtues converge across culture and history.* Unpublished manuscript, University of Pennsylvania, Philadelphia.

Eccles, J. E., & Goorman, J. A. (Eds.). (2002). *Community programs to promote youth development.* Washington, DC: National Academy Press.

Erikson, E. (1963). *Childhood and society* (2nd ed.). New York: Norton.

Frank, J. D. (1974). *Persuasion and healing* (Rev. ed.). New York: Schocken Books.

Greenberger, E., Josselson, R., Knerr, C., & Knerr, B. (1975). The measurement and structure of psychosocial maturity. *Journal of Youth and Adolescence, 4,* 127–143.

Myers, D. G. (1993). *The pursuit of happiness.* New York: Avon Books.

Myers, D. G., & Diener, E. (1995). Who is happy? *Psychological Science, 6,* 10–19.

Nathan, P. E., & Gorman, J. E. (Eds.). (2002). *A guide to treatments that work.* New York: Oxford University Press.

Nisbett, R. E., & Wilson, T. D. (1977). Telling more than we can know: Verbal reports on mental processes. *Psychological Review, 84,* 231–259.

Patrick, C. L., & Olson, K. (2000). Empirically supported therapies. *Journal of Psychological Practice, 6,* 19–34.

Peterson, C. (1992). *Personality* (2nd ed.). Fort Worth, TX: Harcourt Brace.

Peterson, C. (2000). The future of optimism. *American Psychologist, 55,* 44–55.

Peterson, C., & Park, N. (2003a, March 12). *Assessment of character strengths.* Paper presented at the Child Trends Indicators of Positive Development Conference, Washington, DC.

Peterson, C., & Park, N. (2003b). Positive psychology as the even-handed positive psychologist views it. *Psychological Inquiry, 14,* 141–146.

Peterson, C., & Seligman, M. E. P. (2003). Character strengths before and after 9/11. *Psychological Science, 14,* 381–384.

*Peterson, C., & Seligman, M. E. P. (2004). *Character strengths and virtues: A classification and handbook.* Washington, DC: American Psychological Association.

*Ryff, C. D., & Singer, B. (1996). Psychological well-being: Meaning, measurement, and implications for psychotherapy research. *Psychotherapy and Psychosomatics, 65,* 14–23.

Schwartz, S. H. (1994). Are there universal aspects in the structure and contents of human values? *Journal of Social Issues, 50,* 19–45.

*Seligman, M. E. P. (2002). *Authentic happiness: Using the new positive psychology to realize your potential for lasting fulfillment.* New York: Free Press.

Seligman, M. E. P., & Csikszentmihalyi, M. (2000). Positive psychology: An introduction. *American Psychologist, 55,* 5–14.

Smith, M. L., & Glass, G. V. (1977). The meta-analysis of psychotherapy outcome studies. *American Psychologist, 32,* 752–760.

Taylor, S. E., Klein, L. C., Lewis, B. P., Gruenewald, T. L., Gurung, R. A. R., & Updegraff, J. A. (2000). Biobehavioral responses to stress in females: Tend-and-befriend, not fight-or-flight. *Psychological Review, 107,* 422–429.

Walker, L. J., & Pitts, R. C. (1998). Naturalistic conceptions of moral maturity. *Developmental Psychology, 34,* 403–419.

Wolf, S. (1982). Moral saints. *Journal of Philosophy, 79,* 419–439.

Wortman, C. B., Hendricks, M., & Hillis, J. W. (1976). Factors affecting participant reactions to random assignment in ameliorative social programs. *Journal of Personality and Social Psychology, 33,* 256–266.

Yearley, L. H. (1990). *Mencius and Aquinas: Theories of virtue and conceptions of courage.* Albany: State University of New York Press.

CHAPTER 28

Emotional Intelligence in Practice

PETER SALOVEY, DAVID CARUSO, and JOHN D. MAYER

R OSALIND PICARD, AN electrical engineer and computer scientist, is a professor at the Massachusetts Institute of Technology who has spent her life investigating technical challenges such as machine learning and computer pattern recognition. Her work, as reflected in her publications, seems the epitome of logic and rationality. Professor Picard believes that if we want computers to interact naturally with humans in an intelligent manner, we must give them the ability to recognize, understand, and use emotions (Picard, 1997). She came to this view, in part, by reading the neurological literature suggesting that without emotion—or, more particularly, the brain areas involved in the processing of emotions—humans do not make good decisions (e.g., Damasio, 1994). Yet, despite the reasonableness of this claim—the technical challenge of imbuing computers with emotion notwithstanding—many psychologists still have difficulty accepting the idea that emotions are critical to rational cognitive activities and adaptive behavior. Even fewer seem to believe that reliable individual differences in the abilities that Picard wants to program into computers exist, and if they do, that they could or should be measured (see, for example, Shields, 2002, pp. 182–183, in an otherwise excellent book).

James Averill is someone who does. For many years, he has argued that just as intellectual skills are learned and developed, so, too, can we acquire a repertoire of emotional skills that then allows us to achieve, in his words, our full potential (Averill & Nunley, 1992). Likewise, in his model of multiple intelligences, Howard Gardner (1983) described a personal intelligence, which he labeled as "intrapersonal intelligence":

> The core capacity at work here is *access to one's own feeling life*—one's range of affects or emotions: the capacity instantly to effect discriminations among these feelings

Preparation of this chapter was supported by grants from the National Cancer Institute (R01-CA68427), the National Institute of Mental Health (P01-MH/DA56826), the National Institute of Drug Abuse (P50-DA13334), and the Donaghue Women's Health Investigator Program at Yale University.

and, eventually, to label them, to enmesh them in symbolic codes, to draw upon them as a means of understanding and guiding one's behavior. In its most primitive form, the intrapersonal intelligence amounts to little more than the capacity to distinguish a feeling of pleasure from one of pain and, on the basis of such discrimination, to become more involved in or to withdraw from a situation. At its most advanced level, intrapersonal knowledge allows one to detect and to symbolize complex and highly differentiated sets of feelings. One finds this form of intelligence developed in the novelist (like Proust) who can write introspectively about feelings. . . . (p. 239 in paperback edition, original italics)

In the spirit of Gardner, Averill, and others (Leuner, 1966; Payne, 1986), we believe that there is an intelligence involving the processing of affectively charged information (Salovey & Mayer, 1990). We define emotional intelligence (EI) as involving both the capacity to reason about emotions and to use emotions to assist reasoning. We believe emotional intelligence includes abilities to identify emotions accurately in ourselves and in other people, understand emotions and emotional language, manage emotions in ourselves and in other people, and use emotions to facilitate cognitive activities and motivate adaptive behavior (Mayer & Salovey, 1997).

In this chapter, we outline our four-branch model of emotional intelligence and consider some issues in the assessment of emotional intelligence. Then we review research on the application of emotional intelligence in education, human resources management (including an executive coaching case study), politics, marketing, and family dynamics; we consider the key findings, limitations, and opportunities for future research in each of these areas.

A FOUR-BRANCH MODEL OF EMOTIONAL INTELLIGENCE

We began work on a model of emotional intelligence in the late 1980s by reviewing the research literature and asking: What emotion-related skills and abilities have modern investigators of emotion tried—successfully or not—to operationalize over the years (reviewed in Salovey, Woolery, & Mayer, 2001)? Could we pull these skills together into a coherent whole? It seemed that these skills could be grouped into four clusters or "branches" (Mayer & Salovey, 1997): (1) perceiving emotions, (2) using emotions to facilitate thought, (3) understanding emotions, and (4) managing emotions in a way that enhances personal growth and social relations. We view a distinction between the second branch (using emotions) and the other three. Whereas the first, third, and fourth branches all involve reasoning about emotions, the second branch uniquely involves using emotions to enhance reasoning. The four branches form a hierarchy, with identifying emotion in the self and others as the most fundamental or basic-level skill and managing emotions as the most superordinate skill; the ability to regulate emotions in self and others is built up from the competencies represented by the other three branches. We have reviewed the literature concerning individual differences in these four sets of skills elsewhere (e.g., Mayer, Salovey, & Caruso, 2000a, 2000b; Salovey, Bedell, Detweiler, & Mayer, 2000; Salovey, Mayer, & Caruso, 2002; Salovey et al., 2001), although we provide a brief summary of the relevant skills in the following sections and in Table 28.1.

Table 28.1
The Four-Branch "Ability" Model of Emotional Intelligence

Branch Names and Exemplary Skills

Branch 1: Perceiving Emotion
- Ability to identify emotion in a person's physical and psychological states
- Ability to identify emotion in other people
- Ability to express emotions accurately and to express needs related to them
- Ability to discriminate between accurate/honest and inaccurate/dishonest feelings

Branch 2: Using Emotions to Facilitate Thought
- Ability to redirect and prioritize thinking on the basis of associated feelings
- Ability to generate emotions to facilitate judgment and memory
- Ability to capitalize on mood changes to appreciate multiple points of view
- Ability to use emotional states to facilitate problem solving and creativity

Branch 3: Understanding Emotions
- Ability to understand relationships among various emotions
- Ability to perceive the causes and consequences of emotions
- Ability to understand complex feelings, emotional blends, and contradictory states
- Ability to understand transitions among emotions

Branch 4: Managing Emotions
- Ability to be open to feelings, both pleasant and unpleasant
- Ability to monitor and reflect on emotions
- Ability to engage, prolong, or detach from an emotional state
- Ability to manage emotions in oneself
- Ability to manage emotions in others

PERCEIVING EMOTIONS

Emotional perception involves registering, attending to, and deciphering emotional messages as they are expressed in facial expressions, voice tone, or cultural artifacts. Individuals differ in their abilities to discern the emotional content of such stimuli. These competencies are basic information processing skills in which the relevant information consists of feelings and mood states. For example, some individuals, called *alexithymic,* have difficulty expressing their emotions verbally, presumably because they have difficulty identifying those feelings (Apfel & Sifneos, 1979; Bagby, Parker, & Taylor, 1993a, 1993b).

USING EMOTIONS TO FACILITATE THOUGHT

This second branch of emotional intelligence focuses on how emotion affects the cognitive system and, as such, can be harnessed for more effective problem solving, reasoning, decision making, and creative endeavors. Although cognition can be disrupted by emotions, such as anxiety and fear, emotions also can prioritize the cognitive system to attend to what is important (Easterbrook, 1959; Leeper, 1948; Mandler, 1975; Simon, 1982) and even to focus on what it does best in a given mood (e.g., Palfai & Salovey, 1993; Schwarz, 1990).

UNDERSTANDING EMOTIONS

The most fundamental competency at this level concerns the ability to label emotions with words and to recognize the relationships among exemplars of the affective lexicon. The emotionally intelligent individual is able to recognize that the terms used to describe emotions are arranged into families and that groups of emotion terms form fuzzy sets (Ortony, Clore, & Collins, 1988). Perhaps more importantly, the relations among these terms are deduced—for example, annoyance and irritation can lead to rage if the provocative stimulus is not eliminated. This is the branch of emotional intelligence that we would expect to be most related to verbal intelligence.

MANAGING EMOTIONS

The emotionally intelligent individual can repair his or her negative moods and emotions and maintain positive moods and emotions when doing so is appropriate. (It is also sometimes desirable to maintain negative emotional states, such as when a person anticipates having to discipline a child, collect an unpaid bill, or compete against an enemy.) This regulatory process comprises several steps. Individuals must (1) believe that they can modify their emotions; (2) monitor their moods and emotional states accurately; (3) identify and discriminate those moods and emotions in need of regulation; (4) employ strategies to change these moods and emotions, most commonly, to alleviate negative feelings or maintain positive feelings; and (5) assess the effectiveness of those strategies.

Individuals differ in the expectancy that they can alleviate negative moods. Some people believe that when they are upset, they can do something that will make them feel better; others insist that nothing will improve their negative moods. Individuals who believe they can successfully repair their moods engage in active responses to stress, whereas people low in self-efficacy of regulation display avoidance responses, as well as depressive and mild somatic symptoms (Catanzaro & Greenwood, 1994; Goldman, Kraemer, & Salovey, 1996). The ability to help others enhance their moods is also an aspect of emotional intelligence, as individuals often rely on their social networks to provide not just a practical but an emotional buffer against negative life events (Stroebe & Stroebe, 1996). Moreover, individuals appear to derive a sense of efficacy and social worth from helping others feel better and by contributing to their joy.

MEASURING EMOTIONAL INTELLIGENCE

We have been working with two task-based tests of emotional intelligence, the Multifactor Emotional Intelligence Scale (MEIS) and the Mayer-Salovey-Caruso Emotional Intelligence Test (MSCEIT). The MEIS represented an attempt merely to show that measuring emotional intelligence reliably as an ability was feasible (Mayer, Caruso, & Salovey, 1998, 1999). The MSCEIT is a more professional and user-friendly assessment battery and the one that we recommend for research and practice (Mayer, Salovey, & Caruso, 2002; see also www.emotion-aliq.org). It is considerably shorter and better normed than the MEIS, and it can be administered on paper or through a computer interface. Elsewhere, we have tried to make the case that ability-based measures may be a more appropriate way to operationalize our model of emotional intelligence as compared to self-report inventories (Mayer, Caruso, & Salovey, 2000).

The MSCEIT has eight tasks, as depicted in Table 28.2: Two tasks measure each of the four branches of EI. Branch 1, Perceiving Emotions, is measured through (1) faces, for which participants are asked to accurately identify the emotions in faces, and (2) pictures, for which participants are asked to accurately identify the emotions conveyed by landscapes and designs. Branch 2, Using Emotions to Facilitate Thought, is measured by the (3) sensations task, for which participants compare emotions to other tactile and sensory stimuli, and (4) facilitation, for which participants identify which emotions would best facilitate a type of thinking (e.g., planning a birthday party). Branch 3, Understanding Emotions, is measured through (5) changes, which test a person's ability to know which emotion would change into another (e.g., frustration into aggression), and (6) blends, which ask participants to identify which emotions would form a third emotion. Branch 4, Managing Emotions, is measured through (7) emotional management, which involves presenting participants with hypothetical scenarios and asking how they would maintain or change their feelings in them, and (8) emotional relations, which involve asking participants how to manage others' feelings.

The MSCEIT produces a total score, scores at two area levels, and at the four branch levels, as well as scores for the eight individual tasks. When we employ the MSCEIT for validity studies or interpret them in providing case feedback, we exclusively focus on scores at the total, area, and branch levels, especially emphasizing the branch level scores, as they are most consistent with the theory on which

Table 28.2

The Four-Branch Model of Emotional Intelligence as Operationalized by the Mayer-Salovey-Caruso Emotional Intelligence Test (MSCEIT V2.0)

Branch Names and Exemplary Tasks

Branch 1: Perceiving Emotion

- Faces: Identifying emotions expressed in faces
- Pictures: Identifying emotions suggested by photographs of landscapes and abstract artistic designs

Branch 2: Using Emotions to Facilitate Thought

- Sensations: Matching tactile, taste, and color terms to specific emotions
- Facilitation: Indicating how moods and emotions affect cognitive processes such as thinking, reasoning, problem solving, and creativity

Branch 3: Understanding Emotions

- Blends: Identifying the emotions that may encompass a complex feeling state
- Changes: Noticing how feelings and emotions progress or transition from one state to another

Branch 4: Managing Emotions

- Management: Estimating the effectiveness of various strategies that could modify a person's feelings in various situations
- Relations: Estimating the consequences of various strategies for emotional reactions involving other people

the MSCEIT was based (Mayer et al., 2002). Reliabilities at these three levels of the MSCEIT are adequate. In recent work (Mayer, Salovey, Caruso, & Sitarenios, 2001, 2003), we were able to establish that the MSCEIT test's overall reliability is $r = 0.91$ or 0.93 (depending on whether expert-based or general consensus-based scoring is employed; see Mayer et al., 2002), with area reliabilities of $r = 0.86$ to 0.90 and branch scores (representing the four-branch model) of $r = 0.76$ to 0.91. Brackett and Mayer (2003) have reported that the MSCEIT has test-retest reliability of $r = 0.86$ after one month.

PREDICTING OUTCOMES

We have provided more substantial summaries of the relations between MSCEIT scores and important, real-life outcomes elsewhere (Mayer, Salovey, & Caruso, in press), and we are still in the early stages of the use of the MSCEIT in research. However, already, interesting findings are emerging, and we summarize them briefly here. First, we know that emotional intelligence, measured as an ability with the MSCEIT, does not overlap substantially with other psychological constructs such as personality (Big Five) and analytic intelligence (Lopes, Salovey, & Straus, 2003), but this has been a problem for self-report measures of emotional intelligence such as the Bar-On Emotional Quotient Inventory (Bar-On, 1997) and the Schutte et al. (1998) self-report Emotional Intelligence Scale. For instance, Brackett and Mayer (2003) reported multiple R's between the Big Five and the Bar-On scale of 0.75 and the Schutte scale of 0.52; for the MSCEIT, it was only 0.38. The MSCEIT appears to be free of the biasing influences of mood and social desirability as well (Lopes et al., 2003).

Individuals scoring high on the MEIS or MSCEIT have higher grades in school, although these correlations may be accounted for by "third variables" (Barchard, in press; Brackett, Mayer, & Warner, in press; Lam & Kirby, 2002). People higher in emotional intelligence are less likely to engage in violent behavior such as bullying and are less likely to use tobacco, drink alcohol to excess, or take illicit drugs (Brackett & Mayer, 2003; Brackett et al., in press; Rubin, 1999; Swift, 2002; Trinidad & Johnson, 2002). Individuals high in emotional intelligence, measured as an ability with the MEIS or MSCEIT, report more positive interactions and relations with other people (Côté, Lopes, Salovey, & Beers, 2003).

IN PRACTICE

There have been five major areas of application of emotional intelligence theory and measurement: education, human resources management (especially executive coaching), politics, marketing, and family dynamics. We look at these five domains in turn.

EDUCATION

In recent years, the theme of emotional intelligence has been used to organize efforts to teach schoolchildren various kinds of skills that help to build competency in self-management and social relations. In the educational literature, this is usually called "social and emotional learning" (SEL; Elias, Hunter, & Kress, 2001; Payton et al., 2000), and programs range from the teaching of discrete skills in, for example, social problem solving (reviewed in Cohen, 2001; Elias et al., 1997) and conflict management (e.g., Lantieri & Patti, 1996), to larger curricula organized around broader themes in social development.

Three of the broader curricula that are explicit about being especially focused on emotions and emotional intelligence are Self Science (McCown, Jensen, Freedman, & Rideout, 1998), what I term the South Africa Emotional Intelligence Curriculum (de Klerk & le Roux, 2003), and the Innerchoice Publishing activity books (Schilling, 1996). The Self Science curriculum—which was developed independently of and prior to our work on emotional intelligence—is structured around 54 separate lessons organized around 10 goals. Some of these goals are explicitly about emotions—becoming more aware of multiple feelings, developing communications skills for affective states, disclosing thoughts and feelings—and the lessons themselves involve many different subjects in the traditional curriculum. The South Africa curriculum includes 58 activities, the majority of which are focused on feelings, such as the origin of a feeling, feelings and physical symptoms, identifying feelings in animal pictures, feelings that go together, naming the feeling, controlled and uncontrolled ways of expressing your feelings, empathy and validation, and so on. The Innerchoice Publishing activity books include activities for teaching an array of social and emotional competencies, some focused on emotions (managing feelings) and some less so (decision making, self-concept).

Although controlled evaluation studies demonstrating the efficacy of these curricula have not yet been published, reports from teachers, parents, and students suggest that these curricula are appreciated and possible to implement on a large scale. In addition to demonstrating the effectiveness of these programs, the other major challenge is to show that the skills learned in these programs do generalize to real-life situations (Lopes & Salovey, in press).

Zins, Elias, Greenberg, and Weissberg (2000) suggest that to be successful, SEL/ emotional intelligence school-based programs should be comprehensive, multiyear, and integrated into the curriculum and extracurricular activities. They should be theoretically based, as well as developmentally and culturally appropriate. They should promote a caring, supportive, and challenging classroom and school climate; teach a broad range of skills; be undertaken by well-trained staff with adequate, ongoing support; promote school, family, and community partnerships; and be systematically monitored and evaluated.

Difficulties arise, however, when researchers and educators try to identify a set of key skills on which to focus. Payton et al. (2000) list social and emotional competencies under four headings: awareness of self and others, positive attitudes and values, responsible decision making, and social interaction skills. In drawing up any such list of key skills, for a domain as broad as social and emotional functioning, we face several challenges:

- The list is likely to represent a very broad range of skills, and it may be difficult to address all these skills through formal classroom instruction.
- The subskills listed may themselves be fuzzy sets, encompassing a wide array of skills.
- These skills may be partly domain- or context-specific, failing to transfer across situations.
- Some of these skills may depend on other skills, which are not part of the list.

- There may be more common ground between educational programs stressing different key skills than is usually acknowledged, as these programs may operate through similar mechanisms (e.g., enhancing intrinsic motivation).

For all these reasons, the theoretical and empirical rationale for emphasizing one set of skills over another is often difficult to establish (Lopes & Salovey, in press).

HUMAN RESOURCES MANAGEMENT

The workplace has been the most popular domain for applications of emotional intelligence, in part because following Goleman's (1995) best-selling trade book on emotional intelligence, he teamed up with Hay Group, one of the leading human resources development and consulting firms worldwide to promote their measures of workplace competencies and the programs developed to enhance these skills among workers (Goleman, 1998; Goleman, Boyatzis, & McKee, 2002). Some of the extravagant claims about emotional intelligence that can be found in this literature have been criticized quite deservedly (Dulewicz & Higgs, 2000; Zeidner, Matthews, & Roberts, in press). For example, Cooper and Sawaf (1997, p. xxvii) wrote: "if the driving force of intelligence in twentieth century business has been IQ, then . . . in the dawning twenty-first century it will be EQ" or "use of EI for recruitment decisions leads to 90-percentile success rates" (Watkin, 2000, p. 91). This kind of hyperbole notwithstanding, there is a slowly growing literature suggesting that emotional intelligence may matter in the workplace (Ashkanasy & Daus, 2002; Cherniss & Goleman, 2001; Jordan, Ashkanasy, & Härtel, 2003).

From our own work, we have seen, for example, that business students working together in task groups who scored high on the MSCEIT are more likely to be viewed by their peers as developing well-articulated, visionary goals for the group than those students with lower MSCEIT scores (Côté, Lopes, & Salovey, 2003). In a different study, business students working in teams who scored high on the MSCEIT, especially the managing emotions branch, were more likely to have satisfying social interactions and to elicit social support from the other group members (Côté, Lopes, Salovey, & Beers, 2003). In both of these studies, associations with emotional intelligence and the various outcomes held even after controlling for the Big Five personality dimensions. Similarly, students with high MSCEIT scores were more likely to perform well (e.g., on examinations) in an organizational behavior and leadership course (Ashkanasy & Dasborough, 2003) and in their campus jobs (Janovics & Christiansen, 2001).

In real-world studies of organizations and leadership, there have been some hints that emotional intelligence is related to more positive outcomes. For example, Rice (1999) studied the emotional intelligence of teams of claims adjusters working in the insurance industry. Among 164 individuals working in 26 teams, the average EI of the team (measured with the MSCEIT's predecessor, the MEIS) predicted customer satisfaction with the claims adjustment process. And, in a study we just completed among employees of the finance group in a health insurance company, the understanding emotions branch and total MSCEIT scores appear to predict the size of annual salary raises, and the managing emotions branch score appears to predict total compensation. However, these findings should be considered cautiously as we are still analyzing these data and, obviously, have not yet written up the findings nor submitted them for peer review. We hope to have more to report about this study shortly.

Perhaps the workplace application for which emotional intelligence has been most used is in the coaching of executives and other employees. MSCEIT testing often provides a starting point for addressing issues of career development and advancement (Caruso & Wolfe, 2001). For example, consider the following case study from the consulting practice of one of the authors (D. C.) of this chapter.

Case Study

William was muttering under his breath as he ambled down the hallway toward the open conference room door: "I have to communicate better. I need to motivate and inspire my team. People have to feel that they can trust me. I can do this, I can do it." Having just left a meeting with his executive coach, William was energized and ready to tackle his problems head on.

He had asked for a special team meeting to kick off the month. The team meeting, held on the first day of the month, was special for several reasons. For William, it gave him a chance to try out his newly learned skills. For the team, it meant a lost day, as the first of the month fell on a Saturday. Although this was pointed out to William, he had shrugged it off, saying, "The first is the first, no matter what. Think of the symbolism of it. We're starting off the team in the right way."

The group had been assembled for about 15 minutes when William strode into the conference room, smiling and apologizing profusely for being late for the meeting. With his high-energy assertiveness, William launched into a summary of his week's activities, paused for a moment, and then asked his department heads for an update. "That sounded about right," he thought. "Clear and direct communication, an upbeat delivery, full of energy. No problem." But no one said a word. The silence, perhaps more than the looks on the faces of those gathered around the table, finally intruded onto William's attention. "What?" he asked, "You guys look like somebody just died or something. Come on, let's get this meeting going!"

A few throats cleared, there were uncomfortable looks exchanged, and one team member pointed toward the television monitor in the corner. William hadn't noticed it until just then. The sound was turned off, but the image on the screen kept repeating, again and again. William peered at the screen and tried to decipher the caption at the bottom. He looked confused and puzzled, turning his head one way and then another as if to gain a clearer image. It seemed like a few minutes when William finally turned to look at his assembled team and pronounced, "Well, we have some work to do. We can't let this bother us too much, right?" He was proud of his take-charge leadership style, "like the general leading his troops into battle," he thought.

No one responded to his battle cry. Even after directly confronting a few people to give their reports, they just shook their heads and said they'd rather not. By this time, William was no longer his smiling self—he was irritated and angry. He stood up, knocking his chair over, and said, "I can't believe you guys! This is a hell of a way to start off. Just get outta here, the meeting's over." His staff filed out the door without a look back, and William soon found himself alone in the conference room. It had not gone as well as he had planned and hoped. Clearly, something was wrong.

What was wrong was that the meeting began as news of the space shuttle Columbia was being broadcast. The team members were stunned as they silently watched the shuttle break up during its final descent to Florida. They were in no mood for a team meeting or for William's antics that morning.

William is, in essence, a "nice guy." He can be a compassionate person who reaches out to his staff and cares deeply about the welfare of his team. William is not effusively warm, nor is he terribly inspiring. He tends to talk *at* people. It was no surprise that the coaching objectives for William, developed by the firm's CEO and executive VP of human resources, included these general statements:

- Enhance your communication style
- Positively motivate others
- Build a sense of team and trust within your group
- Listen to people

William initially had trouble with some of the objectives. He felt that he was a good listener and that he was always communicating to his team. William had a problem with trust as well—feeling that he was a very trustworthy manager. After a few coaching sessions and some hard-hitting feedback, he began to accept the fact that perhaps he was not the best communicator and that he had not created an atmosphere of trust as best as he could.

While these were not part of his objectives, many people reported that William was "oblivious" and could be impulsive and unpredictable at times. After getting a full report of the aborted weekend meeting, which the coach had not supported, the coach was stumped. The coach felt that he was not addressing the real issues and objectives, but he wasn't sure what these were. William agreed to take the MSCEIT as part of a diagnostic executive assessment. His results on the MSCEIT were as follows:

- *Overall score:* Below average
- *Perceiving emotions:* Well below average
- *Using emotions:* Average
- *Understanding emotions:* Average
- *Managing emotions:* Below average

It was a moment of insight for William's coach. William did not need to learn to listen; he did not fail to understand people. He felt for others and could relate to them (Using Emotions score). William understood people, and as demonstrated during coaching sessions, seemed to have some good insights into issues (Understanding Emotions score). What he missed were the cues and the signals of interpersonal interaction—he couldn't "read" people (Perceiving Emotions score). And, he had trouble integrating his feelings into his thinking and his behavior, felt easily overwhelmed, and tried to be overly rational at times (Managing Emotions score).

The course of coaching changed dramatically after the MSCEIT results were examined. William needed to learn how to decipher the mysterious signals of emotions, mysterious at least to William. It wasn't an issue of attention or awareness—William could attend. He just attended to the wrong cues, or his emotional judgments were totally off base. William started slowly learning emotional cues. But as this might be the work of a lifetime, he enlisted the help of a colleague to be, as William put it, "his seeing-emotion dog." The colleague attended most of William's key meetings, and with the help of the coach, this dynamic duo created a set of signs or signals, like a third-base coach uses to signal to runners or the batter in baseball. The signals were simple at first and not all that subtle. The first set of signals was for positive and negative, and William learned to read the emotional landscape with these basic signs of emotionality of his audience.

He could generate the emotion and match the mood to the task (Using Emotions), and with this accurate, although primitive, data, he was not as "off" as he once was. William learned to leverage the data thus acquired to reason through various emotional what-if scenarios about how people would react and respond (Understanding Emotions). He still struggled with refusing to allow these underlying feelings to influence his decision-making (Managing Emotions), but his analytical skills were appealed to in order to convince him that such a course would often be prudent.

The point of this coaching case study is not really to illustrate the usefulness of putting numbers on William's emotional strengths and weaknesses. Rather, identifying the skills most in need of development provided information allowing the coach and William to get started in their work together. Moreover, merely taking the MSCEIT served to begin a dialogue between the two of them.

POLITICS

As compared to education and human resources management, applications of emotional intelligence in politics are relatively recent. Based loosely on discoveries about the neurological underpinnings of the interactions between emotion and rational decision making (e.g., Adolphs & Damasio, 2001; Damasio, 1994; Jaušovec, Jaušovec, & Gerlič, 2001; LeDoux, 1996, 2000), Marcus, Neuman, and Mackuen (2000) provide a perspective on political judgment that they call "affective intelligence." This is designed to examine how momentary psychological states, such as mood and emotion, interact with ongoing beliefs and values, such as self-interest, in determining political behavior.

Other scholars have looked especially at case examples of political leadership. In a study of all the presidents of the United States from Roosevelt to Clinton, Greenstein (2000) suggests that six qualities are needed for successful presidential leadership: (1) effectiveness as a public communicator, (2) organizational capacity, (3) political skill, (4) vision, (5) cognitive style, and (6) emotional intelligence. In considering emotional intelligence, Greenstein focuses most explicitly on the fourth branch of our model, the management of emotions, and notes that the presidents differed quite a bit in this regard:

> The vesuvian LBJ was subject to mood swings of clinical proportions. Jimmy Carter's rigidity was a significant impediment to his White House performance. The defective impulse control of Bill Clinton led him into actions that led to his impeachment. Richard Nixon was the most emotionally flawed of the presidents considered here. His anger and suspiciousness were of Shakespearean proportions. He more than any other president summons up the classic notion of the tragic hero who is defeated by the very qualities that brought him success. (p. 199)

In the final sentences of his fascinating analysis, Greenstein (2000, p. 200) reveals just how central he believes emotional intelligence is to presidential success: "Beware the presidential contender who lacks emotional intelligence. In its absence all else may turn to ashes."

MARKETING

With the popularization of emotional intelligence through the 1990s, increasingly, marketing and advertising professionals became interested in connecting products to consumers' emotional states through a technique known as *emotional branding*. Although the emotional branding literature is only loosely related to the scientific study of emotional intelligence, there is some sense in that managing the emotions of consumers is part of the way in which products are sold. Emotional connections with potential customers need to be made, and desired emotional outcomes are highlighted in media and other depictions of products.

Emotional branding is based on four principles (Gobé, 2001). First is the idea that consumers want to feel that they have a relationship with the manufacturer of the product or its salesperson and that this relationship is respectful of them. Second is the idea that the consumer wants to have a sensory experience with respect to the product that is rich and memorable. The third idea is that emotional connections with products are best made when the consumer's imagination is peaked through something that is unexpected. Finally, brand loyalty is cultivated when the marketing campaign includes vision, defined as a cohesive brand-emotion connection over time. Some of the more compelling examples of emotional branding suggested by Gobé include Tiffany (prestige, respect, pride), Starbucks (the romance of coffee drinking), and Jet Blue Airlines (feeling cool on a hip airline). Similarly, Martins (2000) considers these kinds of brand-linked emotions as the "magical" element in an effective marketing campaign and points especially to Coca-Cola (joy—"have a Coke and a smile"), McDonalds (playfulness), Harley Davidson (rebellion), and Benetton (empathy and human solidarity). Although many of these themes are not emotions per se, they are connected to identifiable emotional experiences that are then emphasized in advertising. Whether this is an especially effective marketing ploy is unknown at present; there is little empirical literature evaluating these interesting ideas.

FAMILY DYNAMICS

A final domain of application of emotional intelligence concerns effective parenting and avoiding marital dysfunction. Many guidebooks for the general public have been written on the importance of emotion-related competencies and skills in effective parenting and in child development (e.g., Elias, Tobias, & Friedlander, 1999; Gottman, 1997; Shapiro, 1997). For example, through his work with emotion-coaching parents, Gottman discovered that parent-child interactions when strong emotions are being expressed are critical for the child's development. Effective parents seem easily to: (1) become aware of their child's emotions, (2) recognize the emotion as an opportunity for learning and intimacy, (3) listen empathically to their children, (4) help the child label the emotions he or she is experiencing, and (5) set limits while exploring solutions to the problem that gave rise to the emotions.

Recently, studies using the MSCEIT have begun to surface, suggesting strong connections between parental emotional intelligence and social competence in children. For example, Marsland and Likavec (2003) examined a sample of 67 infants and their mothers. They assessed infant attachment at 12 months and obtained mothers' ratings as to the children's socioemotional competence on an extensive rating scale of child behavior. Mothers' emotional intelligence on branches of the MSCEIT (measured by only one task each due to time limits) indicated that maternal EI, especially accurate emotional perception, was highly related to child empathy, prosocial peer relations, and relatedness when their children were 3.5 years of age. Higher maternal EI was also associated with more securely attached infants.

Although there is a large literature on the emotional development of children (e.g., Denham, 1998; Saarni, 1979, 1990, 1999), little work has been done assessing the emotional intelligence of parents and looking at its relation to child-rearing skills and tactics. Considerably more work has been conducted in which emotional competencies in children are assessed, but this is beyond the scope of this chapter as we are only beginning to develop measures, based on our theory of emotional intelligence, that would be suitable for children.

CONCLUSION

In this chapter, we outlined our theory of emotional intelligence, focusing on the four groups of competencies involved in the effective integration of emotion and cognition. We then described the measurement of emotional intelligence as a set of abilities rather than through self-report, especially our measure, the Mayer-Salovey-Caruso Emotional Intelligence Test (MSCEIT). The MSCEIT shows appropriate discriminant and convergent validity, and its four-branch structure produces reliable scale scores. Although predictive validity research with the MSCEIT is in its infancy, it does seem to account for important outcomes, and we emphasized some of those in this chapter. Emotional intelligence is most often put into practice in the design of educational curricula and in organizational development efforts, including executive coaching. However, increasingly, applications in other domains are noted, such as in marketing, politics, and parent skills training. We suspect, though, that the most interesting applications of emotional intelligence have yet to be developed.

REFERENCES

Adolphs, R., & Damasio, A. R. (2001). The interaction of affect and cognition: A neurobiological perspective. In J. P. Forgas (Ed.), *The handbook of affect and social cognition* (pp. 27–49). Mahwah, NJ: Erlbaum.

Apfel, R. J., & Sifneos, P. E. (1979). Alexithymia: Concept and measurement. *Psychotherapy and Psychosomatics, 32,* 180–190.

Ashkanasy, N. M., & Dasborough, M. T. (2003). *Emotional awareness and emotional intelligence in leadership training.* Manuscript submitted for publication.

Ashkanasy, N. M., & Daus, S. D. (2002). Emotion in the workplace: The new challenge for managers. *Academy of Management Executive, 16,* 76–86.

Averill, J. R., & Nunley, E. P. (1992). *Voyages of the heart: Living an emotionally creative life.* New York: Free Press.

Bagby, R. M., Parker, J. D. A., & Taylor, G. J. (1993a). The twenty-item Toronto Alexithymia Scale: I. Item selection and cross-validation of the factor structure. *Journal of Psychosomatic Research, 38,* 23–32.

Bagby, R. M., Parker, J. D. A., & Taylor, G. J. (1993b). The twenty-item Toronto Alexithymia Scale: II. Convergent, discriminant, and concurrent validity. *Journal of Psychosomatic Research, 38,* 33–40.

Barchard, K. A. (in press). Does emotional intelligence assist in the prediction of academic success? *Educational and Psychological Measurement.*

Bar-On, R. (1997). *Emotional Intelligence Quotient Inventory: A measure of emotional intelligence.* Toronto, Ontario, Canada: Multi-Health Systems.

Brackett, M. A., & Mayer, J. D. (2003). Convergent, discriminant, and incremental validity of competing measures of emotional intelligence. *Personality and Social Psychology Bulletin, 29,* 1147–1158.

Brackett, M. A., Mayer, J. D., & Warner, R. M. (in press). Emotional intelligence and the prediction of behavior. *Personality and Individual Differences.*

Caruso, D. R., & Wolfe, C. J. (2001). Emotional intelligence in the workplace. In J. Ciarrochi, J. P. Forgas, & J. D. Mayer (Eds.), *Emotional intelligence in everyday life: A scientific inquiry* (pp. 150–167). Philadelphia: Psychology Press.

Catanzaro, S. J., & Greenwood, G. (1994). Expectancies for negative mood regulation, coping, and dysphoria among college students. *Journal of Consulting Psychology, 41,* 34–44.

Cherniss, C., & Goleman, D. (Eds.). (2001). *The emotionally intelligent workplace: How to select for, measure, and improve emotional intelligence in individuals, groups, and organizations.* San Francisco: Jossey-Bass.

Cohen, J. (Ed.). (2001). *Caring classrooms/intelligent schools: The social emotional education of young children.* New York: Teachers College Press.

Cooper, R. K., & Sawaf, A. (1997). *Executive EQ: Emotional intelligence in leaders and organizations.* New York: Grosset/Putnam.

Côté, S., Lopes, P. N., & Salovey, P. (2003). *Emotional intelligence and vision formulation and articulation.* Manuscript submitted for publication.

Côté, S., Lopes, P. N., Salovey, P., & Beers, M. (2003). *Emotion regulation ability and the quality of social interaction.* Manuscript submitted for publication.

Damasio, A. R. (1994). *Descartes' error: Emotion, reason, and the human brain.* New York: Putnam.

de Klerk, R., & le Roux, R. (2003). *Emotional intelligence: A practical guide for parents and teachers.* Cape Town, South Africa: Human & Rousseau.

Denham, S. A. (1998). *Emotional development in young children.* New York: Guilford Press.

Dulewicz, V., & Higgs, M. (2000). Emotional intelligence: A review and evaluation study. *Journal of Managerial Psychology, 15,* 341–372.

Easterbrook, J. A. (1959). The effects of emotion on cue utilization and the organization of behavior. *Psychological Review, 66,* 183–200.

Elias, M. J., Hunter, L., & Kress, J. S. (2001). Emotional intelligence and education. In J. Ciarrochi, J. P. Forgas, & J. D. Mayer (Eds.), *Emotional intelligence in everyday life: A scientific inquiry* (pp. 133–149). Philadelphia: Psychology Press.

Elias, M. J., Tobias, S. E., & Friedlander, B. S. (1999). *Emotionally intelligent parenting: How to raise a self-disciplined, responsible, socially skilled child.* New York: Three Rivers Press.

Elias, M. J., Zins, J. E., Weissberg, R. P., Frey, K. S., Greenberg, M. T., Haynes, N. M., et al. (1997). *Promoting social and emotional learning—Guidelines for educators.* Alexandria, VA: Association for Supervision and Curriculum Development.

Gardner, H. (1983). *Frames of mind.* New York: Basic Books.

Gobé, M. (2001). *Emotional branding: The new paradigm for connecting brands to people.* Oxford, England: Windsor Books.

Goldman, S. L., Kraemer, D. T., & Salovey, P. (1996). Beliefs about mood moderate the relationship of stress to illness and symptom reporting. *Journal of Psychosomatic Research, 41,* 115–128.

Goleman, D. (1995). *Emotional intelligence.* New York: Bantam Books.

Goleman, D. (1998). *Working with emotional intelligence.* New York: Bantam Books.

Goleman, D., Boyatzis, R., & McKee, A. (2002). *Primal leadership: Realizing the power of emotional intelligence.* Boston: Harvard Business School Press.

Gottman, J. (1997). *The heart of parenting: Raising an emotionally intelligent child.* New York: Simon & Schuster.

Greenstein, F. I. (2000). *The presidential difference: Leadership style from FDR to Clinton.* New York: Free Press.

Janovics, J., & Christiansen, N. D. (2001, April). *Emotional intelligence at the workplace.* Paper presented at the 16th annual conference of the Society of Industrial and Organizational Psychology, San Diego, CA.

Jaušovec, N., Jaušovec, K., & Gerlič, I. (2001). Differences in event-related and induced electroencephalography patterns in the theta and alpha frequency bands related to human emotional intelligence. *Neuroscience Letters, 311,* 93–96.

Jordan, P. J., Ashkanasy, N. M., & Härtel, C. E. J. (2003). The case for emotional intelligence in organizational research. *Academy of Management Review, 28,* 195–197.

Lam, L. T., & Kirby, S. L. (2002). Is emotional intelligence an advantage? An exploration of the impact of emotional and general intelligence on individual performance. *Journal of Sport Psychology, 142,* 133–143.

Lantieri, L., & Patti, J. (1996). *Waging peace in our schools.* Boston: Beacon Press.

LeDoux, J. (1996). *The emotional brain: The mysterious underpinnings of emotional life.* New York: Simon & Schuster.

LeDoux, J. (2000). Cognitive-emotional interactions: Listening to the brain. In R. D. Lane & L. Nadel (Eds.), *Cognitive neuroscience of emotion* (pp. 129–155). New York: Oxford University Press.

Leeper, R. W. (1948). A motivational theory of emotions to replace "emotions as disorganized response." *Psychological Review, 55,* 5–21.

Leuner, B. (1966). Emotional intelligence and emancipation. *Praxis der Kinderpsychologie und Kinderpsychiatrie* [Practice of Child Psychology and Child Psychiatry], *15,* 196–203.

Lopes, P. N., & Salovey, P. (in press). Toward a broader education: Social, emotional, and practical skills. In J. E. Zins, R. P. Weissberg, M. C. Wang, & H. J. Walberg (Eds.), *Building school success on social and emotional learning.* New York: Teachers College Press.

Lopes, P. N., Salovey, P., & Straus, R. (2003). Emotional intelligence, personality, and the perceived quality of social relationships. *Personality and Individual Differences, 35,* 641–658.

Mandler, G. (1975). *Mind and emotion.* New York: Wiley.

Marcus, G. E., Neuman, W. R., & Mackuen, M. (2000). *Affective intelligence and political judgment.* Chicago: University of Chicago Press.

Marsland, K. W., & Likavec, S. C. (2003, June). *Maternal emotional intelligence, infant attachment, and child socioeconomic competence.* Paper presented at the 15th annual meeting of the American Psychological Society, Atlanta, GA.

Martins, J. S. (2000). *The emotional nature of a brand.* Sao Paulo, Brazil: Marts Plan Imagen.

Mayer, J. D., Caruso, D. R., & Salovey, P. (1998). *Multifactor Emotional Intelligence Scale (MEIS)*. (Available from John D. Mayer, Department of Psychology, University of New Hampshire, Conant Hall, Durham, NH 03824 United States)

Mayer, J. D., Caruso, D. R., & Salovey, P. (1999). Emotional intelligence meets traditional standards for an intelligence. *Intelligence, 27, 267–298.*

Mayer, J. D., Caruso, D. R., & Salovey, P. (2000). Selecting a measure of emotional intelligence: The case for ability scales. In R. Bar-On & J. D. A. Parker (Eds.), *The handbook of emotional intelligence* (pp. 320–342). San Francisco: Jossey-Bass.

*Mayer, J. D., & Salovey, P. (1997). What is emotional intelligence? In P. Salovey & D. Sluyter (Eds.), *Emotional development and emotional intelligence: Educational implications* (pp. 3–31). New York: Basic Books.

Mayer, J. D., Salovey, P., & Caruso, D. R. (2000a). Emotional intelligence as Zeitgeist, as personality, and as a mental ability. In R. Bar-On & J. D. A. Parker (Eds.), *The handbook of emotional intelligence* (pp. 92–117). San Francisco: Jossey-Bass.

*Mayer, J. D., Salovey, P., & Caruso, D. R. (2000b). Models of emotional intelligence. In R. J. Sternberg (Ed.), *The handbook of intelligence* (pp. 396–420). New York: Cambridge University Press.

Mayer, J. D., Salovey, P., & Caruso, D. R. (2002). *The Mayer-Salovey-Caruso Emotional Intelligence Test (MSCEIT)*. Toronto, Ontario, Canada: Multi-Health Systems.

Mayer, J. D., Salovey, P., & Caruso, D. R. (in press). Emotional intelligence: Theory, findings, and implications. *Psychological Inquiry.*

Mayer, J. D., Salovey, P., Caruso, D. R., & Sitarenios, G. (2001). Emotional intelligence as a standard intelligence. *Emotion, 1, 232–242.*

*Mayer, J. D., Salovey, P., Caruso, D. R., & Sitarenios, G. (2003). Measuring emotional intelligence with the MSCEIT V2.0. *Emotion, 3, 97–105.*

McCown, K. S., Jensen, A. L., Freedman, J. M., & Rideout, M. C. (1998). *Self science: The emotional intelligence curriculum.* San Mateo, CA: Six Seconds.

Ortony, A., Clore, G. L., & Collins, A. (1988). *The cognitive structure of emotions.* Cambridge, England: Cambridge University Press.

Palfai, T. P., & Salovey, P. (1993). The influence of depressed and elated mood on deductive and inductive reasoning. *Imagination, Cognition and Personality, 13, 57–71.*

Payne, W. L. (1986). A study of emotion: Developing emotional intelligence; self-integration; relating to fear, pain and desire (Doctoral dissertation, Union Graduate School, Cincinnati, OH 1983). *Dissertation Abstracts International, 47(01), 203A.* (UMI No. AAC 8605928)

Payton, J. W., Graczyk, P. A., Wardlaw, D. M., Bloodworth, M., Tompsett, C. J., & Weissberg, R. P. (2000). Social and emotional learning: A framework for promoting mental health and reducing risk behavior in children and youth. *Journal of School Health, 70, 179–185.*

Picard, R. W. (1997). *Affective computing.* Cambridge, MA: MIT Press.

Rice, C. L. (1999). *A quantitative study of emotional intelligence and its impact on team performance.* Unpublished master's thesis, Pepperdine University, Malibu, CA.

Rubin, M. M. (1999). *Emotional intelligence and its role in mitigating aggression: A correlational study of the relationship between emotional intelligence and aggression in urban adolescents.* Unpublished manuscript, Immaculata College, Immaculata, PA.

Saarni, C. (1979). Children's understanding of display rules for expressive behavior. *Developmental Psychology, 15, 424–429.*

Saarni, C. (1990). Emotional competence: How emotions and relationships become integrated. In R. A. Thompson (Ed.), *Nebraska Symposium on Motivation: Vol. 36. Socioemotional Development* (pp. 115–182). Lincoln: University of Nebraska Press.

Saarni, C. (1999). *Developing emotional competence.* New York: Guilford Press.

Salovey, P., Bedell, B. T., Detweiler, J. B., & Mayer, J. D. (2000). Current directions in emotional intelligence research. In M. Lewis & J. M. Haviland-Jones (Eds.), *Handbook of emotions* (2nd ed., pp. 504–520). New York: Guilford Press.

*Salovey, P., & Mayer, J. D. (1990). Emotional intelligence. *Imagination, Cognition and Personality, 9,* 185–211.

*Salovey, P., Mayer, J. D., & Caruso, D. R. (2002). The positive psychology of emotional intelligence. In C. R. Snyder & S. J. Lopez (Eds.), *Handbook of positive psychology* (pp. 159–171). New York: Oxford University Press.

Salovey, P., Woolery, A., & Mayer, J. D. (2001). Emotional intelligence: Conceptualization and measurement. In G. Fletcher & M. Clark (Eds.), *The Blackwell handbook of social psychology: Interpersonal processes* (pp. 279–307). London: Blackwell.

Schilling, D. (1996). *Fifty activities for teaching emotional intelligence: The best from Innerchoice Publishing—Level I: Elementary.* Torrance, CA: Innerchoice.

Schutte, N. S., Malouff, J. M., Hall, L. E., Haggerty, D. J., Cooper, J. T., Golden, C. J., et al. (1998). Development and validation of a measure of emotional intelligence. *Personality and Individual Differences, 25,* 167–177.

Schwarz, N. (1990). Feelings as information: Informational and motivational functions of affective states. In E. T. Higgins & E. M. Sorrentino (Eds.), *Handbook of motivation and cognition* (Vol. 2, pp. 527–561). New York: Guilford Press.

Shapiro, L. E. (1997). *How to raise a child with a high EQ: A parents' guide to emotional intelligence.* New York: HarperCollins.

Shields, S. A. (2002). *Speaking from the heart: Gender and the social meaning of emotion.* Cambridge, England: Cambridge University Press.

Simon, H. A. (1982). Comments. In M. S. Clark & S. T. Fiske (Eds.), *Affect and cognition* (pp. 333–342). Hillsdale, NJ: Erlbaum.

Stroebe, W., & Stroebe, M. (1996). The social psychology of social support. In E. T. Higgins & A. W. Kruglansky (Eds.), *Social psychology: Handbook of basic principles* (pp. 597–621). New York: Guilford Press.

Swift, D. G. (2002). *The relationships of emotional intelligence, hostility, and anger to heterosexual male intimate partner violence.* Unpublished manuscript, New York University, New York.

Trinidad, D. R., & Johnson, C. A. (2002). The association between emotional intelligence and early adolescent tobacco and alcohol use. *Personality and Individual Differences, 32,* 95–105.

Watkin, C. (2000). Developing emotional intelligence. *International Journal of Selection and Assessment, 2,* 89–92.

Zeidner, M., Matthews, G., & Roberts, R. D. (in press). Emotional intelligence in the workplace: A critical review. *Applied Psychology: An International Journal.*

Zins, J. E., Elias, M. J., Greenberg, M. T., & Weissberg, R. P. (2000). Promoting social and emotional competence in children. In K. M. Minke & G. C. Bear (Eds.), *Preventing school problems—promoting school success: Strategies and programs that work* (pp. 71–99). Washington, DC: National Association of School Psychologists.

CHAPTER 29

Gratitude in Practice and the
Practice of Gratitude

GIACOMO BONO, ROBERT A. EMMONS, and MICHAEL E. McCULLOUGH

WHEN A PERSON receives a gift or benefit, a typical emotional response is gratitude directed toward the source of the gift. Research in the psychology of emotion demonstrates that gratitude is a commonly experienced affect. For example, Chipperfield, Perry, and Weiner (2003) reported that feeling grateful was the third most common discrete positive affect experienced in a sample of older adults, reported by nearly 90% of their sample. Gratitude can also represent a broader attitude toward life—the tendency to see all of life as a gift. Gratitude thus has various meanings and can be conceptualized at several levels of analysis ranging from momentary affect to long-term dispositions (Emmons & McCullough, 2004; McCullough, Emmons, & Tsang, 2002). After a brief historical overview of scholarship on gratitude, we describe the relevance of recent research and perspectives on gratitude for issues of applied interest, particularly within the clinical practice of psychology. We contend that gratitude is a key element for sparking positive changes in individuals, families, and organizations.

A BRIEF HISTORY OF GRATITUDE

Throughout history, many cultures have regarded the experience and expression of gratitude as beneficial for both individuals and society. In fact, this is a notion prescribed in Jewish, Christian, Muslim, Buddhist, and Hindu thought (Carman & Streng, 1989). Experiencing gratitude is a highly valued trait (Dumas, Johnson, & Lynch, 2002; Gallup, 1998). Many people would agree that responding with gratitude after receiving some benefit is a moral obligation. One of the first in-depth psychological treatments of gratitude was offered by Adam Smith (1790/1976). He regarded gratitude as a basic and necessary emotion that promotes social stability

Preparation of this chapter was supported by a generous grant from the John Templeton Foundation.

by guiding people to respond to others' goodwill toward them. He also offered a remarkably sophisticated social-cognitive analysis of the situational factors that encourage the experience of gratitude. Beneficiaries are more likely to feel and express gratitude, Smith argued, to benefactors who intend to benefit them (whether they are successful), succeed in benefiting them, and are able to sympathize with the beneficiary's feelings of gratitude.

Expressing gratitude is almost universally considered a virtue, and withholding it seems to be universally regarded as a vice. This is reflected in the scornful connotations universally attached to ingratitude (Amato, 1982). The ubiquitous presence of norms of reciprocity in many cultures may very well be an indication of the fundamental value of expressing gratitude. However, while the regular practice of politeness may help ensure that people give thanks to their beneficiaries, adherence to etiquette alone may not guarantee that people notice many of the things they can be thankful for in the first place. And though religious doctrines may help remind people of the many things to be thankful for, they may still not ensure that people assume a grateful outlook, and thus, be open to the benefits to be had in everyday life. Helping people to realize the gifts for which they could be thankful in everyday life is one important challenge to which gratitude interventions could be fruitfully applied.

Social scientists have touched on the concept of gratitude since the 1930s (Baumgartner-Tramer, 1936, 1938; Bergler, 1945, 1950; Gouldner, 1960; Heider, 1958; Schwartz, 1967; Simmel, 1950). Some considered gratitude to be fundamental, vital for the maintenance of reciprocity obligations between people (Gouldner, 1960; Simmel, 1950). Others considered it evolutionarily adaptive because it forces people to maintain a prosocial orientation in response to altruistic behavior (Schwartz, 1967; Trivers, 1971). However, because psychological research has generally been dominated by a focus on vice rather than virtue (Myers & Diener, 1995), gratitude, along with other phenomena related to the good life, has been neglected. In fact, only recently has research verified that common assumptions about gratitude—namely, that expressing and experiencing it can bring peace of mind, more satisfying personal relationships, and happiness in general—may contain some truth (Emmons & McCullough, 2003; McCullough et al., 2002; Watkins, Woodward, Stone, & Kolts, 2003).

RECENT CONCEPTUALIZATIONS OF GRATITUDE

Research aimed at integrating previous social psychological conceptualizations of gratitude and bringing us closer to an understanding of gratitude and its social implications has emerged only in the past several years. The first earnest attempt to derive such a conceptual view of gratitude was undertaken by McCullough, Kilpatrick, Emmons, and Larson (2001). These researchers defined gratitude as a moral affect because it largely results from and stimulates behavior that is motivated by a concern for another person's well-being—referring to *moral* in a local sense rather than an absolute sense because a recipient may perceive a gift to augment his or her well-being even though it might not be moral or beneficial for other parties. Unlike other moral emotions that operate when an individual falls short of important standards or obligations (i.e., guilt and shame) or when an individual is motivated to help another in need (i.e., sympathy and empathy), gratitude is distinctly operant when the individual is the *recipient* of prosocial behavior.

McCullough et al. (2001) also delineated three moral functions or social aspects of gratitude—gratitude as a moral barometer, as a moral motive, and as a moral reinforcer—and examined the existing empirical research on gratitude and related concepts (i.e., thankfulness, appreciation) to determine how well this conceptualization fit the data. Like a moral barometer, the emotion of gratitude indicates a change in the individual's social relationships; recipients come to regard benefactors as moral agents for having augmented their personal well-being. Gratitude also serves as moral motive because its experience motivates recipients to treat kindness with kindness or inhibit destructive behaviors toward a benefactor either immediately or in the future. (However, note that the reciprocity motivation resulting from gratitude is distinct from motivation sparked by indebtedness and inequity in that it is a pleasant emotion linked to positive psychological states, much like contentment, pride, and hope.) As a moral reinforcer, the expression of gratitude serves to increase the chances that a benefactor will respond with benevolence again in the future, just as the expression of ingratitude can instill anger in benefactors and discourage future prosocial behavior (but McCullough et al., 2002, caution that such expressions of gratitude may not always be pure, in that they can also be driven by self-presentation needs). The research corroborating these three functions is described in the section on gratitude as a moral affect.

REVIEW OF SOCIAL SCIENTIFIC RESEARCH ON GRATITUDE

The empirical research can be broken into three major categories:

1. How gratitude is conceptualized (what it is, as well as when, how, and with whom it happens)
2. What kind of people tend to be grateful
3. How gratitude has been and can be applied to society

Researchers who wish to develop practical applications of gratitude research to improving human health and well-being would benefit from considering all three of these categories of research findings.

Gratitude as Moral Affect

In this section of the chapter, we will review research supporting our contention that gratitude serves as a moral affect—that is, one with moral precursors or consequences.

Gratitude Can Be a Moral Barometer   Grateful emotions and behaviors typically result from the perception that another person has intended to promote your well-being, indicating gratitude's function as a moral barometer (McCullough et al., 2001). (McCullough et al., 2001, also point out that people could experience gratitude for benefits they perceive as being conferred by nonhuman causal agents [e.g., God, fate, or some other intentional force] as well as for benefits based in counterfactual thinking [i.e., when things could easily have been worse].) Tesser, Gatewood, and Driver (1968) found that benefits that were described as intentionally provided, costly to the benefactor, and valuable to the recipient each brought linear increases in the amount of gratitude recipients would expect to experience. People also experienced gratitude when they believed a benefit was caused by other people's efforts (Weiner, Russell, & Lerman, 1979; Zaleski, 1988), and they were even able to correctly identify the cause of other people's gratitude as partly due to the fortunate effort of others (Weiner et al., 1979). In general, people are more grateful for benefits deemed costly to the benefactor, but less grateful when the benefactor was responsible for the circumstances that created the need for the benefit in the first place (Okamoto & Robinson, 1997).

Research demonstrates that gratitude can also signal that a person has been treated in a surprisingly prosocial way by a relationship partner. People appear to experience the most gratitude in response to benefactors who provide unexpected benefits to the beneficiary. For example, benefits received in the context of close communal relationships (e.g., family relationships) led people to feel less gratitude (Bar-Tal, Bar-Zohar, Greenberg, & Hermon, 1977) in part because benefits in such relationships may be considered more obligatory or habitual in nature (Neuberg et al., 1997). Also, beneficiaries may perceive benefits from people higher in relative social status or power (e.g., teachers) as more deliberate than those provided by someone of similar status or power (Hegtvedt, 1990), thereby leading a recipient to express more gratitude (Becker & Smenner, 1986; Okamoto & Robinson, 1997). McCullough et al. (2001) note that such cases may involve more than gratitude because recipients may be unable to reciprocate anything other than expressions of gratitude, or they may be motivated by social desirability (e.g., try to obtain benefits later or deter punishment).

Finally, McCullough et al. (2001) point to evidence that the link between attributions of responsibility for positive outcomes and gratitude probably develops around the age of 7 or 8 (for a review, see Weiner & Graham, 1988). Therefore, a variety of research shows that grateful emotions and behaviors typically result from the perception that another person has intended to promote the individual's well-being, indicating to some degree how and with whom gratitude serves as a moral barometer as well as when during the lifespan this aspect of gratitude may emerge.

Gratitude Can Be a Moral Motive   McCullough et al. (2001) found considerably less evidence for the moral motive function of gratitude. Research by Peterson and Stewart (1996) showed that older adult women who were most cognizant of having been influenced by mentors during their college years (17 years earlier) were more motivated ($r = 0.39$) to be generative (i.e., nurturing toward other people and society) in midlife. However, it was not clear whether gratitude was the affect mediating the observed mentoring-generativity link. Graham (1988) found more direct evidence of a positive correlation between children's expected gratitude for being voluntarily chosen to a team by a captain and the likelihood that they would reciprocate by giving the captain a gift (rs became stronger with age, ranging from 0.34 for the 5- to 6-year-olds, to 0.72 for the 10- to 11-year-olds). With respect to whether gratitude serves to inhibit destructive interpersonal behavior, supportive evidence came from one study by Baron (1984). Undergraduate students were paired with a confederate (who was trained to persuasively disagree with whatever views they may have had) for a task in which they were to simulate a conflict about a work-related matter. Of four conditions introduced by the confederate during a break in the task (i.e., gift, sympathy, humor, and a control), participants in the gift and humor conditions reported that the confederate was more pleasant and that they would be more likely to use collaboration to resolve conflict in the future, compared to participants in the control condition. Again, though, it was not clear whether the gift condition's effect on participants' liking for the confederate was mediated by feelings of gratitude.

Gratitude Can Be a Moral Reinforcer   Finally, McCullough et al. (2001) found extensive support for the notion of gratitude as a moral reinforcer. Research has shown that expressions of gratitude can reinforce kidney donation (Bernstein & Simmons, 1974) and volunteering behavior toward people with HIV/AIDS (Bennett, Ross, & Sunderland, 1996), and field experiments have shown that mere thank-you notes can bring increased tips from customers (Rind & Bordia, 1995), higher response rates on mail surveys (Maheux, Legault, & Lambert, 1989), and more visits from case managers in a residential treatment program (H. B. Clark, Northrop, & Barkshire, 1988). Laboratory experiments likewise corroborated these findings, showing that benefactors who were thanked for their efforts were willing to give more and work harder for others, compared to those who were not thanked for their efforts (R. D. Clark, 1975; Goldman, Seever, & Seever, 1982; McGovern, Ditzian, & Taylor, 1975; Moss & Page, 1972). Conversely, there is evidence that expressions of ingratitude are regarded as aversive (Stein, 1989; Suls, Witenberg, & Gutkin, 1981). Moreover, it appears that people who are high in need for approval, as measured by the Marlowe-Crowne Social Desirability Scale (Crowne & Marlowe, 1960), are more strongly reinforced by beneficiaries' expressions of gratitude (Deutsch & Lamberti, 1986). However, research also shows that selfish ways of expressing gratitude (e.g., saying "thank you" only to entice someone to give even more or thanking someone for his or her patience when it may be more appropriate to apologize for offending him or her) may be detrimental and may cause reactance in benefactors (Carey, Clicque, Leighton, & Milton, 1976; Mehrabian, 1967).

It seems reasonable to conclude from the available empirical evidence that gratitude can indeed be regarded as a moral emotion. The experience of gratitude results from acknowledging the gratuitous role that sources of social support may play in propagating beneficial outcomes in our lives. The experience of gratitude may also help us reciprocate kindness toward those who have been kind to us. Finally, expressing gratitude to people who have been kind to us can validate their efforts and help reinforce such behavior in the future. Therefore, the experience and expression of gratitude is chiefly suited to maximizing positive outcomes in relationships and establishing as well as preserving supportive networks of relationships. Individuals who experience and express gratitude more stand a greater chance of benefiting from their relationships. That is, the more they tune in to how others have helped them along, the more they will do the same in return; and the more frequently such exchanges occur, the more suited the network becomes to maximizing the mutual benefits for those involved.

GRATITUDE AS AN AFFECTIVE TRAIT

Researchers have recently begun to investigate the disposition to experience gratitude (McCullough et al., 2002). Invoking Rosenberg's (1998) multilevel analysis of affect, these researchers defined the disposition to experience gratitude as "a generalized tendency to recognize and respond with grateful emotion to the roles of other people's benevolence in the positive experiences and outcomes that one obtains" (p. 112). They also derived four different facets or qualities of emotional experiences that could distinguish dispositionally grateful people from less dispositionally grateful people. Compared to less grateful individuals, highly grateful individuals may feel gratitude more *intensely* for a positive event, more *frequently* or more easily throughout the day; they may have a wider *span* of benefits or life circumstances for which they are grateful at any given time (e.g., for their families, their jobs, friends, their health), and they may experience gratitude with greater *density* for any given benefit (i.e., toward more people).

In four studies, McCullough et al. (2002) broadly examined the correlates of the disposition toward gratitude. They developed the Gratitude Questionnaire (GQ)-6 (a six-item, self-report measure of the grateful disposition), showed that the GQ-6 converged with observer ratings, and found that the grateful disposition was positively associated with positive affect, well-being, prosocial behaviors/traits, and religiousness/spirituality. They also found that the grateful disposition was negatively associated with envy and materialistic attitudes. They replicated these findings in a large nonstudent sample and showed that these associations persisted even after controlling for social desirability (Paulhus, 1998). Among the Big Five dimensions of personality (John, Donahue, & Kentle, 1991), the disposition to experience gratitude was correlated with extraversion/positive affectivity, neuroticism/negative affectivity, and agreeableness. Moreover, the same associations were obtained using both self-report and peer-report methods.

Specifically, McCullough et al. (2002) found that highly grateful people, compared to their less grateful counterparts, tend to experience positive emotions more often, enjoy greater satisfaction with life and more hope (rs ranged from 0.30 to 0.49, ps < 0.01), and tend to experience less depression, anxiety, and envy (with most rs ranging from 0.18 to 0.39, ps < 0.01). Highly grateful individuals also tend to score higher than do their less grateful counterparts on measures of prosociality. They tend to be more empathic, forgiving, helpful, and supportive as well as less focused on materialistic pursuits than are their less grateful counterparts (with most rs ranging from 0.17 to 0.36, ps < 0.01). Finally, people who are more strongly disposed to experience gratitude tend to be more religiously and spiritually oriented than people lower in gratitude. That is, they tend to score higher on measures of traditional religiousness (e.g., church attendance, prayer) and nonsectarian measures that assess spiritual experiences or sensibilities (e.g., sense of contact with a divine power, belief that all living things are interconnected).

More recently, other researchers seeking to develop another measure of dispositional gratitude have drawn similar conclusions (Watkins et al., 2003). Watkins and colleagues devised the Gratitude, Resentment, and Appreciation Test (GRAT), a self-report measure that conceptualizes dispositional gratitude as a combination of four different characteristics: acknowledgment of the importance of expressing and experiencing gratitude, lack of resentment with respect to benefits received (that is, the person feels a sense of abundance in his or her life rather than deprivation), appreciation for the contributions of others toward benefits received, and appreciation for simple pleasures (e.g., sunsets and seasons, which happen frequently) rather than extravagant pleasures (e.g., vacations and cars, which are likely to happen infrequently). They found evidence of construct validity for their dispositional measure of gratitude and various correlations, which help illuminate its relationship to positive and negative affective states. Across three different undergraduate student samples, scores on the GRAT were positively related to satisfaction with life (as measured by the Satisfaction With Life Scale; Diener, Emmons, Larsen, & Griffin, 1985; rs ranged from 0.49 to 0.62, $ps < 0.0001$) and negatively related to depression (as measured by the Beck Depression Inventory; Beck, 1972; rs ranged from < 0.34 to < 0.56, $ps < 0.01$).

INTERVENTIONS TO PROMOTE GRATITUDE

Researchers have suspected for some time that a person's ability to notice and appreciate the good elements in his or her life can improve well-being (Bryant, 1989; Janoff-Bulman & Berger, 2000; Langston, 1994), and many religious and self-help groups have adopted activities where its members reflect on the gifts that they are grateful for in their lives (e.g., the retreats of various church groups and Alcoholics Anonymous). The belief implicit in these self-help efforts is that the regular practice of grateful thinking should lead to enhanced psychological and social functioning. However, the only way to evaluate unambiguously whether such activity causes increases in well-being is to conduct experiments in which gratitude is manipulated and its effects are observed.

Emmons and McCullough (2003) conducted three experiments investigating the effects of gratitude interventions on psychological and physical well-being. In Study 1, students were randomly assigned to one of three conditions. Participants either briefly described (e.g., in a single sentence) five things they were grateful for in the past week (gratitude condition), five daily hassles from the previous week (hassles condition), or five events or circumstances that affected them in the last week (events condition). Participants completed these exercises along with a variety of other measures once per week for 10 consecutive weeks. A wide range of experiences sparked gratitude; for example, cherished interactions, awareness of physical health, overcoming obstacles, and simply being alive. Participants in the gratitude condition reported being more grateful than those in the hassles condition, thus the induction successfully impacted grateful affect. More importantly, participants in the grateful condition felt better about their life as a whole and were more optimistic about the future than participants in either of the other comparison conditions. In addition, those in the grateful condition reported fewer health complaints and even said that they spent more time exercising than control participants did. Thus, a simple weekly intervention showed significant emotional and health benefits.

In Study 2, Emmons and McCullough (2003) increased the gratitude intervention to a daily practice over a two-week period. As in Study 1, participants were randomly assigned to one of three conditions. The gratitude and hassles conditions were identical to Study 1, but the events condition was changed to a downward social comparison manipulation. In this condition, participants were encouraged to think about ways in which they were better off than others. They added this condition to control for possible demand characteristics. This comparison condition may have inadvertently produced some grateful affect, but even so, the gratitude condition showed an impressive array of benefits. Although the health benefits from Study 1 were not evident in this study (perhaps because of the short duration of the intervention), participants in the grateful condition felt more joyful, enthusiastic, interested, attentive, energetic, excited, determined, and stronger than those in the hassles condition. They also reported having offered others more emotional support or help with a personal problem, indicating that the gratitude induction increased prosocial motivation—and more directly supporting the notion of gratitude as a moral motivator (McCullough et al., 2001). Again, the gratitude manipulation showed a significant effect on positive affect as compared to the hassles condition, but no reliable impact on negative affectivity. In addition, there was some evidence that this daily intervention led to greater increases in gratitude than did the weekly practice that they examined in their first study.

In a third study, Emmons and McCullough (2003) replicated these effects in adults with neuromuscular diseases. Participants were randomly assigned to a gratitude condition or to a "true control condition" in which participants simply completed "daily experience rating forms." Similar to the previous studies, participants in the gratitude group showed significantly more positive affect and satisfaction with life, but, in addition, they showed less negative affect than the control group. Not only did the self-reports of participants in the gratitude condition indicate increased positive affect and life satisfaction, but so did the reports of significant others: Spouses of participants in the gratitude condition reported that the participants had appeared to have higher subjective well-being than did the spouses of participants in the control condition. These studies support the contention that gratitude has a causative influence on subjective well-being and open the door for intervention possibilities with a variety of populations.

To investigate which methods of *expressing* gratitude could enhance positive affect, Watkins et al. (2003) conducted an experiment in which gratitude was manipulated in different ways (i.e., participants were instructed to think about someone to whom they were grateful, write an essay about someone to whom they were grateful, or write a letter to someone to whom they were grateful, which would allegedly be sent to that person). They had participants in the control condition descriptively write about their living rooms. They also measured positive and negative affect before and after the manipulation (using the Positive and Negative Affect Schedule; Watson, Clark, & Tellegen, 1988).

The gratitude conditions led to increases in positive affect, whereas the control condition did not. The grateful thinking condition in particular showed the strongest effect, perhaps because the act itself of writing an essay or a letter of gratitude on demand may have disrupted the experience of positive affect or caused some anxiety. These findings imply that in developing gratitude interventions, developers should consider their targets, the amount of time available for the intervention, and the kind of intervention most appropriate given the circumstances. Watkins and his colleagues also found that gratitude was negatively related to depression in clinical samples (Woodward, Moua, & Watkins, 1998).

GRATITUDE AS A DEPENDENT VARIABLE: CREATIVE ROUTES FOR GRATITUDE INTERVENTIONS

Most of the research studies that we have reviewed were designed to examine the effects of gratitude on psychological, emotional, or interpersonal well-being. In these studies, gratitude is the independent variable, and the various outcomes of interest are the dependent variables. It is also possible to examine changes in gratitude or thankfulness as a function of interventions designed for other purposes, for example, to promote mindfulness (Shapiro, Schwartz, & Santerre, 2002), relaxation (Khasky & Smith, 1999), or forgiveness (Witvliet, Ludwig, & Bauer, 2002).

Gratitude as a quality of mindfulness (Shapiro et al., 2002) appears to be facilitated by a meditation practice referred to as "Intentional Systemic Mindfulness" (p. 639). In another research program, progressive muscle relaxation has been shown to produce a number of positive emotional benefits, including increased feelings of love and thankfulness (Khasky & Smith, 1999). Last, Witvliet et al. found that a forgiveness intervention (imagining yourself being forgiven by your victim) resulted in increased feelings of gratitude, presumably gratitude over being given the gift of forgiveness. These studies demonstrate that a number of innovative psychological interventions have the capacity to engender states of gratitude and its attendant benefits, though they were not designed explicitly for this purpose.

One particular type of psychotherapy originating in Japan, known as *Naikan therapy*, is based in Buddhist philosophy and mobilizes techniques of isolation and meditation to expand clients' awareness of their moral relationships with significant others in their lives. Currently, there are about 40 Naikan centers in Japan, as well as centers in Austria, Germany, and the United States (Krech, 2002). The overall aim of Naikan therapy is to have clients achieve interpersonal balance by realizing a deep sense of connection with the significant others in their lives and to experience a strong sense of gratitude toward people who have provided them with benefits (Hedstrom, 1994; Reynolds, 1983). It is notable that this form of therapy, based so strongly in gratitude, has been used to treat many disorders—including anorexia nervosa (Morishita, 2000), alcoholism (Suwaki, 1985), neuroses, and personality disorders (Sakuta, Shiratsuchi, Kimura, & Abe, 1997)—and it has been applied to the rehabilitation of prisoners and counseling in school and business settings (Krech, 2002).

COPING WITH STRESS: GRATITUDE AS RESILIENCY

In addition to the positive benefits that can accrue from the conscious practice of gratitude, studies have shown that gratitude can buffer a person from debilitating emotions and pathological psychological conditions. Fredrickson, Tugade, Waugh, and Larkin (2003) examined the frequency of positive and negative emotions before and after the tragic events of September 11, 2001. Of 20 emotions, gratitude was the second most commonly experienced (only compassion was rated higher). They found that positive emotions were critical characteristics that actively helped resilient people to cope with the September 11 disaster, suggesting another potential role that gratitude can play in interventions. Indeed, a whole line of research shows that benefit-finding can help people cope with disasters, deadly diseases, and bereavement (Linley & Joseph, 2004; Nolen-Hoeksema & Davis, 2002; Tennen & Affleck, 2002). McAdams & Bauer's (2004) analyses of redemption sequences revealed that even painful experiences could become something for which people are ultimately grateful.

Research is expanding our understanding of the role positive emotions play in sustaining well-being. The experience of positive emotions broadens the scopes of individuals' attention and cognitions and consequently generates an "upward spiral" of improved coping and optimal functioning (Fredrickson, 2001). Thus, the regular experience and expression of gratitude can help build personal and interpersonal resources for coping effectively with stress and adversity.

Gratitude may also be a characteristic that offers protection against psychiatric disorders. A factor-analytically derived measure of thankfulness (which included items explicitly related to gratitude, along with others that seemed to have more in common with love and acceptance) was associated with reduced risk for both internalizing (e.g., depression and anxiety) and externalizing (e.g., substance abuse) disorders in a study involving 2,616 male and female twins (Kendler et al., 2003).

In fact, recent work demonstrates that gratitude may help both cardiovascular and immunological functioning and attempts to explain how such physiological processes contribute to the upward spirals of well-being associated with experiences of appreciation in particular (McCraty & Childre, 2004). These researchers claim that self-generating positive emotions with greater consistency can bring long-term improvements in emotion-regulation abilities, which are conducive to well-being. They argue that "the range of positive emotional experience is limited by the automaticity of historical patterns that operate at a level below conscious awareness to color perception, feelings, and behavior" and suggest that a conscious commitment to practicing positive emotion-focused techniques can facilitate a "repatterning process," which enables "people to cultivate more positive emotions, attitudes, and behaviors in daily life" (p. 243).

McCraty and his colleagues identified patterns of sustained physiological coherence that operate during feelings of appreciation, and they have shown that this may be one of the mechanisms contributing to the positive psychosocial outcomes associated with gratitude. Their term *physiological coherence* refers to the degree of order, stability, and efficiency generated by the body's oscillatory systems (i.e., heart rhythms, respiratory rhythms, blood pressure oscillations, low frequency brain rhythms, craniosacral rhythms, electrical skin potentials, and rhythms in the digestive system; McCraty & Atkinson, 2004). The more people experience sincere feelings of appreciation, the more often this coherence emerges, establishing and reinforcing coherent patterns in the neural architecture as a familiar reference for the brain. This frames gratitude as a way of achieving flow, or optimal experience (Csikszentmihalyi, 1990).

To this end, McCraty and Childre (2004) developed techniques for focusing attention to the area around the heart (the subjective site of positive emotions) and simultaneously engaging in intentional self-inductions of positive emotional states, such as appreciation. Such techniques may be useful tools for interventions seeking to increase gratitude in individuals; that they employ techniques similar to other mind-body interventions may make them particularly useful for fostering gratitude as an attitude or guiding mind-set.

CHALLENGES FOR GRATITUDE APPLICATIONS

Any discussion of the benefits of gratitude would be incomplete without a consideration of factors that render gratitude difficult. Scholars have suggested that a number of attitudes are incompatible with a grateful outlook on life, including perceptions of victimhood (Seligman, 2002), an inability to admit to shortcomings (Solomon, 2002), a sense of entitlement (McWilliams & Lependorf, 1990), envy and resentment (Etchegoyen & Nemas, 2003), and an overemphasis on materialistic values (Kasser, 2002). Interventions to cultivate gratitude cannot ignore these obstacles to gratitude, for it may be necessary to confront these on their own terms before initiating a gratitude focus.

Some of these obstacles are likely to be deeply ingrained in personality. A major personality variable that is likely to thwart gratitude is narcissism (Watkins et al.,

2003). People with narcissistic tendencies erroneously believe they are deserving of special rights and privileges. Along with being demanding and selfish, they exhibit an exaggerated sense of self-importance that leads them to expect special favors without assuming reciprocal responsibilities. The sense of entitlement combined with their insensitivity to the needs of others engenders interpersonal exploitation, whether consciously or unconsciously intended. In short, if a person feels entitled to everything, he or she is thankful for nothing.

Given this situation, people high in narcissism find expressions of gratitude to be highly unpleasant. Furthermore, because narcissistic individuals possess a distorted sense of their own superiority, they might be reluctant to express gratitude in response to benefactors whose generosity or kindness they summarily dismiss as little more than attempts to curry favor. Farwell and Wohlwend-Lloyd (1998) found that in the context of a laboratory-based interdependence game, narcissism was inversely related to the extent to which participants experienced liking and gratitude for their partners.

HOW IS GRATITUDE RELATED TO "THE GOOD LIFE"?

When considering how gratitude is related to the good life, it is useful to bear in mind the various populations whom research has shown to have benefited from expressions or experiences of gratitude or from gratitude interventions. We have already seen that expressing gratitude can help recipients of kidney donations, people caring for others with HIV/AIDS, people in residential treatment programs, servers at restaurants, survey researchers, and volunteers in a soup kitchen. Moreover, victims of profound tragedies (e.g., the September 11 terrorist attacks) who experience gratitude and positive emotions tend to be the ones who recover better. People suffering from disasters, deadly diseases, or human loss appear to cope better as a result of being able to see some benefit in their predicaments. Individuals who are more thankful in their practice of religion seem to fare better in terms of internalizing and externalizing psychiatric disorders.

Gratitude interventions have shown that undergraduate students, adults with neuromuscular diseases, and clinical patients suffering from depression have benefited from increased gratitude in their lives. Use of Naikan psychotherapy techniques suggests that gratitude mind-sets may help students and employees to resolve interpersonal conflicts, prisoners to rehabilitate, and people to recover from various disorders. Finally, appreciation interventions have shown that people (of various ages and religious affiliations) in organizational, educational, and health care settings may likewise benefit from experiences of gratitude (Childre & Cryer, 2000; Childre & Martin, 1999). Informally, church organizations and self-help groups for years have relied on gratitude exercises to help empower individuals.

GUIDELINES FOR THE EMPIRICAL STUDY OF GRATITUDE AND GRATITUDE INTERVENTIONS

To evaluate gratitude interventions and their effectiveness, researchers should adhere to several guidelines. First, if researchers wish to foster well-being by increasing people's gratitude, it is important to make sure that the intervention is successful in fostering gratitude. The degree of gratitude that participants experience can be measured in terms of intensity, frequency, span, and density (McCullough et al., 2002). Including the GQ-6 (McCullough et al., 2002) or the GRAT (Watkins et al., 2003) in the battery of dependent variables will assist to this end. Gratitude as a component of daily emotional and mood experience can also be an important way to evaluate the effects of gratitude interventions on people's experiences of gratitude in everyday life (see McCullough, Tsang, & Emmons, 2004).

Second, the use of daily/weekly diary techniques has proved to be a useful induction for getting individuals to focus on and experience gratitude (Emmons & McCullough, 2003). Having participants write about gratitude-inducing events from their personal lives or even write letters to people to whom they feel grateful may also be useful to this end (Watkins et al., 2003). The letter-writing approach may be especially potent in that it directs attention toward the benefactor and the benefactor's generosity and thus points beyond the concrete benefit received. However, time constraints and considerations of what can reasonably be expected of recipients should be weighed so that the activity of writing a letter itself does not become too demanding or anxiety-producing to induce gratitude in recipients.

Third, researchers are advised to measure dependent variables that reflect the different ways gratitude might influence individual practitioners of gratitude, as well as their relationships with others (McCullough et al., 2002). Thus, to assess individual outcomes, researchers are advised to measure dependent variables corresponding to the different ways gratitude has been shown to benefit individuals in terms of well-being (i.e., increased positive affectivity; decreased negative affectivity, anxiety, depression; satisfaction with life; hope), prosociality (i.e., how much others help them and they help others), and religiousness and spirituality. Most likely, research has not covered all the ways individuals can benefit from increased gratitude. Do people's relationships improve as well? If so, how? Perhaps different relationships benefit in different ways or degrees? Do people reciprocate kindness toward their benefactors? And do they respond prosocially to other people's expressions of gratitude? Researchers may further assess the effects of gratitude on well-being outcomes by assessing whether gratitude buffers targets from life's stressors and whether gratitude has bestowed improved emotion-regulation abilities or increased experiences of flow. The use of daily diary methods may be the best way to assess such individual and relational outcomes.

Fourth, researchers are advised to identify possible moderating factors that may hamper the effectiveness of interventions by assessing dependent variables such as narcissism, resentment, envy, materialism, and personality traits. Moreover, people with high levels of certain traits (i.e., people high in neuroticism or low in extraversion and agreeableness) may have difficulty expressing and experiencing gratitude. Failing to measure these variables may lead intervention researchers to interpret null outcomes as the result of an ineffective intervention, when this may not be true. It may be that such individuals do not benefit from gratitude interventions as much as might less narcissistic and neurotic or more extraverted and agreeable individuals. On the other hand, it might be precisely these people who stand to benefit the most from becoming more grateful. Exploring this issue would be very helpful in clarifying the populations that are likely to benefit the most from gratitude interventions.

FUTURE DIRECTION FOR RESEARCH ON GRATITUDE AND GRATITUDE INTERVENTIONS

There are a number of important avenues to be followed in future research on gratitude and in designing gratitude interventions. The two most critical are (1) identifying promising settings within which to apply gratitude interventions, and (2) examining cross-cultural differences in the experience and expression of gratitude.

SETTINGS AND POPULATIONS THAT STAND TO BENEFIT FROM GRATITUDE

Researchers should investigate other populations that may benefit from the experience and expression of gratitude. Perhaps different types of interventions are effective for different settings. For example, schools and other educational settings are an untapped venue for gratitude interventions. Little research has been conducted on the experience and expression of gratefulness in children. Why wait until adulthood to begin to reap the benefits of grateful living?

Another setting for which gratitude is relevant is the workplace. Emmons (2003) recently proposed that gratitude can benefit organizations in several ways and articulated areas of research that might be useful to this end. Most directly, as a cognitive strategy, gratitude can improve individual well-being and lower toxic emotions in the workplace, such as resentment and envy. Moods are important determiners of efficiency, productivity, success, and employee loyalty. A number of recent studies have demonstrated that employee happiness and well-being are positively associated with performance, commitment, and morale, and negatively associated with absenteeism, burnout, and turnover (e.g., Wright & Staw, 1999). In a society that increasingly relies on teamwork and the culling of diverse strengths from individuals to achieve group and organizational goals, gratitude may very well be a positive emotion that not only buffers individuals from stress but also facilitates the mutual achievements of individuals, groups, and organizations (Emmons, 2003).

THE NEED FOR CROSS-CULTURAL STUDIES

Cross-cultural studies can explore the different ways gratitude is experienced and expressed. It would be surprising if the major attributional processes involved in the production of gratitude were to differ across cultures, but people from various cultures may be grateful for different reasons, depending on the concerns that are most central to them. Studies investigating cross-cultural differences in the determinants and moderators of gratitude across cultures will be crucial for understanding the degree to which experiences of gratitude are universal and diversified. Moreover, it would be useful to explore whether the experience of gratitude leads to different mental, physical, or relational outcomes in some cultures than in others.

One useful distinction that interventions can make is to consider how the identity needs of clients may be different, depending on their cultural orientation. In collectivistic cultures, a sense of relatedness with the communal group is essential for the functioning of the individual, whereas in individualistic cultures, a sense of personal autonomy is essential for the functioning of the individual

(Markus & Kitayama, 1991). By considering these cultural nuances in the design of interventions, researchers can personalize interventions so that they can better focus on the types of benefits that are valued by their recipients. Thus, for example, interventions targeting people with more interdependent selves can focus on benefits that help bring, affirm, or maintain harmony in relationships; and interventions targeting people with more independent selves can focus on benefits that help bring, affirm, or maintain personal autonomy and achievement.

CONCLUSION

In the history of ideas, gratitude has had surprisingly few detractors. Aside from a few harsh words from a small handful of cynics, nearly every thinker has viewed gratitude as a sentiment with virtually no downside. As Comte-Sponville (2001) pointed out, gratitude is "the most pleasant of the virtues, and the most virtuous of the pleasures" (p. 132). It is virtuously pleasant because experiencing it not only uplifts the person who experiences it but also edifies the person to whom it is directed. But the fact that people typically consider gratitude a virtue and not simply a pleasure also points to the fact that it does not always come naturally or easily. Gratitude must, and can, be cultivated. And by cultivating the virtue, it appears that people may get the pleasure of gratitude, and all of its other attendant benefits, thrown in for free.

REFERENCES

Amato, J. A. (1982). *Guilt and gratitude: A study of the origins of contemporary conscience.* Westport, CT: Greenwood Press.

Baron, R. A. (1984). Reducing organizational conflict: An incompatible response approach. *Journal of Applied Psychology, 69,* 272–279.

Bar-Tal, D., Bar-Zohar, Y., Greenberg, M. S., & Hermon, M. (1977). Reciprocity behavior in the relationship between donor and recipient and between harm-doer and victim. *Sociometry, 40,* 293–298.

Baumgartner-Tramer, F. (1936). Gratitude in children and adolescents. *Ethik, 13,* 1–11.

Baumgartner-Tramer, F. (1938). "Gratefulness" in children and young people. *Journal of Genetic Psychology, 53,* 53–66.

Beck, A. T. (1972). *Depression: Causes and treatment.* Philadelphia: University of Pennsylvania Press.

Becker, J. A., & Smenner, P. C. (1986). The spontaneous use of thank you by preschoolers as a function of sex, socioeconomic status, and listener status. *Language in Society, 15,* 537–546.

Bennett, L., Ross, M. W., & Sunderland, R. (1996). The relationship between recognition, rewards, and burnout in AIDS caregiving. *AIDS Care, 8,* 145–153.

Bergler, E. (1945). Psychopathology of ingratitude. *Diseases of the Nervous System, 6,* 226–229.

Bergler, E. (1950). Debts of gratitude paid in "guilt denomination." *Journal of Clinical Psychopathology, 11,* 57–62.

Bernstein, D. M., & Simmons, R. G. (1974). The adolescent kidney donor: The right to give. *American Journal of Psychiatry, 131,* 1338–1343.

Bryant, F. B. (1989). A four-factor model of perceived control: Avoiding, coping, obtaining, and savoring. *Journal of Personality, 57,* 773–797.

Carey, J. R., Clicque, S. H., Leighton, B. A., & Milton, F. (1976). A test of positive reinforcement of customers. *Journal of Marketing, 40,* 98–100.

Carman, J. B., & Streng, F. J. (Eds.). (1989). *Spoken and unspoken thanks: Some comparative soundings.* Dallas, TX: Center for World Thanksgiving.

Childre, D., & Cryer, B. (2000). *From chaos to coherence: The power to change performance.* Boulder Creek, CA: Planetary.

Childre, D., & Martin, H. (1999). *The HeartMath solution.* San Francisco: Harper.

Chipperfield, J. G., Perry, R. P., & Weiner, B. (2003). Discrete emotions in later life. *Journal of Gerontology: Psychological Sciences, 58B,* 23–34.

Clark, H. B., Northrop, J. T., & Barkshire, C. T. (1988). The effects of contingent thank-you notes on case managers' visiting residential clients. *Education and Treatment of Children, 11,* 45–51.

Clark, R. D. (1975). The effects of reinforcement, punishment and dependency on helping behavior. *Bulletin of Personality and Social Psychology, 1,* 596–599.

Comte-Sponville, A. (2001). *A small treatise on great virtues: The uses of philosophy in everyday life.* New York: Henry Holt.

Crowne, D. P., & Marlowe, D. (1960). A new scale of social desirability independent of psychopathology. *Journal of Consulting Psychology, 24,* 349–354.

Csikszentmihalyi, M. (1990). *Flow: The psychology of optimal experience.* New York: HarperCollins.

Deutsch, F. M., & Lamberti, D. M. (1986). Does social approval increase helping? *Personality and Social Psychology Bulletin, 12,* 149–157.

Diener, E., Emmons, R. A., Larsen, R. J., & Griffin, S. (1985). The Satisfaction With Life Scale. *Journal of Personality Assessment, 49,* 71–75.

Dumas, J. E., Johnson, M., & Lynch, A. M. (2002). Likeableness, familiarity, and frequency of 844 person-descriptive words. *Personality and Individual Differences, 32,* 523–531.

Emmons, R. A. (2003). Acts of gratitude in organizations. In K. S. Cameron, J. E. Dutton, & R. E. Quinn (Eds.), *Positive organizational scholarship* (pp. 81–93). San Francisco: Berrett-Koehler.

*Emmons, R. A., & McCullough, M. E. (2003). Counting blessings versus burdens: An experimental investigation of gratitude and subjective well-being in daily life. *Journal of Personality and Social Psychology, 84,* 377–389.

*Emmons, R. A., & McCullough, M. E. (Eds.). (2004). *The psychology of gratitude.* New York: Oxford University Press.

Etchegoyen, R. H., & Nemas, C. R. (2003). Salieri's dilemma: A counterpoint between envy and appreciation. *International Journal of Psychoanalysis, 84,* 45–58.

Farwell, L., & Wohlwend-Lloyd, R. (1998). Narcissistic processes: Optimistic expectations, favorable self-evaluations, and self-enhancing attributions. *Journal of Personality, 66,* 65–83.

Fredrickson, B. L. (2001). The role of positive emotions in positive psychology: The broaden-and-build theory of positive emotions. *American Psychologist, 56,* 218–226.

Fredrickson, B. L., Tugade, M. M., Waugh, C. E., & Larkin, G. R. (2003). What good are positive emotions in crises? A prospective study of resilience and emotions following the terrorist attacks on the United States on September 11th, 2001. *Journal of Personality and Social Psychology, 84,* 365–376.

Gallup, G. (1998). Gallup survey results on "gratitude," adults and teenagers. *Emerging Trends, 20,* 4–5, 9.

Goldman, M., Seever, M., & Seever, M. (1982). Social labeling and the foot-in-the-door effect. *Journal of Social Psychology, 117,* 19–23.

Gouldner, A. W. (1960). The norm of reciprocity: A preliminary statement. *American Sociological Review, 25,* 161–178.

Graham, S. (1988). Children's developing understanding of the motivational role of affect: An attributional analysis. *Cognitive Development, 3,* 71–88.

Hedstrom, L. J. (1994). Morita and Naikan therapies: American applications. *Psychotherapy, 31,* 154–160.

Hegtvedt, K. A. (1990). The effects of relationship structure on emotional responses to inequity. *Social Psychology Quarterly, 53,* 214–228.

Heider, F. (1958). *The psychology of interpersonal relations.* New York: Wiley.

Janoff-Bulman, R., & Berger, A. R. (2000). The other side of trauma: Toward a psychology of appreciation. In J. H. Harvey & E. D. Miller (Eds.), *Loss and trauma: General and close relationship perspectives* (pp. 29–44). Philadelphia: Brunner-Routledge.

John, O. P., Donahue, E. M., & Kentle, R. L. (1991). *The Big Five Inventory—Versions 4a and 54.* Berkeley: University of California, Berkeley, Institute of Personality and Social Research.

Kasser, T. (2002). *The high price of materialism.* Cambridge, MA: MIT Press.

Kendler, K. S., Liu, X., Gardner, C. O., McCullough, M. E., Larson, D., & Prescott, C. A. (2003). Dimensions of religiosity and their relationship to lifetime psychiatric and substance use disorders. *American Journal of Psychiatry, 160,* 496–503.

Khasky, A. D., & Smith, J. C. (1999). Stress, relaxation states and creativity. *Perceptual and Motor Skills, 88,* 409–416.

Krech, G. (2002). *Naikan: Gratitude, grace and the Japanese art of self-reflection.* Berkeley, CA: Stone Bridge Press.

Langston, C. A. (1994). Capitalizing on and coping with daily life events: Expressive responses to positive events. *Journal of Personality and Social Psychology, 67,* 1112–1125.

Linley, P. A., & Joseph, S. (2004). Positive change following trauma and adversity: A review. *Journal of Traumatic Stress, 17,* 11–21.

Maheux, B., Legault, C., & Lambert, J. (1989). Increasing response rates in physicians' mail surveys: An experimental study. *American Journal of Public Health, 79,* 638–639.

Markus, H. R., & Kitayama, S. (1991). Culture and the self: Implications for cognition, emotion, and motivation. *Psychological Review, 98,* 224–253.

McAdams, D. P., & Bauer, J. J. (2004). Gratitude in modern life: Its manifestations and development. In R. A. Emmons & M. E. McCullough (Eds.), *The psychology of gratitude* (pp. 81–99). New York: Oxford University Press.

McCraty, R., & Atkinson, M. (2004). Psychophysiological coherence. In A. Watkins & D. Childre (Eds.), *Emotional sovereignty.* Amsterdam: Harwood Academic.

McCraty, R., & Childre, D. (2004). The grateful heart: The psychophysiology of appreciation. In R. A. Emmons & M. E. McCullough (Eds.), *The psychology of gratitude* (pp. 230–255). New York: Oxford University Press.

*McCullough, M. E., Emmons, R. A., & Tsang, J. (2002). The grateful disposition: A conceptual and empirical topography. *Journal of Personality and Social Psychology, 82,* 112–127.

*McCullough, M. E., Kilpatrick, S. D., Emmons, R. A., & Larson, D. B. (2001). Is gratitude a moral affect? *Psychological Bulletin, 127,* 249–266.

McCullough, M. E., Tsang, J., & Emmons, R. A. (2004). Gratitude in intermediate affective terrain: Links of grateful moods with individual differences and daily emotional experience. *Journal of Personality and Social Psychology, 86,* 295–309.

McGovern, L. P., Ditzian, J. L., & Taylor, S. P. (1975). The effect of positive reinforcement on helping with cost. *Psychonomic Society Bulletin, 5,* 421–423.

McWilliams, N., & Lependorf, S. (1990). Narcissistic pathology of everyday life: The denial of remorse and gratitude. *Contemporary Psychoanalysis, 26,* 430–451.

Mehrabian, A. (1967). Substitute for apology: Manipulation of cognitions to reduce negative attitude toward self. *Psychological Reports, 20,* 687–692.

Morishita, S. (2000). Treatment of anorexia nervosa with Naikan therapy. *International Medical Journal, 7,* 151.

Moss, M. K., & Page, R. A. (1972). Reinforcement and helping behavior. *Journal of Applied Social Psychology, 2,* 360–371.

Myers, D. G., & Diener, E. (1995). Who is happy? *Psychological Science, 6,* 10–19.

Neuberg, S. L., Cialdini, R. B., Brown, S. L., Luce, C., Sagarin, B. J., & Lewis, B. P. (1997). Does empathy lead to anything more than superficial helping? Comment on Batson et al. (1997). *Journal of Personality and Social Psychology, 73,* 510–516.

Nolen-Hoeksema, S., & Davis, C. G. (2002). Positive responses to loss: Perceiving benefits and growth. In C. R. Snyder & S. J. Lopez (Eds.), *Handbook of positive psychology* (pp. 598–606). New York: Oxford University Press.

Okamoto, S., & Robinson, W. P. (1997). Determinants of gratitude expressions in England. *Journal of Language and Social Psychology, 16,* 411–433.

Paulhus, D. L. (1998). Interpersonal and intrapsychic adaptiveness of trait self-enhancement: A mixed blessing? *Journal of Personality and Social Psychology, 74,* 1197–1208.

Peterson, B. E., & Stewart, A. J. (1996). Antecedents and contexts of generativity motivation at midlife. *Psychology and Aging, 11,* 21–33.

Reynolds, D. K. (1983). *Naikan psychotherapy: Meditation for self-development.* Chicago, IL: University of Chicago Press.

Rind, B., & Bordia, P. (1995). Effect of server's "thank you" and personalization on restaurant tipping. *Journal of Applied Social Psychology, 25,* 745–751.

Rosenberg, E. L. (1998). Levels of analysis and the organization of affect. *Review of General Psychology, 2,* 247–270.

Sakuta, T., Shiratsuchi, T., Kimura, Y., & Abe, Y. (1997). Psychotherapies originated in Japan. *International Medical Journal, 4,* 229–230.

Schwartz, B. (1967). The social psychology of the gift. *American Journal of Sociology, 73,* 1–11.

Seligman, M. E. P. (2002). *Authentic happiness: Using the new positive psychology to realize your potential for lasting fulfillment.* New York: Free Press.

Shapiro, S. L., Schwartz, G. E. R., & Santerre, C. (2002). Meditation and positive psychology. In C. R. Snyder & S. J. Lopez (Eds.), *Handbook of positive psychology* (pp. 632–645). New York: Oxford University Press.

Simmel, G. (1950). *The sociology of Georg Simmel.* Glencoe, IL: Free Press.

Smith, A. (1976). *The theory of moral sentiments* (6th ed.). Oxford, England: Clarendon Press. (Original work published 1790)

Solomon, R. C. (2002). *Spirituality for the skeptic.* New York: Oxford University Press.

Stein, M. (1989). Gratitude and attitude: A note on emotional welfare. *Social Psychology Quarterly, 52,* 242–248.

Suls, J., Witenberg, S., & Gutkin, D. (1981). Evaluating reciprocal and nonreciprocal prosocial behavior: Developmental trends. *Personality and Social Psychology Bulletin, 7,* 225–231.

Suwaki, H. (1985). International review series: Alcohol and alcohol problems research: II. Japan. *British Journal of Addiction, 80,* 127–132.

Tennen, H., & Affleck, G. (2002). Benefit-finding and benefit-reminding. In C. R. Snyder & S. J. Lopez (Eds.), *Handbook of positive psychology* (pp. 584–597). New York: Oxford University Press.

Tesser, A., Gatewood, R., & Driver, M. (1968). Some determinants of gratitude. *Journal of Personality and Social Psychology, 9,* 233–236.

Trivers, R., L. (1971). The evolution of reciprocal altruism. *Quarterly Review of Biology, 46,* 35–57.

Watkins, P. C., Woodward, K., Stone, T., & Kolts, R. L. (2003). *Gratitude and happiness: Development of a measure of gratitude, and relationships with subjective well-being.* Manuscript submitted for publication.

Watson, D., Clark, L. A., & Tellegen, A. (1988). Development and validation of brief measures of positive and negative affect: The PANAS Scales. *Journal of Personality and Social Psychology, 54,* 1063–1070.

Weiner, B., & Graham, S. (1988). Understanding the motivational role of affect: Life-span research from an attributional perspective. *Cognition and Emotion, 3,* 401–419.

Weiner, B., Russell, D., & Lerman, D. (1979). The cognition–emotion process in achievement-related contexts. *Journal of Personality and Social Psychology, 37,* 1211–1220.

Witvliet, C. V., Ludwig, T. E., & Bauer, D. J. (2002). Please forgive me: Transgressors' emotions and physiology during imagery of seeking forgiveness and victim responses. *Journal of Psychology and Christianity, 21,* 219–233.

Woodward, K. M., Moua, G. K., & Watkins, P. C. (1998, April). *Depressed individuals show less gratitude.* Paper presented at the annual convention of the Western Psychological Association, Albuquerque, NM.

Wright, T. A., & Staw, B. M. (1999). Affect and favorable work outcomes: Two longitudinal tests of the happy-productive worker thesis. *Journal of Organizational Behavior, 20,* 1–23.

Zaleski, Z. (1988). Attributions and emotions related to future goal attainment. *Journal of Educational Psychology, 80,* 563–568.

CHAPTER 30

Facilitating Curiosity: A Social and Self-Regulatory Perspective for Scientifically Based Interventions

TODD B. KASHDAN and FRANK D. FINCHAM

CURIOSITY IS AN understudied human strength with relevance to domains ranging from creativity, leisure, and social relationships to applications in educational, sport, organizational, and clinical psychology. Although curiosity may be a universal trait, individuals have idiosyncratic interests and differ in their receptivity to novel and challenging activities and the intensity, frequency, and sustainability of curiosity states. Existing research shows that curiosity explains approximately 10% of the variance in achievement and performance outcomes (Schiefele, Krapp, & Winteler, 1992) and 36% in career choices (Lent, Brown, & Hackett, 1994). In the workplace, curiosity-related cognitions and behaviors predict greater adjustment to new occupations (Wanberg & Kammeyer-Mueller, 2000), job-related changes (Wanberg & Banas, 2000), and job-related learning, satisfaction, and performance (e.g., Reio & Wiswell, 2000; Wall & Clegg, 1981). In the clinical realm, individuals with greater curiosity in self-reflection and behavior modification goals show greater clinical gains (e.g., Williams, Gagne, Ryan, & Deci, 2002; Williams, Rodin, Ryan, Grolnick, & Deci, 1998). None of these studies, however, used the term *curiosity*. The construct of curiosity has gone under various labels leading to redundant and isolated research, impeding scientific progress.

Systematic examination of the theories, structure, development, and correlates of curiosity are beyond the scope of this chapter (see Kashdan, in press-a; Silvia, in press, for reviews), which instead focuses on social and self-regulatory factors that enable curiosity to flourish. This analysis serves as a springboard for suggestions to develop empirically informed curiosity interventions. The limitations of existing curiosity research are noted in highlighting new research directions.

THE CONCEPT OF CURIOSITY

Understanding curiosity necessarily requires consideration of its potential overlap with interest, flow, and intrinsic motivation, each of which tends to be used interchangeably within a trait-state individual difference framework (Kashdan, in press-a). In fact, researcher preference often determines which label is used for the construct under study.

We define curiosity as the volitional recognition, pursuit, and self-regulation of novel and challenging opportunities (reflecting intrinsic values and interests). Enduring or *trait curiosity* refers to dispositional differences in curiosity behaviors. A person high in trait curiosity prefers novelty, complexity, uncertainty, and conflict; is more likely to be involved in or actively search for activities with these qualities; is more mindful of discrepancies between what is known and not known in a situation; and has these experiences more readily or chronically. Task or *state curiosity* is a temporary state evoked by an ongoing internal or external activity, implying a transaction between the person and environment. When curious, individuals are actively involved in the pursuit of personal enjoyment. Internal pressures (e.g., guilt and fear) and external pressures (e.g., the demands of other people) cannot induce an individual to appreciate and savor the beauty of a Renee Magritte painting or feel a sense of control and effortlessness while being mindful to the body positioning of an opponent and location of the ball in a tennis match. These examples capture the essence of experiencing curiosity. Reinforcements from momentary curiosity serve as likely precursors to enduring curiosity. Fortunately, curiosity is a malleable psychological state (and perhaps, trait) that is strongly influenced by social contexts and other individual difference variables.

We use the term curiosity because multidimensional curiosity models predate and are implicit in models of intrinsic motivation (e.g., Deci, 1975; Ryan & Deci, 2000) and interest (e.g., Fredrickson, 1998; Krapp, 1999). Berlyne's (1960, 1971, 1978) discussion of contextual properties that induce curiosity—namely, novelty, complexity, uncertainty, and conflict—suggests that research needs to account for person-level curiosity, the interestingness of the specific context, and interactions between person and context. We use this transactional approach to synthesize and expand on relevant curiosity research. The phenomenology of curiosity, interest, and intrinsically motivated states is virtually synonymous and includes positive affect (e.g., vitality, enjoyment), receptivity to new experiences, broadened cognitive processing, task absorption, and active exploration of sources of interestingness. The use of standard curiosity terminology serves to integrate overlapping bodies of work. As evidence of the distinctiveness of curiosity, factor-analytic studies indicate that indexes of positive psychological constructs such as hope, optimism, positive affect, well-being, and life satisfaction all load onto a single global factor whereas curiosity scales load onto an independent factor (Kashdan, 2002, in press-b).

A FRAMEWORK FOR FACTORS THAT SUPPORT CURIOSITY

The propensity and intensity of an individual's curiosity at any given time depend on an individual's personal sensitivities to ongoing activity and the properties of the activity. To specify factors that facilitate and stabilize enhanced levels of curiosity in an activity or domain, we integrate different theoretical traditions. Although several theories offer an account of the social contexts and self-regulatory processes that support the expression of curiosity, we believe self-determination theory (SDT; Deci & Ryan, 1985, 2000) is the most fertile for intervention work. However, to further illuminate methods for intervention, we integrate this with the curiosity-inducing stimulus properties specified by Berlyne (1960), the skills-challenge balance specified by Csikszentmihalyi (1990), and the dynamic interplay among trait curiosity, task curiosity, and situational contexts.

The crux of SDT is that individuals primarily strive to achieve self-determination in their daily activities. Motivation is derived from subjective feelings of self-determination. Self-determination theory covers extensive territory on the social conditions and self-regulatory mechanisms that foster or hinder feelings of self-determination, goal pursuit, and goal attainment, which are integral to well-being and optimal functioning (Deci & Ryan, 2000). We limit our discussion to the mechanisms relevant to curiosity-based activities. Curiosity is given a privileged status in this model:

> Perhaps no single phenomenon reflects the positive potential of human nature as much as intrinsic motivation, the inherent tendency to seek out novelty and challenges, to extend and exercise one's capacities, to explore, and to learn. (Ryan & Deci, 2000, p. 70)

Self-determination theory suggests that the likelihood and strength of curiosity depends on the subjective experience of autonomy and, to a slightly lesser extent, competence. Although SDT affords less attention to feelings of relatedness, we believe social contexts that satisfy this need strongly influence the expression of curiosity. The independent and interactive influence of these psychological needs on task and enduring curiosity is not known.

AUTONOMY

Autonomy hinges on the belief that personal behaviors are self-initiated. In general, people exhibit greater task curiosity (self-report and behavioral measures of persistence during free-choice periods), enjoyment, and deeper cognitive processing when provided greater choice (e.g., Cordova & Lepper, 1996) and when provided greater information and encouragement for personal choices (e.g., Black & Deci, 2000).

Threats, punishment, negative feedback, and surveillance have clear negative effects on task curiosity and performance. These pressures are experienced as internally controlling and tend to result in extrinsic motivation or task disengagement, both of which have adverse effects on performance-related outcomes. There is considerable debate as to the effects of external rewards on curiosity. A meta-analysis found that external rewards have an overall detrimental effect on task-related curiosity (Deci, Koestner, & Ryan, 1999). The undermining effect of external rewards was more robust for interesting, compared to boring, tasks. Extrinsic rewards appear to be useful for motivating individuals to participate in unpleasant or undesirable activities. This is fortunate because monotonous activities, rules, deadlines, evaluations, and social proprieties are vital and integral to schools, organizations, sports, and families. The same rewards that increase motivation in uninteresting tasks undermine motivation in initially interesting tasks because feelings of personal causation shift from internal to external. This underscores a complex relationship:

> That is, a person could feel able to obtain a desired outcome (i.e., have an *internal* locus of *control*) and also feel pressured and controlled by that desired outcome to behave in a certain way (i.e., have an *external* locus of *causality*). (Deci et al., 1999, p. 693)

To sustain or enhance initial task curiosity and enjoyment, the provision of rewards should contribute to an internal locus of causality. The strategies in which rewards (or punishments) are administered affect task-related curiosity (see Ryan, 1982). Informational rewards are used to acknowledge a recipient's mastery and skill development and tend to be unexpected (e.g., a coach encouraging athletes about improvements in their techniques). These rewards let recipients feel that they are the origin of their behavior. Controlling rewards are used to motivate recipients and strengthen their interest (e.g., a coach telling the team that the best performer gets to skip the next practice). These rewards cause recipients to feel like pawns that exchange effort and work for potential rewards.

Feelings of autonomy and the autonomy-supportive behavior of significant others have clear, positive effects on curiosity. As for controlling behaviors such as giving rewards or being critical, the administration tactics are crucial to fostering or hindering curiosity. Controlling tactics may increase immediate task curiosity but are likely to undermine autonomous curiosity and the development of enduring interests. Virtually no empirical attention has been given to the specific mechanisms by which internal pressures are activated and influence curiosity and goal-related outcomes. Overall, curiosity is more likely to be enhanced when control is minimized and feelings of personal choice, meaningfulness, and competence-related processes are emphasized.

COMPETENCE

Events that cause individuals to believe they can interact effectively with the environment (perceived competence) or desire to interact effectively (competence valuation) tend to enhance curiosity and predict achievement gains (e.g., Cury, Elliot, Sarrazin, Da Fonseca, & Rufo, 2002; Elliot et al., 2000). Students with high academic ability but low perceived academic competence report lower academic curiosity, enjoyment, persistence, and grades across a school year than those students with both high academic ability and perceived competence (Miserandino, 1996). Strong abilities are not sufficient, as competency beliefs appear to be the primary mechanism for experiencing high task curiosity and persistence, increasing the likelihood of achievement success.

Appropriate and sincere praise (informational positive feedback) kindles feelings of competence and competence valuation (Deci et al., 1999). The salutary effects of positive task feedback on curiosity in challenging word games were independently mediated by perceived competence and competence valuation (Elliot et al., 2000). However, when using a basketball dribbling task, mediational effects were found only for competence valuation (Cury et al., 2002). These findings highlight the importance of both the administration of positive feedback (informational versus controlling) and the domain specificity of tasks (e.g., academic, challenging cognitive games, sports) in synthesizing curiosity-related research and developing interventions.

Competence valuation is proposed to be more malleable and less stable than perceived competence. Positive feedback following a single task has to contend with substantial personal data (e.g., prior performance) informing beliefs in the certainty of abilities in the task (e.g., math, football). Most of the research on the effects of positive feedback and social contexts on competence-related beliefs and subsequent curiosity have used experimental tasks. More work is needed on the longevity of positive feedback effects and whether changes in competence valuation and task curiosity translate into further participation, engagement, and success in the same domain. The longevity of positive feedback effects is likely to be contingent on the degree to which it is internalized.

Competence-related beliefs are proposed to cause individuals to perceive activities as challenges as opposed to threats. Strong competence-related beliefs can be expected to minimize the disruptive influences of self-consciousness and fears of negative evaluation, and increase feelings of control and task absorption. There is evidence of a sequential relationship from competence valuation to task absorption to task curiosity (Cury et al., 2002). Yet, there are two issues in interpreting these findings: (1) The assessment of competence valuation and task absorption were conducted simultaneously, and (2) task absorption is a structural component of curiosity (Csikszentmihalyi, 1990; Kashdan, in press-a). Refinements in the timing of assessment and greater attention to the differential operationalization of predictors, mechanisms, and outcomes can provide greater understanding of the sequelae of curiosity. Despite these caveats, there is evidence that both autonomy and competence-related beliefs are important antecedents to curiosity. To date, however, there are no data on the potential interplay between these different belief systems.

RELATEDNESS

According to Deci and Ryan (2000), unlike autonomy and competence, satisfying relatedness is not necessary for the expression of task curiosity. However, a sense of connectedness and believing that inner emotional experiences are acknowledged and validated do appear to increase curiosity (Mikulincer & Shaver, 2003, for review of attachment literature). Feelings of relatedness enhance curiosity and performance in athletic, academic, and work contexts (e.g., Grolnick & Ryan, 1989; Hazan & Shaver, 1990; Smoll, Smith, Barnett, & Everett, 1993), producing consequences such as personal growth and less susceptibility to closed-minded cognitions (e.g., ethnic stereotypes, Mikulincer, 1997). Preliminary support exists for reciprocal relationships between curiosity and feelings of relatedness. Feelings of comfort and safety encourage curiosity and exploratory behavior, and curiosity predicts greater feelings of closeness among strangers (Kashdan, Rose, & Fincham, in press; Kashdan & Roberts, in press) and students and teachers (Skinner & Belmont, 1993). Each pathway leads to a broadening of personal resources.

When significant others (e.g., parents, teachers, supervisors, coaches, therapists) are perceived to be sensitive and responsive, concerns about impressing others and being accepted are minimized. Satisfying this fundamental need to belong frees resources to embrace risks and pursue and persist in novel and challenging activities. Infants, children, and adults who feel close to significant others are more likely to explore their environment because the inherent anxiety of novel and ambiguous activity is modulated by beliefs that they can return to a safe comfort zone. Excessive anxieties undermine exploration and increase withdrawal and avoidance behaviors.

We suggest that satisfying feelings of relatedness becomes increasingly important for the initiation, maintenance, and self-regulation of curiosity when activities are conducted in interpersonal contexts. Students, workers, athletes, and clients under the supervision of individuals who satisfy relatedness needs may be inspired to pursue appetitive goals at the potential expense of failure, embarrassment, and rejection.

The Self-Regulatory Strategy of Internalization

Rules, deadlines, assignments, and social mores are necessary for parents to raise young children to be virtuous and productive members of society and for each workplace, school classroom, and athletic team to keep account of what is being learned and to ensure a safe and pleasant environment. Although individuals may initially feel controlled by pressures and obligations to do things that are not self-endorsed, goal-related behaviors can be internalized, thereby producing self-determination and the strongest form of personal investment.

Take the example of a client seeking treatment for impairing social anxiety on the insistence of his or her spouse and work manager (external pressures) as opposed to the desire to be healthier and happier (autonomous reasons). Clients pressured into seeking treatment are likely to be less invested in the treatment process. They may complete treatment-related assignments because of the rationale offered by their therapist: The anxiety experienced during social exposure tasks can be viewed as an investment for a calmer and more pleasurable future. Sometimes clients experience a shift toward greater treatment-related curiosity and personal effort when they recognize positive changes (i.e., competence-related beliefs). Other clients drop out prematurely, which can be a result of discordance between intrinsic values and interests and the treatment process. When treatment-related goals are internalized such that clients begin to understand and value what they are doing, why they are doing it, and begin to invest time and effort of their own accord, their motivation changes. This process leads to increased curiosity in the self-discovery and behavior modification process, subsequently enhancing clinical gains (e.g., Williams et al., 2002).

Considerable data show that autonomy, competence, and relatedness enhance curiosity, initiate internalization, and inform the development of curiosity interventions. But exploration of the salutary effects of treatment-related curiosity and, more importantly, the structure, value, and assessment of internalization has only just begun. There is clinical value in capitalizing on the internalization process to transform lack of motivation and boredom to psychological states closer to curiosity.

ELABORATING THE FRAMEWORK FOR CURIOSITY SUPPORTIVE FACTORS

Domain Specificity of Curiosity

Individuals have idiosyncratic interests and can be expected to react differently to the specific activity (e.g., video game, reading task, documentary on Egyptian pyramids), global domain (e.g., school, sports), or specific content area (e.g., math, philosophy, basketball) under study or target of intervention. Failure to address domain-specific matches between individual interests and specific activities evokes nonrandom error into investigations. On average, girls become less interested in science and math as they get older compared to boys, and individuals in collectivist countries (e.g., China) express less curiosity for solo sports such as mountain biking and rock climbing than individuals in individualistic countries (e.g., United States). Autonomy, competence-related beliefs, and curiosity have shown differential patterns in specific academic subjects and sporting activities (Duda & Nicholls, 1992; Reeve & Hakel, 2000). Most curiosity studies have focused on single content areas or experimental tasks such as pinball games, basketball dribbling drills, and problem-solving tasks (e.g., crossword and jigsaw puzzles). Findings on factors and processes that facilitate curiosity need to be replicated in multiple domains to examine the extent of cross-domain generalizability versus domain-specific patterns and pathways.

A TRANSACTIONAL APPROACH

The transactional work from flow theory (e.g., Csikszentmihalyi, 1990) and Berlyne's (1960, 1971) research on responses to stimuli with varying challenging properties suggest that curiosity behaviors are a function of the person and environment. To augment SDT, these theories share supplemental perspectives on enablers of curiosity. There is substantial support for a quadratic or inverted U-shaped relationship between curiosity and the challenge of ongoing activities. Curiosity will be undermined if activities are too difficult and complex, evoking anxiety and withdrawal, or are too easy, leading to boredom and apathy. Curiosity appears to be inextricably linked to anxiety in predicting the most desirable states and subsequent approach/avoidance behaviors in a given situation (Spielberger & Starr, 1994). To increase the likelihood of heightened curiosity, the challenge of activities should match or slightly exceed the individual's abilities.

Support for this model stems from a considerable number of perceptual tasks in which participants were exposed to stimuli with varying degrees of novelty, complexity, and ambiguity (e.g., bizarre shapes, planes with the wings of a bird). Participants preferred shapes, colors, and pictures with moderate novel, ambiguous, conflicting, and complex properties (inducing greater state anxiety and curiosity) as opposed to neutral or extremely ambiguous stimuli (see Berlyne, 1971; Voss & Keller, 1983, for reviews). These findings are plagued by a narrow operationalization of curiosity and questionable generalizability. However, validation for the quadratic relationship between curiosity and challenge has been replicated in diverse ecological settings such as river kayaking, leisure, and work- and school-related activities (e.g., Csikszentmihalyi & LeFevre, 1989; Jones, Hollenhorst, Perna, & Selin, 2000; Peters, 1978). Using jigsaw puzzle and epistemic tasks, Loewenstein, Adler, Behrens, and Gillis (1992) found that curiosity increased as individuals obtained more information and success toward task completion; however, across each task there was a point of diminishing returns in curiosity and task persistence. Once participants could make well-educated guesses about the final design of jigsaw puzzles, their curiosity dissipated dramatically.

Silvia (in press) has carefully examined much of the research on curiosity and learning and found that a disproportionate number of researchers report only linear analyses or conduct experiments without addressing the quadratic relationship between curiosity and stimulus or task properties. We believe it should become standard practice in the field of curiosity to report the results of quadratic analyses.

CURIOSITY INTERVENTIONS

Curiosity is based on appraisals and emotional reactions to ongoing internal or external activity. Only in rare circumstances would it make sense to directly cultivate curiosity in an intervention. As the prior section makes clear, the best avenue for cultivating curiosity is to create social and contextual conditions that facilitate the perceptions and emotions that lead to greater curiosity. These conditions include satisfying the three psychological needs we have identified, highlighting the personal meaningfulness of activity, producing optimal transactions between person-level characteristics and ongoing activity, and directly manipulating the collative properties of activity.

Table 30.1 presents a list of general strategies for enhancing curiosity based on theory and research on SDT and curiosity-related constructs. The primary targets of intervention include the activities used during sessions, homework assignments, and the interpersonal style and behaviors enacted by leaders or authority figures. For parsimony, we did not include reciprocal feedback loops among activities, psychological needs, and curiosity. Pending the need for supportive data, we would hypothesize that the more needs that are targeted in an intervention, the greater propensity for high levels of task curiosity and the search and attainment of subsequent and enduring curiosity experiences. The task or social environment can be the target of intervention but especially with students, workers, clients, and athletes who have sustained relationships with teachers, managers, therapists, and coaches, respectively. Thus, training authority figures to support self-determination (autonomy, competence, and relatedness) should increase the likelihood of upward spirals among activities, needs, and curiosity, leading to enduring interests. These sorts of multifaceted pathways and relationships should be considered in the design of interventions and analyses of efficacy. Using the targets and strategies in Table 30.1 as a guide, the few existing curiosity interventions are examined along with suggestions for new techniques and modules in the domains of education, work, sports, and health. We begin with an exemplar of interventions targeting both activities and the social environment.

CURIOSITY INTERVENTIONS IN THE HEALTH DOMAIN

Motivational Interviewing (MI)   Originally developed for treating alcohol abuse, for the past 20 years MI has been applied to health-related domains such as smoking cessation, drug use, gambling, domestic abuse, HIV risk reduction, diet and physical activity, and adherence to medical and psychiatric treatment (e.g., Dunn, Deroo, & Rivara, 2001; Miller & Rollnick, 2002). In contrast to authoritarian and confrontational treatments, in MI, therapists gently guide clients in self-directed changes. Expressed motivation to change, articulation of how current behaviors interfere with desired outcomes, and agenda setting during treatment are elicited from clients. Therapists operate at the client's pace and do not use persuasive tactics, refute irrational or maladaptive beliefs, or challenge

Table 30.1

Empirically Informed Targets and Strategies of Curiosity Interventions

Target of Intervention	General Strategies and Techniques	Directly Activated Psychological Needs	Curiosity Outcome
Activity or task	Create tasks that capitalize on novelty, complexity, ambiguity, variety, and surprise.	Direct influence on curiosity	
	Purposely place individuals in contexts that are discrepant with their experience, skills, and personality.	Autonomy	
	Create tasks that can be conducted independently.	Competence	
	Allow opportunities for play.		
	Create tasks that are personally meaningful.	Relatedness	
	Create challenges that match or slightly exceed current skills.		
	Create enjoyable group-based activities.		
Social environment (leadership)	Provide choices and participation in decision-making process.	Autonomy	
	Foster personal responsibility and ownership of actions and successes.		Affect curiosity as a function of activated psychological needs.
	Give clear information about task structure and expectations.		
	Provide encouragement and supportive feedback for efforts.	Competence	
	Focus on improvement and the process of learning and mastery.		
	Elicit and reinforce positive self-talk.		
	Emphasize the meaningfulness of activity and efforts.		
	Aid in goal setting, planning, and monitoring.		
	Avoid threat, judgment, and harsh evaluation and criticism.		
	Foster open dialogue.	Relatedness	
	Express empathy for individuals' emotions, values, and needs.		
	Be warm, accepting, and supportive.		
	Provide clear information about the social structure and other people.		
	Express and model interest in individuals and activities.		

resistance. Motivational interviewing sessions are a forum for clients to openly express thoughts and feelings concerning their desirable and undesirable behaviors and for therapists to help clients explore and resolve conflicts between ongoing behaviors and their interference with intrinsic desires and goals. If clients voice interest, other intervention techniques are also evoked. Motivational interviewing is a brief intervention that has been examined alone or as an adjunct to existing clinical and health interventions.

It is assumed that clients differ in their motivational orientations to change long-standing behaviors and each client's motivation fluctuates as a result of transactions between them and the environment. Despite the use of motivational terminology, we could not find any published work that explicitly tied MI to curiosity or the components of SDT. Motivational interviewing provides a therapeutic environment that supports the psychological needs of autonomy, relatedness, and competence, which facilitate curiosity-related behaviors that lead to positive treatment outcomes. The goal of MI is to foster clients' self-exploration of the meaning, implications, benefits, and costs of their behavioral tendencies. It is believed that a failure to engage in this deep cognitive processing prevents clients from recognizing how their health behaviors disrupt their ability to meet desired outcomes and experience well-being. Motivational interviewing fosters clients' personal accountability and responsibility for their behaviors.

Therapists are trained to enact a specific style compatible with the goals of MI (see Miller & Rollnick, 2002). In support of autonomy, they consistently provide clients with options and the freedom to choose the discussions and agendas of sessions. Therapists help clients perceive conflicts between their ongoing behaviors and their personal short- and long-term goals. For example, engaging in unprotected sex with multiple partners for immediate gratification would conflict with the striving to live a long, healthy life. Upon accentuating clients' mindfulness of these discrepancies, therapists let clients argue both sides of their ambivalent feelings and values in the hopes of resolution. In support of competence, therapists provide continual feedback about the results of formal assessment (e.g., self-report forms, interviews) and their ongoing behavior and its consequences. Treatment goals are elicited from the client and, when necessary, are modified and negotiated with the therapist to ensure they fit the skills and motivation of the client. To cultivate self-efficacy and treatment-related curiosity behaviors, a primary strategy of therapists is to elicit and reinforce self-motivational statements (e.g., recognizing small gains over the course of a week) and behaviors (e.g., rewarding themselves for making progress) made by clients. In support of relatedness, therapists are nonjudgmental, nonconfrontational, and express empathy, validation, understanding, and genuine interest in clients' feelings, values, and concerns. Therapists engage in more listening than talking during sessions, which supports both autonomous behavior and feelings of relatedness. However, when therapists do communicate, it is in a reflective manner to further clients' self-exploration of the aforementioned discrepancies and ambivalence. The training to reach this self-determination supportive interpersonal style taps nearly all of the social environment strategies in Table 30.1.

There is mixed empirical support for the effectiveness of MI (see Dunn et al., 2001), but it is defined as a "probably efficacious" treatment. It appears to be most effective for addictive behaviors, younger clients, and individuals with lower initial motivation for change. Motivational interviewing has been shown to increase curiosity-related behaviors and cognitions in treatment such as active engagement and participation, receptivity to new ideas, and thoughtful processing of different experiences and perspectives. There is evidence that client engagement during treatment mediates the relationship between in-patient treatment (MI versus no-MI) and reduced alcohol use at a three-month follow-up after discharge (Brown & Miller, 1993).

Therapist Training and Treatment Dosage   There is a great deal of variability in how MI is administered, including training of therapists and mode and the length or dosage of treatment. The therapeutic style of MI is distinct from the modal cognitive-behavioral therapy training of psychologists and the noncollaborative decision making in doctor-patient (e.g., directive advice to clients) and teacher-student relationships (e.g., continuous testing and evaluation on preplanned material). Motivational interviewing appears to be used as a standalone intervention or as an adjunct to other programs, administered in individual and group formats, with varying numbers of contact hours (e.g., Dunn et al., 2001). At present, there is no clear standard because results between these modes of delivery differ by the age of client, behavior being treated, and client characteristics. In terms of cost-effectiveness, MI shows great promise as a brief adjunct treatment to initiate client engagement with other programs. Tests of therapist fidelity to the principles of MI should be conducted systematically with independent ratings of audiotaped or videotaped sessions, which should include early and later sessions to assess for behavioral drifts back to initial therapeutic interpersonal styles. The development and evaluation of standardized (e.g., manualized) training and interventions should prevent variability in therapist fidelity and treatment dosage across studies. Learning from the applications of SDT to education (e.g., Williams & Deci, 1996), therapists should be trained in the same self-determination supportive style that they are expected to exhibit to clients. The criterion of therapist training is the effects on trainees' interests in MI, their therapeutic style, and the outcomes of their clients.

Assessment Issues and Suggestions   As for the mechanisms of action in MI, we suggest that future studies examine SDT-related variables such as client autonomy, competence, and relatedness beliefs during treatment sessions and their influence on curiosity and positive health-related outcomes. We emphasize the strong empirical support for the satisfaction of each of these beliefs in predicting curiosity-related outcomes. Additional support stems from a smoking cessation intervention with adults counseled by physicians (Williams et al., 2002). Physicians were trained to provide an intervention similar to MI except that it did not help clients recognize, explore, and resolve discrepancies between what they do and what they would like to be doing and feeling. Results found that the autonomy supportive compared to the control intervention was perceived as more autonomy supportive (as evaluated by independent raters of session audiotapes) and led to greater client efforts and success in smoking cessation. Independent ratings of autonomy support are commendable because they don't contaminate client-rated outcome measures. However, the goal of intervention is to enhance client perceptions of autonomy in the therapeutic setting. We suggest that clinical studies also focus on the satisfaction of needs as rated by clients.

The failure to examine theoretical models and constructs related to curiosity has interfered with examinations of efficacy and process-related mechanisms. A large majority of MI studies have used self-report measures or clinical observations of the broad construct of readiness to change. This complex theoretical construct has less meaning to nonprofessionals than the constructs of curiosity and the psychological needs of SDT. The premise of working with clients with less than ideal motivation for treatment goals begs for instruments that are sensitive to the degree to which treatment goals are pursued because of their own curiosity or internalized extrinsic goals. The single SDT dimension ranging from amotivation to intrinsic motivation is a useful framework for creating specific self-report and interview questions about client curiosity in the current behaviors being treated. Published studies support the use of the Treatment Self Regulation Questionnaire, assessing the degree of clients' self-determined interest in the treatment process (e.g., Williams et al., 2002). To measure the process of change for specific manualized treatments, existing curiosity measures can be modified to address curiosity in the material being presented, therapist-client dialogue, the self-exploration process, and treatment goals (see fourth row in Table 30.2).

The therapeutic approach of creating, maintaining, and resolving personal discrepancies and conflicts in MI appears to be an extension of existing curiosity theoretical models. Clients can be expected to initially experience anxiety and curiosity when discrepancies are developed. However, as information is continually acquired and refinements in clients' sense of self are assimilated or accommodated, anxiety is expected to dissipate. Curiosity may initially abate, but the exploration of new opportunities to enact novel, healthier behaviors and skills can be expected to enhance further curiosity and self-discovery. Similarly, changes in health-related behaviors and feelings of autonomy, competence, and relatedness can be expected to ebb and flow over the course of treatment. Despite the likelihood of nonlinear trajectories, MI studies have primarily used linear analyses.

Besides examining client improvement (or relapse), of interest is whether intra-individual variability in health-related behaviors covary with changes in treatment-related curiosity and constructs such as anxiety and feelings of self-determination. Aggregating changes within treatment to pre- and postdesigns can mask social and self-regulatory factors that facilitate and hinder clinical gains. Constructs can be assessed before and after each session as a dynamic examination of the change, variability, and structure of curiosity within and between individuals (see third row in Table 30.2). Ainley and Hidi (2002) review examples of more dynamic modes of curiosity assessment that have implications for intervention. This methodology allows for better tests of theoretical models, leading to empirical support or the need for model refinements.

Additional Implications for Motivational Interviewing We believe there is merit in using MI as an adjunct to additional areas of study including psychological disorders, the cultivation of positive characteristics such as prosocial behaviors in children, and the beginning of organizational changes in the workplace. It may be particularly useful for programs with universal implementation such as an entire school (e.g., bullying prevention programs) where some students may fail to perceive a need to change and experience initial amotivation. Other unmotivated clients who may benefit from MI include those for whom treatment is court-mandated. Motivational interviewing appears to be useful to gauge and facilitate motivation such that discrepancies between the present and ideal self are highlighted and curiosity for self-discovery and the products of self-discovery are enhanced.

Table 30.2
Suggestions for Assessment in Curiosity Interventions

Assessment Strategies and Techniques	Rationale
Recognize and assess individual differences in trait and task curiosity.	Individuals differ in the desire, recognition, and active pursuit of novelty and challenge. People can prefer difficult cognitive activity, physically manipulating objects, exploring the environment with others, or thinking about their feelings and thoughts. Gauging general tendencies and task curiosity before, during, and after activities can improve tests of the impact of interventions.
Assess theoretically relevant individual differences variables.	Specific individual difference factors moderate relationships between social contexts and curiosity. These variables can offer insight into matching participants to appropriate activities and identifying good or poor responders.
Conduct dynamic assessments of intra-individual variability in curiosity, affect, beliefs, and contextual variables during activity.	Task curiosity, anxiety, and perceptions of skills and challenges can be expected to change over the course of activity. Dynamic measures can further our understanding of curiosity enablers and inhibitors by examining factors that covary with changes in curiosity. Examine quadratic relationships.
Consider modifying existing curiosity scales to address domain-specificity of curiosity for the specific stimuli, content, or domains targeted by interventions.	Greater concordance between outcome measures and study hypotheses will increase the probability of obtaining clinically useful findings (i.e., decrease in measurement error). Interventions are designed to enhance curiosity and goal-related outcomes in domains such as education, sports, or work, or with even greater specificity (i.e., chemistry, baseball). The specificity of scales should be equivalent to the specificity of the domain under study.
Avoid potential contamination effects between curiosity self-report scales and processes and outcomes of interest.	Several curiosity scales are problematic in that items tap domains such as feelings of competency, autonomy, and meaningfulness. Using these scales would contaminate examinations of these same constructs as potential mechanisms of action or outcomes.

Further Suggestions for Cultivating Curiosity in the Health Domain   Clinicians should be creative in using curiosity-enhancing techniques to improve health conditions. Cultivating curiosity-related behaviors may offer adjunctive benefits for patients being treated for degenerative diseases. Patients with Alzheimer's disease have been shown to exhibit a number of cognitive deficits including abilities to process information and consolidate experiences into memories. Specific attentional deficits include difficulties in sustaining attention to external stimulation, tuning out distractions, redirecting resources to novel stimuli, recognition memory of novel stimuli, and visual processing speed (e.g., Rizzo, Anderson, Dawson, Myers, & Ball, 2000). These information-processing difficulties can be expected to interfere with

(1) the active pursuit of novel and challenging opportunities and (2) savoring of pleasurable experiences. These hedonic strategies are contingent on curiosity and exploration of the environment and the self. An experimental study found that early-stage Alzheimer's patients exposed to visual images with intense emotional properties had little difficulty sustaining and redirecting attention to different sections of these pictures compared to their behavior when exposed to less intense images (LaBar, Mesulam, Gitelman, & Weintraub, 2000). Cognitive tasks using visual and audio stimuli with variations in collative properties may serve a restorative function for patients suffering from degenerative diseases by having them practice and improve information-processing skills. One limitation of the LaBar et al. study is that it presented only neutral and negatively valenced images. We believe there is greater benefit in using positively valenced images because the induction of task-positive affect may be more important to the broadening of cognitive processing and building of cognitive resources (Fredrickson, 1998). With computer technology, images can be more fluid and challenging than the two-dimensional pictures used in the experiment. For all clinical innovations, activity-related strategies (see Table 30.1) should be embedded in a framework matching challenges to skills and gently escalating challenges as skills improve.

CURIOSITY INTERVENTIONS IN ORGANIZATIONS: WORK, SCHOOL, AND SPORTS

There are clear distinctions in the purpose, expectations, and relationships between authority figures and participants in occupational, academic, and athletic domains compared to the health domain. Yet we surmise that the intervention and assessment strategies in Tables 30.1 and 30.2 are equally applicable in organizations. To minimize redundancies for intervention suggestions, we examine findings to support specific techniques that cut across domains as well as domain-specific techniques. Only a few existing interventions have directly promoted positive outcomes such as self-esteem and teamwork with curiosity-related behaviors as a secondary focus, if at all. For these reasons, many of our suggestions have been extrapolated from laboratory and field studies.

CULTIVATING SELF-DETERMINATION SUPPORT IN LEADERS

Promotion efforts have focused on training organizational managers (Deci, Connell, & Ryan, 1989), athletic coaches of adolescent ballplayers (Smoll et al., 1993), and student mentors of peer-led teaching groups that supplement faculty lectures (e.g., Tien, Roth, & Kampmeier, 2002). Program components include recognizing and validating the emotions and needs of others, providing information and opportunities for self-initiated choices, engaging in participative decision making, providing genuine encouragement and positive feedback, and avoiding controlling tactics such as threats, punishment, and pressure. These leadership interventions clearly address the three hallmark dimensions of SDT in leadership styles (see Social Environment section of Table 30.1).

Managers, coaches, and peer-teachers exhibited definitive improvements in their promotion of self-determination over the course of training. The transfer from self-determination supportive leaders to self-determined learners to better performance has been found for athletic coaches (Smoll et al., 1993) and peer-led teaching groups (e.g., Tien et al., 2002); without intervention, similar prospective trends were found for professors (Black & Deci, 2000; Williams & Deci, 1996). Leadership changes among athletic coaches (Smoll et al., 1993) influenced child athletes who rated coaches as more reinforcing and encouraging and less controlling compared to the control group. Children in the intervention also reported greater enjoyment, liking, and knowledge of baseball, and feelings of closeness to their coaches and fellow teammates. Children's global self-esteem increased substantially from preseason to postseason in the intervention whereas there were no changes for controls. Well-replicated findings were also found for peer-led intervention groups with students exhibiting greater curiosity and enjoyment in academic material and better grades than comparison classes without peer-led workshops (e.g., Tien et al., 2002). For work managers, the positive influence of intervention-based leadership changes on workers was less conclusive (Deci et al., 1989). Only 1 of 16 variables reflecting workers' attitudes and feelings about their jobs (satisfaction with potential for advancement) changed as a function of the managerial intervention compared to a control group.

GENERAL STRATEGIES TO IMPROVE INTERVENTIONS

Like MI, the peer-led teaching intervention targeted both the social environment and the activities during the workshop. Matching the activity strategies in Table 30.1, the workshop materials were designed to be challenging, personally meaningful and applicable to the overall course, and suitable for group activities. In contrast, the interventions focusing on athletic coaches and work managers targeted the social environment with no formal emphasis on activities. A failure to target work activities could explain the null relationships between the intervention and worker perceptions; as for performance, it was either not assessed or not reported. Prospective studies have shown that the perceived collative properties of occupational tasks predict worker creativity, performance, and satisfaction (Oldham & Cummings, 1996; Wall & Clegg, 1981). We presume that attention to matches between worker skills and occupational challenges and the creation of tasks that are complex, novel, and personally meaningful will strengthen the impact of leadership changes on the curiosity, performance, and satisfaction of workers. The actual activities at work presumably occupy more time in a workday than interactions with managers, thus having a greater impact on work outcomes. There is reason to believe that there will be a reciprocal relationship with greater curiosity and enjoyment in work activities having a contagion effect on relationships with other workers and managers (cf. Kashdan, Fincham, & Rose, 2003). Future interventions targeting the social environment should examine the additive benefits of targeting activities compared to the social environment with the strategies in Table 30.1. This could lead to further work on dismantling the primary targets and strategies that account for leadership, worker, and work climate changes.

As mentioned with MI, the training of leaders and educators should be conducted in a self-determination supportive style. Support for a trickle-down effect stems from studies showing that medical students who perceived their training to be more supportive of their self-determination experienced greater curiosity and competency during their training, and, in the long term, were more supportive of the self-determination of their own patients (Williams & Deci, 1996). Patients under the care of doctors who were more supportive experienced more desirable health outcomes. The promotion of self-determination and curiosity-related positive outcomes stemming from leadership interventions and radiating downward should be replicated in various organizational domains.

FOSTERING MEANINGFULNESS IN ACTIVITIES AND THE PROCESS OF INTERNALIZATION

All human beings have to engage in activities that are incompatible with their personal values and interests. Students are required to complete classes in math, science, literature, social studies, and physical education irrespective of personal interest; workers in rewarding professional careers may abhor administrative responsibilities. The self-regulatory process of internalization can transform activities that are not self-determined into curiosity-inducing activities (Deci & Ryan, 2000).

Internalizing extrinsic sources of meaning (e.g., parental hopes to be more honest, academic value of reading books, athletic value of practice games), in turn, initiates a trajectory from initial to enduring curiosity. Psychological components of internalized activities include feelings of enjoyment and challenge, autonomy, and competence, thus reinforcing greater participation and persistence in the future. Stronger tendencies to integrate goals of psychology classes (learning and applying information presented) into the sense of self have been shown to predict greater enrollment in subsequent psychology classes, better performance, and greater exploration of psychology-related material and opportunities (Harackiewicz, Barron, Tauer, & Elliot, 2002). As an upward spiral of interactive influences, final grades in initial psychology courses moderated the relationship between initial and future curiosity such that students with higher final grades in introductory psychology were more likely to get further involved in the field of psychology than peers with lower grades. Thus, competency beliefs and task curiosity had cyclical effects on enduring curiosity behaviors. To clarify causal relations, prospective investigations are needed that investigate time-lagged associations; for example, the effects of task curiosity during a workday on perceptions of autonomy, competence, and relatedness reported the following workday (as well as the reverse causal pathway of supported needs on subsequent curiosity). The theoretical attention afforded to the self-regulatory process of internalization has far outpaced data. Pending further psychometric attention and assessment, we can only speculate on its importance and how it can be used to enhance positive outcomes.

Increasing the perceived meaningfulness of an activity presumably increases the likelihood of internalization and task curiosity. For students, whenever possible, the real-world applications and personal value of subject matter should be made readily apparent. In classes on mathematics or statistics, teachers can be autonomy-supportive and ask students to vote on themes for upcoming lectures such as supermarket shopping or a record company executive making decisions about new musicians. Using the students' self-selected theme, different analytic techniques can be taught in a real-world context—broach addition, subtraction, multiplication, and division by having students compute the cost of a concert tour of a famous musical artist. In classes such as science or social studies, hands-on activities such as experiments, field trips, reenactments of historical events, and using multimedia technology can bring meaning to potentially mundane activities. There is abundant evidence that academic lectures and reading materials manipulated to be more interesting, challenging, or meaningful induce greater curiosity and learning (see Silvia, in press, for review). These intervention suggestions are made in the knowledge that there is no research on the effects of teachers trained to make classes more meaningful on students' initial and enduring curiosity and the acquisition of enduring competencies.

There is reason to believe that strategies to enhance meaningfulness can be effective in academic and work settings. Although work environments cannot be transformed as easily as classroom settings, workers can be provided with greater information, skills, and participation in the organization. Research has shown that workers provided with exposure to and input in organizational changes report greater openness to changes (i.e., task curiosity) and job satisfaction (Axtell et al., 2002; Wanberg & Banas, 2000). Although MI has focused on clinical problems and health promotion, it can be a useful intervention for exploring, supporting, and validating the emotions, cognitions, and personal discrepancies experienced by employees who may be experiencing initial discomfort during organizational changes that will affect their routine behaviors and responsibilities. There is merit in applying MI to this unexplored terrain, as the strategies of MI counselors are elucidated in published resources (tapping nearly all of Table 30.1).

FOSTERING POSITIVE SOCIALIZATION EXPERIENCES

There is a natural, innocent curiosity when students, workers, and athletes enter new environments where they are exposed to unfamiliar people, rules, and language. However, when individuals enter a new job position, attend the first academic lecture of a class, or begin the first athletic practice of the season, the experience may also be fraught with anxiety. During initial engagement, there is a need to acquire knowledge about activity-related technical skills, responsibilities, autonomy, and the needs and values of authority figures and peers on the same team. Failing to obtain these sorts of information has been shown to increase feelings of ambiguity and anxiety that interfere with job performance and satisfaction (Wanberg & Kammeyer-Mueller, 2000). Surprisingly, socialization experiences have been studied only in the occupational domain and have yet to be the target of intervention. Encouraging positive socialization experiences is presumed to be a useful intervention tool in nearly all organizational domains. Organizations should capitalize on new employees' socialization to increase feelings of personal meaningfulness, which includes providing information about how a worker's job is integral to organizational products, the career trajectories their job can lead to, and the different methods in which their job can be performed. Authority figures can express interest in individuals and assist them in gathering relevant information, helping them make sense of this information, and facilitating social bonds with current organizational members. As shown in Table 30.1, these strategies should activate the psychological needs that induce and sustain heightened curiosity in organizational activity.

ASSESSMENT ISSUES

The potential of organizational techniques for enhancing curiosity has not been adequately examined. Table 30.2, therefore, summarizes rationales and strategies for evaluating the success of curiosity-based interventions in organizations.

Many of these rationales are based on discussions in the first half of this chapter (e.g., section on domain specificity of curiosity).

The design and implementation of curiosity interventions should be conducted within a transactional framework. With relevance to the generation of interventions, the issue of Person (reliable individual difference variables) × Situation interactions on task curiosity deserves much more attention. Achievement orientation has been found to moderate task curiosity such that low achievement-oriented individuals exhibit enhanced curiosity when focusing on their skill development (mastery goals), whereas high achievement-oriented individuals exhibit enhanced curiosity when focusing on their ability (performance goals; e.g., Elliot & Harackiewicz, 1994; Harackiewicz & Elliot, 1993). Each achievement-oriented group had their curiosity undermined in the opposing condition. High achievement-oriented people find activities to be challenging and enjoyable when skills and performance outcomes were made prominent. In contrast, low achievement-oriented individuals react negatively to performance-focused activities and prefer mastery-focused activities that offer a safe environment to challenge their competencies (with less concern about failure).

In other examples of person and situation interactions, (1) when more sociable individuals engaged in problem-solving tasks with others, as opposed to alone, they reported greater short-term and enduring curiosity (Issac, Sansone, & Smith, 1999); and (2) when beginning a new job, individuals with greater trait curiosity were more proactive in seeking new information about their task-related responsibilities, the organization, and performance feedback than low trait curious peers (cf. Wanberg & Kammeyer-Mueller, 2000). By definition, high trait curious individuals experience greater enjoyment in actively exploring and confronting new challenges (Kashdan, in press-a; Kashdan et al., in press). In terms of interventions, these data imply that individual difference variables should be considered in assessment, and attention should be given to the possible need for matching participants to different intervention conditions (i.e., optimize person-environment fits; see Table 30.2, row 2). For example, the mastery-focus strategies in Table 30.1 may be vital to individuals high in achievement motivation and undermine the curiosity of those low in achievement motivation. There appears to be differential value in activating relatedness beliefs based on individuals' interpersonal orientations and promoting internalization and socialization experiences based on individuals' trait curiosity level.

Within this transactional framework, interventions need to move beyond task curiosity to additionally include enduring curiosity as an outcome. We propose that the prediction of subsequent engagement in an activity is the result of reciprocal influences between task curiosity and competency-related, autonomy and relatedness beliefs. For example, task curiosity facilitates greater attention; greater attention leads to greater learning and the development of new skills; the activation of new skills results in increased pleasure and feelings of mastery; and these positive subjective experiences reinforce the pursuit of related future experiences. The majority of research efforts have focused on unidirectional pathways from competency-related (and autonomy and relatedness) beliefs to curiosity. The dynamic interplay of these psychological needs and curiosity offers a more realistic framework for accurately targeting and sustaining change in curiosity interventions. Assessment and analytic approaches to intervention need to mirror the complexity and variability of curiosity and its enabling factors.

CONCLUSION

Most of our strategies, techniques, and suggestions for intervention derive from basic research. A great deal of room remains for innovative experimental curiosity research before turning to intervention. The first half of the chapter discussed in some detail the construct of curiosity and related constructs and offered a framework for understanding factors that might facilitate curiosity. We then offered a number of directions for future research that might increase understanding and promotion of curiosity. Central to developing successful curiosity interventions is the enhancement of task curiosity and the concomitants and consequences of curiosity, such as positive affect, feelings of self-determination, performance enhancement, and the acquisition of skill and knowledge. These changes are likely to reflect relatively rapid responses to interventions. Much slower to respond to intervention and more difficult to define is the impact of enduring curiosity on living a more satisfying and meaningful life. The overarching premise of any curiosity intervention is that changes in curiosity have salutary effects on daily and overall life satisfaction and meaning. This is a missing ingredient of existing interventions that we hope will be included in future scientific pursuits.

REFERENCES

Ainley, M., & Hidi, S. (2002). Dynamic measures for studying interest and learning. In P. R. Pintrich & M. L. Maehr (Eds.), *Advances in motivation and achievement: New directions in measures and methods* (Vol. 12, pp. 43–76). Amsterdam: JAI Press.

Axtell, C., Wall, T., Stride, C., Pepper, K., Clegg, C., Gardner, P., et al. (2002). Familiarity breeds content: The impact of exposure to change on employee openness and well-being. *Journal of Occupational and Organizational Psychology, 75,* 217–231.

Berlyne, D. E. (1960). *Conflict, arousal, and curiosity.* New York: McGraw-Hill.

Berlyne, D. E. (1971). *Aesthetics and psychobiology.* New York: Appleton-Century-Crofts.

Berlyne, D. E. (1978). Curiosity and learning. *Motivation and Emotion, 2,* 97–175.

Black, A. E., & Deci, E. L. (2000). The effects of instructors' autonomy support and students' autonomous motivation on learning organic chemistry: A self-determination theory perspective. *Science Education, 84,* 740–756.

Brown, J. M., & Miller, W. R. (1993). Impact of motivational interviewing on participation and outcome in residential alcoholism treatment. *Psychology of Addictive Behaviors, 7,* 211–218.

Cordova, D. I., & Lepper, M. R. (1996). Intrinsic motivation and the process of learning: Beneficial effects of contextualization, personalization, and choice. *Journal of Educational Psychology, 88,* 715–730.

Csikszentmihalyi, M. (1990). *Flow: The psychology of optimal experience.* New York: HarperCollins.

Csikszentmihalyi, M., & LeFevre, J. (1989). Optimal experience in work and leisure. *Journal of Personality and Social Psychology, 56,* 815–822.

Cury, F., Elliot, A., Sarrazin, P., Da Fonseca, D., & Rufo, M. (2002). The trichotomous achievement goal model and intrinsic motivation: A sequential mediational analysis. *Journal of Experimental Social Psychology, 38,* 473–481.

Deci, E. L. (1975). *Intrinsic motivation.* New York: Plenum Press.

Deci, E. L., Connell, J. P., & Ryan, R. M. (1989). Self-determination in a work organization. *Journal of Applied Psychology, 74,* 580–590.

Deci, E. L., Koestner, R., & Ryan, R. M. (1999). A meta-analytic review of experiments examining the effects of extrinsic rewards on intrinsic motivation. *Psychological Bulletin, 125,* 627–668.

Deci, E. L., & Ryan, R. M. (1985). *Intrinsic motivation and self-determination in human behavior.* New York: Plenum Press.

*Deci, E. L., & Ryan, R. M. (2000). The "what" and "why" of goal pursuits: Human needs and the self-determination of behavior. *Psychological Inquiry, 11,* 227–268.

Duda, J. L., & Nicholls, J. G. (1992). Dimensions of achievement motivation in schoolwork and sport. *Journal of Educational Psychology, 84,* 290–299.

Dunn, C., Deroo, L., & Rivara, F. P. (2001). The use of brief interventions adapted from motivational interviewing across behavioral domains: A systematic review. *Addiction, 96,* 1725–1742.

Elliot, A. J., Faler, J., McGregor, H. A., Campbell, W. K., Sedikides, C., & Harackiewicz, J. M. (2000). Competence valuation as a strategic intrinsic motivation process. *Personality and Social Psychology Bulletin, 26,* 780–794.

Elliot, A. J., & Harackiewicz, J. M. (1994). Goal setting, achievement orientation, and intrinsic motivation: A mediational analysis. *Journal of Personality and Social Psychology, 66,* 968–980.

Fredrickson, B. L. (1998). What good are positive emotions? *Review of General Psychology, 2,* 300–319.

Grolnick, W. S., & Ryan, R. M. (1989). Parent styles associated with children's self-regulation and competence in school. *Journal of Educational Psychology, 81,* 143–154.

Harackiewicz, J. M., Barron, K. E., Tauer, J. M., & Elliot, A. J. (2002). Predicting success in college: A longitudinal study of achievement goals and ability measures as predictors of interest and performance from freshman year through graduation. *Journal of Educational Psychology, 94,* 562–575.

Harackiewicz, J. M., & Elliot, A. J. (1993). Achievement goals and intrinsic motivation. *Journal of Personality and Social Psychology, 65,* 904–915.

Hazan, C., & Shaver, P. (1990). Love and work: An attachment-theoretical perspective. *Journal of Personality and Social Psychology, 59,* 270–280.

Issac, J. D., Sansone, C., & Smith, J. L. (1999). Other people as a source of interest in an activity. *Journal of Experimental Social Psychology, 35,* 239–265.

Jones, C. D., Hollenhorst, S. J., Perna, F., & Selin, S. (2000). Validation of the flow theory in an on-site whitewater kayaking setting. *Journal of Leisure Research, 32,* 247–261.

Kashdan, T. B. (2002). Social anxiety dimensions, neuroticism, and the contours of positive psychological functioning. *Cognitive Therapy and Research, 26,* 789–810.

Kashdan, T. B. (in press-a). Curiosity and interest. In C. Peterson & M. E. P. Seligman (Eds.), *Character strengths and virtues: A handbook and classification.* Washington, DC: American Psychological Association and Oxford University Press.

Kashdan, T. B. (in press-b). The neglected relationship between social interaction anxiety and hedonic deficits: Differentiation from depressive symptoms. *Journal of Anxiety Disorders.*

Kashdan, T. B., Fincham, F. D., & Rose, P. (2003). *The interpersonal dynamics of curiosity: Initial exploration of person, partner, social context, and mechanisms of action.* Manuscript submitted for publication.

Kashdan, T. B., & Roberts, J. E. (in press). Trait and state curiosity in the genesis of intimacy: Differentiation from related constructs. *Journal of Social and Clinical Psychology.*

*Kashdan, T. B., Rose, P., & Fincham, F. D. (in press). Curiosity and exploration: Facilitating positive subjective experiences and personal growth opportunities. *Journal of Personality Assessment.*

Krapp, A. (1999). Interest, motivation, and learning: An educational-psychological perspective. *European Journal of Psychology in Education, 14,* 23–40.

LaBar, K. S., Mesulam, M., Gitelman, D. R., & Weintraub, S. (2000). Emotional curiosity: Modulation of visuospatial attention by arousal is preserved in aging and early stage Alzheimer's disease. *Neruopsychologia, 38,* 1734–1740.

Lent, R. W., Brown, S. D., & Hackett, G. (1994). Toward a unifying social cognitive theory of career and academic interest, choice, and performance. *Journal of Vocational Behavior, 45,* 79–122.

Loewenstein, G., Adler, D., Behrens, D., & Gillis, J. (1992). *Why Pandora opened the box: Curiosity as a desire for missing information.* Unpublished manuscript, Carnegie Mellon University, Pittsburgh, PA.

Mikulincer, M. (1997). Adult attachment style and information processing: Individual differences in curiosity and cognitive closure. *Journal of Personality and Social Psychology, 72,* 1217–1230.

Mikulincer, M., & Shaver, P. R. (2003). The attachment behavioral system in adulthood: Activation, psychodynamics, and interpersonal processes. In M. P. Zanna (Ed.), *Advances in experimental social psychology* (Vol. 35, pp. 53–152). New York: Academic Press.

Miller, W. R., & Rollnick, S. (2002). *Motivational interviewing: Preparing people for change* (2nd ed.). New York: Guilford Press.

Miserandino, M. (1996). Children who do well in school: Individual differences in perceived competence and autonomy in above-average children. *Journal of Educational Psychology, 88,* 203–214.

Oldham, G. R., & Cummings, A. (1996). Employee creativity: Personal and contextual factors at work. *Academy of Management Journal, 39,* 607–634.

Peters, R. A. (1978). Effects of anxiety, curiosity, and perceived instructor threat on student verbal behaviors in the college classroom. *Journal of Educational Psychology, 70,* 388–395.

Reeve, C. L., & Hakel, M. D. (2000). Toward an understanding of adult intellectual development: Investigating within-individual convergence of interest and knowledge profiles. *Journal of Applied Psychology, 85,* 897–908.

Reio, T. G., & Wiswell, A. (2000). Field investigation of the relationship among adult curiosity, workplace learning, and job performance. *Human Resource Development Quarterly, 11,* 5–30.

Rizzo, M., Anderson, S. W., Dawson, J., Myers, R., & Ball, K. (2000). Visual attention impairments in Alzheimer's disease. *Neurology, 54,* 1954–1959.

Ryan, R. M. (1982). Control and information in the intrapersonal sphere: An extension of cognitive evaluation theory. *Journal of Personality and Social Psychology, 43,* 450–461.

Ryan, R. M., & Deci, E. L. (2000). Self-determination theory and the facilitation of intrinsic motivation, social development, and well-being. *American Psychologist, 55,* 68–79.

Schiefele, U., Krapp, A., & Winteler, A. (1992). Interest as a predictor of academic achievement: A meta-analysis of research. In K. A. Renninger, S. Hidi, & A. Krapp (Eds.), *The role of interest in learning and development* (pp. 183–212). Hillsdale, NJ: Erlbaum.

*Silvia, P. (in press). *Exploring the psychology of interest.* New York: Oxford University Press.

Skinner, E. A., & Belmont, M. J. (1993). Motivation in the classroom: Reciprocal effects of teacher behavior and student engagement across the school year. *Journal of Educational Psychology, 85,* 571–581.

Smoll, F. L., Smith, R. E., Barnett, N. P., & Everett, J. J. (1993). Enhancement of children's self-esteem through social support training for youth sports coaches. *Journal of Applied Psychology, 78,* 602–610.

*Spielberger, C. D., & Starr, L. M. (1994). Curiosity and exploratory behavior. In H. F. O'Neil Jr., & M. Drillings (Eds.), *Motivation: Theory and research* (pp. 221–243). Hillsdale, NJ: Erlbaum.

Tien, L., Roth, V., & Kampmeier, J. (2002). Implementation of a peer-led team learning instructional approach in an undergraduate chemistry course. *Journal of Research in Science Teaching, 39*, 606–632.

*Voss, H., & Keller, H. (1983). *Curiosity and exploration: Theories and results*. New York: Academic Press.

Wall, T. D., & Clegg, C. W. (1981). A longitudinal field study of group work redesign. *Journal of Occupational Behavior, 2*, 31–49.

Wanberg, C. R., & Banas, J. T. (2000). Predictors and outcomes of openness to changes in a reorganizing workplace. *Journal of Applied Psychology, 85*, 132–142.

Wanberg, C. R., & Kammeyer-Mueller, J. D. (2000). Predictors and outcomes of proactivity in the socialization process. *Journal of Applied Psychology, 85*, 373–385.

Williams, G. C., & Deci, E. L. (1996). Internalization of biopsychosocial values by medical students: A test of self-determination theory. *Journal of Personality and Social Psychology, 70*, 767–779.

Williams, G. C., Gagne, M., Ryan, R. M., & Deci, E. L. (2002). Facilitating autonomous motivation for smoking cessation. *Health Psychology, 21*, 40–50.

Williams, G. C., Rodin, G. C., Ryan, R. M., Grolnick, W. S., & Deci, E. L. (1998). Autonomous regulation and long-term medication adherence in adult outpatients. *Health Psychology, 17*, 269–276.

CHAPTER 31

Approaches to a Good Life: The Emotional-Motivational Side to Wisdom

UTE KUNZMANN

T HE SEARCH FOR human strengths is a continuous journey with a long history. Since antiquity, one of the guideposts in this search has been the concept of wisdom (e.g., Assmann, 1994; Kekes, 1995). At the core of this concept is the notion of a perfect, perhaps utopian, integration of knowledge and character, mind and virtue.

Because wisdom has been considered an ideal endpoint of human development, the original impetus for psychological work on this concept evolved in the context of lifespan psychology and the study of aging (e.g., Baltes, Smith, & Staudinger, 1992; Baltes, Smith, Staudinger, & Sowarka, 1990; Clayton & Birren, 1980; Sternberg, 1990). Notably, the search for positive human functioning has been a hallmark in this field since its inception (see also Lerner, 2002). For example, Piaget with his characterization of intelligence attempted to capture optimal cognitive development, or Erikson, in his theory of personality development, considered concepts such as generativity and integrity to define progress in personality development during adulthood and old age.

This chapter presents psychological work on wisdom and discusses its role in positive psychology (e.g., Aspinwall & Staudinger, 2003; Seligman & Csikszentmihalyi, 2000; Snyder & Lopez, 2002). Future research in this area could benefit from considering wisdom because of at least three reasons (see also Baltes, Glück, & Kunzmann, 2002; Baltes & Kunzmann, 2003). First, wisdom identifies in the most universal sense the highest forms of expertise that humans can acquire. Studying wisdom helps reveal the strongest qualities of humans as they have evolved

I thank Paul B. Baltes and Fredda Blanchard-Fields for their valuable comments on an earlier version of this chapter.

through the experience of succeeding generations. Certainly, only few achieve wisdom in its higher form; yet, it is those few who hold the key to what humans could be at their best.

Second, even if most of us never acquire higher levels of its manifestation, it seems worth the effort to strive for wisdom. Empirical wisdom research suggests that wisdom can be conceptualized as a more-or-less (i.e., quantitative) phenomenon. Even more to the point, there is a growing body of evidence suggesting that even a little wisdom can make a difference in people's lives (e.g., Kramer, 2000; Kunzmann & Baltes, 2003b; Staudinger, 1999b).

Third, wisdom is a vital component of the three spheres of positive psychology suggested by Seligman and Csikszentmihalyi (2000). Wisdom can be considered a positive personal characteristic; it involves valuable subjective experiences; and it is a life orientation that contributes to productivity and well-being at the individual, social group, and societal levels (e.g., Baltes & Staudinger, 2000; Kramer, 2000; Sternberg, 1998). This chapter illustrates the affective structure and the motivational orientation that go hand in hand with wisdom as it is defined and operationalized in the Berlin wisdom paradigm.

DEFINING WISDOM

Because of its enormous cultural and historical heritage, a comprehensive psychological definition and operationalization of wisdom is extremely difficult, if not impossible. At least three types of explicit conceptualizations of wisdom can be identified in the literature, namely, conceptualizations of wisdom as an aspect of personality development in adulthood (e.g., Ardelt, 2003; Erikson, 1959; Wink & Helson, 1997), conceptualizations of wisdom as postformal dialectic thinking (e.g., Kramer, 1990, 2000; Labouvie-Vief, 1990), and conceptualizations of wisdom as an expanded form of intelligence (e.g., Baltes & Staudinger, 2000; Sternberg, 1998).

Despite their different origins, these three conceptualizations share at least three important ideas about the nature of wisdom. First, wisdom is different from other personal characteristics in that it is integrative and involves cognitive, affective, and motivational elements. Second, wisdom is an ideal: Many people may strive for wisdom, but only few, if any, will ever become truly wise. Third, wisdom sets high behavioral standards; it guides a person's behavior in ways that simultaneously optimize this person's own potential and that of fellow mortals (see also Baltes & Staudinger, 2000; Kramer, 2000; Sternberg, 1998). I return to these three assumptions in the course of this chapter as I discuss the Berlin wisdom paradigm and the research initiated by this paradigm.

THE BERLIN WISDOM PARADIGM

Informed by cultural-historical work on wisdom, the psychological research group of Paul B. Baltes has defined wisdom as an expert knowledge about fundamental questions as to the meaning and conduct of life (e.g., Baltes & Kunzmann, 2003; Baltes & Smith, 1990; Baltes & Staudinger, 2000). Five criteria serve to describe this type of expert knowledge in more detail. The first two general, basic criteria—*factual knowledge* and *procedural knowledge*—are characteristic of all types of expertise. Applied to wisdom-related expertise, these criteria are rich factual knowledge about human nature and the life course and rich procedural knowledge about ways of dealing with fundamental questions about the meaning and conduct of life.

The remaining three metacriteria are considered to be specific for wisdom-related expertise. *Lifespan contextualism* refers to knowledge about the many contexts of life, how they are interrelated, and how they change across the lifespan. The criterion *value relativism and tolerance* describes the acknowledgment of personal and cultural differences in values and life goals and the consideration of these differences when thinking about solutions to problems related to the meaning and conduct of life. Finally, the *awareness and management of uncertainty* refers to an understanding that life decisions, evaluations, or plans will never be free of uncertainty, but must be made as well as the individual can and not be avoided in a resigning manner. Expert knowledge about the meaning and conduct of life is said to approach wisdom, if it meets all five criteria.

As this definition of wisdom suggests, wisdom is neither technical nor intellectual knowledge in the more narrow sense. On the contrary, well-elaborated knowledge about the meaning and conduct of life involves knowledge about human emotions and motivations. For example, outstanding knowledge about life's uncertainties and ways of dealing with them requires knowledge about the emotions intertwined with uncertainty. Value relativism and tolerance reflects an understanding of the nature and development of human motives, and lifespan contextualism includes knowledge about idiographic and normative events that not only shape a person's future but also are a source of deep emotional experiences (e.g., birth of a child, death of loved ones).

In our empirical paradigm, we instruct people to read short vignettes about difficult life problems and to think aloud about these problems (e.g., Baltes & Smith, 1990; Baltes & Staudinger, 2000). For example, a problem related to life review might be: "In reflecting over their lives, people sometimes realize that they have not achieved what they had once planned to achieve. What could they do and consider?" Another dilemma reads: "A 15-year-old girl wants to get married right away. What could she consider and do?" These problems differ from tasks that have been developed in intelligence research in that they are poorly defined and are characterized by multiple potential solutions. High-quality responses to these dilemmas, therefore, require not only exceptional intellectual abilities but also emotional, motivational, and social competence (see also Kramer, 2000; Labouvie-Vief, 1990).

An excerpt from an above-average response to the 15-year-old girl's problem could be: "Well, on the surface, this seems like an easy problem. Marriage for 15-year-old girls typically is not a good thing. Thinking about getting married, however, is not the same as actually doing it. I guess many girls think about it without getting married in the end . . . and there are situations where the average case doesn't fit. Perhaps special life circumstances are involved. The girl may have a terminal illness. She may not be from this country or perhaps she lives in another culture. . . ."

Trained raters evaluate responses such as this by using the five criteria specified as defining wisdom-related knowledge. As demonstrated in our past research, the assessment of wisdom-related knowledge on the basis of these criteria exhibits satisfactory reliability and validity (for recent reviews, see Baltes & Kunzmann, 2003; Baltes & Staudinger, 2000).

THE DEVELOPMENT, STRUCTURE, AND FUNCTIONS OF WISDOM: A THEORETICAL MODEL

The conceptualization of wisdom as expertise and its linkage to lifespan psychology (Baltes, 1987, 1997) suggest a number of conditions under which wisdom is likely to develop. First, as is typical for the development of any expertise, we assume that wisdom is acquired through an extended and intensive process of learning and practice. This process requires a high degree of motivation to strive for excellence as well as supportive environmental conditions.

Second, because wisdom is different from other more circumscribed positive characteristics in that it involves an integration of mind and virtue (i.e., knowledge and character), its development and refinement requires multiple factors and processes, including certain intellectual abilities, the availability of mentors, mastery of critical life experiences, openness to new experiences, and values referring to personal growth, benevolence, and tolerance.

Third, most likely, there are several paths leading to wisdom rather than only one. That is, similar levels of wisdom may result from different combinations of facilitative factors and processes. If a certain coalition of facilitative factors is present, some individuals continue a developmental trajectory toward higher levels of wisdom-related knowledge. Potentially facilitating factors such as a certain family background, critical life events, professional practice, or societal transitions (e.g., the separation and reunion in Germany) may interact in complex additive, compensatory, or time-lagged ways.

These general theoretical perspectives are summarized in our theoretical developmental model of wisdom depicted in Figure 31.1. This model shows that three types of factors and processes are influential for the development of wisdom-related knowledge, namely, *facilitative experiential contexts,* as determined, for example, by a person's age, social context, or culture; *expertise-specific factors,* such as life experience, professional practice, or receiving and providing mentorship; and *person-related factors,* such as intelligence, personality traits, emotional dispositions, and motivational orientations.

These three types of factors are thought to have an influence on the development of wisdom-related knowledge because they determine the ways in which people experience the world and plan, manage, or make sense out of their lives (i.e., the context of developmental regulation). All relations among the three components of our model—facilitative factors, context of developmental regulation, and wisdom-related knowledge—are meant to be bidirectional and accumulative over the life course.

This general theoretical developmental model of wisdom-related knowledge has guided most, if not all, empirical research that members of the Berlin Wisdom Project have conducted during the past two decades. For example, several studies have investigated the role of chronological age in wisdom-related knowledge (e.g., Pasupathi, Staudinger, & Baltes, 2000; Staudinger, 1999a; Staudinger, Smith, & Baltes, 1992). This line of research suggests that wisdom-related knowledge sharply increases during adolescence and young adulthood. During the adult years, wisdom-related knowledge may not change any further in the majority of people. Some readers might find a low association between age and wisdom-related knowledge in adulthood surprising. According to our theoretical model of wisdom, however, this low association is to be expected. As described

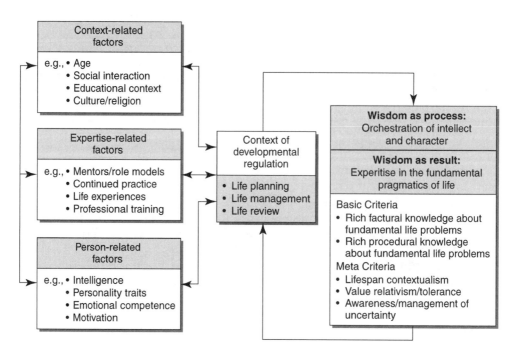

Figure 31.1   The Development, Structure, and Functions of Wisdom: A Theoretical Model

previously, this model states that the development of wisdom-related knowledge requires a coalition of facilitative factors; getting older may be a necessary but not sufficient factor in this process.

In another set of empirical studies, Baltes, Smith, and Staudinger were interested in identifying groups of people with constellations of life experiences that facilitate the acquisition of wisdom-related knowledge (Smith, Staudinger, & Baltes, 1994; Staudinger & Baltes, 1996; Staudinger et al., 1992). Specifically, they investigated the members of a profession where training and professional practice involved continued experience with difficult life problems, namely, clinical psychologists. These clinical psychologists were compared with professionals from fields in which training and everyday job tasks were not specifically dedicated to dealing with difficult life problems. As predicted, the clinical psychologists showed higher levels of wisdom-related performance than the members of other professions. Within the limits of cross-sectional studies, this evidence is consistent with the idea that training and experience in dealing with difficult life problems facilitate the acquisition of wisdom-related knowledge.

There is also experimental work suggesting that the expression of wisdom-related performance, as we have measured it, can be enhanced by social interventions. Boehmig-Krumhaar, Staudinger, and Baltes (2002), demonstrated how a memory strategy—namely, a version of the method of loci—in which participants were instructed to travel on a cloud around the world can be used to focus people's attention on cultural relativism and tolerance. As predicted, following this intervention, participants expressed higher levels of wisdom-related knowledge, especially value relativism and tolerance. Furthermore, Staudinger and Baltes (1996) conducted an experiment in which study participants were asked to think aloud about a wisdom problem under several experimental conditions involving imagined and actual social interactions. Specifically, before responding individually, some participants had the opportunity to discuss the problem with a person they brought into the laboratory and with whom they usually discuss difficult life problems; others were asked to engage in an inner dialogue about the problem with a person of their choice, or to simply think about the problem on their own. Actual social dialogue and the inner-voice dialogue increased performance levels by almost one standard deviation. One important implication of these two studies is that many adults have the latent potential to perform better on wisdom tasks than they actually often do.

In the remainder of this chapter, I focus on our past work on the relationships between person-related factors and wisdom-related knowledge. This work corresponds to the two major research goals we are currently pursuing. One goal is to study the emotional antecedents, correlates, and consequences of wisdom-related knowledge more explicitly than we have done in the past. The other goal is to investigate the links among wisdom-related knowledge, motivational dispositions, and actual behavior (see also Baltes et al., 2002; Kunzmann & Baltes, 2003a, 2003b).

EMOTIONAL-MOTIVATIONAL DYNAMICS OF WISDOM: GENERAL THEORETICAL CONSIDERATIONS

The definition of wisdom as an expert knowledge system about the meaning and conduct of life may suggest to some that our approach to studying wisdom is too cognitive and ignores emotional and motivational competencies that are also central elements of wisdom. Nothing could be further from our intentions. Starting from the notion that knowledge and insight are important characteristics of wisdom, but that the semantic meaning of this concept encompasses more, we have begun to study the interplay between cognitive and emotional-motivational elements of wisdom more explicitly (e.g., Kunzmann & Baltes, 2003a, 2003b).

WISDOM: INTEGRATION OF KNOWLEDGE AND EMOTION

From a developmental point of view, we consider certain emotional experiences and dispositions to be fundamental to the acquisition of wisdom as an expert knowledge system about the meaning and conduct of life. For example, emotional stability and affective sensitivity most likely facilitate the acquisition of wisdom-related knowledge. This idea, as emphasized previously, is a central part of our developmental model of wisdom-related knowledge. Moreover, affective dispositions most likely interact with other developmental factors. For example, stimulating social environments, the availability of good educational systems, or a supportive family potentially contribute to the development of wisdom-related knowledge. The effectiveness of these environmental factors, however, depends not only on a person's intellectual functioning (ability to learn new things, abstract reasoning, or accuracy of information processing) but also on this person's affective dispositions and experiences (e.g., impulsivity, neuroticism, sympathy for others).

It is also likely that the expression of wisdom-related knowledge in a particular situation is moderated by certain emotional dispositions and competencies. An advice giver who is not able or willing to imagine how a needy person feels, for example, is not likely to make an effort to engage in wisdom-related thinking, which would involve careful and detailed analysis of the advice seeker's problem, the weighting and moderation of different parts of the situation, and the consideration of multiple views. Similarly, during a mutual conflict with another person, being able to imagine how this person feels or how we would feel in the other's place may be one steppingstone to value tolerance and a cooperative approach typical of wisdom.

At the same time, however, we can easily think of emotional reactions to difficult and potentially stressful situations that are likely to hinder a wisdomlike approach Candidates are self-centered feelings that indicate personal distress, especially if these negative feelings are intense and long lasting. If people are not able or willing to control their feelings of anger, contempt, or jealousy, for example, they are likely to hurt or enrage others rather than come up with a wise solution to the problem at hand. Similarly, strong and chronic feelings of anxiety might inhibit wisdom-related thinking, which requires distance to the immediate situation, balance, and elaboration. It is in this sense that "cold" cognition and "hot" emotion have been described as two forces that antagonize each other (cf. Keltner & Gross, 1999).

Certainly, the links between other- and self-centered emotions on the one hand and wisdom-related knowledge on the other can take many directions. The idea that certain emotions hinder or facilitate the activation of wisdom-related knowledge and behavior may be less popular in the literature than the notion that it is wisdom that regulates a person's emotional experiences and reactions. In this vein, wisdom researchers have conceptualized wisdom as a resource or personal characteristic that encourages the experiencing of certain positive emotions such as sympathy and compassionate love and decreases the experiencing of other negative emotions (e.g., feelings of hostility, contempt, or personal distress; e.g., Ardelt, 2003; Clayton & Birren, 1980; Helson & Srivastava, 2002; Kramer, 1990; Labouvie-Vief, 1990).

Although empirical research supporting this claim is sparse and correlational in nature, it is reasonable to assume that people with high levels of wisdom-related knowledge experience potentially emotion-evoking events in quite different ways than people with low levels of wisdom-related knowledge. Wisdom, as we have defined it, refers to contextual, historical, dialectical, and holistic knowledge that represents events and phenomena on various levels of abstraction and in different time frames. As a consequence, people with high levels of wisdom-related knowledge should be better able to regard phenomena from a broader viewpoint, to relativize their emotional implications, and to adopt a detached and less emotional attitude than people with low levels of wisdom-related knowledge.

This is not to say that wise people do not experience emotions at all or that their emotional life is reduced and flat. To the contrary, people with higher levels of wisdom-related knowledge may even spontaneously react more strongly to certain events because of their deeper understanding of its significance. Seen over time, however, wisdom-related knowledge should facilitate the down-regulation of emotions so that they do not become dysfunctional. Being able to work with emotions, understand emotions, modify them, and use the information they provide to deal with the environment may be a prerequisite, concomitant, and consequence of wisdom-related knowledge (see also Kunzmann & Baltes, 2003b).

WISDOM: KNOWLEDGE, MOTIVATION, AND BEHAVIOR

Does wisdom-related knowledge guide a person's behaviors in grappling with difficult problems and interacting with others? How do people use their wisdom-related knowledge in everyday life, and what is the motivational orientation that goes hand in hand with this type of knowledge?

Several modern philosophers influenced by the tradition of early Greek philosophy have proposed that wisdom is closely linked to our everyday behaviors. In this tradition, wisdom has been thought to be a resource facilitating behavior aimed at promoting a good life at both an individual and a societal level. For example, Ryan (1996) defined a wise person: "A person S is wise if and only if (1) S is a free agent, (2) S knows how to live well, (3) S lives well, and (4) S's living well is caused by S's knowledge of how to live well" (p. 241). Kekes (1983) wrote, "wisdom is a character trait intimately connected with self-direction. The more wisdom a person has the more likely it is he will succeed in living a good life" (p. 277).

Notably, a good life is not linked exclusively to self-realization and personal happiness but encompasses more, namely, the well-being of others. In this sense, Kekes (1995) has stressed that wisdom is knowledge about ways of developing ourselves not only without violating others' rights but also with coproducing resources for others to develop. Thus, in these philosophical conceptualizations, a central characteristic of a wise person is the ability to translate knowledge into action geared toward the development of self and others.

Psychological wisdom researchers have begun to respond to the longstanding notion that wisdom requires and reflects certain motivational tendencies, which in turn shape the use of wisdom-related knowledge and guide its application in daily life (e.g., Baltes & Staudinger, 2000; Kramer, 2000; Sternberg, 1998). Notably, however, wise persons have been described as being primarily concerned with other people's well-being rather than with their own (e.g., Ardelt, 2003; Holliday & Chandler, 1986). Consistent with this view, Helson and Srivastava (2002) provided evidence that wise persons tend to be benevolent, compassionate, caring, and interested in helping others. The idea that wisdom is different from altruism and prosocial behavior in that it involves a joint consideration of self- and other-related interests, however, has rarely been tested empirically. In the following section, I discuss empirical studies from our lab that can be considered a first step in demonstrating that wisdom is inherently of an intra- and interpersonal nature.

EMOTIONAL-MOTIVATIONAL ELEMENTS OF WISDOM: RELEVANT LINES OF EMPIRICAL RESEARCH

I review three empirical studies that provide empirical evidence for the theoretical idea that wisdom, as we have defined and assessed it, is more than and different from intellectual functioning in the narrow sense. The goal of the first two studies was to demonstrate that wisdom-related knowledge involves not only outstanding intellectual functioning but also certain personality traits, emotional dispositions, and motivational orientations. The third study investigated whether wisdom-related knowledge makes a difference in people's actual emotional reactions when they are confronted with fundamental life problems.

WISDOM: INTELLIGENCE, PERSONALITY, AND SOCIAL-COGNITIVE STYLE?

To test parts of our developmental model of wisdom-related knowledge (see Figure 31.1), Staudinger, Lopez, and Baltes (1997) investigated three general personal factors as correlates of wisdom-related knowledge. These factors were test intelligence, personality traits, and several facets of social-cognitive style. A central goal of this study was to empirically demonstrate that intelligence, as assessed by traditional psychometric tests, would be a relatively weak predictor of wisdom-related knowledge, whereas personality traits and especially a person's social-cognitive style would be more important. This prediction was tested in a study with 125 adults. In a first individual interview session, the authors assessed wisdom-related knowledge by our standard procedure. During a second session, they employed 33 measures to assess multiple indicators of intelligence (e.g., speed of information processing, logical thinking, practical knowledge), personality (e.g., neuroticism, extraversion, openness to new experiences), and social-cognitive style (e.g., social intelligence, creativity, interest in others' needs).

Not all indicators were significant predictors. For example, unrelated to wisdom-related knowledge were speed of information processing and four of the five classic personality traits (i.e., neuroticism, extraversion, agreeableness, and conscientiousness); only openness to experience was related to wisdom-related knowledge. When analyzed separately, the significant intelligence measures accounted for 15% of the variance in wisdom-related knowledge, social-cognitive style accounted for 35% of the variance, and personality for 23%. The simultaneous analyses of all three sets of predictors in hierarchical regression analyses revealed that the unique prediction of intelligence and personality was small (i.e., 2% each), whereas indicators of social-cognitive style contributed a larger share of unique variance, namely 15%.

Together, this evidence supports the notion that wisdom-related knowledge is not simply a variant of intelligence. Certain personality traits and especially social-cognitive style show more overlap with wisdom as we have defined it. This study's correlational evidence may be seen as a first step in testing the prediction that the development of wisdom during adulthood requires not only several cognitive abilities but also noncognitive person-related resources.

EMOTIONAL DISPOSITIONS AND MOTIVATIONAL ORIENTATIONS:
CORRELATES OF WISDOM-RELATED KNOWLEDGE

Extending the study reviewed previously, Kunzmann and Baltes (2003b) provided evidence for links between wisdom-related knowledge and certain emotional and motivational dispositions. These dispositions referred to affective experiences (pleasantness, interest/involvement, and negative affect), value orientations (pleasurable life, personal growth, insight, well-being of friends, environmental protection, societal engagement), and preferred modes of conflict management (dominance, submission, avoidance, cooperation). By highlighting the relations between wisdom-related knowledge and these indicators, we aimed at broadening our understanding of the emotional-motivational side of wisdom.

Our predictions were based on the notion that wisdom-related knowledge requires and reflects a joint concern for developing a person's own and others' potential (see also Sternberg, 1998). In contrast, a predominant search for self-centered pleasure and comfort should not be associated with wisdom. Accordingly, people high on wisdom-related knowledge should report:

- An affective structure that is positive but process- and environment-oriented rather than evaluative and self-centered
- A profile of values that is oriented toward personal growth, insight, and the well-being of others rather than a pleasurable and comfortable life
- A cooperative approach to managing interpersonal conflicts rather than a dominant, submissive, or avoidant style

The findings were consistent with our theory-guided predictions. People with high levels of wisdom-related knowledge reported that they less frequently experience self-centered pleasant feelings (e.g., happiness, amusement) but more frequently process-oriented and environment-centered positive emotions (e.g., interest, inspiration). People with higher levels of wisdom-related knowledge also reported less preference for values revolving around a pleasurable and comfortable life. Instead, they reported preferring self-oriented values such as personal growth and insight as well as a preference for other-oriented values related to environmental protection, societal engagement, and the well-being of friends. Finally, people with high levels of wisdom-related knowledge showed less preference for conflict management strategies that reflect either a one-sided concern with their own interest (i.e., dominance), a one-sided concern with others' interests (i.e., submission), or no concern at all (i.e., avoidance). As predicted, they preferred a cooperative approach reflecting a joint concern for their own and the opponent's interests.

Together, the evidence clearly supports the notion that wisdom, as we have defined and measured this concept, is linked to certain motivational orientations (i.e., a joint concern for developing our own potential and that of others) and affective experiences (i.e., frequent positive, environment-oriented emotions rather than evaluative, self-centered feelings such as happiness or negative feelings such as anger, fear, sadness).

EMOTIONAL REACTIONS TO FUNDAMENTAL LIFE PROBLEMS: WISDOM-RELATED KNOWLEDGE MAKES A DIFFERENCE

A third study that we recently completed in our laboratory was an experimental study in which we exposed people with different levels of wisdom-related knowledge to three fundamental life problems, each presented in a short film clip of about 10 minutes' duration. The problems dealt with an older woman who learns that she has Alzheimer's disease (Alzheimer's film), a young woman who mourns for her husband and young daughter who were killed in a car accident (family loss film), and a middle-age woman who escapes her frustrating family life to travel and find herself (personal growth film). We know from previous studies that these films evoke strong emotional reactions, especially sympathy with the main protagonists, feelings of sadness in response to the family loss and Alzheimer's films, and feelings of happiness in response to the personal growth film (Kunzmann & Grühn, 2004).

The major goal of this study was to provide initial empirical support for the notion that people's wisdom-related knowledge influences their inner feelings and experiences in response to fundamental and existential life problems. We had the following more specific predictions for people with high levels of wisdom-related knowledge:

- Because they are likely to recognize the significance and deeper meaning of events and phenomena, people with high levels of wisdom-related knowledge should first show a salient emotional response when confronted with another person's serious life problem (empathy-hypothesis).
- After further processing of the information, however, people with high levels of wisdom-related knowledge will exhibit effective down-regulation of their emotional responses to distance themselves and to bring their wisdom-related knowledge into foreground (regulation-hypothesis).

Our initial findings are consistent with the empathy prediction. As predicted, people with higher levels of wisdom-related knowledge showed greater emotional reactions to two fundamental life scenarios. They experienced greater pleasantness in response to the personal growth film, and they experienced greater sadness in response to the film dealing with Alzheimer's. In the near future, we will test our second prediction that people with higher levels of wisdom-related knowledge will distance themselves and down-regulate their first emotional response after further processing of the information about the emotion-arousing life scenario.

Together, this initial evidence supports the idea that wisdom as we have defined and measured it influences people's emotional reactions to fundamental life problems in theory-consistent ways. Our findings oppose the view that people with high levels of wisdom-related knowledge generally are emotionally distant and detached (e.g., Erikson, 1959). Rather, people with higher levels of wisdom appear to sympathize with their fellow mortals, regardless of whether they are experiencing life transitions that potentially lead to personal growth or are going through existential problems dealing with their own death and dying.

IMPLICATIONS FOR EDUCATION AND TRAINING

Given that wisdom-related knowledge is related to a number of desirable emotional and motivational dispositions and therefore is likely to foster a successful individual and social development, the question arises as to whether this type of knowledge can be taught (see also Reznitskaya & Sternberg, Chapter 11, this volume; Sternberg, 2001). For example, teaching wisdom-related knowledge could be an important component of professional training and practice. At one time or another in their career, many professionals have to struggle with one or more of the following questions: How can I coordinate my professional career and family development, balance my work load and leisure time, get along with my colleagues, identify my interests, and pursue them cooperatively? From a leadership perspective, we might add questions, such as: How can I maximize a common good rather than optimize the interests of certain individuals or small groups of individuals, get employees involved and motivated, develop and communicate a useful and inspiring vision, and coordinate the long-term and short-term goals of my institution?

What these problems have in common is that they are fundamental, complex, and uncertain; they are poorly defined, have multiple yet unknown solutions, and require coordinating multiple and often conflicting interests within and among individuals. This is precisely why professional knowledge in the narrow sense is typically insufficient to deal with these problems effectively. In contrast, wisdom, as we have defined this concept, is designed to deal especially with problems of this kind. As emphasized previously, wisdom-related knowledge encourages us to embed problems in temporal contexts (past, present, future) and thematic contexts (e.g., family, friends, work) and to consider problems from a broad perspective rather than in isolation. Wisdom-related knowledge also helps to acknowledge the relativity of individual and culturally shared values and to take other values and life priorities into account when thinking about possible problem solutions. Finally, wisdom-related knowledge facilitates decision making under uncertainty.

Although it takes a lifetime of practice and an ensemble of multiple supportive conditions to acquire and maximize our level of wisdom-related knowledge, participating in training programs on wisdom might inspire some people to look in new and constructive ways at the difficulties of life that none of us can avoid.

CONCLUSION

In this chapter, I have argued that even if very few people are able to achieve higher levels of wisdom-related knowledge, it is still worth the effort to strive for it. Certainly, there are many competencies that people can bring to bear when dealing with life's challenges and problems—but no other human capacity will be as integrative as is wisdom. A small but growing body of evidence reviewed previously suggests that wisdom-related knowledge has important implications for our emotional lives as well as for our life priorities and value orientations. Even if the acquisition of wisdom during ontogenesis may be incompatible with leading a predominantly pleasurable, sheltered, and comfortable life, in my view, the field of positive psychology would be incomplete if it failed to consider human strengths such as wisdom. Given their interest in maximizing a common good, wiser people are likely to partake in behaviors that contribute, rather than consume, resources (Kramer, 2000; Kunzmann & Baltes, 2003a; Sternberg, 1998). Moreover, their interest in understanding the complexity of life, including the blending of developmental gains and losses, most likely is associated with affective complexity and sensitivity (e.g., Baltes, 1997; Labouvie-Vief, 1990).

REFERENCES

Ardelt, M. (2003). Empirical assessment of a three-dimensional wisdom scale. *Research on Aging, 25*, 275–324.

Aspinwall, L. G., & Staudinger, U. M. (2003). *A psychology of human strengths: Fundamental questions and future directions for a positive psychology*. Washington, DC: American Psychological Association.

Assmann, A. (1994). Wholesome knowledge: Concepts of wisdom in a historical and cross-cultural perspective. In D. L. Featherman, R. M. Lerner, & M. Perlmutter (Eds.), *Life-span development and behavior* (Vol. 12, pp. 187–224). Hillsdale, NJ: Erlbaum.

Baltes, P. B. (1987). Theoretical propositions of life-span developmental psychology: On the dynamics between growth and decline. *Developmental Psychology, 23*, 611–626.

Baltes, P. B. (1997). On the incomplete architecture of human ontogeny: Selection, optimization, and compensation as foundation of developmental theory. *American Psychologist, 52*, 366–380.

*Baltes, P. B., Glück, J., & Kunzmann, U. (2002). Wisdom: Its structure and function in successful lifespan development. In C. R. Snyder & S. J. Lopez (Eds.), *Handbook of positive psychology* (pp. 327–350). New York: Oxford University Press.

Baltes, P. B., & Kunzmann, U. (2003). Wisdom: The peak of human excellence in the orchestration of mind and virtue. *The Psychologist, 16,* 131–133.

Baltes, P. B., & Smith, J. (1990). Toward a psychology of wisdom and its ontogenesis. In R. J. Sternberg (Ed.), *Wisdom: Its nature, origins, and development* (pp. 87–120). New York: Cambridge University Press.

Baltes, P. B., Smith, J., & Staudinger, U. M. (1992). Wisdom and successful aging. In T. B. Sonderegger (Ed.), *Nebraska Symposium on Motivation 1991: Psychology and aging. Current theory and research in motivation* (Vol. 39, pp. 123–167). Lincoln: University of Nebraska Press.

Baltes, P. B., Smith, J., Staudinger, U. M., & Sowarka, D. (1990). Wisdom: One facet of successful aging. In M. Perlmutter (Ed.), *Late life potential* (pp. 63–81). Washington, DC: Gerontological Society of America.

*Baltes, P. B., & Staudinger, U. M. (2000). Wisdom: A metaheuristic (pragmatic) to orchestrate mind and virtue toward excellence. *American Psychologist, 55,* 122–136.

Boehmig-Krumhaar, S. A., Staudinger, U. M., & Baltes, P. B. (2002). Mehr Toleranz tut Not: läßt sich wert-relativierendes Wissen und Urteilen mit Hilfe einer wissensaktivierenden Gedächtnisstrategie verbessern? [In need of more tolerance: Is it possible to improve value-relativistic knowledge and judgement?]. *Zeitschrift für Entwicklungspsychologie und Pädagogische Psychologie, 34,* 30–43.

Clayton, V., & Birren, J. E. (1980). The development of wisdom across the lifespan: A reexamination of an ancient topic. In P. B. Baltes & O. G. Brim (Eds.), *Life-span development and behavior* (Vol. 3, pp. 103–135). New York: Academic Press.

Erikson, E. H. (1959). *Identity and the life cycle.* New York: International Universities Press.

Helson, R., & Srivastava, S. (2002). Creative and wise people: Similarities, differences, and how they develop. *Personality and Social Psychology Bulletin, 28,* 1430–1440.

Holliday, S. G., & Chandler, M. J. (1986). Wisdom: Explorations in adult competence. In J. A. Meacham (Ed.), *Contributions to human development* (Vol. 17, pp. 1–96). Basel, Switzerland: Karger.

Kekes, J. (1983). Wisdom. *American Philosophical Quarterly, 20,* 277–286.

Kekes, J. (1995). *Moral wisdom and good lives.* Ithaca, NY: Cornell University Press.

Keltner, D., & Gross, J. J. (1999). Functional accounts of emotions. *Cognition and Emotion, 13,* 467–480.

Kramer, D. A. (1990). Conceptualizing wisdom: The primacy of affect–cognition relations. In R. J. Sternberg (Ed.), *Wisdom: Its nature, origins, and development* (pp. 279–313). New York: Cambridge University Press.

*Kramer, D. A. (2000). Wisdom as a classical source of human strength: Conceptualization and empirical inquiry. *Journal of Social and Clinical Psychology, 19,* 83–101.

Kunzmann, U., & Baltes, P. B. (2003a). Beyond the traditional scope of intelligence: Wisdom in action. In R. J. Sternberg, J. Lautry, & T. I. Lubart (Eds.), *Models of intelligence for the next millennium* (pp. 329–343). Washington, DC: American Psychological Association.

*Kunzmann, U., & Baltes, P. B. (2003b). Wisdom-related knowledge: Affective, motivational, and interpersonal correlates. *Personality and Social Psychology Bulletin, 29,* 1104–1119.

Kunzmann, U., & Grühn, D. (2003). *Age differences in emotional reactions to existential life problems: Evidence for greater reactivity in old age.* Manuscript submitted for publication.

Labouvie-Vief, G. (1990). Wisdom as integrated thought: Historical and developmental perspectives. In R. J. Sternberg (Ed.), *Wisdom: Its nature, origins, and development* (pp. 52–83). New York: Cambridge University Press.

Lerner, R. M. (2002). *Concepts and theories of human development.* Mahwah, NJ: Erlbaum.

Pasupathi, M., Staudinger, U. M., & Baltes, P. B. (2000). Seeds of wisdom: Adolescents' knowledge and judgment about difficult life problems. *Developmental Psychology, 37,* 351–361.

Ryan, S. (1996). Wisdom. In K. Lehrer, B. J. Lum, B. A. Slichta, & N. D. Smith (Eds.), *Knowledge, teaching, and wisdom* (pp. 233–242). Dordrecht, The Netherlands: Wolters Kluwer Press.

Seligman, M. E. P., & Csikszentmihalyi, M. (2000). Positive psychology: An introduction. *American Psychologist, 55,* 5–14.

Smith, J., Staudinger, U. M., & Baltes, P. B. (1994). Occupational settings facilitating wisdom-related knowledge: The sample case of clinical psychologists. *Journal of Consulting and Clinical Psychology, 62,* 989–999.

Synder, C. R., & Lopez, S. J. (Eds.). (2002). *Handbook of positive psychology.* New York: Oxford University Press.

Staudinger, U. M. (1999a). Older and wiser? Integrating results on the relationship between age and wisdom-related performance. *International Journal of Behavioral Development, 23,* 641–664.

Staudinger, U. M. (1999b). Social cognition and a psychological approach to the art of life. In T. H. Hess & F. Blanchard-Fields (Eds.), *Social cognition and aging* (pp. 343–375). San Diego, CA: Academic Press.

Staudinger, U. M., & Baltes, P. B. (1996). Interactive minds: A facilitative setting for wisdom-related performance. *Journal of Personality and Social Psychology, 71,* 746–762.

Staudinger, U. M., Lopez, D. F., & Baltes, P. B. (1997). The psychometric location of wisdom-related performance. *Personality and Social Bulletin, 23,* 1200–1214.

Staudinger, U. M., Smith, J., & Baltes, P. B. (1992). Wisdom-related knowledge in a life review task: Age differences and the role of professional specialization. *Psychology and Aging, 7,* 271–281.

Sternberg, R. J. (Ed.). (1990). *Wisdom: Its nature, origins, and development.* Cambridge, England: Cambridge University Press.

*Sternberg, R. J. (1998). A balance theory of wisdom. *Review of General Psychology, 2,* 347–365.

Sternberg, R. J. (2001). Why schools should teach for wisdom: The balance theory of wisdom in educational settings. *Educational Psychologist, 36,* 227–245.

Wink, P., & Helson, R. (1997). Practical and transcendent wisdom: Their nature and some longitudinal findings. *Journal of Adult Development, 4,* 1–15.

PART X

POSITIVE DEVELOPMENT ACROSS THE LIFE SPAN

CHAPTER 32

Fostering the Future:
Resilience Theory and the
Practice of Positive Psychology

TUPPETT M. YATES and ANN S. MASTEN

MORE THAN 30 YEARS ago, investigators studying children in high-risk environments observed that many children achieve positive developmental outcomes despite adverse experiences (Garmezy, 1974; Murphy & Moriarty, 1976; Rutter, 1979; Werner & Smith, 1982). Individuals who achieve these better-than-expected outcomes have been labeled *survivors, resilient, stress-resistant,* and even *invulnerable.* Repeated observations of such youth inspired a generation of research on resilience. As a result, the study of resilience has emerged as a distinct domain of empirical and theoretical inquiry in psychology, particularly in developmental psychopathology (Sroufe & Rutter, 1984). Pioneers in the systematic study of resilience recognized the potential importance of this work for practice. They believed that understanding naturally occurring resilience would inform interventions and policies aimed at fostering successful development among children growing up with heavy burdens of risk or adversity.

Prevention scientists and advocates of a positive approach to psychology have touted the resilience framework for its potential to inform efforts to foster positive developmental outcomes among disadvantaged children, families, and communities. Indeed, the promise of valuable implications for prevention, intervention, and social policy motivates much resilience research. However, there has been little evaluation of progress in applying a resilience framework to practice, and even less consideration of the reciprocal role that practice may play in the advancement of resilience theory and research.

Preparation of this chapter was facilitated by a graduate research fellowship from the National Science Foundation awarded to the first author. The second author's work on resilience has been supported by grants from the National Institute of Mental Health, the National Science Foundation, the William T. Grant Foundation, and the University of Minnesota.

In this chapter, we examine the reciprocal translation between resilience research and the practice of positive psychology. We begin by introducing the resilience framework, its key concepts, and core models. Next, we highlight the implications of a resilience framework for practice and encourage a complementary appreciation for the application of resilience-based practice to the evaluation and refinement of resilience theory. Finally, we discuss several impediments to effective translations between theory and practice, and provide suggestions for surmounting obstacles to a mutually informing relation between the science of resilience and the practice of positive psychology.

A RESILIENCE FRAMEWORK

The resilience framework emerged within a broader transformation in theory and research on psychopathology that created developmental psychopathology (Cicchetti, 1984; Masten, 1989; Sroufe & Rutter, 1984). A core tenet of developmental psychopathology is that investigations of positive and negative adaptation are mutually informative (Sroufe, 1990). A resilience framework is consistent with this perspective in its assertion that the study of developmental processes under extraordinary conditions can inform our understanding of both typical and atypical development.

Scholarly attention to resilience in the late twentieth century rekindled interest in positive psychology because these investigators studied, wrote, and spoke about the human capacity for positive adaptation and achievement in the face of adversity (Masten, 2001). The resilience perspective stressed the importance of *promoting competence* through positive models of intervention and change, in addition to reducing or ameliorating the effects of adversity on children. Thus, these early pioneers encouraged greater attention among researchers and practitioners to positive models and processes, and to the strength of individuals, families, communities, and societies.

KEY CONCEPTS FOR UNDERSTANDING RESILIENCE

The study of risk and resilience sprang from the observation that some individuals in populations exposed to incontrovertible adversity nevertheless achieve positive developmental outcomes. The lives of these individuals exemplify patterns of resilience reflecting "the process of, capacity for, or outcome of successful adaptation despite challenging or threatening circumstances" (Masten, Best, & Garmezy, 1990, p. 426). Resilience is predicated on exposure to significant threat or adversity, and on the attainment of good outcomes despite this exposure (Luthar, Cicchetti, & Becker, 2000). Thus, identifying resilient patterns of adaptation requires the operationalization of several related concepts, including competence, adversity, asset, and risk. Contemporary definitions of these concepts reflect the rising prominence of developmental systems and organizational theories of development in developmental psychology generally (Lerner, 1998), and resilience theory specifically (Luthar, 2003).

Competence and Adversity   Within a developmental perspective, *competence* is conceptualized as the adaptive use of resources, both within and outside the organism, to negotiate age-salient developmental challenges and achieve positive outcomes (Waters & Sroufe, 1983). In studies of resilience, successful outcomes are often evaluated in terms of a track record of success in the age-salient developmental tasks that adults in a particular society, historical time, and culture expect children of a given age period to achieve (Masten & Coatsworth, 1998). Thus, in a Western context, a competent infant may be one who develops a secure attachment in the early caregiving relationship, a competent adolescent may be one who succeeds in the areas of academic achievement and positive peer relationships, and a competent adult may be one who successfully transitions into a romantic partnership and gainful employment.

Adversity refers to negative experiences that have the potential to disrupt adaptive functioning or development. Adverse experiences may operate by temporarily overwhelming all the adaptive resources of an individual, by damaging the adaptive capacity of an individual in the short or long term, or by undermining the development of an individual's adaptive systems, with lasting consequences. Adversity may be acute (e.g., natural disaster) or chronic (e.g., child neglect), arise within the environment (e.g., interparental conflict, political violence) or within the person (e.g., brain tumor), but on some level it has the potential to disrupt development and thwart positive adaptation.

Assets and Risks   In the general population, assets (resources) and risks are associated with positive and negative outcomes, respectively. *Assets* refer to resources in a population that enhance the likelihood of positive developmental outcomes independent of risk status (e.g., good schools, problem-solving skills, family cohesion). Assets can take the form of human capital (i.e., resources within the person) or social capital (i.e., resources stemming from connections and relationships with other people and social organizations). *Risks* refer to events or conditions that increase the probability of an undesired outcome in a group of people with the risk factor (e.g., premature birth, impoverished neighborhood, lead exposure). A risk factor generally predicts worse outcomes in a group of individuals who have the risk factor, but not necessarily for every individual in the group. For example, very low birth weight is generally associated with a variety of developmental problems, but many children go on to develop well despite a history of low birth weight.

Assets and risks rarely occur in isolation in the real lives of children. They tend to pile up, leading to the idea of *cumulative risks or assets* (Seifer & Sameroff, 1987). Risks and assets may counterbalance each other, such that assets may compensate for risks, yielding a kind of *net risk*. As cumulative risk or adversity levels rise, positive outcomes tend to decrease in frequency. Yet, even among individuals whose lives are marked by many risks and adversities, outcomes are often diverse, with some individuals exhibiting positive adaptation. The challenge to account for such variation has led to more complex, interactive models of resilience that emphasize vulnerability and protective processes in development.

Protective Processes and Vulnerabilities   At the level of the individual, protective and vulnerability factors *moderate* the effect of adversity on developmental outcomes. Whereas an asset has a comparably beneficial effect in both high- and low-risk environments, a *protective factor* is disproportionately salient under conditions of adversity. For example, active parental monitoring and restrictive rules may buffer a young adolescent from the risks in a dangerous neighborhood, but such monitoring is not necessary in a safe neighborhood and may even be detrimental to development (Baldwin, Baldwin, & Cole, 1990). A *vulnerability factor* is associated with negative outcomes, particularly when the individual is exposed to adversity. For example, children who encounter frightening and intrusive caregiving in infancy may fail to develop an organized pattern of relating to the caregiver (i.e., disorganized attachment). In the face of future trauma, children with a history of disorganized attachment may be especially susceptible to developing dissociative symptoms (Liotti, 1992). Thus, disorganized attachment is a vulnerability factor for dissociation because its negative influence is magnified in the context of adversity. Protective and vulnerability factors represent interaction effects whereby a given factor has an especially beneficial, or harmful, influence under high-risk conditions. Identifying assets, risks, protective factors, and vulnerabilities is an important first step in understanding resilience. However, to apply a resilience framework in practice or policy, we need to know much more about the *processes* involved in resilience.

PROTECTIVE FACTORS: WHAT MAKES A DIFFERENCE?

Decades of research on a variety of at-risk populations have converged on several specific factors that are consistently associated with resilient patterns of adaptation. As summarized in Table 32.1, a subset of assets and protective factors has coalesced with marked stability over time. Early research identified three categories of resources that protect children in the face of adversity: (1) child characteristics, (2) family characteristics, and (3) community characteristics (Garmezy, 1985; see also Anthony & Cohler, 1987; Rolf, Masten, Cicchetti, Neuchterlein, & Weintraub, 1990). At the level of the child, for example, children who are able to develop flexible coping strategies and a locus of control that allows them to attribute negative experiences to external factors, while retaining the capacity to value their own strengths and assets, fare better in the face of adversity. Intelligence and a sense of humor are associated with flexible problem-solving skills, as well as with academic and social competence. Children who thrive in the face of adversity also tend to be socially responsive and are able to elicit positive regard and warmth from their caregivers. At the level of the family, children who attain positive developmental outcomes emerge from warm, sensitive, and cohesive intrafamilial exchanges and similarly nurturant kinship networks. Protective resources in the community consistently derive from high-quality educational milieus, nurturing and attentive teacher-child relationships, safe housing and neighborhoods, and available adult models of prosocial involvement (e.g., mentors). Surprisingly, though a similar list of assets and protective factors has emerged from diverse studies of risk and resilience, efforts to elucidate the processes that underlie resilience have only recently begun.

ORDINARY ADAPTATION DESPITE EXTRAORDINARY CIRCUMSTANCE: A DEVELOPMENTAL MODEL OF RESILIENCE

Contemporary resilience research departs from a hard-earned recognition that there is no single pattern of resilient adaptation, and that multiple mechanisms and processes are involved in shaping these developmental pathways. Consistent with the tenets of developmental psychopathology, resilience researchers recognize that

Table 32.1

Examples of Assets and Protective Factors That Promote Positive Development

Policy

- Policies that promote universal access to resources that facilitate positive adaptation
  - Preventive healthcare
  - Adequate nutrition
  - Affordable, safe housing
  - Prevention of, and protection from, political violence and persecution
  - Environmental protections (e.g., lead paint, pollution)
  - Equal access to economic and political sources of power and opportunity

Community

- Safe neighborhoods
  - Low community violence
  - Absence of drug trafficking

- Connections to prosocial organizations
  - Boys' and girls' clubs
  - Libraries

- Connections to competent, caring, and prosocial adult models (e.g., mentors)

Education

- High-quality schools
  - Attentive, trained, and compensated teachers
  - After-school programs
  - School recreation resources (e.g., sports, music, art)

Family

- Stable and organized home environment
  - Close relationship to a responsive caregiver
  - Positive sibling relationships
  - Supportive kinship networks

- Socioeconomic advantage

- Faith and religious affiliation

Individual

- A history of positive adaptation
  - Secure attachment in infancy
  - Positive peer relationships
  - Effective emotional and behavioral regulation strategies

- Positive view of self (e.g., self-confidence, self-esteem, self-worth, hopefulness)

- Features valued by society and self (e.g., appealing personality, talents)

- Good intellectual and problem-solving skills

"mechanisms involved in causation might entail dynamic processes operating over time, that indirect chain effects might often be present, and that there might be several different routes to the same outcome" (Rutter & Sroufe, 2000, p. 268). Increasingly, researchers are attempting to identify developmental processes that underlie resilient patterns of adaptation.

Process-oriented studies of resilience consistently implicate fundamental adaptational systems (e.g., attachment and parenting quality, mastery-motivational systems, emotional and behavioral self-regulatory systems) underlying resilient patterns of adaptation (Yates, Egeland, & Sroufe, 2003). These data support recent interpretations of resilience as a reflection of ordinary adaptive processes operating normally under extraordinary conditions (Masten, 2001). An important corollary of this proposition is that adversity will cause the greatest and most enduring damage if it harms or undermines the development of these core systems.

If the road from adversity to maladaptation is mediated by the disruption of basic adaptational processes, the road from adversity to positive developmental outcomes is mediated by factors that preserve, scaffold, or restore these systems (Egeland, Carlson, & Sroufe, 1993; Masten & Coatsworth, 1998). Resilience is not a trait, nor is it a cause of children's faring well in the face of adversity. Rather, resilience is what happens when adaptive systems that have developed in the lives of individual children, within themselves, their relationships, and their environments, work effectively to maintain or restore competence in development. These basic systems have evolved in the course of biological and cultural evolution to protect and promote human development and survival.

Process-oriented models of resilience are especially powerful for two reasons. First, they are more intellectually productive than earlier static trait models because they encourage the elucidation of causal mechanisms in the development of at-risk children. As Rutter (1990) observed:

> We need to ask why and how some individuals manage to maintain high self-esteem and self-efficacy in spite of facing the same adversities that lead other people to give up and lose hope. How is it that some people have confidants to whom they can turn? What has happened to enable them to have social supports that they can use effectively at moments of crisis? Is it chance, the spin of the roulette wheel of life, or did prior circumstances, happenings, or actions serve to bring about this desirable state of affairs? (p. 183)

Second, a better understanding of causal processes in resilient adaptation will contribute to effective practice and policy programs. Identifying causal processes in resilience is essential to effective practice because interventions must manipulate causal processes to effect desired change (Cicchetti & Hinshaw, 2002; Masten & Coatsworth, 1998).

RECIPROCITY BETWEEN RESILIENCE RESEARCH AND THE PRACTICE OF POSITIVE PSYCHOLOGY

The study of positive psychology encourages a shift in emphasis from a preoccupation with the reparation of defect to the building of defense, from a focus on disease and deficit to the strength and virtue in human development (Seligman, 2002; Seligman & Csikszentmihalyi, 2000). Traditional disease models do little to advance this agenda because they emphasize abnormality over normality, maladjustment over adjustment, sickness over health. Although changing gradually, disease models still locate disorder within the individual, rather than within the transactional exchanges between the individual and many other systems at multiple levels (e.g., family, peers, school, media, neighborhood) that could play a role in adaptive and maladaptive developmental pathways. With a growing body of research specifying the processes by which children negotiate salient developmental challenges despite adversity, the resilience framework is ripe for an active role in the applied practice of positive psychology. In turn, the most powerful tests of protective processes will derive from studies of prevention and intervention efforts that aim to alter the course of development.

TRANSLATING RESILIENCE RESEARCH INTO PRACTICE

Prevention and intervention efforts are tools for preventing deviations from adaptive developmental pathways *and* for righting or redirecting maladaptive developmental courses toward more positive outcomes. Resilience research can inform prevention science across multiple levels by clarifying program goals, identifying theoretical variables expected to bring about positive change, guiding the measurement of target variables, and providing a conceptual framework in which findings may be interpreted. Thus, a resilience framework can inform the development, implementation, and evaluation of prevention, intervention, and policy programs to promote positive adaptation among at-risk populations in important ways (Cicchetti & Garmezy, 1993; Cicchetti, Rappaport, Sandler, & Weissberg, 2000; Luthar & Cicchetti, 2000).

Competence-Promoting Interventions   Studies of resilience validate earlier calls to articulate the goals of intervention efforts in terms of promoting health, competence, and wellness, in addition to reducing illness and remediating deficiencies (Cowen, 1985; Strayhorn, 1988; Wyman, Sandler, Wolchik, & Nelson, 2000). A resilience framework recognizes that children possess the potential for positive development if the relational, familial, communal, structural, and sociocultural contexts within which their development is embedded adequately scaffold the development and operation of normative adaptational processes. A competence focus shifts emphasis in intervention toward the promotion and protection of basic adaptational systems that provide the individual with resources to meet the developmental expectations of a given society (Masterpasqua, 1989). Although competence-based interventions continue to address specific threats and vulnerabilities that confer risk for particular problems, they also target desired developmental outcomes and the processes likely to produce them.

Multifaceted Interventions   Cumulative models of risk and protection support interventions that ameliorate multiple risks and promote successful adaptation in several settings (Masten & Wright, 1998; Wyman et al., 2000; Yoshikawa, 1994). A resilience-based approach to practice emphasizes multiple goals, including the amelioration of extant problems, the prevention of new problem development, the prevention of a decline in existing skills and resources, and the promotion of new competencies (Coie et al., 1993). The realization of these varied goals necessitates collaboration among multiple levels of ecological influence ranging from family-focused service provision, to community involvement, to social policy.

Context-Sensitive Interventions   Practical applications of a resilience framework recognize that the effectiveness of a particular intervention will be influenced by the psychosocial context and the nature of the child. The influence of a given factor as either protective- or vulnerability-enhancing is moderated by the context in which it is embedded and the developmental stage at which it is introduced. In Ferguson's (2001) ethnographic study of African American school-boys, a teacher aptly illustrates the contextual specificity of risk and protection when she observes of one boy:

> He's very loud in the classroom, very inappropriate in the class. He has a great sense of humor, but again it's inappropriate . . . But other than that [dry laugh] he's a great kid. You know if I didn't have to teach him, if it was a recreational setting, it would be fine. (p. 92)

The salience of different contexts shifts over development as do individual vulnerabilities and the significance of particular assets and risks. Ultimately, what works for one group of children in a particular context may not work for a similar group of children in a different context, or for different children in the same context. Adaptive outcomes at given stages of development derive from transactional exchanges between the child and her or his environment. Over time, the salient components of that environment evolve from an exclusive emphasis on the parent-child relationship to other influences such as peer networks, school settings, and the broader community (Carlson & Sroufe, 1995). Effective interventions target developmental contexts that are salient for a particular group or subgroup of at-risk individuals.

Empowerment Models of Intervention   In a resilience framework, the promotion of competence involves the strengthening of individuals, as well as of families, communities, and broader social contexts (Cowen, 1991). Moreover, this approach to practice recognizes that powerful sources of healing, strength, restoration, and regeneration are embedded within complex external contexts, not only within individuals. Resilience-based approaches to prevention are consistent with empowerment models, which encourage the incorporation of local assets and resources into practice protocols (Wiley & Rappaport, 2000). This approach recognizes:

> If the "golden child" stands in the ghetto, it is because the ghetto is not a purely negative environment. It is, instead, a rich and complex mixture of family dysfunction and family support, of the breakdown of values and of strong traditions, of both antisocial and prosocial attitudes and beliefs. (Beauvais & Oetting, 1999, p. 102)

It is critical that researchers and practitioners understand that every environment consists of a complex array of potential assets, risks, protections, and dangers. Within a resilience framework, successful prevention and intervention programs direct attention beyond deficits in need of restorative attention to the strengths and potential assets in the child, family, and community (Iscoe, 1974; Luthar & Cicchetti, 2000; Masterpasqua, 1989).

Risk and resilience are operationalized in relation to culturally prescribed expectations for normative behavior. Therefore, it is important to clarify the ways in which adversity and competence vary across different ecological and cultural contexts. Programs that incorporate culturally congruent values, norms, and resources will be more readily accepted, used, and integrated into the community structure (Black & Krishnakumar, 1998; Cicchetti et al., 2000; see also Sagiv, Roccas, & Hazan, Chapter 5, this volume). A resilience framework encourages researchers and practitioners not to speak on behalf of disadvantaged youth and families, but to facilitate the power of these groups and communities to speak for themselves (e.g., through focus groups and community collaboration).

Life-Span Approaches to Intervention   Applied positive psychology is likely to be most efficacious if interventions are initiated early and maintained over time. Positive adaptation in one developmental period provides the child with a foundation that enables successful encounters with subsequent stage-salient challenges (Sroufe, Egeland, & Kreutzer, 1990; Waters & Sroufe, 1983). Conversely, maladaptation at a prior stage of development may compromise the child's capacity to negotiate future developmental challenges successfully. Thus, developmental patterns are magnified across time by virtue of the coherence with which both maladaptive and adaptive behaviors are organized. A corollary to this principle is that the longer an individual is on a particular developmental pathway, the less likely it becomes that he or she will deviate from that course (Sroufe, 1997).

The practical implications of a developmental understanding of resilience are twofold. First, early intervention efforts may exert a disproportionate influence on later development because they can prevent initial derailments from positive adaptive pathways. Second, children require ongoing support, opportunities, and resources to thrive. Therefore, it is unlikely that one-shot interventions in early childhood will ensure positive adaptation over time, particularly if applied to problems that do not arise in early childhood (e.g., AIDS prevention). Interventions must focus on the initiation of positive developmental pathways, as well as on their maintenance over time. Early competence promotion efforts scaffold success that, in turn, provides a platform on which future developmental achievements are built. Yet, resilience at one point does not guarantee resilience at another. Undoubtedly, early intervention is important and powerful, but development can go awry at any time. A resilience framework justifies interventions across the developmental continuum, not just in early childhood. As discussed in the next section, a resilience framework also offers guidance as to when intervention efforts may prove most efficacious.

Developmental Transitions as Intervention Targets   As suggested by developmental theory, organisms may be particularly sensitive to outside influence during major developmental transitions (Lerner, 1998), which may include transitions in context (e.g., school entry), in the self (e.g., puberty), or in social expectations (e.g., adolescence and autonomy). During developmental transitions, the individual undergoes a major reorganization and integration of adaptive capacities, such that new skills are more likely to be incorporated into (or separated out from) the individual's adaptive repertoire (Luthar & Cicchetti, 2000). Thus, efforts to induce positive developmental change may be most potent if implemented during periods of developmental reorganization and integration.

The emergent literature on *turning points* as conduits of resilient adaptation also speaks to the enduring capacity for change throughout development (Rutter, 1996; Wheaton & Gotlib, 1997). Turning point experiences induce lasting alterations (either positive or negative) in a developmental pathway. Lives can take dramatic turns at any point in development, for example, as a result of trauma, a developmental crisis, a conversion experience, or a significant change in physical appearance. Individuals, families, and communities who are destabilized by crisis may be more open to intervention-induced transformational change. Interventions, particularly those that target periods of developmental reorganization, may provide powerful inducements to change, creating turning point experiences. For example, Rutter suggests that interventions in the first five years of life may provide positive turning point opportunities because this period is especially sensitive to the influence of modifiable protective processes (e.g., high-quality caregiving or education). However, while recognizing the value of early intervention efforts for later positive adaptation, a resilience framework also highlights later periods of developmental reorganization (e.g., transitions into adolescence or adulthood) as important opportunities for effective intervention.

Summary   Resilience research has the potential to inform and foster practical applications of positive psychology by highlighting how interventions may operate as protective processes in development. A resilience-based approach shifts the emphasis of intervention research toward primary prevention and competence promotion, in addition to symptom alleviation and disease mitigation. Resilience-based approaches to intervention and prevention complement extant disease/deficit models because they direct practitioners toward mechanisms that may mediate positive developmental change. It is here, perhaps, that we can see the reciprocal connection between developmental psychopathology and resilience theory in that both emphasize the mutually informative relation between typical and atypical development, between the promotion of health and the prevention of disease.

A resilience framework makes explicit guiding principles for practice that effective practitioners implicitly know and use. For example, many of the implications suggested by a resilience framework (e.g., integrating interventions into the community infrastructure; using comprehensive, multilevel intervention approaches; facilitating community participation to promote community capacity building) are subsumed by extant approaches to community intervention (see Altman, 1995, for discussion). In this chapter, we begin to clarify and specify these principles to render them more accessible for the development and training of a new generation of practitioners. Applying a resilience framework to practice will inform future intervention and prevention efforts by emphasizing the value of competence promotion, cumulative protection, contextual specificity and sensitivity, empowerment, and the ongoing garnering of resources to foster positive adaptation among disadvantaged groups.

TRANSLATING RESILIENCE PRACTICE INTO RESEARCH

Optimistic expectations that advancing knowledge about resilient adaptation would contribute to the improvement of interventions that support positive adaptation in adverse conditions have, in large part, fueled the study of resilience. At the same time, however, evaluations of interventions designed to foster resilience offer a powerful way to test causal hypotheses about resilience, and development in general. Scientific progress emerges from the bidirectional influences of theory and practice in a recursive process of theory formulation, testing, data collection, and theory revision (Sameroff, 1983). Theories and conceptual frameworks are often inspired initially by dramatic cases and observations in applied psychology. Systematic research then yields theories and data that can be translated back into practice. Although prevention scientists are increasingly incorporating resilience theory into their missions and models of intervention, the complementary path from practice to theory has been traversed all too infrequently, remaining largely uncharted, since the earliest observations of resilience in development (Howe, Reiss, & Yuh, 2002). In this section, we discuss the role of theoretically guided interventions and carefully conducted evaluations as opportunities to test hypotheses about risk, protection, resilience, and development.

Case Studies   The origin of resilience theory in naturalistic observations of positively developing at-risk youth aptly illustrates how practice can inspire and inform resilience research. Informal translations from dramatic case studies of resilient patterns of adaptation to the beginnings of a resilience framework constituted an early form of practice-to-theory influence. Since this time, however, the translation from practice to research has steadily slowed, and the transition to more advanced levels of practice-to-theory translation has not yet materialized.

Theory-Testing Interventions   Just as improved developmental theories yield more effective interventions, so, too, do theory-testing interventions foster more comprehensive and better informed theories. However, theory-testing interventions must be carefully designed and executed if they are to prove fruitful for resilience research in particular, and the domain of positive psychology broadly. As suggested by Coie and colleagues (1993), interventions "should be guided initially by developmental theory and yield results that reflexively inform and revise the original theory" (p. 1017). All too often, translations from practice to theory derive from overly simplistic, premature conclusions drawn from intervention practices with little or no empirical validation. For example, Hinshaw (2002) observes that researchers often commit a treatment-etiology fallacy, in which they make an erroneous assumption that the mechanism of treatment action (e.g., increasing income) causes observed change in the outcome of interest (e.g., better school attendance). In fact, Hinshaw notes, such relations may be mediated by other factors (e.g., reduced parental conflict due to less financial strain). Understanding causal processes that underlie positive change in children's lives will ensure that our intervention efforts are efficient and effective.

The most convincing evidence for theory comes from studies that demonstrate that changes in a hypothesized causal process (e.g., parenting quality) occur as a result of intervention (e.g., parent training) and are associated with corresponding changes in the outcome of interest (e.g., declining antisocial behavior). Studies that demonstrate the mediating function of conceptually predicted variables (e.g., improved parental discipline practices) in the relation between intervention and outcome (e.g., parent training and reduced antisocial behavior) yield important data for theory testing. Research must establish that the intervention can change both the proposed mediator *and* the outcome of interest. Further, theory confirmation requires that improvements in the outcome variable be explained, at least in part, by changes in the mediator.

Evaluation Research   If practice is to inform and evaluate theory, it must, in its initial conceptualizations, be guided by theory. Similarly, if resilience theory is to inform effective practice, it must be guided by the lessons learned from careful evaluations of extant practice programs. Carefully conducted evaluation research with randomized group assignment and appropriate comparison groups will allow investigators to experiment with altering the course of human development in the context of identifiable and quantifiable adversity, and to evaluate causal hypotheses about resilience and development (Cicchetti & Toth, 1992; Kellam & Rebok, 1992; Luthar & Cicchetti, 2000; Sandler, Wolchik, MacKinnon, Ayers, & Roosa, 1997).

BUILDING CONNECTIONS AMONG SCIENCE, PRACTICE, AND INDIVIDUALS

The mutually informing relation between science and practice has been articulated by many scholars (Cicchetti & Hinshaw, 2002; Masten, 1989; Rutter & Sroufe, 2000; Sameroff, 1983). However, translations of this appreciation into real-world implications for practice and theory have been slow to develop. Moreover, there remains little recognition of the valuable contributions that community-based resources and leaders may offer to intervention protocols and research.

In this chapter, we have outlined the implications of resilience theory for enhancing the well-being of at-risk populations. We have argued that practical applications of resilience theory can advance our knowledge of protective processes in adverse conditions. Finally, we have suggested that both practice and theory will be enhanced by the adoption of culturally sensitive, empowerment-oriented methods. As observed by Rutter (1993), however, "knowing what end you want to bring about and knowing *how* to achieve that objective are two very different things" (p. 630, *original italics*). In this final section, we offer suggestions to help researchers, practitioners, and other stakeholders (e.g., children, families, teachers) foster effective translations among resilience research, the practice of positive psychology, and, by extension, the well-being of at-risk youth, families, and communities.

COLLABORATION

Ultimately, "a system dependent on outside experts, who prescribe culturally and ecologically irrelevant mental health services, has more risks than benefits for vulnerable children" (Fantuzzo & Mohr, 2000, p. 346). The connection between science and prevention must be forged through collaborative endeavors involving scientists, practitioners, and community members from diverse settings (Cowen, 1991). However, fostering these relationships remains a formidable challenge.

Traditionally, practitioners and researchers train in isolation from one another. Growing efforts to bridge this chasm through scientist-practitioner training programs and collaborative learning environments represent one avenue toward fostering connections between science and practice. However, fundamental differences remain between scientist and practitioner paradigms. For example, scientists operate on extended time schedules with rigid adherence to protocols and methods. In contrast, practitioners typically focus on here-and-now solutions with little patience for the time and rigidity required to empirically validate applied work through systematic research and evaluation. More challenging still are the barriers that prevent scientists and practitioners from connecting with the individuals they seek to understand and assist.

The challenge to transcend longstanding barriers among scientists, practitioners, and community stakeholders is formidable, but much can be learned from exemplar projects that have successfully moved toward collaborative and integrative models of research and practice. The Child Development-Community Policing (CD-CP) Program is an excellent example of collaborative efficacy (Marans, Berkowitz, & Cohen, 1998). In this program, the Yale University Child Study Center combined forces with the New Haven Department of Police Service to improve service delivery to child perpetrators, witnesses, and victims of violent crime. This collaborative approach to practice is now being replicated in several communities across the United States. Programs such as the CD-CP recognize that no single group of professionals is able to address the multiple needs of high-risk children and families (Marans et al., 1998).

Methodological Fidelity versus Ecological Validity

One of the quandaries that researchers and practitioners face is the invariable tradeoff between methodological fidelity and ecological validity (Sandler et al., 1997). A resilience framework recognizes that the importance of methodological fidelity and manualized intervention strategies is tempered by the need for bottom-up development efforts that depart from a collaborative relationship with the community to ensure cultural and ecological validity (Cicchetti et al., 2000). Methodologically sound evaluation research may help resolve the fidelity versus validity dilemma. Evaluation research may distinguish the core constituents of an intervention that require methodological fidelity to ensure efficacy from those components that may be modified to fit the needs of a particular population without compromising effectiveness.

Conceptual Clarification

A competence-promotion agenda requires consistent definitions of adversity and competence, as well as clear specification of target variables. Many studies assume risk status without verifying the magnitude of risk exposure (Richters & Weintraub, 1990). Similarly, the identification of competence and, by extension, of resilient patterns of adaptation, depends on how positive adaptation is operationalized. Given the multidimensional nature of competence, it is important to specify the domains to which we are referring when we label various states of adaptation as positive (or, in the context of adversity, resilient; Luthar et al., 2000). Researchers and practitioners must also clearly operationalize specific factors targeted by a given study or intervention. Perhaps most importantly, however, these target variables must encompass sources of protection and vulnerability that are relevant to the population of interest.

Methodologically Sound Evaluation Research

The growth in research on risk and protective factors has contributed to preventive interventions aimed at enhancing adaptation under conditions of adversity. However, questions remain as to how and why they work, for whom they are most effective, and to what extent their positive influences endure over the developmental course (Sandler et al., 1997). Although applying a resilience framework to intervention and prevention allows for the integration of theoretically modifiable mediators into intervention protocols, these interventions must be carefully evaluated to ascertain their efficacy and to test developmental hypotheses (Mrazek & Haggerty, 1994).

Evaluation research fosters increased accuracy, efficiency, and efficacy in both science and practice. First, evaluation research provides important scientific information about mediating and moderating processes in resilience. Thus, evaluation research offers a tool with which scientists can test causal hypotheses about adaptive processes in high-risk environments. Second, empirically sound efficacy evaluations inform cost-benefit analyses that encourage and justify federal and state expenditures for practical applications of positive psychology (Luthar & Cicchetti, 2000). Finally, evaluation research may reveal moderators of treatment effects and provide insight into subgroups of individuals who may respond more or less favorably to a particular intervention (Hinshaw, 2002). In these varied ways, evaluation research has the capacity to benefit all stakeholders in the process of promoting competence among children, families, and communities.

PROTECTION AND VULNERABILITY AS UNIVERSAL PROCESSES

A resilience framework recognizes that all communities, families, and individuals are composed of multiple assets, risks, protective factors, and vulnerabilities that interact and transact to shape the course of development. Still, classist, racist, and gendered assumptions direct current research allocation either toward or away from needy populations, depending on the issue. We must attend to all children, including those in populations that have been historically viewed as low risk. Children from groups that are traditionally considered "privileged" may exhibit substantial psychopathology and maladaptation in response to significant life adversity (Luthar & D'Avanzo, 1999). Similarly, all youth, even those who appear competent at a given time, require guidance and nurturance to achieve their potential.

The recognition that all persons encounter a unique compilation of assets and risks may advance our understanding of resilience. Studies including low-risk comparison groups (rather than just adaptive and maladaptive groups within a high-risk sample) are needed to evaluate differences between competent (i.e., low adversity and positive adaptation) and resilient groups (i.e., high adversity and positive adaptation). Comparisons of resilient and competent individuals who differ only with respect to their prior adversity exposure are rare, but such analyses will allow us to better understand the processes underlying resilience.

CAVEATS

A competence-based approach to practice and research avoids controversial taxonomic definitions of health and illness because it negates popular misconceptions of resilience as a pick-yourself-up-by-the-bootstraps trait. Thus, it provides a less pejorative and more clinically relevant system of practice (Masterpasqua, 1989). Still, resilience has the potential to become yet another marker by which people are judged as fit or unfit, good or bad, special or banal. We must recognize that resilience reflects basic developmental processes operating normally under extraordinary circumstances, not individual strength or deficiency.

Mounting evidence indicates that interventions can effect positive change in the lives of young people. We must be cognizant, however, that applying a resilience framework to practice carries the risk of suggesting that, if given appropriate services, children can surmount adversity and achieve resilient adaptation. Worse yet, some policymakers may erroneously conclude that resilience arises from within the child and use this misconception to justify the withdrawal of social welfare services. Interventions may foster positive developmental trajectories in the context of adversity, but no intervention can make a child *resilient*. There is no such thing as the resilient child. We must not revert to the conceptualization of decades past when terms such as *invulnerability* gained popularity at the expense of vulnerable youth.

As researchers, clinicians, parents, policymakers, and educators, we stand in awe of individuals who appear to overcome seemingly insurmountable odds, though research shows that they do not rise on their own. The urge to allow the remarkable capacities for human adaptation under adversity to distract us from the plight of children living in high-risk environments is tempting. However, the capacity for children to overcome adversity under the right circumstances does not justify either our continued collusion in the perpetuation of risk, or our omission of needed protections and supports for youth. Resilience is not a characteristic of the individual; it is a developmental process that is fostered or thwarted by the scaffolding provided by the individual's sociocultural and structural contexts, and ensuing transactions between the individual and multiple levels of ecological influence (Egeland et al., 1993; Luthar et al., 2000; Masten, 2001; Yates et al., 2003).

CONCLUSION

Positive psychology emphasizes the study of human strength and virtue with the aim of understanding and facilitating positive developmental outcomes (Seligman & Csikszentmihalyi, 2000). A resilience framework offers a powerful tool for realizing the goals of positive psychology through research and practice because it justifies prior calls for wellness enhancement and competence promotion (Cicchetti et al., 2000; Cowen, 1991). This chapter has traced the origin of contemporary resilience theory and research from its roots in case studies and construct definitions to its current emphasis on developmental and interactive processes that highlight the reciprocal relation between the science and practice of resilience.

A resilience framework offers compelling implications for the design, implementation, and evaluation of intervention efforts with high-risk youth. Contemporary interventions routinely incorporate competence promotion into their stated missions (Masten, 2001). Many programs strive to enhance the asset base of children, as well as to reduce their adversity exposure. Evaluation outcomes often include measures of positive adaptation in addition to more traditional measures of distress and psychopathology. These changes are apparent in recent descriptions of contemporary intervention models, such as "cumulative competence promotion and stress protection" (Wyman et al., 2000). However, as efforts to promote the health and competence of future generations expand, they must be met with commensurate evaluative research to ascertain the specific features of interventions that are effective and the validity of the theoretical hypotheses on which they were grounded.

Self-righting tendencies are a central feature of all living organisms (Sameroff & Chandler, 1975). As such, resilience, or at least the striving for it, is an expected feature of development in high-risk environments. Indeed, the absence of positive strivings among children, regardless of risk status, is atypical. Resilience describes patterns of positive adaptation that reflect the normative operation of fundamental developmental processes under nonnormative conditions. The enduring impact of adversity on development is mediated by disruptions in basic adaptational systems; therefore, interventions must aim to protect, restore, redirect, or reactivate such systems.

Resilience-informed practice recognizes that there is more to helping children than treating problems. As Seligman and Csikszentmihalyi (2000) have argued: "It is about identifying and nurturing their strongest qualities, what they own and are best at, and helping them find niches in which they can best live out these strengths" (p. 6). Based on a comprehensive science of adaptation and development, a resilience framework transcends pathology-focused models to promote basic adaptational systems that enable children to achieve positive developmental outcomes.

REFERENCES

Altman, D. G. (1995). Strategies for community health intervention: Promises, paradoxes, pitfalls. *Psychosomatic Medicine, 57*(3), 226–233.

Anthony, E. J., & Cohler, B. J. (Eds.). (1987). *The invulnerable child.* New York: Guilford Press.

Baldwin, A. L., Baldwin, C., & Cole, R. E. (1990). Stress-resistant families and stress-resistant children. In J. Rolf, A. S. Masten, D. Cicchetti, K. H. Nuechterlein, & S. Weintraub (Eds.), *Risk and protective factors in the development of psychopathology* (pp. 257–280). New York: Cambridge University Press.

Beauvais, F., & Oetting, E. R. (1999). Drug use, resilience, and the myth of the golden child. In J. L. Johnson (Ed.), *Resilience and development: Positive life adaptations* (pp. 101–107). New York: Kluwer Academic/Plenum Press.

Black, M. M., & Krishnakumar, A. (1998). Children in low-income, urban settings: Interventions to promote mental health and well-being. *American Psychologist, 53*(6), 635–646.

Carlson, E. A., & Sroufe, L. A. (1995). The contribution of attachment theory to developmental psychopathology. In D. Cohen (Ed.), *Developmental processes and psychopathology: Vol. 1. Theoretical perspectives and methodological approaches* (pp. 581–617). New York: Cambridge University Press.

Cicchetti, D. (1984). The emergence of developmental psychopathology. *Child Development, 55,* 1–7.

Cicchetti, D., & Garmezy, N. (Eds.). (1993). *Development and psychopathology: Vol. 5. Milestones in the development of resilience* [Special issue]. New York: Cambridge University Press.

*Cicchetti, D., & Hinshaw, S. P. (Eds.). (2002). *Development and psychopathology: Vol. 14. Prevention and intervention science: Contributions to developmental theory* [Special issue]. New York: Cambridge University Press.

Cicchetti, D., Rappaport, J., Sandler, I., & Weissberg, R. P. (Eds.). (2000). *The promotion of wellness in children and adolescents.* Washington, DC: Child Welfare League of America Press.

Cicchetti, D., & Toth, S. L. (1992). The role of developmental theory in prevention and intervention. *Development and Psychopathology, 4,* 489–493.

Coie, J. D., Watt, N. F., West, S. G., Hawkins, J. D., Asarnow, J. R., Markman, H. J., et al. (1993). The science of prevention: A conceptual framework and some directions for a national research program. *American Psychologist, 48,* 1013–1022.

Cowen, E. L. (1985). Person centered approaches to primary prevention in mental health: Situation focused and competence enhancement. *American Journal of Community Psychology, 13,* 31–48.

Cowen, E. L. (1991). In pursuit of wellness. *American Psychologist, 46,* 404–408.

Egeland, B., Carlson, E., & Sroufe, L. A. (1993). Resilience as process. *Development and Psychopathology, 5*(4), 517–528.

Fantuzzo, J. W., & Mohr, W. K. (2000). Pursuit of wellness in Head Start: Making beneficial connections for children and families. In R. P. Weissberg (Ed.), *The promotion of wellness in children and adolescents* (pp. 341–369). Washington, DC: Child Welfare League of America Press.

Ferguson, A. A. (2001). *Bad boys: Public schools in the making of black masculinity.* Ann Arbor: University of Michigan Press.

Garmezy, N. (1974). The study of competence in children at risk for severe psychopathology. In C. Koupernik (Ed.), *The child in his family: Children at psychiatric risk* (Vol. 3, pp. 77–97). New York: Wiley.

Garmezy, N. (1985). Stress resistant children: The search for protective factors. In J. E. Stevenson (Ed.), *Recent research in developmental psychopathology* (pp. 213–233). Oxford, England: Pergamon Press.

Hinshaw, S. P. (2002). Prevention/intervention trials and developmental theory: Commentary on the Fast Track special section. *Journal of Abnormal Child Psychology, 30*(1), 53–59.

Howe, G. W., Reiss, D., & Yuh, J. (2002). Can prevention trials test theories of etiology? *Development and Psychopathology, 14,* 673–694.

Iscoe, I. (1974). Community psychology and the competent community. *American Psychologist, 8,* 607–613.

Kellam, S. G., & Rebok, G. W. (1992). Building developmental and etiological theory through epidemiologically based preventive intervention trials. In R. E. Tremblay (Ed.), *Preventing antisocial behavior: Interventions from birth through adolescence* (pp. 162–195). New York: Guilford Press.

Lerner, R. M. (Ed.). (1998). *Handbook of child psychology: Theoretical models of human development* (Vol. 1). New York: Wiley.

Liotti, G. (1992). Disorganized/disoriented attachment in the etiology of the dissociative disorders. *Dissociation, 4,* 196–204.

*Luthar, S. S. (Ed.). (2003). *Resilience and vulnerability: Adaptation in the context of childhood adversities.* New York: Cambridge University Press.

Luthar, S. S., & Cicchetti, D. (2000). The construct of resilience: Implications for interventions and social policies. *Development and Psychopathology, 12,* 857–885.

Luthar, S. S., Cicchetti, D., & Becker, B. (2000). The construct of resilience: A critical evaluation and guidelines for future work. *Child Development, 71*(3), 543–562.

Luthar, S. S., & D'Avanzo, K. (1999). Contextual factors in substance use: A study of suburban and inner-city adolescents. *Development and Psychopathology, 11,* 845–867.

Marans, S., Berkowitz, S. J., & Cohen, D. J. (1998). Police and mental health professionals: Collaborative responses to the impact of violence on children and families. *Child and Adolescent Psychiatric Clinics of North America, 7*(3), 635–651.

Masten, A. S. (1989). Resilience in development: Implications of the study of successful adaptation for developmental psychopathology. In D. Cicchetti (Ed.), *The emergence of a discipline: Vol. 1. Rochester Symposium on Developmental Psychopathology* (pp. 261–294). Hillsdale, NJ: Erlbaum.

*Masten, A. S. (2001). Ordinary magic: Resilience processes in development. *American Psychologist, 56*(3), 227–238.

Masten, A. S., Best, K. M., & Garmezy, N. (1990). Resilience and development: Contributions from the study of children who overcome adversity. *Development and Psychopathology, 2,* 425–444.

Masten, A. S., & Coatsworth, J. D. (1998). The development of competence in favorable and unfavorable environments. *American Psychologist, 53*(2), 205–220.

Masten, A. S., & Wright, M. O. (1998). Cumulative risk and protection models of child maltreatment. *Journal of Aggression, Maltreatment, and Trauma, 2*(1), 7–30.

Masterpasqua, F. (1989). A competence paradigm for psychological practice. *American Psychologist, 44*(11), 1366–1371.

Mrazek, P. J., & Haggerty, R. J. (1994). *Reducing risks for mental disorders: Frontiers for preventive intervention research.* Washington, DC: National Academy Press.

Murphy, L. B., & Moriarty, A. E. (1976). *Vulnerability, coping and growth: From infancy to adolescence.* New Haven, CT: Yale University Press.

Richters, J., & Weintraub, S. (1990). Beyond diathesis: Toward an understanding of high-risk environments. In S. Weintraub (Ed.), *Risk and protective factors in the development of psychopathology* (pp. 67–96). New York: Cambridge University Press.

Rolf, J., Masten, A. S., Cicchetti, D., Neuchterlein, K. H., & Weintraub, S. (Eds.). (1990). *Risk and protective factors in the development of psychopathology.* New York: Cambridge University Press.

Rutter, M. (1979). Protective factors in children's responses to stress and disadvantage. In J. E. Rolf (Ed.), *Primary prevention of psychopathology: Social competence in children* (pp. 49–74). Hanover, NH: University Press of New England.

*Rutter, M. (1990). Psychosocial resilience and protective mechanisms. In S. Weintraub (Ed.), *Risk and protective factors in the development of psychopathology* (pp. 181–214). New York: Cambridge University Press.

Rutter, M. (1993). Resilience: Some conceptual considerations. *Journal of Adolescent Health, 14,* 626–631.

Rutter, M. (1996). Transitions and turning points in developmental psychopathology: As applied to the age span between childhood and mid-adulthood. *International Journal of Behavioral Development, 19,* 603–626.

Rutter, M., & Sroufe, L. A. (2000). Developmental psychopathology: Concepts and challenges. *Development and Psychopathology, 12,* 265–296.

Sameroff, A. J. (1983). Developmental systems: Contexts and evolution. In W. Kessen (Ed.), *Handbook of child psychology: Vol. 1. History, theory, methods* (pp. 237–294). New York: Wiley.

Sameroff, A. J., & Chandler, M. J. (1975). Reproductive risk and the continuum of caretaking casualty. In G. Siegel (Ed.), *Review of child development research* (Vol. 4, pp. 187–243). Chicago: Chicago University Press.

Sandler, I. N., Wolchik, S. A., MacKinnon, D., Ayers, T. S., & Roosa, M. W. (1997). Developing linkages between theory and intervention in stress and coping processes. In I. N. Sandler (Ed.), *Handbook of children's coping: Linking theory and intervention* (pp. 3–40). New York: Plenum Press.

Seifer, R., & Sameroff, A. J. (1987). Multiple determinants of risk and vulnerability. In B. J. Cohler (Ed.), *The invulnerable child* (pp. 51–69). New York: Guilford Press.

Seligman, M. E. P. (2002). Positive psychology, positive prevention, and positive therapy. In C. R. Snyder & S. J. Lopez (Eds.), *Handbook of positive psychology* (pp. 3–9). New York: Oxford University Press.

Seligman, M. E. P., & Csikszentmihalyi, M. (2000). Positive psychology: An introduction. *American Psychologist, 55,* 5–14.

Sroufe, L. A. (1990). Considering normal and abnormal together: The essence of developmental psychopathology. *Development and Psychopathology, 2*(4), 335–347.

Sroufe, L. A. (1997). Psychopathology as an outcome of development. *Development and Psychopathology, 9,* 251–268.

Sroufe, L. A., Egeland, B., & Kreutzer, T. (1990). The fate of early experience following developmental change: Longitudinal approaches to individual adaptation in childhood. *Child Development, 61,* 1363–1373.

Sroufe, L. A., & Rutter, M. (1984). The domain of developmental psychopathology. *Child Development, 55,* 17–29.

Strayhorn, J. M. (1988). *The competent child.* New York: Guilford Press.

Waters, E., & Sroufe, L. A. (1983). Social competence as developmental construct. *Developmental Review, 3,* 79–97.

Werner, E. E., & Smith, R. S. (1982). *Vulnerable but invincible: A longitudinal study of resilient children and youth.* New York: McGraw-Hill.

Wheaton, B., & Gotlib, L. H. (1997). Trajectories and turning points over the life course: Concepts and themes. In B. Wheaton (Ed.), *Stress and adversity over the life course* (pp. 1–25). New York: Cambridge University Press.

Wiley, A., & Rappaport, J. (2000). Empowerment, wellness, and the politics of development. In D. Cicchetti, J. Rappaport, I. Sandler, & R. P. Weissberg (Eds.), *The promotion of wellness in children and adolescents* (pp. 59–99). Washington, DC: CWLA Press.

*Wyman, P. A., Sandler, I., Wolchik, S., & Nelson, K. (2000). Resilience as cumulative competence promotion and stress protection: Theory and intervention. In R. P. Weissberg (Ed.), *The promotion of wellness in children and adolescents* (pp. 133–184). Washington, DC: Child Welfare League of America Press.

Yates, T. M., Egeland, B., & Sroufe, L. A. (2003). Rethinking resilience: A development process perspective. In S. S. Luthar (Ed.), *Resilience and vulnerability: Adaptation in the context of childhood adversities* (pp. 234–256). New York: Cambridge University Press.

Yoshikawa, H. (1994). Prevention as cumulative protection: Effects of early family support and education on chronic delinquency and its risks. *Psychological Bulletin, 115*(1), 28–54.

CHAPTER 33

Organized Youth Activities as Contexts for Positive Development

REED LARSON, ROBIN JARRETT, DAVID HANSEN, NICKKI PEARCE, PATRICK
SULLIVAN, KATHRIN WALKER, NATASHA WATKINS, and DUSTIN WOOD

SOCIAL REFORMERS IN the late nineteenth and early twentieth centuries developed a new set of contexts for youth that were specifically aimed at the
goals of positive psychology. Community youth programs (scouts, Y's,
youth clubs) and school-based extracurricular activities were created with the
objective of preparing young people to be psychologically vibrant adults who
contribute to the well-being of society. Advocates argued that these organized
activities would promote youth's development of fundamental personal and social resources that are typically not acquired in school, such as initiative, motivation, connections to adults, and, more recently, multicultural competency. As
we enter the pluralistic and rapidly changing global world of the twenty-first
century, these personal and social resources are more important to adulthood
than ever (Larson, 2002; Larson, Wilson, Brown, Furstenberg, & Verma, 2002;
Parker, Ninomiya, & Cogan, 1999). But school curricula remain focused on promoting a limited set of individual cognitive skills that can be measured by
exams (Youniss & Ruth, 2002). Thus, organized youth activities have an important role to play in adolescents' preparation for adulthood, and developmental
researchers—who have given limited attention to these contexts—have an important responsibility to provide theories and research on how they facilitate
the growth of these diverse resources.

Existing research suggests that participation in organized youth activities is
related to general indicators of positive development, but it provides little evidence on how development occurs. Controlled longitudinal studies show that
participation in youth programs is associated with increased self-esteem, later
educational achievement (Eccles & Barber, 1999; Marsh, 1992), participation in

We are deeply indebted to the youth and adult leaders who shared their experiences with us and to
the William T. Grant Foundation for its support of this research.

voluntary associations at age 30 (Hanks & Eckland, 1978), and occupational attainment at age 40 (Glancy, Willits, & Farrell, 1986). Some studies suggest that effects are greater for disadvantaged youth (Mahoney, 2000; Marsh & Kleitman, 2002). A fundamental limitation of nearly all of this research, however, is that it has treated youth programs as a "black box." Most studies provide little or no assessment of what goes on inside programs: what youth experience, how development occurs, or what effective youth practitioners do to support development (Eccles & Templeton, 2002; National Research Council and Institute of Medicine, 2002). As a result, we lack the *theories of change* that are needed for useful evaluation research, and we have little information that is helpful for the designers and practitioners of youth programs because research findings are not related to variables that they control.

This chapter describes our program of research aimed at understanding the *developmental processes* occurring within organized youth activities. What happens inside the activities that leads to positive change in young people? A guiding premise of our work is that youth programs are a context in which youth are active producers of their own development. We and others have found that when adolescents are signaled across the hours of the day, organized activities stand out as settings in which they report a psychological state of high motivation, attention, and challenge (Csikszentmihalyi, Rathunde, & Whalen, 1993; Larson, 2000). Youth experience themselves as deeply engaged and agentic in a way that rarely happens in other parts of their daily lives. These are psychological conditions under which they can be expected to be active learners: to be self-organizing. Indeed, in a preliminary focus group study, we found that youth described themselves as actively engaging in a wide range of development experiences within organized activities (Dworkin, Larson, & Hansen, 2003). Furthermore, adolescents in our survey research reported higher rates of personal and social learning experiences (related to identity, initiative, emotion regulation, teamwork, and adult networks) in youth programs than during their daily school work and interactions with friends (Hansen, Larson, & Dworkin, 2003). So organized youth activities appear to be a particularly fertile context for self-generated change.

In our current research, we are developing grounded theory on how this change unfolds. What are the developmental processes that young people engage in within organized activities, and how do effective adult leaders of activities support these processes? In the first section of the chapter, we describe the longitudinal qualitative methods we are using to do this. In the middle section, we report the processes of change we have found in five domains of development. Last, we examine the role that adult leaders of youth programs (often called *youth practitioners* or *youth workers*) play in facilitating these developmental processes.

FOLLOWING DEVELOPMENTAL CHANGE IN THREE YOUTH PROGRAMS

To study these developmental processes, we carried out in-depth investigations of three high-quality youth programs. Participants and adult leaders in the programs were interviewed and observed over a 3- to 4-month natural cycle of program activity. Heath (1998) has found that effective youth programs engage young people in activities that they describe as "work," and the youth in all three programs were engaged in working toward some type of goal or goals.

Three Programs

Clarkston FFA: A Rural School-Based Program　The first program we studied was a local chapter of the National FFA organization. This is an after-school program for high school students in the United States, oriented toward promoting leadership and preparing youth for careers in agriculture, food, fiber, and natural resource systems. We chose the Clarkston FFA chapter, located in a nearly all-White rural high school, because the two agriculture teachers who were its advisors placed high value on youth leadership and had reputations as effective mentors. The structure of the program provides many leadership roles and ways for youth to actively contribute. We studied this program during a 16-week period when the youth were involved in planning a summer day camp for fourth graders. The goal of the day camp was to teach these children about agriculture and to interest them in joining FFA when they reached high school. During this period, youth also participated in several regional and state FFA competitions (e.g., in poultry judging) and undertook several community service projects.

Art-First: An Urban Arts Program　We chose the second program, Art-First, because it was recognized in the youth development community as providing high-quality art education to disadvantaged youth in a large city. The program draws ethnically and racially diverse students from all over the city. In addition to studio courses in visual arts, Art-First offers programs to help young people prepare for college, gain practical job skills, and learn about careers in the arts. We studied youth participating in Art-First's two-part summer career development program, coordinated by a dedicated young social worker with extensive experience working with teens. The first part of this program was a six-week course in which high school-age youth participated in various hands-on activities aimed at developing job skills related to arts careers. In the second six-week part of this program, students worked 20 hours a week in two principle activities: an arts-related internship in a business or nonprofit organization and a group arts project. This year, the arts project was creating a set of murals to be mounted on the local train platform.

Youth Action: An Urban Civic Program　The third program was a youth activist organization in the same large city, which also had a positive reputation in the youth development community. Students in this program undertake action campaigns, often to alter policies in the city's public high schools. During the four months of study, their efforts were largely targeted toward changing the schools' zero tolerance policy and expanding sexuality education. Youth spend a considerable amount of time researching issues and learning about activism; then they put this knowledge to work. Participants in the program are primarily youth of color, including Latino, African American, and biracial teens. The adult leader was a committed Arab American young man who has earned the respect of the diverse youth he works with. We followed members in this program as they organized a city-wide Youth Summit, during which 300 youth from across the city took part in all-day, youth-led workshops. A panel in which youth voiced concerns and demands for school reform to a state senator and a representative from the school system was also included in the Summit. In addition, during this period, members of Youth Action were involved with a coalition that organized a rally for fair school funding, and they held a meeting with the superintendent of the city's schools.

GATHERING DATA ON DEVELOPMENTAL PROCESSES

Our primary objective was to understand developmental experiences in these programs over the cycle of program activity. Because we are interested in youth as producers of their development, interviews were the method of choice. We wanted to understand how the young people experienced and conceptualized processes of change. At each program, we asked the adult leaders to select a sample of 10 to 13 representative participants, including approximately equal numbers of girls and boys. Our staff members then conducted biweekly phone interviews with each youth as well as longer face-to-face interviews at the beginning, at midpoint, and at the end of the study period. The open-ended interview protocols were developed from focus groups conducted with youth workers, the youth development literature, and a prior study with high school students (Dworkin et al., 2003). All interviews were audiotaped and transcribed. Across the three programs, 206 youth interviews were conducted with 34 youth.

To help understand the adult leaders' role in facilitating this change, we also carried out biweekly interviews with the adult leaders and observed program sessions. The interviews with the leaders followed the same schedule as the interviews with the youth. A total of 33 leader interviews were conducted with the four adult leaders (including both FFA leaders). The observations were conducted biweekly or weekly, using techniques of participant observation. Observers took detailed notes following standard ethnographic protocols. Twenty-four observations were conducted across the three programs.

FROM DATA TO THEORY

Our analysis of the interviews and observations was guided by the grounded theory approach. This approach involves generation of coding schemes from the data that profile the themes and concepts and then conducting further steps of analyses to identify the relationships among concepts. Used by researchers across many disciplines, the purpose of grounded theory is to construct inductively derived theory that is grounded in qualitative data (Glaser & Strauss, 1967; Strauss & Corbin, 1998).

The analyses were carried out by five analysis teams that focused on five distinct domains of development and by a sixth team that focused on the actions of the adult leaders. The first stage of analysis entailed coding and sorting out all material from the transcripts that fit into the domains of each team. NVivo, a qualitative data management program (QSR International, 2001), was used to aid in this process. In the second stage, the teams carried out a process of discovery focused on the material in their domain. Team members read the text for themes and underlying concepts in the participants' and leaders' interviews and in the ethnographic notes from the observations (Glaser & Strauss, 1967; Taylor & Bogdan, 1998). Team members also kept notes on issues, themes, and ideas that arose from their work.

The final stages were then aimed at testing and further refining these preliminary concepts. The teams developed coding schemes for classifying themes and constructs in the narrative data (Charmaz, 1983) and then used grounded theory methods to examine how the different themes and constructs related to each other (Strauss & Corbin, 1998). As new material became available, they tested whether the new data fit with prior codes, concepts, and theories and modified the latter as appropriate. This process allowed them to refine and verify the emerging conceptual ideas. We turn now to providing summary accounts of the teams' findings, first, on the five developmental processes, then, on what adult leaders did to support these processes.

DEVELOPMENTAL PROCESSES IN ORGANIZED YOUTH ACTIVITIES

PROCESS 1: DEVELOPING INITIATIVE

Initiative is the capacity to get things done—to organize your efforts over time to achieve a goal. This capacity is becoming increasingly important in the global twenty-first century. The greater fluidity of society requires that adults be more able to direct their lives and that communities have people capable of social and economic entrepreneurship (Larson, 2000). But obtaining the capacity for initiative is no easy achievement. Youth have limited skills for developing and executing plans (Gauvain & Perez, in press); indeed, the majority of adults are not very good at sticking with and achieving instrumental goals (Gollwitzer, 1999). Our survey research (Hansen et al., 2003) and the current study suggest that youth programs are a context where adolescents have some of their best opportunities to develop and practice components of initiative.

All three of the programs we studied engaged members in working toward goals, and youth's development of initiative skills appeared to grow from the challenges they encountered in striving toward these goals. We asked the youth at each biweekly interview what "challenges and obstacles" they were facing in their work. At a basic level, they repeatedly reported struggling with the challenges of "just doing it," of mobilizing their time and effort. Students in the Clarkston FFA, for example, encountered difficulties with finding time and not being sidetracked by other distractions in their lives (Larson, Hansen, & Walker, in press), challenges that were frequently encountered in the other two programs as well. Youth in Art-First reported being daunted by the size of the canvas they were given and challenged to get their murals done with a tight deadline.

As the weeks progressed, the youth recounted developing strategies for addressing this basic challenge of mobilizing their time and effort. The most frequently reported learning experiences in this domain involved learning that success in their projects was related to starting early, managing their time, and working hard. One youth in Art-First reported, "I basically learned how to just keep at it, you know, and once in awhile, just step back, and clear your head, and then get back at it." Similarly, Rosa, at Youth Action, said she learned:

> Not to give up, oh my god, you know, how many times? It was just like, let's just forget it and start something new. It's not going to work. It's too hard, you know. But, I mean we just kept going and pushed forward and we got it!

The underlying insight reported by many youth was, "Hard work pays off"— success in a project is correlated with the effort invested. In close analysis of the Clarkston data, we found that the youth were beginning to think about time and effort as *quantities* that can be deliberately allocated to achieve a goal; they were beginning to think about future time—the days and weeks ahead—as an arena in which their effort can be deployed (Larson, Hansen, et al., in press).

Several youth in Art-First and Youth Action articulated a more advanced level of strategic thinking, which they developed in response to the logistical challenges of their work. These youth reported gaining insights on how to problem-solve, consider contingencies, and organize steps in the work to effectively accomplish an end. A student at Youth Action, Leon, recounted the steps the group followed in their campaign to change the school system's uniform discipline code. First, they did research: They surveyed students in the schools and gathered data through the school board's office of accountability:

> After we got the research, we started having proposals with members of the board. And some were warm toward us; some didn't really care. But after we kept doing it and doing it and getting more and more concrete facts and solid figures, after awhile [it was] too obvious to ignore. If you have research and analysis, then it's like you can't ignore solid research. So eventually they changed it and modified some things.

In contrast to Leon's account of a methodical progression of steps, a student in Art-First reported learning that reaching a goal is often a nonlinear process. He had an internship at a toy company that developed new toys, and said, "There's a lot of going back to the beginning. After you work, you get to step ten, [then] 'Oh, something happened,' so you gotta go back to step zero (laughs)."

At this more advanced level, youth were learning to think logistically about how to organize the multiple steps and components in their work. Research shows that adolescents are just acquiring the cognitive abilities to think about complex, interacting systems (Mascolo, Fisher, & Neimeyer, 1999). These youth reported learning to develop plans that took into account the dynamics of multiple systems: their group, adult organizations (e.g., the school board), and other levels of analysis (e.g., what would be of interest to fourth graders at a day camp). Consistent with this, Heath (1999) found that teens in effective youth programs develop linguistic tools related to this kind of logistic thinking, such as scenario building and use of if-then sentence constructions.

Youth in these programs, then, appeared to be both learning to mobilize their time and effort and acquiring more advanced logistic strategies for organizing this effort. For several students, this increased ability for initiative appeared to transfer to other parts of their lives, including to their career planning. Rosa from Youth Action, who was from an immigrant working-class family, described how their achievements as a group had made her decide to pursue a career in law:

> I didn't think I could be a lawyer. I'm like, it's got a lot of schooling, but I think it's really made me say yes, it's a possibility. You can make anything, you know, we've done things. We started out, like a really dinky organization, but now a lot of people are looking to us and they're like: how do you do this and how do you do that? So we've gotten to be, hopefully, one of the greater organizations. And so I believe anything's possible.

The success that Rosa and others experienced through youth programs appeared to build initiative skills and confidence in those skills that they carried into the future. Although these results are preliminary, we suspect that these developmental changes contribute to the finding that participation in youth programs predicts later educational achievement and adult occupational attainment (Eccles & Templeton, 2002).

Process 2: Transformations in Motivation

Interrelated with the development of initiative skills were changes in youth's motivation. Time sampling research has shown that a large number of American adolescents are chronically bored, with the highest rates of boredom occurring during activities that are challenging and require sustained effort such as schoolwork (Larson & Richards, 1991). Yet, to thrive as adults, young people need to learn to be motivated by challenge: They must learn to enjoy work. Because organized activities are the one context in teens' lives where motivation, challenge, and attention consistently co-occur, it has been hypothesized that they provide youth with unique opportunities to learn to enjoy serious, adultlike challenges (Kleiber, Larson, & Csikszentmihalyi, 1986).

As we followed youth's participation in the three programs, we witnessed this type of transformation in adolescents' motivation and began to see how it occurs. We found that many participants joined the programs for extrinsic reasons. They reported entering the programs to please their parents or to hang out with other teens. Many of the students in Youth Action said that they joined because participation provided the community service hours that were required for high school graduation; for a few who were being paid, the money was an incentive for joining. As they participated in the programs, however, most indicated that their motives for participation changed. Rosa from Youth Action said:

> When I first started, I wasn't really too interested. One of the things that kept me interested was being paid; I was a youth apprentice. Then I started realizing that I like this kind of work. I'm helping people.

In fact, Rosa and many Youth Action students, including those not being paid, continued participation well after they had fulfilled their required high school service hours. Across the three programs, youth reported that their reasons for participating had shifted. Despite the hard work involved, the great majority of youth we interviewed indicated that they remained in the program because the work had become intrinsically rewarding.

What accounted for the development of intrinsic motivation in this work? When asked to explain week-to-week elevations in their motivation, first, many youth emphasized the special opportunities that the programs provided. They reported that their motivation was raised because they were able to engage in activities that were novel, fresh, and personally enticing: They got to do things that they were not able to do outside the program. Several FFA members pointed to the freedom they had to choose from a wide range of activities; one reported having tried every activity that the program offered. An Art-First student, Marsha, compared her experience in the program with art classes at her school:

> My school is so restricted because we're going to be graded; you are always worried about it. But our teacher here said, "Just experiment." So I went crazy, it's all abstract and I had never done that before; I'm enjoying the program very much.

The key idea for Marsha and other youth seemed to be that they were voluntarily choosing activities that were novel and personally interesting.

Second, they described their change in motivation as emerging from the experience of involvement in the activity itself. From week-to-week, they reported getting caught up in preparing for the FFA competitions, working on their Art-First murals, and planning the Youth Action rally. When asked what it was about organizing a workshop that made him so motivated, a boy at Youth Action replied simply: "I've been doing a lot of work, I'm really psyched." Participants repeatedly explained their motivation by saying that the work they were doing was "exciting," "fun," and "enjoyable." A boy at Art-First said, "The more and more I get involved, the more and more I'm like anticipating the next time I get to come back." In short, participation in the activities appeared to be self-reinforcing.

This transformation in motivation—this new experience of enjoying work—can be provisionally explained with Csikszentmihalyi's (1975, 1990) theory of flow, which presents intrinsic motivation as growing out of the experience of challenge. These youth programs provided a range of activity choices that allowed students to select activities that, in Csikszentmihalyi's terms, had personally engaging "opportunities for action" or challenges. In the FFA, a number of youth emphasized the regional and state competitions as the source of challenge, and across programs many youth were engaged by the challenges of doing well: creating a beautiful mural, having an effective rally, and organizing a successful day camp. Taking on these challenges required concerted effort and, as youth got into the work, a number reported discovering that they were skilled at it. The core of Csikszentmihalyi's theory, supported by much research, is that when people experience their skills as *matched to* the challenges of an activity, they have the experience of absorption and enjoyment, an experience evident in the students' repeated reports of excitement, fun, and "being psyched."

What is important for our purposes is that this enjoyment of challenge is self-reinforcing. It creates the desire to repeat the experience. And when people are in conditions where they experience a sequence or channel of meaningful challenges that are matched to their skills, Csikszentmihalyi finds that they experience sustained deep enjoyment or *flow,* which is repeated each time they participate in the activity. Our data suggest that youth programs allow young people to learn to enjoy work because they provide flexible and supportive conditions for youth to find this channel—to discover and sustain this matching of challenges with their skills.

Having discovered this capacity to enjoy work and challenge, a few youth reported that it carried over to others areas of their lives. Excited by his experience in working on FFA projects, a boy stated: "I'm going to turn my attention toward other things that I like and work toward them." By his account, the experience of enjoyment in FFA had roused to life a capacity for deep absorption in working toward other types of challenges.

Process 3: Acquiring Social Capital

Adolescent development consists not only in the acquisition of new skills and dispositions but also in the formation of personal relationships, including those with adults. Youth need and benefit from relationships with members of adult worlds who provide *social capital*—who provide information and resources that connect them to these adult worlds (Benson, 1997; National Research Council and Institute of Medicine, 2002). Social capital is also considered to be good for communities, because the exchange of knowledge, resources, and trust creates a healthy civil society (Putnam, 2000). Involvement in youth programs can offer adolescents opportunities to build social capital and tap into the expertise of highly resourced adults.

Youth from all three programs we studied described how activities of the programs brought them into contact with adults from the community. Participants in Art-First developed relationships with adults in professional settings through their internships. Members of Youth Action interacted with community leaders and school administrators as part of their campaign for school reform. In FFA, a student leader, Jeff, described how they interacted with members of the community through their outreach activities:

> One good thing that we do is foundation collection. That's when we go around to all the agribusinesses and try to collect money for the state. I really didn't know anyone in this town until I got into there. And we just go around and talk to them and say who you are and say like can we have your money (laughs). But, it's let me meet new people. And this past year as being president, I talked to a lot more people in the community.

As a result of these interactions, Jeff reported that he now would sometimes speak with these adults when he saw them at a store or at community events.

Some of the youth described using these contacts and relationships for information or other purposes. Leon, at Youth Action, explained how he drew on the relationships with adults he met through the program:

> I talk to them and, if I have a question about an issue, they'll be able to help me out with it. Since I got to know some of 'em, I had a problem with my computer, and one of them just happened to be skilled at fixing computers. So, I was able to talk to him and he actually fixed my computer free of charge.

In the same vein, a member of the Clarkston FFA described how he was able to draw on his relationship with a local banker developed through FFA to assist in organizing a trap shoot: "The banker in town is a big shooter and stuff—a big hunter. I just called up the bank and he got everything pretty much lined up for us. I called him twice and he called all the rest of the people."

Most significantly, youth at all three programs reported using these relationships in connection to their education and career paths. This was illustrated when a member of Youth Action was told by his school that he had to come back for one class after his senior year, and he would be required to go full time and take a full load. But the boy talked with a person at central administration whom he had met through Youth Action, and this person explained that he could take the course through night school and made sure that this arrangement was worked out. Many students reported learning from adults about college and career choices and sometimes using these adults for letters of reference. An academically talented youth at Art-First, Marco, described the relationship with the supervisor at his internship:

My supervisor has friends at Dartmouth College, which is one of my college choices, and the fact that I'm creating connections—this sounds evil, I don't mean to sound manipulative or anything—to people who know other people that can get to know me can help me achieve my goal of getting into the college that I want.

The contacts that Marco gained were so helpful that he felt like he was doing something wrong, but they were extremely valuable in his ultimate success in gaining admission to a first-rate college.

Across programs, the students repeatedly described their relationships with these adults as "opening new worlds." They had their "eyes opened," had "doors opened," and been brought "out of their shell." They reported learning what a given career world is "really like," as well as learning how real people manage the challenges of those worlds. One student said that these experiences made her more trusting of the adult world; another spoke of having her hopes for the future raised. School and career choices that had been abstract and unreal became tangible possibilities. An FFA member said, "It's definitely given me new options that I've never even thought about or I wouldn't have thought about had I not joined this organization." By developing relationships with adults through these programs, youth were able to draw on the experience of these experts in ways that provided social capital and opened new opportunities for their future.

PROCESS 4: BRIDGING DIFFERENCE

Another type of interpersonal capital, gained largely through peers, involved developing relationships and understanding across dimensions of human difference. The contemporary world increasingly brings people from diverse groups into contact; therefore, it is essential that young people learn to *bridge difference*—to understand, respect, and forge relationships across religious, ethnic, and other dimensions of human diversity. Yet high rates of racial intolerance and hate crimes by youth (Southern Poverty Law Center, 2000; Youniss et al., 2002) and a rising tide of ethnic conflicts across the world (Brubaker & Laitin, 1998) indicate that many young people are not developing competencies to understand and appreciate human diversity. Youth programs have been identified as potentially unique and important contexts for teenagers to develop these competencies (National Research Council and Institute of Medicine, 2002), and our data provided evidence of how this developmental process occurs.

The data suggested that youth learn to bridge difference through a three-step process. The first step involved interaction with youth who were different in some way. At the Clarkston FFA, which was all White, the salient differences that were bridged were those between different cliques and crowds: jocks, brains, punks, and hicks (Watkins, 2003). At Youth Action and Art-First, where students were diverse, we observed interactions across ethnic groups and sexual orientations. The students reported that these cross-group interactions often resulted from work toward the shared goals in the program. An FFA member, Jamie, said:

Cliques will have their different ideas on the small tiny details. You give each a major goal, and then give them each their own part to work on to reach that goal. They're still working together, while having their own individual likes and dislikes.

The FFA youth were not always enthused about working with teens from different cliques, but their individual and group success depended on it. At Youth Action, the students described coming together with youth from different ethnic groups to "basically act as a family and work together for a certain goal." The shared goals provided a common ground for youth with different backgrounds to build trust and have sustained, meaningful interactions.

As a result of these interactions, the second step involved learning about these others and beginning to see them in more human terms. Youth in the programs worked in small groups on specific tasks or projects. The high levels of close interactions and interdependency that characterized the small groups allowed youth to learn about and become familiar with one another. A girl in FFA remarked, "We know each other better because we've worked with each other." Youth were active in this learning process and often initiated learning about one another's interests, values, family backgrounds, and perspectives on different issues. A girl at Youth Action said, "Now I see different races and I try to talk to them and try to be as friendly as I [would] be to my own race." A couple of youth reported the experience of what we have called "discovering the personhood" in someone from a different group. At FFA, a girl reported the change in this way: "Jack, he's a big punk; [but], there's a person inside of him that's completely different from what you see." Similarly, a boy described a friendship he had formed with a bisexual teen at Youth Action, "It's the same person inside. He's really bi and he's cool." These youth learned to look past outward appearance and group affiliation and came to understand the humanity of others. Through meaningful interactions over time, the youth came to know others more deeply and realized that *difference* is only one aspect of a person.

At a third step, youth reported changes in thinking that affected how they interacted with members of other groups. The insights gained in step two seemed to facilitate youth being considerate of differences that had once impeded genuine interaction. A student at Youth Action stated, "I'm a lot more sensitive to issues that affect people than before. I didn't really understand, but now I want to understand why certain people feel this way." This sensitivity was related to changes in their behavior. An FFA member recounted how the level of respect across cliques had risen to the point that, on a weekend trip, they found themselves all hanging out together in one person's hotel room, "Usually we split up, but we were all in the room laughing. It was weird. You just learn to respect people's different ways." Program members also learned to curtail comments that would be hurtful to others. Latasha at Youth Action reported:

> The program has showed me to be sensitive to this boy that had a sex change. I used to make fun of him at school like all the other kids do. We had a speaker [talk] to us about queer people. They told us [to] put ourselves in their shoes. I didn't like the feeling of it, so I decided to change and I started talking to him.

The developmental process entailed in these three steps of bridging difference was not always easy. When confronted with differences, youth often struggled, resisted, or denied that they had anything to learn. The adult leaders of the programs worked hard to provide conditions for positive intergroup interactions. These conditions were closely similar to those cited in the research on facilitating relationships between cultural groups: equal status, cooperative interaction, individualized contact across groups, and support from the adults in the setting (Allport, 1954; National Research Council, 2000). In this environment, youth struggled, but many actively and intentionally engaged in interactions, made discoveries about different groups, and changed how they thought about and behaved toward youth who were different in some way. The sequence of three steps, and the role of programs in facilitating them, is encapsulated in the description from a Latino youth, Miguel:

> Youth Action's a cool place to come to. A lot of ethnic groups come together and you meet a lot of people. Like certain people you're going to like, certain people you're not going to like, so you always come together on a certain issue. You might not like them, but when it comes to [reforming] school, you come together. And it opens up the way you think about other people and your skills, the way you talk, your shyness, everything, like it kind of goes away. It starts fading and you make like a better person of yourself.

Process 5: Newfound Responsibility

If you ask youth what they must gain to be adults, becoming responsible is one of the primary qualities they mention (Arnett, 2000). Indeed, evidence suggests that the development of responsible behavior is strongly related to success and satisfaction across the spheres of adult life, from family to work; for example, an employee's level of conscientiousness is found to be the personality trait most predictive of work outcomes after general intelligence (Barrick & Mount, 1991; Judge, Heller, & Mount, 2002). All three of the programs we studied turned over major task responsibility to youth, and in all three many participants reported a process of coming to feel and act more responsible as a result of this experience.

Compared to adolescents in other cultures, Western youth are rarely in situations where their performance impacts people other than themselves (Schlegel & Barry, 1991). But the three programs we studied were an exception. At the Clarkston FFA, youth took responsibility as members of work groups preparing for the competitions and service projects. At Art-First, youth had duties at their internship. At Youth Action, members took responsibility for facilitating workshops and conducting research to be used for meetings with school administrators. Sometimes youth volunteered for these tasks, and sometimes they were recruited into them by the adult leaders. Often their desire to perform well for the adult leader made them take the task more seriously, as expressed by a student at Youth Action: "That is like another responsibility; I did not want to disappoint Jason."

Our data suggested that the development of responsibility from these demands (as with bridging difference) can be described as a three-stage process. The first stage was characterized by youth's taking on a task and being surprised in their capacity to be successful in meeting its demands. At the beginning, they often reported feeling nervous or anxious that the task might be beyond their capabilities. A girl in Youth Action, who had been assigned to lead a group discussion, said, "It's scary to think that I should take over. What do I do? I'm still a little [scared], although I try, and then Jason said he'll help me." Therefore, when youth later executed the tasks successfully, they were often impressed by what they had accomplished. For example, after setting up a meeting and giving a presentation to an important public school official, Gabriella, at Youth Action, reported:

> I didn't know that I was capable of doing some of the activities we do here, like setting up meetings with the Board of Education. That's big, you know? I have never been a part of anything like that.

For this girl and others in this situation, there was a sense of surprise and pride that they were able to accomplish what they did.

Over time, the students' continued successes in taking responsibility for tasks were less likely to elicit surprise, and they entered a second stage where they came to see their success as indicative of a stable characteristic of how they are when they are in the program. In other words, they experienced an emerging responsible self that was specific to the program—it described their role identity inside the program but was distinct from their general way of seeing themselves (Wood & Roberts, 2003). This stage was more evident among youth who had been in the program over several years. Jeff, a student leader at the Clarkston FFA, illustrated this stage when he stated:

> I'm more disciplined here. A lot of my friends outside FFA seem to get kinda wild sometimes. And, of course, I have to go with 'em. [But] I'd have to say I work harder when I'm in the program.

At this stage, acting responsibly becomes a mode of behavior that youth are comfortable turning on when they are involved with the program but may not employ in other parts of their lives.

The third stage involved generalizing responsibility to other domains. Jeff experienced his responsible behavior carrying over to how he acted at his job, and he anticipated his qualities in the program would eventually be integrated into his general character. After admitting that he was "kinda wild" with his friends, the interviewer asked him which "self" he would be most like in 6 or 10 years. Jeff responded, "I'll probably be more like the FFA [self]. Slowed down and more responsible." In a similar vein, an Art-First youth reported feeling "older" as a result of what he had accomplished there. And a student at Youth Action reported that, although he used to really want to have his own car, his new sense of being responsible, gained through the program, had led him to see saving for college as more important. As a result of repeatedly succeeding in tasks that required responsibility, these youth had come to internalize a general sense of themselves as responsible.

This three-stage developmental process evolved through an interaction between the youth's commitment to the goals of the programs and the support they received from the adult leaders and other youth. Roberts and Wood (in press) show how people's bonds to social institutions facilitate, encourage, and demand development of self-control. Thus, the youth reported that they acted responsibly partly because they did not want to let their peers or the adult leaders down. At the same time, their motivation and capacity to act responsibly was nurtured and directed by the adult leaders. As discussed in the next section, the adult leaders guided youth into tasks they could handle. In some cases, the leader of Youth Action described pairing youth with an older group member who could provide mentoring and support. Thus, although it was the youth who made the discovery that they were capable of acting responsibly, the adult leaders often played a role in shaping conditions for these discoveries to be made.

CREATING CONDITIONS FOR POSITIVE DEVELOPMENT: THE ROLE OF ADULT LEADERS

When we turn to examining the role of adult leaders in supporting these developmental processes, we observed what could be seen as a paradox. Across the five domains of development, youth described themselves as the agents of their own development. They learned about difference through an active process of interacting with others and then reformulating their beliefs and behavior. They came to view themselves as responsible through a process of self-discovery. Yet, at the same time, it is apparent from our data that the adult leaders were active and intentional in creating the conditions to support these processes of youth-driven change. Indeed, we found that when adult leaders backed off and gave youth complete control, the youth's work could stall or become disorganized due to the youth's inexperience, which could then undermine their motivation and learning (Larson, Hansen, et al., in press; see also Camino, 2000). The paradox, then, is that if adult leaders completely stand back, learning can get off track, but if adult leaders take over control, youth will not experience the ownership and agency that drives the developmental changes we have described.

The adult leaders of these three programs, we found, were highly skilled at avoiding the horns of this paradox: balancing youth agency and adult direction. Our data suggest that the adults employed a set of techniques to cultivate youth ownership *at the same time* they were providing guidance and structure to help keep things on track. Elsewhere we described how the two Clarkston FFA advisors used several techniques to maintain this balance in ways that supported development of initiative (Larson, Hansen, et al., in press). Here we describe how the adult leaders used these same and other techniques to sustain this balance in ways that facilitated a wider range of developmental experiences. To provide focus, we give primary attention to how these techniques were used by Jason Massad, the Youth Action leader.

TECHNIQUE 1: FOLLOWING YOUTH'S LEAD

A first technique involved supporting goals and directions that the youth set for the program's activities. At Youth Action, Jason expected the youth to determine what their next action would be. It was the youth who decided to hold a Youth Summit, and, afterwards, to plan a rally to protest a new citywide high school exam. Jason provided support activities to help youth prepare for these events—typing handouts, providing transportation, and coaching several members on how to give a presentation. But he insisted that ownership and "the creative work" for executing these events remain in the hands of the youth. The Clarkston FFA advisors demonstrated the same strategy of following youth's lead (Larson, Hansen, et al., in press).

By reinforcing youth ownership, this technique reinforced youth's role as active agents of their development. Because youth had set the goals for Youth Action, they experienced the challenges of the work as their own; thus, they had to generate solutions to these challenges. As described previously, it was through the process of generating these solutions that teens developed initiative skills. Because youth set the direction, they also owned the mistakes, which induced the process of reflecting on what to do better the next time. After the Youth Summit, the students in Youth Action articulated a catalog of things they did right and things they would do differently for their next event.

Following youth's lead is not easy for many adult leaders because it requires a great deal of forbearance and adaptability. At the last minute, for example, the youth decided to completely redesign one of their Youth Summit workshops. Jason emphasized, however, that for a program to be youth-driven, it was important that he be comfortable with loose ends and teenage spontaneity: "Like if they wanna wing parts of it, they can wing parts of it, and they'll learn from that." He was clear that it was the process, not the product, that was important. By having their goals and directions supported, youth in these programs were more likely to engage in the developmental processes of learning initiative, internalizing responsibility, and other growth experiences.

TECHNIQUE 2: CULTIVATING A CULTURE OF YOUTH INPUT

Another technique used by Jason and other adult leaders involved cultivating norms that emphasized youth input and leadership. All of the organizations we studied had a distinct culture, passed on across cohorts, and from the first day that youth walked in the door, they learned expectations, aphorisms, and norms that reinforced their role in providing input. At Youth Action, this culture included expectations that youth direct events and that their voices be expressed (e.g., through doing raps or reading poetry at events). The strength of this culture was demonstrated when the youth were working with a woman from another organization who expected the youth to follow a plan she had developed. In Jason's words:

> She just kind of came in with like, "We have expertise on this issue, we can like provide you with this information, we'll do this for you." And my youth were like, "We've been researching this all summer, we have the information we need, we just want your support."

The adult-directed approach of this woman did not fit the Youth Action culture, and the youth firmly rejected it.

The adult leaders of the programs helped cultivate these cultures in ways that encouraged not only youth ownership but also the responsibilities that go with this ownership. The culture at FFA included structured leadership roles (president, secretary, etc.), along with a history of expectations that individuals in those roles took on. These organizational cultures, then, legitimized youth leadership while providing norms for how it is exercised. They created demand conditions for youth to learn responsibility. Thus, these cultures stressed youth input, but they were also a vehicle through which adults supported a climate for youth-driven learning experiences.

TECHNIQUE 3: MONITORING

While the first two techniques were often directed at encouraging the ownership part of the adult leaders' balancing act, other techniques were directed more at keeping youth on track. Monitoring involved ongoing attentiveness to how the work of the group was proceeding, and intervening as needed. Adult leaders made ongoing decisions about how much they could let youth wing it and when they needed to provide guidance or intervene in some way because the costs of letting things get off course were too great. Jason had a laid-back approach and provided the youth with many opportunities to drive the work, but if they let things lag, he would speak up:

> Like Tuesday, they wanted to goof around (laughs) and I was like, "You guys, we gotta get serious, we have two weeks left before this Youth Summit, we're gonna have hundreds of people coming." But it's okay, they're youth. My role is to make sure that we're serious when we need to be.

When Jason felt things needed to be brought back on track, he would do it. He made many phone calls to check in with youth to make sure they were present at key meetings. If something was not done, he would sometimes do it himself so that the overall momentum was not stopped due to some critical missing piece.

For adult leaders, deciding when to intervene and play this role can be difficult. Adult leaders debate among themselves when they should let youth fail versus rescuing them to ensure the success of an activity (Zeldin & Camino, 1999). An important concern is that when adults step in too assertively, it can undermine youth ownership (Soep, 1997). Jason's interventions, however, were carefully oriented to encourage rather than undercut the work and the goals of the youth. One teen, Aisha, said Jason was:

> Always making sure that you had your plan out just 110%, like know that this is exactly what you were going to do; go for step A and then go for step B. He always made sure that it made sense, like if you had a problem with getting a situation, "Okay, I can see how I can do this."

In a sense, Jason was holding up a mirror to help students see their work better and see what needed to be done. Through monitoring the progress of youth's work and intervening as he saw fit, he and the other expert adult leaders not only kept youth on track but, by doing so in discreet ways, helped reinforce youth ownership (Larson, Hansen, et al., in press).

TECHNIQUE 4: CREATING INTERMEDIATE STRUCTURES

At a higher level of intervention, the adult leaders sometimes structured or reconfigured tasks to make them more manageable for youth. They created structures that helped fit tasks to what they perceived to be the youth's abilities. Thus, Jason would often prepare a calendar that organized the group's preparations for an event or write out the shell of a script for a student conducting a meeting. When Youth Action members met with several other groups, one of the adult leaders came prepared with a set of flip charts that gave the agenda for the meeting and had empty boxes for decisions that the youth needed to make. Although the students might have been able to create the agenda on their own, the adult's structure permitted them to spend the meeting time focused on concrete planning. This kind of adult structuring was most common at Art-First, where, for example, the adult leader carried out the negotiations with the city transit authority to get approval for doing the murals. Although some practitioners might have chosen to include youth in this process, the Art-First leader felt that the complexity of these negotiations and the limited patience of the city required that she handle it. This prior work allowed her to be able to present a defined and manageable task to the youth on the first day of the program.

Accurately gauging what youth can and cannot do requires experience, and many leaders either overestimate or underestimate youth's capabilities (Zeldin & Camino, 1999). In certain situations, the introduction of an appropriate level of structure appeared to be necessary to allow youth to keep the work from breaking down (Larson, Hansen, et al., in press). Using Csikszentmihalyi's model, adult leaders used this technique to define challenges that were matched to youth's skills and, hence, create conditions for sustained intrinsic motivation.

TECHNIQUE 5: STRETCHING AND PUSHING YOUTH

But the adult leaders did not just match tasks to youth's abilities; they often encouraged, provoked, and pushed the youth to try out new roles and ideas. They nudged youth to go beyond their comfort zones. This included taking on not only new levels of responsibility, as discussed previously, but also new topics. For example, when Youth Action initiated a campaign for comprehensive sexual education in the schools, Jason invited a gay man to talk with the youth about being gay, an opportunity that most of the youth had never had. Many members described this encounter as eye-opening and as a stimulus for changes in the domain of "bridging difference." This pushing was adapted to what the leaders felt youth could handle. Jason recognized that sometimes he pushes too much, and the youth might not be ready for that level of responsibility:

> Maybe they weren't ready to do something, you know, and they needed more talent or skill development. Part of it is being able to read people and knowing when to say, "Will you do this?" and they're like, "No, I don't wanna do that," and is it that they really don't wanna do it, or do they just need that push?

Jason reported that he periodically steps back and asks, "Okay, what are people's just everyday human needs?" In sum, these attempts at stretching were created and adjusted in ways that encouraged youth to make new discoveries but without overwhelming them.

THE ART OF PRACTITIONERS

Adult leaders' challenge of balancing youth ownership with guidance and support is not easy. As in other service fields, practitioners face the challenge of reconciling the conflicting professional inclinations to do what their expertise says people need versus empowering them to engage in self-change (Rappaport, 1981). In programs with youth, this means finding a balance between being the adult, who knows more and can do things more expeditiously, and relating to young people as partners—who are likely to be more motivated and learn more when they experience agency. Faced with this choice, the typical tendency is for adults to place greater emphasis on control—on keeping things on track—rather than allowing youth input and ownership (Camino, 2000).

But what was evident from these three programs was that keeping things on track and youth ownership are not inevitably at odds. Jason Massad, as well as the adult leaders of the Clarkston FFA and Art-First, had developed skills for balancing the two. They supported youth ownership in ways that reinforced youth responsibility. When they created structures or intervened to keep things on track, they did so in ways that often shored up rather than undercut youth ownership. From week to week, they would deploy one technique or another, as they felt necessary, to maintain or restore the balance. In effect, they were helping create a channel for youth's exercise of agency—and thus youth's sense of ownership—that was within the youth's capabilities. In Vygotsky's theory, they were providing scaffolding that helped keep youth within their "zone of proximal development" (i.e., within a level of learning matched to their abilities). In Csikszentmihalyi's theory, they were helping create conditions in which the challenges were matched to youth's skills, conditions in which youth could experience self-sustaining intrinsic motivation in the process of learning.

It was our observation that what adult leaders did was more art than a science. Their balancing act was not achieved by prescription, but by responding improvisationally to the ongoing situation. Expert practitioners learn from experience, build from their own personal strengths, and are responsive to the context and conditions at hand (Larson, Hansen, et al., in press; Walker, Marczak, Blyth, & Bordon, in press). It should also be recognized that different balances of youth ownership and adult intervention may be appropriate for programs with different developmental goals, in different situations, and for different groups of youth. As compared to the Clarkston FFA and Youth Action, Art-First and a theater production we studied recently had a greater balance of adult direction relative to youth ownership, a balance that was better suited to their emphasis on talent development (Larson, Walker, & Pierce, in press). It should also be recognized that we have presented only one of the many balancing acts that the adult leaders performed. They play diverse roles for youth—as mentors, teachers, parents, and friends—thus, their improvisation includes trying to juggle many types of, sometimes competing, goals and imperatives.

CONCLUSION

Human development involves a process of dialectic interaction between the environment and the developing person. A distinctive feature of youth programs is that they provide environments characterized by the types of constraints and contingencies that are typical of adult worlds (Heath, 1998; Larson, 2000). Youth in the three programs we studied confronted the sort of obstacles and challenges people must overcome to reach long-term goals. They were subject to the norms of adult professional worlds (e.g., in their arts internships and dealing with school officials), they encountered the realities of ethnic differences, and they encountered the weight and duties of responsibility to others. These were contexts in which actions mattered.

The important finding of our research was that the youth responded to these environments as active agents in the dialectic process. They made choices, pursued goals, and changed how they thought about and acted on the world. They were active producers of their own development across multiple domains of learning. They responded to obstacles and challenges by developing insights that allowed them to better reach goals. They actively drew on adults to develop knowledge and find their way in adult career worlds. Through collaborative interactions with youth from different backgrounds, they gained understanding and learned modes of communication for bridging these differences. And through successful experiences in taking on responsibility, they progressively changed their self-concepts to that of being responsible persons. Organized youth programs, our data suggest, can be a fertile context for active processes of positive development in multiple domains.

Effective adult leaders, we have seen, are active as well and play important roles in facilitating this dialectic process. On the one hand, they are representatives of the adult world. They translate, help articulate constraints, or intervene to keep youth's engagement on track. On the other hand, they support youth's ownership of their work in ways that facilitate youth's active processes of development.

In further work, we plan to study additional programs to better test, confirm, revise, and expand the descriptions of processes we have described here. Research using other methods will ultimately be important to filling out and providing fuller evaluation for these findings. Important tasks for the future include understanding how young people's self-selection into programs influences the patterns seen here and evaluating how these processes vary across contexts, types of adult leaders, and the full array of organized youth programs. We are hopeful that information on the processes of development in this context will provide knowledge to better design youth programs and better train youth practitioners so that more youth will be prepared to be psychologically versatile and vibrant adults who make positive contributions to society.

REFERENCES

Allport, G. (1954). *The nature of prejudice.* Cambridge, MA: Addison-Wesley.

Arnett, J. (2000). Emerging adulthood: A theory of development from the late teens through the twenties. *American Psychologist, 55,* 469–480.

Barrick, M. R., & Mount, M. K. (1991). The Big Five personality dimensions and job performance: A meta-analysis. *Personnel Psychology, 44,* 1–26.

Benson, P. L. (1997). *All kids are our kids: What communities must do to raise caring and responsible children and adolescents.* San Francisco: Jossey-Bass.

Brubaker, R., & Laitin, D. (1998). Ethnic and nationalist violence. *Annual Review of Sociology, 24,* 423–452.

Camino, L. A. (2000). Youth-adult partnerships: Entering new territory in community work and research. *Applied Developmental Science, 4,* 11–20.

Charmaz, K. (1983). The grounded theory method: An explication and interpretation. In R. Emerson (Ed.), *Contemporary field research* (pp. 109–126). Prospect Heights, IL: Waveland Press.

Csikszentmihalyi, M. (1975). *Beyond boredom and anxiety: The experience of play in work and games.* San Francisco: Jossey-Bass.

Csikszentmihalyi, M. (1990). *Flow: The psychology of optimal experience.* New York: HarperCollins.

Csikszentmihalyi, M., Rathunde, K., & Whalen, S. (1993). *Talented teenagers: The roots of success and failure.* Cambridge, England: Cambridge University Press.

Dworkin, J., Larson, R., & Hansen, D. (2003). Adolescents' accounts of growth experiences in youth activities. *Journal of Youth and Adolescence, 32,* 17–26.

Eccles, J. S., & Barber, B. L. (1999). Student council, volunteering, basketball, or marching band: What kind of extracurricular involvement matters? *Journal of Adolescent Research, 14,* 10–43.

*Eccles, J. S., & Templeton, J. (2002). Extracurricular and other after-school activities for youth. In W. S. Secada (Ed.), *Review of educational research* (Vol. 26, pp. 113–180). Washington, DC: American Educational Research Association Press.

Gauvain, M., & Perez, S. (in press). Not all hurried children are the same: Children's participation in planning their after-school activities. In J. E. Jacobs & P. Klaczynski (Eds.), *The development of judgment and decision-making in children and adolescents.* Mahwah, NJ: Erlbaum.

Glancy, M., Willits, F., & Farrell, P. (1986). Adolescent activities and adult success and happiness: Twenty-four years later. *Sociology and Social Research, 70,* 242–250.

Glaser, B., & Strauss, A. (1967). *The discovery of grounded theory.* Chicago: Aldine.

Gollwitzer, P. M. (1999). Implementation intentions: Strong effects of simple plans. *American Psychologist, 54,* 493–503.

Hanks, M., & Eckland, B. (1978). Adult voluntary associations and adolescent socialization. *Sociological Quarterly, 19,* 481–490.

*Hansen, D., Larson, R., & Dworkin, J. (2003). What adolescents learn in organized youth activities: A survey of self-reported developmental experiences. *Journal of Research on Adolescence, 13,* 25–56.

Heath, S. B. (1998). Working through language. In S. M. Hoyle & C. T. Adger (Eds.), *Kids talk: Strategic language use in later childhood* (pp. 217–240). New York: Oxford University Press.

Heath, S. B. (1999). Dimensions of language development: Lessons from older children. In A. S. Masten (Ed.), *Cultural processes in child development: The Minnesota Symposium on Child Psychology* (Vol. 29, pp. 59–75). Mahwah, NJ: Erlbaum.

Judge, T. A., Heller, D., & Mount, M. K. (2002). Five-factor model of personality and job satisfaction: A meta-analysis. *Journal of Applied Psychology, 87,* 530–541.

Kleiber, D., Larson, R., & Csikszentmihalyi, M. (1986). The experience of leisure in adolescence. *Journal of Leisure Research, 18,* 169–176.

Larson, R. (2000). Toward a psychology of positive youth development. *American Psychologist, 55,* 170–183.

*Larson, R. (2002). Globalization, societal change, and new technologies: What they mean for the future of adolescence. *Journal of Research on Adolescence, 12,* 1–30.

Larson, R., Hansen, D., & Walker, K. (in press). Everybody's gotta give: Adolescents' development of initiative within a youth program. In J. Mahoney, R. Larson, & J. Eccles (Eds.), *Organized activities as contexts of development: Extracurricular activities, after-school and community programs.* Mahwah, NJ: Erlbaum.

Larson, R., & Richards, M. (1991). Boredom in the middle school years: Blaming schools versus blaming students. *American Journal of Education, 91,* 418–443.

Larson, R., Walker, K., & Pierce, N. (in press). A comparison of high quality youth-led and adult-led youth programs: Balancing inputs from youth and adults. *Journal of Community Psychology.*

Larson, R., Wilson, S., Brown, B. B., Furstenberg, F. F., & Verma, S. (2002). Changes in adolescents' interpersonal experiences: Are they being prepared for adult relationships in the twenty-first century? *Journal of Research on Adolescence, 12,* 31–68.

Mahoney, J. (2000). School extracurricular activity participation as a moderator in the development of antisocial patterns. *Child Development, 71,* 502–516.

Marsh, H. (1992). Extracurricular activities: Beneficial extension of the traditional curriculum or subversion of academic goals? *Journal of Educational Psychology, 84,* 553–562.

Marsh, H., & Kleitman, S. (2002). Extracurricular school activities: The good, the bad, and the nonlinear. *Harvard Educational Review, 72,* 464–511.

Mascolo, M., Fisher, K., & Neimeyer, R. (1999). The dynamic codevelopment of intentionality, self, and social relations. In J. Brandstädter & R. M. Lerner (Eds.), *Action and self-development: Theory and research through the life span* (pp. 133–166). Thousand Oaks, CA: Sage.

National Research Council. (2000). *Improving intergroup relations among youth.* Washington, DC: National Academy Press.

*National Research Council and Institute of Medicine. (2002). *Community programs to promote youth development.* Washington, DC: National Academy Press.

Parker, W. C., Ninomiya, A., & Cogan, J. (1999). Educating world citizens: Toward multinational curriculum development. *American Educational Research Journal, 36,* 117–146.

Putnam, R. D. (2000). *Bowling alone: The collapse and revival of American community.* New York: Simon & Schuster.

QSR International. (2001). *NVivo for Microsoft Windows.* Melbourne, Australia: Author.

Rappaport, J. (1981). In praise of paradox: A social policy of empowerment over prevention. *American Journal of Community Psychology, 9,* 1–25.

Roberts, B. W., & Wood, D. (in press). The cumulative continuity model of personality trait development. In D. Mroczek & T. Little (Eds.), *Handbook of personality development.* Mahwah, NJ: Erlbaum.

Schlegel, A., & Barry, H. (1991). *Adolescence: An anthropological inquiry.* New York: Free Press.

Soep, E. (1997). Walking on water and knocking on doors. *New Designs for Youth Development, 13,* 32–35.

Southern Poverty Law Center. (2000). Hate goes to school. *Intelligence report* [online]. Retrieved from www.SPLCENTER.org.

Strauss, A., & Corbin, J. (1998). *Basics of qualitative research: Techniques and procedures for developing grounded theory* (2nd ed.). Thousand Oaks, CA: Sage.

Taylor, S. J., & Bogdan, R. (1998). *Introduction to qualitative research methods: A guidebook and resource* (3rd ed.). New York: Wiley.

Walker, J., Marczak, M., Blyth, D., & Bordon, L. (in press). Designing youth development programs: Toward a theory of developmental intentionality. In J. Mahoney, R. Larson, & J. Eccles (Eds.), *Organized activities as contexts of development: Extracurricular activities, after-school and community programs.* Mahwah, NJ: Erlbaum.

Watkins, N. D. (2003, June). *Bridging difference in a rural youth program: Hicks and outsiders.* Poster presented at the Society for Community Research and Action, Las Vegas, New Mexico.

Wood, D., & Roberts, B. (2003). *Cross-sectional and longitudinal tests of the personality and role identity structural model (PRISM).* Unpublished manuscript, University of Illinois, Urbana-Champaign.

Youniss, J., Bales, S., Christmas-Best, V., Diversi, M., McLaughlin, M., & Silbereisen, R. (2002). Youth civic engagement in the twenty-first century. *Journal of Research on Adolescence, 12,* 121–148.

Youniss, J., & Ruth, A. (2002). Approaching policy for adolescent development in the twenty-first century. In J. Mortimer & R. Larson (Eds.), *The changing adolescent experience: Societal trends and the transition to adulthood* (pp. 250–271). New York: Cambridge University Press.

Zeldin, S., & Camino, L. (1999). Youth leadership: Linking research and program theory to exemplary practice. *New Designs for Youth Development, 15,* 10–15.

CHAPTER 34

Positive Aging

GEORGE E. VAILLANT

ALFRED PAINE WAS a model of the Sad-Sick. True, he did not acknowledge either his alcoholism or his depression. Like Pollyanna, Voltaire's Dr. Pangloss, and *Mad Magazine's* Alfred E. Neuman, Paine was a master of denial. On pencil-and-paper tests of neuroticism, he scored very low on the depression subscale. On questionnaires, he described himself as close to his children and in good physical health. Thus, it was only by interviewing him personally, talking with his wife, examining his objective medical record, reading the disappointed questionnaires from his children—and then, finally, by reading his obituary—that Alfred Paine's misery could be fully appreciated. The uncomplaining nature of Paine's written replies did not alter the fact that his life story had always been terribly sad.

On the other hand, Richard Luckey was a well-loved child who took excellent care of himself, but unlike Alfred Paine, Luckey had come from more modest beginnings. None of his four grandparents had gone beyond grade school. One grandfather had been a police officer and the other a self-made owner of a large baking company. His father graduated from high school and went on to become a successful businessman, so Richard Luckey, like Alfred Paine, had gone to an excellent boarding school. After college, Luckey became head of two successful businesses (one of which he created)—at the same time. Always careful to take care of himself, Luckey married well. Unlike Paine, he knew how to take care of his money, how to appreciate his wife, and how to make his own luck. More on these two characters later.

As we contemplate surviving until old age, a common worry is that we will spend decades helpless and/or in pain. We forget to look at the positive. Our problem is that there have been many longitudinal studies of physical longevity (e.g., Baltes & Mayer, 1999; Dawber, 1980; Fries, 1980; Rowe & Kahn, 1999) but very few studies that have examined psychological longevity.

The mission of positive aging is very clear: to add more life to years, not just more years to life. For example, we worry that impotence is an inevitable consequence of old age, but Simone de Beauvoir (1972) cheers us. She offers the hopeful example of an admittedly exceptional 88-year-old man. He reported intercourse with his 90-year-old wife one to four times a week. True, at 75 to 80, for most surviving husbands and wives in good health, the average is more likely to be once every 10 weeks (Bortz, Wallace, & Wiley, 1999).

To begin with, it is as profoundly misleading to look at the average old person as it is to look at the average 20-year-old car. Careful driving and maintenance are everything. Often, old cars evolve into cripples not because of aging but because of poor maintenance, poor driving, and misuse. So, too, with humans. Much of what we view as the inexorable decay of aging between ages 70 and 90 is a result of accident and disease. Proper maintenance is everything.

Eventually, the years take their toll, but an aging octogenarian can do almost everything a young person can do; it just takes a little longer and must begin a little earlier. Such limitations, however, did not impede Will Durant from winning the Pulitzer Prize for history at 83, or Frank Lloyd Wright from designing the Guggenheim Museum at 90, or 80-year-old marathoners being able to run 26 miles faster than 99% of 20-year-olds. While performing his daily routine of cello practice, the 91-year-old Pablo Casals was once asked by one of his students, "Master, why do you continue to practice?" Casals answered, "Because I am making progress" (Heimpel, 1981).

True, from age 30 on, nominal aphasia (our inability to remember names) steadily worsens, but this does not lead to Alzheimer's. Over time, we also become less adept at remembering spatial cues, so, by 80, we lose our cars in parking lots. But we remain just as adept at remembering emotionally nuanced events as we did when we were much younger; and in the healthy, a majority of facets of intelligence have not declined.

A major difficulty in studying positive aging is measurement. Good health, both psychological and physical, is a very real and very tangible boon. But the quantification of good health is by no means easy. Two men have colostomies; for one man, it is only a minor inconvenience; for the other, it is a devastating blow to self-image. Why? To understand positive aging, we need to be able to answer this question. Most observers can agree on illness. But as soon as positive health is raised, a multitude of voices, often quite heated voices, cry value judgment.

In this chapter, I try to measure successful aging by assessing health—physical health and psychosocial health, both subjective health and objective health. Only when all four facets of health are present will *good* health be declared. First, with the passage of time, progressively diminished physical reserves are an inevitable part of aging, but the rate at which these diminished reserves occur is variable. Biologically, you can be young or old for your chronological age. Second, physical health involves experiencing the biological ravages of age without feeling sick. Good self-care, high morale, intimate friends, mental health, and coping strategies often make the difference between being ill and feeling sick. Third, age and social class are important. To control for age, all the participants reported in this chapter have been studied for 60 years, and each participant's health was known at every age from 20 to 80. To control for social class, the health of two homogeneous cohorts at opposite ends of the social spectrum—a College cohort and an Inner-City cohort—was studied. Within-cohort differences and between-cohort similarities are those emphasized. Fourth, in 1948 the founders of the World Health Organization (WHO) defined health as "physical, mental and social well-being, not merely the absence of disease or infirmity" (WHO, 1952). Thus, measuring objective psychosocial health is more difficult than measuring physical health but an equally important task. At age 90, some people not only are active and still climb mountains but also are able to do so in good cheer and with close friends. That is even more desirable. Clearly, subjective mental health is as important to aging as are objective indicators. Healthy aging, then, is being both contented *and* vigorous as well as being not sad or sick or dead.

The College cohort included 268 Harvard University sophomores selected for physical and mental health c. 1940 (Vaillant, 1977). The socially disadvantaged Inner-City cohort included 456 nondelinquent schoolboys with a mean IQ of 95 and a mean education of 10 years (Glueck & Glueck, 1950, 1968). The details of the study have been well described in previous reports (Vaillant, 1995, 2002; Vaillant, Meyer, Mukamal, & Soldz, 1998).

To increase the chances of successful contrast and to minimize value judgment, the study, called the Study of Adult Development, focused on men at the ends of the health spectrum. In each cohort, I contrast the one-fourth of the men who lived out the past decade feeling the healthiest—the Happy-Well—with the one-half who spent most of the past decade either feeling both sad and sick or being dead. To reduce argument, I deliberately exclude the one man in four who fell somewhere in the gray zone of being either healthy or sick depending on the criteria chosen. In short, three-quarters of the men reflect black and white categories of aging—the Happy-Well, the Sad-Sick, and the Prematurely Dead—and one-quarter, the Intermediate group, are excluded (see Table 34.1).

Of 268 College men originally admitted to the study at about ages 19 to 20, 31 men (12%) died before age 50 or withdrew from the study. This left 237 College men. All men who died between 50 and 75 were classified as dead. The three-quarters who survived until 75 were classified *Happy-Well, Intermediate,* and *Sad-Sick* (see Table 34.1).

Of 456 Inner-City men originally admitted to the study at ages 12 to 16, 44 (10%) died by age 50 and 80 (17.5%) withdrew. This left 332 men in the study. Although they were 10 years younger than the College men, their objectively rated health (i.e., the proportion physically well, chronically ill, disabled, or dead) at 70 was the same as that of the College men at 80. Much of this variance came from

Table 34.1
Definition of Positive Aging

	College Age 80 N = 237		Inner-City Age 70 N = 332	
	N	%	*N*	%
Happy-Well	62	26	95	29
Intermediate	75	32	114	34
Sad-Sick	40	17	48	14
Prematurely Dead	60	25	75	23

Note: The Happy-Well, the Intermediate, and the Sad-Sick all survived until age 75 if College men and until age 65 if Inner-City men. However, at the time that the data for this chapter were analyzed, not all of the College men were quite 80 and not all of the Inner-City sample were quite 70.

differences in education, which, in turn, predicted obesity, cigarette and alcohol abuse, diabetes, and blood pressure. The variance did not depend on differences in parental social class per se. Part of the variance came from the fact that poor physical, and especially poor mental health, led to downward social mobility. Thus, adult social class is powerfully associated with physical health.

To differentiate the Happy-Well unambiguously from the Sad-Sick, I chose six contrasting dimensions of health. These measures are described in detail in Vaillant (2002) and Vaillant and Mukamal (2001):

1. *Absence of objective physical disability (at age 75 for College Cohort or at age 65 for Inner-City Cohort):* Every five years, the study sought from each College and Inner-City man a complete physical exam including chest x-rays, routine blood chemistries, urinalysis, and an electrocardiogram. A study internist, blind to psychosocial adjustment, then rated all of these physical examinations on a four-point scale (Vaillant, 1979). He rated the men as "1" if they were still without any irreversible illness and "2" if they were afflicted with an irreversible illness that was neither life shortening, nor disabling. Such illnesses might be mild glaucoma, treatable hypertension, or noncrippling arthritis. If in the judgment of the study internist, the College men suffered from an irreversible life-threatening illness, they were called a "3" or chronically ill. This category refers to illnesses that could be expected to be progressive and to shorten life or eventually to affect daily living, but which were not in the eyes of the study internist disabling. Examples of such illnesses are coronary thrombosis or diabetes or hypertension not fully controlled by medication.

Finally, the internist rated the men "4" if they suffered both irreversible illness and, in his judgment, significant disability. Examples are multiple sclerosis, chronic congestive heart failure, and disabling arthritis of the hip. Only this category "4" reflected unsuccessful aging. The men, after all, were 75 to 85 years old and could be expected to have some illnesses.

2. *Subjective physical health at age 75:* Since human beings are remarkably adaptable and suggestible, physical disability is in part subjective. When asked to rate their health subjectively, some depressed people may whine that their health is bad even when it is quite good, and some happy stoical people may boast that their health is excellent when in fact it is objectively poor. In public life, the severely physically ill John F. Kennedy and Franklin D. Roosevelt offer such examples. Still others were rated objectively *disabled* by their physicians and denied subjective disability not from stoicism and good cheer but by dissociating themselves from reality. The most common ailments of men and women who saw themselves as *disabled* but who were called *not* disabled by study physicians were arthritis and depression. Health is anything but black or white.

The rating for this second dimension of successful aging was subjective and was based on a 15-point scale of self-reported "Instrumental Activities of Daily Living" (Vaillant, 2002). The scale measured whether at 75 the men believed that they could still carry out most daily tasks as before. Such men reported that they still took part in activities such as tennis singles or downhill skiing or chopping wood. They could climb two flights of stairs without resting, carry their suitcases through airports, and walk two miles with their grandchildren although they might perform all of these tasks more slowly than in the past. Finally, they could still drive, care for the yard, travel, and shop without assistance.

3. *Length of undisabled life:* A third dimension of successful physical aging was how many years of living the men lost by subjective and/or by objective physical disability or from premature death. By definition, none of the Happy-Well had spent any time prior to age 80 disabled—either objectively or subjectively. By way of contrast, before age 80, the Prematurely Dead (those men dying between ages 50 and 75) had spent an average of 18 years either dead or disabled. Before age 80, the Sad-Sick had all spent at least 5 and an average of 9 years irreversibly disabled.

4. *Objective mental health (range 9 to 23):* There is not much fun in living to old age if you are unhappy, thus, this fourth dimension of successful aging was considered. At age 65, independent raters assessed the College and Inner-City men's objective global mental health with good interrater agreement (Vaillant & Vaillant, 1990). Good objective mental health reflected late midlife success in four areas: work, love, play, and avoiding psychiatric care. A "mentally healthy" man continued to grow in and to enjoy his career until long after 50. Over the past 15 years, his marriage through his eyes and those of his wife would have been clearly happy. He had played games with friends and taken enjoyable vacations. He neither consulted psychotherapists nor took psychiatric medicines. On average, he took less than five days of sick leave a year. A low score on any single item was still consistent with excellent mental health, but some men, often those with alcohol abuse or major depression before age 50, fared badly in most or all areas and, therefore, fell into the bottom quartile (range 15 to 23). By definition, none of the Happy-Well and a majority of the Sad-Sick fell in the bottom quarter of mental health.

5. *Objective social supports (range 2.5 [best] to 14.0 [worst]):* Social supports are a crucial dimension of healthy aging. Good social supports were defined as being closely connected with wives, children, siblings, playmates (e.g., bridge and golf), a religious group, social networks (e.g., clubs and civic organizations), and confidantes. Two independent raters made these judgments by reviewing at least 10 questionnaires—including those from wives and children—and usually at least one 2-hour interview (Vaillant et al., 1998). This variable was not available for the Inner-City sample. A score of 10.5 to 14.0 reflected social supports in the worst quartile.

6. *Subjective life satisfaction (range 10 to 40):* The study developed a scale to quantify joy—a subjective life satisfaction scale to measure this sixth dimension of healthy aging. Nine facets of life were assessed on two consecutive questionnaires. Each item was rated over the past *20 years* as to how the men regarded their marriage, for example, as highly satisfying (2.0 points), generally satisfying (1.5 points), somewhat satisfying (1.0 points), not very satisfying (0.5 points), not at all satisfying, or "does not apply to my life" (0 points). The same question was asked for income-producing work, children, friendships, hobbies, community service activities, religion, recreation, and other. The score was the total of the four underlined items plus the most satisfying score from the other five. To meet criteria for being among the Happy-Well on the last two biennial questionnaires, a study member needed to regard at least *two* of the five activities selected as "very satisfying" or have a total score of 7.0 or more.

Sometimes, evidence for enjoyment of life was utterly unambiguous. For example, as a means of describing his life, an Inner-City man marked four facets as "very satisfying." He marked three additional facets—friendship, social contacts, and recreation/sports—"very satisfying" with *two* checks. Among the nine facets, the only exception was his marriage. Here, rather than check an answer, he wrote, "hard to answer as I have been divorced a long time, but I have a super relationship with my ex-wife." He then ad-libbed, "I just love being with people and family and helping them when needed as well as traveling and having the health and enough money to be satisfied." Positive psychology happens.

A RESEARCH DEFINITION OF HEALTHY AGING

Each of the six dimensions of aging was significantly associated with all others—roughly as strongly as height correlates with weight. Of the 237 College men active in the study, 62 men were categorized as *Happy-Well*. These were men who had experienced, objectively *and* subjectively, biologically *and* psychologically good health in all six dimensions. Such Happy-Well men could be defined as follows: Before age 80, they spent no years physically disabled—either objectively or subjectively. In addition, compared to their peers in the study, their social supports were in the top three-quarters; their mental health was in the top three-quarters, and their life satisfaction was in the top two-thirds.

Forty of the 237 men were classified *Sad-Sick*. These were men who by age 80 had experienced at least five years of subjective or objective physical disability. In addition, all of these 40 Sad-Sick men were classified as psychosocially unhappy in at least one of the three psychosocial dimensions: mental health, social support, or life satisfaction.

Sixty of the 237 men died after age 50 and before age 75. They were classified as *Prematurely Dead*. We often think of death, especially premature death, as an act of God—a tumor striking down the innocent in the flower of youth. (This was one reason that the 12 deaths from the College sample before 50 were excluded: 6 men were killed in action in World War II and the others in freak accidents or from rare genetic illnesses.) There were other early deaths even more senseless and tragic, but these deaths were the exceptions. That is, before death, the 60 College men who died prematurely (i.e., after 50 and before age 75) were almost as psychosocially impaired as the surviving Sad-Sick men. Before death, all but 18 of these 60 men had suffered poor social supports or poor mental health or were dissatisfied with their lives.

I followed the same procedure for categorizing the health of the 332 participating Inner-City men who survived past 50 and for whom the study had complete records. In contrast to the College sample, half of the 44 early (i.e., before age 50) deaths were due to some form of self-neglect. At ages 65 to 70, there were 95 Happy-Well, 114 Intermediate, 48 Sad-Sick, and 75 Prematurely Dead by age 65. Although the proportions of Inner-City men in each outcome category were almost identical to the College men, it should be noted that the Inner-City men were 10 years younger.

CLINICAL EXAMPLES

I hope the life stories of Alfred Paine and Richard Luckey, who introduced this chapter, make my operational definitions of the Happy-Well and the Sad-Sick come alive, so that the concept of positive aging becomes more than mere platitude or value judgment. (Names and identifying details have been altered to protect anonymity.)

The ancestors of Alfred Paine had been successful New England clipper ship captains. All his grandparents had graduated from high school. One grandfather became a merchant banker, and the other, president of the New York Stock Exchange. His father had graduated from Harvard, and his mother, from a fashionable boarding school. From childhood on, however, Paine was the unlucky owner of a handsome trust fund—unlucky because of how he obtained it.

When Alfred Paine was only 2 weeks old, his mother died from the complications of childbirth. When he was only 2 years old, his father died, too. So it was that the orphaned Paine became an heir. As an only child, Paine was bottle-fed by a variety of surrogates and raised by his grandmother and aunt. They were old and did not enjoy the challenge of dealing with an energetic young boy who was also a head-banger. In adolescence, Paine was a lone wolf.

In college, Alfred Paine was often in love. But it appeared to the study staff that, for Paine, being in love meant having someone to care for him. His multiple marriages were all unhappy—in part, because of the alcoholism that he maintained that he did not have and, in part, because he was frightened of intimacy. At 50, Paine answered "true" to the statement, "Sexually most people are animals" and "I would have preferred an asexual marriage." But he did not complain. Thus, of his second marriage he could write, "I have doubts about the real value of marriage . . . the state of my own marriage, which is excellent, has nothing to do with my philosophizing." But his "excellent" marriage soon ended in divorce. Positive psychology must be assessed by what people do, not what they say. In old age, Paine's third wife was protective and loving toward him. In return, he was disrespectful and uncaring toward her. Before he died, I asked how Paine and his wife collaborated. He replied, "We don't. We lead parallel lives."

At 47, Alfred Paine recalled the ages from 1 to 13 as the unhappiest in his life. At age 70, Paine changed his story and believed that the ages from 20 to 30 were the unhappiest. But there had never been a time that Paine was happy. It was only that Paine, as I have suggested, was not a complainer. He had never sought psychotherapy, and none of his doctors ever called him mentally ill. Early on, however, his wife volunteered, "I wish he'd be analyzed not only for our sex life but for his ulcer and to give me someone to talk to."

Subjectively, Paine described his own physical health as excellent; objectively, his health was anything but. In fact, by age 68 he was seriously overweight, afflicted by hypertension and gout, and he suffered from obstructive pulmonary disease—the result of lifelong smoking. On paper, he could sound assertive. For example, in 1947, he favored a preventive war with Russia, "Let's go all out and get it done"; and during the Vietnam War, he was in favor of using hydrogen bombs. But his occupational life documented his real life timidity. "Security was the brightest part of my job," he confided. "I haven't the guts to go out on my own as a man of the world."

When I interviewed Paine at 73, he appeared to me like an old man in a nursing home. Both his kidneys and his liver were failing; and he was cursed with a mild dementia, the result of a drunken automobile accident. He was at least 30 pounds overweight and looked 10 years older than his age. There was no question that he was physically disabled. He was the only College man in the study to have lost all his teeth.

Although he had made a good living in middle management over the years, Paine's handsome trust fund had evaporated; and his pension had eroded through multiple divorces and tax troubles. His house looked as if furnished from yard sales. The only exception was the elegant Cantonese porcelain umbrella stand that stood guard by the front door, in mute testimony to the fact that his New England ancestors had waxed rich in the China clipper trade. Little other than television now absorbed Paine. He rarely left his sofa. At no time in his life had he ever had hobbies or learned to play.

Alone of all the men who returned the age 75 questionnaire, Paine refused to answer the part that dealt with life enjoyment. Thus, his unacknowledged lack of joy in life could be inferred from his behavior. Over the past 20 years, there was no area of his life, other than his religious activities, in which he had expressed satisfaction. Admittedly, in questionnaires, he said nice things about his children, but during the interview when I asked him what he had learned from them, he responded irritably, "Nothing. I hardly see my children. They hardly let me see my grandchildren." Turning to questionnaires from his children, one daughter saw him only every three years; one daughter saw him once a year and viewed her father as having "lived an emotionally starved life," and at age 35, Alfred Paine's only son believed that he had never been close to his father.

In terms of social supports, Paine, orphaned at 2, had no siblings, and he was close to no relative. Since the age of 50, he had engaged in no pastimes with friends. When I asked him at 73 to describe his oldest friend, he growled, "I don't have any." He rarely talked to anybody on the telephone. His only confidante was, occasionally, his wife.

Only Paine's religious affiliation was strong. He was proud that he was a committed Episcopalian, and he went on religious retreats, which brought him real satisfaction. Sadly, although these retreats reflected the only social network he possessed, after age 72 he could no longer afford to go on them. Paine could not care for his teeth, his money, or his soul.

At age 73, Paine could climb stairs only with difficulty. He had great difficulty walking even 100 yards; he was unable to drive at night, and he had to give up golf because of his gout. On his last questionnaire, in a shaky hand, Paine, age 75, referred to his general health as "very good" and reported that he had no difficulty in physical activities. Both his wife and his doctor, however, saw him as seriously impaired. The very next year, Paine was placed in a nursing home; a year later, he died from his multiple illnesses. (For research purposes, Paine was classified with the Sad-Sick rather than with the Prematurely Dead because he survived past his 75th birthday.)

Having followed the easy path and described negative aging, I next describe positive aging. Richard Luckey tells a different story. At 70, when looked at through the eyes of their internists, Richard Luckey's objective physical health had seemed actually worse than Alfred Paine's. Luckey had high blood pressure, atrial fibrillation, a cardiac pacemaker, pancreatitis, and was "status post-back surgery." He was even more overweight than Paine. On the basis of all this, the study internist classified the 70-year-old Luckey disabled. But being ill is very different from feeling sick. Truth is revealed through follow-up.

From age 70 to 80, Paine sickened unto death, while Luckey's health only got better. Luckey not only said his health was excellent but, by age 75, his objective health could no longer be classified by the study internist as disabling. Luckey had completely recovered from his pancreatitis. His "status post-back surgery"—which loomed so ominously to the study internist when Luckey was 70—turned out to have been 30 years in the past. Indeed, at age 76, Luckey spent two months downhill skiing in Vail. True, he still wore a pacemaker, and, true, his blood pressure remained high. But in his doctor's words—not just his own—"Mr. Luckey continues to enjoy relatively good health . . . he continues to be active physically and also mentally. He is now writing a book on the Civil War." As Luckey himself expressed it, "I have done less chain sawing, but I still split wood."

Another crucial difference between Paine and Luckey was that Luckey had friends with whom he exercised regularly. In addition, he had never smoked, and he used alcohol in moderation. But, as the song suggests, it is easier to "button up your overcoat" and "take good care of yourself" if you belong to someone, and Luckey had always enjoyed social supports. At the risk of oversimplification, Richard Luckey's mother had loved him as a child; and a half century later, "Almost everything we do," he trumpeted, "is family oriented. We have practically no social calendar." His wife amplified, "We rarely go out, but we will have groups for supper such as the church fellowship group or the basketball team for a weekend of skiing or a vestry meeting at the house." Without a social calendar, Luckey was also commodore of his distinguished West Coast yacht club. Actions speak louder than pencil-and-paper questionnaires—a fact that future research workers in positive psychology must learn to embrace.

In its efforts to define positive aging, the study asked each man to describe his relative satisfaction over the past 20 years with eight different facets of living. Remember, Alfred Paine had chosen to leave that part of his biennial questionnaire blank. In contrast, Richard Luckey described not only his hobbies, his religion, and his income-producing work as "very satisfying," but, more important, he experienced his relationships with his wife and with his children as "very satisfying." His wife and children's questionnaires revealed a similar satisfaction with him. Luckey's daughter had described her parents' marriage as "better than my friends"; then, for good measure, she had added two pluses. Luckey's wife gave her marriage a "9" out of "9" and, clearly, the marriage had worked even better for her husband. Luckey was close to his brother with whom he skied regularly in the winter and fished regularly in the summer. He stayed in very close touch with, and took great pleasure from, his children and grandchildren. His recreational activities included active involvement not only with his brother and children but also with the other sailors of his yacht squadron. Subjectively, Luckey perceived himself with relatively few close friends and would have liked more. Objectively, his friendship network was very rich.

It was so easy for Luckey to take in, to "metabolize," any love that he was offered. When he was 60, he wrote of his father, who had died 20 years before, "I have never completely gotten over Dad's death. I will always remember him as the finest man I ever knew."

Wondering how the Luckeys still played together while the Paines led "parallel lives," I asked how his marriage had lasted for 40 years. With Churchillian simplicity, Luckey replied, "I really love Chrissie and she loves me. I really respect her, highly esteem her, and she is a real person." On her recent questionnaire, Chrissie wrote the study, "My husband is my best friend; I like looking after him. We have grown closer and fonder every year." There were 50 years of stable marriage to back up their words. In 1970, Luckey and his wife had sailed by themselves from San Francisco to Bali. The trip led to many months of close co-operation and shared physical labor. On the journey, Luckey illustrated his sailing journal with his own watercolors.

All during his 15 years, Luckey had loved writing and painting for fun. At 77, he had put on a solo exhibition of his marine watercolors. "With painting," he added dreamily, "You forget everything, and that is why it is so very relaxing." In church, Luckey sang both solo and in the choir. "I don't have a day when I don't have something to do that I want to do . . . creativity is absolutely necessary for someone to be healthy." Ten years before, with no more intelligence than Paine, Luckey, at age 67, told the study that he had "just finished a screen play and sent it to a literary agent." No, it was never performed, and, to my knowledge, his book on the Civil War is still unpublished. But as Luckey had written to the study at age 70, "I am living in the present—enjoying life and good health while it lasts. I think very little about the past or future, and I don't take myself very seriously."

THE PREDICTORS OF HEALTHY AGING

To many, it seems as if heart attacks and cancer are visitations from malicious fate and that much of the pain of old age seems in the hands of a cruel god—or at least of cruel genes. The whole process of growing old sometimes feels completely out of our control. In addition, there is much data well represented by "The Whitehall II Study" (Marmot et al., 1991), which emphasizes the importance of social class to successful aging. But blessed with prospectively gathered data, I was astonished that fate was relatively unimportant. Much of a septuagenarian's positive aging or lack of it is determined by factors already established before age 50. What seemed even more astonishing was that these factors are more or less controllable.

Ten years ago, a leading gerontologist, Paul Baltes, acknowledged that research had not yet reached a stage where there was good causal evidence for predicting healthy aging (Baltes & Baltes, 1990, p. 18). True, there have been several distinguished 10- to 20-year prospective studies of physical aging (Baltes & Mayer, 1999; Busse & Maddox, 1988; Rowe & Kahn, 1999; Shock, 1984; Thomae, 1987). All have contributed valuable understanding about the course of old age. But none of these studies have followed their subjects for more than 25 years, and few knew what their members were like before 50. In contrast, the Study of Adult Development has illuminated predictors that at 50 could foretell whether a man would be enjoying his 70th or 80th year. I identify these predictors one by one. But first, I note variables that, surprisingly, did not predict successful aging.

SIX VARIABLES THAT *DID NOT* PREDICT POSITIVE AGING

ANCESTRAL LONGEVITY

Lacking lifetime studies of humans, scientists have studied aging in fruit flies. You can breed and study many generations of fruit flies in a year; and in the longevity of fruit flies, it appears that genes are very important. Therefore, one of the first variables the study looked at was ancestral longevity. For the College men, ancestral longevity was estimated by computing the age at death of the subjects' parents and their four grandparents. For the Inner-City men, only the longevity of parents could be computed with accuracy. At age 60, the longevity of the ancestors of study members who died young was significantly shorter than the ancestral longevity of those who still survived. But to my surprise, by age 75, the average life spans of the ancestors of the Happy-Well and of the Sad-Sick were identical (see Table 34.2). In a replication study on 90 women who were 75 to 79 years old in the Terman Study (Vaillant, 2002), ancestral longevity was only weakly correlated with vigorous late-life adaptation. The longevity of the Inner-City men's parents contributed not at all to whether they were aging well or poorly at 70. The most likely explanation for the insignificant effect of ancestral longevity is the sheer number of genes involved. Obviously, specific genes are very important in predicting specific illnesses that shorten life; there may be other genes that facilitate longevity. But in a given individual, there may be so many good and bad longevity genes that ancestral effects tend to average out.

CHOLESTEROL

Everyone worries about cholesterol, especially in popular magazines. But these magazines would lose valuable advertising revenues if they chose to worry their readers about really significant risks to health—such as smoking and alcohol abuse. It is perfectly true that for young men or for those who have already had a heart attack, lowering high cholesterol is beneficial. It was equally true, however, that cholesterol levels at age 50 did not distinguish the Happy-Well from the Sad-Sick or even from the Prematurely Dead (see Table 34.2). This finding has been confirmed by much larger, more representative studies (Krumholz et al., 1994).

Table 34.2
Correlation of Uncontrollable < Age 50 Predictors with Five
Outcomes of Positive Aging 15 to 25 Years Later

Variables (Range)	Successful Aging College/ Inner-City 1–4	Physical Health			Mental Health	
		Mean Number of Years Disabled <80/<70 0–40	Dead <75/ Dead <65 0–1		Subjective Satisfaction College/ Inner-City 10–40	Objective College/ Inner-City 9–25
"Fate" (Ages 10–49)						
Ancestral longevity (40–100)	.15/ns	.16/.01	−.19/−.11		ns/ns	ns/ns
Cholesterol mg/100 ml	ns/ns	ns/ns	ns/ns		ns/ns	ns/ns
Parental social class (1–5)	ns/ns	ns/ns	ns/ns		ns/ns	ns/ns
Warm childhood environment (5–25)	.18/ns	ns/ns	ns/ns		ns/ns	.19/.14
Stable childhood temperament (1–5)	ns/ns	ns/ns	ns/ns		ns/.18	ns/.20

Notes: For all dependent and independent variables, a low score is "healthy" with the exception of ancestral longevity. All values and variables (if different) for the two samples are presented as College/Inner-City.
$n = 237$ (College sample); $n = 332$ (Inner-City sample); ns = Not significant; otherwise, all correlations $p < .05$, but $p > .01$; Spearman rho (two-tailed) used throughout.

Parental Social Class

Interest in the importance of social class and mental health has been fostered by many studies showing the strong cross-sectional association between job prestige and social class with physical health. But in our prospective study, parental social class was unassociated with late-life physical health. For example, at age 47, the social class of the Inner-City men (I = upperclass, V = underclass; Hollingshead & Redlich, 1958) was powerfully associated with physical heath at age 70. Forty percent of the men in classes I through III were still not dead or disabled, and 37% fell in the Happy-Well. In contrast, only 9% of the men in Class V were not disabled, and only 3% were among the Happy-Well. But the relationship was not causal. Rather, both poor social class and poor health were a function of alcohol abuse, mental illness, and poor education. However, there was no significant correlation between *parental* social class of the men at 14 and their health at 70 (see Table 34.2).

Warm Childhood Environment

Surprisingly, by age 70, stability of parental marriage, parental death in childhood, family cohesion, and warm childhood environment—variables important to health in young adulthood—were no longer predictive of outcome (see Table 34.2). This was true for both the College and Inner-City study cohorts. For both cohorts, two research assistants, blinded to all subsequent data, rated five facets of the men's childhood environmental strengths (global impression, family cohesion, and relations with mother, father, and siblings) on scales from 1 to 5 (range: 5 = warmest environment, 25 = bleakest environment; Vaillant, 1974, 1995).

Stable Childhood Temperament

Likewise, stable childhood temperament (rated by parental report of childhood temperament: 1 = easy baby and toddler; 3 = minor problems; 5 = phobias, shyness, tantrums, enuresis; Vaillant, 1974, 1995) was unrelated to physical and mental health and successful aging in the College men. However, it did show a small association with mental health alone in the Inner-City men (see Table 34.2).

Stress

Stress did not appear to be an important predictor. Many believe that stress or multiple physical symptoms secondary to stress are detrimental to health. For the psychologically minded, an attractive contrarian hypothesis is that men who "hold stress in" age poorly. Neither of these hypotheses was supported by the study data. The number of physical symptoms under stress before age 50 did not correlate with physical health at age 75. The number of illnesses, thought by some to be psychosomatic, such as ulcers, asthma, and colitis that the men had endured between 20 and 65, did not affect physical health at age 75. The number of serious negative life events before 65 did not predict physical health at 75 (Cui & Vaillant, 1996). Over the short term, stress can seriously affect health, but over the long term, how you deal with stress seems more important.

SEVEN FACTORS THAT *DID* PREDICT
POSITIVE AGING

Table 34.3 illustrates the factors that did predict positive aging. Five factors assessed prior to age 50 did predict healthy aging for both cohorts. A sixth protective factor, education, was important to aging well for both Inner-City men but was not really applicable to the College cohort, whose education was too homogeneous to be a differential predictor. A seventh independent predictor, exercise, was available for the College men but not for the Inner-City men. The univariate importance of these predictors is illustrated in Table 34.3, but each variable was important to positive aging when the others were controlled (Vaillant, 2002).

NOT BEING A SMOKER OR STOPPING SMOKING YOUNG

Smoking was calculated in pack-years (packs per day × years smoking) by age 50. In both male cohorts, not being a heavy smoker before the age of 50 was the most important single predictive factor of healthy physical aging. Among the College men, heavy smoking (more than a pack a day for 30 years) was 10 times more frequent among the Prematurely Dead than among the Happy-Well. Yet, if a man had stopped smoking by about age 45, the effects of smoking (as much as one pack a day for 20 years) could no longer be discerned at 70 or 80.

ADAPTIVE COPING STYLE (MATURE DEFENSES)

The second most powerful predictor of positive aging among the Happy-Well was an adaptive involuntary coping style. Independent raters—blinded to the men's current physical health and ignorant of their future—had reviewed each individual's entire record to rate his defenses. An adaptive coping style is referred to as the use of *mature defenses*. For each man, the mean maturity of defensive behaviors,

Table 34.3

Correlation of Relatively Controllable < Age 50 Predictors with
Five Outcomes of Positive Aging 15 to 25 Years Later

	Successful Aging College/ Inner-City 1–4	Physical Health		Mental Health	
Self-Care Predictors (Range)		Length of Active Life Years Disabled < 80 0–40	Dead < 75/ Dead < 65 0–1	Subjective Satisfaction College/ Inner-City 10–40	Objective College/ Inner-City 9–25
Pack-years of smoking (0–90)	**.35/.31**	**.30/.31**	**.30/.23**	ns/ns	**.26**/.14
Maturity of defenses (1–9)	**.32/.23**	**.27**/.17	ns/ns	**.34/.28**	**.41/.46**
Alcohol abuse (*DSM-III*) (1–3)	**.42/.19**	**.38/.18**	**.40/.15**	**.21**/ns	**.32/.21**
Healthy weight (1–2)	.14/.11	.14/ns	ns/ns	ns/ns	ns/ns
Exercise (1–2)/education (6–19)	**.22/.20**	.18/**.20**	ns/ns	ns/ns	**.24/.25**
Stable marriage (1–2)	**.27/.22**	.15/.13	ns/.17	**.33/.27**	**.39/.33**

Notes: For all dependent and independent variables, a low score is "healthy." All values and variables (if different) for the two samples are presented as College/Inner-City.

$n = 237$ (College sample); $n = 332$ (Inner-City sample); ns = Not significant; unbold correlations $p < .05$; bold correlations $p < .001$; Spearman rho (two-tailed) used throughout.

largely identified from the age of 47 (*SD* 2 years), were scored on a nine-point scale consistent with the *DSM-IV* Defensive Functioning Scale (American Psychiatric Association [APA], 1994): 1 = most adaptive, 9 = most maladaptive. In everyday life, the term mature defenses refers to our capacity to turn lemons into lemonade and not to turn molehills into mountains. Analogous to immune and clotting mechanisms, the choice of defense mechanisms is relatively involuntary. The term *mature* refers to the fact that when adults are followed over 60 years (Vaillant, 1977; Vaillant & Mukamal, 2001), immature coping styles of passive aggression, dissociation, projection, and acting out decline, and the coping styles of altruism, sublimation, suppression (stoicism), and humor increase. In both samples, mature defenses were common among the Happy-Well and virtually absent among the Sad-Sick. This strong association resulted because mature defenses at 50 predicted mental health in older age. Mature defenses did not predict the men's future objective physical health, but mature defenses often did keep objectively disabled men from feeling subjectively disabled.

ABSENCE OF ALCOHOL ABUSE

DSM-III criteria (APA, 1980) were used to assess alcohol abuse (scored 1 = no abuse; 2 = alcohol abuse, 3 = alcohol dependence). Absence of alcohol abuse was the only protective factor in this study that powerfully predicted both psychosocial and physical health. Alcohol abuse was defined as the evidence of multiple alcohol-related problems (with spouse, family, employer, law, and health). Until now, most major longitudinal studies of health, for example, The Framingham Study (Dawber, 1980) in Massachusetts and the Marmot et al. (1991) Whitehall studies in England, have controlled only for reported alcohol *consumption*, not abuse. Unfortunately, reported alcohol consumption reflects alcohol abuse (loss of voluntary control and/or adverse consequences from alcohol abuse) almost as poorly as reported food consumption reflects obesity. Neither reported alcohol nor calorie consumption is a useful predictor of poor aging, while obesity and symptomatic alcohol abuse are.

Prospective studies reveal that alcohol abuse is a *cause*—not a result—of increased life stress (Cui & Vaillant, 1996), of depression (Vaillant, 1995), and of downward social mobility. In addition, alcohol abuse causes death for many reasons other than liver cirrhosis and motor vehicle accidents. Alcohol abuse causes suicide, homicide, cancer, heart disease, and a depressed immune system. Indeed, alcohol abuse was almost as bad for health in nonsmokers as heavy smoking was bad for health among social drinkers (Vaillant, Schnurr, Baron, & Gerber, 1991).

HEALTHY WEIGHT

Healthy weight was measured by the body-mass index (BMI; kg/m2): At age 50, men with a BMI > 28 (overweight) or a BMI < 22 (underweight) = 2; men with BMI < 29 and > 21 (healthy weight) = 1.

STABLE MARRIAGE

Stable marriage was defined as 1 = married without divorce, separation, or serious problems until age 50; otherwise = 2.

EXERCISE

Exercise (recorded for College men only), defined as exercise that burned more than 500 kilocalories per week, was classified as regular exercise (Schnurr, Vaillant, & Vaillant, 1990). Less than 500 kilo/calories of exercise a week was recorded as exercise absent.

YEARS OF EDUCATION

Years of education was a continuous variable from 6 to 19. Because the range of education for the College men was truncated, education was used as a predictor for Inner-City men only. For the Inner-City men, years of education were an important protective variable. Although length of education is often viewed as merely a manifestation of social class and intelligence, its association with healthy aging depended on neither of these factors. The components of education that appeared to correlate with physical health in old age were self-care, future orientation, and perseverance—not IQ and paternal income. The effect of education on health was indirect. The more education the Inner-City men obtained, the more likely they were to stop smoking, eat sensibly, and use alcohol in moderation. Thus, a major reason that the health of the Inner-City men declined so much more rapidly than the College men was that the Inner-City men not only were much less educated but also led far less healthy lifestyles. The Inner-City men were almost twice as likely as the College men to abuse alcohol and cigarettes, and they were more than three times as likely to be overweight. In Table 34.4, the contrast in physical health between the Inner-City men who did not attend college and the College men who attended graduate school is dramatic.

A crucial piece of evidence supports the fact that education predicts positive aging for reasons independent of parental social class and intelligence. True, the physical health of the 70-year old Inner-City men was as poor as that of the College men at 80. But remarkably, the health of the *college-educated* Inner-City men at 70

Table 34.4
The Relation of Health at Age 70 to
Years of Education

	Education of Men (Years)			
	Inner-City		College	
	< 16	16[a]	16	17+
	$n = 302$	$n = 26$[b]	$n = 78$[c]	$n = 156$
Health	(%)	(%)	(%)	(%)
Excellent	0	0	8	12
Good	7	23	30	30
Chronic illness	20	43	24	34
Disabled	22	12	11	8
Dead	51	2	27	16

[a] Three men attended graduate school.
[b] Four men did not yet have health rated at age 70.
[c] Three men were excluded because they did not graduate.

Table 34.5
Contrast of the Social Class of College Men and
Inner-City Men with 16 Years of Education

	Inner-City Men $n = 30$	College Men $n = 78$
IQ	104 ±11	133 ± 12
Height	69.6 ± 2.3	70.8 ± 2.4
Parental social class I or II	0%	68%
Income at age 47	27K ± 5K	63K ± 57K
Social class at age 47	20%	37%

was as good as that of the College (Harvard) men at 70 (see Table 34.4). This was in spite of the fact that the college-educated Inner-City men's childhood social class, their tested IQ, their income at age 47, and the prestige of their colleges and jobs were markedly inferior to the College (Harvard) men (see Table 34.5). Parity of education alone was enough to produce parity in physical health.

CONCLUSION

The protective factors in Table 34.3—a stable marriage, the ability to make lemonade from lemons, avoiding cigarettes, modest use of alcohol, regular exercise, persevering with education, and maintaining normal weight—allow us to predict positive health *30 years* in the future.

Sixty-six College men—still in good health at age 50—possessed less than four protective factors. At age 80, not one—not a single one—of these men was among the Happy-Well; and 21, or almost a third, were among the Sad-Sick, and three times as many as expected were dead. All 7 men who, like Alfred Paine, had less than two protective factors at age 50, were dead by age 80. In contrast, 44 College men had all six factors present; 25 were among the Happy-Well, and only 1 was among the Sad-Sick.

Although the average Inner-City man at age 50 tended to have fewer protective factors than the College men, the power of these protective factors was the same. For example, there were 52 Inner-City men who at age 50 enjoyed both good health and five or more protective factors. Twenty years later, only 2% of such men were among the Sad-Sick or Dead, and 33 were among the Happy-Well. There were 37 Inner-City men who were not disabled at age 50 but who possessed less than two protective factors. At 70, 25 were among the Sad-Sick or Prematurely Dead and only 3 were among the Happy-Well. In other words, positive aging to an extraordinary degree is controllable and thus teachable by positive psychology.

There are exceptions. Some people are struck by lightning; others are crippled by someone else's stupidity or die from malignant genes. But the vast majority—at least in these two White male cohorts—of septuagenarians are products of their own, often involuntary, behavior.

The good news, however, is that most of us—if we start young and try hard—can voluntarily control our weight, our exercise, and our abuse of cigarettes—at least by the time we are 50. And with hard work and with the help of able intervention, we can improve our relationships with our most significant other, achieve abstinence from alcohol, and use fewer maladaptive defenses. Indeed, the fellowship of Alcoholic's Anonymous offers a valuable object lesson to positive psychology. I do not wish to blame the victim, but I do wish to accentuate the positive. Whether we live to a vigorous old age lies not so much in our stars or in our genes, as in ourselves.

REFERENCES

American Psychiatric Association. (1980). *Diagnostic and statistical manual of mental disorders* (3rd ed.). Washington, DC: Author.

American Psychiatric Association. (1994). *Diagnostic and statistical manual of mental disorders* (4th ed.). Washington, DC: Author.

Baltes, P. B., & Baltes, M. M. (1990). *Successful aging.* Cambridge, England: Cambridge University Press.

*Baltes, P. B., & Mayer, K. V. (Eds.). (1999). *The Berlin Aging Study.* Cambridge, England: Cambridge University Press.

Bortz, W. M., Wallace, D. H., & Wiley, D. (1999). Sexual function in 1,202 aging males: Differentiating aspects. *Journals of Gerontology: Series A, Biological Sciences and Medical Sciences, 54,* M237–M241.

Busse, E. W., & Maddox, G. L. (1988). *The Duke Longitudinal Studies of Normal Aging: 1955–1980.* New York: Springer.

Cui, X. J., & Vaillant, G. E. (1996). Antecedents and consequences of negative life events in adulthood: A longitudinal study. *American Journal of Psychiatry, 152,* 21–26.

Dawber, T. R. (1980). *The Framingham Study.* Cambridge, MA: Harvard University Press.

de Beauvoir, S. (1972). *The coming of age.* New York: G. P. Putnam & Sons.

*Fries, J. F. (1980). Aging: Natural death and the compression of morbidity. *New England Journal of Medicine, 303,* 130–135.

Glueck, S., & Glueck, E. (1950). *Unraveling juvenile delinquency.* New York: Commonwealth Fund.

Glueck, S., & Glueck, E. (1968). *Delinquents and nondelinquents in perspective.* Cambridge, MA: Harvard University Press.

Heimpel, H. (1981). Schlusswort. In Max Planck Institut für Geschicte (Ed.), *Hermann Heimpel zum 80 Geburtstag.* Göttingen, Germany: Hubert & Co.

Hollingshead, A. B., & Redlich, F. C. (1958). *Social class and mental illness.* New York: Wiley.

Krumholz, H. M., et al. (1994). Lack of association between cholesterol and coronary heart disease mortality and morbidity and all-cause mortality in persons older than 70 years. *Journal of the American Medical Association, 272,* 1335.

Marmot, M. G., Smith, G. D., Stansfeld, S., Patel, C., North, F., Head, J., et al. (1991). Health inequalities among British civil servants: The Whitehall II Study. *Lancet, 337,* 1387–1393.

*Rowe, J. W., & Kahn, R. L. (1999). *Successful aging.* New York: Dell.

Schnurr, P. P., Vaillant, C. O., & Vaillant, G. E. (1990). Predicting exercise in late midlife from young adult personality characteristics. *International Journal of Aging and Human Development, 30,* 153–161.

Shock, N. (1984). *Normal human aging.* Washington, DC: U.S. Government Printing Office.

Thomae, H. (1987). Conceptualizations of responses to stress. *European Journal of Personality, 1,* 171–191.

Vaillant, G. E. (1974). The natural history of male psychological health: II. Some antecedents of healthy adult adjustment. *Archives of General Psychiatry, 31,* 15–22.

*Vaillant, G. E. (1977). *Adaptation to life.* Boston: Little Brown.

Vaillant, G. E. (1979). Natural history of male psychological health: Effects of mental health on physical health. *New England Journal of Medicine, 301,* 1249–1254.

Vaillant, G. E. (1995). *Natural history of alcoholism revisited.* Cambridge, MA: Harvard University Press.

*Vaillant, G. E. (2002). *Aging well.* New York: Little, Brown.

Vaillant, G. E., Meyer, S. E., Mukamal, K., & Soldz, S. (1998). Are social supports in late midlife a cause or a result of successful physical aging. *Psychological Medicine, 28,* 1159–1168.

Vaillant, G. E., & Mukamal, K. (2001). Positive aging in two male cohorts. *American Journal of Psychiatry, 158,* 839–847.

Vaillant, G. E., Schnurr, P. P., Baron, J. A., & Gerber, P. D. (1991). A prospective study of the effects of cigarette smoking and alcohol abuse on mortality. *Journal of General Internal Medicine, 6,* 299–304.

Vaillant, G. E., & Vaillant, C. O. (1990). Natural history of male psychological health: XII. A 45-year study of successful aging at age 65. *American Journal of Psychiatry, 147,* 31–37.

World Health Organization. (1952). Constitution of the World Health Organization. In *World Health Organization handbook of basic documents* (5th ed.). Geneva, Switzerland: Palais des Nations.

PART XI

BUILDING COMMUNITY THROUGH INTEGRATION AND REGENERATION

CHAPTER 35

Bringing Subjectivity into Focus: Optimal Experiences, Life Themes, and Person-Centered Rehabilitation

ANTONELLA DELLE FAVE and FAUSTO MASSIMINI

Bishnu is a smart and active boy. He is 15 years old and lives with his parents and two siblings in Bhaktapur, an ancient town in Nepal. He is very good at school, he can read both Nepali and English fluently, and he is especially talented in drawing. Sometimes he plays chess and soccer with his friends. The principal of his school, during an interview with a representative of Redd Barna—the Norwegian section of Save the Children International—stated: "Bishnu is one of the most brilliant students of this school. He is an asset for our society." Bishnu performs everything with his feet because cerebral palsy prevents him from using upper limbs and hands, from speaking fluently, and from running and walking long distances. Nevertheless, he can perform almost all daily activities, except putting on clothes. He describes himself as a very sociable boy: "I love my friends, parents, teachers . . . my friends help me." In the future, he wants to become an artist and to work with computers.

Five years ago, Caterina got a position as a clerk in a health service. She had studied foreign languages and planned to work as an interpreter, but she generally feels good about her job. She is 30, lives with her husband, and is fond of table tennis. She practices regularly, and she has won several national tournaments. She considers this activity a sport, a demanding task, and an opportunity

We would like to thank the people who collaborated in this work for their invaluable contributions: the participants, for devoting a conspicuous amount of their time to complete our questionnaires and for providing highly personal and, therefore, precious information on their life history and daily experience; the researchers, Walter Bosio, Manuela Lombardi, Pier Paola Pifferi, and Lorella Santoro, for being able to build an authentic research alliance with the participants during the data collection and for actively taking part in the coding phase; and the members of Bhaktapur CBR Organization, for introducing us to the Nepalese participants and their families and for the enthusiasm and commitment they transmitted us.

to develop personal skills through constant training. Her husband shares this interest and supports her. Caterina does not like to talk about her childhood; she remembers herself as a deceitful and unsatisfied little girl living in a problematic family environment. An accident, which occurred as a consequence of these difficult circumstances, changed her life when she was 14. Today, she plays table tennis in a wheelchair, but she is a satisfied woman, who perceives a good balance among her different life domains: family, work, and sport. As to future goals, Caterina aims at being always satisfied with herself and at progressing in her personal growth. She describes herself as sociable, versatile, and a person undergoing a ceaseless evolution.

Giovanni is 40 years old. He earned a university degree in pedagogy, and he presently teaches humanities in a secondary school. He is not satisfied with his professional life: He finds the job too repetitive and the students too young and not much interested in literature and history. However, he gets deeply engaged while preparing lessons because he can learn new things and transmit them to the students. Giovanni would like to go on studying, but his salary is the main family income (he is married and has a son). Although he is aware of this responsibility, he perceives family as a basic resource, and he quotes being with his wife and playing with his son among the most pleasant activities of his daily life. He married at 28 and, some years later, became the father of an adopted child. Despite the difficulties and the emotional stress he and his wife faced to achieve this goal, they overcame the perplexities of judges and social workers. As a matter of fact, the situation was unusual: Giovanni has been blind since he was 16; his wife and son are blind as well. He pursues three main goals in his life: being a good husband and father, studying to enrich his culture, and growing at personal and spiritual levels. He describes himself as an optimist, a person who trusts life and people, and a person who wants to grow, who is searching.

DISABLEMENT AND FUNCTIONING: INDIVIDUALS IN CONTEXT

In 1980, the World Health Organization (WHO) launched the International Classification of Impairments, Disabilities and Handicaps (ICIDH). It represented the first attempt to integrate the biomedical model of disease with the social perspective and to take into account the role of environmental factors in the production of disablement. The ICIDH defined *impairment* as an observable and measurable loss or abnormality of a biological structure or function. *Disability* referred to the limitation in the daily activities caused by impairments. Impairments and disabilities constituted a *handicap* if they led to disadvantages that limited or prevented a person from fulfilling socially expected roles. However, ICIDH did not address two main issues: cultural differences and individual psychological characteristics.

As to the first issue of cultural differences, the social representation of the body and its pathologies is strongly related to cultural norms and beliefs, widely differing across societies and influencing the opportunities for action and integration available for disabled citizens. As stated by Ingstad (1999), the status and social roles of a person are not necessarily determined by health and physical conditions. Disabled persons will be disadvantaged only in a social, cultural, or attitudinal environment in which their condition brings about disadvantageous consequences (Bickenbach, Chatterji, Badley, & Üstün, 1999). In the native languages of American

Indians, for example, there is no word for disability. People are evaluated for what they can do, rather than for their limitations (Marshall & Largo, 1999). In non-Western cultures, disabled people are often more integrated in society. Together with social cohesion and low levels of individualism, lack of facilities and specialized institutions paradoxically facilitates their active participation in community life (Agarwal, 1995; Brown et al., 1998; Tanaka-Matsumi & Draguns, 1997).

The second issue, individual psychological characteristics, refers to the increasing need for an approach to disablement focused on the subjective perspective and on perceived quality of life. This approach can help avoid the mistake of looking for psychological and behavioral differences between the people with disablement and the other citizens: Many people with disabilities perceive themselves as ordinary persons coping with extraordinary circumstances (Saravanan, Manigandam, Macaden, Tharion, & Bhattacharji, 2001).

The revised International Classification of Impairments, Disabilities and Handicaps (ICIDH-2) and its evolution, the International Classification of Functioning (ICF; WHO, 2001), have brought about significant advancements in the interpretation of disablement. They are centered on the biopsychosocial model, developed by Engel (1977) and presently considered the best framework to deal with health issues (Gatchel & Bell, 2000). In ICF, each dimension of health and disease is conceptualized as a dynamic interaction between individual features and social and physical environment. Cross-cultural issues have been addressed through careful translation and testing of the evaluation instruments in 15 different countries (Üstün et al., 2001). In addition, rather than emphasizing the consequences of disease (such as impairments and handicaps), this classification focuses on the components of health: *body functions, activities,* and *participation,* and on their variations among individuals. Disablement is considered a variation in functioning from this threefold perspective.

However, despite this Copernican revolution at the conceptual level, the dominant model in health care and rehabilitation practice is still biomedical (Mathew, Ravichandran, May, & Morsley, 2001). Empirical work tends to explore the medical management of the physical problems associated with disablement. Most scales and questionnaires investigating health-related quality of life analyze complaints rather than positive aspects, pain and shortcomings rather than well-being, with only a few exceptions (Hyland & Kenyon, 1992; Salmon, Manzi, & Valori, 1996). Health professionals are trained to focus on the physical components of disease and on the associated disadvantages and activity restrictions.

Nevertheless, studies show that life satisfaction is not at all incompatible with disease. Albrecht and Devlieger (1999) found that 54.3% of people with serious disablement rated their quality of life as excellent or good. Kerr and Stephens (1997) asked deaf people to report their positive experiences after hearing loss, thus verifying that disease can have a positive impact on life. Sodergren and Hyland (2000) investigated the positive consequences of illness among people currently sick or recovering from disease, and they identified major recurring answer categories, such as improved interpersonal relationships, positive personality changes, reappraisal, and restructuring of life.

Several factors influence the outcomes of disablement. As suggested in the ICF model, both environmental and personal features can mediate the impact of disablement on the quality of life (Johnston & Pollard, 2001). At the environmental level, attitudes and behavior of caregivers and family members play a primary role

(Kreuter, 2000; Saraswathi, 1992; Ünalan et al., 2001). Social relationships, education and job opportunities, and structural and interpersonal facilitators and barriers remarkably affect the quality of life of people with disablement (Fougeyrollas, 1995; Meyers, Anderson, Miller, Shipp, & Hoenig, 2002). At the personal level, studies have highlighted the mediating function of psychological adaptation to disability (Menzel, Dolan, Richardson, & Olsen, 2002), perception of control (Fisher & Johnston, 1996b; Plahuta et al., 2002), emotional distress (Fisher & Johnston, 1996a), and coping style (Galvin & Godfrey, 2001).

FOCUSING ON RESOURCES: PSYCHOLOGICAL SELECTION AND WELL-BEING

We propose an approach to the study of disablement centered on individuals' subjective reports and personal way of interacting with the environment. Specifically, our approach focuses on perceived well-being, optimal experiences, self-determination in setting life goals, and developmental trajectories.

Individuals can be more or less effective in exploiting the environmental opportunities for action available to them. Being an open and self-organizing system, the person actively exchanges information with the environment, attaining progressively higher levels of order and integration, at both the biological and psychological levels (Delle Fave, 1996; Massimini & Delle Fave, 2000). In their daily lives, individuals differentially reproduce a subset of the available environmental information—activities, interests, relationships, values, behavioral norms—through their preferential allocation of attention. This process, *psychological selection,* is related to the biological constraints that allow humans to simultaneously perceive and elaborate only a limited number of environmental stimuli (Csikszentmihalyi & Massimini, 1985).

Several studies have shown that psychological selection is guided by the quality of subjective experience associated with the interaction with the environment. The identification of optimal experience has been particularly relevant. This is a state of consciousness characterized by the perception of high environmental challenges, adequately high personal skills, high concentration, involvement, enjoyment, control of the situation, and intrinsic motivation, that is, involvement in the task for its own sake, regardless of extrinsic rewards (Csikszentmihalyi, 1975, 1985; Csikszentmihalyi & Csikszentmihalyi, 1988). Most daily activities can be associated with optimal experience. However, the situation should be sufficiently complex to require active engagement and to promote satisfaction in the use of personal skills.

The perception of high environmental challenges fosters the increase of related skills. This dynamic structure of optimal experience leads to the preferential cultivation of competencies in specific activities. Thus, this experience can be considered the compass directing psychological selection and supporting the development of the life theme, which comprises the basic life goals and lifelong targets each person uniquely selects for preferential cultivation (Csikszentmihalyi & Beattie, 1979; Csikszentmihalyi & Massimini, 1985).

As to disability, research studies have emphasized the importance of optimal experience in promoting individuals' physical as well as social functioning. This has been assessed for congenital or early occurring diseases, in the case of disabilities acquired during adolescence or adulthood, consequent to chronic or progressive diseases, or disability caused by traumas or accidents (Delle Fave, 1996; Delle Fave & Maletto, 1992; Delle Fave & Massimini, 2003; Negri, Massimini, & Delle Fave, 1992). In the following sections, we discuss findings from studies we have recently conducted in Italy and Nepal, which highlight the role of optimal experiences in coping with disability, maximizing individual resources, and promoting the cultivation of self-selected developmental tasks (life theme) and goals.

Participants

The participants were people from Italy and Nepal with different kinds of sensory or motor impairments. Among them, 51 (30 women and 21 men, ranging in age from 12 to 92) were blind from birth (29.4%) or because of diseases occurring during adolescence or adulthood (70.6%). Of the 33 participants with spinal cord injury (SCI; 25 males and 8 females, ages 18 to 57), 29 were paraplegic and 4 were quadriplegic. We also interviewed 20 young Nepalese people (12 females and 8 males, 14 to 29 years old) with motor impairments either due to hereditary diseases such as osteogenesis imperfecta and Duchenne's muscular dystrophy or acquired at birth and during infancy because of poliomyelitis, intrapartum asphyxia, or premature birth.

As in other developing countries, health care and disease prevention in Nepal are officially claimed as goals to be pursued, but in practice they are still far from being achieved. In spite of recent improvements in the legislation and policy concerning disability, the rights of Nepalese disabled people are far from being met. Only 15.3% of these citizens benefit from health services, more than 70% have no education and literacy, 78% within the economically active age range are unemployed, and 77% fully depend on their families. Because material and technological resources are scarce, there is great need for low cost rehabilitation (Nepal South Asia Centre [NESAC], 1998). Several nongovernmental organizations (NGOs) provide health services, but they are mostly located in big towns, and their intervention programs are often standardized, rather than being tailored to local community needs and individual demands.

In the effort to effectively promote health in spite of severe resource restrictions, many developing countries have adopted intervention strategies based on decentralization and involvement of local communities (Atkinson, Rolim Medeiros, Lima Oliveira, & Dias de Almeida, 2000). One of the core features of this approach is represented by community-based rehabilitation (CBR) programs, which are often supported by local and international nongovernmental organizations. These CBR projects are designed to provide medical treatment, as well as psychosocial support to ill and disabled people. Training courses are offered to parents and family members to compensate for the shortage of physiotherapists, at the same time enhancing the effectiveness of the therapeutic intervention. Disabled people are also provided with vocational training and job opportunities (Werner, 1987). Resources are devoted to advocacy campaigns against discrimination of people with disabilities and to disease-prevention programs. Community-based rehabilitation projects represent a prominent tool for health promotion in that they are strongly connected to the local culture, they often compensate for the lack of primary health care structures, and they contribute to community development as well.

The disabled young people we met in Nepal benefited from a CBR project first launched in 1986 by a group of Jaycees volunteers in the area of Bhaktapur in the

Kathmandu Valley. The intervention program started with 11 children and today has grown into an organization providing a variety of need-based services to more than 1,000 children and young people (SCN-CBR, 2000). Bhaktapur CBR typically uses already-existing family and community resources. Therapists and nurses are involved as consultants, and they pass on their competencies to the family and to the community, promoting home-based rehabilitation.

PROCEDURES

To investigate optimal experience and life themes, we used two instruments designed to explore the subjective evaluation of daily life opportunities and future expectations. The first, the Flow questionnaire (Delle Fave & Massimini, 1988, 1991; Massimini, Csikszentmihalyi, & Delle Fave, 1988), opened with three quotations describing optimal experience. Participants were asked whether they had ever felt optimal experience in their life, and, if yes, they were invited to list the associated activities or situations (also called optimal activities). No limitations were given on the number of activities to be quoted. Subsequently, participants were invited to select from their list the activity associated with the most pervasive and intense optimal experiences and to rate on Likert-type scales the level of cognitive, affective, and motivational variables perceived during this activity. Additional open-ended questions investigated the phenomenological features of optimal experience, participants' wishes, pleasant activities, situations of disengagement and apathy, and the environmental factors influencing the cultivation of the optimal activities. Participants who acquired disability during adolescence or adulthood answered most of the questions twice: referring to their present condition and referring to the period before disablement. The answers to the open-ended questions were coded and included in broader functional categories, covering the major life domains (Csikszentmihalyi, 1997). The second instrument, the Life Theme questionnaire, investigated the person's history and future expectations. Information was collected about events and people perceived as relevant positive and negative influences, about present challenges and accomplishments, and about future goals (Csikszentmihalyi & Beattie, 1979).

OPTIMAL EXPERIENCE: ASSOCIATED ACTIVITIES AND PSYCHOLOGICAL FEATURES

Figure 35.1 shows the activities participants associated with optimal experiences. In the cases of acquired impairments, results refer to the period of life following the onset of disablement. Most participants reported at least one activity: Only three blind people and three people with spinal cord injuries stated that they had never felt optimal experiences.

Among blind people, the most frequent category of answers was "media," comprising activities such as reading in Braille, listening to music and to radio news, and watching [sic] TV. Work ranked second in frequency, followed by leisure, mostly referring to playing music. As for people with SCI, the first category in rank was leisure, followed by health care and work. Young people with motor impairment quoted work as the most frequent opportunity for optimal experience. Media and study ranked second and third, respectively.

The prominent association of optimal experience with the use of media among blind participants is apparently only paradoxical. These people learned to acquire

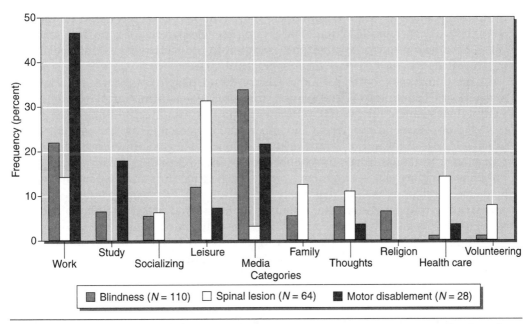

Figure 35.1 Activities Associated with Optimal Experience. Percentage distribution of answers among people with blindness (*N* participants = 48, *N* answers = 110), with SCI (*N* participants = 30, *N* answers = 64), and among youths with motor impairment (*N* participants = 19, *N* answers = 28).

information and to interact with their environment through sensorial paths alternative to sight, such as touching and hearing. Reading in Braille requires specific and complex skills, which are difficult to acquire even for people born blind. Mauro, a boy of 12 with congenital blindness, stated: "I like to read, but for me it's difficult; I am not very good at it. My main challenge now is to learn to read well, because it's important. I want to read faster, and therefore I practice a lot. Now I am reading *Robinson Crusoe,* and I enjoy it."

The same is true of watching TV. Programs are not designed for a blind audience. A great amount of information comes from images, and it is only implicitly referred to through words and sounds. Giorgio, 26, born blind, described his strategy to meet this challenge as follows: "I sit in front of the television, I listen to the words, and I build mental images on the story that is described: I look for messages; I identify myself with the characters."

The challenge is even higher for people with acquired blindness, who later in life had to learn to read through fingers instead of eyes, to "watch" TV using ears. Marzia, who became blind at the age of 23 and who was 39 years old when she completed the questionnaires, quoted both reading and watching TV as opportunities for optimal experiences. She explained: "Reading means acquiring culture, opening up yourself to the world. Now it is hard for me, because I have to read in Braille. I read less frequently, but when I do, I get really involved. Watching TV sometimes is a way to get in touch with the world, to learn . . . now. When I could see, I had no TV at home."

Work as an opportunity for optimal experiences mostly referred to handicrafts and manual activities among people born blind: Knitting, working as physiotherapists or bookbinders, and bottoming chairs with straw were reported. On the contrary, people with acquired blindness mostly quoted activities based on intellectual skills, such as teaching. These competencies, developed during school years, became a resource for their integration into productive life, counterbalancing the difficulties faced in performing practical tasks.

In the domains of both work and leisure, blind people frequently associated music—both listening to it and playing instruments—with optimal experiences. Again, the use and cultivation of prominently auditory and tactile skills were perceived as occasions for enjoyment and engagement. Piero, 30 years old, had started to study music at the age of 20 after becoming blind. He got a diploma in classical guitar, and he taught music in schools. He described studying music as follows: "Besides being my job, it's a source of self-actualization. It is an inner incentive, it helps me develop my technical and artistic skills, but it's a means to attain experiences, rather than an end in itself." Giulia, 21, born blind, started to play piano at the age of 6. She describes music as ". . . a source of life and a refuge. It gives me the opportunity to know new people and things. I'd like to devote myself to the history of music, maybe to become a researcher at the university."

People with spinal lesions, on the contrary, associated optimal experience with media in only 3% of the answers. This is not surprising. Our cross-cultural findings showed that media and, especially, watching TV are only rarely reported as occasions for optimal experiences among people who can see, at least in Western countries, where TV is part of daily life and of every household's equipment (Massimini & Delle Fave, 2000; Massimini, Delle Fave, & Borri Gaspardin, 1992). As Figure 35.1 shows, paraplegic and quadriplegic people most frequently associate optimal experience with leisure activities, followed by health care and work. Leisure primarily included sports such as archery, basketball, table tennis, athletics, and horseback riding. For Davide, 27, paraplegic, playing basketball and practicing athletics represented ". . . a way to give vent to all what I have inside, to actualize what I promised myself to do. It's also a hobby, and a revenge. Sport is good for the body and for the mind; it keeps you away from bad habits. It helps shape your temperament. For me, it's a struggle with myself . . . When I finish the training, I feel actualized; I don't have any more wishes. I feel I was able to achieve what I intended to do."

Health care ranked second in frequency, mostly referring to physiotherapy sessions and rehabilitation exercises. Federico, 28, paraplegic, provided the following description of physiotherapy: "For me it means to do whatever I can, as hard as I can. When I finish the session, I feel good, light."

As for work, most participants highlighted its multifaceted role: Work was perceived as an opportunity to improve personal skills and performance, but also a way to actively participate in productive and social life. Ferruccio, 45, has an incomplete quadriplegia: His spinal cord is damaged, but not severed. He can still perform some movements with his arms and hands. Ferruccio associated optimal experience with working as bookkeeper and cashier in his family's butchery. He described this activity as "exerting control over the business, improving it, coping with bureaucracy, but also getting socialization opportunities. Work, when it's perceived as enjoyable, empowers a person both at the mental and at the economic levels."

Young people with motor impairments quoted work, media, and study as the prominent opportunities for optimal experiences. Work was by and large the most frequent category, comprising 47% of the answers. It included activities such as woodcarving, knitting, repairing radio and TV sets, and working at the offset press and with the computer. Rakesh, 28, whose lower limbs became paralyzed because of poliomyelitis when he was a baby, ran his own business as an electrician. When asked about the quality of experience at work, he said: "I chose this job because when I was younger I had a tape recorder, and I opened it . . . repairing TV sets you can learn new things and also earn money." Ambika, 20, could not walk because of osteogenesis imperfecta. However, she found in knitting both an opportunity for optimal experience and a source of income for the whole family: "Learning to knit was one of my most enjoyable experiences, about seven years ago . . . I get the wool from an NGO; when I complete the work, they take it. Every morning I plan what to do, and when I work I only think to what I'm doing. When the wool finishes, I get bored, and I watch TV or spend time with my siblings."

Media, mostly watching films, ranked second among the activity categories Nepalese youth associated with optimal experience. Most participants—like most people in Nepal—did not have a television set at home. Therefore, watching TV was a rather rare opportunity. Study ranked third and was quoted prominently by adolescents who still attended school. Bishnu, 15, provided such a description of learning activities: "School is important because it provides knowledge, teachings, many things. I enjoy doing homework and reading; I feel happy in doing them."

Table 35.1 shows the psychological features of optimal experience, as reported by the participants in the three groups.

Most variables' values showed no significant differences across groups, except for perceived absence of boredom and clear goals. However, it is difficult to interpret these isolated differences because both variables scored above 6 on average on a 0 to 8 scale in all three groups. These findings globally shed light on the recurring structure of optimal experience and on the role of optimal activities in

Table 35.1
Psychological Features of Optimal Experience as
Described by the Three Groups of Participants

Variables	Blindness $N = 48$		Spinal Cord Injury $N = 30$		Motor Disability $N = 19$		F	p
	M	SD	M	SD	M	SD		
Challenges	7.5	1.2	7.1	1.5	7.0	1.8	1.9	ns
Skills	7.0	1.5	6.5	1.5	6.3	1.7	1.8	ns
Involvement	6.7	1.4	6.7	1.3	7.3	1.1	1.4	ns
Clear feedback	7.3	1.6	6.6	1.8	6.9	1.6	1.8	ns
Intrinsic motivation	6.7	2.5	7.4	1.7	6.9	2.2	1.0	ns
No boredom	7.5	1.1	7.4	1.0	6.3	1.7	7.4	<.01
Enjoyment	7.0	1.7	7.0	1.4	7.4	1.1	0.7	ns
No distraction	6.6	1.8	5.9	2.1	6.6	1.6	1.6	ns
No anxiety	6.1	2.5	6.5	1.9	6.0	2.0	0.5	ns
Clear goals	7.8	1.1	6.7	1.5	7.3	1.2	7.2	<.01
Control of situation	6.8	1.9	5.9	1.9	6.5	1.8	1.9	ns

Note: Not significant (ns) indicates that no significant difference between variables' values was detected across the three groups through ANOVA comparison.

supporting development through creative engagement in self-selected tasks, independently of performance outcomes or social expectations.

Positive and Negative Life Influences

Table 35.2 shows the percentage distribution of the positive and negative life influences quoted by the three groups of participants in the Life Theme questionnaire. The first remark concerns the number of respondents who provided at least one answer. While only two blind people and one person with SCI reported no positive influences, seven blind people (13.7%), five people with SCI (15.2%), and three youths with motor impairment (15%) stated that they could not detect any event or experience having negatively affected their life.

Blind participants and people with SCI quoted their families as the major positive influence, as a source of help, support, and trust: "The family atmosphere was very serene, despite poverty and work difficulties. It provided me with a good base to cope with life, and this helped me later, when I was 31 and I had to face gradual sight loss" (Rita, 45). Gabriele, 34, paraplegic, referred to his wife and son: "They are fundamental components of my life. They brought order in me. My son gives me stimuli to act; he makes me feel useful."

Study and social relations followed in rank among the answers of blind people. Gustavo, 51, reported: "The major positive influence in my life was school, especially the university. It allowed me to do what I wanted: Now I teach; I have a job I like, thanks to my previous education." Marcella, 40, who became blind at the age of 23, quoted: "When I lost sight, the relationship with other people, blind and not blind ones, taught me that I could live anyway."

Table 35.2
Percentage Distribution of Positive and Negative Life Influences
Reported by People with Blindness and Spinal Cord
Injury and by Youths with Motor Impairment

Categories	Blindness		Spinal Cord Injury		Motor Disability	
	Positive $N = 49$	Negative $N = 44$	Positive $N = 32$	Negative $N = 28$	Positive $N = 20$	Negative $N = 17$
Work	8,1	4,0	9,3	11,3	25,0	31,8
Study	17,7	5,3	8,1	1,6	28,1	4,5
Social relations	16,9	34,7	20,9	14,5	3,1	—
Leisure	3,2	—	9,3	1,6	3,1	—
Money, SES	0,8	—	—	—	—	—
Family	31,5	25,3	30,2	29,0	3,1	—
Self	8,9	10,7	10,5	6,5	6,3	—
Religion	10,5	—	2,3	—	—	—
Health	1,6	16,0	7,0	32,3	31,3	59,1
Society, values	0,8	4,0	2,3	3,2	0,0	4,5
N of answers	124	75	86	62	32	22

Note: Dashes indicate that no answers were reported within the category.

For participants with SCI, social relations were second in rank. Caterina, 30, paraplegic, described the support of friends as follows: "They helped me deal with my dark side; they gave me the love I could not get from my family."

Young people with motor impairments prominently reported health-related factors: The most frequent answers referred to CBR intervention, which contributed to improve their health conditions through surgical operations, rehabilitation, physiotherapy, and technological aids: "Before I could not walk. Now I can do whatever I want, I go to school, and I attend a vocational training course. The training site is located five kilometers from here; I have to take a bus and to walk for a while. CBR provided me with physiotherapy and vocational training, and my parents always supported and encouraged me" (Rakesh, 20). Studying and getting a job closely followed. Krishnaram, 29, who works as a teacher in a village close to Bhaktapur, quoted: "The most positive influence in my life was teaching: I wanted this job and now I have it. I became independent and in addition I contribute to children's education."

As to negative life influences, blind people mostly listed social relations and family. Dario, 32, born blind, quoted: "The major negative experience was the difficulty in having friends when I was a child. But this taught me that you have to do something to get in touch with people; you have to disclose yourself to others to cultivate relations." Martina, 27, referred to her family as follows: "My parents tolerated everything I did, because . . . 'she is a poor blind girl.' They didn't teach me to love others. I grew up very selfish, and now I understand the reason why I have difficulties in getting friends, in building social relations. I am trying to change my attitudes and my behavior."

Blindness was not frequently quoted among negative influences. This finding can be better understood through the words of Dario, 32: "I'd like to quote blindness. But I cannot do it, because I don't know what seeing means; even though I know it's an impairment, for me it's quite a normal thing." The perspective of people who lost sight later in life is different. For example, Marcella, 40, reported: "The contact with other people is more problematic. Those who can see can easily establish even occasional relations with people on the bus. Now I cannot approach other people; they have to do it first. Some people want to help you, but then they don't know how to behave, how to deal with you. In addition, I had to stop studying for two years in order to learn to write and read in Braille."

People with SCI prominently quoted the accident or disease causing their disablement. Silvio, 34, tetraplegic after a road accident, explained: "I had to cope with problems related to my physical and moral survival, to my dignity. Looking inside me and around me, I am trying to find a solution, fighting to improve my condition as much as possible, working, and cultivating intimate relationships. My major challenge is to be able to do something again, to accept myself again." And Luigi, 30: "With paraplegia I was born twice. I had to learn all what I already knew, but in a different way. I had to learn to put on clothes, to make a better use of my mind, to pay more attention to my physical health. I had to develop commitment, will, patience. But I am not sure this will negatively affect my future. It depends on how my life will unfold; I plan to build a family, to find a gratifying job, to become autonomous."

Family followed closely, ranking second in frequency. Answers mostly referred to two issues: conflicts with parents during childhood and adolescence and difficulties with partner or spouse, often as a consequence of SCI. Flora, 22, paraplegic, quoted: "My boyfriend said that he had pity on me, and I told him to get lost. This made me feel insecure and mistrustful; I am afraid of suffering again." As for social interactions, ranking third among the negative influences, Beatrice, 26, complained about "people's prejudices. They made things more difficult to me after the accident. I felt refused, but I learned to ignore it. I tried to talk, to discuss the problem, but it was often useless."

Young people with motor impairment prominently quoted physical constraints among the negative influences. They especially emphasized activity limitations due to disablement: "I cannot perform all the activities that require the use of legs. I cannot run. But I am trying everything I can do to become independent" (Deepa, 28).

Work was second in rank among negative influences, but again in terms of activity limitations: "I have difficulties with housework, I get backache, I cannot wash clothes" (Laxmi, 16). "I can't do heavy works . . . but I can work in the kitchen" (Gauri, 22).

LIFE ACCOMPLISHMENTS

In the Life Theme questionnaire, participants were asked: "What would you consider a real success or accomplishment in your life up till now?" Only five blind people, one person with SCI, and three young participants with motor impairments did not provide any answer.

Figure 35.2 shows the answer distribution in the three groups.

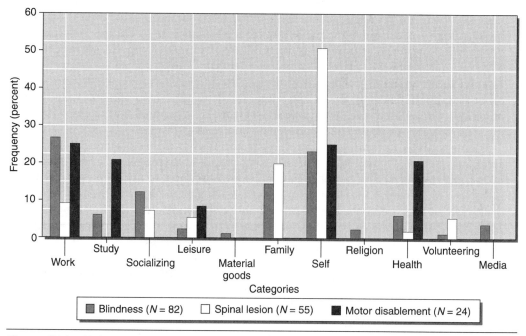

Figure 35.2   Major Life Accomplishments. Percentage distribution of answers reported by people with blindness (*N* participants = 40, *N* answers = 82), with SCI (*N* participants = 32, *N* answers = 55), and by youths with motor impairment (*N* participants = 17, *N* answers = 24).

Blind people's perceived accomplishments were mostly included in two categories: work and self-growth: "My major accomplishment is to face the challenge of getting to know and improve myself. To think that, despite some attainments, I am not on the top of the mountain, I have not finished yet" (Piero, 30). "Having become more self-confident. Having overcome the obstacle of being blind, having accepted myself: before I did not, and I didn't want to learn anything" (Teresa, 18). "My greatest accomplishment is having found peace and joy in blindness. You can do many things even without seeing: You can play music, find a job, live like other people" (Rita, 45).

Personal growth was largely prominent among people with SCI: "Many new experiences I had. It seems to me that I started a second life" (Federico, 28). "I accepted my handicap" (Nicola, 30). "I testified that it's possible to live despite great problems. I have decided to live and not to survive. If you choose to live you have to do your best, without putting burdens on others" (Clelia, 57). "Having developed self-criticism and the capability to laugh" (Sergio, 38). "Before the accident, I had a satisfying family life and I had achieved all the material goals I had set to me. Now, my accomplishment is having preserved a creative will" (Silvio, 34).

Young people with motor impairments quoted work, self-growth, study, and health in similar percentages: "My major accomplishments are practicing regular physiotherapy exercises, going to school, and undertaking a vocational training to learn woodcarving. I'd like to become a trainer, to teach woodcarving to other people" (Dipendra, 20). "My major accomplishment is to have a positive life. I work with disabled children; I suffered from the same problems they have and I can help them" (Purushottam, 29).

OPTIMAL EXPERIENCE AND DEVELOPMENT: SUGGESTIONS FOR PRACTICE

Researchers, practitioners, and policymakers agree that health cannot be simply considered as the absence of physical deviations from the normal condition. Within the notion of health, we should include the possibility for people to exploit their own resources and to develop their skills according to the environmental opportunities.

The findings presented show that optimal activities play a prominent role in disabled people's chances of integration in the active life, in that their cultivation contributes to the maximization of their residual sensory-motor skills and to the implementation of vicarious motor abilities and sensorial channels. The enjoyment, high challenges, and intrinsic motivation reported in doing such activities are substantial prerequisites for their preferential replication and for the achievement of higher levels of complexity in behavior, through the progressive increase of related skills and the acquisition of new information. This is especially true of productive activities such as work and study and activities requiring complex skills such as sports and arts.

The findings also showed that development can be successfully pursued through disablement. Physical constraints can help discover new opportunities in daily life, foster personal growth, and enhance individual strengths and resources. Although most participants reported disablement among the negative life influences, they also stressed their effort to effectively overcome the related social, behavioral, and biological constraints, focusing on the positive and constructive components of their life history and daily experience.

Despite the cultural and socioeconomic discrepancies between the Italian and Nepalese samples, no differences were found in the availability of optimal activities, their experiential features, their relevance for individuals' integration in productive life, and the role of family in supporting disabled members' development and autonomy.

Information on disabled persons' subjective perception of daily life, available opportunities for action and development, and social relations is essential to design intervention programs centered on individual resources and not on social expectations. We attempted to investigate these issues through the collection of information from adults and adolescents with motor disabilities. In particular, our findings provide some suggestions for intervention:

- The quality of subjective experience associated with daily activities and contexts can be treated as an indicator of quality of life from the person's perspective. In designing intervention programs, attention should be paid to the subjectively perceived opportunities for optimal experiences and to their role in mobilizing individual resources and in promoting the cultivation of self-selected developmental tasks and goals. Individual differences in coping with disability could be analyzed from this perspective, thus allowing the development of intervention programs tailored on individual needs and resources.
- The effectiveness of the family and cultural environment in fostering autonomy and integration should be explored through the analysis of the occurrence and frequency of daily activities and social settings—on one side—and the associated quality of experience—on the other side. Disabled people's job position and career perspectives, educational opportunities and future goals, leisure and interaction opportunities, and associated experience should be investigated from the subjective perspective to assess the degree of overlapping between the cultural expectations concerning disabled citizens and their perceived needs and goals.
- Intervention programs should aim at promoting optimal experiences and engagement in subjectively meaningful and socially relevant tasks to foster individual development and integration as well. From a biopsychosocial perspective, attention should be paid to aspects of the social environment that could be implemented, removed, or changed to empower the status of disabled citizens.

CONCLUSION

Demosthenes, one of the most famous orators and statesmen of ancient Greece, lived in Athens during the fourth century b.c. He was described as a very shy boy, suffering from stammer. Nevertheless, he determined to actively take part in politics, and he engaged in a systematic struggle with himself. He declaimed long and difficult speeches while carrying little stones in his mouth; he learned to control his breathing and modulate voice tones. Eventually, he succeeded.

However, Demosthenes' life is wrapped up in the veil of anecdotes and legends, while the people who answered our questionnaires are living examples of the amazing resource potential of human beings. Goffredo, a 21-year-old paraplegic man, stated: "Life is a challenge itself. I realized that humans cannot decide about future events, but that it is important to control and improve their consequences. You need courage to start facing this challenge, then you need perseverance and constancy in order not to give up, and also optimism to look at the future. But the more difficult the challenges, the greater the satisfaction in overcoming them. I did everything I could do. I completed my studies, I have a job, I searched for—and I found—a good relationship with a girl. I seized all the opportunities starting from the first one on the list: the opportunity to react."

REFERENCES

Agarwal, A. (1995). Mass-media and health promotion in Indian villages. *Psychology and Developing Societies, 7,* 217–236.

*Albrecht, G. L., & Devlieger, P. J. (1999). The disability paradox: High quality of life against all odds. *Social Science and Medicine, 48,* 977–988.

Atkinson, S., Rolim Medeiros, R. L., Lima Oliveira, P. H., & Dias de Almeida, R. (2000). Going down to the local: Incorporating social organization and political culture into assessments of decentralised health care. *Social Science and Medicine, 51,* 619–636.

Bickenbach, J. E., Chatterji, S., Badley, E. M., & Üstün, T. B. (1999). Models of disablement, universalism and the international classification of impairments, disabilities and handicaps. *Social Science and Medicine, 48,* 1173–1187.

Brown, A. S., Varma, V. K., Malhotra, S., Jiloha, R. C., Conover, S. A., & Susser, E. S. (1998). Course of acute affective disorders in a developing country setting. *Journal of Nervous and Mental Diseases, 186,* 207–213.

Csikszentmihalyi, M. (1975). *Beyond boredom and anxiety: The experience of play in work and games.* San Francisco: Jossey-Bass.

Csikszentmihalyi, M. (1985). Emergent motivation and the evolution of the self. In D. Kleiber & M. H. Maher (Eds.). *Motivation in adulthood* (pp. 93–113). Greenwich, CT: JAI Press.

Csikszentmihalyi, M. (1997). Activity, experience and personal growth. In J. Curtis & S. Russell (Eds.), *Physical activity in human experience: Interdisciplinary perspectives* (pp. 59–88). Champaign, IL: Human Kinetics.

Csikszentmihalyi, M., & Beattie, O. (1979). Life themes: A theoretical and empirical exploration of their origins and effects. *Journal of Humanistic Psychology, 19,* 677–693.

Csikszentmihalyi, M., & Csikszentmihalyi, I. S. (Eds.). (1988). *Optimal experience: Psychological studies of flow in consciousness.* New York: Cambridge University Press.

Csikszentmihalyi, M., & Massimini, F. (1985). On the psychological selection of biocultural information. *New Ideas in Psychology, 3,* 115–138.

Delle Fave, A. (1996). Il processo di 'trasformazione di flow' in un campione di soggetti medullolesi [The process of flow transformation in a sample of people with medullary lesions]. In F. Massimini, P. Inghilleri, & A. Delle Fave (Eds.), *La selezione psicologica umana* [Human psychological selection] (pp. 615–634). Milano, Italy: Cooperativa Libraria IULM.

Delle Fave, A., & Maletto, C. (1992). Processi di attenzione e qualità dell'esperienza soggettiva nei non vedenti [Attention processes and quality of subjective experience in blind people]. In D. Galati (Ed.), *Vedere con la mente: Processi cognitivi, affettivi e strategie adattative* [Seeing through the mind: Cognitive processes, affects and adaptive strategies] (pp. 321–353). Milano, Italy: Franco Angeli.

Delle Fave, A., & Massimini, F. (1988). Modernization and the changing contexts of flow in work and leisure. In M. Csikszentmihalyi & I. S. Csikszentmihalyi (Eds.), *Optimal experience: Psychological studies of flow in consciousness* (pp. 193–213). New York: Cambridge University Press.

Delle Fave, A., & Massimini, F. (1991). Modernization and the quality of daily experience in a southern Italy village. In N. Bleichrodt & P. J. D. Drenth (Eds.), *Contemporary issues in cross-cultural psychology* (pp. 110–119). Amsterdam: Swets & Zeitlinger.

Delle Fave, A., & Massimini, F. (2003). Making disability into a resource. *The Psychologist, 16,* 133–134.

Engel, G. L. (1977). The need for a new medical model: A challenge for biomedicine. *Science, 196,* 129–136.

Fisher, K., & Johnston, M. (1996a). Emotional distress as a mediator of the relationship between pain and disability: An experimental study. *British Journal of Health Psychology, 1,* 207–218.

Fisher, K., & Johnston, M. (1996b). Experimental manipulation of perceived control and its effect on disability. *Psychology & Health, 11,* 657–669.

Fougeyrollas, P. (1995). Documenting environmental factors for preventing the handicap creation process: Quebec contributions relating to ICIDH and social participation of people with functional differences. *Disability and Rehabilitation, 17,* 145–153.

Galvin, L. R., & Godfrey, H. P. D. (2001). The impact of coping on emotional adjustment to spinal cord injury (SCI): Review of the literature and application of a stress appraisal and coping formulation. *Spinal Cord, 39,* 615–627.

Gatchel, R., & Bell, G. (2000). The biopsychosocial approach to spine care and research. *Spine, 25*(20), 2572.

Hyland, M. E., & Kenyon, C. A. P. (1992). A measure of positive health-related quality of life: The Satisfaction with Illness Scale. *Psychological Reports, 71,* 1137–1138.

Ingstad, B. (1999). The myth of disability in developing nations. *Lancet, 354,* 757–758.

Johnston, M., & Pollard, B. (2001). Consequences of disease: Testing the WHO International Classification of Impairments, Disabilities and Handicaps (ICIDH) model. *Social Science and Medicine, 53,* 1261–1273.

Kerr, P. C., & Stephens, D. (1997). The use of an open-ended questionnaire to identify positive aspects of acquired hearing loss. *Audiology, 36,* 19–28.

Kreuter, M. (2000). Spinal cord injury and partner relationships. *Spinal Cord, 38,* 2–6.

Marshall, C. A., & Largo, H. R. H., Jr. (1999). Disability and rehabilitation: A context for understanding the American Indian experience. *Lancet, 354,* 758–760.

Massimini, F., Csikszentmihalyi, M., & Delle Fave, A. (1988). Flow and biocultural evolution. In M. Csikszentmihalyi & I. S. Csikszentmihalyi (Eds.), *Optimal experience: Psychological studies of flow in consciousness* (pp. 60–81). New York: Cambridge University Press.

Massimini, F., & Delle Fave, A. (2000). Individual development in a bio-cultural perspective. *American Psychologist, 55,* 24–33.

Massimini, F., Delle Fave, A., & Borri Gaspardin, M. (1992). Televisione e qualità dell'esperienza soggettiva: L'integrazione tra dati quantitativi e qualitativi [TV and the quality of subjective experience: Integration of quantitative and qualitative data]. *Ikon, 24,* 5–30.

Mathew, K. M., Ravichandran, G., May, K., & Morsley, K. (2001). The biopsychosocial model and spinal cord injury. *Spinal Cord, 39,* 644–649.

*Menzel, P., Dolan, P., Richardson, J., & Olsen, J. A. (2002). The role of adaptation to disability and disease in health state valuation: A preliminary normative analysis. *Social Science and Medicine, 55,* 2149–2158.

Meyers, A. R., Anderson, J. J., Miller, D. R., Shipp, K., & Hoenig, H. (2002). Barriers, facilitators and access for wheelchair users: Substantive and methodological lessons from a pilot study of environmental effects. *Social Science and Medicine, 55,* 1435–1446.

Negri, P., Massimini, F., & Delle Fave, A. (1992). Tema di vita e strategie adattative nei nonvedenti [Life theme and adaptive strategies in blind people]. In D. Galati (Ed.), *Vedere con la mente: Processi cognitivi, affettivi e strategie adattative* [Seeing through the mind: Cognitive processes, affects and adaptive strategies] (pp. 355–380). Milano, Italy: Franco Angeli.

Nepal South Asia Centre (NESAC). (1998). *Nepal Human Development Report 1998.* Kathmandu, Nepal: Author.

Plahuta, J. M., McCulloch, B. J., Kasarskis, E. J., Ross, M. A., Walter, R. A., & McDonald, E. R. (2002). Amyotrophic lateral sclerosis and hopelessness: Psychosocial factors. *Social Science and Medicine, 55,* 2131–2140.

Salmon, P., Manzi, F., & Valori, R. M. (1996). Measuring the meaning in life for patients with incurable cancer: The Life Evaluation Questionnaire (LEQ). *European Journal of Cancer, 32*(A), 755–760.

Saraswathi, T. S. (1992). Child survival and health and their linkages with psycho-social factors in the home and community. *Psychology and Developing Societies, 4,* 73–87.

Saravanan, B., Manigandam, C., Macaden, A., Tharion, G., & Bhattacharji, S. (2001). Re-examining the psychology of spinal cord injury: A meaning centered approach from a cultural perspective. *Spinal Cord, 39,* 323–326.

SCN-CBR. (2000). *The rights of the children with disabilities.* Mid-term review report [internal publication only]. Bhaktapur, Nepal: Save the Children Norway and CBR-Bhaktapur.

*Sodergren, S. C., & Hyland, M. E. (2000). What are the positive consequences of illness? *Psychology & Health, 15,* 85–97.

Tanaka-Matsumi, J., & Draguns, J. (1997). Culture and psychopathology. In J. W. Berry, M. H. Segall, & C. Kagitçibasi (Eds.), *Handbook of cross-cultural psychology: Vol. 3. Social behavior and applications* (pp. 449–492). Needham Heights, MA: Allyn & Bacon.

Ünalan, H., Gençosmanoglu, B., Akgün, K., Karamehmetoglu, S., Tuna, H., Önes, K., et al. (2001). Quality of life of primary caregivers of spinal cord injury survivors living in the community: Controlled study with short form-36 questionnaire. *Spinal Cord, 39,* 318–322.

*Üstün, T. B., Chatterji, S., Bickenbach, J. E., Trotter, R. T., II, Room, R., Rehm, J., et al. (Eds.). (2001). *Disability and culture: Universalism and diversity.* Göttingen, Germany: Hogrefe & Huber.

Werner, D. (1987). *Disabled village children.* Palo Alto, CA: Hesperian Foundation.

World Health Organization. (2001). *International classification of functioning, disability and health* [Endorsed by the Fifty-Fourth World Health Assembly for international use on May 22, 2001]. Retrieved March 8, 2002, from http://www.who.int/icidh.

CHAPTER 36

Good Lives and the Rehabilitation of Offenders: A Positive Approach to Sex Offender Treatment

TONY WARD and RUTH MANN

THE TREATMENT OF sex offenders in the past two decades has focused on reducing the psychological and social deficits associated with each individual's offending. The rehabilitation model associated with this approach has been called the *risk-need approach* and is concerned with decreasing the likelihood that offenders will engage in behavior that will prove harmful to the community (Andrews & Bonta, 1998; Ward & Stewart, 2003a). The expectation is that by identifying and managing dynamic risk factors (e.g., antisocial attitudes and deviant sexual arousal), offending rates will be reduced. The primary goal of treatment is always reducing and managing risk, not enhancing the quality of offenders' lives (Ward, 2002).

The major form this theory takes in the sexual-offending domain is that of relapse prevention (RP). A number of clinicians and researchers have argued that the treatment of sexual offenders ought to be based on an understanding of the process of relapse (e.g., Pithers, 1990). It has been suggested that there are clear patterns evident in the behavior of sexual offenders, which translate into distinct clusters of cognitive, affective, and behavioral offense variables (Ward, Louden, Hudson, & Marshall, 1995). Models of the relapse process set out to provide a rich description of the cognitive, behavioral, motivational, and contextual risk factors associated with a sexual offense (Ward & Hudson, 2000). Theory at this level typically includes an explicit temporal factor and focuses on proximal causes or the *how* of sexual offending. The aim in treatment is to ensure that individuals acquire skills to cope with risk factors in a nonabusive manner. The different stages of an individual's offense process are typically linked to distinct treatment strategies.

We propose that treatment based on removing deficits or risk factors is unlikely to sufficiently motivate offenders in treatment and does not pay enough attention to the issue of psychological agency and personal identity. Rather than adopting an RP-type of program, we recommend locating or embedding it within a more constructive, strength-based capabilities approach—what we have called the *good lives model* of offender rehabilitation (Ward, 2002; Ward & Stewart, 2003a, 20003b, 2003c). In the good lives model (GLM), risk factors are viewed as obstacles that erode individuals' capacity to live more fulfilling lives. Essentially, risk factors function as indicators or markers that an individual's pursuit of primary human goods is compromised in some way. That is, the internal and external conditions necessary to achieve valued outcomes may be missing or incomplete. Thus, the therapeutic focus should be on implementing offenders' good lives conceptualization as well as managing risk. The modification of criminogenic needs, or dynamic risk factors, will occur because of implementing a good lives plan.

In this chapter, we propose that the GLM of rehabilitation has the necessary conceptual resources to provide therapists with comprehensive guidelines for treating sex offenders. The good lives model grounds or underpins the risk management approach and provides an explanation of why risk factors are problematic for the person and society and accounts for their interrelationships. First, we discuss the required features of a good rehabilitation theory; then we outline the GLM and examine its application to the assessment and treatment of sex offenders.

WHAT SHOULD A REHABILITATION THEORY LOOK LIKE?

A good theory of offender rehabilitation should specify the aims of therapy, provide a justification of these aims in terms of its core assumptions about etiology and the values underpinning the approach, identify clinical targets, and outline how treatment should proceed in the light of these assumptions and goals (Ward & Marshall, in press). Thus, etiological theories and practice models are conceptually linked by an overarching theory of rehabilitation, which functions as a bridging theory. The bridge is between factors that are thought to cause offending and the way treatment strategies are implemented. For example, there is a close relationship between deficit models of sexual offending and problem-based clinical practice by virtue of the risk-need theory of rehabilitation and its attendant RP treatment framework. The risk-need theory connects assumptions about the causes of sexual offending (i.e., psychological deficits), the type of interventions that should be used (i.e., problem reducing), and, most significantly, the way these interventions should be implemented (i.e., to reduce or manage risk). In RP, the focus is on moderating or reducing risk factors, not enhancing an individual's capacity to live a more fulfilling life.

A good rehabilitation model should also specify the style of treatment (e.g., skills based, structured), inform therapists about the appropriate attitudes to take toward offenders, address the issue of motivation, and clarify the role and importance of the therapeutic alliance. A number of these features of treatment are either ignored by standard RP approaches or regarded as external to treatment. That is, they are seen as a set of concerns about process rather than substance or content.

The good lives model fits in well with a constructive view of punishment because it is based on a more positive view of human nature and the intrinsic value of human beings. This point has been powerfully argued by Margalit (1996):

Even if there are noticeable differences among people in their ability to change, they are deserving of respect for the very possibility of changing. Even the worst criminals are worthy of basic human respect for the possibility that they may radically reevaluate their past lives and, if they are given the opportunity, may live the rest of their lives in a worthy manner. (p. 70)

An adequate theory of rehabilitation should have the conceptual resources to create a bridge between etiology and treatment, specify treatment targets, provide a rationale and theoretical basis for the importance of forming positive attitudes toward offenders and thereby clarify the role of a therapeutic alliance, deal with agency and identity, be strength based, explain the relationship between risk and goods—adopt the twin foci of seeking to equip offenders to live good lives but also to minimize and control risk—have rich conception of human nature and the related issues of values and motivation, and provide concrete suggestions for the assessment and treatment of sex offenders.

THE RISK-NEED MODEL

We do not have the space to offer a systematic exposition and critique of the risk management rehabilitation model (for a comprehensive critique, see Ward & Brown, 2003; Ward & Stewart, 2003a). Our aim is merely to outline the basic assumptions of this approach to rehabilitation and to provide an appropriate context for the GLM.

Three general principles underpin the risk-need approach to the treatment of offenders (see Andrews & Bonta, 1998). First, the *risk principle* is concerned with the match between level of risk and the actual amount of treatment received. Second, according to the *need principle,* programs should primarily target criminogenic needs, that is, dynamic risk factors associated with recidivism that can be changed. Third, the *responsivity principle* is concerned with a program's ability to reach and make sense to the participants for whom it was designed. In other words, will offenders be able to absorb the content of the program and subsequently change their behavior?

The treatment form this model has taken in the sexual offending domain is commonly that of relapse prevention. The goal is to help sex offenders understand their offense pattern and cope with situational and psychological factors that place them at risk for reoffending (Ward & Hudson, 2000). The basic idea underpinning this approach is that the best way to reduce recidivism rates is to identify and reduce or eliminate an individual's array of dynamic risk factors. These factors constitute clinical needs or problems that should be explicitly targeted. Thus, treatment programs for sexual offenders are typically problem-focused and aim to eradicate or reduce the various psychological and behavioral difficulties associated with sexually abusive behavior. These problems include intimacy deficits, deviant sexual preferences, cognitive distortions, empathy deficits, and difficulties managing negative emotional states.

It is clear that the risk management and related RP models have resulted in more effective treatment and lower recidivism rates (Hollin, 1999; Laws, Hudson, & Ward, 2000). In addition, the emphasis on empirically supported therapies and accountability is a laudable goal. However, alongside these undoubted strengths are some areas of weakness. The majority of these concerns revolve around the issue of offender responsivity and point to the difficulty of motivating offenders using this approach.

In brief, we argue that as a theory of rehabilitation, it lacks the conceptual resources to adequately guide therapists and to engage offenders (Ward & Stewart, 2003c). More specifically, it adopts a "pin cushion" model of treatment and views offenders as disembodied bearers of risk. Second, it does not address the issue of human agency and personal identity and, in effect, adopts a rather reductionist approach to human behavior. Third, it disregards the crucial importance of human needs and their influence in determining offending behavior. Related to this is a failure to explicitly focus on the establishment of a strong therapeutic relationship with the offender; it is silent on the question of therapist factors and attitude toward offenders. Fourth, the risk-need model does not systematically address the issue of offender motivation and tends to lead to negative or avoidant treatment goals. Finally, this perspective often results in a mechanistic, one-size-fits-all approach to treatment and does not really deal with the critical role of contextual factors in the process of rehabilitation.

GOOD LIVES MODEL OF OFFENDER REHABILITATION

The GLM of offender rehabilitation is essentially a strength-based approach and, as such, seeks to give offenders the capabilities to secure primary human goods in socially acceptable and personally meaningful ways (Kekes, 1989; Rapp, 1998; Ward & Stewart, 2003a). Primary goods are actions, states of affairs, characteristics, experiences, and states of mind that are viewed as intrinsically beneficial to human beings and are sought for their own sake rather than as means to some more fundamental ends (Deci & Ryan, 2000; Emmons, 1999; Schmuck & Sheldon, 2001). From the perspective of this model, humans are by nature active, goal-seeking beings who are consistently engaged in the process of constructing a sense of purpose and meaning in their lives. This is hypothesized to emerge from the pursuit and achievement of a number of primary human goods (valued aspects of human functioning and living), which collectively allow individuals to flourish, that is, to achieve high levels of well-being. According to the GLM, the identification of risk factors simply alerts clinicians to problems (obstacles) in the way offenders are seeking to achieve valued or personally satisfying outcomes. Therefore, the identification of risk elements is a critical part of assessment because it flags the existence of problems in the way individuals seek primary human goods. Different categories of risk factors point to problems in the pursuit of different types of human goods. For example, the existence of social isolation indicates difficulties in the way the goods of intimacy and community are sought and may indicate skill deficits and/or a lack of social opportunities and resources.

Thus, the core idea is that all meaningful human actions reflect attempts to achieve primary human goods (Emmons, 1999; Ward, 2002).

There is a consensus (in Western culture, at least) about the lists of primary human goods noted in psychological and social science research (Cummins, 1996; Emmons, 1999), evolutionary theory (Arnhart, 1998), practical ethics (Murphy, 2001), and philosophical anthropology (Nussbaum, 2000; Rescher, 1990). Derived from these various research endeavors (especially the work of Murphy, 2001) is the following list of nine primary human goods:

1. Life (including healthy living and optimal physical functioning, sexual satisfaction)
2. Knowledge
3. Excellence in play and work (including mastery experiences)
4. Excellence in agency (i.e., autonomy and self-directedness)
5. Inner peace (i.e., freedom from emotional turmoil and stress)
6. Relatedness (including intimate, romantic, and family relationships) and community
7. Spirituality (in the broad sense of finding meaning and purpose in life)
8. Happiness
9. Creativity

This list is comprehensive and is consistent with much recent work on human motivation, well-being, and social policy. Each of these primary goods can be broken down into subclusters or components; in other words, the primary goods are complex and multifaceted. For example, the primary good of relatedness contains the subcluster goods of intimacy, friendship, support, caring, reliability, honesty, and so on.

The possibility of constructing and translating conceptions of good lives into actions and concrete ways of living depends crucially on the possession of *internal* (skills and capabilities) and *external* conditions (opportunities and supports). The specific form that a conception will take depends on the actual abilities, interests, and opportunities of each individual and the weightings he or she gives to specific primary goods. The weightings or priorities allocated to specific primary goods is constitutive of an offender's *personal identity* and spells out the kind of life sought and the kind of person he or she would like to be. The assumption here is that personal identity is derived from our commitments and resultant ways of life. However, because human beings naturally seek a range of primary goods or desired states, it is important that all classes of primary goods be addressed in a conception of good lives; they should be ordered and coherently related to one another. If an offender decides to pursue a life characterized by service to the community, a core aspect of his or her identity will revolve around the primary goods of relatedness and community. The offender's sense of mastery, meaning, and agency will reflect the overarching goods of relatedness and community and its associated subclusters of goods (e.g., intimacy, caring, reliability, honesty). The resulting good lives conceptions should be organized in ways that ensure each primary good has a role to play and can be secured or experienced by the individual concerned. A conception that is fragmented and lacks coherency is likely to lead to frustration and harm to the individual concerned, as well as to a life lacking an overall sense of purpose and meaning (Emmons, 1996). Additionally, a conception of good lives is always *context dependent*; there is no such thing as the right kind of life for an individual across every conceivable setting. Therefore, all individuals are hypothesized to live their lives according to a GLM, either explicitly or implicitly, or, rather, GLM in the plural sense because each general GLM can be deconstructed into a number of distinct, although related, forms. That is, there is no such thing as the right kind of life for any specific person; there are always a number of feasible possibilities, although there are limits defined by circumstances, abilities, and preferences (Kekes, 1989; Ward & Stewart, 2003b, 2003c).

Psychological, social, and lifestyle problems emerge when these GLMs are faulty in some way. When they do not achieve what they set out to, the well-being of individuals living according to such GLM is reduced. In the case of criminal behavior, it is hypothesized that there are four major types of difficulties:

1. Problems with the *means* used to secure goods
2. A lack of *scope* within a good lives plan
3. The presence of *conflict* among goals (goods sought) or incoherence
4. A lack of the necessary *capacities* to form and adjust a GLM to changing circumstances (e.g., impulsive decision making)

Taking into account the type of GLM problem an offender has, a treatment plan should be *explicitly* constructed in the form of a good lives conceptualization that, taking into account an offender's preferences, strengths, primary goods, and relevant environments, specifies exactly what competencies and resources are required to achieve these goods. This crucially involves identifying the internal and external conditions necessary to implement the plan and designing a rehabilitation strategy to equip the individual with these required skills, resources, and opportunities. Such an approach to offender rehabilitation is significantly contextualized and promotes the importance of personal identity and its emergence from daily living (and actions). It is also clearly value laden in the sense that primary human goods represent outcomes that are beneficial to human beings and their absence is harmful (to the individual and to others). Therefore, rehabilitation should be tailored to individual offenders' particular GLM and should seek to install only the internal and external conditions that will enable its realization. The detection of dynamic risk factors or criminogenic needs signals that there are problems of scope, coherence, inappropriate means, and planning deficits in the distinct domains of a person's life. Risk analysis simply informs therapists that there are problems in the way offenders seek human goods. Treatment should proceed on the assumption that effective rehabilitation requires the acquisition of competencies and external supports and opportunities to live a different kind of life.

IMPLICATIONS FOR THE ASSESSMENT OF SEXUAL OFFENDERS

If the GLM is to be adopted as a foundation for sexual offender treatment, the first area to consider is that of sex offender assessment—*assessment* meaning any structured or unstructured activity that is intended to discover more about the sexual offender, in particular, the offender's risk, treatment needs, and responsivity factors (i.e., the personal factors such as IQ, personality, and learning style that affect the way in which the offender responds to treatment). For example, a typical assessment package for sexual offenders might include structured interviews focusing on personal history, relapse knowledge (e.g., Mann, Beckett, Fisher, & Thornton, 2002), and personality (e.g., the PCL-R; Hare, 1991); a battery of psychometric tests measuring areas related to risk of sexual recidivism such as impulsivity, offense-supportive attitudes, and socioaffective functioning; a psychophysiological assessment such as phallometric testing (Marshall & Fernandez, 2000); IQ testing; and behavioral observation.

Often, assessment procedures are conducted by technicians or assistant psychologists who might think of their work as separate from the process of treatment. Assessors may be trained in the technical aspects of psychometric assessment, such as the importance of not acting in any way that could influence the client's responses. To adhere to these principles, the assessor often does not attempt to build a relationship with the sexual offender, but presents the assessment tasks in as neutral a way as possible. Sexual offender clients often respond to this presentation with suspicion, because they have no indication that the process of assessment is adapted to their personal needs or issues. In the 1980s, most sexual offender specialists learned that sex offenders were likely to manipulate the assessment and treatment process and were guided to expect that "the client will have goals that the therapist does not share and the therapist is expected to override the client's wishes" (Salter, 1988, p. 87). In practice, this assumption could lead to reluctance by the therapist or assessor to discuss the purpose of assessment or to invite clients' thoughts and ideas about their needs.

Such an approach to assessment is not consistent with the GLM. The GLM leads to a prediction that people are most responsive to an intervention when that intervention is tailored to their own personal goals and needs. Sexual offender assessment should be seen as an intervention in its own right because it is a process that is capable of bringing about change. For instance, a well-conducted collaborative risk and need assessment (see next section) can in itself lead a client to start thinking about change or to gain insight into problems not previously recognized. Assessment can also lead to change in a person's environment. For example, an assessment that concludes that a particular offender is both high risk and high need (or "high deviancy" as it is sometimes called) can lead to the offender's being moved to more secure conditions or receiving an increased level of social punishment. Therefore, the assessment process should be treated with the same level of care as the treatment intervention. In doing so, attention should be paid both to the style of assessment and to the content.

ASSESSING PERSONAL GOALS AND PRIORITIES

First, we examine the content of an assessment package that would be consistent with the GLM. We continue to believe that risk, needs, and responsivity are three major issues to be explored through assessment. However, we also recommend a fourth area for exploration: *priorities*. Risk-need principles should be nested or embedded within a good lives framework; that is, it is essential to assess a client's own goals, life priorities, and aims for the intervention. In particular, it is essential to understand how a client prioritizes and operationalizes the primary human goods such as those outlined by Ward (2002) and described earlier in this chapter. If this fourth area is not explored, sexual offender assessment concentrates only on vulnerabilities and fails to recognize the importance of understanding how an individual can become fulfilled. We, therefore, recommend that assessment of risk and vulnerability be balanced with an assessment of how each individual constructs his or her conception of a good life (Ward & Stewart, 2003b, 2003c).

There is no psychometric measure that can make this assessment, and a reliance on questionnaires may limit the depth of data gathered, so a clinical interview is the recommended approach. We have tried, and found ineffective, the method of presenting a list of primary human goods to offenders and asking them to choose their priorities. In our experience, such a task has been approached as if it were a test rather than an opportunity for self-exploration. In consequence, we recommend instead that an open-ended interview be conducted, where the assessor's intentions and the rationale for the interview are made transparent. For example, the interview could be introduced in the following way:

> Researchers have suggested that there are a number of activities and experiences that human beings need if they are to have a good (fulfilling) life. I want to talk about these things with you and find out which you feel you have achieved in your life and which you don't. We can then talk about how treatment can help you focus on the things that you don't have in your life and how you can go about building up those areas. We can also play to your strengths—the areas where you have achieved happiness or satisfaction—and build on those positives. The outcome for you from treatment should be that you feel your life to be more rewarding, satisfying, and balanced. It is my hope and expectation that this would also mean that you don't experience the problems you had before when you were offending.

The exploratory interview should address a number of different issues with respect to each human good:

- What does this mean to you?
- How important is this to you? Has your view of its importance changed over time—for example, do you currently see this as a more important area than you used to?
- How have you gone about achieving this in your life? Which strategies have worked the best? Which have worked least well?
- Would you like to have more of this in your life?
- What do you think has prevented you from achieving this in your life as much as you could have done?
- Where would you like to be with respect to this in one year's time? Five years' time? Ten years' time?

Such questions allow for the assessment of each individual's conception of a good life. They also facilitate an understanding of the individual's strategies for realizing primary goods. To make a more comprehensive assessment of each individual's potential for achieving a good life, the assessing clinician should have an understanding of the following areas, so that answers to the previous questions can be probed in line with the theory behind the GLM. The following four issues, taken from Ward and Stewart (2003b), could form the basis for a final good lives formulation:

1. Is there restricted scope? That is, is the individual focusing on some goods to the detriment of other goods, so that his or her life seems to lack adequate balance and range of priorities? For instance, the individual may overemphasize mastery and underemphasize relationships or favor knowledge but not pursue any form of creativity.
2. Are some human goods pursued through inappropriate means? That is, has the individual chosen strategies for achieving goods that have turned out to be counterproductive? For example, the individual may have chosen

to pursue the goal of intimacy by adopting extremely controlling behaviors toward partners.

3. Is there conflict among the goals articulated? For instance, does the individual state priorities that cannot coexist easily, such as wanting emotional intimacy with a romantic partner but also wanting sexual freedom and variety of partners? Or does the individual predominantly engage in everyday behaviors inconsistent with his or her higher order goals, such as an individual who desires autonomy but is required to display considerable loyalty to an employer? Emmons (1999) has clearly described the stress that results from a lifestyle that is inconsistent with an individual's most valued goods.

4. Does the person have the capacity or capabilities to enact his or her plan—implicit or explicit? Is the plan realistic, taking into account the individual's abilities, likely opportunities, deep preferences, and values?

An exploration of a sexual offender's good lives conception can assist the clinician in formulating a treatment plan that provides the opportunity for the individual to achieve greater satisfaction and well-being. If offenders are able to see how the treatment plan will directly benefit them in terms of goods that they value, we argue that they are far more likely to engage enthusiastically in treatment. Given that we know that men who reoffend despite receiving sex offender treatment were consciously unengaged with the treatment process (Webster, in press), it seems reasonable to assume that high perception of treatment relevance will be associated with reduced risk of further offending.

ASSESSMENT STYLE

Recently, it has become fashionable to approach sexual offender assessment with a primary intention of assessing risk (Hart, Laws, & Kropp, 2003). An understanding of risk is the primary preoccupation for most of those involved professionally with the sexual offender—from the sentencing authority to the treatment provider and the policymaker to those engaged in monitoring and offense prevention. However, an understanding of risk is *not* the primary preoccupation of most sexual offenders. Instead, offenders tend to be more concerned about their links with family and friends, their physical circumstances, their position within their immediate and wider community, and the relief of stress and other negative personal symptoms. For instance, a recent survey of sex offenders who refuse treatment in Her Majesty's (HM) Prison Service (Mann & Webster, 2003) established that maintaining family support was the most important priority for this group. Denial or treatment refusal was seen as necessary to maintain important relationships.

Given that the risk assessor's priority is in conflict with the offender's priority as revealed during risk assessment, it is often unlikely that such assessment will uncover the full picture of a person's functioning. For instance, the offender who is not motivated to work with the risk assessor is likely to conceal or minimize areas related to risk that are unpleasant to reveal, such as deviant sexual interests. Assessment is more accurate and more productive if both parties share goals and priorities. With this issue in mind, Mann and Shingler (2002) produced a set of guidelines for collaborative risk assessment, which attempts to reconcile the needs and goals of clinician and offender. The collaborative approach reconceptualizes risk assessment as need assessment and involves the therapist's working with the client to define together the nature of the client's problems and to agree on a process for working toward solutions. The collaborative approach to assessment is entirely consistent with the GLM, emphasizing as it does the fundamental autonomy and dignity of the human being, even though the individual has committed crimes or other harmful acts on others.

In essence, the collaborative approach involves a genuine commitment from the therapist to work transparently and respectfully and to emphasize that the client's best interests are to be served by the assessment process. Potential issues of risk and need are presented to the client as areas for collaborative investigation. Results of assessment procedures such as phallometric and psychometric testing are discussed and the client is invited to collaborate in drawing conclusions from them. Perhaps most relevant of all to the GLM, the client's strengths and life achievements are considered to be as important as the client's offense-related needs in determining prognosis and treatment plan. Where the collaborative risk assessment process has been introduced as a conscious strategy, the early indicators are that relationships between treatment staff and clients are greatly improved, with a subsequent positive effect on motivation and retention in treatment (Mann & Shingler, 2002).

In conclusion, then, the GLM approach to assessing sexual offenders must be seen in both the content and style of the assessment procedure. Assessment of sexual offenders must continue to examine risk, need, and responsivity factors but must also involve a full consideration of the individual's good lives conceptualization. Assessment of all these areas should be achieved using the collaborative approach wherever possible to convey the professional's commitment to respecting the client. The treatment plan arising from such an assessment will be individualized, consistent with the individual's priorities, and, therefore, less likely to conflict with the client's personal goals. This sets an individual up to enter treatment with a sense that treatment is a relevant and important activity to engage in.

IMPLICATIONS FOR THE TREATMENT OF SEXUAL OFFENDERS

Applying the GLM to sex offender treatment requires the delineation of several principles that must underlie the construction of a treatment program:

- Many sex offenders are likely to have experienced adversarial developmental experiences as children and should, therefore, be seen as individuals who have lacked the opportunities and support necessary to achieve a coherent good lives plan.
- Consequently, sexual offenders lack many of the essential skills and capabilities necessary to achieve a fulfilling life.
- Sexual offending represents an attempt to achieve human goods that are desired, but the skills or capabilities necessary to achieve them are not possessed. Alternatively, sexual offending can arise from an attempt to relieve the sense of incompetence, conflict, or dissatisfaction that arises from not achieving valued human goods.
- The absence of certain human goods seems to be more strongly associated with sexual offending: agency, inner peace, and relatedness.

- The risk of sexual offending may be reduced by assisting sexual offenders to develop the skills and capabilities necessary to achieve the full range of human goods, with particular emphasis on agency, inner peace, and relatedness.
- Treatment is, therefore, seen as an activity that should *add to* sexual offenders' repertoire of personal functioning, rather than an activity that simply *removes* a problem or is devoted to *managing* problems, as if a lifetime of restricting their activity is the only way to avoid offending. Like contemporary medical treatment, sex offender treatment should aim to return individuals to as normal a level of functioning as possible and should place restrictions only on activities that are highly related to the problem behavior. Thus, a man who raped an adult woman might be encouraged to avoid certain situations in his future life, but he should not be encouraged to give up any hopes of developing an intimate relationship by being told to avoid all situations where single women might be present.

The GLM conceptualization of sexual offending, therefore, differs in several important ways from the traditional sexual offender treatment model. These differences are elaborated next.

AIMS OF THE GOOD LIVES MODEL TREATMENT

The aims of GLM treatment are always specified as "approach goals" (Emmons, 1996; Mann, 2000; Mann, Webster, Schofield, & Marshall, 2004). That is, the aims of treatment are defined in terms of what clients will achieve and gain, rather than in terms of what they will cease to think or do. There are several advantages to specifying the goals of treatment in this way. First, the goals are more likely to resonate with the client's intrinsic motivation to change, in that change is more appealing if the results appear obviously life enhancing. Second, the goals are more likely to fit with offenders' own preoccupations following conviction. Much as we would like to think that most sexual offenders are preoccupied with avoiding future offending, the truth is they are more preoccupied with their own quality of life. An approach-goal-focused program offers a better quality of life, while still focused on achieving what most programs are funded to achieve: reductions in recidivism. Third, an approach-goal-focused program is pragmatically more likely to work: Research with alcohol abusers has demonstrated that people working toward approach goals are less likely to lapse than those working toward avoidance goals (Cox, Klinger, & Blount, 1991). In our own work, we have been able to demonstrate that sexual offenders undergoing an approach-focused self-management intervention showed greater compliance with treatment compared to a more traditional avoidance-focused relapse prevention program. Even so, they emerged with an equally clear idea of their personal risk factors and warning signs (Mann et al., 2004).

MANUALIZED OR FORMULATION-BASED TREATMENT?

A treatment approach based on the GLM may struggle to find the right balance of structure and flexibility. Traditionally, sexual offender treatment programs have been highly structured psychoeducational programs, where skills are taught in a series of modules such as emotion management, victim empathy, and so forth. Such programs may not be consistent with the GLM's emphasis on person-centered values (Drake & Ward, 2003). On the other hand, unstructured treatment programs have been found to have no impact on recidivism rates and, therefore, presumably, are not sufficiently targeting offense-relevant areas of pathology. Drake and Ward argue for a formulation-based treatment approach, where the intervention covers topics relevant to an individual formulation of the client, based on the kind of assessment procedure described previously. It must, however, be emphasized that formulation-based interventions are not the same as unstructured programs. Although challenging, it is our contention that it is possible to manualize a formulation-based program. For example, a program run by William Marshall and his colleagues in Canada (Marshall, Anderson, & Fernandez, 1999) adopts a rolling format, where group members work through a series of assignments at their own pace. Assignments include both offense-related topics, such as victim empathy assignments, and topics related to achieving human goods, such as intimacy, attachment, and emotional management. Although one way to deliver such a program is for each group member simply to complete each assignment, it is also possible to tailor the program for each individual, based on a formulation of the member's needs. In such an approach, one group member might, for example, spend only one session examining self-esteem but several sessions examining the issue of other-esteem. Another group member might complete more victim empathy assignments than usual, if this was a particular area of deficit. To operate a manual-based program according to individual formulations, it is necessary to have considered all possible areas of need within the program, from which a selection will be drawn for each individual, and to have a careful system of recording work undertaken so that evaluations of treatment efficacy can still be conducted. It would also be necessary to have some clear guidelines that specify conditions under which each possible area of treatment would be either offered or deemed unnecessary. Such manualized but individualized programs are rare within today's state of the art, but there is evidence of programs moving in this direction; and we encourage further consideration of such treatment design.

RECONCEPTUALIZING SEX OFFENDER TREATMENT TARGETS ACCORDING TO THE GOOD LIVES MODEL

Essentially, treatment involves two steps. First, offenders must construe themselves as people who can secure all the important human goods in socially acceptable and personally rewarding ways (Ward & Stewart, 2003b). Maruna (2001) has presented convincing evidence that such a construal of self is a feature of offenders who successfully desist from further criminal behavior.

Second, the treatment program should endeavor to assist offenders in developing the scope, capacities, coherence, and strategies necessary for a healthy personal good lives plan. For sex offenders, it is suggested that the personal goods that tend most often to have been corrupted or neglected are agency, relatedness, and inner peace. To achieve a GLM-consistent treatment approach, the goals of treatment need to be considered and aligned with the good lives model. In this section, we examine some of the best-established goals of sexual offender treatment and reinterpret them in terms of the GLM. Table 36.1 displays 14 treatment need areas defined by Thornton (2002) and offers suggestions for how relevant

Table 36.1
Good Lives Model of Treatment

Treatment Need Area	GLM Conceptualization	GLM Treatment Approach
1. Sexual preoccupation	Offender is limited in alternative strategies for achieving the human goods of agency, or inner peace. Or, intimacy and sex are seen as blurred rather than independent goals. Or, offender's GLM lacks scope: too much emphasis placed on the achievement of one secondary good. Another possibility is overvaluing goods of physical satisfaction (health/living good) and play.	Develop wider range of strategies for achieving agency and inner peace. Increase scope of offender's GLM so that secondary goods other than sexual activity increase in importance. Seek other means of achieving physical stimulation, pleasure, and sense of adventure/play.
2. Sexual preference for children	Offender has not developed alternative strategies for achieving the secondary goods of sexual satisfaction and sexual intimacy. Or, lack of scope within offender's GLM: too much emphasis placed on achieving sex/intimacy at any cost. Or, corruption of agency/mastery good: agency considered to be achieved through sexual domination of a minor.	Develop wider range of strategies for achieving secondary goods of sexual satisfaction and sexual intimacy. Increase strategies for achieving agency and mastery in nonsexual situations.
3. Sexual preference for rape	Conflict between goals of relatedness, agency, and sexual activity. A corruption of the agency good: The offender achieves a sense of autonomy by humiliating or dominating others while neglecting the secondary goods of emotional and sexual intimacy.	Increase strategies for achieving agency; realign GLM to separate agency from relatedness. Increase importance of emotional and sexual intimacy within the good lives plan.
4. Adversarial sexual attitudes	Problems in the way the good of relatedness is sought and/or frustration arising from failure to achieve this good through inappropriate means. Women are viewed as unreliable or untrustworthy.	Seeking to establish appropriate means of seeking good of relatedness and managing feelings of anger and frustration (mood management skills).
5. Sexual entitlement	Tendency to value own needs above those of others; competence and agency linked to asserting self over others. Lack of scope of GLM, lack of attention to establishing relationships, intimacy, good of community and, therefore, failure to appreciate needs and rights of others.	Focus on broadening scope of GLM to include goods of relatedness and community. Learn that establishing own competence and agency through asserting own needs over others is likely to be counterproductive in the long run.

Table 36.1 *Continued*

Treatment Need Area	GLM Conceptualization	GLM Treatment Approach
6. Offense-supportive beliefs	Refers to offenders' representations of their own goals and the beliefs that support them. For example, children are sexual beings or women are unknowable. Offense-supportive beliefs function as maps that help offenders to make sense of their life, partially confer identity, and stipulate way to achieve goals.	Clarify that primary goods are not the problem but rather the way they are sought. Therefore, focus on selecting ways of achieving human goods that take into account offenders' preferences, abilities, contexts, and values while ensuring outcome is ethically acceptable and personally satisfying.
7. Belief that women are deceitful	This belief is likely to be related to intimacy failures and resulting emotional turbulence (failure of inner peace): anger, resentment, and so on.	Therapy to concentrate on providing greater understanding of the source of this belief and associated emotional states. Encourage offenders to understand the relationship between this belief and frustrated pursuit of human goods in their circumstances. Then develop GLM that can rectify problems.
8. Inadequacy (low self-esteem, external locus of control, loneliness)	Lack of capacity to achieve agency (autonomy, self-directedness) and mastery (excellence in work/play).	Teach skills to enhance achievement of agency and mastery (e.g., skills of self-directedness, emotional management). Assess and enhance aspects of life that result in mastery good being achieved (i.e., areas where skill, knowledge, or ability already exist or are potentially achievable).
9. Distorted intimacy balance	Goods of intimacy sought through associations with children because of lack of capacity (e.g., confidence, skill) to achieve intimacy/relatedness with adults. Or, lack of social connectedness with community and, therefore, lack of access to social opportunities.	Teach skills and increase confidence necessary to achieve relatedness successfully with adults. Increase access to social relationships and institutions that appeal to offenders (e.g., hobby classes, work opportunities).
10. Grievance schema	Obstacle to achieving inner peace, likely to be caused by lack of access to number of other goods, especially overarching good.	Work to assist in dismantling grievance beliefs and replace with strategies to achieve inner peace. Identify problems in implementation of GLM and seek to install internal and external conditions required to successfully implement it within offenders' unique contexts.

(Continued)

611

Table 36.1 *Continued*

Treatment Need Area	GLM Conceptualization	GLM Treatment Approach
11. Lack of emotional intimacy	Either neglect of intimacy as a human good within the individual's GLM, lack of capacity to achieve intimacy/relatedness, or problems regulating emotions (i.e., achieve inner peace).	Consider role of intimacy within GLM; teach skills to assist better achievement of relatedness. Help to modulate and manage emotions more effectively.
12. Lifestyle impulsivity	Lack of necessary capacity to form and adjust a GLM to changing circumstances. Lack of capacity to achieve good of agency because of difficulties inhibiting desires, planning, and implementation.	Teach skills of decision making, adapting to changing circumstances, considering longer term consequences before acting. Acquire basic self-control strategies.
13. Poor problem solving	Lack of capacity to achieve agency (autonomy and self-directedness).	Teach skills of problem solving, negotiation, conflict resolution.
14. Poor emotional control	Lack of capacity to achieve agency (autonomy and self-directedness) and inner peace.	Teach emotional management skills.

Note: Treatment need areas adapted from Sinclair Seminars Conference on Sex Offender Re-Offense Prediction, by D. Thornton, 2002, *Structured Risk Assessment.*

offense-related psychological characteristics may be understood and treated within a good lives approach. The table, however, outlines only possible links to human goods and therapy options and is not meant to be rigidly prescriptive. According to the etiological assumptions underlying the GLM, individuals vary in terms of the specific goods related to their offending behavior and, therefore, the problems inherent in their GLM.

From this table, it is clear that the specific activities of a GLM-based treatment program for sexual offenders are not significantly different from those of a conventional treatment program. What differs is that the goal of each intervention component is explicitly linked to the GLM theory. In other words, a more holistic treatment perspective is taken, based on the core idea that the best way to reduce risk is by helping offenders live more fulfilling lives. In addition, therapy is tailored to each offender's GLM while still being administered in a systematic and structured way. It is envisaged that offenders need only undertake those treatment activities that provide the ingredients of their particular plan. In addition to this focus on a better fit between therapy and offenders' specific issues, abilities, preferences, and contexts, greater attention is played to the development of a therapeutic alliance and the process of therapy. Basic respect for the offender is derived from the GLM assumptions about the value of persons and their pursuit of primary goods. This view stipulates that therapists should aim to establish themselves as trustworthy individuals who can be relied on to address offenders' concerns and care for their welfare. Furthermore, risk factors are regarded as internal and external obstacles that make it difficult for an individual to implement a GLM in a socially acceptable and personally fulfilling manner. Thus, a major focus is on the establishment of skills and competences needed to achieve a better kind of life, alongside the management of risk. This twin focus incorporates the strengths of the relapse prevention and capabilities approaches to treatment. It is also much easier to motivate offenders if they are reassured that the goods they are aiming for are acceptable; the problems reside in the way they are sought. Sometimes, however, individuals mistake the means (secondary goods) for the end (primary goods), and it may be necessary to spend much time exploring the goods that underlie their offending behavior and the specific problems in their GLM. In the GLM approach, the goal is always to create new skills and capacities within the *context* of individuals' good lives plans and to encourage fulfillment through the achievement of human goods.

A recent exercise in HM Prison Service has confirmed that sexual offenders are more likely to respond positively to treatment targets that are formulated according to the GLM. In this exercise, three focus groups of sexual offenders were convened to discuss their ideas for a new booster treatment program.[1] The offenders consulted were all graduates of a conventional cognitive-behavioral treatment program, which had involved cognitive restructuring, victim empathy, and approach-focused relapse prevention work. When discussing the idea of booster treatment, all three groups stressed that the focus of such a group should be positive and based on the future. They did not want to spend more time "going over" the past because this was experienced as demoralizing. They wanted the program to be a place where they could get support and practice new skills. They suggested that the following topics felt most important and relevant to them: improving relationships and intimacy, building self esteem, learning how to deal with emotions such as jealousy, practicing coping strategies, developing a support network, and considering how to disclose their offending to others. Each one of these suggestions is consistent with the GLM of sexual offender treatment, suggesting that the GLM is likely to be perceived as highly relevant by offenders.

CHANGING THE LANGUAGE OF TREATMENT

It has been suggested that a GLM reformulation of sex offender treatment probably affects the aims and principles of treatment more than it affects the content of modern programs. Another area in need of attention is the language of treatment. Modern texts on sexual offender treatment constantly use language such as *deficit, deviance, distortion, risk,* and *prevention.* All such words are associated with negative evaluations or negative expectancies. The GLM is a positive model, based on assumptions that people are more likely to embrace positive change and personal development, so the kinds of language associated with such an approach should be future-oriented, optimistic, and approach-goal focused. Thus, we make the following suggestions.

Language associated with avoidance goals should be changed to language associated with approach goals. *Relapse prevention* could be re-termed *self-management* or *change for life;* problems and deficits should be rephrased as approach goals: Thus, the term *intimacy building* should be used in preference to *intimacy deficits.*

---

[1] The authors wish to gratefully acknowledge the contribution of Rebecca Milner, who facilitated these focus group sessions.

Program names should be changed to reflect the future orientation of treatment; thus, we would no longer have programs named STOP (a popular acronym) or *Sex Offender Risk Management*, but we would have names such as *healthy sexual functioning*. The use of positive language has a compelling effect on those we treat. For example, in HM Prison Service, changing the term *dynamic risk factor* to *treatment need* has greatly facilitated collaboration in assessment and treatment (as well as being a more accurate description of the results of therapeutic assessment).

CONCLUSION

In this chapter, we presented a new theory of offender rehabilitation and applied it to sex offenders. The good lives model is a strength-based approach and proposes that the major aim of treatment is to equip offenders with the necessary internal and external conditions required to implement a good lives plan in their particular set of circumstances. In the GLM, risk factors are viewed as distortions in these conditions and are not expected to provide the sole focus of rehabilitation. Instead, there is a twin focus on establishing good lives and avoiding harm. In our view, this theory has the conceptual resources to provide a comprehensive guide for therapists in the difficult task of treating sex offenders and making society a safer place.

Seligman (2002) has powerfully argued for the need for psychology to adopt a more constructive, strength-based approach to basic and applied research. His plea for the development of strength-based theories and the execution of rigorous empirical work is timely and reminds us that positive psychology does not have to be naive or wooly minded. He states: "We need to ask practitioners to recognize that much of the best work they already do in the consulting room is to amplify their clients' strengths rather than repair their weaknesses" (p. 5).

We think the best way to lower sexual offending recidivism rates is to equip offenders with the tools to live more fulfilling lives rather than to simply develop increasingly sophisticated risk management measures and strategies. At the end of the day, most offenders have more in common with us than not and, like the rest of humanity, have needs to be loved, valued, to function competently, and to be part of a community. To lose sight of this fact is to court disaster as well as to risk becoming agents of punishment rather than facilitators of hope.

REFERENCES

Andrews, D. A., & Bonta, J. (1998). *The psychology of criminal conduct* (2nd ed.). Cincinnati, OH: Anderson.

Arnhart, L. (1998). *Darwinian natural right: The biological ethics of human nature.* Albany: State University of New York Press.

Cox, M., Klinger, E., & Blount, J. P. (1991). Alcohol use and goal hierarchies: Systematic motivational counseling for alcoholics. In W. R. Miller & S. Rollnick (Eds.), *Motivational interviewing: Preparing people to change addictive behavior* (pp. 260–271). New York: Guilford Press.

Cummins, R. A. (1996). The domains of life satisfaction: An attempt to order chaos. *Social Indicators Research, 38,* 303–328.

Deci, E. L., & Ryan, R. M. (2000). The "what" and "why" of goal pursuits: Human needs and the self-determination of behavior. *Psychological Inquiry, 11,* 227–268.

Drake, C. R., & Ward, T. (2003). Treatment models for sex offenders: A move toward a formulation-based approach. In T. Ward, D. R. Laws, & S. M. Hudson (Eds.), *Sexual deviance: Issues and controversies* (pp. 226–243). Thousand Oaks, CA: Sage.

Emmons, R. A. (1996). Striving and feeling: Personal goals and subjective well-being. In P. M. Gollwitzer & J. A. Bargh (Eds.), *The psychology of action: Linking cognition and motivation to behavior* (pp. 313–337). New York: Guilford Press.

Emmons, R. A. (1999). *The psychology of ultimate concerns.* New York: Guilford Press.

Hare, R. (1991). *Manual for the Hare Psychopathy Checklist-Revised.* Toronto, Ontario, Canada: Multi-Health Systems.

Hart, S., Laws, D. R., & Kropp, P. R. (2003). The promise and peril of sex offender risk assessment. In T. Ward, D. R. Laws, & S. M. Hudson (Eds.), *Sexual deviance: Issues and controversies* (pp. 207–225). Thousand Oaks, CA: Sage.

Hollin, C. R. (1999). Treatment programs for offenders: Meta-analysis, "what works" and beyond. *International Journal of Law and Psychiatry, 22,* 361–372.

Kekes, J. (1989). *Moral tradition and individuality.* Princeton, NJ: Princeton University Press.

Laws, D. R., Hudson, S. M., & Ward, T. (Eds.). (2000). *Remaking relapse prevention with sex offenders: A sourcebook.* Newbury Park, CA: Sage.

*Mann, R. E. (2000). Managing resistance and rebellion in relapse prevention. In D. R. Laws, S. M. Hudson, & T. Ward (Eds.), *Remaking relapse prevention with sex offenders* (pp. 187–200). Thousand Oaks, CA: Sage.

Mann, R. E., Beckett, R., Fisher, D., & Thornton, D. (2002). Relapse prevention interview. In D. M. Doren (Ed.), *Evaluating sex offenders: A manual for civil commitment and beyond* (pp. 201–209). Thousand Oaks, CA: Sage.

Mann, R. E., & Shingler, J. (2002, April). *Collaborative risk assessment.* Paper presented at Tools to Take Home conference, Cardiff, Wales. (Available from the authors, H. M. Prison Service, Room 725, Abell House, John Islip Street, London, SW1P 4LH, England)

Mann, R. E., & Webster, S. D. (2003, April). *Why do some sex offenders refuse treatment?* Workshop presented at Tools to Take Home conference, Birmingham, England. (Available from the authors, Her Majesty's Prison Service, Room 725, Abell House, John Islip Street, London, SW1P 4LH, England)

Mann, R. E., Webster, S. D., Schofield, C., & Marshall, W. L. (2004). Approach versus avoidance goals in relapse prevention with sexual offenders. *Sexual Abuse: A Journal of Research and Treatment, 16,* 65–74.

Margalit, A. (1996). *The decent society.* Cambridge, MA: Harvard University Press.

Marshall, W. L., Anderson, D., & Fernandez, Y. M. (1999). *Cognitive behavioral treatment of sexual offenders.* Chichester, England: Wiley.

Marshall, W. L., & Fernandez, Y. M. (2000). Phallometric testing with sexual offenders: Limits to its value. *Clinical Psychology Review, 20,* 807–822.

Maruna, S. (2001). *Making good: How ex-convicts reform and rebuild their lives.* Washington, DC: American Psychological Association.

Murphy, M. C. (2001). *Natural law and practical rationality.* New York: Cambridge University Press.

Nussbaum, M. C. (2000). *Women and human development: The capabilities approach.* New York: Cambridge University Press.

Pithers, W. D. (1990). Relapse prevention with sexual aggressors: A method for maintaining therapeutic gain and enhancing external supervision. In W. L. Marshall, D. R. Laws, & H. E. Barbaree (Eds.), *Handbook of sexual assault: Issues, theories and treatment of the offender* (pp. 346–361). New York: Plenum Press.

Rapp, C. A. (1998). *The strengths model: Case management with people suffering from severe and persistent mental illness.* New York: Oxford University Press.

Rescher, N. (1990). *Human interests: Reflections on philosophical anthropology.* Stanford, CA: Stanford University Press.

Salter, A. C. (1988). *Treating child sex offenders and victims: A practical guide.* Thousand Oaks, CA: Sage.

Schmuck, P., & Sheldon, K. M. (Eds.). (2001). *Life goals and well-being.* Toronto, Ontario, Canada: Hogrefe & Huber.

Seligman, M. E. P. (2002). Positive psychology, positive prevention, and positive therapy. In C. R. Snyder & S. J. Lopez (Eds.), *Handbook of positive psychology* (pp. 3–9). New York: Oxford University Press.

Thornton, D. (2002). *Structured risk assessment* Madison, WI: Sinclair Seminars Conference on Sex Offender Re-Offense Prediction. Videotape available from www.sinclairseminars.com.

*Ward, T. (2002). Good lives and the rehabilitation of offenders: Promises and problems. *Aggression and Violent Behavior, 7,* 513–528.

Ward, T., & Brown, M. (2003). The risk-need model of offender rehabilitation: A critical analysis. In T. Ward, D. R. Laws, & S. M. Hudson (Eds.), *Sexual deviance: Issues and controversies* (pp. 338–353). Thousand Oaks, CA: Sage.

Ward, T., & Hudson, S. M. (2000). A self-regulation model of relapse prevention. In D. R. Laws, S. M. Hudson, & T. Ward (Eds.), *Remaking relapse prevention with sex offenders: A sourcebook* (pp. 79–101). Thousand Oaks, CA: Sage.

Ward, T., Louden, K., Hudson, S. M., & Marshall, W. L. (1995). A descriptive model of the offense chain in child molesters. *Journal of Interpersonal Violence, 10,* 452–472.

Ward, T., & Marshall, W. L. (in press). Good lives, etiology, and the rehabilitation of sex offenders: A bridging theory. *Journal of Sexual Aggression.*

*Ward, T., & Stewart, C. A. (2003a). Criminogenic needs and human needs: A theoretical model. *Psychology, Crime, & Law, 9,* 125–143.

*Ward, T., & Stewart, C. A. (2003b). Good lives and the rehabilitation of sexual offenders. In T. Ward, D. R. Laws, & S. M. Hudson (Eds.), *Sexual deviance: Issues and controversies* (pp. 21–44). Thousand Oaks, CA: Sage.

*Ward, T., & Stewart, C. A. (2003c). The treatment of sex offenders: Risk management and good lives. *Professional Psychology: Research and Practice, 34,* 353–360.

Webster, S. D. (in press). Pathways to sexual offense recidivism following treatment: An evaluation of the Ward and Hudson self-regulation model of relapse. *Journal of Interpersonal Violence.*

CHAPTER 37

Facilitating Forgiveness: Developing Group and Community Interventions

FRANK D. FINCHAM and TODD B. KASHDAN

> The weak can never forgive. Forgiveness is the attribute of the strong.
>
> —Mahatma Ghandi (2000, p. 301)

ONE OF LIFE'S few certainties is that everyone will, at some point, feel hurt, let down, betrayed, disappointed, or wronged by another human being. In the face of such injury, negative feelings (e.g., anger, resentment, disappointment) are common. Motivation to avoid the source of the harm, or even a desire to retaliate or seek revenge, is also typical. Indeed, some have argued that retaliation in such circumstances "is deeply ingrained in the biological, psychological, and cultural levels of human nature" (McCullough & Witvliet, 2002), a position consistent with Aristotle's view of anger as "a longing, accompanied by pain, for a real or apparent revenge for a real or apparent slight" (Aristotle, 1939, p. 173). Although it is perhaps arguable whether revenge is one of a few *fundamental* human motivations, as Reiss and Havercamp (1998) assert, its corrosive effects are undeniable. Retaliatory impulses may motivate the victim to reciprocate the transgression in kind, but reciprocated harm is usually perceived to be greater than the original offense by the transgressor, who, in turn, may retaliate to even the score. Given such escalating cycles of vengeance, it is not surprising that revenge is implicated in many of our most ignominious acts as a species, including homicide, suicide, terrorism, and genocide.

Considerable evidence documents the corrosive effects of reciprocated harm in relationships; responding to a partner's transgression with negative behavior is the most reliable overt signature of marital dysfunction, and key determinants of such responses (e.g., attributions for the transgression) have been thoroughly investigated (Fincham, 2003). In contrast, relatively little data exist on how people manage to inhibit the tendency to respond negatively to a partner's bad behavior and respond constructively instead, a process called *accommodation*. Some initial data suggest that such responses are related to relationship commitment, greater interdependence between persons, and having plentiful time, rather than a limited time, to respond (e.g., Yovetich & Rusbult, 1994). Although important, such findings provide only a partial understanding of how relationships are maintained in the face of partner transgressions. Consider the case of an extramarital affair where the perceived reason for the affair is the adulterous spouse's selfish focus on his or her own immediate wishes. Assuming equal levels of commitment, what happens in one marriage that allows the betrayed partner to overcome his or her anger and resentment and behave in a conciliatory manner toward the spouse whereas in another marriage the relationship remains tense for years? As they remain constant in this example, neither the major relationship macro-motive (commitment) nor the proximal determinant (reasons for the event) identified in research on accommodation can help in providing an answer. This example highlights the need for a new category of relationship process that may follow a transgression and the initial hurt engendered by it but that may also influence the aftermath of the event. One such process is forgiveness, a construct that has recently engaged the attention of psychologists[1] and that, as we argue, is an important human strength that can contribute to the good life and, for some, the meaningful life.

WHAT IS FORGIVENESS?

This simple question does not have a simple answer. Although it is a complex construct without a consensual definition, at the center of various approaches to forgiveness is the idea of a freely chosen motivational transformation in which the desire to seek revenge and to avoid contact with the transgressor is lessened, a process sometimes described as an altruistic gift (e.g., Enright, Freedman, & Rique, 1998; Worthington, 2001). This core feature immediately distinguishes forgiveness from constructs such as denial (unwillingness to perceive the injury), condoning (removes the offense and, hence, the need for forgiveness), pardon (granted only by a representative of society such as a judge), forgetting (removes awareness of offense from consciousness; to forgive is more than not thinking about the offense), and reconciliation (which restores a relationship and is, therefore, a dyadic process). Thus, the common phrase "forgive and forget" is misleading because forgiveness is possible only in the face of remembered wrongs or hurt.

There is less agreement among researchers on whether forgiveness requires a benevolent or positive response (e.g., compassion, empathy, affection, approach behavior) to the offender or whether the absence of negative responses (e.g., hostility, anger, avoidance) is sufficient (Exline, Worthington, Hill, & McCullough, 2003; Fincham, 2000). Both cross-sectional and longitudinal data show that the

---

[1] Although scientists have paid remarkably little attention to forgiveness, research on this topic has recently mushroomed. The five studies available prior to 1985 have since increased by over 4,000% (PsycINFO, July 2002), and several research-based texts on the topic have appeared (e.g., Enright & North, 1998; McCullough, Pargament, & Thoresen, 2000; Worthington, 1998; for a bibliography, see McCullough, Exline, & Baumeister, 1998).

two dimensions may function differently; spouses' retaliatory motivation following a transgression is related to partner reports of psychological aggression and, for husbands, to ineffective arguing whereas benevolence motivation correlates with partner reports of constructive communication and, for wives, partners' reports of ineffective arguing (Fincham & Beach, 2002a; Fincham, Beach, & Davila, 2003). An initial longitudinal study showed that in the first few weeks following a transgression, avoidance and revenge motivation decreased whereas benevolence motivation did not change (McCullough, Fincham, & Tsang, 2003). To complicate matters further, forgiveness is conceptualized at different levels, as a response to a specific transgression, a personality trait, and a characteristic of social units (e.g., families, communities).

What is becoming clear, however, is that laypeople may use and conceptualize interpersonal forgiveness in ways that differ from researchers. For example, Kantz (2000) found laypersons believe that reconciliation is a necessary part of forgiveness, an element explicitly rejected by many definitions of forgiveness used in research. In this study, subjects also endorsed the view that forgiveness could cause emotional problems, which again runs counter to the salutary effects attributed to forgiveness in most research. This finding raises the legitimate question of whether forgiveness is harmful or, as we have claimed, a human strength.

IMPLICATIONS OF DEFINING FORGIVENESS FOR APPLIED WORK

Because lay conceptions appear to confuse forgiveness and related constructs, conceptual clarity is particularly important in applied work that attempts to facilitate forgiveness. For example, the lay conception that forgiveness involves reconciliation may lead some who forgive to place themselves in danger of future harm. Thus, attempts to facilitate forgiveness should include an educational component to ensure that participants understand fully what forgiveness does and does not entail. It may also be necessary to assess perceived negative consequences of forgiving before making an attempt to encourage forgiveness. Before turning to applied work, we first examine whether forgiveness is associated with positive outcomes.

FORGIVENESS AND WELL-BEING

The presumed benefits of forgiveness for well-being have been the single most important stimulus for the upsurge of research on forgiveness in the past 20 years. In fact, there is now even some fMRI evidence to show that forgiveness activates a specific region of the brain (posterior cingulated gyrus) that is distinct from that activated by empathy (Farrow et al., 2001). The existence of a distinct functional anatomy for forgiveness points to its potential evolutionary advantage.

PHYSICAL HEALTH

The view that forgiveness can improve physical health is found in religious writings and in the recommendations of some health professionals (see Thoresen, Harris, & Luskin, 2000). Much of the evidence pertaining to this issue is indirect and focuses on the adverse effects of one type of unforgiving response, namely, hostility. Forgiveness decreases hostility, and a meta-analysis of 45 published studies shows that hostility is an independent risk factor for coronary heart disease and premature death (Miller, Smith, Turner, Guijarro, & Hallett, 1996). There is also anecdotal evidence that learning to cultivate a forgiving heart decreases hostility (Kaplan, 1992).

In a similar vein, forgiveness can facilitate the repair of supportive close relationships, and such relationships are known to protect against negative health outcomes. For example, marital conflict is associated with poorer health (Burman & Margolin, 1992; Kiecolt-Glaser et al., 1988) and with specific illnesses such as cancer, cardiac disease, and chronic pain (see Schmaling & Sher, 1997). Hostile behaviors during conflict relate to alterations in immunological (Kiecolt-Glaser et al., 1997), endocrine (Kiecolt-Glaser et al., 1997), and cardiovascular (Ewart, Taylor, Kraemer, & Agras, 1991) functioning. It has even been suggested that forgiveness may be associated with well-being because it helps people maintain stable, supportive relationships (McCullough, 2000). Consistent with this view, married couples report that the capacity to seek and grant forgiveness is one of the most important factors contributing to marital longevity and marital satisfaction (Fenell, 1993).

Initial studies on physiological reactivity provide more direct evidence on forgiveness and physical functioning. For example, Witvliet, Ludwig, and Van der Laan (2001) demonstrated that engaging in unforgiving imagery (rehearsing hurtful memories and nursing a grudge) produced more negative emotions and greater physiological stress (significantly higher EMG, skin conductance, heart rate, and blood pressure changes from baseline), which endured longer into recovery periods. On the other hand, forgiving imagery (engaging in empathic perspective taking and imagining forgiveness) produced lower physiological stress levels. In a second study, Lawler, Younger, Piferi, and Jones (2000) found that people exhibited lower physiological reactivity (e.g., forehead EMG activity, diastolic blood pressure) during an interview about a transgression when they had forgiven the transgressor than when they had not forgiven the transgressor. They also found that forgiving people reported fewer physical symptoms. Berry and Worthington (2001) provided additional evidence of a relation between the disposition to forgive and physical health. These investigators also showed that the tendency to forgive predicted cortisol reactivity (indicating higher stress) following imagination of typical relationship events, thereby suggesting that hormonal factors may also be implicated in any link between forgiveness and health. It is not difficult to imagine how such physiological or hormonal reactivity could over time adversely influence health.

Two studies, however, suggest a more complicated picture. First, in a nationally representative probability sample of 1,423 respondents, Toussaint, Williams, Musick, and Everson (2001) found that the relationship between forgiveness and self-rated health, controlling for sex, race, education, marital status, and religiousness, varied as a function of age. Specifically, self-forgiveness was related to health in younger groups (18 to 44, 45 to 64 years) but not in persons over 65 years of age. In contrast, forgiveness of others was related to health in the oldest group but not the younger groups. (Comparisons across age showed that the coefficients for 18 to 44 and 65+ year groups were significantly different for other-forgiveness and were marginally significant for self-forgiveness.) More important in the present context is the second study concerning the motivation for forgiving. This study compared those who forgave out of a sense of religious obligation to those who forgave out of love. During descriptions of the offense, people who forgave out of obligation showed more anger-related responses (e.g., masking smiles, downcast eyes) and elevated blood pressure compared to those who forgave out of love (Huang & Enright, 2000). This suggests that what forgiveness means to a person may be critical for his or her physiological and behavioral responses. This study alerts us to the fact that only freely given forgiveness that conforms to the criteria outlined earlier is relevant to the good life. Forgiveness born of obligation, pain avoidance, manipulation, and so on is neither a strength nor virtue.

MENTAL HEALTH

Several studies provide data suggesting a link between forgiveness and mental health. Wuthnow (2000) surveyed 1,379 people in small religious groups (e.g., prayer groups, Bible studies) and found that being a member who had been "helped to forgive someone" was related to attempts and successes in overcoming an addiction, overcoming guilt, and perceiving encouragement when feeling down. Similarly, Toussaint et al. (2001), using their nationally representative sample, found that both self-forgiveness and forgiveness of others was inversely related to a measure of psychological distress in all age groups investigated. However, only the tendency to forgive others was related to overall life satisfaction. In developing a measure of forgiveness, Mauger et al. (1992) found that forgiveness of both self and of others was inversely related to indicators of psychopathology as measured by the Minnesota Multiphasic Personality Inventory in a sample of clients at a Christian outpatient counseling center. Tangey, Fee, and Lee (1999) found a negative relation between a dispositional tendency to forgive others and depressive symptoms and hostility: Forgiving self as a transgressor was also inversely related to depressive symptoms and positively related to overall psychological adjustment. In contrast, Subkoviak et al. (1995) found in a sample of adolescents and their parents that lower forgiveness scores were unrelated to depressive symptoms but were related to greater anxiety. Symptoms of anxiety, depression, and anger have also been shown to decline following a forgiveness intervention (e.g., Freedman & Enright, 1996). Improved existential well-being has also been found following forgiveness intervention (Rye & Pargament, 2002). But a longitudinal study conducted over eight weeks showed that changes in forgiveness toward specific offenders were unrelated to change in overall life satisfaction, which remained stable over the course of the study (test-retest $r = 0.79$, McCullough, Bellah, Kilpatrick, & Johnson, 2001).

Likewise, to the extent that forgiveness helps enhance relationship quality, a possibility supported by numerous studies documenting a robust association between forgiveness and relationship satisfaction (e.g., Fincham, 2000), forgiveness may be associated with improved mental health because of links between overall relationship quality and mental heath.[2] For example, the link between relationship

---

[2] McCullough, Rachal, et al. (1998) found that a composite measure of relationship commitment and satisfaction was negatively related to reported avoidance and revenge following a recent hurt and the worst relationship hurt as identified by participants in a romantic relationship. Fincham (2000) also found that forgiveness and marital satisfaction were related and showed that forgiveness accounted for variance that was independent of marital satisfaction in predicting overall behavior toward the partner and in reported retaliatory and conciliatory responses to a partner transgression. Moreover, forgiveness fully mediated the relationship between responsibility attributions for partner behavior and reported behavior toward the partner. Importantly, McCullough, Rachal, et al. showed that pre- and posttransgression closeness are related, in part, through forgiveness. Thus, forgiving does appear to promote reconciliation (closeness).

quality and depression is increasingly well established (see Beach, Fincham, & Katz, 1998), and a link with eating disorders has been documented (see Van den Broucke, Vandereycken, & Norre, 1997). There is also some direct evidence that forgiveness is linked to relationship destructive factors in that lower levels of forgiving predict psychological aggression and protracted conflict in marriage (Fincham & Beach, 2002a; Fincham et al., 2003).

CRITIQUE

Compelling, direct evidence documenting a *causal* link between forgiveness and physical and mental health is lacking. Experimental or longitudinal research that might address the issue of causality is rare in the literature on forgiveness. An exception is McCullough et al.'s (2001) study, which showed no relation between change in forgiveness and life satisfaction, a finding that could reflect disparity in level of measurement of the two constructs (e.g., forgiveness for a specific event versus a global measure of functioning), the existence of a causal lag that is different from the eight-week period investigated, or limited variability in life satisfaction over this short period. It would be premature to conclude that forgiveness improves individual well-being. Nonetheless, recognition of the negative physical and mental health outcomes associated with processes that can occur in the absence of forgiving (e.g., preoccupation with blame, rumination) appears to sustain theoretical attempts to identify processes linking forgiveness and physical and mental health.

Applied studies that attempt to facilitate forgiveness currently provide the only direct evidence about the effects of forgiveness on well-being. Because such studies are often experimental in design, they are an important test of the hypothesis that facilitating forgiveness actually influences well-being rather than merely being associated with it. We, therefore, begin our discussion of applied research by reviewing the evidence it provides on the impact of forgiveness on well-being.

APPLIED RESEARCH ON FORGIVENESS

Since Close (1970) published a case study on forgiveness in counseling, various models of forgiving have emerged in the counseling/psychotherapy literature. However, with the exception of Enright's work (e.g., Enright & Coyle, 1998), the impact of these models on clinical practice has been questioned (McCullough & Worthington, 1994). Where there has been an impact, model builders have skipped the task of validating their models and proceeded directly to intervention outcome research (Malcolm & Greenberg, 2000). Perhaps more importantly, the psychotherapy literature has far outstripped empirical data on forgiveness, leaving us in the awkward position of attempting to induce forgiveness without knowing a great deal about how it operates in everyday life.

Of the 14 available studies, all but two (Coyle & Enright, 1997; Freedman & Enright, 1996) are group interventions. Worthington, Sandage, and Berry (2000) summarized these interventions (delivered to 393 participants) by showing a linear dose-effect relationship for the effect sizes they yielded. Specifically, clinically relevant interventions (defined as those of six or more hours' duration) produced a change in forgiveness (effect size = 0.76) that was reliably different from zero, with nonclinically relevant interventions (defined as one or two hours' duration) yielding a small but measurable change in forgiveness (effect size = 0.24). These authors tentatively conclude, "amount of time thinking about forgiveness is important in the amount of forgiveness a person can experience" (p. 234). Because effect size and proportion of males in the study were negatively related, they also conclude that men are more "substantially at risk for holding onto unforgiveness than are women" (p. 241). Finally, they noted that one study produced a negative effect (Al-Mubak, Enright, & Cardis, 1995; Study 1), most likely because participants were given time to think about their hurt without being induced to think about forgiveness.

The analyses previously summarized demonstrate that we have made good progress in devising interventions to induce forgiveness. But this is analogous to focusing on a manipulation check in experimental research. What about the dependent variable; does inducing forgiveness produce positive psychological outcomes? Here results are more mixed. For example, Hebl and Enright (1993) showed that their forgiveness intervention produced significantly greater forgiveness in elderly females than a placebo control group but that both groups showed significant decreases in symptoms of anxiety and depression. In contrast, Al-Mubak et al. (1995) found that, relative to a placebo control group, their forgiveness intervention produced significant increases in forgiveness and hope and a significant decrease in trait anxiety among college students emotionally hurt by a parent. However, the groups did not differ in depressive symptoms following intervention. A problem with these, and many of the other available studies, is that the interventions are delivered to samples that are either asymptomatic or show limited variability in mental health symptoms, making it difficult to demonstrate intervention effects on these variables.

It is, therefore, encouraging that in an intervention study where participants (adults who had experienced sexual abuse as children) were screened to show psychological distress before the intervention (Freedman & Enright, 1996), the intervention produced significantly greater forgiveness, hope, and self-esteem and decreased anxiety and depression relative to a wait list control group. Intervention with the wait list control group showed a significant change for the group relative to the time the group had served as a control condition and made the group indistinguishable from the experimental group. These changes were maintained over a 12-month period.

CRITIQUE

Because interventions are a relatively blunt experimental manipulation that may influence a number of variables, it will be important in future intervention studies to show that changes in forgiveness are correlated with changes in psychological well-being. Perhaps most importantly in the current context, intervention research has thus far focused on the individual experience of forgiving and not the interactions that occur around forgiveness. The result is that most intervention research tells us little about how to help people negotiate forgiveness (Worthington & Wade, 1999). This is an important omission because repentance and apology (phenomena that involve interpersonal transactions) facilitate forgiveness and because, in the context of an ongoing relationship, forgiveness may involve numerous transactions. Additional challenges for future research on group-based forgiveness interventions are summarized by Worthington et al. (2000).

The limitations of the available data are more understandable when we recall that less than 15 years ago, pioneering publications did not contain reference to any published empirical research on forgiveness (e.g., Hebl & Enright, 1993; Mauger et al., 1992). Research on forgiveness is in its infancy, and the jury is still out on the case for the importance of forgiveness in maintaining and promoting well-being. This is not to imply that the case lacks evidentiary support. However, it is clear that attempts to promote forgiveness have been limited in conceptualization and scope. In particular, they reflect the traditional assumptions made in psychotherapy/counseling, namely, that people (patients, clients) wronged by another need to seek help from professionals (therapists/counselors) in a special environment divorced from their natural setting (the clinic). In the remainder of the chapter, we, therefore, offer a much expanded view for research on facilitating forgiveness.

TOWARD A COMPREHENSIVE, EVIDENCE-BASED MODEL FOR FACILITATING FORGIVENESS

We begin this section by examining the implications of positive psychology for attempts to facilitate forgiveness; then we identify the premises that underlie the approach that we offer. Finally, we discuss the facilitation of forgiveness in terms of two dimensions, breadth of reach and intensity, and relate them to delivery formats.

FORGIVENESS THROUGH THE LENS OF POSITIVE PSYCHOLOGY

Viewing forgiveness through the lens of positive psychology (e.g., McCullough & Witvliet, 2002) has implications for a more complete understanding of the construct and for evaluating efforts to facilitate forgiveness. As a human strength, forgiveness has the potential to enhance functioning and not simply protect against dysfunction. But because measurement of forgiveness has focused on its negative dimension (avoidance, retaliation, e.g., McCullough, Rachal, et al., 1998), most of what has been learned about forgiveness rests on inferences made from the absence of the negative (dysfunction). Here there is the danger of falling prey to a logical error—the absence of a negative quality (e.g., vengeance) is not equivalent to the presence of a positive quality (e.g., benevolence). Like psychology itself, forgiveness research has (unwittingly) focused on human dysfunction in opposition to which positive psychology was born. What positive emotions, strengths, and virtues (other than empathy) correlate with forgiveness? Our inability to answer this question immediately points to the need to broaden the nomological network in which forgiveness is situated to include strengths and virtues. Similarly, attempts to facilitate forgiveness should not simply be evaluated in terms of the prevention or amelioration of dysfunction but also in terms of their ability to promote optimal functioning. We advocate a focus on the positive in forgiveness research as a complement to, rather than a substitute for, existing work mindful of the admonition that "a positive approach cannot ignore pathology or close its eyes to the alienation and inauthenticity prevalent in our society" (Ryan & Deci, 2000, p. 74).

Awareness of possible, positive correlates of forgiveness also directs attention to the positive dimension of forgiveness, benevolence. As noted, forgiveness cannot be understood completely by studying unforgiveness, just as marital quality cannot be fully understood by the study of marital distress or optimism by the study of learned helplessness (Fincham, 2000). Thus, we must remain open to the possibility that negative and positive dimensions of forgiveness may have different determinants, correlates, and consequences. For example, it can be hypothesized that negative and positive dimensions predict avoidance/revenge and conciliatory behaviors, respectively. Similarly, different intervention efforts may be needed for reducing retaliatory and avoidance motivations versus increasing benevolence.

Finally, the lens of positive psychology alerts us to different ways in which forgiveness may function in relation to optimal human experience. Thus far, we have noted that the exercise of forgiveness facilitates gratification in one of the main realms of life (the interpersonal) and thus contributes to the good life (Seligman, 2002a). But forgiveness may also promote a meaningful life. All three of the major monotheistic religions emphasize forgiveness, and the practice of forgiveness in Judaism, Christianity, and Islam can easily be seen as serving something much larger than the forgiver and, therefore, contributing to the meaningful life. However, two very important caveats must be added. First, forgiveness does not necessarily contribute to a meaningful life among the faithful; it will do so only when exercised freely and not as the mindless exercise of a religious obligation (cf. earlier described study by Huang & Enright, 2000). Second, the exercise of forgiveness can also contribute to the meaningful life for nonreligious forgivers. However, to do so, it is likely to require the forgiver to be consciously motivated by a desire to create a better community or society and to view his or her action as contributing to the realization of this goal. At an applied level, the implication is that, where appropriate, efforts should be made to show the link between the individual's action and the service of something greater than the individual, such as God's will for the faithful, or for the secular, the betterment of a social unit (e.g., family, neighborhood, school) or the community as a whole (e.g., through the establishment of more humane norms). In short, the lens of positive psychology alerts us to an important but relatively unexplored issue pertaining to forgiveness, its meaning for the forgiver.

UNDERLYING PREMISES

The approach that we offer reflects a number of premises that shape its form, which are, therefore, briefly articulated. First, it is informed by an integrated prevention and treatment perspective. It moves beyond the positive psychology approach toward prevention, which focuses on strengths in people at risk (Seligman, 2002b). Laudable as such an expanded view of prevention might be, it suffers from *decontextualizing* risk and ignoring cultural and structural factors that maintain risk behavior. For example, facilitating forgiveness for someone who has a strong social network that encourages a hostile response may deprive the person of social support and, at worst, set him or her in conflict with support providers. A comprehensive model, therefore, needs to encompass change in collectives and not only individuals.

A second premise is that persons who might benefit from forgiving may not be seeking help. This means that the traditional *waiting mode* familiar to psychologists needs to be replaced by the *seeking mode* embraced by the community mental health movement (Rappaport & Chinsky, 1974). In contrast to waiting for clients to present at the office for diagnosis and treatment, in seeking mode we move into the community taking on nontraditional roles such as developer of community programs, consultant to local groups, and evaluator of community-based intervention efforts. In the present context, this is particularly important because many potential beneficiaries of forgiveness are likely to be reached through natural community groups (e.g., religious organizations).

Third, persons who might benefit from forgiving may not have the financial resources to obtain professional help or be located in areas served by mental health care providers. Therefore, any forgiveness intervention should be designed to reach people in a variety of settings (including rural and geographically isolated settings) and be viable for use in these settings. Thus, at a minimum, the intervention should be easily implemented, reasonably brief, and economic to implement. Ideally, it should involve a familiar process that occurs naturally in the community. This means that there is likely to be a need to look to a broader range of persons (e.g., media specialists) and modes of delivery (e.g., distance learning) than is typical in traditional psychological interventions.

Finally, we operate from the premise that any attempt to facilitate forgiveness should represent best practice in terms of what is currently known scientifically about forgiveness and its facilitation. A corollary is that any intervention must lend itself to evaluation, for without evaluation no program can be assumed to be effective. The notion that "something is better than nothing" is simply misguided, no matter how well intentioned, and, as Bergin (1963) reminds us, anything that has the potential to help also has the potential to harm. We now consider forgiveness facilitation in a two-dimensional framework.

DIMENSION 1: BREADTH OF REACH

Forgiveness interventions have been limited to those delivered by a professional to an individual or a small group of individuals. Given the observation made in the chapter opening that everyone will, at some point, feel hurt, let down, betrayed, disappointed, or wronged, these interventions are inadequate to reach everyone for whom forgiveness is relevant. Moreover, in asking about the nature of forgiveness, we noted that it can be applied to social units. By facilitating forgiveness in such units, we not only provide a more complete approach to facilitating forgiveness but also begin to address the problem of decontextualized interventions. Broadening our approach in this manner is clearly a radical departure from the traditional clinical model that has informed prior intervention efforts.

The importance of including community-level intervention in a comprehensive approach to facilitating forgiveness is emphasized by the observation: "A large number of people exposed to a small risk may generate more cases than a small number exposed to a high risk" (Rose, 1992, p. 87). But the inclusion of community-level intervention in our approach brings with it new challenges. It needs to be recognized, for example, that outcome for individuals is alone insufficient to evaluate such interventions because the unit of intervention and evaluation is the community or organization. How do we assess the community or organization environment? This is not the context in which to address such questions. These kinds of questions are beginning to be addressed in the field of public health where community-level intervention has recently taken root. Readers interested in these challenges are referred to analyses of methodological issues arising from community-level and community-based intervention (Sorensen, Emmons, Hunt, & Johnson, 1998; Thompson, Coronado, Snipes, & Puschel, 2003).

DIMENSION 2: INTENSITY

It is a truism that the intensity of interventions differs, and we use this dimension to order prevention, enhancement, and remediation efforts. Prevention and enhancement are appropriate for those who are not manifesting levels of distress that impair their normal functioning, whereas remediation is targeted at those experiencing clinical levels of distress.

As to prevention, we distinguish among *universal* preventive measures, considered desirable for everyone in the population; *selective* preventive measures, considered desirable for subgroups of the population at higher than average risk; and *indicated* preventive measures, desirable for individuals who are known to be at high risk (Mrazek & Haggerty, 1994). In universal prevention, benefits outweigh the minimal costs and risks for everyone. In contrast, indicated interventions are not minimal in cost (e.g., time, effort). This reflects the fact that recipients of an indicated prevention may be experiencing some (subclinical) level of distress associated with the transgression.

Determining the place of enhancement on the intensity continuum is difficult. On the one hand, persons appropriate for enhancement should not be motivated by an experienced transgression but rather the desire to improve their life experience. As such, they most closely resemble recipients of universal or selective prevention. On the other hand, the minimal preventions provided in these cases do not match the motivation that prompts their involvement in intervention. As a result, we place enhancement between prevention and remediation on the intensity dimension.

Having briefly described the two dimensions integral to our approach to facilitating forgiveness, we next discuss the interventions to which they give rise.

FACILITATING FORGIVENESS

Table 37.1 illustrates our framework for facilitating forgiveness. Reflecting our premise that intervention should reflect best practice, we derive two important implications from the forgiveness literature. First, interventions should include an educational component about what forgiveness does and does not entail with both appropriate and inappropriate examples of forgiveness (e.g., use of forgiveness as a means—to manipulate, assert moral superiority—rather than an end) and their consequences. This can serve both to avoid dangers likely to result from misconceptions about forgiveness (e.g., returning to a dangerous situation because reunion is confused with forgiveness) and to relieve psychological distress when individuals feel the need to forgive a transgressor but find themselves unable to do so because forgiveness is confused with something they may not want to do either consciously or, more often, unconsciously (e.g., condone transgressor's action). Second, when interventions address forgiveness of a specific transgression, they should require the participants to spend time thinking about forgiveness, which seems to be

Table 37.1
An Expanded Framework for Facilitating Forgiveness

Intensity of Intervention	Breadth of Reach		
	Individual	Group	Social Unit/Institution in Community
Prevention			
Universal	Forgiveness information campaign		
Selective	Psychoeducation		
Indicated	Psychoeducation with forgiveness implementation		
Enhancement	Psychoeducation with relationship skills training		
Remediation	Forgiveness-focused therapeutic intervention		

related to the occurrence of forgiveness (with the corollary that simply exposing people to the transgression they experienced without facilitating forgiveness may be iatrogenic, Worthington et al., 2000).

The first level of intervention shown is an information campaign to promote awareness of forgiveness and describe what it does and does not involve, its correlates, and it status as a human strength. Although we advocate use of the mass media for this purpose, the campaign does not preclude some contact with professional staff (e.g., telephone information line).

We advocate use of the mass media for a forgiveness information campaign because the media has played a useful role in disseminating health information to the public. Here we can envision a cross-media promotion strategy that includes newspapers, posters, billboards, informational pamphlets, and television. Television in particular has proved useful in modifying potentially harmful behaviors such as cigarette smoking and poor diet (Biglan, 1995; Sorensen et al., 1998), and we envision it as the core around which the campaign is organized. In particular, skilled use of infotainment (e.g., a feature story in which forgiveness themes are embedded, followed by a celebrity interviewed about overcoming a hurt in his or her life) is preferred over the more traditional public health announcement for two reasons. First, a television series, if well executed, is likely to gain greater attention. Second, such a series can become a longer term resource that offsets campaign costs. Finally, it needs to be recognized that the success of such a campaign should not be judged in terms of its impact on forgiveness per se, but rather on its ability to raise awareness and to produce a climate in which forgiveness is supported.

At the next level of intervention is psychoeducation. What distinguishes this level from the last is that factors that facilitate forgiveness, described in generic terms, are added to the intervention. Hence, topics such as empathy and humility, which have been emphasized in existing interventions, will garner attention. In addition, recipients of the intervention will be directed to recall instances in which they were forgiven as a vehicle to draw attention to our common frailty as human beings and to elaborate on the virtue of gratitude (McCullough, Emmons, & Tsang, 2002). This level of intervention does not include exercises designed to bring about forgiveness of a specific transgression. Rather, its goal is to create conditions propitious to consideration of forgiveness as a possible response when a transgression is experienced. Both levels of intervention described thus far are intended to entail relatively low cost for the recipients.

Greater recipient time and effort are required for the third level of intervention, psychoeducation with forgiveness implementation. It is only at this level that response to a specific transgression in the recipient's life is addressed. An important element of this level of intervention is screening of recipients because not everyone who has experienced a transgression (and, therefore, at risk) will be a suitable candidate. At the most fundamental level, recipients need to be screened for clinical disorder. However, even in the absence of such disorder, when the transgression occasions a traumatic response (shatters basic beliefs about the world, etc.; see Gordon, Baucom, & Snyder, 2000), this level of intervention is not appropriate, even if the response does not reach the level of diagnosable posttraumatic stress disorder. This level of intervention is most similar to the majority of extant group interventions for forgiveness (see Worthington et al., 2000). However, these interventions have yet to capitalize on a growing body of research showing that writing about past traumatic experiences has beneficial effects on mental and physical health (see Esterling, L'Abate, Murray, & Pennebaker, 1999). Our approach to facilitating forgiveness, therefore, makes extensive use of writing exercises. We have described this intervention in detail elsewhere (Fincham & Beach, 2002b).

The next level of intervention is enhancement. Participants in enhancement programs generally are self-selected; hence, their motivation is likely to be high. At this level, recipients learn forgiveness as a general skill without targeting a specific transgression. Ripley (1998) provides the lone example of such an approach. Community couples participated in this intervention with the goal of increasing intimacy and preventing future problems in their relationships. Many of the couples in Ripley's program denied having any unresolved hurts, which supports our decision not to target specific participant transgression at the level of enhancement. As an interpersonal process, forgiveness as a general skill is difficult to imagine in the absence of more general relationship skills (e.g., communication skills). Hence, intervention at the level of enhancement includes training in such relationship skills.

Finally, remedial interventions are targeted at persons whose functioning has been impaired by a transgression or series of transgressions. Little is known about interventions for severe and long-lasting harms because these have not been the subject of the group interventions that have dominated the forgiveness intervention literature. However, there are notable examples of such interventions for individuals (e.g., Coyle & Enright, 1997). Whether forgiveness in this situation simply becomes a component of a broader intervention or can be sustained as an independent self-contained intervention is open to question. The answer to this question may rest on the extent to which the transgression and the response to it are part of a chronic pattern of functioning in the person's life. It is conceivable that self-contained forgiveness interventions are viable to the extent that they deal with single, precisely defined harms (e.g., marital infidelity). Most of what is known about this level of intervention derives from clinical experience and is largely anecdotal. This has not prevented the emergence of more formal process models of forgiveness (e.g., Enright & Coyle, 1998) to inform intervention, but these models have not been subject to empirical evaluation that demonstrates forgiveness unfolds in the manner specified. Nonetheless, outcome studies based on interventions using these models (e.g., Coyle & Enright, 1997; Freedman & Enright, 1996) make useful contributions to our knowledge about the benefits of promoting forgiveness in the context of psychotherapy. However, there is no evidence yet on whether facilitating forgiveness of a transgression confers advantages over interventions that do not deal with forgiveness per se.

DELIVERY FORMAT

Consistent with our broadened view of facilitating forgiveness, we advocate diverse delivery formats for forgiveness interventions. We have already discussed use of the mass media in a forgiveness information campaign. Use of mass media need not be limited to this level of intervention, however. Indeed, we can conceive of judicious use of this delivery format for all levels of intervention except remediation. For example, there already exists a competitive market of trade books dealing with forgiveness, some of which take the form of self-help (e.g., Klein, 1995), but, as is too often the case, this self-help domain is relatively uninformed by research on forgiveness. Thus, this delivery format is ripe for development of evidence-based material.

Delivery of interventions via the print medium is necessarily limited as compared to audiovisual presentation. More information can be presented more vividly in a shorter time frame using the audiovisual medium. Given this advantage, as well as its ability to engage attention, we advocate the development of audiovisually based interventions. However, both of these delivery formats provide minimal control over the delivery of the intervention because readers can access pages in whatever order they choose, and viewers can fast forward videotapes at the click of a button. The issue of control becomes important where interventions include programmatic, cumulative exercises designed either to facilitate forgiveness of a specific transgression or to develop a relationship skill. Everything presented via the print or audiovisual medium can be delivered in a more controlled manner through the digital medium. Delivery of an intervention on a CD or DVD can control access to later parts of the intervention by making it contingent on performing earlier parts. Mastery of material can also be assessed once it has been accessed and immediate feedback given with further progress through the intervention dependent on a minimal level of mastery. Programs can also be written to individualize the intervention by tailoring what material is presented dependent on a participant's answers to relevant questions.

Almost anything that can be delivered via CD and DVD can also be delivered via the Internet. This latter medium of delivery is particularly exciting because of its growing penetration of households throughout the world and because it allows greater control over the delivery of the intervention (e.g., time spent on writing exercises can be monitored precisely, writing can be analyzed online, and so on). The possibility of delivering an intervention to millions of people throughout the world via the Internet makes the road ahead both an exciting and daunting path to travel.

We would be remiss if we did not comment on the face-to-face delivery format with individuals and groups. In our judgment, this medium is the sine qua non of the remedial level of intervention, though it is also an option for other levels. But even here, our vision is broader than that traditionally found. Consistent with our premises on a seeking mode of intervention and participant resources not necessarily enabling access to professionals, we see a critical role for paraprofessionals in facilitating forgiveness. Indeed, there has long been data to suggest that psychotherapy interventions delivered by professionals and paraprofessionals do not differ in effectiveness (e.g., Christensen, Miller, & Munoz, 1978). This brings us to the issue of starting points for implementing our vision of facilitating forgiveness.

STARTING POINTS

Rather than approach the task de novo and reinvent the wheel, we believe that a useful starting point is to look for existing interventions in the community that might include forgiveness as well as those that might be enhanced by including a focus on forgiveness. We identify an example of each before highlighting limitations of the approach advocated in this chapter.

An unlikely but promising starting point is the legal system where forgiveness is gaining attention in both criminal (e.g., Nygaard, 1997) and civil contexts (e.g., Feigenson, 2000). Two entry points are particularly promising from our perspective. First is the recent emergence of problem-solving courts, particularly community courts, which use judicial authority to solve legal and nonlegal problems that arise in individual cases and consider outcomes that go beyond mere application of the law. Denckla (2000) describes the role and impact of forgiveness in problem-solving courts. Two obvious next steps might be to (1) index the degree to which forgiveness operates in particular courts and relate this to relevant outcomes (e.g., recidivism), and (2) compare jurisdictions in which such courts do and do not operate.

Perhaps more obvious as a point of entry for forgiveness research are restorative justice programs. There is a diversity of views on what is meant by *restorative justice* (Johnstone, 2002), but several themes underlie this diversity, including attention to what should be done for the victim, relating to offenders differently (not seeing them as enemies from the outside but as "one of us"), and the community's willingness to be involved in conflict resolution between victim and offender (Johnstone, 2002). By allowing for forgiveness, restorative justice programs empower the victim and allow the perpetrator to be affirmed both by the victim and the community as a person of worth and to regain—or for many gain for the first time—their respect and be reintegrated—or integrated—into society. Recognizing these themes does not give rise to a particular method but rather offers a set of purposes and values to guide responses to crime (Morris & Young, 2000; see also Ward & Mann, Chapter 36, this volume). We now briefly consider one form in which restorative justice has been implemented, victim offender mediation (VOM), sometimes called victim-offender reconciliation programs.

Victim offender mediation programs began in the 1970s in Canada, and there are now hundreds of programs throughout the world (focused largely on juvenile offenders), evaluation of which yields salutary findings, including participant satisfaction, perceived fairness of restitution agreement, restitution completion, and recidivism (see Umbreit, 2001). Note, however, that forgiveness is not an explicit goal of such programs. Indeed, good mediators avoid use of terms such as *forgiveness* and *reconciliation* because they "pressure and prescribe behavior for victims" (p. 25). But this does not preclude forgiveness from taking place in VOM. This provides the opportunity to compare outcomes in cases where forgiveness does and does not take place. An obvious additional need is to examine the features of cases where forgiveness occurs in an attempt to identify its potential determinants.

Finally, we identify a widely accepted program that does not make reference to forgiveness—peer mediation in educational institutions. There is evidence that peer mediation in schools helps students resolve their conflicts constructively, which tends to result in reducing the numbers of student-student conflicts referred to teachers and administrators, which, in turn, tends to reduce suspensions (Johnson & Johnson, 1996). The outcomes of such programs might well be enhanced in educational institutions in which a forgiveness information campaign has been conducted, compared to matched institutions that have not experienced such a campaign. Alternatively, inclusion of educational material on forgiveness in such peer mediation programs themselves seems appropriate provided it does not implicitly pressure students to engage in forgiveness but only outlines forgiveness as one of many possible outcomes. Once introduced, an outcome evaluation of programs that do and do not include this enhancement would be needed. These suggestions alert us to an important consideration: the need for developmentally appropriate materials in facilitating forgiveness in people of different ages as the understanding of forgiveness changes with age.

LIMITATIONS

Our suggestions exhibit the same major weakness of extant forgiveness programs: They do not speak to the issue of forgiveness transactions between people. Indeed, they do not capitalize on the fact that the transgressions often occur in ongoing relationships where the victim has direct access to the transgressor. We know that transgressor and victim usually engage in systematic, but differing, distortions of the original event (see Stillwell & Baumeister, 1997), setting the stage for conflict around the issue of forgiveness. This observation draws attention to the perspective of the transgressor. Acknowledging wrongdoing and accepting forgiveness may itself be a human strength, but they have not been the topic of this chapter, which has focused instead on the granting of forgiveness. This is not to suggest that the facilitation of forgiveness is entirely independent of the transgressor. On the contrary, there is strong evidence that transgressor behavior (e.g., apology, offers of restitution) facilitates forgiveness. Thus, supplemental materials or even a set of interventions parallel to those described that emphasize the perspective of the transgressor need to be developed.

In addition, while we have incorporated social units/groups into our analysis, we have not addressed the issue of forgiveness between such units. Forgiveness at this level of analysis raises its own set of thorny problems, which are beyond the scope of this chapter (see Worthington, 2001, for a discussion of forgiveness at the social and societal levels). Finally, we have outlined a systematic program for research on facilitating forgiveness in global terms, a necessary limitation given space constraints.

CONCLUSION

In this chapter, we identified forgiveness as a human strength, analyzed evidence on the benefits of forgiving, and summarized research on forgiveness interventions.

We analyzed forgiveness with a positive psychology focus and offered a much broader conception of how forgiveness might be facilitated. A next step is to develop detailed protocols for the levels of intervention identified and to investigate the efficacy of each, not only in preventing distress but also in enhancing optimal human functioning. Such a remit is clearly beyond that of a single investigator and will require our collective efforts. The enormity of the challenge is matched only by the potential payoff of work that, with the help of modern technology, has the potential to enhance the lives of millions of fellow humans.

REFERENCES

Al-Mubak, R., Enright, R. D., & Cardis, P. (1995). Forgiveness education with parentally love-deprived college students. *Journal of Moral Education, 14*, 427–444.

Aristotle. (1939). *Rhetoric.* Cambridge, MA: Harvard University Press.

Beach, S. R., Fincham, F. D., & Katz, J. (1998). Marital therapy in the treatment of depression: Toward a third generation of outcome research. *Clinical Psychology Review, 18*, 635–661.

Bergin, A. E. (1963). The effects of psychotherapy: Negative results revisited. *Journal of Counseling Psychology, 10*, 244–250.

Berry, J. W., & Worthington, E. L. (2001). Forgivingness, relationship quality, stress while imagining relationship events, and physical and mental health. *Journal of Counseling Psychology, 48*, 447–455.

Biglan, A. (1995). Translating what we know about the context of antisocial behavior into a lower prevalence of such behavior. *Journal of Applied Behavior Analysis, 28*, 479–492.

Burman, B., & Margolin, G. (1992). Analysis of the association between marital relationships and health problems: An interactional perspective. *Psychological Bulletin, 112*, 39–63.

Christensen, A., Miller, W. R., & Munoz, R. F. (1978). Paraprofessionals, partners, peers, paraphernalia and print: Expanding mental health service delivery. *Professional Psychology, 9*, 249–270.

Close, H. T. (1970). Forgiveness and responsibility: A case study. *Pastoral Psychology, 21*, 19–25.

Coyle, C. T., & Enright, R. D. (1997). Forgiveness intervention with postabortion men. *Journal of Consulting and Clinical Psychology, 65*, 1042–1046.

Denckla, D. A. (2000). Forgiveness as a problem-solving tool in the courts: A brief response to the panel on forgiveness in criminal law. *Fordham Urban Law Journal, 27*, 1613–1619.

Enright, R. D., & Coyle, C. T. (1998). Researching the process model of forgiveness within psychological interventions. In E. L. Worthington (Ed.), *Dimensions of forgiveness: Psychological research and theological perspectives* (pp. 139–161). Philadelphia: Templeton Press.

Enright, R. D., Freedman, S., & Rique, J. (1998). The psychology of interpersonal forgiveness. In R. D. Enright & J. North (Eds.), *Exploring forgiveness* (pp. 46–62). Madison: University of Wisconsin Press.

Enright, R. D., & North, J. (Eds.). (1998). *Exploring forgiveness.* Madison: University of Wisconsin Press.

Esterling, B. A., L'Abate, L., Murray, E. J., & Pennebaker, J. W. (1999). Empirical foundations for writing in prevention and psychotherapy: Mental and physical health outcomes. *Clinical Psychology Review, 19*, 79–96.

Ewart, C. K., Taylor, C. B., Kraemer, H. C., & Agras, W. S. (1991). High blood pressure and marital discord: Not being nasty matters more than being nice. *Health Psychology, 103,* 155–163.

Exline, J. J., Worthington, E. L., Hill, P., & McCullough, M. E. (2003). Forgiveness and justice: A research agenda for social and personality psychology. *Personality and Social Psychology Bulletin, 7,* 337–348.

Farrow, T. F. D., Zeng, Y., Wilkinson, I. D., Spence, S. A., Deakin, J. F. W., Tarrier, N., et al. (2001). Investigating the functional anatomy of empathy and forgiveness. *Neuroreport, 12,* 2433–2438.

Feigenson, N. R. (2000). Merciful damages: Some remarks on forgiveness, mercy and tort law. *Fordham Urban Law Journal, 27,* 1633–1649.

Fenell, D. (1993). Characteristics of long-term first marriages. *Journal of Mental Health Counseling, 15,* 446–460.

*Fincham, F. D. (2000). The kiss of the porcupines: From attributing responsibility to forgiving. *Personal Relationships, 7,* 1–23.

Fincham, F. D. (2003). Marital conflict: Correlates, structure and context. *Current Directions in Psychological Science, 12,* 23–27.

Fincham, F. D., & Beach, S. R. (2002a). Forgiveness in marriage: Implications for psychological aggression and constructive communication. *Personal Relationships, 9,* 239–251.

Fincham, F. D., & Beach, S. R. (2002b). Forgiveness: Toward a public health approach to intervention. In J. H. Harvey & A. E. Wenzel (Eds.), *A clinician's guide to maintaining and enhancing close relationships* (pp. 277–300). Mahwah, NJ: Erlbaum.

Fincham, F. D., Beach, S. R., & Davila, J. (2003). *Forgiveness and conflict resolution in marriage.* Manuscript submitted for publication.

Freedman, S. R., & Enright, R. D. (1996). Forgiveness as an intervention goal with incest survivors. *Journal of Consulting and Clinical Psychology, 64,* 983–992.

Ghandi, M. (2000). *The collected works of Mahatma Gandhi* (2nd ed., Vol. 51, pp. 301–302). Mahatma Ghandi Young India. New Deli: Government of India, Publications Division.

Gordon, K. C., Baucom, D. H., & Snyder, D. K. (2000). Forgiveness in marital therapy. In M. E. McCullough, K. I. Pargament, & C. E. Thoresen (Eds.), *Forgiveness: Theory, research and practice* (pp. 203–227). New York: Guilford Press.

Hebl, J. H., & Enright, R. D. (1993). Forgiveness as a psychotherapeutic goal with elderly females. *Psychotherapy, 30,* 658–667.

Huang, S. T., & Enright, R. D. (2000). Forgiveness and anger-related emotions in Taiwan: Implications for therapy. *Psychotherapy, 37,* 71–79.

Johnson, D. W., & Johnson, R. T. (1996). Conflict resolution and peer mediation programs in elementary and secondary schools: A review of the research. *Review of Education Research, 66,* 459–506.

Johnstone, G. (2002). *Restorative justice: Ideas, values, debates.* Cullumpton, Devon, England: Willan.

Kantz, J. E. (2000). How do people conceptualize and use forgiveness? The Forgiveness Attitudes Questionnaire. *Counseling and Values, 44,* 174–186.

Kaplan, B. H. (1992). Social health and the forgiving heart: The Type B story. *Journal of Behavioral Medicine, 15,* 3–14.

Kiecolt-Glaser, J. K., Glaser, R., Cacioppo, J. T., MacCullum, R. C., Snydersmith, M., Kim, C., et al. (1997). Marital conflict in older adults: Endocrine and immunological correlates. *Psychosomatic Medicine, 59,* 339–349.

Kiecolt-Glaser, J. K., Kennedy, S., Malkoff, S., Fisher, L., Speicher, C. E., & Glaser, R. (1988). Marital discord and immunity in males. *Psychosomatic Medicine, 50,* 213–229.

Klein, C. (1995). *How to forgive when you can't forget.* New York: Berkley Books.

Lawler, K. A., Younger, J., Piferi, R. A., & Jones, W. H. (2000, April). *A physiological profile of forgiveness.* Paper presented at the annual meeting of the Society for Behavioral Medicine, Nashville, TN.

Malcolm, W. M., & Greenberg, L. S. (2000). Forgiveness as a process of change in individual psychotherapy. In M. E. McCullough, K. I. Pargament, & C. E. Thoresen (Eds.), *Forgiveness: Theory, research, and practice* (pp. 179–202). New York: Guilford Press.

Mauger, P. A., Perry, J. E., Freeman, T., Grove, D. C., McBride, A. G., & McKinney, K. E. (1992). The measurement of forgiveness: Preliminary research. *Journal of Psychology and Christianity, 11,* 170–180.

McCullough, M. E. (2000). Forgiveness as human strength: Theory, measurement, and links to well-being. *Journal of Social and Clinical Psychology, 19,* 43–55.

McCullough, M. E., Bellah, C. G., Kilpatrick, S. D., & Johnson, J. L. (2001). Vengefulness: Relationships with forgiveness, rumination, well-being, and the Big Five. *Personality and Social Psychology Bulletin, 27,* 601–610.

McCullough, M. E., Emmons, R. A., & Tsang, J. (2002). The grateful disposition: A conceptual and empirical topography. *Journal of Personality and Social Psychology, 82,* 112–127.

McCullough, M. E., Exline, J. J., & Baumeister, R. F. (1998). An annotated bibliography of research on forgiveness and related concepts. In E. L. Worthington (Ed.), *Dimensions of forgiveness: Psychological research and theological perspectives* (pp. 193–317). Philadelphia: Templeton Press.

McCullough, M. E., Fincham, F. D., & Tsang, J. (2003). Forgiveness, forbearance, and time: The temporal unfolding of transgression-related interpersonal motivations. *Journal of Personality and Social Psychology, 84,* 540–557.

McCullough, M. E., Pargament, K. I., & Thoresen, C. E. (Eds.). (2000). *Forgiveness: Theory, research, and practice.* New York: Guilford Press.

McCullough, M. E., Rachal, K. C., Sandage, S. J., Worthington, W. L., Brown, S. W., & Hight, T. L. (1998). Interpersonal forgiving in close relationships. II: Theoretical elaboration and measurement. *Journal of Personality and Social Psychology, 75,* 1586–1603.

*McCullough, M., & Witvliet, C. V. (2002). The psychology of forgiveness. In C. R. Snyder & S. J. Lopez (Eds.), *Handbook of positive psychology* (pp. 446–458). New York: Oxford University Press.

McCullough, M., & Worthington, E. L. (1994). Encouraging clients to forgive people who have hurt them: Review, critique, and research prospectus. *Journal of Psychology and Theology, 22,* 3–20.

Miller, T. Q., Smith, T. W., Turner, C. W., Guijarro, M. L., & Hallett, A. J. (1996). Meta-analytic review of research on hostility and physical health. *Psychological Bulletin, 119,* 322–348.

Morris, A., & Young, W. (2000). Reforming criminal justice: The potential for restorative justice. In H. Strang & J. Braithwaite (Eds.), *Restorative justice: Philosophy to practice* (pp. 11–31). Aldershot, England: Ashgate/Dartmouth.

Mrazek, P. J., & Haggerty, R. J. (Eds.). (1994). *Reducing risks for mental disorders: Frontiers for preventive intervention research.* Washington, DC: National Academy Press.

Nygaard, R. L. (1997). On the role of forgiveness in criminal sentencing. *Seton Hall Law Review, 27,* 980–1022.

Rappaport, J., & Chinsky, J. M. (1974). Models for delivery of service from a historical and conceptual perspective. *Professional Psychology, 5,* 42–50.

Reiss, S., & Havercamp, S. M. (1998). Toward a comprehensive assessment of fundamental motivation: Factor structure of the Reiss profiles. *Psychological Assessment, 10,* 97–106.

Ripley, J. S. (1998). *The effects off marital social values on outcomes of forgiveness: Couples enrich-ment psychoeducational groups or communication couples enrichment psychoeducational groups.* Unpublished doctoral dissertation, Virginia Commonwealth University, Richmond.

Rose, G. (1992). *The strategy of preventive medicine.* New York: Oxford University Press.

Ryan, R. M., & Deci, E. L. (2000). Self-determination theory and the facilitation of intrin-sic motivation, social development, and well-being. *American Psychologist, 55,* 68–78.

Rye, M. S., & Pargament, K. I. (2002). Forgiveness and romantic relationships in college: Can it heal the wounded heart? *Journal of Clinical Psychology, 58,* 419–441.

Schmaling, K. B., & Sher, T. G. (1997). Physical health and relationships. In W. K. Halford & H. J. Markman (Eds.), *Clinical handbook of marriage and couples intervention* (pp. 323–345). New York: Wiley.

Seligman, M. E. P. (2002a). *Authentic happiness: Using the new positive psychology to realize your potential for lasting fulfillment.* New York: Free Press.

Seligman, M. E. P. (2002b). Positive psychology, positive prevention, and positive therapy. In C. R. Snyder & S. J. Lopez (Eds.), *Handbook of positive psychology* (pp. 3–9). New York: Oxford University Press.

Sorensen, G., Emmons, K., Hunt, M., & Johnston, D. (1998). Implications of the results of community intervention trials. *Annual Review of Public Health, 19,* 379–416.

Stillwell, A. M., & Baumeister, R. F. (1997). The construction of victim and perpetrator memories: Accuracy and distortion in role-based accounts. *Personality and Social Psy-chology Bulletin, 23,* 1157–1172.

Subkoviak, M. J., Enright, R. D., Wu, C., Gassin, E. A., Freedman, S., Olson, L. M., et al. (1995). Measuring interpersonal forgiveness in late adolescence and middle adulthood. *Journal of Adolescence, 18,* 641–655.

Tangey, J., Fee, R., & Lee, N. (1999, August). *Assessing individual differences in the propensity to forgive.* Paper presented at the 107th annual conference of the American Psychologi-cal Association, Boston.

Thompson, B., Coronado, G., Snipes, S. A., & Puschel, K. (2003). Methodological advances and ongoing challenges in designing community-based health promotion programs. *Annual Review of Public Health, 24,* 315–340.

Thoresen, C. E., Harris, A. H. S., & Luskin, F. (2000). Forgiveness and health: An unan-swered question. In M. E. McCullough, K. I. Pargament, & C. E. Thoresen (Eds.), *Forgive-ness: Theory, research, and practice* (pp. 254–295). New York: Guilford Press.

Toussaint, L. L., Williams, D. R., Musick, M. A., & Everson, S. A. (2001). Forgiveness and health: Age differences in a U.S. probability sample. *Journal of Adult Development, 8,* 249–257.

Umbreit, M. S. (2001). *The handbook of victim offender mediation: An essential guide to practice and research.* San Francisco: Jossey-Bass.

Van den Broucke, S., Vandereycken, W., & Norre, J. (1997). *Eating disorders and marital rela-tionships.* London: Routledge.

Witvliet, C. V., Ludwig, T. E., Van der Laan, K. L. (2001). Granting forgiveness or harbor-ing grudges: Implications for emotion, physiology, and health. *Psychological Science, 121,* 117–123.

Worthington, E. L. (Ed.). (1998). *Dimensions of forgiveness.* Philadelphia: Templeton Foun-dation Press.

Worthington, E. L. (2001). Unforgiveness, forgiveness, and reconciliation and their implica-tions for societal interventions. In R. G. Helmick & R. L Petersen (Eds.), *Forgiveness and reconciliation: Religion, public policy, and conflict transformation* (pp. 161–182). Philadelphia: Templeton Press.

*Worthington, E. L., Sandage, S. J., & Berry, J. W. (2000). Group interventions to promote forgiveness. In M. E. McCullough, K. I. Pargament, & C. E. Thoresen (Eds.), *Forgiveness: Theory, research, and practice* (pp. 228–253). New York: Guilford Press.

*Worthington, E. L., & Wade, N. G. (1999). The psychology of unforgiveness and forgiveness and implications for clinical practice. *Journal of Social and Clinical Psychology, 18*, 385–418.

Wuthnow, R. (2000). How religious groups promote forgiving: A national study. *Journal for the Scientific Study of Religion, 36*, 124–137.

Yovetich, N. A., & Rusbult, C. E. (1994). Accommodative behavior in close relationships: Exploring transformation of motivation. *Journal of Experimental Social Psychology, 30*, 138–164.

PART XII

PUBLIC POLICY INITIATIVES: GOOD GOVERNANCE AND THE GOOD LIFE

Human Connections and the Good Life: Balancing Individuality and Community in Public Policy

DAVID G. MYERS

HUMANS HAVE A need to belong, to connect, to bond. When those needs are met, through intimate friendships and equitable marriages, self-reported happiness runs high and children generally thrive. The 1960 to early 1990s era of heightened individualism was accompanied by a fraying of human bonds and, despite increasing affluence, by declining indicators of communal health and well-being. This chapter describes the need to belong, documents the links between close relationships and subjective well-being, identifies some benefits and costs of modern individualism, and suggests how communitarian public policies might respect both essential liberties and communal well-being.

WHO IS HAPPY?

Who lives with the greatest happiness and life satisfaction? The last quarter century has offered some surprising, and some not-so-surprising, answers. Self-reported well-being is *not* much predicted from knowing a person's age or gender (Myers, 1993, 2000b; Myers & Diener, 1996). Despite a smoothing of the emotional terrain as people age, and contrary to rumors of midlife crises and later life angst, happiness is about equally available to healthy men and women of all ages. At all of life's ages and stages, there are many happy and fewer unhappy. Moreover, despite striking gender differences in ailments such as depression (afflicting more women) to alcoholism (afflicting more men), happiness does not have a favorite gender.

So, who *are* the relatively happy people?

- As Ed Diener (2000) indicates, some *cultures* (especially those where people enjoy abundance and political freedom) are conducive to increased satisfaction with life.

641

- Certain *traits* and temperaments appear to predispose happiness. Some of these traits, such as extraversion, are genetically influenced, which helps explain David Lykken and Auke Tellegen's (1996) finding that about 50% of the variation in current happiness is heritable. Like cholesterol levels, happiness is genetically influenced but not genetically fixed.
- National Opinion Research Center (2002) surveys of more than 40,000 Americans over three decades indicate that people active in *faith communities* more often report being "very happy" (as have 47% of those attending religious services more than weekly and 27% of those never attending).

MONEY AND HAPPINESS

Does money buy happiness? Many people presume there is some connection between wealth and well-being. From 1970 to 2002, the number of entering American collegians who consider it "very important or essential" that they become "very well off financially" rose from 39% to 73% (Sax, Astin, Korn, & Mahoney, 2002).

Are people in rich nations, indeed, happier? National wealth does predict national well-being up to a certain point, with diminishing returns thereafter (Myers, 2000b). During the 1980s, the comparatively affluent West Germans expressed more happiness than the very poor Bulgarians, but not more than the moderately affluent Irish. But national wealth rides along with confounding factors such as civil rights, literacy, and years of stable democracy.

Within any nation, are rich people happier? Yes, again, especially in poor countries where low income threatens basic human needs (Argyle, 1999). In affluent nations, the income-happiness correlation persists. But some analysts find it "surprisingly weak" (Inglehart, 1990, p. 242). Moreover, the human capacity for adaptation has made happiness nearly equally available to the richest Americans, to lottery winners, to middle income people, and to those who have adapted to disabilities (Myers, 2000b).

Does economic growth boost happiness? The happiness boost that comes with increased money has a short half life. Over the past four decades, Americans' per person income, expressed in constant dollars, has doubled (thanks to increased real wages into the 1970s, the doubling of women's employment, and increasing nonwage income). Although income disparity has also increased, the rising economic tide has enabled today's Americans to own twice as many cars per person, to eat out more than twice as often, and to mostly enjoy (unlike their 1960 counterparts) dishwashers, clothes dryers, and air conditioning. So, believing that it is "very important" to be very well off financially and having seen their affluence ratchet upward, are Americans now happier? As Figure 38.1 indicates (updated from Myers, 2000b), their self-reports suggest not. Moreover, before a late 1990s rebound, the third of a century after 1960 was marked not only by spiraling affluence but also by plummeting social well-being. The divorce rate doubled. Teen suicide tripled. Reported violent crime nearly quadrupled. The prison population quintupled. And the proportion of babies born to unmarried parents sextupled. The National Commission on Civic Renewal (1998) combined 22 such social trends to create its "Index of National Civic Health," which plunged southward from 1960 to the early 1990s, even as affluence rose. I have called this conjunction of upward material prosperity and downward social recession *The American Paradox* (Myers, 2000a).

The same conclusion—that economic growth has *not* produced increased personal or social well-being—is true of European countries and Japan, according to

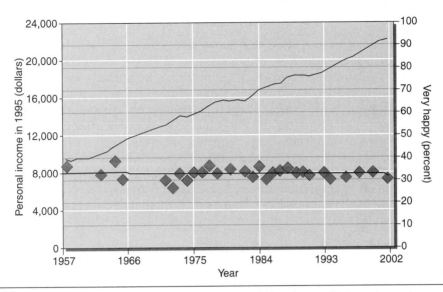

Figure 38.1 Economic Growth and Self-Reported Happiness. *Data sources:* Income, U.S. Commerce Department; Happiness, National Opinion Research Center.

Richard Easterlin (1995). In Britain, for example, sharp increases in the percentages of households with cars, central heating, and telephones have not been accompanied by increased happiness.

Not only does wealth not boost well-being, those individuals who strive the hardest for wealth tend to have lower-than-average well-being—a finding that "comes through very strongly in every culture I've looked at," reported Richard Ryan (quoted in Kohn, 1999; see Kasser & Ryan, 1996). His collaborator, Tim Kasser, concludes from their studies that those who instead strive for "intimacy, personal growth, and contribution to the community" experience a higher quality of life (Kasser, 2000). Ryan and Kasser's research echoes an earlier finding by H. W. Perkins: Among 800 college alumni surveyed, those with "Yuppie values"—who preferred a high income and occupational success and prestige to having very close friends and a close marriage—were twice as likely as their former classmates to describe themselves as "fairly" or "very" *un*happy (Perkins, 1991).

We know the perils of materialism, sort of. In a nationally representative survey, Princeton sociologist Robert Wuthnow found that 89% of more than 2,000 participants felt "our society is much too materialistic." *Other* people are too materialistic, that is. For 84% also wished they had more money, and 78% said it was "very or fairly important" to have "a beautiful home, a new car and other nice things" (Wuthnow, 1994).

You have to wonder, what's the point? What's the point of accumulating stacks of unplayed CDs, closets full of seldom-worn clothes, garages with luxury cars? What's the point of corporate and government policies that inflate the rich while leaving the working poor to languish? What's the point of leaving huge estates for your children, as if inherited wealth could buy them happiness, when that wealth could do so much good in a hurting world? (If self-indulgence can't buy us happiness and cannot buy it for our kids, why not leave any significant wealth we accumulate to bettering the human condition?)

THE NEED TO BELONG

Aristotle would not be surprised that those who value intimacy and connection are happier than those who lust for money. He called us "the social animal." Indeed, noted Roy Baumeister and Mark Leary (1995), we humans have a deep need to belong,[1] to feel connected with others in enduring, close, supportive relationships. Soon after birth, we exhibit powerful attachments. We almost immediately prefer familiar faces and voices. By eight months, we crawl after our caregivers and wail when separated from them. Reunited, we cling.

Adults, too, exhibit the power of attachment. Separated from friends or family—isolated in prison, alone at a new school, living in a foreign land—people feel their lost connections with important others. If, as Barbara Streisand sings, "People who need people are the luckiest people in the world," then most people are lucky.

AIDING SURVIVAL

Social connections serve multiple functions. Social bonds boosted our ancestors' survival rate. By keeping children close to their caregivers, attachments served as a powerful survival impulse. As adults, those who formed attachments were more likely to come together to reproduce and to stay together to nurture their offspring to maturity.

Cooperation in groups also enhanced survival. In solo combat, our ancestors were not the toughest predators. But as hunters they learned that six hands were better than two. Those who foraged in groups also gained protection from predators and enemies. If those who felt a need to belong were also those who survived and reproduced most successfully, their genes would in time predominate. The inevitable result: an innately social creature. People in every society on earth belong to groups.

WANTING TO BELONG

The need to belong colors our thoughts and emotions. We spend a great deal of time thinking about our actual and hoped-for relationships. When relationships form, we often feel joy. Falling in mutual love, people have been known to feel their cheeks ache from their irrepressible grins. Asked, "What is necessary for your happiness?" or "What is it that makes your life meaningful?" most people mention—before anything else—close, satisfying relationships with family, friends, or romantic partners (Berscheid, 1985). Happiness hits close to home.

ACTING TO INCREASE SOCIAL ACCEPTANCE

When we feel included, accepted, and loved by those important to us, our self-esteem rides high. Indeed, say Leary, Haupt, Strausser, and Chokel (1998), our self-esteem is a gauge of how valued and accepted we feel. Much of our social behavior, therefore, aims to increase our belonging—our social acceptance and inclusion. To avoid rejection, we generally conform to group standards and seek to

---

[1] This section and the next draw, with permission, from my *Psychology*, 7th edition (New York: Worth Publishers, 2004).

make favorable impressions. To win friendship and esteem, we monitor our behavior, hoping to create the right impressions. Seeking love and belonging, we spend billions on clothes, cosmetic products and surgeries, and diet and fitness aids—all motivated by our quest for acceptance.

Maintaining Relationships

For most of us, familiarity breeds liking, not contempt. We resist breaking social bonds. Thrown together at school, at summer camp, or on a vacation cruise, people resist the group's dissolution. Hoping to maintain our relationships, we promise to call, to write, to come back for reunions. Parting, we feel distress.

When something threatens or dissolves our social ties, negative emotions overwhelm us. The first weeks living on a college campus away from home distress many students. But if feelings of acceptance and connection build, so do self-esteem, positive feelings, and desires to help rather than hurt others (Buckley & Leary, 2001). When immigrants and refugees move, alone, to new places, the stress and loneliness can be depressing. After years of placing such families individually in isolated communities, today's policies encourage "chain migration" (Pipher, 2002). The second refugee Sudanese family that settles in a town generally has an easier time adjusting than the first.

For children, even a brief time-out in isolation can be an effective punishment. For adults as well as children, social ostracism can be even more painful. To be shunned—given the cold shoulder or the silent treatment, with others' eyes avoiding yours—is to have your need to belong threatened, observe Kipling Williams and Lisa Zadro (2001). People often respond to social ostracism with depressed moods, initial efforts to restore their acceptance, and then withdrawal. "It's the meanest thing you can do to someone, especially if you know they can't fight back. I never should have been born," said Lea, a lifelong victim of the silent treatment by her mother and grandmother. "I came home every night and cried. I lost 25 pounds, had no self-esteem and felt that I wasn't worthy," reported Richard, after two years of silent treatment by his employer.

If rejected and unable to remedy the situation, people sometimes turn nasty. In a series of studies, Jean Twenge and her collaborators (Twenge, Baumeister, Tice, & Stucke, 2001; Twenge, Catanese, & Baumeister, 2002; also see Baumeister, Twenge, & Nuss, 2002) told people (based on a personality test) that either they would have "rewarding relationships throughout life" or "everyone chose you as someone they'd like to work with." They told other participants that they were "the type likely to end up alone later in life" or that others whom they had met didn't want them in a group that was forming. Those excluded became much more likely to engage in self-defeating behaviors and underperform on aptitude tests. They also exhibited more antisocial behavior, such as by disparaging someone who had insulted them or aggressing (with a blast of noise) against them. "If intelligent, well-adjusted, successful university students can turn aggressive in response to a small laboratory experience of social exclusion," noted the research team, "it is disturbing to imagine the aggressive tendencies that might arise from a series of important rejections or chronic exclusion from desired groups in actual social life" (p. 1068).

Most socially excluded teens do not commit violence, but some do. Charles "Andy" Williams, described by a classmate as someone his peers derided as "freak, dork, nerd, stuff like that," went on a shooting spree at his suburban California high school, killing 2 and wounding 13 (Bowles & Kasindorf, 2001).

Exile, imprisonment, and solitary confinement are progressively more severe forms of punishment. The bereaved often feel life is empty and pointless. Children reared in institutions without a sense of belonging to anyone or locked away at home under extreme neglect become pathetic creatures—withdrawn, frightened, speechless. Adults denied acceptance and inclusion may feel depressed. Anxiety, jealousy, loneliness, and guilt all involve threatened disruptions of our need to belong. Even when bad relationships break, people suffer. In one 16-nation survey, separated and divorced people were only half as likely as married people to say they were "very happy" (Inglehart, 1990). After such separations, feelings of loneliness and anger—and sometimes even a strange desire to be near the former partner—are commonplace.

CLOSE RELATIONSHIPS AND HAPPINESS

So far, we have seen that age, gender, and a rising economic tide are but modest predictors of happiness. Valuing intimacy and connection more than increasing material possessions *does* predict well-being. It's no wonder, given our human need to belong. So, if that need is met, are people happier? Healthier?

FRIENDSHIPS AND WELL-BEING

Attachments with intimate friends have two effects, believed Francis Bacon (1625): "It redoubleth joys, and cutteth griefs in half." "I get by with a little help from my friends," sang John Lennon and Paul McCartney (1967).

Indeed, people report happier feelings when with others (Pavot, Diener, & Fujita, 1990).

Asked by National Opinion Research Center interviewers, "How many close friends would you say you have?" (excluding family members), 26% of those reporting fewer than five friends and 38% of those reporting five or more said they were "very happy."

MARRIAGE AND WELL-BEING

Worldwide, 9 in 10 people will experience marriage, reports the United Nations' *Demographic Yearbook.* Do the attachments (and constraints) of marriage more often stifle or feed happiness?

Mountains of data reveal that most people are happier attached. Compared with those who never marry, and especially compared with those who have separated or divorced, married people report greater happiness and life satisfaction. This marriage-happiness correlation extends across countries and (contrary to some pop psychology) both genders (see Figure 38.2).

Why are married people happier? Does marriage breed happiness? Or is happiness conducive to marriage? The marriage-happiness traffic appears to run both ways. First, happy people, being more good-natured, outgoing, and sensitive to others, may be more appealing as marital partners. Unhappy people experience more rejection. Misery may love company, but company does not love misery. An unhappy (and, therefore, self-focused, irritable, and withdrawn) spouse or roommate

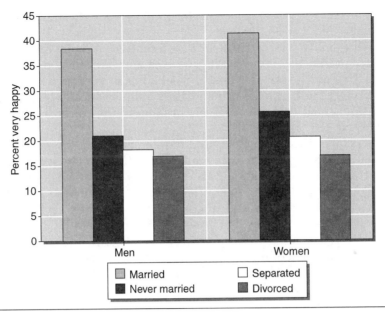

Figure 38.2   National Opinion Research Center Surveys of 40,605 Americans (1972 to 2000)

is generally not fun to be around (Gotlib, 1992; Segrin & Dillard, 1992). For such reasons, positive, happy people more readily form happy relationships.

Yet, "the prevailing opinion of researchers," noted Arne Mastekaasa (1995), is that the marriage-happiness correlation is "mainly due" to the beneficial effects of marriage. Consider: If the happiest people marry sooner and more often, then as people age (and progressively less happy people move into marriage), the average happiness of both married and never-married people should decline. (The older, less happy newlyweds would pull down the average happiness of married people, leaving the unhappiest people in the unmarried group.) However, the data refute this prediction, which suggests that marital intimacy, commitment, and support do, for most people, pay emotional dividends. Marriage offers people new roles that produce new stresses, but it also offers new rewards and sources of identity and self-esteem. When marked by intimacy, marriage (friendship sealed by commitment) reduces loneliness and offers a dependable lover and companion (Hendrick & Hendrick, 1997).

CLOSE RELATIONSHIPS AND HEALTH

Linda and Emily had much in common. When interviewed for a study conducted by UCLA psychologist Shelley Taylor (1989), both Los Angeles women had married, raised three children, suffered comparable breast tumors, and recovered from surgery and six months of chemotherapy. But there was a difference. Linda, a widow in her early 50s, was living alone, her children scattered in Atlanta, Boston, and Europe. "She had become odd in ways that people sometimes do when they are isolated," reported Taylor. "Having no one with whom to share her thoughts on a daily basis, she unloaded them somewhat inappropriately with strangers, including our interviewer" (pp. 139–142).

Interviewing Emily was difficult in a different way. Phone calls were interrupted. Her children, all living nearby, were in and out of the house, dropping things off with a quick kiss. Her husband called from his office for a brief chat. Two dogs roamed the house, greeting visitors enthusiastically. All in all, Emily "seemed a serene and contented person, basking in the warmth of her family" (Taylor, 1989, pp. 139–142).

Three years later, the researchers tried to reinterview the women. Linda, they learned, had died two years before. Emily was still lovingly supported by her family and friends and was as happy and healthy as ever. Because no two cancers are identical, we can't be certain that different social situations led to Linda's and Emily's fates. But they do illustrate a conclusion drawn from several large studies: Social support—feeling liked, affirmed, and encouraged by intimate friends and family—promotes not only happiness, but also health.

Relationships can sometimes be stressful, especially in living conditions that are crowded and lack privacy (Evans, Palsane, Lepore, & Martin, 1989). "Hell is others," wrote Jean-Paul Sartre. Peter Warr and Roy Payne (1982) asked a representative sample of British adults what, if anything, had emotionally strained them the day before. Their most frequent answer? "Family." Even when well-meaning, family intrusions can be stressful. And stress contributes to heart disease, hypertension, and a suppressed immune system.

On balance, however, close relationships more often contribute to health and happiness. Asked what prompted yesterday's times of pleasure, the same British sample, by an even larger margin, again answered, "Family." For most of us, family relationships provide not only our greatest heartaches but also our greatest comfort and joy. Moreover, seven massive investigations, each following thousands of people for several years, revealed that close relationships affect health. Compared with those having few social ties, people are less likely to die prematurely if supported by close relationships with friends, family, fellow workers, members of a church, or other support groups (Cohen, 1988; House, Landis, & Umberson, 1988; Nelson, 1988). Some additional examples:

- In a study that followed leukemia patients preparing to undergo bone marrow transplants, only 20% of those who said they had little social support from their family or friends were still alive two years later. Among those who felt strong emotional support, the two-year survival rate was nearly triple—54% (Colon, Callies, Popkin, & McGlave, 1991).
- A study of 1,234 heart-attack patients found nearly a doubled rate of a recurring attack within six months among those living alone (Case, Moss, Case, McDermott, & Eberly, 1992).
- A study of 1,965 heart disease patients revealed a five-year survival rate of 82% among those married or having a confidant, but only 50% among those having no one (R. B. Williams et al., 1992).

It has long been known that married people live longer, healthier lives than the unmarried. A seven-decade-long Harvard study found that a good marriage at age 50 predicts healthy aging better than does a low cholesterol level at 50 (Vaillant, 2002; see also Vaillant, Chapter 34, this volume). But why? Is it just that healthy people are more likely to marry and stay married? Two recent analyses conclude, after controlling for various possible explanations, that marriage does get under the skin. Marriage "improves survival prospects" (Murray, 2000) and "makes people" healthier and longer-lived (Wilson & Oswald, 2002). What also matters is marital functioning. Positive, happy, supportive marriages are conducive to health; conflict-laden ones are not (Kiecolt-Glaser & Newton, 2001).

There are several possible reasons for the link between social support and health (Helgeson, Cohen, & Fritz, 1998). Perhaps after symptoms appear family members who offer social support also help patients to receive medical treatment more quickly. Perhaps people eat better and exercise more because their partners guide and goad them into adhering to treatment regimens. Perhaps they smoke and drink less. One study following 50,000 young adults through time found that such unhealthy behaviors drop precipitously after marriage (Marano, 1998). Perhaps supportive relationships also help us evaluate and overcome stressful events, such as social rejection. Perhaps they help bolster our self-esteem. When we are wounded by someone's dislike or by the loss of a job, a friend's advice, assistance, and reassurance may be good medicine (Cutrona, 1986; Rook, 1987).

Environments that support our need to belong also foster stronger immune functioning. Given ample social support, spouses of cancer patients exhibit stronger immune functioning (Baron, Cutrona, Hicklin, Russell, & Lubaroff, 1990). Social ties even confer resistance to cold viruses. Sheldon Cohen and his collaborators (Cohen, Doyle, Skoner, Rabin, & Gwaltney, 1997) demonstrated this after putting 276 healthy volunteers in quarantine for five days after administering nasal drops laden with a cold virus. (The volunteers were paid $800 each to endure this experience.) The cold fact is that the effect of social ties is nothing to sneeze at. Age, race, sex, smoking, and other health habits being equal, those with the most social ties were least likely to catch a cold and they produced less mucus. More than 50 studies further reveal that social support calms the cardiovascular system, lowering blood pressure and stress hormones (Uchino, Cacioppo, & Kiecolt-Glaser, 1996; Uchino, Uno, & Holt-Lunstad, 1999).

Close relationships also provide the opportunity to *confide* painful feelings, a social support component that has now been extensively studied. In one study, James Pennebaker and Robin O'Heeron (1984) contacted the surviving spouses of people who had committed suicide or died in car accidents. Those who bore their grief alone had more health problems than those who could express it openly. Talking about our troubles can be open heart therapy. Older people, many of whom have lost a spouse and close friends, are somewhat less likely to enjoy such confiding. So, sustained emotional reactions to stressful events can be debilitating. However, the toxic impact of stressful events can be buffered by a relaxed, healthy lifestyle and by the comfort and aid provided by supportive friends and family.

DOES RADICAL INDIVIDUALISM SUBVERT OUR NEED TO BELONG?

We humans have a deep need to belong, which, if met, helps sustain our happiness and health. Yet consider some contemporary advice from Western pop psychology:

> Do your own thing. If it feels good, do it. Shun conformity. Don't force your values on others. Assert your personal rights (to sell and buy guns, to sell and buy

pornography). To love others, first love yourself. Listen to your own heart. Prefer solo spirituality to communal religion. Be self-sufficient. Expect others likewise to believe in themselves and to make it on their own.

Such sentiments define the heart of economic and social individualism, which finds its peak expression in modern America.

All post-Renaissance Western cultures to some extent express the triumph of individualism as what Elizabeth Fox-Genovese (1991, p. 7) calls *"the* theory of human nature and rights." But contemporary America is the most individualistic of cultures. One famous comparison of 116,000 IBM employees worldwide found that Americans, followed by Australians, were the most individualistic (Hofstede, 1980). We can glimpse America's individualism in its comparatively low tax rates. Taxes advance the common good through schools, roads, parks, and health, welfare, and defense programs that serve and protect all—but at a price to individuals. And in the contest among American values, individual rights trump social responsibilities.

Individualism is a two-sided coin. It supports democracy by fostering initiative, creativity, and equal rights for all individuals. But taken to an extreme, it becomes egoism and narcissism—the self above others, the individual's own present above posterity's future. Shunning conformity, commitment, and obligation, modern individualists prefer to define their own standards and do as they please, noted Robert Bellah and his colleagues (Bellah, Madsen, Sullivan, Swidler, & Tipton, 1985) in their discernment of modern *Habits of the Heart.* And as Putnam (2000) has massively documented, we are becoming more, not less, individualistic. Compared to a half century ago, we are more often bowling alone, and voting, visiting, entertaining, car-pooling, trusting, joining, meeting, neighboring, and giving proportionately less. Social capital—the family and community networks that nurture civility and mutual trust—has waned.

The celebration and defense of personal liberty lies at the heart of the American dream. It drives our free market economy and underlies our respect for the rights of all. In democratic countries that guarantee basic freedoms, people live more happily than in those that don't. Migration patterns testify to this reality. Yet for today's radical individualism, we pay a price: a social recession that has imperiled children, corroded civility, and slightly diminished happiness. *When individualism is taken to an extreme, individual well-being can become its ironic casualty.*

A VISION OF A MORE CONNECTED FUTURE

To counter radical individualism and the other forces of cultural corrosion, a social renewal movement is emerging—one that affirms liberals' indictment of the demoralizing effects of poverty and conservatives' indictment of toxic media models; one that welcomes liberals' support for family-friendly workplaces and conservatives' support for committed relationships; one that agrees with liberals' advocacy for children in all sorts of families, and conservatives' support for marriage and coparenting. "Anyone who tunes in politics even for background music can tell you how the sound has changed," observed Ellen Goodman (1994). Yesterday's shouting match over family values has become today's choir, she added. When singing about children growing up without fathers, "Politicians on the right, left and center may not be hitting exactly the same notes, but like sopranos, tenors and baritones, they're pretty much in harmony." We are recognizing that liberals' risk factors (poverty, inequality, hopelessness) and conservatives' risk factors (early sexualization, unwed parenthood, family fragmentation) all come in the same package.

Without suppressing our differences, do most people not share a vision of a better world? Is it not one that rewards initiative but restrains exploitative greed? That balances individual rights with communal well-being? That respects diversity while embracing unifying ideals? That is accepting of other cultures without being indifferent to moral issues? That protects and heals our degrading physical and social environments? In our utopian social world, adults and children will together enjoy their routines and traditions. They will have close relationships with extended family and with supportive neighbors. Children will live without fear for their safety or the breakup of their families. Fathers and mothers will jointly nurture their children; to say, "He fathered the child" will parallel the meaning of, "She mothered the child." Free yet responsible media will entertain us with stories and images that exemplify heroism, compassion, and committed love. Reasonable and rooted moral judgments will motivate compassionate acts and enable noble and satisfying lives.

Harbingers of this renewal are emerging. The dialogue is shifting—away from further expansion of personal rights and toward enhancement of communal civility. Signs of what Everett Carll Ladd (1998) called a "silent revolution"—a renewal of civic life—are springing up. People are beginning to understand the costs as well as the benefits of the unbridled pursuit of the old American dream—individually achieved wealth. In increasing numbers, neighborhoods are organizing, foundations are taking initiatives, youths are volunteering, scholars are discerning, faith-based institutions are tackling local problems, and civic renewal organizations are emerging. Government and corporate decision makers are becoming more agreeable to family supportive tax and benefit policies.

By the late 1990s, evidence was mounting that America's post-1960 social recession was ending and social renewal was underway. Various indicators of teen social pathologies peaked around 1994 and began abating. Child (under age 18) poverty, teen pregnancy, teen suicide, and teen violence all were subsiding from earlier peaks (see Figure 38.3).

THE COMMUNITARIAN MOVEMENT

Supported by research on the need to belong, on the psychology of women, and on communal values in Asian and Third-World cultures, many social scientists are finding renewed appreciation for human connections. A communitarian movement offers a "third way"—an alternative to the individualistic civil libertarianism of the left and the economic libertarianism of the right. It implores us, in the words of Martin Luther King Jr., "to choose between chaos and community," to balance our needs for independence and attachment, liberty and civility, me-thinking and we-thinking. The Communitarian Platform "recognizes that the preservation of individual liberty depends on the active maintenance of the institutions of civil society" and that a "fragile social ecology" supports the family and communal life that underlies civility.

Typically, conservatives are economic individualists and moral collectivists. Liberals are moral individualists and economic collectivists. Third-way communitarians advocate moral and economic policies that balance rights with communal responsibility. "Democratic communitarianism is based on the value of the

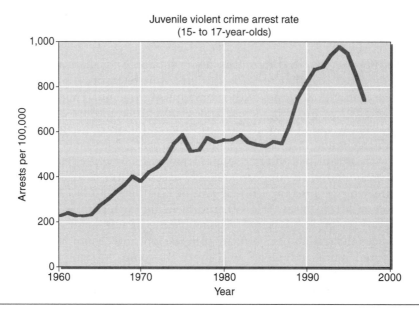

Figure 38.3   Arrest Rate for Juvenile Violent Crime. Data provided by FBI statistician Jodi M. Brown drawing from *Uniform Crime Report* records and reported in *The American Paradox: Spiritual Hunger in an Age of Plenty* by D. G. Myers, 2000b, New Haven, CT: Yale University Press.

sacredness of the individual, which is common to most of the great religions and philosophies of the world," explained Robert Bellah (1995/1996). But it also "affirms the central value of solidarity . . . that we become who we are through our relationships." Agreeing that "it takes a village to raise a child," communitarians remind us of what it takes to raise a village.

Listen to communitarians talk about European-style child benefits, extended parental leaves, flexible working hours, campaign finance reform, and ideas for "fostering the commons" and you'd swear they are liberals. Listen to them talk about covenant marriages, divorce reform, father care, and character education and you'd swear they are conservatives.

Communitarians welcome incentives for individual initiative and appreciate why Marxist economies have crumbled. "If I were, let's say, in Albania at this moment," said Communitarian Network cofounder Amitai Etzioni (1991, 1999), "I probably would argue that there's too much community and not enough individual rights." In communal Japan (where "the nail that sticks out gets pounded down"), Etzioni says he would again sing a song of individuality (Etzioni, 1999). In the individualistic Western context, he sings a song of social order, which in times of chaos (as in crime-plagued or corrupt countries) is necessary for liberty (Etzioni, 1994). Where there is chaos in a neighborhood, people may feel like prisoners in their homes.

Opposition to communitarians comes from civil libertarians of the left, economic libertarians of the right, and special interest libertarians (such as the American National Rifle Association). Much as these organizations differ, they are branches of the same tree—all valuing individual rights in the contest with the common good. Communitarians take on all such varieties of libertarians.

Unrestrained personal freedom, they say, destroys a culture's social fabric; unrestrained commercial freedom exploits workers and plunders the commons. Etzioni (1998) sums up the communitarian ideal is his *New Golden Rule:* "Respect and uphold society's moral order as you would have society respect and uphold your autonomy."

To reflect on your own libertarian versus communitarian leanings, consider what restraints on liberty you support: Luggage scanning at airports? Smoking bans in public places? Speed limits on highways? Sobriety checkpoints? Drug testing of pilots and rail engineers? Prohibitions on leaf burning? Restrictions on TV cigarette ads? Regulations on stereo or muffler noise? Pollution controls? Requiring seat belts and motorcycle helmets? Disclosure of sexual contacts for HIV carriers? Outlawing child pornography? Banning AK-47s and other nonhunting weapons of destruction? Required school uniforms? Wire taps on suspected terrorists? Fingerprinting checks to protect welfare, unemployment, and Social Security funds from fraud?

All such restraints on individual rights, most opposed by libertarians of one sort or another, aim to enhance the public good. When New York City during the 1990s took steps to control petty deviances—the panhandlers, prostitutes, and sex shops—it made the city into a more civil place, with lessened crime and fear. "It is better to live in an orderly society than to allow people so much freedom they can become disruptive"; two-thirds of Canadians but only one half of Americans have agreed (Lipset & Pool, 1996).

Libertarians often object to restraints on guns, panhandlers, pornography, drugs, or business by warning that such may plunge us down a slippery slope leading to the loss of more important liberties. If today we let them search our luggage, tomorrow they'll be invading our houses. If today we censor cigarette ads on television, tomorrow the thought police will be removing books from our libraries. If today we ban handguns, tomorrow's Big Brother government will take our hunting rifles. Communitarians reply that if we don't balance concern for individual rights with concern for the commons, we risk chaos and a new fascism. The true defenders of freedom, contends Etzioni, are those who seek to balance rights with responsibilities, individualism with community, and liberty with fraternity.

THE MARRIAGE MOVEMENT

Communitarians are among the scholars and civic leaders—"women and men, liberals and conservatives"—who signed a 2000 statement on "The Marriage Movement" (www.marriagemovement.org). This is not a nostalgia movement that aims to stuff Jeannie back in the bottle and gays and lesbians back in the closet. Nor does it argue that everyone should marry and no one should divorce. Rather, it documents the price that Westerners pay for the post-1960 collapse of marriage. American trends—with the population of unmarried adults up from 25% to 41% and the proportion of children not living with two parents up from 12% to 32%—mirror social changes in Britain, Canada, Australia, and elsewhere in the Western world.

But aren't some clinicians right to suppose that it is better to replace unhappy present marriages with future happier ones? Here comes another paradox: If divorce ends unhappy marriages, then shouldn't the remaining marriages be happier? Yet today, though freer to escape bad marriages, we are somewhat less satisfied with the marriages we have. As new psychological research shows, people express greater satisfaction with irrevocable choices (like those made in an "all purchases final" sale) than with reversible choices (refunds or exchanges allowed; Gilbert & Ebert, 2002). When feeling bound to something or someone, we're more likely to love that thing or person than when we are freer to contemplate alternatives.

Despite our occasional doubts, research shows that committed marriages are associated with health, happiness, and reduced poverty, and with better-educated, healthier, and more successful children. Moreover, research indicates that marriage doesn't just ride along with social, psychological, and economic well-being; it contributes to them. Controlling for parental race, education, and income does not eliminate the marriage effect (Myers, 2000a). Therefore, say the "marriage movement" signers, government, schools, churches, counselors, and the media should make marriage renewal a priority.

CONCLUSION

The Communitarian initiative and the marriage movement are but two facets of a blossoming social ecology movement that may become a counterpart to earlier civil rights, environmental, and women's movements. The Center for the New American Dream (www.newdream.org) is challenging materialistic excess. The National Parenting Association (www.parentsunite.org) encourages family supportive corporations, workplaces, schools, and tax policies. The ecumenical Call to Renewal (www.calltorenewal.com) unites churches in efforts to "overcome poverty, dismantle racism, promote healthier families and support communities and reassert the dignity of each human life." The nonpartisan National Marriage Project (www.marriage.rutgers.edu) aims to strengthen the state of our unions. And, yes, the positive psychology movement (www.positivepsychology.org) seeks to advance human happiness, strengthen character, and promote civic health.

This broadly based social ecology movement affirms liberals' concerns about income inequality and their support for family-friendly workplaces and children in all family forms. It affirms conservatives' indictments of toxic media models and their support for marriage and coparenting. And it found encouragement in the last decade's subsiding of teen violence, suicide, and pregnancy, and its increase in volunteerism. Recognizing our need to belong and having a vision for positive communal life, practitioners of positive psychology will likewise take heart and will join the effort to promote a social ecology that nurtures happiness, health, and civility.

REFERENCES

Argyle, M. (1999). Causes and correlates of happiness. In D. Kahneman, E. Diener, & N. Schwartz (Eds.), *Well-being: The foundations of hedonic psychology* (pp. 353–373). New York: Russell Sage Foundation.

Bacon, F. (1625). Of friendship. *Essays.*

Baron, R. S., Cutrona, C. E., Hicklin, D., Russell, D. W., & Lubaroff, D. M. (1990). Social support and immune function among spouses of cancer patients. *Journal of Personality and Social Psychology, 59,* 344–352.

Baumeister, R. F., & Leary, M. R. (1995). The need to belong: Desire for interpersonal attachment as a fundamental human motivation. *Psychological Bulletin, 117,* 497–529.

Baumeister, R. F., Twenge, J. M., & Nuss, C. K. (2002). Effects of social exclusion on cognitive processes: Anticipated aloneness reduces intelligent thought. *Journal of Personality and Social Psychology, 83,* 817–827.

Bellah, R. N. (1995/1996, Winter). Community properly understood: A defense of "democratic communitarianism." *Responsive Community,* 49–54.

Bellah, R. N., Madsen, R., Sullivan, W. M., Swidler, A., & Tipton, S. M. (1985). *Habits of the heart: Individualism and commitment in American life.* Berkeley, CA: University of California Press.

Berscheid, E. (1985). Interpersonal attraction. In G. Lindzey & E. Aronson (Eds.), *The handbook of social psychology* (pp. 413–484). New York: Random House.

Bowles, S., & Kasindorf, M. (2001, March 6). Friends tell of picked-on but 'normal' kid. *United States Today,* p. 4A.

Buckley, K. E., & Leary, M. R. (2001, February). *Perceived acceptance as a predictor of social, emotional, and academic outcomes.* Paper presented at the Society of Personality and Social Psychology annual convention, San Antonio, TX.

Case, R. B., Moss, A. J., Case, N., McDermott, M., & Eberly, S. (1992). Living alone after myocardial infarction: Impact on prognosis. *Journal of the American Medical Association, 267,* 515–519.

Cohen, S. (1988). Psychosocial models of the role of social support in the etiology of physical disease. *Health Psychology, 7,* 269–297.

Cohen, S., Doyle, W. J., Skoner, D. P., Rabin, B. S., & Gwaltney, J. M., Jr. (1997). Social ties and susceptibility to the common cold. *Journal of the American Medical Association, 277,* 1940–1944.

Colon, E. A., Callies, A. L., Popkin, M. K., & McGlave, P. B. (1991). Depressed mood and other variables related to bone marrow transplantation survival in acute leukemia. *Psychosomatics, 32,* 420–425.

Cutrona, C. E. (1986). Behavioral manifestations of social support: A microanalytic investigation. *Journal of Personality and Social Psychology, 51,* 201–208.

Diener, E. (2000). Subjective well-being: The science of happiness, and a proposal for a national index. *American Psychologist, 55,* 34–43.

Easterlin, R. (1995). Will raising the incomes of all increase the happiness of all? *Journal of Economic Behavior and Organization, 27,* 35–47.

Etzioni, A. (1991, May/June). The community in an age of individualism. *The Futurist,* 35–39.

*Etzioni, A. (1994). *The spirit of community: The reinvention of American society.* New York: Simon & Schuster.

Etzioni, A. (1998). *The new golden rule.* New York: Basic Books.

Etzioni, A. (1999, February). Address to the Communitarian Summit, Washington, DC.

Evans, G. W., Palsane, M. N., Lepore, S. J., & Martin, J. (1989). Residential density and psychological health: The mediating effects of social support. *Journal of Personality and Social Psychology, 57,* 994–999.

Fox-Genovese, E. (1991). *Feminism without illusions: A critique of individualism.* Chapel Hill, NC: University of North Carolina Press.

Gilbert, D. T., & Ebert, J. E. T. (2002). Decisions and revisions: The affective forecasting of changeable outcomes. *Journal of Personality and Social Psychology, 82,* 503–514.

Goodman, E. (1994, September 24). Where family values begin—and end. *Washington Post,* A-27.

Gotlib, I. H. (1992). Interpersonal and cognitive aspects of depression. *Current Directions in Psychological Science, 1,* 149–154.

Helgeson, V. S., Cohen, S., & Fritz, H. L. (1998). Social ties and cancer. In J. C. Holland (Ed.), *Psycho-oncology* (pp. 730–742). New York: Oxford University Press.

Hendrick, S. S., & Hendrick, C. (1997). Love and satisfaction. In R. J. Sternberg & M. Hojjat (Eds.), *Satisfaction in close relationships* (pp. 56–78). New York: Guilford Press.

Hofstede, G. (1980). *Culture's consequences.* Beverly Hills, CA: Sage.

House, J. S., Landis, K. R., & Umberson, D. (1988). Social relationships and health. *Science, 241,* 540–545.

Inglehart, R. (1990). *Culture shift in advanced industrial society.* Princeton, NJ: Princeton University Press.

Kasser, T. (2000). Two versions of the American dream: Which goals and values make for a high quality of life. In E. Diener & D. R. Rahtz (Eds.), *Advances in quality of life: Theory and research* (Vol. 1, pp. 3–12). Dordrecht, The Netherlands: Kluwer Press.

Kasser, T., & Ryan, R. M. (1996). Further examining the American dream: Differential correlates of intrinsic and extrinsic goals. *Personality and Social Psychology Bulletin, 22,* 280–287.

Kiecolt-Glaser, J. K., & Newton, T. L. (2001). Marriage and health: His and hers. *Psychological Bulletin, 127,* 472–503.

Kohn, A. (1999, February 2). In pursuit of affluence, at a high price. *New York Times.* Available from via www.nytimes.com.

Ladd, E. C. (1998). *Silent revolution: The rebirth of America's civic life and what it means for all of us.* New York: Free Press.

Leary, M. R., Haupt, A. L., Strausser, K. S., & Chokel, J. T. (1998). Calibrating the sociometer: The relationship between interpersonal appraisals and state self-esteem. *Journal of Personality and Social Psychology, 74,* 1290–1299.

Lennon, J., & McCartney, P. (1967). *Sgt. Pepper's lonely hearts club band* [Beatles]. On [Record]. Capital Records.

Lipset, S. M., & Pool, A. B. (1996, Summer). Balancing the individual and the community: Canada versus the United States. *Responsive Community,* 37–46.

Lykken, D., & Tellegen, A. (1996). Happiness is a stochastic phenomenon. *Psychological Science, 7,* 186–189.

Marano, H. E. (1998, August 4). Debunking the marriage myth: It works for women, too. *New York Times.* Available from www.nytimes.com.

Mastekaasa, A. (1995). Age variations in the suicide rates and self-reported subjective well-being of married and never married persons. *Journal of Community and Applied Social Psychology, 5,* 21–39.

Murray, J. E. (2000). Marital protection and marital selection: Evidence from a historical-prospective sample of American men. *Demography, 37,* 511–521.

Myers, D. G. (1993). *The pursuit of happiness.* New York: Avon Books.

*Myers, D. G. (2000a). *The American paradox: Spiritual hunger in an age of plenty.* New Haven, CT: Yale University Press.

Myers, D. G. (2000b). The funds, friends, and faith of happy people. *American Psychologist, 55,* 56–67.

Myers, D. G., & Diener, E. (1996, May). The pursuit of happiness. *Scientific American, 274,* 54–56.

National Commission on Civic Renewal. (1998). *Index of national civic health: A nation of spectators* (Final Report). New York: Free Press.

National Opinion Research Center. (2002). *General social survey data for 1972 to 2000.* Retrieved from http://csa.berkeley.edu:7502.

Nelson, N. (1988). *A meta-analysis of the life-event/health paradigm: The influence of social support.* Unpublished doctoral dissertation, Temple University, Philadelphia.

Pavot, W., Diener, E., & Fujita, F. (1990). Extraversion and happiness. *Personality and Individual Differences, 11,* 1299–1306.

Pennebaker, J. W., & O'Heeron, R. C. (1984). Confiding in others and illness rate among spouses of suicide and accidental death victims. *Journal of Abnormal Psychology, 93,* 473–476.

Perkins, H. W. (1991). Religious commitment, Yuppie values, and well-being in postcollegiate life. *Review of Religious Research, 32,* 244–251.

Pipher, M. B. (2002). *The middle of everywhere: The world's refugees come to our town.* San Diego, CA: Harcourt Brace.

*Putnam, R. D. (2000). *Bowling alone: The collapse and revival of American community.* New York: Simon & Schuster.

Rook, K. S. (1987). Social support versus companionship: Effects on life stress, loneliness, and evaluations by others. *Journal of Personality and Social Psychology, 52,* 1132–1147.

Sax, L. J., Astin, A. W., Korn, W. S., & Mahoney, K. M. (2002). *The American freshman: National norms for Fall 2002.* Los Angeles: UCLA, Higher Education Research Institute.

Segrin, C., & Dillard, J. P. (1992). The interactional theory of depression: A meta-analysis of the research literature. *Journal of Social and Clinical Psychology, 11,* 43–70.

Taylor, S. E. (1989). *Positive illusions: Creative self-deception and the healthy mind.* New York: Basic Books.

Twenge, J. M., Baumeister, R. F., Tice, D. M., & Stucke, T. S. (2001). If you can't join them, beat them: Effects of social exclusion on aggressive behavior. *Journal of Personality and Social Psychology, 81,* 1058–1069.

Twenge, J. M., Catanese, K. R., & Baumeister, R. F. (2002). Social exclusion causes self-defeating behavior. *Journal of Personality and Social Psychology, 83,* 606–615.

Uchino, B. N., Cacioppo, J. T., & Kiecolt-Glaser, J. K. (1996). The relationship between social support and physiological processes: A review with emphasis on underlying mechanisms and implications for health. *Psychological Bulletin, 119,* 488–531.

Uchino, B. N., Uno, D., & Holt-Lunstad, J. (1999). Social support, physiological processes, and health. *Current Directions in Psychological Science, 8,* 145–148.

Vaillant, G. E. (2002). *Aging well: Surprising guideposts to a happier life from the landmark Harvard study of adult development.* Boston: Little, Brown.

Warr, P., & Payne, R. (1982). Experiences of strain and pleasure among British adults. *Social Science and Medicine, 16,* 1691–1697.

Williams, K. D., & Zadro, L. (2001). Ostracism: On being ignored, excluded, and rejected. In M. R. Leary (Ed.), *Interpersonal rejection.* New York: Oxford University Press.

Williams, R. B., Barefoot, J. C., Califf, R. M., Haney, T. L., Saunders, W. B., Pryor, D. B., et al. (1992). Prognostic importance of social and economic resources among medically treated patients with angiographically documented coronary artery disease. *Journal of the American Medical Association, 267,* 520–524.

Wilson, C. M., & Oswald, A. J. (2002). *How does marriage affect physical and psychological health? A survey of the longitudinal evidence.* Working paper, University of York and Warwick University.

Wuthnow, R. (1994). *God and mammon in America.* New York: Free Press.

CHAPTER 39

Happiness as a Public Policy Aim: The Greatest Happiness Principle

RUUT VEENHOVEN

A TTEMPTS TO IMPROVE the human lot begin typically with treating compelling miseries, such as hunger and epidemics. When these problems are solved, attention shifts to broader and more positive goals; we can see this development in the history of social policy, the goal of which has evolved from *alleviating poverty* to providing *a decent standard of living* for everybody. The field of medicine has witnessed a similar shift from assisting people to *survive* to, in addition, promoting a good *quality of life*. This policy change has put some difficult questions back on the agenda, such as: "What is a good life?" and "What good is the best?" The social sciences cannot provide good answers to these questions, since they have also focused on misery. Yet, a good answer can be found in a classic philosophy, and it is one that is worth reconsidering.

THE GREATEST HAPPINESS PRINCIPLE

Two centuries ago, Jeremy Bentham (1789) proposed a new moral principle. He wrote that the goodness of an action should not be judged by the decency of its intentions, but by the utility of its consequences. Bentham conceived final *utility* as human *happiness*. Hence, he concluded that we should aim at the "greatest happiness for the greatest number." Bentham defined happiness in terms of psychological experience, as "the sum of pleasures and pains." This philosophy is known as *utilitarianism* because of its emphasis on the utility of behavioral consequences. *Happyism* would have been a better name, since this utility is seen as contribution to happiness.

When applied at the level of individual choice, this theory runs into some difficulties. Often, we cannot foresee what the balance of effects on happiness will be. In addition, the theory deems well-intended behavior to be amoral if it happens to pan out adversely. Imagine the case of a loving mother who saves the life of her sick child, a child that grows up to be a criminal; mothers can seldom foresee a child's future and can hardly be reproached for their unconditional motherly love.

The theory is better suited for judging general rules, such as the rule that mothers should care for their sick children. It is fairly evident that adherence to this rule will add to the happiness of a great number. Following such rules is then morally correct, even if consequences might be negative in a particular case. This variant is known as *rule-utilitarianism.*

Rule-utilitarianism has been seen as a moral guide for legislation and has played a role in discussions about property laws and the death penalty. The principle can also be applied to wider issues in public policy, such as the question of what degree of income inequality we should accept. The argument is that inequality is not bad in and of itself; it is only so if it reduces the happiness of the average citizen. The greatest happiness principle can also be used when making decisions about health care and therapy. Treatment strategies can be selected on the basis of their effects on the happiness of the greatest number of patients.

OBJECTIONS AGAINST THE PRINCIPLE

The greatest happiness principle is well known, and it is a standard subject in every introduction to moral philosophy. Yet the principle is seldom put into practice. Why is this? The answer to this question is also to be found in most introductory philosophy books: Utilitarianism is typically rejected on pragmatic and moral grounds.

Pragmatic Objections   Application of the greatest happiness principle requires that we know what happiness is and that we can predict the consequences of behavioral alternatives on it. It also requires that we can check the results of applying this principle; that is, we can measure resulting gains in happiness. At a more basic level, the principle assumes that happiness can be affected by what we do. All of this is typically denied. It is claimed that happiness is an elusive concept and one that we cannot measure. As a consequence, we can only make guesses about the effects of happiness on behavioral alternatives and can never verify our suppositions. Some even see happiness as an immutable trait that cannot be influenced. Such criticism often ends with the conclusion that we would do better to stick to more palpable seasoned virtues, such as justice and equality.

Moral Objections   Another objection is that happiness is mere pleasure or an illusionary matter and hence not very valuable in and of itself. It is, therefore, not considered as the ultimate ethical value. Another moral objection is that happiness spoils; in particular, it fosters irresponsible consumerism and makes us less sensitive to the suffering of others. Still another objection holds that the goal of advancing happiness justifies amoral means, such as genetic manipulation, mind control, and dictatorship. Much of these ethical qualms are featured in Huxley's (1932) *Brave New World.*

THE PLAN FOR THIS CHAPTER

The preceding discussion is armchair theorizing, mainly by philosophers and novelists. How do these objections stand up to empirical tests? I first introduce modern empirical research on happiness, then consider the qualms mentioned previously in the light of the findings. I start with the claim that happiness is no practicable goal and next inspect the evidence for the idea that happiness is not a desirable outcome.

RESEARCH ON HAPPINESS

Empirical research on happiness started in the 1960s in several branches of the social sciences. In sociology, the study of happiness developed from social indicators research. In this field, *subjective* indicators were used to supplement traditional *objective* indicators, and *happiness* became a main subjective indicator of social system performance (Andrews & Withey, 1976; Campbell, 1981).

In psychology, the concept was used in the study of mental health. Jahoda (1958) saw happiness as a criterion for positive mental health, and items on happiness figured in the pioneering epidemiological surveys on mental health by Gurin, Veroff, and Feld (1960) and Bradburn and Caplovitz (1965). At that time, happiness also figured in the groundbreaking cross-national study of *human concerns* by Cantril (1965) and came to be used as an indicator of successful aging in gerontology (Neugarten, Havinghurst, & Tobin, 1961). Twenty years later, the concept appeared in medical outcome research. Happiness is a common item in questionnaires on health-related quality of life such as the much-used SF-36 (Ware, 1996). More recently, economists such as Oswald (1997) and Frey and Stutzer (2000) have also picked up the issue.

Most empirical studies on happiness are based on large-scale population surveys, but there are also many studies of specific groups, such as single mothers, students, or lottery winners. The bulk of these studies revolves around one-time questionnaire studies, but there are a number of follow-up studies and even some experimental studies. To date, some 3,000 research reports have been published, and the number of publications is increasing exponentially.

The study of happiness has been institutionalized rapidly over the past few years. Most investigators have joined forces and formed the International Society for Quality of Life Studies (ISQOLS; www.cob.vt.edu/market/isqols). In addition to this social science association, there is a health science-oriented association, the International Society for Quality of Life Research (www.isoqol.org). The *Journal of Happiness Studies* (www.wkap.nl/journals/johs) is a specialized academic journal, and the research findings are presented in the *World Database of Happiness* (www.eur.nl/fsw/research/happiness).

This collaboration has created a considerable body of knowledge, which I use in the following discussion to determine the reality value of philosophical objections against the greatest happiness principle.

IS HAPPINESS A PRACTICAL GOAL?

Pragmatic objections against the greatest happiness principle are many. The most basic objection is that happiness cannot be defined; therefore, all talk about happiness is mere rhetoric. The second objection is that happiness cannot be measured, so we can never establish an absolute degree and number for happiness. A third objection holds that lasting happiness of a great number is not possible; at best, we can find some relief in fleeting moments of delusion. The last claim is that we cannot bring about happiness. I next discuss these objections individually.

CAN HAPPINESS BE DEFINED?

The word *happiness* has different meanings. These meanings are often mixed up, which gives the concept a reputation for being elusive. Yet, a confusion of tongues about a word does not mean that no substantive meaning can be defined. Let us consider what meanings are involved and which of these is most appropriate as an end goal.

Four Qualities of Life   When used in a broad sense, the word happiness is synonymous with quality of life or well-being. In this meaning, it denotes that life is good but does not specify what is good about life. The word is also used in more specific ways, which can be clarified with the help of the classification of qualities of life presented in Table 39.1.

This classification of meanings depends on two distinctions. Vertically, there is a difference between chances for a good life and actual outcomes of life. Chances and outcomes are related but are certainly not the same. Chances can fail to be realized, because of stupidity or bad luck. Conversely, people sometimes make much of their life in spite of poor opportunities. This distinction is common in the field of public health research. Preconditions for good health, such as adequate nutrition and professional care, are seldom confused with health itself. Yet, means and ends are less well distinguished in the discussion on happiness.

Horizontally, there is a distinction between external and internal qualities. In the first case, the quality is in the environment; in the latter, it is in the individual. Lane (2000) made this distinction clear by emphasizing "quality of persons." This distinction is also commonly made in public health. External pathogens are distinguished from inner afflictions, and researchers try to identify the mechanisms by which the former produce the latter and the conditions in which this is more or less likely. Yet again, this basic insight is lacking in many discussions about happiness.

Table 39.1
Four Qualities of Life

	Outer Qualities	*Inner Qualities*
Life chances	**Livability of environment**	**Life-ability of the person**
Life results	**Utility of life**	**Satisfaction**

Together, these two dichotomies mark four qualities of life, all of which have been denoted by the word *happiness*.

Livability of the Environment   The top-left quadrant denotes the meaning of good living conditions. Often the terms *quality of life* and *well-being* are used in this particular meaning, especially in the writings of ecologists and sociologists. Economists sometimes use the term *welfare* for this meaning. *Livability* is a better word, because it refers explicitly to a characteristic of the environment and does not carry the connotation of paradise. Politicians and social reformers typically stress this quality of life.

Life-Ability of the Person   The top-right quadrant denotes inner life chances, that is, how well we are equipped to cope with the problems of life. This aspect of the good life is also known by different names. Especially doctors and psychologists use the terms *quality of life* and *well-being* to denote this specific meaning. There are more names, however. In biology, the phenomenon is referred to as *fitness*. On other occasions, it is denoted by the medical term *health,* in the medium variant of the word. (There are three main meanings of health: The maxivariant is all the good [WHO, 1985, definition], the medium variant is life-ability, and the minivariant is absence of physical defect.) Sen (1993) calls this quality of life variant *capability*. I prefer the simple term *life-ability,* which contrasts elegantly with *livability*. This quality of life is central in the thinking of therapists and educators.

Utility of Life   The bottom-left quadrant represents the notion that a good life must be good for something more than itself. This presumes some higher value, such as ecological preservation or cultural development. In fact, there are myriad values on which the utility of life can be judged. There is no current generic for these external turnouts of life. Gerson (1976) referred to these kinds as *transcendental* conceptions of quality of life. Another appellation is *meaning of life,* which then denotes *true* significance instead of mere subjective sense of meaning. I prefer the more simple *utility of life,* admitting that this label may also give rise to misunderstanding. (A problem with this name is that the utilitarians used the word *utility* for subjective appreciation of life, the sum of pleasures and pains.) Moral advisors, such as your pastor, emphasize this quality of life.

Satisfaction with Life   Finally, the bottom-right quadrant represents the inner outcomes of life, that is, the quality in the eye of the beholder. As we deal with conscious humans, this quality boils down to subjective appreciation of life, commonly referred to by terms such as *subjective well-being, life satisfaction,* and *happiness* in a limited sense of the word. Life has more of this quality, the more and the longer it is enjoyed. In fairy tales, this combination of intensity and duration is denoted with the phrase, "They lived happily ever after." There is no professional interest group that stresses this meaning, and this seems to be one of the reasons for the reservations surrounding the greatest happiness principle.

Which of these four meanings of the word *happiness* is most appropriate as an end goal? I think the last one. Commonly, policy aims at improving life chances by, for example, providing better housing or education, as indicated in the upper half of Table 39.1. Yet, more is not always better, and some opportunities may be more critical than others. The problem is that we need a criterion to assign priorities among the many life chances policymakers want to improve. That criterion should be found in the outcomes of life, as shown in the lower half of Table 39.1. There, *utility* provides no workable criterion, since external effects are many and can be valued differently. *Satisfaction with life* is a better criterion, since it reflects the degree to which external living conditions fit with inner life-abilities (see also Pavot & Diener, Chapter 40, this volume). Satisfaction is also the subjective experience Jeremy Bentham (1789) had in mind.

Four Kinds of Satisfaction   This brings us to the question of what *satisfaction* is precisely. This is also a word with multiple meanings. We elucidate these meanings in Table 39.2, which is based on two distinctions: vertically, between satisfaction with *parts* of life versus satisfaction with life *as a whole,* and horizontally, between *passing* satisfaction and *enduring* satisfaction. These two bipartitions yield again a fourfold taxonomy.

PLEASURES   Passing satisfaction with a part of life is called *pleasure.* Pleasures can be sensory, such as a glass of good wine, or mental, such as the reading of this text. The idea that we should maximize such satisfactions is called *hedonism.* Epicurus is renowned as an advocate of this view, though he focused on peace of mind.

PART SATISFACTIONS   Enduring satisfaction with a part of life can concern a domain of life, such as working life, and an aspect of life, such as its variety. Sometimes, the word *happiness* is used for such part satisfactions, in particular for satisfaction with your career.

TOP EXPERIENCE   Passing satisfaction can be about life as a whole, in particular when the experience is intense and oceanic. This kind of satisfaction is usually referred to as *top experience.* When poets write about happiness, they usually describe an experience of this kind. Likewise, religious writings use the word happiness often in the sense of a mystical ecstasy. Another word for this type of satisfaction is *enlightenment.*

LIFE SATISFACTION   Enduring satisfaction with your life as a whole is called *life satisfaction* and also commonly referred to as *happiness.* This is the kind of

Table 39.2
Four Kinds of Satisfaction

	Passing	Enduring
Part of Life	**Pleasure**	**Part satisfaction**
Life as a Whole	**Top experience**	**Life satisfaction**

satisfaction Bentham seems to have had in mind when he described happiness as the "sum of pleasures and pains." Elsewhere, I have delineated this concept in more detail and defined it as "the overall appreciation of one's life-as-a-whole" (Veenhoven, 2000).

Life satisfaction is most appropriate as a policy goal. Enduring satisfaction is clearly more valuable than passing satisfactions, and satisfaction with life as a whole is also of more worth than mere part satisfaction. Moreover, life satisfaction is probably of greater significance, since it signals the degree to which human needs are being met. I return to this point later.

In sum, *happiness can be defined as the overall enjoyment of your life as a whole.*

CAN HAPPINESS BE MEASURED?

A common objection to the greatest happiness principle is that happiness cannot be measured. This objection applies to most of the previously discussed meanings of the word, but does it apply to happiness in the sense of life satisfaction?

Happiness in this sense is a state of mind, which cannot be assessed objectively in the same way as weight or blood pressure. Happiness cannot be measured with access to merit goods, since the effect of such life chances depends on life abilities. Though there is certainly a biochemical substrate to the experience, we cannot as yet measure happiness using physical indicators. The "hedometer" awaits invention. Extreme states of happiness and unhappiness manifest in nonverbal behavior, such as smiling and body posture, but these indications are often not well visible. This leaves us with self-reports. The question is then whether happiness can be measured adequately in this way.

Self-Reports   There are many reservations about self-report measures of happiness: People might not be able to oversee their lives, self-defense might distort the judgment, and social desirability could give rise to rosy answers. Thus, early investigators experimented with indirect questioning. Happiness was measured by a clinical interview, by content analysis of diaries, and by using projective methods such as the Thematic Apperception Test. These methods are laborious, and their validity is not beyond doubt. Hence, direct questions have also been used from the beginning. A careful comparison of these methods showed that direct questioning yields the same information at a lower cost (Wessman & Ricks, 1966).

Direct Questioning   Direct questions on happiness are often framed in larger questionnaires, such as the much-used 20-item Life Satisfaction Index (LSI) of Neugarten et al. (1961). There are psychometric advantages with the use of multiple-item questionnaires, in particular, a reduction of error due to difference in interpretation of key words. Yet, a disadvantage is that most of the happiness inventories involve items that do not quite fit the concept defined previously. For instance, the LSI contains a question on whether the individual has plans for the future, which is clearly something other than enjoying current life.

The use of multiple items is common in psychological testing because the object of measurement is mostly rather vague. For example, *neuroticism* cannot be sharply defined and is, therefore, measured with multiple questions about topics that are likely to be linked to that matter. Yet, happiness is a well-defined concept (overall enjoyment of life as a whole) and can, therefore, be measured by one question. Another reason for the use of multiple items in psychological measurement is that respondents are mostly unaware of the state to be measured. For instance, most respondents do not know how neurotic they are, so neuroticism is inferred from their responses to various related matters. Yet, happiness is something of which the respondent is conscious. Hence, happiness can also be measured by single direct questions, which is common practice and one that works.

Common Survey Questions   Because happiness can be measured with single direct questions, it has become a common item in large-scale surveys among the general population in many countries. A common question reads:

Taking all together, how satisfied or dissatisfied are you currently with your life as a whole?

1   2   3   4   5   6   7   8   9   10

Dissatisfied   Satisfied

Many more question and answer formats have been used. All acceptable items are documented in full detail in the "Item bank" of the *World Database of Happiness* (Veenhoven, 2002).

Validity   Though these questions are fairly clear, responses can be flawed in several ways. Responses may reflect how happy people think they should be rather than how happy they actually feel, and it is also possible that people present themselves as happier than they actually are. These suspicions have given rise to numerous validation studies. Elsewhere I have reviewed this research and concluded that there is no evidence that responses to these questions measure something other than what they are meant to measure (Veenhoven, 1984, Chapter 3, 1998). Though this is no guarantee that research will never reveal a deficiency, we can trust these measures of happiness for the time being.

Reliability   Research has also shown that responses are affected by minor variations in wording and ordering of questions and by situational factors, such as the race of the interviewer or the weather. As a result, the same person may score six in one investigation and seven in another. This lack of precision hampers analyses at the individual level. It is less of a problem when average happiness in groups is compared, since random fluctuations tend to balance, typically the case when happiness is used in policy evaluation.

Comparability   Still, the objection is made that responses on such questions are not comparable, because a score of six does not mean the same for everybody. A common philosophical argument for this position is that happiness depends on the realization of wants and that these wants differ across persons and cultures (Smart & Williams, 1973). Yet, it is not at all sure that happiness depends on the realization of idiosyncratic wants. The available data are more in line with the theory that it depends on the gratification of universal needs (Veenhoven, 1991). I return to this point in the discussion later on the signal function of happiness.

A second qualm is whether happiness is a typical Western concept that is not recognized in other cultures. Happiness appears to be a universal emotion that is recognized in facial expression all over the world (Ekman & Friesen, 1975) and for which words exist in all languages. A related objection is that happiness is a unique experience that cannot be communicated on an equivalent scale. Yet, from an evolutionary point of view, it is unlikely that we differ very much. As in the case of pain, there will be a common human spectrum of experience.

Last, there is methodological reservation about possible cultural bias in the measurement of happiness, due to problems with translation of keywords and cultural variation in response tendencies. Elsewhere I have looked for empirical evidence for these distortions but did not find any (Veenhoven, 1993, Chapter 5).

All these objections imply that research using these measures of happiness will fail to find any meaningful correlations. Later, we see that this is not true.

In sum, *happiness as life satisfaction is measurable with direct questioning and well comparable across persons and nations.* Hence, happiness of a great number can be assessed using surveys.

IS HAPPINESS POSSIBLE?

Aiming at happiness for a great number has often been denounced as *illusionary* because long-term happiness, and certainly happiness for a great number, is a fantasy. This criticism has many origins. In some religions, the belief is that man has been expelled from Paradise: Earthly existence is not to be enjoyed; we are here to chasten our souls. Classic psychologists have advanced more profane reasons.

Freud (1929/1948) saw happiness as a short-lived orgasmic experience that comes forth from the release of primitive urges. Hence, he believed that happiness is not compatible with the demands of civilized society and that modern man is, therefore, doomed to chronic unhappiness. In the same vein, Adorno believed that happiness is a mere temporary mental escape from misery, mostly at the cost of reality control (Rath, 2002).

The psychological literature on adaptation is less pessimistic, but it, too, denies the possibility of enduring happiness for a great number. It assumes that aspirations follow achievements and, hence, concludes that happiness does not last. It is also inferred that periods of happiness and unhappiness oscillate over a lifetime, and the average level is, therefore, typically neutral. Likewise, social comparison is seen to result in a neutral average, and enduring happiness is possible only for a "happy few" (Brickman & Campbell, 1971).

Enduring Happiness   Figure 39.1 presents the distribution for responses to the 10-step question on life satisfaction in the United States. The most frequent responses are 7, 8, and 9 and less than 2% scores below neutral. The average is 7.46. This result implies that most people must feel happy most of the time. That view has been corroborated by yearly follow-up studies over many years (Ehrhardt, Saris, & Veenhoven, 2000) and by studies that use the technique of experience sampling (Schimmack & Diener, 2003).

Happiness for a Great Number   The high level of happiness is not unique to the United States. Table 39.3 shows similar averages in other Western nations. In fact, average happiness tends to be above neutral in most countries of the world. So happiness for a great number is apparently possible. Table 39.3 also shows that average happiness was below neutral in Russia in 1995. A similar pattern is observed in most other former Soviet states, probably as a result of the social

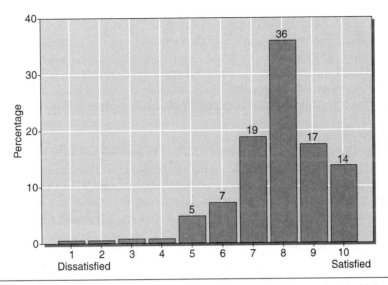

Figure 39.1   Life-Satisfaction in the United States, 1995. *Source: World Values Study Group, 1997* (Computer file, ICPSR 6160) by the World Values Study Group, 1997, Ann Arbor, MI: Institute for Social Research.

transformations in this era. Possibly, average happiness is also below neutral in some of the countries not investigated, in particular, war-stricken countries in Africa such as Uganda and in Middle East nations such as Iraq. All this is in flat contradiction to Freudian theory, which predicts averages below four everywhere and defies adaptation theory that predicts universal averages around five.

In sum, *enduring happiness for a great number of people is possible.*

Table 39.3
Life Satisfaction in
Nations in the 1990s

Switzerland	7.95
Sweden	7.52
Netherlands	7.51
United States	7.46
Belgium	7.39
Germany (West)	6.92
France	6.43
Japan	6.36
India	6.15
Poland	6.03
Hungary	5.60
Russia	4.51

Note: Average scores on scale 0–10.
Source: World Database of Happiness, Happiness in Nations, Rank Report 2002, by R. Veenhoven, retrieved from www.eur .nl/fsw/research/happiness.

CAN HAPPINESS BE MANUFACTURED?

The observation that people *can* be happy does not mean that they can be *made* happier by public policy. Like the wind, happiness could be a natural phenomenon beyond our control. Several arguments have been raised in support of this view.

A common reasoning holds that happiness is too complex a thing to be controlled. In this line, it is argued that conditions for happiness differ across cultures and that the dynamics of happiness are of a chaotic nature and one that will probably never be sufficiently understood.

The claim that happiness cannot be created is also argued with a reversed reasoning: We understand happiness sufficiently well to realize that it cannot be raised. One argument is that happiness depends on comparison and that any improvement is, therefore, nullified by "reference drift" (VanPraag, 1993). Another claim in this context is that happiness is a traitlike matter and hence not sensitive to any improvement in living conditions. All this boils down to the conclusion that planned control of happiness is an illusion (but see Sheldon & Lyubomirsky, Chapter 8, this volume).

Table 39.4
Happiness and Society in 65 Nations in the 1990s

Characteristics of Society	Correlation with Happiness[a]	N
Affluence[b]	+.64	60
Rule of law		
–Civil rights[c]	+.36	62
–Absence of corruption[d]	+.54	40
–Murder rate[e]	–.66	52
Freedom		
–Economical[f]	+.62	54
–Political[g]	+.30	62
–Personal[h]	+.34	49
Equality		
–Income equality[i]	–.00	45
–Gender equality[j]	+.16	46

[a] Happiness: *World Database of Happiness,* Catalog of Happiness in Nations, question type 111b.
[b] Income per capita of the population in U.S. dollars, corrected by differences in local purchasing power. *Human Development Report 1998,* Table 1.
[c] Index of Civil Rights, by Freedom House, 2000.
[d] Expert rating of presence of corruption, by Transparency International, 1995.
[e] Medical registration of murder as cause of death in percentage of all deaths. *Source: United Nations Demographic Yearbook,* Table 21, by the United Nations, 1998, New York: Author.
[f] Index of Economic Freedom, Fraser Institute, 1995. *Source: Economic Freedom in the World 1975–2000,* by J. D. Gwartney and R. A. Lawson, 2001, retrieved from www.fraserinstitute.ca /publications.
[g] Index Political Rights, by Freedom House, 1996.
[h] Index composed of legal guaranteed freedoms to organize one's life in one's own way (settlement, partner choice, family planning) and public acceptance of it (divorce, homosexuality, suicide). These data refer to 1990.
[i] Ratio part in national income of the poorest 20% and the richest 20%. *World Cultural Report 1998,* Table 12.
[j] Index based on gender differences in (1) education, (2) life span, (3) labor market, (4) executive posts, and (5) seats of the parliament. *Source: A Larger Pie through a Fair Share? Gender Equality and Economic Performance* [Working Paper No. 315], by G. Dijkstra, 2000, Den Haag, The Netherlands: Institute of Social Studies.

Table 39.4 *Continued*

Characteristics of Society	Correlation with Happiness[a]	N
Citizenship		
−Participation in voluntary associations[k]	+.50	60
−Preference for participative leadership[l]	+.39	57
Cultural plurality		
−Percent migrants[m]	+.32	43
−Tolerance of minorities[n]	+.57	61
Modernity		
−Schooling[o]	+.32	60
−Informatization[p]	+.66	51
−Urbanization[q]	+.31	60
Explained variance (R^2)		83%

[k] Active participation in clubs. Participation in 16 kinds of associations, churches, sportclubs, unions, for example, World Value Surveys items 19-52 (WVS2) and 28-36 (WVS3).
[l] Opinions of middle-level managers. *Source:* "Culture Specific and Cross-Culturally Generalizable Implicit Leadership Theories: Are Attributes of Charismatic/Tranformational Leadership Universally Endorsed?" Table 5, by DenHartog et al., 1999, *Leadership Quarterly, 10,* pp. 219–256.
[m] Percentage of allochtones in the population. *World Culture Report,* 1998, Table 6.
[n] Number of kinds of people, of whom an individual says not to prefer as neighbors. World Value Survey items 69-82 (WVS2) and 51-60 (WVS3).
[o] Participation in education. *Human Development Report 1998,* Table 1.
[p] Number PCs per 100,000 inhabitants. *Human Development Report 1998,* Table 34.
[q] Percentage of the population living in an urban environment. *Human Development Report 1998,* Table 21.
Sources: "States of Nations," World Database of Happiness: Ongoing Register of Scientific Research on Subjective Enjoyment of Life, by R. Veenhoven, 2002, retrieved from www.eur.nl/fsw /research/happiness; *Human Development Report 2000,* by the United Nations Development Program, 2000, New York: Oxford University Press; *TI-Corruption Perception Index 1997,* by Transparency International, 1997, Berlin, Germany: Author; *Freedom in the World 2000,* by Freedom House, 2000, retrieved from www.freedomhouse.org/research; *World Culture Report,* by UNESCO, 1998, Paris: Author; and *World Values Survey, 1980–1996* (Computer file, ICPSR 6160), by the World Values Study Group, 1997, Ann Arbor, MI: Institute for Social Research.

As in the case of health, the conditions for happiness can be charted inductively using epidemiological research. Many such studies have been performed over the past decade. The results are documented in the *World Database of Happiness* (Veenhoven, 2002) and summarized in reviews by Argyle (2002); Diener, Suh, Lucas, and Smith (1999); and Veenhoven (1984, 1997). What does this research tell us about conditions for happiness?

External Conditions   Happiness research has focused very much on social conditions for happiness. These conditions are studied at two levels: At the macro level, there are studies about the kind of society where people have the most happy lives, and at the micro level, there is much research about differences in happiness across social positions in society. As yet, there is little research at the meso level. Little is known about the relation between happiness and labor organization, for example.

LIVABILITY OF SOCIETY   In Table 39.3, we have seen that average happiness differs greatly across nations. Table 39.4 shows that these are systematic differences. People live happier in rich nations than in poor ones, and happiness is also higher in nations characterized by the rule of law, freedom, good citizenship, cultural plurality, and modernity. Not everything deemed desirable is related, however. Social equality in nations appears to be unrelated to average happiness.

There is much interrelation between the societal characteristics in Table 39.2; the most affluent nations are also the most free and modern ones. It is, therefore, difficult to estimate the effect of each of these variables separately. Still, it is evident that these variables together explain almost all the differences in happiness across nations; R^2 is 0.83!

The relationship between happiness and material affluence is presented in more detail in Figure 39.2. Note that the relationship is not linear, but follows a convex pattern. This indicates that economic affluence is subject to the economic law of diminishing returns, which means that economic growth will add to average happiness in poor nations, but not in rich countries.

This pattern of diminishing returns is not general. Figure 39.3 shows that the relationship with corruption is linear, which suggests that happiness can be improved by combating corruption even in the least corrupt countries.

These findings fit the theory that happiness depends very much on the degree to which living conditions fit universal human needs (livability theory). They do not fit the theory that happiness depends on culturally variable wants (comparison theory) or that happiness is geared by cultural-specific ideas about life (folklore theory). I have discussed these theoretical implications in more detail elsewhere (Veenhoven & Ehrhardt, 1995).

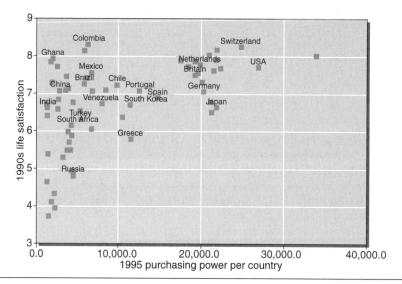

Figure 39.2   Affluence and Happiness in 60 Nations in the 1990s. *Data sources:* Affluence: "Income per Capita of the Popuplation, Corrected for Local Differences in Purchasing Power," *Human Development Report, 1998*, Table 1, by the United Nations Development Program, New York: Oxford University Press; Happiness: "Distributional Findings in Nations," question type 121b, *World Database of Happiness: Ongoing Register of Scientific Research on Subjective Enjoyment of Life*, by R. Veenhoven, 2002, retrieved from www.eur.nl/fsw/research/happiness.

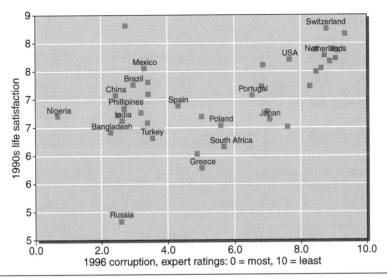

Figure 39.3   Absence of Corruption and Happiness in 40 Nations in the 1990s. *Data sources:* Corruption: *TI-Corruption Perception Index 1997,* Expert ratings, by Transparency International, 1995, Berlin, Germany: Transparency International; Happiness: "Distributional Findings in Nations," question type 121b, *World Database of Happiness: Ongoing Register of Scientific Research on Subjective Enjoyment of Life,* by R. Veenhoven, 2002, retrieved from www.eur.nl/fsw/research/happiness.

POSITION IN SOCIETY   Many studies have considered the relationship between happiness and position in society. The main results are summarized in Table 39.5. Happiness is moderately related to social rank in Western nations, and in non-Western nations, the correlations tend to be stronger. Happiness is also related to social participation, and this relationship seems to be universal. Being embedded in primary networks appears to be crucial to happiness, in particular, being married. This relationship is also universal. Surprisingly, the presence of offspring is unrelated to happiness, at least in present-day Western nations. These illustrative findings suggest that happiness can be improved by facilitating social participation and primary networks (see Myers, Chapter 38, this volume).

Internal Conditions   Happiness depends on the livability of the environment and on the individual's ability to deal with that environment. What abilities are most crucial? Research findings show that good health is an important requirement and that mental health is more critical to happiness than physical health. This pattern of correlations is universal. Intelligence appears to be unrelated to happiness, at least school intelligence, as measured by common IQ tests.

Happiness is strongly linked to psychological autonomy in Western nations. This appears in correlations with inner control, independence, and assertiveness. We lack data on this matter from non-Western nations.

Happiness has also been found to be related to moral conviction. The happy are more acceptant of pleasure than the unhappy, and they are more likely to endorse social values such as solidarity, tolerance, and love. Conversely, the happy tend to

Table 39.5
Happiness and Position in Society

Characteristic	Correlation *within* Western Nations[a]	Similarity *across* All Nations[b]
Social rank		
–Income	+	–
–Education	±	–
–Occupational prestige	+	+
Social participation		
–Employment	±	+
–Participation in associations	+	+
Primary network		
–Spouse	++	+
–Children	0	?
–Friends	+	+

[a] ++ = Strong positive; + = Positive; 0 = No relationship; – = Negative; ? = Not yet investigated; and ± = Varying.
[b] + = Similar; – = Different; and ? = No data.
Source: "Catalog of Correlational Findings," *World Database of Happiness: Ongoing Register of Scientific Research on Subjective Enjoyment of Life*, by R. Veenhoven, 2002.

be less materialistic than the unhappy. It is as yet unclear whether this pattern is universal (see Table 39.6).

In sum, *conditions for happiness can be charted empirically; the available data is already very informative.*

Can Happiness Levels Be Raised?

Findings suggest that happiness can be advanced systematically. Public policy can create conditions that appear conductive to happiness, such as freedom, while therapy and education can foster personal characteristics such as independence. Yet, these empirical data will not convince the critics who believe in a theory that holds happiness as immutable (see also Sheldon & Lyubomirsky, Chapter 8, this volume).

One such theory is that happiness depends on comparison and that standards of comparison adjust to success and failure, although with some delay. In this view, happiness can at best be raised temporarily. Though this theory applies for some kinds of satisfaction, it does not apply for satisfaction with life as a whole. It appears that life satisfaction is not *calculated* cognitively, but rather *inferred* from unreasoned affective experience, which in its turn is related to the gratification of basic needs. The theory that happiness is relative is simply wrong (Veenhoven, 1991).

Another theory holds that we are born either happy or unhappy and that policy interventions can change little as far as this is concerned. A collective variant of this theory is that happiness is a national character trait, for instance, that Russians are chronically unhappy because of a cultural tradition of melancholy. This theory is also wrong; follow-up of individuals show marked changes over the long

Table 39.6
Happiness and Personal Characteristics

Characteristic	Correlation *within* Western Nations[a]	Similarity *across* All Nations[b]
Abilities		
–Physical health	+	++
–Mental health	++	++
–IQ	0	?
Personality		
–Internal control	++	?
–Extraversion	+	?
–Aggression	–	+
Values		
–Hedonism	+	?
–Materialism	–	?
–Social	++	?

[a] ++ = Strong positive; + = Positive; 0 = No relationship; – = Negative; and ? = Not yet investigated.
[b] + = Similar; – = Different; and ? = No data.
Source: "Catalog of Correlational Findings," *World Database of Happiness: Ongoing Register of Scientific Research on Subjective Enjoyment of Life,* by R. Veenhoven, 2002. Retrieved from www.eur.nl/fsw/research/happiness.

term, and trend studies of nations show also profound changes. Figure 39.4 dramatically demonstrates that Russian unhappiness is not a national character trait. This matter is discussed in more detail in Veenhoven (1994).

From an evolutionary view, it is also unlikely that happiness is a traitlike matter. If so, happiness could not be functional, and neither could be the affective signals on which it draws. It is more plausible that happiness is part of our adaptive equipment and that it serves as a compass in life. Mobile organisms must be able to decide whether they are in the right pond or not and hedonic experience is a main strand of information when determining the answer. If the animal is in a biotype that does not fit its abilities, it will feel bad and move away. This seasoned orientation system still exists in humans, who, moreover, can estimate how well they feel over longer periods and reflect on the possible reasons for their feeling. In this view, happiness is an automatic signal that indicates an organism or person's thriving. In this view it is logical that we can raise happiness by facilitating conditions in which people thrive.

In sum, *happiness of the great number can be raised, just like public health can be promoted.* At best, there is an upper limit to happiness, analogous to the ceiling of longevity.

IS HAPPINESS A DESIRABLE OUTCOME?

The fact that public happiness *can* be raised does not mean that happiness *should* be raised. Several arguments have been brought against this idea. Happiness has

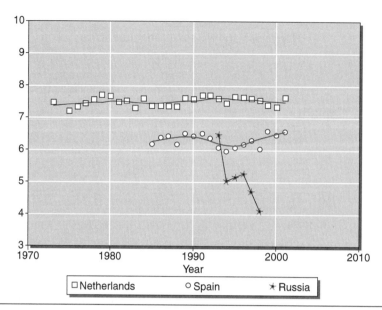

Figure 39.4 Trend in Average Happiness in Nations. *Source:* "Distributional Findings in Nations, Trend Report 2002," *World Database of Happiness: Ongoing register of scientific research on subjective enjoyment of life,* by R. Veenhoven, 2002, retrieved from www.eur.nl/fsw/research/happiness.

been denounced as trivial and of less worth than other goal values. It has also been argued that happiness will spoil people and that the promotion of happiness requires objectionable means. Much of this criticism has been advanced in discussions about different concepts of happiness. The question here is whether these objections apply for happiness as life satisfaction.

IS HAPPINESS REALLY DESIRABLE?

In his *Brave New World,* Huxley (1932) paints a tarnished picture of mass happiness. In this imaginary model society, citizens derive their happiness from uninformed unconcern and from sensory indulgence in sex and a drug called *soma*. This is indeed superficial enjoyment, but is this enjoyment happiness? It is not. This kind of experience was classified as pleasures on the top left in Table 39.2 and distinguished from life satisfaction on the bottom right. Enduring satisfaction with life as a whole cannot be achieved by mere passive consumption. Research shows that it is typically a by-product of active involvement.

Likewise, Adorno depicted happiness as a temporary escape from reality and rejected it for that reason (Rath, 2002). Here, happiness is mixed up with top experience. Life satisfaction is typically not escapism. Research shows that it is linked with reality control.

Happiness has also been equated with social success and, on that basis, rejected as conformist rat-race behavior. This criticism may apply to satisfaction in the domain of career (top-right quadrant in Table 39.2) but not to satisfaction with life as a whole. In fact, happy people tend to be independent rather than conformist.

Happiness has also been denounced on the basis of assumptions about its determinants. As noted earlier, it is commonly assumed that happiness depends on social comparison. In this view, happiness is merely thinking to be better off than the Joneses. Likewise, it is assumed that happiness depends on the meeting of culturally determined standards of success and that the happiness of present-day Americans draws on their ability to live up to the models presented in advertisements. Both these theories see happiness as cognitive contentment and miss the point that happiness is essentially an affective phenomenon that signals how well we thrive.

In sum, *there are no good reasons to denounce happiness as insignificant.*

Is Happiness the Most Desirable Value?

Agreeing that happiness is desirable is one thing, but the tenet of utilitarianism is that happiness is the *most* desirable value. This claim is criticized on two grounds: First, it is objected that it does not make sense to premise one particular value, and second, there are values that rank higher than happiness. There is a long-standing philosophical discussion on these issues (Sen & Williams, 1982; Smart & Williams, 1973), to which the newly gained knowledge about happiness can add the following points.

One new argument in this discussion is in the previously mentioned signal function of happiness. If happiness does indeed reflect how well we thrive, it concurs with living according to our nature. From a humanistic perspective, this is valuable.

Another novelty is in the insight that quality of external living conditions depends on inner life abilities and vice versa (Table 39.1). Democracy is generally deemed to be good, but it does not work well with anxious and uneducated voters. Likewise, conformity is generally deemed to be bad but can be functional in collectivist conditions. This helps us to understand that general end values cannot be found in the top quadrants. Instead, end values are to be found in the bottom quadrants, in particular, the bottom-right quadrant (Table 39.1). Happiness and longevity indicate how well a person's life abilities fit the conditions in which that person lives and, as such, reflects more value than is found in each of the top quadrants separately. Happiness is a more inclusive merit than most other values, since it reflects an optimal combination.

A related point is that there are limits to most values, too much freedom leads to anarchy, and too much equality leads to apathy. The problem is that we do not know where the optimum level lies and how optima vary in different value combinations. Here again, happiness is a useful indicator. If most people live long and happily, the mix is apparently livable. I have elaborated these points in more detail elsewhere (Veenhoven, 1996, 2000).

In sum, *if one opts for one particular end value, happiness is a good candidate.*

Will the Promotion of Happiness Be at the Cost of Other Values?

Even if there is nothing wrong with happiness in itself, maximization of it could still work out negatively for other valued matters. Critics of utilitarianism claim this will happen. They foresee that greater happiness will make people less caring and responsible and fear that the premise for happiness will legitimize amoral means. This state of affairs is also described in *Brave New World* (Huxley, 1932), where citizens are concerned only with petty pleasures and the government is dictatorial.

Does Happiness Spoil?   Over the ages, preachers of penitence have glorified suffering. This sermonizing lives on in the idea that happiness does not bring out the best of us. Happiness is said to nurture self-sufficient attitudes and to make people less sensitive to the suffering of their fellows. Happiness is also seen to lead to complacency and thereby to demean initiative and creativeness. It is also said that happiness fosters superficial hedonism and that these negative effects on individuals will harm society in the long run. Hence, promotion of happiness is seen to lead into societal decay; Nero playing happily in a decadent Rome that is burning around him.

There is some literature on the positive effects of happiness, recently in the context of *positive psychology*. This writing suggests that happiness is an activating force and facilitates involvement in tasks and people. Happiness is seen to open us to the world, while unhappiness invites us to retreat (Fredrickson, 2000). This view fits the theory that happiness functions as a go signal.

Research findings support this latter view of the consequences of happiness. Happiness is strongly correlated with activity and predicts sociable behaviors, such as helping. Happiness also has a positive effect on intimate relations. There is also good evidence that happiness lengthens life (Danner, Snowdon, & Friesen, 2001). Thus, happiness is clearly good for us. I have reviewed this research in more detail elsewhere (Veenhoven, 1988, 1989). All this does not deny that happiness may involve some negative effects, but apparently the positive effects dominate.

Does a Premise for Happiness Excuse Amoral Means?   The main objection against utilitarianism is that the greatest happiness principle justifies any way to improve happiness and hence permits morally rejectable ways, such as genetical manipulation, mind control, and political repression. It is also felt that the rights of minorities will be sacrificed on the altar of the greatest number.

The possibility of such undesirable consequences is indeed implied in the logic of radical utilitarianism, but is it likely to materialize? The available data suggest this is not true. As seen in Table 39.4, citizens are happiest in nations that respect human rights and allow freedom. It also appears that people are happiest in the most educated and informatized nations. Likewise, Table 39.4 shows that happy people tend to be active and independent. In fact, there is no empirical evidence for any real value conflict. The problem exists in theory, but not in reality.

In sum, *there is no ground for the fear that maximalization of happiness will lead into consequences that are morally objectionable.*

CONCLUSION

The empirical tests falsify all the theoretical objections against the greatest happiness principle. The criterion appears practically feasible and morally sound. Hence, the greatest happiness principle deserves a more prominent place in policy making.

REFERENCES

Andrews, F. M., & Withey, S. B. (1976). *Social indicators of well-being: Americans' perceptions of life quality.* New York: Plenum Press.

*Argyle, M. (2002). *The psychology of happiness* (3rd ed., rev.). London: Methuen.

Bentham, J. (1789). *Introduction to the principles of morals and legislation.* London: Payne.

Bradburn, N. M., & Caplovitz, D. (1965). *Reports on happiness: A pilot study of behavior related to mental health.* Chicago: Aldine.

Brickman, P., & Campbell, D. T. (1971). Hedonic relativism and planning the good society. In M. H. Appley (Ed.), *Adaptation-level theory: A symposium* (pp. 287–302). New York: Academic Press.

Campbell, A. (1981). *The sense of well-being in America.* New York: McGraw-Hill.

Cantril, H. (1965). *The pattern of human concern.* New Brunswick, NJ: Rutgers University Press.

Danner, D. D., Snowdon, D. A., & Friesen, W. V. (2001). Positive emotions in early life and longevity: Findings from the nun study. *Journal of Personality and Social Psychology, 80,* 804–819.

DenHartog, D. N. (1999). Culture specific and cross-culturally generalizable implicit leadership theories: Are attributes of charismatic/transformational leadership universally endorsed? *Leadership Quarterly, 10,* 219–256.

*Diener, E., Suh, E. M., Lucas, R. E., & Smith, H. L. (1999). Subjective well-being: Three decades of progress. *Psychological Bulletin, 125,* 276–302.

Dijkstra, G. (2000). *A larger pie through a fair share? Gender equality and economic performance* [Working Paper No. 315]. Den Haag, The Netherlands: Institute of Social Studies.

Ehrhardt, J. J., Saris, W. E., & Veenhoven, R. (2000). Stability of life-satisfaction over time: Analysis of ranks in a national population. *Journal of Happiness Studies, 1,* 177–205.

Ekman, P., & Friesen, P. W. (1975). *Unmasking the face.* Englewood Cliffs, NJ: Prentice-Hall.

Fredrickson, B. L. (2000). Cultivating positive emotions to optimize health and well-being. *Prevention and Treatment, 3,* article 1a.

Freedom House. (2000). *Freedom in the world 2000.* Retrieved from www.freedomhouse.org /research.

Freud, S. (1948). *Das Unbehagen mit der Kultur, Gesammte Werke aus den Jahren 1925–1931* [Culture and its discontents]. Frankfurt-am-Main, Germany: Fisher Verlag. (Original work published 1929)

Frey, B. S., & Stutzer, A. (2000). Happiness prospers in democracy. *Journal of Happiness Studies, 1,* 79–102.

Gerson, E. M. (1976). On quality of life. *American Sociological Review, 41,* 793–806.

Gurin, G., Veroff, J., & Feld, S. (1960). *Americans view their mental health.* New York: Basic Books.

Gwartney, J. D., & Lawson, R. A. (2001). *Economic freedom in the world 1975–2000.* Retrieved from www.fraserinstitute.ca/publications.

Huxley, A. (1932). *Brave new world.* Stockholm, Sweden: Continental Books.

Jahoda, M. (1958). *Current concepts of positive mental health.* New York: Basic Books.

Lane, R. (2000). *The loss of happiness in market democracies.* New Haven, CT: Yale University Press.

Neugarten, B. L., Havinghurst, R. J., & Tobin, S. S. (1961). The measurement of life satisfaction. *Journal of Gerontology, 16,* 134–143.

Oswald, A. J. (1997, November). Happiness and economic performance. *Economic Journal,* 1815–1831.

Rath, N. (2002). The concept of happiness in Adorno's critical theory. *Journal of Happiness Studies, 3,* 1–21.

Schimmack, U., & Diener, E. (Eds.). (2003). Experience sampling methodology in happiness research [Special issue]. *Journal of Happiness Studies, 4*(1).

Sen, A. (1993). Capability and well-being. In M. Nussbaum & A. Sen (Eds.), *The quality of life* (pp. 30–53). Oxford, England: Clarendon.

Sen, A., & Williams, B. (Eds.). (1982). *Utilitarianism and beyond.* Cambridge, England: Cambridge University Press.

Smart, J. J., & Williams, B. (1973). *Utilitarianism, for and against.* Cambridge, England: Cambridge University Press.

Transparency International. (1997). *TI-Corruption Perception Index 1997.* Berlin, Germany: Author.

United Nations. (1998). *United Nations demographic yearbook* (UN-DY). New York: Author.

United Nations Development Program. (2000). *Human Development Report 2000* (UN-DP). New York: Oxford University Press.

United Nations Educational, Scientific and Cultural Organization (UNESCO). (1998). *World culture report.* Paris: Author.

VanPraag, B. M. (1993). The relativity of welfare. In M. Nussbaum & A. Sen (Eds.), *The quality of life* (pp. 362–385). Oxford, England: Clarendon Press.

Veenhoven, R. (1984). *Conditions of happiness.* Dordrecht, The Netherlands: Kluwer Academic.

Veenhoven, R. (1988). The utility of happiness. *Social Indicators Research, 20,* 333–354.

Veenhoven, R. (1989). *How harmful is happiness? Consequences of enjoying life or not?* The Hague, The Netherlands: Rotterdam University Press.

Veenhoven, R. (1991). Is happiness relative? *Social Indicators Research, 24,* 1–34.

Veenhoven, R. (1993). *Happiness in nations: Subjective appreciation of life in 56 nations, 1946–1992.* Rotterdam, The Netherlands: RISBO—Erasmus University.

Veenhoven, R. (1994). Is happiness a trait? Test of the theory that a better society does not make people any happier. *Social Indicators Research, 32,* 101–160.

Veenhoven, R. (1996). Happy life-expectancy: A comprehensive measure of quality-of-life in nations. *Social Indicators Research, 39,* 1–58.

Veenhoven, R. (1997). Progrès dans la compréhension du bonheur [Advances in understanding happiness]. *Revue Québécoise de Psychologie, 18,* 29–74. English version available on www.eur.nl/fsw/research/veenhoven.

Veenhoven, R. (1998). Vergelijken van geluk in landen [*Comparing happiness in nations].* Sociale Wetenschappen, 42*(4), 58–84.

Veenhoven, R. (2000). The four qualities of life: Ordering concepts and measures of the good life. *Journal of Happiness Studies, 1,* 1–39.

*Veenhoven, R. (2002). *World Database of Happiness: Ongoing register of scientific research on subjective enjoyment of life.* Retrieved from www.eur.nl/fsw/research/happiness.

Veenhoven, R., & Ehrhardt, J. (1995). The cross-national pattern of happiness: Test of predictions implied in three theories of happiness. *Social Indicators Research, 43,* 33–86.

Ware, J. E., Jr. (1996). The SF-36 health survey. In B. Spilker (Ed.), *Quality of life and pharmaco-economics in clinical trials* (pp. 337–345). Philadelphia: Lippincott-Raven.

Wessman, A. E., & Ricks, D. F. (1966). *Mood and personality.* New York: Holt, Rhinehart and Winston.

World Health Organization. (1985). *Targets for health for all.* Copenhagen, Denmark: Author.

World Values Study Group. (1997). *World Values Survey, 1980–1996* [Computer file, ICPSR 6160]. Ann Arbor, MI: Institute for Social Research.

CHAPTER 40

Findings on Subjective Well-Being: Applications to Public Policy, Clinical Interventions, and Education

WILLIAM PAVOT and ED DIENER

A S AN AREA of study within psychology, the study of happiness, or subjective well-being (SWB), has grown remarkably in the past 25 years. Evidence of this trend is increasingly apparent; for example, in 1999, a substantial edited volume on SWB was published (Kahneman, Diener, & Schwarz, 1999), and in 2000, a special millennium issue of the *American Psychologist* devoted exclusively to "positive psychology" (Seligman & Csikszentmihalyi, 2000, p. 5) was published. Attaining a greater understanding of human happiness, well-being, and optimal functioning has become a major goal for the field.

Parallel to this rising interest in SWB, there has been an increase in the sophistication and reliability of instruments designed to assess SWB, and a general increase in the empirical rigor of methodology that SWB researchers employ. Simple survey methodologies have been enhanced with nonself-report measures and retrospective reports of emotional experiences have been supplemented with experiential sampling methods (Diener, 2000, p. 35). Cross-sectional research designs have been reinforced with longitudinal studies. As a consequence, the findings from research on SWB have become increasingly reliable and valid indicators of the SWB of individuals. Moreover, as a result of several large-scale studies (e.g., Diener, Diener, & Diener, 1995), a growing database focused on the SWB of nations has also been established.

Advances in the quality and quantity of research devoted to SWB have led to both a sizeable database and a set of replicable findings related to the causes and consequences of the experience of SWB. Several of these findings have implications for areas such as clinical intervention, education, and public policy. This chapter provides a brief sketch of some of these findings and social applications.

We first briefly review the definition of SWB and discuss some of the major findings to date. Then, we discuss the potential positive utility of a national index of SWB (Diener, 2000) and present some examples of how such an index could be applied to policy decisions in areas such as unemployment, clinical interventions, industrial/organizational interventions, and education.

DEFINING SUBJECTIVE WELL-BEING

Generally, researchers investigating aspects of SWB tend to view it as a broad, multifaceted domain, rather than as a specific, narrow, unidimensional construct. For example, Diener, Suh, Lucas, and Smith (1999) offered the following definition: "Subjective well-being is a broad category of phenomena that includes people's emotional responses, domain satisfactions, and global judgments of life satisfaction" (p. 277). Most investigators break down emotional responses into the two relatively independent dimensions of positive affect (PA) and negative affect (NA). Emotional or affective responses, whether experienced as moods or emotions, tend to represent "on line" (Diener, 2000, p. 34) information and evaluations of relevant events in their environment. Global judgments of life satisfaction represent more cognitively based evaluations of a person's life as a whole (Pavot & Diener, 1993b). Using multitrait-multimethod analyses, Lucas, Diener, and Suh (1996) demonstrated that pleasant affect, unpleasant affect, and life satisfaction are separable constructs, and it is therefore desirable to conceptualize (and assess) these components of SWB separately. Domain satisfactions represent more specific evaluations of important aspects of a person's life, for example, marital satisfaction or satisfaction at work. Some researchers have approached satisfaction judgments from the perspective of discrepancies between a person's perceived state and specific standards, such as past conditions and aspirations (e.g., Michalos, 1985). Overall, domain satisfactions tend to be correlated with life satisfaction but it is likely that at least some domains might represent areas of desired change and perhaps sources of low satisfaction, whereas others may represent sources of fulfillment and meaning, and therefore these domains are a source of high satisfaction.

Subjective well-being is a necessary but not sufficient condition for good quality of life and well-being (Diener & Biswas-Diener, 2003). A sense of SWB is an essential component of a positive quality of life. Regardless of environmental, material, or social advantage, if an individual is experiencing strong dissatisfaction, anxiety, or depression, it would be hard to characterize that individual as having attained a good quality of life. Conversely, SWB alone is not sufficient for a good quality of life; it is conceivable that an individual's temperament might predispose him or her to the experience of positive emotions, even under circumstances where justice, dignity, and other essential qualities of a good life were absent.

In sum, SWB represents people's judgments or evaluations of their own lives, and those judgments can be based on both cognitive and emotional responses. Such judgments or evaluations are essential information to determine an individual's overall well-being and quality of life, but they are not sufficient to "cause" a good quality of life if basic elements of human dignity and freedom are absent.

MEASUREMENT ISSUES

As noted, methods of measuring SWB have become increasingly sophisticated. Early researchers relied almost exclusively on brief, often single-item, self-reported assessments of SWB. Although quite simple in format, responses to these survey items appear to have moderate validity and have been demonstrated to correlate with other methods of assessment (Pavot & Diener, 1993a). However, brief self-reported measures are vulnerable to biases and methodological artifacts (Schwarz & Strack, 1999). Memory biases, presentational biases, and even the placement of an item within a larger survey instrument can potentially introduce error of measurement into the responses people make to a brief self-report measure of SWB.

Mindful of the potential vulnerability of these simple methods of assessing SWB, investigators have devoted attention to developing increasingly sophisticated techniques of measurement. One improvement has been the evolution of early, single-item self-report measures of SWB into multiple-item, often multiple-factor instruments (for examples, see Pavot & Diener, 2003). Advances have also been made in the development of alternative methods to supplement traditional self-reports of SWB. For example, Experience-Sampling Methodology (ESM; Diener, 2000) involves random sampling of a respondent's thoughts and moods over time, with the aid of a palm computer, which signals the respondent to complete a report and records his or her responses. By sampling the ongoing experiences of the individual, ESM can overcome many of the shortcomings of measures that are completed on a single occasion, such as the mood or emotional state of the respondent at the particular moment of response. ESM data can be averaged across many occasions, effectively canceling out momentary mood fluctuations or transient situational circumstances that might produce deviations from the respondent's long-term level of SWB. Another frequently used strategy is to gather informant reports from the family and friends of a target individual. Such reports can provide external validation for self-reported measures completed by the target individual. Sandvik, Diener, and Seidlitz (1993) incorporated one-time, self-reported measures of life satisfaction with ESM measures and informant reports within a single study and found moderate-to-strong intercorrelations among these methodologies. Other methodological options include physiological measures, interviews, reaction-time measures presented on a computer, and ratings of facial expression (e.g., smiling).

Because of these developments, it is now possible to assemble complex assessment batteries to measure SWB and related constructs. Such batteries could include an array of measures utilizing distinct methodologies, and providing cross-method convergence and validation, thereby minimizing the potential biases inherent to any particular method used alone.

SOME CAUSES AND CORRELATES OF SWB

A sizable number of variables have been identified as correlates of SWB. It would be difficult to provide a complete listing and discussion of all of these relations in the present chapter. However, a relatively small number of factors have emerged over time as consistent, significant predictors of SWB. These correlates include temperament, traits and other personality characteristics, social relations, income, unemployment, and societal/cultural influences.

The relation between SWB and temperament is one of the most consistent and substantial relations that has been identified. Temperament is usually conceptualized as the basic and pervasive tone of the personality, considered by most to be heritable, and demonstrated to be a stable factor within the personality of individuals. Two particular personality traits, extraversion and neuroticism, have been shown to have moderate to strong correlations with SWB (see DeNeve & Cooper, 1998, for a review). Extraversion has consistently been shown to have at least a moderate correlation with pleasant affect (Lucas & Fujita, 2000), and neuroticism has shown a similar, if not stronger, correlation with negative affect (Fujita, 1991). Many researchers view temperament, as captured by the traits of extraversion and neuroticism, as the primary connection between personality and SWB.

In addition to extraversion and neuroticism, other personality dimensions have been correlated with SWB constructs. Two more of the "Big Five" personality dimensions, agreeableness and conscientiousness (DeNeve & Cooper, 1998), and a number of other, somewhat narrower personality traits, such as dispositional optimism and self-esteem (Lucas et al., 1996), are related to SWB.

When compared to the influence of personality, the effects of many life changes and life events appear to have a limited long-term effect on an individual's level of SWB. One explanation for the modest impact of most life events is the process of adaptation (Brickman & Campbell, 1971). When people experience a good event or positive change in their lives, it typically brings them a brief period of increased happiness. However, over time, we tend to habituate or adapt to our improved situation, and eventually we may return to our typical level of SWB (influenced by temperament). In a study of both lottery winners and accident victims with spinal cord injuries, Brickman, Coates, and Janoff-Bulman (1978) found the effects of these powerful life events on long-term SWB were not as strong as expected. Negative or aversive events, unless extreme, often produce a similar effect; we are less happy for a relatively brief period, but slowly return to a "set-point" level of happiness. This "hedonic treadmill" (Brickman & Campbell, 1971) of adaptation provides some level of explanation as to why life events and life changes, both good and bad, often seem to have little impact on an individual's long-term level of SWB.

One model relating to SWB combines the effects of personality and adaptation. The dynamic equilibrium model (Headey & Wearing, 1992) proposes that people have baseline levels of positive and negative affect that are established by their personality characteristics, particularly extraversion and neuroticism, respectively, that cause a recurring level of good and bad events. Random and uncontrollable good or bad events may temporarily move people away from these personal baselines, but people will return to these levels over time. The effects of adaptation tend to make the role of temperament-based personality characteristics more salient.

Although adaptation tends to cancel out the effects of many life events on SWB, in some instances, life events do exert a long-term impact on SWB. For example, Stroebe, Stroebe, Abakoumkin, and Schut (1996) found higher than average levels of depression among widows than among nonbereaved persons. Caregivers of Alzheimer's patients have deteriorating SWB over time (Vitaliano, Russo, Young, Becker, & Maiuro, 1991). Periods of unemployment can have a long-term detriment to the SWB of some individuals, even after becoming re-employed (Clark, Georgellis, Lucas, & Diener, 2003). At a national level, conditions within a society can significantly influence SWB. Within most nations, the typical finding is that most people are happy (Diener & Diener, 1996). However, data from the World Values Survey (World Values Study Group, 1994) indicate that considerable variance between nations is possible. In Bulgaria, for example, 60% of survey respondents were below the mid-point of the scale for life satisfaction, and 40% of the sample reported more negative than positive emotions (Diener, 2000). The social and political policies of a nation can exert a powerful influence on the SWB experienced by its citizens. Although adaptation to life events typically does occur, the process is not complete in all circumstances.

Several researchers have examined the influence of goals on SWB. Cantor (1990) has noted that commitment to specific goals can provide an individual with a sense of agency and purpose. Emmons (1986) demonstrated that the mere existence of important, valued goals, and progress toward achieving those goals, were associated with higher life satisfaction; conflict between goals or ambivalence toward goals were correlated with negative affect. Other efforts (e.g., Cantor & Sanderson, 1999; Scheier & Carver, 1993) have examined how the method of approaching a person's goals influences well-being. Within individualist cultures, personal goals can exert strong influences on SWB, although the importance of such goals may be diminished within other cultural contexts (Suh, 1999).

Another influential factor in the experience of SWB is the quality of an individual's social relationships. In a study of the characteristics of very happy people, Diener and Seligman (2002) found that self-ratings of relationships and peer-ratings of relationships were higher for individuals identified as "very happy" (p. 83), than similar ratings for individuals reporting lower levels of happiness. In fact, all members of the very happy group reported good-quality social relationships, prompting the authors to conclude that good social relationships ". . . form a necessary but not sufficient condition for high happiness—that is, they do not guarantee high happiness, but it does not appear to occur without them" (p. 83).

Another important point to take from the research on highly happy people is that very happy people are not ecstatic. Among the very happy group studied by Diener and Seligman (2002), 92 moments of experience were sampled, but none of these moments was rated by the respondents as "ecstatic," or at the very top of a 10-point scale. Generally, the highly happy group reported moods such as "7" or "8" on the same scale. Further, all individuals in the very happy group reported occasional unhappy or neutral moods (Diener & Seligman, 2002). Thus, even very happy individuals report mood variability, and some negative mood states. High SWB individuals can experience and express negative emotion when it is appropriate to do so.

A number of studies have consistently found a positive relation between marriage and SWB. A meta-analysis of such studies by Haring-Hidore, Stock, Okun, and Witter (1985) revealed an average correlation of 0.14 between marital status and SWB. However, the findings of Lucas, Clark, Georgellis, and Diener (2003) indicate that one cause of the marriage-SWB relation is the selection of happier people into marriage, in contrast to the lower level of happiness on average of those who do not marry.

The sociocultural environment surrounding each person is another significant influence on that individual's SWB. Most studies focused on examining cultural differences are in fact cross-national rather than cross-cultural, because the relevant data is collected within a given country, and cultures may be more or less encompassing than national boundaries. In a recent review, Diener, Oishi, and Lucas (2003) estimated that 18% of the variance in positive emotions and 11% of the variance in negative emotions, along with 12% of the variance in life satisfaction, were due to between-nation differences. Among the predictors of these differences, one of the strongest is the wealth of a nation (Diener et al., 1995). This relation may be somewhat over-determined, because human rights, longevity, and democracy tend to co-vary with national wealth (Diener et al., 2003).

OUTCOMES OF SWB

A sizable amount of research has examined the outcomes of people with varying levels of SWB. This is a critical issue; if there are no discernable differences in life outcomes, adaptation to stress, and mastery of their environment between people who report different levels of SWB, or if in fact these outcomes are less positive for those with high SWB, then the importance of SWB as a desirable goal is significantly diminished. Although the impact of SWB has been examined across many life domains, in this chapter we will focus on three: The quality of social relationships, work life, and mental health.

Several studies have focused on the quality of social relationships. Diener and Seligman (2002) found that individuals reporting high SWB had stronger romantic and other social relationships than less happy groups. Extraversion has consistently been found to correlate with SWB, and extraversion has in turn been linked with affiliation, life satisfaction, and chronic positive affect (e.g., Emmons & Diener, 1985; Lyubomirsky & Lepper, 2001; Pavot, Diener, & Fujita, 1990). Eventual marriage is a significant life experience for 90% of people worldwide (Myers, 2000), and people who do marry tend to report more happiness than those who are divorced, widowed, or single (Diener et al., 1999; Mastekaasa, 1994). Until recently, most of the data on the marriage-SWB relation has been correlational in nature, obtained in cross-sectional studies; under such circumstances it would be equally as plausible to conclude that marriage causes happiness as that happiness causes marriage. But two large-scale longitudinal studies, one in Australia (Marks & Fleming, 1999) and another in Germany (Lucas et al., 2003) have demonstrated that higher levels of SWB were predictive of an increased likelihood of marriage at a later measurement. It seems reasonable to conclude that the benefits of marriage add to the SWB of the individuals within the marriage, but it is now clear that people with higher levels of SWB are more likely to marry. Another important concern is the quality of the relationship once a couple marries. Marital satisfaction is more strongly related to global individual happiness than satisfaction in any other domain (Glenn & Weaver, 1981). Positive affect is a predominant emotional tone for those with high SWB, and the expression of positive affect in the marital relationship, especially when attempting to resolve conflict, is predictive of marital satisfaction and less risk for divorce (Gottman, Coan, Carrere, & Swanson, 1998). High-quality social relationships are significant assets throughout the lifespan. The preponderance of evidence suggests that individuals high in SWB have an advantage in this domain by virtue of their ability to cultivate and maintain satisfactory friendships, romantic relationships, and marital bonds.

Another significant life domain for most people involves their experiences in their working life. Not only is working a source of income, but it also provides meaningful activity for individuals, and productivity for society. A number of studies have examined the relation between SWB and a successful working life. As a beginning, happy people report higher levels of job satisfaction (Tait, Padgett, & Baldwin, 1989). Moreover, Staw, Sutton, and Pelled (1994) examined positive emotion in the workplace, and found that employees higher in dispositional positive affect received better pay and higher supervisor ratings. It appears that positive affect leads to better performance, and conversely, good performance leads to positive affect (Côté, 1999). In addition, happy people are better able to solve conflicts on the job (Baron, Fortin, Frei, Hauver, & Shack, 1990). Going beyond the basic requirements of the work, job satisfaction predicts good organizational citizenship (e.g., aiding coworkers; George & Brief, 1992). On the other end of the spectrum, job satisfaction showed less relation with undesirable behaviors such as sabotage (Mangoine & Quinn, 1975).

A number of other aspects of work life have been examined with regard to their relation to SWB, and the pattern is consistent: Subjective well-being is associated with good success in the workplace. Happy workers are productive, satisfied workers, and their positive affect is associated with good organizational citizenship, good relations with coworkers, and improved conflict resolution.

A third major life domain is mental health. Each year millions of people seek treatment for mood disorders, anxiety disorders, somatoform disorders, and numerous other clinical problems. Thousands commit suicide as a consequence of severe depression. Although the etiology of such disorders often appears to be at least partially biological, the current diathesis-stress model (Holmes, 2001) is a recognition that environmental stressors, and our ability or inability to cope with them, play a major role in determining the onset and severity of many disorders.

Diener and Seligman (2002), in their survey of the characteristics of very happy people, found that individuals high in SWB did not score in the clinical range of the MMPI, with the exception of a handful of people with elevated scores on the Hypomania scale. This same group had lower neuroticism scores, indicating lower levels of negative emotional reactivity, relative to groups lower in SWB. Moreover, the high SWB group scored lower on an interview suicide measure, which measured suicidal thoughts and behaviors (Diener & Seligman, 2002).

Chronic stress can have serious consequences for both the psychological and physical well-being of people. At the physical level, chronic stress breaks down the immune system (Andersen, Kiecolt-Glaser, & Glaser, 1994), which in turn increases the vulnerability of the body to disease and physical breakdown. The effects of stress have been implicated as risk factors for diseases as diverse as rheumatoid arthritis (Zautra, Burleson, Matt, Roth, & Burrows, 1994), and cancer (Kiecolt-Glaser, 1999). At the psychological level, there is consistent evidence that chronic stress can lead to learned helplessness and depression (Hiroto & Seligman, 1975). But several constructs, such as optimism (Segerstrom, Taylor, Kemeny, & Fahey, 1998) and hardiness (Maddi & Kobasa, 1984), represent traits that promote positive emotions and have been shown to be related to more positive health outcomes. Fredrickson and Joiner (2002) demonstrated that positive affect is associated with more effective coping and better overall outcomes. Thus, it appears that SWB and positive affectivity can act as key buffers to the effects of chronic stress, and reduction of the effects of chronic stress can in turn reduce the risks of both psychological and physical illness and distress.

Successful outcomes in other life domains have been associated with high SWB, but the previous examples demonstrate that SWB is a valuable outcome: People high in SWB tend to have a number of positive qualities. Subjective well-being promotes good interpersonal relations and connectedness to others; employees with high SWB are assets and positive contributors to the workplace; and high SWB can act as a significant buffer against the effects of chronic stress, being associated with better physical and psychological health outcomes. The vast preponderance of evidence indicates that high SWB is a desirable condition that produces positive outcomes for both the individual and society.

A NATIONAL INDEX OF SWB INDICATORS

Evidence from a number of studies suggests that, although temperament has a strong influence on an individual's SWB, social and political conditions within a nation can significantly influence SWB as well. There is no systematic, nationwide database from which policy makers and others can seek information about the level of SWB among citizens of the United States. Diener (2000) proposed the creation of a national index of SWB indicators, and we reiterate that proposal here. A national index could include a battery of SWB indicators that could be used to track levels of SWB over time. A national index of SWB would make it possible to compare the SWB of individuals representing various age groups, occupational categories, income levels, and regions of the country. An annual survey could allow trends in SWB to be observed. The impact of events (e.g., terrorist attacks, major policy changes) on SWB could be more clearly determined, and national productivity could be assessed in relation to SWB. National economic indicators (the gross domestic product index, unemployment rates, the consumer price index) and social indicators (crime rates, infant mortality, literacy) have long been recognized as sources of critical information for policy makers. Subjective indicators represent the third leg on the stool—indicating the subjective well-being of the nation. The British government, for example, has started to take an interest in the state of the nation's happiness (see Donovan & Halpern, 2002).

The established economic and social indicators have strong influence, in part, because they become focal points for people's attention, highlighting the particular factor being measured. For example, monthly unemployment figures not only provide specific numbers, but they have the effect of focusing people's attention on the issues and policies surrounding unemployment rates. In the same way, a national index of SWB could focus attention on the subjective experiences of citizens. Measuring people's feelings of fulfillment, meaning, positive affect, spirituality, positive emotions at work, and other subjective experiences will help bring focus to goals beyond money (such as personal income or GDP). In addition, it will give us a way of tracking national policies, such as universal health care or other major changes, which might be put in place over the next decades if they have a strong impact on SWB.

A prototype for a possible survey instrument is presented in Appendix A. Items assessing life satisfaction, domain satisfactions, and emotional experiences could form the core of a national survey. Additional items, presented on a rotating basis, would give periodic samples of the subjective reaction of people to longer term social issues, and special items could be included to assess people's reactions to particular events or newly developed social concerns (e.g., homeland security).

APPLICATIONS OF SWB RESEARCH

A considerable amount of research on SWB has already been completed; a much larger body of knowledge would be available if a national index was implemented. Still another concern, however, is the issue of finding specific applications for this information. What life domains could readily benefit from a better understanding of the causes and benefits of SWB? We briefly examine three possible areas of application: Public information/education, applications in industrial and organizational settings, and applications related to clinical interventions.

One way that psychologists can influence people's well-being is through their efforts to educate the public, both students and adults alike, in our knowledge of what makes for a life high in SWB. People high in chronic positive affect seem to have a number of desirable characteristics. Not only do high SWB individuals make more money; they tend to have better marriages and other social relationships, and they exhibit higher levels of community involvement. For these reasons, it appears that helping people to have high SWB might be a worthwhile goal. That is not to say that everyone will be elated all of the time; such a goal would not be realistic and, indeed, would not be desirable. Instead, a more desirable goal would be a population of people who are happy most of the time, with only modest levels of negative affect.

Psychologists could provide a step toward improving the SWB of the population by educating the public about key findings from research. Some examples of information could include findings on materialism and realistic expectations. Although a common American pursuit is the accumulation of material wealth, research indicates that materialism can be toxic to happiness, particularly if people begin to value money more highly than other values such as family and friends (e.g., Kasser & Ryan, 1993). It is important to maintain a process orientation; that is, to view happiness as an ongoing process of active involvement, rather than some utopian place where one has everything. Good social relations are necessary for high SWB (Diener & Seligman, 2002), luxury cars and summer villas are not. If material accumulation becomes a primary goal, the maintenance of social relationships can become secondary, and the prospects of happiness are diminished (e.g., Kasser & Ryan, 1993; see also Kasser, this volume).

Another area of potential education is related to promoting the cultivation of realistic expectations. Very happy people are not always a 10 on a 10-point happiness scale. We can try to be happier, but nobody can remain constantly elated. It is functional for people to have some bad moods when such emotions are appropriate, and it is important to have some emotional variation. So the goal of achieving constant high happiness for everyone at all times is not only unrealistic, but it could ultimately be harmful if people expect to be constantly happy, and consider themselves failures when they are unable to achieve constant high happiness. Emotional constancy is not a functional state; in fact, emotional invariance is a possible criterion for disorder.

Another focal point for education might be the implications that the findings from SWB research have for work and organizational settings. People experiencing high SWB tend to become more engaged and involved in their work, earn more money, have better relations with supervisors and coworkers, and in general are better organizational citizens (George & Brief, 1992). The challenge is to create new work environments that foster involvement and provide opportunities to be challenged, and that foster positive social interactions (see Henry, this volume). Automation has already eliminated many repetitive and unfulfilling work settings, and that process will continue. But care should be taken to ensure that the new work settings created by technology and information systems are engaging, and that electronic interactions do not completely preclude positive, face-to-face interactions with coworkers.

A third area of potential application of the findings from SWB research involves psychological interventions in the clinical area. One possibility would involve using SWB measures as outcome indicators for therapy (see also Ruini &

Fava, this volume). Typically, measures of distress are used for such assessments. For example, an assessment of depression or anxiety might be given to a client in the initial stages of therapy, and then that same assessment might be repeated over the course of treatment. If the assessments that the client completes after a course of therapy show lower levels of depression or anxiety, such indications are taken as a measure of the success of therapy. But including measures of SWB would introduce a new dimension; not only could the reduction of symptoms be measured, but the increase in SWB could be another index of improvement. Some promising results in this area have already been reported (Pavot & Diener, 1993b). Another application in therapy settings might be to provide education of clients with regard to SWB findings, providing alternative behavioral possibilities based on such research. High SWB is clearly not sufficient for good mental health (Diener, 2000), but it does appear to add an additional approach to consider within the scope of a larger program of clinical intervention. It is also noteworthy that very happy individuals seem to have low levels of psychopathology (Diener & Seligman, 2002).

CONCLUSIONS

The scientific study of SWB has advanced considerably over the past quarter-century. In many respects, our knowledge of happiness is tentative and limited, but a good empirical foundation has been laid. A set of reliable sources of SWB have been identified, including personality characteristics, social relationships, and goals, along with societal, cultural, and political factors.

A number of beneficial outcomes of SWB have been established: People high in SWB tend to have more success in their social relationships and marital life, they tend to be successful and positively oriented in work settings, they are involved in their communities and care about other people. High SWB tends to provide a buffer for the effects of chronic stress and is an asset in the maintenance of good psychological and physical health.

A national index of SWB indicators could provide an important additional perspective on the quality of life in the United States. Unlike economic and social indicators, subjective indicators of well-being could provide policy makers with insights as to how people actually perceive the quality of their lives, apart from economic or social trends and conditions. Establishing a national index of SWB would also have the effect of focusing people on the issues surrounding SWB and might open the door to allow psychologists to better disseminate the accumulated findings on SWB to the public.

Virtually all evidence to date identifies the experience of positive emotion and SWB as beneficial. High SWB people are not constantly ecstatic, oblivious to changing conditions around them, and invariant in their emotions; rather, they are flexible, adaptive individuals, successfully coping with ongoing changes in their environments, able to make appropriate emotional reactions in the face of negative or threatening situations. Thus, SWB is an important asset, both to individuals and to societies, and an expanded and intensified study of this phenomenon seems well justified.

APPENDIX A

Prototype Survey, National Index of Subjective Well-Being

(Questions on Life Satisfaction)

A. Thinking about your own life and personal circumstances, how satisfied are you with your life as a whole?

_____ Very satisfied   _____ Somewhat dissatisfied
_____ Satisfied   _____ Dissatisfied
_____ Somewhat satisfied   _____ Very dissatisfied
_____ Neutral

B. Your life is:

_____ Very close to ideal   _____ Somewhat distant from ideal
_____ Close to ideal   _____ Distant from ideal
_____ Somewhat close to ideal   _____ Very distant from ideal
_____ Neutral

(Domain Satisfactions)

Using the following scale:

7 = Very satisfied
6 = Satisfied
5 = Slightly satisfied
4 = Neutral
3 = Slightly dissatisfied
2 = Dissatisfied
1 = Very dissatisfied

Please indicate how satisfied you are with:

_____ Your personal relationships   _____ Your work
_____ Your health   _____ Your leisure time
_____ Your standard of living   _____ Your spiritual life

(Mood questions)

Using a number between 1 and 7, where 1 = Did not have this feeling, and 7 = Felt this very strongly, indicate the degree to which you have felt each of the following:

_____ Happy   _____ Bored
_____ Sad   _____ Energetic
_____ Angry   _____ Unsafe
_____ Stressed   _____ Loved by others
_____ Affectionate   _____ Lonely

If you work at a paying job, during the past week, indicate the degree to which you felt each of the following, using the same scale as above (1 = Did not have this feeling; 7 = Felt this very strongly):

_____ Happy at work   _____ Engaged and interested in your work
_____ Unhappy at work   _____ Bored

Note: In addition to these questions, a set of rotating questions could be included in the survey. These questions might focus on areas where satisfaction is unlikely to change rapidly. From a pool of 20 rotating questions, for example, perhaps 5 might appear each year, so that all questions would appear once every four years. Issues such as traffic congestion, taxes, and leisure time are potential domains. One or two special questions relevant to changing social concerns (e.g., homeland security) may provide important additional data.

REFERENCES

Andersen, B. L., Kiecolt-Glaser, J. K., & Glaser, R. (1994). A biobehavioral model of cancer stress and disease course. *American Psychologist, 49*, 389–404.

Baron, R. A., Fortin, S. P., Frei, R. L., Hauver, L. A., & Shack, M. L. (1990). Reducing organizational conflict: The role of socially induced positive affect. *International Journal of Conflict Management, 1*, 133–152.

Brickman, P., & Campbell, D. T. (1971). Hedonic relativism and planning the good society. In M. H. Appley (Ed.), *Adaptation-level theory* (pp. 287–305). New York: Academic Press.

Brickman, P., Coates, D., & Janoff-Bulman, R. (1978). Lottery winners and accident victims: Is happiness relative? *Journal of Personality and Social Psychology, 36*, 917–927.

Cantor, N. (1990). From thought to behavior: "Having" and "doing" in the study of personality and cognition. *American Psychologist, 45*, 735–750.

Cantor, N., & Sanderson, C. A. (1999). Life task participation and well-being: The importance of taking part in daily life. In D. Kahneman, E. Diener, & N. Schwarz (Eds.), *Well-being: The foundations of hedonic psychology* (pp. 230–243). New York: Russell Sage Foundation.

Clark, A. E., Georgellis, Y., Lucas, R. E., & Diener, E. (2003). *Unemployment alters the setpoint for life satisfaction.* Manuscript in preparation.

Côté, S. (1999). Affect and performance in organizational settings. *Current Directions in Psychological Science, 8*, 65–68.

DeNeve, K. M., & Cooper, H. (1998). The happy personality: A meta-analysis of 137 personality traits and subjective well being. *Psychological Bulletin, 124*, 197–229.

*Diener, E. (2000). Subjective well-being: The science of happiness and a proposal for a national index. *American Psychologist, 55*, 34–43.

Diener, E., & Biswas-Diener, R. (2003, February 4–5). *Findings on subjective well-being, and their implications for empowerment.* Paper presented at the World Bank Conference, Measuring Empowerment: Cross-Disciplinary Perspectives, Washington, DC.

Diener, E., & Diener, C. (1996). Most people are happy. *Psychological Science, 7*(3), 181–185.

Diener, E., Diener, M., & Diener, C. (1995). Factors predicting the subjective well-being of nations. *Journal of Personality and Social Psychology, 69*, 851–864.

Diener, E., Oishi, S., & Lucas, R. E. (2003). Personality, culture, and subjective well-being: Emotional and cognitive evaluations of life. *Annual Review of Psychology, 54*, 403–425.

Diener, E., & Seligman, M. E. P. (2002). Very happy people. *Psychological Science, 13*, 81–84.

*Diener, E., Suh, E. M., Lucas, R. E., & Smith, H. L. (1999). Subjective well-being: Three decades of progress. *Psychological Bulletin, 125*, 276–302.

Donovan, N., & Halpern, D. (2002). *Life satisfaction: The state of knowledge and implications for government.* London: Downing Street Strategy Unit. Retrieved from http://www.strategy.gov.uk/2001/futures/attachments/ls/paper.pdf.

Emmons, R. A. (1986). Personal strivings: An approach to personality and subjective well-being. *Journal of Personality and Social Psychology, 51*, 1058–1068.

Emmons, R. A., & Diener, E. (1985). Personality correlates of subjective well-being. *Personality and Social Psychology Bulletin, 11*, 89–97.

Fredrickson, B. L., & Joiner, T. (2002). Positive emotions trigger upward spirals toward emotional well-being. *Psychological Science, 13*, 172–175.

Fujita, F. (1991). *An investigation of the relation between extraversion, neuroticism, positive affect, and negative affect.* Unpublished master's thesis, University of Illinois at Urbana-Champaign.

*George, J. M., & Brief, A. P. (1992). Feeling good—doing good: A conceptual analysis of the mood at work—organizational spontaneity. *Psychological Bulletin, 112,* 310–329.

Glenn, N. D., & Weaver, C. N. (1981). The contributions of marital happiness to global happiness. *Journal of Marriage and the Family, 43,* 161–168.

Gottman, J. M., Coan, J., Carrere, S., & Swanson, C. (1998). Predicting marital happiness and stability from newlywed interactions. *Journal of Marriage and the Family, 60,* 5–22.

Haring-Hidore, M., Stock, W. A., Okun, M. A., & Witter, R. A. (1985). Marital status and subjective well-being: A research synthesis. *Journal of Marriage and the Family, 47,* 947–953.

Headey, B., & Wearing, A. (1992). *Understanding happiness: A theory of subjective well-being.* Melbourne, Australia: Longman Cheshire.

Hiroto, D. S., & Seligman, M. E. P. (1975). Generality of learned helplessness in man. *Journal of Personality and Social Psychology, 31,* 311–327.

Holmes, D. S. (2001). *Abnormal psychology* (4th ed.). Boston: Allyn & Bacon.

*Kahneman, D., Diener, E., & Schwarz, N. (Eds.). (1999). *Well-being: The foundations of hedonic psychology.* New York: Russell Sage Foundation.

Kasser, T., & Ryan, R. M. (1993). A dark side of the American dream: Correlates of financial success as a central life aspiration. *Journal of Personality and Social Psychology, 65,* 410–422.

Kiecolt-Glaser, J. K. (1999). Stress, personal relationships, and immune function: Health implications. *Brain, Behavior, and Immunity, 13,* 61–72.

Lucas, R. E., Clark, A. E., Georgellis, Y., & Diener, E. (2003). Re-examining adaptation and the set point model of happiness: Reactions to changes in marital status. *Journal of Personality and Social Psychology, 84,* 527–539.

Lucas, R. E., Diener, E., & Suh, E. M. (1996). Discriminant validity of well-being measures. *Journal of Personality and Social Psychology, 71,* 616–628.

Lucas, R. E., & Fujita, F. (2000). Factors influencing the relation between extraversion and pleasant affect. *Journal of Personality and Social Psychology, 79,* 1039–1056.

Lyubomirsky, S., & Lepper, H. S. (2001). *What are the differences between happiness and self-esteem?* Manuscript submitted for publication.

Maddi, S. R., & Kobasa, S. C. (1984). *The hardy executive: Health under stress.* Homewood, IL: Dow Jones-Irwin.

Mangoine, T. W., & Quinn, R. P. (1975). Job satisfaction, counterproductive behavior, and drug use at work. *Journal of Applied Psychology, 60,* 114–116.

Marks, G. N., & Fleming, N. (1999). Influences and consequences of well-being among Australian young people: 1980–1995. *Social Indicators Research, 46,* 301–323.

Mastekaasa, A. (1994). Marital status, distress, and well-being: An international comparison. *Journal of Comparative Family Studies, 25,* 183–205.

Michalos, A. C. (1985). Multiple discrepancies theory (MDT). *Social Indicators Research, 16,* 347–413.

Myers, D. G. (2000). The funds, friends, and faith of happy people. *American Psychologist, 55,* 56–67.

Pavot, W., & Diener, E. (1993a). The affective and cognitive context of self-reported measures of subjective well-being. *Social Indicators Research, 28,* 1–20.

Pavot, W., & Diener, E. (1993b). Review of the Satisfaction with Life Scale. *Psychological Assessment, 5,* 164–172.

Pavot, W., & Diener, E. (2003). Well-being (including life satisfaction). In R. Fernandez-Ballesteros (Ed.), *Encyclopedia of psychological assessment* (Vol. 2, pp. 1097–1101). London: Sage.

Pavot, W., Diener, E., & Fujita, F. (1990). Extraversion and happiness. *Personality and Individual Differences, 11*, 1299–1306.

Sandvik, E., Diener, E., & Seidlitz, L. (1993). Subjective well-being: The convergence and stability of self-report and nonself-report measures. *Journal of Personality, 61*, 317–342.

Scheier, M. F., & Carver, C. S. (1993). On the power of positive thinking: The benefits of being optimistic. *Current Directions in Psychological Science, 2*, 26–30.

Schwarz, N., & Strack, F. (1999). Reports of subjective well-being: Judgmental processes and their methodological implications. In D. Kahneman, E. Diener, & N. Schwarz (Eds.), *Well-being: The foundations of hedonic psychology* (pp. 3–25). New York: Russell Sage Foundation.

Segerstrom, S. C., Taylor, S. E., Kemeny, M. E., & Fahey, J. L. (1998). Optimism is associated with mood, coping, and immune change in response to stress. *Journal of Personality and Social Psychology, 74*, 1646–1655.

*Seligman, M. E. P., & Csikszentmihalyi, M. (2000). Positive psychology: An introduction. *American Psychologist, 55*, 5–14.

Staw, B. M., Sutton, R. I., & Pelled, L. H. (1994). Employee positive emotion and favorable outcomes at the workplace. *Organization Science, 5*, 51–71.

Stroebe, W., Stroebe, M., Abakoumkin, G., & Schut, H. (1996). The role of loneliness and social support in adjustment to loss: A test of attachment versus stress theory. *Journal of Personality and Social Psychology, 70*, 1241–1249.

Suh, E. M. (1999). Culture, identity consistency, and subjective well-being. *Dissertation Abstracts International, 60*(09), 4950-B.

Tait, M., Padgett, M. Y., & Baldwin, T. (1989). Job and life satisfaction: A reevaluation of the strength of the relationship and gender effects as a function of the date of the study. *Journal of Applied Psychology, 74*, 502–507.

Vitaliano, P. P., Russo, J., Young, H. M., Becker, J., & Maiuro, R. D. (1991). The screen for caregiver burden. *Gerontologist, 31*, 76–83.

World Values Study Group. (1994). *World Values Survey, 1981–1984 and 1990–1993* [Computer file, ICPSR version]. Ann Arbor, MI: Institute for Social Research.

Zautra, A. J., Burleson, M. H., Matt, K. S., Roth, S., & Burrows, L. (1994). Interpersonal stress, depression, and disease activity in rheumatoid arthritis and osteoarthritis patients. *Health Psychology, 13*, 139–148.

CHAPTER 41

A Population Approach to Positive Psychology: The Potential for Population Interventions to Promote Well-Being and Prevent Disorder

FELICIA A. HUPPERT

THIS CHAPTER ARGUES for the value of assessing and understanding psychological processes in representative samples of the population. Population-based studies allow us not only to establish how traits, capabilities, and conditions are distributed throughout the population, but also to establish the demographic, psychosocial, health, and biological variables that are associated with them. To date, the focus of population-based health research has been overwhelmingly negative and disease-oriented. It is proposed that by adopting theoretical concepts developed in the field of epidemiology, combined with theoretical and empirical developments in positive psychology, psychologists can both promote positive well-being in the general population and, as a direct consequence, reduce the prevalence of many common physical and mental disorders. This chapter examines the empirical foundations on which population approaches rest and compares the potential efficacy of interventions targeted at individuals who have a disorder (or are at high risk of a disorder) with universal interventions aimed at shifting the whole population in a desirable direction. Several universal intervention programs are described, followed by a review of population studies that specifically measure subjective well-being rather than the absence of disorder, to establish which health and socio-demographic variables are associated with positive psychological states.

I am very grateful to John Helliwell (Vancouver, Canada) and Peter Jones (Cambridge, United Kingdom) for their careful reading of the draft manuscript and their thoughtful comments. My warm thanks to Julian Huppert for preparing the figure.

Some limitations of the research approaches to date, and recommendations for future research and practice conclude the chapter.

INDIVIDUAL VERSUS POPULATION APPROACHES

There are two main approaches to understanding the causes of a disease or disorder. One is an individual-based approach and the other is a population-based approach. The individual-based approach involves the careful definition of a disorder, followed by an investigation of individual characteristics and experiences that may have led to the disorder. The disorders that form the focus of psychological enquiry may be either mental (including both affective and cognitive disorders) or physical, such as cardiovascular disease, obesity, or cancers. The individual factors that psychologists investigate may include aspects of the early environment (e.g., attachment), IQ, temperament, education, social relationships, stress, life events, and genotype. Individual-based research seeks to establish what causes the disorder in the individual by examining such individual differences.

In contrast, population-based research seeks to understand why some populations have more disorder than others. For example, cardiovascular disease is far more common in the United States and the United Kingdom than in Japan and Italy (e.g., Khaw, 1997). Within a nation, cardiovascular disease is strongly related to social inequality, with more disadvantaged groups showing higher prevalence levels of disease. The common mental disorders such as depression and anxiety are also strongly related to social inequality (e.g., D. Melzer, Tom, Brugha, Fryers, & Meltzer, 2002). Epidemiologists (from the Greek "epi" and "demos" meaning "about the people") seek the causes of disorder by examining differences between populations or groups, rather than differences between individuals, an approach shared by some areas of health psychology. The factors under investigation include income distribution, employment rate, environmental toxins, divorce rate, and general lifestyle variables such as dietary patterns and average levels of alcohol consumption and cigarette smoking.

These two contrasting approaches to understanding the causes of disorder bring with them contrasting approaches to treatment. The aim of the individual-based approach is to alleviate symptoms in the individual; the aim of the population-based approach is to reduce the number of individuals who have the disorder. Pharmacological, behavioral, and surgical techniques may be extremely effective in controlling disorders such as heart disease at an individual level. However, for most common disorders, there are community-level as well as individual-level risk factors. By establishing the social and environmental risk factors for heart disease, epidemiologists and health psychologists can play a vital role in reducing the number of people who have the disorder. The treatment method preferred here is population prevention. Reducing the risk factors for disorders in the whole population may sound like a heroic and costly exercise compared to targeting treatment on just those individuals who have the disorder. However, the effectiveness of the population approach has already been demonstrated. For example, the substantial drop in cardiovascular disease in the United States, the United Kingdom, and other developed countries has not arisen primarily from better individual treatments. Rather, it has arisen largely from reducing blood pressure and cholesterol levels in the whole population, as a consequence of successful health promotion measures advocating the importance of exercise, healthy diet, and smoking cessation (Puska, Vartiainen, Tuomilehto, Salomaa, & Nissinen, 1998).

DISTRIBUTION OF RISK FACTORS AND PREVALENCE OF DISORDER

The success of the epidemiological approach in reducing the prevalence of disorder in a population relies on one important property of the risk factors; that they form a continuous distribution in the population. This can be clearly demonstrated using the example of cardiovascular disease. One of the principal risk factors for cardiovascular disease is hypertension, and hypertension is just one extreme of the normal distribution of blood pressure in the population. This general point is illustrated in Figure 41.1. In this case, "threshold for disorder" refers to hypertension which has been defined by the World Health Organization (WHO) as being in excess of specified values of systolic and diastolic blood pressure (more than 160/95 mm Hg; WHO, 1978). Individuals with these very high levels of blood pressure are at much higher risk of developing heart disease. However, even individuals who fall just below the threshold are at increased risk of heart disease compared to individuals whose blood pressure is well below the threshold. So across the full spectrum of blood pressure, the higher the blood pressure, the higher the risk of developing heart disease. Individual-based approaches treat only those individuals who are above the cutpoint, that is, who have diagnosed hypertension.

The population-based approach is radically different. It tries to shift the whole population, so that the population mean of the underlying risk factors (e.g., blood

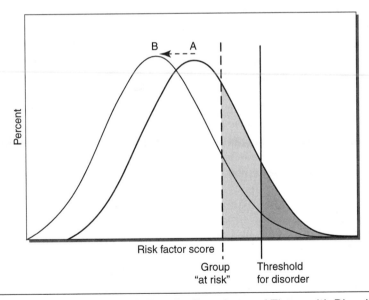

Figure 41.1 Model to Illustrate (a) That the Prevalence of Those with Disorder Is Related to the Population Distribution of Risk Factor Scores and (b) That a Small Downward Shift in the Mean Score from A to B Results in a Large Decrease in the Prevalence of Disorder

pressure) is decreased and, hence, there are many fewer people in the tail of the distribution. Even a tiny shift in the mean of the risk factor can lead to a major decrease in the prevalence of the disorder. This, too, can be seen in Figure 41.1. As the mean risk factor score of population A is shifted downward to the mean of population B, the number of cases of disorder (the tail of the distribution) is sharply reduced. But there is an even greater benefit of the population approach. Paradoxically, the majority of people who develop a disorder come not from the group at highest risk (e.g., those with diagnosed hypertension) but from the group with a lower risk, since they are far more numerous (see Figure 41.1). By lowering the mean risk of the whole population, the total number of cases may be drastically reduced.

This approach does not work for disorders where the underlying risk factors are not continuously distributed in the population. Huntington's disease is an example of where this approach would not work, since it is strongly under genetic control, with half the offspring of an affected parent developing the disorder. However, for most common diseases, the underlying risk factors form a continuous distribution in the population, probably because there are multiple underlying causes of vulnerability. So the epidemiological technique of shifting the population toward a healthier state should be given serious consideration in the realm of mental health.

THE EMPIRICAL CASE FOR A POPULATION APPROACH TO IMPROVING MENTAL HEALTH

The population-based approach to reducing the numbers of people who have a disorder arose from the work of the eminent U.K. epidemiologist Geoffrey Rose. In his landmark book, Rose (1992) demonstrated that the prevalence of many common diseases in a population or subgroup of a population is directly related to the population mean of the underlying risk factors. Therefore, by changing the mean, we should be able to change the prevalence. Rose believed that his approach had relevance for psychiatric disorder as well as for physical disorder, and his hypothesis was first tested by Anderson, Huppert, and Rose (1993). This study examined the distribution of scores on a mental health questionnaire in subpopulations of a nationally representative U.K. sample who took part in the Health and Lifestyle Survey (Cox et al., 1987). Anderson et al. found that the prevalence of clinically significant, above threshold scores on a well-known measure of psychological distress, the General Health Questionnaire (GHQ-30; Goldberg, 1978), was directly related to the mean number of symptoms in the subpopulation. That is, the higher the mean number of symptoms, the higher the prevalence of people in the abnormal category. Moreover, this relationship was evident even when the group with above-threshold scores was excluded when calculating the mean. Anderson et al. also found that the data for any subpopulation lay along a single continuous distribution of symptoms with no excess of cases or evidence of bimodality.

This was a very important discovery since a priori it was entirely possible that we would find a distinct pathological group, with an excess of cases in the high end of the symptom scale, similar to the excess of cases at the low end of the IQ distribution representing the distinct pathologies of severe learning disability. The fact that the mental health data were best described by a dimensional model shows there is no clear boundary between the presence and absence of pathology in relation to common mental disorders (predominantly depression and anxiety). The unidimensionality of symptoms of common mental disorders, and the direct relationship between the population mean and the number of cases, has recently been confirmed by D. Melzer et al. (2002) who analyzed data from almost 10,000 respondents to the OPCS (Office of Population, Census and Surveys) National Household Psychiatric Morbidity Survey (H. Meltzer, Gill, Petticrew, & Hinds, 1995). The dimensional model does not imply the absence of biological or other individual factors in the development of the condition, but does imply that there is a uniform distribution of susceptibility in the population, and that there are population-level factors which influence the development of the condition. Based on their seminal study, Anderson et al. (1993) drew the following conclusions:

> Populations thus carry a collective responsibility for their own mental health and well-being. This implies that explanations for the differing prevalence rates of psychiatric morbidity must be sought in the characteristics of their parent populations; and control measures are unlikely to succeed if they do not involve population-wide changes. (p. 475)

A similar analysis has been undertaken of the relationship between mean alcohol consumption and the prevalence of heavy or problem drinking. Using cross-sectional data on over 32,000 adults who took part in the Health Survey for England, Colhoun, Ben-Shlomo, Dong, Bost, and Marmot (1997) showed that regional mean alcohol consumption of those who do not drink heavily is strongly correlated with the regional prevalence of heavy drinking and also of problem drinking. They conclude that factors that increase mean consumption in light or moderate drinkers are likely to result in an increase in heavy drinking and related problems. Conversely, a small reduction in the mean consumption of light or moderate drinkers (for example by increasing the cost of alcohol or discouraging binge drinking) is likely to result in a substantial decrease in serious alcohol-related problems.

A major policy implication of establishing a population dimensional model of pathology is that reducing prevalence requires population intervention (Rose, 1992). Longitudinal studies can give an indication of the relationship between change in the population mean and change in prevalence. Using a regression analysis on their cross-sectional data, Anderson et al. (1993) predicted that the prevalence of disorder in the overall population would fall by approximately 7% for every unit fall in the population mean GHQ. If the mean population GHQ score fell by one standard deviation, this would correspond to a fall of approximately 40% in the prevalence of disorder.

The basic prediction was tested directly some years later by Whittington and Huppert (1996), who re-interviewed the original population seven years after the initial survey. They showed, for the first time, that changes in the prevalence of psychiatric disorder in a subpopulation were related to changes in the mean number of psychiatric symptoms in that population. They further demonstrated that the relationship is linear and confirmed the earlier prediction: That is, a one point decrease in mean scores on the GHQ was associated with a 6% decrease in prevalence of disorder. The Whittington and Huppert study was observational, but it implies that if population interventions were developed they could potentially have a substantial effect on reducing prevalence of common mental disorder.

A further analysis of the longitudinal data investigated the relationship between baseline scores on the GHQ and subsequent mortality. Numerous studies in the literature had shown that individuals with diagnosed psychiatric disorder had a shorter life expectancy than those without disorder. Huppert and Whittington (1995) established that this relationship between life expectancy and mental health applied right across the distribution of GHQ scores, not only in those with disorder. They found a linear relationship between baseline GHQ score and seven-year survival. The effect was greater for men than for women; for every one point increase in the GHQ score at baseline, there was a 12% increase in the risk of the men dying over the subsequent seven years, when physical health, lifestyle and demographic variables were controlled for. Therefore, interventions that reduce the mean number of psychological symptoms in the population should not only reduce the number of people with common mental disorders, but also reduce premature deaths.

POPULATION PREVENTION STRATEGIES FOR IMPROVING MENTAL HEALTH

Prevention strategies are usually targeted at groups with a disorder or those believed to be at high risk for a disorder. In the former case, the aim is to reduce the severity, duration, or relapse rate of the disorder; in the latter case, the aim is to reduce the likelihood that the disorder will occur. However, in this chapter, the focus is on *population prevention*, that is, measures that are regarded as desirable for everyone in the population. In the physical health domain, such measures include compulsory wearing of seatbelts, fluoridation of drinking water and advocating healthy diet, exercise, sensible drinking, and smoking cessation. In the mental health domain, such measures would include encouragement of positive self-perceptions, social skills, stress reduction, and coping behaviors.

Population prevention measures may be either universal, being applied to every member of the community, or selective, being applied to every member of a subgroup of the community (Jenkins, 1994). These subgroups are usually defined by sociodemographic factors such as age, sex, and occupation. Examples include good antenatal care for pregnant women, and health and social interventions for socially isolated elderly people. We can regard such groups as being at increased risk of certain physical and mental disorders, but the population measures apply to everyone in the subgroup and not just targeted individuals. While the aim of population prevention approaches is usually to reduce pathology, they can have a double payoff, in promoting and enhancing adaptability and healthy functioning for the majority, as well as preventing pathology.

The method of delivering population interventions is obviously a key factor in their success. Educational or health promotion approaches can be offered through organizations such as schools, workplaces, health clinics, or community centers. The media also have a major role to play, both in providing reliable information and in modeling desirable patterns of behavior. In a recent review, Gould (2001) showed a very strong link between media presentations of actual or fictional suicides and the subsequent suicide rate. In Germany, Schmidtke and Hafner (1988) found that each of two showings of a television drama depicting a young man's fictional suicide on a railway track was followed by a significant increase in railway suicides by young men. The media's power for good should also not be underestimated. For example, soap operas which currently portray "life as it is" and thereby appear to condone aggressive behavior, eating disorders, drug taking, or teenage suicide, could as readily promote values such as compassion, self-efficacy, tolerance, and activities that encourage sustainable happiness and fulfillment. Whether population interventions are conducted through community-based organizations or via the media, it is essential to learn from both the successes and failures of health promotion methods in the past to ensure their maximal effectiveness (see Taylor, this volume).

Depression and conduct disorders, such as violence or aggression, are among the behavioral and mental health problems, which may be amenable to being tackled successfully through a population prevention approach. New forms of medication and some of the newer talking therapies (e.g., cognitive therapy) can be extremely effective in alleviating the suffering experienced by an individual when they are in a depressed state, and some forms of cognitive and psychodynamic therapy have been shown to reduce the relapse rate (Paykel et al., 1999). Recent years have seen a huge increase in rates of depression in many countries, as well as rates of suicide, particularly among young people (Cutler, Glaeser, & Norberg, 2000). We can either go on administering effective treatments to ever larger numbers of individuals, or we can try to reduce the prevalence of depression in the population.

Depressive disorder meets the criteria for population prevention, since both the symptoms of depression and many of the major risk factors (e.g., stress, self-esteem) are continuously distributed in the population. The clinical diagnosis of depression can be regarded as an arbitrary cutpoint along a distribution of symptoms; that is, a point at which the symptoms have become so numerous and so disabling that the individual can no longer manage their normal activities. Individuals who do not quite meet diagnostic criteria for depressive disorders may nevertheless be struggling in their daily life. While many valuable interventions are targeted at those "at risk" individuals (e.g., Jaycox, Reivich, Gillham, & Seligman, 1994), individuals without a diagnosed disorder often receive little or no help, and their struggle may have serious effects on their family life, work, and health. By reducing the mean number of depressive symptoms in the population, the whole population could be shifted in a healthy direction, and there would be fewer people in the tail of the distribution who meet the criteria for depressive disorder.

Likewise, Rose (1992) has suggested that deviant behaviors such as violence are "simply the tail of the population's own distribution" (p. 64). Therefore, reducing the mean level of violence or the mean of its risk factors in a population will reduce the prevalence of serious violence and related crime. Thus, the population approach has the huge advantage that the mental health and behavior of the entire population can be improved, and not just that of individuals at high risk or those with diagnosable disorder.

SAMPLE POPULATION PREVENTION PROGRAMS

There is a wealth of programs for the prevention of mental health disorders in at-risk groups (e.g., Gillham, Shatte, & Freres, 2000; Greenberg, Domitrovich, & Bumbarger, 1999; Seligman, Schulman, DeRubeis, & Hollon, 1999; Stathakos & Roehrle, 2003) and some are administered through universal organizations such as schools (e.g., Jaycox et al., 1994). However, such approaches not only miss the opportunity of improving mental health and functioning for everyone, but they may stigmatize the targeted individuals. Fortunately, there are a growing number of universal interventions for young people that are usually school-based, and some are described in the next section. At the present time, however, it is hard to find mental health interventions that specifically target the adult population. One valuable initiative is reviewed here.

POSITIVE PARENTING PROGRAM

In view of the fundamental importance of child development in the early years, and the evidence for a sensitive period with respect to the effects of stress on the developing nervous system and behavioral outcomes (Dawson, Ashman, & Carver, 2000), a series of linked programs in Australia has focused on parental education (Sanders, 1999; Sanders, Montgomery, & Brechman-Toussaint, 2000; Sanders, Turner, & Markie-Dadds, 2002). This program, known as Triple P (Positive Parenting Program), is administered in a variety of ways, including both community-based and media interventions. Sanders and his colleagues report on the effects of a 12-episode television series, *Families,* on disruptive child behavior and family relationships. The initial report was based on only 56 parents of children aged between 2 and 8 years, who were randomly assigned to either watching the television series or to a waiting list control group. Compared to the control group, parents in the television viewing condition reported significantly lower levels of disruptive child behavior and higher levels of perceived parenting competence, and as measured by a 36-item child behavior inventory, the prevalence of disruptive behavior dropped from around 43% to 14%. The authors also report that all postintervention effects were maintained at six-month follow-up.

The Triple P intervention has now been extended so that all parents of preschool children in the region are eligible to participate. A shortened version of the program is delivered through community health services. It involves an eight-week parenting skills training program consisting of group sessions followed by telephone consultations. In Western Australia, over 4,000 families have participated in the program. Program evaluation has documented an increase in the use of positive parenting strategies as opposed to harsh, punitive strategies, a decrease in parental reports of the number and intensity of child behavior problems, a decrease in parental depression, anxiety, and stress, and an increase in marital or relationship satisfaction. It has been estimated that if carried out at a universal level and if all eligible families enrolled, Triple P would reduce the total proportion of preschool children with significant behavior problems by around 40% (Lewis, 1996).

Such initiatives should be applauded; they produce valuable outcomes in the short term and probably in the long term, and are unlikely to do harm. However, an unavoidable limitation is that, although the program was offered to all members of the specific population (parents of preschool children), it was only taken up by some parents, who are likely to be unrepresentative of the population as a whole. Hence, it may miss those who have the most to gain. Intervention via the mass media probably provides the best vehicle for the general adult population.

SCHOOL-BASED INTERVENTIONS

The universality of schooling (at least in developed countries) makes schools the ideal place for the delivery of mental health interventions for children. This has been recognized in a number of programs, some of which teach cognitive and emotional skills, while others emphasize interpersonal relationships. In one large program from Virginia, adolescents are taught life skills by high school students in interactive classroom sessions. The program is called "Going for the Goal" and involves adolescents learning how to identify positive life goals, focus on the process of goal attainment rather than the outcome, identify behaviors which facilitate or compromise goal attainment, and find or create social support (Danish, 1996). The program has been administered to tens of thousands of adolescents in numerous cities in the United States.

While potentially very effective, such programs have not always been evaluated against matched control groups. The Penn Resiliency Program is an exciting school-based initiative that aims to prevent depression in adolescents. It involves 12 two-hour sessions of cognitive behavior therapy and its effectiveness compared with controls has recently been demonstrated (Freres, Gillham, Reivich, & Shatte, 2002). An excellent review of universal interventions for the prevention of mental health disorders in school-age children has been carried out by Greenberg et al. (1999). They identified 14 universal preventive interventions that had undergone a quasi-experimental or randomized evaluation and had been found to produce positive outcomes in either symptom reduction or reduction of risk factors. One of the largest such programs was the Norwegian nationwide intervention campaign to prevent school bullying. Both bullying and being a victim of bullying are major risk factors for mental health problems, as well as being undesirable in their own right. The program involved extensive information for teachers describing current knowledge on the nature, causes, and effects of school bullying and detailed suggestions for its reduction and prevention. Videos and questionnaires were provided for the children, and written information was provided for all Norwegian families with school-age children. Olweus (1991) conducted a quasi-experimental study of this campaign with approximately 2,500 pupils, and reports a reduction of around 50% in bullying and related problems, with more marked effects after two years than after one year. There was also a reduction in general anti-social behavior such as vandalism, theft, truancy, and drunkenness.

A recent Special Issue of the American Psychologist (Weissberg & Kumpfer, 2003) presents the most up-to-date information on prevention of mental health and behavioral problems in children, and includes examples of universal interventions. While authors of universal intervention studies acknowledge the value of promoting competence and positive mental health among all children, the measured outcomes commonly focus on reductions in psychopathology rather than positive benefits for the whole population. Testing the applicability of the Rose (1992) model described earlier, following these programs would be a valuable exercise.

EXPLORING THE POSITIVE IN POPULATION STUDIES

The content of an effective population intervention program needs to be solidly based on epidemiological evidence concerning the demographic, social, and environmental factors that confer risk or protection. There is a wealth of data related to risk factors for mental disorders and impaired functioning, particularly those affecting early childhood development and adolescence, the working population and the elderly. However, there have been surprisingly few population-based studies of what characterizes individuals who are mentally healthy and well-functioning, nor of the factors that protect individuals from developing disorders despite adverse circumstances. This point has been eloquently made by Ryff and Singer (1998a, 2000).

However, there are some notable exceptions that have investigated positive well-being in representative population samples and we will focus on just a few. These include Canada's National Population Health Survey, the British Health & Lifestyle Survey, and the National Study of Midlife Development in the United States (MIDUS). These studies have used a variety of measures of positive psychological well-being and have examined the relationship between these measures and a range of demographic, social, and environmental factors. The principal findings are summarized next.

ILLUSTRATIVE POPULATION STUDIES

The National Population Health Survey in Canada administered measures of both positive and negative mental health to almost 18,000 participants aged 12 and above (Stephens, Dulberg, & Joubert, 1999). The measures included sense of coherence (Antonovsky, 1993), self-esteem (Rosenberg, 1965), sense of mastery (Pearlin, Lieberman, Menaghan, & Mullan, 1981), and a single item assessing happiness and interest in life.

The Health & Lifestyle Survey in Britain examined positive and negative well-being in a nationally representative sample of over 6,000 community residents aged 18 and above (Cox et al., 1987). Both positive and negative measures were derived from the General Health Questionnaire (GHQ-30; Goldberg, 1978), a widely used and well-validated mental health measure. Positive well-being was based on positive responses to the 15 positively worded items, and negative well-being was based on a standard GHQ measure of symptoms of psychological distress (Huppert & Whittington, 2003).

MIDUS administered a measure of psychological well-being developed by Ryff and her colleagues (Ryff & Singer, 1996) to a nationally representative sample of around 3,000 adults aged 25 to 74. They assessed six dimensions of psychological well-being: self-acceptance, positive relations with others, autonomy, environmental mastery, purpose in life, and personal growth.

There have also been many large economic and social surveys that include measures of well-being. They tend to use single items measuring happiness or life satisfaction, but their findings are relevant here and some are reported next.

DEMOGRAPHIC AND SOCIAL INFLUENCES ON WELL-BEING

Gender   It has long been known that compared with men, women have a higher prevalence of psychological disorder as well as reporting a higher number of symptoms of psychological distress. But what is the relationship between gender and positive measures of well-being? Large social surveys that have included a single item on happiness or life satisfaction tend to find little evidence of gender differences (e.g., Donovan & Halpern, 2002; Helliwell, 2003). In the Canadian study, men obtained higher scores than women on all the positive measures with the exception of happiness/interest in life where there was no difference (Stephens et al., 1999). Similar findings were obtained in the British Health & Lifestyle Survey, where men obtained higher total scores on the positive items than did women (Huppert & Whittington, 2003). However, GHQ items load on five robust and replicable factors, and on one of these, social functioning (which contains only positive items), women had higher scores than men (Huppert, Walters, Day, & Elliott, 1989). This is consistent with data from the MIDUS study that showed that scores for men and women were largely similar on all dimensions with the major exception that women scored higher on positive social relations with others (Ryff & Singer, 1998b).

Age   The association between age and well-being has also been examined in all the large surveys. The findings depend on what aspect of well-being is being assessed. In the Health and Lifestyle Survey, the total score on the positive items decreased with advancing age, as did the scores on the positive subfactors social functioning and self-efficacy (Huppert & Whittington, 2003). In contrast, the Canadian and U.S. studies found that on some measures, the scores improved with advancing age. Stephens et al. (1999) reported that sense of coherence increased progressively with advancing age, while self-esteem, sense of mastery, and happiness/interest in life were highest in midlife. In the Canadian study, younger people had the lowest prevalence of positive mental health overall and the highest prevalence of mental health problems. In the MIDUS study, scores improved with age on two of the dimensions (autonomy, environmental mastery), declined with age on two dimensions (personal growth, purpose in life), and showed no change on the two remaining dimensions (positive relations, self-acceptance).

Education   The MIDUS study shows an interesting relationship between psychological well-being and education. Individuals with college education rated themselves higher on all dimensions than those with less than a college education, and this was particularly marked for the dimensions of environmental mastery, positive relations with others, and self-acceptance. The educational differences were particularly prominent for women. Autonomy was the single dimension of well-being that showed no educational differences. Similarly, the Canadian study showed that self-esteem, mastery, and happiness/interest in life all increased with increasing formal education. However, caution is needed in the interpretation of these findings. In a review of the literature on subjective well-being, Diener, Suh, Lucas, and Smith (1999) concluded that most of the relationship between education and subjective well-being can be explained by the fact that the more highly educated tend to have higher incomes, better health, and more social contacts. Once these factors are controlled for, the relationship tends to diminish or disappear. On this basis, we might expect that occupational social class, which is highly correlated with education and income, would be related to subjective well-being measures, but data from the Health & Lifestyle Survey failed to find such a relationship (Huppert & Whittington, 2003).

Income   There is a relationship between income and well-being such that those with higher income tend to report being happier or more satisfied with their life. However, over recent decades, average income has increased substantially, while happiness levels have remained fairly static (Helliwell, 2003). Cross-national studies show a steep rise in reported happiness/satisfaction as GDP increases, but only up to the point at which income is sufficient for basic needs to be met;

beyond that point, the curve flattens out and higher national income does not increase national happiness (Layard, 2003).

Social Relationships   All the evidence suggests that social factors have a much greater effect on mental health than do demographic factors or income. The Canadian study showed social support was strongly associated with all positive and negative measures (in opposite directions). The Health & Lifestyle Survey found that perceived social support and number of social roles were related to measures of both positive and negative well-being, although their effect was greater on negative scores. Research using a wide range of sampling techniques and assessment methods confirms that social relationships (having friends, workmates, supportive relatives, and being engaged in the community) are a very important determinant of happiness and subjective well-being (Argyle, 2002; Diener et al., 1999; Helliwell, 2003). Social relationships appear to have a dual effect on well-being; they have both a direct effect which is probably related to our evolutionary origin as social animals, and an indirect effect which involves buffering the adverse behavioral and physiological responses to stress (House, Landis, & Umberson, 1988). In this context, it is interesting that a school-based intervention program that focused on developing supportive social interactions with peers and teachers proved to be more effective in adjustment to school change and academic performance than a program that focused on coping and problem-solving skills (Felner et al., 1993).

STRESS, PHYSICAL HEALTH, AND WELL-BEING

Stress   Stress appears to have a very powerful effect on well-being, whether defined in terms of adverse life events, chronic stressors, or daily hassles. However, studies have not always separated the effects of stress on positive and negative measures. In the Canadian National Population Health Survey, a measure of current stress was one of the strongest correlates of mental health status, being strongly related to all the positive and negative measures. This study also obtained information about the number of childhood traumas, and this measure was strongly associated with a sense of coherence and to a lesser extent with mastery and happiness, but interestingly it was unrelated to self-esteem. Childhood trauma was also strongly related to negative measures of depression and distress. The Health and Lifestyle Survey included a measure of recent life events and how stressful they were perceived to be. Stress was one of the strongest determinants of symptoms of psychological distress but was less strongly related to measures of positive well-being. An interesting finding from the Health & Lifestyle Survey is that unemployment, a typical stressor, is more strongly related to the absence of good feelings than to the presence of psychological symptoms (Huppert & Whittington, 2003). This is an important observation because in many studies these two different phenomena are not distinguished and hence erroneous conclusions may be reached.

Physical Health   With regard to the relationship between physical health and well-being, it seems obvious that psychological well-being is reduced when our physical health is acutely or chronically compromised. Indeed, many studies report an association between measures of subjective well-being and physical health in the expected direction (e.g., Ryff & Singer, 1998a). However, it is often impossible to disentangle to what extent the relationship arises primarily from an association between low scores on the well-being scale and physical health problems, rather than between high scores on the well-being scale and good physical health. This is because most well-being scales have a response range from very positive to very negative. To establish the true relationship between positive well-being and physical health, we need to look at positive responses to positive well-being items. For example, in the Canadian study, positive well-being was defined categorically, in terms of scores above a cutpoint on the positive mental health scales. A strong association was found between reports of physical health problems and scores on the negative mental health scales, but physical health was unrelated to any of the indices of positive mental health. The extensive social survey literature using happiness and life satisfaction measures shows only a weak relationship between these measures and self-reports of physical health problems. However, there is a very strong relationship between these measures and global self-reported health; that is, replies to the questions "In general, would you say your health is excellent, very good, good, fair or poor?" (Donovan & Halpern, 2002). Yet, the strength of the association with global self-reported health may reflect a response bias, rather than a true association between objective physical health and subjective well-being. Consistent with the weak relationship between reported health problems and positive measures of well-being, Huppert and Whittington (2003) have found that current illness symptoms and chronic conditions or disability while being related to both positive and negative measures of well-being, were more strongly related to the negative measures. Their positive measure comprised positive responses to positive items. Indeed there are reports that even individuals with a very serious physical disability such as paraplegia show an initial reduction in happiness and life satisfaction, but return to their normal levels within a relatively short period (Kahneman, 1999). Such findings point to the central importance of including genuinely positive measures of subjective well-being in research studies.

This point is further reinforced in a recent re-analysis of the relationship between scores on a psychological symptom scale and mortality in the following seven years (Huppert & Whittington, 1995, 2003). In the original study, mortality was found to be linearly related to the number of psychological symptoms reported on the GHQ-30. However, this study used a standard GHQ symptom score that did not differentiate between positive and negative scores. In the re-analysis reported in Huppert and Whittington (2003), it was found that 7-year mortality was associated with the absence of positive well-being rather than the presence of psychological symptoms. This finding highlights the need to improve well-being for normal people in the population, rather than always focusing on those with problems.

FUTURE DIRECTIONS

As stated earlier, effective population interventions require evidence-based strategies for enhancing mental health. This brief review of data from representative population samples demonstrates, however, that we seem to know a great deal more about what impairs mental health than what enhances it. Factors such as social support, stress, and physical health problems all appear to exert a larger effect on negative measures of well-being than on positive ones. In other words, the absence of chronic or acute stressors, the absence of physical health problems, or the presence of social support does not appear to do much to enhance our well-being and enjoyment of life. This may be because we have been looking at the wrong kinds of variables. As others have noted (e.g., Ryff & Singer, 1998a), the absence of physical health problems is not the same as physical thriving, but constructs such as physical energy or vitality are rarely measured. Likewise, social support, while invaluable for helping us through times of stress or illness, may play a little role in positive experiences such as joy or creativity. We need to find better ways of measuring social relationships that are more relevant to positive affect and positive behaviors. The richer concept of "positive social relations with others" (Ryff & Singer, 1996) offers a valuable alternative.

CONCLUSION

Clinical and health psychologists have developed and refined a range of techniques for improving the psychological well-being of patients with mental and physical disorders. Psychological well-being has been linked to a variety of beneficial physiological processes including reductions in levels of the stress hormone cortisol and improvements in immune function (Seeman, Singer, Rowe, Horwitz, & McEwen, 1997). Thus, improving the psychological well-being of individuals with a disorder not only reduces symptoms of the disorder but initiates a positive spiral of processes that decrease morbidity and increase survival (Ryff & Singer, 2000).

Many interventions also target individuals who are at high risk of a disorder such as those with a family history of disorder or individuals who are socially disadvantaged or have experienced a major trauma. These early interventions to prevent mental health problems or reduce their impact (e.g., by providing support and developing coping skills) can have long-lasting beneficial effects on the individual and their family.

This chapter has taken the further step of advocating that many of the techniques developed by clinical and health psychologists can be used to improve the psychological well-being of the whole population. Moreover, it is argued that by focusing on interventions at the population level, we will reduce the number of people in the population who have mental disorders, as well as reducing the numbers of those at high risk of disorder. These claims are based on the Rose (1992) model of disease that underpins much of modern epidemiology. The relevance of the model to mental health has been demonstrated in population studies showing that symptoms or risk factors for common mental disorders form a continuous distribution throughout the population, and that the prevalence of disorder is related to the mean level of symptoms in the population (Anderson et al., 1993; Colhoun et al., 1997; D. Melzer et al., 2002; Whittington & Huppert, 1996). Therefore, reducing symptoms or risk factors in the population should reduce the prevalence of disorder.

To date, the mental health studies demonstrating this relationship have been observational, both cross-sectional and longitudinal. But there is every reason to suppose that population interventions that succeed in reducing mean symptoms or risk factors will also reduce prevalence of disorder. Durlak (1995) has pointed out that if only 8% of normal children go on to have serious adjustment problems as adults (as against 30% of clinically dysfunctional children), the normal children would account for the great majority of maladjusted adults, simply because there are so many more of them. There is clearly a strong case for prevention programs that promote well-being and enhance resilience in the whole population. However, studies that examine the long-term effects of population intervention programs are much needed. Targeted interventions will still be required for individuals with disorder or those at high risk, but there should be many fewer individuals in these categories.

When combined with insights from positive psychology, it can be argued that the aim of the population approach is to improve the lives of normal people in terms of their psychological well-being, their vitality, their capabilities, and their social relationships. This may sound utopian, but some population interventions that are already in place, suggest that many of these goals are feasible and practical. Policymakers both within the health field and beyond (e.g., Layard, 2003) are beginning to take a real interest in population interventions to improve psychological well-being because of the benefits to society, both in the short-term and the long-term. Population-based positive psychology may well be in the forefront of health and social reforms in the coming decades.

REFERENCES

Anderson, J., Huppert, F. A., & Rose, G. (1993). Normality, deviance and minor psychiatric morbidity in the community. *Psychological Medicine, 23,* 475–485.

Antonovsky, A. (1993). The structure and properties of the Sense of Coherence Scale. *Social Science and Medicine, 36,* 725–33.

Argyle, M. (2002). *Psychology of happiness.* New York: Routledge.

Colhoun, H., Ben-Shlomo, Y., Dong, W., Bost, L., & Marmot, M. (1997). Ecological analysis of collectivity of alcohol consumption in England: Importance of average drinker. *British Medical Journal, 314,* 1164–1168.

Cox, B. D., Blaxter, M., Buckle, A. L. J., Fenner, N. P., Golding, J. F., Gore, M., et al. (1987). *The Health and Lifestyle Survey: Preliminary report of a nationwide survey of the physical and mental health, attitudes and lifestyle of a random sample of 9003 British adults.* London: Health Promotion Research Trust.

Cutler, D. M., Glaeser, E., & Norberg, K. (2000). *Explaining the rise in youth suicide* (NBER Working Paper No. 7713). Cambridge, England: National Bureau of Economic Research.

Danish, S. J. (1996). Going for the goal: A life skills program for adolescents. In G. W. Albee & T. P. Gullotta (Eds.), *Primary prevention works* (pp. 291–312). Newbury Park, CA: Sage.

Dawson, G., Ashman, S. B., & Carver, L. J. (2000). The role of early experience in shaping behavioral and brain development and its implications for social policy. *Development and Psychopathology, 12,* 695–712.

Diener, E., Suh, E. M., Lucas, R. E., & Smith, H. L. (1999). Subjective well-being: Three decades of progress. *Psychological Bulletin, 125,* 276–302.

Donovan, N., & Halpern, D. (2002). *Life satisfaction: The state of knowledge and implications for government.* London: Downing Street Strategy Unit. Retrieved from http://www .strategy.gov.uk/2001/futures/attachments/ls/paper.pdf.

Durlak, J. A. (1995). *School-based prevention programs for children and adolescents.* Thousand Oaks, CA: Sage.

Felner, R. D., Brand, S., Adan, A. M., Mulhall, P. F., Flowers, N., Sartain, B., et al. (1993). Restructuring the ecology of the school as an approach to prevention during school transitions: Longitudinal follow-ups and extensions of the school transitional environment project (STEP). *Prevention in Human Services, 10,* 103–136.

Freres, D. R., Gillham, J. E., Reivich, K., & Shatte, A. J. (2002). Preventing depressive symptoms in middle school students: The Penn Resiliency Program. *International Journal of Emergency Mental Health, 4*, 31–40.

Gillham, J. E., Shatte, A. J., & Freres, D. R. (2000). Preventing depression: A review of cognitive-behavioral and family interventions. *Applied and Preventative Psychology, 9*, 63–88.

Goldberg, D. P. (1978). *Manual of the General Health Questionnaire.* London: NFER-Nelson.

Gould, M. S. (2001). Suicide and the media. *Annals of the New York Academy of Sciences, 932*, 200–221.

*Greenberg, M. T., Domitrovich, C., & Bumbarger, B. (1999). *Preventing mental disorders in school-age children: A review of the effectiveness of prevention programs.* Hyattsville, MD: U.S. Department of Health and Human Services, Report for Center for Mental Health Services.

Helliwell, J. F. (2003). How's life? Combining individual and national variables to explain subjective well-being. *Economic Modelling, 20*, 331–360.

House, J. S., Landis, K. R., & Umberson, D. (1988). Social relationships and health. *Science, 241*, 540–545.

Huppert, F. A., Walters, D. E., Day, N., & Elliott, B. J. (1989). The factor structure of the General Health Questionnaire (GHQ-30): A reliability study on 6317 community residents. *British Journal of Psychiatry, 155*, 178–185.

Huppert, F. A., & Whittington, J. E. (1995). Symptoms of psychological distress predict seven-year mortality. *Psychological Medicine, 25*, 1073–1086.

*Huppert, F. A., & Whittington, J. E. (2003). Evidence for the independence of positive and negative well-being: Implications for quality of life assessment. *British Journal of Health Psychology, 8*, 107–122.

Jaycox, L., Reivich, K., Gillham, J. E., & Seligman, M. E. P. (1994). Prevention of depressive symptoms in school children. *Behavior Research and Therapy, 32*, 801–816.

Jenkins, R. (1994). Principals of prevention. In E. S. Paykel & R. Jenkins (Eds.), *Prevention in psychiatry* (pp. 11–24). London: Gaskell.

Kahneman, D. (1999). Objective happiness. In D. Kahneman, E. Diener, & N. Schwarz (Eds.), *Well-being: The foundations of hedonic psychology* (pp. 3–25). New York: Russell Sage Foundation.

Khaw, K.-T. (1997). Epidemiological aspects of aging. *Philosophical Transactions of the Royal Society: Biological Sciences, 352*, 1829–1835.

*Layard, R. (2003). *Happiness—Has social science a clue?* [Lionel Robbins Memorial Lectures 2002/3]. London School of Economics and Political Science.

Lewis, J. (1996). *Triple P—Positive Parenting Program: Evidence based action in child health promotion.* Perth, Australia: Report of the Eastern Perth Public and Community Health Unit.

Meltzer, H., Gill, B., Petticrew, M., & Hinds, K. (1995). *OPCS Surveys of Psychiatric Morbidity in Great Britain, Report: 1. The prevalence of psychiatric morbidity among adults living in private households.* London: Her Majesty's Stationery Office.

Melzer, D., Tom, B. D. M., Brugha, T. S., Fryers, T., & Meltzer, H. (2002). Common mental disorder symptom counts in populations: Are there distinct case groups above epidemiological cutoffs? *Psychological Medicine, 32*, 1195–201.

Olweus, D. (1991). Bully/victim problems among school children: Basic facts and effects of an intervention program. In D. J. Pepler & K. H. Rubin (Eds.), *The development and treatment of childhood aggression* (pp. 411–448). Hillsdale, NJ: Erlbaum.

Paykel, E. S., Scott, J., Teasdale, J. D., Johnson, A. L., Garland, A., Moore, R., et al. (1999). Prevention of relapse in residual depression by cognitive therapy. *Archives of General Psychiatry, 56,* 829–835.

Pearlin, L. I., Lieberman, M., Menaghan, E., & Mullan, J. (1981). The stress process. *Journal of Health and Social Behavior, 22,* 337–358.

Puska, P., Vartiainen, E., Tuomilehto, J., Salomaa, V., & Nissinen, A. (1998). Changes in premature deaths in Finland: Successful long-term prevention of cardiovascular diseases. *Bulletin of the World Health Organization, 76,* 419–425.

*Rose, G. (1992). *The strategy of preventive medicine.* Oxford, England: Oxford University Press.

Rosenberg, M. (1965). *Society and the adolescent self-image.* Princeton, NJ: Princeton University Press.

*Ryff, C. D., & Singer, B. H. (1996). Psychological well-being: Meaning, measurement, and implications for psychotherapy research. *Psychotherapy and Psychosomatics, 65,* 14–23.

Ryff, C. D., & Singer, B. H. (1998a). Contours of positive human health. *Psychological Inquiry, 9,* 1–28.

Ryff, C. D., & Singer, B. H. (1998b). Middle age and well-being. In H. S. Friedman (Ed.), *Encyclopedia of mental health* (Vol. 2, pp. 707–719). San Diego, CA: Academic Press.

Ryff, C. D., & Singer, B. H. (2000). Interpersonal flourishing: A positive health agenda for the new millennium. *Personality and Social Psychology Review, 4,* 30–40.

Sanders, M. R. (1999). Triple P-Positive parenting program: Toward an empirically validated multilevel parenting and family support strategy for the prevention of behavior and emotional problems in children. *Clinical Child and Family Psychology Review, 2,* 71–90.

Sanders, M. R., Montgomery, D. T., & Brechman-Toussaint, M. L. (2000). The mass media and the prevention of child behavior problems: The evaluation of a television series to promote positive outcomes for parents and their children. *Journal of Child Psychology and Psychiatry, 41,* 939–948.

Sanders, M. R., Turner, K. M., & Markie-Dadds, C. (2002). The development and dissemination of the Triple P-Positive Parenting Program: A multilevel, evidence-based system of parenting and family support. *Prevention Science, 3,* 173–189.

Schmidtke, A., & Hafner, H. (1988). The Werther Effect after television films: New evidence from an old hypothesis. *Psychological Medicine, 18,* 665–676.

Seeman, T. E., Singer, B. H., Rowe, J. W., Horwitz, R., & McEwen, B. S. (1997). The price of adaptation: Allostatic load and its health consequences, MacArthur Studies of Successful Aging. *Archives of Internal Medicine, 157,* 2259–2268.

Seligman, M. E. P., Schulman, P., DeRubeis, R. J., & Hollon, S. D. (1999). The prevention of depression and anxiety. *Prevention and Treatment, 2*(8), 1–22.

Stathakos, P., & Roehrle, B. (2003). The effectiveness of intervention programs for children of divorce—a meta-analysis. *International Journal of Mental Health Promotion, 5,* 31–37.

Stephens, T., Dulberg, C., & Joubert, N. (1999). Mental health of the Canadian population: A comprehensive analysis. *Chronic Diseases in Canada, 20,* 118–126.

Weissberg, R. P., & Kumpfer, K. L. (2003, June/July). Prevention that works for children and youth [Special issue]. *American Psychologist, 58.*

Whittington, J. E., & Huppert, F. A. (1996). Changes in the prevalence of psychiatric disorder in a community are related to changes in the mean level of psychiatric symptoms. *Psychological Medicine, 26,* 1253–1260.

World Health Organization. (1978). *Arterial hypertension: Report of a WHO expert committee* (WHO Technical Report Series No. 628). Geneva, Switzerland: Author.

PART XIII

SIGNPOSTS FOR
THE PRACTICE OF
POSITIVE PSYCHOLOGY

CHAPTER 42

Toward a Theoretical Foundation for Positive Psychology in Practice

P. ALEX LINLEY and STEPHEN JOSEPH

I N THIS CONCLUDING chapter, our objectives are to draw together some of the key issues that arise for us through considering the foundations of positive psychology as it moves toward practice. In considering some of these fundamental issues, applied positive psychology will be able to proceed from a solid theoretical, empirical, and epistemological foundation. While we cannot always provide answers, at least by highlighting what we see as some of the key issues, we may hold them up for scrutiny and consideration by others. In this way, we hope that applied positive psychology may evolve as a self-reflective practice, mindful of its fundamental assumptions, explicit about its value position, and integrative in its approach and application.

One of the things that became clear to us in editing the chapters of this volume was the rich but diverse traditions from which positive psychology is drawn. This is undoubtedly a strength, but this diversity has also restricted the development of a theory that may account for and synthesize the research findings from the positive psychology tradition. In grappling with the question of a theory of positive psychological practice, we have identified five core issues. We begin by describing how it is inevitable that any approach to working with people is premised—often implicitly—on a fundamental assumption about human nature. Hence, we start with the core assumption that we believe positive psychology holds about human nature and consider the implications of this for practice.

This fundamental assumption raises a number of further questions, which we consider in the following sections. First, what is the value position that positive psychology adopts and what does this mean for practice? Second, whose agenda should we be working to, as we seek to apply positive psychology? Third, how might a theory of positive psychology serve to integrate the positive and negative aspects of human experience? Fourth, we consider the ramifications of these questions for the nature of knowledge as it is viewed within positive psychology.

In concluding, we review the key points of the preceding sections and propose that it is incumbent upon positive psychology to be self-reflective. We argue that positive psychology should be mindful of its fundamental assumptions, aware of and open to its value position, and cognizant of what each of these mean for us as individual researchers and practitioners in the field.

FUNDAMENTAL ASSUMPTIONS ABOUT HUMAN NATURE

Any practice of psychology rests on a fundamental assumption about human nature. These assumptions do not lend themselves to straightforward empirical inquiry, and hence may be considered as questions of value and morality—and thus individual ethics and preference. Further, these assumptions are typically implicit, and therefore are often uncritically accepted by practitioners trained in a particular model and a particular way of working. It is precisely because these fundamental assumptions are implicit that they are so often taken for granted and unchallenged, assuming the position of the status quo. Importantly, these fundamental assumptions are inevitably formed within a particular social, cultural, and historical context (cf. Marcus & Fischer, 1986; Prilleltensky, 1994). This social, cultural, and historical boundedness, fixed as it is to a particular place and time, may limit the relevance of the fundamental assumptions formed within it as times change.

As Seligman (2002, 2003) notes, much of modern psychology has been dominated by the doctrines of Freud, "the ghost in the machine" of psychology and psychotherapy (Hubble & Miller, Chapter 21, this volume), and yet rarely do psychologists stop and reflect on where and why this view arose. Seligman further explicitly states that it is this view that positive psychology seeks to overthrow (Seligman, 2003).

Positive Psychology's Fundamental Assumption about Human Nature

If positive psychology as a discipline rejects the Freudian, "rotten to the core" view of human nature, what perspectives remain? Implicit within positive psychology is the idea that human beings have the potential for "good," and that we are motivated to pursue a "good life." Thus, our implicit notion of value and morality requires that positive psychology's fundamental assumption about human nature take account of these implicit values (the potential for "good" and the desire for a "good life").

In considering how views of human nature fundamentally influenced our perspective on the promotion of living a good life (or a *morality of evolution*), Horney (1951) delineated three possible positions in trying to understand core human nature. The first position was that people are by nature sinful or driven by primitive instincts (this accords with the Freudian "rotten to the core" view). From this first position, the goal of society must be to contain these destructive impulses. The second position was that inherent within human nature was both something essentially "good" and something essentially "bad," sinful, or destructive. From this second position, the goal of society must be to ensure that the "good" side of human nature triumphs over the "bad" side. The third position was that inherent within people are evolutionary constructive forces that guide people toward realizing their potentialities. Horney was careful to note that this third position did *not* suggest that people were inherently good (since this would presuppose a knowledge of what constitutes good and bad). Rather, the person's values would arise from their striving toward their potential, and these values would thus be constructive and prosocial in their nature (and hence may be considered "good.").

From this third position, the goal of society must be therefore to cultivate the facilitative social-environmental conditions that are conducive to people's self-realization. When people's tendency toward self-realization is allowed expression, Horney (1951) argued that:

> . . . we become free to grow ourselves, we also free ourselves to love and to feel concern for other people. We will then want to give them the opportunity for unhampered growth when they are young, and to help them in whatever way possible to find and realize themselves when they are blocked in their development. At any rate, whether for ourselves or for others, the ideal is the liberation and cultivation of the forces which lead to self-realization. (pp. 15–16)

THE LINEAGE OF THIS FUNDAMENTAL ASSUMPTION

This constructive force for self-realization formed the basis of Horney's (1951) therapeutic approach. A similar position was taken by Rogers (1959, 1964) in describing the concepts of the actualizing tendency and the organismic valuing process, which are at the core of the person-centered model. The actualizing tendency refers to the constructive, directional, developmental force that is believed to reside within all of us. The organismic valuing process (OVP) refers to the ongoing valuing and choices that we make throughout our lives, and the extent to which those values and choices accord with our intrinsic, organismic nature. Similar views have also been expressed by a number of other influential theorists and writers (see Joseph & Linley, Chapter 22, this volume).

One of the earliest proponents of this view was Aristotle, who believed that within each individual there was a unique *daimon*, or spirit, that would guide them to pursue the activities and goals that were right for them. Acting in accordance with a person's daimon would lead to *eudaimonia*, or well-being, while acting against a person's daimon would lead to ill-being (Aristotle, n.d.; see also Kekes, 1995). The daimon would always lead the person in a constructive direction that also facilitated, rather than undermined, the well-being of others.

These three perspectives proposed by Aristotle, Horney, and Rogers all agree that there is a constructive developmental tendency within human nature, and that this tendency, when given appropriate expression, leads to the well-being of both the individual and their wider community and society. They are also consistent in the way in which they each account for ill-being or psychopathology, suggesting that ill-being and psychopathology arise to the extent that the individual has lost contact with their innate directional force.

It is this assumption, that people possess an innate constructive directional tendency, we argue, that positive psychology has (implicitly) adopted. It is this directional tendency that motivates us to pursue a "good life," and our "positive" values arise from our strivings toward this "good life." Arguably the best articulation of this position was put forward by Rogers (1959) and since has been developed by other theorists and researchers who have been informed by the humanistic, and particularly the person-centered psychology tradition (see, e.g., Sheldon & Kasser, 2001). Hence, we use terminology here that respects and integrates this lineage of positive psychology.

EVIDENCE CONSISTENT WITH THIS FUNDAMENTAL ASSUMPTION

What evidence is consistent with this organismic valuing process? We then go on to consider the implications of this for practice (see also Joseph & Linley, Chapter 22, this volume). At the core of this concept is the distinction between the internal locus of evaluation and the external locus of evaluation. The internal locus is reflected in motivations and behaviors that arise from within and are the result of the individual's intrinsic directional force (i.e., the actualizing tendency). The external locus is reflected in motivations and behaviors that arise from outside of the individual and are the result of the perceived influence of other people, whether real or imagined. These ideas are developed more fully in Rogers' work on the internal locus of evaluation (e.g., Rogers, 1951, 1964) and the self-determination theory perspectives on the range of sources for motivation (see, e.g., Brown & Ryan, Chapter 7, this volume; Deci & Ryan, 1985; Ryan & Deci, 2000).

In reviewing research within the positive psychology tradition, it is clear that the weight of evidence falls squarely in support of this internal-external distinction. It is also clear that well-being is consistently associated with internal, rather than external pursuits. Our views of a good life are inherently our own, they cannot be imposed by others (King, Eels, & Burton, Chapter 3, this volume). Intrinsic motivation for tasks leads to flow and optimal experience (Csikszentmihalyi, 1990; Delle Fave & Massimini, Chapter 35, this volume). Intrinsic valuing leads to subjective and psychological well-being (Kasser, 2002; Kasser, Chapter 4, this volume), and this holds even when the goals themselves are external, but the motivation for pursuing them is internal (Carver & Baird, 1998; Sagiv, Roccas, & Hazan, Chapter 5, this volume). Pursuing goals that are self-concordant (i.e., that fit with our intrinsic values and aspirations) leads to both goal attainment and increased well-being (Sheldon & Elliot, 1999; Sheldon & Houser-Marko, 2001). Further, as people shift their goals over time, they are more likely to do so in ways that reflect the OVP (Sheldon, Arndt, & Houser-Marko, 2003). Healthy self-regulation is facilitated by mindfulness and autonomy—that is, being aware of, open to, and choosing our own directions (Brown & Ryan, 2003; Brown & Ryan, Chapter 7, this volume). The sources of our happiness lie within us, whether through reference to our genetic makeup or the intentional activities that we undertake (Sheldon & Lyubomirsky, Chapter 8, this volume).

Within the clinical setting, it is the client who is the engine of therapeutic change—not the therapist or their therapeutic model (Hubble & Miller, Chapter 21, this volume; Wampold, 2001). Similarly, hope, posttraumatic growth, and psychological well-being are not imposed from without, but are facilitated from within (Lopez et al., Chapter 24, this volume; Ruini & Fava, Chapter 23, this volume; Tedeschi & Calhoun, Chapter 25, this volume). The existential approach pays particular attention to the individual and their way of "being in the world" (Bretherton & Ørner, Chapter 26, this volume). When the needs of offenders are recognized and these needs built into treatment and rehabilitation programs, re-offending is significantly reduced (Ward & Mann, Chapter 36, this volume).

Within the work setting, leadership works when it fits with the needs and aspirations of the individuals being led (Sivanathan, Arnold, Turner, & Barling, Chapter 15, this volume). Employees perform best when their strengths are being used (Hodges & Clifton, Chapter 16, this volume). Executive coaching is most effective when it assimilates with the coachee (Kauffman & Scoular, Chapter 18, this volume). Organizations are at their most positive and creative when they empower their staff through recognizing and supporting them in their strengths and differences (Henry, Chapter 17, this volume). In terms of the financial bottom line, workers who have their needs met by the organization are not only more satisfied, but also more productive (cf. Judge, Thoresen, Bono, & Patton, 2001).

Consider the role of an internal locus in curiosity, gratitude, forgiveness, and spirituality. We cannot be genuinely curious because of external forces (Kashdan & Fincham, Chapter 30, this volume), or genuinely grateful because we are compelled to be so (Bono, Emmons, & McCullough, Chapter 29, this volume). Forgiveness only works when it comes from within (Fincham & Kashdan, Chapter 37, this volume), just as spirituality or religion confer benefits through people's intrinsic identification with them (Pargament & Mahoney, 2002).

At the heart of positive psychology is its explicit focus on strengths and virtues (see Peterson & Park, Chapter 27, this volume). In describing human strengths, Peterson and Seligman (2003) wrote that a person's signature strengths convey a sense of ownership and authenticity in their use, an intrinsic yearning to use them and a feeling of inevitability in doing so. Hence, using our signature strengths is considered to be concordant with our intrinsic interests and values.

The fundamental message of this is clear. Implicit throughout positive psychology is a position on human nature that speaks directly to the ideas of the OVP. To function optimally, people need to function intrinsically. This intrinsic valuing, motivation, and behavior accords with people's innate actualizing tendency and OVP, and affords them well-being (i.e., eudaimonia), one of the goals of applied positive psychology.

EVIDENCE THAT QUESTIONS THIS FUNDAMENTAL ASSUMPTION

However, it is clear from the irresponsibility and suffering in the world that people do not always follow their OVP. Criticisms of this approach are not new, and Rogers was often criticized for what some people saw to be his "Pollyanna theorizing." However, he argued that:

> I am certainly not blind to all the evil and the terribly irresponsible violence that is going on . . . There are times that I think I don't give enough emphasis on the shadowy side of our nature, the evil side. Then I start to deal with a client and discover how, when I get to the core, there is a wish for more socialization, more harmony, more positive values. Yes, there are all kinds of evil abounding in the world, but I do not believe this is inherent in the human species any more than I believe that animals are evil. (cited in Zeig, 1987, p. 202)

In asking the question as to whether the current evil and suffering in the world are evidence that might be used to dismiss the idea of this constructive directional force, we are left with a consideration of the presence or absence of the facilitative social-environmental conditions. Just as an acorn will develop into an oak tree with the right environmental conditions (soil, water, light), so people will grow and develop in socially constructive directions, provided that the social-environmental conditions are facilitative of their growth. Hence, this view locates "evil" within the absence of facilitative social-environmental conditions, rather than as an inherent aspect of human nature per se. In this way, far greater emphasis is placed on the social-environmental context in which an individual is embedded.

THE IMPORTANCE OF A FACILITATIVE SOCIAL-ENVIRONMENTAL CONTEXT

Positive psychology is thus inevitably drawn toward understanding the individual within his or her social-environmental context. This approach requires a different way of thinking about people than is prevalent in current mainstream (cognitive) psychology where the emphasis is on the individual and their internal processes. To understand the individual more fully, they must be seen as but a small part of a much larger social-environmental context, which likely has a strong influence over their attitudes, behaviors, and cognitions.

In recognizing the role of powerful social-environmental forces in shaping our individual experience, it becomes clear that the OVP may be inevitably distorted by powerful but nonfacilitative social-environmental conditions. A central issue then rests on what would constitute facilitative social-environmental conditions, and what applied positive psychologists may do to promote and maintain them. This question is beyond the scope of this chapter, but the interested reader is referred to Rogers (1959), as well as the self-determination theory perspectives provided by Deci and Ryan (2000), Ryan (1995), and Ryan and Deci (2000).

As positive psychology seeks an integrative theory of optimal human functioning, we propose that the idea of an organismic valuing process provides that theory and has much empirical support to underpin it. The implications of this for practice in terms of our value position, the agenda to which we are working, our understanding of positive and negative functioning, and the epistemologies that we consider appropriate, all follow from this fundamental assumption. It is to these that we turn next.

VALUE ASSUMPTIONS

Just as our way of working with people assumes a fundamental view about human nature, it also assumes a value position. Again, more often than not, this value position is implicit, and rarely held up to scrutiny or criticism, but it is nonetheless still inescapable (Christopher, 1996). In posing this question for positive psychology and the practice of positive psychology, it is our intention to make explicit the value assumptions that positive psychologists have typically adopted and to recognize them both for what they offer and what they restrict.

VALUE ASSUMPTIONS WITHIN THE NAME "POSITIVE PSYCHOLOGY"

First, within the name of the discipline itself, we find a value assumption. *Positive psychology* suggests a value assumption of the *positive* (whatever it may be). Implicit within that assumption is the view that the *positive* is both good and desirable. We do not dispute any of these points. However, as some criticisms suggest (Held, 2003; Norem, 2003), *positive* psychology could be taken to imply that anything that is not positive psychology is *negative* psychology. This is a position we explicitly disavow. Rather, we agree with the view espoused by Sheldon and King (2001, p. 216) that "positive psychology is simply psychology." While this position is not conveyed by the name of the discipline, like Diener (2003), we suggest that "positive psychology" is likely here to stay. The time has passed for debates about alternative descriptors (e.g., strengths psychology), and the time has arrived for us to be explicit about what we mean in using the term.

Positive psychology came about in response to the predominant late twentieth-century orientation of mainstream psychology to disease and the medical model. As such, it is entirely understandable that in this early phase of its history, there was the need for an emphasis on what was different about this approach. However, five years on, the pendulum has now swung away from an exclusive focus on the positive and is resting at the place of a more integrative approach that includes both the positive and negative aspects of human functioning. (This represents the idea of synthesis in Hegel's 1807/1931 work on the development of ideas as they move from *thesis* [i.e., traditional mainstream psychology] to *antithesis* [i.e., positive psychology], to *synthesis* [i.e., the integration with which we are now concerned].) As such, positive psychology's current position accords with calls for a new integrative psychology (Sternberg & Grigorenko, 2001).

The "Good" in Positive Psychology

The fundamental value assumption of positive psychology is that the *positive* (however defined) is good (cf. Christopher, 2003). However, the crux of this issue rests precisely on how we define the *positive*. Seligman and Csikszentmihalyi (2000) propose three levels of positive psychology: positive subjective experiences; positive individual characteristics, and; positive institutions. But what is the value position that underpins these three levels of the *positive*? As demonstrated by Christopher (1999), many Western values are implicitly imbued with the liberal individualism that characterizes the current Western cultural and historical epoch. Thus, the Western way of understanding the world thinks primarily in terms of the individual as distinct from his or her community, culture, and cosmos, a view that is very different to many non-Western cultures (Shweder & Bourne, 1984).

Positive Psychology as Culturally Informed

A clear implication of this is that positive psychology research findings, at least as developed within a Western liberal individualistic context, are not prototypically exportable to countries or cultures that do not share our modern cultural identity. This should not be taken as a criticism, but rather as an open and reflective stance on the limits and scope of positive psychology, and especially the practice of positive psychology. Indeed, recognizing our inevitable cultural embeddedness is the basis on which a full understanding of positive psychology rests. In being aware of these limits, we are able to be more fully respectful and tolerant of different traditions and approaches, especially in the recognition that we have as much to learn from them as they have from us. In terms of practice, these issues are fundamental as positive psychology seeks to extend its foundations further into Europe and Asia, and also in being mindful of the practice of positive psychology in diverse multicultural settings within our own societies (cf. Eisenberg & Ota Wang, 2003; Lopez et al., 2002).

WHAT IS GOOD AND DESIRABLE WITHIN POSITIVE PSYCHOLOGY?

The value assumptions implicit within positive psychology are also fundamental for the prescriptions we make on what is good and desirable. Especially as attention moves from basic research to practice, and the science of positive psychology moves from being descriptive to prescriptive, these values critically inform the directions that our interventions and facilitative work takes. Again, it is worth noting at this point that this position is no different than that of any other applied psychology discipline. Just as all of clinical psychology, counseling psychology, and industrial/organizational psychology operate from a (typically implicit) value position, so too does applied positive psychology. Our intention here, however, is to render this value position explicit, and hence open to scrutiny, criticism, and revision as appropriate.

Seligman (e.g., 2002; Seligman & Csikszentmihalyi, 2000) has defined the "desired outcomes" (i.e., valued goods) of positive psychology as happiness and well-being. This could be taken to suggest that in any value hierarchy within positive psychology, happiness and well-being would be found at the head of such a hierarchy. However, we suggest that this was not necessarily Seligman's intent, and we go on to demonstrate why.

THE MEANING OF WELL-BEING

First, what is meant by *happiness* and *well-being* is crucial. If my *happiness* is to be found, for example, through exploiting others, is that a legitimate aim for positive psychology? Of course, it is not, and Seligman and Csikszentmihalyi (2000) address this through reference to what they term "collective well-being." Hence, implicitly, the further value position is adopted that the happiness and well-being of any given individual should not be at the detriment and cost of others. Indeed, if it were, how would one decide who merited happiness, and who merited suffering for that person's happiness? These questions concern the first of the three levels of positive psychology, that is, valued subjective experiences. Hence, we may have valued subjective experiences that are not in keeping with the third level of positive civic virtues, such as civility, tolerance, and responsibility. If anything, these may restrain our happiness. However, here the definition of happiness is crucial.

Subjective Well-Being   Happiness defined within the scientific term of subjective well-being is the sum of life satisfaction and affective balance (i.e., positive affect minus negative affect). In this regard, Seligman and Csikszentmihalyi (2000) raised the issue of "the calculus of well-being"—what can we do to be consistently more happy? Yet, as Kahneman (1999) notes, this may be largely impossible (but see Sheldon & Lyubomirsky, Chapter 8, this volume, for a contrasting perspective). However, what would it mean if positive psychology had been looking at the wrong type of happiness? There may be much merit to the argument that increases in happiness are unsustainable because of the "hedonic treadmill" (Brickman & Campbell, 1971). This is in accord with much of the research evidence.

Psychological Well-Being   In contrast, psychological well-being (defined as "engagement with the existential challenges of life," Keyes, Shmotkin, & Ryff, 2002) provides a much broader and more rounded context of well-being. It is also more fully compatible with the positive psychological functioning that results from acting concordantly with our organismic valuing process, which we established to be a fundamental assumption of positive psychology. The well-being described by Aristotle (eudaimonia), Horney (growth), and Rogers (fully functioning) is also captured much more fully by this concept of psychological well-being. Indeed, throughout the psychological literature, a number of authors have drawn this distinction both empirically (Compton, Smith, Cornish, & Qualls, 1996; Keyes et al., 2002; McGregor & Little, 1998; Ryff, 1989; Waterman, 1993) and theoretically (Ryan & Deci, 2001; Ryff & Singer, 1996). This distinction has important implications for positive psychology, and especially applied positive psychology.

First, as we noted, the "calculus of well-being" does not suggest how happiness may be sustainably increased—in contrast, much of the research evidence points to the transitory and fleeting nature of this subjective experience (Kahneman, 1999). Even Sheldon and Lyubomirsky's (Chapter 8, this volume) work on sustainable boosts in happiness is characterized, we suggest, by activities that are more in keeping with a psychological well-being perspective (i.e., practicing gratitude, performing acts of kindness) than a strictly subjective well-being perspective. (Although we also note that the two concepts are typically moderately correlated; Compton et al., 1996; Keyes et al., 2002; Waterman, 1993.)

The Nature of Well-Being as a Desired Outcome

Having emphasized these distinctions between subjective well-being and psychological well-being, we further suggest that the exclusive pursuit of subjective well-being (i.e., the more common "happiness") is likely a futile and contradictory pursuit. In contrast, psychological well-being, taken as representative of the positive psychological functioning espoused by Aristotle (eudaimonia), Horney (growth), and Rogers (fully functioning), is more appropriately adopted as a desired outcome of positive psychology, and hence a legitimate goal of applied positive psychology.

What all these conceptions have in common, and which is implicit within the concept of psychological well-being, is its location in the context of the individual within community and culture, rather than the individual in isolation. Thus, psychological well-being as we understand it, and as we propose it within applied positive psychology, is concerned as much with collective well-being as it is with individual well-being. In this way, psychological well-being can be viewed to be at the head of the applied positive psychology value hierarchy, but not at the expense of civic virtues such as tolerance, civility, and responsibility. Rather, we would argue, psychological well-being could not occur except within a context that respected the "desired goods" of the third level of positive psychology, positive institutions and civic virtues. This position thus reflects Sternberg's (1998) extrapersonal dimension of wisdom; the value relativism in wisdom as described by Baltes (e.g., Baltes, Glück, & Kunzmann, 2002; Baltes & Staudinger, 2000); and the permanent adversities (i.e., contingency, conflict, and plurality within values) that inhibit the path to the good life described by Kekes (1995).

When well-being as a desired outcome of positive psychology is made explicit and conceptualized in this way, it is more fully consistent with the fuller understanding of the goals of applied positive psychology. This more easily allows their interrelationships to be documented and understood, rather than being seen as inconsistent and potentially incompatible.

IMPLICATIONS OF THE SWB-PWB DISTINCTION FOR PRACTICE

The implications of this distinction for practice are considerable. If subjective well-being were the goal of applied positive psychology, should we sanction ever-greater experience of momentary positive affect and avoidance of negative affect? On this basis, ever more consumption and greater luxury should serve to boost our momentary hedonic states. Yet, the evidence clearly indicates the contrary: More money, more materialism, more possessions, all singularly fail to make us any happier (Csikszentmihalyi, 1999; Kasser, 2002; Myers, 2000). In contrast, they may have even the reverse effect, leading to psychological ill-being (Kasser, Chapter 4, this volume; Kasser & Ryan, 1993, 1996) and greater ecological costs that are a detriment to our long-term environmental well-being and survival (Sheldon & McGregor, 2000).

Further, in being guided by our organismic valuing process, it is clear that the positive psychological functioning outcomes that arise are outcomes of psychological well-being (personal growth and fulfillment) rather than subjective well-being (the pursuit of pleasure and the avoidance of pain). We may also draw the distinction that subjective well-being is typically an external pursuit, influenced in large part by our exterior circumstances, whereas psychological well-being springs from within, being an inherently intrinsic outcome.

As noted by theorists such as Maslow (1968) and Rogers (1959), we can infer that psychological well-being does not fall prey to the problems of the calculus of well-being as does subjective well-being. There is no hedonic treadmill for psychological well-being, which is more appropriately viewed as an ongoing process rather than a fixed state, whereas subjective well-being is of its nature limited by how much pleasure we can experience at any given passing moment.

THE AGENDA FOR PRACTICE

A third question that arises following positive psychology's fundamental assumption of the organismic valuing process is: Whose agenda should we be working to in applying positive psychology? Again, this question is typically implicit, yet it remains fundamental to the nature, direction, and goals of practice.

WHOSE AGENDA?

To illustrate this point, consider each of these possible agendas for the major domains of professional practice. Should the goal of the therapist (whether within the remit of clinical psychology, counseling psychology, counseling, or psychotherapy) be to assimilate the person into their society, thus working to the agenda of society, and acting as an agent of social control? Or should their goal be to facilitate the organismic valuing process of the client, thus working to the agenda of the client, and possibly acting as an agent for social change to the extent that the client wishes to go against the values espoused by society (cf. Hubble & Miller, Chapter 21, this volume; Joseph & Linley, Chapter 22, this volume)?

Should the goal of the educational psychologist be to guide the student to fit in with his or her educational-social context or to try and change the educational-social context so that it better meets the needs of the individual, thus working to that person's agenda (cf. Cohn, Chapter 14, this volume)? Should the goal of the forensic psychologist be concerned with the treatment of the offender and the prevention of further offending, thus working to the agenda of the victim and the broader society which should be protected? Or should the goal of the forensic psychologist be to facilitate the organismic valuing process of the offender, to equip them with appropriate ways of meeting their needs and aspirations that are more socially constructive, thus working to the agenda of the offender (see Ward & Mann, Chapter 36, this volume)?

Should I/O psychologists be working on behalf of the company or organization to guide personnel selection, training, product development, marketing, or customer relations? Or should they be more concerned with the well-being of employees and consumers and business practices that are socially and environmentally responsible (cf. Henry, Chapter 17, this volume; Hodges & Clifton, Chapter 16, this volume)? Should health psychologists work to influence the health of the population or subgroups of the population, according to the agenda of policymakers (cf. Huppert, Chapter 41, this volume)? Should psychologists with input to government and public policy be working to the agenda of the government, or to the agenda of the populace, seeking to promote the choices and values that would be right for the populace (cf. Kasser, Chapter 4, this volume; Myers, Chapter 38, this volume; Veenhoven, Chapter 39, this volume)?

THE ISSUES ARISING FROM THE QUESTION: "WHOSE AGENDA?"

We do not provide answers to these fundamental questions of whose agenda we should be working to. Rather, we simply raise these issues as necessary for any agenda of positive psychology in practice. However, two key points do arise from this consideration. First, that there may be cases when the agenda being pursued is at odds with the OVP of individuals. In these instances, making the agenda explicit at least allows it to be open to consideration, criticism, and revision. Second, to the extent that the agenda of the broader context is concordant with the agenda of the individual and their OVP, the more likely it is to be successful.

Consider, for example, that people satisfied at work are more productive (Judge et al., 2001), that people who use their strengths and talents in the workplace make higher profits for their organization (Hodges & Clifton, Chapter 16, this volume), and that executive coaching is most effective when it harnesses the inner resources of the coachee (Kauffman & Scoular, Chapter 18, this volume). Psychotherapy works only because of, and not in spite of the client (Hubble & Miller, Chapter 21, this volume). Recognising the needs and aspirations of offenders and facilitating them in finding legitimate ways to meet these needs and aspirations leads to lower rates of re-offending (Ward & Mann, Chapter 36, this volume). Health strategies are only effective if they serve the needs of the target population to at least a minimal extent (Huppert, Chapter 41, this volume; Taylor & Sherman, Chapter 19, this volume). Governments (at least in democratic societies) only remain in power if their policies are judged effective and appropriate by the voting public. Hence, the overall message is that if the agenda for practice is not the agenda of the individuals it is intended to target, it is far less likely to succeed than if it accords with the agenda of those individuals.

INTEGRATING THE POSITIVE AND NEGATIVE

Positive psychology rejects the categorical approach to psychopathology that is current within clinical psychology and the *DSM* (Maddux, 2002; Maddux, Snyder, & Lopez, Chapter 20, this volume). Instead, positive psychology proposes that psychopathology is instead best represented as a continuum, rather than a category that is absolutely present or absent. However, there is not a positive psychological theory that can account for this position. The organismic valuing process, on the other hand, accounts for both psychopathology and well-being through its premise that psychopathology is manifest to the extent that people are not acting in accord with their OVP. Well-being arises, in contrast, to the extent that people are intrinsically and organismically valuing in their choices and behaviors (see Joseph & Linley, Chapter 22, this volume). This theory therefore provides a natural continuum that accounts for the varying extents of human experience of psychopathology and well-being, hence, the categorical distinction between positive and negative is viewed as inappropriate, since they are both part of the same vein of human experience.

The Nature of Ill-Being and Well-Being

The key implications of this for practice are that the goals of intervention, within a therapeutic context at least, do not begin and end with the target of the client being symptom-free. Rather, the applied positive psychologist, working to facilitate the client's OVP, would not consider their work done when the disorder had been treated. Instead, they would continue through the zero point of neither ill-being nor well-being, and work with the goal of the facilitation of well-being (cf. Joseph, Linley, Harwood, Lewis, & McCollam, in press). These ideas have been explored in the context of posttraumatic stress disorder (Joseph, 2004; Linley & Joseph, 2002a).

It is further the case that the facilitation and promotion of well-being is believed to provide an effective buffer against subsequent psychosocial stressors. For example, Fredrickson's broaden-and-build theory of positive emotions postulates that experiencing positive emotions undoes the damaging effects of negative emotions. Positive emotions also serve to build resources against future stressors, such that as and when they arise, their effects are more easily and effectively dissipated (Fredrickson, 1998, 2001; Fredrickson & Levenson, 1998).

An Integrative View of the Human Condition

This integration of the positive and negative in positive psychology also importantly recognizes both sides of the human condition, the experience of positive and negative emotions, which are inescapably part of what it means to be human (Linley & Joseph, 2003). Larsen, Hemenover, Norris, and Cacioppo (2003) have delineated how the brain systems that underlie positive and negative emotions are distinct but may also be co-activated. This co-activation may be experienced as unstable, unpleasant, and disharmonious, but it may be key to working through and transcending major life stressors: In essence, one must be able to confront adversity, but also accept and find meaning in it.

In a similar vein, Ryff and Singer (2003) describe how good lives are effortful and challenging and arise from zest and engagement in living. Thus, for a life to be considered good, it would not be characterized by ease, but rather by an active and determined quest to overcome obstacles, to live being mindful of our mortality, and appreciating life therefore all the more. It is for this reason that we (e.g., Linley & Joseph, 2002b, 2002c) have referred to posttraumatic growth as the "apotheosis of positive psychology." Posttraumatic growth represents the psychological well-being that positive psychology aspires to, but within a context of suffering and adversity that debunks any criticism of positive psychology's "Pollyanna theorizing" (cf. Linley & Joseph, 2004; Linley, Joseph, Cooper, Harris, & Meyer, 2003). Hence, in integrating the positive and the negative within the context of posttraumatic growth, we have described a tragic hopefulness that encapsulates both a recognition of our existential position and inevitable mortality, and described how wisdom may be one positive outcome of the struggle with trauma (Linley, 2003). Despite this, we still maintain a desire to live and grow and make the most of what we have (Linley, 2000; Linley & Joseph, 2002b, 2002c).

POSITIVE PSYCHOLOGY AND THE NATURE OF KNOWLEDGE

From the outset, Seligman (e.g., 2001) attempted to ensure that positive psychology is a discipline characterized by good empirical science. This is a position that we support, and fully agree that scientific pedigree should be a hallmark of positive psychology research and practice. However, we must also be mindful about the nature of the questions that we are asking. In considering the organismic valuing process for example, or the value stance that positive psychology adopts, we are left with questions of values (which are relative) and morality (which is a matter of personal ethics). Neither of these can be scientifically proven right or wrong, since they are not empirical questions per se, but rather reflect the standpoint from which we have chosen to operate. Hence, while the empirical method has taught us much and guards against conjecture and anecdote being accepted in place of scientific research, we must be aware that it cannot tell us everything. Some questions are not reducible to empirical questions that fit neat experimental methodologies.

POSITIVE PSYCHOLOGY AND THE LIMITS OF EMPIRICAL SCIENCE

These caveats notwithstanding, advances in our methodological and statistical knowledge do allow important questions to be answered with a degree of empirical sophistication that was not previously possible. Hence, it is not our intention to suggest that the nonempirical nature of some of these questions be used as an excuse for "bad science"—far from it. We only wish to note that empirical methodologies may not be equipped to answer all our questions, and hence we should be receptive to a variety of methods of inquiry, being careful to recognize the appropriate place and value of each.

For example, recent developments in experience sampling methodologies and diary studies have been used to lend greater validity to self-report data. The growing array of qualitative methodologies (e.g., interpretative phenomenological analysis; grounded theory; discourse analysis) have already allowed us insights into aspects of human experience that would not have been detected through directive questionnaires or artificial laboratory settings. (See Larsen et al., 2003, for an example of the co-activation of positive and negative affect that was detected only through using an experience sampling methodology.)

Human experience is at the core of much positive psychology, and as Rathunde (2001) notes, researchers could learn much from the "experiential turns" of such early psychological pioneers as James, Dewey, and Maslow, who focused on immediate subjective experience in trying to understand optimal human fulfillment. In seeking to objectify psychology in the positivist scientific tradition, Rathunde argues that much rich data from subjective experience has been unnecessarily excluded from psychological discourse. It would be eminently regretable if this were allowed to continue.

The questions that positive psychology and the practice of positive psychology lead us to ask may be beyond the remit of our current experimental designs and abilities. However, we should not thereby exclude the questions as not worth asking, but should rather seek to answer them in the most appropriate way that we can. Our guiding ethos should not be which questions fit with our scientific methods, but what methods, scientific or otherwise, may be most appropriate for answering the questions of interest to us. These are far from issues that will be easily resolved, but the questions are fundamental as we develop the further practice of positive psychology.

POSITIVE PSYCHOLOGY IN PRACTICE AS A REFLECTIVE ENDEAVOR

In conclusion, our call is for positive psychology in practice to be a reflective endeavor. Too often psychology can proceed without a full awareness of its inherent assumptions, values, and biases. Hence, we have tried to delineate what these may be for positive psychology as a basic science, and particularly applied positive psychology as a professional practice.

First, the assumptions that positive psychology makes about human nature fit with the tradition of an innate constructive directional force, one of the earliest proponents of which was Aristotle. We made a core distinction in this regard between an intrinsic locus of evaluation and an external locus of evaluation. Intrinsic valuing and behavior are in accord with our organismic valuing process, our innate constructive directional force, and lead to eudaimonic well-being. This perspective is consistent with a wide range of research within positive psychology and beyond.

Second, the value position of positive psychology is that the positive is good, and that well-being is a desired outcome. However, this value position should not be taken to suggest that the negative should be ignored, rather, there is a place for both in the integrative psychology that positive psychology aspires to. Further, the well-being that is held to be a desired outcome of positive psychology is best conceptualized as psychological well-being or eudaimonia, a well-being that accords with the civic and extrapersonal values of broader community, society, and ecology as much as it does with the individual. Relatedly, this value position is implicitly informed by the tenets of liberal individualism, and hence caution is merited if we seek to apply positive psychology beyond the contexts in which it has been developed. However, being mindful and reflective of these issues should facilitate an open attitude and tolerance that will serve the discipline well.

Third, positive psychology as a professional practice should be reflective of the agendas that it pursues. While it may not always be appropriate to follow the agenda of the individual, a self-reflective stance guards against the distortion or uncritical perpetuation of an agenda that may be deficient or unjust.

Fourth, applied positive psychology should not ignore the negative valences of human experience, but should rather seek to understand and facilitate optimal human functioning within the context of both the light and darkness of living. Indeed, it is likely that any perspective on human functioning that was focused on either the positive or the negative would be insufficient. Rather, it is necessary that the two valences of human experience should be seen as sides of the same coin: One cannot be understood without reference to the other.

Fifth, we have noted and support the call for positive psychology, whether basic or applied, to be founded on good scientific practice. However, we have also described how some of the questions in which positive psychologists may be interested may not be reducible to units of empirical scrutiny. Often in the practice of positive psychology, we may find ourselves grappling with questions of value and morality that do not lend themselves to experimental investigation. We call upon positive psychologists, therefore, to be reflective of these issues and ensure that it is the questions they wish to ask that shape their methodologies, rather than limiting the scope of their inquiries to the available methodologies. This will likely lead to some thorny issues, but will allow the discipline to genuinely advance.

Overall, the practice of positive psychology has much to offer for the well-being and optimal functioning of individuals and their societies at all levels, from the person themselves, through the group, community, and organization, to the society and culture as a whole. In being reflective of the assumptions and values on which it rests, positive psychology in practice may be more fully aware of the strengths and limitations of its approach, using this knowledge mindfully in the quest for genuine progress and scientific discovery. We stand at the beginning of exciting times in the practice of positive psychology as we look for new ways to facilitate good lives for all.

REFERENCES

Aristotle. (n.d.). *The nicomachean ethics of Aristotle* (D. P. Chase, Trans.). London: J. M. Dent & Sons.

Baltes, P. B., Glück, J., & Kunzmann, U. (2002). Wisdom: Its structure and function in regulating successful lifespan development. In C. R. Snyder & S. J. Lopez (Eds.), *Handbook of positive psychology* (pp. 327–350). New York: Oxford University Press.

Baltes, P. B., & Staudinger, U. M. (2000). Wisdom: A metaheuristic (pragmatic) to orchestrate mind and virtue toward excellence. *American Psychologist, 55,* 122–136.

Brickman, P., & Campbell, D. T. (1971). Hedonic relativism and planning the good society. In M. H. Appley (Ed.), *Adaptation-level theory: A symposium* (pp. 287–305). New York: Academic Press.

Brown, K. W., & Ryan, R. M. (2003). The benefits of being present: Mindfulness and its role in psychological well-being. *Journal of Personality and Social Psychology, 84,* 822–848.

Carver, C. S., & Baird, E. (1998). The American dream revisited: Is it *what* you want or *why* you want it that matters? *Psychological Science, 9,* 289–292.

Christopher, J. C. (1996). Counseling's inescapable moral visions. *Journal of Counseling and Development, 75,* 17–25.

Christopher, J. C. (1999). Situating psychological well-being: Exploring the cultural roots of its theory and research. *Journal of Counseling and Development, 77,* 141–152.

Christopher, J. C. (2003, October). *The good in positive psychology.* Paper presented at the Second International Positive Psychology Summit, Washington, DC.

Compton, W. C., Smith, M. L., Cornish, K. A., & Qualls, D. L. (1996). Factor structure of mental health measures. *Journal of Personality and Social Psychology, 71,* 406–413.

Csikszentmihalyi, M. (1990). *Flow: The psychology of optimal experience.* New York: Harper & Row.

Csikszentmihalyi, M. (1999). If we are so rich, why aren't we happy? *American Psychologist, 54,* 821–827.

Deci, E. L., & Ryan, R. M. (1985). *Intrinsic motivation and self-determination in human behavior.* New York: Plenum Press.

Deci, E. L., & Ryan, R. M. (2000). The "what" and "why" of goal pursuits: Human needs and the self-determination of behavior. *Psychological Inquiry, 11,* 227–268.

Diener, E. (2003, October). *Critiques and limitations of positive psychology.* Roundtable discussion at the Second International Positive Psychology Summit, Washington, DC.

Eisenberg, N., & Ota Wang, V. (2003). Toward a positive psychology: Social developmental and cultural contributions. In L. G. Aspinwall & U. M. Staudinger (Eds.), *A psychology of human strengths: Fundamental questions and future directions for a positive psychology* (pp. 117–129). Washington, DC: American Psychological Association.

Fredrickson, B. L. (1998). What good are positive emotions? *Review of General Psychology, 2,* 300–319.

Fredrickson, B. L. (2001). The role of positive emotions in positive psychology: The broaden-and-build theory of positive emotions. *American Psychologist, 56,* 218–226.

Fredrickson, B. L., & Levenson, R. W. (1998). Positive emotions speed recovery from the cardiovascular sequelae of negative emotions. *Cognition and Emotion, 12,* 191–220.

Hegel, G. W. F. (1931). *The phenomenology of mind.* (J. B. Baillie, Trans., 2nd ed.). London: Allen & Unwin. (Original work published 1807)

Held, B. S. (2003, October). *Critiques and limitations of positive psychology.* Roundtable discussion at the Second International Positive Psychology Summit, Washington, DC.

Horney, K. (1951). *Neurosis and human growth: The struggle toward self-realization.* London: Routledge & Kegan Paul.

Joseph, S. (2004). Client-centred therapy, posttraumatic stress disorder, and posttraumatic growth: Theoretical perspectives and practical implications. *Psychology and Psychotherapy: Theory, Research, and Practice, 77,* 101–119.

Joseph, S., Linley, P. A., Harwood, J., Lewis, C. A., & McCollam, P. (in press). Rapid assessment of well-being: The Short Depression-Happiness Scale. *Psychology and Psychotherapy: Theory, Research, and Practice.*

Judge, T. A., Thoresen, C. J., Bono, J. E., & Patton, G. K. (2001). The job satisfaction-job performance relationship: A qualitative and quantitative review. *Psychological Bulletin, 127,* 376–407.

Kahneman, D. (1999). Objective happiness. In D. Kahneman, E. Diener, & N. Schwarz (Eds.), *Well-being: The foundations of hedonic psychology* (pp. 3–25). New York: Russell Sage Foundation.

Kasser, T. (2002). *The high price of materialism.* Cambridge, MA: MIT Press.

Kasser, T., & Ryan, R. M. (1993). A dark side of the American dream: Correlates of financial success as a central life aspiration. *Journal of Personality and Social Psychology, 65,* 410–422.

Kasser, T., & Ryan, R. M. (1996). Further examining the American dream: Differential correlates of intrinsic and extrinsic goals. *Personality and Social Psychology Bulletin, 22,* 280–287.

Kekes, J. (1995). *Moral wisdom and good lives.* Ithaca, NY: Cornell University Press.

Keyes, C. L. M., Shmotkin, D., & Ryff, C. D. (2002). Optimizing well-being: The empirical encounter of two traditions. *Journal of Personality and Social Psychology, 82,* 1007–1022.

Larsen, J. T., Hemenover, S. H., Norris, C. J., & Cacioppo, J. T. (2003). Turning adversity to advantage: On the virtues of the coactivation of positive and negative emotions. In L. G. Aspinwall & U. M. Staudinger (Eds.), *A psychology of human strengths: Fundamental questions and future directions for a positive psychology* (pp. 211–225). Washington, DC: American Psychological Association.

Linley, P. A. (2000). Transforming psychology: The example of trauma. *The Psychologist, 13,* 353–355.

Linley, P. A. (2003). Positive adaptation to trauma: Wisdom as both process and outcome. *Journal of Traumatic Stress, 16,* 601–610.

Linley, P. A., & Joseph, S. (2002a). Posttraumatic growth. *Counseling and Psychotherapy Journal, 13,* 14–17.

Linley, P. A., & Joseph, S. (2002b, October). *Posttraumatic growth: The apotheosis of positive psychology.* Poster presented at the First International Positive Psychology Summit, Washington, DC.

Linley, P. A., & Joseph, S. (2002c, June). *Posttraumatic growth: The positive psychology of trauma.* Paper presented at the First European Positive Psychology Conference, Winchester, England.

*Linley, P. A., & Joseph, S. (2003). Putting it into practice. *The Psychologist, 16,* 143.

Linley, P. A., & Joseph, S. (2004). Positive change following trauma and adversity: A review. *Journal of Traumatic Stress, 17,* 11–21.

Linley, P. A., Joseph, S., Cooper, R., Harris, S., & Meyer, C. (2003). Positive and negative changes following vicarious exposure to the September 11 terrorist attacks. *Journal of Traumatic Stress, 16,* 481–485.

Lopez, S. J., Prosser, E. C., Edwards, L. M., Magyar-Moe, J. L., Neufeld, J. E., & Rasmussen, H. N. (2002). Putting positive psychology in a multicultural context. In C. R. Snyder & S. J. Lopez (Eds.), *Handbook of positive psychology* (pp. 700–714). New York: Oxford University Press.

Maddux, J. E. (2002). Stopping the "madness": Positive psychology and the deconstruction of the illness ideology and the *DSM.* In C. R. Snyder & S. J. Lopez (Eds.), *Handbook of positive psychology* (pp. 13–25). New York: Oxford University Press.

Marcus, G. E., & Fischer, M. M. J. (1986). *Anthropology as cultural critique: An experimental moment in the human sciences.* Chicago: University of Chicago Press.

Maslow, A. H. (1968). *Toward a psychology of being* (2nd ed.). New York: Van Nostrand Reinhold.

McGregor, I., & Little, B. R. (1998). Personal projects, happiness, and meaning: On doing well and being yourself. *Journal of Personality and Social Psychology, 74,* 494–512.

Myers, D. G. (2000). The funds, friends, and faith of happy people. *American Psychologist, 55,* 56–67.

Norem, J. K. (2003, October). *Critiques and limitations of positive psychology.* Roundtable discussion at the Second International Positive Psychology Summit, Washington, DC.

Pargament, K. I., & Mahoney, A. (2002). Spirituality: Discovering and conserving the sacred. In C. R. Snyder & S. J. Lopez (Eds.), *Handbook of positive psychology* (pp. 646–659). New York: Oxford University Press.

Peterson, C., & Seligman, M. E. P. (2003). *Values in Action (VIA) classification of strengths* [Draft dated January 4, 2003]. Retrieved January 15, 2003, from the www .positivepsychology.org/strengths.

Prilleltensky, I. (1994). *The morals and politics of psychology: Psychological discourse and the status quo.* Albany: State University of New York Press.

Rathunde, K. (2001). Toward a psychology of optimal human functioning: What positive psychology can learn from the "experiential turns" of James, Dewey, and Maslow. *Journal of Humanistic Psychology, 41,* 135–153.

Rogers, C. R. (1951). *Client-centered therapy: Its current practice, implications and theory.* London: Constable.

*Rogers, C. R. (1959). A theory of therapy, personality, and interpersonal relationships, as developed in the client-centered framework. In S. Koch (Ed.), *Psychology: A study of a science* (pp. 184–256). New York: McGraw-Hill.

*Rogers, C. R. (1964). Toward a modern approach to values: The valuing process in the mature person. *Journal of Abnormal and Social Psychology, 68,* 160–167.

Ryan, R. M. (1995). Psychological needs and the facilitation of integrative processes. *Journal of Personality, 63,* 397–427.

*Ryan, R. M., & Deci, E. L. (2000). Self-determination theory and the facilitation of intrinsic motivation, social development, and well-being. *American Psychologist, 55,* 68–78.

Ryan, R. M., & Deci, E. L. (2001). On happiness and human potentials: A review of research on hedonic and eudaimonic well-being. *Annual Review of Psychology, 52,* 141–166.

Ryff, C. D. (1989). Happiness is everything, or is it? Explorations on the meaning of psychological well-being. *Journal of Personality and Social Psychology, 57,* 1069–1081.

Ryff, C. D., & Singer, B. (1996). Psychological well-being: Meaning, measurement, and implications for psychotherapy research. *Psychotherapy and Psychosomatics, 65,* 14–23.

Ryff, C. D., & Singer, B. (2003). Ironies of the human condition: Well-being and health on the way to mortality. In L. G. Aspinwall & U. M. Staudinger (Eds.), *A psychology of human strengths: Fundamental questions and future directions for a positive psychology* (pp. 271–287). Washington, DC: American Psychological Association.

Seligman, M. E. P. (2001, October). *Welcome to positive psychology.* Address to the Positive Psychology Summit, Washington, DC.

Seligman, M. E. P. (2002). *Authentic happiness: Using the new positive psychology to realize your potential for lasting fulfilment.* New York: Free Press.

*Seligman, M. E. P. (2003). Positive psychology: Fundamental assumptions. *The Psychologist, 16,* 126–127.

*Seligman, M. E. P., & Csikszentmihalyi, M. (2000). Positive psychology: An introduction. *American Psychologist, 55,* 5–14.

Sheldon, K. M., Arndt, J., & Houser-Marko, L. (2003). In search of the organismic valuing process: The human tendency to move toward beneficial goal choices. *Journal of Personality, 71,* 835–869.

Sheldon, K. M., & Elliot, A. J. (1999). Goal striving, need satisfaction, and longitudinal well-being: The Self-Concordance Model. *Journal of Personality and Social Psychology, 76,* 482–497.

Sheldon, K. M., & Houser-Marko, L. (2001). Self-concordance, goal-attainment, and the pursuit of happiness: Can there be an upward spiral? *Journal of Personality and Social Psychology, 80,* 152–165.

*Sheldon, K. M., & Kasser, T. (2001). Goals, congruence, and positive well-being: New empirical validation for humanistic theories. *Journal of Humanistic Psychology, 41,* 30–50.

Sheldon, K. M., & King, L. (2001). Why positive psychology is necessary. *American Psychologist, 56,* 216–217.

Sheldon, K. M., & McGregor, H. A. (2000). Extrinsic value orientation and the tragedy of the commons. *Journal of Personality, 68,* 383–411.

Shweder, R. A., & Bourne, E. J. (1984). Does the concept of the person vary cross-culturally. In R. A. Shweder & R. A. LeVine (Eds.), *Culture theory: Essays on mind, self, and emotion* (pp. 158–199). New York: Cambridge University Press.

Sternberg, R. J. (1998). A balance theory of wisdom. *Review of General Psychology, 2,* 347–365.

Sternberg, R. J., & Grigorenko, E. L. (2001). Unified psychology. *American Psychologist, 56,* 1069–1079.

Wampold, B. E. (2001). *The great psychotherapy debate: Models, methods, and findings.* Mahwah, NJ: Erlbaum.

Waterman, A. S. (1993). Two conceptions of happiness: Contrasts of personal expressiveness (eudaimonia) and hedonic enjoyment. *Journal of Personality and Social Psychology, 64,* 678–691.

Zeig, J. K. (1987). *The evolution of psychotherapy.* New York: Brunner/Mazel.

Author Index

Subject Index